PSYCHOLOGICAL ASSESSMENT WITH THE MMPI-2

PSYCHOLOGICAL ASSESSMENT WITH THE MMPI-2

Alan F. Friedman, PhD
Northwestern University Medical School
Independent Practice

Richard Lewak, PhD
Del Mar Clinic

David S. Nichols, PhD
Oregon State Hospital

James T. Webb, PhD
Gifted Psychology Press, Inc.

LEA
LAWRENCE ERLBAUM ASSOCIATES, PUBLISHERS
2001 Mahwah, New Jersey London

Lawrence Erlbaum Associates, Inc., Publishers
10 Industrial Avenue
Mahwah, NJ 07430

Cover design by Kathryn Houghtaling Lacey

Library of Congress Cataloging-in-Publication Data

Psychological assessment with the MMPI-2 / Alan F. Friedman ... [et al.].
p. cm.
Includes bibliographical references and index.
ISBN 0-8058-1444-2 (cloth : alk. Paper) — ISBN 0-8058-3869-4 (pbk. : alk. paper)
1. Minnesota Multiphasic Personality Inventory.
I. Friedman, Alan F.
RC473.M5 P79 2000
155.2'83—dc21 99-087193
CIP

Books published by Lawrence Erlbaum Associates are printed on acid-free paper, and their bindings are chosen for strength and durability.

Printed in the United States of America
10 9 8 7 6 5 4 3 2 1

In loving memory of my father and to his grandchildren,
Emily Lauren and Benjamin Arthur, my precious children.
To Goldine Gleser, my mentor, colleague, and treasured friend
A. F. F.

To my daughter, Rachel Levak
R. W. L.

To my beloved godson, Benjamin David Bowman
D. S. N.

To my mentor, Raymond Fowler, and to my niece, Nadia E. Webb,
who continues the tradition of quality assessment
J. T. W.

Contents

Code-Pattern Look-Up Table xv
List of Figures xxi
List of Tables xxiii
List of Appendix Tables xxv
Foreword xxvii
W. Grant Dahlstrom
Foreword xxix
Robert P. Archer
Preface xxxi

CHAPTER 1 DEVELOPMENT OF THE MMPI AND MMPI–2 1
General Description of the MMPI/MMPI–2 *1*
Historical Development of the MMPI *3*
MMPI Restandardization: The MMPI–2 *9*
Experimental Form (AX) and the MMPI–2 Booklet *10*
New Normative Sample *12*
Uniform *T*-Scores *16*
Notes *22*

CHAPTER 2 MEASURES OF PROFILE VALIDITY 25
The Traditional Measures and Their Derivatives *25*
Cannot Say Score (*?*) *26*
Variable Response Inconsistency Scale (*VRIN*) *28*
True Response Inconsistency Scale (*TRIN*) *32*
Infrequency Scale (*F*) *33*
F-Back Scale [*FB*] *35*

Additional Measures of Response Style *39*
Self-Unfavorable Scales *39*
Infrequency-Psychopathology Scale: *F(p)* *39*
Dissimulation Scale (*Ds*) *43*
Self-Favorable Scales *46*
Lie Scale (*L*) *47*
Correction Scale (*K*) *49*
Superlative Self-Presentation Scale (*S*) *53*
Positive Malingering Scale (*Mp*) *55*
Social Desirability Scale (*Sd*) *56*
Socioeconomic Status Scale (*Ss*) *57*
Validity Indices *59*
F—FB *59*
Dissimulation Index (*F – K*) *60*
Notes *67*

CHAPTER 3 THE CLINICAL SCALES AND THEIR DERIVATIVES 70
Clinical Scale Development and Use *70*
Harris–Lingoes Subscales *73*
Subtle–Obvious Subscales *76*
Overlapping Item Content *79*
Scale 1: Hypochondriasis (*Hs*) *80*
Scale 2: Depression (*D*) *83*
Harris–Lingoes Subscales *85*
D1: Subjective Depression *86*
D2: Psychomotor Retardation *86*
D3: Physical Malfunctioning *87*
D4: Mental Dullness *88*
D5: Brooding *88*
Scale 2: Subtle–Obvious Subscales *89*
Scale 3: Hysteria (*Hy*) *90*
Harris–Lingoes Subscales *95*
Hy1: Denial of Social Anxiety *95*
Hy2: Need for Affection *96*
Hy3: Lassitude–Malaise *97*
Hy4: Somatic Complaints *98*
Hy5: Inhibition of Aggression *98*
Scale 3: Subtle–Obvious Subscales *99*
Scale 4: Psychopathic Deviate (*Pd*) *101*
Harris–Lingoes Subscales *106*

Familial Discord: *Pd1* *106*
Authority Problems: *Pd2* *107*
Social Imperturbability: *Pd3* *108*
Social Alienation: *Pd4* *109*
Self-Alienation: *Pd5* *110*
Scale 4: Subtle–Obvious Subscales *111*
Scale 5: Masculinity–Femininity (*Mf*) *112*
Scale 6: Paranoia (*Pa*) *119*
Harris–Lingoes Subscales *122*
Ideas of external Influence (*Pa1*) *123*
Poignancy: *Pa2* *124*
Moral Virtue: *Pa3* *124*
Scale 6: Subtle–Obvious Subscales *125*
Scale 7: Psychasthenia (*Pt*) *127*
Scale 8: Schizophrenia (*Sc*) *130*
Harris–Lingoes Subscales *135*
Social Alienation: *Sc1* *136*
Emotional Alienation: *Sc2* *136*
Lack of Ego Mastery, Cognitive: *Sc3* *137*
Lack of Ego Mastery, Conative: *Sc4* *138*
Lack of Ego Mastery, Defective Inhibition: *Sc5* *139*
Sensorimotor Dissociation: *Sc6* *140*
Scale 9: Hypomania (*Ma*) *141*
Harris–Lingoes Subscales *146*
Amorality: *Ma1* *146*
Psychomotor Acceleration: *Ma2* *147*
Imperturbability: *Ma3* *148*
Ego Inflation: *Ma4* *148*
Scale 9: Subtle–Obvious Subscales *149*
Scale 0: Social Introversion (*Si*) *151*
Notes *157*

CHAPTER 4 ADMINISTRATION AND SCORING 160
Forms of the MMPI–2 *160*
Abbreviated and Short Forms *161*
Foreign Translations *162*
Test Instructions *163*
Test Conditions *167*
Participants' Requirements *168*
Test Scoring and Profile Plotting *172*
Coding the Profile *173*

MMPI/MMPI–2 Code Pattern Correspondence *176*
Notes *182*

CHAPTER 5 INTERPRETING THE VALIDITY SCALES 185
? (Cannot Say) Score *186*
Variable Response Inconsistency Scale (*VRIN*) *187*
True Response Inconsistency Scale (*TRIN*) *189*
Infrequency Scale (*F*) *190*
F-Back Scale [*FB*] *193*
Self Unfavorable Scales *194*
Infrequency-Psychopathology Scales: *F(P)* Scale *194*
Dissimulation Scale (*Ds*) *195*
Self Favorable Scales *196*
Lie Scale (*L*) *196*
Correction Scale (*K*) *197*
Superlative Scale (*S*) *203*
Positive Malingering Scale (*Mp*) *204*
Social Desirability Scale (*Sd*) *204*
Socioeconomic Status Scale (*Ss*) *205*
Validity Indices *205*
F – FB Index *205*
Dissimulation Index (*F – K*) *206*
Issues in Determining Validity *207*
Basic Validity Scale Configurations *209*
Random Response Set *209*
Notes *209*
Report Language *209*
All-True Response Set *209*
Notes *214*
Report Language *214*
All-False Response Set *214*
Notes *214*
Report Language *214*
Common Validity Scale Patterns *214*

CHAPTER 6 INTERPRETING THE MMPI–2 CLINICAL SCALES 231
Introduction *231*
Clinical Scales and Codes (also see *Code Pattern Look-up Table*) *232*

Scale 1 (*Hs*) *232*
Treatment *234*
Scale 2 (*D*) *253*
Treatment *255*
Scale 3 (*Hy*) *279*
Treatment *281*
Scale 4 (*Pd*) *295*
Treatment *299*
Scale 5 (*Mf*) *316*
Treatment *318*
Scale 6 (*Pa*) *320*
Treatment *322*
Scale 7 (*Pt*) *326*
Treatment *326*
Scale 8 (*Sc*) *329*
Treatment *330*
Scale 9 (*Ma*) *333*
Treatment *334*
Scale 0 (*Si*) *336*
Normal Code, High *K* (*K*+) *337*

CHAPTER 7 INTERPRETING THE CONTENT OF THE MMPI–2: CRITICAL ITEMS, CONTENT SCALES, AND SUBSCALES 338
Critical Items *338*
Content Scales *345*
Anxiety Scale (*ANX*) *354*
Fears Scale (*FRS*) *355*
Obsessiveness Scale (*OBS*) *357*
Depression Scale (*DEP*) *358*
Health Concerns Scale (*HEA*) *360*
Bizarre Mentation Scale (*BIZ*) *361*
Anger Scale (*ANG*) *362*
Cynicism Scale (*CYN*) *364*
Antisocial Practices Scale (*ASP*) *365*
Type A Behavior Scale (*TPA*) *366*
Low Self-Esteem Scale (*LSE*) *368*
Social Discomfort Scale (*SOD*) *370*
Family Problems Scale (*FAM*) *371*
Work Interference Scale (*WRK*) *373*
Negative Treatment Indicators (*TRT*) *374*

General Principles for the Interpretation of Content Scales *376*
The Personality Psychopathology Five (PSY–5) 379
Negative Emotionality/Neuroticism Scale (*NEN*) *381*
Psychoticism Scale (*PSY*) *381*
Disconstraint Scale (*DIS*) *382*
Aggressiveness Scale (*AGG*) *384*
Low Positive Emotionality/Extraversion Scale (*LPE*) 386
Effects of Response Styles on the *PSY–5* Scales *387*

CHAPTER 8 INTERPRETING THE SUPPLEMENTARY SCALES 388
Introduction *388*
Factor Scales *A* and *R* *391*
Ego Strength Scale (*Es*) *395*
Overcontrolled–Hostility Scale (*O-H*) *397*
Dominance Scale (*Do*) *399*
Social Responsibility Scale (*Re*) *400*
College Maladjustment Scale (*Mt*)
Keane et al.'s Post-Traumatic Stress Disorder Scale (*PK*); and Schlenger and Kulka's Post-Traumatic Stress Disorder Scale (*PS*) *402*
Gender Role–Masculine (*GM*) and Gender Role–Feminine (*GF*) Scales *404*
Substance Abuse Measures: The MacAndrew Alcoholism scale (*MAC/MAC–R*), The Addiction Potential Scale (*APS*), and The Addiction Acknowledgment Scale (*AAS*) *406*
Marital Distress scale (*MDS*) *412*

CHAPTER 9 INTERPRETATION AND REPORT WRITING 414
Clinical And Actuarial Approaches to Interpretation *414*
Development of Actuarial Rules *415*
Actuarial Data and Base Rates *417*
The Importance of Referral Data *419*
Demographic Variables *421*
Age *421*

Gender 422
Education 423
Race 424
Socioeconomic Variables 425
Interpretive Steps 426
Common Code Patterns 429
Code-Patterns, Elevation, and Additional Scales 438
Organizing the Data 442
Writing the Report 443
Guidelines for Beginning a Report: 444
Organization of the Report 457
Symptoms, Complaints, and Personality Traits 459
Self-Concept 459
Perception of the Environment 460
Interpersonal Relationships 460
Behaviors 460
Emotional Control and Response To Stress 461
Psychological Resources 462
Dynamics/Etiology 462
Diagnostic Impressions 463
Treatment Implications 466
Interpretation of "Complex Profiles" 468
Scale 5 470
Scale 0 470
Energizers and Suppressors 470
Strategies for Providing Feedback to the Client 471
Guidelines for Giving Feedback 473
Evaluating Feedback 476

CHAPTER 10 COMPUTERIZED INTERPRETATION OF THE MMPI–2 477
Computer-Based Test Interpretation (CBTI) 477
Computerized Interpretation of the MMPI/MMPI–2 480
Caldwell Report 482
MMPI–2 Adult Interpretive System by Roger Greene 492
MMPI–2 Minnesota Report, Adult Clinical System—Revised, by James N. Butcher 503

Marks (and Lewak) Adult Feedback and Treatment Report for MMPI–2 and MMPI *522*

APPENDIX A 532
Scoring Keys and Norms for MMPI–2 Scales and Critical Items

APPENDIX B 577
MMPI–2 Uniform and Linear *T*-Score Conversions for Validity, Clinical, Supplementary, Content, Content Component, Subscales, and Special Scales

APPENDIX C 633
Item Overlap and Intercorrelations Among the Standard MMPI–2 Validity and Clinical Scales in the Caldwell Clinical Data Set

APPENDIX D 634
***K*- and Non-*K*-Corrected *T*-Score Values for the MMPI–2 Basic Scales Based on the Original Minnesota Normative Group (*N* = 225 Men, 315 Women)**

REFERENCES 645

AUTHOR INDEX 667

SUBJECT INDEX 675

ABOUT THE AUTHORS 687

Code-Pattern Look-Up Table

Scale 1 232

Spike 1 code 232
High 1, low 4 codes (for men) 234
High 1, low 5 code (for women) 234
12/21 codes 234
123/213 codes 235
1234/2134 codes 237
1237/2137 codes 237
128/218 codes 238
129/219 codes 238
120/210 codes 239
13/31 codes 240
Conversion V code 242
13/31 high *K* codes 243
132/312 codes 243
134/314 codes 244
136/316 codes 244

137 code 245
138/318 codes 246
1382 code 247
139 code 247
14/41 codes 248
15/51 codes 249
16/61 codes 250
17/71 codes 251
18/81 codes 251
19/91 codes 252
10/01 codes 253

Scale 2 253

Spike 2 code 254
Spike 2, low 9 code 255
21/12 codes 256
213/231 codes 256
23 codes 258
24/42 codes 260
243/423 codes 262
247/427/472/742 codes 262
248 codes 264
25/52 codes 265
26/62 codes 266
27/72 codes 267
273/723 codes 269
274/724 codes 269
275/725 codes 270
278/728 codes 271
28/82 codes 273
281/821 codes 274
284/824 codes 274
287/827 codes 276

29/92 codes 276
20/02 codes 278

Scale 3 279

Spike 3 codes 280
Spike 3, high K codes 280
31 codes 281
32 codes 281
321 codes 283
34/43 codes 284
345/435/534 codes 286
346/436 codes 287
35/53 codes 288
36/63 codes 289
37/73 codes 290
38/83 codes 292
39/93 codes 293
30/03 codes 294

Scale 4 295

Spike 4 codes 296
High 4, low 5 codes 298
41/14 codes (see 14/41 codes) 298
42/24 codes (see 24/42 codes) 298
43/34 codes (see 34/43 codes) 298
45/54 codes 298
46/64 codes 300
462/642 codes 301
463/643 codes 302
468/648 codes 304
469 codes (see 496/946 codes) 305
47/74 codes 305

478 codes 306
48/84 codes 307
48/84, High *F*, low 2 codes 309
482/842/824 codes 309
486/846 codes 310
489/849 codes 310
49/94 codes 311
493/943 codes 313
495/945 codes 314
496/946 codes 314
498/948 codes 315
40/04 codes 315

<u>*Scale 5*</u> 316

Spike 5 codes 316
51/15 codes (see 15/51 codes) 318
52/25 codes (see 25/52 codes) 318
53/35 codes (see 35/53 codes) 318
54/45 codes (see 45/54 codes) 318
56/65 codes 318
57/75 codes 318
58/85 codes 319
59/95 codes 319
50/05 codes 320

<u>*Scale 6*</u> 320

Spike 6 codes 320
61/16 codes (see 16/61 codes) 321
62/26 codes (see 26/62 codes) 321
63/36 codes (see 36/63 codes) 321
64/46 codes (see 46/64, 462/642, 463/643, and 468/648 codes) 321
65/56 codes (see 56/65 codes) 321

68/86 codes 322
69/96 codes 323
698/968 codes 325
60/06 codes 325

Scale 7 326

Spike 7 codes 326
71/17 codes (see 17/71 codes) 327
72/27 codes (see 27/72 codes) 327
73/37 codes (see 37/73 codes) 327
74/47 codes (see 47/74 codes) 327
75/57 codes (see 57/75 codes) 327
76/76 codes (see 67/76 codes) 327
78/87 codes 327
79/97 codes 328
70/07 codes 329

Scale 8 329

Spike 8 codes 330
81/18 codes (see 18/81 codes) 331
82/28 codes (see 28/82 codes) 331
83/38 codes (see 38/83 codes) 331
84/48 codes (see 48/84 codes) 331
85/58 codes (see 58/85 codes) 331
86/68 codes (see 68/86 codes) 331
87/78 codes (see 78/87 codes) 331
89/98 codes 331
80/08 codes 332

Scale 9 333

Spike 9 codes 333

High 9, High *K* codes 334
91/19 codes (see 19/91 codes) 335
92/29 codes (see 29/92 codes) 335
93/39 codes (see 39/93 codes) 335
94/49 codes (see 49/94 codes) 335
95/59 codes (see 59/95 codes) 335
96/69 codes (see 69/96 codes) 335
97/79 codes (see 79/97 codes) 335
98/89 codes (see 89/98 codes) 335
90/09 codes 335

Scale 0 336

Spike 0 codes 336
01/10 codes (see 10/01 codes) 336
02/20 codes (see 20/02 codes) 336
03/30 codes (see 30/03 codes) 337
04/40 codes (see 40/04 codes) 337
05/50 codes (see 50/05 codes) 337
06/60 codes (see 60/06 codes) 337
07/70 codes (see 70/07 codes) 337
08/80 codes (see 80/08 codes) 337
09/90 codes (see 90/09 codes) 337
Normal code, High *K* (*K*+) 337

List of Figures

Figure		Page
1.1.	Mean MMPI–2 profiles for men by educational level.	15
1.2.	Mean MMPI–2 profiles for women by educational level.	16
1.3.	Mean MMPI–2 profiles for men by occupational level.	17
1.4.	Mean MMPI–2 profiles for women by occupational level.	18
5.1.	Random response set for men.	210
5.2.	Random response set for women.	211
5.3.	All-true response set for men.	212
5.4.	All-true response set for women.	213
5.5.	All-false response set for men.	215
5.6.	All-false response set for women.	216
5.7.	"Most open" to "most closed" validity configurations.	218
5.8.	"Most closed" validity configuration.	219
5.9.	"Most open" validity configuration.	220
5.10	Admitting serious problems while attempting to cope and preserve self-esteem.	221
5.11.	Good ego strength, but experiencing problems.	222
5.12.	Validity pattern A.	223
5.13.	Naïve but open validity configuration.	224
5.14.	Naïve, but non-defensive disturbed configuration.	227
5.15.	Distress in a candid, self-critical person.	228
5.16.	Unusual or paradoxical validity configuration.	229
5.17.	"The college-educated" validity configuration.	230
9.1.	Conversion V.	430
9.2.	Paranoid valley or psychotic V.	431
9.3.	Spike 4 profile.	433
9.4.	Positive or psychotic slope.	434
9.5.	Negative or neurotic slope.	435
9.6.	Passive aggressive V.	436
9.7.	K + profile.	437
9.8.	"Floating" profile.	439
9.9.	26 code pattern.	458

List of Tables

Table		Page
1.1	Item Changes and Deletions and Their Effects on Standard Scales	12
1.2	Original MMPI Items Changed in the MMPI–2	13
1.3	T-Score Equivalents of Percentiles: Ranges of btained Linear and Uniform T (*UT*) Scores	21
1.4	Percentile Equivalents of Uniform T (*UT*) Scores	21
2.1	MMPI–2 *F* – *K* Scores at the Lower and Upper Extremes of Different Diagnostic and Participant Groups	66
3.1	*T*-Score Classifications and Percentile Values	71
5.1	Raw *?* Score Summary	188
5.2	*L* Scale Summary	199
7.1	A Comparison of the Content Contained Within Three Sets of Critical Items	341
7.2	The MMPI–2 Content Scales With Numbers of Items and Patterns of Item Overlap	348
7.3	Item Overlap between MMPI–2 Content and Component Scales and the Wiggins Content Scales	349
7.4	Intercorrelations of Similar MMPI–2 and Wiggins Content Scales for Restandardization Men (and Women)	352
7.5	Similarities and Differences for the MMPI–2 and Wiggins Content Scales	353
9.1	Code Patterns and Associated Stressors	463
9.2	Notes for the Clinical Use of the Goldberg Rules	464
9.3	Mean Goldberg (*N* – *P*) Index Values by Codetype	467
9.4	MMPI–2 Scales and Associated Fear-Conditioned Defensive Responses	474

LIST OF APPENDIX TABLES

A.1	Standard Validity Measures and Other Measures of Response Style	533
A.2	Standard Clinical Scales and Their Derivatives	539
A.3	MPI–2 Content Scales and Content Component Subscales	554
A.4	The Personality Psychopathology Five (PSY–5)	563
A.5	Supplementary Scales	565
A.6	Critical Item Sets	569
B.1	Linear *T*-Score Conversions for Standard Validity Scales and Other Measures of Response Style for Men	578
B.2	Linear *T*-Score Conversions for Standard Validity Scales and Other Measures of Response Style for Women	583
B.3	Uniform and Linear *T*-Score Conversions for Standard Clinical Scales With *K* Corrections	588
B.4	Uniform and Linear *T*-Score Conversions for Standard Clinical Scales Without *K* Corrections	593
B.5	Linear *T*-Score Conversions for Harris–Lingoes Subscales for Men and Women	598
B.6	Linear *T*-Score Conversions for Wiener–Harmon Subtle–Obvious Subscales for Men and Women	606
B.7	Linear *T*-Score Conversions for Finn–Martin Masculinity–Femininity Subscales	609
B.8	Linear *T*-Score Conversions for *Si* Subscales	611
B.9	Uniform *T*-Score Conversions for Content Scales	612

B.10 Uniform *T*-Score Conversions for the Content Component Scales for Men 617

B.11 Uniform *T*-Score Conversions for the Content Component Scales for Women 619

B.12 Linear *T*-Score Conversions for Personality Psychopathology Five (PSY–5) Scales for Men and Women 621

B.13 Linear *T*-Score Conversions for Supplementary Scales for Men 623

B.14 Linear *T*-Score Conversions for Supplementary Scales for Women 627

B.15 *T*-Scores Below 30 for Six MMPI–2 Scales Based on MMPI–2 Normative Data 631

C.1 Item Overlap and Intercorrelations Among the Standard MMPI–2 Validity and Clinical Scales in the Caldwell Clinical Data Set 633

D.1 *K*-Corrected *T*-Score Values for the MMPI–2 Basic Scales Based on the Original Minnesota Normative Group (*N* = 225 Men, 315 Women) 635

D.2 Non-*K*-Corrected *T*-Score Values for the MMPI–2 Basic Scales Based on the Original Minnesota Normative Group (*N* = 225 Men, 315 Women) 639

Foreword

For the student of personality assessment who is taking his or her first look at one of the current versions of the Minnesota Multiphasic Personality Inventory (the MMPI–2 or the MMPI–A [Adolescent]), the task of mastering the relevant background literature and interpretive lore is daunting, to say the least. A beginner facing this challenge is fortunate, indeed, to have in hand the present text. Covering as it does developments in the MMPI over the more than 50-year span from its publication by the University of Minnesota Press in 1942 to its present-day applications in numerous fields of personality appraisal, this volume serves the new student well.

From the first appearance of the MMPI in the form of a box of item cards to be sorted into one of three categories (a version very friendly to the test taker but often burdensome to the clinician), the inventory began to take on descriptive terminology and analytic techniques that became increasingly specialized, much to the chagrin of Starke Hathaway, one of the developers of the MMPI. As the MMPI versions proliferated (during World War II with the very first booklet version, later with newer booklets, and finally even computer-based versions), the task of mastering these concepts became increasingly difficult. The authors of the present volume have imposed order and sense on this array of material for the student new to personality assessment. Until now, it has been hard to find this information in a single source.

While preserving the core of the knowledge derived from the original MMPI, this text also summarizes the rapidly growing literature on the newer versions. Information about new scales as well as about classic profile patterns have been brought together in a manageable format. Thus, the experienced user of these inventories is equally well served by this volume. The busy clinician who needs a summary of recent developments of the MMPI–2 will appreciate the efforts of the authors in tracking down and summarizing new material on the inventory.

—W. Grant Dahlstrom
Kenan Professor of Psychology
University of North Carolina

Foreword

Friedman, Lewak, Nichols, and Webb have done a masterful job of creating an extensively revised and expanded second edition of their guide to the MMPI. With David Nichols added to the distinguished team of authors, the text introduces many new topics and issues, includes fuller descriptions of the clinical, content, and supplementary scales, and incorporates 245 new references. It will certainly be useful as a reference for MMPI–2 beginners, but it will also be of strong interest to researchers and experienced clinicians attempting to maximize their MMPI–2 informational yields.

Readers will find all of the basic and essential information expected in this type of guide book. The authors provide an important series of clear administration guidelines and a thorough review of the literature on administration. They describe all of the numerous MMPI–2 scales; their summaries of the complex literature on these scales are outstanding. They provide code pattern look-up tables that include treatment recommendations for numerous two- and three-point configurations based on a balanced combination of empirical evidence and their own extensive clinical expertise. In addition, they give crucial "hands-on" information about the validity scales for the MMPI–2, including such new scales as the *F*(*p*) scale. The text consistently suggests recommended cut-off scores for each validity scale, and offers guidance on the often confusing and ambiguous cut-off issue. It also includes two new chapters on the MMPI–2 content scales (chap. 7) and the MMPI–2 supplementary scales (chap. 8). Readers will appreciate the authors' detailed guidance on psychological report writing and the integration of test findings, their fair and well-balanced discussion of the controversial question of the extent to which research findings and clinical data derived from the MMPI can be generalized to the MMPI–2, and their sound and thoughtful feedback strategy for clinicians providing clients with test information. This attention to feedback issues helped distinguish the authors' 1989 text, and their MMPI–2 treatment is considerably more refined.

Moving beyond the basic and essential information, Friedman and his colleagues address a variety of clinicians' and researchers' special concerns. For example, they take frequent opportunities to comment on potential forensic applications of MMPI–2 data, especially the interpretation of validity scales in determining protocol validity. They also present detailed appendices with the means, standard deviations, item composition, and *T*-score conversions for all of the useful MMPI–2 scales, and numerous tables and graphs illustrating various profiles likely to be encountered in a clinical setting. They offer a rich and balanced overview of four adult computer interpretation reports, which is complimented by the complete reproduction of these report products. Chapter notes enable the interested reader to delve more deeply into the topic area (e.g., the information on translations available for the MMPI–2).

In summary, Friedman, Lewak, Nichols, and Webb have created an invaluable and comprehensive guide for the MMPI–2. Their magisterial overview balances a researcher's need for extensive references and detailed information with a clinician's need for usable strategies and approaches. *Psychological Assessment With the MMPI–2* is an important addition to the libraries of all those individuals who wish to use the MMPI–2 for clinical purposes, research investigations, and in forensic assessment settings.

—Robert P. Archer
Eastern Virginia Medical School

Preface

Recent research findings coupled with the important changes to the Minnesota Multiphasic Personality Inventory (MMPI) necessitated the rewriting of this book. Our original text came out in the Summer of 1989, about the same time the MMPI–2 was published by the University of Minnesota Press. From a timing standpoint, this was a frustrating coincidence for us as authors; although aware of the MMPI–2's imminent publication, we did not expect to contemplate a revision of our textbook as soon as we did. It was immediately apparent on the publication of the MMPI–2 that the restandardization committee had produced a useful improvement over the original instrument, an achievement to be applauded and appreciated. Following several years of new work with the MMPI–2, we set out to rewrite our original text, recruiting a fourth colleague, incorporating the modifications to the original MMPI, and including new interpretative information, such as treatment recommendations and new validity considerations. This was no small task as the research literature on the MMPI–2 quickly swelled. The continuing expansion of the MMPI–2 into the forensic arena since the publication of our original book also motivated us to include more information about self-favorable and self-unfavorable responding in medicolegal contexts.

The original MMPI, although familiar as an old friend, has grown to a new level of maturity while retaining its original character and integrity. The addition of extensive descriptive correlates for the validity, clinical, and various supplementary and additional scales distinguishes this edition from its predecessor. Additionally, readers will notice in the appendices expanded coverage of scales, including psychometric data for the restandardization normative sample across a variety of scales.

This book has two broad purposes. The first is to provide beginning MMPI–2 users with a basic understanding of the construction and application of the test. The second is to provide more experienced MMPI/MMPI–2 users with a reference guide that will be useful in applied practice. In the service of these purposes, the book covers a broad range of material. Some readers may elect to use only the Code-Pattern Look-Up Table, which provides psychological descriptions of various MMPI–2 patterns. Others may use the book to assist in their personality assessment report writing or in their research efforts. Our desire was to bridge the gap between books reviewing the important research literature and books explaining the rich clinical wisdom that many professionals bring to the task of interpreting MMPI–2 profiles.

The reader should note that when we discuss the original MMPI, the term *MMPI* is used; when we discuss information or concepts that are applicable to both the MMPI and the MMPI–2, the term *MMPI–2* is used. The reader should also note that, wherever possible, the term *code pattern* has replaced the traditional term *codetype* (e.g., Code-Pattern Look-Up Table).

ACKNOWLEDGMENTS

Several people extended themselves to us for this edition and without whose assistance and generosity this book would not have been possible. Roger Greene, our friend and colleague, was always available to provide his insight and thoughts about our material and unflinchingly gave of his time for the production of tables and appendix information, as well as clarification of many important issues. Roger epitomizes the concept and practice of collegiality. Goldine Gleser lent her scholarly ear and hand in discussing key statistical issues and assisted in much of the *T*-score discussion in the text. Her encouragement, wisdom, and support were as steadfast for this text as it was for the first edition. Auke Tellegen reviewed much of the *T*-score material, and his comments and friendship throughout this project will always be valued. Bob Colligan's interest and assistance in the accurate production of various normative data enhance the utility of this text; his sharing of critical material is much appreciated. Beverly Kaemmer at the University of Minnesota Press was patient and helpful in granting the permission requests, and her knowledge and expertise with the MMPI–2 was again invaluable in the writing of this text. Alex Caldwell answered many questions throughout this project, and his clinical wisdom and penetrating insights into the test enhanced our understanding of many important psychometric and clinical issues. Steve Rothke and Phil Marks provided support and valuable discussion, and their interest throughout this project is greatly valued. Alan Jaffe's understanding of personality dynamics and psychotherapy greatly enriched the quality of the clinical discussion in this text and his comradeship was of immense importance to me. Steve Weiss, my former professor and current colleague and close friend, has been a source of continued support throughout this project and beyond, and I have the deepest gratitude for him. Steve Patt's wise counsel and friendship are held in the highest regard. Cindy Wiertel typed and helped edit most of the manuscript, and her patience and persistence contributed to the completion of this book. Linda Rock contributed her skills and time in editing portions of this text; her efforts are greatly appreciated. Grant Dahlstrom was always available to discuss any questions we had during the rewriting of this text, and his expertise and scholarliness have always been, and will always be, treasured. We thank the University of Minnesota Press, National Computer Systems, Inc., the American Psychological Association,

Psychological Assessment Resources, and Western Psychological Services for their permission to reproduce various materials important in the making of this book.

Finally, I wish to express my gratitude to Richard Pechter for his friendship, guidance, and support over the years.

—Alan F. Friedman, PhD
Chicago

1

Development of the MMPI and MMPI–2

GENERAL DESCRIPTION OF THE MMPI/MMPI–2

The Minnesota Multiphasic Personality Inventory (MMPI) is the most widely used objective personality inventory in the world (Greene, 2000; Lubin, Larsen, & Matarazzo, 1984; Lubin, Larsen, Matarazzo, & Seever, 1985). Even from its beginnings, the MMPI has enjoyed popularity and has been ranked as a leading personality instrument (Archer, 1997). Taught in the majority of clinical psychology training programs (Dahlstrom & Moreland, 1983; Watkins, 1991), the test is used by most psychologists who conduct assessments as part of their clinical and consulting practice (Dahlstrom, 1992b; Moreland & Dahlstrom, 1983). The MMPI has also been the subject of extensive research interest. According to Butcher and Owen (1978), 84% of the research in the personality inventory domain has been with the MMPI. The test has been the undisputed leader in the number of test references produced each year (Reynolds & Sundberg, 1976), and Dahlstrom, Welsh, and Dahlstrom (1975) listed close to 6,000 MMPI references in their *MMPI Handbook*. More recently, an examination of the *Eleventh Mental Measurements Yearbook*, published in 1992, reveals 2,913 published refereed MMPI journal articles since the last published review in the 1978 *Yearbook*, an average of about 4 MMPI articles per week for 14 years! Butcher (1987b) counted over 10,000 books and articles produced on the test, and that estimate is certainly higher now given the continued pace of publications.

The widespread use of this test is attributable to several factors, including its simplicity of scoring and administration, an objective response format important for research designs, a large item pool (from which at least 800 additional scales have been derived), many useful applications, and thousands of empirically established correlates. In fact, it is difficult to imagine many settings in which psychologists perform assessment and treatment functions where the MMPI has not been used. Inpatient and outpatient mental health facilities often employ psychologists to make diagnostic and treatment decisions, and the MMPI is typically included in psychological test batteries or even administered independently. Many clinical practitioners routinely use the MMPI to screen new patients in their office practice for maladjustment and to help formulate treatment plans. Psychologists use the test in medical settings to evaluate the presence of psychological components in physical complaints and to assist in predicting response to various treatments (Osborne, 1979).

Industrial-organizational and clinical psychologists, whose responsibilities involve matching individuals to particular employment positions or screening individuals for psychopathology, also use the MMPI. For example, because the MMPI is sensitive to emotional maladjustment in individuals other than identified patient groups, it is often used in personnel selection situations in which high-risk occupations require careful screening of applicants. People in positions of public trust, such as airline flight crews, law enforcement officers, nursing staff, ministerial candidates, and nuclear power plant operators, are typically administered the MMPI (Butcher, 1979). Research applications with the MMPI, either as the sole subject of study or as one of the major dependent measures in an investigation, range from cross-cultural studies of response patterns to evaluating treatment effects to making forensic decisions (Friedman, Webb, & Lewak, 1989; Rothke & Friedman, 1994; Rothke et al., 1994).

The original MMPI consists of 566 numbered statements,[1] each of which can be answered true or false on an answer sheet, or, in the original card deck form, the test takers sort their responses into "T" for true, "F" for false, or Cannot Say categories. An item is scored as Cannot Say if it is marked both true and false on the answer sheet, left blank, or sorted into the Cannot Say category in the card deck form.

There are several methods for scoring a completed test. The answer sheet is either hand scored or read by a special scanner machine. Some MMPI users enter the responses from the answer sheet into a computer that is programmed to score, and sometimes to interpret, the test. More recently, some test takers enter their responses using a keyboard directly into a computer, which instantly scores the test.

For the original MMPI thirteen standard scales are scored, regardless of the scoring method. The following are the original 3 validity scales and 10 *standard* clinical scales. Note that the convention adopted here is that the eight scales numbered 1–4 and 6–9 will be referred to as the *basic* clinical scales or, more simply, as the *basic scales*. When speaking of the entire set of clinical scales given on the main profile form, including Masculinity–Femininity (*Mf*, or Scale 5) and Social Introversion (*Si*, or Scale 0), we refer to the *standard clinical scales* or more simply, the *standard scales*.

VALIDITY SCALES

Lie (*L*)
Infrequency (*F*)
Correction (*K*)

CLINICAL SCALES

Scale 1 Hypochondriasis (*Hs*)
Scale 2 Depression (*D*)
Scale 3 Hysteria (*Hy*)
Scale 4 Psychopathic Deviate (*Pd*)
Scale 5 Masculinity–Femininity (*Mf*)
Scale 6 Paranoia (*Pa*)
Scale 7 Psychasthenia (*Pt*)
Scale 8 Schizophrenia (*Sc*)
Scale 9 Hypomania (*Ma*)
Scale 0 Social Introversion (*Si*)

The validity scales were developed to assist in recognizing test records produced by uncooperative or deceptive participants with various test-taking attitudes (e.g., faking good or faking bad) or participants who had difficulty comprehending or reading the test items. The clinical scales were developed primarily to assist in identifying the type and severity of abnormal psychiatric conditions. A secondary goal was to provide an objective means of estimating therapeutic effects and other changes in the status of patients' conditions across time (Dahlstrom, Welsh, & Dahlstrom, 1972). The raw scores on each of the validity and clinical scales are converted to *T* scores by plotting them onto a profile sheet, thereby yielding a series of comparable scores. It is the pattern of these scale scores that is usually interpreted. The *T* scores provide the clinician an opportunity to examine how the test taker compares to different populations, including, most importantly, a standardized group of normal individuals. A more detailed description of *T* scores is provided later in this chapter.

HISTORICAL DEVELOPMENT OF THE MMPI

In an important historical overview of the MMPI, W. Grant Dahlstrom (1992b), summarized a series of studies by C. Landis and his colleagues at the New York State Psychiatric Institute in the 1930s (Landis & Katz, 1934; Landis, Zubin, & Katz, 1935; Page, Landis, & Katz, 1934; see also Greene, 1980, 2000); these studies strongly reinforced the skepticism at that time of professionals relying on personality testing as an aid in assessment and diagnosis because the existing personality tests, according to Landis, lacked validity. Specifically, those objective tests relied on individuals' willingness and capacity to accurately report their feelings and experiences and also depended on their reading and intellectual ability to comprehend the inventory. These concerns sensitized clinicians to the need for improving the validity of objective personality tests.

Despite the tenor of the times, or perhaps because of it, Starke R. Hathaway and J. C. McKinley teamed up to develop a new inventory capable of overcoming the limitations inherent in the existing personality tests. Hathaway, a clinically experienced physiological psychologist, and McKinley, a neuropsychiatrist, both at the Medical School at the University of Minnesota, were joined in their later efforts by Paul E. Meehl, also a psychologist. Hathaway and McKinley were originally motivated to design a test that could serve as an aid "in diagnosing persons classified as constitutional psychopathic inferiors" (Hathaway, 1939, p. 117); assist "in assessing the psychological factors associated with physical problems or disease seen in a medical practice" (McKinley & Hathaway, 1943, p. 161); and as a corollary, "measure the effectiveness of insulin therapy" (Hathaway, 1964, p. 204) in schizophrenia, which was in widespread use by the late 1930s. The test also came to be seen as an aid in determining levels of psychiatric impairment and changes in the patients' condition over time, as well as in measuring the effects of psychotherapy (Dahlstrom et al., 1972).

Although the MMPI was originally published in 1942 (David S. Nichols, personal communication, January 13, 2000) by the University of Minnesota Press, the authors actually began their work on the test in the late 1930s. There were several subsequent revisions of the MMPI manual through 1983. Colligan, Osborne, Swenson, and Offord (1989) reported that the first article describing the inception of the MMPI was provided by Hathaway and McKinley in a 1940 publication entitled "A Multiphasic Personality Schedule (Minnesota): I. Construction of the Schedule." Hathaway and McKinley strove to correct many of the problems hampering the effectiveness of previously existing personality inventories. Previous personality inventories were constructed using a rational basis with a focus on content validity, and lacked scales designed to measure the participant's test-taking attitude (e.g., defensiveness or overreporting of symptoms). An example of one such psychological inventory is the Woodworth (1920) Personal Data Sheet, also called the Psychoneurotic Inventory. World War I created a strong need to screen for maladjustment among draftees, and Woodworth developed a 116-item self-rating scale to detect neurotic maladjustment. The items consisted of statements that Woodworth believed reflected neurotic symptoms. If a participant answered a certain number of items in the deviant direction, a psychiatric interview was conducted. A fundamental assumption inherent in the test was that the items measured what Woodworth assumed they measured. Items were chosen on rational grounds; that is, if the items appeared content-relevant to neuroticism, they were included in the scale. Over time, it became clear that items selected on a rational basis did not always indicate deviant behavior in the way Woodworth expected. Another unwarranted assumption in the Woodworth Personal Data Sheet, and similar tests, was that the participant would, and could, honestly and accurately describe him- or herself. This is not always the case; self-deception and social desirability factors operate to influence the person's responses to test items. Although the Woodworth Personal Data Sheet was not completed early enough to allow its use before World War I ended, it did set the stage for other similarly constructed inventories that achieved widespread use after the war (Anastasi, 1982). The Bell (1934) Adjustment Inventory and the Bernreuter (1933) Personality Inventory were derived from the Woodworth Personal Data Sheet and were also criticized for their excessive reliance on a rational approach to test construction and for the face valid nature of the test items (Colligan et al., 1989).

Because of Hathaway's reservations about the rational approach to inventory construction, he used an empirical method (the criterion keying method) to construct the MMPI. As Anastasi (1982) noted, the MMPI represents the outstanding example of this test construction methodology. In this method, test items are administered to two or more groups of participants—a criterion group selected for homogeneity with respect to a certain diagnosis, cluster of features, traits, or other characteristics (e.g., schizophrenia) and a normal comparison group that does not share the same characteristics or shares them only in base-rate amounts. Items to which the criterion and comparison groups respond differently are included on the scale being developed, and items to which the responses of the two groups are similar are not included. Scales constructed in this fashion are typically named after the criterion group. Scoring the scales is accomplished by assigning 1 point to each item answered in the direction that is marked significantly more frequently by the criterion participant; that is, if a higher proportion of individuals with hysteria than normals answered true to an item, a response of true to that item would be given 1 point on the Hysteria scale, and a response of false would be given 0 points. The higher the raw score a person receives on a scale, the more items he or she has answered in the direction of the criterion group.

Using this criterion keying method, Hathaway and McKinley began their construction of the MMPI by compiling more than 1,000 self-reference statements from a wide variety of sources, including psychiatric examination forms, psychiatric textbooks, previously published attitude and personality scales, clinical reports and case summaries, and their own clinical experience.[2] From these resources, they eventually adopted an item pool of 550 separate statements that could be answered true or false.[3] The statements were judged to be easily readable, and ranged in content from phobias, religious attitudes, and general health to social attitudes and affects (Dahlstrom et al., 1972). Using this pool of 550 items, Hathaway and McKinley proceeded to construct scales by contrasting the responses of normal and clinical criterion groups.

The normal reference group consisted of 724 friends and relatives of patients being seen at the University of Minnesota Hospital outpatient department who were willing to complete the test. The normals were all White, belonged to what was termed "the underprivileged" classes, and came from all parts of Minnesota (McKinley & Hathaway, 1940). According to Dahlstrom and Welsh (1960), "the subjects were approached in the halls and in waiting rooms of the hospital, and invited to participate in the research project" (p. 44). Additional normal and patient groups consisted of high school graduates attending pre-college conferences at the University of Minnesota (n = 265), medical patients from the University of Minnesota Hospital (n = 254), skilled Work Project Administration (WPA) personnel (n = 265), and inpatients with varied diagnoses in the psychiatric unit (then called the Psychopathic Unit) at the University of Minnesota Hospital (n = 221). Normal participants (other than the medical patients) who were then under the care of a physician were excluded from the normative samples; all other participants were included. Dahlstrom et al. (1972) pointed out the importance of the normal reference groups by stating that

> the performance of these men and women on each of the component scales in the MMPI is used as the basis for the norms in the test profile. Each subject taking the MMPI, therefore, is being compared to the way a typical man or woman endorsed

> those items. In 1940, such a Minnesota normal adult was about 35 years old, was married, lived in a small town or rural area, had had eight years of general schooling, and worked at a skilled or semiskilled trade (or was married to a man with such an occupational level). (pp. 7–8)

Hathaway and McKinley found their original sample of normals to correspond well in age, gender, and marital status to the Minnesota population in the 1930s census (Dahlstrom, et al. 1972).[4] However, it is now generally accepted that "the original MMPI norm group appears to have over-represented lower educational and occupational groups" (Dahlstrom, 1993, p. 9). We address this important limitation later in this chapter.

The clinical criterion (abnormal) groups consisted of carefully selected psychiatric patients and participants representing the following major diagnostic categories: hypochondriasis, depression, conversion hysteria, psychopathy, paranoia, psychasthenia, schizophrenia, and hypomania. Two other groups were later added to develop two additional scales for the MMPI. One of these groups consisted of normal college women used to develop a Social Introversion scale (*Si*), and the other group consisted of "homosexual invert males" (Hathaway, 1956/1980, p. 110) used to develop the Masculinity–Femininity scale (*Mf*).

Very shortly after the MMPI gained widespread acceptance, criticisms were made regarding the narrowness of the original standardization group used to obtain normal values for the scales. The 724 normals who were recruited as participants while accompanying patients to the hospital consisted of Whites, disproportionately of Scandinavian, German, and Irish descent, who were almost exclusively from the Minnesota, North Dakota, South Dakota, Iowa, and Wisconsin areas. Nichols (1992b) stated that "the phrase 'Minnesota farmers' became the standard term of opprobrium for this largely rural, eighth-grade-educated skilled or semi-skilled northern Midwestern group of Scandinavian origins" (p. 562). The generalizability of such norms to other areas of the country was repeatedly questioned, and the implications of such limited norms have been well described by Pancoast and Archer (1989). In general, normal groups that have taken the MMPI since its original publication have typically scored about 0.5 *SD*s (5 *T*-score points) above the mean, causing test users to have to downwardly calibrate the scores of most normals so as to avoid overinterpreting or overpathologizing their test results. Pancoast and Archer combined various MMPI samples for normal men and women from over 5 decades to demonstrate the inadequacy of the original norms. Their data demonstrate the relative elevation of all other normal samples above the mean of the original normals. Their results also suggest that the scores of normals subsequent to those used in the original standardization generally have not changed across 5 decades of MMPI use, which when considered along with the relative elevation, underscores the fact that the original norms were not an adequate representation of the U.S. population.[5]

Colligan and his colleagues (Colligan, Osborne, Swenson, & Offord, 1983; Colligan et al., 1989), at the Mayo Clinic in Rochester, Minnesota, attempted to provide more contemporary and accurate norms than those provided by the original group of normals. Colligan et al. (1983) tested a contemporary sample of normal individuals in rural Minnesota to compare the results with the original standardization group. In a critique of their work, Greene (1985) noted important differences between the mean scores on the standard MMPI scales for their contemporary and original samples, generally ranging from 1 to 6 *T*-score points.[6]

Colligan and his colleagues have provided norms for a variety of scales in addition to the basic validity and clinical scales, including Wiggins' (1966) content scales (Colligan & Offord, 1988), Barron's (1953) Ego Strength scale (Colligan & Offord, 1987b), and MacAndrew's (1965) Alcoholism scale (Colligan & Offord, 1987a). Although their norms have not been widely adopted, their efforts further sensitized other MMPI researchers to the need for contemporary norms. Readers interested in using the Colligan et al. data can do so by referring to their useful text (Colligan et al., 1989) containing numerous conversion tables that compare the old norms with their contemporary sample. Readers using their norms, however, must remember that their sampling is not representative of the U.S. population. For a more representative national sample of the nation, the reader is advised to use the recently restandardized MMPI, which will soon be described.

The expansion of the MMPI into settings such as general medicine, forensic and child custody evaluations, outpatient psychotherapy, assessment of disability, and personnel screening has accentuated the inadequacy of the original norms. It appears that the original normals reflected a fixed reference group rather than a true normative sample, and practical implications of such a major deficiency are important to consider. For example, because so-called normals would score slightly higher on the test, they were vulnerable to being "screened out" of sensitive employment positions (e.g., flight crew or nuclear power plant operators) where strict cutoff scores (*T* score above 70) were used. Another problem in the use of the original normal groups was the double duty they were forced to perform. That is, although the item responses by the normals provided the needed contrast for the original criterion groups on which the MMPI clinical scales were developed, this use made the normals inappropriate for the establishment of test norms:

> By making the Minnesota normals serve as both a source of contrast for pathological samples and the reference for normative standards, the latter function was compromised. Forcing the normals to perform this double duty, in effect, purged them of their normal levels of abnormality. (Nichols, 1992b, p. 562; see also Pancoast & Archer, 1989)

By not using a new sample of normals to establish the normative standard, Hathaway and McKinley introduced a serious constructional deficiency in the design of the test.[7] The importance of proper cross-validation is well recognized, but the test constructors did not cross-validate the original keying of items (Helmes & Reddon, 1993). An important consequence of omitting a cross-validation sample involves the basic metric or measurement unit that the MMPI uses to indicate deviation from the norm. Dahlstrom and Tellegen (1993) stated,

> The effect of such an omission would be to anchor the T-score values on each of the basic scales *too low* and to employ a T-score unit that was *too short*, because the

> standard deviations would be artificially small on these scales. The impact of inappropriate anchoring and scaling on the scales of the MMPI would be to introduce an excess of false positive scores (i.e., some individuals who are not pathological would earn significantly elevated *T*-scores on one or more of the profile scales. (p. 3)

Another factor that seems to have slightly affected the original MMPI norms relates to the frequency of omitted items by the original normals. Pancoast and Archer (1989) reported a high rate of item omissions (14 items for men and 15 items for women) as calculated from the item endorsement frequencies presented by Dahlstrom and Welsh (1960). The original MMPI test instructions permitted participants to omit items, whereas later users of the test discouraged such omissions. Later samples of adult normals probably reflect an increased compliance with these later instructions, given that participants omit very few items (e.g., Clopton & Neuringer, 1977). The effects on the original norms from item omissions is estimated to have lowered mean *T* scores by about 1 *T*-score point (Pancoast & Archer, 1989). This would still leave about a 4-*T*-score-point difference, on average, between the subsequent groups of normals and the original group, thereby supporting the idea that the original normals were atypical of the general population. Regarding the new sample of contemporary normals assembled for the restandardization of the MMPI, Dahlstrom and Tellegen (1993) stated that

> it is possible that the adults in the MMPI–2 re-standardization samples were more willing to give definitive answers to the component items in the inventory than was the case in the original normative groups. If so, this effect would also serve to raise the raw scores and lower the T-scores in the norms for the MMPI–2. (p. 3)

Finally, the decision to exclude from the normal sample anyone "under a physician's care" may have contributed to the sample's problematic nature. As Nichols (1992b) pointed out, this criterion was not operative in the revision of the MMPI leading to the MMPI–2. Excluding all participants under a physician's care introduces more atypicality into the original normal group.

In addition to inappropriate and obsolete norms, other internal problems affected contemporary use of the MMPI. Many items had become outdated and difficult to understand or were objectionable to individuals completing the test. For example, many test takers found some items pertaining to bodily functions to be intrusive or offensive (e.g., "I have had no difficulty in starting or holding my bowel movements"). Many items asking test takers about their religious beliefs (e.g., "I believe there is a God") were also experienced as offensive by some people. The need to modernize the language (e.g., eliminate sexist language) or improve the grammar in many items has also long been recognized. Another complaint voiced by some test takers referred to the 16 repeated items (Gallucci, 1986); these test takers were irked by their perception that these items were put into the test to entrap them (actually the items were repeated to facilitate early machine scoring).

A problem invisible to test takers but noticeable to test interpreters was the lack of percentile equivalency across the linear *T* distributions for the standard scales, thereby making it difficult to make percentile inferences from scale elevations

(Caldwell, 1991; Tellegen & BenPorath, 1992; Ward, 1991). The need for a means to directly compare scores across different scales was evident but was not appropriate with the original MMPI (see *"Uniform T Scores"* later in this chapter for a more detailed explanation of *T* scores).

Finally, the last reason for revising the MMPI stemmed from the need to revitalize the existing item pool by introducing items and scales that reflect more current diagnostic and therapeutic concerns (Duckworth, 1991a). For example, items relevant to substance abuse, family functioning, readiness for treatment or rehabilitation, and one's ability to return to work were needed. Additionally, scales that could augment the existing validity scales in detecting unreliable and invalid profiles would enhance the usefulness of the instrument. Toward all these ends, the MMPI restandardization project was initiated.

MMPI RESTANDARDIZATION: THE MMPI–2

The project to restandardize the MMPI began in 1982, and the MMPI–2 was published in 1989, along with new test materials that consisted of hand-scoring templates, new answer and profile sheets, new test booklets, and different computer-scoring options, all of which are described in chapter 3.[8] A new MMPI–2 test manual was also published (Butcher et al., 1989, p. 1). It describes the MMPI–2 as "a broad-band test designed to assess a number of the major patterns of personality and emotional disorders."[9] The MMPI–2, which is the first revision of the test since its original publication in 1942, is intended for use with adults aged 18 and older.[10]

The MMPI–2 is not intended for use with adolescents. It was recognized by the MMPI–2 committee that adult norms would not be applicable to an adolescent form (Archer, 1984, 1987, 1988, 1997). A separate revision of the test was conducted for the sole purpose of developing an adolescent instrument derived from the MMPI–2 and was named the MMPI–A (Adolescent).[11] The test was released in 1992. A normative sample representative of the general teenage population was recognized as important for standardizing the MMPI–A, and a shorter version of the test was also considered to be an improvement given that the basic validity and clinical scales were essentially uncompromised. The MMPI–A manual contains detailed information on this instrument (Butcher et al., 1992). Readers seeking a comprehensive treatment of the MMPI–A may consult Robert Archer's *MMPI–A: Assessing Adolescent Psychopathology* (2nd ed.).[12]

The 478-item MMPI–A is intended for adolescents between the ages of 14 and 18, although some individuals who are less than 14 years old can be administered the MMPI–A if they possess the necessary reading level and comprehension abilities, as well as the necessary tolerance and willingness to complete a lengthy inventory. Archer's (1997) textbook should be consulted for administration guidelines for adolescents using the MMPI–A. Because the adolescent norms include 18-year-olds, a clinician who is testing an 18-year-old could use either the adolescent or the adult versions of the MMPI. A general rule as to which test to administer involves assessing characteristics such as the person's reading level and ability, as well as whether the adolescent is living at home. In general, if the 18-year-old is living outside of the home and working or attending college, the adult version of the test is indicated, whereas if the person is not emancipated from his or her home environment, the MMPI–A should be considered.

To summarize, the MMPI–2 restandardization project ensured continuity with the original MMPI by minimizing changes in the composition of the original validity and clinical scales (Archer, 1997). This meant leaving the *K*-correction factor intact. A contemporary sample of normals replaced earlier outdated norms with new clinical data collected concurrently to assess the validity of new and modified scales. Items were replaced or modified in accordance with the mission of modernizing the language in the test (BenPorath & Butcher, 1989). New scales were created in order to measure contemporary clinical problems, and for this reason new items replaced many rarely scored or obsolete items. An improved metric replaced linear *T* scores to allow test interpreters to more accurately compare scale scores with each other.

It appears that the restandardization project was successful in meeting its goal of maintaining continuity with the original test. Despite initial concerns about the MMPI–2 revision, practitioners generally have adopted the modified test. In a survey of the entire membership of the Society of Personality Assessment regarding its use of the MMPI–2, Webb, Levitt, and Rojdev (1993) found a significant adoption of the MMPI–2 since its publication, with a trend they interpreted as suggesting that the majority of practitioners would be using the instrument within 6 months of their survey. Indeed, it does appear that the majority of individuals are taking advantage of the changes offered by the MMPI–2 (BenPorath, 1993).

EXPERIMENTAL FORM (AX) AND THE MMPI–2 BOOKLET

An experimental booklet (Form AX) was developed for the purpose of testing a new group of normal participants and was the basis for developing the new MMPI–2 booklet. Form AX included all 550 original MMPI items followed by an additional 154 new experimental items.[13] The restandardization committee identified several items that required modification to improve clarity. Eighty-two of the original MMPI items were rewritten for Form AX in order to improve or modernize their language and were empirically studied by BenPorath and Butcher (1989) to assess the psychometric impact of the modifications. These authors administered Form AX to college students along with the original MMPI 1 week later (in a counterbalanced design) to determine the effects of the item changes. They also administered the original test twice to a separate group of participants to serve as a baseline for comparison purposes. Although there were some minor shifts in item endorsements (only nine items), "no significant changes were noted among items rewritten due to sexist language, minor rewording, grammatical changes, ambiguous items, or religious content" (BenPorath & Butcher, 1989, p. 650). Their data also showed that no item–scale correlations changed significantly as a result of rewriting the items. In effect, they found that they could improve the face validity of many items without unduly affecting the operating characteristics of the scales. Ultimately, 14 of the 82 rewritten items were eliminated, leaving 68 of the empirically studied items intact in the final MMPI–2 booklet. It should also be noted that 47 of the 154 experimental items in Form AX did not survive into the final MMPI–2 booklet (Nichols, 1992b).

The MMPI–2 booklet also dropped the 16 repeated items originally contained in the MMPI (Buechley & Ball, 1952; Friedman et al., 1989a). Often used as a measure for test response consistency (the test–retest [TR] index), these repeated items were replaced with a new scale named the Variable Response Inconsistency scale (*VRIN*) designed to assess inconsistent responding. This scale is described in chapter 2.

The basic validity and clinical scales were essentially unaffected by item deletions, even though 13 items were eliminated from the following clinical and validity scales: 4 items were deleted from the *F* scale, 1 item was deleted from Scale 1 (*Hs*), 3 items were deleted from Scale 2 (*D*), 4 items were deleted from Scale 5 (*Mf*), and 1 item was deleted from Scale 0 (*Si*). Table 1.1 allows the reader to inspect the MMPI–2 changes and deletions and their effects on the standard scales. Table 1.2 illustrates examples of item modifications in the MMPI–2.

The restandardization committee decided that many original MMPI items that were not scored on any basic validity or clinical scale should be eliminated and replaced with newer items that would allow additional scales to be constructed. Therefore, 77 items contained in the last 167 items on the MMPI were dropped and replaced with 89 items intended for use with new scales (Greene, 1991a). The total number of items in the MMPI–2 is 567 (1 item more than the original test), and 21 of the items are so-called nonworking or nonscored items, that is, items not scored on any of the scales listed in the MMPI–2 manual (Butcher et al., 1989). These extra items were included as "possible replacements for problematic items or as enhancements to the existing item pool" (Dahlstrom, 1993, p. 3).

The reader is reminded that it was the 704-item Form AX that was administered to the sample of normal participants in the restandardization project. Although the revised item pool in the MMPI–2 is considered a definite improvement by most test users, the revision is not without its critics. Nichols (1992b) stated,

> Although the new items expand clinically important areas of content like substance abuse, marital relations, and suicide, their phrasings do not always reflect the smooth, worn quality of common speech. The three new suicide statements, for example, employ the fixed operative expression, "kill(ing) myself," in preference to more varied and less violent locutions like "want to die," "end it all," "commit suicide," "get it over with." Most of the hundreds of scales developed from the original item pool are relatively intact unless they included significant religious content or were drawn mainly from the last 200 items of the original MMPI. In order to be scored, however, the older keys must be translated into MMPI–2 item numbers, a process aided by an appendix in the manual (Butcher, Dahlstrom, Graham, Tellegen, & Kaemmer, 1989). (p. 563)

The loss of certain items in the MMPI–2 booklet has affected, as noted by Nichols (1992a, 1992b), some special scales that were used in the original test. Some of the affected scales are discussed in chapter 8, where the supplementary scales are described in detail. Readers interested in more detailed information about

TABLE 1.1
Item Changes and Deletions and Their Effects on Standard Scales

	Number of Items			*Types of Changes*			
Scale	*Deleted*	*Remaining*	*Changed*	*A*	*B*	*C*	*D*
L		15	2	1	1		
F	4	60	12	1	5	6	
K		30	1		1		
Hs	1	32	5		1	3	1
D	3	57	2	1	1		
Hy		60	9		4	2	3
Pd		50	4		2	1	1
Mf	4	56	6	1	2	1	2
Pa		40	2	1			1
Pt		48	2			1	1
Sc		78	13		1	7	5
Ma		46	7	4	2	1	
Si	1	69	6		3	2	1
Not on any basic scale			16	3	7	3	3

Note. A = elimination of possibly sexist wording; B = modernization of idioms and usage; C = grammatical clarification (tense, voice, minor additions, and deletions); D = simplifications.

From *Minnesota Multiphasic Personality Inventory–2 Manual for Administration and Scoring* (p. 8), by J. N. Butcher, W. G. Dahlstrom, J. R. Graham, A. Tellegen, & B. Kaemmer, 1989, Minneapolis: University of Minnesota Press.

MMPI–2 item characteristics are encouraged to consult Dahlstrom's (1993) supplement to the MMPI–2 manual.

NEW NORMATIVE SAMPLE

The most significant change in the MMPI–2 is the replacement of the earlier outdated norms. The MMPI–2 norms are based on the responses of 2,600 adults (1,462 women and 1,138 men) between the ages of 18 and 84 who were paid volunteers recruited by a variety of methods, including newspaper advertisements and random mailing solicitations from directories and advertising lists (Butcher et al., 1989). Initially, approximately 2,900 participants were tested, but the following participants were eliminated: those who omitted 40 or more of the 704 items in

Form AX or those who had a very high score on the *F* scale (20 or more) or a high score on a new "back page" *F* scale, called the *F*-Back (F_B), which was designed for Form AX (the *F*-back scale is described in chap. 2). Participants who did not provide adequate biographical information or omitted other informational forms were also excluded from the final sample. The 2,600 participants were selected from the following seven states: California, Minnesota, North Carolina, Ohio, Pennsylvania, Virginia, and Washington. A small proportion of the sample also included participants selected from military bases and a federal Indian Reservation. Heterosexual couples (823 men, 832 women) were included in the sample and were administered collateral data that included a measure of significant recent life changes (which the total sample completed) and an instrument designed to measure

TABLE 1.2

Original MMPI Items Changed in the MMPI–2

MMPI Item Number	*MMPI Contents*	*Scale Scored On*	*MMPI–2 Item No.*	*MMPI–2 Contents*
17	My father was a good man.	F, Sc	6	My father is a good man, or (if your father is dead) my father was a good man.
29	I am bothered by acid stomach several times a week.	Hs	28	I am bothered by an upset stomach several times a week.
83	Any man who is able and willing to work hard has a good chance of succeeding.	F	108	Anyone who is able and willing to work hard has a good chance of succeeding.
250	I don't blame anyone for trying to grab everything he can get in this world.	Ma	227	I don't blame people for trying to grab everything they can get in this world.
304	In school I found it very hard to talk before the class.	Pt, Si	275	In school I found it very hard to talk in front of the class.
410	I would certainly enjoy beating a crook at his own game.		406	I would certainly enjoy beating criminals at their own game.
466	Except by a doctor's orders I never take drugs or sleeping powders.		429	Except by doctor's orders I never take drugs or sleeping pills.

Note. From *Manual Supplement: The Items in the MMPI–2: Alterations in Wording, Patterns of Interrelationship, and Changes in Endorsements* (pp. 20–28), by W. G. Dahlstrom, 1993, Minneapolis: University of Minnesota Press. "MMPI–2" and "Minnesota Multiphasic Personality Inventory–2" are trademarks owned by the University of Minnesota. Reprinted with permission.

their perception of their partner or spouse and their level of relationship satisfaction (Butcher et al., 1989).

The ethnic diversity of the new sample is greater than the original sample, as it includes African Americans, Hispanics, and Native Americans. However, in comparison with the 1980 census data reported in the MMPI–2 manual, it appears that Asian Americans, Native Americans, and Hispanics are underrepresented. The age distribution also shows that men and women in the age range of 18 to 19 are underrepresented, as are older adults between the ages of 70 and 84.

The most notable difference between the restandardization group and the 1980 census data centers on the educational differences and the generally higher socioeconomic status (SES) of the restandardization sample. Examination of Table 4 in the MMPI–2 manual shows that well-educated participants are notably overrepresented in the new sample (as compared with the 1980 census data) at the expense of individuals with a high school education or less. For example, 27.2% of the male participants were college graduates compared with 9.8% of the general population in 1980; 26.7% of the female participants were college graduates compared with 7.5% of the general population in 1980. The average educational level in the new sample was close to 2.5 years of college. This level of education is not only higher than the 1980 census data, but is vastly higher than the original norm group, which overrepresented lower educational and occupational groups (Dahlstrom, 1993) and is about 2 years higher than the most recent estimates of the mean years of education (12.7) for adults over the age of 24 (Schinka & LaLone, 1997). The general skew in the new sample toward upper socioeconomic levels in the normative group is well recognized by researchers and expert users of the test. However, different concerns have been expressed about the meaning of this skew. The MMPI–2 manual (Butcher, Dahlstrom, Graham, Tellegen, & Kaemmer, 1989) attempts to minimize the importance of the skew by stating that "the distributions of the normative samples on these various indexes of socioeconomic status appear to be closer to those of the typical subjects currently being asked to take the MMPI in various settings around the United States" (p. 5). Although precisely what constitutes the "typical" participant being asked to complete the MMPI–2 is not specified in the manual and is not otherwise known, participants being tested for Social Security benefits, or supplementary security income, as well as clients in various public agencies and in state mental hospitals, typically are of a lower SES and will not match very well to the socioeconomic characteristics of the current standardization group (Caldwell, 1991; Duckworth, 1991a, 1991b).

Recently, in a supplement to the MMPI–2 manual Dahlstrom and Tellegen (1993) published data showing the distinct differences between the various socioeconomic levels of normal participants. Using a multivariate technique, they were able to estimate the influence of the differences in age, education, gender, race, and occupational level on the basic clinical and validity MMPI–2 scale scores. For 6 of the 13 standard scales (*F*, *K*, *Hs*, *Pt*, *Sc*, *Si*) Dahlstrom and Tellegen found that the largest component of variance came from the educational-level differences. For example, men and women with less education scored higher on the *L* and *F* scales and lower on the *K* scale, whereas on the clinical scales, men and women with less education scored significantly higher on Scales 1, 7, 8, and 0. Men and women's scores on Scale 5 (*Mf*) are also noticeably affected by occupational and educational status. Men with higher SES and women with less education tend to produce higher Scale 5 scores (Dahlstrom, 1993).[14] The reader is referred to Figs. 1.1–1.4 reprinted from Dahlstrom. These figures graphically show the differences in scores for men and women across different educational and occupational levels.

Even so, while these differences between the groups do exist, they are generally small, and personality differences are more likely to account for any given MMPI–2 profile than are general background factors (Dahlstrom & Tellegen, 1993).

More recently, Schinka and LaLone (1997) conducted scale comparisons between the restandardization sample and a more current census-matched subsample with estimates of educational level for 1993 provided by the U.S. Bureau of the Census. The census-matched subsample drawn from the larger

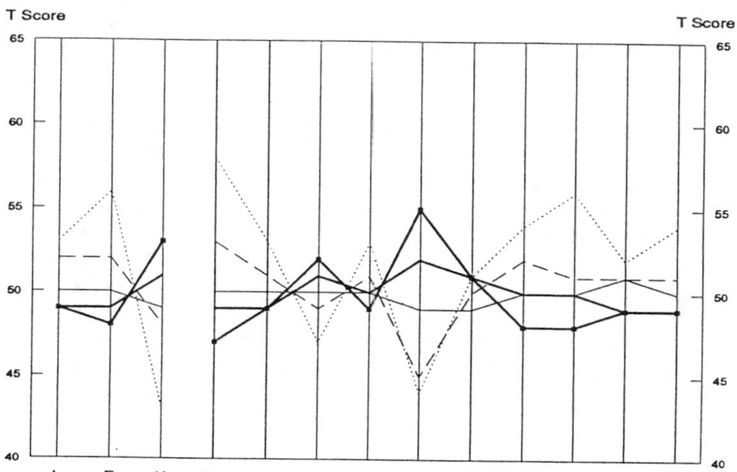

	L	F	K	Hs 1	D 2	Hy 3	Pd 4	Mf 5	Pa 6	Pt 7	Sc 8	Ma 9	Si 0
Under 12 yrs, n=61	53	56	43	58	53	47	53	44	51	54	56	52	54
High school, n=242	52	52	48	53	51	49	51	45	50	52	51	51	51
Some college, n=272	50	50	49	50	50	50	50	49	49	50	50	51	50
College grad, n=310	49	49	51	49	49	51	50	52	51	50	50	49	49
Post-graduate, n=253	49	48	53	47	49	52	49	55	51	48	48	49	49

FIG. 1.1. Mean MMPI–2 profiles for men by education level. From *Manual Supplement: Socioeconomic Status and the MMPI–2: The Relation of MMPI–2 Patterns to Levels of Education and Occupation* (pp. 40–41, 46–47), by W. G. Dahlstrom & A. Tellegen, 1993, Minneapolis: University of Minnesota Press. "MMPI–2" and "Minnesota Multiphasic Personality Inventory–2" are trademarks owned by the University of Minnesota. Reprinted with permission.

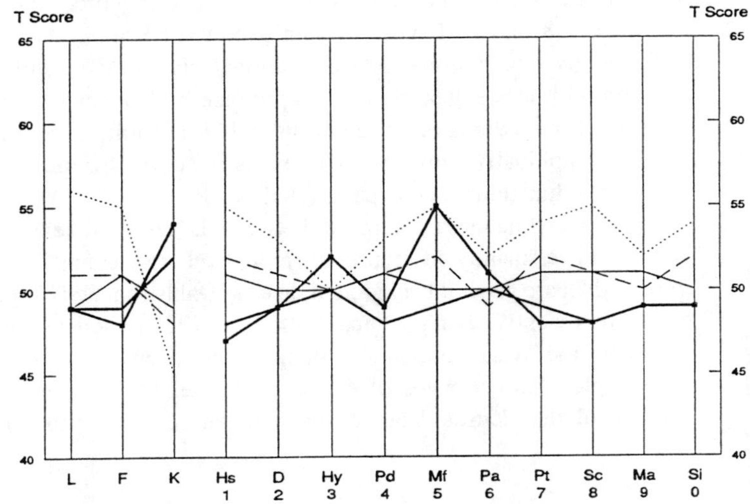

		L	F	K	Hs 1	D 2	Hy 3	Pd 4	Mf 5	Pa 6	Pt 7	Sc 8	Ma 9	Si 0
Under 12 yrs, n=67	······	56	55	45	55	53	50	53	55	52	54	55	52	54
High school, n=398	— —	51	51	48	52	51	50	51	52	49	52	51	50	52
Some college, n=380	——	49	51	49	51	50	50	51	50	50	51	51	51	50
College grad, n=390	——	49	49	52	48	49	50	48	49	50	49	48	49	49
Post-graduate, n=227	—•—	49	48	54	47	49	52	49	55	51	48	48	49	49

FIG. 1.2. Mean MMPI–2 profiles for women by education level. From *Manual Supplement: Socioeconomic Status and the MMPI–2: The Relation of MMPI–2 Patterns to Levels of Education and Occupation* (pp. 40–41, 46–47), by W. G. Dahlstrom & A. Tellegen, 1993, Minneapolis: University of Minnesota Press. Copyright © 1993 by the Regents of the University of Minnesota. All rights reserved. "MMPI–2" and "Minnesota Multiphasic Personality Inventory–2" are trademarks owned by the University of Minnesota. Reprinted with permission.

restandardization sample appears to accurately reflect an acceptable representation of the current U.S. population, despite the overestimates of education previously described.

UNIFORM *T* SCORES

Linear Versus Uniform *T*-Scores

The raw scores of the basic MMPI/MMPI–2 scales all have different means and standard deviations as well as different ranges of scores in any normative sample. These statistics reflect differing numbers of items in the several scales as well as the frequency of item endorsement. Thus, to evaluate the clinical significance of an individual's set of scores, it is necessary to compare each score to its mean and judge the size of the difference using the standard deviation. Furthermore, to compare scores on different scales, it is desirable to transform the scores to a common metric. This has been done traditionally with the MMPI scales by converting the scores on each scale to standardized *T* scores having a mean of 50 and a standard deviation of 10. That is to say,

$$T = 50 + 10(X - M)/SD, \tag{1}$$

where X is the score of a participant on the scale in question, M is the mean, and SD is the standard deviation of the scale in the normative or reference sample.

The reference sample used for the computation of the *T* scores determines the elevation and the extent of the *T*-score spread. To the extent that the normative or reference sample is inadequate, the *T* scores will be inappropriate (Dahlstrom & Tellegen, 1993). As noted previously, the original normative sample differed from later normative samples, both demographically and with respect to the means and standard deviations of a number of scales.

The linear *T*-score transformation of raw scores has a number of advantages: (a) It is easy to use computationally and quickly conveys some notion of where the score stands in reference to the normative sample; (b) equal raw score differences on a particular scale are maintained as equal differences on its transformed scale; (c) all scales expressed in *T* scores are equated with respect to their mean and standard deviation and, hence, are to some extent comparable; (d) and the linear

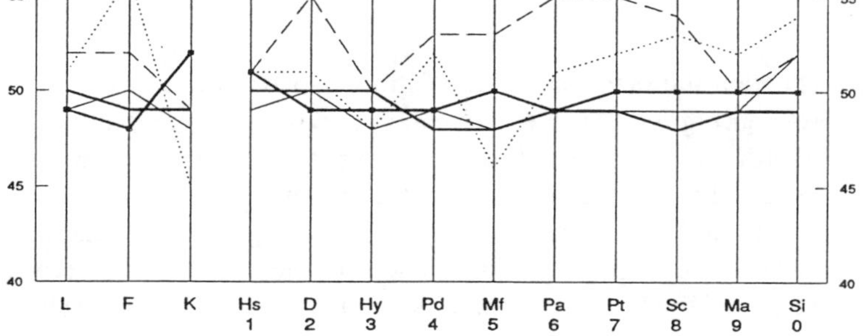

	L	F	K	Hs 1	D 2	Hy 3	Pd 4	Mf 5	Pa 6	Pt 7	Sc 8	Ma 9	Si 0
Laborer, n=132	51	56	45	51	51	48	52	46	51	52	53	52	54
Clerical, n=37	52	52	49	51	55	50	53	53	55	55	54	50	52
Skilled, n=164	49	50	48	49	50	48	49	48	49	49	49	49	52
Managerial, n=168	50	49	49	50	50	50	48	48	49	49	48	49	49
Professional, n=479	49	48	52	51	49	49	49	50	49	50	50	50	50

FIG. 1.3. Mean MMPI–2 profiles for men by occupational level. From *Manual Supplement: Socioeconomic Status and the MMPI–2: The Relation of MMPI–2 Patterns to Levels of Education and Occupation* (pp. 40–41, 46–47), by W. G. Dahlstrom & A. Tellegen, 1993, Minneapolis: University of Minnesota Press. "MMPI–2" and "Minnesota Multiphasic Personality Inventory–2" are trademarks owned by the University of Minnesota. Reprinted with permission.

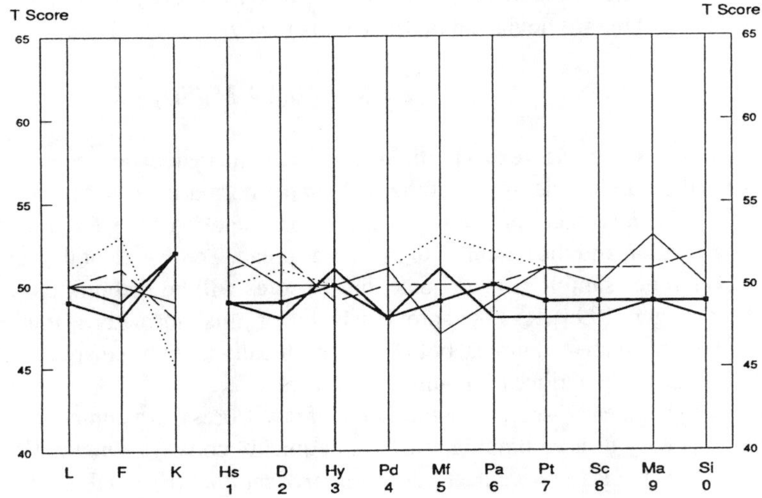

		L	F	K	Hs 1	D 2	Hy 3	Pd 4	Mf 5	Pa 6	Pt 7	Sc 8	Ma 9	Si 0
Laborer, n=73	······	51	53	45	50	51	50	51	53	52	51	51	51	52
Clerical, n=328	— —	50	51	48	51	52	49	50	50	50	51	51	51	52
Skilled, n=51	——	50	50	49	52	50	50	51	47	49	51	50	53	50
Managerial, n=109	——	50	49	52	49	48	51	48	51	48	48	48	49	48
Professional, n=581	—•—	49	48	52	49	49	50	48	49	50	49	49	49	49

FIG. 1.4. Mean MMPI–2 profiles for women by occupational level. From *Manual Supplement: Socioeconomic Status and the MMPI–2: The Relation of MMPI–2 Patterns to Levels of Education and Occupation* (pp. 40–41, 46–47), by W. G. Dahlstrom & A. Tellegen, 1993, Minneapolis: University of Minnesota Press. "MMPI–2" and "Minnesota Multiphasic Personality Inventory–2" are trademarks owned by the University of Minnesota. Reprinted with permission.

equation allows for easy extrapolation beyond those scores actually obtained in the reference group. Such extrapolation is extremely important for tests such as the MMPI that are intended for use with pathological groups whose scores may be expected to go much higher than the reference group.

Linear *T* scores have two major disadvantages: (a) Standardized *T*-score scales are not fully equivalent (differences in the shapes of the raw distributions as measured by skewness and kurtosis remain after the linear transformations) and (b) assumptions based on a normal distribution to the effect that a *T* score of 70 or higher encompasses only about 2.5% of the reference population do not usually hold. Furthermore, the percentage meeting this criterion is not the same from one scale to another when they differ in terms of skewness. The same linear *T* score can signify different percentile standings for different scales. In other words, linear *T* scores from different scales are not "percentile comparable."

Normalized *T* Scores

Because of the above difficulties and limitations, Colligan et al. (1980) suggested that it would be advisable to normalize scores on the clinical scales of the MMPI and developed such scores on a new reference sample of 1,408 normal men and women living in the Midwest (Colligan et al., 1983). This transformation involves fitting the raw scores of the sample to a normal distribution and then converting these scores to a mean of 50 and standard deviation of 10. They handled the problem of providing normative values for raw scores falling outside the range of values in the reference sample by using a special conversion formula based on the power transformation methods suggested by Box and Cox (1964).

The main problem with the normal transformation of scores from a raw score distribution skewed to the right (a characteristic of MMPI scores) is that it spreads out scores at the lower end of the scale while crunching together those at the upper end. Thus, the differentiation among high scores found in clinical populations is reduced.

Uniform *T* Scores

The MMPI–2 restandardization committee (Butcher et al., 1989) decided to continue using the linear rather than the normalized *T*-scale transformation, but with some modification to improve the percentile comparability of scores across scales. Changing to normalized scores would be too radical, necessitating "substantial changes in the frequencies and clinical implications of elevated *T*-scores and *T*-score profiles" (Tellegen & Ben-Porath, 1992, p. 147).

Hence, they derived a new standardized score, called the uniform *T* score to make the percentile values of the *T* scores more similar across the eight clinical scales (Scales 1–4 and 6–9) and between men and women, but with as little departure as possible from the original linear *T* scores. Scales 5 and 0 were not considered clinical scales and hence were omitted from these computations. The reason given by Tellegen and Ben-Porath (1992, p. 146) for omitting these scales was that these two scales do not represent clinical constructs. They were also derived differently than were the clinical scales and are less skewed. These two scales, as well as the traditional validity scales (*L*, *F*, and *K*), continue to be transformed to linear *T* scores. Their use in conjunction with uniform *T* scores creates no problem according to Tellegen and Ben-Porath.

Three major steps were involved in the uniform *T*-score transformation.

1. The 16 raw-score distributions, eight scales each for men and women, were first transformed to the traditional linear *T* scores. Then for each of the 101 percentile values (0.5, 1.0, 2.0, 3.0, ..., 97.0, 98.0, 99.0, 99.5), the corresponding linear *T* score for each of the 16 scales was obtained by interpolation. The 16 *T* scores for each percentile value were then averaged to obtain composite scores. These 101 average *T*-score values essentially define the prototypical linear *T*-score distribution to be approximated by the uniform *T* scores.

2. The scores resulting from Step 1 were inadequate without further work. It was necessary to obtain the raw scores corresponding to the *T* scores derived in Step 1. Then, by interpolation, the raw-score estimates corresponding to integer *T*-score values were derived. A round of interpolations were conducted to obtain

the raw scores for each scale corresponding to the 52 integer composite scores ranging from 31 to 82 in the normative sample.

3. If uniform *T* scores were needed for only those raw scores that actually occurred in the normative sample, it could have been accomplished at this point by further interpolation to provide integer *T* scores for each integer raw score. However, scores well outside this range (e.g., *T* values above 90) are common in clinical samples and could not have been derived. To handle all possible raw scores, a regression equation was needed for each scale that would adequately fit the 52 target values obtained in Step 2 and would allow for extrapolation for more extreme raw-score values. For this purpose, a polynomial regression equation was sought that would become linear for high values of *X*. The equation used was as follows:

$$\textbf{Uniform } T \textbf{ score} = B_0 + B_1X + B_2D^2 + B_3D^3, \qquad (2)$$

where X is the raw score to be transformed; B_0 is the intercept; B_1, B_2, and B_3 are regression weights, and $(D = C - X)$ if X is less than C and 0 if X is greater than or equal to C. The value of C selected was the raw score for each scale corresponding to a composite T score of 60. Putting it differently, the quadratic and cubic components of the above equations cease having any effect on the uniform *T* scores above $T = 60$ and thereafter the uniform *T* values are linearly related to the raw scores.

The 16 regression equations represented by Equation 2 applied to the raw scores on each scale provide very good fits to the 52 scores of the prototype uniform *T* scale. The multiple correlations were all .998 or higher. These equations provided the non-*K*-corrected uniform *T*-score look-up tables included in the MMPI–2 manual. The same method was used to derive the *K*-corrected clinical scale scores and the new content scale scores, in each case using the same target composite linear *T*-score values.

The uniform *T* scores, like the linear *T* scores, of the eight clinical scales are skewed to the right; unlike the linear *T*-score scales, they are all skewed approximately to the same moderate degree. It can be argued that the moderate skew of the uniform *T* scores is appropriate because some skew is to be expected for scales designed to tap dysfunctional attributes when used on a nonscreened sample (Tellegen & Ben-Porath, 1992, pp. 150–154).

Equivalence in percentile values has been especially improved for the extremes of the distribution (see Table 1.3). For example, linear *T* scores at the 95th percentile varied from 66 on Scale 3 to 70 on Scale 8 for men and 71 on Scale 8 for women. The corresponding range for uniform *T* scores is 67 to 69. As Tellegen and Ben-Porath (1992) pointed out, comparability has been achieved "without requiring the marked departures from traditional linear *T*-score distributions that would have been imposed by normalization" (p. 154).

It should be noted that uniform $T = 70$ is at the 96th percentile, whereas uniform $T = 65$ is at the 92nd. Table 1.4 shows different uniform *T*-score values with the corresponding percentile equivalents. Butcher and Williams (1992) recommended

TABLE 1.3

T-Score Equivalents of Percentiles: Ranges of Obtained Linear and Uniform *T* (*UT*) Scores

Percentile	*Range of Linear T Scores*	*Range of UT Scores*
10	37–40	38–39
20	41–42	41–42
30	43–45	44
40	45–48	46–47
50	48–50	48–50
60	50–52	51–52
70	53–55	54–55
80	57–59	57–59
90	62–64	62–64
95	66–71	67–69
99	73–83	77–80

Note. The ranges are those of the non-*K*-corrected *T* scores obtained for Scales 1–4 and 6–9 in the MMPI–2 normative samples. From "The New Uniform *T* Scores for the MMPI–2: Rationale, Derivation, and Appraisal," by A. Tellegen & Y. S. Ben-Porath, 1992, *Psychological Assessment: A Journal of Consulting and Clinical Psychology, 4,* 145–155. Copyright © 1992 by the American Psychological Association. Reprinted with permission.

TABLE 1.4

Percentile Equivalents of Uniform *T* (*UT*) Scores

UT Score	*Percentile Equivalent*
30	<1
35	4
40	15
45	34
50	55
55	73
60	85
65	92
70	96
75	98
80	>99

Note. The percentiles are those of the targeted *UT* scores. From "The New Uniform *T* Scores for the MMPI–2: Rationale, Derivation, and Appraisal," by A. Tellegen & Y. S. Ben-Porath, 1992, *Psychological Assessment: A Journal of Consulting and Clinical Psychology, 4,* 145–155. Copyright © 1992 by the American Psychological Association. Reprinted with permission.

that a uniform *T* score of 65 or greater be used to demarcate the "clinical range." This recommendation stems from studies showing 65 to be the optimal score level for separating known clinical groups from the new MMPI–2 normative sample.

Although derivation of the uniform *T* scores appears complicated, their distribution is essentially that of a composite linear MMPI *T* score. It has been shown that relatively small differences occur, as was intended, when traditional linear *T* scores are compared with uniform *T* scores on the MMPI–2 for both normals (Dahlstrom & Tellegen, 1993, Figs. 1–16) and clinical participants (D. W. Edwards, Morrison, & Weissman, 1993). Much larger differences occur when linear *T*-score values derived from the original Hathaway MMPI norms are compared with either the linear *T* scores or the uniform *T*-score values derived from the MMPI–2 normative sample.

NOTES

[1]Sixteen of the 550 statements on the original MMPI were repeated, bringing the item total to 566. The repeated items originally were included to assist in the mechanical scoring of the inventory but actually are scored only once for the clinical scales on which they appear (Scales 6, 7, 8, and 0).

[2]The Humm–Wadsworth Temperament Survey (Humm & Wadsworth, 1935) appears to be a methodological precursor of the MMPI and was cited in Hathaway's (1939) article, "The Personality Inventory as an Aid in the Diagnosis of Psychopathic Inferiors." Examination of the Humm–Wadsworth scale items shows a remarkable resemblance to at least 27% of the 550 MMPI items (D. S. Nichols, personal communication, April 1, 1999). Meehl (1989) also noted that many items on the MMPI were adapted from the 318-item Humm–Wadsworth inventory.

[3]The item pool originally consisted of 504 items, to which McKinley and Hathaway (1943) later added 55 items primarily related to masculinity–femininity, but eventually eliminated 9 more items, resulting in a final pool of 550 separate items. Because 16 items were repeated to facilitate early machine scoring, the final published booklet version of the MMPI contains 566 items, with the 16 repeated items scored no more than once each on any scale.

[4]Hathaway and Briggs (1957), in the course of providing normative data on a number of additional MMPI scales, replaced many incomplete or defective protocols of the original normals, and their modified sample of 226 men and 315 women became the basis for the *T* scores printed on the MMPI standard profile sheet. *T* scores derived from norms in *An MMPI Handbook* (Dahlstrom et al., 1972, 1975) and other MMPI reference works do not necessarily match precisely the *T* scores on the standard profile sheet for the original MMPI because of the "purified" sample.

[5]Greene (1990b) questioned whether similar findings would be obtained with psychiatric patients. He examined the scores of psychiatric patients over a 40-year span of time with the intention of discovering any appreciable changes in profiles as a function of time. Four frequently occurring code patterns were identified (Spike 4, 24/42, 27/72, and 68/86), as were the means and medians across four periods of time (1950, 1960, 1970, and 1980). The results show that the code patterns differed very little over time in the means and medians. His results were similar to that of Pancoast and Archer (1989), who found strong stability on the MMPI scale scores of normal adult samples across 40 years. Although Greene (1990b) did not assess the existence of similar correlates across time for these samples, he did demonstrate in part that the "MMPI may not be as outdated as many people have thought" (Greene, 1991a, p. 12).

[6]Greene (1985) also pointed out that Colligan, Osborne, and Offord (1980) used normalized *T* scores versus linear *T* scores, which are used with the traditional profile sheet. Colligan et al. used normalized *T* scores because the original norm *T*-score distributions of most MMPI scales have varying degrees of positive skew, making it difficult to accurately compare *T* scores across scales (Colligan et al., 1980; Miller & Streiner, 1986). Normalized *T* scores are comparable across scales. Miller and Streiner found an absence of correspondence when code patterns using the original norms were compared with the new norms; this was found for linear transformations and for normalized *T* scores. They recommended Colligan et al.'s norms be used only in conjunction with the original norms until the clinical relevance of the differences are determined. More recently, Greene (1991a) commented on the incongruent profiles produced by the different norm sets. He stated that although it is important to know the concordance between codetypes generated by the two sets of norms, the basic issue remains as to whether the original or contemporary norms more accurately reflect external correlates. Greene's concern is valid and remains valid for the new contemporary sample of normals used in restandardizing the MMPI–2.

[7]There was a dearth of funds available to Hathaway and McKinley to develop an adequate normative sample and to pursue further cross-validation studies because of the economic depression (Butcher, Dahlstrom, Graham, Tellegen, & Kaemmer, 1989).

[8]The University of Minnesota Press represented by Beverly Kaemmer appointed a committee to oversee and direct the revision of the test. The committee consisted of James Butcher and Auke Tellegen of the University of Minnesota, W. Grant Dahlstrom of the University of North Carolina, and John Graham of Kent State University.

[9]Nichols (1992b) described the MMPI–2 manual in a recent review of the MMPI–2 in the *Eleventh Mental Measurements Yearbook*. We minimally modified the following excerpt to reflect the current status of the MMPI–2 manual:

> The MMPI2 manual is five times the size of its predecessor, and is divided between text and appendices in a ratio of 1:2. It is clearly written and strikes an appropriate balance between clinical and psychometric values. The restandardization is well described and tables are provided to compare the normative sample against the 1980 census data. For the clinician, there are scoring keys and interpretative information for each scale mentioned in this review, a section on protocol validity, and a pair of interpreted protocols. Tables are provided that give interpretive implications of four or five levels of elevation for the standard scales. This feature serves a very useful orienting purpose, but these tables may be quite misleading when moderate to extreme response sets are present. Tables for converting raw scores to linear or uniform T-scores are provided for the standard scales, with and without K-corrections. For the psychometrician, there are test–retest and internal consistency values, itemmetric and codetype concordance data, and external correlates for most scales. Conversion tables for translating MMPI item numbers into MMPI–2, and vice-versa, are provided. Three scoring keys and a few other errors have been discovered so far and have been noted in forthcoming errata. A final appendix, K-1 and K-2, is given for converting K-corrected and non-K-corrected *T*-scores on MMPI–2 profiles into MMPI values. By an unfortunate oversight, the *T*-score values reported in these tables did not reflect the adjustments to the original normative data made by Hathaway and Briggs (1957). Corrected tables appear in the manual revision. (Nichols, 1992b, p. 564)

[10]The restandardization project included adults as old as 84 years of age, but the age range between 80 and 84 represented only 0.8% of the total sample, as compared with 2.2% and 4% of

the 1980 census data for men and women, respectively. It appears that older adults were generally underrepresented in the new sample. Test users are cautioned to be aware that as clients approach age 60, the normative data tends to be underrepresentative of the true numbers of that age cohort, according to the 1980 census.

Friedman, Webb, and Lewak (1989) and Colligan and Offord (1992) summarized the findings related to the impact of age on MMPI scores. In general, they reported that peaks on Scales 1 (*Hs*) and 2 (*D*) are relatively uncommon early in life but become more common later. The reverse is true for Scales 4 (*Pd*) and 8 (*Sc*). These base-rate shifts appear to reflect the normal process of concern with physical health that is associated with aging and with the common problems of impulse control and identity concerns affecting younger populations. These findings have been replicated in normal adult samples reported by Dahlstrom, Lachar, and Dahlstrom (1986), who examined four age groups. In general, because older individuals obtain higher scores on scales measuring physical health concerns, a profile with moderate to marked elevations on the Depression scale and/or the Hypochondriasis scale should be adjusted and interpreted less pathologically than the same profile from a young adult. Colligan et al. (1989) expressed similar concerns, and the reader is referred to their data because their contemporary normative sample much more closely matches the 1980 U.S. census data, especially as it pertains to older adults.

[11]The basic committee charged with developing the instrument consisted of James N. Butcher, Caroline L. Williams, John R. Graham, Robert P. Archer, Auke Tellegen, and Yossef S. BenPorath.

[12]The MMPI–A is available from National Computer Systems under license from the University of Minnesota Press.

[13]It should be noted that although for the most part the 154 experimental items followed the original 550 MMPI items, some item order changes occurred. Specifically, the 16 repeated items were eliminated in the Form AX, leaving gaps in the item slots that were filled in with some of the experimental items. This was done to preserve the traditional scoring keys for the original scale (W. G. Dahlstrom, personal communication, October 29, 1994). Therefore, the flow of the original items was slightly interrupted by the introduction of the new items, although probably without much consequence.

[14]Duckworth (1991a, 1991b) and Caldwell (1991) suggested that the higher average educational and occupational level of the new normative sample may handicap the utility of the MMPI–2 in populations with low SES. Caldwell proposed using the MMPI–2 booklet to capitalize on the improvements in the readability of the items but plotting the resultant raw scores on both the MMPI and MMPI–2 profile sheets. In this fashion, a visual comparison can be made between the two sets of norms regarding the consequences of using two quite different fixed reference groups. Alan Friedman and his colleague, Alan Jaffe, studied a sample of 291 disability-benefit applicants (Rothke et al., 1994), who had a mean educational level of 10.5 years for men and 11.0 years for women. The mean MMPI–2 *F* linear *T* score for men was 110 and 96 for women. However, when Table K in the MMPI–2 manual was used to transform MMPI–2 *T* scores into MMPI linear *T* scores, the *T* score on the *F* scale fell to 97 and 84 for men and women, respectively; this use of the transformation table substantially reduced the disability-benefit participants' *F* scores. SES correlated negatively with *F* scale elevations, a finding consistent with Dahlstrom and Tellegen's (1993) recent data. When testing a low SES individual, the reader is advised to be aware that the positive skew in the MMPI–2 normative sample toward upper SES inflates the impression of psychopathology.

2

Measures of Profile Validity

THE TRADITIONAL MEASURES AND THEIR DERIVATIVES

The traditional validity measures are Cannot Say (*?*), *L*, *F*, and *K*. Three additional validity scales were published with the MMPI–2 and are named the Variable Response Inconsistency scale (*VRIN*), the True Response Inconsistency scale (*TRIN*), and the *F*-Back scale (*FB*). Most recently, the Infrequency-Psychopathology scale *F(p) and the Superlative (S)* scales were added to the profile sheet for interpretation. All of these scales are described in this chapter. The original intent of Hathaway and McKinley in developing the traditional validity scales was to aid in determining the test-taking attitude of the subject. Some individuals are motivated to distort their responses to the test items, either to minimize the presentation of their psychological problems or to exaggerate their psychopathology. Others may present a distorted picture of themselves by answering the items without fully comprehending their meaning or perhaps by simply not reading the items and responding randomly or with a true or false response bias. It is, therefore, important to ascertain the participant's test-taking disposition before interpreting the clinical scales. Although the validity scales were designed for this purpose, they have also been shown to correlate with personality traits and behaviors. Hence, the validity scales can enrich the clinical interpretation of the profile by providing the clinician with other psychological descriptors as well as an index of self-description accuracy.

The accurate assessment of a participant's test-taking attitude on the MMPI–2 (or any other personality inventory) is a complex issue. Some individuals believe they are giving an honest picture of themselves through their responses but in fact are distorting their presentations by overly positive self-evaluations, exaggerated perceptions of control or mastery, or unrealistic optimism (S. E. Taylor & Brown, 1988). These self-illusions may serve them well in coping with life's stresses but will affect their responses to inventory items. Paulhus (1984) referred to those participants who believe in their positive self-reports as engaging in self-deception and those who consciously attempt to manipulate others' views of themselves as "impression managers." There appears to exist a continuum of accurate self-reporting that ranges from underreporting to overreporting psychological problems and concerns, although Lanyon, Dannebaum, Wolf, and Brown (1989) conceptualized underreporting and overreporting as independent dimensions. It is up to the clinician to assess the validity of the participant's self-report before making a detailed analysis of the clinical and supplementary scale scores. To this end, the following validity scales should be considered as indispensable in assessing the individual's self-report style and test-taking attitude (see chap. 5 for detailed information on the interpretation of the validity scales).

The composition of the validity scales with the keyed responses is presented in Appendix A (see Table A1). The *T*-score conversions for the validity scales are presented in Appendix B (see Tables B1–B2).

Cannot Say Score (?)

The Cannot Say score is the number of items an individual did not answer or double marked, thereby leaving the response unscorable. A response could also be unscorable if it is uncertain to the test scorer whether a true or false response was given to the item. On the original MMPI, Cannot Say was plotted as a scale and assigned an arbitrary *T*-score value.[1] However, technically it did not qualify as a *scale* because scales have a set number of items or a consistent item pool (Friedman, Webb, & Lewak, 1989). On the MMPI–2 profile sheet, a space exists for recording the raw score value of omitted or double-marked or unscorable items, but the score is not transferred to the clinical profile as it was for the MMPI. The MMPI–2 manual (Butcher et al., 1989) considers a profile invalid with a Cannot Say score of 30 or higher, whereas raw scores between 11 and 29 are of questionable validity. Scores between 0 and 10 are probably valid, but the psychologist should examine the content of omitted items.

The reasons for the lack of a response to an item are numerous. Perhaps some of the items lack personal relevance, or an individual filling out an answer sheet could accidentally skip an item. Different motivational factors, such as test-taking resistance or suspiciousness, have been associated with high Cannot Say scores (Dahlstrom et al., 1972). Not answering an item may be related to decisional ambiguity, which is the inability of the participant to decide how to respond to an item (Fulkerson & Willage, 1980). In addition, intellectual or reading deficits may make it difficult to comprehend an item, leading to its omission (Ball & Carroll, 1960). However, most test takers respond to all of the items, although some individuals may object to various items (Clopton & Neuringer, 1977). For example, those in personnel selection situations are more likely to react negatively to items if they feel there is no job relevance. If participants omit items, it is always desirable to encourage them to complete the omitted ones, and to assess why they chose to leave them out. Although in many cases the omission may have occurred accidentally, other omissions may have occurred because the item was ambiguous or offensive to the reader or, as implied earlier in the case of adolescence, semantically confusing. It is likely, however, that the improved item wording on the MMPI–2 will lead to fewer item omissions.

Archer (1992) summarized the findings of Ball and Carroll (1960), who examined correlates of Cannot Say scores among 262 ninth-grade, public school students in Kentucky. Archer stated that, in general, the adolescents who omitted greater numbers of MMPI items also had lower IQ scores and grades that were below average. This seems to suggest that intelligence and reading limitations are associated with Cannot Say scores as much as negativistic attitudes toward the testing. An inverse relationship between reading grade level and raw scores on the Cannot Say measure was also found by Archer and Gordon (1991). In a sample of 495 normal adolescents who were administered the MMPI–A and the Ohio Literacy Test, a measure of reading comprehension, they found that adolescents who have difficulty reading MMPI or MMPI–A items tend to omit items at a higher frequency than other adolescents. Archer also pointed out that, unfortunately, many adolescents also attempt to respond to items that they have difficulty reading or understanding, which often results in invalid test protocols. This emphasizes the necessity to evaluate carefully an individual's reading ability before he or she is administered the MMPI–2 (see chap. 3).

Usually 10 or fewer omitted items or less will not affect the validity of the profile. When between 5 and 30 items are omitted, Greene (1980, 1991a) recommended a procedure called "augmenting" the profile. In this procedure, the items that were omitted are endorsed in the deviant direction, scored, and reinterpreted. The test should also be scored without the items marked in the deviant direction so that the two profiles can be compared. More than 30 item omissions renders the test record highly suspect, if not completely invalid (Butcher et al., 1989). If items are omitted, then the scale on which they are scored will be lowered,[2] thus compromising the validity of the profile. The omission of items can also change the MMPI's high-point pairs (highest clinical scales), which could significantly alter the interpretation of the profile (Clopton & Neuringer, 1977). It should be noted that the validity and clinical scale items are all contained within the first 370 items of the test. Thus, if the item omissions occur after Item 370, the standard scales will not be affected. However, the supplementary and content scales, which are scored after Item 370, could be affected.

Clopton and Neuringer (1977) conducted a two-phase study to address the issue of item omission and its effects on profile configuration. In the first phase, they examined the occurrence of omitted MMPI items from Veterans Administration (VA) psychiatric patients being admitted to the hospital, outpatients at a regional mental health center (MHC), and police and firefighter applicants who had completed the MMPI. In each of these three groups, the majority of test participants completed all 566 items, with the percentage of participants omitting 5 or fewer items being 93.7% for the job applicants, 88.9% for MHC clients, and 85.6% for the VA patients. The corresponding number of mean items omitted was 2.45 for job applicants, 2.24 for MHC clients, and 4.68 for the VA patients.

The second phase of Clopton and Neuringer's (1977) study involved inspecting the effects of randomly omitted items on profile elevation and configuration (high-point pairs). A subset of 180 randomly selected VA patient MMPI profiles, which were completely filled out, were then rescored with 5, 30, 55, 80, 105, and 130 items randomly omitted. The original MMPI profiles were compared with the different rescored profiles with different levels of omitted items. As more MMPI items were omitted, there was a corresponding reduction in the profile elevation and, perhaps more importantly, changes occurred in profile configurations. The mean reductions in *T* scores across the clinical scales for the six levels of omitted items fell an average of 0.45, 2.74, 5.61, 7.70, 9.09, and 11.54 points, respectively. Randomly eliminating 30 MMPI items from complete answer sheets in their study led to a change in the high-point pair in more than 25% of the profiles and an average reduction of nearly 3 *T*-score points in the clinical profile. Thus, profile configuration, rather than specific *T*-scale scores, is more importantly affected by a large number of item omissions.

Although most people rarely omit a significant number of items, the consequences of doing so are such that the clinician should inspect the answer sheet carefully for a completed test record. Failure to check an answer sheet having a large number of item omissions can mislead the test interpreter to underestimate the degree of psychopathology revealed in the profile. As suggested earlier, whenever possible it is good practice to ask examinees why items were omitted and to encourage them to complete those items. A recent example illustrates the importance of checking the answer sheet for item omissions. An MMPI had been completed by a security guard applicant during a preemployment screening. The clinical psychologist who interpreted the profile failed to examine the answer sheet and instead relied exclusively on the profile for making his recommendations. The profile was well within the normal limit range. However, the applicant had omitted approximately 77 items from the first 370 items on the MMPI. Because the psychologist failed to look at the answer sheet, he recommended that the security guard be hired for employment. The numerous item omissions came to the attention of this text's first author when the security guard later became involved in a shooting incident that led to litigation in which the guard was sued for brutal and aggressive force. Clearly, the MMPI should have been either considered invalid or given back to the job applicant to complete his responses to the items. This kind of oversight can be avoided if clinicians routinely look at the Cannot Say score on the profile sheet or, if it is not reported, examine the answer sheet directly.

Variable Response Inconsistency Scale (*VRIN*)

The *VRIN* scale is a 67-item scale designed to detect inconsistent or contradictory responding. It is a new scale designed for the MMPI–2 and resembles the function of the shorter Carelessness scale on the MMPI developed by Greene (1978).[3] One major difference between the *VRIN* scale and the Carelessness scale is the greater scale length of the former. The *VRIN* scale is also seen as a replacement for the TR index on the MMPI, which consisted of 16 repeated items and for which four or more inconsistent responses raised the question of profile invalidity due to inconsistent responding.[4]

The content of the *VRIN* item pairs have similar or opposite meaning (Butcher et al., 1989). Some pairs of items are scored as inconsistent if one item receives an opposite endorsement (true or false as the case may be) from the other item in the pair, whereas others are scored as inconsistent if both pairs are scored as either true or false. As Butcher et al. (1989) has stated, "the score in the *VRIN* scale is the total number of item pairs answered inconsistently" (p. 28). High scores raise the possibility that the test taker did not respond carefully to the content of the inventory, thereby rendering the profile uninterpretable. The scoring direction for the *VRIN* items is based on the frequency of item endorsements by the contemporary normal sample; hence, many apparently contradictory response patterns are not scored. The following examples from the *VRIN* scale illustrate the scoring directions for inconsistency and the item content of the *VRIN* scale (see Table A.1 for a complete listing of the *VRIN* items and the scoring key).

3. I wake up fresh and rested most mornings. (True)
39. My sleep is fitful and disturbed. (True)

If an individual answered true to both Items 3 and 39, he or she would receive a raw score point of 1 on the *VRIN* scale.

9. My daily life is full of things that keep me interested. (False)
56. I wish I could be as happy as others seem to be. (False)

Both Items 9 and 56 need to be endorsed false in order to receive 1 point on the *VRIN* scale.

349. I am never happier than when I am alone.
515. I am never happier than when I am by myself.

Both Items 349 and 515 need to be oppositely endorsed (True–False or False–True) in order to be scored on the *VRIN* scale. Greene (1991a) pointed out that the *VRIN* scale actually consists of 49 pairs of unique items because two separate response patterns (i.e., True–False or False–True) are scored for 18 of these 67 item pairs, as with Items 349 and 515.

Because scoring is configural for the *VRIN* scale, the user must be especially careful if hand scoring the scale because mistakes could easily be made. Iverson and Barton (1999) recently investigated the hand-scoring accuracy of the *VRIN* and *TRIN* scales and compared these results to the reliabilities of the other clinical and validity scales. Despite high reliabilities across most of the scales, clerical errors were common (7% of the scales were scored inconsistently), although for the most part these errors only "represented one or two raw score points and did not affect the clinical interpretation of the scales" (Iverson & Barton, 1999, p. 69). However, there were three times as many scoring disagreements for the *VRIN* scale than for any other scale, suggesting that the configural nature of the scale is much less of a scoring handicap if a computer-scored program is used. If this is not possible, clinicians should carefully check their hand scoring of this scale.

For the MMPI–2 to be clinically interpretable, it is necessary for the individual to respond to semantically similar items in similar ways (Nichols & Greene, 1995). A high rate of inconsistent responses usually indicates difficulties in understanding the content of the inventory or a lack of cooperation (noncontent responding). The *VRIN* scale (along with the *TRIN* scale) was designed to complement the interpretation of the *L*, *F*, and *K* validity scales. The MMPI–2 manual states that, for example

> a high F score combined with a high *VRIN* score is more likely to indicate a profile that is uninterpretable owing to carelessness, confusion, etc. than if *VRIN* is not elevated. On the other hand, in the case of high F and low *VRIN*, carelessness, etc. can be ruled out and a high F score can be interpreted in terms of its actual content which could, then, reflect either true psychopathology or deliberate efforts to fake bad. (Butcher et al., 1989, p. 28)

More recent research findings also support this strategy of interpreting an elevated *F* scale by referring to the *VRIN* score (Wetter et al., 1992).

Note that a participant could shift his or her test-taking attitude at any point during the test administration. For example, an individual could become fatigued and less motivated to read the content and then resort to random, all-true, or all-false responding. If the participant answered cooperatively during at least the first 370 items, all of the clinical and validity scales could be accurately interpreted. However, after Item 370, if a participant adopts a random-response bias, the content and supplementary scales could be unduly affected. Greene (1991a) pointed out that the *VRIN* scale items are fairly evenly distributed throughout the MMPI–2. If the clinician wanted to take the care and time to score the validity scales in blocks of items rather than for the entire test, it could be determined where a participant began randomly or inconsistently responding. This approach would be particularly helpful for intermediate scores on the *VRIN* scale.

The MMPI–2 manual suggests that a raw score of 13 ($T = 80$) on the *VRIN* scale indicates inconsistent responding, which is consistent with more recent research focusing on validity scale cutoff scores (Berry, Wetter, et al., 1991). Greene (1991a, 1991b), however, suggested a more graduated interpretation. He suggested a raw score cutoff of 16 for the *VRIN* scale and that scores between 8 and 15 could indicate either consistent or inconsistent responding, thereby necessitating the examination of other measures. More recently, Nichols and Greene (1995) stated the following:

> Unfortunately for *VRIN* raw scores in the range of 11 to 16, a relatively large number of inconsistent cases may be inappropriately judged consistent, whereas many consistent cases, particularly in psychiatric samples, may be inappropriately judged inconsistent. In some cases, especially where there is a large imbalance between the proportion of items marked "true" and those marked "false," lower *VRIN* raw scores (e.g., 7–12) may lead to incorrect judgments of consistency. In these cases, *TRIN* (true response inconsistency) may prove to be a more appropriate indicator of response consistency because of its greater sensitivity to extremes and "true" versus "false" responding.

> Additional indices of consistency may usefully supplement *VRIN* and should always be used when *VRIN* falls within the indeterminant range of 11 to 16, inclusive, and we encourage their examination when *VRIN* exceeds a raw score of 6. (p. 21)

(See the section in this chapter entitled "Additional Measures of Response Style" for a discussion of other measures that can be used in conjunction with the *VRIN* scale.)

The main number of *VRIN* items earned by men and women in the MMPI–2 standardization group was approximately 5 (*SD* = 2.5). Test–retest correlation coefficients for these participants over about a 1-week interval was .54 for men and .51 for women.

Recent research data supports the validity of the *VRIN* scale. Berry et al. (1992) recently investigated the tendencies of normal participants who completed the MMPI–2 to randomly respond, although they were given the test with standard instructions. The participants were asked to estimate the extent to which they randomly responded to questions, and their self-reports were compared with their *VRIN*, *F*, and *FB* scores. The major findings showed that partial random responding occurred with some frequency and that self-reports of random responding correlated significantly with MMPI–2 random-responding measures. This study supports the construct validity of the *VRIN* scale and its sensitivity to random responding.

In another investigation of the sensitivity of the validity scales to detect random responding and malingering, Wetter et al. (1992) instructed college students to either randomly respond to the entire MMPI–2 or to fake various levels of psychiatric disturbance. Their results showed that the *VRIN* scale was elevated only in the random-responding group. The *F* and *FB* scales were elevated in both the random and malingering groups. It appears that the *VRIN* scale is essential to examine when the *F* or *FB* scale is elevated.

Although random responding elevates the *VRIN* scale, a high or intermediate *VRIN* score may not always indicate carelessness or uncooperativeness. Bond (1986, 1987) suggested that individuals with higher inconsistencies scores tend to endorse more maladjustment items. This view is consistent with data presented by Greene (1991a), who demonstrated that 43% of 68/86 codetypes could result from inconsistency. In fact, he pointed out that most code patterns that include Scale 8 frequently could result from inconsistency. This makes sense, given that seriously thought-disturbed individuals such as those obtaining the 86 or 68 profile (e.g., individuals with schizophrenia) are likely to have difficulty maintaining the consistent set that normals have during testing. Another possible explanation for indeterminant range scores on the *VRIN* scale (raw scores of 7 to 13) involves not carelessness or lack of cooperation but rather indecisiveness (Bond, 1987; Fulkerson, & Willage, 1980). If an item is clearly applicable or inapplicable to an individual, it will be relatively easy to respond with certainty and consistency. However, an item with ambiguous application to the person involves a complex judgment process that can change on a repeated presentation of an item. Bond (1986) studied the MMPI responses of college students and found that indecision, rather than carelessness, may be a more important determinant of inconsistency on repeated items. Even though Bond (1986) was studying the repeated items on the Carelessness scale and the TR index, it may be valid to generalize his findings about semantic inconsistency to the item pairs on the *VRIN* scale. Bond (1987) offered three possible reasons for which items may elicit indecision: (a) the degree of ambiguity in an item perceived by the respondent, (b) the perceived degree of relevance an item has to the respondent, and (c) the degree of conflict aroused in a respondent by an item that is applicable but of an undesirable nature. Whereas carelessness may be one factor for elevated scores or inconsistency measures, other factors, such as indecision and maladjustment, could also be important contributing determinants.

Examination of the MMPI–2 manual (Butcher et al., 1989) shows that for the contemporary normal men and women there is a small but significant correlation between the *VRIN* scale and recent life changes and a social readjustment rating scale. There is also a small but significant correlation between dysphoria and hostility and the *VRIN* scale for a subsample of men and women, as rated by their life partners on an adjustment scale. The implications raised by Bond (1986, 1987) and gleaned from the MMPI–2 manual data are that indeterminant scores of normals and psychiatric patients on the *VRIN* scale may not reveal inconsistent or careless responding as much as indecisive responding, a result that would suggest quite different empirical correlates and meaning. This issue needs more study in order to make interpretive sense out of scores in the indeterminant range on the *VRIN* scale.

True Response Inconsistency Scale (*TRIN*)

The *TRIN* scale is a new scale consisting of 23 item pairs designed to assist in the interpretation of the traditional validity indicators. Like the *VRIN* scale, the *TRIN* scale reflects the tendency of a participant to respond to items in a contradictory or inconsistent fashion (Butcher et al., 1989). Although *VRIN* items can have either similar or opposite content, *TRIN* items consist exclusively of pairs that are opposite in content. According to the MMPI–2 manual, inconsistency is scored as follows:

> If a participant responds inconsistently by answering true to both items of certain pairs, one point is added to the *TRIN* score; if the participant responds inconsistently by answering false to certain item pairs, one point is subtracted. Consequently, a very high *TRIN* score indicates a tendency for the test participant to give true answers to the items indiscriminately ("acquiescence") and a very low *TRIN* score indicates a tendency to answer false indiscriminately ("non-acquiescence")(negative *TRIN* scores are avoided by adding a constant to the raw score). In other words, very low or very high *TRIN* scores are warning that the test participant may have been answering the inventory indiscriminately so that the profile may be invalid and uninterpretable. (Butcher et al., 1989, p. 28)

The following examples of *TRIN* items, with the scored direction in parentheses, illustrate the scoring characteristics of the scale.

3. I wake up fresh and rested most mornings. (True)
39. My sleep is fitful and disturbed. (True)

This pair of items is one of the 14 item pairs to which the inconsistent response is "true." A test participant endorsing both of these items would receive 1 raw score point. The following pair of items illustrates an inconsistent response if both items are answered "false." A total of nine pairs of items are scored in the false direction.

9. My daily life is full of things that keep me interested. (False)
56. I wish I could be as happy as others seem to be. (False)

For this pair, or any pair of items scored false on the *VRIN* scale, 1 point is subtracted from the total raw score. A score of 9 points is always added to the final score to avoid the possibility of negative scores. For example, a client endorsing only falsely scored pairs of items on the *TRIN* scale and no scored items in the true direction would obtain a negative score if it were not for the constant being added. (See Table A.1 for a complete listing of the *TRIN* items and the scoring key).

The MMPI–2 manual shows that the contemporary sample of men and women averaged approximately 9 raw score points on the *TRIN* scale. Test–retest reliability data in the MMPI–2 manual for about a 1-week interval show normal men and women to have a correlation coefficient of .34 and .52, respectively. The manual also recommends that a *TRIN* score of 5 or less or 13 or greater would suggest inconsistent responding. A low raw score reflects a false-response bias, whereas higher scores reflect a true-response bias. The contemporary normal sample is used as a reference group for converting the raw scores on the *TRIN* scale to linear *T* scores.

Interpretation of the *TRIN* scale often can clarify the validity of a particular profile. For example, a high *F* score in conjunction with the markedly elevated *TRIN* score suggests indiscriminate responding, whereas an elevated *T* score with a low to moderate *TRIN* score reveals a possible magnification of symptoms or marked psychopathology. The *TRIN* scale, like the *VRIN* scale, should always be assessed when interpreting the validity of any MMPI–2 profile.

Infrequency Scale (F)

The *F* scale was designed to measure the tendency of an individual to respond to the test items in an unusual manner, such as in the case of not comprehending the items. On the MMPI–2, it consists of 60 items (64 items on the MMPI) to which at least 90% of the normals in the original standardization group responded in the same direction (either true or false). Whether an *F* scale item is answered true or false is irrelevant; the point is that the items are said to have high community agreement in most cases.[5] According to Marks, Seeman, and Haller (1974), "every time a participant responds in a rare direction, they are deviating from the community on some participant in which it is in exceedingly high agreement"(p. 12). For this reason, the scale has come to be called the Frequency or Infrequency scale. Because the probability is .90 or better that for any given item the normal participant will answer in the popular direction, it is not surprising that the mean number of deviant responses for the *F* scale is relatively low for the MMPI–2 normative sample (mean score for men = 4.5, mean score for women = 3.7).[6] Normal individuals responding to the test with the usual care and understanding usually will not obtain raw score values above 6 or *T*-score values higher than 55 on the MMPI–2 (Butcher et al., 1989). However, individuals suffering from situational distress (e.g., loss of a loved one or relationship or job-related problems) or psychopathology often will elevate their *F* scale score as high as *T*-score values of 65 or greater.

The *F* scale items represent a broad range of content that obviously suggests deviant behavior, making it relatively easy for individuals either to deny symptoms or to overclaim problems, depending on their motives. The item composition of the *F* scale with the scoring direction is presented in Appendix A. Examples of *F* scale items, with the item numbers and keyed responses, are as follows:

24. Evil spirits possess me at times. (True)
30. I have nightmares every few nights. (True)
36. When I am with people, I am bothered by hearing very queer things. (True)
78. I am liked by most people who know me. (False)
126. I believe in law enforcement. (False)
168. I have had periods in which I carried on activities without knowing later what I had been doing. (True)

The *F* scale underwent some changes in the restandardization, with 12 modifications to the 60 items, including six grammatical changes, five modernizations of idioms and usage, and one change in sexist wording (Dahlstrom, 1993). The content of the *F* scale remains diverse and includes psychotic-type experiences and strange sensations, social maladjustment, poor physical health, hostility, and unconventional beliefs. Because 25 of the 60 items overlap other scales, and because about one third of the scale items are scored on the so-called psychotic tetrad scales (Scales 6, 7, 8, and 9), increasing elevations on the *F* scale are usually associated with increasing psychotic scale elevations. Greene (1991a) pointed out that 15 *F* scale items overlap with Scale 8 (Schizophrenia) and 9 items overlap with Scale 6 (Paranoia). (See Appendix C for a table presenting the amount of item overlap content on the *F* scale.)

The *F* scale—when elevated—is considered one of the most sensitive scales of the test for indicating severity of maladjustment and generally tends to correspond to the overall elevation of the clinical scales. For this reason, seriously or acutely disturbed individuals tend to obtain elevated scores on this scale. Also, people who exaggerate their concerns and psychological problems by overclaiming symptoms elevate the *F* scale, whereas individuals wishing to appear free of psychological problems tend to produce low scores (Friedman, Webb, & Lewak, 1989; Rothke et al., 1994). Numerous studies have supported the validity of the *F* scale in detecting people who overclaim symptoms or malinger, with the general result that the *F* scale is elevated above a *T* score of 90. Cutoffs vary for this scale according to the setting, but scores above 90 generally should raise the concern of the clinician to look for other indications in the MMPI–2 of exaggeration or random responding as well as in nontest data, such as interviews, life history data, and observations from people familiar with the participant. In a recent review of the MMPI with a focus on the validity scales, Berry, Baer, and Harris (1991) meta-analytically reviewed 28 studies that used the MMPI to detect malingering. The multiple comparisons contrasting malingering and honest groups on the raw and *T*-scaled *F* scores showed that this scale (particularly raw score values of *F*) is one of the most powerful measures on the test in detecting faking. The *F* scale was elevated slightly over 2 *SD*s above scores of participants answering honestly. Although their study identified other measures in the test for detecting malingering, the *F* scale was clearly the measure of choice for detecting "faking bad." It is recommended, however, that the reader not rely on any one scale in deciding about an individual's test-taking attitudes. Rather, a combination of measures coupled with nontest data should be considered in the clinical decision-making/inference process.

Elevated *F* scale scores may result from either a single factor, such as poor comprehension, random responding, severe psychosis or malingering, or a combination of these factors. Therefore, it is important to consider the *F* scale as serving three important functions (Graham, 1990). First, the scale should be considered as an indication of the openness or guarded approach of the test taker. Next, if the profile appears valid and the *F* scale score is in the patient range, it may roughly indicate the person's level of distress or maladjustment. Last, scores on the scale can serve to suggest behavioral correlates about the individual. (Specific behavioral, emotional, and cognitive correlates for the *F* scale are described in chap. 5). Numerous recent studies and reviews have provided useful guidelines for interpreting elevations on this scale (Bagby, Rogers, & Buis, 1994; Bagby, Rogers, Buis, & Kalemba, 1994; Berry, Baer, & Harris, 1991; Berry, et al., 1995; Lamb, Berry, Wetter, & Baer, 1994; Rogers, Bagby, & Chakraborty, 1993; Rogers, Sewell, & Salekin, 1994; Rothke et al., 1994; Sivec, Lynn, & Garske, 1994; Wetter, Baer, Berry, Robinson, & Sumpter, 1993).

Test–retest correlation coefficients for 82 men and 111 women from the contemporary normative sample are reported in the MMPI–2 manual (Butcher et al., 1989). These participants were retested at an average interval of 8.58 days (*Mdn* = 7 days), with men and women showing test–retest values of .78 and .69, respectively. Although the MMPI–2 manual does not present similar data for psychiatric patients, Dahlstrom et al. (1975) reported test–retest coefficients for psychiatric cases on the *F* scale that range from .80 to .81 with a 1- to 2-day interval between tests and from .63 to .76 with a 1-year interval between tests. In a large-scale meta-analysis of MMPI reliability studies using a wide variety of populations conducted between 1970 and 1981, Hunsley et al. (1988) found an average internal consistency of .77 across 70 studies of the *F* scale. They also reported an average test–retest reliability of .70 for 15 studies, with time intervals from 1 day to 2 years.

F-Back Scale *(FB)*

The *FB* scale was developed on the MMPI–2 to operate in a manner similar to the *F* scale, but the items appear later in the inventory. The 60-item *F* scale is scored within the first 361 items, with 82% of the items scored between Items 1 and 299. The last *F* scale item is 361, which indicates that this sensitive scale prematurely stops its measurement function short of the entire instrument. Therefore, the restandardization committee for the MMPI–2 designed a 40-item *F*-Back scale (so named because of the location of the items in Form *Ax*) to pick up where the *F* scale left off (Butcher et al., 1989). *FB* begins at Item 281. Although the basic validity and clinical scales are all scored within the first 370 items, many of the content and supplementary scale items occur after Item 370. Therefore, a scale similar to the *F* scale was needed for the latter part of the test to detect random or faking-bad/faking-good tendencies that could affect the content and supplementary scale scores.

Items on the *FB* scale were selected if they were endorsed by less than 10% of the contemporary normative sample in the deviant direction. The majority of *FB* scale items (95%) are concentrated between Items 300 and 567, making the scale sensitive to a response set or shift in responding due to fatigue or a change in cooperation during the latter part of an MMPI–2 administration. In this regard, the *FB* scale serves a parallel function to the earlier occurring *F* scale, with a wideband sensitivity to different response sets, including symptom magnification or fabrication, random responding, and severe psychopathology (Berry et al., 1992). The following are examples of *FB* scale items, with the scoring direction indicated in parentheses (see Table A1 for a complete listing of the *FB* content and the scoring key):

281. I dislike having people around me. (True)
291. I have never been in love with anyone. (True)
303. Most of the time I wish I were dead. (True)
311. I often feel as if things are not real. (True)
407. I deserve severe punishment for my sins. (True)
463. Several times a week I feel as if something dreadful is about to happen. (True)
383. When things get really bad, I know I can count on my family for help. (False)
404. I have no trouble swallowing. (False)

It should be noted that the *FB* scale, although similar in its construction to the *F* scale, is somewhat different in its content. The predominant content theme in the *F* scale appears to be psychoticism, whereas the main theme for the *FB* scale appears to be acute distress and depression (Nichols & Greene, 1995). Therefore, clinicians should consider this content difference when making any interpretive inferences from the two scales.

Because the *FB* scale was constructed to appear later in the test, it shares little item overlap with the standard clinical scales. The *FB* scale shares two items each with Scales 6 (Paranoia) and 7 (Psychasthenia) and nine items with Scale 8 (Schizophrenia). However, because most of the items are scored between Items 300 and 567, there is significant overlap with the content scales and, to a lesser degree, with the supplementary scales. For example, the *FB* scale shares as many as

6 items with the content scales *DEP* (Depression) and *FRS* (Fears) and as few as one item with *SOD* (Social Discomfort), *ANX* (Anxiety), *ANG* (Anger), and *HEA* (Health Concerns).

As mentioned above, although some content differences exist between the *FB* and the *F* scales, examination of the partner ratings in the contemporary normative sample shows that the *FB* scale is similar to the *F* scale in that it shows significant positive correlations with dysphoria, hostility, impulsivity, and antisocial behavior and negative correlations with sociability and conformity (Butcher et al., 1989). It should be noted that almost the entire *FB* scale is keyed in the "true" direction (37 of the 40 items), so a "true" response bias will tend to elevate the scale. A very high score should be checked against the *TRIN* score, *VRIN* score, and the answer sheet itself.

Internal consistency estimates (Cronbach's coefficient alpha) for the *FB* scale is .71 for a subsample of 82 men in the normative sample and .75 for a subsample of 111 women. Test–retest reliability coefficients for the same participants are .86 for men and .71 for women, with a mean test–retest interval of 8.5 days. *F* scale test–retest correlation coefficients are much lower for men (.78) and about the same for women (.69; Butcher et.al., 1989).

Although the construction method was similar for the *F* and *FB* scales, the same raw score values will yield more extreme *T* scores on the *FB* scale than on the *F* scale because the *FB* scale has a smaller standard deviation than the *F* scale. This is, in part, because the *FB* scale has fewer items (40 items vs. 60 on the *F* scale) and, more importantly, because the *FB* scale, unlike the *F* scale, has been derived on the basis of the contemporary MMPI–2 norms and as a result has a higher proportion of items with extreme endorsement frequencies (Arbisi & Ben-Porath, 1995b; A. Tellegen, personal communication, March 5, 1999).

Berry et al. (1991) found that a raw score of 9 on the *FB* scale outpredicted the ability of the *VRIN* scale to detect random profiles (the *VRIN* scale is described later in this chapter). Berry et al. (1991b) had 180 college students complete the MMPI–2 under standard instructions prior to having their test booklets removed and the remaining blanks on the answer sheet randomly completed. Groups of students had their booklets removed after 100, 200, 300, 400, or 500 items were completed. The more random responses that were given, the higher the *FB* scores (as well as those for the *F* and *VRIN* scales). Thus, the scale appears to be sensitive to random responding. Berry et al. (1992) also found the *FB* scale to be sensitive to random responding in job applicants and community volunteers; a significant number of these normal participants taking the MMPI–2 admitted to answering some of the MMPI–2 items in a random manner. The range of average random responses was between 12 and 38. Positive correlations between the *FB* scale (and other validity scales) and the participant's self-estimations of random responding support the sensitivity of the *FB* scale to noncontent responding.

Further support for the sensitivity of the FB scale to detect not only random responding but also malingering comes from an investigation by Wetter, Baer, Berry, Smith, and Larsen (1992). These researchers explored the effects of both random responding and malingering on the validity scales of the MMPI–2 using four groups of college students. One group completed the answer sheet in a random manner, two other groups were told to complete the MMPI–2 so as to appear moderately or severely disturbed, and the last group answered honestly. The *FB* scale was sensitive to all four conditions and performed as well as the *F* scale. The *FB* scale scores increased in elevation with the level of feigned disturbance. The fake-severe disturbance group produced the highest *FB* score (*M* =119, *SD* = 4.2), followed by random responders (*M* = 116.5, *SD* = 6.0). The values for the *F* scale followed the same pattern and were only slightly higher, except for the fake-severe group, which had an almost identical value (*M* =119.4, *SD* =3.7) to the *FB* scale.

The efficacy of the *FB* scale to detect the overreporting of symptoms is further illustrated in a study by Wetter et al. (1993), who instructed two groups of normal adults about the characteristics of posttraumatic stress disorder (PTSD) and paranoid schizophrenia and then asked them to simulate these disorders on the MMPI–2. To determine if the information about the disorders helped them to feign a realistic profile, Wetter et al. compared their scores with actual groups of paranoid schizophrenic and PTSD patients. Having specific information about the psychological disorder did not enable the fakers to simulate actual patient profiles with the validity scales, including the *FB* scale. Specifically, the PTSD patients produced a mean *FB* *T*-scale score of 85 (*SD* = 23.6), whereas the simulators produced a mean *T*-score value of 110 (*SD* = 20.3). The paranoid schizophrenic patients produced a mean *T*-score value of 74.2 on the *F*(*B*) scale (*SD* = 19.0), with the simulators earning a mean *T*-score value of 119.3 (*SD* = 2.0). Clearly, the fakers tended to grossly overclaim symptoms relative to the actual patients, a trend consistently seen in the faking-bad literature. Malingerers reliably score in the upper *T*-score ranges on both the *F* and *FB* scales.

Although the *FB* scale is a new scale, it has received significant research attention since its publication and appears to be a useful and valuable addition to the MMPI–2. In a recent meta-analysis of malingering scales and indexes on the MMPI–2, Rogers et al. (1994) found that the *FB* scale yielded strong effect sizes for controls and psychiatric comparison groups. They did point out that large ranges of cutting scores exist for the *FB*, suggesting that clinicians need to exercise the same caution in interpreting this scale as they do for the other validity measures. Greene (1991a) suggested interpreting the elevation on the *FB* scale in a similar manner to the *F* scale because the construction of the two scales is so similar. This appears to be a practical suggestion, but readers should be aware that they could encounter profiles in which the *FB* scale may be significantly more elevated than the *F* scale (e.g., a participant may produce an *FB* scale *T* score of 110 with an *F* scale *T* score of 65). Such a difference suggests the possibility of fatigue, uncooperativeness, or random responding in the latter portion of the MMPI–2 rendering the content and supplementary scales uninterpretable. However, because the person responded consistently in the earlier part of the test, the standard clinical scales can be meaningfully analyzed. It is rare to see the converse situation—a high *F* scale score but a within-normal-limit-range *FB* scale score. Such a protocol would suggest standard interpretation of the content or supplementary scales, but caution should be exercised in interpreting the clinical scales. In general, a multivariate approach to profile validity is suggested, with the examination of the *FB* scale being an important part of this process. It is important to recall that the difference in content between the *F* scale (which emphasizes psychoticism) and the *FB* scale (which emphasizes acute distress) may also account for discrepancies between elevations on these scales.

Cutoff scores for validity measures in the MMPI–2 vary from study to study as a function of local base rates and participant characteristics, such as educational level and intelligence. Therefore, the psychologist would be wise to examine each protocol on an individual basis while considering different factors, including, but not limited to, the participant's motivation or test-taking attitude (e.g., overreporting in an attempt to gain sympathy or monetary gain as in a personal-injury litigation case), socioeconomic factors, reading ability (which could affect comprehension), and psychopathology (which can operate independently or in concert with any of the above-mentioned factors). Guidelines for determining an invalid profile are described in this chapter and in chapter 5; however, in general, the same *T*-score values that apply for the *F* scale should be used for the *FB* scale in suggesting profile invalidity.

Additional Measures of Response Style

The usefulness of the standard validity scales can be enhanced by examining additional measures of reporting or response styles, which can be distinguished as self-favorable or self-unfavorable in nature. Self-deception and impression management tendencies are factors important to consider in clinical, forensic, and personnel settings, where motivation can affect the test results. (See Nichols & Greene, 1997, for a comprehensive overview on the subject of deception as it relates to the MMPI–2.)

The *Ds* and *F(p)* scales are categorized as measuring the reporting of self-unfavorable traits, attributes, and dispositions that the participant believes to be false. Scales *L*, *K*, *S*, *Mp*, *Sd*, and *Ss* are measuring the displaying or mimicking of self-favorable traits, attributes, and dispositions. These scales are not meant to be inclusive of all available scales for use but rather represent what we recognize to be the mainstream measurements or those with the potential to develop into useful adjuncts to the standard validity scales.

SELF-UNFAVORABLE SCALES

The Infrequency–Psychopathology Scale: *F(p)*

The *F(p)* scale was designed by Arbisi and Ben-Porath (1995a, 1995b) for the MMPI–2 as an additional self-unfavorable or over reporting measure, particularly for use with patient populations in which a high rate of endorsement of psychological disturbance is expected. They suggested that the *F(p)* scale be used to understand elevations on the *F* scale, which may be elevated for several reasons, including random responding, poor reading comprehension of the items, genuine psychopathology, or an attempt to fake bad (i.e., attempt to portray one's self as more impaired than is actually the case). As previously described, the *F* scale contains items that were endorsed by less than 10% of the normal standardization group of the original MMPI (Hathaway & McKinley, 1943); it was not constructed of items that were endorsed infrequently by psychiatric patients (a common misconception about the scale). Therefore, an elevated *F* scale score cannot automatically be assumed to be an indication of malingering of illness or of an invalid profile (Friedman, Webb, & Lewak, 1989). The *F(p)* scale was constructed of items endorsed rarely (20% or less in the keyed direction) by two separate groups of patients with known psychiatric disturbance and by members of the MMPI–2 restandardization sample. As noted by Arbisi and Ben-Porath (1997), there are overlapping items between the *F(p)* scale and certain clinical scales, especially Scale 8 (*Sc*), with which it shares five items in common. The item overlap between the *F(p)* scale and the other clinical scales is substantially less than that between the *F* and *FB* scales and the clinical scales. The *F(p)* scale contains 27 items, of which 15 overlap with the *F* scale. The following items represent examples of the content on this new scale, with the direction of scoring following the item in parentheses:

66. It would be better if all laws were thrown away. (True)
93. Sometimes when I am not feeling well I am irritable. (False)
162. Someone has been trying to poison me. (True)
252. Everything tastes the same. (True)
478. I hate my whole family. (True)

Arbisi and Ben-Porath (1995b) suggested that when the *F(p)* scale is elevated along with the *F* scale, the clinician can more confidently attribute the high scores to a patient's attempt to overreport psychopathology if other validity measures such as the *VRIN* and *TRIN* scales are not elevated significantly. More recent investigations have found that the *F(p)* scale is less influenced by diagnostic membership and the confounding effects of distress and psychopathology than is the *F* scale and is more effective than the *F* scale in distinguishing groups with genuine psychopathology from those asked to feign psychiatric impairment (Arbisi & Ben-Porath, 1997; Frueh et al., 1997; Ladd, 1998; Rothke et al., 2000). However, Bagby, Rogers, Buis, et al. (1997) found that the *F(p)* scale was more effective in distinguishing patients with schizophrenia from participants feigning that disorder whereas the *F* and *FB* scales were better able to identify patients with depression from participants feigning depression. This finding is not surprising, given that the *F(p)* item content is more relevant to psychoticism than it is to major depression. Nicholson et al. (1997) found that the *F(p)* scale failed to outperform the *F* scale in their malingering comparisons. Even so, Nicholson et al. (1997) noted "that *F(p)* may be the preferred index of fake bad responding when the two indicators perform comparably because interpretation of elevated scores appears more straight-forward in the case of *F(p)* than *F*" (p. 476).

Rothke et al. (in press) provided normative data for the *F(p)* scale with a large variety of clinical and forensic samples, including psychiatric inpatients with borderline personality disorder (BPD), paranoid schizophrenia, PTSD, and alcoholism, as well as pain management patients, TBI patients, and Social Security disability-benefit applicants. In addition, data were provided for nonlitigating TBI patients and normals simulating BPD, PTSD, and paranoid schizophrenia. The results showed that elevations on the *F(p)* scale are infrequent in most clinical samples; elevations are much more common when malingering or exaggeration of psychopathology is expected. Consistent with the findings of Arbisi and Ben-Porath (1997), Rothke et al.'s study supports the finding that the *F*(*p*) scale is relatively independent of psychiatric diagnoses and is less sensitive than scale the *F* or *FB* scale to specific psychopathology.

It is recommended that the *F*(*p*) scale be studied further, but its applied use should be governed by using a sequence of steps, as well as observing cautions about its potential limitations. Arbisi and Ben-Porath (1995b) recommended that the following sequence be followed in interpreting an elevated *F* scale: (a) Rule out random responding and acquiescence by eliminating profiles with elevated *VRIN* ($T \geq 100$) or *TRIN* ($T \geq 80$) scores; (b) rule out malingering or exaggeration by considering whether *F*(*p*) is elevated; and (c) if the results of steps a and b are negative, then a high *F* scale can be considered consistent with psychopathology. An elevated *FB* score should be interpreted with the same sequence.

When an elevated *F*(*p*) scale is encountered, we recommend that an examination be made of which items are endorsed before a conclusion about exaggeration or malingering is made. For example, four of the items on the *F*(*p*) scale (Items 90, 192, 276, and 478) deal with participants' views of their mother and father and whether they love (loved) their parents and family. Rothke et al. (in press) reported a case of a patient with no other signs of malingering or secondary gain issues who endorsed all four of these items, consistent with a very significant history of impaired family relationships. Despite the fact that these items were rarely endorsed by the clinical derivation sample or the normal standardization group, we suggest that the clinician be mindful of a history of significant family problems before interpreting an *F*(*p*) score inflated by the endorsement of two or more of these four items. Given that it takes very few item endorsements to inflate an *F*(*p*) score, these types of concerns should be addressed to avoid overinterpreting the meaning of an elevated *F*(*p*) score.

It is important to recognize that because the *F*(*p*) items extend almost throughout the inventory (up to Item 555), an elevated *F*(*p*) score could be due to item endorsements fairly evenly distributed or concentrated early or late or even in the middle of the instrument. To address these types of concerns, the MMPI–2 restandardization committee added the *FB* scale to cover infrequently endorsed items that occur later in the MMPI–2 (as described earlier, the *F* scale stops its measurement function at Item 361). This was done with the awareness that individuals may change their approach (e.g., because of fatigue, uncooperativeness, or boredom) to answering the items during the test administration. The utility of the *FB* scale lies in the fact that many important scales (e.g., content and supplementary) occur later in the inventory and warrant interpretive caution should the *FB* scale be significantly elevated.

Similarly, Arbisi and Ben-Porath (1995a) and Arbisi, McNulty, Ben-Porath, and Boyd (1999) recognized that the *F(p)* scale could be applied in a similar way as the *F* and *FB* scales. That is, by dividing the *F(p)* item content into items occurring earlier versus later in the test, they could identify differences on these subcomponent scales, which could help explain an elevated *FB* or *F* score. These component subscales are named *F(p)1* and *F(p)2*. The *F(p)1* subscale begins with Item 51 and ends with Item 252; the *F(p)2* subscale begins with Item 270 and ends with Item 501. The following examples should help illustrate how scoring for the *F(p)1* and *F(p)2* subscales could assist in the interpretive process. Consider a participant who obtains an acceptable *VRIN* and *TRIN* score, indicating consistent responding, but significantly elevates the *FB* scale with a normal-range *F* score. Examination of the *F(p)* score for possible exaggeration might reveal a slightly elevated scale score (e.g., raw score of 3 or 4) but not one which is considered exceedingly high in terms of a *T-score* value. By scoring the *F(p)1* and *F(p)2* subscales, the clinician could discover that all three or four items were endorsed on the *F(p)2* subscale, thereby raising the distinct possibility that the respondent began exaggerating his or her complaints in the latter part of the inventory. This should alert the clinician to be careful to not overinterpret the content and supplementary scales that occur later in the inventory. When the *F* and *F(p)* scales are elevated without the *FB* scale also being elevated, an inspection of the *F(p)* subscales can help the clinician feel confident to interpret the content and supplementary scales if the *F(p)2* subscale is not significantly elevated.

Clearly, research is needed to better understand the operating characteristics of these new components subscales, but they appear to have promise in assisting test interpreters to identify response sets occurring early or late in the test administration process.

It is important to remember that specific clinical settings reflect different base rates of psychopathology; it is therefore critical that clinicians understand the nature of their population with regard to frequency and type of psychopathology before interpreting the *F(p)* scale or any other scale score. Arbisi and Ben-Porath (1997) recommended that additional studies be conducted in settings in which clear incentives to feign symptoms exist. Rothke et al. (in press) suggested that future investigations of samples of psychiatric or injured patients control for motivation to appear impaired (as might be the case in patients involved in litigation, seeking disability compensation, or attempting to avoid criminal prosecution) by carefully interviewing the patient or by record review as the *F(p)* scale appears sensitive to efforts to overreport symptoms. In the Rothke et al. study, participants who were either in the process of litigation and seeking compensation, or feigning psychiatric conditions produced elevated *F(p)* scores, supporting the construct validity of the scale. This is not to suggest, however, that all litigating participants exaggerate their complaints. When used with clinical judgment, the *F(p)* scale can be a useful addition to the assessment of MMPI–2 profile validity. (See Table A.1 for a listing of the *F(p)* item composition and direction of scoring; see Tables B.1 and B.2 for the raw-score-to-*T*-score conversions for the MMPI–2 standardization group.)

Dissimulation Scale (*Ds*)

Gough (1954) developed the 74-item *Ds* scale by identifying MMPI items that empirically differentiated a group of patients classified as psychoneurotic from a group of test normals (college students and professional psychologists) instructed to take the MMPI simulating the role of a neurotic patient. The items separating the simulators from the patients were further studied in a cross-validation procedure. The simulators tended to score much higher than the actual neurotic patients, suggesting that individuals prevailing stereotypes about neuroticism were not a good fit to the actual construct of neuroticism as measured by the MMPI. (For a more current study of prevailing stereotypes about mental illness, see Rapport, Todd, Lumley, & Fisicaro, 1998.) The *Ds* scale is intended to be used for assessing the intentional overstatement of psychological disturbance or faking sick. The function of the scale is similar to the *F* and *FB* scales, although the content of the *Ds* scale is much more subtle than the latter scales, where "what is the rare and atypical response" (Caldwell, 1997, p. 17) is consistently obvious. The *Ds* scale does not have the extreme or psychotic-related item content of the *F* and *FB* scales and overlaps neurotic exaggeration as much as psychotic malingering. It is therefore useful in assessing the intentional exaggeration of a variety of symptoms for financial gain or manipulative intent (Caldwell, 1997). Rogers et al. (1994) also pointed out that the scale is multifaceted and extends beyond neurotic symptoms. Gough indicated that the *Ds* items covered the following: physical complaints and dysfunctions; feelings of victimization, injustice, and discouragement; irritability,fear, and anxiety; lack of independence and self-sufficiency; discontent with childhood and family background; sexual conflicts and preoccupations; and bizarre ideation and religiosity.

The MMPI–2 has retained 58 of the original 74 *Ds* items (78.4%) of which 19% were altered (Rogers et al. 1994).[7] Table A1 lists the item composition and scoring key for the 58- item MMPI–2 *Ds* scale (sometimes referred to as *Ds2* for purposes of clarity by some researchers); Tables B1 and B2 list the raw-score-to-*T*-score conversions for the scale. The following items are examples of the *Ds* scale content, with the direction of scoring in parentheses. Note that the majority of the scale items are scored as "true" (48), with 10 items scored as "false."

17. I am sure I get a raw deal from life. (True)
22. No one seems to understand me. (True)
57. I hardly ever feel pain in the back of my neck. (False)
72. My soul sometimes leaves my body. (True)
75. I usually feel that life is worthwhile. (False)

In providing a general review of the *Ds* scale with a few specific research examples, we wish to convey the point that the basic findings are consistent across studies; that is, that the *Ds* scale appears to measure exaggerated claims of psychopathology. There are a number of recent and older studies and reviews supporting the construct validity of the scale (e.g., Anthony, 1971; Bagby et al.,

1997; Berry, Baer, & Harris, 1991; Frueh, Gold, & de Arellano, 1997; Gough, 1954, 1957; Greene, 1991a, 2000; Nichols & Greene, 1997; Rogers et al., 1994; Walters, White, & Greene, 1998; Wetter et al., 1992).

Anthony (1971) instructed 40 nonpsychotic U.S. Air Force male clients, after taking the MMPI under usual administration conditions, to exaggerate the troubles that had brought them to treatment so that their readministered MMPI would reflect a more severe condition than they were actually experiencing. They were also asked to exaggerate in a way that was not clearly obvious. The 74-item *Ds* scale was scored, and the results showed an optimum hit rate of 86% in identifying exaggerated MMPI profiles. This hit rate was higher than the $F - K$ (81%) and F raw-score (81%) hit rates. The findings support the utility of the *Ds* scale in discriminating exaggerated MMPIs from authentically produced deviant profiles. In support of Anthony's findings, Greene (1991a) stated that the *Ds* scale appears useful in identifying fake-bad profiles.

Walters et al. (1988) found support for the use of the *Ds-r* scale, an abbreviated version of the *Ds* scale (see Note 10), in an inmate population for identifying genuinely disturbed inmates. In the first part of a two-phase study, Walters et al. were interested in how the standard validity and clinical scales performed against the *Ds-r* scale (and other indexes). The participants were 72 male inmates with maximum security status at a U.S. penitentiary. A structured psychiatric interview was administered to the inmates, generally within one day of an administered MMPI. A 4-point rating scale was created to evaluate an inmate's proneness to exaggerate psychiatric symptomatology. The ratings were made by two psychologists familiar with both the inmates and their contact with others (e.g., work supervisors). The average length of time between the psychiatric interview and the rating assignment was 7.6 months. A rating of 1 on the scale reflected malingering, whereas a rating of 4 indicated no malingering or embellishment of symptomatology. The base-rate estimate for psychopathology in this setting was estimated to be 60%. An abbreviated MMPI was scored (first 400 items of Form R), so only 28, rather than 40, *Ds-r* items could be scored. Therefore, prorated T-scores were calculated for the *Ds-r* scale. The results showed that the MMPI validity and clinical scales (with the exception of Scale 1) could not accurately discriminate the malingerers from the nonmalingerers. Although the *Ds-r* scale failed to improve on the base-rate criterion in the study without the assistance of an indeterminant category, it could differentiate malingering from genuine psychopathology. Low scores on the *Ds-r* scale were predictive of authentic pathology, but high scores failed to correlate with malingering.

More recently, Berry, Baer, and Harris (1991) meta-analytically reviewed 28 studies that used the original MMPI to detect malingering. The contrasting of several malingering and honest groups on several reporting measures showed the original *Ds* scale to be one of the most effective measures in detecting overreporting and one of the indexes of choice for identifying malingering. The mean effect size in *T*-scale value was approximately 2 *SD*s ($d = 2.17$) for the *Ds* scale. For the original Dissimulation scale (*Ds*), a raw cutting score of 35 was common across studies and had a hit rate of about 88%. The revised Dissimulation scale (*Ds-r*) had much lower effect sizes when contrasting faking and honest groups, suggesting caution in its use (Berry, Baer, & Harris 1991).

Whereas Berry, Baer, and Harris (1991) focused on findings with the original MMPI, Rogers et al. (1994) examined different faking indicators specifically for the MMPI–2. Rogers et al. reported that although the meta-analysis by Berry, Baer, and Harris demonstrated the efficacy of the *Ds* scale in assessing malingering, unfortunately most of the MMPI–2 studies had relied on the shortened 34-item version of the Dissimulation scale, sometimes referred to as *Ds- r2*. The *Ds-r2* yielded only a moderate effect size in the meta-analysis. The longer 58-item version of the scale is likely to be more discriminating in its detection of dissimulated profiles. Berry et al. (1995) found the *Ds2* scale (58 items) to be effective in detecting the overreporting of closed-head injury symptoms by nonclinical participants instructed to fake such a syndrome and by compensation-seeking (vs. non-compensation-seeking) closed-head injury patients. Berry et al. (1995) cautioned that an unelevated overreporting scale score, such as on the *Ds-r2*, does not automatically rule out the possibility of feigning of neuropsychological problems.was administered to the inmates, generally within one day of an administered MMPI. A 4-point rating scale was created to evaluate an inmate's proneness to exaggerate psychiatric symptomatology. The ratings were made by two psychologists familiar with both the inmates and their contact with others (e.g., work supervisors). The average length of time between the psychiatric interview and the rating assignment was 7.6 months. A rating of 1 on the scale reflected malingering, whereas a rating of 4 indicated no malingering or embellishment of symptomatology. The base-rate estimate for psychopathology in this setting was estimated to be 60%. An abbreviated MMPI was scored (first 400 items of Form R), so only 28, rather than 40, *Ds-r* items could be scored. Therefore, prorated T-scores were calculated for the *Ds-r* scale. The results showed that the MMPI validity and clinical scales (with the exception of Scale 1) could not accurately discriminate the malingerers from the nonmalingerers. Although the *Ds-r* scale failed to improve on the base-rate criterion in the study without the assistance of an indeterminant category, it could differentiate malingering from genuine psychopathology. Low scores on the *Ds-r* scale were predictive of authentic pathology, but high scores failed to correlate with malingering.

More recently, Berry, Baer, and Harris (1991) meta-analytically reviewed 28 studies that used the original MMPI to detect malingering. The contrasting of several malingering and honest groups on several reporting measures showed the original *Ds* scale to be one of the most effective measures in detecting overreporting and one of the indexes of choice for identifying malingering. The mean effect size in *T*-scale value was approximately 2 *SD*s (d = 2.17) for the *Ds* scale. For the original Dissimulation scale (*Ds*), a raw cutting score of 35 was common across studies and had a hit rate of about 88%. The revised Dissimulation scale (*Ds-r*) had much lower effect sizes when contrasting faking and honest groups, suggesting caution in its use (Berry, Baer, & Harris 1991).

Whereas Berry, Baer, and Harris (1991) focused on findings with the original MMPI, Rogers et al. (1994) examined different faking indicators specifically for the MMPI–2. Rogers et al. reported that although the meta-analysis by Berry, Baer, and

Harris demonstrated the efficacy of the *Ds* scale in assessing malingering, unfortunately most of the MMPI–2 studies had relied on the shortened 34-item version of the Dissimulation scale, sometimes referred to as *Ds- r2*. The *Ds-r2* yielded only a moderate effect size in the meta-analysis. The longer 58-item version of the scale is likely to be more discriminating in its detection of dissimulated profiles. Berry et al. (1995) found the *Ds2* scale (58 items) to be effective in detecting the overreporting of closed-head injury symptoms by nonclinical participants instructed to fake such a syndrome and by compensation-seeking (vs. noncompensation-seeking) closed-head injury patients. Berry et al. (1995) cautioned that an unelevated overreporting scale score, such as on the *Ds-r2*, does not automatically rule out the possibility of feigning of neuropsychological problems.

> It is possible that a participant fabricating or exaggerating closed-head injury symptoms might not conceptualize the syndrome as including psychiatric, as opposed to physical and cognitive problems. Thus, they might feign deficits on neuropsychological testing but not on the MMPI–2 and hence not elevate overreporting scales. (p. 522)

We suggest that the 58-item version of the Dissimulation scale (*Ds*) is a useful additional scale in evaluating the validity of an MMPI–2 profile. However, more research is needed, especially with adolescents and actual samples of malingerers versus analogue study participants. Research findings vary regarding cut scores as a function of the population studied, the methodology used, and the sample size employed. For these reasons, it is recommended that an assessment of protocol validity be based on the examination of multiple MMPI–2 measures as well as rely on other clinical data beyond the MMPI–2, such as record reviews, life history data, and interview findings.

SELF-FAVORABLE SCALES

Factor studies of various measures of self-favorable responding to the MMPI have repeatedly produced findings indicating that defensiveness cannot be subsumed under a single dimension. In Wiggins' (1964) analysis and expansion of these reports, he distinguished between Alpha (Block, 1965), a dimension consistent with A. L. Edwards' (1957) interpretation of faking good on personality inventories without special instructions to do so (p. 57), and Gamma, which Wiggins (1964) interpreted as "social desirability in role-playing" (p. 555). Nichols and Greene (1988), for example, found a strong tendency for scales developed under fake-good instructional sets to be highly correlated with each other but only weakly associated with scales like *K* and *A*. Paulhus (1984, 1986) proposed a two-factor model of social desirability responding that distinguishes between self-deception, the tendency to bias inventory responses brought about by the person's belief that such responses are true and justified, and impression management ("other deception"), a self-conscious and deliberate attempt to tailor responses so as to create a favorable impression and mislead the clinician in the direction of an overly benign personality description from test results. The Gamma dimension has been labeled variously as "lying" (A. L.

Edwards, Diers, & Walker, 1962), "propagandistic bias" (Damarin & Messick, 1965) and "impression management" (Paulhus, 1984, 1986); these labels converge on the theme of a self-conscious, or intentional, motivation to promote a favorable impression of the self. The Alpha dimension is largely coextensive with the first factor of the MMPI/MMPI–2, with the high end of this dimension being marked by scales that reflect distress, discomfort, and maladjustment (e.g., *A*, *Pt*, and *DEP*) and the negative pole marked by scales such as *K*, *Es*, *S*, and *Ss*. In the Wiggins (1964) and Paulhus (1984, 1986) analyses, this factor was marked by the *K* scale and Edwards' Social Desirability scale (*So-r*). Two of the scales described later, Butcher and Han's (1995) Superlative Self-Presentation scale (*S*) and S. E. Nelson's (1952) Socioeconomic Status scale (*Ss*), also are related to this dimension. The other two scales, Cofer, Chance, and Judson's (1949) Positive Malingering scale (*Mp*) and Wiggins' (1959) Social Desirability scale (*Sd*) marked, along with the *L* scale, the Gamma dimension in the Wiggins and Paulhus studies.

Lie Scale (*L*)

The *L* scale consists of 15 items, all of which are scored in the false direction. The scale was designed as a validity indicator to detect intentional efforts to underreport problems. Underreporting of problems can occur in many settings and is often referred to as "faking good" or as defensive or socially desirable responding. Circumstances and settings that "promote" this response set include personnel selection situations, child custody litigation and other forensic cases, prison inmates wishing a transfer to a more desirable setting, patients wanting a release from a forced hospitalization, and clients coerced into marital or family treatment who want to look psychologically healthy (Baer, Wetter, & Berry, 1992).

The *L* scale items had their origin in previous research on honesty and deceit by Hartshorne and May (1928). Because the items for the *L* scale were borrowed from previous work and rewritten, they compose the only scale in the original MMPI that was not empirically constructed. The *L* scale provides 15 opportunities throughout the test for the participant to endorse certain virtues. The items represent socially virtuous behaviors (e.g., denial of dishonesties or aggressive feelings) that may be desirable for many people but are rarely true for most people. For this reason, the "items constituted a fairly subtle trap for anyone who wanted to give an unusually good impression of himself" (Meehl & Hathaway, 1946, as cited in Dahlstrom & Dahlstrom, 1980, p. 97). The following are examples of *L* scale items, with the direction of scoring following the item in parentheses:

41. I do not always tell the truth. (False)
51. I do not read every editorial in the newspaper every day. (False)
102. I get angry sometimes. (False)
203. I gossip a little at times. (False)
260. Once in a while I laugh at a dirty joke. (False)

Individuals are expected to claim some feelings of virtue, and most do, in fact, answer some items in the "lie" direction. The mean number of items answered in this direction by the contemporary normative sample was 3.5 for both men and women. The original MMPI Lie scale *T*-score values were arbitrarily established and did not provide separate validity scale values for men and women. However, the MMPI-2 Lie scale (and other validity scales) *T*-score values were established according to the new normative data with separate *T*-scores by gender.

Most often, higher raw scores on the *L* scale reflect the tendency to put oneself in a favorable light. Consequently, the clinical scales are expected to be suppressed because the individual is tending to deny basic human frailties and "look good." In addition to its sensitivity to detect obvious efforts at looking good, the *L* scale is also related to psychopathology when elevated, especially paranoid symptoms in some cases (Coyle & Heap, 1965; Fjordbak, 1985) and certain neurotic conditions (Friedman, Webb, & Lewak, 1989). Interpretive guidelines for the *L* scale are further discussed in chapter 5.

Because all the items on the Lie scale are scored in the false direction, an all-false response set will elevate the *L* scale as well as Scales 1, 2, and 3, for which the deviant response is usually false. An extremely low raw score on the *L* scale could likewise reflect an all-true response bias. When this is suspected, the *TRIN* scale should be investigated. In the MMPI–2 revision, the *L* scale lost no items, although the sexist wording on some items was changed and one item was changed to reflect more modern usage. The majority of the items on the *L* scale ($n = 9$) do not overlap the other MMPI–2 scales. The largest overlap occurs with Scales 2 and 9, each sharing two items in common with the *L* scale. The reader is referred to Appendix C for a presentation of the overlap content of the *L* scale, Appendix A (see Table A1) for a listing of the *L* scale items and direction of scoring, and Appendix B (see Tables B1 and B2) for the *T*-score conversions for the Lie scale and other validity measures.

Moderator variables (e.g., SES, education, and occupation) can greatly affect scores on the *L* scale. The item content of the scale is fairly obvious, and sophisticated individuals rarely elevate the scale, perhaps because they realize it would be unconvincing to give such a distorted response to the items. College educated individuals and those with a higher SES infrequently obtain *T* scores above 50; thus, elevated *L* scale score for a college-educated individual should be carefully evaluated. Individuals of lower SES with less education tend to earn higher scores on the *L* scale because the items reflect a more obvious form of test-taking defensiveness (Dahlstrom & Tellegen, 1993).

Test–retest reliability coefficients on the *L* scale for the MMPI–2 over an approximate 1-week interval shows coefficients of .77 for men and .81 for women in a subset of the contemporary normal sample (Butcher et al., 1989). Retest data are not available in the manual for psychiatric patients on this scale. However, the earlier data on the original MMPI can be applied to the present MMPI–2 scale because its composition has not changed significantly. On the MMPI *L* scale, test–retest correlation coefficients for psychiatric cases range between .74 and .78 with a 1- to 2-day interval between tests and between .35 and .61 with a 1-year interval between administrations (Dahlstrom et al., 1975). In a large-scale meta-analysis of MMPI reliability using a wide variety of populations conducted between 1970 and 1981, Hunsley, Hanson, and Parker (1988) reported an average internal consistency of .77 across 70 studies of the *L* scale. They also reported an average test–retest reliability of .63 for eight studies with time intervals from 1 to 2 years.

Additional reliability data on the MMPI–2 are presented by Matz, Altepeter, and Perlman (1992), who examined the temporal stability and internal consistency of the MMPI–2 in a sample of 128 students. Moderate to high stability coefficients were obtained (range = .60 to .90, *Mdn* = .74), with alpha coefficients ranging from .39 to .91 (*Mdn* = .62).

In a recent meta-analysis of 25 studies in which participants who responded honestly were compared with participants who underreported psychopathology, Baer et al. (1992) found that the *L* scale, relative to other special scales or indexes designed to detect underreporting, is a valid measure. In general, their review indicates that participants known to be underreporting problems tend to score about 1 *SD* above average on the *L* scale.

Correction Scale (*K*)

The original purpose for developing the *K* scale was to improve the sensitivity of the clinical scales to detect psychopathology by adding a correction or suppressor factor to the scaled scores. Without this correction factor there were too many false negatives or low-ranging MMPI scores among psychiatric patients whose psychopathology should have elevated certain clinical scales. The efforts of Meehl, Hathaway, and McKinley (e.g., McKinley, Hathaway, & Meehl, 1948; Meehl, 1945b) in the development of the *K* scale were directed primarily toward the reduction of false negatives without significantly affecting the number of accurate diagnostic identifications, or test hits.[8] Experience with the MMPI also demonstrated that although the *L* and *F* scales were adequate in detecting extreme test-taking attitudes or distortions, they were less sensitive to more subtle expressions of defensiveness or the underreporting of problems. Recognizing that test scores are considerably influenced by test-taking attitudes, Meehl, Hathaway, and McKinley identified two important general test-taking approaches: (a) the tendency to be self-critical and overly self-disclosing ("plus getting") usually referred to as faking bad, and (b) the tendency to be defensive or to overportray one's virtues, often referred to as *faking good* (Meehl & Hathaway, 1946, as cited in Dahlstrom & Dahlstrom, 1980, p. 120). Proper interpretation of the validity scales, particularly the *K* scale, should aid in assessing the presence of a fake-bad or fake-good test attitude. Another way to conceptualize the function of the validity scales is along a continuum: One end measures an individual's willingness or capacity to be open to admitting problems, including an overdeclaration of symptoms, and the other end measures the strong tendency to minimize problems or to be closed to admitting any problems at all (Friedman, Webb, & Lewak, 1989).

The *K* scale was developed by selecting 25 male and 25 female psychiatric inpatients who obtained normal scale elevations (no *T* score over 70). These patients had *L* scale *T* scores of at least 60, indicating test-taking defensive and psychiatric diagnoses (e.g., alcoholism, personality disorders, or behavioral disturbances) rather than psychotic or neurotic disorders. The responses of these patients (who apparently were answering these test items in a defensive manner) were compared with those of some of the Minnesota normative cases used in the original standardization group. Item analysis yielded 22 items (common to men and women) that discriminated the "true and false negative profiles and their item endorsements by at least 30%" (Dahlstrom et al., 1972, p. 124). High scores on these items indicated more defensiveness and a greater likelihood of a false negative (e.g., a patient who should have generated an abnormal profile but who actually obtained a normal one). Low scores on these items were important in detecting false positives (i.e., cases in which normals obtained abnormal test scores). Because the 22-item *K* scale was insensitive to some depressed and schizophrenic patients who tended to produce normal-looking profiles, an additional 8 items were included to assist in separating the original normative group from these two patient groups and resulted in a final scale of 30 items. In addition to meeting the criterion of differentiating the normals from the abnormals (e.g., schizophrenic and depressive patients), the items also had to meet another criterion. Specifically, these items also had to be insensitive to participants who were instructed to fake good or fake bad, thereby implying that their content was not obvious.

By adding differential proportions of raw *K* scores to five of the clinical scales, Meehl, Hathaway, and McKinley were able to improve the ability of these scales to differentiate between the normal and criterion groups. The standard profile sheet is based on *T* scores corrected for the *K* additions, and test users are advised to make certain that they add the *K*-correction factor to five clinical scales. However, the MMPI–2 manual provides conversion tables for plotting non-*K*-corrected profiles, and many computer programs provide both *K* and non-*K*-corrected profiles for the test user. The raw *K* scale addition for Scale 1 (*Hs*) is 0.5 and 0.4 for Scale 4 (*Pd*), Scale 7 (*Pt*) and Scale 8 (*Sc*) have 1 full raw score value of *K* added, and Scale 9 (*Ma*) receives 0.2 *K*. The *K*-correction values remain unchanged in the MMPI–2. It is important to note that the *K*-correction value for any given clinical scale is related to the proportion of subtle items contained in the scale (McKinley et al., 1948).

Because the *K* corrections were developed with adult psychiatric patients, it may not always be appropriate to use the *K* corrections with dissimilar populations. Greene (2000) reviewed the literature on the use of the *K* scale in various settings and concluded that, in general, little research justifies the continued widespread use of the *K* correction of the clinical scales. Greene stated that clinicians probably need to avoid using *K* corrections in settings in which normal persons are being evaluated with the MMPI-2, but they should use the *K* corrections in settings in which psychopathology is suspected, keeping in mind the potential inaccuracies that *K* corrections may introduce. More recently, Butcher (1994b) studied the MMPI–2 profiles of airline pilot applicants. He noted that the majority of these participants tended to score above the clinical cutoff of $T = 65$ on the *K* scale, suggesting an overly favorable response pattern in a group of well-adjusted individuals. Because high *K* scale scores are common in many other personnel selection populations, the addition of the *K* correction to the profile may be inappropriate in situations assessing normals, given that the scale was developed to detect defensiveness in psychiatric populations. However, it does appear that most clinicians—and most researchers—continue to use the *K* correction despite this limitation (Colby, 1989). It is recommended for adults (e.g., those 18 years and older) that the reader apply the *K* correction and plot *T* scores with and without the *K* correction with normal populations until future research clarifies the appropriate parameters of its use. As Archer (1992) noted, "the raw score *K*-correction is not used in profiling *T*-scores for adolescents with either the original test instrument or the MMPI–A" (p. 84). It appears that adolescent MMPI profiles are more accurate without the *K* correction (Colligan & Offord, 1991).

Most recently, Archer, Fontaine, and McCrae (1998) examined the accuracy of the *K* correction procedure in a large sample of psychiatric inpatients. Their results indicated that the *K* correction procedure with the MMPI and the MMPI–2 did not result in higher correlations with external criteria in comparison with non-*K*-corrected scores. They suggested that the reason that the original *K*-correction weights were retained for use in the MMPI–2 was because the massive research literature generated for the original MMPI was based on *K*-corrected scores. This raises a considerable dilemma, as researchers and clinicians can either use the *K*- or non-*K*-corrected scores:

> They can use *K*-correction procedures with standard weights, which link their results to a large research literature, or the non-*K*-corrected scores, which relates to a much smaller literature but produces stronger evidence of concurrent validity. This dilemma can be resolved if future researchers report results of analyses using non-*K*-corrected scores (perhaps in addition to *K*-corrected scores), so that a comprehensive non-*K*-corrected research literature can eventually be developed for the MMPI–2. (Archer, Fontaine, & McCrae, 1998, p. 98)

As pointed out by Putzke, Williams, Daniel, and Boll (1999), there is a relative dearth of studies examining the effectiveness of the *K*-correction procedure. Investigations are needed to examine various adult patient populations, as well as different clinical settings that vary in regard to the prevalence of defensiveness.

Twenty-nine of the 30 items on the *K* scale are scored in the "false" direction making the scale sensitive to the effects of an all-false or all-true response set, as well as reflecting the scale's function to measure the denial of problems. The mean number of *K* scale endorsements for men and women in the contemporary normative sample was approximately 15. The *K* scale contains five unique (nonoverlapping) items, with the remaining 25 items distributed somewhat equally across the clinical scales. The *K* scale content is wide-ranging and covers issues of self-control, family and interpersonal relationships, and the denial of problems. The following items from the *K* scale illustrate the wide-ranging content; the scored responses are indicated in parentheses (see Table A.1 for a complete listing of the item composition of the *K* scale with the scoring key):

29. At times I feel like swearing. (False)
83. I have very few quarrels with members of my family. (True)
116. Often I can't understand why I have been so irritable and grouchy. (False)
127. Criticism or scolding hurts me terribly. (False)
167. I find it hard to make talk when I meet new people. (False)

The *K* scale did not lose any items in the MMPI–2 revision, although one item was slightly altered for modernization purposes.

Test–retest correlation coefficients based on the MMPI–2 contemporary normative sample for the *K* scale are .84 for men and .81 for women over an average interval of about 1 week. Internal consistency estimates (Cronbach's coefficient alpha) for the MMPI–2 *K* scale are .73 for men and .71 for women. The MMPI–2 *K* scale does not appear to have lost any reliability in the revision process as the *K* scale is essentially unchanged. As expected, reliability coefficients for psychiatric patients are lower than those of normals. Test–retest correlation coefficients for psychiatric cases on the MMPI *K* scale range between .46 and .56 for a 1- to 2-day interval between tests and between .42 and .72 for a 1-year interval between tests (Dahlstrom et al., 1975). In Hunsley et al.'s (1988) large-scale meta-analysis of MMPI reliability studies using a wide variety of populations conducted between 1970 and 1981, an average internal consistency of .82 across 71 studies of the *K* scale was reported. They also reported an average test–retest reliability of .77 for 15 studies with time intervals from 1 day to 2 years.

Various elevations on the *K* scale are associated with different interpretations or personality correlates. Very-high-scoring participants (*T* score greater than or equal to 65) are generally described as maintaining a defensive posture and unwilling to admit to psychological problems. However, well-functioning individuals also describe themselves in similar terms, which may simply reflect that their lives are in order (Butcher et al., 1989). For this reason, it is critical that the *K* scale score be assessed in the context of as much other information as possible, including the referral context and the person's past and current life situation. In general, elevated *K* scale scores are positively correlated with SES. The MMPI–2 manual (Butcher et al., 1989) points out that individuals with more status stand to lose more by making disclosures that reveal incompetence, ineffectiveness, and insecurities. Therefore, these individuals may try to slant their responses in such a way as to protect their self-esteem and the impressions that others will form about them. The use of the *K* scale weights serve to correct for this type of defensiveness. Very-low-scoring participants on the *K* scale are often seen as being overly self-critical in confessing many psychological difficulties. In general, elevated *K* scores are associated with lower ranging clinical scale scores, whereas the converse is true for underelevated *K* scores (Friedman, Webb, & Lewak, 1989). When there are clinical elevations in a high *K* profile, they tend to be associated with a neurotic triad (Dahlstrom et al., 1972). Individuals faking bad tend to overclaim symptomatology, and the resulting low *K* scores are often associated with peaks on the psychotic tetrad scales (Scales 6, 7, 8, and 9; Dahlstrom et al., 1972). Socioeconomic factors, age, race, culture, and intelligence all affect the interpretation of the clinical and validity scales and must be considered when interpreting a profile. These important moderator factors are discussed in chapter 9.

It is important to recognize that a high *T* score on a clinical *K*-corrected scale could be due to the addition of a large *K* correction or due to a high raw score on that scale. Therefore, it is critical to examine the raw score values on the elevated scales. For example, a *T* score of 65 on Scale 7 (*Pt*) could be achieved in several ways. One way could consist of a male participant endorsing (a) 20 Scale 7 items in the deviant direction and 13 *K* scale items or (b) 10 Scale 7 items and 23 *K* scale items. The latter endorsement pattern reflects significantly more defensiveness or ability to cope with symptoms than does the former pattern. Inferring worry or tension from the *T* score values of 65 in the latter case may be misleading because the individual with the lower raw score value on Scale 7 is less likely to be experiencing worry and tension.

Interpretation of the validity scales is discussed more completely in chapter 5, but it should be pointed out that general psychiatric patients with bonafide disorders tend to score higher on the *K* scale than do normals instructed to feign a psychiatric disorder (Graham, Watts, & Timbrook, 1991; Wetter et al., 1992). A number of studies have supported this finding, with the implication being that scores on the *K* scale below a *T* score of 35 should be checked against other validity measures to ascertain the possibility of a faked or "overreported" profile. A recent study (Lamb et al., 1994) also illustrates that when test participants are instructed to fake a closed-head injury and are given specific information on how to manipulate the validity scales (including the *K* scale), they are able to lower their validity scale scores. Although these results show that coaching can have an important impact on MMPI–2 results in analogue-malingering participants, the implication is that test instructions and test-taking attitudes can greatly affect the scores that clinicians interpret. The importance of test instructions is described in chapter 4.

Superlative Self-Presentation Scale (*S*)

Since the restandardization of the MMPI (i.e., the MMPI–2), Butcher and Han (1995) developed a new scale to assess "the presentation of self in a superlative manner" (p. 25). This scale, *S*, was developed by contrasting the item responses of 274 male airline pilot applicants with the 1,138 men from the MMPI–2 restandardization sample. Fifty items were identified that both differed significantly (.001) in their endorsement frequency between the two groups and contributed to the internal consistency of the scale. In separate factor analyses of the *S* scale items for the men and women of the MMPI–2 restandardization sample, Butcher and Han developed and named five component subscales: Belief in Human Goodness (*S1*, 15 items), Serenity (*S2*, 13 items), Contentment with Life (*S3*, 8 items), Patience and Denial of Irritability and Anger (*S4*, 8 items), and Denial of Moral Flaws (*S5*, 5 items).

The component subscales afford a good idea of the content of the *S* scale, with their emphasis on benevolence, serenity, and freedom from impatience and irritability. Butcher and Han (1995) presented external correlates gleaned from the couple's data collected in the restandardization project. These portray the high scorer as emotionally stable and well controlled, calm and relaxed, and patient and easygoing, as well as agreeable, cooperative, and trusting in relations with others.

These descriptors suggest a close relationship between the *S* scale and the *K* scale. Indeed, the two scales share 10 items (5 on *S1*, 3 on *S2*, and 1 each on *S3* and *S4*) and intercorrelate in the .80s. Butcher and Han (1995) found additional positive correlations between the *S* scale and the *R*, *Es*, *Re*, *O-H*, and *L* scales, and negative correlations with the *A*, *Pt*, *CYN*, *Mt*, *ANG*, *ANX*, and *Sc* scales. These correlates indicate that the *S* scale, like the *K* scale, incorporates high levels of first-factor and, to a lesser extent, second-factor variance. Both the *S* and *K* scales are negatively correlated with all of the MMPI–2 content scales (Butcher, Graham, Williams, & Ben-Porath, 1990), but the correlations are generally somewhat higher for the *S* scale than for the *K* scale. Moreover, judging from the 39 items of the *S* scale and the 30 items of the *K* scale for which social desirability ratings are available (Dahlstrom et al., 1975), the *S* scale appears to indicate slightly (9% or 10%) more social desirability than the *K* scale. These factors would suggest that the *S* scale is somewhat more likely than the *K* scale to suppress content scale scores and the endorsement of obvious items in general. In this sense, the *S* scale appears to possess good construct validity.

Although the empirical strategy used to develop the *S* scale is not, as such, especially objectionable, it does tend to conflate the means and motives by which the pilot applicants manifested their "superlative" adjustments. Thus, some may have emphasized a deliberate strategy of claiming extraordinary adjustment; others of denying relatively common weaknesses, character flaws, worries, and habits; and still others, those of truly superior adjustment, may have merely marked the items in a manner consistent with that adjustment, without seeking to overstate it. Moreover, for those participants who may have exaggerated their adjustment, some may have approached the task in a self-conscious fashion, whereas others may have achieved similar results through less conscious, self-deceptive means (Nichols & Greene, 1997). In this sense, then, the construct validity of the *S* scale remains ambiguous.

Although the availability of subscales for the *S* scale affords some degree of insight into the content of the items favored by particular respondents, these subscales do not necessarily correspond well to the strategies of response undertaken by the pilot applicants to yield the different rates of endorsement that determined which items would compose the scale as a whole. Regardless of these potential problems and their implications for the interpretation of *S* scores, the *S* scale has performed well in several research trials involving the discrimination of a variety of samples instructed to fake good on the MMPI–2 from samples given standard instructions. Among these, two studies incorporated features that permitted the evaluation of the incremental contribution of several scales and indices that have been proposed for the detection of underreporting. In hierarchical regression analyses, Baer, Wetter, Nichols, et al. (1995) found that only 2 of the 11 underreporting scales and indexes they investigated demonstrated incremental validity beyond the *L* and *K* scales: the *S* scale and Wiggins' *Sd* scale. A similar analysis by Bagby, Rogers, Nicholson, et al. (1997) found that, depending on the samples compared, only *S*, *Sd*, *So-r* (Edwards' Social Desirability scale), and Nichols and Greene's (1991) Other Deception scale (*Od*) could demonstrate incremental validity over the *L* and *K* scales. Furthermore, in both studies, the *S* scale was among those scales showing the largest effect sizes. More recently, Bagby, Nicholson, Buis, Radovanovic, and Fidler (1999) found that a composite based on the raw score sum of the *S* and *Sd* scales substantially outperformed the *L* and *K* scales in a study of underreporting and nonunderreporting child custody litigants.

As already noted, the *S* scale belongs to a class of scales that are known to be saturated with the first factor. As such, it is likely to suppress most of the clinical and content scales, bias the profile toward a negative slope, and push up *K*, *Es*, *GM*, and similar scales. Butcher and Han (1995) presented several empirical correlates for *S* scores gleaned from spousal ratings gathered during the MMPI–2 restandardization project. Partners of high *S* scorers tend to describe them as pleasant and relaxed, as slow to express annoyance, as disinclined to worry or fret about minor matters or to become irritable or grouchy over such things, as not moody, and as not suspicious or argumentative in their approach to others. In other words, the unusual freedom from emotional discomfort and interpersonal conflict claimed by high *S* scorers tended to be confirmed as realistic attributes in ratings by their spouses. It will require further investigation to establish reliable empirical correlates in other samples, both normal and abnormal, and to ascertain more precisely its position in relation to other, better established response-style measures. For the time being, however, the *S* scale does show promise in the detection of certain common types of underreporting of psychopathology. (See Table A.1 for the item composition and scoring key for this scale. Tables B.1 and B.2 list the *T*-score conversions from the raw-score values for the *S* scale.

Positive Malingering Scale (*Mp*)

Cofer et al. (1949) had 81 male and female college students complete the MMPI under three instructional sets: under standard instructions (i.e., honestly) and then (a) under instructions to malinger (to avoid induction into the Army), (b) under instructions to create the best possible impression of themselves (to be accepted into a midshipman training program), and (c) under standard instructions a second time. The second administration intended to eliminate the regression-toward-the-mean effect of the trend of slightly greater normality on the average that is expected on a second standard administration. Thirty-four items (one a duplicate) were found to be stable under the two standard administrations and the fake-bad instructions but to be endorsed more frequently under the fake-good instructions. These constitute the 33 items of the original *Mp* scale. In keeping with the tendency of these items to change only under fake-good instructions, the *Mp* items can be understood as flaws that most people admit when responding candidly but deny when seeking to create a highly favorable impression.

In their meta-analysis of MMPI underreporting scales, Baer et al. (1992) found an average effect size of 1.42 across 11 studies, making it among the best performers among the 10 scales and indexes examined and substantially better than the *L* scale (.94), the *K* scale (.90), and the *F* – *K* scale (.71). For example, Otto, Lang, Megargee, and Rosenblatt (1988) found that the *Mp* scale correctly classified 80% of a sample of alcoholic participants, half of whom were instructed to conceal psychopathology and half of whom followed standard instructions, the best of several measures that included *L*, *K*, *F* – *K*, and *Sd*.

The MMPI–2 version of *Mp* is reduced by 7 items to 26. It overlaps the *Sd* scale by 13 items, the *L* scale by 6, the *S* scale by 6 (4 of these on *S2*), and the *K* scale by 4 items. Correlations between the *Mp* scale and these scales in a large psychiatric sample were .75, .65, .56 (.66), and .50, respectively.

Content is quite variable, with masculine interests; freedom from worries, fears, and internal struggles or changes of heart; sexual inhibition or circumspection; and high confidence in oneself and in one's leadership potential emerging as discernable themes.

High scores are best considered in relation to scores on the *L*, *K*, *Sd*, *Ss*, and *S* scales. Scores at or above $T = 60$ should raise the question of a deliberate effort to exaggerate one's level of adjustment, especially when accompanied with similar elevations on the *Sd* scale. When both the *Mp* and *Sd* scales exceed $T = 65$ or are higher than the *K* scale, and when *Ss* scores are average or low, a conscious attempt to fake good is strongly suggested. High *L* scores tend to push up the *Mp* and *Sd* scales. When scores on the *L* scale are significantly higher than those for the *Mp* and *Sd* scales, however, the respondent's approach may be more naive than deliberate, a reaction to the fear of moral judgment rather than an attempt to mislead the examiner into a belief or judgment that the respondent is free of maladjustment and psychopathology. *S* scores exert considerably greater upward pressure on the *K* and *Mp* scales than on the *L* or *Sd* scales, such that the *S* scale is usually high, along with the *K* scale, when the *Mp* scale is significantly elevated but the *Sd* and *L* scales are not. (See Table A.1 for the scoring key and item composition for the *Mp* scale; Tables B.1 and B.2 present the raw-score-to-*T*-score conversions for this scale.)

Social Desirability Scale (*Sd*)

The responses of 72 male and 106 female Stanford University undergraduates instructed to answer each item in terms of whether people in general would consider a true or a false response more desirable were compared separately with 55 male and 85 female Stanford University controls following standard instructions. Participants given the desirability instructions were further given to understand that they were to make their judgments on the basis of "the general values of American culture." Wiggins (1959) found 40 items that separated the desirability group from the standard instruction group at .001 or less, for both men and women. In their meta-analysis, Baer et al. (1992) found an average effect size for the *Sd* scale of 1.60 across six studies making it the best performing of the scales and indexes they reviewed.

The MMPI–2 version of the *Sd* scale is reduced by 7 items to 33. It overlaps the *Mp* scale by 13 items, the *L* scale by 7, the *S* scale by 2 (both on *S2*), and the *K* scale by 1 item. Correlations with these scales of .75, .54, .35 (.49), and .28, respectively, were found in a large psychiatric sample.

Whereas the items of the *Mp* scale are biased toward the denial of shortcomings and distress, the items of the *Sd* scale tend to emphasize the assertion of positive attributes. The content of the *Sd* scale affirms broad interests: conventional, if not conservative, socially responsible moral values; a high level of drive and energy; persistence and decisiveness; sociability, extraversion, and an absence of self-consciousness; and an absence of health concern. In keeping with the instructions to judge desirability in terms of the values of people in general, the content of the *Sd* scale converges on a portrait of an idealized model citizen, one who is extraverted and outgoing, free of worry and self-doubt, assertive, self-directed and in full control of his or her mental faculties; who is orderly, confident, capable, decisive, cool under pressure, and oriented to success; and who is composed but friendly, buoyant, energetic, up-to-the-task, and actively engaged in living; but one who is also overconventional, hypervirtuous, prudish, and unrealistic in terms of self-portrayal.

Unlike the *S* scale and other Alpha-type scales, which appear to conceal psychopathology directly by suppressing test expressions of neuroticism and psychoticism, the *Mp* and *Sd* scales, as scales of the Gamma dimension, appear to achieve their results by somewhat different and more indirect means. Although these means are not thoroughly understood, both scales appear to mask psychopathology through the substitution of a highly favorable social image. High scorers on the *Mp* and *Sd* scales deny flaws and assert virtues that most people do not feel the need to deny or assert when taking the MMPI–2. In the case of the *Mp* scale, this image emphasizes virtue and stability in the context of relaxed, pacific, quiet self-assurance, and a placid if not imperturbable emotionality, whereas the image conveyed by the *Sd* scale emphasizes virtue and vitality in the context of a strong-willed, outgoing, constructive, engaged, and poised social presence.

As with the *Mp* scale, scores at T = 60–65 on the *Sd* scale should raise the question of a deliberate attempt to portray oneself in terms of an idealized social image, and *Sd* scores that exceed the *K* scale strongly suggest such, especially when *Ss* scores are average or low. (See Table A.1 for the item composition and scoring key for the *Sd* scale; Tables B.1 and B.2 list the *T*-score conversions from the raw-score values for the *Sd* scale.)

Socioeconomic Status Scale (*Ss*)

Rescued from obscurity by Alex Caldwell, S. E. Nelson's (1952) *Ss* scale was inspired by the insight that various aspects of abnormal psychology and symptomatic behavior may be related to social stratification. As an example, Nelson mentioned that such behaviors as wife beating, heavy drinking, improvident spending habits, siding with and covering for his children vis-à-vis school authorities, and relocating the family's domicile to avoid creditors may be easily construed as psychopathic by mental health service providers, a group typically if not uniformly of high social status, even though such behaviors may be all but normative in some segments of the lower-lower class.

From an initial sample of 710 male patients who had been treated at the Ft. Snelling VA Hospital, S. E. Nelson (1952) simultaneously rated patients for years of education and occupational level, as determined by the Warner seven-step scale of occupational status categories. Forty-one participants with 13 or more years of education and occupations within the highest two status categories (e.g., engineer or manager) constituted the high-status group; 43 participants with 8 or fewer years of education and occupations within the lowest status category (e.g., laborer or dishwasher) constituted the low-status group. Eighty-seven items were found to separate the two groups at the .01 level or less, and these became the *Ss* scale; 73 of these items remain on the MMPI–2.

The scale was validated on new samples of patients for which highly significant correlations were found with education (.47), occupational level (.45), and intelligence (.41). The *Ss* scale was unrelated to age in both the scale development and later validation samples. In a cross-validation sample, the *Ss* scale misclassified only half as many participants as Gough's (1948a, 1948b) Status scale (*St*), although both scales correctly classified most of the participants. W. L. Jenkins (1952) found that the *Ss* scale was related to better prognosis in paranoid schizophrenia.

Nelson divided his scale into 12 groups of items according to content: physical complaints (13 items), sleep difficulties (3 items), psychological deficit (4 items), phobias and obsessive–compulsive traits (9 items), delusions and misperceptions (6 items), paranoid traits (5 items), affective states (5 items), self-insight (3 items), rigid moral code (2 items), interest in intellectual pursuits (2 items), other interests (6 items), and a miscellaneous category (15 items). The direction of scoring is such that high scorers tend to deny somatic complaints; dysphoric mood; fears and phobias; cynicism, suspiciousness, paranoia, and psychoticism; problems with cognitive functioning; nonintellectual interests and occupations that depend largely on physical (vs. mental) activity; introversion; and impulsiveness. They portray themselves as alert, concerned about their social presentation, fallible, inclined toward candor, mature, discreet, and morally flexible and tolerant.

A scale of the Alpha type, the *Ss* scale shares considerable variance with both the *K* and *S* scales, correlating with both at about .65, despite sharing only two items with each. Although such correlations would naturally raise the question of defensiveness, albeit of a rather subtle kind, there is little doubt that higher status members of society, in general, possess a degree of insulation from stresses and sources of instability that is unavailable to those at lower socioeconomic levels. Their better reputations and the greater financial resources and respect they command confer considerable flexibility and a wider range of alternatives for managing interpersonal conflict, situational difficulties, and economic reverses—indeed hardships and misfortunes of most kinds. Moreover, and in the main, such people tend to possess the kinds of abilities, intelligence, knowledge, and skills that enabled them to attain higher SES in the first place, as compared with those who fail to attain such status. In the face of difficulty, then, the higher status person tends to have a wider network and greater access to social support; better and more reliable problem-solving skills; greater access to information and expertise; more money and more discretion as to how it is spent; and more time to assess, plan, and implement measures for its alleviation. In the light of such advantages, it is not surprising that such persons would have a higher threshold for experiencing feelings of inadequacy and insecurity, developing symptoms of maladjustment and psychopathology, and expressing distress over their problems, even when present, than would persons lacking these advantages.

Although the validity and performance characteristics of the *Ss* scale have been little explored since its initial development, Caldwell (1988) has argued that this scale can play a helpful role in the interpretation of *K* scores, along with the Gamma scales *L*, *Mp*, and *Sd*. When high *K* scores are accompanied by high *Ss* scores, and *L*, *Mp*, and *Sd* scores are unelevated or low, Caldwell suggested that the elevation on the *K* scale should not be construed as a deliberate attempt to mislead the examiner or to frustrate the purposes of the evaluation; rather, the elevation should be understood to reflect the portrayal of favorable adjustment over which the examinee has little conscious control. By an extension of this reasoning, a deceptive or defensive interpretation of elevated scores on the *S* scale should be attenuated when these are accompanied by high *Ss* scores. When the *K* score is high along with elevations on the Gamma scales and the *Ss* score is average or low, Caldwell recommended that the *K* score be interpreted as indicating an intentional fake-good approach to the evaluation.

Conversely, when the *K* and *Ss* scores are both low, the *Mp*, *Sd*, and *Ds* scores are average, and the *F* score is not higher than T = 80, "a low-status candor, lack of sophistication, and genuine self-negativity in the absence of any 'faking bad'" (Caldwell, 1988, p. 95) is suggested. When the *K* and Gamma scale scores are low, the *F* and/or *Ds* score is high, and the *Ss* score is within an average range, Caldwell (1988) argued that there existed "an excessive self-criticalness or deliberate faking bad with the low K not being due to low socioeconomic status" (p. 95).

In keeping with Caldwell's (1988) view that the *Ss* scale achieves its positivizing of test performance without any conscious effort to convey a more favorable impression on the MMPI–2, it is noteworthy that its correlations with the Gamma scales are close to 0, the highest being with the *Mp* scale at .17. (See Table A.1 for the item composition and scoring key for the *Ss* scale; Tables B.1 and B.2 present the *T*-score conversions from the raw-score values for the *Ss* scale.)

VALIDITY INDICES

F–FB

In a valid profile, the *F* and *FB* scales should have similar scores, given that both scales consist of infrequently endorsed items. Nichols and Greene (1995) recommended that the absolute raw score difference between the *F* and *FB* scales provides a crude measure of consistency of item endorsement on both halves of the test. If the raw score for the *FB* scale exceeds the *F* scale by 6 or more and there are no content reasons to explain the difference, it becomes important to consider that the second half of the test may be invalid. As stated earlier, the *F* scale ends with Item 361 and the *FB* scale begins at item 281. The *FB* scale is useful for detecting random or faking-bad/faking-good tendencies that could affect, for example, the content scales concentrated in the last 150 items of the inventory.

On the basis of a random sort of scores for the *VRIN*, *F*, and *FB* scales, Greene (2000) reported that 75% of these random sorts had a raw score of 7 or higher on the *F–FB* index. With *VRIN* scores in the intermediate range (8–15), he reported that less than 26% of the random sorts had scores of 6 or lower on this index. Greene (1991a) stated that the "clinician can be fairly confident that the client has endorsed the items consistently if this index is 6 or lower when *VRIN* is in the intermediate range of 8–15" (p. 70). It is recommended that the *F–FB* raw difference score be routinely examined in assessing the validity of an MMPI–2 profile (see chap. 5 for specific recommendations regarding this measure).

Dissimulation Index (*F* – *K*)

The *F* – *K* index was derived by Harrison Gough (1947, 1950) as an additional validity indicator for the original MMPI to assist in determining whether an individual completed the test in an appropriate manner or attempted to simulate or exaggerate psychopathology. Gough found the *F* – *K* index to be a more accurate classifier of simulated or faked profiles than the *F* or *K* scale alone. The *F* – *K* index is derived by subtracting the raw *K* score from the raw *F* score. When the raw *F* score is greater than the *K* score, the index takes on a positive numerical value; when the reverse is true, the index takes on a negative numerical value. According to Baer et al. (1992), "individuals overreporting psychopathology should obtain elevated F and low *K* scores, resulting in positive scores on this index, while those underreporting psychopathology should obtain low F and high *K* scores, resulting in negative scores" (p. 510). In general, elevated *F* scores have been attributed, in part, to psychotic conditions, cries for help, general maladjustment, random responding, and partial or pure malingering. Participants with low *F* scores have been described as free of psychological problems or denying difficulties (faking good) when the *K* scale is significantly elevated (e.g., Friedman, Webb, & Lewak, 1989). Elevated *K* has usually been interpreted as suggesting defensiveness, cautiousness, or emotional reserve, with low *K* scores reflecting a tell-all attitude and lack of emotional modulation or reserve (Caldwell, 1988; Lewak, Marks, & Nelson, 1990).

In creating the index, Gough (1947) had a group of 11 clinical workers feign two psychiatric syndromes:

> The first syndrome was defined as "an acute, severe, anxiety neurosis which would lead to separation from the service, but not to commitment to a mental hospital," and the second as "a non-deteriorated, acute, paranoid schizophrenic psychosis." Skilled judges were able to identify eight of the eleven psychoneurotic patterns which intermixed with 68 authentic psychoneurotic records, and were able to identify all of the psychotic simulations when they were intercalated with 24 authentic profiles. At the same time, a simple combination of the *F* raw score minus the *K* raw score was able to pick out ten of the eleven simulated records in each of the two situations. The *F* – *K* cutting scores proposed at that time were plus 4 and over for neurotic profiles, and plus 16 and over for psychotic profiles. (p. 408)

Gough (1950) later suggested that $F - K$ scores of more than 9 indicated a fake-bad attitude (i.e., the participant attempted to present him- or herself with serious psychopathology). Scores of less than 0 on the $F - K$ index indicated a fake-good profile, whereby the participant attempted to deny the presence of any type of psychological disturbance. Gough (1950) stated that the $F - K$ index was less efficient in detecting fake-good profiles as compared with fake-bad profiles at any particular cutoff score. He pointed out that the problem in establishing an $F - K$ cutting score is one of minimizing false positives and false negatives.

What is considered to be over versus underreporting is often subject to the interpretative skills of the clinician as cutoff guidelines using clinical and normal groups have varied considerably among researchers and reference groups. Most investigations on the $F - K$ index have used analogue participants who were asked to simulate various disorders or normalcy and whose profiles were then compared with those of authentic normal and patient profiles. College students have constituted the majority of these participants, and Dahlstrom et al. (1972) noted the differences in conducting faking studies with college students. For example, it is known that well-educated individuals tend to score higher on the *K* scale by almost 1 *SD*. Therefore, their elevated *K* scores will tend to bias their $F - K$ index scores in the fake- good direction. Greene (2000) indicated in his review of the $F - K$ index that it has been difficult to identify any specific $F - K$ score for the detection of students instructed to fake good under usual administration instructions for the MMPI. Presumably, students who are for the most part free of psychopathology find it difficult to look even better than they already are when instructed to fake good. Greene also acknowledged that another problem in detecting fake-good profiles in college students (or any one else) is that a person who is effectively handling his or her problems and who is well-adjusted would be expected to score low on the *F* scale and high on the *K* scale, indicating an absence of distress. Therefore, Greene stated that normal persons taking the MMPI often will be inappropriately classified as producing underreported profiles.

Greene's review contains some important conclusions. He stated that the usefulness of the $F - K$ index in detecting fake-bad profiles may be more limited with actual clinical patients who exaggerate their problems than with students. He recommended interviewing those who obtain a high *F* score and hence a high $F - K$ index, to determine if their self-report of distress is accurate or exaggerated. He also questioned the utility of the index in detecting fake-good profiles among psychiatric patients. He pointed out that psychiatric patients and inmates have difficulty producing normal-appearing profiles when instructed to do so (Grayson & Olinger, 1957; Lawton & Kleban, 1965). Recently, Bagby, Rogers, Nicholson, et al. (1997) found that a sample of schizophrenic outpatients in the residual phase were in fact able under fake-good instructions to reduce their clinical scale elevations as well as, if not better than, students, thereby suggesting that patients are as capable as students to manipulate their MMPI–2 clinical scale scores. The Marks et al. (1974) study of projected discharged profiles seems to supports Greene's call for additional research to examine whether normal profiles produced by clinical participants instructed to fake good are generally positive prognostic signs.

Clear limitations have also been reported on the utility of the index for separating profiles of patients simulating or exaggerating illness from authentic patient profiles (Anthony, 1971). Hedlund and Won Cho (as cited by Greene, 1988b) found that psychiatric patients achieved a mean *F* – *K* index score near 0 compared to the –10 noted with normals (Osborne & Offord, 1986), which is clearly in contrast to what Gough (1950) had indicated earlier about the index not being affected by the presence of psychiatric disturbance per se. In light of this, interpretation of a profile as that of malingering or exaggerating psychopathology must be made with caution as it does appear that the presence of psychiatric disturbance has a bearing on the resulting *F* – *K* score.

It is generally reported that scores on the *F* – *K* index increase significantly as the degree of simulated disturbance increases (Greene, 1988a; Wetter et al., 1992). Berry, Baer, and Harris (1991) conducted a meta-analysis on 28 studies that used the original MMPI to detect malingering in order to quantify how much higher malingerers or simulators score on the various overreporting scales and indexes, including the *F* – *K* index. They noted a wide variability in cut scores used across studies, with cut scores between 7 and 16 yielding the highest classification rates. On the basis of their review of various scales and indexes, the *F* – *K* index was recommended as a choice for identifying malingerers. Overall, the results showed that participants malingering or overreporting their symptoms scored almost 2 *SD*s higher on the *F* – *K* index than participants answering honestly. Rogers et al. (1994) also found the *F* – *K* index to be a powerful indicator of malingering in their meta-analytic study of MMPI–2 fake-bad measures and recommended that it be used in conjunction with the *F* scale and the obvious–subtle subscale differences as a screening indicator.

Along the same lines as the above-reported investigation, Baer et al. (1992) meta-analytically reviewed the empirical literature on the detection of underreporting psychopathology (faking good) on the original MMPI. Twenty-five studies in which participants were responding honestly were compared with participants underreporting psychopathology. Several indexes were examined, including the *F* – *K* index. By computing mean overall hit rate (percentage of total participants correctly classified) for each index of underreporting by collapsing across cutting scores, the investigators were able to gain a general impression of which measure best detected underreporting participants. The *F* – *K* index correctly classified 77% of the participants, and the highest mean overall hit rate of 84% was obtained for the *Sd* scale (Wiggins, 1959). As with the malingering participants reported earlier, there was considerable variability in hit rates; the percentage of honest participants correctly classified ranged from 62% to 100% with the best overall hit rate being 95% with an *F* – *K* index score of –11. In general, the results indicated that underreporting participants and honest participants differ on the *F* – *K* index by just less than 1 *SD* ($d = 0.71$). It appears that the *F* – *K* index is less accurate in correctly classifying underreporters versus overreporters of psychopathology, a finding consistent with other investigations (Bagby et al., 1997a). The considerable overlap in distributions between honest and underreporting participants is likely an important factor in these differences. The reader interested in more details about methodologies used in these type of studies is referred to the studies by Baer et al. (1992); Baer, Wetter, and Berry (1995); Berry, Baer, and Harris (1991); and Baer, Wetter, Nichols, Greene, and Berry (1995).[9]

Note that the study and use of the $F - K$ index is primarily focused on adults. Adolescent inpatient respondents score significantly higher on the F scale than adult psychiatric inpatients, and outpatient adolescents score similarly to adult inpatients on the F scale. Given the higher F scale value among teenagers, Archer (1997) suggested that the $F - K$ index criterion should be used very cautiously with these respondents when the MMPI–A is administered.

The revision of the MMPI necessitates the establishment of new norms for the $F - K$ index for several reasons. Four items were deleted from the original F scale (resulting in a scale of 60 items), and 12 modifications were made to the remaining items, including 6 grammatical changes, 5 modernizations of idioms and usage, and 1 change in sexist wording (Butcher et al., 1989; Dahlstrom, 1993). The K scale was less affected, as it lost no items in the revision and only one item on the scale was modified. Participants in the contemporary group of normals were screened out if their item endorsements on the F scale were too elevated (raw score greater than 20). No such limitations were imposed on the collection of participants for the normative sample of the original MMPI. Inspection of the item endorsement frequencies of the contemporary and original normative groups shows distinct differences on many items, especially on the K scale, which may reflect societal and cultural changes since the time of the development of the original MMPI.

The purified standardization sample of the original MMPI (Hathaway & Briggs, 1957) contained 225 men and 315 women from which the T-score conversions for clinical profiling were derived. The male group had a mean age of 33.1 years, a mean level of education of 9.7 years, and a mean $F - K$ score of –8.56. The female group had a mean age of 33.9 years, a mean level of education of 10.0 years, and a mean $F - K$ score of –8.91. For the standardization sample of the MMPI–2 consisting of 1,138 men and 1,462 women, the mean age of the combined sample was 41.0 years, with mean level of education of 14.7 years. The mean $F - K$ score was –10.77 for men and –11.37 for women. This is about 2 full points more in the negative direction for both groups compared with the purified standardization sample on the original MMPI and about 1 full point more in the negative direction for men. It is also about the same for women compared with the recent norms of Osborne et al. (1986)[10] for the original MMPI (Rothke et al., 1994).

Data are now available from several investigations on the $F - K$ index from the MMPI–2. Graham, Watts, and Timbrook (1991) examined the utility of the MMPI–2 validity scales and the $F - K$ index for identifying fake-bad and fake-good profiles. A cutoff score of 12 or higher for women and 17 or higher for men correctly classified 90% of fake-bad profiles by college students but also misclassified approximately 16% of psychiatric patients as having produced a fake-bad profile. For detecting fake-good profiles, the index was not as useful, a finding consistent with previous research with the original MMPI. As previously stated, recent meta-analyses (Baer et al., 1992; Baer, Wetter, Nichols, et al., 1995; Berry et al., 1991a) on the original MMPI corroborates the finding that the $F - K$

index is much more useful for detecting fake-bad than fake-good profiles. Iverson, Franzen, and Hammond (1993) examined the ability of the new *FB* scale and the *F* – *K* index to discriminate prison inmates instructed to malinger mental illness from actual psychiatric patients. The inmates instructed to malinger psychopathology produced much higher scale scores, including higher *F* and lower *K* scores than inmates and psychiatric patients who were given standard instructions. The mean *F* – *K* index was 24.8 (*SD* = 13.0) for malingerers, –4.9 (*SD* = 8.1) for inmates given standard instructions, and –4.5 (*SD* = 8.9) for psychiatric patients. The *F* – *K* index and the *F* scale produced comparable overall rates of correct classification, and both were more effective than was the *FB* scale.

With the revision of the MMPI–2, Rothke et al. (1994) reported MMPI–2 norms for the new standardization group on the *F* – *K* index and presented data for samples of psychiatric patients, head-injured patients who were litigating and not litigating, individuals seeking disability benefits, job applicants for police and priest positions, and substance abusers. These investigators chose to approach the establishment of normative guidelines for detecting over- or underreported profiles by selecting scores that separated the upper 2.5% and lower 2.5% from the overall score distribution (i.e., ±2 *SD*s from the mean, assuming a normal distribution of scores). This approach is viewed as preferable to the use of cutoff scores derived from analogue studies (i.e., those in which participants are asked to fake bad or fake good), in which the assumption is made that analogue participants actually reflect how malingerers would respond. Wetter et al. (1993) noted that analogue participants often are not given specific information about the diagnosis they are attempting to feign, nor are they told that successful malingering involves selective and not mass endorsement of symptoms. This may result in analogue malingerers obtaining an overly positive *F* – *K* index value, leading to exaggerated cutoff scores. Rothke et al.'s approach of setting guideline scores based on the extremes from the distribution of scores of a particular diagnostic or applicant group is similar to the concept of using local norms as a way of enhancing the generalizability of cutoff scores to a particular participant. This is an important point because the *F* – *K* index is not only used for clinical decision making but also for making decisions about whether a participant may be malingering in a litigation or forensic context or whether someone should be denied a job because they excessively denied psychological weaknesses or difficulties in an employment context. Thus, these interpretations have real-life implications for individuals.

Table 2.1 lists the MMPI–2 *F* – *K* scores (from Rothke et al., 1994) at the approximate lower and upper 2.5 percentile of the distribution reported for various samples. This should allow a specific comparison of a participant's score to the general population from which the individual derived:

> These scores should not be viewed as specific cutoffs for fake good or fake bad profiles. This is due, in part, to the fact that some of the samples are small in size and these "cutoff" scores could easily be affected by a single extreme score. These scores should serve as a reminder that *F* – *K* scores will differ across clinical samples

necessitating future normative studies on these clinical populations. (Rothke et al., 1994, p. 10)

The importance of comparing a single participant's score to an appropriate reference group is suggested by Table 2.1:

> For example, in a competency-to-stand trial evaluation in which the defendant presumably would have an interest in appearing impaired, it would be important to consider using *F* – *K* scores for psychiatric patients (if that individual had a history of psychiatric disturbance) as they may differ from those of the normative population. Thus, an interpretation of the validity of the profile should not be based solely on the guidelines for the normative population. The same would hold true of a patient with traumatic brain injury (TBI) involved in personal injury litigation; the sample scores for patients with TBI should be considered. (Rothke et al., 1994, p. 13)

As can be seen in Table 2.1, very different conclusions would be drawn about whether a participant was feigning or exaggerating a disorder if cutoffs based on the normative sample were used, as opposed to making adjustments from the specific diagnostic group. Rothke et al. (1994) suggested that the clinician use the guidelines from the normative group but make adjustments for the specific diagnostic group in order to address how a participant's score compares with that of the general population in a manner that is mindful of the impact of a particular condition on the *F* – *K* index score. This is similar to the practice of using general cutoff scores on neuropsychological tests for identification of impairment and then modifying interpretations based on adjustments for age and education, which are well known to affect neuropsychological test performance (e.g., Heaton, Grant, & Matthews, 1991).

The Rothke et al. (1994) data show that the scores on the *F* – *K* index are generally more in the negative direction (underreporting direction) on the MMPI–2 than on the original MMPI, where comparison scores were available, except for the psychiatric sample. This could be due in part to the fact that the mean raw *K* scale scores for the MMPI–2 normative group were approximately 15 (for both men and women) compared with approximate means of 13 for the original normative group. This is likely to have been an effect of the MMPI–2 normative group having a higher mean level of education than the original normative group. Rothke et al.'s findings also indicate the need to maintain separate guidelines for male and female participants in fake-bad assessments, a finding consistent with other studies. For example, Graham, Watts, and Timbrook (1991) found that a cutoff score of 12 for women and 17 for men produced the highest correct classification rates.

In summary, the research to date with the *F* – *K* index for both the MMPI and the MMPI–2 suggests that the index is much more useful for identifying fake-bad than fake-good profiles. The cutoff scores derived from the original MMPI that exist in the clinical lore should be replaced with cutoffs from the MMPI–2 research (see chap. 5 for suggested cutoff scores).

TABLE 2.1

MMPI–2 $F - K$ Scores at the Lower and Upper Extremes of Different Diagnostic and Participant Groups

Participant Group and Gender	*N*	*Approximate Lower 2.5% (Fake Good)*	*Approximate Upper 2.5% (Fake Bad)*
Normals			
Male	1,138	–22	4[a]
Female	1,462	–22	3[a]
Psychiatric			
Male	215	–18	27
Female	241	–20	22
Substance dependent			
Male	168	–19	10
Female	96	–22	10
Traumatic brain injury			
Male	50	–23	17
Female	29	–22	–1
SSD/SSI benefit applicants			
Male	217	–11	37
Female	74	-22	30
Police applicants			
Male	49	-25	-11[b]
Female	12	-24	13[b]
Priest applicants			
Male	38	-25	-8[b]
Female	30	-24	-7[b]

Note. SSD = Social Security disability; SSI = supplemental security income.

[a]These "cutoffs" might have been higher had the normative group not excluded participants with raw *F* scores of 320.

[b]Scores in this direction more likely reflect a willingness to acknowledge difficulties (in these participant groups) than an attempt to feign a disorder.

From "MMPI–2 Normative Data for the $F - K$ Index: Implications for Clinical, Neuropsychological, and Forensic Practice," by S. E. Rothke, A. F. Friedman, W. G. Dahlstrom, R. L., Greene, R. Arrendondo, and A. W. Mann, 1994, *Assessment, 1*, 1–15.

It is recommended that a determination of profile validity not be made on the basis of a single score or index value alone. Rather, an examination of various measures, as well as of overall clinical scale elevation (mean profile elevation), in conjunction with interview findings and the participant's history and current circumstances is recommended. Future research should focus on specific diagnostic groups in order to maximize generalizability to individual cases. This would also minimize the potential impact of differing base rates of elevated and low index scores within different groups on the sensitivity and specificity of guideline scores (Glaros & Kline, 1988). Research exploring the outcome (e.g., treatment, job selection, and litigation status) and recovery correlates of the $F - K$ index would make it a much more useful clinical tool. Specifically, Rothke et al. (1994) suggested that

> investigations on the use of the $F - K$ index as a validity indicator need to include independent measures (either other tests or criterion measures if available) of malingering, exaggeration of illness, defensiveness, denial of illness, and effects of litigation and/or of the job selection process on test performance. (p. 14)

NOTES

[1]The *T*-score values for the original MMPI Cannot Say scale, as well as for the *L* and *F* scales, were set arbitrarily by Hathaway and Mc*K*inley and do not accurately reflect the frequency with which a specific raw score will be obtained. For example, the MMPI profile sheet shows that a raw score of 30 on the Cannot *S*ay scale corresponds to a *T*-score value of 50. This is a gross inaccuracy, as omitting 30 items would be highly unusual. In fact, no study has reported a mean number of omitted items close to 30 (Clopton & Neuringer, 1977). Greene (1980) pointed out in a review of four population samples (clinic clients, medical patients, prison inmates, and university students) that no more than 5% of the participants in any given sample omitted more than 30 items. Clopton and Neuringer recommended that changes be made in the norms on the MMPI standard profile sheet so that a raw score of 5 would be set equal to a *T* score of 50 to reflect that most participants omit fewer than five items. They also suggested that the next level of *T* score, 60, be equivalent to a raw score of 30 omitted items, which should indicate caution in interpreting a profile with such a score. Greene also suggested using adjusted *T* scores to more accurately indicate the frequency with which a specific Cannot Say raw score will be obtained. He showed raw scores between 1 and 5 to correspond to *T*-score values between 45 and 49, raw scores between 6 and 30 to correspond to *T*-score ranges between 60 and 69, and raw scores of 31 and above to correspond to *T* scores of 70 and higher. For the Cannot Say scale, as well as for the other validity scales, male and female norms are equivalent on the MMPI but different on the MMPI-2.

[2]The one exception to this rule is women's scale 5 (Masculinity–Femininity) scores that are artificially raised by low raw scores resulting from unanswered (omitted) items (Butcher et al., 1989).

[3]Greene (1978) developed a Carelessness scale for the MMPI to determine "whether the client is willing or able to complete the MMPI in an appropriate manner" (p. 410). The Carelessness scale consists of 12 pairs of psychologically opposite items selected on an empirical basis. The items for the scale were chosen by examining the responses of 150 participants to the 566 items of the MMPI. The responses of 50 VA patients, 50 clients at a university psychology clinic, and 50 introductory psychology college students were all placed in a 566 × 566 matrix. According to Greene (1978), a computer program

> selected all possible nonredundant pairs of items that were answered in a consistent direction more than 90% of the time. That is, a pair of items was selected if 46 out of the 50 individuals within a group answered the first item of the pair either true or false and the other item reached the same criterion with either the same or opposite answer as the first item of the pair. This procedure resulted in the selection of 271 pairs of items in the VA sample, 643 pairs of items in the psychology clinic sample, and 140 pairs of items in the college student sample. (p. 407)

Pair of items overlapping with the *L* or *K* scales were excluded, whereas pairs of items overlapping with the *F* scale were excluded only when the content was evaluated to be deviant or bizarre. The empirical selection of the items thus far was based on their being answered in a consistent direction. The next step was to select pairs of these items that were psychological opposites. Two graduate students in clinical psychology and Greene separately selected pairs of items judged to be opposite and that had been selected empirically in at least two of the three samples. Pairs of items were retained for the Carelessness scale only if all three judges agreed that the pairs were psychologically opposite. Twelve pairs of items were identified. (For the item numbers with directions of scoring see Friedman, Webb, & Lewak, 1989.)

The maximum score individuals can receive on the carelessness scale is 12 if they answer all 12 pairs inconsistently. Greene (1980) suggested a cutting score of four or more inconsistent responses for identifying invalid profiles. Greene pointed out that this cutting score is not based on any external criteria to validate the score. However, a cutting score of 4 or more (corresponding to a *T* score of 70) classified from 10% to 18% of the profiles in his sample as being of "questionable validity." The mean scores or number of inconsistent responses by each of the three samples used in the study were as follows: 1.76 (SD = 1.45) for VA psychiatric patients, 2.20 (SD =1.28) for psychology clinic clients, and 1.48 (SD = 1.34) for university students. The Carelessness scale may be misnamed, as it appears to measure inconsistent responding due to several possible sources. (For a more complete review of the Carelessness scale, see Friedman, Webb, & Lewak, 1989.)

[4]Many MMPI users employ the TR index to further assess the test-taking attitude of the respondent. The TR index consists of the total number of items answered oppositely when the 16 repeated items are presented (Buechley & Ball, 1952; Dahlstrom et al., 1972). The 16 repeated items are drawn from Scales 6, 7, 8, and 0 and were added to the group booklet form to assist in the mechanical scoring of the inventory. The 16 items are actually scored only once on the test. The TR index can be scored on both the group booklet form and the abbreviated version of Form R, as the latter contains all of the necessary items for scoring the clinical and validity scales within the first 399 items. (For a listing of TR index items and a discussion of this measure, see Friedman, Webb, & Lewak, 1989.)

[5]Greene (1991a) pointed out that eight *F* scale items (Items 12, 48, 120, 132, 204, 222, 264, and 288) do not meet the 10% or below criterion for either men or women in the MMPI–2 normative sample, with four other items for men also not meeting this criterion.

[6]The slightly higher mean values for men and women in the MMPI–2 normative sample on the *F* scale provides further support for the renorming of the original MMPI. In other words, the endorsement frequency for some items has changed on the MMPI–2.

[7]The 74-item *Ds* scale was revised when Gough (1957) published the California Psychological Inventory (CPI). Gough (1957) included the *Ds* scale on the CPI (approximately 200 items on the CPI were taken from the MMPI) in a shortened 44-item version with the direction of scoring reversed and renamed the well-being (*Wb*) scale. As already mentioned, the rationale for reducing the scale length was that the original scale was considered to be too long, and it contained too many items with extreme declarations of psychopathology for the CPI (Gough, 1987a). The *Wb* scale was eventually reduced to 38 items for the 1987 version of the CPI. The *Ds* scale, as described in Dahlstrom and Welsh's (1960) *An MMPI Handbook* (p. 53), has 74 items, with the revised *Ds* scale (*Ds-r*) containing 40 items. The change from 44 to 40 items is due to modifications in the

MMPI items when they were included in the CPI booklet. Four of the *Wb* items were modified from the MMPI wording, which means that the *Ds-r* is in effect only 40 items long.Of the 40 *Ds-r* items, 34 are retained on the MMPI–2 and are sometimes referred to as *Ds-r2* (Rogers et al., 1994). The reader should be aware that Gough's (1987a) revision of the *Ds* scale to 40 items was made to accommodate the needs of the CPI and does not imply that the abbreviated version was an improvement over the original scale.

[8]A *test hit* is defined as a normal person or psychiatric patient yielding a normal or abnormal profile respectively. A test hit is when a test accurately classifies a participant. When a normal individual obtains a nonelevated MMPI–2 profile, his or her test is said to be a true negative because it indicates the absence (negative) of psychopathology. When the clinical status of a patient indicates abnormality and the corresponding MMPI–2 profile is elevated, the results are congruent with the observed clinical status, and a true-positive result is obtained. This means that the test is accurately detecting the presence (positive) of abnormal behavior. A *test miss* is defined as a normal or abnormal individual yielding an abnormal or normal profile, respectively. It is a test miss because the MMPI–2 is incorrectly classifying a participant. When a normal individual obtains an elevated or abnormal MMPI–2 profile, he or she is being falsely identified on the test as having present (positive) psychopathology. His or her test is said, therefore, to be a false positive. When an abnormal person generates a normal profile, the test is falsely identifying the absence (negative) of abnormality and is therefore called a false negative.

[9]The first attempt to apply the $F-K$ index to the detection of participants attempting to present an overly favorably test profile (fake good) was by Hunt (1948), who found that a cutting score of equal to or less than –11 identified 62% of a prison sample asked to fake good but also resulted in a 93% false-positive rate with psychology undergraduate students asked to produce an authentic profile. Much better results were obtained for the identification of simulators of psychiatric disorder (fake bad) using a cutoff of equal to or greater than 11 (only a 12% false-positive rate). Gough (1950) reanalyzed data from several studies not initially involving the $F-K$ index and found the index much more useful for correctly separating fake-bad simulators from normal and patient groups than for the discrimination of simulated fake good profiles from authentic normal and psychiatric profiles. He also noted that the mean $F-K$ index score did not differ between normals and authentic psychiatric patients from university and VA hospital settings, suggesting that the index was not susceptible to distortion on the basis of psychiatric disturbance (a critical element for the establishment of an empirical index used to discriminate simulators of illness or wellness from genuine normal and impaired populations). Gough reported $F-K$ index data for the original normative sample of the MMPI (294 men and 397 women), noting that scores were roughly normally distributed (M = –8.96, SD = 6.97 for the composite sample; separate means by gender were not reported). Only 11% of the participants had an $F-K$ index equal to or greater than 0, although this may have been, in part, an artifact of the normative sample having included participants with many missing item responses (to disturbing or embarrassing questions), thus lowering the potential F score. This was one of the issues addressed by Hathaway and Briggs (1957) in their "purification" of the original normative sample. When Gough pooled his data with data from other clinical and analogue simulator groups, he found a cutting score of 7 or higher correctly identified 95% of normals and 75% of fake-bad simulators.

[10]More recent normative data for the $F-K$ index on the original MMPI was provided for 305 men and 335 women by Osborne et al. (1986). Men were found to have a mean index score of –9.77 (SD = 6.63), and the mean score for women was –11.22 (SD = 6.19). The mean for the combined group was –10.53 (SD = 6.43), which, in contrast to that (–8.96) found earlier by Gough (1950), indicated the need for updated norms. A score of 0 or higher for women and 1 or higher for men identified the 5% of highest scores (the fake-bad direction), and scores of –21 or below for women and –20 or below for men were at the lowest 5% (the fake-good direction) for this newer normative group. Similar results were summarized by Greene (1988a).

3

The Clinical Scales and Their Derivatives

CLINICAL SCALE DEVELOPMENT AND USE

The MMPI–2 has 10 standard clinical scales that are universally scored when the test is administered. These scales, numbered 1 through 9 plus 0, were originally named after the diagnostic criterion groups (hypochondriasis, depression, etc.) but currently are indicated by their numbers. The original diagnostic labels that named the scales are misleading, as the behaviors expected to be associated with the diagnostic labels on specific scales are not always observed. Therefore, the naming of the scales by numbers is less misleading in terms of what the scales are measuring. Table A.2 contains the item composition of each clinical scale with the keyed responses. Tables B.3 and B.4 present the *T*-score conversions for the clinical scales.

The clinical scales were the first scales to be constructed from the test items and have been the focus of most of the MMPI research done in the past 50-plus years. They form the basis of all of the coding systems (see chap. 4) and the core of all the clinical uses of the MMPI–2. Traditionally, Scales 1, 2, and 3 are referred to as the *neurotic triad*, and Scales 6, 7, 8, and 9 are referred to as the *psychotic tetrad*. The modifications made in the restandardized MMPI–2 left the clinical scales essentially intact, with only nine deleted items from Scales 1, 2, 5, and 0.

Once the clinician has ascertained through an analysis of the validity measures that a profile is valid, an interpretation of the clinical scales is possible. Interpretation of the clinical scales is primarily focused on scale elevations and configuration with attention to item content being an important adjunct in the process. Typically, clinicians examine each scale elevation to form an initial impression of the test taker prior to examining the score combinations and the profile code (Butcher et al., 1989). After examining the clinical scales, the psychologist typically examines the different content scale scores, usually the

TABLE 3.1
T-Score Classifications and Percentile Values

Uniform T Score	*Classification Percentile*	*Equivalent*
30	Very low	<1
35		4
40	Moderately low	15
45		34
50	Average	55
55		73
60	Moderately high	85
65		92
70	High	96
75		98
80	Very high	>99
85		
90	Extremely high	

Note. From "The New Uniform *T* Scores for the MMPI–2: Rationale, Derivation, and Appraisal," by A. Tellegen & Y. S. Ben-Porath, 1992. *Psychological Assessment: A Journal of Consulting and Clinical Psychology, 4*, 145–155. Copyright © 1992 by the American Psychological Association. Adapted with permission.

Harris–Lingoes and Subtle–Obvious subscales. These subscales were derived from many of the clinical scales in order to help clarify the meaning of individual scale elevations. Because these subscales are discussed within the context of the clinical scales, we present an overview of their derivation and meaning before the clinical scale descriptors. Moderator variables, such as age, education, and SES are discussed in relationship to MMPI–2 profiles in chapter 9.

The *T*-score value at which clinical significance is generally assumed is at 65 and above (as compared with 70 on the original MMPI). This does not mean that individuals with scores below 65 are always free of psychopathology or concerns. The guideline cutoff score of 65 should be considered a demarcation to assist the clinician in interpreting the MMPI–2 profile rather than as an absolute standard. Although considerably less research has been conducted on low-scale elevations, it is still important to examine the lowest scores in a profile to ascertain if there is significance attached to the score (Friedman, Webb, & Lewak, 1989; Greene, 2000, 1991a). Keiller and Graham (1993) studied partner ratings in a subsample of the MMPI–2 standardization sample and compared low, medium, and high scores on the MMPI–2 clinical scales. They reported that for this nonclinical sample, low scores on most MMPI–2 scales provided valuable information. In general, low-scoring nonclinical participants showed positive characteristics and greater than average adjustment, which will usually be the opposite of those traits typically associated with high scores on a particular scale. Their findings did not suggest that low scores indicate negative characteristics or adjustment problems that were poorer than average.

More recently, Graham, Ben-Porath, and McNulty (1997) recognized that Keiller and Graham's (1993) findings might not generalize to the clinical settings in which the MMPI–2 is most typically used. They therefore, studied the meaning of low scores on both the clinical and supplementary scales in an outpatient mental health population. Low scores were defined as being below a *T* score of 41. Graham et al. (1997) reported the following results:

> Our results indicate that the meaning of low scores on the MMPI–2 scales that we were able to study differs from one scale to another. For some scales, low scores seemed to provide no useful information. For other scales, low scorers appeared to have fewer symptoms and negative characteristics than within normal limit scorers. In some cases, these characteristics are specifically related to the construct that the scales were designed to measure; in others, they indicate better overall adjustment. Perhaps the most consistent finding was that for none of the scales that we studied did low scores indicate more negative characteristics or poorer overall adjustment than within normal limit scorers. (p. 390)

Graham et al. recommended that low MMPI–2 scales in an outpatient mental setting be interpreted cautiously; it should not be assumed that a low score necessarily indicates the converse of a high score on that scale.

It is clear that more research in multiple populations is needed concerning the correlates of low scores on the clinical and supplementary scales. We believe it is important to note unusually low scores on any of the clinical or supplementary scales in any population as it can raise important interpretive hypotheses. For example, if a psychiatric patient who recently suffered multiple losses obtained a very low score on the Depression scale, the clinician should consider whether the patient is pathologically attempting to deny depression and whether suicide precautions should be considered. Any statistically deviant score is worthy of consideration and should be attempted to be understood in the particular context of the individual's situation.

On the profile sheet where MMPI–2 scores are plotted, the scales have been limited to a *T* score of 30, so it is not possible to plot a lower score. However, Table B.15 provides a table developed by Ward (1994) that provides *T*-score values below 30 for select scales.[1]

The reader is reminded that for the basic clinical Scales 1, 2, 3, 4, 6, 7, 8, and 9, uniform *T* scores are used in plotting a profile, whereas Scales 5 and 0 still use the linear *T*-score conversions from the original MMPI. Describing various elevations on the scales as "high," "very high," and so on is a subjective process that varies across different interpretative manuals and clinical situations. This text uses the *K*-corrected *T*-score ranges in Table 3.1 for describing standard clinical scale elevations on the MMPI–2. These elevation descriptions are approximations for the clinical scales and relatively rough, sometimes very rough, approximations for all of the other scales. Scores on the border between classifications are particularly open to judgment.

Once a profile has been scored and plotted onto a profile sheet, it can be coded. Coding is a procedure used to summarize the elevation and rank order of scales using a notation system. Coding is provided by most computerized report services and is easy to accomplish by hand. Coding is useful for research purposes and profile classification, such as finding a similarly matched profile. This topic, as well as scoring procedures, is described in detail in chapter 4.

Harris–Lingoes Subscales

Elevations on certain clinical scales often can be better understood by examining the subscale components to the parent scale. To this end, Harris and Lingoes (1955; 1968) devised subscales that are used routinely in the analysis of an MMPI–2 profile. The MMPI–2 item pool is heterogeneous, and many clinical scales have diverse content. Therefore, a particular scale score can reflect different item endorsement patterns for different individuals. For example, two individuals with the exact *T*-score elevation of 70 on Scale 2 (Depression) could have endorsed different content areas of depression items. One person may have endorsed many items related to depressed mood, whereas the other person may have emphasized items related to vegetative symptoms, both areas having different clinical implications for the treatment and description of depression. Dissimilar endorsement patterns of items within a scale are thought to be related to particular behavioral patterns or correlates. Harris and Lingoes developed subscales for Scales 2, 3, 4, 6, 8, and 9 after inspecting the item content of each clinical scale and grouped these items into categories that appeared homogeneous. That is, items that appeared to reflect a single trait or attribute were grouped into new subscales, which Harris and Lingoes named on the basis of the item content. They did not develop subscales for Scales 1 and 7 as the items on these scales appeared to be related to single constructs. Scale 1 content is obvious in nature and relates to bodily concerns, whereas Scale 7, also obvious in content, relates to anxiety, worry, and tension. Scales 5 and 0 are multidimensional in nature, but Harris and Lingoes chose not to develop subscales for these scales, presumably because they were added later to the instrument and were not included among the original clinical scales. Scales 5 and 0 have been factor analyzed and broken down into component subscales and are discussed later in this chapter.

The Harris–Lingoes subscales for Scales 2, 3, 4, 6, 8 and 9 are described under the appropriate clinical parent scale in this chapter. The scale composition and direction of scoring for the Harris–Lingoes subscales is presented in Table A.2. Linear *T*-score conversions for the Harris–Lingoes subscales for men and women based on the restandardization sample (Butcher et al., 1989) are presented in Table B.5. It should be noted that the Harris–Lingoes subscale items are contained within the first 370 items of the MMPI–2, so a clinician wishing to administer an abbreviated test can still derive the scores for these subscales. In the restandardization of the MMPI, only one item (MMPI Item 95) was dropped that affected any of the Harris–Lingoes subscales. Specifically, the Psychomotor Retardation subscale (*D2*), a Depression subscale, lost 1 item, leaving *D2* with 14 items instead of 15 items on the MMPI–2 (Levitt, 1990). Most interpretive and scoring services provide scores for all of the Harris–Lingoes subscales, but when hand scoring the test, the clinician is advised to score for the subscales when the clinical scales are between a *T* score of 60 and 80. Scores much higher or lower are unlikely to reveal any significant scatter between the subscales.

The 28 subscales derived from the clinical scales for the Harris–Lingoes subscales vary in their length, with 11 of the subscales possessing 10 or fewer items, resulting in low internal consistency values for several of the subscales (Krishnamurthy, Archer, & Huddleston, 1995). However, most of the subscales have a high degree of internal consistency. The reader is referred to Graham (1990) for a listing of the internal consistency (alpha) coefficients for men and women in the MMPI–2 restandardization. Graham also presented data on the temporal stability of the subscales. These data show that the subscales are generally less stable than the parent scales.

There are also considerable intercorrelations between some of the subscales because the scale constructors made no effort to eliminate item overlap. Some items may overlap up to four different subscales (Caldwell, 1988). It is reasonable to assume that the high intercorrelations among the subscales are a result of this structural redundancy: "For example, all 10 items on the Brooding subscale also appear on the Subjective Depression subscale, and 12 of the 15 items on the Mental Dullness subscale are on the Subjective Depression subscale" (Greene, 1991a, p. 140). Research conducted by Childs, Dahlstrom, Kemp, and Panter (1992) suggest that the Harris–Lingoes subscales are also likely to be multidimensional in nature. Harris and Lingoes (1968) presented their intercorrelations in mimeographed materials, and Graham (1990) presented intercorrelations for the subscales based on responses by the restandardization sample (Butcher et al., 1989).

Most recently, McGrath, Powis, and Pogge (1998) found that scores on the subscales covaried significantly as a function of code-pattern. The MMPI–2 profiles of 483 psychiatric inpatients were analyzed, with the results indicating that code-pattern was found to be a predictor of every Harris–Lingoes subscale. McGrath et al. provided a useful table presenting the Harris–Lingoes subscale mean values across 14 code-patterns, thereby giving the user a basis for comparing their data against a large psychiatric sample. The value in this table lies in its ability to give the reader an opportunity to compare their individual Harris–Lingoes subscale scores to normative data for a particular code-pattern, thereby indicating whether or not the subscale scores are consistent with a prototypic code-pattern. Clearly, however, more research is needed with psychiatric patients, as well as other populations, with three- and four-point code-patterns to make these data generalizable to clinical and nonclinical settings.

Most interpretive guidebooks suggest 65 as the *T*-score value at or above which a subscale score should be interpreted, although some researchers suggest a score of 70 as more appropriate (e.g., Chojnacki & Walsh, 1994; Greene, 1991a). This text suggests 65 or greater as the cutoff for interpreting most of the subscales, although there are exceptions to this recommendation.[2]

Because the Harris–Lingoes subscales have been used to supplement, and not replace, the interpretation of the clinical scales, clinicians have generally found the Harris–Lingoes subscales to be helpful in interpreting MMPI/MMPI–2 profiles. However, there are several concerns about the reliability and validity of the subscales. The most important problems are related to the ways in which the subscales were constructed. The rational method of forming the subscales by clustering items into content areas is a subjective process, the success of which may vary. Factors contributing to this success can include the number of candidate items and the adequacy of the definition of content areas selected. However, Harris and Lingoes made no attempt to cross-validate their subscales nor to relate them to external criteria. This type of research is greatly needed. One attempt to link behavioral correlates to the subscales failed (Calvin, 1975). A more recent attempt (Miller & Streiner, 1985) to reproduce the Harris–Lingoes subscales, by clinicians who were asked to rationally group the items, failed to duplicate more than about one third of these subscales. This suggests that the subscales' reliability is poor and that the interpretation of the subscales may be as subjective as their development.

Another recent investigation (Foerstner, 1986) of the factor structure of various MMPI scales (including, but not limited to, the Harris–Lingoes subscales) showed that 10 factors accounted for the majority of variance. The first factor was named Depression. The three highest factor loadings on depression were *D1* (Subjective Depression), *D4* (Mental Dullness), and *D5* (Brooding). However, *D2* (Psychomotor Retardation) and *D3* (Physical Malfunctioning) did not load at all on the first factor. This suggests that these subscales may not be related to the construct of depression in the specific way Harris and Lingoes (1955; 1968) assumed. For example, *D2* and *D3* may be more associated with the vegetative than the depressed mood aspects of depression syndromes. Likewise, the study showed that other subscales failed to appear with significant factor loadings, as would be expected from their parent scales. Therefore, this and other studies suggest that the subscales under a given parent scale may be associated with heterogeneous constructs.

Krishnamurthy et al. (1995) suggested generally reexamining the utility of the subscales and their limitations. We agree with this suggestion and note that there is a conspicuous lack of diverse norms in different settings, which are needed to aid in the interpretation process with the subscales. Also, because many of the subscales are short (e.g., fewer than 10 items), a change in the response to even 1 item can produce a large shift in the *T*-score value for that particular subscale (Caldwell, 1988). Wrobel (1992) found support for 16 of the 28 subscales in an empirical study using clinicians' ratings of outpatient therapy clients; however, 12 subscales were not supported. Wrobel pointed out that many of the unsupported subscales consisted of subtle content, again raising the concern that subtle items may hurt, not help, certain scales. Overall, however, his study provided support for the validity of the majority of the Harris–Lingoes subscales. But until reliability and validity studies more clearly and consistently support the use of the subscales, the clinician is urged to be cautious about the practical application of the Harris–Lingoes subscales.

Subtle–Obvious Subscales

Another important component of the clinical scales are the Subtle–Obvious subscales developed by Wiener and Harmon (1946) and later published under Wiener's name (Wiener, 1948, 1956). By rationally grouping items into categories obviously reflective of psychopathology, Wiener and Harman found that they could provide additional measures useful in determining the test-taking attitude of a respondent. They created Subtle and Obvious subscales for Scales 2, 3, 4, 6, and 9. For these particular scales, the addition of the Subtle raw score to the Obvious raw score should equal the non-*K*-corrected raw score. Scales 1, 7, and 8 consist of mostly obvious items, which made it difficult for Wiener and Harmon to create Subtle subscales. The Subtle–Obvious subscales do not contain an equal amount of items, and no efforts were made to balance them. The subscales contain 108 subtle items and 145 obvious items. Greene (1991a) stated that the

> empirically determined deviant response for 65 (59%) of these subtle items was in the opposite direction from what would be expected by merely inspecting item content, whereas only 8 (5%) of these obvious items were scored in the opposite direction. These findings substantiate the subtle and obvious nature of these two groups of items, respectively. (p. 79)

A complete listing of the subscales' composition can be found in Table A.2, and the linear *T*-score conversions from raw scores can be found in Table B.6. In their scheme, subtle items refer to being less obvious measures of psychopathology or, said another way, items that are lacking in face validity.

Although Wiener and Harmon (1946) defined item obviousness and subtlety according to the items' relationship to psychopathology, other researchers have defined the distinction in different terms. For example, Jackson (1971) defined item subtlety as involving the respondent's ability to determine the specific trait or scale to which an item corresponds. Christian, Burkhart, and Gynther (1978) defined subtle–obvious items by having college students rate all of the MMPI items in relationship to psychopathology on a 5-point scale ranging from 1 (*very subtle*) to 5 (*very obvious*) with the midpoint termed neutral items. For example, the mean obviousness ratings for all of the MMPI scales showed that the *F* scale and Scale 8 had the highest ratings, indicating their items are obvious in nature. The mean obviousness ratings were lowest, thereby indicating subtlety, for the *Mf* and *K* scales. In still another attempt to classify subtle–obvious items, Wales and Seeman (1968) made the distinction using a statistical assignment method. They called items obvious or *X items* if a minority of the normative group's endorsements on the items were exceeded by a larger proportion of psychiatric cases. Subtle items were referred to as *0 (zero) items* when items endorsed frequently by the normative participants were exceeded in endorsement frequency by the psychiatric cases. *X* (obvious) items were therefore scored as pathological when answered in the converse direction of the majority of the normative group, and 0 (subtle) items were scored as pathological because more psychiatric cases endorsed the items.

Clearly, many different subtle–obvious distinctions have been made, and Dubinsky, Gamble, and Rogers (1985) provided a useful overview of the subtle–obvious literature. They stated that regardless of the item sets used, participants instructed to manipulate their MMPI scores tend to increase or decrease their obvious item scores, but their scores for subtle items tend to move in the opposite direction. In other words, it is easier for participants to more effectively manipulate the obvious rather than the subtle items. This so-called paradoxical effect "is a fairly robust phenomenon and occurs with fake bad and fake good instructions with normal and psychiatric (inpatient, outpatient, and forensic) populations, and with all three of the major S/O [subtle–obvious] item sets" (Hollrah, Schlottman, Scott, & Brunelti, 1995, p. 288).

Although most of the subtle–obvious research has been conducted with the MMPI, it appears safe to generalize the research findings from the MMPI to the MMPI–2, given that only 3 of the 13 items dropped from the original test were on the Subtle–Obvious subscales of Wiener and Harmon (all 3 items were on Scale 2; Hollrah et al., 1995). Specifically, Scale 2 lost one item on the Obvious subscale and two items on the Subtle subscale.

The subtle–obvious distinction has been used for two main purposes. The first is to assess the test-taking attitude of the participant. This is generally done by examining the difference scores between the Subtle and Obvious subscales. Participants who overreport or magnify their problems may substantially elevate their Obvious scores over their Subtle scores, whereas the converse is true for participants underreporting their problems. Greene (2000) suggested that a participant who obtains *T* scores of 90 or more on all five Obvious subscales, and *T* scores close to 40 on all five Subtle scales, may be attempting to overreport, whereas the converse relationship between scores on the subscales should suggest a possible underreporting response set. By summing the differences between the Obvious and Subtle subscales, a single overall measure can be used to determine reporting styles. Greene described this simple method as follows: Subtract the Subtle and Obvious *T*-score values for each of the five subscales, and add them together. The mean total *T*-score difference in normal samples is in the range of 0 to –30, whereas in psychiatric samples it is in the range of 50 to 60. There is more variability in psychiatric samples because patients admit to more problems, thereby increasing their scores on the Obvious subscales. (Note that because the majority of MMPI–2 items are scoreable [i.e., pathological], when endorsed "true," the percentage of items marked "true" provides a gross index of psychopathology that corresponds with the sum differences between the Obvious and Subtle subscales.) As Greene noted, it is crucial that a high score suggestive of overreporting be verified so as not to overlook genuine psychopathology. The second way in which the subscales are used is to provide personality correlates associated with the subscale scores. To this end, Dahlstrom (1991) has provided correlates for each of the Subtle and Obvious subscales derived from partner ratings on the Katz (1968)

Adjustment Scales for the 841 couples in the MMPI–2 restandardization sample. Some of these correlates are described under the appropriate scale descriptions in this chapter.

The issue of Subtle–Obvious subscale effectiveness has been the focus of much controversy. Some researchers have strongly suggested that the subtle items actually diminish the efficacy of the parent scale and fail to provide valid correlates of behavior (L. D. Nelson, 1987; L. D. Nelson & Cicchetti, 1991; Weed, Ben-Porath, & Butcher, 1990). Unfortunately, many of the studies suggesting such evidence are deeply flawed conceptually, regardless of their varying merits in terms of execution. The typical format for such studies is to select some obvious criterion such, as the Beck Depression Inventory (BDI), the Symptom Checklist—90 Depression scale, or the Profile of Mood State Depression scale, and to then compare the success of, say, the Depression–Obvious or Depression–Subtle subscale (and sometimes the full Depression scale) in predicting to this criterion. The typical finding, of course, is that the obvious component of the Depression scale best predicts such an obvious criterion, the subtle component predicts poorly if at all, and the full scale is somewhere in the middle.

Although the Subtle and Obvious subscales are known to have different, in some cases widely different, social desirability values, this factor has rarely been addressed, much less controlled, in this rather long series of studies. Each Subtle and Obvious subscale has its own unique operating characteristics and should be assessed as such. Until recently, there has not been sufficient impartial analysis of this body of obvious–subtle research. Fortunately, the situation has recently changed with the publication of Hollrah et al.'s (1995) exhaustive and balanced review of the convergent and discriminant validities of the Subtle–Obvious subscales. They also raised important questions responding some of the recent contributions to the "negative" subtle items literature, such as the article by Weed et al. (1990). The following statements summarize Hollrah et al. (1995) findings, which we endorse:

> After a thorough review of the literature, some uncertainty still remains regarding the validity of the MMPI subtle items. Support for the subtle item validity varies depending on the methodology used and the particular subtle subscale investigated. Of even greater clinical relevance, addressing the empirical method of test construction, and in response to the hypothesis that the subtle items were included by sampling error (e.g. Jackson, 1971), there is as yet no consistent evidence that removing the subtle items would result in MMPI scales with greater clinical validity.
>
> It is likely that some of the subtle items were indeed included by sampling error. However, some of the subtle items may belong on the respective scales. Likewise, many obvious items may be on their scales due to sampling error, as some studies do not support their discriminative validity. Analyses to determine validity for specific items, or at least specific scales, seems more appropriate than declaring either all or none of the subtle items as valid measures. (p. 295)

Hollrah et al. also stated that the main support in the literature for subtle–obvious items lies in their ability to detect fake-good profiles in psychiatric settings.

Overlapping Item Content

Many of the items on the clinical scales are scored on other clinical scales, whereas some items are not. The items that are unique to a particular validity or clinical scale are referred to as *nonoverlapping items*, whereas those scored on more than one scale are called *overlapping items*. The overlapping items within the MMPI–2 have been a source of concern to clinicians and researchers alike. The empirical criterion approach to test construction allows the total item pool to be used repeatedly with different criterion groups. An item is retained for inclusion in the scale if it discriminates a criterion group from a normal group. The number of scales that can be derived from this method is only limited by the number of available criterion groups (K. B. Stein, 1968). The concern that arose from this construction method is that although the standard MMPI scales were capable of differentiating the normals from each of the psychiatric criterion groups, the psychiatric criterion groups were not contrasted with each other. Hence, there is overlap in item content between the criterion scales. This structural redundancy, however, does not appear to be a trivial artifact of the test construction method; many of the scales share a common variance, which is reflected by the presence of overlapping items (Friedman, Gleser, Smeltzer, Wakefield, & Schwartz, 1983; Friedman, Webb, & Lewak, 1989; Gentry, Wakefield, & Friedman, 1985).[3] (For a review of the methodological concerns about the item overlap, see the text by Friedman, Webb, & Lewak, 1989. See also Appendix C for a table describing the amount of item overlap and the intercorrelations based on overlap.)

Considerable range exists in the amount of item overlap among the clinical scales, and there are many more overlapping items than nonoverlapping items on each scale. Some items (e.g., MMPI–2 Items 9 and 31) overlap as many as five and six different scales, whereas other items overlap as few as two scales (e.g., MMPI–2 Items 11 and 34). Scale 8 (*Sc*), which is the longest scale on the MMPI–2 with 78 items, has 62 overlapping items, the greatest number for any of the clinical scales, whereas Scales 1(*Hs*) and 3 (*Hy*) share 20 items in common, the largest number shared by any two scales. Scales 7 (*Pt*) and 8 overlap almost as much, with 17 items in common. The neurotic triad consisting of Scales 1, 2, and 3 has 24, 47, and 50 overlapping items, respectively, leaving only 8, 10, and 10 items, respectively, that are unique to each of these scales. The traditional psychotic tetrad, consisting of Scales 6, 7, 8, and 9, has 33, 39, 62, and 31 overlapping items, respectively, and 7, 9, 16, and 15 nonoverlapping items, respectively. Of the 13 items dropped from the original MMPI for the restandardization leading to the MMPI–2, none of the items were overlap items; all were unique to the particular scale on which they were scored. A perusal of the items belonging to the basic clinical scales indicates that the traditional neurotic and psychotic scales share a considerable amount of item overlap. Thirty-five items appear concurrently on at least one neurotic and one psychotic scale. Within the neurotic triad, and exclusive of other psychotic scales, there are 30 items that appear on at least two of the three scales and in some instances all three (MMPI–2 Items 2, 10, 18, 39, 45, 141, and 175). Within the psychotic tetrad of scales, there are 18 items shared by at least two of the four scales that are exclusive of the neurotic scales and one item that overlaps all four psychotic scales (MMPI–2 Item 23).

Only seven pairs of scales have no items in common: *L* and *Hs*, *Hs* and *K*, *Pd* and *L*, *Hs* and *Mf*, *Hs* and *Ma*, *L* and *Si*, and *F* and *Si* (Dahlstom et al., 1972; Wheeler et al., 1951).

SCALE 1: HYPOCHONDRIASIS (*Hs*)

Scale 1 was the first scale to be published on the MMPI and measures the number of bodily complaints claimed by an individual or, said another way, the degree to which a person is denying good physical health. Hypochondriasis is a disturbance involving an unrealistic interpretation of physical signs or sensations as abnormal, which leads the person to fear that he or she has a serious disease (American Psychiatric Association, 1994). Hypochondriasis was a clinical syndrome studied by Hathaway and McKinley (1940) to construct Scale 1, and the criterion group consisted of 50 inpatients with only pure, uncomplicated hypochondriasis. Patients with other coexisting disorders, like a psychosis or other physical disease, were excluded from the criterion group. Hypochondriasis was selected for study because of the large numbers of patients with this disorder, and because it was a relatively easy diagnosis to establish (McKinley and Hathaway, 1940).

Several revisions of the scale were required before it could satisfactorily make discriminations. After the criterion group was selected, the next step in the construction of the scale was to specify the normals. Various samples within the normal group used in constructing Scale 1 were also included in assembling subsequent clinical scales. The first sample consisted of 109 men and 153 women, ranging in age from 26 to 43, who were visitors at the University of Minnesota Hospitals. As noted earlier (chap. 1) , participants were eliminated if they were under the care of a physician at the time. The second normal sample consisted of 265 unmarried entering freshmen who were receiving precollege guidance counseling at the University of Minnesota Testing Bureau. Unfortunately, more is known about the demographics of the normals used in constructing Scale 1 than for the criterion participants, whose proportion of gender or other information is unreported. McKinley and Hathaway (1940), however, did state that participants "were deleted, however, to exclude the extremes of age or other obviously disturbing influences" (p. 256).

The empirical method was primarily used to identify items that discriminated the normals and physically ill people from the 50 patients in the hypochondriacal criterion group. An item was considered for inclusion on the scale if the normals and patients in the criterion group differed in the frequency of responding to the item by at least twice the standard error of the proportions of true–false responses of the two groups (Greene, 1991a). However, McKinley and Hathaway (1940) did reject a few of the items in a nonempirical manner if they thought the item drifted too far from the construct of hypochondriasis.

An initial version of the scale consisted of 55 items, but further work was required to refine the scale because of the high numbers of psychiatric patients without clinically observed hypochondriasis who also obtained significant Scale 1 elevations. To correct for this occurrence, 50 patients without hypochondriacal complaints, but with high scores on the initial version of Scale 1, were compared with the original group of 50 hypochondriacal patients. Items that discriminated these two groups became known as the CH (Correction for Hypochondriasis) scale. The *CH* scale consisted of 48 items. Experimentation with the *CH* items by assigning them different weights failed to improve the performance of the scale. Ultimately, the maximum discrimination was achieved when *CH* was subtracted from the preliminary Hypochondriasis scale. As Greene (1980) described it, "for each of these correction items where an individual answers in the non-hypochondriacal direction, one point was subtracted from the total score on Scale 1" (p. 9). Cross-validation with the $H-C$ scale reliably separated normals from hypochondriacal patients. The hospitalized medical sample demonstrated that the presence of physical disease did not significantly raise scores on the scale.

A final version of Scale 1 occurred when McKinley and Hathaway attempted to improve the separation between Scales 1 and 3. Many *C* items were dropped, as were original Scale 1 items that did not stand up on further analysis. The addition of a 0.5 *K* value helped to improve the ability of the scale to make accurate diagnostic discriminations, and commercially available profile sheets provide a space to add the 0.5 *K* value to Scale 1.

The final scale consisted of 33 items related to various aspects of bodily functions, including generalized aches and pains and concerns about different body regions. The restandardization leading to MMPI–2 prompted the omission of one objectionable item, the modification of three items for grammatical clarification (e.g., tense), the modernization of one item for idiom or usage, and the simplification of one item. Therefore, the MMPI–2 Scale 1 has 32 items. The content of the scale is considered obvious, with no subtle items, meaning that an individual wishing to deny good health can easily do so. Given the face validity of the items, Wiener and Harmon (1946) did not categorize the item content of Scale 1 into their Subtle–Obvious subscales. Because all of the items relate to physical health and sensation, Harris and Lingoes (1955) did not discover enough item heterogeneity to form different subscales. As Greene (2000; 1991a) pointed out, factor analyses of the items in several different populations have consistently identified poor physical health and gastrointestinal difficulties as the two major factors in this scale.

The following items are examples of Scale 1 content, with the item number preceding the statement and the direction of scoring in parentheses (see Table A.2 for a complete listing of the Scale 1 items with their direction of scoring):

2. I have a good appetite. (False)
28. I am bothered by an upset stomach several times a week. (True)
53. Parts of my body often have feelings like burning, tingling, crawling, or like "going to sleep." (True)
57. I hardly ever feel pain in the back of my neck. (False)

141. During the past few years I have been well most of the time. (False)

The deviant direction for 66% (21 of the 32 items) of the items is "false." Therefore, a false response set tends to elevate the scale. Most items on Scale 1 overlap the other neurotic scales, *D* and *Hy*. Only four items overlap Scale 8 (Schizophrenia); one item overlaps Scale 6 (Paranoia). Twenty of the 32 items on Scale 1 are also scored on Scale 3 (*Hy*); therefore, an elevated score on either scale tends to raise the other one. Only eight items are unique (nonoverlapping) to Scale 1. (See Appendix C for a table describing the overlapping content for Scale 1.)

Greene (2000) stated that the construct validity of Scale 1 is supported by the fact that both older, well-researched scales and newer scales overlap with Scale 1. Specifically, Wiggins' (1966) Poor Health and Organic Symptoms content scales from the MMPI both have 13 items, respectively, in common with MMPI–2 Scale 1. The Health Concerns content scale from the MMPI–2 (Butcher, Graham, Williams, & Ben-Porath, 1990) shares 23 of its 36 items in common with Scale 1.

Increasing elevations on Scale 1 correspond to increasing bodily complaints. Neurotic individuals with bodily preoccupations tend to endorse a diffuse set of complaints about the body, whereas actually ill patients without psychological disturbance contain their item endorsements to the specific physical areas concerning them. Greene (2000) reported that physically ill patients usually obtain only moderate *T*-score elevations between 58 and 64. Patients with actual physical illness are more likely to elevate Scale 2 (Depression) than Scale 1.

The normals in the restandardization sample averaged a raw-score value of approximately 5 and 6 for men and women, respectively, on Scale 1. As normal people age, their Scale 1 scores tend only to increase slightly, approximately two to three items over the life span (Colligan et al., 1989). Scale 1 elevations have also been noted to occur in chronic pain patients (who also elevate Scale 3) and have been associated with high posttreatment pain intensity and a failure to return to normal activity levels (Prokop, 1988). Generally, a high elevation on Scale 1 is a negative predictor of treatment response (Prokop, 1988). If the clinician sees an excessively low Scale 1 score, such as a raw score of 0, interpretation can range from the individual simply being unusually free of bodily complaints and concerns to being pathologically unconcerned with or unaware of his or her bodily functions. The lack of psychological mindedness so often cited with high scores on this scale has been seen in a few rare cases with unusually low *Hs* raw scores. Such scores may also indicate the denial of any physical problems because of a counterphobic defense.

When examining Scale 1 in a profile, it is important to note the amount of *K* being added. Because a 0.5 *K* is added to Scale 1, a person may have important hypochondriacal concerns, despite a nonelevated score, because of a low *K* value.

Although some MMPI experts consider that Scale 1 elevations may reflect transient symptoms, such as the flu or a cold (Duckworth, 1979), it is generally considered a stable scale, with test–retest coefficients for psychiatric cases ranging from .79 to .86 for up to a 2-week period and from .38 to .65 for a 1-year interval (Dahlstrom et al., 1975).

Hunsley et al.'s (1988) large-scale meta-analysis of MMPI reliability studies using a wide variety of populations conducted between 1970 and 1981 found an average internal consistency of .79 across 70 studies. They also reported an average test–retest reliability of .78 for 16 studies, with time intervals from 1 day to 2 years. More recently, Butcher et al. (1989) reported reliability data for a subset of the restandardization sample that included 82 normal men and 111 normal women retested at an average interval of 8.5 days (*Mdn* = 7 days) and found test–retest correlation coefficients for men and women of .84 and .85, respectively, again illustrating the stability or characterologic nature of this scale. Internal consistency estimates (Cronbach's coefficient alpha) of .77 and .81 were reported for men and women, respectively.

SCALE 2: DEPRESSION (*D*)

Scale 2 was designed to measure the presence and depth of symptomatic depression, which is a mood state characterized by low morale, feelings of hopelessness or worthlessness, slowing of thought and action, and sometimes preoccupations with death and suicide (Dahlstrom et al., 1972). Scale 2 is considered to be a mood scale and is, therefore, sensitive to transient and even very brief emotional states. For this reason, it is useful in measuring response to treatment. It is the most frequently elevated scale in the MMPI–2 and the most frequent high point in adult psychiatric populations (Nichols, as cited in Greene, 1988b). In adolescent patients, Scale 2 appears second only to Scale 4 (Psychopathic Deviate) in high-point frequency on the MMPI (Marks et al., 1974).

Five participant groups were used to construct the scale. However, most of the 60 items contained on the original scale were derived by comparing normals (i.e., participants without observable depression) with a group of 50 patients who were carefully diagnosed as being in the depressed phase of a manic–depressive psychosis (Hathaway & McKinley, 1942). Because some nondepressed participants obtained elevated scores, a correction factor was derived (as was done in the construction of Scale 1) by comparing item endorsement patterns of 40 normal individuals, who earned elevated depression scores on an early version of the scale, with a group of 50 patients without observable depressive signs but who scored high on the early Depression scale. Eleven items differentiating these two groups became correction items that were included in the final scale. A depressed normal group was also used in the derivation of the scale "to help establish the meaning of more intermediate scale values between the normal and criterion groups, which would have been impossible if only the two extreme groups were contrasted" (Greene, 1980, p. 73). Hathaway and McKinley (as cited in Dahlstrom & Dahlstrom, 1980) described the final selection of scale items in the following way:

> First, each depressive item had to show a progressive increase in frequency from the normal groups through the depressed normal group to the criterion group since it was assumed that the depressed normals would be less than the criterion cases but more

than the general normals. In all items primarily indicating depression, the difference in percentage between the normal and the criterion was 2.5 or more times its standard error. Second, the non-depressed group percentage for the item was required to approach that for normals. After careful analysis of all percentages for each of the 504 items, 60 items were chosen as the final depression scale. (p. 26)

Although the criterion group for Scale 2 consisted of individuals afflicted with a severe depressive illness characterized as psychotic, Hathaway and McKinley considered depression to be the cardinal feature of their disturbance. Dahlstrom et al. (1972) stated that "although the scale was devised on a largely psychotic group of patients, it became clear in the early research that the items reflected depressive mood changes on a neurotic basis—in fact, any depressive reaction, no matter what the underlying character structure or adjustment status of a patient might be" (p. 187).

The original MMPI Depression scale had 60 items, but the revision leading to the MMPI–2 deleted 3 items pertaining to religious matters (e.g., "I go to church almost every week"). The resulting 57-item MMPI–2 scale also underwent modifications on two items, one that eliminated sexist wording and one that modernized its usage (MMPI–2 Item 57; "I am a good mixer" became "I am a very sociable person"). Approximately two thirds of the 57 items (37 false; 20 true) on Scale 2 are keyed in the "false" direction. Therefore, all false-response sets will inflate Scale 2 scores, as well as the other scales in the neurotic triad (Scales 1, 2, and 3). Scale 2 shares 47 of its 57 items fairly evenly with the other clinical scales (Dahlstrom et al., 1972). Only 10 items are unique to the scale. The MMPI–2 Depression scale shares only nine items in common with MMPI–2 *DEP* content scale. These two scales measure different aspects of depressive symptoms, so they should not be used interchangeably. The overlapping item content of Scale 2 is presented in Appendix C. The item composition of Scale 2 with the direction of scoring is presented in Table A.2.

Test–retest reliability data for Scale 2, as reported in the MMPI–2 manual (Butcher et al., 1989), were based on 82 normal men and 111 normal women, retested at about 1 week, which yielded correlation coefficients of .75 and .77, respectively. Dahlstrom et al. (1972) reported lower test–retest stability data on clinical groups, which is expected, given the greater emotional instability of clinical patients. In Hunsley et al.'s (1988) large-scale meta-analysis of MMPI reliability studies using a wide variety of populations conducted between 1970 and 1981, an average test–retest reliability of .78 was reported for 16 studies, with time intervals from 1 day to 2 years. Hunsley et al. also reported an average internal consistency of .81 across 74 studies of Scale 2. More recently, internal consistency estimates for Scale 2 were derived from the MMPI–2 restandardization sample (Butcher et al., 1989) and yielded correlation coefficients of .77 and .81 for men and women, respectively.

The items in the scale reflect a number of concerns related to depression, including a lack of interest in things, denial of happiness or personal worth, and physical symptoms (e.g., sleep disturbance and gastrointestinal complaints). The following are examples of items from Scale 2, with the item number preceding the statement and the direction of scoring following the items in parentheses:

2. I have a good appetite. (False)
5. I am easily awakened by noise. (True)
18. I am troubled by attacks of nausea and vomiting. (True)
31. I find it hard to keep my mind on a task or job. (True)
75. I usually feel that life is worthwhile. (False)
95. I'm happy most of the time. (False)
109. I seem to be about as capable and as smart as others around me. (False)

In general, as Scale 2 scores elevate into the clinically significant range ($T \geq 65$), the greater the probability the person is suffering depressive symptoms. Severity is often a function of scale elevation, but it is also reflected in other clinical scale elevations. Rarely is Scale 2 elevated in isolation. Analysis of other clinical scale elevations, as well as subscales and supplementary scales, helps to determine the nature of the depression. Scale 2 not only reflects the presence and degree of various forms of symptomatic depression but also reflects the basic personality features of hyperresponsibility, high personal standards, and intropunitiveness, which can predispose an individual to experience depression (Butcher et al., 1989; Dahlstrom et al., 1972). Individuals scoring in the extremely high range ($T \geq 91$) likely have endorsed a wide range of depressive content that most likely reflects severe withdrawal, a dependent state, and serious suicidal risk.

Although several studies have provided correlates for high-scoring psychiatric patients on Scale 2, very low scores ($T < 40$) should not be interpreted in psychiatric patients as reflecting the converse of depression, such as an active, enthusiastic, optimistic, socially outgoing person. These very-low-score descriptors are more likely to apply to normals than psychiatric patients. (Keiller & Graham, 1993). However, Venn (1988) reported pathological correlates in a sample of low-scoring adult men on Scales 2 and 0 (Social Introversion) who took the MMPI as part of an employment screening process. Low-scoring participants on Scale 2, with concurrent low scores on Scale 0, had indications of probable character pathology (e.g., impulsive behavior and arrest record). As stated earlier, Keiller and Graham suggested that low scores may have different meanings for psychiatric outpatients and inpatients and that low scores may be more likely associated with unfavorable characteristics in psychiatric samples. Further research on low scores in different samples across settings (e.g., forensic, medical, and employment) is called for in order to understand the generalizability of their findings.

Harris–Lingoes Subscales

Harris and Lingoes (1955) developed five subscales for the Depression scale on the MMPI, which are identical on the MMPI–2. The five subscales for the Depression scale are: Subjective Depression (*D1*), Psychomotor Retardation (*D2*), Physical

Malfunctioning (*D3*), Mental Dullness (*D4*), and Brooding (*D5*). The scoring key and item composition for the Harris–Lingoes subscales for Scale 2 can be found in Table A.2. Table B.5 presents the linear *T*-score conversions for the raw-score values.

D1: Subjective Depression (32 Items)

The longest of the subscales, this subscale indicates obvious distress, such as feeling unhappy, suicidal, joyless, worrying, having sleeping and concentration difficulties, and generally not feeling worthwhile. Other descriptors include feeling easily hurt by criticism and a lack of energy for coping with problems (Caldwell, 1988; Nichols & Greene, 1995). Dysphoria is the mood state typified by this subscale and diagnoses of depression or dysthymia often accompany elevations on this subscale as well as the other depression subscales (Graham, Ben-Porath, & McNulty, 1999). Caldwell (1988) stated that this subscale captures the "general misery of depression" (p. 16). The worrying aspect of the scale is found in the fact that all 10 of the items on the brooding subscale (*D5*) are contained within *D1*. Wrobel (1992) reported the following correlates to be applicable to high *D1* scorers: pessimism, poor morale, low self-esteem, lack of energy for coping, feelings of psychological inertia, and a lack of joy in doing things. Graham et al. (1999) also reported that high *D1* scorers feel overwhelmed and unable to cope with stress.

Low scorers on this subscale tend not to report a loss of interest or general depressive feelings.

The following items are examples from *D1* with the MMPI–2 item numbers and direction of scoring in parentheses. Seventeen of the items are scored in the "false" direction, and 15 items are scored in the "true" direction:

2. I have a good appetite. (False)
39. My sleep is fitful and disturbed. (True)
43. My judgment is better than it ever was. (False)
56. I wish I could be as happy as others seem to be. (True)
75. I usually feel that life is worthwhile. (False)

D2: Psychomotor Retardation (14 Items)

The items on this subscale reflect inhibited aggression and a lack of energy, vigor, and initiative (Nichols & Greene, 1995). Wrobel (1992) found a low but significant correlation with a lack of participation in social interactions. Psychiatric outpatient women in the Graham et al. (1999) study sample were also described as not being very competitive. Nichols and Greene (1995) suggested that *D2* emphasizes social withdrawal and rigid controls against hostile or aggressive expressions. In essence, this subscale is tapping a dimension of passivity and submissiveness. Caldwell (1988) asserted that elevations on this subscale may reflect indecisiveness at least as much as physiologic slowing. This is consistent with the moderate correlation Nichols and Greene reported between the Mental Dullness (*D*4) subscale and *D2*.

Levitt (1989) suggested that a low *D2* score, when other depression indexes are high, may point to a suicide potential, presumably because the person has the energy to act on his or her suicidal feelings. However, Graham et al. (1999) also found that females with high scores on the *D2* subscale were described by their therapists as having suicidal ideation.

Four of the items on this subscale are scored in the "true" direction, and 10 items are scored in the "false" direction. The following items illustrate the content of this subscale, with the MMPI–2 item numbers and direction of scoring in parentheses:

9. My daily life is full of things that keep me interested. (False)
29. At times I feel like swearing. (False)
37. At times I feel like smashing things. (False)
170. I am afraid of losing my mind. (True)
233. I have difficulty in starting to do things. (True)

D3: Physical Malfunctioning (11 Items)

Seven of the 11 items overlap Scales 1 and 3, reflecting feelings of weakness, loss of appetite, weight changes, and constipation (Caldwell, 1988). High scores most likely reflect a preoccupation with oneself (Wrobel, 1992). A sense of feeling unrelieved from one's discomforts and pessimistic about ever feeling well is suggested. *D3* is probably the most specific indicator of depressive somatization (Nichols & Greene, 1995). It is not surprising that the Lassitude–Malaise subscale (*Hy3*) and *D3* correlate strongly in a group of psychiatric inpatients and outpatients (Nichols & Greene, 1995).

Graham et al. (1999) reported that women psychiatric outpatients were described by their therapists as lacking energy and having a low sex drive. Furthermore, they were described as lacking interest and aspirations. Both men and women who score high on *D3* were seen as having difficulty with concentration although it is interesting to note that concentration difficulties were not generally reported by Graham et al. (1999) for patients scoring high on the Mental Dullness (*D4*) subscale.

Low *D3* scores most likely reflect that the individual does not feel physically handicapped and may, in fact, feel very good.

Four of the 11 items on this subscale are scored in the "true" direction, and 7 items are scored in the "false" direction. The following items illustrate the content of this subscale:

18. I am troubled by attacks of nausea and vomiting. (True)
20. I am very seldom troubled by constipation. (False)
45. I am in just as good physical health as most of my friends. (False)
175. I feel weak all over much of the time. (True)

D4: Mental Dullness (15 Items)

Caldwell (1988) referred to this scale as the "mental fog" (p. 17) of depression. The themes he reported in the subscale consist of (a) "losing one's mind", that is, being easily distracted, unable to comprehend what one reads, and suffering memory and judgment problems (this is consistent with Wrobel's, 1992, finding of a distrust of one's psychological functioning accompanying high scores on this subscale;) However, it is of interest to note that the Graham et al. (1999) investigation of psychiatric outpatients did not reveal any marked concentration difficulties in high *D4* scorers; (b) trouble getting started on tasks, reduced energy, and a lack of confidence; (c) a feeling of diminished interest and involvement in life (this is consistent with Wrobel's, 1992, findings of feelings of unresponsiveness and distrust of one's psychological functioning being associated with high *D4* scores). *D4* and *D2* share five items in common. *D4* also shares four items with the Lack of Ego Mastery, Cognitive subscale (*Sc3*) and 5 items with the Lack of Ego Mastery, Conative subscale (*Sc4*), both reflecting mental insufficiency (Nichols and Greene, 1995). Graham et al. (1999) reported that for high *D4* scorers both men and women outpatients reported a history of physical abuse, while men reported being sexually abused. Women outpatients were also described as suspicious and as being overly sensitive to criticism.

According to Caldwell, low *D4* scorers do not complain that their judgment is impaired or that they are unable to be as cognitively efficient as others.

Eight of the items on this subscale are scored in the "true" direction, and seven items are scored in the "false" direction. The following items illustrate the item content of *D4*:

10. I am about as able to work as I ever was. (False)
31. I find it hard to keep my mind on a task or job. (True)
43. My judgment is better than it ever was. (False)
73. I am certainly lacking in self-confidence. (True)
147. I cannot understand what I read as well as I used to. (True)

D5: Brooding (10 Items)

All 10 of these items overlap with *D1*. The content suggests that one feels unworthwhile and useless and, when elevated in conjunction with a high Scale 2 score, adds to the hopelessness of the depression (Caldwell, 1988). Irritability and a proneness to rumination are likely correlates (Wrobel, 1992). Interestingly, men but not women in the Graham et al (1999) study of psychiatric outpatients were described as worriers. *D5* and the *DEP* content scale for the MMPI–2 share eight items in common. Nichols and Greene (1995) stated that *D5* is a measure of general distress and is sensitive to anhedonia. They also stated that *D5* can predict the intensity and pervasiveness of guilt, which may be reflected in the Self-Alienation subscale (*Pd5*). Specifically, guilt will be more clearly identifiable when *D5* and *Pd5* are both elevated above the *OBS* content scale, as well as above the level of other distress scales, such as Anxiety (*A*) and the following content scales: Anxiety (*ANX*), Fears (*FRS*), Depression (*DEP*), Work Interference (*WRK*), and Negative Treatment Indicators (*TRT*). Nichols and Greene underscored the fact that *D5* is saturated with first-factor variance (i.e., general maladjustment), which places an emphasis on feeling miserable and upset.

Caldwell indicated that a low *D5* score, especially with an accompanying low *T* score on Scale 2, may indicate a capacity to respond resiliently to life's stresses.

Eight of the items are scored in the "true" direction, and two items are scored in the "false" direction. The following items illustrate the item content of *D5*.

56. I wish I could be as happy as others seem to be. (True)
92. I don't seem to care what happens to me. (True)
130. I certainly feel useless at times. (True)
146. I cry easily. (True)
170. I am afraid of losing my mind. (True)

Scale 2: Subtle–Obvious Subscales

The Wiener–Harmon Depression–Obvious subscale (*D-O*) for the MMPI–2 has 39 items, of which 17 are scored in the "true" direction and 22 items are keyed in the "false" direction. The Depression–Subtle subscale (*D-S*) has 18 items, of which 3 items are scored in the "true" direction and 15 are scored in the "false" direction. The following items are examples of subtle–obvious items on Scale 2, with the scoring direction and obvious or subtle distinction in parentheses. The items are preceded by the MMPI–2 number. The item composition and scoring key for the Subtle–Obvious subscales can be found in Table A.2. The linear *T*-score conversions for the Wiener–Harmon subscales for men and women are presented in Table B.6.

15. I work under a great deal of tension. (True–Obvious)
31. I find it hard to keep my mind on a task or a job. (True–Obvious)
33. I seldom worry about my health. (False–Obvious)
37. At times I feel like smashing things. (False–Obvious)
55. I sometimes keep on at a thing until others lose their patience with me. (False–Obvious)
181. I do not have spells of hayfever or asthma. (True–Obvious)

Caldwell (1988) described the 39 *D-O* subscale items of Wiener and Harmon (1946) as covering a "broad depressive spectrum" (p. 15), including feeling unhappy, worried, and useless; crying easily; and having sleep and appetite problems. The 18 subtle items include a cluster pertaining to the inhibition of anger, aggression, and self-assertion. Nichols and Greene (1995) reported a similar description, adding that the *D-S* subscale reflects an inhibition or suppression of irritability and sadism in emotional life and fantasy. Other subtle items report lacking perseverance and "never feeling euphoria or even unusually good" (Caldwell, 1988, p. 15). W. G. Dahlstrom (personal communication, 1997) suggested that the subtle items may reflect a predisposition to develop the disorder that the parent scale is measuring. For example, an individual scoring low on the *D-O* items but high on the *D-S* items may have a tendency to develop depression. In general, individuals with greater levels of maladjustment tend to endorse more obvious items, whereas defensive responders or persons with milder forms of psychopathology tend to endorse primarily subtle items in describing their feelings (Dahlstrom et al., 1972).

Hollrah et al.'s (1995) review of the subtle-obvious convergent validity literature led them to caution that the *D-S* subscale is not a valid measure of depression. They stated, however, that the decision to use only the *D-O* subscale should be evaluated with caution. They found the *D-O* subscale to be better than the full *D* scale when measuring obvious depression symptoms. They also reviewed studies that show support for both the full *D* scale and the discriminant validity of the *D-S* subscale.

Dahlstrom (1991) reported several correlates for men and women for each of the Subtle–Obvious subscales derived from partner ratings in the MMPI–2 restandardization sample. For the *D-O* subscale, trouble sleeping, unrealistic attitude about abilities, worries about health, a lack of energy, multiple fears, a tendency to get sad, a lack of confidence, and complaints of body aches all characterize male and female participants. For women scoring high on the *D-O* subscale, the following descriptors were generated: nervous, not cheerful, not pleasant or relaxed, cries easily, concerned about death, and avoiding contact with others.

D-S subscale elevations were associated with the following descriptors for both men and women: does not swear or curse, dislikes flirting, cooperative, thoughtful of others, pleasant and relaxed, and attends religious functions. Specific to women only, the following descriptions were given: self-confident, few fears and bad dreams, does not break things when angry, not lacking in emotional control, not stubborn, does not worry about the future and gets along well with others. Men were described as follows: not moody or bossy, friendly, does not take prescription drugs, not argumentative or critical of others, and does not get angry and yell.

Caldwell (1988) reported that low *D-O* scores reflect an individual who has ample self-confidence and feels that life is worthwhile. Low *D-S* scores reflect willfulness and assertion and the capacity to feel anger as it is situationally appropriate.

SCALE 3: HYSTERIA (*Hy*)

The diagnosis of hysteria, although common in the 1930s, was difficult to establish because clear-cut criteria in the clinical concept were lacking, hysterical phenomenon were concurrent with other neurotic symptoms in the same individual, and there was diagnostic uncertainty of hysterical reactions in individuals who were suspected of having organic disease (McKinley &

Hathaway, 1944, as cited in Dahlstrom & Dahlstrom, 1980). Thus, the 60-item *Hy* scale was originally developed to aid in the diagnosis of hysteria and to measure the degree to which a patient is likely to develop symptoms of conversion. The restandardization of the MMPI–2 left the scale composition intact with no item deletions, although nine items were modified regarding modernization of idioms and usage, grammatical clarifications, and simplifications.

The participants in the criterion group were taken primarily from the inpatient service of the psychiatric unit at the University of Minnesota Hospitals. McKinley and Hathaway (1944, as cited in Dahlstrom & Dahlstrom, 1980) described the criterion participants as follows:

> They had each received the diagnosis psychoneurosis, hysteria, or had been especially noted as having characteristic hysterical components in the personality disturbance. In the assignment of these diagnostic terms, the neuropsychiatric staff followed, as closely as possible, current clinical practice. Where cases showed a simple conversion symptom such as aphonia, an occupational cramp, or a neurologically irrational anesthetic area, the diagnosis was usually well agreed upon. In some cases, there remained a doubt as to whether there was a true organic illness such as multiple sclerosis present or whether the syndrome reflected hypochondriasis or an early schizophrenic reaction. (p. 46)

Participants with less dramatic symptomatology made psychodiagnosis a more difficult and less certain task. After several attempts, a final criterion group consisting of 50 cases was selected. Although no modal description or demographic data for the Scale 3 criterion hysteric patients were provided (Colligan et al., 1983), the 50 patients included in the criterion group did manifest the "neurotic defenses of the conversion form of hysteria" (Dahlstrom et al., 1972, p. 191) or hysteric personality features. In individuals who had developed an involuntary psychogenic loss or disorder of function, the physical symptoms allowed them to evade responsibilities and to escape from stressful and unpleasant situations. It was thought that patients whose personality organization revolves around hysterical defenses tend to function adequately or even well under ordinary circumstances, but when faced with difficult situations the tenuous nature of their personality organization is taxed beyond its capacity to cope and symptoms emerge reflecting an overburdened self (e.g., emotional lability, emotional intensity, and modulation difficulties). Dahlstrom, et al. noted that a need to detect such a predisposition for breakdown was necessary and was in part the motivation for the development of Scale 3. It was immediately apparent to McKinley and Hathaway that two major categories of items existed within the scale. One group referred to somatic complaints; the other group referred to an extraverted social style. The bodily complaint items related to such symptoms as headaches, dizzy spells, and hand tremor. As McKinley and Hathaway (as cited in Dahlstrom & Dahlstrom, 1980, p. 46) pointed out, the declaration of social well-being was illustrated by the frequent endorsement of "false" to items such as "I frequently have to fight against showing that I am bashful" (MMPI–2 Item 161), "I get mad easily and get over it soon" (MMPI–2, Item 213), and "Some people are so bossy that I feel like doing the opposite of what they request even though I know they are right" (MMPI–2, Item 98). Despite the predominance of these two types of items, several other items referred to feelings of dysphoria ("blue" or "unhappy"). Specifically, MMPI–2 Item 65, "Most of the time, I feel blue," is keyed in the "true" direction, whereas MMPI–2 Item 95, "I'm happy most of the time," is keyed in the "false" direction. The subsets of items describing somatic complaints and feelings of well-being and comfort are usually independent of each other or negatively correlated in normals, but tend to be positively correlated in patients whose personality functioning is organized around hysteric psychodynamics. Generally, the more elevated and prominent the role of Scale 3 in a code type, the less insightful the individual tends to be and the more likely it is that physical symptoms will emerge when the individual experiences stress.

Greene (1991a) reviewed the relation of Scale 3 item content to other scales and underscored the correspondence of its content to the independent clusters of items reported by K. B. Little and Fisher (1958). The two clusters, *admission of physiologic symptoms* and *denial of symptoms*, were used to construct the Admission (*Ad*) and Denial (*Dn*) scales. Greene (1991a) stated that:

> The Ad scale correlates positively (.89–.90) with Scale 1, which is logical since the two scales have 18 items in common. The Dn scale correlates positively (.78-.88) with the K scale, with which it has 9 items in common. Clients who score high on the Ad scale complain about their somatic functioning and have poor interpersonal relationships. High scorers on the Dn scale are described as lacking insight into their own behavior and are morally virtuous. Little and Fischer (1958) believe that when both of these scales are elevated, the person should have conversion reaction dynamics. (p. 145)

Note that the *Ad* and *Dn* scales virtually overlap the obvious and subtle components of Scale 3, respectively.

The normal group used in the construction of Scale 3 consisted of 200 women and 139 men, all married and between the ages of 26 and 43, who typically had 8 years of schooling, with few being educated beyond high school. The second group of normals consisted of 114 women and 151 men who were entering college students and were included to control for age and intelligence (McKinley & Hathaway, 1944, as cited in Dahlstrom & Dahlstrom, 1980).

McKinley and Hathaway viewed the *Hy* scale as measuring a variable trait closely related to the construct measured by Scale 1 (Hypochondriasis). There is considerable overlap between Scales 1 and 3, 20 items to be precise, representing the most item overlap shared by any two clinical scales. The positive correlation between Scales 1 and 3 motivated McKinley and Hathaway to attempt to decrease this correlation by eliminating as many of the overlapping somatic items as possible. The results of this effort are best summarized by McKinley and Hathaway (1944, as cited in Dahlstrom & Dahlstrom, 1980), who stated that

> Elimination of the somatic items resulted in a marked drop in the number of test cases identified and introduced another disturbing difficulty; if only the nonsomatic items

> were used, there was a strong relation with age and education. The mean score was more than a half sigma higher for the college group than for older persons. These results forced the inclusion of some somatic items in the final scale with consequent high correlation (r = .52 normals and r = .71 clinic cases) between Hs (hypochondriasis) and Hy (hysteria). Some relation still remains between age and intelligence and the Hy score. The relation seems valid clinically. (p. 47)

It appears that the positive correlation that exists between Scales 1 and 3 is not a simple artifact of the item overlap but reflects a common psychological dimension in the elevation of these two scales, apparently somatization (Friedman et al., 1983; Marks & Seeman, 1963). It is important to note that McKinley and Hathaway distinguished clinical differences between individuals when both scales were elevated but with one score higher than the other. Specifically, they identified a different prognosis and treatment for these patterns of scores:

> Where Hs was higher, the physical complaints were diffuse and frequently required much less study to establish the presence of an important psychological factor in the disability. On the other hand, when Hy was dominant, the person frequently appeared normal psychologically and his physical complaints were likely to mimic closely or be accompanied by some common physical syndrome of the type now called "psychosomatic" (McKinley & Hathaway, 1944, as cited in Dahlstrom & Dahlstrom, 1980, p. 49).

More generally, Duckworth and Anderson (1995) pointed out that denial and repression are the primary mechanisms of defense being tapped by Scale 3. Therefore, although symptoms associated with scale scores above Scale 3 may be acknowledged by the individual, those indicated by scales with *T* scores below Scale 3 may not be acknowledged and the person may show a distinct absence of insight. Greene (1991a) suggested that this rule should be used cautiously, given the lack of research to support it.

The scoring direction for the majority of the items on Scale 3 is "false." Forty-seven (78%) of the items are scored as "false," with 13 items (22%) scored as "true." As with Scales 1 and 2 in the neurotic triad, a tendency to endorse the items in the "false" direction will also elevate Scale 3 (see chap. 5 for a description of an all-false response set profile). Scale 3 has fairly evenly distributed overlap with the other clinical scales. Although there is no *K* correction added to Scale 3, there is, in effect, a built-in *K* correction factor since Scale 3 has 10 items in common with the *K* scale (Greene, 1991a). The following items illustrate the varied content in Scale 3. The scoring direction for each item is in parentheses, with the MMPI–2 item number preceding the item. For a complete listing of items on Scale 3, with the direction of scoring, see Table A.2. The overlapping item content of Scale 3 is presented in Appendix C.

2. I have a good appetite. (False)
3. I wake up fresh and rested most mornings. (False)
11. There seems to be a lump in my throat much of the time. (True)
18. I am troubled by attacks of nausea and vomiting. (True)

29. At times I feel like swearing. (False)
95. I am happy most of the time. (False)

High scores on Scale 3 are obtained by individuals often described as childishly self-centered with a high need for approval and affection. They will seek reassurance that they are likeable and will try to elicit it by flattering, rewarding, and complimenting others (Lewak et al., 1990). Conformity and naivete are characteristic, along with the absence of insight due to the predominance of denial and repression in their personality organization. Fearful of emotional and physical pain, they tend to limit their awareness, which can result in impaired reality testing under stressful circumstances (Caldwell, 1974). Lewak et al. suggested that it is helpful to look for what these individuals explicitly deny because that is often at the center of their conflict. Sociable, but shallow in their relationships, high Scale 3 scorers can become resentful of perceived demands and develop somatic concerns to remove themselves from responsibilities they resent or fear being unable to handle. It is rare for high scorers to develop psychotic symptoms, although their symptom pictures can be quite pronounced when they feel overwhelmed. Although the behaviors measured by Scale 3 are traitlike in appearance, the item content reflects behaviors that can change over time. The phrasing of the items in the present tense also allows test takers to interpret the items according to their current circumstances. For these reasons, Dahlstrom et al. (1972) stated that the scale may show less test–retest agreement relative to other scales and that split-half estimates of reliability are inappropriate or misleading for Scale 3.

The test–retest correlation coefficients for psychiatric patients on Scale 3 ranged between .66 and .80 for intervals between 1 and 2 weeks and between .36 and .72 for a 1-year interval between tests (Dahlstrom et al., 1975). More recently, Butcher et al. (1989) provided test–retest reliability coefficients for 82 normal men and 111 normal women retested at an average interval of about 1 week, with the men and women obtaining coefficients of .72 and .75, respectively. Hunsley et al.'s (1988) large-scale meta-analysis of reliability studies using a wide variety of populations conducted between 1970 and 1981 reported an average internal consistency of .78 across 70 studies of Scale 3 and also reported an average test–retest reliability of .74 for 15 studies with time intervals from 1 day to 2 years. In contrast to the Hunsley et al. internal consistency findings, Butcher et al. reported much lower estimates of internal consistency; specifically, they reported coefficient alpha values of .58 and .56 for men and women, respectively, in their restandardization sample. The much lower values reported by Butcher et al. is most likely due to the greater diversity in participants used in the Hunsley et al. meta-analysis, which included college students, psychiatric patients, medical patients, alcohol and/or drug abusers, and incarcerated criminals.

Although various correlates for Scale 3 are reported in the literature, it is important that the clinician be selective in choosing the descriptors to be applied to any one individual. Some correlates, for example, although reported to be valid, may not have the validity always ascribed to them. Hedlund (1977), in comparing the results of seven independent studies that attempted to empirically identify the behavioral or symptom correlates of individual MMPI clinical scales for psychiatric patients, found that Scale 3 did not always correlate with specific items of dissociation, amnesia, or conversion symptoms, items that might be assumed to be relevant to the construct of hysteria. He did find, however, that Scale 3 was regularly related to a number of somatic complaints (e.g., diarrhea, loss of appetite, and sleep disturbance) and significantly correlated with a number of depression-related complaints. It is recommended that the clinician assess individuals on a case-by-case basis that includes an understanding of their psychosocial history and context in which they are being evaluated, as well as carefully inspect the various subscales and supplementary scales to better understand the meaning of the particular clinical scale elevation.

Harris–Lingoes Subscales

Harris and Lingoes (1955, 1968) developed the following five subscales for Scale 3: Denial of Social Anxiety (*Hy1*), Need for Affection (*Hy2*), Lassitude–Malaise (*Hy3*), Somatic Complaints (*Hy4*), and Inhibition of Aggression (*Hy5*). The specific item composition of these subscales is listed in Table A.2. Table B.5 lists the linear *T*-score conversion for the raw-score values.

The Harris–Lingoes subscales for the MMPI are identical in the MMPI–2. No items were deleted in Scale 3 for the restandardization, so the composition of the Harris–Lingoes subscales has remained intact.

Hy1: Denial of Social Anxiety (6 Items)

This short, 6-item subscale is keyed entirely in the "false" direction. The items on *Hy1* are contained completely in K. B. Little and Fischer's (1958) *Dn* scale and the *Hy-S* subscale. The subscale appears to reflect the denial of social shyness and inhibition and never tends to be elevated when Scale 0 (*Si*) is elevated (reflecting introversion; Caldwell, 1988). Caldwell (1988) described high scorers as manifesting an "over-socialized friendliness" (p. 19) toward unfamiliar others. Nichols and Greene (1995) described high *Hy1* individuals as seeking attention, approval, support, and affection in the context of their interactions with others. Levitt (1989) described low scorers as socially maladjusted and anxious, shy, and easily embarrassed. It appears that *Hy1* taps the personality dimension of social extraversion (when elevated) and social introversion (when submerged). Nichols and Greene suggested examining *Hy1* in the context of its relation to other measures of introversion to determine if the introversion is situational or long term. Specifically, when *Pd3* (Social Imperturbability), *Hy1*, and *Hy-S* are all low, they should be examined in relation to the *SOD* content scale, Scale 0, and *Si1* (Shyness/Self-Consciousness). Nichols and Greene (1995) stated the following configural guidelines for interpreting introversion as a state versus a trait:

> High scores on SOD, Si and Si_1 when in the context of low scores on Pd_3, Hy_1 and Hy-S, suggest long term or congenital trends toward shyness and social withdrawal.

> When SOD, Si, and Si_1 are high, but Pd_3, Hy_1 and Hy-S are in an average range, an acute or temporary withdrawal secondary to loss or distress is suggested. (p. 37)

It should be noted that Wrobel (1992) did not find that social introversion was linked to *Hy1* per therapist ratings of clients in psychotherapy. He suggested that the short length of the subscale or the nature of the outpatient sample may have attenuated his results.

The following 6 items represent the entire scale content for *Hy1*. The MMPI–2 item number precedes the item with the scoring direction in parentheses following each item:

129. My conduct is largely controlled by the behavior of those around me. (False)
161. I frequently have to fight against showing that I am bashful. (False)
167. I find it hard to make talk when I meet new people. (False)
185. I wish I were not so shy. (False)
243. When in a group of people, I have trouble thinking of the right things to talk about. (False)
265. I am likely not to speak to people until they speak to me. (False)

Hy2: Need for Affection (12 Items)

The items in this subscale appear to emphasize a faith and trust in others and reflect a denial of resentment or suspicion toward others (Caldwell, 1988; Greene, 2000; 1991a; Wrobel, 1992). It appears that high scorers prefer to avoid interpersonal conflicts. Graham et al. (1999) found high scoring *Hy2* psychiatric men and women outpatients to be more empathic than low scorers and this correlate was unique to *Hy2* among the *Hy* subscales. They also reported that high scoring women were seen as moralistic by their therapists. There is a strong element of unconflicted passivity and submissiveness in *Hy2* which reflects a "go along to get along" social spirit according to Nichols and Greene (1995), high scorers believe that the consequences of self-assertion are generally not socially constructive:

> High scorers seem to believe that, if one thinks the best of others, others will oblige by behaving in accordance with a benign and benevolent set of expectations, and that argument, disagreement, challenge, and confrontation are to be rejected because they can only serve to make social relations unpleasant, create hurt feelings, and foster alienation. (p. 40).

They also view *Hy2* as related to an aspect of cynicism, with low scorers "disclaiming self-traits of trustworthiness and social constructiveness" (Nichols & Greene, 1995, p. 33). Caldwell (1988) described low scorers as perceiving the world as "combative" (p. 19) where one has to take care of oneself and fight for what one wants and believes.

The following items represent examples of the subscale, with the scoring direction following the item and the MMPI–2 item number preceding the item. Eleven of the 12 items are scored in the "false" direction with only 1 item scored as "true":

58. I think a great many people exaggerate their misfortunes in order to gain the sympathy and help of others. (False)
76. It takes a lot of argument to convince most people of the truth. (False)
81. I think most people would lie to get ahead. (False)
124. I often wonder what hidden reason another person may have for doing something nice for me. (False)
213. I get mad easily and then get over it soon. (False)
230. I can be friendly with people who do things which I consider wrong. (True)

Hy3: Lassitude–Malaise (15 Items)

Although 10 of the 15 items on this scale overlap with Scale 2, Caldwell (1988) suggested that the scale taps less of the generalized devaluation of the self that is seen in depression and is more of a measure of having been made to feel weak, tired, sleepless and less interested in life by life's aggravations or one's own poor health. High scorers report not feeling like themselves physically and mentally. Nichols and Greene (1995) described *Hy3* as reflecting some depressive somatization, like *D3* (Physical Malfunctioning), but having a greater emphasis on moods than on somatic difficulty. In a sample of psychotherapy patients, Wrobel (1992) found that complaints about physical and mental functioning, and feelings of needing attention and reassurance, positively correlated with elevated *Hy3* scores, whereas efforts to keep up a good front negatively correlated with *Hy3* scores. Graham et al. (1999) found high scoring *Hy3* psychiatric men and women outpatients to have suicidal ideation.

Prokop (1986) investigated the Harris–Lingoes subscale patterns for Scale 3 in a low-back pain sample. Prokop (1986, 1988) recommended that if *Hy3* and *Hy4* are elevated (but not *Hy1*, *Hy2*, and *Hy5*), in a low-back pain population, it may be appropriate to describe the individual as abnormally focusing on his or her physical symptoms. It should be noted that *Hy1*, *Hy2*, and *Hy5* all overlap with the K. B. Little and Fischer's (1958) *Dn* scale (except that *Hy5* has one item not appearing on the *Dn* scale according to Greene (1991a). Prokop (1988) cautioned against inferring the presence of conversion dynamics when only *Hy3* and *Hy4* are elevated in low-back pain patients, stating that the patient may be attempting to express his or her distress about confusing or frightening symptoms. Such patients are often diagnosed with a nonconversion-based somatoform disorder. Consistent with Prokop's (1988) contention of an abnormal focus on one's bodily functioning is Greene's (1991) description of *Hy3* having 14 of its 15 items in common with the Little and Fischer' *Ad* scale. As noted earlier, Little and Fischer suggested that conversion reaction dynamics should be suspected if both the *Dn* and *Ad* scales are elevated.

Five of the items on this subscale are scored in the "true" direction, and 10 items are scored in the "false" direction. The following items are examples of the *Hy3* content, with the scoring direction in parentheses following the item. The MMPI–2 item number precedes the item:

2. I have a good appetite. (False)
3. I wake up fresh and rested most mornings. (False)
9. My daily life is full of things that keep me interested. (False)
31. I find it hard to keep my mind on a task or job. (True)
65. Most of the time, I feel blue. (True)
175. I feel weak all over much of the time. (True)

Hy4: Somatic Complaints (17 Items)

Caldwell (1988) described this subscale as generally characterizing the "somatic conversion" (p. 19) component of Scale 3. Twelve of the 17 items are also scored on Scale 1 (*Hs*). The five items that are not scored on Scale 1 have elements of anxiety (e.g., fainting spells and "lump in my throat") that are in noteworthy contrast to the reporting of somatic dysfunction, without the explicit anxiety that characterizes Scale 1 (Caldwell, 1988, p. 20). Graham et al. (1999) reported that 17% of 305 psychiatric women outpatients who scored above $T = 65$ on *Hy4* reported current anxiolytic medication usage. Greene (1991a) pointed out that 16 of the 17 items in this scale overlap with K. B. Little and Fischer's (1958) *Ad* scale and that the *Ad* scale correlates positively (r = .89–.90) with Scale 1. The only items missing from *Hy4* (and Scale 3) that are Scale 1 items relate to gastrointestinal complaints. The single exception is MMPI–2 Item 18, which reports attacks of nausea and vomiting (Caldwell, 1988). Whereas Scale 1 and the *HEA* content scale represent general physical complaints, *Hy4* (and *Hy-O*) emphasize specific, as opposed to vague, symptoms (Nichols & Greene, 1995). Low scores should be interpreted as reflecting a person free of excessive somatic concerns.

The following items are examples of *Hy4* content. The scoring direction follows each item in parentheses with the MMPI–2 item number preceding the item. Six of the items in this subscale are scored in the "true" direction, and 11 items are scored in the "false" direction:

11. There seems to be a lump in my throat much of the time. (True)
18. I am troubled by attacks of nausea and vomiting. (True)
40. Much of the time my head seems to hurt all over. (True)
47. I am almost never bothered by pains over my heart or in my chest. (False)
91. I have little or no trouble with my muscles twitching or jumping. (False)
159. I have never had a fainting spell. (False)
224. I have few or no pains. (False)

Hy5: Inhibition of Aggression (7 Items)

The seven items in this scale appear to reflect the inhibition or suppression of aggression, irritability, and anger in emotional life and fantasy (Nichols & Greene, 1995). Caldwell (1988) reported that high scorers "get upset" (p. 20) by aggression in others and have a "hysteroid abhorrence of violence" (p. 20) that is likely to be quite prominent if *Hy5* is elevated with a high Scale 5 score in the "feminine" direction by men or women. Nichols and Greene (1995) pointed out that although *Hy5* moderately correlates with measures of denial of anger or hostility, it "appears to operate more as a disgust with anger and hostility than a denial scale per se" (p. 30). Low scores suggest an ability to experience anger directly; in fact, very low scores (e.g., raw score of 0 or 1) suggest an interest or fascination with anger or violence with its potential consequences, as well as a lowered threshold for experiencing morbid or violent fantasies. Very low *Hy5* scores may particularly indicate hostility when accompanied by elevations on *ANG2* (Irritability), *TPA1* (Impatience), and *TPA2* (Competitive Drive; Nichols & Greene, 1995). It is important to carefully note other indicators of impaired empathy when *Hy5* is very low, such as the particular code pattern and other measures (e.g., *ASP1* and *CYN*). Inspection of the item content of *Hy5* shows it to be subtle in nature, with six of its seven items overlapping with the *Hy-S* subscale (Wrobel, 1992).

The following items represent the entire scale membership for *Hy5*. The MMPI–2 item number is provided, with the direction of scoring in parentheses. All of the items on *Hy5* are keyed in the "false" direction:

7. I like to read newspaper articles on crime. (False)
14. I enjoy detective or mystery stories. (False)
29. At times I feel like swearing. (False)
115. The sight of blood doesn't frighten me or make me sick. (False)
116. Often I can't understand why I have been so irritable and grouchy. (False)
135. I have often lost out on things because I couldn't make up my mind soon enough. (False)
157. What others think of me does not bother me. (False)

Scale 3: Subtle–Obvious Subscales

Wiener and Harmon (1946) developed Subtle and Obvious subscales for Scale 3. The MMPI–2 Hysteria–Obvious subscale (*Hy-O*) has 32 items, of which 12 items are keyed in the "true" direction and 20 are scored in the "false" direction. The Hysteria–Subtle subscale (*Hy-S*) has 28 items, of which 27 items are scored in the "false" direction and 1 item is keyed in the "true" direction. The following items are examples of these subscale items, with the direction of scoring and subtle–obvious distinction in parentheses. The MMPI–2 item number precedes the item. See Table A.2 for a listing of the Subtle–Obvious subscales and the scoring key. The linear *T*-score conversions for the Wiener–Harmon subscales for men and women is presented in Table B.6.

11. There seems to be a lump in my throat much of the time. (True–Obvious)
31. I find it hard to keep my mind on a task or job. (True–Obvious)
45. I am in just as good physical health as most of my friends. (False–Subtle)
58. I think a great many people exaggerate their misfortunes in order to gain the sympathy and help of others. (False–Subtle)
76. It takes a lot of argument to convince most people of the truth. (False–Subtle)
230. I can be friendly with people who do things I consider wrong. (True–Obvious)

The *Hy-O* items appear to emphasize specific, as opposed to vague, symptoms (Nichols & Greene, 1995). In fact, as Caldwell (1988) indicated, the composition of the *Hy-O* subscale is almost identical to *Hy3* and *Hy4*, as well as K. B. Little and Fischer's (1958) *Ad* scale. The numerous physical concerns reflected in this subscale include some items related to the construct of hysteria, such as fainting spells and hand tremors. The *Hy-O* subscale appears to reflect somatic problems and discomforts that may also antagonize normal sleep (Nichols & Greene, 1995). A low score contraindicates depleted energies due to physical discomfort and distress.

Dahlstrom (1991) derived correlates for the *Hy-O* subscale from partner ratings on the Katz Adjustment Scales (Butcher et al., 1989) in the MMPI–2 restandardization sample. Men and women with high *Hy-O* scores were described as having trouble sleeping; worrying about their health; lacking energy and appearing worn out; lacking an interest in things; not appearing self-confident, cheerful, or pleasant; and complaining about body aches and ailments. Women in particular were seen as restless, self-blaming, worried about the future, and feeling like others do not care about them. Men in particular were seen as having a poor sense of humor; getting easily upset by small, unexpected events; having difficulty making decisions; lacking ambition; and not willing to try new things.

Caldwell (1988) pointed out that the *Hy-S* subscale is very similar in item content to the *Hy1*, *Hy2*, and *Hy5* subscales, as well as virtually identical to K. B. Little and Fischer's (1958) *Dn* scale. Nichols and Greene (1995) viewed the *Hy-S* subscale as measuring a subtle and complex disposition to claim freedom from problems in adaptation, hostile feelings and impulses, cynicism and distrust, and social discomfort. An elevated *Hy-S* score usually is not the result of an intentional effort to mislead the psychologist. Nichols and Greene (1995) generated several hypotheses for an elevated *Hy-S* score (as well as an elevated *K* score): These elevations

> may be the product of honest but erroneous self-appraisal (self-deception); above-average adjustment, resourcefulness and resiliency; or a social advantage that confers protection or insulation from major stresses or challenges to adjustment such as great wealth, high socioeconomic status, or a close, active, and committed circle of friends or family. (p. 34)

They also pointed out that the full *Hy* scale is a somewhat less satisfactory measure of the repression construct than *Hy-S*, mostly because of the dysphoric content in *Hy3*.

Low *Hy-S* scores are likely to indicate mild cynicism. Admission to feeling somewhat beleaguered, uncomfortable with strangers, and having a view of the world as antagonistic would also characteristic low scorers.

Dahlstrom (1991) provided the following correlates for the *Hy-S* subscales. Both men and women are perceived as being self-confident, lacking shyness, willing to try new things, getting along well with others, not being suspicious of or avoiding others, friendly, and not lacking in emotional control. Women in particular were rated as not getting very sad or bored, not lacking in energy or having many fears, being able to laugh with others, not worrying about the future, and not getting their feelings easily hurt. Men were described as not arguing about minor things, being constructive or helpful, affectionate, generous, not bossy, cooperative, and not demanding attention.

SCALE 4: PSYCHOPATHIC DEVIATE (*Pd*)

Scale 4 was developed to measure the "personality characteristics of the amoral and asocial subgroup of persons with psychopathic personality disorders" (Dahlstrom et al., 1972, p. 195). The scale is named Psychopathic Deviate because McKinley and Hathaway (1944, as cited in Dahlstrom & Dahsltrom, 1980) did not expect it to differentiate all the cases of psychopathic personalities; rather, the scale was successful in identifying half or somewhat more of the cases repeatedly classed as clinical psychopathic personalities. The scale name implies "a variation in the direction of psychopathy" (p. 63), in keeping with the psychopathic personality classification of the American Psychiatric Association in use at that time, which was broad and included pathological emotionality and sexuality as well as asocial or amoral trends (McKinley & Hathaway, 1944, as cited in Dahlstrom & Dahlstrom, 1980).

The criterion group consisted of more women than men ranging in age from 17 to 22, but the sample size was not reported. The criterion participants were referred by the courts for study in a psychiatric setting. McKinely and Hathaway (1944, as cited in Dahstrom & Dahlstrom, 1980) provided the following description of these participants:

> The symptomatic backgrounds of the criterion cases were highly varied but can be characterized in several ways. Most often the complaint was stealing, lying, truancy, sexual promiscuity, alcoholic over-indulgence, forgery, and similar delinquencies. There were no major criminal types. Most of the behavior was poorly motivated and poorly concealed. All the criterion cases had long histories of minor delinquency. Although many of them came from broken homes or otherwise disturbed social backgrounds, there were many in whom such factors could not be seen as particularly present. (pp. 57–58)

The common denominator across the participants seemed to be that they had low anticipation of the consequences of their behavior and could not seem to "learn those anticipatory anxieties which operate to deter most people from committing antisocial behavior" (Marks et al., 1974, p. 25). Essentially, individuals with psychopathic traits were seen as lacking in their ability to form warm and stable bonds to others, to appreciate social customs and abide by societal rules, and to profit from experiences that had negative consequences. They were, in essence, psychologically immature (McKinley, 1944). These individuals may appear free from disabling anxiety and not be perceived as particularly troubled or disturbed until found in a situation demanding the use of inner resources that the psychopathic individual lacks. The general social maladjustment that characterizes these individuals leads to dissatisfaction with the self and others and often results in strong feelings of social and self-alienation.

The normal comparison participants (294 men and 397 women) used to construct the 50-item *Pd* scale consisted of college freshmen receiving guidance counseling at the University of Minnesota and married Minnesota residents who were considerably older. The average age of these latter participants was 35, so the college sample introduced some balance. Cross-validation procedures involved 100 prisoners and 78 psychiatric inpatients diagnosed with "psychopathic personality." The scale was expected to identify only the asocial individuals. McKinley and Hathaway (1944, as cited in Dahlstrom & Dahlstrom, 1980, p. 61) reported that among the prisoners, 59% obtained *T* scores at or above 70 on the *Pd* scale, whereas 45% of the psychiatric cases obtained scores above that level.

Five preliminary scales were developed before the final items were selected for inclusion on the *Pd* scale. The MMPI–2 *Pd* scale did not lose any items in the recent revision, although four items were changed (two items were modernized in language, one item was grammatically clarified, and the wording of one item was simplified).

The item content of Scale 4 is diverse. McKinley and Hathaway (1944, as cited in Dahlstrom & Dahlstrom, 1980) initially identified the following three general groupings of item content: (a) social maladjustment items, (b) depression items, and (c) paranoid-trend items. The mixed factor content of the scale is reflected in factor analytic studies of the scale. For example, Dahlstrom et al. (1972) described the results of Comrey's (1958) and Astin's (1959, 1961) factor analytic investigations. They reported that hypersensitivity, poor impulse control, social maladjustment, and emotional deprivation were four of the many factors emerging from their work. Nichols and Greene (1995) captured these factors in their poignant description of how the high *Pd* scorer tends to manifest his or her psychopathology in the environment:

> In Pd, an impoverished emotional life and feelings of emptiness lead the individual to make his/her mark on the social environment and to force others to acknowledge an autonomy that the individual experiences internally as incomplete and poorly consolidated. The usual result is a series of scrapes, broken promises, under-achievement, lost employment, ephemeral relationships, and legal difficulties. (p. 35)

Harris and Lingoes (1955) also identified different subgroupings of items on Scale 4, which we describe shortly.

The critical scoring direction is about evenly split between true and false responses (24 true, 26 false) for this 50-item scale. A *K*-correction factor of 0.4 added to the *Pd* scale improved its ability to make diagnostic discriminations, and this value is generally added to the raw score on the *Pd* scale. Ten out of 50 items are non-overlapping or unique to Scale 4, with the remaining 40 overlapping items being distributed over the clinical scales and the *F* and *K* scales. Scale 4 shares five and seven items with the *F* and *K* scales, respectively, and only one overlapping item with Scale 1 (*Hs*). It shares 1 or 2 items with Scale 5 (*Mf*), depending on whether male or female norms are being used. Scales 3 (*Hy*) and 8 (*Sc*) both share 10 items with Scale 4, and Scale 2 shares 7 items with Scale 4. (See Appendix C for a table describing the overlapping item content of Scale 4.) The fact that there are 7 Scale 4 items overlapping with Scale 2 (*D*) may be consistent with the situational or state condition of the criterion participants at the time of testing. Greene (1980, 1991a) noted that because all the members of the criterion group were involved in legal proceedings and/or incarcerated, it is likely that they may have manifested depressive moods more reflective of their situation rather than an inherent tendency to feel depressed.

McKinley and Hathaway (1944, as cited in Dahlstrom & Dahlstrom, 1980) originally reported a test–retest correlation coefficient of .71 for Scale 4 obtained on a normal sample of 47 cases, with a time interval of a few days to more than a year. Butcher et al. (1989) reported test–retest reliability data for their community (normal) sample of 82 men ($r = .81$) and 111 women ($r = .79$) *retested at an average interval of 8.6 days (Mdn* = 7 days).

In psychiatric cases on the MMPI Scale 4, test–retest correlation coefficients for 1- to 2-day intervals ranged between .69 and .75 and between .48 and .49 for 1-year intervals between tests (Dahlstrom et al., 1972). Hunsley et al.'s (1988) large-scale meta-analysis of MMPI reliability studies using diverse populations conducted between 1970 and 1981, reported an average test–retest reliability of .71 for 16 studies, with time intervals from 1 day to 2 years.

Internal consistency estimates for Scale 4 were derived from the MMPI–2 restandardization sample (Butcher et al., 1989) and yielded coefficients of .60 and .62 for men and women, respectively. Hunsley et al. (1988) reported higher internal consistency values for Scale 4, but used a wider variety of populations (abnormal and normal) in their meta-analysis. They reported an average internal consistency value of .81 across 71 studies for Scale 4.

The following items from Scale 4 illustrate the broad content of the scale. The MMPI–2 item numbers precede the item, with the direction of scoring in parentheses (Table A.2 provides the item composition of Scale 4 with the direction of scoring):

9. My daily life is full of things that keep me interested. (False)
21. At times I have very much wanted to leave home. (True)
22. No one seems to understand me. (True)
32. I have had very peculiar and strange experiences. (True)

35. Sometimes when I was young, I stole things. (True)
95. I am happy most of the time. (False)
264. I have used alcohol excessively. (True)
266. I have never been in trouble with the law. (False)

Individuals with high Scale 4 scores, especially when it is the highest or second highest scale elevation in the profile, typically have shallow emotional lives that may go undetected by others until the "situation demands evidence of a sense of responsibility, appreciation of social patterns, or personal and emotional loyalties" (Dahlstrom et al., 1972, p. 195; McKinley & Hathaway, 1944, as cited in Dahlstrom & Dahlstrom, 1980). These individuals can be described as having feeling deficits as they have developed the coping mechanism of numbing out their vulnerable feelings (Lewak et al., 1990). Prolonged exposure to abusive or neglectful caregivers in early life often sets the stage for the development of a constellation of personality traits that include poor frustration tolerance, impulsiveness, antisocial attitudes, and a reduced capacity for empathy toward others. Traumatogenic experiences, such as dysfunctional childrearing, could often lead to the development of a cognitive style that allows these individuals to recognize and intellectually understand their experiences but feel emotionally cut off from their own vital resources, thereby limiting or handicapping their ability to have genuine reciprocal exchanges with others. In fact, Rathvon and Holmstrom (1996) recently found that Scale 4 showed a significant positive correlation with a narcissistic depletion factor. Even in so-called normal populations, such as police applicants, or among sensation seekers, such as sky divers, where the *Pd* score is the highest score but still within the normal limit range, some of the *Pd* characteristics or trends are still observed. For example, instead of being overtly antisocial, an individual may be somewhat cynical or immature in relation to authority figures.

In the normative sample for the restandardized MMPI–2, partner ratings revelaed that Scale 4 appears sensitive to distress and recent life changes (Butcher et al., 1989). Participants from this sample who scored high on the *Pd* scale were perceived by their partners to be dysphoric, antisocial, hostile, impulsive, and nonconforming. Hathaway and Meehl (as cited in Dahlstrom et al., 1972), reported a large number of adjectives characteristic of normals with high *Pd* scores that were generated by friends of the normal participants. Overall, these high Scale 4 scorers tended to be quite socially visible. Typical descriptors applied to these normals obtaining normal range *Pd* scores included extraverted, adventurous, enthusiastic, sarcastic, exhibitionistic, talkative, high-strung, assertive, active, energetic, immature, and irritable.

Several normal groups score in the high–normal and low–moderate range on Scale 4, including social activists, mental health professionals, and adolescents (Greene, 1991a). Although a high Scale 4 score is often associated with a personality disorder diagnosis, such as narcissistic, passive–aggressive, borderline, or antisocial (Morey & Smith, 1988), the presence of a high Scale 4 elevation does not always indicate that an individual will manifest antisocial behaviors, especially if there is not a history of such actions. If Scale 9 is elevated, along with Scale 4, as a primary high point, then the probability is increased for overt expression of antisocial behavior. The reader is cautioned to be aware that negative emotionality as reflected in feelings of alienation (see *Pd4* and *Pd5* descriptions in this chapter) is often more prominent in high Scale 4 scorers than is antisocial behavior, especially if the individual is not being assessed in the context of the correctional system. Butcher and Williams (1992) underscored this point by stating that the *ASP* content scale (see chap. 7) is only modestly correlated (.37) with the *Pd* scale. Scale 4 is a mixed content scale that includes, but is not limited to, measuring antisocial behavior; the *ASP* scale is a more direct measure of that construct (Butcher et al., 1990).

Duckworth and Anderson (1995) viewed "fighting something" (p. 164) as a cardinal feature of an elevated Scale 4. They suggested that the individual may be in conflict with his or her parents, friends, spouse, society, or school and that it is essential to examine the context in which the person is being assessed in order to better understand the significance of the Scale 4 elevation. Lower elevations on the scale suggest that the "fighting out" may not be expressed directly but may reflect instead a covert attitude or feeling that something or someone other than the client needs to be changed. Duckworth and Anderson also emphasized the importance of recognizing that moderate *Pd* elevations may reflect situational stress, such as marital difficulties rather than a personality trait disturbance.

Alcohol, drug, and polydrug abuse and addiction are often associated with high Scale 4 scores and can be conceptualized as a remedial stimulant for the feeling deficits that these individuals experience (Craig, 1984a, 1984b, 1984c, 1988; Jaffe, 1992; Jaffe & Jaffe, 1992). See the chapter by Greene and Garvin (1988) for a comprehensive review of the MMPI in relation to drug and alcohol abuse. Although additional diagnoses, such as depression, are often given to drug and alcohol dependent individuals, it should be pointed out that if indicators in the MMPI–2 (e.g., *DEP* content scale and Scale 2) do not support such a diagnosis, a high Scale 4 scorer may not be experiencing a typical depressive feeling state, such as a sense of sadness and loss, but rather may be experiencing feelings of emptiness and alienation (Lewak et al., 1990).

It appears that scores on Scale 4 decrease with age in men and women in all populations (Colligan et al., 1983, 1989; Colligan, Osborne, Swenson, & Offord, 1948; Friedman, Webb, & Lewak, 1989; Greene, 1991a). Greene suggested that this pattern most likely reflects the slow maturational changes that occur in persons with elevated scores. Archer (1997) noted that there is also clear evidence that Scale 4 scores also differ as a function of adolescence versus adulthood in both normal and clinical populations. He pointed out that adolescents tend to endorse more Scale 4 items than do adults and that the normal adolescents in the MMPI–A sample would produce a mean *T*-score value of approximately 55 if scored using MMPI–2 norms. It is, therefore, not surprising that adolescent codetypes typically include prominent Scale 4 elevations (Archer, Gordon, & Klinefelter, 1991; Marks et al., 1974).

Harris–Lingoes Subscales

As previously noted, the Harris–Lingoes subscales can help identify the particular pattern of item content that characterizes a high score on the MMPI–2 parent scale. Scale 4 is particularly well served by a subscale pattern analysis as the scale is rich and varied in its content. Several *Pd* subscales assess very different aspects of psychopathy; consideration of these differences may have significant implications for clinical practice and assessment (Lilienfeld, 1999). Harris and Lingoes (1955) developed five subscales for Scale 4: Familial Discord (*Pd1*), Authority Problems (*Pd2*), Social Imperturbability (*Pd3*), Social Alienation (*Pd4*), and Self-Alienation (*Pd5*). Unlike the majority of Harris–Lingoes subscales that were unaffected by the MMPI–2 revision, several item changes and deletions on the *Pd* subscales called into question the consistency between the MMPI and the MMPI–2 for these subscales (Chojnacki & Walsh, 1994). In the original construction of their subscales, Harris and Lingoes, for unexplained reasons, added from two to six items to each of the *Pd* subscales taken from an unpublished earlier version of Scale 4 (Greene, 1991a; Levitt, 1990). For reasons that are also unclear, the MMPI–2 revision deleted these items from the *Pd* subscales. The only rationale provided was that these items were not included in the final version of Scale 4 (Butcher et al., 1989, p. 29), and questions about the possible advantages of retaining these "off-scale" items on the basis of their content or their contribution to enhanced subscale reliability were not addressed. The MMPI–2 manual (Butcher et al., 1989, p. 75, Table B2) provides normative data for the reduced *Pd* subscales.

In examining the consistency between the original MMPI and the MMPI–2, Chojnacki and Walsh (1994) concluded that the shortened *Pd* subscales do not materially affect the *T* scores for these subscales. On the revision of the MMPI–2, *Pd1*, *Pd2*, *Pd3*, *Pd4*, and *Pd5* lost two, three, six, five, and three items, respectively. Table A2 lists the composition and scoring direction for the *Pd* subscales, and Table B5 presents the raw-score conversions to linear *T* scores for the subscales.

Familial Discord: Pd1 (9 Items)

The items in this subscale reflect current and historical problems with one's family and the accompanying feeling that one wishes to escape a loveless home (Caldwell, 1988). Levitt (1989) reported that high scorers reject a family situation that they consider affectionless, stressful, and lacking in emotional support. Wrobel's (1992) study of clinician descriptions for *Pd1* elevations showed feelings of struggle against family control to be significant. Graham et al. (1999) reported that high scoring psychiatric outpatient women on *Pd1* tended to blame their families for their difficulties, demanded much attention, and appeared argumentative. Given the item content for this subscale, it is not surprising that Pancoast and Archer (1988) found that adolescents, in contrast to adults, are particularly likely to endorse items on this subscale. Nichols and Greene (1995) report that *Pd1* is biased toward conflict and alienation in the family of origin and viewed it as a general measure of family alienation. In fact, when *F*, *Sc1* (Social Alienation), and *Pd1* are all elevated, there is likelihood of the respondent making explicit statements concerning toward one or both parents. Caldwell reported that low scores re supportive family with genuine compatibility and strong ties or possibly to minimize and deny family problems.

The following items are examples of *Pd1* content, with the scoring di in parentheses and the MMPI–2 item number preceding the item. Five i this subscale are scored in the "true" direction, and four items are scored "false" direction:

21. At times I have very much wanted to leave home. (True)
83. I have very few quarrels with members of my family. (False)
125. I believe that my home life is as pleasant as that of most people I (False)
202. My parents often objected to the kind of people I went around with. (
214. I have been quite independent and free from family rule. (False)
283. My parents and family find more fault with me than they should. (

Authority Problems: Pd2 (8 Items)

The content of *Pd2* reflects an opposition to authority figures, dislike of sc and a lack of constraint. The items have a strong historical bias, with an emp on past delinquent behavior, legal involvement, and trouble with authority. may account for why they seem not to be suppressed by elevated *K* s (Caldwell, 1988). Lilienfeld (1999) found *Pd2* to be more highly correlated other *Pd* subscales with most indexes of antisocial behavior, a finding that i surprising, given that several items refer explicitly to illegal actions. He reported that *Pd2* may be the better marker of primary psychopathy as comp with the other *Pd* subscales, a finding generally consistent with those of Meloy Gacono (1995) and Graham et al. (1999). High scores reflect a lack of behav control or impulsivity, either in the form of "clear violations of social norms rules or attitudes that clearly suggest a lower threshold for behavior that vio rules and brings one into conflict with others, especially those in author (Nichols & Greene, 1995, p. 27). Wrobel (1992) found the descriptor "res demands and convention of parent and/or society" to apply to his sampl outpatients scoring high on *Pd2*. Levitt (1989) described high *Pd* scorers rebellious and having difficulty accepting standards of behavior that imp responsibilities and interfere with personal gratification. The clinician should t careful note of elevated *Pd2* scores, especially if elevated with other indicator social disinhibition, such as the *ASP* content scale or its component subsc Antisocial Behavior (*ASP2*). *Pd2* and *ASP2* imply the direct expression antisocial conduct, but the prediction of antisocial behavior is higher when *ASP* greater than *Pd2*, *Pd2* is greater than *ASP*, and *ASP* is greater than *CYN* (Cynicis Nichols & Greene, 1995). It should be noted that *Pd2* and the MMPI–2 *ASP* cont scale share three items.

Graham et al. (1999) found that psychiatric men and women outpatients who scored high on the *Pd2* subscale reported recent alcohol and substance abuse and dependence problems. This finding is consistent with the above description of impulsive individuals with low frustration tolerance.

Low *Pd2* scorers do not admit having difficulties with authority and tend to be socially conforming. They have a capacity for constraint that high scorers lack, and this may reflect a "mature submission to the rules and regulations that make for a sense of community with orderly and harmonious social relations among citizens" (Nichols & Greene, 1995, p. 40).

The following items are examples of the *Pd2* content, with the scoring direction in parentheses and the MMPI–2 item number preceding the item. Two items on this subscale are scored in the "true" direction, and six items are scored in the "false" direction:

34. I have been in trouble because of my sex behavior. (False)
105. In school, I was sometimes sent to the principal for bad behavior. (True)
129. My conduct is largely controlled by the behavior of those around me. (False)
160. I liked school. (False)
266. I have never been in trouble with the law. (False)

Social Imperturbability: Pd3 (6 Items)

Originally a 12-item subscale, the removal of 6 items from the MMPI–2 version of the subscale left it with 6 items, all of which overlap the *Pd-S* subscale (Caldwell, 1988). This subscale appears to reflect a strong extraversion tendency but without the need for affection and approval from others. Nichols and Greene (1995) stated that "Pd_3 reflects a highly aggressive and insouciant sociability consistent with a desire to use interpersonal relationships to manipulate, intimidate, exploit, and otherwise extract goods and services from others. There is little emphasis on social approval" (p. 37). There is a socially aggressive or impervious nature to high *Pd3* scorers that is especially pronounced if signs of cynicism, hostility, and antisocial trends are present in the MMPI–2 profile. High *Pd3* scorers (raw scores of 5 or greater on the MMPI–2) tend to be pushy and insensitive in their social interactions or even aggressive or overbearing (Nichols & Greene, 1995). The Denial of Social Anxiety subscale (*Hy1*) and *Pd3* now share 67% of their item content, making their interpretation similar. The elimination of the earlier mentioned six items in the MMPI–2 version of the *Pd3* (because the items were not part of the final *Pd* scale) accounts for this increased proportion of item overlap. In effect, these two subscales reflect a social insensitivity that may constitute part of a narcissistic syndrome.

Low *Pd3* scorers are likely to feel uncomfortable in social situations and experience difficulty taking social initiative. When *Pd3*, *Hy1*, and *Hy-S* are all low, and there are high scores on the *SOD* content scale, *Si*, and *Si2* (Social Avoidance), there may be long-term or congenital (temperamental) trends toward shyness and social withdrawal. If, however, *Pd3*, *Hy1*, and *Hy-S* are within normal limits, but *SOD*, *Si*, and *Si1* are significantly elevated, the individual may be experiencing a temporary social withdrawal in reaction to a loss or other distress (Nichols & Greene, 1995).

The following items represent the *Pd3* subscale in its entirety. The MMPI–2 item number precedes the item, with the scoring direction in parentheses. All of the items are scored in the "false" direction:

70. I am easily downed in an argument. (False)
129. My conduct is largely controlled by the behavior of those around me. (False)
153. It makes me uncomfortable to put on a stunt at a party even if others are doing the same sort of thing. (False)
167. I find it hard to make talk when I meet new people. (False)
185. I wish I were not so shy. (False)
243. When in a group of people, I have trouble thinking of the right things to talk about. (False).

Social Alienation: Pd4 (13 Items)

This subscale has six items that overlap with Scale 6 (*Pa*) and reflects a general feeling of "paranoid flavored resentments" (Caldwell, 1988, p. 22; e.g., MMPI–2 Item 99, "Someone has it in for me"). Nichols and Greene (1995) classified *Pd4* under their paranoid thought process category in their structural summary as it reflects severe alienation from others and a sense of felt deprivation and of being given a "bum deal." There is an element of residual sadness and longing in *Pd4* that indicates a vulnerable, lonely, and unhappy self. High *Pd4* scorers have a pervasive mistrust of others, who are viewed as more depriving than hostile. Consequently, they feel that others are uncaring and cannot be counted on (Nichols & Greene, 1995). This sense of emotional deprivation is supported by Wrobel's (1992) findings that anchored clinician ratings to patient characteristics associated with elevated *Pd4* scores. Those characteristics consisted of feeling socially isolated, a lack of gratification in social relationships, a lack of feeling of belongingness, and externalizing blame. The finding of sadness from the Graham et al. (1999) study for psychiatric men outpatients is consistent with the lonely and unhappy individual just described. Levitt (1989) suggested examining *Pd1* when *Pd4* is elevated to ascertain if family members and intimates are the source of failed support. To this end, the clinician would want to also examine other measures, such as the *FAM* content scale. If only *Pd4* and *Pd5* (Self-Alienation) are elevated relative to the other *Pd* subscales, particularly *Pd2*, the individual may prove to be more likely to benefit from psychotherapy. However, research is needed to substantiate this conjecture (Lilienfeld, 1999).

Low *Pd4* scorers feel understood, fairly treated, and enjoy a sense of belongingness in their social environments (Caldwell, 1988).

The following items are examples of *Pd4* content, with the direction of scoring in parentheses and the MMPI–2 item number preceding the item. Ten of the items on this subscale are scored in the "true" direction, and 3 items are scored in the "false" direction:

12. My sex life is satisfactory. (False)
22. No one seems to understand me. (True)
42. If people had not had it in for me, I would have been much more successful. (True)
56. I wish I could be as happy as others seem to be. (True)
157. What others think of me does not bother me. (False)
225. My way of doing things is apt to be misunderstood by others. (True)

Self-Alienation: Pd5 (12 Items)

Wrobel (1992) described feelings of despondency as a correlate of the high *Pd5* scorer, and Caldwell (1988) and Graham et al. (1999) described a similar feeling state underscoring the guilt and self-blame, regretful feelings, and feelings of hopelessness and unhappiness so typical of these individuals. The subscale appears sensitive to the anhedonia elements inherent in Scale 4 that McKinley and Hathaway (1944, as cited in Dahlstrom & Dahlstrom, 1980) viewed as an important component of the parent scale. Nichols and Greene (1995) believed that guilt, which can negatively effect one's capacity to enjoy life in a spontaneous and fluent fashion, is best assessed using *Pd5*. They pointed out that the level or intensity of guilt as measured by *Pd5* can be estimated from scores on *D5* (Brooding) and the *LSE* content scale. Nichols and Greene (1995) elaborated by stating that

> it is important to discriminate guilt as a specific emotional state from states of more general upset in which guilt is only a component of distress and dysphoria. Many individuals experience guilt, regret, and remorse in the context of other, mostly unpleasant, emotions such as anxiety, fearfulness, apathy, depression, worry, and so forth. Such experiences often so obscure or obstruct the assessment of guilt per se that this emotional state and its role in the individual's psychic life are left uncertain. Guilt is most readily identified when Pd_5 and D_5 are elevated above OBS, as well as above the level of other distress scales such as A, ANX, FRS, DEP, WRK, and TRT. (p. 29)

The level or severity of the expressed guilt in high *Pd5* scorers approximates a theme of self-flagellation (with elevated *LSE*) with "exaggerated culpability and ostentatious remorse" (Nichols & Greene, 1995, p. 38). Caldwell (1988) and Nichols and Greene agreed that *Pd5* may also reflect the characteristic remorse seen in some alcoholic patterns (e.g., MMPI–2 code-patterns 247/274, 427/472, and 724/742).

Low *Pd5* scorers do not report feeling unhappy, can in fact experience pleasures in life, find daily life stimulating and rewarding, do not express guilt or remorse about past misdeeds, and deny excessive use of alcohol (Graham, 1990).

The following items are examples of *Pd*5 content, with the scoring direction in parentheses and the MMPI–2 item number preceding the item. Ten of the items on this subscale are scored in the "true" direction, and 2 items are scored in the "false" direction:

9. My daily life is full of things that keep me interested. (False)
31. I find it hard to keep my mind on a task or job. (True)
52. I have not lived the right kind of life. (True)

56. I wish I could be as happy as others seem to be. (True)
82. I do many things which I regret afterwards. (I regret things more than others seem to) (True)
89. My hardest battles are with myself. (True)

Scale 4: Subtle–Obvious Subscales

Wiener and Harmon (Wiener, 1948) developed Subtle and Obvious subscales for Scale 4 of the MMPI. The MMPI–2 Psychopathic Deviate–Obvious subscale (*Pd-O*) has 28 items, of which 20 are scored in the "true" direction and 8 items are keyed in the "false" direction. The Psychopathic Deviate–Subtle subscale (*Pd-S*) consists of 22 items, of which 4 are keyed in the "true" direction and the remaining 18 items keyed in the "false" direction. The following items are examples of subtle–obvious items on Scale 4, with the scoring direction and obvious or subtle distinction in parentheses. See Table A.2 for a listing of the subtle–obvious items and the scoring key. The linear *T*-score conversions for the Wiener–Harmon subscales for men and women is presented in Table B.6.

9. My daily life is full of things that keep me interested. (False–Obvious)
17. I am sure I get a raw deal from life. (True–Obvious)
35. Sometimes when I was young, I stole things. (True–Obvious)
95. I am happy most of the time. (False–Obvious)
113. I know who is responsible for most of my troubles. (True–Subtle)
129. My conduct is largely controlled by the behavior of those around me. (False–Subtle)
157. What others think of me does not bother me. (False–Subtle)
219. I have been disappointed in love. (True–Subtle)

The *Pd-O* items reflect various subjective discomforts that include feeling misunderstood, feeling unhappy, and feeling unfairly treated, and having gotten into trouble (Caldwell, 1988). Examining the convergent validity literature, Hollrah et al. (1995) concluded that methodological problems with the MMPI subtle–obvious studies make it difficult to summarize the validity of the Subtle and Obvious subscales as the results of their research reveals different findings for different scales. They reported, however, that in isolated studies, the *Pd-O* subscale does correlate with discomfort and the admission of social nonconformity. The content of the *Pd-O* subscale suggests feeling unhappy and at odds with others and with life. Low scores suggest a closeness and warmth with others and social conformity (Caldwell, 1988).

Dahlstrom (1991) examined the correlates of the Subtle and Obvious subscales derived from partner ratings on the Katz Adjustment Scales used in the MMPI–2 restandardization (Butcher et al., 1989). For both men and women, the following descriptions emerged as significant for high *Pd-O* scorers: lacks interest in things, feels others do not care about him or her, gets very sad or blue, has many fears, moody, worries about the future, takes nonprescription drugs, has been arrested or had legal difficulties, lacks social judgment, and whines and demands attention.

For women only, the following represents a partial list of significant findings: poor sense of humor, restless, not affectionate, lacks energy, feelings easily hurt, easily annoyed, lacks self-confidence, lacks emotional control, argues about minor things, suspicious of others, has difficulty making decisions, and does not get along well with others. There were no significant descriptors derived for men only.

Caldwell (1988) pointed out that some subtle items on the *Pd-S* subscale appear nearly as obvious as the *Pd-O* items. These items report family quarrels, getting little sympathy, and wanting to leave home. The more subtle items are those that report an absence of social anxieties, ease in talking to others, and a denial of manipulation.

Dahlstrom (1991) derived the following correlates for the *Pd-S* subscale for men and women from the partner ratings made in the MMPI–2 restandardization sample: moody, stubborn, easily annoyed, swears or curses, not passive and obedient, talks too much, makes big plans, and has conflicts over sex. For men only, the following correlates were derived: trouble sleeping, not shy, lacks energy, gets very sad, and has been arrested or had legal troubles. For women only, the following correlates were derived: temper tantrums, resents being told what to do, argues about minor things, nags, feels others do not care about her, gets bossy, is uncooperative, lacks emotional control, and drinks excessively.

Low *Pd-s* scores suggest self-confidence, a sense of inner calmness, and a restraint or shyness with strangers (Caldwell, 1988).

In reviewing the literature on the Subtle subscales, Hollrah et al. (1995) were unable to find studies that supported the discriminative validity of the *Pd-S* subscale. Therefore, appropriate caution is warranted.

SCALE 5: MASCULINITY–FEMININITY (*MF*)

The exact motivation of Hathaway and McKinley for developing Scale 5 could be somewhat unclear to readers consulting different texts, given that various accounts are given to explain this scale's origins. For example, Dahlstrom et al. (1972), generally considered the most reliable historical chroniclers of the MMPI, stated that

> Scale 5 was designed to identify the personality features related to the disorder of male sexual inversion.... Persons with this personality pattern often engage in homoerotic practices as part of their feminine emotional makeup; however, many of these men are too inhibited or full of conflict to make any overt expression of their sexual preferences. (p. 201)

As Colligan et al. (1983) indicated, the 1943 MMPI manual describes the *Mf* scale as intending to measure "the tendency toward masculinity or femininity of interest pattern in the direction of the opposite sex" (p. 40). Clearly, the original manual's description differs from the more psychopathological account given by Dahlstrom et al. (1972) in describing the origins and intent of Scale 5. Hathaway and McKinley discovered that it was too difficult then to obtain a large enough group of homosexual men and women possessing enough similar qualities to classify into a single criterion group (Hathaway, 1956/1980). At least three subgroups of homosexuals were identified with different etiologies for their homosexuality. One subgroup was a pseudohomosexual type with neurotic features related to inferiority; another subgroup was a psychopathic type who tended to elevate Scale 4 (*Pd*), and a third subgroup became the final reference criterion group. This group consisted of 13 homosexual inverted men (Hathaway, 1956/1980). Although no demographic data were reported for these participants, they were screened for gross psychological abnormalities, like psychosis, and any clear-cut neurotic tendencies. They were also considered free of psychopathy (Dahlstrom & Welsh, 1960). These individuals were seen as having a feminine emotional makeup; however, many were considered too inhibited or conflicted to express their homoerotic sexual preferences. Their feminine disposition was believed to be apparent in their expressive styles, interests, and attitudes, as well as in their sexual relationships (Dahlstrom et al., 1972). Greene (1991a) stated that "such persons were thought to engage in homoerotic behavior as a part of their feminine (i.e. inverted) personality characteristics" (p. 155).

Many items used to develop Scale 5 were added after the original Minnesota normative group had already participated in the various scale constructions; consequently, newly formed normal groups were selected for comparison purposes. These groups consisted of 67 female airline employees and 54 soldiers. Three basic comparisons resulted in the addition of 55 new items in the MMPI pool. When an item differentiated a soldier from a criterion group participant (homosexual inverted men), the item was said to be a trend in the direction of femininity on the part of homosexual inverted men (Hathaway & McKinley, 1943). A second comparison step in item selection involved identifying a group of men scoring in the "feminine" direction on an Invert scale derived by Terman and Miles (1936). The item endorsements of these inverted men were then compared with a group of normals. The use of the invert scale from Terman and Miles' (1936, as cited in Colligan et al., 1983) Attitude Interest Analysis Test "represents the first time that items from one diagnostic test were used to select a contrast group that was employed as an additional criterion group used for selecting items on an MMPI scale" (p. 44). A third comparison step, which appears to have been conducted initially but is considered the least important by Hathaway (1956/1980), involved comparing the normal men (soldiers) with normal women (airline employees) to determine their response frequencies by gender.

The 60 items that persevered through all three comparison steps became Scale 5. Twenty-three of the Scale 5 items are borrowed from Terman and Miles (1936), whereas the other 37 items came from the MMPI item pool.

Despite some preliminary efforts, Hathaway and McKinley were unable to successfully construct an independent scale measuring female homosexual inversion. A number of subsequent studies have demonstrated that despite the efforts of the scale constructors, Scale 5 does not adequately discriminate male homosexuals from male nonhomosexuals, which was the original intent of the scale (Wong, 1984). Therefore, it is important not to infer homosexuality based solely on an elevated Scale 5 score. In fact, it is difficult to predict homosexuality from MMPI or MMPI–2 data. The final *Mf* scale was believed to measure masculinity at one pole and femininity at the opposite pole; therefore, this scale was seen as being bipolar. However, as other researchers (e.g., Bem, 1974) suggested, masculinity and femininity may be more accurately assessed using separate scales for each dimension. They may each represent a different construct. On the other hand, Bem's measures of gender role are not independent of masculinity versus femininity scales, such as Scale 5 of the MMPI (Wakefield, Sasek, Friedman, & Bowden, 1976). Also, the psychometric adequacy of Bem's Femininity scale has been criticized (Kimlicka, Wakefield, & Friedman, 1980; Kimlicka, Wakefield, & Goad, 1982). Recent studies (e.g., Kimlicka, Sheppard, Wakefield, & Cross, 1987) suggest that bipolar masculinity–femininity scales have not yet been, and may not be, replaceable with separate masculine and feminine factors. However, the *MMPI–2 Manual* (Butcher et al., 1989) describes two recently developed gender-role scales developed by Peterson and Dahlstrom (1992). These scales, named *GM* (Gender Role—Masculine) and *GF* (Gender Role—Feminine), were designed as independent measures of the masculine and feminine factors in Scale 5. Developed on data provided by the normative sample for the MMPI–2, these new scales can be useful adjuncts to aid in the interpretation of Scale 5. However, more research is needed to assess their clinical utility. Chapter 8 provides more interpretive information on these new scales; Table A.5 provides the item composition and scoring key for these scales.

Factor analytic studies of Scale 5 indicate that the scale is composed of multiple factors (Graham, Schroeder, & Lilly, 1971; Sines, 1977). Given its multidimensional character, inferences about masculinity and femininity drawn from Scale 5 elevations should be made cautiously. The item content of the scale is varied and, to a degree, does seem to reflect, among other things, stereotypic masculine and feminine interest patterns. Items reflecting masculine–feminine interests appear to have the highest correlation with overall scale scores and are therefore considered the most differentiating items on the scale (Dahlstrom et al., 1972). Although the interest-type items are obvious or face valid in nature, there are other items on the scale with more subtle meaning. For example, MMPI–2 Item 193, "In walking, I am very careful to step over sidewalk cracks," is keyed in the "false" direction for both men and women. A "true" response would earn both men and women a point in the "masculine" direction. Apparently, this item empirically differentiated the criterion groups and no obvious theoretical explanation (except perhaps post hoc) can be offered.

Because Scales 5 and 0 were added after the publication of the MMPI, it took time for their assimilation into the mainstream of research and clinical practice. It was soon recognized that Scale 5 (and Scale 0) was an important measure, and research attention was eventually paid to the scale, although Harris and Lingoes (1955) and Wiener and Harmon (1946) did not develop subscales for Scale 5 (or

Scale 0). As mentioned previously, the content of Scale 5 is diverse and has been studied fairly extensively. The item content covers "a range of emotional reactions, interest, attitudes, and feelings about work, social relationships, and hobbies on which men and women in general differ" (Butcher et al., 1989, p. 29). Graham et al. (1971) factor analyzed the responses to MMPI Scale 5 (and Scale 0) from 422 psychiatric inpatients, outpatients, and normals. Their six factors were then used by Serkownek (1975) to develop subscales in order to provide additional content information for the interpretation of Scale 5: Narcissism–Hypersensitivity (*Mf1*), Stereotypic Feminine Interest (*Mf2*), Denial of Stereotypic Masculine Interests (*Mf3*), Heterosexual Discomfort–Passivity (*Mf4*), Introspective–Critical (*Mf5*), and Socially Retiring (*Mf6*). [4] Graham (1987) reported test-retest reliability coefficients for men and women (over a 6-week interval) provided by Moreland (1985). For men on the *Mf* subscales (Serkownek, 1975), test–retest reliability coefficients range from .67 to .83, with an average of .78. For women, test–retest reliability coefficients range from .69 to .83, with an average of .76.

In a large-scale study, Foerstner (1986) investigated the interrelationships among the 63 MMPI subscales developed by Serkownek (1975), Harris and Lingoes (1955), Wiggins (1966), and Wiener and Harmon (1946). The stability of her factor structure was also studied across different populations. Nine hundred MMPIs for male and female psychiatric inpatients, chemical-dependent residents, and private practice outpatients were analyzed. Ten factors were identified that accounted for 75.5 % of the total variance. The 10 factors were named (a) Depression, (b) Agitated Hostility, (c) Social Introversion, (d) Cynical Distress, (e) Health Concerns, (f) Ideas of Reference, (g) Traditional Feminine Interests, (h) Family Conflict, (i) Inner Directedness, and (j) Qvetch—Vague Dysphoria or Hypersensitivity. Most of the factor structures were similar for the samples, although a difference existed between the factor structure of psychiatric inpatient samples and private practice outpatients. Of interest in this discussion of Scale 5 are Foerstner's findings for the Serkownek subscales. *Mf1* loaded positively on the depression factor (.57), with *Mf4* loading negatively on the Social Introversion factor (–.50). *Mf2* loaded on the expected Traditional Feminine Interest factor.

It is clear from the data reported in Foerstner's (1986) study that Scale 5 (and Scale 0) is multifactorial in nature; therefore, its composition is not limited to masculine–feminine factors. Scale 5 scores, whether high or low, may be achieved by item endorsements affecting any of a combination of at least six factors (Wong, 1984). Schuerger, Foerstner, Serkownek, and Ritz (1987) pointed out that the subscale correlates for Scale 5 are generally personological and nonpathological in nature. That is, the only subscale for Scale 5 that suggests psychopathology is *Mf1*. This is in contrast to the findings for the Scale 0 subscales, described under the Scale 0 heading in this chapter. Most of the Serkownek subscales for Scale 0 are psychopathological in nature.

A new set of seven *Mf* subscales has been developed for the MMPI–2 by Martin and Finn (Martin, 1993) using factor analytic procedures. The normative sample used in constructing these subscales was the MMPI–2 community participants (Butcher et al.,

1989). These subscales are free of item overlap and have internal consistency coefficients high enough to suggest that these subscales are cohesive measures. The first subscale, Denial of Stereotypical Masculine Interests, is a measure of lack of interest in activities typically considered male or masculine. The second subscale, Hypersensitivity–Anxiety, is a measure of self-focused worry and sensitivity. Stereotypical Feminine Interests is the third subscale and is a measure of activities typically considered female of feminine. Low Cynicism, the fourth subscale, is a measure of the lack of cynicism and suspiciousness about human motivations. Aesthetic Interest is the fifth subscale and is a measure of interest in the arts and written expression. The sixth subscale, Feminine Gender Identity, measures the wish to be female and to have interests traditionally associated with women. Restraint is the seventh subscale and is a measure of restraint from loud and aggressive interests and behaviors. Martin and Finn also provided a composite bipolar femininity–masculinity scale that is a combination of the three subscales that they believe to be the most central to the construct of masculinity–femininity (E. H. Martin, personal communication, April 8, 1996). These subscales are: *Denial of Stereotypical Masculine Interests*, *Stereotypical Feminine Interests*, and *Feminine Gender Identity*. Table A.2 in this text provides the item composition for these new subscales, the scoring direction for the items, and the means and standard deviations for the MMPI–2 normative sample. Table B.7 provides the linear *T*-score conversions for these new subscales.

In the MMPI–2, Scale 5 lost four items in the revision, leaving it with 56 items. The four dropped items (MMPI Items 69, 70, 249, and 295) were either outdated or often considered offensive on a religious or sexual bases. Fifty-two of the items on this scale are scored in the same direction for men and women. An endorsement of any of these items in the keyed direction gives the respondent a point in the direction of femininity. Four of the items in the scale deal with clear sexual concerns and represent a scoring exception in that they are keyed in the opposite direction for women and men. For example, Item 121, "I have never indulged in any unusual sexual practice," is keyed "true" for women and "false" for men. The other three items dealing with sexual concerns are keyed "true" for men and "false" for women (MMPI–2 Items 166, 209, and 268.) Because of the obvious nature of these four *Mf* items dealing with sexual concerns, someone wishing to conceal his or her sexual interests could easily do so. If using hand-scoring templates, it is important to use the appropriate male or female template for scoring the record sheet. For men, 25 of the items on the *Mf* scale are keyed in the "true" direction, whereas 31 items are keyed in the "false" direction. For women, 23 of the items are keyed in the "true" direction, whereas 33 items are scored in the "false" direction.

Scale 5 uses linear *T* scores rather than uniform *T*-score conversions. This is also the case for Scale 0 and the *L*, *F*, and *K* scales as well. For women, high *T* scores on the profile sheet are associated with low raw scores, indicating a response to the items in a "masculine" direction. For men, the converse is true, with high raw scores associated with high *T* scores. Therefore, a man with a high raw score or high *T* score is said to be endorsing Scale 5 items the way in which women stereotypically respond. Low *T* scores in men reflect a low endorsement of feminine-type items and indicates a more masculine interest pattern. The reason for reversing the raw scores on the profile sheet is to maintain uniformity with the other scales, in that high scores represent a form of deviation. In the case of Scale 5, elevated *T* scores represent endorsement patterns similar to the opposite gender.

The following items are examples of Scale 5, with the scoring direction in parentheses and the item numbers preceding the item. Table A2 presents the item composition for Scale 5, with the direction of scoring for the items. Appendix C presents a table describing the overlapping item content of Scale 5. Scale 5 shares one, two, and three items with the *L*, *F*, and *K* scales, respectively, and shares the most items with Scale 0 (nine items).

1. I like mechanics magazines. (False)
4. I think I would like the work of a librarian. (True)
19. When I take a new job, I like to find out who it is important to be nice to. (False)
26. I feel that it is certainly best to keep my mouth shut when I'm in trouble. (False)
64. I enjoy reading love stories. (True)
137. I used to keep a diary. (True)
271. I think that I feel more intensely than most people do. (True)

For Scale 5 on the MMPI, test–retest correlation coefficients for psychiatric cases range between .79 and .83 for a 1- to 2-day interval and between .77 and .99 for college students. The correlation coefficients for 1- to 2-week intervals between test administrations in psychiatric cases range between .76 and .79; the corresponding correlation coefficient for male college students is .72 (Dahlstrom et al., 1975).

In Hunsley et al.'s (1988) large-scale meta-analysis of MMPI reliability studies using a wide variety of populations conducted between 1970 and 1981, an average internal consistency of .73 across 39 studies of Scale 5 was reported. They also reported an average test–retest reliability of .69 for 10 studies, with time intervals from 1 day to 2 years. For MMPI–2 Scale 5, the *MMPI–2 Manual* (Butcher et al., 1989) reports reliability data for a subset of the recent normative sample (82 men and 111 women). An average interval of about 1 week shows Scale 5 to have a test–retest correlation of .82 and .73 for men and women, respectively. Internal consistency estimates (coefficient alpha) for Scale 5 for men and women were .58 and .37, respectively.

Scale 5 is one of the scales most affected by the revision of the MMPI. It appears that men in the new normative group have answered more items in the "feminine" direction as compared with the original fixed reference group. This has resulted in the lowering of most men's *T* scores on the *Mf* scale by about 10 *T*-score points (Dahlstrom & Tellegen, 1993; Duckworth & Anderson, 1995; Friedman, 1990; Strassberg, 1991). For women, there is much less change in the endorsement frequencies of the items and women's *T* scores are less dramatically affected. Another factor that influences MMPI–2 elevations on Scale 5 is education level. In the MMPI–2 normative sample, less educated men earned lower *T*- score means on Scale 5 and less educated women obtained higher average *T*-score values.

Investigations of the correlates for high and low Scale 5 scores in normals have been conducted by Hathaway and Meehl (as cited in Dahlstrom et al., 1972) and Gough, McKee, and Yandell (1955). Hathaway and Meehl found that high Scale 5 normal men were described by their peers as sensitive and prone to worry, idealistic and peaceable, sociable and curious, and having general aesthetic interests. Women with high *Mf* scores did not have corresponding similar descriptors, although they were described as adventurous. Low-scoring men on the *Mf* scale were described by their peers as practical, balanced, cheerful, self-confident, and independent, whereas low-scoring women on the *Mf* scale were seen as sensitive, responsive, modest, grateful, and wise.

Gough et al. (1955, as cited in Dahlstrom et al., 1972) described the high Scale 5 man as inner-directed and intellectually curious. Work and achievements provided these men significant gratification, and they were seen as mature, self-aware individuals. They had good judgment and common sense. They could communicate effectively and were quite verbal. Some of the adjectives typical of these high Scale 5 men included ambitious, clear-thinking, effeminate, imaginative, nervous, organized, sensitive, and submissive. Low-scoring men on Scale 5 were seen as lacking insight into their motives, preferring action to thought, and having narrow interests. They did not appear to have the psychological complexity or inner-directedness that the high Scale 5 men had. Nichols and Greene (1995) provided a good summary of high *Mf* scores in men (low scores in women). They stated that the *Mf* scale emphasizes passivity, sensitivity, and aesthetic and/or intellectual interests: "Sedentary activities and pastimes are preferred over those involving movement, competition, and the out-of-doors. *Mf* seems to reflect intellectualization over rationalization" (Nichols & Greene, 1995, p. 35).

More recently, Long and Graham (1991), using ratings provided by significant others, studied the descriptions of normal men with various levels of scores on Scale 5. The participants were 819 heterosexual couples who were included in the normative samples of the MMPI–2 (Butcher et al., 1989). In contrast to previous literature indicating high Scale 5 men to be passive, dependent, and submissive, they found that men with higher Scale 5 scores actually tended to be less passive and obedient. They found that level of education was a better predictor of certain behaviors and personality characteristics than *Mf* scores in normal men.

The correlates for high and low *Mf* scale scores vary as a function of the type of individuals being assessed. For example, high Scale 5 scores are frequently obtained by normal married men, although not for women (Dahlstrom et al., 1972). Although relatively frequent among normal men, Scale 5 is not often a high point among psychiatric patients (Tanner, 1990). Given that much of the *Mf* item content suggests mild maladjustment, Ward and Dillon (1990) investigated whether emotional distress is a correlate of the *Mf* scale in clinical populations. In studying the *Mf* raw scores and symptom ratings obtained on psychiatric patients, emotional distress correlates for Scale 5 were identified. Anxiety, depressed mood, guilt feelings, and tension were associated with high raw scores ("feminine" direction) in both men and women. It is interesting to note that Ward and Dillon found these correlates to be largely independent of other MMPI clinical scales.

It is clear that high Scale 5 scorers, particularly men, vary in their behavioral descriptions or diagnoses as a function of their normal versus psychiatric status. High *Mf* scores in men (low *Mf* scores in women) in a normal population may indicate sensitivity, as well as aesthetic or intellectual interests, particularly if the person is college educated. Traditionally, the literature has emphasized the passivity or submissiveness often noted in high Scale 5 men, although Long and Graham (1991) found opposite trends. An underlying dimension of Scale 5 has been hypothesized to be role flexibility (Kunce & Anderson, 1976, 1984). The high Scale 5 man is able to appreciate a diversity of interests and show tolerance for differences in others. Traditional masculine interests are likely to be expressed by men who score in the $T =$ 46–55 range. Scores below 46 begin to suggest "macho" orientations, with very low scores ($T < 40$) strongly suggestive of an activity-oriented, nonverbally expressive type of individual who may be perceived as insensitive, competitive, aggressive, independent, and possibly crude, with traditional masculine–feminine views and possible underlying doubts about his own masculinity. High Scale 5 women are likely to be seen in many ways similar to low Scale 5 men, that is, as aggressive, competitive, dominating, energetic, and confident. The low Scale 5 woman may be described as hyperfeminine if her score is below a *T* score of 40 and if she is not college educated (Graham, 1990). Between a *T* score of 40 and 55, she is likely to be described as having stereotypically feminine interests.

Clearly, high and low *Mf* scores vary greatly in their correlates for men and women. More interpretive information on Scale 5 is provided in chapter 6.

SCALE 6: PARANOIA (*Pa*)

There is no available information describing the exact way the paranoid criterion group was selected, nor do data exist about the demographic characteristics of the participants used in the construction of this 40-item scale. It is assumed that the usual item selection procedures were used as with the other MMPI scales. The criterion patients, according to Hathaway (1956/1980), had a diagnosis of paranoid state, paranoid condition, or paranoid schizophrenia, and the scale was developed to assess paranoid symptoms and features. The patients studied in the criterion group manifested various signs of paranoia, including ideas of reference, feelings of persecution, grandiose self-concepts, hypersensitivity, rigid thinking, and suspiciousness. There were attempts to improve the operating characteristics of the scale, but Hathaway (1956/1980) stated that the results were disappointing:

> As with other scales, several different scales were derived and tested by cross-validation. This cross-validation was always disappointing and the published scale was considered weak although it was the best that could be developed. One factor that seemed to justify at least temporary use of the scale was that there were few false positives. When a person had

> a high score, he tended to be diagnosed as paranoid or at least he was felt to be sensitive and rigid in personal relationships. (p. 73)

Hathaway (1956/1980) went on to state that, as was true with Scale 8, the hope that Scale 6 could be improved was not realized. "Even the K variable failed to sharpen the differentiation. It was felt that the K correction did not help because more than 20% of the Scale 6 items were already subtle in character" (as cited in Dahlstrom & Dahlstrom, 1980, p. 73) Consequently, there is no added fraction of *K* to Scale 6 on the profile sheet as there is for other clinical scales.

Scale 6 measures a range of chronic and acute paranoid mentation and attitudes that include frank psychotic ideation, oversensitivity, and rigid denials of cynicism. The scale also taps externalizing processes, such as projection, hypervigilance, and scanning for "evidence" of hostile intentions or actions. According to Nichols and Greene (1995), Scale 6 is "the most general measure of projection and is sensitive to both implicit and explicit operations to place or locate motives, responsibility, and other, especially undesirable, personal attributes outside the self" (p. 36). This is consistent with Ihilevich and Gleser's (1986, 1991) definition of projection, which involves the attribution of negative intent or characteristic to others without substantiating evidence.

To help determine the nature of the psychopathology, it is critical to examine the Harris–Lingoes subscales from this scale when a score is elevated. For example, an individual with no clear-cut thought disorder (e.g., ideas of reference or feelings of persecution) may in fact be clinically paranoid if he or she is pathologically oversensitive to others' slights or failures of consideration. Often these individuals may be diagnosed with paranoid character traits or a paranoid personality disorder. However, Morey and Smith (1988), in their comprehensive review of personality disorders, pointed out the rarity of a diagnosis of paranoid personality disorder in clinical populations with base-rate ranges between 0.9% and 1.4%. They stated that it has not been conclusively demonstrated that increasing elevations on Scale 6 are associated with a paranoid personality disorder. Because individuals with this disorder are characterized as mistrustful and suspicious, it may be that they are unlikely to endorse the face-valid (obvious) items reflecting paranoia. For this reason, the *K*+ profile described by Marks et al. (1974) may reflect paranoid symptomatology in psychiatric inpatients. In this *K*+ code pattern, all of the clinical scales are below a *T* score of 70, with six or more scales below a *T* score of 60. The only prominent scale is an elevated *K*. Marks et al. found in their psychiatric inpatient sample that 18% of the participants with the 86/68 code pattern were diagnosed with paranoid personality disorder, whereas 68% were diagnosed with paranoid schizophrenia. Another code pattern that may include paranoid personality disorder features is the 248 profile, with elevated *L* and *K* scales suggesting guardedness (Tarter & Perley, 1975). It is important to note that Scale 6 may not always be elevated in paranoid-personality disordered patients, and other scales should be examined for indications of blame, anger, and mistrust (Morey & Smith, 1988).

Nichols and Greene (1995) described the cognitive operations of the high Scale 6 scorer. They stated that:

> *Pa* emphasizes the rationalization of anger, resentment, and the loss of control. One sees rigid self-justification, the accumulation and hostile or self-justifying use of "evidence" or authorization for accusation, suspicion, and attack. *Pa* seems to reflect rationalization over intellectualization. (Nichols & Greene, 1995, p. 35)

Typically, high scorers on Scale 6 fear moral and/or physical attacks, feel easily misunderstood, and unfairly criticized and treated, as well as self-righteous, opinionated, suspicious, and self-dissatisfied (Friedman, Webb, & Lewak, 1989; Lewak et al., 1990). Additionally, they are seen as argumentative, stubborn, self-centered and lacking in social skills. Normal men with high MMPI Scale 6 elevations in their profile have been described as sensitive, sentimental, loyal, trustful, cooperative, kind, and submissive, whereas normal women have been described as emotional, soft-hearted, and sensitive (Dahlstrom et al., 1972). Individuals scoring in the normal range on Scale 6 (*T* = 46–57) may either lack paranoid symptoms or have well-ingrained paranoid traits with sufficient reality testing to avoid endorsing the obvious items on the scale (Greene, 1991a, 1991b).

The recent MMPI–2 restandardization project examined the meaning of elevated *Pa* scores for normals. Women in the MMPI–2 normative sample who scored high on Scale 6 were described by their husbands as moody with a tendency to get sad and blue, lacking emotional control, having a tendency to cry easily, and being susceptible to bad dreams (Butcher & Williams, 1992). Men were not clearly differentiated in the way their partners described them, and no significant correlates were reported for men.

There is mixed information on the meaning of low scores on Scale 6. Some authors contend that low scores actually reveal the hidden presence of paranoia, as a respondent who is trying to conceal his vulnerabilities may deny any suspiciousness or hypersensitivity whatsoever (e.g., Butcher & Williams, 1992; Duckworth & Anderson, 1995; Endicott, Jortner, & Abramoff, 1969; Friedman, Webb, & Lewak, 1989; Lewak, 1993). Other researchers failed to find a consistent relationship between Scale 6 scores and paranoid symptomatology (Vestre & Watson, 1972). In our experience, we have observed clinically paranoid individuals attempting to look good to obtain very low scores on Scale 6. A very low score on this scale should alert the clinician to look for other measures of suspiciousness or cynicism, such as a low score on the *Pa3* (Moral Virtue) subscale and/or high scores on the *CYN* (Cynicism) content scales, especially *CYN 2* (Interpersonal Suspiciousness).

Dahlstrom et al. (1972) reported the descriptions of Hathaway and Meehl's low-scoring normals on Scale 6. Men were described by their acquaintances as cheerful, balanced, and decisive but also as conscienceless. These men perceived themselves as orderly and as good social mixers. Women were seen by others as serious, mature, reasonable, and trusting. They saw themselves as self-controlled, persevering, wise, loyal, and modest. W. Anderson (1956, as cited in Dahlstrom et al., 1972) found that college students in counseling with MMPI Scale 6 scores below a *T* score of 40 tended to be underachievers with low grades and reported difficulties with their parents.

All 40 of the original items in Scale 6 have been retained in the MMPI–2 (Butcher et al., 1989). However, two items were modified to eliminate sexist wording and to simplify the item meaning. The following items illustrate the range of content in Scale 6. The MMPI–2 item numbers precede the item, with the direction of scoring in parentheses. Table A.2 provides the item composition of the scale with the keyed direction for the items. See Appendix C for a table describing the overlapping item content of Scale 6.

16. Once in a while I think of things too bad to talk about. (True)
22. No one seems to understand me. (True)
24. Evil spirits possess me at times. (True)
42. If people had not had it in for me, I would have been much more successful. (True)
95. I am happy most of the time. (False)
314. I have no enemies who really wish to harm me. (False)

Twenty-five of the items on Scale 6 are scored in the "true" direction, and 15 items are scored in the "false" direction. Because more items are endorsed in the "true" direction, as is the case with the other psychotic clinical scales, an all-true response set will tend to elevate this scale. Thirty-three of the items on Scale 6 overlap other scales, with the *F* scale and Scales 4 and 8 sharing 9, 8, and 13 items, respectively, with Scale 6. Seven items on Scale 6 do not overlap with other scales. Dahlstrom et al. (1972) reported early itemetric research of J. W. Little (1949) examining which Scale 6 items were the most discriminating with the highest item–total scale (biserial) correlations. The frankly paranoid item "I believe I'm being plotted against" (MMPI–2 Item 138) was the most differentiating item for his college-level participants with a biserial correlation of .77. Other items tended to be less related to the total scale scores.

For MMPI Scale 6, the test–retest correlation coefficients for psychiatric cases ranged between .61 and .71 for a 1- to 2-day interval between testing and between .59 and .65 for a 1-year interval between testing (Dahlstrom et al., 1975). In Hunsley et al.'s (1988) large-scale meta-analysis of MMPI reliability studies using various populations conducted between 1970 and 1981, an average internal consistency of .73 across 70 studies of Scale 6 was reported. They also reported an average test–retest reliability of .69 for 15 studies for time intervals of 1 day to 2 years. On the MMPI–2, Butcher et al. (1989) reported test–retest reliability data on Scale 6 for their community (normal) sample of 82 men ($r = .67$) and 111 women ($r = .58$) retested at an average interval of 8.6 days (*Mdn* = 7 days). Scale 6 has the lowest test–retest values for the clinical scales as well as the lowest internal consistency estimates (Cronbach's coefficient alpha) for the clinical scales (excluding the *Mf* scale for women) with alpha coefficients of .34 and .39 for men and women, respectively.

Harris–Lingoes Subscales

Harris and Lingoes developed three subscales for Scale 6: Ideas of External Influence (*Pa1*), Poignancy (*Pa2*), and Moral Virtue (*Pa3*). The scoring key and item composition for these subscales can be found in Table A.2. Table B.5 presents the linear *T*-score conversions for the raw-score values for men and women.

Ideas of External Influence: *Pa1* (17 Items)

Sixteen of the 17 items on *Pa1* (formerly Persecutory Ideas) are scored in the "true" direction and mostly reflect the open persecutory content of Scale 6 (Caldwell, 1988). Ward, Kersh, and Waxmonsky (1998) suggested that *Pa1* is the only MMPI–2 scale or subscale that measures uniquely paranoid ideas. These researchers derived a three-factor structure for the Scale 6 using substance abuse patients and found that *Pa1* and the Paranoid factor had 14 of 16 items in common, thereby supporting the construct of validity of this subscale. It should be noted that although *Pa1* "does have substantial item overlap with the Bizarre Mentation content scale, Bizarre Mentation intermixes explicitly paranoid items with more general psychotic symptoms" (Ward et al. 1998, p. 295). Wrobel (1992) found projection to be a defense associated with patients having high *Pa1* scores. Nichols and Greene (1995) stated that their paranoid thought process category is best represented by *Pa1* "which emphasizes persecutory ideas, resentment, and convictions of having been unfairly treated, and delusional ideas of being attacked, influenced, subverted, or undermined" (p. 32). They also noted that the *Pa-O* subscale is highly redundant with *Pa1*. High *Pa1* scorers tend to feel that the world is an unsafe or hostile place and that others are not to be trusted. It is not surprising that *Pa1* and *Pd4* (Social Alienation) share six items in common and are highly intercorrelated in a sample of psychiatric inpatients and outpatients (Nichols & Greene, 1995). Caldwell stated that raw scores as low as 5 or 6 may point to a paranoid process. High scorers tend to blame others for their problems, feel that others have unfairly blamed or punished them, and feel misunderstood (Graham, 1990). It is not surprising to learn that high male *Pa1* scorers in the Graham et al. (1999) investigation of psychiatric outpatients tended to report a history of being physically abused as well as reporting a history of committing domestic violence, a finding generally supportive of the clinical lore and empirical data linking the two.

Low scorers do not endorse items suggesting externalization of their problems or the use of projection as their main mechanism of defense and tend not to externalize their problems.

The following items represent the *Pa1* content, with the direction of scoring in parentheses and the MMPI–2 item number preceding the item. Only one item is scored in the "false" direction:

17. I am sure I get a raw deal from life. (True)
22. No one seems to understand me. (True)
42. If people had not had it in for me, I would have been much more successful. (True)
113. I know who is responsible for most of my troubles. (True)
138. I believe I am being plotted against. (True)
314. I have no enemies who really wish to harm me. (False)

Poignancy: Pa2 (9 Items)

This subscale appears to measure how sensitive or thin-skinned an individual is in reaction to others. It reflects a facet of the mood or feeling aspect of depression (Nichols & Greene, 1995). Individuals with high scores report an unusual intensity of feelings, angry resentment, a painful sensitivity to criticism, cry easily, feel misunderstood, and feel lonely even in the presence of others (Caldwell, 1988; Graham et al. 1999). These individuals tend to see themselves as taking a longer time to heal from emotional hurts compared to others and they recognize that they are easily wounded (Levitt, 1989). Feeling more high-strung than others, high scorers may tend to look for risky or exciting activities to make them feel better (Graham, 1990).

Low scorers feel understood and accepted and do not experience themselves as more sensitive than others (Caldwell, 1988; Graham, 1990).

Seven of the nine items in this subscale are scored in the "true" direction. The following items are example of the *Pa2* content, with the MMPI–2 item number preceding the item and the direction of scoring is in parentheses:

22. No one seems to understand me. (True)
100. I have never done anything dangerous for the thrill of it. (False)
146. I cry easily. (True)
271. I think I feel more intensely than most people do. (True)
285. I am more sensitive than most other people. (True)

Moral Virtue: Pa3 (9 Items)

This subscale primarily measures how one perceives other people in terms of their trustworthiness. High scorers tend to have optimistic and naive attitudes about others and themselves and may have difficulty experiencing forgiveness when they feel they have been deceived or treated unfairly (Caldwell, 1988; Graham, 1990). There appears to be an underlying rigidity of opinions and attitudes that translates into a judgmental orientation toward others' behavior (e.g., good/bad; right/wrong, and moral/immoral). For this reason, Caldwell thought that the scale is better named as Moral Righteousness. High scorers endorse items reflecting firm expectations regarding the honesty and trustworthiness of others. Endorsement of *Pa3* items could also "represent a tendency by some paranoid patients to deny cynical attitudes" (Ward et al., 1998, p. 295). Meehl and Hathaway (1946, as cited in Ward et al., 1998) speculated that "paranoid deviates are characterized by a tendency to give two sorts of responses, one of which is obviously paranoid, the other 'obviously' not" (p. 555).

Low scorers view others as untrustworthy and motivated by self-interest and are likely to be suspicious of their motives. Nichols and Greene (1995) suggested that a low *Pa3* score coupled with a high *Hy2* (Need for Affection) score reflects cynicism of a competitive, narcissistic, or suspicious variety.

All of the items except one are scored in the "false" direction for this subscale. The following items are examples of *Pa3* contents with the MMPI–2 item number preceding the item, and the direction of scoring in parentheses.

16. Once in a while I think of things too bad to talk about. (True)
81. I think most people would lie to get ahead. (False)
104. Most people are honest chiefly because they are afraid of being caught. (False)
286. Most people inwardly dislike putting themselves out to help other people. (False)
315. I tend to be on my guard with people who are somewhat more friendly than I had expected. (False)

Scale 6: Subtle–Obvious Subscales

Wiener and Harmon (1946) developed Subtle and Obvious subscales for Scale 6 on the MMPI. The MMPI–2 Paranoia–Obvious subscale (*Pa-O*) has 23 items, of which 20 items are keyed in the "true" direction and 3 items are keyed in the "false" direction. The Paranoia–Subtle subscale (*Pa-S*) has 17 items, of which 5 items are keyed in the "true" direction and 12 items are keyed in the "false" direction. The following items are examples of subtle–obvious items on Scale 6, with the MMPI–2 item number preceding the item and the scoring direction and obvious or subtle distinction in parentheses. See Table A.2 for a listing of the subtle–obvious items and the scoring key. The linear *T*-score conversions for the Wiener–Harmon subscales for men and women are presented in Table B.6.

17. I am sure I get a raw deal from life. (True–Obvious)
24. Evil spirits possess me at times. (True–Obvious)
113. I know who is responsible for most of my troubles. (True–Subtle)
145. I feel that I have been often punished without cause. (True–Subtle)
244. Something exciting will almost always pull me out of it when I'm feeling low. (False–Subtle)
314. I have no enemies who really wish to harm me. (False–Obvious)

Caldwell (1988) categorized the 23 items in the *Pa-O* subscale into three categories: (a) persecutory paranoid items (e.g., feeling personally mistreated and knowing who your enemies are), (b) feelings of loneliness and social isolation, and (c) self-awareness of a distressingly low threshold for emotional reactions (e.g., hypersensitivity). *Pa1* overlaps greatly with *Pa-O*, sharing 15 of its 17 items with *Pa-O*. Not surprisingly, Nichols and Greene (1995) reported a high correlation $r = .94$) between *Pa1* and *Pa-O* in a sample of psychiatric inpatients and outpatients. Overall, *Pa-O* appears to emphasize the operation of blaming and attributing hostility to others, as well as including a few oversensitive/depressive items from *Pa2*. Hollrah et al. (1995) reviewed

Wrobel and Lachar's (1982) results and reported that *Pa-O* correlated positively with measures of discomfort and reality distortion. Dahlstrom et al. (1972) reported that Wiener and Harmon (1946) found that the original Minnesota normal men endorsed the *Pa-O* items much less frequently than they did those of the other Obvious subscales. A perusal of the mean number of item endorsements for the Obvious subscales in the recent MMPI–2 restandardization sample (see Butcher et al., 1989, pp. 81–83, Table B3) shows that both men and women again endorse the *Pa-O* items much less frequently than those of the other Obvious subscales, although *Pa-O* has significantly fewer items than the other Obvious subscales. An elevated *Pa-O* score in a "normal" participant warrants a careful assessment of potential paranoid symptoms or paranoid character traits.

Dahlstrom (1991) examined the correlates of the Subtle and Obvious subscales derived from partner ratings on the Katz Adjustment Scales used in the MMPI–2 restandardization (Butcher et al., 1989). For both men and women, the following descriptions emerged as significant for high *Pa-O* scorers: suspicious of others, poor sense of humor, lacks interest in things, feels others do not care about him or her, has many fears, experiences bad dreams, frets over little things, moody, not cheerful, complains of body aches, overly sensitive to rejection, does not show sound judgment, and gives up too easily. For men, some of the descriptions included the following: whines and demands attention, lacks affection, bossy, unpleasant, hostile, and unfriendly. For women, some of the descriptors included the following: gets very sad, thinks others are talking about her, cries easily, lacks energy, appears worn out, lacks emotional control, worries about the future, does not get along with others, and acts helpless.

Caldwell (1988) suggested that low *Pa-O* scores may reflect an absence of resentments, successful social engagement, a comfort with one's own feelings, and possibly a high threshold for aggravation.

The *Pa-S* items, although classified as subtle, appear to have some obvious items (e.g., "I know who is responsible for most of my troubles"). Nine of the 17 items on this subscale overlap with *Pa3*, moral virtue, and therefore there may be some interpretive redundancy between high scores on these two subscales. The male and female normal participants in the restandardization sample (Butcher et al., 1989) tended to obtain a lower mean score on *Pa*-S versus the other Subtle subscales. Although this could be due in part to the relatively shorter length of *Pa-S*, or to particular features of the restandardization sample, among psychiatric patients a high score on *Pa-S*, like *Pa-O*, warrants a careful assessment of potential paranoid symptoms or paranoid character traits.

Dahlstrom (1991) found that both men and women in the MMPI–2 restandardization sample who had elevated *Pa-S* scores were described by their partners as not being nervous, passive, or obedient. Women were described as not suspicious of others, showing sound judgment, not overeating, and thoughtful of others. Men were described as not lying, having a good sense of humor, not lacking an interest in things, not worrying over small things, being cooperative, and not overly sensitive to rejection.

SCALE 7: PSYCHASTHENIA (*Pt*)

Scale 7 was designed to measure a neurotic pattern called *psychasthenia*, a term introduced by Pierre Janet (Marks et al., 1974) but which is no longer generally used. Psychasthenia involves an inability to resist undesired, maladaptive behaviors, which McKinley and Hathaway (1942) described as deriving from the concept of a "weakened will" (p. 616). Preceding this concept of a weakened will was the idea of a weakened (asthenic) nervous system that was commonly referred to as neurasthenia. The catch-all diagnosis of neurasthenia applied to a syndrome with vague and variable symptoms, "particularly manifesting as extreme fatigue, insomnia, depression, headaches, dyspepsia, and a variety of non-verifiable physical complaints" (Gosling, 1987, p. 2). This diagnosis, one of the most common diagnoses in the late 19th and early 20th centuries, was given to individuals unable to keep up their former pace of life and, in fact, appeared in the second edition of the *DSM* (American Psychiatric Association, 1968) as *neurasthenic neurosis* but was subsequently dropped from the third edition of the *DSM* (American Psychiatric Association, 1980). The emphasis in this syndrome was on physical manifestations, with exhaustion, easy fatigability, and chronic weakness as the cardinal features, although proponents of the syndrome were unable to discover the pathological basis of the so-called disease (Gosling, 1987).

Rather than emphasizing physical problems, individuals classified as having psychasthenic tendencies in the initial MMPI development were described as having excessive self-doubts and worries, leading to tension, difficulty in making choices, various fears, obsessive preoccupations, compulsive urges and acts (e.g., hand washing), vague anxieties, and feelings of low self-confidence and insecurity. These individuals might find themselves ruminating about meaningless facts (like repeatedly counting unimportant objects) in an attempt to control their high anxiety levels. In the past, psychasthenic conditions were often referred to as compulsion neuroses, obsessive–compulsive states, or obsessive–ruminative tension states (McKinley, 1944).

Scale 7 does not contain items reflecting specific phobias and compulsions because individual differences between participants probably failed to permit an item to be endorsed with sufficient frequency to survive an item analysis (Marks et al., 1974). It is believed, therefore, that the underlying personality structure of psychasthenia, rather than specific fears and/or phobias, is reflected in the content of Scale 7. Marks et al. (1974) stated that "although the specific fears, preoccupations, and compulsive acts are different from individual to individual and are potentially innumerable, the personality makeup of such persons has sufficient homogeneity to comprise a recognizable common pattern" (p. 28).

Scale 7 consists of 48 items that were derived by using the usual empirical method of contrasting the criterion group to a mixed group of normals. Because the resultant number of items selected in this fashion was small, the scale was augmented by selecting additional items that correlated with the total scale score. In the revision of the MMPI, Scale 7 did not lose any items but did have two of its items slightly rewritten (e.g., grammatical clarification).

In constructing the original scale, 20 psychiatric inpatients with a diagnosis of psychasthenia were selected as criterion participants, a relatively small sample. It was apparently very difficult to locate outpatients with this syndrome, and few patients were so severely handicapped by their condition as to require hospitalization. McKinley and Hathaway (1942) admitted that even with the small group of carefully examined inpatients, there was at least one, and possibly more, incorrectly diagnosed participants. The item endorsements of the 20 criterion cases were compared with a group of 139 normal married men ranging in age from 26 to 43 and 200 normal married women ranging in age from 26 to 43. Additionally, 265 college students were included in a separate comparison to ascertain the effects of age on item endorsements. Once items were identified as differentiating the criterion group from the two normal groups, an additional item analysis was performed correlating each item with the total scale score in a sample of 100 randomly selected psychiatric patients and 100 normal persons. Because of the small number of criterion cases studied, the scale was not cross-validated at the time it was published (McKinley & Hathaway, 1942). However, the scale is internally consistent with split-half values that are almost as high as the test-retest coefficients. The content of the scale seems to indicate a trait underlying the various psychasthenic symptoms it is measuring. For example, as cited in Duckworth and Anderson (1995), "Kunce and Anderson (1976, 1984) have hypothesized an underlying dimension of organization for this scale that in the normal individual with moderate elevations is shown as the ability to organize and to be punctual and methodical" (p. 230).

Because the items on Scale 7 clearly reflect maladjustment, the lack of item subtlety did not permit Wiener and Harmon (1946) to construct Subtle and Obvious subscales. Similarly, Harris and Lingoes did not categorize the items on this scale as the items cannot be easily separated into subcategories. "True" is the scoring direction for 81% of the 48 items on Scale 7, and therefore an all-true response set would tend to elevate this scale. The addition of a full *K* value (the entire raw *K* score) to Scale 7 helps to correct for a defensive response set affecting Scale 7 scores, and a space is provided on the profile sheet to add 1.0 *K* to the *Pt* raw score. Scale 7 has 9 nonoverlapping items, with most of its overlapping content being shared with Scales 8 (17 items) and 2 (13 items). The following items illustrate the content of Scale 7. The MMPI–2 item number is presented before the item, and the scoring direction is in parenthesis. Table A.2 lists the scale composition and the scoring key for Scale 7.

3. I wake up fresh and rested most mornings. (False)
11. There seems to be a lump in my throat much of the time. (True)
31. I find it hard to keep my mind on a task or job. (True)
56. I wish I could be as happy as others seem to be. (True)
73. I am certainly lacking in self-confidence. (True)
140. Most nights I go to sleep without thoughts or ideas bothering me. (False)

Scale 7 measures many of the tendencies and traits of the obsessive–compulsive and anxiety disorder. High scores reflect negative emotionality characterized by feelings of low self-confidence and self-doubts about one's abilities, self-blame, heightened sensitivity, rigid efforts to control impulses, moodiness, and general maladjustment or Subjective distress. In fact, Scale 7 on the MMPI/MMPI–2 is the best marker for the first factor among the basic scales that is usually identified in factor analytic studies. This first factor is typically named *general maladjustment* or *subjective distress.* Scale 7 is highly correlated with Welsh's *A* scale (.90 for non-*K*-corrected *T* scores and .55 for *K*-corrected *T* scores), which is the classic marker for the first factor (Nichols & Greene, 1995). It is for this reason that Scale 7 (and Scale 2) is often referred to as a distress scale (e.g., Lachar, 1974). In general, Scale 7 is sensitive to a general dimension of cognitive inefficiency and worrying that leads to tension and the inability to relax (Friedman, Webb, & Lewak, 1989; Lewak et al., 1990). It appears that Scale 7 emphasizes a fear or dread of some external catastrophe against which an individual might try to prepare or insulate him- or herself by rumination, obsession, and worry (Nichols & Greene, 1995). It is, therefore, not surprising that high Scale 7 scores can be associated with sleep disturbances. Duckworth and Anderson (1995) viewed Scale 7 as a measure of long-term distress (trait anxiety) rather than as situational stress (state anxiety). McKinley (1944) stated that the symptoms of psychasthenia become ingrained into the individual's personality, and thus they tend to last for years, although periods of acute discomfort commonly occur. Although high Scale 7 scorers are often seen as agitated, the specific clinical manifestation will depend on other scale elevations. For example, Scale 7 is frequently elevated in the profiles of psychiatric patients (e.g., 278/728 and 87/78 profiles). When significantly elevated with Scale 2, depression and indecision are often observed, and when coupled with Scale 8 (e.g., 78/87), confusion, disorganized thinking, and feelings of depletion are manifested (Duckworth & Anderson, 1995; Friedman, Webb, & Lewak, 1989; Greene, 1991a; Rathvon & Holmstrom, 1996). In psychiatric inpatient settings, Scale 7 elevations reflect severe guilt, low energy, depressed mood, and sometimes hallucinations (Graham & Butcher, 1988).

There is no single source of variance in Scale 7; thus, individuals scoring high on this scale can manifest any number of aspects of maladjustment, ranging from poor concentration and agitation to psychotic tendencies (Comrey, 1958). High-scoring normals are generally described in more favorable terms than psychiatric patients, although women have more neurotic features typically than men. Dahlstrom et al. (1972) described peer ratings reported by Hathaway and Meehl using MMPI Scale 7. High Scale 7 men were described as sentimental, peaceable, good-tempered, verbal, and dissatisfied whereas women were rated as sensitive, prone to worry, emotional, and high-strung. More recently, the restandardization participants with high Scale 7 scores were rated by their spouses as having many fears, being nervous, being indecisive, lacking in self-confidence, and having sleep problems (Butcher & Williams, 1992).

Low-scoring individuals on Scale 7 are often seen as relaxed and able to handle their responsibilities without distress. They appear self-controlled, realistic, and able to organize themselves.

Test–retest coefficients for psychiatric patients on MMPI Scale 7 range from .83 to .86 for 1- to 2-week intervals between administrations and from .49 to .58 for

1-year intervals between tests (Dahlstrom et al., 1975). In Hunsley et al.'s. (1988) large-scale meta-analysis of MMPI reliability studies using several diverse populations conducted between 1970 and 1981, an average internal consistency of .84 across 70 studies of Scale 7 was reported. They also reported an average test-retest reliability of .82 for 16 studies for time intervals of 1 day to 2 years. More recently, Butcher et al. (1989) reported test–retest reliability data for their community (normal) sample of 82 men (r =. 89) and 111 women (r = .88) retested at an average interval of 8.6 days (*Mdn* = 7 days). Internal consistency estimates (Cronbach's coefficient alpha) for Scale 7 were also derived from the restandardization sample (Butcher et al., 1989) and yielded coefficients of .85 and .87 for men and women, respectively.

SCALE 8: SCHIZOPHRENIA (*Sc*)

Schizophrenia, first identified as a syndrome by Kraepelin (1893; see Kraepelin, 1919) and later named *schizophrenia* by Bleuler (1950) in 1911, is currently recognized as a group of disorders with a biogenic etiological basis (Eysenck, Wakefield, & Friedman, 1983; Gallagher & Jones, 1987). Diagnostic criteria for a schizophrenic disorder, according to the fourth edition of the *DSM* (American Psychiatric Association, 1994), include impairment in various psychological processes involving thinking, perceiving, feeling, and behaving, with no specific feature considered pathognomonic of the disorder. Often a deterioration from a previous level of functioning is observed, with continuous signs of the disorder necessary for at least 6 months during the individual's life. Various symptoms precede the illness (prodromal phase) or remain (residual) after the active phase of the disorder. These symptoms often vary between individuals and include social withdrawal; inappropriate affect; bizarre ideation; odd behavior; and digressive, vague, circumstantial speech, which, according to Marks and Seeman (1963), can lead the clinician talking to a schizophrenic patient to often wonder "How did we get to this?" because logical thought is so circuitous and frequently interrupted.

It is not surprising that the development of Scale 8 was the most difficult of all the clinical scales to construct because schizophrenia involves diverse behavioral, emotional, and cognitive symptoms. Although more research time was devoted to this scale than the others, it is still considered one of the weaker diagnostic scales (Marks & Seeman, 1963). Despite many efforts at refinement, the ability of the *Sc* scale to separate the criterion schizophrenic participants from the normals (hit rate) could not be made to exceed 60% (Hathaway, 1956, 1980). As many as a dozen variations of the scale were attempted from four preliminary scales before the final version of the *Sc* scale was accepted and cross-validated. These preliminary scales were derived from two partly overlapping groups of 50 patients with varying subtypes of schizophrenia (catatonic, paranoid, simple, and hebephrenic). About 60% of the participants were women and 40% were men. Hathaway (1956, 1980) did not offer more specific definitional features of the criterion participants, but Dahlstrom et al. (1972) gave the following description of schizophrenic individuals:

> Most commonly, persons showing this psychiatric reaction are characterized as constrained, cold, and apathetic or indifferent. Other people see them as remote and inaccessible, often seeming sufficient unto themselves. Delusions of varying degrees of organization, hallucinations, either fleeting or persistent and compelling, and disorientation may appear in various combinations. Inactivity or endless stereotypy, may accompany the withdrawal of interest from other people or external objects and relationships. These persons frequently perform below the levels expected of them on the basis of their training and ability. (p. 215)

Nichols (1988) pointed out that the criterion schizophrenic group very likely was contaminated, with a large minority of affectively disordered participants. Historically, schizophrenia had been grossly overdiagnosed in this country, whereas affective disorders had been underdiagnosed, especially in relation to each other. Because there is much symptom overlap between the two syndromes, many affectively disordered participants were probably inaccurately classified as schizophrenic. In contrast, few false-positive classifications were likely made in constructing the criterion group for Scale 9 (Hypomania), as manic patients with schizophrenic-like symptoms were excluded. Therefore, Nichols (1988) stated that Scale 9 was probably rendered an "unusually valid measure of the core features of the manic syndrome" (p. 80).

Despite the many efforts to improve the detection ability of Scale 8, it was not until the *K* scale was developed by Meehl and Hathaway (1946; as cited in Dahlstrom & Dahlstrom, 1980) and used as a device to improve the discriminative ability of Scale 8 that it was considered complete. As indicated earlier, about 60% of the cross-validation cases could be correctly identified with the scale when 1 full *K* value was added to Scale 8. The addition of 1 full *K* value helped to reduce the number of false positives or high-scoring normals from 15% to 2%. Hathaway (1956, 1980) pointed out, however, that even with the correction, a considerable number of the 91 cross-validation cases (all of which were psychiatric patients diagnosed as schizophrenic) remained below a *T* score of 61 on MMPI Scale 8.

The *K* value appears to work in improving the operation of Scale 8 in the following way. By adding *K* to the raw score on Scale 8, the *T* scores for the criterion participants (schizophrenics) and normals were both raised, but the *T* scores of the criterion group increased more relative to the normals. Presumably, the reason the schizophrenic participants failed initially to be identified was due to the denial or minimizing of psychopathology associated with *K*. Adding *K* to their scores is intended to correct for this minimizing tendency, which is less pronounced in the normals, who presumably have less psychopathology to minimize.

It is now customary to add the value of 1.0 raw *K* to the raw score of Scale 8 before plotting the standard score on the profile sheet. It is recommended that clinicians continue to use the *K* correction factor for Scale 8, especially with psychiatric patients, as the vast majority of research conducted on Scale 8 has used *K*-corrected rather than non-*K*-corrected scores (Walters, 1988). Note that because 1 full *K* value is added to Scale 8, it is possible to obtain an elevated Scale 8 score ($T \geq 65$), with approximately 20 Scale 8 items endorsed in the deviant direction and an average score on the *K* scale. Therefore, it is important to examine the raw score on

Scale 8 as well as the endorsed item content before inferring a diagnosis of psychosis from a high score on Scale 8 considered in isolation. A diagnostic conclusion of schizophrenia cannot be made solely on the basis of a Scale 8 elevation. The relationship of other scale elevations and patterns must be examined, as well as special indexes, in the context of the referral question and other clinical information in order to accurately identify an individual with schizophrenia or schizophrenic-like symptoms. Many individuals with elevated Scale 8 scores as the most prominent high point in a profile are not psychotic; in some cases, an individual may be suffering from severe depression, perhaps with psychotic features and acute distress, a severe personality disorder, an organic brain disorder, or some extreme sensory impairment, or have an unconventional, rebellious orientation toward society (Butcher & Williams, 1992).

Scale 8 does appear to operate in a differentiating fashion in psychiatric settings. Walters (1984) found that Scale 8 elevations differentiated schizophrenic and schizophrenic-spectrum disorders in general psychiatric patients. In a nonpsychiatric setting, a moderately elevated Scale 8 score should be interpreted with attenuated descriptors as many individuals will not present psychopathology suggestive of a schizophrenic disorder. For example, Anderson and Kunce (1984) found that in a sample of university counseling center clients with Scale 8 as their highest score and a *T* score above 70, the majority of clients tended to feel socially isolated and had interpersonal difficulties, but only a minority were assessed as having bizarre thoughts. The case notes in the files of all of these participants indicated that the significantly elevated *Sc* scale reflected stressful identity or personal crises rather than chronic or severe psychopathological conditions. Although this study demonstrates the lack of expected psychopathology associated with a Scale 8 elevation, other research has shown that although "normal" or nonpsychiatric participants with high Scale 8 scores may not carry a diagnosis of schizophrenia, they often share certain characteristics with the schizophrenic participants (e.g., Fine, 1973; S. P. Keane & Gibbs, 1980), thereby providing construct validity for the scale. For example, S. P. Keane and Gibbs tested the hypothesis that participants (university students) with elevated Scale 8 scores would exhibit qualitatively different word associations from those with normal MMPI profiles. Students with elevated profiles exhibited associations similar to those frequently observed in hospitalized schizophrenic patients, such as perseverations, self-references, and blocking. Although the students were not described as manifesting any form of a severe disturbance, Keane and Gibbs hypothesized that their associational deficits, as detected by Scale 8 elevations, could exhibit themselves in a subtle way on tasks that tap organizational ability, grammatical structure, and conventional associative linkages.

In general, researchers have found that prominent Scale 8 elevations, especially in psychiatric settings, do predict a schizophrenic diagnosis, especially if there is a concurrent elevation on Scale 6 (*Pa*) or on scores in the psychotic/schizophrenic direction on certain MMPI indexes (i.e., Taulbee-Sisson signs and the Goldberg index; Walters, 1988). Marks et al. (1974) found that 68% of their 86/68 code pattern participants were diagnosed as psychotic (schizophrenic/paranoid), whereas 18% were diagnosed as having paranoid personality disorders. Seventy percent of their 89/98 code pattern participants were described as psychotic (schizophrenic/mixed), whereas 58% of their 278/872 participants and 70% of their 28/82 participants were diagnosed as schizophrenic and schizophrenic/ schizoaffective, respectively. Greene (2000) reported the frequency of MMPI code patterns in a large sample (*N* = 8,727) of psychiatric inpatients and outpatients collected by Hedlund and Won Cho (1979) in the 1970s. For women, some of the most frequently occurring codes were the 86, 48, and 84 code patterns (Spike 4 was the most frequent code pattern); for men, the 86 was one of the most frequently occurring code patterns. Greene (2000) provided detailed data on the frequency with which each MMPI–2 code pattern occurred in the sample of patients collected by Hedlund and Won Cho. This comparison was accomplished by eliminating the omitted 13 items from the MMPI–2 and rescoring the data using uniform *T* scores. Many changes in the frequency of scale elevations and code patterns resulted, but in general Scale 8 occurred less frequently in both the male and female patients. (See Greene, 2000, for a more detailed description of the code pattern frequencies for the MMPI–2 and Walters, 1988, for a review of the relation between Scale 8 and schizophrenia.) Greene (1988b; 2000) pointed out that there is considerable heterogeneity in psychiatric diagnoses within a given code pattern as the Marks et al. (1974) data indicate. However, it does appear that Scale 8 is useful in describing the behavior of and, to a certain extent, deriving a diagnosis for individuals scoring high on this scale. Studies (e.g., Walters, 1984) consistently show that schizophrenic patients earn higher mean scores on Scale 8 relative to normals and other nonschizophrenic psychiatric patients.

As with certain other clinical scales, it is important to examine the Harris–Lingoes subscales to help determine the meaning of a particular scale elevation. Wiener and Harmon (Wiener, 1948) did not develop Subtle and Obvious subscales for Scale 8.

Disorganized thinking, impaired reality testing, and communication problems appear to be cardinal features of high Scale 8 scorers (Friedman, Webb, & Lewak, 1989). As scores increase, the individual's logic appears less coherent, and at markedly high levels, individuals tend to have impaired communications between themselves and others. Duckworth and Anderson (1995) also indicated that at increasing levels of Scale 8 individuals are likely to manifest poor judgement that lands them into difficulties. Extremely high elevations ($T > 100$) usually reflect situational stress rather than chronic disorganization and typically individuals with identity crises ("Who am I?") score in this range. Coupled with an elevated Scale 0, the person tends to show even greater communication disturbance because of a lack of social contact with others. Nichols and Greene (1995) viewed Scale 8 as a measure of a tendency to withdraw into fantasy and, at high levels ($T = 85$), to prefer the world of fantasy to real-world relationships. They provided detailed and useful information on the relation of Scale 8 to the *F* scale and to the *BIZ* content scale stating that

> when BIZ (especially BIZ1 [Psychotic Symptomatology]) is elevated along with Sc, the fantasy tends toward the psychotic and bizarre, with a significant breach in reality

> testing and in the ability to discriminate external from internal events. When Sc is not accompanied by elevations on BIZ, fantasy tends to be of a compensatory, wish fulfillment type, in which reality adherence is relatively well preserved. These inferences may be fortified with reference to the difference between F and BIZ scores: F substantially greater than BIZ suggests social deviance and poor reality testing without bizarre aspects; a large negative difference suggests bizarre fantasy but with relatively less impaired reality contact. A similar relationship between F and Sc scales also bears upon the expression of psychoticism. When the elevation of both scales is nearly equivalent or F is slightly higher than Sc, psychotic manifestations are apt to be public, including interpersonal bizarreness with evident emotional and motivational dyscontrol. When Sc is elevated, to the extent that it exceeds F, psychotic manifestations are apt to be of an internalized kind, such as bizarre fantasies and autism, with interpersonal detachment and withdrawal. (Nichols & Greene, 1995, p. 36)

Individuals with significant Scale 8 elevations tend to feel mistrustful toward others and think that people will dislike them. Lewak et al. (1990) and Caldwell (1984) hypothesized that Scale 8 elevations are associated with a childhood of being despised and rejected by a person on whom life and security depended:

> Perhaps in some instances the child expressed some peculiar habit or eccentricities or was physically inept which led others to express anger, hatred, and resentment towards him or her. The assumption is that the child, in an act of self-protection, would shut down, that is, not think or not pay attention, which would lead in turn to faulty cognitive and emotional functioning. (Lewak et al., 1990, p. 246)

With high Scale 8 elevations, individuals might experience hallucinations, confusion, panic, or anxiety and possibly be delusional. Scale 8 is associated with feeling unhappy, moody, inferior, and alienated, as well as with immaturity, impulsivity, and reclusion. High Scale 8 scorers are viewed by others as odd or peculiar and shy, even schizoid at times. Low Scale 8 scorers are seen as friendly, responsible, cautious, and unimaginative in their approach to problem solving and as practical and concrete in their thinking (Graham, 1990).

Hathaway and Meehl (as cited in Dahlstrom et al., 1972) found that the normal men in their study who had elevated scores on this scale were not seen by their peers as withdrawn or deviant. Social difficulties were not perceived, although these men were seen as self-dissatisfied and prone to worry. Overall, they were described as good-tempered, verbal, enthusiastic, and having wide aesthetic interests. Peaceable, kind, and sentimental were emotional descriptors given to them. Women were described as sensitive and high-strung, as well as frank, kind, and modest. Other descriptors for normal men in a different sample provided by Gough et al. (1955, as cited in Dahlstrom et al., 1972) are much more negative. Terms like *hostile* and *irritable* suggest difficulties in handling aggression and imply a certain lack of control in modulating emotions.

Scale 8 on the MMPI–2 lost no items in the restandardization project, but 13 of the scale's 78 items were modified, with mostly grammatical clarifications and simplifications. As the longest clinical scale, there is considerable item overlap with other scales. Scale 8 shares the most items with Scales 7 (17 items) and the *F* scale (15 items) and has more items in common with the other psychotic scales that it does with the neurotic scales. There are only 16 items unique (nonoverlapping) to Scale 8. As is the case for other psychotic scales, the deviant direction of endorsement for the majority of Scale 8 items is "true;" specifically, 59 (76%) of the 78 items are scored as "true" and 19 (24%) items are scored as "false." J. W. Little (1949) found that the item "I hear strange things when I am alone" has the highest correlation (*r* = .70) to the total scale, with the next highest item having a value of .67 ("I cannot keep my mind on one thing"). The following items demonstrate the diversity of content on Scale 8. The MMPI–2 item number precedes the item, and the scoring direction is in parentheses. Table A.2 provides the item composition of the scale and the scoring direction for the items. See Appendix C for a table describing the overlapping item content of Scale 8

9. My daily life is full of things that keep me interested. (False)
12. My sex life is satisfactory. (False)
17. I am sure I get a raw deal from life. (True)
21. At times I very much wanted to leave home. (True)
22. No one seems to understand me. (True)
32. I have had very peculiar and strange experiences. (True)
138. I believe I am being plotted against. (True)

MMPI Scale 8 test–retest coefficients for psychiatric cases ranged from .75 to .82 for a 1- to 2-day interval between tests and from .56 to .64 for a 1-year interval between tests (Dahlstrom et al., 1975). Test–retest correlation coefficients for a subsample of the MMPI–2 restandardization group (82 men and 111 women) retested at about a 1-week interval were .87 and .80 for men and women, respectively (Butcher et al., 1989). In Hunsley et al.'s (1988) large-scale meta-analysis of MMPI reliability studies using a wide variety of populations conducted between 1970 and 1981, an average test–retest reliability of .78 for 17 studies was reported for time intervals for 1 day to 2 years. They also reported an average internal consistency (Cronbach's coefficient alpha) of .82 across 73 studies of Scale 8. More recently, Butcher et al. reported internal consistency estimates for Scale 8 on the MMPI–2 of .85 and .87 for men and women, respectively. Scales 8 and 7 had almost identical alpha coefficients, the highest for all of the validity and clinical scales. Clearly, Scale 8 appears to be an internally consistent scale with good test-retest reliability.

Harris–Lingoes Subscales

Harris and Lingoes developed the following subscales for Scale 8: Social Alienation (*Sc1*); Emotional Alienation (*Sc2*); Lack of Ego Mastery, Cognitive (*Sc3*); Lack of Ego Mastery, Conative (*Sc4*); Lack of Ego Mastery, Defective Inhibition (*Sc5*); and Sensorimotor Dissociation (*Sc6*). The specific item composition of the subscales is listed in Table A2; Table B5 provides the linear *T*-score conversions for the raw-score values.

Social Alienation: Sc1 (21 Items)

This subscale consists of items reflecting emotional deprivation. Specifically, the items reflect feeling misunderstood, insulted, punished unfairly, plotted against, and detached from one's own family and others and a sense of loneliness around others (Caldwell, 1988). High *Sc1* scorers tend to lack a viable support system (Levitt, 1989). Graham et al. (1999) reported that the men in their outpatient psychiatric sample tended to report that their families lacked love and that there was a history of physical abuse. Women, in particular, admitted to more suicide attempts if they were a high versus a low scorer on *Sc1*. Although an individual may also concurrently score high on *Pd1* (Familial Discord) and *Pd4* (Social Alienation), it is important to assess these and other subscale scores separately as the clinical implications can vary. For example, a high *Sc1* score, coupled with relatively low *Sc2* (Emotional Alienation) and *Pd5* (Self-Alienation) scores, suggests that the person's sense of pessimism and hopelessness may be confined to other people, although he or she is still able to derive gratification from activities of nonsocial interests (Nichols & Greene, 1995). High *Sc1* scorers feel they have been given a "bum deal" but do not feel the residual sadness or longing that appears in *Pd4* (Nichols & Greene, 1995). To a large extent, high *Sc1* individuals prefer noninvolvement with others. *Sc1* also measures an element of paranoia in that high scorers are generally mistrustful of others. When the *F* scale and/or *Pd1* are also elevated, the person may express hatred toward one or both parents (Nichols & Greene, 1995).

Low *Sc1* scorers tend to like others, feel attached to them, feel understood, respected, well treated, and deny feelings of hatred/resentment toward family members (Caldwell, 1988; Graham, 1990).

Sixteen of the items on this subscale are scored in the "true" direction, and 5 items are scored in the "false" direction. The following items illustrate the content of *Sc1*. Preceding the item is the MMPI–2 item number, with the direction of scoring in parentheses:

17. I'm sure I get a raw deal from life. (True)
21. At times I have very much wanted to leave home. (True)
22. No one seems to understand me. (True)
138. I believe I am being plotted against. (True)
278. I get all the sympathy I should. (False)
280. I seem to make friends about as quickly as others do. (False)

Emotional Alienation: Sc2 (11 Items)

This subscale consists of items reflecting an existence devoid of interests, engagement, or aspiration (Nichols & Greene, 1995). Levitt (1989) thought the scale basically measured depression, and in fact, the scale does appear to measure an emotional withdrawal from life. Graham et al. (1999) reported a similar description of the high *Sc2* scorer suggesting a greater likelihood of depression as well as having few or no friends. Caldwell (1988) described high scorers as experiencing life as an "ungratifying strain" (p. 28) and as taking pleasure in hurting loved ones or being hurt by them. Graham (1990) also described high scorers as feeling apathetic and frightened. Wrobel (1992) provided correlates for *Sc2* that included feeling a lack of rapport with oneself, a flat or distorted affect, and a feeling of oneself as strange. Nichols and Greene (1995) described emotional alienation as reflecting a "pathological disengagement from life that discounts future interests, prospects, and engagements to the extent that they can no longer serve as incentives for continuing to live" (p. 29). In this regard, the high *Sc2* scorer is seen as lacking an investment in the future, which raises the possibility of suicidal behavior and thoughts, which should be further evaluated by examining critical items (MMPI–2 Items 150, 303, 506, 520, and 524) and the suicidal ideation component *DEP4* of the *DEP* content scale (Ben-Porath & Sherwood, 1993; see chap. 7). Although *Sc2* does have items reflective of unconventional thought processes, the items tend not to be as strongly suggestive of psychosis as other measures, such as Psychotic Symptomatology (*BIZ1*) or Sensorimotor Dissociation (*Sc6*; Nichols & Greene, 1995).

Low *Sc2* scorers deny feelings of depression and despair, feel that life is worthwhile, and deny sadistic or masochistic needs (Graham, 1990).

Eight of the 11 items on this subscale are scored in the "true" direction, whereas 3 items are scored in the "false" direction. The following items illustrate the content of *Sc2*, with the MMPI–2 item number preceding the item and the scoring direction in parentheses:

9. My daily life is full of things that keep me interested. (False)
65. Most of the time I feel blue. (True)
92. I don't seem to care what happens to me. (True)
273. Life is a strain for me much of the time. (True)
303. Most of the time I wish I were dead. (True)
323. Sometimes I enjoy hurting persons I love. (True)

Lack of Ego Mastery, Cognitive: Sc3 (10 Items)

This short subscale contains items that reflect cognitive deficits in the areas of memory, attention, and concentration. Although similar to *D4* (Mental Dullness), *Sc3* emphasizes a disruption of thought processes by the intrusion of troubling thoughts, whereas the *D4* content emphasizes disability that interferes with the completion of mental work (Nichols & Greene, 1995). The MMPI–2 *HEA* content scale contains items sensitive to cognitive deficits, such as confusion and impaired judgment, but *Sc3* should exceed the score on the *HEA* scale before giving an interpretation specific to *Sc3*. The high *Sc3* scorer tends to have a sense of disability where thinking is concerned (Nichols & Greene, 1995). High *Sc3* scorers tend to experience more distress or discomfort by their cognitive deficits than high *D4* scorers although the two scales frequently elevate as a pair (Levitt, 1989). High *Sc3* scores generally indicate individuals who feel they are losing their minds, report strange thought processes and feelings of unreality, and have trouble with concentration and memory functions (Graham, 1990). Graham et al. (1999) reported in their outpatient psychiatric sample, that the high *Sc3* scorer was described by their therapist as suffering acute psychological turmoil and as not coping well with stress.

Low scorers generally deny any difficulty with their thinking processes (Caldwell, 1988).

Nine of the 10 items on this subscale are scored in the "true" direction, with 1 item scored as "false." The following items illustrate the content of *Sc3*, with the MMPI–2 item number preceding the item and the scoring direction in parentheses:

31. I find it hard to keep my mind on a task or job. (True)
32. I have had very peculiar and strange experiences. (True)
165. My memory seems to be all right. (False)
170. I'm afraid of losing my mind. (True)
180. There's something wrong with my mind. (True)
299. I cannot keep my mind on one thing. (True)

Lack of Ego Mastery, Conative: Sc4 (14 Items)

Conation means an inclination to act purposively, which is exactly what high *Sc4* scorers lack. This subscale consists of items that reflect the degree of lost motivation to behave in a constructive and productive fashion (Levitt, 1989). High scorers have a sense of malfunction in their cognitive operations, such as attention, concentration, judgment, and memory, along with a withdrawal of interest, that leads to a lack of pleasure and interest in daily life (Nichols & Greene, 1995). Caldwell (1988) stated that the items reflect an inability to mobilize one's energy, that it is tough to get going and focus one's mental energy. Indeed, this subscale appears to measure the psychic equivalent of psychomotor retardation (*D2*); in fact, Nichols and Greene (1995) viewed this subscale as being sensitive to a "general psychic disability" (p. 40). Wrobel (1992) found that clinician raters found feelings of psychological weakness to be a significant correlate for high *Sc4* scorers. Typically, high scorers feel that life is a strain and may be experiencing depression, in that they have given up hope of things ever getting better (Butcher et al., 1989; Graham, 1990; Graham et al., 1999). Some items reflect a tendency to withdraw into fantasy and daydreaming as an escape from stress, and one item (MMPI–2 Item 303, "Most of the time I wish I were dead") raises the question of suicidal apathy or despair. The inertia and lack of initiative high scorers experience lead to severe emotional alienation, in fact *Sc4* overlaps heavily (eight items) with *Sc2*. High *Sc4* scorers, however, can differ from the pure emotional alienation that high *Sc2* scorers experience, in that *Sc4* measures a lack of sustained mental focus and passive distractibility, which proceeds more from anergy and indifference than from the cognitive disruption that is often seen in the case of *Sc3* (Nichols & Greene, 1995).

Sc4 may capture much of the essence of the Sc parent scale, as the two measures correlate highly (*r* = .84) in a sample of psychiatric inpatients and outpatients (Nichols & Greene, 1995). Low *Sc4* scores reflect a feeling that life is worthwhile, a denial of depression and suicidal ideation, and the feeling that one has enough energy for spontaneously initiating actions. Generally, the person is happy to be alive and does not complain of cognitive deficits (Caldwell, 1988; Graham, 1990).

The following items are examples of *Sc4* content, with the MMPI–2 item number preceding the item and direction of scoring in parentheses. Eleven of the items are scored in the "true" direction, and 3 items are scored in the "false" direction:

9. My daily life is full of things that keep me interested. (False)
31. I find it hard to keep my mind on a task or job. (True)
32. I've had very peculiar and strange experiences. (True)
43. Most any time I would rather sit and daydream than do anything else. (True)
65. Most of the time I feel blue. (True)
210. I like to visit places where I have never been before. (False)
290. I worry over money and business. (False)

Lack of Ego Mastery, Defective Inhibition: Sc5 (11 Items)

This subscale consists of items that emphasize a fear or dread of internal disintegration or loss of control (Graham, 1990; Nichols & Greene, 1995). Graham reported that high scorers may feel restless, hyperactive, and irritable and may have periods of laughing/crying that they cannot control, as well as have episodes during which they did not know what they were doing. Caldwell (1988) noted that *Sc5* shares six items with Scale 9 (*Ma*) and that *Sc5* is often elevated when Scales 8 and 9 are both elevated. Therefore, the potential for eruptions of uncontrollable rage are high when *Sc5* is elevated. When *Sc5* is elevated, the person may be vulnerable to being overwhelmed with rage affect and other scales should be examined in relation to this subscale to assess the potential for rageful expressions of emotions. Nichols and Greene (1995) addressed this issue and made the following statement about how content scales in relation to *Sc5* can be useful in this assessment:

> Relative to ANG, TPA and Sc5 reflect a more chronic condition, one closer to concepts of hostility, rage, and resentment. Thus, ANG scores well above scores on TPA and Sc5 imply a more state-like anger. When elevations on TPA and Sc5 equal or exceed the ANG score, however, anger is likely to operate in a trait-like fashion, with the respondent appearing to seek opportunities for discharge or to anticipate situations in which anger in one or more of the parties involved will be stimulated, if not expressed. The relations among the three scales (ANG, TPA, and Sc5) provide some basis for predicting the degree of focus that will characterize angry feelings and expressions: If ANG is greater than TPA and TPA is greater than Sc5, anger is likely to be tightly focused on specific issues, perceived offenses, or persons. The reverse pattern (Sc5 > TPA > ANG) implies blind or diffuse rage with appropriate targets determined largely by opportunity and convenience. (p. 30)

Graham et al. (1999) findings of women clients with high *Sc5* scores having a higher likelihood of a borderline personality disorder diagnosis is consistent with the rage and hostility associated with elevated *Sc5* scores.

Low *Sc5* scores reflect the self-perception that it takes a lot to get oneself excited, that one is well controlled and not restless or irritable (Caldwell, 1988; Graham, 1990). In essence, a low *Sc5* score may indicate good control over one's impulses.

The following items are examples of *Sc5* content with the scoring direction in parentheses and the MMPI–2 item number preceding the item. All 11 items on this subscale are scored in the "true" direction and are obvious (vs. subtle) making *Sc5* vulnerable to response-style distortions (e.g., all true or all false response sets or fake-good or fake-bad response sets).

23. At times I have fits of laughing and crying that I cannot control. (True)
85. At times I have a strong urge to do something harmful or shocking. (True)
168. I have had periods in which I carried on activities without knowing later what I had been doing. (True)
218. I have periods of such great restlessness that I cannot sit long in a chair. (True)
274. I am so touchy on some participants that I can't talk about them. (True)
322. I am afraid of using a knife or anything very sharp or pointed. (True)

Sensorimotor Dissociation: Sc6 (20 Items)

This subscale covers a range of content that includes unexplainable bodily changes, like twitchings, unusual weakness or numbness, blank spells, voice changes, loss of taste, ringing in the ears, feelings of depersonalization, and fits of laughing and crying (Caldwell, 1988). *Sc6* is primarily focused on motor, sensory, and dissociative symptoms, and it is recommended that the content component scales (Ben-Porath & Sherwood, 1993), such as Gastrointestinal Symptoms (*HEA1*), Neurological Symptoms (*HEA*2), and General Health Concerns (*HEA3*), be examined to determine both the range of symptoms claimed and their level of intensity (Nichols & Greene, 1995). It appears that high *Sc6* scores reflect a deterioration of control in the way impulses are inhibited; the items reflect a certain loosening of ties to reality. However, the original name of the scale—Bizarre Sensory Experiences—does not appear to represent the scale content in its entirety. For this reason, the scale has been renamed Sensorimotor Dissociation, which appears to more accurately capture the nature of the subscale items. Nichols and Greene (1995) provided some much-needed clarification of this issue, stating that

> in the 1955 edition of their subscale manuscript, Harris and Lingoes designated Sc6 (Sc3 at that time) "bizarre sensory experiences." In their 1968 revision, however, the authors renamed this subscale "sensorimotor dissociation." The revised designation corresponds far more closely to the actual content of the items comprising Sc6. While many of the items on this subscale are unusual and a few reflect psychoticism (311, 319, 355), only one item (355) has possible bizarre connotations. The remaining items

> mostly reflect soft neurologic signs: sensory (252, 247, 255, 298), motor (23, 91, 106, 177, 179, 182, 295), and possible dissociation (168, 182, 229, 296, 311). (p. 31)

In general, high *Sc6* scorers feel their bodies are changing in strange and unusual ways. They may report skin sensitivities, voice changes, muscle twitchings, clumsiness, balance difficulties, ringing in their ears, and feelings of weakness and paralysis (Graham, 1990). Wrobel (1992) reported that a feeling of depersonalization was a significant correlate for the high *Sc6* scorer in his sample of clients in therapy in a private outpatient facility. Low scorers tend to not report the occurrence of these symptoms and experiences.

The following items are examples of the *Sc6* content, with the direction of scoring in parentheses and the MMPI–2 item number preceding the item. Fourteen of the items are scored in the "true" direction and 6 items are scored in the "false" direction:

23. At times I have fits of laughing and crying that I cannot control. (True)
32. I've had very peculiar and strange experiences. (True)
44. Once a week or oftener I suddenly feel hot all over for no real reason. (True)
91. I have little or no trouble with my muscles twitching or jumping. (False)
168. I have had periods in which I carried on activities without knowing later what I had been doing. (True)
177. My hands have not become clumsy or awkward. (False)
255. I do not often notice my ears ringing or buzzing. (False)

SCALE 9: HYPOMANIA (*Ma*)

Scale 9 consists of 46 items measuring the aspects of a mildly elevated mood that often is accompanied by a flight of ideas, affective lability, and psychomotor excitement. The personality pattern the scale reflects is the affective disorder termed *hypomania* (Dahlstrom et al., 1972). Hypomania indicates heightened activity levels with accompanying symptoms or traits such as easy distractibility, insomnia, overoptimism, occasional grandiosity, suspiciousness, and irascibility. McKinley and Hathaway (1944, as cited in Dahlstrom & Dahlstrom, 1980) selected a group of 24 inpatients at the University of Minnesota Hospital as their criterion participants for constructing this scale. Unfortunately, no available demographic data are reported on the criterion participants (Colligan et al., 1983). According to McKinley and Hathaway (as cited in Dahlstrom & Dahlstrom, 1980), only patients with less than a full-blown manic syndrome were usable, because the more severe cases could not participate fully in the task of sorting inventory items into the appropriate true, false, and Cannot Say categories: "The clinical diagnoses were either hypomania or mild acute mania, depending on the severity of the case" (p. 52). Hence, the scale name *Hypomania* reflects this measure of a less than full-blown manic condition. It was important to derive a measure of more subtle or moderate cases of mania so that the condition could be identified early on to improve the prognosis and treatment options for the patient. Patients were excluded from study if they were delirious, confused, schizophrenic, or depressed with agitation. McKinley and Hathaway (as cited in Dahlstrom & Dahlstrom, 1980) recognized the small number of cases in their criterion group and conceded that "in spite of the small number of criterion and test cases available, a scale for *Hypomania* is presented. It is the best that we could derive from the patients seen over a 5-year period" (p. 57).

Scale 9 is sensitive to expansive, elated, and euphoric mood states. Additionally, Nichols and Greene (1995) stated that "Ma reflects the ease of access that thoughts, feelings, and impulses have to the motor system. When Ma is elevated, motor readiness is high" (p. 36). The higher the elevation on Scale 9, the more energetic a person tends to be and the more compelled the individual feels to act in using that energy (Duckworth & Anderson, 1995). In fact, as scale elevations increase, the more likely the person is to get overcommitted or overinvolved in activities. Nichols (1988) provided an excellent description of manic affect that can be useful in understanding Scale 9 elevations:

> Affect is characteristically elated, euphoric, enthusiastic, expansive, triumphant, and disinhibited. The patient may present as playful, jocular, quick-witted, and high-spirited, free of all normal cares and concerns, in tip-top shape, and ready for action. This picture is unstable, however, and may change suddenly into one of anger and hostility if the patient is blocked in the pursuit of some goal, has his or her self-esteem challenged, experiences a rebuff, or in some other way feels thwarted. The patient often feels highly vulnerable to real or implied personal criticism even though he or she may be quite imperturbable regarding other matters. For a large minority of patients the dominant mood is one of irritability rather than elation and affect may be somewhat dysphoric. The patient may seem cantankerous and constantly in transit between flare-ups of litigiousness, contentiousness, and antagonism. Fear may emerge in some cases, usually relatively late in the manic episode, and may be related to reverses, rejections, and alienation, secondary to the reactions of friends, family, or staff to the patient's obnoxiousness. Major lapses in judgment, including sexual or financial indiscretions occurring early in the episode, which become clear to the patient, may also stimulate a fearful response. Finally, fear may be a reaction to the realization that the manic flight will soon expire and be supplanted by depression. Not uncommonly, such fears may reach delusional proportions and involve themes of retribution or of being poisoned (by medication, i.e., being slowed down to the point that depression may catch up). (p. 76)

High scores on Scale 9 tend to reflect a proclivity to distance oneself from personal distress either by running away or by acting out. There is a tendency to deny emotional distress and to shift these feelings to the motor sphere (Nichols & Greene, 1995). Lewak et al. (1990) hypothesized that the high Scale 9 scorer is protecting him- or herself against frustration and unhappiness associated with failure. They hypothesized that these individuals may have had parents with excessively high expectations, which led to internalized, anxious strivings. A significant Scale 9 elevation energizes behaviors, particularly those associated with other clinical scale elevations. For example, when the *Ma* scale is elevated with the *Pd* scale, acting out will occur with a possible antisocial focus. However, other scales, such as the *Hy* scale, need to be considered as the *Ma* scale "appears to play a role in determining both the frequency of acting out and the extent to which it will take an antisocial direction" (Nichols & Greene, 1995, p. 35). Specifically, the *Hy* scale, when elevated with the *Ma* scale, tends to augment the expression of social interest such as through the observance of social propriety and approval seeking.

Caldwell (1984) viewed Scale 9 elevations as reflecting the degree of fear of future frustrations, which leads to a diminished capacity to enjoy the here and now. The person cannot relax as his or her future depends on maintaining an increasing activity level in attempt to maintain his or her reward schedule or avoid deprivation or failure (Friedman, Webb, & Lewak, 1989).

The *Ma* scale content is heterogeneous and covers the classic features of a hypomanic syndrome, such as excitement, heightened activity levels, expansiveness, and overambitiousness or high aspirations (Butcher et al., 1989). Other items describe extraversion, moral attitudes, family relationships, and bodily concerns. The following items illustrate the content of Scale 9. The MMPI–2 item number precedes the item, and the scoring direction is in parentheses. See Table A.2 for a complete listing of Scale 9 items and the direction of scoring. The overlapping item content of Scale 9 is presented in Appendix C.

15. I work under a great deal of tension. (True)
21. At times I have very much wanted to leave home. (True)
23. At times I have fits of laughing and crying that I cannot control. (True)
55. I sometimes keep on at a thing until others lose their patience with me. (True)
85. At times I have a strong urge to do something harmful or shocking. (True)
100. I have never done anything dangerous for the thrill of it. (False)
154. I am afraid when I look down from a high place. (False)
169. When I get bored I like to stir up some excitement. (True)
263. I am always disgusted with the law when a criminal is freed through the arguments of a smart lawyer. (False)

Patients with only mild affective symptoms may be difficult to distinguish from ambitious, energetic normals. Therefore, it is important to observe periods of euphoria, increased irritability, and unproductive activity to assist in making an accurate diagnosis (Lachar, 1974). Nichols (1988) pointed out the importance of retesting individuals suspected of having an affective disorder as the variability in their mood state will influence their MMPI–2 profile. For example, a psychiatric inpatient may initially test without a Scale 9 elevation if he or she is depressed but, on later retesting, may show an elevated Scale 9 score suggestive of mood instability. Scale 9 does in fact figure prominently in code patterns associated with mood disorders, especially those with manic correlates. Code patterns 49/94, 69/96, and 89/98 all contribute to a diagnosis of mania (Nichols, 1988). The setting can often determine the diagnoses associated with MMPI–2 profiles. For example, Marks et al. (1974) classified approximately 70% of their female psychiatric inpatients with the 89/98 code pattern as psychotic (schizophrenic/mixed) and 17% of them were diagnosed as psychoneurotic (depressive reaction). Raskin and Novacek (1989) administered MMPIs and the Narcissistic Personality Inventory to undergraduate students. The highest scorers on the measure of narcissism were best represented by the 98/89 code pattern (with an average elevated *F* score of $T = 65$). This code pattern in a normal population appears to reflect narcissism and manic defenses rather than mania per se.

Low scores on Scale 9 reflect a low energy or activity level. Kunce and Anderson (1976, 1984) viewed zest as an underlying dimension of Scale 9. Therefore, low Scale 9 scores reflect a lack of vitality or even depression (Friedman, Webb, & Lewak, 1989). Low Scale 9 scorers may feel chronically tired, have trouble performing their work, or even be temporarily ill (Duckworth & Anderson, 1995). Low Scale 9 scorers are not likely to stir up excitement or be too talkative (Keiller & Graham, 1993). They may feel empty or depleted, and lack self-confidence and motivation (Lewak et al., 1990).

Dahlstrom et al. (1972) reported the correlates of Hathaway and Meehl's investigation of normal men and women. Sociability, energy, and openness appeared to be the major theme characterizing men, which is consistent with the optimism factor that McKinley and Hathaway (1944, as cited in Dahlstrom & Dahlstrom, 1980) described as a stable factor in normals. These men were further described as talkative, impulsive, adventurous, curious, generous, affectionate, and sentimental. Women were described similarly and were also seen as frank, courageous, idealistic, and possessing high energy as reflected by the adjectives *talkative*, *enthusiastic*, and *versatile*.

Butcher and Williams (1992) reported data from the couples rating study in the MMPI restandardization project (Butcher et al., 1989). Husbands of high Scale 9 scorers viewed their wives as wearing unusual clothes, talking too much, stirring up excitement, taking many risks, getting excited or happy for little reason, and telling people off. Wives viewed their high Scale 9 husbands as acting bossy, talking too much, whining and demanding attention, and taking drugs other than those prescribed by a doctor.

As Duckworth and Anderson (1995) noted, it is common to see peak Scale 9 (and Scale 5 in men) scores in college students. It is important to examine the elevation of Scale 9 in making an appropriate interpretation. When a person with a high score is generally well-adjusted, the appropriate descriptors for Scale 9 would be enthusiastic, eager, talkative, versatile, driven to be successful and involved, and friendly and happy. As scores increase, however, expect to see maladaptive hyperactivity and agitation.

Scores on Scale 9 tend to be related to age, with older individuals obtaining lower scores (reflecting lower energy and activity levels and more body concerns) and late-adolescent or younger participants, such as teenagers, tending to score in the upper normal to moderate range, which could be considered indicative of impulse control problems (Greene, 2000). Age should, therefore, be considered when examining Scale 9. Consistent results have not emerged regarding the effects of race on scale scores. But Gynther (1979) described various demographic effects on MMPI scales, and African Americans do appear to score higher than Whites, although not dramatically so.

Scale 9 did not lose any items in the restandardization project. However, seven items were changed; four items had sexist wording modified, two items were modernized, and one item had a grammatical clarification. Thirty-five of the 46 items are scored in the "true" direction, and 11 items are scored in the "false" direction. As the predominant deviant response to the items is "true," as it is for the other psychotic scales, an all true-response set would elevate Scale 9 with the other scales in the psychotic tetrad. Other than Scale 8, with which it shares 11 overlap items, Scale 9 shares few overlapping items relative to the other scales. Fifteen of the 46 items are unique to the scale. According to J. W. Little (1949, as cited in Dahlstrom et al., 1972), the highest biserial correlation for any item was .48 on the item "At times I have very much wanted to leave home" (MMPI–2 Item 21), with two other items tied with similar correlations of .45. These items were "I don't blame anyone for trying to grab everything they can get in this world" (MMPI–2 Item 227) and "I do not blame a person for taking advantage of people who leave themselves open to it" (MMPI–2 Item 248). It is likely that these low correlations reflect the heterogeneity of the scale (Dahlstrom et al., 1972).

It should be noted that an examination of the mean lexile values (lexile is a special index of reading difficulty and comprehension) for the basic scales shows Scale 9 to have the most difficult items to read and understand of all the clinical scales. For example, the Harris–Lingoes subscale Amorality (*Ma1*) has a reading level of about the ninth grade. Reading level requirements are discussed in chapter 4, but in general the MMPI–2 manual (Butcher et al., 1989) recommends an eighth grade reading level for taking the MMPI–2. According to Paolo, Ryan, and Smith (1991),

> for clinicians who are working with populations whose members possess average reading skills of eighth or ninth grade, the Hypomania (Ma) subscales, and possibly the Hypomania clinical scale itself, should be interpreted cautiously. At the very least, clinicians should determine whether individual patients are able to read and comprehend adequately the more difficult items on these scales. (p. 532).

Commercially available profile sheets provide for adding 0.2 *K* to Scale 9 as this value has been shown to increase the ability of the scale to make accurate diagnostic discriminations.

Internal consistency estimates (alphas) for MMPI–2 Scale 9 based on the restandardization sample (Butcher et al., 1989) are .58 for men and .60 for women. Test–retest correlation coefficients for Scale 9 in the restandardization sample over an interval of about 1 week were .83 for men and .68 for women. Test–retest correlation coefficients for MMPI Scale 9 for psychiatric cases with a 1- to 2-day interval between tests ranged from .71 to .81 and from .43 to .52 with a 1-year interval between tests (Dahlstrom et al., 1975). Hunsley et al.'s (1988) large-scale meta-analysis of MMPI reliability studies using a diversity of populations conducted between 1970 and 1981 reported an average internal consistency of .71 across 73 studies of Scale 9.

They also reported an average test-retest reliability of .65 for 17 studies with time intervals from 1 day to 2 years.

Harris–Lingoes Subscales

Harris and Lingoes developed four subscales for Scale 9: Amorality (*Ma1*), Psychomotor Acceleration (*Ma2*), Imperturbability (*Ma3*), and Ego Inflation (*Ma4*). The specific item composition of these subscales and the direction of scoring are listed in Table A.2; Table B.5 lists the linear *T*-score conversions for the raw-score values.

Amorality: Ma1 (6 Items)

This short six-item subscale has five items scored in the "true" direction. Caldwell (1988) believed that the scale is better named as Opportunism, given that high scorers on this subscale see others as selfish, dishonest, and opportunistic and feel justified to behave in a similar fashion. They also tend to derive vicarious gratification from the exploitative ways of others (Butcher et al., 1989). Nichols and Greene (1995) viewed *Ma1* as reflecting a kind of "thoughtless expediency" (p. 33) that can put others at a disadvantage and as a somewhat subtle measure of cynicism. According to Levitt (1989), high scorers believe that a person is foolish not to take every possible advantage of every situation and, as selfish people, see life as an endless series of minor skirmishes in which the person who is not overburdened with scruples is usually victorious.

Graham et al. (1999) reported the following information for high scorers ($T \geq 65$) on *Ma1* in their sample of psychiatric outpatients. Both men and women reported a history of alcohol abuse within the last 6 months preceding their intake interview; women patients were more likely to have an Axis I diagnosis (DSM III-R) of substance abuse or dependence and an Axis II diagnosis of antisocial personality disorder. During intake interviews, men with high scores were described as having an angry mood and their therapists indicated that they had tendencies to act out. This is consistent with their higher frequency of being physically abusive, committing domestic violence, and the greater likelihood of having a domestic violence conviction.

Low *Ma1* scorers (0 or a raw score of 1) may have moral values emphasizing individual responsibility and control over oneself (Caldwell, 1988) and may also reflect a lack of cynicism in the individual.

The following six items represent the entire *Ma1* content. The MMPI–2 item number precedes the item, with the scoring direction in parentheses:

131. When I was a child, I belonged to a group of friends that tried to be loyal through all kinds of trouble. (True)
227. I don't blame people for trying to grab everything they can get in this world. (True)
248. I do not blame a person for taking advantage of people who leave themselves open to it. (True)

250. At times I have been so entertained by the cleverness of some criminals that I have hoped that they would get away with it. (True)
263. I am always disgusted with the law when a criminal is freed through the arguments of a smart lawyer. (False)
269. If several people find themselves in trouble, the best thing for them to do is to agree upon a story and stick to it. (True)

Psychomotor Acceleration: Ma2 (11 Items)

Although the items in this subscale are manic in nature, they do not appear to reflect a negative tension state or unwanted arousal (Caldwell, 1988). The Wiggins (1966, 1969) *HYP* content scale is a better measure of excessive or undesired excitability. Although the behaviors implied by the items in this subscale are unusual in nature, the item content is not strongly suggestive of psychosis (Nichols & Greene, 1995). Generally, high scorers report accelerated speech, thought processes, and motor activities and may report tension, restlessness, and excitement (Butcher et al., 1989). High scorers are easily bored and may look for stimulation in order to change their mood state. Wrobel (1992) reported hyperactivity as a significant correlate for this subscale. Levitt (1989) viewed *Ma2* as a sensation-seeking measure, with high scorers having a high optimal stimulation level. These individuals may have a significant need for a variety of experiences. If Scale 9 is significantly elevated, it is likely that *Ma2* will also be elevated (Caldwell, 1988).

Graham et al. (1999) found in their sample of psychiatric outpatients that high scoring women on *Ma2* ($T \geq 65$) were more likely to have a diagnosis of borderline personality disorder. Male patients were more likely to report a history of being physically abusive and to have a history of committing domestic violence.

Low *Ma2* scores may reflect a slow, cautious pace or tempo and may be indicative of a low general level of excitement in one's life. Nichols and Greene (1995) suggested that a low *Ma2* score may indicate psychomotor retardation, whereas a low Scale 9 score, with an elevated *Ma2* score, may not report a loss of energy. Low *Ma2* scorers may also deny any tension or hyperactivity and not desire excitement. In fact, they may altogether avoid situations or activities involving risk or danger (Graham, 1990).

The following items illustrate the item content of *Ma2*. Nine of the 11 items are scored in the "true" direction, and 2 items are scored in the "false" direction:

15. I work under a great deal of tension. (True)
85. At times I have a strong urge to do something harmful or shocking. (True)
100. I have never done anything dangerous for the thrill of it. (False)
106. My speech is the same as always (not faster or slower, no slurring or hoarseness). (False)
122. At times my thoughts have raced ahead faster than I could speak them. (False)
169. When I get bored I like to stir up some excitement. (True)

Imperturbability: Ma3 (8 Items)

The items on this subscale suggest that one is not bothered by interruptions, distractions, and tensions (Caldwell, 1988), and a certain quality of imperviousness is reflected in the items (Nichols & Greene, 1995). *Ma3* could be considered as subtle in nature as seven of the eight items are scored on the *Ma-S* subscale. Five of the eight items are scored in the "false" direction. High *Ma3* scorers deny social anxiety in a manner similar to high *Hy1* (Denial of Social Anxiety) scorers (Levitt, 1989). High *Ma3* scores reflect a socially comfortable person who feels secure interacting with others with little concern about the opinions, values, and attitudes of others (Butcher et al., 1989). Extraversion appears to be related to high *Ma3* scores, although *Ma3* is not a direct measure of this factor. Nichols and Greene described the high *Ma3* scorer as not being afraid to be socially visible. They also saw *Ma3* as reflecting dispassion ("cool") and composure under difficult social stresses. Successful individuals may elevate this scale. Caldwell (1988) said that "Ma3 is often the predominant subscale in controlled striving and performance-oriented patterns such as a relatively unelevated code 39/93 with K up" (p. 32). Likewise, the Graham et al. (1999) investigation of MMPI–2 correlates in a psychiatric outpatient population failed to identify pathological correlates for elevated *Ma3* scores.

Low scores may reflect an impatience at being interrupted or distracted and a self-conscious hesitation in groups (Caldwell, 1988). Low scorers often feel uncomfortable in the presence of others and are easily influenced by people's opinions, values, and attitudes. Levitt (1989) viewed low scores as reflecting anxious, shy, easy-to-embarrass individuals who are uncomfortable in social situations.

The following items illustrate the item content of *Ma3*. The MMPI–2 item number precedes the item, and the scoring direction is in parentheses:

93. Sometimes when I am not feeling well I am irritable. (False)
136. It makes me impatient to have people ask my advice or otherwise interrupt me when I am on something important. (False)
167. I find it hard to make talk when I meet new people. (False)
220. I never worry about my looks. (True)

Ego Inflation: Ma4 (9 Items)

The nine items of this relatively short subscale are all scored in the "true" direction; therefore, a "true" response bias could inflate this subscale. This subscale reflects the grandiosity so typical of the manic or hypomanic individual, and high scorers usually have unrealistic appraisals of their own abilities and self-worth. They tend to become resentful when people make demands on them (Butcher et al., 1989) or are bossy toward them. The items on this subscale appear to suggest anger when one's importance is not appreciated and there is an underlying theme of "willful stubbornness" (Caldwell, 1988, p. 33). Nichols and Greene (1995) reported that *Ma4* reflects a quality of willfulness and bravado and often the individual appears to be defending him- or herself against passivity and dependency by behaving in a counterdependent or countersubmissive fashion (e.g., asserting dominance in an overt fashion). High *Ma4* scores also connote a sense of superiority and contempt for others. Graham et al. (1999) found that female psychiatric outpatients with high scores on *Ma4* ($T \geq 65$) were viewed as sociopathic by their therapists with narcissistic and histrionic features. Difficult to motivate, they were described as easily bored and impatient.

Low scores reflect interpersonal submissiveness with a willingness to accept arbitrary treatment from others. A low *Ma4* score, coupled with an elevated *Sc2* (Emotional Alienation) score, suggests apathy and psychological impotence (Nichols & Greene, 1995). The low scorer is more likely to show a willingness to tolerate domineering behavior in others. There is also a certain modesty regarding their self-importance, making it easier for them to accept orders without objection (Caldwell, 1988). Low *Ma4* scores may reflect an individual who is also very self-critical (Graham, 1990).

The following items are examples of the *Ma4* content. The MMPI–2 item number precedes the item, and the scoring direction is in parentheses.

50. I have often had to take orders from someone who did not know as much as I did. (True)
55. I sometimes keep on at things until others lose their patience with me. (True)
61. I am an important person. (True)
98. Some people are so bossy that I feel like doing the opposite of what they request, even though I know they are right. (True)
190. My people treat me more like a child than a grownup. (True)
211. I have been inspired to a program of life based on duty which I have since carefully followed. (True)

Scale 9: Subtle–Obvious Subscales

Wiener and Harmon (1946) developed Subtle and Obvious subscales for Scale 9 in the MMPI. The MMPI–2 Hypomania–Obvious subscale (*Ma-O*) has 23 items, of which 20 items are scored in the "true" direction and 3 items are scored in the "false" direction. The Hypomania–Subtle subscale (*Ma-S*) also consists of 23 items, of which 15 items are scored in the "true" direction and 8 items are scored in the "false" direction. The following items are examples of the subtle–obvious items on Scale 9, with the scoring direction and obvious or subtle distinction in parentheses; the MMPI–2 item number precedes the item. See Table A.2 for a listing of the subtle–obvious items and the scoring direction for each subscale. The linear *T*-score conversions for the Wiener–Harmon subscales for men and women is presented in Table B.6.

15. I work under a great deal of tension. (True–Obvious)

23. At times I have fits of laughing and crying that I cannot control. (True–Obvious)
100. I have never done anything dangerous for the thrill of it. (False–Obvious)
106. My speech is the same as always (not faster or slower, no slurring or hoarseness). (False–Subtle)
113. I know who is responsible for most of my troubles. (True–Subtle)
169. When I get bored I like to stir up some excitement. (True–Subtle)
263. I am always disgusted with the law when a criminal is freed through the arguments of a smart lawyer. (False–Subtle)

The majority of obvious items on the *Ma-O* subscale pertain to episodes of intense excitement and periods of great restlessness, with excitement, impulse pressures, and vigilance predominating (Caldwell, 1988). Hollrah et al. (1995) reviewed the research of Wrobel and Lachar (1982), which examined the correlates for the Subtle and Obvious subscales. The *Ma-O* subscale correlated positively with the factors labeled Discomfort and Sociopathy, although discomfort was a less than optimal scale descriptor, as it correlated with all of the obvious subscales. Nevertheless, the description of the *Ma-O* item content given by Caldwell is consistent with the finding of Discomfort and, to a lesser extent, with Sociopathy. Clearly, other MMPI–2 measures, such as Antisocial Practices (*ASP*), Cynicism (*CYN*) (Butcher et al., 1989), and Antisocial Attitudes (*ASP1*; Ben-Porath & Sherwood, 1993; see chap. 7), should be examined to help establish the presence of sociopathy.

Dahlstrom (1991) examined the correlates of the Subtle and Obvious subscales derived from partner ratings on the Katz Adjustment Scales used in the MMPI–2 restandardization (Butcher et al., 1989). For both men and women, the following descriptors emerged as significant for high *Ma-O* scorers: nervous, does not go to religious functions, moody, and does not show sound judgment. For men only, the following descriptors were given: takes nonprescription drugs, whines and demands attention, prone to temper tantrums, suspicious of others, swears and curses, not pleasant and relaxed, upset by small unexpected events, talks back, acts without thinking, and is not thoughtful of others. For women only, the following descriptors were given: restless, has many fears, does strange things, has bad dreams, lacks emotional control, gets excited or happy for no reason, worries about the future, not helpful or constructive, talks too much, bored and restless, takes too many risks, cries easily, wears strange clothes, gives up too easily, and tells others off about their faults.

Low *Ma-O* scorers suggest a constrained sense of self-importance, an absence or careful avoidance of intense excitement in one's life, and possibly a strict but integrated individual conscience (Caldwell, 1988).

Although some of the *Ma-S* items clearly reflect hypomania (e.g., "When I get bored I like to stir up some excitement"), other items indicating a denial of anxiety (mostly occurring on *Ma3*) appear to be more subtle in nature (Caldwell, 1988). Examples of such items include "I never worry about my looks" (scored as "true"), and "I find it hard to make talk when I meet new people" (scored as "false"). The variety in the content of the *Ma-S* subscale makes it difficult to summarize, but Caldwell (1988) stated that much of the content relates to a "heightened level of arousability and interpersonal assertiveness that is similar to but less disruptive than *Ma-O*" (p. 31)

Hollrah et al. (1995), in a thorough review of the validity of the subtle items in the MMPI, stated that of all the subtle subscales the *Ma-S* subscale showed the best validity: "Ma-S was consistently related to scale-appropriate external measures and occasionally had more validity than Ma-full and Ma-O" (p. 293). He suggested that the convergent validity of the *Ma-S* subscale is due to the subtle items obvious relationship to hypomania.

Dahlstrom (1991) derived the following correlates for the *Ma-S* subscale for both men and women from the partner ratings made in the MMPI–2 restandardization sample: not shy, talks too much, makes big plans, talks back, tells others off about their faults, stubborn, gets excited or happy for no reason, takes too many risks, and gives advice too freely. For men only, the following correlates were derived: bossy, craves attention, does not lack energy, does strange things, has temper tantrums, reports bad dreams, resents being told what to do, apathetic about others' feelings, does the opposite of what is asked, takes nonprescription drugs, has been arrested or had trouble with the law, likes to flirt, acts without thinking, stirs up excitement, expresses a belief in strange things, whines and demands attention, laughs and jokes with others, volunteers for projects, and enjoys parties and friends. For women only, the following correlates were derived: wears strange clothes, tries too hard, resents being told what to do, does not avoid contact with others, does not show sound judgment, stirs up excitement, brags too much, threatens to harm others, and takes advantage of others.

A low *Ma-S* score suggests a high level of interpersonal constraint and social caution consistent with a slow personal pace (Caldwell, 1988).

SCALE 0: SOCIAL INTROVERSION (*Si*)

The original 70-item Social Introversion scale was designed to evaluate an individual's degree of introversion–extraversion (Drake, 1946). The *Si* scale is the only clinical scale in the MMPI for which the criterion group was composed of a nonpsychiatric (normal) sample. Its construction was motivated by the use of a test being routinely administered in the guidance program at the University of Wisconsin. This test, developed by C. Evans and McConnell (1941), was designated as the Minnesota T-S-E (Thinking–Social–Emotional) Inventory. Evans and McConnell separated the character traits of introversion-extraversion into areas of thinking, social activity, and emotional expression. An individual could be considered as introverted or extraverted in any of these three areas. Because the MMPI was also part of the standard battery of tests being administered to students, Drake decided to devise a scale measuring social introversion from the MMPI that would produce data similar to the T-S-E Inventory. Two criterion groups were selected. The first group consisted of 50 female students ranking at the

65th percentile or higher on the social introversion–extraversion dimension of the T-S-E Inventory; the second group consisted of 50 female students who scored below the 35th percentile.[5] Three participants scoring high on the *L* scale of the MMPI were excluded from the criterion groups. Although the scale was constructed with all of the female students, it was later validated with men. Because men and women scored so similarly, Drake combined them as a single group for purposes of establishing the norms. The items in the MMPI pool that differentiated these two groups (after removing items with very high or very low endorsement frequencies in either or both groups) became the 70-item Social I.E. scale (Drake, 1946), later known as Scale 0 on the MMPI.

After the 70 items were identified that discriminated the two criterion groups, a new group of MMPI record sheets were scored with the new scoring key for social introversion–extraversion. As Drake (1946, as cited in Dahlstrom & Dahlstrom, 1980) noted, "these MMPI record sheets contain the responses of a group of students who had cleared through the testing office after the group of students who provided the data for the item analyses" (p. 77). The scores were then correlated with the Social I.E. scores obtained on the T-S-E Inventory and yielded a correlation coefficient of –.72 for a sample of 87 female students and –.71 for a sample of 81 male students. The correlation coefficients yielded negative values because a low score on the T-S-E Inventory indicates introversion, whereas a high score on the MMPI/MMPI–2 indicates introversion.

Norms were reported in terms of linear *T* scores and were based on the test records of 193 male students and 350 female students. As stated previously, men's and women's scores were so similar that the norms were combined for both genders (Drake, 1946). In a subsequent study, Drake and Thiede (1948) obtained additional cross-validation for Scale 0 by examining the level of high school and college activity participation in a sample of 594 female college students. Students tending to participate in more activities scored higher on extraversion, whereas those with lower activity participation scored higher on introversion. The developers of the Minnesota T-S-E Inventory conceptualized social introversion as indicating a withdrawal from social responsibilities and contacts, with little real interest in people, and social extraversion as involving an interest in social contact, with a strong interest in others (Dahlstrom et al., 1972). The final *Si* scale may be limited by any of the biases inherent in the T-S-E Inventory because the criterion groups of social introverts and extraverts were derived from scores on the Social I.E. scale (Dahlstrom et al., 1972).

Elevated scores on Scale 0 ($T > 50$) indicate introversion tendencies, whereas scores below a *T* score of 50 indicate extraversion tendencies. The item content of the scale broadly reflects a dimension of introversion–extraversion that emerges as a primary dimension from statistical studies of the MMPI (Friedman, 1982; Gentry et al., 1985; Wakefield et al., 1975). The items reflect uneasiness in social situations; feelings of inferiority and discomfort; unhappiness, shyness, and hypersensitivity. Two broad content domains of Scale 0 have been identified as shyness and self-consciousness, which is the Subjective aspect of introversion, and social avoidance, the objective or socially visible part of introversion (Nichols &

Greene, 1995). As described in the Scale 5 section of this chapter, Graham et al. (1971) factor analyzed the responses to Scale 0 (and Scale 5) from 422 psychiatric inpatients, outpatients, and normals. They identified seven Scale 0 factors, of which six were used by Serkownek (1975) to construct subscales for Scale 0 (and Scale 5). The seventh factor, Demographic Variables, was not used to construct a subscale. The Scale 0 subscales were named Inferiority–Personal Discomfort (*Si1*), Discomfort With Others (*Si2*), Staid–Personal Rigidity (*Si3*), Hypersensitivity (*Si4*), Distrust (*Si5*), and Physical–Somatic Concerns (*Si6*). As Greene (1991a) pointed out, clinicians can continue to use the Serkownek (1975) subscales on the MMPI–2 as only 1 item has been dropped from Scale 0, which reduced *Si2* from 14 to 13 items. Graham (1987) reported test–retest reliability coefficients for men and women (over a 6-week interval) provided by Moreland (1985). For men, on all of the Serkownek subscales, the coefficients range from .68 to .89, with an average of .77. For women, the range is from .63 to .87, with an average of .76. C. L. Williams (1983) reported 1-week test–retest reliabilities for *Si* subscales averaging .84 for women and .68 for men.

In a large-scale study, Foerstner (1986) investigated the interrelationships among the 63 MMPI subscales developed by Serkownek (1975), Harris and Lingoes (1955), Wiggins (1966), and Wiener and Harmon (1946). (Note that neither Harris and Lingoes, nor Wiener and Harmon developed subscales for Scale 0 or Scale 5.) Nine hundred MMPIs from male and female psychiatric inpatients, chemical-dependent residents, and private practice outpatients were analyzed by Foerstner. Ten factors were identified that accounted for 75.5% of the total variance. *Si4* (Hypersensitivity) loaded on the first factor, Depression (.67), as did *Si1* (Inferiority–Personal Discomfort; .65) and *Si5* (Distrust; .44). *Si3* (Staid–Personal Rigidity) loaded negatively on the factor named Social Introversion. *Si1* also loaded on the third factor, Agitated Hostility (.64). *Si5* loaded on the factor Cynical Distrust (.63). It is clear from the data in Foerstner's investigation that Scale 0 (like Scale 5) is multifactorial and that maladjustment is a major component of the scale. A Scale 0 score, whether high or low, may be achieved by item endorsements affecting any of a combination of at least six factors (Wong, 1984). In contrast to the nonpathological correlates for the Serkownek *Mf* subscales, the *Si* subscales, with the exception of *Si3*, appear pathology related.

More recently, Ben-Porath, Hostetler, Butcher, and Graham (1989) developed three new content-homogeneous subscales for the MMPI–2 *Si* scale. They used a multistage approach involving a series of empirical and rational procedures to develop the subscales. These subscales—named Shyness/Self-Consciousness (*Si1*), Social Avoidance (*Si2*), and Self–Other Alienation (*Si3*)—were developed with data provided by college students. Data analysis with this and the MMPI–2 normative sample demonstrated that these new measures combined to contribute to the assessment of nearly 90% of the variance in the full Si scale. Validation of these MMPI–2 *Si* subscales was provided by the results of Sieber and Meyers (1992). These investigators compared results on the Si subscales against self-report measures of constructs that were believed to be differentially related to the three subscales. They stated that:

> specifically, measures of self-esteem, public self-consciousness, social anxiety, and shyness were expected to correlate with Si1; measures of self-esteem, public self-consciousness, social anxiety, and social avoidance were expected to correlate with Si2; finally, measures of self-esteem, alienation, anomia, loss of control, and personal and social identity were expected to correlate with Si3. (Sieber & Meyers, 1992, p. 185)

These hypotheses were generally supported by the data. It appears that elevated *Si1* scores reflect shyness around others, uneasiness in social surroundings, and discomfort in unfamiliar situations. High *Si*2 scores appear to reflect an active avoidance of others, a dislike of group situations, and an aversion to social events. High *Si*3 scorers appear to have low self-esteem, a lack of interest in activities, low self-confidence, and to not feel in control of their life outcomes.

Most recently, Ward and Perry (1998) investigated the *Si* subscales and found that, as in previous research, the three *Si* subscales accounted well for variance in *Si* scores in clinical samples. *Si3* items were found to be less obvious indicators of social introversion as compared with *Si1* and *Si2* items; *Si3* appears to be more of a measure of the general maladjustment factor of the MMPI–2. Ward and Perry cautioned users of the *Si* subscales to recognize that *Si1* and *Si2* are purer measurements of the social introversion construct and are not reflective of negative emotionality. In fact, they pointed out that the item content of *Si1* and *Si2* is virtually the same as that from the *SOD* content scale. Table A.2 lists the composition and scoring direction for the *Si* subscales; Table B.8 provides the raw-score-to-*T*-score conversions.

Although Scale 0 lost only one item in the revision of the MMPI–2, six items were modified to modernize idioms and usage of words, improve grammatical clarification, simplify wording in the items. There is a fairly even balance of "true" and "false" scoring for this scale, with 34 of the 69 items scored in the "true" direction and 35 items scored in the "false" direction. For both men and women the assignment of 1 raw point increases a person's score in the direction of introversion. In other words, the higher one's raw score, the more introverted one tends to be.

The following items represent the broad content of Scale 0. The MMPI–2 item number precedes each item, and the scoring direction is in parentheses. Table A.2 lists the complete item composition and direction for scoring of Scale 0.

25. I would like to be a singer. (False)
49. I am a very sociable person. (False)
56. I wish I could be as happy as others seem to be. (True)
79. I do not mind being made fun of. (False)
100. I have never done anything dangerous for the thrill of it. (True)
135. I have often lost out on things because I couldn't make up my mind soon enough. (True)
161. I frequently have to fight against showing that I am bashful. (True)
207. I would like to belong to several clubs. (False)

Scale 0 has proportionately fewer overlapping items than any other validity or clinical scale (Greene, 2000; 1991a). Forty-three of the items on the scale overlap other scales, with the *Pd* and *Mf* scales sharing the most items with the *Si* scale (11 and 9 items, respectively). The *L* and *F* scales share no items in common with Scale 0. Twenty-six of the items are non-overlapping items. It should be noted that, like Scale 5, Scale 0 uses linear, rather than uniform, *T* scores. Appendix C provides a table listing the overlapping item content of Scale 0.

Many researchers and clinicians believe strong constitutional and biological factors contribute to the introversion–extraversion dimension of personality (e.g., Eysenck, 1967; Meyer, 1983; Wakefield, Wood, Wallace, & Friedman, 1978). The stability of scores on this scale over time seem to reflect this biological and/or constitutional component. Test–retest correlation coefficients support this contention, with generally high test–retest coefficients for the scale. For psychiatric patients, the coefficients range from .80 to .88 for a 1- to 2-week interval between MMPI administrations and from .63 to .64 for a 1-year interval between tests (Dahlstrom et al., 1975). In Hunsley et al.'s (1988) large-scale meta-analysis of MMPI reliability studies using a wide variety of populations conducted between 1970 and 1981, an average test–retest reliability of .86 for 16 studies with time intervals from 1 day to 2 years was reported. More recently test–retest reliability data were reported for the MMPI–2 scales over about a 1-week interval (Butcher et al., 1989). Scale 0 test–retest correlation coefficients were .92 for men and .91 for women, and were the highest correlation coefficients reported for any of the validity or clinical scales.

In the Hunsley et al. (1988) meta-analysis study of the MMPI, an average internal consistency of .81 across 41 studies of Scale 0 was reported. The *MMPI–2 Manual* (Butcher et al., 1989) reports internal consistency estimates (coefficient alpha) of .82 and .84 for men and women, respectively, on Scale 0.

Scale 0 reflects how comfortable an individual is around other people. High scores (introversion) reflect a preference for being alone, whereas low scores (extraversion) reveal a preference for being with others (Drake & Thiede, 1948; Duckworth & Anderson, 1995; Friedman, Webb, & Lewak, 1989). It is important to examine other clinical scales when Scale 0 is high or low because Scale 0 can operate as an activator or inhibitor for certain behaviors. For example, a high Scale 8 score will indicate more social isolation and communication problems when Scale 0 is also elevated. A very low Scale 0 score will accentuate the impulsivity often seen in high Scale 4 scorers and indicate a superficiality and shallowness in relationships. Individuals with impoverished social relations, as is often seen in schizoid or certain other personality disorders, tend to elevate Scale 0. Lewak et al. (1990) stated that elevated *Si* scores

> may reflect a childhood characterized by an absence of warmth and physical contact from others. Elevated scores suggest that these people have extinguished their feeling response to physical touch and affection. They suffer from a form of "affect hunger" and yet, they feel conflicted about close, intimate relationships. (p. 273)

Lewak et al. also suggested that low *Si* scores reflect more than just social extraversion. Rather, a low score ($T < 40$) suggests an intense need for social stimulation driven more by insecurity than a proclivity for intense social experiences.

Hathaway and Meehl (as cited in Dahlstrom et al., 1972), examined the descriptions of high Scale 0 scorers. Men were described by their acquaintances with only one typical adjective, modest. Dahlstrom et al. suggested that perhaps the introverted personality style of these men made it difficult for others to get to know them and, therefore, characterize them more fully. In contrast, women scoring high on the *Si* scale were described as modest, shy, self-effacing, and sensitive. They showed emotional warmth and had home and family interests. Dahlstrom et al. made the important point that the personality styles of these individuals appear to reflect the basic preference for a style of life in keeping with their emotional needs, rather than individuals who are inhibited or thwarted in their efforts to have broader social contacts.

Dahlstrom et al. (1972) also presented the research descriptions of high- and low-scoring men on Scale 0 provided by Gough et al. (1955). More maladjustment appears inherent in the following description as compared with the Hathaway and Meehl (as cited in Dahlstrom et al., 1972) depiction of the introvert:

> The high 0 men were described as slow in personal tempo, stereotyped, and lacking originality in approach to problems. The implication seems to be that these men showed such qualities as part of a general insecurity. They were also described as unable to make decisions without vacillation, hesitation, or delay. They were seen as rigid and inflexible in thought and action, as overly controlled and inhibited, and as lacking confidence in their own abilities. They were conforming and followed prescribed methods in the things they did. They became fussy and pedantic in even minor matters.
>
> In their relations with others, they were seen as lacking poise and social presence, as becoming rattled and upset in a social situation. Perhaps as a consequence, these men were rated as cold and distant. They were not affected in this aloofness, but appeared free of pretense and conscientiousness and dependable in their responsibilities. They seemed to derive personal reward and pleasure from their work and placed a high value on productive achievement for its own sake. Toward authority, these men were submissive, compliant, and overly accepting. They tended to sidestep as a way of handling troublesome situations. They either made concessions to avoid unpleasantness or passively resisted pressures by not getting involved in things. They were generally permissive and accepting, however, in their relations with others, respecting other people, and not making judgments. As a result, these high 0 men kept out of trouble and showed socially appropriate behavior. They get along well in the world as it is. (p. 228)

Low-scoring men (extraverts) in the normal group examined by Hathaway and Meehl (as cited in Dahlstrom et al., 1972) were described as versatile and sociable, whereas low-scoring women, also described as mixing well with others, were also seen as enthusiastic, talkative, assertive, and adventurous. Gough et al. (1955, as cited in Dahlstrom et al., 1972) described men scoring low on Scale 0 in more unfavorable terms than did Hathaway and Meehl. Although male low scorers were seen as expressive and colorful, they were also described as ostentatious and exhibitionistic. They focused on success as a means for achieving status and power. Competitive and vigorous, they were dominant in relation to others. They could be opportunistic in that they viewed others only in terms of what they could get from them, rather than being sensitive to their feelings. Self-indulgent and unable to delay gratification, they were often impulsive, acting without sufficient deliberation. Their actions could easily stimulate hostility and resentment around them. Chapter 6 further elaborates on these descriptions of high and low scorers on Scale 0.

NOTES

[1]As Ward (1994) pointed out, the *T*-score cutoff of 30 truncates the distributions of positive traits and clinical populations. Ward made the valid point that although the MMPI–2 is basically a measure of psychopathology and is therefore sensitive to the presence of psychiatric symptoms and maladaptive personality traits, there are a few MMPI–2 supplementary scales that measure *positive* personality attributes, such as the Dominance scale, the Social Responsibility scale, and the Ego Strength scale (Butcher et al., 1989). Additionally, two new scales, the Gender Role–Masculine and Gender Role–Feminine, were designed to measure aspects of gender role. Because conversion tables in the MMPI–2 manual limit scores to 2 *SD*s below the mean (no lower than 30), Ward (1994) stated that a *T* score of 30 will be automatically assigned to any raw score that is more than 2 *SD*s below the mean. Although this is unlikely to be important with the clinical scales (except for Scale 5), the positive attribute scales named above may be better interpreted when they are very low by using the more accurate *T*-score table constructed by Ward and presented in Table B.15.

[2]Krishnamurthy et al. (1995) recently discussed the psychometric problem that poses substantial interpretative limitations for two of the Harris–Lingoes subscales. Specifically, *Hy1* (Denial of Social Anxiety) and *Pd3* (Social Imperturbability) are short subscales consisting of six items each with relatively high-mean raw-score values in the MMPI–2 normative sample. Consequently, as reflected in the normative table in the MMPI–2 table, it is not possible for an individual (male or female) to produce a *T* score greater than 61 on the *Hy1* subscale or for a man to score higher than a *T* score of 64. Likewise, a woman cannot score higher than 65 on the *Pd3* subscale. Krishnamurthy et al. correctly concluded that using a cutoff score of $T = 65$ for interpreting all of the Harris–Lingoes subscales will therefore eliminate the possibility of interpreting these particular subscales which cannot elevate beyond a *T* score of 65. Krishnamuthy et al. (1995) recommended dropping these two subscales from standard use because they are vulnerable to misinterpretation. Although we agree that the *Hy1* and *Pd3* subscales are susceptible to misinterpretation, the clinician can still use these subscales by carefully examining the raw-score values.

[3]It appears that in several studies, the overlapping item content of the MMPI relates to the personality dimensions of psychoticism and neuroticism. However, until recently no researcher had used clinical criterion groups to test the hypothesis that the overlapping items could differentiate psychotic and neurotic participants (Friedman et al., 1983; Gentry et al., 1985; Wiederstein, 1986). The implications of such a study go beyond methodological interest. The MMPI has been considered by many as generally unsuccessful in distinguishing between different categories of abnormality beyond the grossest levels (Rodgers, 1972; Wheeler, Little, & Lehner, 1951). Possibly, as Wakefield, Bradley, Doughtie, and Kraft (1975) suggested, the mixture of overlapping items measuring more general personality characteristics and

nonoverlapping items purportedly measuring more specific traits within a type category may impede the differential diagnostic effectiveness of the test.

Following the suggestions made by H. E. Anderson and Bashaw (1966) and Wakefield et al. (1975) that items common to two or more scales measure common dimensions, Friedman et al. (1983) developed three new scales for the purpose of differentiating groups of neurotic, psychotic, and normal individuals. These scales are collectively referred to as the Friedman Overlap scales (FOS). The individual scales are named the Psychotic Overlap scale (POS), the Neurotic Overlap scale (NOS), and the Maladjustment Overlap scale (MOS). These scales were derived in a rational manner, and the *L*, *F*, *K*, *Si*, *Pd*, and *Mf* scales were excluded from consideration in the construction of these new scales. Items that are scored on the traditional psychotic scales (*Pa*, *Sc*, and *Ma*) were counted as items on the POS if they occurred on at least two scales within the psychotic triad and did not occur on any of the neurotic scales (*Hs*, *D*, *Hy*, and *Pt*). This produced 18 items that are scored on the POS. Similarly, the NOS consists of items occurring on at least two scales within the traditional neurotic triad (*Hs*, *D*, *Hy*) plus the *Pt* scale and on none of the psychotic scales. This produced 30 items that are scored on the NOS. A third scale, the MOS, was developed for purposes of discriminating normals from psychotic and neurotic patients. This consists of 35 items occurring on at least one neurotic and one psychotic scale. All 83 items on the FOS were scored in the standard critical direction and were included only if they were scored in the same direction on the relevant scales.

Friedman et al. (1983) hypothesized that the NOS and the POS would discriminate normals from neurotic and psychotic individuals, and neurotic and psychotic individuals from each other. MMPI data from four groups of participants were studied. Group 1 consisted of 101 patients hospitalized in the psychiatric unit at Ohio State University Hospital with functional psychotic diagnoses (45 men, 56 women). Group 2 consisted of 85 patients with neurotic diagnoses (30 men, 55 women) from the same patient population. Group 3 consisted of 76 outpatients receiving treatment at the Mayo Clinic in Rochester, Minnesota, for strictly medical (nonpsychiatric) problems (37 men, 39 women). Group 4 consisted of 38 college students taking introductory psychology classes at a technical institute in a large Midwestern city (12 men, 26 women).

Discriminant analyses of the criterion groups were performed separately for the MMPI and the FOS. The standard MMPI (566 items) correctly classified 62% of both the neurotic and psychotic participants, whereas the shorter FOS (83 items) correctly classified 54% of the neurotic participants and 52% of the psychotic participants.

The MMPI and the FOS were equally effective in correctly classifying 88% of the normal controls. It appears that based on this study and others (e.g., Gentry et al., 1985; Wiederstein, 1986) that the POS and the NOS appear to measure the general constructs of psychoticism and neuroticism. However, further research in a clinical setting is needed before they can be considered useful for differential diagnosis.

The clinician should be cognizant that the overlapping content appears to represent more than just a methodological artifact associated with the empirical criterion group construction strategy; rather, the overlapping items, especially as they pertain to the dimensions of psychoticism and neuroticism, represent valid factors common to the scales.

[4]*Mf2*, *Mf4*, and *Mf5* lost only two, one, and one items, respectively, in the revision of the MMPI–2, thereby leaving the Serkownek subscales essentially intact and available for use. Although the Serkownek subscales could still be scored in the MMPI–2, psychometric and methodological concerns led the restandardization committee to not include them in the MMPI–2. Graham (1993) provided the following rationale for not recommending the use of the Serkownek subscales in the MMPI–2:

> One major concern about Serkownek's Scale 5 subscales was that the factor analysis on which they were based may have had methodological problems. Graham et al. (1971) combined male

> and female data in their analysis, and this could have produced artificially the masculine interest and feminine interests factors. Another concern was that some of the items in the Serkownek subscales were scored in the opposite direction from the parent scales. Finally, for women, the raw scores on the Scale 5 subscales were transformed to T-scores in the opposite direction from the parent scale. High raw scores on Scale 5 subscales yielded high T-scores, whereas for Scale 5 itself, higher raw scores yield lower T-scores. (p. 117)

[5]The female students were studied in 1944 and 1945, and men were not included in further validation studies because of the danger that the war would most likely have left an extremely biased and atypical male sample on college campuses (Drake & Thiede, 1948).

4

Administration and Scoring

FORMS OF THE MMPI–2

The most commonly used version of the MMPI–2 is the printed booklet form, which appears in either softbound or hardcover form, and which consist of 567 items. Both the softbound and hardcover booklets are reusable and are commonly used for individual or group administrations. The hardcover booklet is more commonly used for laptop administration when hard surfaces such as a desk are not available. Whereas the softcover booklet requires a separate answer sheet, the hardcover booklet uses an answer sheet that is inserted over two pegs at the back of the book and follows a step-down format whereby each consecutive page reveals another column of answer spaces matched with the booklet column of corresponding questions. The columns use alternating colors of purple and black to assist the reader in matching the answer sheet to the appropriate page in the booklet. Because the step-down format reveals only one column of questions and answer spaces, the likelihood of misplacing a response to a specific question is reduced. This is especially useful when testing confused patients or individuals unaccustomed to taking tests. The order of the items are the same in the softcover and hardcover booklets, which was not the case with the original MMPI forms (see Friedman, Webb, & Lewak, 1989). Separate sets of templates are needed for hand scoring both of these forms of the MMPI–2. Note, however, that the answer sheets for the soft- and hardcover forms are not interchangeable for hand-scoring purposes. The MMPI–2 is available in Spanish in both the softcover and audiotape forms but not in the hardbound booklet version.

The audiotape version of the MMPI–2, available in English and Spanish, is intended for individuals with visual impairment, reading difficulties, and physical handicaps (a proctor can record the responses, if necessary).[1] In a group administration, headphones and separate tape machines are recommended to prevent noise distraction and to allow an individual to replay unanswered items at a later time. It is also important to ensure that the participant is taught how to operate the tape machine in order to stop it, for whatever reason, or to return to a previous item. Careful proctoring should be conducted in situations in which individuals (e.g., adolescents) are listening to the MMPI–2 audiotape with headphones. In one instance, a Social Security disability applicant being administered the MMPI–2 audiotape (with headphones) replaced the MMPI–2 cassette with a music tape, which the applicant found much more entertaining!

Computer-based administrations are common today, and administration time varies between 1 hr to 1 hr and 15 min. As for the printed forms, screening for readability by selecting sample items is suggested. One major advantage to a computer-administered MMPI–2 is the ease of scoring and efficiency, although not all participants are comfortable with this type of administration. Spinhoven, Labbe, and Rombouts (1993) reported that although most patients feel favorable about using a computer in a clinical setting, little research has been conducted to assess patient characteristics that could pose potential difficulties in computerized assessments. They suggested conducting a precomputer assessment interview to learn how a participant feels about interacting with a computer because this may have particular importance, for example, in a case of a psychotic patient with delusions about thought insertions or broadcasting.

In general, clinicians' attitudes toward computer-based testing are quite positive (Spielberger & Piotrowski, 1990), although some questions about the comparability between computer and booklet administrations have been raised. The results suggest that mean scale scores may be slightly lower when using a computerized administration. Although the differences generally are small, some authors have suggested a need for separate norms and profile sheets for computer-administered protocols (Watson et al., 1990; Watson, Thomas, & Anderson, 1992). More research is needed with varied populations, however, before implementing these suggestions. More recently, there has been interest in computerized adaptive testing, which involves the application of the countdown method to reduce the number of administered MMPI/MMPI–2 items in order to save administration time. This technique involves the presentation of scale items until the participant endorses a predetermined number that indicates that he or she is either elevated or not elevated on a particular scale. Although preliminary in nature, several studies have shown that adaptive testing may have promise in the future (e.g., Ben-Porath, Slutske, & Butcher, 1989; Butcher, Keller, & Bacon, 1985; Clavelle & Butcher, 1977; Roper, Ben-Porath, & Butcher, 1991; see chap. 10 for a discussion on computer-generated psychological reports.)

ABBREVIATED AND SHORT FORMS

Because the full-length MMPI/MMPI–2 can take up to 2 hours or longer to complete, some test users have considered the length of the test prohibitive for practical application, especially with physically disabled or easily fatigued participants. The term *abbreviated form* refers to administering the first 370 items of the MMPI–2 or the first 399 items in the original MMPI in order to score all of the standard validity and clinical scales. Abbreviating the MMPI–2 to the first 370 items can reduce the test-taking time, on average, from 20 to 40 min. Abbreviating the test administration in this fashion may be indicated when an elderly or enfeebled participant is physically unable to complete a longer sitting or becomes less cooperative over the course of the testing. Likewise, a poor reader may struggle for an excessive length of time over a test booklet before completing all of the items. A major disadvantage in eliminating the remaining items, however, is that many of the supplementary and new MMPI–2 content scale items occur later in the booklet. It is recommended, whenever possible, that the individual complete the entire inventory, even if this requires multiple sittings, unless obvious reasons contraindicate such an effort.

Short forms of the test refer to reduced sets of items on different scales that are thought to be a valid substitute for full-scale scores. Most short forms were developed with the original MMPI rather than MMPI–2. At least 14 short forms were developed with the original MMPI (Butcher & Hostetler, 1990), but no effort was made by the MMPI restandardization committee (Butcher et al., 1989) to preserve any of the MMPI short forms in the MMPI–2.[2] Butcher and Hostetler concluded that short forms for the MMPI–2 were inadequate measures of the constructs assessed by the full scales. If, however, one decides to use a short form for research purposes, it is important to report that shortened measures, rather than the full scales, were used. In our opinion, too many factors mitigate against the use of any of the short forms for routine clinical use. For example, the codetype correspondence to the full-length MMPI–2 is generally poor, and in shortening the test, many items are eliminated that are needed for scoring the supplementary scales, the Harris–Lingoes subscales, and various other special scales.

More recently, Dahlstrom and Archer (in press) developed a 180 item short form based on the MMPI–2 restandardization sample and psychiatric patients. While the above described concerns regarding poor correspondence between full scale score profiles and estimated profiles appear to apply to this study, there may be value in using this shortened MMPI–2 form for screening psychopathology rather than completely identifying it. Future research will determine the utility of this MMPI–2 180 item short form.

FOREIGN TRANSLATIONS

The MMPI is used in over 65 countries and has more than 115 translations (Butcher & Graham, 1989). The first translation of the original test occurred in Italy in 1948. Since the MMPI was restandardized in 1989, at least 15 translation projects have been initiated, including several Asian language projects and at least 5 Spanish translations of the MMPI–2 have been completed or are in progress (Argentina, Chile, Mexico, Spain, and Puerto Rico; Butcher, 1992). The most frequently used Spanish translation in Latin America, developed by Rafael Nuñez (1967), has been criticized as tending to overpathologize individuals (e.g., Fuller & Malony, 1984; Lucio & Reyes-Lagunes, 1994). This tendency to produce higher Spanish mean scores on the clinical scales led Lucio and Reyes-Lagunes to develop normative data on a Mexican transliterated version of the MMPI–2 (see also Whitworth, 1988; Whitworth & McBlaine, 1993). Transliteration techniques invoke the concept that the psychological meaning of the item is more important than its literary equivalency. (For a comprehensive guide and description of general strategies for developing foreign translations of the test, see Butcher & Pancheri, 1976.) More recently, Butcher (1996) edited a comprehensive book entitled *International Adaptations of the MMPI–2*, which addresses important methodological issues in translating and adapting the MMPI–2 in foreign countries, as well presents the results of several translation projects in Belgium, China, France, Greece, Iceland, Israel, Korea, the Netherlands, Norway, Russia, Thailand, Turkey, and Vietnam. Recently, French Canadian and Hmong translations of the MMPI–2 have been made available from National Computer Systems.[3]

A version of an MMPI translation that is not commonly thought of, but of great practical importance, is the translation into American Sign Language (ASL) for the hearing impaired. Brauer (1992) stated that "this language of the deaf is spatial and motile, characteristics that do not lend the language to expression in written form. Therefore, an ASL translation must be captured on videotape or film" (p. 381). Results from a recent investigation into the effectiveness of this ASL version of the MMPI–2 holds promise for its future use with the 500,000 to 1 million deaf individuals in the United States (Brauer, 1988, 1992).

TEST INSTRUCTIONS

Because administering the MMPI–2 is a relatively easy task, many professionals overlook important factors that influence the participants test-taking attitude and hence contribute to invalid results. Clinicians are urged to familiarize themselves thoroughly with the *MMPI–2 Manual* (Butcher et al., 1989) before administering, scoring, and interpreting the test. The MMPI–2 should be presented to the test taker in a serious manner; too often clinicians minimize the importance of the test in an attempt to alleviate any performance anxiety. As a result, participants often believe the test is not important and thereby compromise their cooperation by reading the items too quickly, carelessly, skipping some, and generally lessening their investment in the task. A clear explanation of how the results will be used can help increase cooperation, as well as fulfill the ethical responsibilities of the psychologist to inform consumers about the nature and purpose of an evaluation. Finn (1996) presented a model for involving the client in the assessment task and suggested ways to increase the client's cooperation, including encouragement of questions for the examiner to jointly formulate questions that the test results might address. As Finn pointed out, the latest set of ethical principles of psychologists (America Psychological Association, 1992) now specifies that all clients be given feedback about test results in a way that they can understand those results. Finn emphasized that if clients are treated as collaborators in the assessment process, they are more likely to give accurate and useful information when completing the test.

Psychologists unfamiliar with professional assessment guidelines should consult the following resources: *Ethical Principles of Psychologists and Code of Conduct*

(American Psychological Association, 1992); *Guidelines for Providers of Psychological Services to Ethnic, Linguistic, and Culturally Diverse Populations* (American Psychological Association, 1993); *Guidelines for Child Custody Evaluations in Divorce Proceedings* (American Psychological Association, 1994); *Standards for Providers of Psychological Services* (American Psychological Association, 1977); *Standards for Educational and Psychological Testing* (American Psychological Association, 1985); and *Guidelines for Users of Computer-Based Tests and Interpretations* (American Psychological Association, 1986).

Instructions are printed on the softcover and hardcover test booklet forms, and the audiotape instructions are presented at the beginning of the audio tape format. These instructions basically direct the test taker to decide whether an item is mostly true or mostly false as it applies to him- or herself, and also encourage the test taker to try and respond to every statement. A question that commonly arises is, "Do I answer as I am currently feeling?" Most examiners encourage participants to answer as they are currently feeling, but sometimes, under special circumstances, an examiner may want to learn how participants wish to perceive themselves when they feel better or are leaving the hospital or concluding psychotherapy. The examiner then may ask the participant to fill out the test looking ahead toward the completion of a therapy or hospital program and answer the items in the way that he or she would expect to feel at that time. In some situations, the participant who is able to produce a less disturbed profile under such looking-ahead instructions (*projected discharge profile*), as compared with his or her admission or initial profile taken under the usual instructions, is considered to have a better prognosis (Marks et al., 1974).

In addition to the standardized instructions printed on the MMPI–2 forms, some test users and researchers use supplemental instructions and information to help answer commonly asked questions, to alleviate test anxiety, and to reduce the proportion of invalid profiles due to the over- or underreporting of psychological strengths or problems, respectively. For example, Butcher, Morfitt, Rouse, and Holden (1997) found that a group of male job applicants for pilot positions who produced defensive MMPI–2 profiles were able, upon readministration, to produce valid profiles after being given new test instructions. These instructions were designed to inform them that defensiveness can invalidate the test. The participants produced higher content scale scores without producing higher clinical scale scores. This study demonstrates that specialized instructions in preemployment settings could reduce invalid profiles because of underreporting tendencies. Additional research is needed with other populations in which the base rates for dissimulation or simulation are high. Examples include forensic settings, where pleas of insanity or diminished capacity are seen, or in disability and insurance compensation proceedings where claims of injury or disability are alleged.

The following example of supplemental instructions for taking the MMPI–2 is adapted from the Caldwell Report (Caldwell, 1977):

1. Answer every question as truthfully you can; that's very important for accuracy and the best use of the results.

2. Be sure to mark the correct number on the answer sheet for the question you are answering. Remember that a question marked as both "true" and "false" may be scored as "not answered," or as answered in both directions.
3. If a question seems confusing, as if it could mean different things, answer it according to the meaning that is best for you at this time.
4. Phrases like *some of the time* and words like *often* and *seldom* should be answered according to how you feel about them; it's how *you* feel about the words that matters.
5. When you have finished, take a few minutes to check your answer sheet for any missing answers, incomplete erasures, or double-answered questions.
6. Above all, relax. Numerous people have taken the MMPI–2, and all have survived.

The following answers to commonly asked questions are adapted from Lewak et al. (1990) and from the Caldwell Report (Caldwell, 1977):

1. "What is the MMPI–2?"
   Answer: The MMPI–2 is short for the Minnesota Multiphasic Personality Inventory. It is a tool used for the assessment of personality. It is approximately 50 years old and is psychology's most researched instrument.
2. "How long will this take?"
   Answer: About an hour to two hours, usually. Some people take longer, whereas some people finish in 45 to 50 minutes.
3. "I'm tired and not feeling well; will that affect how I do on the inventory?"
   Answer: Probably not. But answer the statements in terms of how you feel most of the time. How you feel now may make you take a little longer to finish, but the results will be essentially the same as long as you answer truthfully.
4. "How do I answer the questions?"
   Answer: When you take the test, answer the questions as you currently feel. Work quickly, because no one answer is "vital." It is the pattern of answers that make the difference.
5. "Do I have to answer all of the questions even if I don't know the right answer?"
   Answer: Answer all of the questions. If you cannot answer all of the questions, leave no more than a few unanswered. If you are unsure of an answer, use the following rule: If the answer to a question is more true than false, answer it true. If it is more false than true, answer false. For example, the item "I get headaches often" could be answered as follows: I get headaches but not that often; therefore, I answer false.
6. "Will it make any difference if I skip some questions and come back to them?"
   Answer: If you do it carefully, skipping some questions and returning to them probably will not make any difference. But it is easy to get mixed up

in marking your answers, and that will make a difference. So it is better to do them in order, if possible.

7. "What if I do not have time to finish all the questions right now?"
Answer: That is perfectly all right. But try to do them all now, or as soon as possible. Brief interruptions do not matter and will not change the results.
8. "Suppose I cannot answer all of the questions?"
Answer: Try to answer all of them. If you omit a few items, it will not matter, but try to do them all.
9. "Why do so many questions seem irrelevant or just plain stupid or silly?"
Answer: Many may seem that way, but the wording of the question often has little to do with how the answer is scored. Your answer is simply compared with those of others who have answered the same questions.
10. "Why am I taking this test? Does it mean that something is wrong with me?"
Answer: We have asked you to take the test because it helps us to get to know you better in less time, and thus is cost-effective. Many who come to the clinic are asked to take it for this reason.
11. "But I don't have any problems. It is my child, whom I brought to the clinic, who has the problems. Why do I have to take the test?"
Answer: You are asked to take the test so we know what kind of psychological environment your child lives in. For example, your child may possess extremely high energy and be very active, and you as a parent may have energy that is more in the average range. Knowing this helps us (and you) understand how your interactions with your child are affecting you both.
12. "If my wife and I take the test, I'm afraid that you will blame one of us for the problems we're having, and that will make things worse."
Answer: That is a reasonable concern, but the MMPI–2 is not used to find out who has the most problems. What the MMPI–2 can do is help us see how two people might be inadvertently "pushing each others sensitive area" and so be unable to communicate. The test interpretation is not meant to judge either person or to leave either person feeling blamed.
13. "I think I can outsmart the test. I probably can tell what the questions are getting at."
Answer: The pattern of answers to questions rather than individual responses is what is important to the psychologist. Being as honest as possible will serve to make the test results more valid and useful to you and the psychologist interpreting the test. In fact, many questions that appear to be obvious are not measuring what people think they are measuring. People who try to outsmart the test might make it invalid, but often not in the direction they think and not without revealing their intention to do so.
14. "Why does the test ask so many questions that clearly don't apply to me?"
Answer: The test was constructed as a general inventory, so many questions may not apply to you. If a question does not apply to you, simply answer false or true, whichever direction is most applicable for you.
15. "How can you tell anything about me from all those questions anyway?"
Answer: After your answer sheet is finished, it is scored, and a graph is drawn to see how you scored on different dimensions of personality and

how your scores compare to others. There are also scales that tell how you answered the test (cautiously, candidly, denying problems, or even exaggerating them). Your configuration or pattern of scores is what is important to us.

16. "Will I get feedback from my test?"
    Answer: The actual test protocol and the graph will not be given to you in order to maintain test security. However, an explanation of the results will be provided.
17. "What is the cost of the test?"
    Answer: See the clinic fee schedule. The fee covers administration and scoring. Feedback will probably come in a regular session for which you pay your usual fee to your therapist.
18. "What if I disagree with the feedback?"
    Answer: That is something you and your therapist can discuss. When you get feedback, you may want to bring a tape recorder so that you can listen to the feedback and take some time to formulate questions that you might want to ask your therapist. Remember, the test is for your own benefit.

TEST CONDITIONS

The testing environment should be comfortable, with as few distracting influences as possible. Extraneous noise should be minimized, and the participant should be isolated from others not involved in simultaneous testing. Testing is a matter involving personal or confidential issues, and whenever possible, the participant is entitled to adequate privacy. To prevent inadvertent answer disclosure and to maintain a consistent test environment, only the test administrator and test taker should be able to see the test items and responses (American Psychological Association, 1986). Lighting should be adequate and seating comfortable, and a desk or tabletop is preferable to holding the booklet on the lap. If a participant is bedridden (e.g., hospitalized), the hardcover booklet is most helpful. Test administrators using computer equipment to administer the test should consult the *Guidelines for Users of Computer-Based Tests and Interpretations* (American Psychological Association, 1986) as well as a recent review by Bersoff and Hofer (1995) of legal issues in computerized psychological testing. If a monitor screen is used to present the items, correct positioning of the equipment can reduce glare or reflections from windows. An obvious, but frequently neglected, point is the importance of informing the participant ahead of time to bring reading glasses if they are needed.

Whether a test is group or individually administered or presented on a monitor screen, a proctor should be available to monitor the test completion and provide assistance when necessary and appropriate. A trained assistant to the examiner can successfully answer questions a participant raises during the examination. Proctoring is especially necessary in group administrations to ensure the privacy of responses, to help in writing answers in the appropriate places, and to discourage conversations. Proctors should be careful not to linger near any particular individual for too long, so that the individual does not become overly concerned that his or her responses are being monitored. When questions are asked about the specific meaning of a statement or a word, the proctor or examiner should be helpful but neutral. Specifically, dictionary definitions should be given for commonly misunderstood words as *constipation, nausea, dramatics, journalist,* and *brood.* (Dahlstrom et al., 1972). When participants question the meaning of an item itself, it is best to encourage them to interpret it in their own way. Even though the MMPI–2 is considered to be an objective instrument, the items pull from each participant a particular meaning that leads to an endorsement that is ultimately compared to a normative base of participants who have responded to the same items.

A commonly asked question in private practice and in evaluation settings is, "Can I take the test home and complete it?" Although it may be convenient to allow this practice, it is not recommended because psychologists ethically are bound to make reasonable efforts to maintain the integrity and security of tests (see Ethical Principle 2.10 of the American Psychological Association's, 1992, "Ethical Principles of Psychologists and Code of Conduct") as well as to ensure a valid result of the assessment. The psychologist cannot control the test environment when the test is taken out of the professional setting, and there is no guarantee that the designated test taker even completed the instrument him- or herself. This could be particularly important in assessment when the evaluation results are used in a legal proceeding. In fact, unmonitored test administrations may not be admissible in a legal proceeding; such nonstandard administrations involve a breach in the chain of evidence because the connection between the individual and the item responses cannot be established. Another factor for avoiding an unmonitored test administration is that the presence of an individual proctoring the test is consistent with one of the elements of standardization (Pope, Butcher, & Seelen, 1993). Whenever there is a departure from the standardized procedure in establishing the test norms, one runs the risk of losing the valid inferences drawn from the test.

PARTICIPANTS' REQUIREMENTS

There are many important determinants for completing a valid MMPI–2. In addition to the cooperation of the test taker, one of the most important factors to assess before administering the test is the reading level of the test taker. The manual for the original MMPI (Hathaway & McKinley, 1983) recommended that at least a sixth-grade reading level be required. This guideline was based on studies conducted after the test was published that showed that a few of the items required a sixth-grade reading level (Butcher et al., 1989). In constructing the MMPI, Hathaway and McKinley intended the wording of the component items to be well within the reading capacity of most American men and women with a fifth-grade education (Dahlstrom, Archer, Hopkins, Jackson, & Dahlstrom, 1994).

Subsequent evaluations of the MMPI word content have resulted in even higher reading level recommendations; Ward and Ward (1980) suggested at least a seventh-grade reading level. Blanchard (1981) analyzed the MMPI for reading difficulty using readability formulas. Using a criterion for comprehension of items between 90% and 100%, he found several items requiring 10th-grade reading skills and recommended that alternative forms of presentation be used for participants with less than 10th-grade reading skills.[4]

The MMPI–2 manual (Butcher et al., 1989) recommends that test takers have at least an eighth-grade education for a valid test administration. Although subsequent studies generally have supported this recommendation (Paolo et al., 1991; Schinka & Borum, 1993), a detailed investigation of the MMPI–2 items using different reading indexes led Dahlstrom et al. (1994) to conclude that the average difficulty level of MMPI–2 (and MMPI and MMPI–A) items is at about the sixth-grade level. They also noted that the instructions in the MMPI–2 booklet are somewhat more difficult to read than the component items; therefore, the test administrator should ensure that the participant fully understands the task. The clinician might request the test taker to read the instructions aloud and explain the meaning of the task to ensure compliance, or the clinician may elect to read the instructions aloud with the participant reading along silently.[5]

Although we acknowledge that a sixth-grade level is sufficient for the MMPI–2, it is important to note Greene's (2000) caveat that simply using completed years of education to estimate reading ability may result in gross overestimates. Similarly, Dahlstrom et al. (1994) noted the limitations of exclusively relying on "years of education" to indicate reading ability:

> Background data on most test participants typically include summaries of their schooling. For example, the number of years of education is often employed as a gauge of the subject's level of reading competence; unfortunately, this index is quite unreliable. Subjects may distort their prior school history in reporting their background to the examiner or may fail to indicate that their achievement was far below the average of their class. As a result, reported grade-level may be a poor index of the subject's ability to read with sufficient comprehension to complete the test in a satisfactory manner. (p. 33)

There are also instances in which some participants with less than a sixth-grade education possess the reading ability to complete the instrument.

Although the *F*, *Fb*, *VRIN*, and *TRIN* scales help identify MMPI–2 test administrations that were compromised by failing to understand some or all of the items, it is obviously more desirable to anticipate and screen for any comprehension problems ahead of time.

Exceeding a required sixth-grade reading level increases the probability of a valid administration. Schinka and Borum (1993) suggested using an eighth-grade level of formal education with at least average grades to ensure that participants will understand the content of the MMPI–2. If a participant has less than 8 years of formal education, is not fluent in English, or is otherwise English language compromised, the examiner can either administer readability measures—such as the Gray Oral Reading Test, Forms A and B (Wiederholt & Bryant, 1986); the Woodcock-Johnson Test—Revised, Form A, Passage Comprehension; the Wechsler Individual Achievement Test, Reading Comprehension (1992); and the California Achievement Test, Reading Battery A (1993)—or the examiner can select certain items from the MMPI–2 booklet for the participant to read aloud and explain. It is not recommended that the potential test taker merely read aloud the first several items in the inventory as these items tend to be easier to read than later items. Simply reading an item may mask a problem in item comprehension; instead, more difficult items should be selected for screening purposes. Dahlstrom et al. (1994, Table D.5) provided a list of the most difficult MMPI–2 items arranged by lexile scores. The following items from this table were selected because they were ranked as difficult items and appear on either the validity or clinical scales:

114. Sometimes I am so strongly attracted by the personal articles of others, such as shoes, gloves, etc., that I want to handle or steal them, though, I have no use for them.
212. I have at times stood in the way of people who are trying to do something, not because it amounts to much but because of the principle of the thing.
262. "In a group of people I would not be embarrassed to be called upon to start a discussion or give an opinion about something I know well."
283. The person who provides temptation by leaving valuable property unprotected is about as much to blame for the theft as the one who steals it.

For persons with suspected marginal reading levels, these items could be presented prior to test administration in order to assess the participant's comprehension. If the audiotape form of the test is being administered to an illiterate participant or someone who cannot complete the written form, difficult items could also be read by the examiner. As with the MMPI–2 booklet, the examiner should not merely present the first few items from the audiotape form as these tend to be relatively easy items. It is also impractical to locate these sample items on the tape before testing, so reading them in a manner similar to the presenter's voice on the tape will suffice for screening purposes. In any case, the examiner will want to ensure that the participant adequately understands the task of listening to the tape and recording his or her responses and should observe the first few items being recorded on the answer sheet by the participant.

The audiotape form is preferred to actually reading each item aloud to the participant as the audiotape presentation of items is paced and uniform, thereby reducing inflections and fatigue in the presenter's voice. If for some reason the audiotape version is unavailable to the test administrator, or the participant requires direct supervision to ensure compliance with responding to each item, it is unlikely that an oral reading by the examiner will seriously compromise the results, provided the items are read clearly and slowly. In fact, the oral administration allows the clinician the advantage of observing the client and noting any indicators of psychological functioning, such as hesitancies, emotional responses, confusion, or indecision (E. L. Edwards, Holmes, & Carvajal, 1998). An investigation of the effects of orally administering the MMPI showed that although statistical differences occurred between the standard and oral administration in a split-half design, clinically significant differences appeared minimal (Kendrick & Hatzenbuehler, 1982). Most recently, E. L. Edwards et al. (1998) administered the

MMPI–2 twice to college students under two formats: standard booklet administration and oral presentation with the examiner reading the items to the students and recording their answers. No significant differences were found when comparing oral and booklet presentation for either men or women. Clinicians administering the test orally most likely will obtain results comparable with the standard administered test, although more research is needed to confirm this conclusion. Specifically, it is not known if the recording of responses by the participant versus the examiner makes a difference in the accuracy of the results.

Psychiatric impairment usually does not interfere with the administration of the MMPI–2 unless the participant is too confused or agitated to cooperate. Even so, the MMPI–2 manual (Butcher et al., 1989) cautions the test administrator to be alert to any of the following physical conditions or emotional states that could impair the capacity of the participant to complete the MMPI–2 in a valid manner:

> Limited visual acuity, dyslexia or receptive aphasia, learning disorder, drug or alcohol intoxication or withdrawal states, toxic reactions to various infectious agents or other organic deliria, disorientation arising from brain injury or confusion, post-seizure confusion in an epileptic disorder, residual neurological impairment from prolonged polydrug regimes, confusional states during catatonic episodes or bouts of hallucinations, the profound psychomotor retardation of a major depressive condition, or the extreme distractibility of a manic reaction. (p. 14)

Because depressed patients or cognitively impaired participants may take longer than usual to complete the test, it is important to note the test-taking time. Too much or too little time can be of diagnostic significance for all participants (e.g., too little time may indicate impulsiveness or uncooperativeness, whereas too much time may indicate obsessiveness, psychomotor retardation, or motivational difficulties). Hospitalized psychiatric patients may require several sittings to complete the inventory because of distractability or fatigue or because of interruptions for treatment, medication, meals, visitations, and similar events that are common in the hospital milieu. Such interruptions can add 2 hr or even several days to the test administration. Very lengthy administrations raise the question of reliability as such patients may undergo significant change in symptoms and mental status in the course of a few days.

Usual administration time for the completion of the audiotape MMPI–2 is about 1.5 hr to 2 hr. A computer administration may be somewhat shorter (by 15 to 30 min). Participants taking the written booklet form usually complete the inventory in 1 to 2 hr, although limited reading ability or noncooperative attitudes may extend the test-taking time. Subaverage intellectual ability may also extend the time to complete any of the forms of the test.

Functional intelligence as measured by a standardized IQ test, such as the Wechsler Adult Intelligence Scale-Revised (WAIS–R) or the WAIS–III, should be at least in the low-average range (80–89), although participants in the borderline range (70–79) of impairment may be able to complete the task if they are properly motivated, monitored, and evaluated ahead of time for reading and comprehension abilities. In general, an IQ score should be considered in relation to other variables (e.g., attention and concentration factors and reading ability). For example, an individual with a Full Scale IQ (FSIQ) score of 75 without any history of central nervous system disease or brain injury may be developmentally impaired and therefore unable to complete the task, especially if he or she has reading deficits. On the other hand, an individual with an FSIQ score of 75 who premorbidly had a considerably higher IQ (perhaps as estimated from educational attainment, work record, or previous testing) is more likely to have retained the necessary reading ability to complete the MMPI–2 (S. E. Rothke, personal communication, January 1, 1997). Participants with disabilities such as blindness, deafness, or even paralysis can successfully complete the MMPI–2 under certain conditions. However, special versions of the test may be necessary, such as the audiotape form, usually with additional proctoring assistance. *An MMPI Handbook* (Dahlstrom et al., 1975) should be consulted before testing participants with disabilities.

TEST SCORING AND PROFILE PLOTTING

Scoring the MMPI–2 can be accomplished using handheld plastic templates or with the aid of a scanner and a computer. The National Computer Services is the official distributor of the University of Minnesota trademark materials. Other scoring and interpretive services exist, such as the Caldwell Report and Psychological Assessment Resources.[6] National Computer Systems provides scoring templates for the hard- and softcover MMPI–2 booklets. As previously mentioned, these scoring templates are not interchangeable. Hence, when scoring the MMPI–2, it is necessary to have the appropriate templates to match the soft- or hardcover form of the tests. The answer sheet designed for the softcover booklet should be used for an audiotape administration. National Computer Systems provides scoring templates for the basic validity and clinical scales; the supplementary, content, and content component scales, and the Harris–Lingoes subscales. There are 14 scoring templates for either the hard- or softcover MMPI–2 answer sheet. Scale 5 (*Mf*) has two scoring templates, one for men and one for women and the scorer should be careful to select the template that matches the participant's gender.

When using the hard- or softcover scoring keys, the marks on the bottom of the key should coincide with the marks on the answer sheets. The number of marks appearing through the transparent squares on the scoring key should be counted and recorded as the raw score in the proper place on the profile sheet. Double-marked or omitted items are tallied by inspecting the answer sheet and should be recorded as Cannot Say (*?*) responses in the appropriate space provided on the profile sheet for the standard scales. Double-marked items (items marked as both true and false) are scored as a deviant response; a line should be drawn through the item so it is not inadvertently counted when the template is placed over the answer sheet. When a participant double marks or omits between 5 and 30 items, an augmented profile can be drawn to assist in interpretation (Greene, 1991a).[7] Erasures usually contraindicate random responses because participants by their modified response, are demonstrating a careful reading of the item content.

After the answer sheet has been scored for the basic validity and clinical scales, the raw scores must be carefully transferred to the profile sheet and converted to *T* scores. Because *T* scores differ by gender for the various scales, it is important that raw scores be transferred to the appropriate side of the profile sheet identified as male or female. After raw scores are recorded under each scale, a different proportion of the *K* scale is added to the appropriate scales. The fraction of *K* to be added is easily computed by consulting the table listed on the MMPI–2 profile sheet showing all raw-score values of *K* and different proportions of those values (see chap. 2 for a listing of the appropriate values of *K* to be added to each scale). The scorer should draw a line under the raw score of *K* on the profile sheet, so that the appropriate fractions can be added to the clinical scales. The raw score plus the *K* scale addition is then plotted onto the profile sheet. Test users who do not wish to use the *K* correction can consult Table B.4 to convert the non-*K*-corrected raw scores into appropriate *T* scores. Simply omitting *K* and directly plotting the value(s) onto the profile sheet will result in an incorrect conversion, as the MMPI–2 profile sheet is based on adult norms with the *K*-correction factor.

Within the profile matrix, the marks or dashes represent raw-score values. Each dash represents a raw-score value of 1. Each scale, except for Scale 5 (*Mf*), shows an increase in *T*-score value for each raw-score point added. The final raw score is indicated on the profile sheet by plotting the raw-score placement on the appropriate scale. After all the scale scores are plotted in this fashion, a solid line is drawn between the clinical scales to connect them. Likewise, the validity scales are connected. The clinical and validity scales, however, have a partition between them, and traditionally they are not connected.

By drawing the profile, the psychologist is provided with a raw score and corresponding *T* score for each scale. The *T*-score values are located at the extreme left and right columns of the profile matrix. MMPI–2 *T* scores have a mean of 50 and a standard deviation of 10 (see chap. 2 for a detailed discussion of *T* scores). For example, if a male participant obtains a raw score of 39 on Scale 0 (*Si*), this indicates that his *T* score is 65, 1.5 *SD*s above the mean.

The profile sheets for the MMPI–2 show a darkened line for all scales at a *T*-score value of 65 to indicate scores that are within 1.5 *SD*s of the mean. Scores above this range indicate a significant deviation from the standardization group pattern of responding and are considered abnormal values. Chapter 1 provides the equation for deriving *T* scores, but the conversions from raw scores to *T* scores already are provided on the printed profile sheets for all of the officially published scales.

CODING THE PROFILE

Soon after publication of the MMPI, two systems were developed to codify information yielded by the scoring process. The first system, developed by Hathaway (1947), is summarized in *An MMPI Handbook* (Dahlstrom et al., 1972) and in *Psychological Assessment With the MMPI* (Friedman, Webb, & Lewak,

1989). One of the earliest uses of the Hathaway system was in the original *Atlas* (Hathaway & Meehl, 1951), a book of clinical case summaries grouped according to elevated scales or coded profile high points. However, the Hathaway system is not used with the MMPI–2. The second system, designed by Welsh (1948), is the only coding system used with the MMPI–2, and it has been slightly modified to correspond to the $T = 65$ cutoff on the MMPI–2 profile sheet (Butcher et al., 1989).

The function of coding is to provide a convenient means of identifying salient characteristics of the profile, especially with respect to the profiles elevation and pattern. Although single-scale elevations are important to examine and interpret, the emphasis in clinical use of the test has been to interpret profile patterns; a profile pattern is the configuration of scale scores relative to each other. By coding a profile, a test user can organize the data into a simple-to-read summary for clinical and research use. From the coded profile, the psychologist should be able to interpret the entire profile with all of its information, including the following: configuration or pattern of the component scores, the overall elevation of the test pattern, the range or scatter of score values, the highest and lowest scales in the profile, and the standard configuration of the validity scales (Dahlstrom, 1992a).

The first step in the modified Welsh (1948) coding system substitutes numbers 1–0 for the 10 standard scales, in the standard profile arrangement:

Hs 1	*Pa* 6
D 2	*Pt* 7
Hy 3	*Sc* 8
Pd 4	*Ma* 9
Mf 5	*Si* 0

The writing of the modified Welsh code begins by identifying the highest clinical scale *T*-score value and writing the number assigned to that scale (as in the preceding list) as the first number of the code, with the remaining scale numbers following in descending order of elevation. When two or more scales share the same elevation, they should be recorded in ordinal sequence from left (Scale 1) to right (Scale 0) in the profile. The next step is to indicate the relative elevation of all scales in the profile. The *T*-score values and corresponding elevation symbols for this system are as follows (Butcher et al., 1989):

T-Score Values	Symbols
≥120	!!
110–119	!
100–109	**
90–99	*
80–89	‘ ‘
70–79	‘
65–69	+
60–64	-
50–59	/
40–49	:

30–39 #

≤29 (to the right of #)

In this coding system, a double exclamation mark (!!) follows all scores at a *T* score of 120 or above. Scores between 110 and 119 are followed by a single exclamation mark (!). A double asterisk (**) follows all scales between 100 and 109. Scores between 90 and 99 are followed by a single asterisk (*). Scores between 80 and 89 are followed by a double prime (‘ ‘). A single prime (‘) follows score between 70 and 79. A new notation sign, a plus sign (+), follows scores between 65 and 69. A dash sign (-) follows scores between 60 and 64. A slash (/) follows score between 50 and 59. A colon (:) follows scores between 40 and 49. The pound sign (#) follows scores between 30 and 39. Scores of 29 and below are recorded to the right of the pound sign (#). It should be noted that the validity scales are recorded to the right of the clinical scales. Traditionally, the validity and clinical scales should be separated by a space or two. Scale scores that are the same or are within 1 *T*-score point of each other are underlined. If no scale score falls within a given interval of elevation, the appropriate symbol for the missing range is, nevertheless, recorded. When scales fall into two different ranges but remain within 1 *T*-score point, they and the elevation symbol should be underlined (Dahlstrom et al., 1972). Note that it is not necessary to include a symbol to the left of the scale with the highest score or to the right of the elevation symbol following the lowest score.

The following examples illustrate the application of the modified Welsh coding system for two MMPI–2 profiles:

Example 1

	L	*F*	*K*	1	2	3	4	5	6	7	8	9	0
T score	40	60	46	34	56	56	90	63	50	90	73	91	43

Modified Welsh code: 947*“ 8‘+5-236/0:1# F-/KL:

Example 2

	L	*F*	*K*	1	2	3	4	5	6	7	8	9	0
T score	44	61	49	50	89	62	51	60	62	79	63	38	70

Modified Welsh code: 2“ 70‘+8365-41/:9# F-/KL:

Although the code summarizes the pattern of the MMPI–2 scores, a shorthand method is often used to describe the test record instead of the total code. Dahlstrom (1992a) stated that the pattern may be briefly designated by the following:

> (a) the highest single scale (the high-point code); (b) the highest and lowest scales (the cross-point code); (c) the highest two scales (the two-point high code), either in order (e.g., 12 or 87) or without regard to order (e.g., 12/12, 78/87, etc.); or (d) the highest three scales (three-point high-point code). On the basis of such abbreviations (sometimes including elevation indicators as well), test records identical in respect to the highest or lowest scales but differing in other parts of their codes can be grouped together and studied for common nontest implications or

> correlates (e.g., similar symptoms, diagnoses, or personality attributes). However, it should be obvious that such shorthand designations of the test patterns necessarily disregard a great deal of useful information.
>
> Some writers refer to these code designations or abbreviations as *codetypes*, rather than simply as two-point codes, high-point codes, and so on. There is a legitimate use for the term *codetype* (as distinct from code) when a number of different code patterns are grouped into a more general set (e.g., Lachar's, 1974, neurotic codetype, psychotic codetype, or character disorder codetype). Applying ... *codetype* [italics added] to specify individual code combinations or patterns needlessly confuses the two different uses of MMPI coding procedures. (p. 154)

Dahlstrom raised a valid point in differentiating *codetypes* from *codes* and *code patterns*, and his recommended conventions are followed in this book.

MMPI/MMPI–2 CODE PATTERN CORRESPONDENCE

While administering, scoring, and coding an MMPI–2 is straightforward, interpreting the profile requires attention to the fact that there are sometimes differences in the way an MMPI–2 pattern of scores corresponds to the original MMPI pattern. Since 1990, over 40 studies have been published on the concordance between MMPI–2 and MMPI code patterns (Greene, Gwin, & Staal, 1997) and have important practical implications. Specifically, individuals who complete the MMPI–2 and have their scores plotted on both the original and new norms, may have different profile patterns. Because different profile patterns would have different correlates and interpretations, the practical question becomes which profile should the psychologist interpret. Greene (1991a) described two different procedures for assessing congruence or concordance between the MMPI and the MMPI–2.

> First, MMPI data can be quickly transformed to simulate the MMPI–2 by dropping the 13 items that were not retained on the MMPI–2 and converting the raw scores into the appropriate T-scores. This procedure assumes that the changes made at the item level on the MMPI–2 will not have a systematic effect on the data. It is also possible to score both the MMPI–2 and the MMPI if Form AX, the form used to collect the restandardization data, was administered since it contains all of the items on the MMPI and the MMPI–2.
>
> Second, the MMPI and the MMPI–2 can be administered to the same clients with some interval of time between the two test administrations (e.g. Honaker, 1990). This latter method has been used infrequently, because it requires a significant amount of time and effort on the part of the clinician. It also tends to confound test-retest reliability changes with the differences between the MMPI and the MMPI–2. (p. 246)

Note that the concordance rates vary as a function of the norm shift direction; thus, the MMPI–2 and the MMPI are not expected to have perfect concordance.

Greene (1991a) gave the following illustration of how the norm shifts can affect code-pattern concordance:

> For example, 4-8/8-4 codetypes on the MMPI have a concordance rate of 35% on the MMPI–2 in men and women, whereas 4-8/8-4 codetypes on the MMPI–2 have a concordance rate over 90% on the MMPI in men and women. Thus, 4-8/8-4 codetypes on the MMPI–2 should be a very homogeneous subset of 4-8/8-4 codetypes on the MMPI, and it would be expected that 4-8/8-4 codetypes on the MMPI–2 should have more reliable correlates since the codetype is more homogeneous.
>
> The opposite pattern for concordance rates between the MMPI–2 and the MMPI also can be found. For example, 1-3/3-1 codetypes on the MMPI have a concordance rate over 90% on the MMPI–2 in men and women, whereas 1-3/3-1 codetypes on the MMPI–2 have a concordance rate around 50% on the MMPI in men and women. Thus, 1-3/3-1 codetypes on the MMPI–2 are a more heterogeneous subset of 1-3/3-1 codetypes on the MMPI, and it would be expected that 1-3/3-1 codetypes on the MMPI–2 should have less reliable correlates since the codetype is more heterogeneous. (p. 249)

Recently, Dahlstrom (1992a) demonstrated that shifting from the original Minnesota-based norms (published in 1951) to the new MMPI–2 national norms (published in 1989) changes the profile patterns obtained for the restandardization sample on the two-point high-code patterns. Dahlstrom analyzed the Form AX test booklet (see chap. 1) consisting of 704 items completed by the restandardization sample. Because this form included both the original MMPI items and the MMPI–2 items, the answer sheets could be scored for both the original MMPI and the MMPI–2 using different norms to plot the resulting profiles.

Appreciable differences, for both men and women, occurred when their MMPI–2 scores were converted to MMPI norms. For men, Scales 1, 3, 6, and 7 appeared as the first or second high points more frequently when using the MMPI–2 norms versus the original norms. Scales 2, 4, 8, and 9 were less frequently displayed in the MMPI–2 profiles as the high point or second highest scale, and Scale 5 dropped the most in the shift. For women, similar trends were observed with Scales 1, 3, 5, 7, and 0 (particularly Scale 5), appearing more frequently as the first or second high points when using the MMPI–2 norms. Scales 2, 4, 6, 8, and 9 decreased in prominence in their profile patterns.

Some code patterns also showed substantial shifts in frequency of occurrence, and others did not; the most unstable patterns for men were 24/42, 25/52, 27/72, 28/82, 34/43, 45/54, 48/84, 57/75, 58/85, 59/95, and 89/98; the most unstable patterns for women were 34/43, 38/83, 30/03, 46/64, 48/84, 49/94, 40/04, 68/86, and 69/96. High-point pairs that were more stable were, for men, 12/21, 13/31, 20/02, 39/93, and 69/96 and, for women, 13/31, 26/62, 27/72, 36/63, 59/95, 70/07, and 89/98. Dahlstrom (1992a) noted that "the single largest increase in frequency from the original to the new norms occurred for the 13/31 code, from 28 (2.5%) to 61 (5.4%). Correspondingly, the largest drop in frequency occurred for the 59/95 code pattern, from 122 (10.7%) to 42 (3.7%)" (p. 159).

Note that these community samples did not show either marked elevation or wide ranges of scatter in their profiles. Therefore, as Dahlstrom (1992) stated "they are less likely to demonstrate as much stability in their code patterns in shift in norms as would be true in records from more deviant participants with wide-ranging scores" (p. 161). Individuals such as psychiatric patients tend to produce more deviant and wide-ranging scores and therefore produce more stability in their code patterns when shifts in norms occur. The data in the MMPI–2 manual (Butcher et al., 1989) show that about two thirds of patients obtained the same two-point high-point codes when the norm shift occurred (Dahlstrom, 1992a).

Greene (1991a) provided data on the concordance of specific MMPI–2 and MMPI code patterns in a sample of psychiatric inpatients and outpatients. When the two highest clinical scales had to be in the same order, the average concordance rate across all of the MMPI–2 code patterns was approximately 50%; this rate increased to about 65% when the two highest clinical scales could be in either order. Greene found the following high-point pairs in men had high concordance: 24/42, 28/82, 48/84, and 49/94. In women, the following high-point pairs had high concordance between the original and new norms: Spike 2, Spike 3, Spike 4, 48/84, 49/94, Spike 7, and Spike 0. Two-point high pairs that had very low concordance rates in both men and women were the 16/61 and 26/62 patterns; 20/02, 40/04, and 69/96 were patterns of low concordance rates in men. Greene's data show that the concordance rates for specific code patterns can vary drastically as a function of whether the MMPI–2 or the MMPI is used as the criterion.

More recently, Humphrey and Dahlstrom (1995) examined the stability of *T*-score patterns across both the MMPI and the MMPI–2 in a small sample of 53 individuals under court review at a forensic unit of a state hospital. These individuals completed both the MMPI and the MMPI–2 within an interval of a few days. They found that the otherwise stable raw scores for the two administrations changed drastically when converted into *T* scores on their respective norms. Humphrey and Dahlstrom raised an important issue by showing that not only did the high-point pairs shift between administrations, but the lowest scale score was also the same in less than half of the MMPI patterns. Because clinicians who skillfully interpret the instrument should rely on all of the scores in the MMPI/MMPI–2 profile, "the important shifts that may appear further down in the profile must also be brought into consideration" (Humphrey & Dahlstrom, 1995, p. 430).

Tellegen and Ben-Porath (1996) criticized the results of Humphrey and Dahlstrom (1995). First, they pointed out that the *Q* correlations used were

> potentially misleading similarity indicators because they do not reflect profile differences in either elevation or scatter. Thus, when a person's MMPI–2 and MMPI T-score profiles are very similar by virtue of being essentially normal, small and insignificant score differences between the two can result in a low Q correlation. (Tellegen & Ben-Porath, 1996, p. 642)

Second, they criticized Humphrey and Dahlstrom's results as neglecting the fact that raw-score profile correlations tend to inflate because of substantial differences between the raw-score means of the scales included in the profile; therefore, their comparison of the *T*-score profile correlations with the much higher corresponding raw-score profile correlations of the same participants ws flawed. The major factor that Tellegen and Ben-Porath attributed to the low correlations between same-person MMPI and MMPI–2 *T*-score profiles is the fundamental difference between raw scores and "means-equating" *T* scores. They believed that there is no reason to identify normative differences as the only or primary reason for the shifts that occur.

In general, it is clear that the MMPI–2 results in lower T-score values (Blake et al., 1992; Friedman, 1990; Harrell, Honaker, & Parnell, 1992; Humphrey & Dahlstrom 1995; Ward, 1991). Dahlstrom (1992a) suggested three sources of change that contribute to the differences between the original and new norms: (a) reworded or omitted items that probably do not appreciably affect any changes in code concordance, (b) uniform *T*-score values computed for the eight clinical scales, and (c) new means and standard deviations for each scale. Dahlstrom (1992a) noted that "the overall impact on the T-score distributions for scales 1–4 and 6–9 of the uniform T-score transformations was minimal, affecting primarily scores at the very ends of the distributions of T-scores" (p. 156). The restandardization sample did, however, differ from the original Minnesota normative group in terms of item endorsement frequencies, which did affect the way in which the new *T*-score values were established for the MMPI–2. Dahlstrom (1992) stated that

> In turn, these shifts affected the scaling by means of which the new T-score values were established for MMPI–2. That is, the raw-score means tended to be at least ½ SD more deviant than the values obtained by the participants in the original Hathaway and McKinley sample. Therefore, as reported in the MMPI–2 *Manual*, overall comparisons of the T-score distributions on the original MMPI and on the MMPI–2 revealed that the anchoring points of the basic clinical scales have been raised several raw-score points. This shift reduced the general elevation of T-score values across the profile for particular raw-score values on the component scales. In addition, the raw-score standard deviations from the more heterogeneous normative groups that were collected for the MMPI–2 proved to be somewhat larger, thereby reducing the extent of deviation of any given raw-score value on the scales. This effect also contributed to the general lowering of profile elevations on MMPI–2. (p. 156)

A major issue emerging from all of the concordance studies revolves around which set of *T* scores provides the most valid pattern format from which to address the extant interpretive literature on code patterns. This issue has raised a significant controversy; some researchers (e.g., Caldwell, 1997; Humphrey & Dahlstrom, 1995) have recommended plotting the raw scores on both sets of norms and examining both sets for interpretive information or simply interpreting the MMPI–2 on the basis of original norms. Others, in an effort to ameliorate the concordance problem, have recommended that well-defined code patterns be the only basis for the configural interpretation of MMPI–2 profiles. Well-defined code patterns tend to produce high concordance rates and, therefore, are more reliable and valid to interpret (e.g., Graham, 1990; Graham, Timbrook, Ben-Porath, &

Butcher, 1991; Tellegen & Ben-Porath, 1993, 1996). *Well-defined codetype* or code pattern means that, for example, in a two-point code, the third scale is lower than the second scale in the high-point pair by some arbitrary value, usually 5 *T*-score points. If such separation does not exist between the second and third scales, the profile would not be interpretable as a two-point code according to proponents of this rule. Instead, they propose that the interpretation of such profiles would be limited to a scale-by-scale strategy. Dahlstrom (1992a) has objected to the limitation imposed by this rule on the grounds that

> few, if any, of the research investigations that furnished the code correlates for MMPI interpretation themselves utilized such refinements in the definition of the research groups. The vast majority of studies of code patterns based on high points or high-point pairs, which presently provide the guidelines for profile pattern interpretation were carried out without regard to such restrictions on third-scale elevation in the formation of their groupings. (p. 155)

Dahlstrom (1992a) also stated that "there is little empirical justification for the imposition of any arbitrary elevation gap between the first and second or the second and third or third and fourth scales in the profile code" (p. 155). A disadvantage in using such restrictive rules is that the number of interpretable profiles often drops to an impractical level for the clinician. For example, D. W. Edwards, Weissman, and Morrison (1993) found that when using well-defined code patterns, the number of classifiable profiles decreased from 75% to 36%. Tellegen and Ben-Porath (1993) argued that limiting interpretation to well-defined code patterns does not appear to exclude most profiles. They stated that

> Graham and colleagues (1991) reported that in their two psychiatric samples an average of 83% of the MMPI–2 profiles belonged to 1- or 2- or 3-point codetypes that have a 5 point definition. The corresponding average for their two normative samples is 71%. The analysis reported by Graham and colleagues (1991) did not include a fourth possible classification of codetypes as falling within normal limits (i.e., all 10 clinical scores are less than 65). When this option is added to the well-defined 1- or 3-point codetypes, the percentage of classified profiles rises to 87 in the psychiatric sample and 92 in the normative sample, where 59% of the profiles were within normal limits. (p. 492)

Graham, Timbrook, et al. (1991) clearly did not think that using well-defined code patterns to interpret MMPI–2 profiles is an exclusionary process.

Greene et al. (1997) reviewed the concordance literature and noted that "there are a wide range of opinions on the degree of code pattern comparability between the MMPI and MMPI–2 ranging from 50% to 90% using well-defined codetypes, and 40% to 70% for nonrestrictive codetypes" (p. 28). A nonrestrictive two-point code, for example, is based on the two highest scales, regardless of other elevations. An important process to help resolve the issue of which profile is more valid is to conduct research that focuses on whether the specific empirical correlates of well-defined MMPI–2 code patterns differ from nonrestrictive code patterns, (Greene et al., 1997; Staal & Greene, 1998). McNulty, Ben-Porath, and Graham (1998) have addressed this concern by examining the effects of profile definition on the correlates of four common MMPI–2 code patterns (13/31, 24/42; 27/72, and 46/64). The participants were 301 community mental health center outpatients with a wide range of diagnoses and diverse backgrounds. Their findings suggested that the use of more restrictive classification rules yielded more valid codetype descriptors. Although conceptually valid descriptors would also apply to nonrestrictive two-point code patterns, there were more spurious correlates. McNulty et al. (1998) stated that

> [for] profiles that are not well-defined, the list of conceptually relevant descriptors may be overinclusive. Further, the less similar the profile is to well-defined criteria, the less likely it is that such descriptors would apply. The implication for test interpretation is that clinicians should place greater confidence in the accuracy of correlates when interpreting a well-defined codetype than when interpreting a not defined one. Descriptors of individuals who produce profiles that are not well-defined should be more tenuous. (p. 407)

These results are important and need to be replicated with larger samples and additional code patterns.

Because the norms that are used can change profile patterns dramatically, it is recommended that the clinician administer the MMPI–2 booklet but plot two profiles, one with the MMPI–2 norms and one with the original norms. It is a quite straightforward task to translate the MMPI–2 raw scores into MMPI *T* scores by using Appendix K in the MMPI–2 manual (Butcher et al., 1989) or Appendix D in this text. This method allows each profile to be interpreted separately to determine their differences and similarities (Caldwell, 1997; D. W. Edwards, Weissman, & Morrison, 1993; Humphrey & Dahlstrom, 1995). Having both profiles will enrich the range of interpretive hypotheses. In some cases, the original profile may appear to be the better match to the test taker, whereas in other cases the MMPI–2 will be the better fit. Although we endorse the plotting of both profiles, we cannot state unequivocably that either is more accurate.

When the profile is well-defined, it is easier and more reliable to interpret the code pattern than one that is not well-defined. On the other hand, that level of definition inevitably reduces the level of coverage; that is, some profiles may not be classifiable because they do not meet the specific definition of the five *T*-score point criterion.

Caldwell (1997) pointed out the need for pattern research on the correlates of the MMPI–2. He recommended interpreting the original MMPI configuration for personality characteristics and behavioral prediction purposes, to draw on the 50-plus years of pattern research from the original MMPI profile. In our opinion, however, this should be considered only as an interim suggestion. Research already is under way to collect empirical correlates of MMPI–2 profile patterns. As this research grows, the development of code-pattern data will become sufficiently available to supplant, enrich, or reinforce those correlates developed for code patterns within the original MMPI. Initial efforts in this direction have appeared recently that provide information for MMPI–2 code patterns in both outpatient settings (Graham, Ben-Porath, & McNulty, 1999) and inpatient settings (Archer, Griffin, & Aiduk, 1995). The data from these studies are incorporated into the relevant code-pattern descriptions in chapter 6 of this text. Based on these study findings, it appears in general that the correlates of MMPI–2 profiles that replicate corresponding patterns in the MMPI are similar. For those MMPI code patterns that have not yet been replicated in samples using the MMPI–2, it may be preferable to use the original MMPI profile as the basis for interpretation.

NOTES

[1]Both the English and Spanish audiotape recording present all 567 MMPI–2 items, which are spoken twice. The inventory is recorded on two cassettes, in both the English and Spanish versions. In the English version, cassette 1, Side A, contains Items 1–143 and Side B contains Items 144–296; Cassette 2, Side A, contains Items 297–440 and Side B contains Items 441–567. In the Spanish version, cassette 1, Side A, contains Items 1–187 and Side B contains Items 188–359; Cassette 2, Side A contains Items 360–460 and Side B contains Items 461–567.

[2]Butcher and Hostetler (1990) described the three most widely researched of the MMPI short forms, the Mini-Mult, the Faschingbauer Abbreviated MMPI (FAM) and the MMPI–168. The Mini-Mult (Kincannon, 1968) consists of 71 items and is scored for the standard clinical and validity scales, except for Scale 0. The FAM (Faschingbauer, 1974) consists of 166 items and was primarily developed using item factor clusters to create short scales. The MMPI–168, developed by Overall and Gomez-Mont (1974), involves scoring the first 168 items of the MMPI, as the authors believed that these items sufficiently represented the MMPI scales. (For a detailed comparative analysis, see Butcher & Hostetler, 1990.)

Other abbreviated versions of the MMPI include the 86-item Midi-Mult (Dean, 1972), the 173-Item Hugo (1971) Short Form, the Maxi-Mult 104 (Spera & Robertson, 1974), and the Maxi-Mult 94 (McLachlan, 1974).

Recent investigations of short-form versions of the MMPI continue to support Alker's (1978) statement in the *Eighth Mental Measurements Year Book* review (Buros, 1978) that "virtually no convincing evidence is available that the short forms make contributions to clinical decision-making in a fashion that compares favorably on statistical criteria with the full MMPI" (p. 934). Alker (1978) also stated that no one version is clearly superior over any other (p. 934). Willcockson, Bolton, and Dana (1983) compared six MMPI short forms for their ability to identify code patterns and indexes of psychopathology obtained from the full-length MMPI using renal dialysis and paranoid schizophrenic patients. Their results suggest that the accuracy of the short forms differs for different patient populations and diagnostic criteria. One problem common to all the short forms is the failure to recapture the exact profile obtained from the full-length MMPI (McLaughlin, Helms, and Howe, 1983). Whenever a test is shortened, the issue of the effect on its reliability is raised. In an examination of short forms, Streiner and Miller (1986) stated, "From the limited evidence that is available, it appears that there is some reduction in reliability of short forms due to shortening the individual scales" (p. 111). These authors concluded that no shortened scale will ever favorably compare to the full-length MMPI. Greene (1982) suggested that we treat shortened MMPI versions as new tests and attempt to validate them individually.

[3]The following list of published translations of the MMPI–2, with ordering information, was provided by the University of Minnesota Press.

- Chinese (Mandarin): Chinese University Press, Shatin, N. T. Hong Kong; 852-609-6508 (telephone), 852-603-6692 (fax)
- Dutch/Flemish: Jan Derksen PEN Test Publishers, P.O. Box 6537, 6503 GA Nymegen, the Netherlands; 31-24-3240884 (telephone), 31-481-465867 (fax)

- French: Mireille Simon, ECPA, 25 rue de la Plaine, 75980 Paris, Cedex 20, France; 33-1-40-09-62-62 (telephone), 33-1-40-09-62-80 (fax)
- Hebrew: University of Haifa, Faculty of Social Sciences, Mount Carmel, Haifa 31905, Israel; 972-4-240-111(telephone), 972-4-246814 or 972-4-240966 (fax)
- Hmong: Customer Service, National Computer System, P.O. Box 11416, Minneapolis, MN 55440, 800-627-7271 (telephone), 612-939-5199 (fax)
- Italian: Roberto Mattei, Organizzazioni Speciali, Via Scipone Ammirato 37, 50136 Firenze, Italy; 55-660-997 (telephone), 55-669-446 (fax)
- Spanish (for Mexico): Manual Moderno, Av Sonora 206, Col. Hipodromo, 06100 Mexico, D.F. 52-5-265-1100 (telephone), 52-5-265-1162 (fax)
- Spanish (for Spain): TEA Ediciones, Fray Bernardino de Sahagun, 24, Madrid 28036, Spain, 91-359-83-11 (telephone), 91-345-86-08 (fax)
- Spanish (for the United States): Customer Service, National Computer Systems Authority, P.O. Box 1416, Minneapolis, MN 55440; 800-627-7271 (telephone), 612-939-5199 (fax)

[4]Using the 550 MMPI item pool, Blanchard (1981) found that the MMPI contained 6,317 words, of which 4,467 are monosyllabic, 1,422 disyllabic, and 320 trisyllabic. Average sentence length was 11.2 words, with an average number of syllables per sentence being 15.4. There was about one polysyllabic word per sentence.

[5]Paolo et al. (1991) pointed out that it is possible for participants to generate valid clinical profiles but at the same time generate invalid scores on the additional scales. They investigated and reported the reading requirements of 61 MMPI–2 special scales and subscales that contained a high percentage of items requiring a reading proficiency level beyond the eighth grade. Many of the items on these scales could be difficult to understand for those individuals possessing only the minimum requisite reading level for taking the MMPI–2. Paolo, Ryan, and Smith identified the following nine scales on which at least 25% of the total number of items required more than an eighth-grade reading level: *ASP* (Antisocial Practices), *TPA* (Type A Behavior), *Hy2* (Need for Affection), *Pa3* (Naivete), *Sc5* (Lack of Ego Mastery, Defective Inhibition), *Sc6* (Sensory Motor Dissociation), *Ma1* (Amorality), *Ma3* (Imperturbability), and *Ma4* (Ego Inflation). Paolo, Ryan, and Smith suggested that the Hypomania clinical scale itself be cautiously interpreted with individuals possessing less than an eighth- or ninth-grade education; 66.7% of the *Ma1* items, 37.5% of the *Ma3* items, and 33.3% of the *Ma4* items require greater than an eighth-grade reading level. The following items taken from the *Ma1* subscale illustrate the extent of the demands that these items make on the reader:

250. At times I have been so entertained by the cleverness of some criminals that I have hoped that they would get away with it. (True)
Lexile value: 1,199. Approximate reading level: 11th grade.
263. I am always disgusted with the law when a criminal is freed through the arguments of smart lawyer. (False)
Lexile value: 1,132. Approximate reading level: 10th grade.
269. If several people find themselves in trouble, the best thing for them to do is to agree upon a story and stick to it. (True)
Lexile value: 1,105. Approximate reading level: 10th grade.

[6]The following resources can be contacted for scoring and interpretation services, as well as for providing test materials and literature on the MMPI/MMPI–2:

- National Computer Systems, Customer Service, P.O. 1416, Minneapolis, MN 55440; 800-627-7271 (telephone), 612-939-5199 (fax)
- Caldwell Report, 1545 Sawtelle Blvd., Los Angeles, CA 90025; 310-478-3133 (telephone)

- Professional Assessment Resources, P. O. Box 998, Odessa, Florida 33556; 800-331-8378 (telephone)

[7]Greene (2000; 1991a) described a procedure called *augmenting* the profile, when between 5 and 30 items have been unanswered by a participant in an MMPI–2 administration. Although not studied empirically, this procedure may have some practical benefits to the psychologist if he or she is cautious about not overinterpreting the results from this procedure. Usually, it is preferable to have a participant retake the omitted or double-marked items, but this may not always be possible (e.g., client may have left the office). The basic method assumes that the omitted items were being avoided and that if endorsed, the items would have been scored in a deviant direction. It is always important to inspect the omitted items for any content themes before augmenting the profile. The first step in this process is to determine which scales the omitted items are scored on, keeping in mind that some items overlap multiple scales and may be scored in opposite directions on some scales (see Dahlstrom, 1993, for a listing of the item overlap of various MMPI–2 scales). The clinician adds 1 point for each omitted item to the raw score of the appropriate scale. Before plotting this corrected or augmented profile on the standard profile sheet, Greene (2000, 1991a) cautioned that if the *K* scale has been augmented, it is important to augment all of the *K*-corrected scales if a *K*-corrected profile is being plotted. This method could change the code pattern that is interpreted, so it is important to note on the profile sheet if the augmented or nonaugmented code pattern is being interpreted, if in fact they differ.

A second method described by Greene (2000; 1991a) for augmenting a profile involves determining the scales with the omitted items and determining the percentage of items actually endorsed in the deviant direction on those scales. For example, if a client answered 20 of the 60 items on the *F* scale in the deviant direction and omitted 10 *F* items, the clinician would calculate the proportion of endorsed *F* items and add to that value the same proportion of omitted items on that scale. In this example, the participant endorsed 33% (20 out of 60 items) of the *F* items, and .33 of the omitted 10 items is about 3 items. Three items would then be added to the *F* score and plotted as an augmented *F* scale. As with the first method, it is also important to note on the profile sheet whether the augmented or nonaugmented code pattern is being interpreted.

5

Interpreting the Validity Scales

Several methods and a number of special scales are available to assess complex validity issues on the MMPI–2, many of which are discussed later in this chapter, as well as in chapter 2. However, nine basic validity measures provide the clinician with the essential frame of reference for interpreting the clinical and supplementary scales. These nine basic validity measures (*?*, *VRIN*, *TRIN*, *F*, *FB*, *F(p)*, *L*, *K*, and *S*) give some indications of (a) whether the client understood and answered all the items; (b) the extent to which the client is endorsing items claiming the experience of psychological pain and unusual, bizarre experiences, behaviors, or ideas; (c) the extent to which the client might be trying to consciously or unconsciously give a favorable or unfavorable self-portrayal; and (d) the extent to which the client was consistent or inconsistent in reporting. In other words, the basic validity scales are useful in determining the *consistency* and *accuracy* of reporting. In addition to measuring validity, some of the validity scales also have personality correlates. The interpretations that follow, then, focus both on the *validity* aspects of the validity scales and, where applicable, the *personality* aspects.

As previously described in chapter 2, the MMPI was constructed with three basic validity scales: *L*, *F*, and *K* scales. The *VRIN*, *TRIN*, *FB*, *and F(p) and S* scales were developed for the MMPI–2 to assist in evaluating the consistency and accuracy of a given protocol. Except for some slight differences in cutoff scores, minor rewordings, and the loss of four items on the *F* scale, the three original validity scales (*L*, *F*, and *K*) are the same for the MMPI–2 as they were for the MMPI. The contemporary normative sample did slightly alter the *T*-score values for the *L*, *F*, and *K* scales.

Chapter 2 provides a detailed description of the construction methodology, psychometric operating features, and reliability and validity research for all of the scales described in this chapter. Table A.1 provides the item composition and scoring keys for all of the following validity scales. Tables B.1 and B.2 provide the linear *T*-score conversions for the standard validity scales and other measures of response style.

? (CANNOT SAY) SCORE

The *?* Scale is misnamed in that it is not a scale in any sense of the word; rather, it is a reporting of the number of unscorable items (i.e., double-marked or omitted items). Consequently, we refer to it as a Cannot Say score rather than as a scale.

On the MMPI–2, the number of unscorable items is recorded on the bottom left of the profile sheet, and no *T*-score value is given. The test instructions are different for the MMPI–2 than for the MMPI in that test takers are asked to answer all of the questions, if possible, so the mean number of omitted items on the MMPI–2 is even smaller than on the MMPI. The significance of omitted items on the MMPI–2, therefore, is heightened because the test taker has been specifically asked to answer all of the questions.

Normal Range: Five or Fewer Unscorable Items

Little, if any, validity significance is associated with the omission of five or fewer items, although examining omitted items may yield clinical hypotheses. In forensic settings, every omitted item could be significant and should be noted by the expert witness, as the opposing attorney might question the omission(s) during cross-examination. In such settings, a protocol could be returned for completion even if only four or five items are left unanswered. The psychologist should be aware that a cross-examining attorney could ask, "Did the defendant answer all the questions?" and, if the answer is no, "Which questions were not answered?" Thus, the client should be encouraged to complete omitted items on the test if this is feasible.

Moderate to High Range: 6 to 29 Unscorable Items

Raw scores of 6 to 29, if reading or comprehension difficulties can be ruled out, generally indicate idiosyncratic and contentious interpretation of items and/or obsessional indecision, often with extreme intellectualization. This process may be seen in the legalistic overcautiousness of some paranoid clients or the indecision of anxious, obsessive–compulsive ones. In other individuals, this range may reflect a reticence to respond openly to test items that probe personal experiences or private feelings and experiences in particularly sensitive areas for that person.

Marked Elevation (Possibly Invalid Profile): 30 or More Unscorable Items

If more than 30 items are omitted, the elevation and the code pattern of the clinical profile is likely to be significantly lowered (except for Scale 5 for women, which could be elevated), reducing the probability of obtaining an accurate picture of the person's unique personality characteristics. Extremely high raw scores can occur among severely emotionally impaired persons, who are unable to perform the decision-making task because of profound depression, intrusive thoughts, extreme preoccupation with the exact meaning of the questions, or apprehension that the questions' dichotomous nature will unfairly put them in some negative or inaccurate category. It is probable, however, that such a high score indicates a resistive, uncooperative person or a person with substantial reading or comprehension problems.

The clinician should attempt to discover the reasons for the individual's Cannot Say propensity when so many items are omitted before asking the individual to retake the test. The clinician should sensitively probe the reasons for items being unanswered (or double marked) and reassure the individual that the assessment process is collaborative in nature. Even, so it is possible to interpret profiles with limited accuracy when as many as 30 items are omitted, although the attenuating effect on the profile must be considered because clinical scales can drop significantly and the code pattern can also change. Note that if the omitted items all or mostly occur after Item 370, the basic validity and clinical scales will not be affected (see chap. 2, Footnote 1, and chap. 4, Footnote 7).

If up to 30 items are omitted, Greene (1991a; 2000) suggested the following procedure: First, score all omitted or double-marked items in the pathological direction and plot the profile, then plot a second profile with the items omitted. Once this has been done, compare both profiles and write a report discussing the two profiles and the nature of the omitted items. The report will be speculative but could be valuable nonetheless. If there is some consistency among the omitted items, the test interpreter can speculate as to possible explanations, given the two profiles. This should be carefully considered in a forensic setting, however, as the data will likely be ruled as speculative (Pope et al., 1993). In general, if more than 30 items have been omitted, the profile is likely invalid.

Please see Table 5.1 for an interpretive summary of the Cannot Say score values.

Variable Response Inconsistency Scale *(VRIN)*

This 67 item MMPI–2 scale was designed to detect inconsistent responding. It is particularly useful when the *F* and/or *FB* scale (or both) is elevated and there is uncertainty as to whether the elevations reflect severe psychopathology, random, or careless responding, or symptom magnification. In such cases, an elevated *VRIN* scale would suggest that the *F* and *FB* elevations are due to confusion or careless responding, whereas a low *VRIN* score would suggest that the high *F* or *FB* score (or both) is due to severe psychopathology or careful exaggeration of psychopathology. Cutoff scores for invalidity are inexact, but the following ranges provide cut-off guidelines.

Consistent Responding: Raw Scores Between 0 and 8, *T* Scores Between 30 and 65

Because the determination of validity is a multivariate process, it is important to examine other indicators of response consistency when assessing the validity of the profile. Raw scores between 0 and 8 on the *VRIN* scale typically reflect consistent

TABLE 5.1
Raw *?* Score Summary

Raw Score	*Description*
0–1	In most cases, this is the expected number of unscorable items.
2–5	Normal range. Little distortion to the profile, unless all of the omitted items are from a particular content area, and even then the distortion will be small. Usually either occurs because of oversight by the test taker or is due to a particularly individualized interpretation of the items. If possible, inquire about the omitted items, as the client may have misunderstood the instructions to answer all of the items. In a forensic setting, be aware that the omitted items may be the subject of cross-examination.
6–29	Moderate to high elevation. Look for any pattern to the omitted items, and determine whether there is resistance, confusion, or idiosyncratic interpretation of the items. In a forensic setting, this is a significant number and should be returned for completion and the reasons for noncompletion should be explored. Be aware that the individual's reasons for not answering the items may be the subject of cross-examination. If possible, inquire about the omitted items, as the client may have misunderstood the instructions to answer all of the items.
> 30	Profile is probably not valid and should not be interpreted until the omitted items are subsequently completed. Ascertain the likely cause for the item omissions. The client may be resistant, psychotic, confused, or angry about a particular life area reflected in the items, or the client may not have heard the test instructions to answer all of the items. Whenever asking the client to answer omitted items, explain that no one item is important on its own; rather, it is the pattern of scores that is relevant. Also deal with any anxiety about how the test results are going to be used and/or feelings that some of the test items may not seem relevant. As scores approach 30, profile elevation and code pattern may be affected. Examine omitted items for any particular pattern, and follow up with further questioning. Construct an augmented profile if the client is unable or unwilling to complete the protocol. Do not do this in a forensic setting, unless you can justify it under cross-examination.

responding, with a raw score of 8 equaling a *T* score of 65. However, we suggest that a cutoff raw score of 8 is too conservative and could lead to many false identifications of inconsistent responding.

Profile Indeterminate: Raw Scores Between 9 and 16, *T* Scores Between 69 and 101

In this range, the profile could reflect either inconsistent or consistent responding. The MMPI–2 manual suggests that a raw score of 13 or higher (*T* score of 85 for men, 87 for women) should be the cutoff for determining inconsistent responding. Examine the *TRIN* score and the other measures of responding to further determine the validity of the profile. Severely disturbed individuals whose confusion and uncertainty is part of their symptom picture often score in this range on the *VRIN* scale. However, if the *VRIN* score is in the upper end of this large range, it is unlikely that the MMPI–2 profile validly reflects the individual's stable personality.

Inconsistent Responding : Raw Scores Greater Than 16, *T* Scores of 85 or Greater

Raw scores over 16 on the *VRIN* scale strongly suggest that the profile is invalid due to inconsistent responding. Even if the profile is valid by *F*, *FB*, *L*, and *K*, criteria, the high *VRIN* score suggests so much inconsistency that the profile's validity is compromised. A raw score of 16 should be considered very high in clinical samples, suggesting a highly unusual response set, even among clinical patients.

True Response Inconsistency Scale *(TRIN)*

This 23-item scale developed for the MMPI–2 measures a participant's tendency to answer "True" or "False" to the MMPI–2 items without careful consideration of the meaning of the items. Some individuals may answer the items with a tendency to acquiesce, responding "True" (yea-saying) to the items even if their answers are inconsistent. Others respond with resistance or defensiveness, responding "False" (nay-saying) without full regard for the meaning of an item.

A majority of MMPI–2 items are scored in the pathological direction when marked "true"; thus, severely disturbed individuals will produce high *F* scores, high clinical scale scores, and a higher percentage of "true" responses. The exception, however, are somatizing profiles (e.g., 123/321 and 13), where more of the pathological responses are "false." These individuals, like others who are approaching the test with a highly positive self-presentation, will produce a higher "false" than "true" response percentage.

The *TRIN* scale can be useful in determining a yea- or nay-saying response set, especially when "true" or "false" percentages are high. The *TRIN* score is computed by adding a point for every "true" *TRIN* item endorsed and subtracting a point for every "false" *TRIN* item. Nine is added to the equation to ensure there are no negative numbers. A profile is showing no evidence of yea- or nay-saying with a *TRIN* score of 9 (0 "true" items endorsed + 0 "false" items endorsed + 9 = 9). A score of 13 or greater suggests considerable yea-saying, and a score of 5 or less suggests nay-saying.

Raw Scores Between 8 and 10

If other validity indicators suggest the profile is valid, then *TRIN* scores in this range confirm it.

Raw Scores of 11 to 12 and 6 to 7

The profile is revealing significant yea-saying or nay-saying and may be invalid. The individual's response set should be investigated, and the test could be retaken or cautiously interpreted, depending on the setting.

Raw Scores of 5 and Less and 13 and Greater

The profile is invalid because of excessive yea- or nay-saying and should be retaken with appropriate test-taking instructions and/or proctoring.

Infrequency Scale (*F*)

The *F* items reflect the degree to which thoughts, attitudes, and experiences reported by a person are different from the normative population. Persons who randomly mark items, who cannot comprehend item content, or who consciously attempt to portray a negative image of themselves endorse *F* items to a higher degree than the general population and also to a higher degree than genuinely disturbed populations. However, individuals who are authentically disturbed and unhappy also elevate the *F* scale, as would persons with unusual attitudes (e.g., sociopaths) or alienating experiences (e.g., minority populations). Because about one third of the *F* items overlap with Scales 6, 7, 8, and 9, elevations on the *F* scale are often accompanied by elevations on these clinical scales, particularly Scales 6 and 8. The following descriptions deal primarily with validity issues and, to some extent, address clinical correlates. The clinical information, however, is minor compared with the validity information and should be ignored if contradicted by the information from the basic clinical scales.

Low Scores: Raw Scores of 2 or Less, *T* Scores Between 36 and 44

Raw scores of 2 or less on the *F* scale suggest a person who is conventional in that the person is reporting few, if any, unusual thoughts, beliefs, or behaviors and is in no particular distress at the time of testing. Individuals without elevations on the clinical scales, then, may be described as calm, dependable, sincere, unpretentious, and honest, attributes one would expect from a person who is basically psychologically healthy. For some individuals, however, the possibility exists that they are denying or minimizing problems and that they have systematically avoided admitting to distressing or unusual feelings or thoughts. The other validity scales, however, would provide a clue to the source of the low *F* scores; thus a low *L* score and a normal *K* score would suggest that the low *F* score is, in fact, reflecting mental health rather than positive malingering. Sometimes an individual obtains a very low *F* score but also obtains a moderately elevated clinical profile. This would suggest that the individual's disturbance is not acute but more long-standing and perhaps not psychologically disorganizing.

Moderate Scores: Raw Scores Between 3 and 7, *T* Scores Between 45 and 61

Raw scores between 3 and 7 indicate acknowledgment of a number of unusual experiences, attitudes, feelings, and behaviors that differ somewhat from the norm. With adolescents, college populations, creative persons, or moderately disturbed people, such *F* elevations are not atypical. Similarly, when persons become intensely involved in religious, political, or social causes that are different from the mainstream, the scores on the *F* scale tend to be slightly elevated. Occasionally, however, particularly in mental health settings, such scores will occur in persons with some psychopathology, but who have adjusted to experiencing chronic problems, and therefore are not in great immediate distress. Their problems are "contained" and perhaps ego-syntonic.

High Scores: Raw Scores Between 8 and 16, *T* Scores Between 61 and 92

Valid raw scores between 8 and 16 suggest distress, increasing significantly toward the middle and high end of this range. Scores in this range indicate unusual or markedly unconventional thinking and attitudes, as well as psychological distress. Identity and self-esteem issues, as well as psychopathology, are indicated, and the person is likely to be described as moody, changeable, restless, unstable, dissatisfied, talkative, and opinionated but self-deprecating, all descriptions associated with psychological disturbance. The clinical scales are almost always elevated when the *F* scale is in this range, so the basic personality picture is described by the code pattern. The personality descriptors associated with *F* elevations in this range reflect general disturbance and distress. Young people struggling with identity problems and a need to define themselves through nonconformity frequently score in this range on the *F* scale. Generally, as *F* scores approach 16, the profile almost always reflects a serious, often panicked disturbance. *F* scores between 8 and 12 are typically seen in individuals with a long-standing and serious disturbance.

Borderline Valid Scores: Raw Scores Between 17 and 25, *T* Scores Between 88 and 113 (for Men) and Between 88 and 120 (for Women)

Raw scores between 17 and 25 are in an indeterminate range and suggest the following possibilities: (a) failure of the client to understand the items; (b) resistance or lack of cooperation; (c) random or haphazard reporting of numerous *F* items because of delusional thinking, confusion, or other psychotic processes; (d) conscious distortion and exaggeration of psychological symptom for secondary gain; (e) panicked overendorsement of *F* items, perhaps to draw attention to current fear, pain, and distress; or (f) seriously disturbed individuals, perhaps in inpatient, or prison settings. As the *F* scale approaches 17, the importance of all the other validity indicators to rule out symptom magnification becomes even more critical. With scores this high, the examiner should suspect that the profile is invalid and should check this by considering the characteristics of the remainder of the profile, the actual test-taking and interview behavior, and possible motivations for exaggeration that might derive from the client's current situation. Even profiles with *F* scores of 25 may be occasionally interpreted in a psychiatric setting in some cases. An interpretable *F* score in this range is almost always associated with a profound disturbance, disorganized thinking and psychotic symptoms, although sometimes it may be a "cry for help." A clinical interview usually reveals very atypical thought processes, poor judgment, and distortion of reality, often accompanied by confusion, withdrawal, and lack of cooperation.

Interpreting a profile with an *F* score between 22 and 25 is hazardous. Certainly, in a forensic setting, the clinician would have to be armed with solid supportive evidence to withstand a cross-examination and show that such a profile is validly interpretable. Information would have to be presented from other tests, history, and interviews to paint an integrated picture of the individual so that the elevated profile has some context. For example, an expert witness psychologist might say, "Yes, by standard criteria this *F* score of 25 suggests invalidity. However the other tests suggest a serious psychotic disturbance and the patient's history confirms it. In light of such data this MMPI–2 may reflect his current psychosis." Although *F* scores in the very high range can be interpreted in some situations, they should not be interpreted if the scales showing confusion and inconsistency or a biased response set (i.e., *VRIN*, *TRIN*, *F(p)*, and *Ds*) are also significantly elevated. Increasingly, it has been our experience that attorneys send, through a psychologist, their clients or opponent clients' MMPI–2 to one of the computer-generated report services. These services tend to be conservative in validity cutoff scores so that an *F* score over 18 is ruled invalid. This may be too conservative in some cases, but the psychologist would need to be prepared to defend a claim of validity as the *F* score reaches 18 and above. It can be difficult to explain under cross-examination why a respected computer-generated report is inaccurate in suggesting that a profile is malingered or invalid and why the psychologist is accurate in suggesting it is valid. Consequently, the expert witness needs to be well prepared and have the ability to integrate the MMPI–2 data with other persuasive data if claiming an elevated MMPI–2 *F* score is valid.

Very High/Invalid Scores: Raw Scores of 26 or Greater, *T* Scores of 116 or Greater (for Men) and 120 or Greater (for Women)

Although *F* scores in the very high range (raw scores of 26 and above) sometimes can be very cautiously interpreted in situations in which there appears no motivation for malingering and a serious disturbance is suspected, generally such high scores should be considered invalid or seriously exaggerated. Information from *F* scores this high is probably not stable because it reflects an acute disturbance. Nevertheless, the test data will give information about how the individual is experiencing the world right now and how the person is presenting himself to the psychologist. Once the individual has stabilized, it may help to have the person retake the test for a more valid evaluation of his or her personality organization.

F-Back Scale (*FB*)

As described earlier in chapter 2, this scale was developed with the new MMPI–2 normative sample using the same rationale as the original *F* scale. This scale is an attempt to identify persons whose concentration or motivation decreases during the last half of the test and who may even begin randomly marking items with little or no attention to item content. Any item answered by 10% or fewer of the new normative group that was not an *F* item became an *FB* item. It is important to note that the *T* scores for the *FB* scale rise much more quickly for a given raw score than the *T* scores for the *F* scale. A raw score of 16 on the *FB* scale, for example, yields a *T* score of 108, whereas the equivalent raw score on the *F* scale is a *T* score of 85 (see chap. 2). Most items on the *FB* scale have an acute distress and depression theme, whereas the major theme of the *F* items reflects psychoticism. Consequently, profiles may show quite different raw scores on the two *F* scales, depending on the kind of disturbance being evaluated. In some cases, the *FB* scale is significantly higher than the *F* scale, but this does not necessarily mean that the individual became more disturbed over the course of the test or necessarily exaggerated his or her symptoms toward the end of the test. An *FB* score higher than an *F* score may instead reflect individuals, for example, who are experiencing distress associated with drug and/or alcohol problems, and the resulting disorganization of their life and support system, rather than the psychotic-like disorganization reflected in *F* elevations. Defining exact cutoff scores, although reassuring to the clinician, is not possible for the *FB* scale, as it is not possible for any of the validity scales. Validity has to be ascertained using a multivariate approach, taking into account all validity data, the setting, and other test data. However, the following cutoff guidelines may provide a framework for determining validity.

Low Scores: Raw Scores Between 0 and 3, *T* Scores Between 42 and 55

Raw scores between 0 and 3 would suggest a well-adjusted individual if the clinical scales are not elevated and the other validity scales suggest validity. It could also reflect a possible denial of problems, especially if the other validity scales suggest underreporting. Psychopathology, if present and reflected on the profile with an *FB* score in this range, tends to be long-standing, ego-syntonic, and nonpsychotic in nature

High Normal to High Range: Raw Scores Between 4 and 14, *T* Scores Between 58 and 100

In a valid, unelevated profile, the low end (e.g., *FB* = 4) could reflect normal range comfort and distress, occasioned by perhaps, for example, chemical dependency problems. If obtained in an elevated profile, *FB* scores in the lower part of this range suggest that the disturbance is long-standing and may be ego-syntonic. As the *FB* score approaches a raw score of 14, the severity of the disturbance increases and the importance of making sure that other validity indicators are within acceptable parameters increases.

Very High Range: Raw Scores Between 15 and 19, *T* Scores Between 101 and 120

This range is often associated with chronically maladjusted and acutely disturbed individuals, as well as the range for malingered and random profiles. As scores approach 19, the probability increases that the individual is malingering, especially in cases in which there is clear secondary gain from doing so. In rare cases, scores in this range could also reflect chronic psychopathology, borderline personality functioning, panic, and chemical addiction and abuse. As described earlier, 37 of the 40 *FB* items are scored as "true," so an acquiescing response bias would elevate the *FB* scale, but not without also elevating the TRIN score to unacceptable levels in most cases.

Extremely Elevated Scores: Raw Scores of 20 or Greater, *T* Scores of 120 or Greater

The profile is very probably invalid, especially if there is any secondary gain, as in forensic and disability cases. In some psychiatric settings, *FB* scores may be as high as 21 to 24 raw-score points and reflect a severe disturbance; additionally, the accompanying profile code pattern is probably not stable. Scores in this range in a *clinical* population suggest a high degree of response unusualness, even among clinical groups. As raw scores range from 20 to 24, the probability increases that the individual is overreporting regardless of the setting, or that the individual is panicked, pleading for help, or severely disturbed. Other validity scales should confirm the determination of whether the profile is valid.

SELF-UNFAVORABLE SCALES

Infrequency-Psychopathology Scales: *F(p)* Scale

The *F(p)* scale (see chap. 2.) consists of very rarely endorsed items among both psychiatric patients and normals and is useful in detecting the overreporting of psychopathology.

Normal Range: Raw Scores of 3 and Below, T Scores of 65 and Below. Raw scores of 3 and below suggest a lack of obvious overreporting. If the other validity scales suggest invalidity, a low *F(p)* score would not change that determination.

Indeterminate Range: Raw Scores Between 4 and 9, T Scores Between 71 and 113. Raw Scores between 4 and 9 are in the indeterminate range, depending on the setting. If other validity indicators suggest invalidity, then *F(p)* scores in this range would confirm it. This scale is most useful when the validity indicators show marginal validity. In these cases, raw scores of 5 and above on the *F(p)* scale would suggest invalidity.

High/Invalid Range: Raw Scores of 10 or More, T Scores of 114 or Greater. If the *F(p)* score is a raw score of 10 or greater, the profile is probably *exaggerated, even if the other validity scales suggest validity.*

Dissimulation Scale (*Ds*)

As discussed earlier in chapter 2, this is a useful scale in detecting a self-unfavorable bias or overreporting. When the *F* scale is elevated above a raw score of 14, it is often difficult to determine how much of the disturbance is severe psychopathology, with little or no exaggeration, and how much is due to overreporting. The overreporting may be due to dramatization and panic, or it may be due to conscious dissimulation. The 58-item Dissimulation scale is very helpful in determining the degree or presence of symptom magnification.

Valid Range: Raw Scores of 18 and Below, T Scores of 63 and Below (for Women) and 65 and Below (for Men). Raw scores on the *Ds* scale of 18 and below suggest an absence of malingering. Any psychopathology evidenced is likely accurate, even if the other validity scales suggest some exaggeration (e.g., raw $F = 20$ and $K = 10$).

Moderately Elevated Range: Raw Scores Between 19 and 27, T Scores Between 65 and 82. Raw scores between 19 and 27 suggest some exaggeration and a tendency to present oneself from the perspective of feeling one's worst. If the other validity scales suggest validity, then the profile is likely still valid, even as scores on the *Ds* scale approach a raw score of 27, especially in seriously disturbed and psychotic individuals. Even so, some exaggeration is likely present as raw scores approach 27. If the other validity scales suggest invalidity or exaggeration, then raw scores on the *Ds* scale toward the end of this range support invalidity.

High Range: Raw Scores Between 28 and 33, T Scores Between 81 and 93. Raw scores between 28 and 33 suggest the likelihood of exaggeration, even if the profile is valid by other validity criteria. Scores this high suggest that persons are consciously presenting themselves as mentally ill, and the clinician needs to determine why. Even so, in severely impaired psychiatric patients, scores this high do not always invalidate the profile, although exaggeration is likely taking place.

Very High Range: Raw Scores Between 34 and 37, T Scores Between 92 and 101. Raw scores between 34 and 37 are high and, in almost all cases, suggest malingering, especially if the other validity scales confirm it. Even if the profile is determined valid by other validity measures, raw scores in this range suggest conscious self-unfavorable reporting and malingering.

Invalid Range: Raw Scores of 38 and Above, T Scores Equal to or Greater Than 99. Raw scores above 38 strongly suggest that the profile is malingered, even if the other validity scales are solidly in the interpretable range. If the other validity scales suggest self-unfavorable responding, scores in this range would make a diagnosis of malingering difficult to refute.

SELF-FAVORABLE SCALES

Lie Scale (*L*)

As described in chapter 2, the *L* scale consists of 15 items, which give the respondent 15 opportunities to claim desirable virtues that almost everyone would like to have, although almost nobody does. This scale, when elevated, reflects naive or obvious attempts by a person to look unusually virtuous, culturally conservative, overly conscientious, and above moral reproach. Because frank, self-aware persons so rarely endorse such statements, *L* scale scores above a *T* score of 65 are unusual, except in persons who have cultural backgrounds that require strict cultural conformity, are in occupations (e.g., clergy) that stress narrow personal and professional virtues, or are in situations (such as a job interview or child custody evaluation) that prompt them to present themselves in their "best light." It is not surprising to observe that the mean number of *L* items reported for airline pilot applicants is about 5 (Butcher, 1994b).

Education and age must be considered when interpreting an *L* score. Individuals of less than average intelligence or less than high school education tend to score slightly higher (about 5 *T*- score points) than a *T* score of 50. Individuals above age 50 likewise tend to endorse more *L* items, perhaps associated with age-related increases in conservative attitudes.

Although elevation on the *L* scale measures an individual's claim to unrealistically high moral virtues, it is generally adept at measuring purposeful distortion only in naive, unsophisticated people or in situations in which the motivation to present oneself in an overly positive light is very high, such as in a personnel (e.g., fitness for duty or preemployment selection) or custody evaluation. Psychologically sophisticated individuals, particularly persons with a college education, are often able to "see through" the items on this scale and therefore not endorse them. These psychologically sophisticated individuals generally are able to admit to certain understandable moral "flaws" and understand that to deny them would make them look as if they were not being honest. They may still attempt to portray themselves as unusually virtuous on other portions of the test, which would change elevations on some of the other validity scales, but the *L* scale would likely remain within normal limits. Elevated *L* scores in persons with broadly educated backgrounds can be difficult to interpret. In some cases, it may reflect a person who, although being educationally sophisticated, is quite morally and psychologically constricted and judgmental. Consider the following:

Ms. F., a successful attorney and MBA, was given the MMPI–2 as part of her treatment plan subsequent to a painful divorce. Her husband had complained in therapy prior to the divorce that his wife was a very judgmental person who had little patience with his recent business difficulties. When asked about this, Ms. F. admitted that she believed that failure was a sign of weakness and that she had little patience for people who got the "wrong answer" in life. Her MMPI–2 profile was within the normal range, but her *L* score was elevated at a *T* score of 65. She was rigid in her views, perfectionistic, and had difficulty admitting to mistakes. She was clearly apprehensive about being judged by the therapist and stated that she thought psychological problems were a sign of weakness.

Such attributes are associated with elevated *L* scores in educated individuals who are not taking the test as part of a job evaluation or divorce custody evaluation. In these latter cases, an *L* elevation also could reflect some defensiveness and an attempt to put one's best foot forward rather than (or as well as) personality attributes. Educated individuals with high *L* scores lack insight and generally are psychologically naive. When they seek treatment, it is usually only for advice for a specific problem. Insight therapy is particularly threatening to them because they feel that probing questions by the therapist are somehow searches for what is "wrong" with them. Interestingly, educated individuals with high *L* scores tend to lack anxiety (Matarazzo, 1955), perhaps reflecting the inner peace associated with moral certitude. Please see Table 5.2 for an interpretive summary of the Lie Scale Values.

Correction Scale *(K)*

This 30-item scale was not significantly altered on the MMPI–2 except for the minor rewording of one item. Although primarily considered a validity scale, it contains substantial clinical information about ego strength, reality contact, and coping abilities, as well as about defensiveness, guardedness, and test-taking posture. The *K* scale is an empirically derived "correction" scale developed to sharpen the diagnostic accuracy of Scales 1, 4, 7, 8, and 9 with adult inpatients. Note that the *K* items are not as obvious as the *L* items.

Despite the addition of the *K* corrections to these clinical scales, high *K* scores are usually associated with defensiveness and therefore lowered profiles, whereas low *K* scores are more often associated with more elevated clinical profiles. This is because elevations on the *K* scale in general reflect poise, emotional sophistication, and an unwillingness to admit to being "knocked off balance" or distressed by emotional problems. If an individual is guarded, as reflected by an elevated *K* scale, he or she is unlikely to admit to psychopathology. It is important for the clinician to examine the contribution of *K* to Scales 7 and 8 because the full amount of obtained raw *K* is added to these clinical scales. The individual with an elevated Scale 8 score due to the *K* addition is different from a person whose Scale 8 score is elevated due to the contribution of mostly Scale 8 items with a small added *K* value. The high *K* person is likely to be more in control of whatever pathology exists and is often able to mask it, especially in structured situations.

The *K* scale can be thought of as representing emotional control and coping capacity. At higher elevations, it also reflects emotional constrictedness. It is instructive to read the following *K* items to gain a "feel" for the scale. In answering the items in the scored direction, the individual reveals a cautiousness about admitting extremes of emotions, whether positive or negative, or any loss of emotional control:

29. "At times I feel like swearing." (False)
127. "Criticism or scolding hurts me terribly." (False)
136. "It makes me impatient to have people ask my advice or otherwise interrupt me when I am working on something important." (False)
148. "I have never felt better in my life than I do now." (False)

The respondent is keeping a very emotionally middle-of-the-road response set, responding in a measured and emotionally cautious way. People of higher SES tend to score higher on the *K* scale because emotionally modulated responding is socially appropriate. Extremes of emotions, "making a fuss," and being too emotional are seen as inappropriate. Not all upper SES individuals have a high *K* score, however. One challenge that clinicians, especially forensic experts, encounter is how to distinguish when a high *K* score is due to genuine upper SES, poise, and emotional control and when is it due to a conscious attempt by respondents to distort and portray themselves as psychologically healthy and emotionally balanced.

Very Low Scores: Raw Scores of 7 or Below, *T* Scores Below 35

Very low scores ($T < 35$) can stem from several possibilities. If there is any secondary gain from being diagnosed with a psychiatric disturbance and other validity scales suggest self-unfavorable responding along with elevated clinical scales, consider that the profile may be intentionally exaggerated. Typically, the profile would also show exaggerated *F* and *F*B Scale scores and the overendorsement of critical items. In valid profiles in which the clinical scales are elevated, such a low *K* score suggests severe disturbance with little capacity to modulate feelings and behaviors. The individual would likely need a very supportive and involved intervention, and any suicidal and/or homicidal threats should be taken seriously. These individuals experience their symptoms as frightening and feel a sense of panic and loss of control. They are self-critical and need directive, supportive, esteem-building psychotherapy.

TABLE 5.2

L Scale Summary

T Score	*Raw Score*	*Description*
33–43	0–2	Suggests candidness and willingness to admit to common human failings. However, if the other validity scales suggest an exaggeration of psychopathology, this low score could be part of an attempt to present oneself as disturbed and without resources to be moral. In some exaggerated profiles, clients overendorse pathological items (high *F* score), claim to have no defenses (very low *K* score), and have very low *L* scores.
47–57	3–5	This is the "normal" range for individuals taking the test in normal situations. Individuals taking the test in forensic or job evaluation settings would typically score higher. At a *T* score of 55, there is already a slight tendency to be putting one's best foot forward, unless the individual is from an unsophisticated background. A *T* score of 55 might be seen in an educated although mildly cautious, defensive individual and/or in a mildly moralistic individual. Individuals from lower SES backgrounds score in this range and the *L* score reflects traditional, if somewhat unsophisticated views.
61–67	6–7	Suggests concern and some rigidity over matters of self-control and moral values, as well as a tendency to be conforming and conventional. Such preoccupation with high moral standards usually is attached to a fear of being found unacceptable by others, unless the person scrupulously adheres to rules. The defense mechanism of denial may be characteristic of these individuals. People show some lack of self-awareness and insight when *L* elevations in this range are present. In an educated individual or in a custody or job evaluation setting, this *L* elevation also suggests an attempt to look one's best and to deny unacceptable human impulses. The validity of the test may be somewhat compromised by elevations towards the high end of this range. Airline pilot applicants score in the lower end of this range.

(continued on next page)

T Score	*Raw Score*	*Description*
70–81	8–10	Uncommon. If scoring errors or a systematic denial response set can be ruled out, the person is denying many of the most common and obvious human faults. Such individuals have intense needs to present a good front and do so with rigidity, repression, and denial. Moral issues, as well as their own integrity and concern with scruples, permeate their lives to the point that they are typically seen as self-righteous and uncompromising. Their self-perception and lifestyle are bound by rigid moral rules, and they are sensitive to social disapproval. Some see psychological problems as a sign of moral weakness. They tend to be naively defensive, as though worried that their "life rules" might be "wrong" and therefore vulnerable to judgment. They deny or gloss over unfavorable traits in themselves, repress foibles or unacceptable urges, and have little insight into their motives or behaviors. Sometimes the elevated *L* score is a manifestation of extreme naivete in a person from a culturally restricted environment. Other times it reflects a conscious attempts to distort the MMPI–2 profile. In either cases, such persons typically make poor candidates for insight-oriented psychotherapy. Strategic or directive approaches are likely to work best. In forensic settings, these elevations would bring into doubt the veracity of the profile. The burden of proof would be on the expert witness in claiming, for example, that an MMPI–2 profile of a divorcée seeking custody of her children was valid with a raw *L* score of 10. If the protocol is valid, then the *L* scale suggests a very moralistically rigid and psychologically naive individual.
83–105	11–15	These scores are rare. Although the profile is probably invalid, the reasons for such an elevated *L* scale need to be ascertained. If the profile is an original MMPI, then look for a scoring error because scoring the *L* scale on the MMPI involves counting items without a template, so errors can occur. Also, be aware that the *T* score for a given raw score is higher on the MMPI–2. Valid scores in this range may reflect (a) an overcontrolled, rigid, repressed individual lacking insight; (b) the black-and-white moralistic thinking associated with some religious orders although having strong religious convictions will not necessarily raise the *L* score, it is the rigidity and lack of sophistication about knowing how others really behave); (c) an unsophisticated or even panicked attempt to look unusually virtuous (often found in forensic or personnel situations); or (d) a psychotic individual who has an unelevated profile although usually the clinical profile will be close to $T = 65$. In this last case, the high *L* score reflects a paranoid rigidity and apprehension about being criticized. However, in these cases, there are usually other signs of a serious disturbance, such as the endorsement of items on the BIZ content scale and/or elevations on the Harris–Lingoes subscales and endorsement of relevant critical items.

Low Scores: Raw Scores Between 8 and 13, *T* Scores Between 35 and 45 (for Men) and Between 35 and 46 (for Women)

Low scores suggest that the person's coping abilities are compromised. Their defenses may be immature, and their emotional conflicts are destabilizing. Emotional–behavioral controls are likely to be poor. The low *K* score suggests that the disturbance reflected on the clinical scales will be behaviorally manifested, thus, the client is also likely to admit to the symptoms and complaints associated with the profile. These individuals tend to be self-critical, have poor self-esteem, and lack confidence that they have the skills to deal with their problems. A similar nondefensiveness and self-criticality is sometimes evident in persons engaged in the self-examination involved in insight-oriented psychotherapy. In cases in which the clinical scales show an absence of elevation, such low K scores would suggest candor and healthy openness, although often with a tendency to "wear one's feelings on one's sleeve."

Normal Elevations: Raw Scores Between 14 and 18, *T* Scores Between 47 and 56

A normal *K* elevation indicates a person who exhibits culturally appropriate emotional control and manifests a balance between emotional spontaneity and emotional constraint. These individuals generally feel in control of their emotional life. Even if the clinical scales are elevated, *K* scores in this range, especially toward $T = 55–56$, suggest some coping ability; psychological symptoms associated with the clinical scale elevations are likely to be at least somewhat under volitional control. In general, the closer the scale approaches a *T* score of 50 and higher, the more functional are the defenses and coping system. The prognosis is better for successful therapeutic interventions as the *K* scale approaches a *T* score of 55 to 56 and above until about a *T* score of 65, when emotional overcontrol and defensiveness can inhibit therapeutic insights.

Moderate Elevations: Raw Scores Between 19 and 22, *T* Scores Between 58 and 65

Moderate *K* elevations in the absence of elevations on the clinical scales are found in people generally described as independent, enterprising, ingenious, resourceful, enthusiastic with wide interests, and having a variety of interpersonal relationships, all attributes suggesting good mental health. Their lives are generally well managed, and they feel in control. *K* scores in this range, even in elevated profiles, generally contraindicate loss of control or uncontrollable acting out. The prognosis for psychological insight and change is generally better when *K* is in this moderate range rather than when *K* is below 45 or above 65. When *K* is below 40 to 45, the individual is likely to be overwhelmed by the feelings and psychopathology associated with the clinical scale elevations. If *K* is elevated above $T = 65$, poise and control tend to become emotional constriction and the individual resists psychological insights. If the clinical scales suggest psychopathology, moderate *K* scores suggest an ability to cope, with many areas of practical self-sufficiency and compensated functioning. For example, if an individual obtained a profile suggesting a serious depression with anxiety, low self-esteem, and guilt (e.g., high elevations on Scales 2, 7, and 8) but his or her *K* score is at a *T* score of 64, the individual might be able to successfully mask the full extent of his or her discomfort and work reasonably well. Such individuals can function with extended periods of efficiency and competence, even though their disturbance would be experienced by them as a loss of pleasure, underlying but managed anxiety, and periods of deep, but controlled, unhappiness.

High Scores: Raw Scores of 23 and Greater, *T* Scores of 66 and Greater

High scores in clinical populations reflect people who are particularly defensive and have difficulty tolerating suggestions that they might have psychological problems. Although they may see others as having psychological problems, they view their own emotional difficulties as "under control." They tend to be uncomfortable and rejecting of unconventional or nonconformist behavior in others and are often subtly judgmental of such behavior. Although quite concerned with being socially appropriate, they are relatively insightless concerning their emotional effect on others. Many such persons are rigidly managerial in their attempts to control their "world" as though disorganization would create a catastrophic unraveling of their life. They show reluctance to be seen as psychotherapy patients and reject suggestions that they might need assistance in understanding or managing their feelings or behaviors. Generally, they avoid examining problem areas because they view themselves as rational, normal, and balanced. They feel uncomfortable with any uncontrollable surges of emotion that can arise in the process of psychotherapy and the exploration of past experiences. If they seek psychotherapy, they gravitate toward intellectual types of therapy, such as psychoanalysis, which makes few unpredictable cathartic demands on them. *K* scores in this high range can also be obtained in forensic (e.g., child custody) and personnel evaluation situations. In these settings, *K* scores of 65 to 66 and above reflect the defensiveness that is somewhat expected, and the profile is likely to underestimate psychopathology. Long-range predictions from the profile could be inaccurate.

Some individuals, usually from higher socioeconomic groups, can score at or above a *T* score of 65 on the *K* scale and obtain nonelevated clinical scales that accurately reflect a lack of psychopathology. In these cases, the *K* score is often reflecting the "stiff upper lip" of a basically nonpathological individual from a cultural background that frowns on any uncontrolled displays of emotion and emphasizes that "one should always have one's life in order." *K* is correlated with education and upper SES, and people of upper SES tend to value emotional control and etiquette over impulsive expressions of affect. It is difficult to differentiate an elevated *K* scale due to high SES and nonconscious defensiveness from an elevated *K* scale due to conscious defensiveness. Scores on the Positive Malingering Scale (*Mp*), the Socioeconomic Status Scale (*Ss*), and the Social Desirability Scale (*Sd*) could be useful in making that differentiation and are discussed later in this chapter as well as in chapter 2.

Superlative Scale (*S*)

Butcher and Han (1995) developed this new scale by contrasting the item responses of 274 male airline pilot applicants with the 1,138 men of the MMPI–2 restandardization sample. The scale has good external validity and appears to measure mental health, contentment with life, and an ability to get along effectively with others. Although mentally healthy people will exhibit some of these attributes, it is unlikely that many will exhibit all of them to a high degree Consequently, high *S* scores ($T > 65$, raw score > 38) suggest that claims of superlative adjustment likely are exaggerated.

Butcher and Han (1995) suggested that the *S* scale may work similarly to the *F* scale. For example, moderate *F* scores suggest true distress and disturbance, but extreme scores suggest exaggeration. In the same way, moderate *S* scores ($T =$ 50–60) could suggest good adjustment and mental health, but as *T* scores rise above 60, the claims of good adjustment may be exaggerated. A raw score of 38 equals a *T* score of 65. Butcher and Han also factorially identified five subscales for the *S* scale.

S1: Belief in Human Goodness

This 15-item subscale appears to measure the exact opposite of the Cynicism content scale (*CYN*) with items pertaining to a belief that people are decent, helpful, loyal, and fair. A raw score of 13 and 14 equals a *T* score of 65 for men and women, respectively. Because this subscale contains only 15 items, it tops out at a *T* score of 70. Consequently, *T* scores over 60 (raw score > 11) could be considered high.

S2: Serenity

This 13-item subscale appears to measure a sense of inner peace, lack of internal conflict, social comfort, and integrity. A raw score of 10 equals a *T* score of 64 for men and 67 for women. A raw score of 13 equals a *T* score of 75 for men and 79 for women, so *T* scores between 64 and 79 should be considered high.

S3: Contentment With Life

This eight-item subscale measures a sense of contentment with one's life choices and achievements. A raw score of 7 equals a *T* score of 65 for men and 68 for women so the scale has a low ceiling. Scores above a *T* score of 60 should be considered high.

S4: Patience and Denial of Irritability and Anger

This eight-item subscale includes items pertaining to being patient, not irritable or grouchy, not needing to win points with difficult people, and being accommodating when being hurried or made to wait. A raw score of 7 equals a *T* score of 63 for both men and women and endorsement of all eight items yields a *T* score of 68, so scores over a *T* score of 60 should be considered high.

Subscale S5: Denial of Moral Flaws

This very short five-item subscale deals mainly with a denial of alcohol or marijuana abuse, denial of unusual sex practices, and claiming no secrets of which one is ashamed. Four endorsed items yield a *T* score of 53 for women and 58 for men. Five endorsed items yield a *T* score of 65 for men and 61 for women.

In cases in which self-favorable responding is suspected with high *K* scores and elevations on the *Mp* and *Sd* scales, elevations on some of the *S* subscales could validate the assumption of underreporting and exaggeration of superlative adjustments.

Future research should provide cutoff scores for different settings and populations, but until then, clinicians should cautiously factor scores on the *S* scale into their validity decision.

Positive Malingering Scale (*Mp*)

The *Mp* scale (Cofer et al., 1949) has been found useful in determining how much of the *K* elevation may be due to intentional self-favorable responding versus upper SES and self-deception. At present, only the Caldwell computerized report scores the *Mp* scale and uses it as an essential part of the validity write-up. Although little research exists on cutoff scores for the *Mp* scale, the following scores could serve as guidelines (Caldwell, 1988):

1. If both the *K* and *Mp* scales are elevated above *T* scores of 60, then the individual may be consciously attempting to make a good impression; the moderately elevated *Mp* score reflects some conscious underreporting and attempts to look socially virtuous.
2. If the *K* scale is elevated above a *T* score of 60 and the *Mp* scale is below 60, then the high *K* scale is probably the result of a genuine lack of introspective self-awareness and/or the "stiff upper lip" approach to life associated with upper SES. The lower the *Mp* score in association with a high *K* score, the more likely the *K* score is reflecting a nonconscious positive self-presentation.

Social Desirability Scale (*Sd*)

This scale was developed by Wiggins (1959) by asking Stanford University students to respond to the MMPI as "people in general would consider desirable" (Caldwell, 1988, p. 92). The scale operates similarly to the *Mp* scale, which accounts for its high correlation of .74 with that scale.

Caldwell (1988) argued that high scores above raw scores of 18 to 20 (T = 73–86) in the presence of a low *K* score suggest a person of lower SES who was attempting to consciously look his or her best, whereas low scores in the presence of a high *K* score suggest that the person's *K* score is reflecting mostly upper SES identification, with little, if any, conscious underreporting. If the *K* score is elevated and both the *Mp* and *Sd* scales are at a *T* score of 55 or lower, then the *K* elevation may well reflect education, social poise, and nonaware positive self-presentation. If both the *Mp* and *Sd* scales are elevated above a *T* score of 60, then the elevated *K* is probably reflecting self-favorable responding. The higher the *Mp* and/or *Sd* score, the more the individual is attempting to consciously look his or her best.

Socioeconomic Status Scale (*Ss*)

This scale, developed by S. E. Nelson (1952), is described by Caldwell (1988), who viewed it as reflective of "current 'earned' (socio-economic) status" (p. 94). This scale, together with the *Mp* and *Sd* scales, is used by Caldwell to fine-tune the validity section of the Caldwell Report by determining how much of a particular *K* elevation is due to SES and how much is due to conscious or unconscious underreporting. Caldwell reported that the scale correlates about .50 with independent measures of SES, and about .40 with IQ scores.

Although there is limited empirical research, Caldwell (1988) has made a convincing argument for using the *Ss* scale as part of the process to partial out an elevated *K* score of genuine emotional restraint associated with upper SES versus conscious defensiveness. For example, when the *K* scale is elevated (e.g., $T = 65$), he suggested that if the *Ss* scale is also elevated (e.g., $T = 65$, raw score = 67), reflecting upper SES, and the *Mp* and *Sd* scales are low (e.g., $T = 53$ and 54, respectively), suggesting a lack of a conscious positive self-presentation, then the high *K* score reflects the genuine emotional control and poise associated with upper SES without conscious positive malingering. On the other hand, if a *K* score is high but the *Ss* score is low (e.g., $T = 50$–55) and the *Mp* and *Sd* scores are high, then the elevated *K* score reflects someone who is intentionally responding self-favorably or underreporting.

VALIDITY INDICES

F – FB Index

In a valid profile, typically the *F* and *FB* scores will be elevated in more or less the same *T*-score range because both scales reflect disturbance, psychological distress, and unusual responding. As mentioned earlier, sometimes there is a valid discrepancy between *F* and *FB* scores, wherein the *FB* score is higher than the *F* score because the individual's disturbance is associated with serious depression and its resulting distress. However, if the *FB* score is between 15 and 19 raw-score points and greater than the *F* score by 8 raw-score points, and the content items do not clearly reflect drug and alcohol abuse issues or acute panic-like distress, then the second half of the test may be invalid. Therefore the content scales should not be interpreted although the clinical scales could be interpreted, if the other validity scales are not unduly elevated.

Dissimulation Index (*F* – *K*)

The *F* – *K* index is a useful further check on validity. The *F* scale measures severity of psychopathology and the *K* scale measures defensiveness. Most bona fide psychopathology involves some attempt at compensated functioning. A very high *F* score and a very low *K* score indicates that the individual is grossly disturbed and defenseless, a condition that is rarely true. Schizophrenic individuals typically will obtain raw *F* scores between 10 and 18 but usually with at least some elevation on the *K* scale. Conceptually, the usefulness of the *F* – *K* index reflects the fact that psychopathology usually is associated with some functioning defenses, so an individual claiming extreme distress (high *F*) and no defenses (low *K*) is probably exaggerating their disturbance. Cut off scores for the *F* – *K* index, like all cutoff scores, vary according to the setting, so the following are to be used only as guidelines.

Low *F* – *K* Scores

The *F* – *K* index is less accurate in correctly identifying self-favorable responders (see chap. 2). The mean *F* – *K* score is –10.77 and –11.37 for men and women, respectively, in the MMPI–2 restandardization group. The approximate lower 2.5% range for the restandardization sample is –22 for both men and women. Table 2.1 provides a range of scores across diagnostic groups for self-favorable (fake-good) responding. As the research to date with this index indicates that *F* – *K* is much more useful in identifying fake-bad versus fake-good profiles, it is recommended that the reader rely upon the *F* – *K* index for assistance in assessing self-unfavorable responding rather than self-favorable responding. The reader is referred to the *S*, *Mp*, *Sd*, and *Ss* scales in this chapter and in chapter 2 for assistance in interpreting self-favorable responding.

Normal Range: Raw Scores *F* – *K* Between 0 and 11

Scores in this range suggest the profile is valid, especially if the other validity indicators suggest validity. If other validity measures suggest exaggeration, then an *F* – *K* score of 11 and below would argue for a valid, but pathological, profile.

High Range: Raw Scores Between 12 and 16

Scores in this range suggest exaggeration or malingering, except in psychiatric patients, where *F* – *K* scores up to 16 would not be uncommon. If there appears to be no secondary gain from appearing pathological, *F* – *K* scores in this range may reflect the extreme pain and lack of psychological resources associated with severe psychopathology. In cases in which there could be secondary gain from appearing disturbed, *F* – *K* scores in this range should act as a red flag, alerting the clinician to the possibility of symptom magnification or severe distress.

Invalid Range: Raw Scores of 17 or Greater

Scores in this range suggest invalidity, especially if there is any secondary gain from overreporting. If the other validity indicators suggest exaggeration, scores in this range would confirm it.

Issues in Determining Validity

Determining the validity of a profile is often a difficult task for seasoned and novice practitioners alike. The problem is aggravated by the fact that exact cutoff scores are rarely given in the major textbooks on the MMPI–2, and when they are given, they are accompanied by the necessary disclaimers about how cutoff scores vary according to the setting and the motivation to over- or underreport problems. Given the expanded use of the MMPI–2 in forensic and employment settings, as well as its traditional use in diagnosis and treatment planning, it is remarkable how robust the original and supplementary scales have proved to be in determining test-taking attitudes across a wide range of settings. Nevertheless, it is a very complex task to be able to factor in the issues of setting and motivation with the covarying of a number of validity scales in determining the various test-taking attitudes. The following is a summary of validity issues to remember when venturing into the challenging task of determining test-taking response sets:

1. In private practice settings, if the individual taking the test has little motivation to distort his or her adjustment, the basic validity scales, *VRIN*, *TRIN*, *F*, *FB*, *F(p)*, *L*, *K*, and *S* are often sufficient in determining the test-taking attitude. In these nonforensic, mainly treatment-oriented settings, the clinician can be more liberal with cutoff scores before suggesting that a profile is invalid. For example, a self-referred client taking the MMPI–2 test as part of treatment evaluation obtains an *FLK* configuration as follows: *F* at $T = 43$, *L* at $T = 64$, *K* at $T = 65$, with *VRIN* and *TRIN* valid. In a forensic situation, this validity configuration would suggest an underreporting style. However, in a private practice setting, if there is little motivation to self-favorable report, the clinician needs to also consider that the validity scales may be accurately portraying a rigid, emotionally constricted individual who lacks psychological insight and self-awareness, rather than somebody who is consciously underreporting. In this setting, the test feedback process with the client would be helpful in arriving at a diagnosis and treatment plan, irrespective of whether the profile appeared to reflect an over- or underreporting style, and the clinician could be less concerned about strict cutoff scores for validity.

2. In settings in which other data (e.g., setting and history) suggest extreme psychopathology and distress (e.g., a crisis house), the validity cutoff scores need to be adjusted upward. For example, in such a setting, a raw *F* score of 28 might not be unusual, and the *VRIN* and *TRIN* scales as well as the *Ds* scale, may be elevated, reflecting real confusion, panic, and yea-saying in the direction of pathology. Although the profile is unlikely to be a stable reflection of the indi-

vidual's personality, it may not always be consciously exaggerated. In such settings, extreme endorsements of psychopathology may be reflecting genuine panic, disorientation, and extreme self-criticism, with some conscious exaggeration, reflecting a plea for help. In these cases, strict cutoff scores that might be used in a forensic setting would clearly be inappropriate.

3. In forensic situations in which there is high motivation to appear or not appear psychologically impaired, yet socially and morally above reproach, cutoff scores become more important and the need to use the additional measures of response style becomes more pressing. In these cases, the *Ds*, *F(p)*, *Mp*, *Sd*, *Ss*, and *S* scales, as well as the traditional validity scales, become very useful. Clinicians should also be aware that there is sometimes a borderline area where it is difficult to tell solely from MMPI–2 data whether a profile is clearly malingered or accurate.

4. In work settings (e.g., preemployment screenings, fitness-for-duty evaluations, and workers' compensation assessments), motivation may be high to appear psychologically healthy and morally above reproach, so cutoff scores are more important and the usefulness of scores on the additional measures of response style increases. Unfortunately, giving exact cutoff scores is difficult. Sometimes a profile that appears underreported is, in fact, accurately reflecting an individual from an upper socio-economic background and a cultural milieu that values emotional control, denial of emotions, and "getting on with life" in the face of an emotional crisis. This would be reflected in a high *K* score, some *L* elevation, and perhaps an unelevated clinical profile. Typically, the *Mp* and *Sd* scales would also be low and the *Ss* scale would be elevated, with only moderate scores on the *S* scale. It is also important to be cautious about using these supplementary validity scales until more extensive research data is available. Until that time, they should be used as helpful adjuncts in determining the direction of validity. The clinician also has to weigh the evidence from interviews and other test data to determine whether a particular profile in the borderline area is likely invalid or likely valid. In many cases, of course, the profile is clearly invalid or valid. It is the indeterminate forensic cases that are the most difficult with which to deal. Validity is determined by examining not only all the basic and supplemental validity scales but also the likelihood that the person is motivated to malinger, the elevation of the profile, and the number of critical items endorsed. It is the overall direction of validity that is relevant. The good news for the clinician is that rarely will one validity indicator invalidate a profile; usually, there is a pattern of responses. For example, an individual may have a yea-saying response set in which he or she is saying "true" to many psychopathological items. This will lead to an elevated profile, a high "true" percentage, a high *TRIN* score, perhaps some *VRIN* elevation if the individual is contradictory in some of his or her responses, and high *F* and *FB* scores. The *Ds* scale would likely show an elevation, and there would be a high number of critical items endorsed. There would be many indicators that the profile was not an accurate clinical portrayal, so the task of determining validity is not as daunting as it may appear.

Basic Validity Scale Configurations

An important validity consideration is whether a client simply marked the items at random, tended to mark most or all of them as being true, or all as being false. Early in the MMPI's development, these response sets were examined to see how effective the validity scales were in detecting such test-taking behaviors. The configurations of the validity scales show distinctive patterns for each response bias, as do the clinical scales.

RANDOM RESPONSE SET

Random marking results in the patterns shown in Figs. 5.1 and 5.2. However, some actual clinical situations result in a similar-looking validity scale configuration, so clinicians need to examine the actual raw scores and *T* scores for each of the validity scales before determining validity. Although the elevated clinical scales and the high *F* scale looks similar to the "most open" validity scale pattern described later, it is important to note that the *L* and *F* scales are far more elevated in the randomly marked profile.

Notes

The validity configuration resulting from a random response set of an adult client shows that the *F* scale is much greater than *T* = 100, that the *L* scale is at *T* = 65–66, and that the *K* scale is about *T* = 50. The clinical scales are characterized by a generally elevated profile with all of the clinical scales except Scale 0 at or above *T* = 65 and Scale 5 at *T* scores of 54 and 69 for men and women, respectively. A psychotic slope with a spike on Scale 8 and a subspike on Scale 6 is evident. A person responding in a random manner may adopt an idiosyncratic response pattern, such as marking a block of four or five items as true followed by another block of four items as false, or the person may mark "true" and "false" randomly. The *VRIN* scale is the most useful scale in determining randomness (see this chapter for cutoff scores). The *F*B, *VRIN*, and *TRIN* scales are at *T* scores of 124, 96, and 71, respectively, for men and 120, 98, and 73, respectively, for women.

Report Language

The profile is invalid because the respondent answered the items in a random manner. The respondent may have done this out of confusion, anger, or resistance to the testing situation. After the clinician has determined the reasons for this response pattern, the respondent should retake the test.

ALL-TRUE RESPONSE SET

An all-true response set (see Figs. 5.3 and 5.4) has as its most discerning features elevated *F* and *F*B scores, with subaverage scores on the *L* and *K* scales (usually at or below a *T* score of 35).

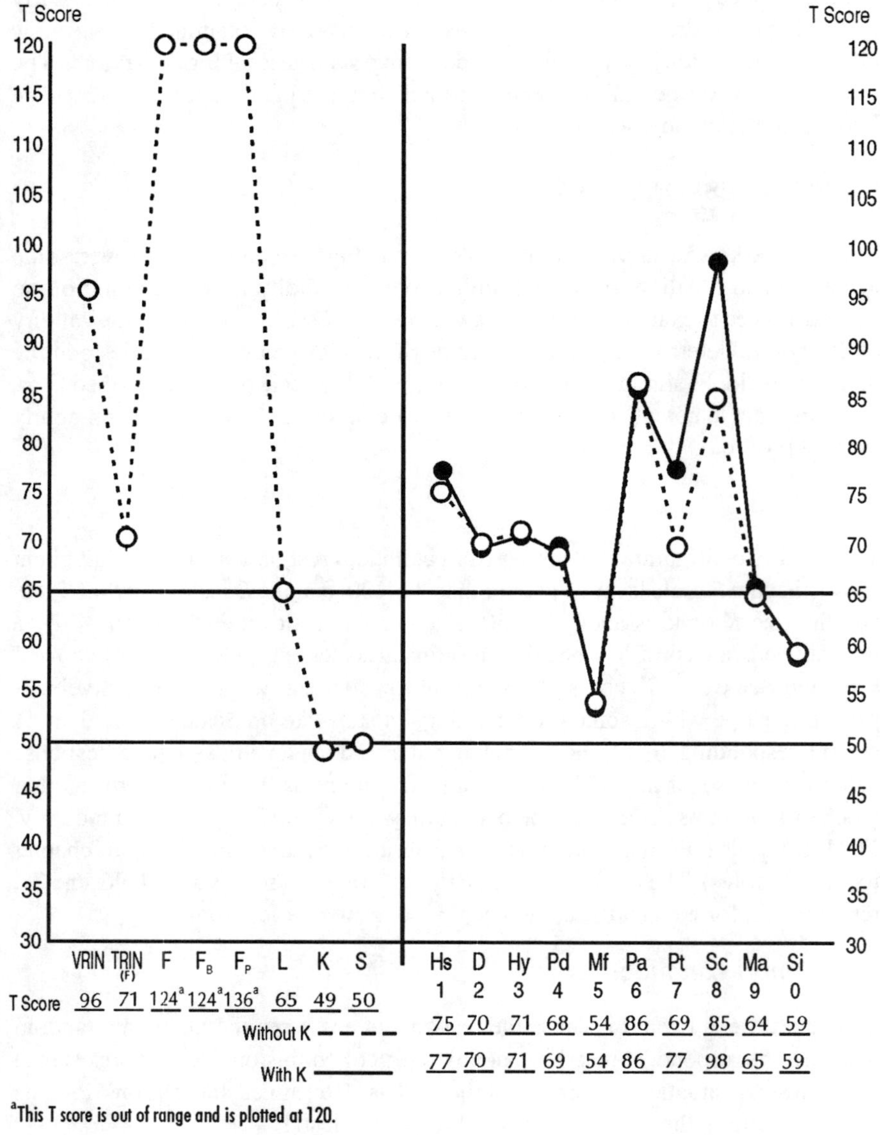

FIG. 5.1. Random response set for men. Adapted from *Manual Supplement: Corrected Graphs for the Items in the MMPI–2: Alterations in Wording, Patterns of Interrelationship, and Changes in Endorsements* (pp. 10–15), by W. G. Dahlstrom, 1994, Minneapolis: University of Minnesota Press. Copyright 1994 by the Regents of the University of Minnesota.

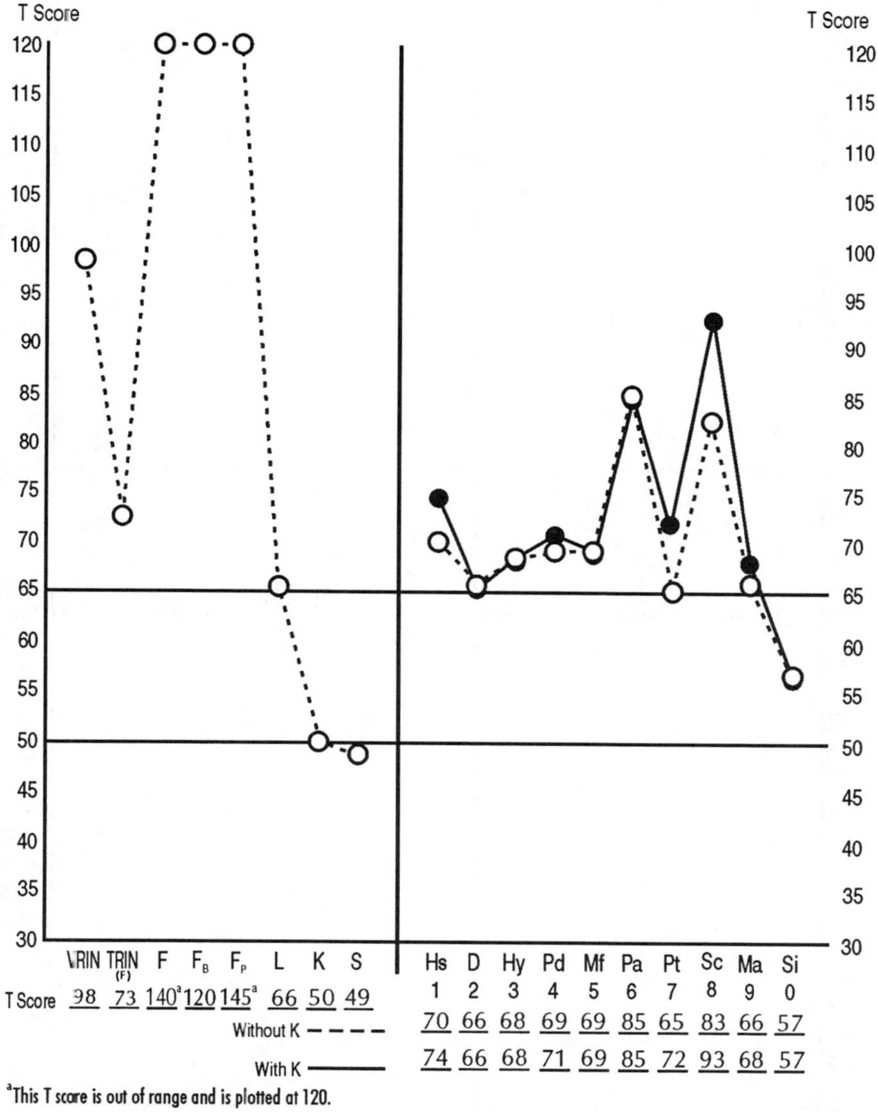

FIG. 5.2. Random response set for women.

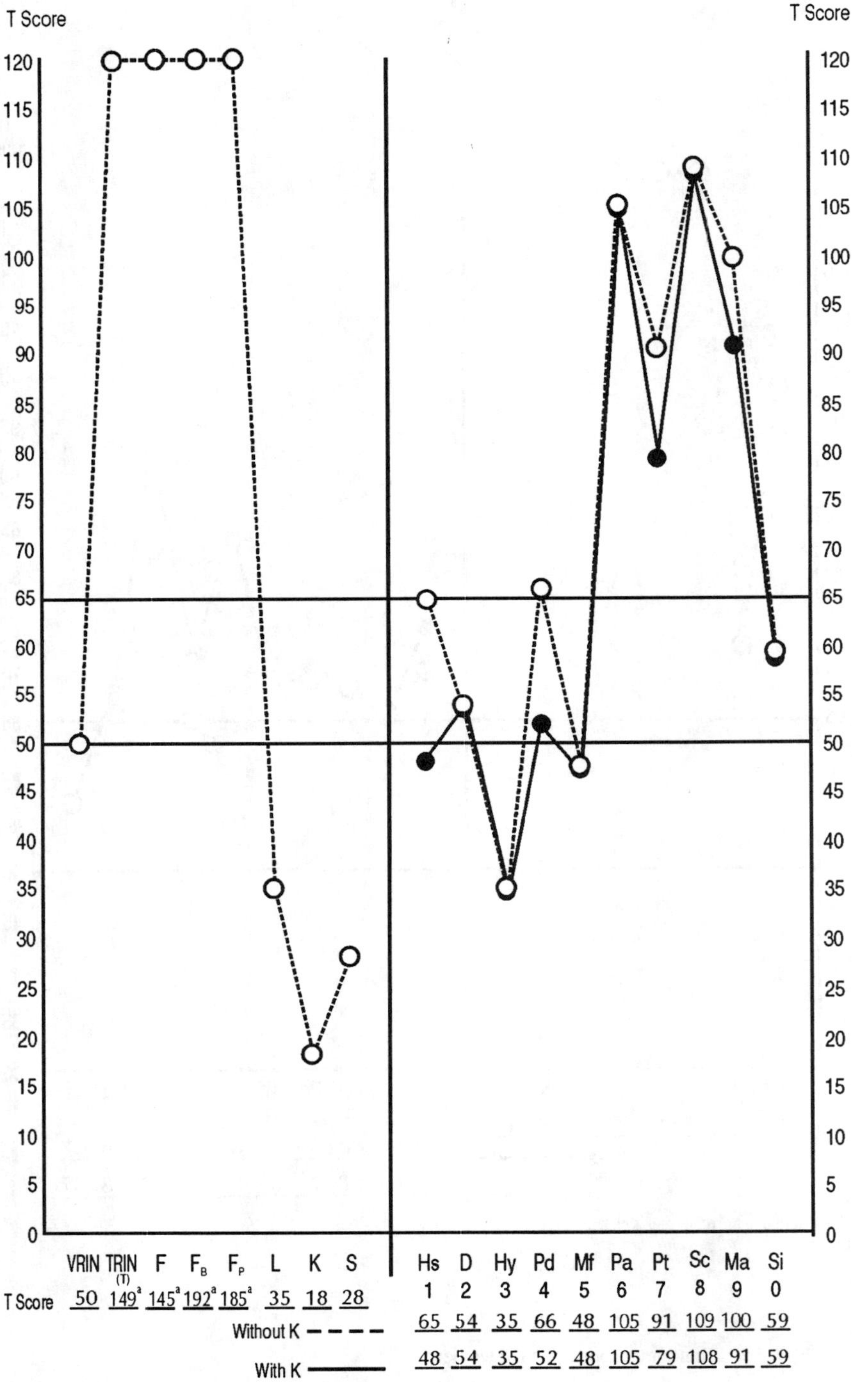

[a] This T score is out of range and is plotted at 120.

FIG. 5.3. All-true response set for men.

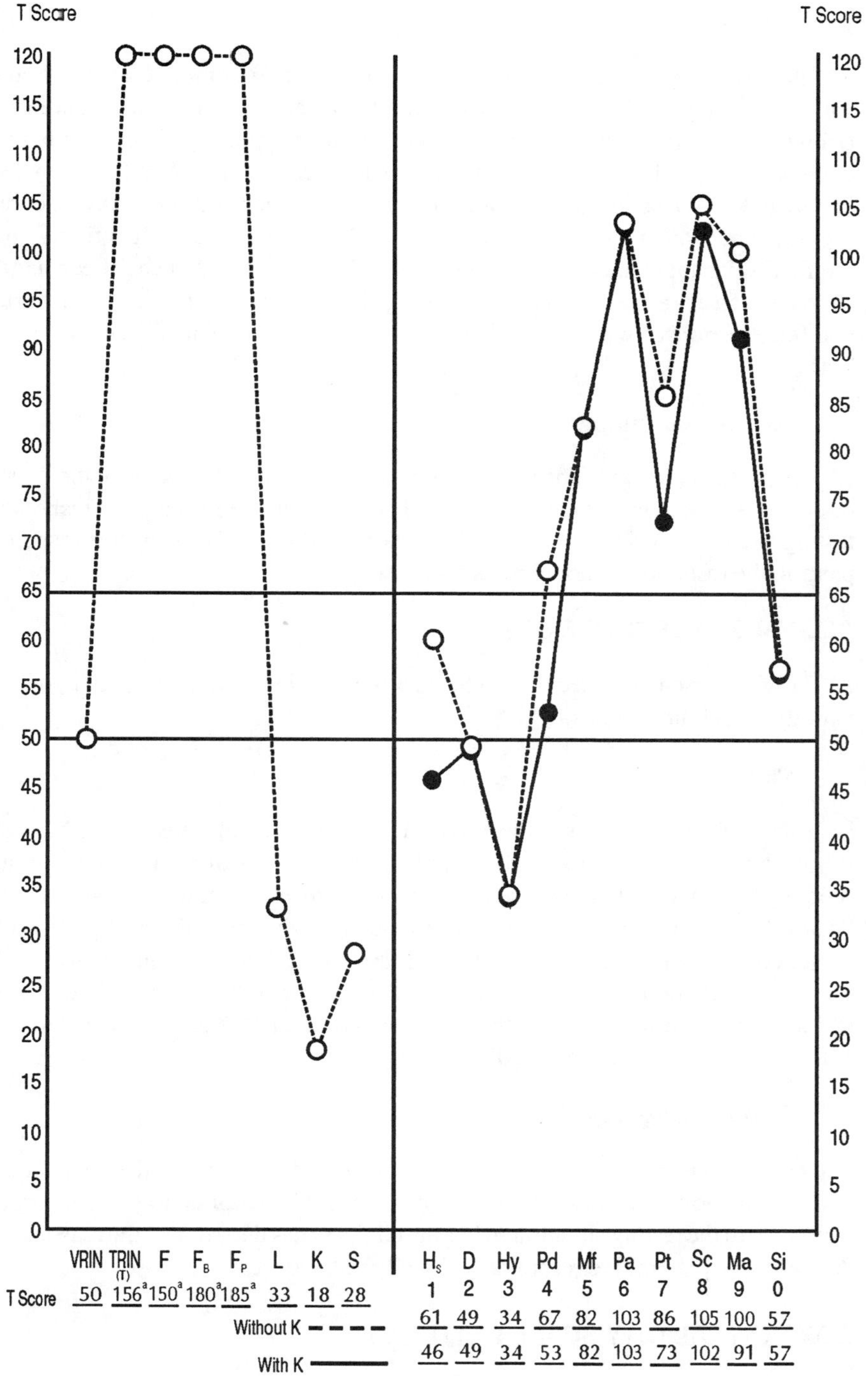

[a]This T score is out of range and is plotted at 120.

FIG. 5.4. All-true response set for women.

Notes

The discerning features of this configuration are extremely elevated *F* and *FB* scores, usually off the top of the profile sheet, and the *L* and *K* scores are well below 50. On the clinical scales, a psychotic slope typically occurs, with a 68 code pattern. Scales 1, 2, 3, and 4 tend to be low relative to Scales 6, 7, 8, and 9. Whereas *VRIN T* scores are 50 for both men and women, *FB* and *TRIN T* scores are 192 and 149, respectively, for men and 180 and 156, respectively, for women. A visual examination of the answer sheet (if the profile has been hand-scored) or an examination of the computer printout to see the percentages of true and false responses would quickly confirm the presence of an all-true response bias.

Report Language

The profile is invalid. The patient has answered most of the items in the "true" direction. The respondent may have done this out of confusion, anger, or fear of the testing situation. After the clinician has determined the reasons for this response pattern, the respondent should retake the test.

ALL-FALSE RESPONSE SET

All-false endorsements (see Figs. 5.5 and 5.6) result in a distinctive pattern on the validity and clinical scales.

Notes

In an all-false response set, the *F*, *L*, and *K* scales are all elevated with *L* highest, followed by *F* and *K*. This elevation on the *L* scale is not surprising as *L* items are scored when endorsed as false, so all the *L* items are endorsed in this response set. Scales 1, 2, and 3 (neurotic scales) are elevated above Scales 6, 7, 8, and 9 (psychotic scales). Whereas *VRIN T* scores are 50 for both men and women, *FB T* scores are at 55 for men and 54 for women. The *FB* score is low because 37 of the 40 items on this scale are scored in the "true" direction. *TRIN T* scores are at 114 and 118 for men and women, respectively.

Report Language

The profile is invalid because the respondent tended to answer the items in the "false" direction. The respondent may have done this out of confusion, anger, or resistance to the testing situation. After the clinician has determined the reasons for this response pattern, the respondent should retake the test.

COMMON VALIDITY SCALE PATTERNS

People's responses to being questioned about various intimate aspects of their lives vary. As some TV talk shows attest, some people relish sharing even intimate

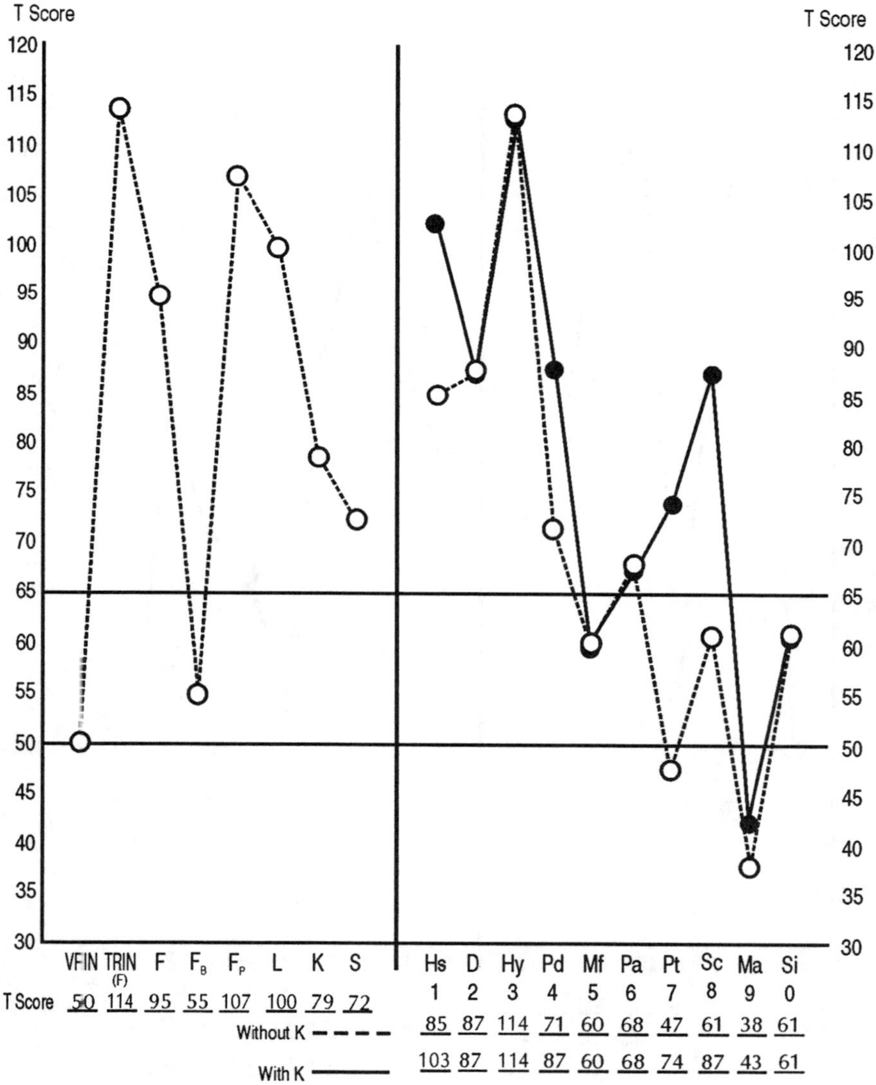

FIG. 5.5. All-false response set for men.

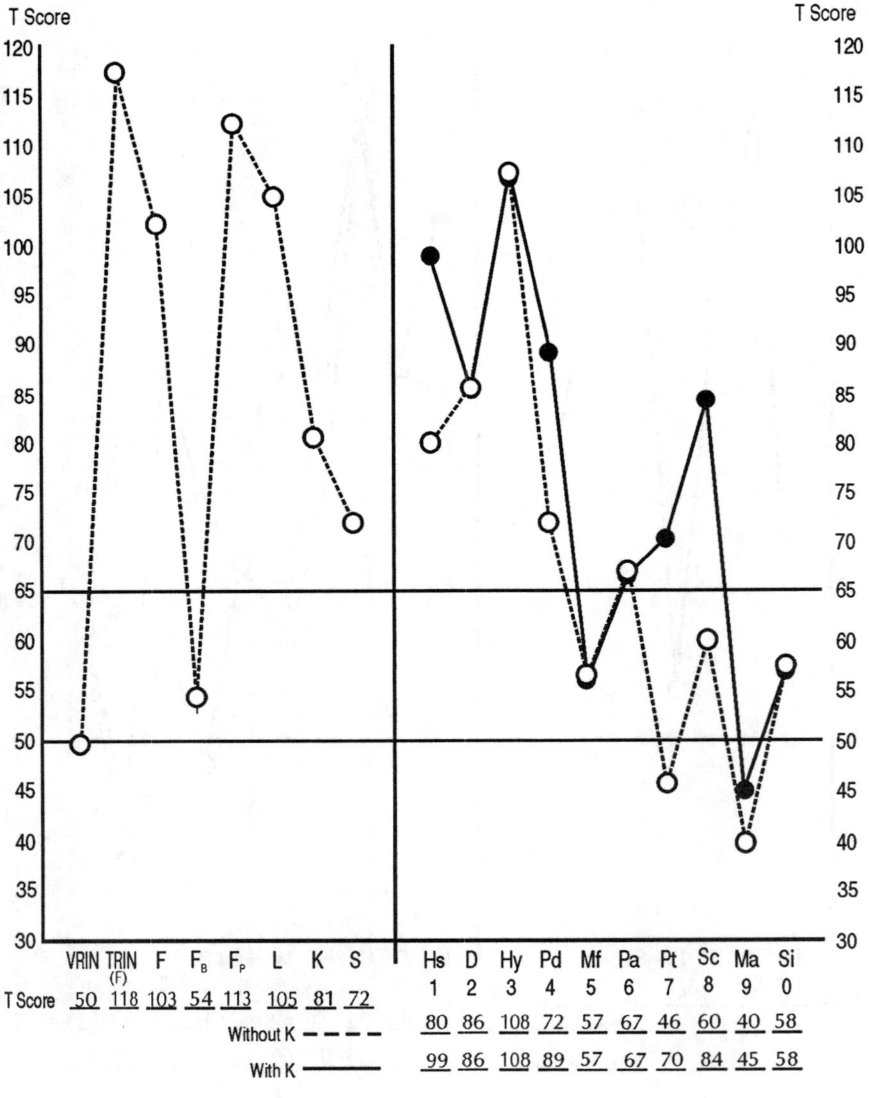

FIG. 5.6. All-false response set for women.

aspects of their lives to the point of exaggeration, whereas other people react defensively when questioned about basic human habits, foibles, or behaviors. The MMPI–2 validity scales can reflect a number of response sets on a continuum from a response set that is open to the point of exaggeration to a very closed response set so extreme that no useful information is revealed except a reluctance to reveal information. The following descriptions and examples represent various validity configurations on this continuum from "most open" to "most closed" (see Fig. 5.7) in terms of admitting emotional and psychological difficulties and human vulnerabilities. The descriptions given apply to both men and women.

The following four basic validity scale configurations are important because they occur frequently and add substantially to the interpretations obtained through considering each validity scale separately. After these basic configurations are shown and described, additional variants of these patterns are presented with notes and suggested report-writing language. To make these validity illustrations realistic, we have added ages and educational levels to each example. This should also remind the report-writing clinician that demographic variables are important starting points for the interpretation process.

These four configurations are:

- "Most closed" validity configuration (see Fig. 5.8)
- "Most open" validity configuration (see Figs. 5.9–5.11)
- Validity Pattern "A" configuration (see Fig. 5.12)
- Naïve but Open validity configuration (see Fig. 5.13)

"Most Closed" Validity Configuration

This pattern occurs when the *L* and *K* scales are above a *T* score of 65, with the *F* scale at or below $T = 50$ (see Fig. 5.8). The more elevated the *L* and *K* scales, the more likely the profile is invalid and the more confidence can be put in the interpretation that such persons were strongly attempting to present themselves in an extremely favorable light by minimizing or denying problems, unacceptable impulses, or feelings. A similar, although lower, *T*-score validity configuration occurs often among job applicants or persons in situations (e.g., child custody evaluations) in which they wish to appear particularly well-adjusted. In inpatient settings, however, this validity scale pattern can be found sometimes in psychotic patients who are using massive denial, repression, or strong attempts at self-control. Other diagnostic groups characterized by denial and lack of insight (such as individuals with hysteria, hypochondriasis, or alcoholism, or other substance abuse problems) may occasionally show a similar pattern.

In some cases, this pattern is found in normals or clients in outpatient settings (although at a lower *T*-score level) who are out of touch with any emotional difficulties, who emphasize self-control, and who are repressed and inhibited. For example, they may seek therapy as part of a marriage problem, but they tend to lack any psychological mindedness and are often naïve and morally judgmental. It is hard to claim that this validity configuration invalidates a profile if it has been obtained by a bright professional who is self-referred for a marriage problem. More

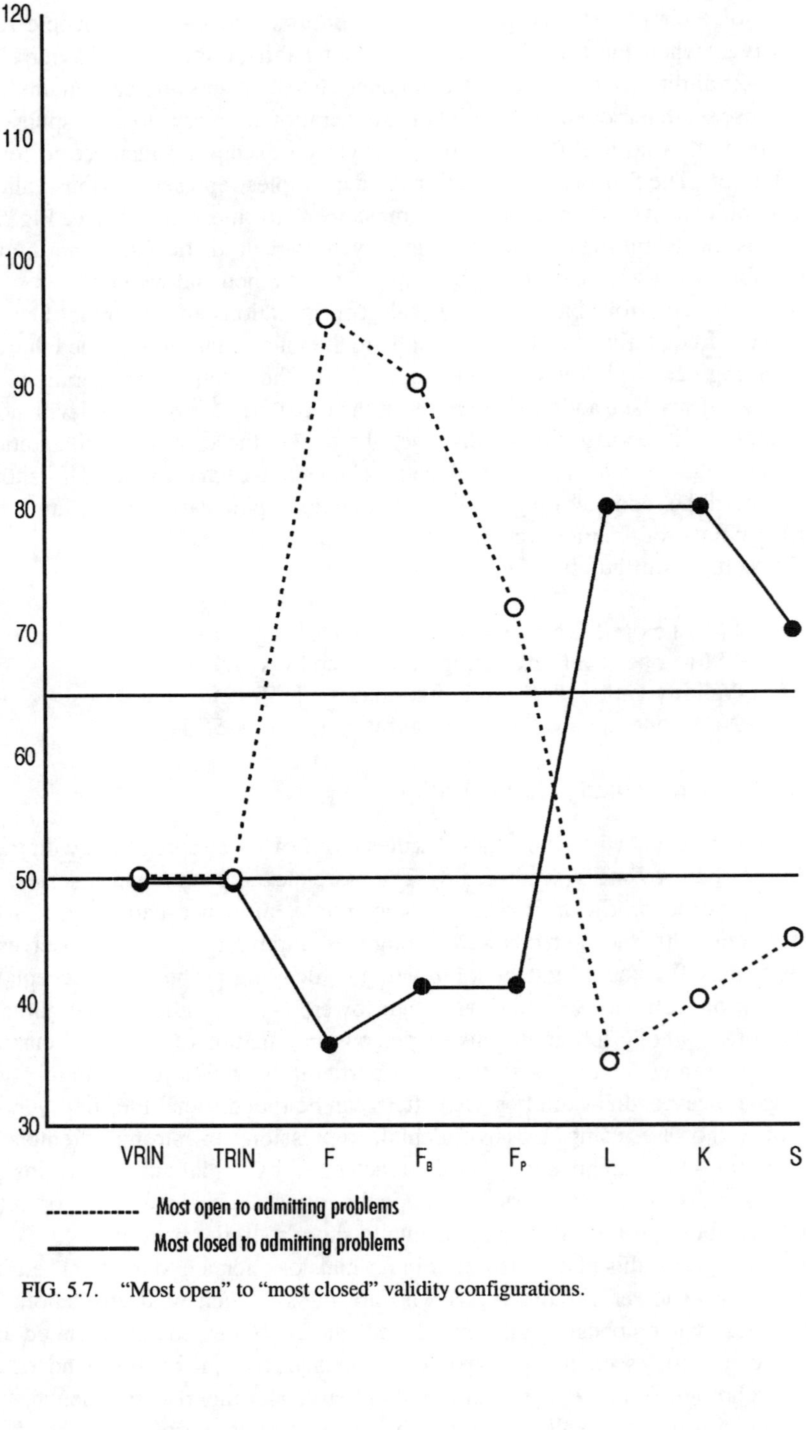

FIG. 5.7. "Most open" to "most closed" validity configurations.

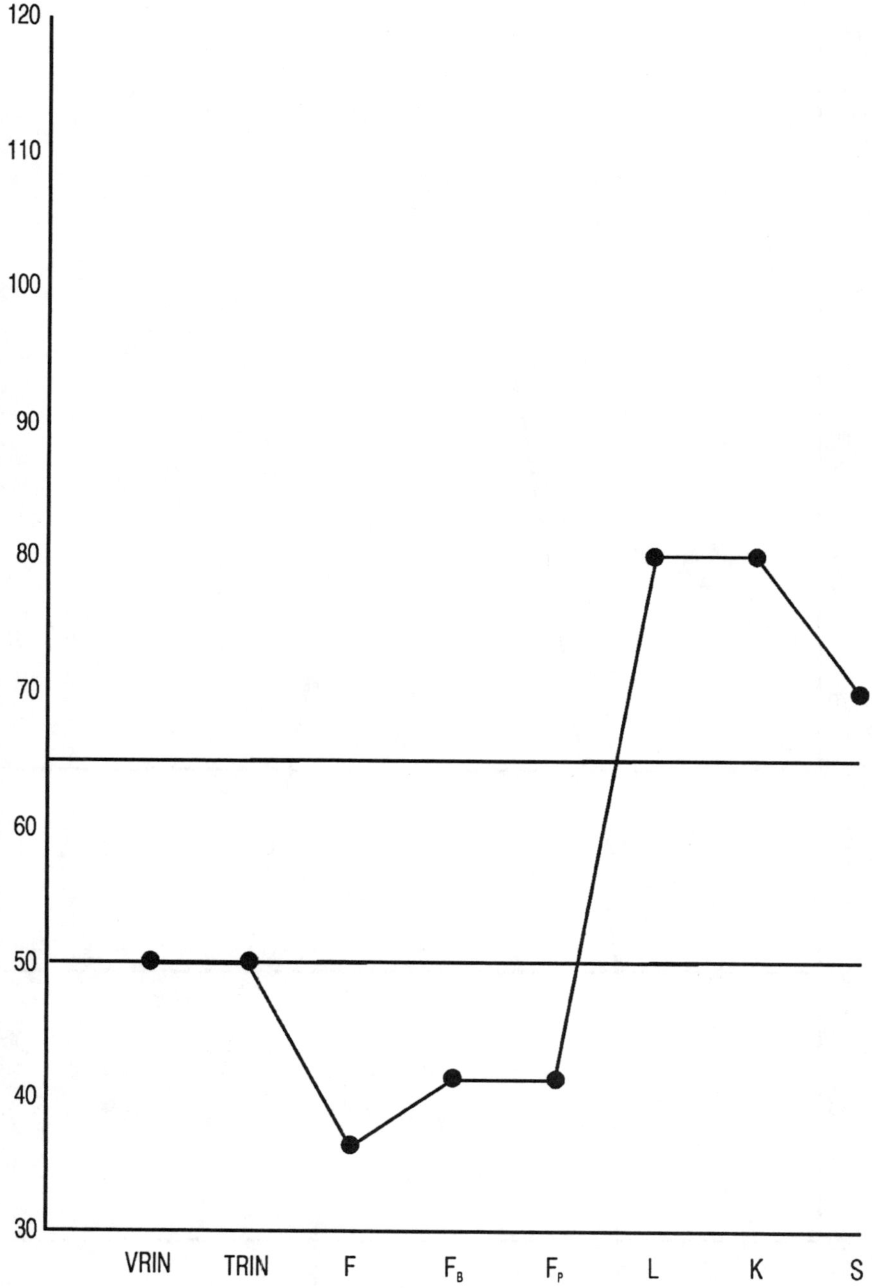

FIG. 5.8. "Most closed" validity configuration.

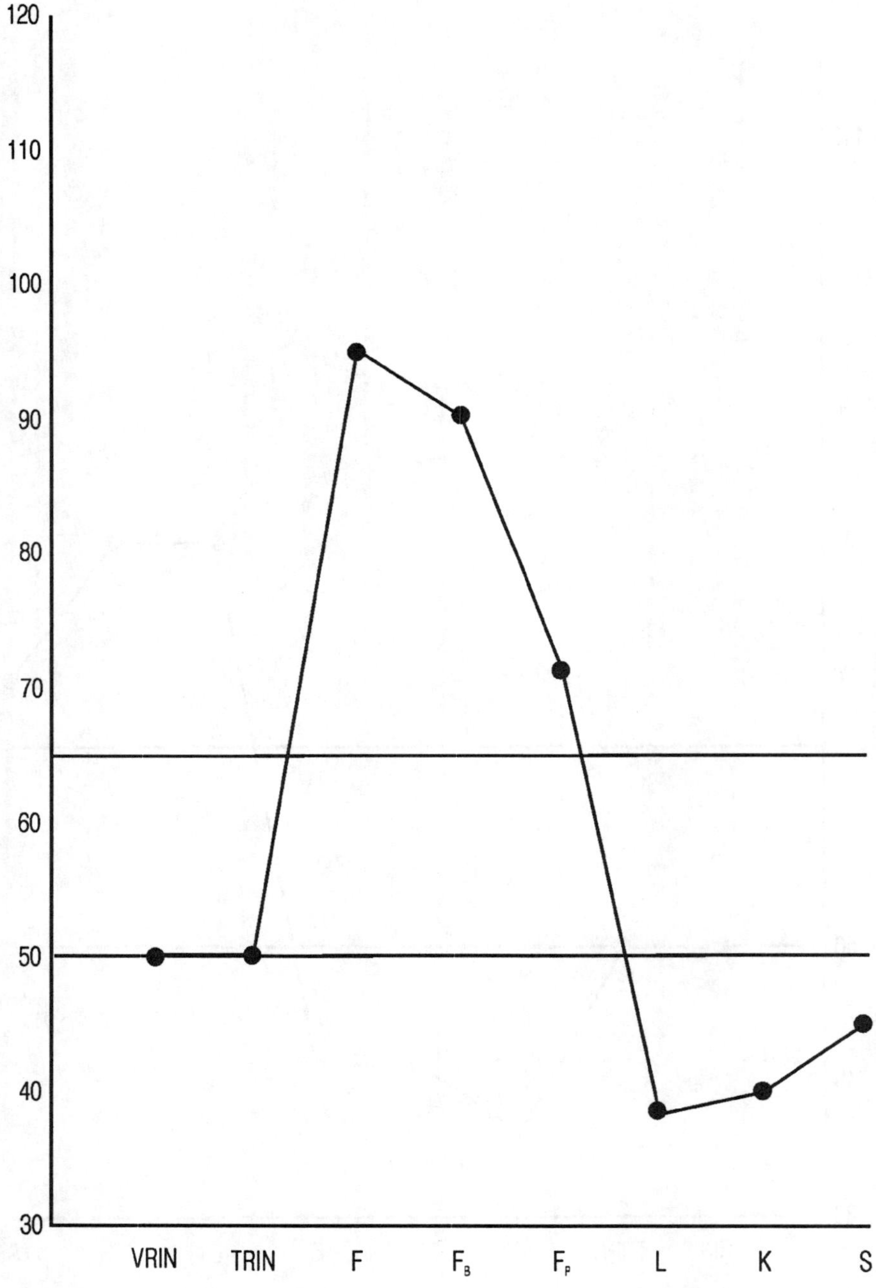

FIG. 5.9. "Most open" validity configuration.

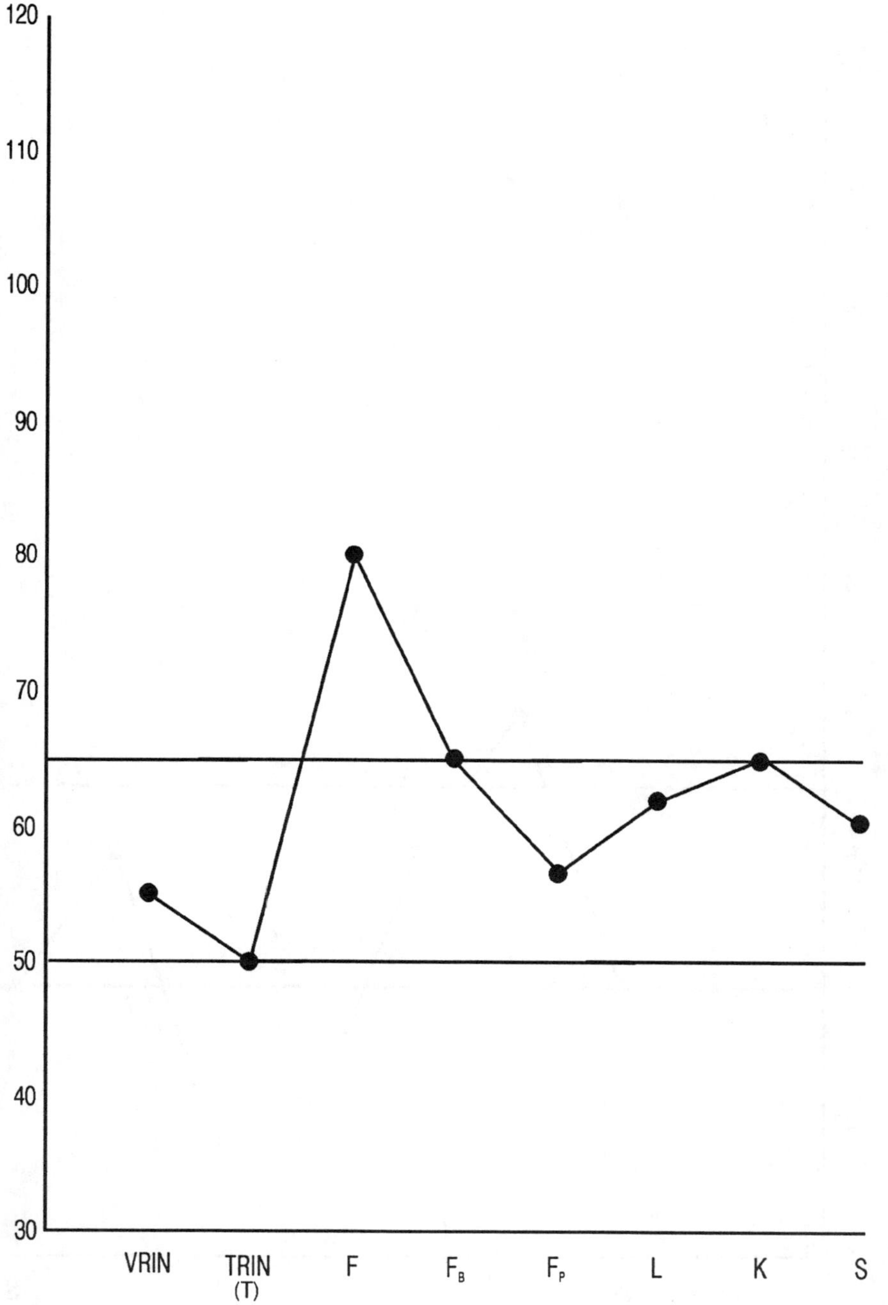

FIG. 5 10. Admitting serious problems while attempting to cope and preserve self-esteem.

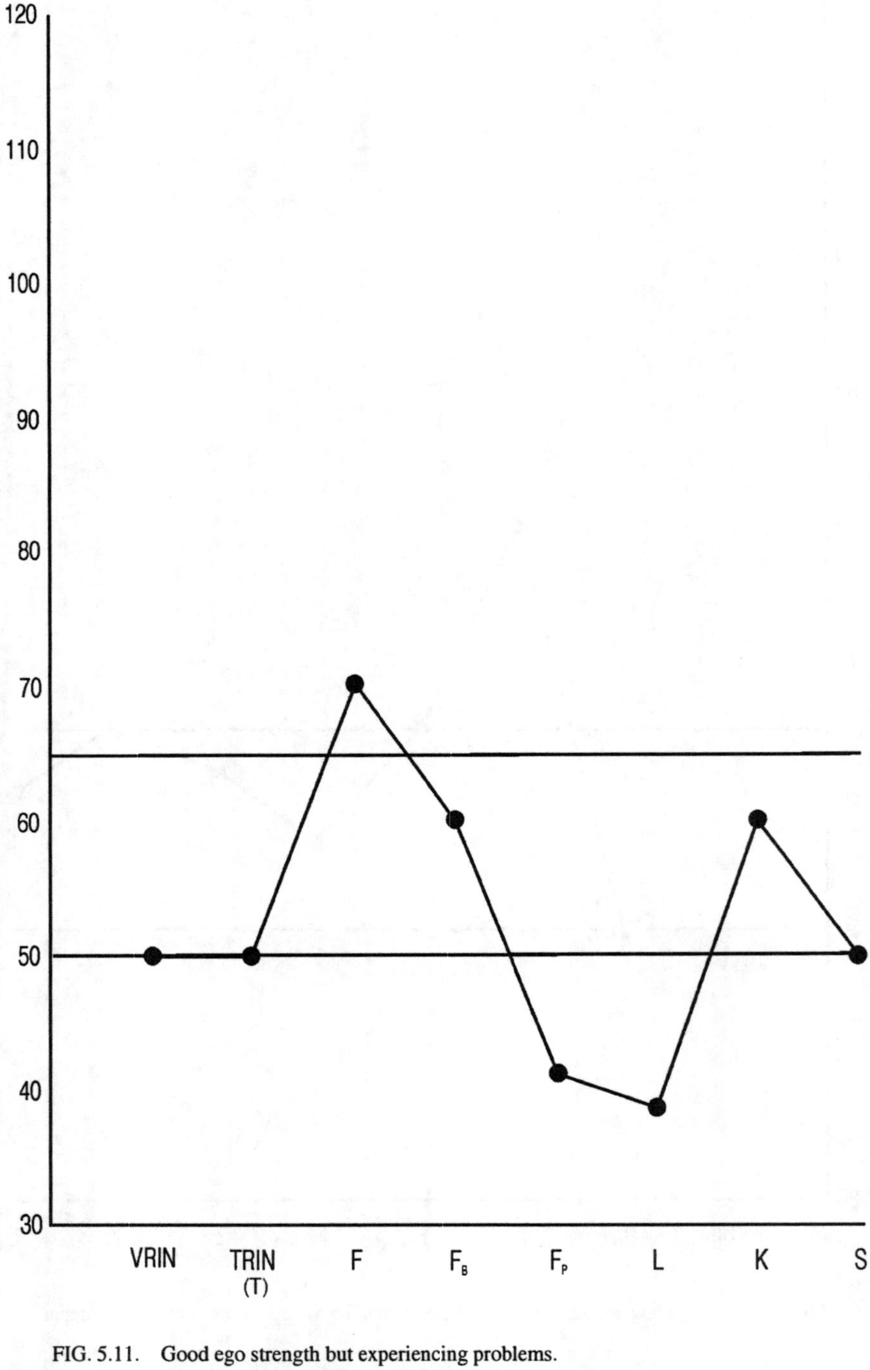

FIG. 5.11. Good ego strength but experiencing problems.

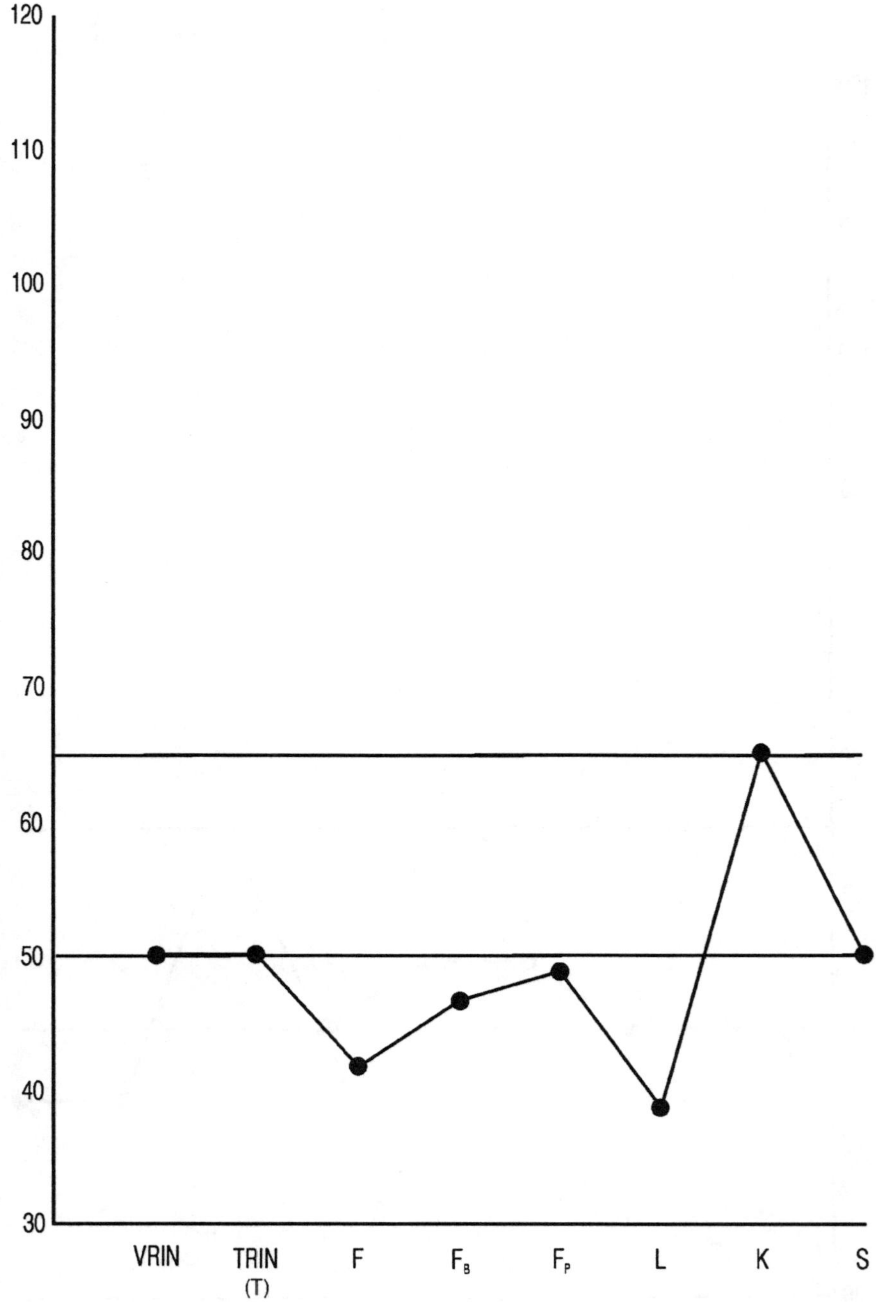

FIG. 5.12. Validity Pattern A (see also Fig. 5.17).

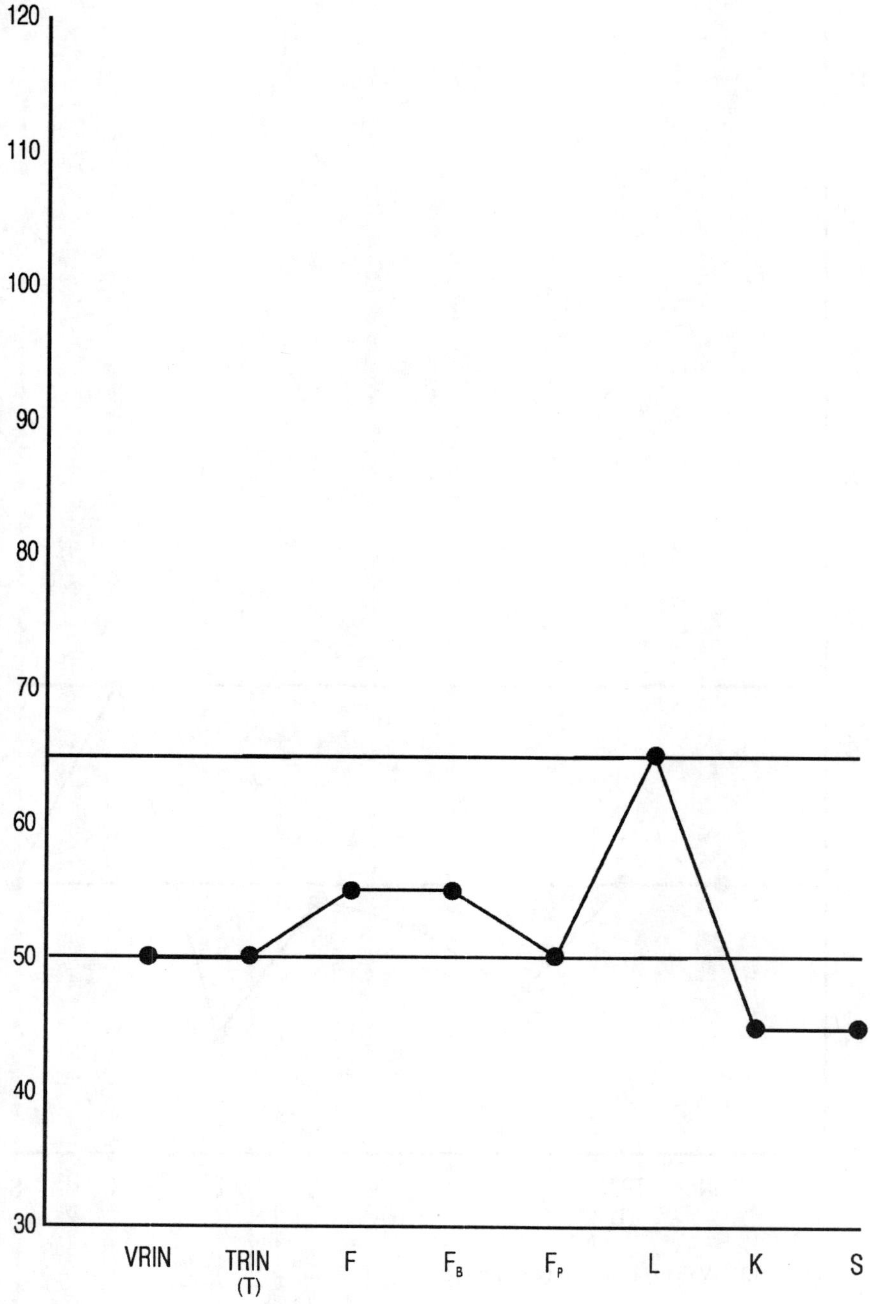

FIG. 5.13. Naïve but open validity configuration.

likely, the validity configuration reflects a rigid, inhibited, and naive individual who lacks insight but presents with a good social facade. However, the same validity configuration in a person seeking custody of his or her children in a forensic setting would raise red flags for invalidity.

The minimizing effect reflected on the validity scales would also be reflected on the clinical scales, which would tend to be suppressed. In some cases in which defensiveness is to be expected, as in a job screening, norms have been collected to serve as a base for expected levels of defensiveness (e.g. Pope, Butcher, & Seelen, 1993). Defensive MMPI–2 profiles may be interpreted cautiously in settings in which the cost of making an error may not be high and when the test results are not likely to be subject to significant challenge. In other settings, however, defensive profiles need to be carefully integrated with historical and other data to partial out how much of the variance is accounted for by conscious distortion versus self-deception and personality attributes. The *Mp*, *Sd*, *S*, and *Ss* scales, among others discussed earlier, can also be helpful in making validity determinations.

Individuals with the "most closed" validity pattern are often self-favorably reporting. To the extent that situational causes for this pattern can be ruled out, such as job applications, fitness-for-work assessments, or child custody evaluations, this pattern is associated with persons who value control, are rigid in their views, cling to rules and regulations, and view the world and the behaviors of others in terms of extremes of value judgments (e.g., "good" vs. "bad" or "strong" vs. "weak").

"Most Open" Validity Configuration

This configuration, also referred to as an "open and self-critical," "in pain," or "plea for help" configuration, occurs when the *F* scale is above a *T* score of 65, and the *L* and *K* scales are at or less than a *T* score of 50 (see Fig. 5.9). Such persons are openly admitting to psychological difficulties, doubt their ability to handle stress, and generally are amenable to professional help.

As *F* increases above a *T* score of 80 and/or *K* decreases below a *T* score of 45, these individuals are reporting acute and pervasive distress and an absence of coping abilities. Their level of psychological disorganization is so extreme that they are unlikely to benefit from insight-oriented therapy until crisis intervention has achieved some stability and the immediate stress is alleviated. With such a high *F* score, however, the possibility should also be considered that the person may be exaggerating his or her psychological conflicts, stress, and personal problems, sometimes as a "cry for help" in order to obtain the most immediate attention (see also Fig. 5.15). He or she may also be attempting to simulate psychopathology. The cutoff scores for the validity scales are discussed earlier in this chapter.

Two subtypes of the "most open" validity pattern (formerly referred to as the "Inverted V" configuration by Greene, 1991a) frequently occur. In Subtype 1 (see Fig. 5.10) the *L* and *K* scales are between 50 and 60 and the *F* scale is greater than 65, and sometimes much higher. These clients, although admitting problems, are also exhibiting the defenses of denial and repression. They are often not well educated and they lack psychological mindedness (reflected in the elevated *L* score). Often the coping attempts of such persons are limited in effectiveness, and they may have a stable but chronically maladjusted lifestyle. If the *Mp* scale and/or the *Sd* and *S* scales are also elevated, then the elevations on the *L* and *K* scales are likely reflecting some conscious attempts to minimize the considerable pathology being manifested.

Subtype 2 can be referred to as the "good ego strength, but experiencing problems" profile (see Fig. 5.11). In this configuration, the *K* scale is above a *T* score of 55, the *F* scale is at least equal to the *K* scale, and the *L* scale is less than a *T* score of 50. Persons with this pattern typically cope well, as would be expected given their moderate psychopathology (moderate *F*) and good emotional control (moderate *K*). Although they may have long-standing problems, these individuals may have adjusted to them as a chronic lifestyle so that they experience few feelings of disorganizing distress. Even as the *F* scale rises above $T = 65–70$, such persons have a functioning defense system as reflected in the elevated *K* scale, but simultaneously are describing a variety of problems that may be severe. If the *K* scale is moderately elevated in the presence of a high *F* score, the score on the Ego Strength scale (*Es*) can be helpful in determining the stability or fragility of the individual's coping style. For example, if the *K* scale is at a *T* score of 60 and the *Es* scale is at *T* score of 35, then the exterior poise and control reflected in the *K* score is probably somewhat brittle and fragile.

Validity Pattern "A" is characterized by a validity configuration wherein the *K* scale is greater than the *F* and *FB* scales which in turn are greater than the *L* scale (see Fig. 5.12). Generally, the *F* and *FB* *T* scores are between 50 and 55, the *L* score is about 40 to 45, and the *K* score is about 60 to 65. Persons with such patterns usually are not in distress and have appropriate resources for dealing with their current stress. If they do have problems, they do not feel overwhelmed by them. College-educated or other widely experienced persons are somewhat more likely to show this pattern, and it reflects the array of their coping resources. Some job applicants or normal persons in marital conflict situations may also obtain this pattern, but in such cases this may represent an attempt to portray themselves in a somewhat overly favorable light.

The "naïve but open" (see Fig. 5.13) validity profile, is one where the *T* scores decrease from *L* to *F* to *K*, resulting in a linear trend downward. Generally, the *L T* score is about 60 to 65, the *F T* score is about 55, and the *K T* score is about 45.

Although such persons may be experiencing some mild situational, emotional, or interpersonal difficulties, they are usually psychologically naïve and unsophisticated, often have limited educational backgrounds, and often have lowered expectancies about the extent to which they can control or have an impact on their own feelings, impulses, or life situations. They usually are poor candidates for insight-oriented psychotherapy, preferring practical solution-oriented approaches.

Figures 5.14–5.17 represent variants of the four basic configurations. Notes and report language are provided for each of these additional validity configurations.

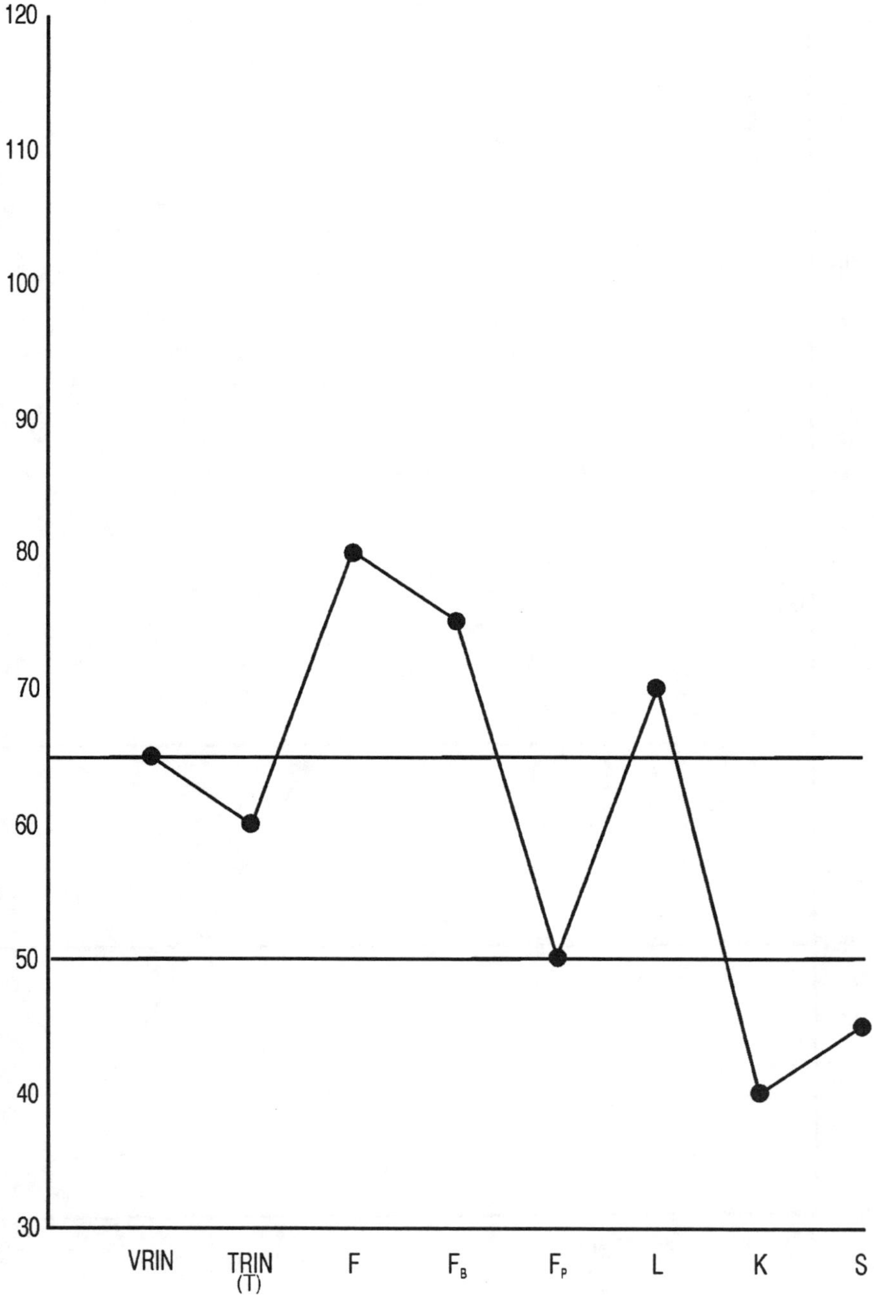

FIG. 5.14. Naïve but non-defensive disturbed configuration.

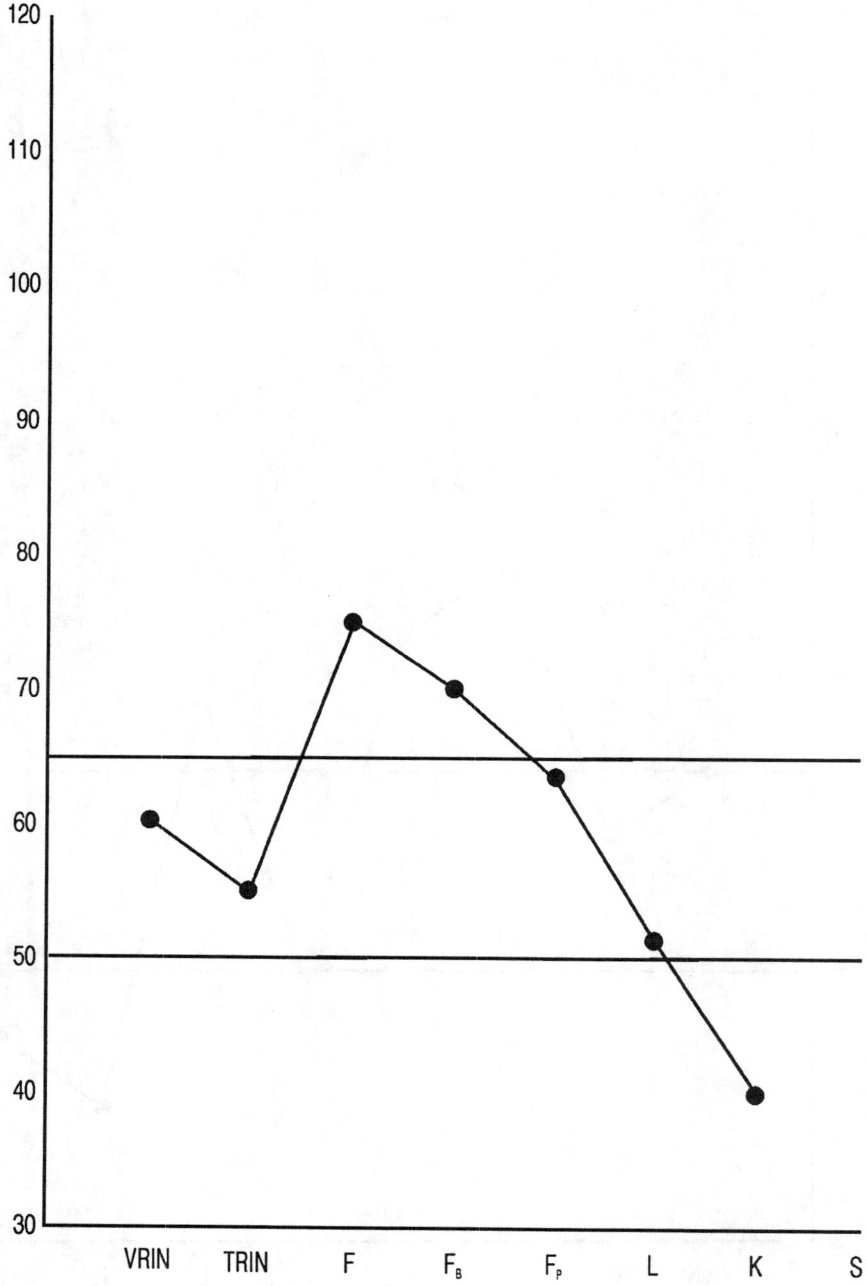

FIG. 5.15. Distress in a candid, self-critical person.

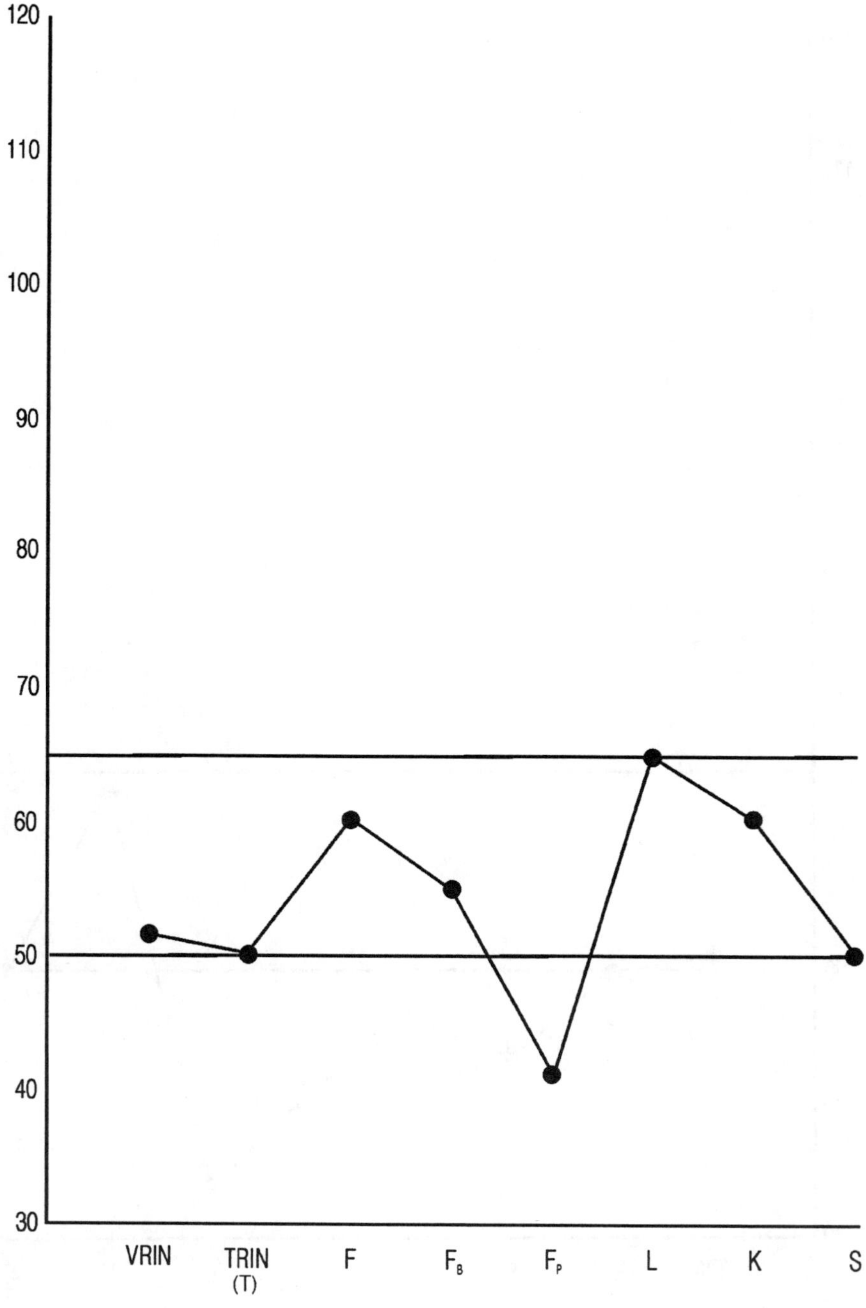

FIG. 5.16. Unusual or paradoxical validity configuration.

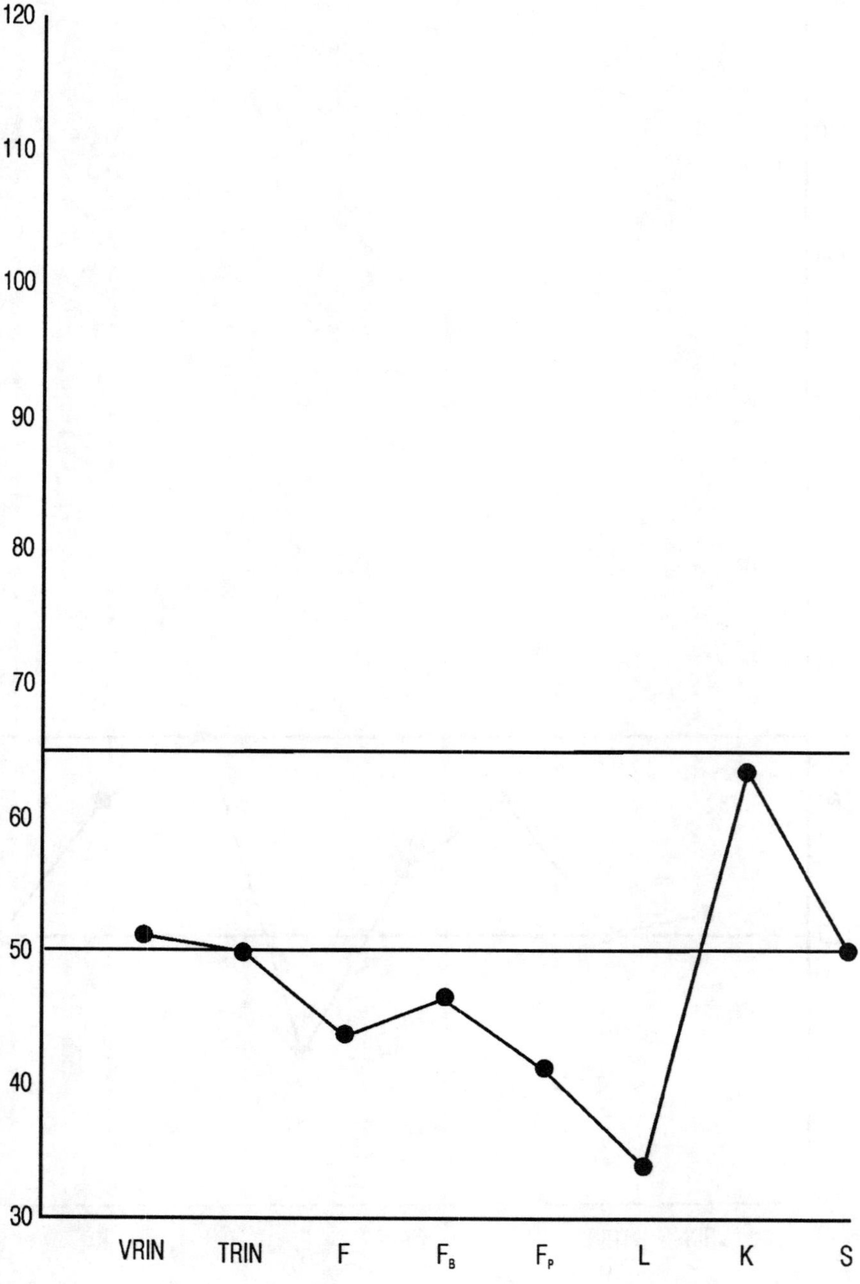

FIG. 5.17. "The college-educated" validity configuration.

6

Interpreting the MMPI–2 Clinical Scales

INTRODUCTION

The following code-pattern information represents an admixture of actuarial and clinical information. Actuarial data do not exist concerning all possible clinical configurations of the MMPI–2 and MMPI; however, clinical data based on observation and historical use do exist. Thus, we have integrated different sources so that the maximum number of diverse MMPI–2 profiles can be interpreted. By combining these two approaches, but using the actuarial knowledge as the basic matrix, it is possible to interpret all single and two-point codes, many three-point scale combinations, and even some four-point combinations. Because 18- and 19-year-old participants typically complete the MMPI–2, code patterns with importance to late adolescence are described when relevant.

Interpretations of code patterns are presented in a convenient lookup format, (i.e., in order of the clinical scales). In addition, there is a Code-Pattern Look-Up Table immediately following the Table of Contents so that readers seeking an interpretation about a specific MMPI–2 pattern can quickly locate the pages containing interpretations associated with that pattern.

The primary sources for the present interpretations are, in alphabetical order, Archer (1992a, 1997); Archer, Griffin, and Aiduk (1995); Butcher (1990b); Butcher et al. (1989); Butcher and Williams (1992); Caldwell (1988, 1997); Carkhuff, Barnett, and McCall (1965); Carson (1969); Dahlstrom et al. (1972, 1986); Drake and Oetting (1959); Duckworth and Anderson (1995); Fowler (1966); Friedman, Webb, and Lewak (1989); Friedman, Webb, Smeltzer, and Lewak (1989); Gilberstadt and Duker (1965); Graham (1990, 1993); Graham, Ben-Porath, and McNulty (1999); Graham and McCord (1985); Greene (1991a; 2000); Hovey and Lewis (1967); Lachar (1974); Lewak et al. (1990); Marks et al. (1974); Seeman (1963); Swenson, Pearson, and Osborne (1973); Van de Riet and Wolking (1969); Webb (1970a, 1970b); and Webb, McNamara, and Rodgers (1981/1986). These are recommended as additional sources offering more background as well as the documentation of the research bases for various interpretations.

It should be noted that the recently described correlates of the Graham et al. (1999) investigation and the Archer et al. (1995) study are based on psychiatric outpatients and psychatric inpatients, respectively. These two extensive investigations of MMPI–2 correlates are the most comprehensive studies to date; it appears that the correlates of the MMPI–2 code patterns are similar in outpatient and inpatient psychiatric settings. Graham et al. also reported that the correlates of most MMPI–2 scales and code patterns in their study are clearly comparable with those previously identified for the original MMPI. Thus, the code descriptions in this chapter, which are based on past MMPI research coupled with recent findings, should assist the clinician in accurately describing his or her client.

The interpretation of elevated code patterns is the primary focus of this chapter. Interpretation of normal-range *T* scores are not described in this chapter. Normal-range correlates for the clinical scales can be found in the text by Lewak et al. (1990) and, to some extent, in chapter 3 of this textbook. Low points on several scales, however, are addressed where relevant. Although little empirical study has been done on the meaning of low elevations and although there is some debate regarding the interpretation of low points, low scores on some scales nevertheless can change the interpretation of a profile (see chap. 3). As discussed previously, clinicians generally emphasize interpretation of the two, three, or four-point code patterns; however, elevations on other individual scales expand, modify, and color their interpretation. As described in chapter 3, the scale elevations given here are based on *K*-corrected *T*-score ranges and are approximations for the clinical scales; scores on the border (e.g., $T = 65$) between classifications are particularly open to clinical judgment.

Generally, MMPI interpretations have been developed on White participants with an IQ of 80 or above and/or education above sixth grade. Modifications of interpretations based on the different characteristics and base rates of behaviors of these various groups are sometimes included in this chapter. Even so, the reader is encouraged to become familiar with the *MMPI Patterns of American Minorities* (Dahlstrom et al., 1986).

CLINICAL SCALES AND CODES

Scale 1 (*Hs*)

This scale reflects fears and preoccupations about physical functioning and body damage. The more elevated the scale, the more intense and all-consuming are these preoccupations, the more immature and dependent the individual, and the more lacking in psychological insight. The lower the scale below $T = 50$, the more the individual will have a tendency to be cavalier about physical illnesses and ailments.

Spike 1

High scores ($T \geq 65$) and Spike 1 codes occur in persons who are preoccupied with numerous physical complaints, fears, and anxieties. They generally lack joy, see themselves as physically infirm and view their bodies as sources of pain, fear, and discomfort rather than as sources of any pleasure. Others describe them as whiny, complaining, and egocentric, perhaps because they use their complaints to impose demands or to control the behavior of others. Generally, they have difficulty openly expressing anger, which instead tends to be expressed symbolically through their symptoms. Others describe them as stubborn, pessimistic, generally sour on life, unambitious, and lacking in drive. Although individuals with Scale 3 elevations also exhibit numerous physical complaints, they are different from individuals with high scores on Scale 1, in that they are more cheerful, blasé, and denying in the face of their complaints of pain.

Certain demonstrable neurological disorders can elevate Scale 1 into this range. However, it is not clear how much elevation is due to psychological factors and how much is due to neurological factors. Even in individuals with bona fide physical problems, these elevations predict a defeatist and cynical attitude toward life and caregivers. Their symptoms and hypochondriacal patterns typically are longstanding and resistant to change. Although stress can aggravate their physical symptoms, generally their complaints are not a reaction to immediate stress but rather the result of a long-standing personality style of dealing with life's difficulties. As clients, these people can be frustrating because they tend to not follow through completely with suggested treatments, quickly becoming discouraged. Often shopping from doctor to doctor, their anxieties are shaped by the doctors' concerns. Note that although elevations on Scale 1 increase with age, they do not reach an elevation above $T = 65$ purely due to age. When Scale 1 is above $T = 75$, the somatic concerns are so pervasive and all-consuming that they dominate the individual's life.

Moderately high ($T = 55–65$) scorers may be reacting to a bona fide physical disorder, although in such cases they are more likely to have an accompanying elevation on Scale 2. Some physical illnesses (e.g., Lyme's disease) have physical symptoms that can elevate Scale 1 into this range. Even in this moderate range, there is a tendency to be somewhat pessimistic, to somatize under stress, and to be somewhat repressed and inhibited in expressing negative affects.

Moderately low ($T = 35–45$) scores suggest a person who is not overly concerned with bodily function issues and who is likely to generally be effective in daily living (if no other scales are elevated above $T = 60$). Such individuals are seen as resilient, alert, and energetic.

Very low ($T \leq 35$) scores can be obtained for a number of reasons: (a) The individual is reacting to a family member who hypochondriacally used illnesses in a manipulative way and now is overreacting by rejecting even normal aches and pains; (b) the individual is an extremely health-conscious person who takes pride in health to the point of ignoring aches, pains, or illnesses until they are quite severe; or (c) the individual was reared in a family in which health was not an issue. Note, however, that very low scores on Scale 1 may be particularly meaningful in elevated depressed profiles, (e.g., 278 codes), where the low Scale 1 score may reflect a disinterest in one's physical well-being to the point of passive resignation and a feeling of not caring what happens to one's body.

Relations With Other Scales

High 1, Low 4 Codes (for Men), High 1, Low 5 Codes (for Women)

Pessimism, whining, and complaining typically are found in individuals with high Scale 1 scores. The low Scale 4 scores would predict conformity, passivity and low sex drive. Low Scale 5 scores in women would predict an overidentification with stereotypic traditional feminine roles related to a yielding passivity. In either case, the dependent self-centeredness of Scale 1 is aggravated by the passivity and difficulties expressing or dealing with anger predicted by the low scores on Scale 4 or 5. This pattern is particularly distinctive when Scale 1 is the highest elevated scales, but it can also be interpreted as a secondary configuration, even when other scales are more elevated.

Treatment. Assertiveness training and education around how to deal with anger often are appropriate with this code pattern. Have the individual keep a diary of when physical symptoms seem to increase in severity and to look for links between emotional stresses and physical discomfort. Supportive, nonconfrontive therapies appear to work best. Look for childhood experiences of early losses or illnesses and/or a family style of discouraging the expression of negative affect, which may have conditioned these individuals into developing physical responses to stress.

12/21 Codes (See Also 21/12 Codes When Scales 1 and 2 Are Within 5 T-Score Points)

These persons exhibit multiple physical symptoms and complaints and show great concern over their physical functioning. Generally, there is no demonstrable organic pathology, but when real physical problems exist, they exaggerate their severity. Their numerous somatic complaints likely will focus on pain (e.g., headaches, stomach aches, and backaches), cardiac complaints, or gastrointestinal difficulties (e.g., anorexia, nausea, vomiting, or ulcers). Fatigue, weakness, and dizziness are often present, along with irritability and depression. In fact, diagnoses of depression or dysthymia are common. Physical tension and anxiety may also occur, particularly if Scale 7 or 9 is elevated. These persons tend to be restless and prone to worry about many things.

Persons with this code pattern usually are dependent and immature yet can be hardworking and driven. They are often conflicted about assuming responsibilities but tend to do so, although in a whiny and complaining way. They generally have continuing doubts about their own abilities and tend to be indecisive. Repression and denial of emotional problems is characteristic; they lack insight and resist implications that symptoms are related to emotional causes or conflicts. They tend to turn angry feelings inward rather than toward others, and excessive use of alcohol may be present. Major clinical depression is not common for persons with this code pattern. Similarly, feelings of depersonalization or suicidal impulses are not likely, unless Scale 8 is also elevated (see 128/218 codes).

Medical clients with 12/21 patterns are difficult to treat because they often have learned to live with their symptoms and to manipulate others with their complaints. Generally, they tend to react to life's stresses with physiological symptoms and lack aggressiveness and a strong sex drive. Typically, they have a stable work and marital history. There is often a high frequency of sleep and wake disturbance, especially if Scale 9 is below $T = 50$.

College students with 12/21 codes are generally shy, tense, introverted, unhappy, worried, and insecure and feel quite self-conscious, particularly in dealings with the opposite gender. Tension, insomnia, and social discomfort are usually more prominent than the bodily manifestations seen in older persons with this pattern. College women in particular tend to be indecisive, seek continued reassurance, and "freeze up" on academic examinations. Headaches are particularly likely in these women when Scale 5 also is low.

Treatment. The essence of elevated 12/21 codes is an underlying fear that one is hopelessly physically damaged, with a certainty of increasing physical illness and death. These clients can respond well to antidepressants, although they have to be convinced first that their depression is "inevitable," given their histories of combating pain and physical infirmity. Secondary elevations on Scales 7 and 9 may require medications that also would treat the agitation accompanying these added elevations. These individuals are vulnerable to developing dependencies on medication. Elective surgery should be avoided until the hypochondriacal aspects of the profile have been treated. Traditional psychotherapy tends not to work well with these clients because they often have learned to live with and to use their complaints and tolerate high levels of discomfort before becoming motivated to change. Although they may show good response to short-term treatment, symptoms are likely to return. A combination of behavioral deconditioning, Gestalt, and supportive psychotherapy seems to work best. For example, having the client's aches and pains "do the talking" may help in the ventilation and catharsis of blocked emotional responses. Working through early childhood losses in a supportive reparenting modality could be useful. Initially, the therapist needs to develop a therapeutic alliance by helping the client manage medical treatment and helping them avoid doctor shopping and repeating medical treatments. When giving feedback to these individuals, discuss how debilitating fear and pain can be and begin treatment by having them keep a diary on how their physical symptoms increase with stress, so that they can begin behavioral ways of reducing stress.

123/213 Codes (See Also 1234/2134 and 1237/2137 Codes; See Also 213/231 Codes If Scale 3 Is Within 5 T-Score Points of Scale 1)

The elevation of Scale 3 changes the interpretation of the 12/21 code pattern by adding hysterical defenses; the individual shows more "niceness," repression and inhibition, and a sense of long-suffering acceptance of physical ailments, with less of the whiny, complaining cynicism of the pure 12/21 pattern. These persons express multiple physical complaints, especially abdominal–visceral pain, weakness, fatigue, low energy, and sleep disturbance. Their history shows chronic longstanding hypochondriasis. They are prone to develop physical symptoms in response to stress. Strong somatization, anxiety, and depression are primary characteristics associated with this code pattern. They may present their complaints with substantial irritability, even though a passive dependence also is likely to be present. Often there is real physiological breakdown because of years of tension and apprehensiveness. For men, especially, there is often a sense of sexual inadequacy. Confused or psychotic thinking, suicidal thoughts, obsessions, and compulsions are not likely. However, they generally are depressed, pessimistic, hopeless, apathetic, lacking in assertiveness, unlikely to take risks, and may feel "over the hill" or in declining health. They often feel that life is a strain. They also tend to feel unappreciated by others.

Where Scale 4 is the low point, the 123/213 pattern suggests even more passivity, lack of heterosexual drive, and sexual difficulties. With a low Scale 9, (T < 50), it suggests a low energy level, a lack of vocational aggressiveness, and a strong tendency to "take to bed" when stresses accumulate.

Women with low Scale 5 scores and men with high Scale 5 scores are long-suffering in their assumption of duties, sacrifices, and unnecessary burdens to the point of guilt-inducing masochism. Low Scale 5 scores in women or high Scale 5 scores in men add to the passivity and inhibition already present in the 123/213 code pattern.

If the *L* scale is elevated, these individuals are more likely to have sexual or marital difficulties because of their moral rigidity and lack of psychological mindedness. Although they tend to be extremely conscientious at work, the *L* elevation suggests even more fears and concerns about social disapproval already present in the 123/213 code pattern. Marks and Seeman (1963) reported that 85% of their sample had at least average school performance. Very few were either above or below average, suggesting that these individuals worked hard to fit in and not take risks or "make waves," even during their school years. In contrast, Graham et al. (1999) reported that their participants showed an achievement orientation.

Treatment. Therapeutic techniques should be similar to the those used with the 12/21 code pattern, with assertiveness training and helping them learn to express anger to unblock the repressed anger and sadness around past losses and deprivations. Look for childhood experiences with early losses of loved ones and perhaps frightening physical illnesses in the client or someone close to them. These individuals may have dealt with these early losses by attempting to be brave, by trying to "look on the bright side," or by denying and repressing any normal negative emotions, perhaps out of fear of further loss of emotional support. Helping them to learn to recognize and express anger directly would be an important therapeutic goal.

1234/2134 Codes The addition of Scale 4 changes the interpretation of the 123/213 code pattern. The hostility and alienation indicated by Scale 4 are overcontrolled by the 123/213 pattern, leading to explosive episodes as the overcontrol or the physiological responses reflecting the overcontrol (e.g., ulcers) break down. Scale 4 in the 1234/2134 pattern also predicts manipulativeness, demandingness, self-centeredness/ and addiction proneness, even if the *MAC–R* scale remains unelevated. These individuals are extremely dependent, manipulating others to get their dependency needs met, yet highly insecure, reflecting the basic mistrust associated with an elevated Scale 4. They will show many of the symptoms common to the 123/213 code pattern, as well as the additional ones described here.

Some of these persons are heavy drinkers or alcoholics who can be combative when intoxicated. Men with this profile show hostility toward women (sometimes abusively so), particularly when their strong dependency needs are frustrated or not met. Poor work and marital adjustment are characteristic, accompanied by physical complaints (usually digestive difficulties, such as ulcers, nausea, vomiting, or anorexia), hostility, depression, tension, and perhaps insomnia. For many of these men, their underlying yearnings to be dependent on women appear to be related to histories of feeling rejected by their mothers.

Treatment. In addition to the therapeutic techniques indicated with the 123/213 code pattern, these clients need to recognize when tension and frustration are building and to find more adaptive and less explosive and impulsive ways to express it. Because they are highly dependent, they need much support combined with limit setting to help them see how their impulsive need for instant gratification is self-defeating. Insight therapy, along with behavior modification for the anger management, can help them understand how their anger is related to their unmet dependency needs in early childhood.

1237/2137 Codes. In addition to the 123/213 code pattern correlates noted earlier (see 123/213 code interpretations), the addition of Scale 7 predicts increased anxiety, tension, fearfulness, inability to be assertive, feelings of inadequacy, and dependent interpersonal relations, usually in addition to psychophysiological ailments. Back and chest pains, as well as epigastric complaints, are particularly common. These people are seen as weak, moody, fearful, highly inadequate, and unable to cope with everyday stress and responsibility (particularly if *K* and *ES* are below $T = 50$). This pattern predicts individuals who internalize conflict and anxiety. Men with this profile frequently marry a dominant woman and in this relationship perpetuate a role of dependency. Chronic unemployment and alcohol dependency may occur. These individuals are extremely subservient and have chronic difficulties expressing anger. They lack psychological mindedness and are highly inhibited and repressed.

Treatment. Because of their use of repression and denial (as expected from elevations on Scales 3 and 7), there often are difficulties with accurate history reporting. Assertiveness training and rehearsing the expression of anger, as well as supportive psychotherapy, are indicated. As with any code pattern in which depression and anxiety are components, medications usually are helpful. These individuals often have a pleasant social presentation because of their ability to role-play and to deny and repress negative affects and because of their strong needs to please authority figures. They are quick to interpret any pushing by the therapist as a rejection or displeasure with them. This could result in premature termination. Behavioral therapies to teach them self-soothing could be useful given that many experienced chaotic childhoods with unpredictable emotional support. In their childhood, they may have experienced unpredictable rages directed toward them where they feared for their lives or the lives of their loved ones. Help them reengage the experience, learning to express anger, and then learn to self-soothe and relax in the face of induced emotionally arousing situations.

128/218 Codes

This is primarily a depression profile, with both psychotic and somatizing features. The bizarreness of the physical complaints reflects the depth of the individual's depression, as well as the damaged self-esteem. The physical complaints usually have a bizarre component ranging over the entire upper body, and are accompanied by complaints of fatigue, weakness, tension, and insomnia, which are typical of the 12/21 code pattern. The Scale 8 elevation adds the likelihood of disturbances in thinking, such as difficulties with thinking, memory, and concentration, as well as feelings of alienation from others that occur in 28/82 code patterns. Many individuals with the 128/218 code pattern reveal histories of notable dependency on others. Some are acutely prepsychotic or psychotic and have somatic delusions, but most are not psychotic. Rather, the code pattern suggests a severe depression with feelings of physical and psychological disintegration.

Treatment. Antidepressant medications usually are indicated. Explorative and insight psychotherapy generally should be avoided or used with caution as this type of therapy tends to be disorganizing and confirming of their negative self-esteem. Childhood histories often show cold, withdrawn caretakers and emotional deprivation. Supportive, motherly therapies that reparent the individual can be effective, although short-term treatment strategies, such as cognitive restructuring, self-esteem building, and assertiveness training, could be useful. These individuals suffer from a profound negative self-image and feelings that they are hopelessly emotionally and physically damaged and unlovable, so therapies that enhance self-esteem quickly are most likely to be helpful. Do not expect, however, a quick, positive transference, as these individuals fear that closeness will lead to abandonment and rejection.

129/219 Codes

If Scales 1, 2, and 9 are all elevated at about the same level, it is difficult to discern whether this is a primary affective disorder with mood instability creating secondary psychosomatic complaints or whether this is a somatizing depression with agitation (reflected in the Scale 9 elevation) as a secondary component. As one would expect given the 29 part of the elevation, there is substantial mood instability and agitation. Concern about bodily functions and ailments is greatly distressing to such persons, who respond to them as virtual emergencies. Acute distress, tension, agitation, and restlessness are prominent. Headaches, insomnia, and complaints such as spastic bowel are frequent. A neurological etiology for their problems should be considered because in a small minority of cases this pattern has been associated with organic brain syndromes. It is also possible that the elevation on Scale 9 reflects a hypomanic defense in which the person is conflicted or passive dependent, as reflected in the elevation of Scales 1 and 2.

Treatment. This code pattern is complicated for psychotherapy because somatizing defenses are mixed with elements of a mood disorder. Where emotional lability and depressive symptoms are primary, antidepressant medications may be useful, although caution is needed because some clients may develop a manic episode. Where a history of mood instability exists, antimanic agents should be considered. Treatment strategies involve helping the individual (a) deal with fears of loss and failure and (b) distinguish between their own wants and internalized parental expectancies for great achievement. Usually, this profile reflects fears of failure and the expected resulting emotional abandonment and disapproval. Some of these clients are prone to alcoholism or other addictions, and appropriate cautions are needed.

120/210 Codes

If Scales 1, 2, and 0 are all elevated at about the same level, a distinction must be made as to whether this is a somatizing profile in an introverted individual or whether it is a depressed, introverted, schizoid individual with somatizing features. Typically, the 20/02 pattern is a very stable code pattern, as is the 12/21 code pattern. Taken together, these elevations predict depression, withdrawal, indecisiveness, interpersonal avoidance, and feelings of inadequacy and guilt. These symptoms are accompanied by diverse somatic complaints and a defeatist attitude. Such persons are distinctly lacking in joy and most often are seen as aloof and passive and sometimes withdrawing in a misanthropic or schizoid fashion (particularly if Scale 6 or 8 is also elevated).

Treatment. Assertiveness training and cognitive restructuring could serve to help these individuals deal with their pessimistic and negative outlook. It may also be useful to ask the client to have their symptoms "do the talking" to help them ventilate some of their repressed feelings and to help them engage in emotional connecting. Antidepressants, as with all depressive profiles, could help alleviate their dysphoria, although medication should be given in small doses, as these disorders tend to be long-standing and any rapid change tends to be experienced as uncomfortable. Childhood histories often reveal parental emotional and physical aloofness, distance, and a lack of warmth, although without overt hostility. Many of these clients experienced a loss of childhood carefreeness because of demands on them to be prematurely adult and responsible, perhaps because of illness in themselves or others.

13/31 Codes (See Also Conversion V)

The 13/31 code pattern is more common in women and in older persons, and somatoform diagnoses are often given. These persons are typically preoccupied with numerous physical problems. The most typical complaint is one of pain, which usually centers on the extremities: head, back, neck, arms, eyes, and legs. They are vulnerable to developing physical symptoms in response to stress. Other frequent problems involve eating such as nausea or discomfort after eating, and sometimes anorexia or bulimia. Often fatigue, dizziness, numbness, and tremors also are found. Severe anxiety or depression usually are absent, although some patients may report depression. Sleep disturbances and low sex drive are complaints associated with this code, as are histrionic features. The elevation on Scale 3 generally tempers the pessimistic, complaining cynicism shown by high Scale 1 individuals. If Scale 2 is coded third, then depression and pessimism are evidenced, although coated over with a veneer of resignation. If Scale 7 is elevated along with the 13/31 pattern, then anxiety, tension, and guilt also are present, with even more fears of conflict and the expression of anger. If Scale 8 is the third most elevated scale, the client also may complain of dizziness, losses of consciousness, and bizarre physical symptoms. If Scale 9 is elevated along with the 13/31, then there is more emotionality, approval seeking, denial, and explosiveness. Note, however, that some 139 code patterns have been associated with chronic brain syndromes.

Few clients with 13/31 codes are incapacitated by their symptoms and continue functioning, albeit at a reduced level of efficiency. Unless the *K* scale is low, they present themselves as normal and responsible and often will object to psychological examination or referral and will resent "having their minds probed." They have a high need for social approval, and have strong values about being seen as cheerful, contented, and "brave in the face of their pain." If the *L* and *K* scales are elevated, then there is even more repression, denial, and fears of being judged. As a result, these individuals are difficult to engage in psychotherapy. They seek medical explanations for their problems and lack insight into psychological factors that may underlie or influence their problems. Some, particularly those older than 40, will have demonstrable physical pathology, perhaps reflecting how prolonged stress leads to eventual physical breakdown. In many cases, the extreme inhibition and unconscious fear of dealing with emotionally charged material leads to physical pathology and preoccupations that are clearly psychological in origin.

These persons show strong needs for attention, affection, and sympathy and feel insecure without it. Often their physical complaints produce secondary gains, such as caretaking behavior from others, particularly if the pattern is a Conversion V. Other secondary gains may include avoiding responsibilities and duties and/or control of others through inducing sympathy from them. Not surprisingly, then, these people are described by others as immature, egocentric, dependent, and selfish.

Although generally outgoing and sociable (particularly if Scale 0 is below $T =$ 50), their social relations tend to be superficial and focused on meeting their needs for reassurance. Given their extreme fears regarding body damage, it is surprising that many are described as optimistic (especially if Scales 2 and 7 are within the normal range), but the description reflects their use of repression, denial, rationalization, and projection wherein they blame others or situations for difficulties. Seldom do they express negative feelings, such as anger, in a direct fashion. Instead, they either repress and deny these feelings so that they get expressed somatically as tension and somatic symptoms or express them in a passive–aggressive fashion. Establishing enduring, realistic relations with members of the opposite gender is characteristically a problem, as one would expect with an individual whose primary defenses are so immature. However, these people seek these relations because of their needs for emotional support and because such relations are socially appropriate.

It is helpful to note whether Scale 1 is substantially higher than Scale 3, or vice versa. A 13 code predicts clear hypochondriacal features with associated complaining and pessimism, whereas a 31 code will predict more immaturity, dependency, and needs for social approval, with the hypochondriacal complaints stoically suffered and perhaps only developing when faced with stressful situations.

The 13/31 code is the second most common among both fathers and mothers of child psychotherapy clients. It is associated with mothers who are overprotective, extraverted, and suggestible. When mothers have this code, it is associated with some improvement both for the mother and the child. When fathers have this code, the prognosis is less favorable. Among fathers, this profile is associated with immature dependency, strong needs for acceptance, and the use of subtle and indirect strategies to gain affection and attention.

College women (5% of whom show this code) describe themselves as affectionate and thoughtful. Their peers, however, see them as selfish, self-centered, dependent, attention seeking, irritable, emotional, high-strung, and with frequent physical complaints. Often there is a strong orientation toward marriage but far less interest toward academic concerns, which often then emerge as problem areas.

College men likewise are seen as selfish, dependent, self-centered, and demanding. One of their primary complaints is that they do not get enough consideration from their families. Most appear socially at ease, fluent, expressive, and confident (particularly if K is high and 0 is low). In psychological settings, they often assertively insist on knowing their test results and on being given definite answers to their problems. Typically, however, they do not return for professional help after the first or second session. They rationalize, blame others, and generally avoid self-examination.

Treatment. Although these persons generally are reluctant to talk about possible psychological factors, it may be possible to do so if no direct link is made between their physical symptoms and the current emotional stressors. Clients with this code often terminate treatment prematurely if they are pressured to examine their emotional lives. Clients with 13/31 code patterns are highly suggestible, and they expect therapists to provide definite answers and solutions. Their symptoms can be shaped by the kinds of medical attention they receive.

It is interesting to note (Marks & Seeman, 1963) that 60% of the persons with 13/31 codes experienced the early death of a parent. This code pattern predicts the learning of withholding of feelings, being "brave" in the face of loss, and blocking the expression of anger surrounding these losses. These individuals need to learn to recognize when anger and sadness are building so that they can find constructive ways to express them. Assertiveness training, which can help them learn to deal with conflict, and Gestalt therapy, which allows their symptoms to do the "talking," can help them learn to ventilate their feelings. If early parental illness or death occurred, help the client finish any grieving for past losses, observing in the therapy session how fears of being emotionally flooded leads to somatic complaints as a way to shift attention away from emotionally overwhelming material.

Conversion V Code

A Conversion V occurs when Scales 1 and 3 are elevated above a *T* score of 65 and Scale 2 is approximately 8 or more *T*-score points lower than Scales 1 and 3. Persons with Conversion V patterns show strong needs to interpret their psychological or interpersonal problems in ways that are socially acceptable. They deny troubles or inadequacies, and lack the expression of pessimism and depressive feelings seen in the 123/213 code pattern. They seem almost indifferent or even jovial in their presentation, presenting their numerous somatic complaints in a positive, almost cheerful manner. They deny troubles or inadequacies, and the anxiety and depression often found in 13/31 persons without a Conversion V pattern is typically absent. If Scale 9 is distinctly elevated, then the possibility must be considered that manic defenses are being used to ward off depression and the Conversion V pattern is likely to be somewhat less stable and likely to change when the manic defenses are insufficient for the person to cope.

Many people with Conversion V patterns develop somatic complaints or psychological symptoms of a highly reasonable and socially acceptable type that allow them to displace and externalize inadequacies or problems. They emphasize their somatic symptoms and can discuss their level of pain without the accompanying affect usually associated with people who are experiencing pain. Their physical problems almost always are characterized by "secondary gains," wherein the person is able to avoid responsibilities and/or to manipulate or control situations or the behaviors of others.

A Conversion V pattern, if contained within a normal-limits profile, reveals a socially outgoing person who is cheerfully optimistic. Because of their repressive tendencies, they frequently appear immature or even flighty. Under stress, they may develop psychophysiological complaints, but ordinarily they appear exceedingly normal, responsible, helpful, and sympathetic, although overcontrolled and lacking in insight.

Treatment. See treatment section under the 13/31 code.

13/31, High K Codes

The elevation on the *K* scale within the 13/31 profile predicts even more overcontrol, inhibition, denial, and need for social acceptance. These individuals have difficulty with the expression of negative feelings, so the therapist will have to multiply the intensity of what they say in order to get a true sense of empathy for what they are really experiencing. These individuals are unaware of their negative impulses and emotions and are concerned with being seen as normal, responsible, helpful, and sympathetic. Often their lives are organized around ideals of service to others and contribution to community. They are genuinely caring individuals, uncomfortable with conflict to such a degree that repression of unacceptable impulses may lead to physical breakdown. They are threatened by any suggestion that they might have psychological difficulties, which they see as weaknesses, or even that they have unconventional behaviors. They do not tolerate the role of psychiatric client well. Whatever physical symptoms might exist are unlikely to be debilitating (see also Conversion V).

Treatment. Although unlikely to profit from traditional psychotherapy, these persons do benefit from professional reassurance. Therapists may be tempted to confront clients out of a feeling that they are not doing their job if they are in some way "sympathetic" to the clients' physical complaints. However, aggressive pushing or confrontation by the therapist will lead to quick termination. The elevation on the *K* scale particularly predicts that the client will be apprehensive to opening up and experiencing any catharsis. Assertiveness training, emotional support, and helping the client finish grieving about past losses, if done in a gradual manner, could be useful therapeutic strategies. Remember that these individuals can develop real physical symptoms because of the stress placed on their musculoskeletal and organ systems by the inhibition of feelings.

132/312 Codes

The addition of Scale 2 as the third highest scale changes some characteristics of the 13/31 code pattern only slightly. The depression is still masked by the 13/31 somatizing and denial but is manifested as episodes of tension, distress, and complaints of weakness and fatigue. Some of these individuals deny any experience of depression, although for others it is more palpable. Others experience periods during which their pain seems to disappear, reflecting the interplay between depressive symptoms and hysterical defenses. In addition, they typically show many of the 13/31 code-pattern characteristics, such as being conventional, conforming, anxious to be liked by others, and passive, especially if Scale 4 is low. If Scale 7 is elevated, they are even more conforming, with strong needs for approval and apprehension about conflict.

Treatment. With the addition of Scale 2 coded third, clients may be open to hearing how their physical symptoms have "worn them out" and led to an underlying depression, which could be treated with medications. Psychotherapy should focus on how current losses and stresses replicate past childhood losses. In a supportive, nonjudgmental environment, these individuals can be open to relaxation training and, because of their hysterical defenses, some are amenable to hypnosis. In the process of relaxing, they may become aware of repressed feelings, such as sadness, which then could provide the necessary material for helping them deal with past losses. See also the psychotherapy section for the 13/31 code pattern.

134/314 Codes

Somatic complaints may be less prominent in such persons as compared with their behavior pattern, which is opinionated, snobbish, and even cocky, argumentative, or belligerent. The addition of an elevated Scale 4 to the 13/31 code pattern predicts anger, manipulative dependency, occasional impulsiveness, and emotional distrust. These individuals can manifest some of the characteristics of the 34/43 code pattern, such as being explosive and manipulative. Usually the *O-H* scale will also be elevated, reflecting the overcontrol of feelings. They also will exhibit other 13/31 code-pattern characteristics, including a bland indifference toward their symptoms, role-playing for social approval, and numerous physical symptoms, which can be used to manipulate others into satisfying their dependency needs. Conflicts between their desires for independence and their fears of abandonment lead to approach–avoidance conflicts in their relations. These individuals seldom have insight into why they alienate others. Their somatic complaints reflect overcontrolled feelings, especially anger, that are not openly expressed in a modulated fashion; instead, their feelings are expressed either in episodic outbursts or indirectly through passive–aggressive means.

Treatment. In addition to the therapeutic strategies outlined for the 13/31 code pattern, these individuals need help in learning to recognize and express anger as it builds rather than overcontrolling it out of fear of rejection and abandonment. Pay attention to what these individuals deny, as it often is the source of their conflict. Look for childhood experiences of abuse and/or rejection, which may have made them phobic about expressing anger directly toward others. In some cases, this code pattern reflects an emotional shutting down, perhaps in response to some profound emotional pain. This leads these individuals to develop a role-playing approach to life whereby they fit into others' role expectations and develop physical symptoms in response to their general overcontrol and the bottling up of feelings.

136/316 Codes

The addition of Scale 6 to the 13/31 code pattern predicts a hypersensitivity to criticism and to any demands made on them by others. These individuals exhibit many characteristics of the 13/31 pattern, but the addition of Scale 6 suggests some characteristics of a 36/63 code/ such as paranoid defenses and a tendency to project their anger onto others.

These individuals are very tense and sensitive to criticism or even to requests by others that could be construed as demands. They are particularly sensitive to being judged by others as "mentally ill." Paradoxically, they tend to be rigid and stubborn themselves, often even being egocentric or even narcissistic, and often have a strong sense of pride and a rigid morality. They are particularly concerned about their social image and have a strong need to be seen as attractive and conforming.

Physical problems, particularly gastrointestinal problems or headaches, may develop during stressful situations. Despite their physical symptoms, these individuals (particularly men with this profile) are competitive. Their competitiveness may come from a feeling that they need to be in control of situations, as well as somehow have to prove themselves and "be better than others" in order to be above others' criticisms. Sometimes their need for control is so intense that they engage in ruthless power operations, with little insight into how others might see their behaviors. Although their anger tends to be overcontrolled, when they feel wronged, they can be particularly focused on seeking "justice" but tend to egocentrically rationalize their behaviors.

When Scale 6 is within 8 *T*-score points of Scale 3 and both are elevated significantly above a *T* score of 65, then suspiciousness and anger will be more marked and the possibility of early paranoid schizophrenia might be considered. When Scale 3 is higher than Scale 6 by 8 or more *T*-score points, overt paranoid features are less likely and physical complaints will be more prominent. The paranoid traits will be more subtle, with a tendency toward unreasonable jealousies and a sensitivity to feeling criticized or unfairly treated but with a veneer of niceness and socially correct behavior.

Treatment. See also therapeutic strategies outlined for the 13/31 and 36/63 code patterns. These individuals are particularly sensitive to anything that could be construed as criticism or judgement. Before insight and catharsis can develop, these individuals need to feel that the therapist is "on their side." Explore for childhood histories of criticism or judgment with parents' rigid adherence to high moral standards. These individuals tend to internalize their parents' strict values and have difficulty developing empathy for themselves as children who may have been severely punished for minor moral transgressions. Watch for these individuals as parents to replicate their own childhood experiences and to be somewhat punitive, moralistic, and rigid with their own children. The primary focus in therapy should be in helping them verbalize their wants directly to others before they allow resentments to develop rather than passive–aggressively forming moral judgements. Relaxation training and self-esteem building also can be helpful.

137 Codes

Severe anxiety and panic attacks are common, accompanied by cardiac complaints, such as tachycardia and/or epigastric distress, particularly if Scale 9 is also elevated. Under stress, they develop numerous somatic complaints; although anxiety attacks are the most common, fears and phobias about illnesses are also found. The addition of Scale 7 to the 13/31 code pattern adds anxiety, guilt, and profound fears of rejection to an already dependent code-pattern. These individuals are extremely uncomfortable with conflict and are dependent to the point that they are easily bullied or controlled. They tend to be ingratiatingly subservient.

Persons with this profile are rigid and adapt poorly to situational changes. Often they are unrealistically insecure about work and finances and depend on a dominant spouse to take responsibility for managing their lives and to discipline the children. Poor vocational adjustment due to underachievement is likely.

Treatment. These individuals can be best understood by thinking of them as panicked, dependent children. Because they are agreeable and ingratiating, they are likable. However, they can exhaust the therapist because of their constant need for reassurance, which has only a transitory effect on lowering their anxiety. If they perceive the therapist as impatient or angry with them, they become anxious and clinging. Look for childhood histories of unpredictably explosive and/or rejecting parents or situations. The profile reflects an individual who is constantly on guard against the onset of unpredictable overwhelming emotional and/or physical pain. Look for traumatic experiences in which they feared for their lives, and use deconditioning therapies, such as systematic desensitization and implosion therapies, to lower their anxiety. Help them develop self-soothing strategies, perhaps using therapy techniques to help them reparent their "inner child."

138/318 Codes (See Also 1382 Codes)

These persons tend to have eccentric and unusual ideas and beliefs, particularly about religious and sexual topics, as well as numerous vague and bizarre somatic complaints. These complaints often resemble the kinds of complaints associated with neurological damage, such as tremors, amnesia, blurred vision, and dizziness. Their response to their physical symptoms reflects the interplay of the 13/31 and 38/83 code patterns. For example, sometimes they respond blandly about their physical symptoms, as one would expect with a 13/31 code pattern; at other times, they respond with panic and extreme anxiety, as one would expect with high Scale 8 elevations. This is an intuitively odd code pattern in that it mixes both neurotic and psychotic elements. The hypochondriacal concerns may act as an "anchor," grounding the individual in realistic concerns, preventing the eruption of more floridly psychotic symptoms.

These individuals are quite changeable both in their moods and in their belief systems. When threatened, they may experience brief psychotic episodes, which disappear abruptly once the threat is removed. Religiosity and even religious delusions may be present. The religious preoccupations may represent a defense against the development of "looser" thinking.

These individuals have great difficulty concentrating, and their responses to open-ended questions tend to be confused, with loose associations, so that the flow of conversation appears somehow oddly connected. Many would be considered borderline personalities, and their childhood histories often show a family background of psychosis and/or emotional deprivation. In men, fears regarding homosexuality are common, even though traditionally masculine occupations are usually chosen. These persons function best in structured situations, and their bizarre symptoms may occur only when such structure is absent. They tend to have unusual sex histories; although often sexually preoccupied, many are sexually naïve and inhibited.

Treatment. Individuals with this code pattern typically have severely disturbed family histories and many unresolved dependency needs. As elevations on Scale 3 would predict, they have strong needs for reassurance and closeness but also experience great fears of rejection. Their tendency toward loose associations could be a barometer for how stressful particular avenues of psychotherapy are becoming. Therapy should be highly structured and proceed slowly. Reparenting type of therapies in a highly structured situation would most likely be useful.

1382 Codes

In addition to the 138/318 interpretation, notable depression, confused thinking, heavy drinking, and suicidal preoccupation are likely. Such persons usually are single or have poor marital adjustment. Typically, they float from one job to another.

Treatment. See treatment section under the 138/318 Codes. This disturbed code-pattern reflects a mixture of somatic, psychotic, hysterical, and depressive traits and symptoms. In such a mixed symptom picture, whichever complaints and symptoms are most prominent could be taken and dealt with initially, dealing with the symptoms step by step. Antidepressant and antianxiety medications could be useful in conjunction with a reparenting supportive type of therapy, providing structure and assertiveness training as well as self-esteem building.

139 Codes

Some of these persons are diagnosed as having an organic brain disorder. More often, however, the etiology is personality based. Extremely needy for approval, these individuals tend to lack self-awareness. Their role tends to be that of performer and approval seeker, often with manic defenses of overcommitment in their attempts to please. They have difficulties expressing anger, often allowing it to accumulate and then explode. After they have exploded, they tend to deny or repress the importance of the explosive episode and go back to being cheerful and in denial. Numerous somatic complaints are present (e.g., headaches, hearing and visual complaints, tremor, and coordination difficulties), about which the person is quite upset but with little awareness of any emotional component. These persons have a low frustration tolerance, are irritable, and show temper outbursts, often becoming combative or destructive (particularly if Scale 4 is also elevated and/or if K is low).

Interpersonal relations are stormy, and divorces are frequent. Often these persons have histories of demanding perfection from their families and showing little outward affection for them. Hostility often may be shown directly, particularly following ingestion of alcohol. Most often this code is associated with personality disorders or with brain syndromes associated with trauma. Sometimes, although less often, they are associated with anxiety–reaction diagnoses.

Treatment. Look for a family history of domineering parents whose approval was dependent on performance. These individuals often internalize their parents' expectations, wherein they simultaneously resent their controlling parents and internalize their values. The physical symptoms reflect their overcontrol and lack of awareness of negative emotions. Because of their increased needs for approval, they respond well to supportive, approving therapists, who can then help them distinguish what their wants are versus the internalized expectations of their parents. Help them see how their strong needs for approval lead to their feeling controlled and dominated, replicating their childhood experiences with their parents. Help them learn to recognize when anger and irritability are building, and help them rehearse ways of expressing it so that negative emotions do not build, leading to explosive episodes.

14/41 Codes

This is a relatively rare code pattern, particularly for women. The primary feature tends to be somatic in nature rather than psychopathic. Scale 1 substantially reduces the aggressive acting out usually associated with Scale 4 elevations. Rather, the acting out will come through as a subtle, manipulative dependency, with a tendency to manipulate others through physical illnesses. The addition of Scale 4 to Scale 1 aggravates the cynicism, bitterness, and pessimism already manifested by the elevation of Scale 1. These individuals are highly dependent and at the same time distrustful. They often show histories of inadequacies in fitting in with groups generally and often become upset with rules, regulations, or restrictions. They tend to be negative, complaining, self-pitying, and easily upset when their immediate needs are not met. They approach life with a "what will you do for me today?" attitude, centered on their physical illnesses and disabilities. They feel entitled and are highly dependent, although they simultaneously anticipate being let down and emotionally abandoned. Their negativism will manifest itself more as a stubbornness and a passive resistance to being controlled in any way. Their self-centered and demanding style usually is accompanied by physical complaints, particularly nonspecific headaches and reports of general pain, although few specific symptoms. They tend not to report any type of emotional distress, such as depression or anxiety, as a result of their physical symptoms; rather, they express their distress in an angry negativity and defeatedness.

They often have a pattern of socially unacceptable behavior and inadequacy in meeting the usual stresses and responsibilities of life. Excessive alcohol use is also usually present. In school or on the job, they show a history of indecision and poorly defined goals and have difficulties in establishing enduring relations with members of the opposite gender. Their family relations are characterized by some tension, turmoil, and chronic complaining.

The most common three-point codes are 143/413 and 142/412. When Scale 3 is also elevated, family and marital problems are suggested, centering on feelings of anger, which are intermingled with feelings of social inadequacy and conflicts over dependence and independence. The presence of Scale 3 predicts overcontrol, a tendency to mask the hostility and alienation suggested by Scale 4, and an increased likelihood that the physical symptoms reflect the overcontrol of negative impulses. Usually such code patterns would also show an elevation on the *O-H* scale.

Treatment. Although they may show a good response to short-term symptomatic treatment, persons with 14/41 codes tend not to stay in treatment long enough to make significant personality changes because they quickly become resistant to any demands placed on them by the therapist. They tend to be demandingly dependent individuals who want to be taken care of but at the same time are angry and distrustful. These feelings tend to be expressed in passive ways rather than overtly. Their tendency is to approach the therapist with a "what are you going to do for me today?" attitude because they see themselves as suffering and immobilized by their physical ailments. They feel entitled to quick relief and are angry when they do not experience it.

Treatment could focus on their tendency to distrust that others really care and consequently their tendency to feel that they must manipulate others into taking care of them. They want to be taken care of but are angry, anticipate abandonment, and feel justified in manipulating others as the only way they can get their basic needs met. Look for early childhood histories of emotional let-downs and abandonment that left them insecure about getting their basic emotional needs met. Sometimes this occurs in the context of a history of illness in themselves or in someone they were dependent on. Conceptually, this code pattern reflects an immature, dependent individual who psychologically is "very young." They need help in learning to be more self-sufficient. Family therapy, combined with some limit setting by the therapist, could help the family learn not to be codependent with the individual's manipulations.

15/51 Codes (See Also Scales 1 and 5)

This is an uncommon code for men and an extremely rare code for women. Most commonly, Scale 3, 4, or 2 is the third highest scale for men.

Men with this code usually are fussy, complaining, and cynical and have a basically passive lifestyle. Somatic difficulties frequently are the focus of their complaints. Overt acting out is generally contraindicated, and seldom do they engage in open conflict or disagreement. Usually, they are of above-average intelligence, and their SES is middle class or higher.

In women, the interpretation of this uncommon code depends on the person's social class background. Middle-class, educated women with a 15/51 code exhibit the attributes of Scale 1 elevations, such as pessimism, complaining, and being somewhat immature. Yet, paradoxically, they are interpersonally competitive and even aggressive with many traditional masculine interests, sometimes emotionally dominating in their relations with men. Women of lower socioeconomic backgrounds also are described as pessimistic, complaining, and immature but less aggressive, although they still exhibit traditional male interests and occupational pursuits. For both men and women, this code pattern is associated with multiple surgeries.

When interpreting 15/51 codes, always examine the third highest scale in combination with Scales 1 and 5. For example, a 153 code would be described first as a 15 code, then as a 13 code, and then perhaps as a 53 code (if Scales 5 and 3 are within a few *T*-score points of each other).

Treatment. In working with 15/51 men, assertiveness training, as well as carthartic techniques to help them express their bottled-up anger, could help reduce their stress level and resulting somatic symptoms. Women with a 15/51 pattern would not need assertiveness training, although they would need help to understand how their physical symptoms may be related to the blocking of the expression of emotions. They would benefit from learning to recognize when stress is building and how they tend to repress and deny their emotions. With 15/51 women, explore if there have been conditioning experiences that may have led them to reject traditional feminine roles and values.

16/61 Codes

The addition of Scale 6 to Scale 1 adds hypersensitivity; vigilance for criticism; and a tendency to rationalize, project blame onto others, and use paranoid defenses. These people are described as rigid, grouchy, and stubborn, and they resent demands being made of them. They are evasive, fearful of emotional involvement, defensive, overly sensitive, and quick to anger. Typically, they are unaware of their irritability and hostility and usually attribute their feelings to the way that others treat them. As expected with Scale 1 elevations, they also may manifest some form of somatization disorder.

Conceptually, the code pattern reflects an individual who feels sick and physically infirm, feels unfairly treated, and blames the world and others for their difficulties. They are ready to defend themselves, as if anticipating being criticized or judged for their symptoms, and are quick to feel unfairly treated or unreasonably misunderstood.

If Scale 8 is coded third, unusual somatic preoccupations and, in some cases, somatic delusions may reflect an underlying psychotic breakdown, which is being defended against through bodily preoccupations. Actual psychotic behaviors rarely are reported, however, in a 16/61 code pattern. This is a rare code pattern both for men and women. The most common third highest scale for men tends to be Scales 2 and 4 and for women, Scales 3 and 8.

Treatment. In treatment settings, these individuals anticipate criticism and judgment. As a result, they are defensive, resentful, and bitter, perhaps in anticipation of such criticism, which elicits anger and resentment from others, thereby confirming their suspicion. Look for childhood experiences of being criticized, judged, or even physically abused. These individuals are extremely sensitive to anything that can be construed as a criticism or a demand, which suggests conditioning experiences of having been criticized or dominated. Psychotherapy should concentrate on helping them feel secure while learning to express their anger directly rather than allowing rationalized resentments to accumulate. Suggest that they keep a diary of when their physical symptoms increase in intensity to see if it is linked to the buildup of their anger and/or resentments.

17/71 Codes

Chronically tense and anxious, as well as guilty and ruminative, these individuals manifest many tension-related complaints and symptoms. Obsessive overconcern with body functions and disorders, along with extreme intellectualization, is common. Underlying feelings of guilt, inferiority, pessimism, and difficulties in being assertive are typical symptoms. Their physical complaints reflect their tension and their anxiety. In addition to feeling insecure, inhibited, inferior, and guilty, obsessive thoughts, fears, and panic that they are "losing their mind and/or health" are common. Usually, Scale 2 is also elevated, with associated depressive features. Typically, these individuals are shy, introverted, and retiring, and they tend to worry about their lack of interpersonal skills. This code is more commonly obtained by men than women. For both genders, the most common threepoint codes are 172/712 and 173/713.

Treatment. This essentially is a neurotic disorder. Consequently, these insecure and anxious individuals profit from reassurance, supportive psychotherapy, thought-stopping techniques, assertiveness training, and relaxation training. They tend to be responsible, conscientious individuals who follow recommendations. Implosive-type therapies, Gestalt therapies, and insight therapy can be useful for these individuals. Look for childhood conditioning experiences of unpredictable illnesses in them or in someone close to them. The profile reflects a constant apprehensiveness about the onset of some unpredictable physical illness.

18/81 Codes

Individuals with this pattern are likely to present with somatic complaints, some of which may be bizarre. In some cases, they are somatic delusions; in other cases, the somatic complaints may represent a defense against the emergence of an actual psychotic episode. Easily distracted and confused, they report difficulties with concentration, thinking, and memory. They may show a flat affect with generalized unhappiness and vague depression. Poor social adjustment characterizes these persons, particularly with members of the opposite gender. They lack trust in others, feel alienated from others, keep others at a distance, and generally feel isolated (even more so when Scale 0 is likewise elevated). Some show a nomadic lifestyle with a poor work history. Particularly when under stress, these persons are distractible and confused in their thinking and periods of disorientation are possible. Emotionally, they are constricted and bottled up, although this may alternate with episodes of sudden belligerence if they feel cornered or threatened by hostility from others. Their home life is often severely disrupted by their emotional style. They do not appear to have learned ways of expressing feelings in a modulated fashion, particularly angry, assertive, or emotionally vulnerable feelings. The most common three-point codes are 182/812, 183/813, and 187/817.

Treatment. These clients tend to show little response to reassurance and tend not to do well with insight types of therapies. Look for childhood conditioning experiences of being subjected to hostility from people on whom they depended. Early immaturity, along with severe teasing, put-downs, or other kinds of identity-damaging experiences, would be common with this kind of profile. Supportive, re-parenting-type therapies would be recommended for these individuals, who tend to feel overwhelmed by insights and are especially vulnerable to taking new insights as confirming their negative self-image. Antipsychotic medication may be necessary, particularly during upsets associated with new insights or with confrontive experiences. These individuals could also profit from assertiveness training to help them learn to recognize and express angry feelings directly.

19/91 Codes (See Also 129/219 and 139 Codes If Scales 2 and 3 Are Within 5 T-Score Points of Scale 9)

This rarely occurring code is associated with tense and restless persons, usually in acute turmoil and mental distress, who exhibit multiple somatic complaints as well as a high energy level and agitation. They show clear overconcern with bodily functions and possible disabilities, even though this overconcern may be expressed in the form of verbal denial or attempts to conceal (or avoid confronting) physical dysfunctions. This pattern may reflect central nervous system or endocrine dysfunction expressed in the form of a high energy level (perhaps agitation) combined with numerous physical complaints.

Where physical etiology has been ruled out, consideration should be given to the hypothesis that the person is attempting to mask an underlying depression (particularly if Scale 2 is below $T = 45$) and that the distress stems from strong dependency needs that the person finds frightening. Such persons, on the surface, appear extraverted and aggressive, but underneath they are usually passive and dependent. Although they appear to be ambitious, they characteristically lack definite goals, or jump from goal to goal. Most commonly, Scale 3 or 4 is the third highest.

Treatment. These individuals are driven, ambitious, and insecure. Psychotherapy could help them define their own goals versus the internalized goals set for them by, perhaps, ambitious parents. In some cases, these individuals come from disadvantaged childhoods, where they developed a strong need to prove themselves because of fears of failure and social disapproval. In other cases, their background is one of being constantly driven and motivated by ambitious parents. Many of them have internalized their parents' strong values around achievement to the point where they develop somatic symptoms reflecting their inner pressure and constant level of anxious strivings.

Conceptually, this profile can be understood as reflecting a constant need to be productive and to protect against future frustration, perhaps out of fear of slowing down or experiencing a loss and then becoming depressed. The physical complaints and anxieties could be a result of extreme tension, and the physical symptoms become sources of secondary anxiety as the hypomanic individual becomes concerned about physical impediments to maintaining control over their reward system. Deconditioning-type therapies to help them deal with their fears of being trapped without an effective reward system could be useful in modulating their high-drive state.

10/01 Codes

This rare code is associated with persons who are socially uncomfortable and withdrawn, aloof, cynically distrustful, passive, and unassertive. They report a limited number of physical complaints, and they do not complain of psychological discomfort or emotional distress. These highly conventional, law-abiding individuals tend to acquiesce to their discomfort, perhaps accepting it as their "lot" in life. When Scale 8 is also elevated as the third highest scale, schizoid withdrawal and social inadequacies are strongly suggested, usually combined with numerous somatic complaints. Most often Scale 2 is the third highest scale, and when elevated above $T = 65$, the person is likely to show depression, accompanied by the lack of a social support system. Look for childhood experiences of deficient socialization and a lack of parental warmth (but usually no overt hostility or anxiety).

Treatment. These individuals seem to have accepted their symptoms and consequently have few complaints. Assertiveness training, social skill building, and teaching them to recognize anger and express it directly could be helpful in dealing with their tendency toward passivity and withdrawal.

Scale 2 (*D*)

Scale 2 is one of the most frequently elevated scales in clinical populations and is usually elevated together with other scales, reflecting the fact that psychopathology of any kind tends to be distressing. In addition, Scale 2 generally is highly sensitive both to current mood and mood changes. Thus, interpretation of Scale 2 elevations depends on the configuration of the rest of the profile. Most often Scales 7, 1, 8, or 0 are elevated along with Scale 2, with Scale 7 suggesting added anxiety, Scale 1 suggesting a somatic component, Scale 8 suggesting feelings of alienation and aloneness, and Scale 0 indicating social withdrawal. Scale 2 increases somewhat with age, perhaps reflecting an increased seriousness about life as one ages or perhaps reflecting the inevitable accumulation of unresolved losses.

High scores ($T \geq 65$) reflect people who are depressed, anxious, worried, and who experience low self-esteem and are pessimistic in their general outlook. Typically, they show a narrowing of interests, low frustration tolerance, and poor morale and generally feel discouraged, sad, useless, and guilty. Elevations of $T = 65–85$ sometimes suggests a good prognosis for therapy, especially if no other scales are elevated, because the person is likely to be quite motivated to seek relief. On the other hand, high elevations can also suggest a serious, long-term, and more difficult-to-treat depression.

The higher Scale 2 is above $T = 65$, the more depressed and self-deprecating the person is likely to be, in addition to difficulties with concentrating, memory, and general efficiency. Scores above $T = 80$ suggest individuals who feel so dejected that they are unable to concentrate, think clearly, and make effective decisions.

Moderately high (T = 55–65) scores suggest individuals who are somewhat inhibited, serious, and introspective, with a tendency to take setbacks badly and with a quickness to feel guilty and self-blaming when things go wrong. They tend to lack self-confidence and to be acquiescing and passive in the face of conflict. Generally, they are responsible, analytical people who avoid risks and characteristically think in terms of good and bad or right and wrong, particularly if the L scale is also elevated.

Moderately low to very low scores ($T \leq 45$), if no other scales are elevated, suggest persons who are alert, cheerful, active, and self-confident, with a good sense of humor, and are seen by others as enthusiastic and socially outgoing (particularly if Scale 0 is low). In some people, however, a low Scale 2 score can also indicate a lack of inhibition and perhaps even impulsiveness, especially if Scale 9 is elevated, the K scale is low, and/or Scale 4 is mildly elevated. Low scores on Scale 2 are often found in younger people.

T scores below 40 can indicate a denial of depression in a cyclothymic, labile person, particularly if Scale 9 is also high. Caution, therefore, should be exercised before dismissing a low Scale 2 as insignificant.

Spike 2

Spike 2 occurs when Scale 2 is the only scale elevated beyond $T = 65$. These individuals are likely to be experiencing a current depression, which may be a reactive depression or a chronic one. Typically, the person feels inadequate and lacking in self-confidence and is often anxious, self-critical, and quick to feel guilty. These individuals experience all the typical symptoms of depression, including disturbances in sleep, appetite, sex drive, concentration, and memory and may attempt to expiate guilt feelings by mental self-punishment. They tend to be serious individuals who are highly responsible and somewhat passive. This is especially true if no other scales are significantly elevated.

In college students, Spike 2 profiles generally are clinically less significant and more often reflect concern over situational problems (usually, relations with the opposite gender, learning issues, or vocational choices). Spike 2 college students typically resist efforts to probe deeply into the origins of their problems and instead seek to get advice from a parent surrogate.

As in all depressive profiles, suicidal ideation and plans should be routinely evaluated, although suicide cannot be predicted by the MMPI–2 alone. The client's responses to Items 150, 506, 520, and 524 on the MMPI–2 may be significant because these items refer directly to suicidal ideation and/or suicide attempts. In some cases, Spike 2 code patterns are highly stable ones; the individuals have come to terms with their depression and may not even be aware of how depressed they are.

Prognosis is generally good within a short time; these individuals often respond well to medication and to a directive approach helping them finish grieving over past losses as well as learning to change their self-evaluations. There are several well-researched treatments for simple depressive disorders. Cognitive restructuring, psychotropic medication, assertiveness training, relaxation training, self-esteem building, and dealing with grief over past losses are all useful therapeutic modalities. (See also treatment section under the Spike 2, low 9 codes.)

Relations With Other Scales

Spike 2, Low 9 Codes

When Scale 2 is elevated, no other clinical scales are significantly elevated, but Scale 9 is below $T = 50$ and sometimes below $T = 45$, then the depression is typified by fatigue, low energy, lack of assertiveness, and a quickness to "give up" in the face of obstacles. The depression is likely to be moderate to severe, and in some cases the Spike 2, low 9 profile can reflect a long-standing personality adjustment. These individuals are often serious, circumspect people who guard their energy resources carefully. They are careful not to overcommit to tasks and activities, and their personality may lack "color." These people may complain of low energy, of feeling easily fatigued, and of feeling overwhelmed by too much to do. Because of this, they may postpone responsibilities because of feeling unable to cope, although this often is accompanied by guilt. If Scale 4 is at or below $T = 50$, even greater passivity, low aggressiveness, low sex drive, and a rigid adherence to rules, regulations, and responsibilities are likely. With a low Scale 4 score, one generally can predict a life based on duty, with accompanying feelings of being burdened, responsible, worried, and guilt prone.

Treatment Psychotherapy with Spike 2 individuals tends to be fairly uncomplicated, as many traditional approaches to treatment of depression are effective. Cognitive restructuring, directive approaches, relaxation training, psychotropic medications, and the finishing of grieving over past losses all would be effective therapeutic strategies. These individuals, especially in the normal and moderately elevated ranges, are motivated and follow instructions. These ranges predict the ability to form supportive, trusting relations with their therapist without undue fear of loss, which would block such a relationship, and treatment progresses rapidly.

Energizing antidepressants may be indicated for a Spike 2, low 9 profile, although individuals whose history suggests a long-term personality adjustment with chronic depression tend to expect any changes due to the medication to be experienced as uncomfortable. Consequently, if prescribed, medication should start in small doses.

With a Spike 2, low 9 profile, first rule out a depressive phase of a bipolar disorder. In any Spike 2 profile, look for childhood experiences of too much responsibility with deficits of age-appropriate carefreeness. These individuals tend to be hyperresponsible and may have experienced periods where they were expected prematurely to take on adult roles. Cognitive restructuring, thought stopping, relaxation training, and assertiveness training are all useful with this code pattern. Teach these individuals to relax and "stop their guilty thoughts" whenever they are relaxed, and help them set up a reinforcement schedule for themselves after they have completed some of their responsibilities. As with any depression profile, suicidality should be assessed.

21/12 Codes (See Also 12/21 Codes; See Also 123/213 Codes If Scale 3 Is Within 5 T-Score Points of Scale 1)

The interpretation is similar to that of the 12/21 code, except that depression and tension–anxiety are more prominent features. The depression usually is of a restless, rather than an apathetic, nature. As with 12/21 codes, acting out is contraindicated (except with 1234/2134 codes). These individuals tend to have a strong work ethic, often reflected in their puritanical, self-pitying style. Oral-dependent and sometimes alcoholic, these individuals exhibit many of the physical symptoms associated with a 12/21 code but exhibit more complaining and pessimism, as one would expect with elevations on Scale 2. This code occurs more frequently as age increases and is more common among men than women. Most often Scales 3 and 7 are the third highest elevation.

Treatment. See also treatment section under the 12/21 codes. With Scale 2 elevated above Scale 1, some individuals may complain more of depressive features and be more amenable to working on finishing grieving over any past losses. Others with this code, however, may be poorly motivated for psychotherapy despite their obvious distress. Therapy techniques may help clients turn their somatic complaints into emotional expression. These individuals may be more open to antidepressants, especially if presented from the perspective of needing medication because they are "worn out" by their physical symptoms. Assertiveness training may also be useful.

213/ 231 Codes (See Also 123/213 Codes)

Although interpretation basically is similar to the 21/21 code, the elevation of Scale 3 predicts hysterical defenses, such as repression, denial, and strong needs for social approval. These clients manifest depression and hypochondriacal concerns, such as headaches, chest pain, or nausea and vomiting. Their depression, however, may be a *smiling depression*, where they literally smile as they cry yet appear unaware of the apparent contradiction in their affective state. They deny anger, are inhibited, and have an exaggerated need for affection. They show conflicts over emotional dependency, craving affection and emotional support, yet fearing loss and abandonment. Although they often demand sympathy and get secondary gains from their symptoms, they feel dissatisfied and worry over becoming too dependent.

Typical symptoms and complaints are depression, with all the accompanying features of sleep and eating problems, eating problems, loss of libido, and difficulties with concentration or memory. They are tense, nervous individuals with numerous somatic complaints. Many complain of nausea or vomiting, weight loss, heart complaints, chest pains, and forgetfulness. Often there may be a cyclical nature to these individuals' complaints. The hysterical defenses associated with Scale 3 elevations appear to operate intermittently so that the individual may go from being outwardly smiling and well-functioning to being incapacitated by depression. Initially, this may appear to be a cyclothymic disorder, but the moodiness with this code pattern reflects the operation of hysterical defenses and related flights into health followed by periods of depression and gloominess as the hysterical defenses collapse. There also tends to be genuine somatic involvement, especially in more elevated profiles or in older people as years of stress and tension take their toll physically on the individual.

When Scale 7 is also elevated, worry is a notable part of the clinical picture. These individuals often have histories of indifference or outright rejection from their fathers, and many experienced the loss through death or divorce of one of their parents during childhood. Interestingly, their childhoods were characterized by social participation rather than withdrawal and they tend to live socially responsible lives. These people are often highly conscientious, although self-sacrificing, and therefore have a tendency to induce guilt in others. As parents, they give a great deal to their families, often in self-sacrificing ways, with a sense of feeling unappreciated. Although this is an attempt to manipulate others into caring for them by "giving too much," they are likely to end up feeling unloved and unappreciated as others take them for granted. In some cases, family members act out, perhaps in reaction to the dependent manipulativeness of the individual as a parent.

Treatment. These individuals exhibit approach–avoidance conflicts in their primary relations. Although dependent and wanting nurturing and emotional support, they fear emotional abandonment. Look for childhood histories of an early death of a parent and/or experiences of rejection or emotional withdrawal from a father figure. In the presence of such a history, these individuals may be repeating their childhood experiences of craving emotional support from a nurturing figure but at the same time fearing another abandonment. They go through life wanting to please others but attempt to elicit others' nurturing behavior through their physical symptoms, thereby causing them to feel constantly tense and fearful of emotional loss and abandonment. The holding in of feelings eventually leads to physiological breakdown. Because these individuals use denial and repression, they tend to deny parental emotional abuse. Consequently, insight therapy moves slowly. Pushing by the therapist will lead to premature termination. Go with the resistance: Agree with them about how loving and supportive their caregivers were, but also remind them how, in spite of how much love they had as children, there were periods where they occasionally might have felt hurt and let down; then explore these periods in order to obtain emotional catharsis. Relaxation training, assertiveness training, and catharsis around past losses, as well as teaching them to express anger, all are helpful therapeutic strategies. Help them deal with their anger and sadness around early rejections or parental death and to get a sense of empathy for themselves as abandoned or rejected children. Both the anger and sadness parts of the mourning process appear to be blocked as they struggle to be "nice" and acceptable to the therapist and to others, believing that if they are in any way displeasing, they will be rejected.

These individuals can exhibit a "flight into health," hysterical defenses that suddenly operate so that they report feeling "great" and then terminate prematurely. If during therapy these individuals begin to criticize other medical professionals, be aware they may be ventilating frustration with their current therapist. It is important to deal with the transference for therapy to continue. Catharsis and helping them express resentment, perhaps about the therapeutic process, could help model how the expression of anger and resentment does not lead to the therapist's withdrawal. Because these individuals are strongly conscientious (especially men), they may elicit support initially in their work environments but then can irritate coworkers because of their self-sacrificing martyrdom. Although likely begun in an attempt to gain approval from others, their conscientiousness backfires as others feel they have been made to feel guilty.

As with all depression code patterns, suicide assessment is important, although these individuals tend not to commit suicide. Antidepressant medications can be useful.

23 Codes (See Also See 213/231 Codes; See Also 32 Codes If Scale 3 Is Within 5 T-Score Points of Scale 2)

The 23 code is essentially similar to the 231/213 code pattern, although some differences exist given that Scale 1 is lower. The major characteristics associated with the 23 code pattern are depression, helplessness, apathy, fatigue, multiple somatic complaints (especially in response to stress), emotional overcontrol, and fatigue and sleep disturbances. Low sex drive may be reported. Feelings that might lead to conflict tend not to be expressed directly. Marked episodes of anxiety are infrequent. With the hysterical defenses, the underlying depression is positivized and denied, so these individuals present as bottled up, filled with self-doubts and insecurities, and exhibit a lack of interest or involvement in their surroundings. They generally have difficulty expressing their feelings in any direct or precise way and present vaguely as dissatisfied and unhappy. Typically, they are immature and dependent, exhibiting difficulties with confrontation and the expression of anger. Often they feel weak or exhausted, and their depression is typically long-standing. If Scale 9 is low, this predicts even more complaints of fatigue and exhaustion. Physical illness is sometimes a precipitating factor for evaluation and treatment of individuals with this code. As one would expect with Scale 3 elevations, there are difficulties expressing anger or sadness, which tend to be expressed more as hurt feelings, being unappreciated, and being unrecognized. Persons with a 23 code tolerate unhappiness and have accepted that they will function at a low level of efficiency, unable to start tasks readily or complete them when started. These individuals can appear depressed, but the operation of hysterical defenses more often suggest that they have a pleasant and somewhat flat demeanor. They also may exhibit the smiling depression and "laughing through their tears" aspects of the 213/231 profile. The most frequent three-point codes are 231/321, 234/324, and 237/327.

Paradoxically, men with 23 codes are superficially very achievement-oriented but often complain of a lack of recognition on their jobs. Although they may seek added responsibilities, they also dread them because what they really want is the recognition without the fear of loss and failure. Such men (particularly those with 237 or 239 codes) seem particularly serious, driven, industrious, or competitive but are also both dependent and immature in the strength of their desire to be recognized.

Women with 23 codes (particularly with a low Scale 5 or 9) show weakness, apathy, insecurity, and prominent depression, along with energy and assertiveness problems. Unhappiness and general inefficiency at work and home typically are chronic, with a long history of marital and family maladjustment. Marital problems may relate to these women having little interest in sex, and some complain of physical pain during intercourse. Despite their insecurity and distress, they show little sustained effort to seek help.

Although this code is more frequent among persons beyond age 25, it nonetheless occurs in adolescents and is associated with poor peer relations. These adolescents typically are lonely individuals with few friends either inside or outside of school settings. Generally, they are seen as passive, compliant, and obedient. Family patterns often show an underinvolved father in a professional occupation and an overinvolved mother. Sexual acting out and drug abuse is not notably associated with this pattern for adolescents. (For more information on adolescent profiles, see Archer, 1997.)

Treatment. These individuals have difficulty dealing with conflict and confrontation both at work and home because of the possible rejection by others, and often tolerate much unhappiness before becoming motivated toward change. These persons are not introspective, and response to insight-oriented therapy may be poor. Catharsis generally is helpful because so much negative affect is denied and bottled up. However, they tend to stay positive and deny anger or conflict, so it is often hard to engage their negative affects. It is important initially to "go with the resistance" and agree with their positivizations of childhood, family, and current relations. Once they feel their relations are not going to be "threatened" by the probing of their negative feelings, the therapist can gently probe how certain past experiences may have produced some negative responses in them. Techniques may be useful that can help them learn to ventilate anger they feel over past hurts. When a particularly painful memory is engaged, they may resist and deny feeling any anger around that event; nonetheless, insist on their role-playing a confrontation, "even though you may not feel any of the anger." Usually after such a role-play, they do feel relief. It is important, initially, that their relations with loved ones are not in any way threatened by the therapy, as they are highly dependent. As with any depression profiles, antidepressants can be useful if the client can see them as not humiliating.

24/42 Codes

This code may reflect either a chronic 24/42 lifestyle or a high Scale 4 individual who recently has experienced a situational setback and is feeling trapped, angry, and defeated. In either case, the person at the time of testing likely felt depressed, angry, frustrated, dissatisfied, resentful, critical, argumentative, and restless. Associated with it is self-defeating behavior, wherein they will act out in a socially unacceptable manner and then feel distress. Most often they show periods when anger is turned outward, with a feeling of being the unfortunate victim of circumstance that they feel prevented them from accomplishment. At other times, the anger will be turned inward, causing them to feel reprehensible and unworthy, with a tendency to be self-defeating, if not self-destructive. For individuals with a high Scale 4 history but are currently dealing with the adverse consequences of their behavior, the 24/42 profile reflects someone who has had difficulty maintaining control over their impulses and who is currently experiencing situational and transient depression and remorse. After acting out and getting caught, they feel distress. However, this distress is the result of being caught and punished, rather than any impulse-restraining guilt. Although their apparent conscience pangs may be severe (even out of proportion to the event), their acting-out behaviors are likely to recur in the future in a cyclic fashion.

Home and family problems, loss of employment, and histories of social problems typically accompany the 24/42 pattern, and they are resentful of demands placed on them by others. Heavy drinking, substance abuse, or alcoholism is frequent. In some cases, legal difficulties are also frequent; in other cases, these individuals manifest numerous relationship problems and career instabilities without any legal difficulties. Many show an inadequate and passive–dependent adjustment pattern. For persons beyond age 40, their failure to achieve accomplishments or satisfaction in life results in self-blame, depression, and distress about failures to achieve past goals or sometimes results in projecting blame. Most often with this code, Scale 7, 3, or 8 is the third highest scale.

Adolescents with this pattern show marked disregard for accepted social standards and are particularly resentful of authority figures, argumentative, afraid of involvement with others, blameful, and frequently involved with drugs. Legal violations (arrest, detention, conviction, and probation) are common, as is running away from home or treatment centers. Most adolescents with this pattern feel alienated from other family members and wish to escape from their intolerable and highly conflicted home situations. They perceive their caregivers as unaffectionate and inconsistent. Difficulties in school are common and are usually related to difficulties in concentrating and truancy. This is a frequent profile pattern of unmarried mothers and is associated with promiscuous sexual behavior.

Overall, 24/42 code individuals feel depressed, frustrated, dissatisfied, and restless. They are pessimistic about the future, experience low self-esteem and express distress about failures to achieve past goals. This distress oscillates between self-blame and blaming others for making them a victim. Because these individuals tend to be self-defeating, self-destructive, and emotionally labile, a suicide evaluation is imperative, particularly when Scales 2 and 4 are highly elevated. Often their suicidal behaviors represent an attempt to punish others or to make them feel guilty.

Treatment. Psychotherapy will depend upon what kind of 24/42 individual is being evaluated. The antisocial individual who is currently caught may need to "hit bottom" in order to effectively examine his or her life and change. One subgroup of 24/42 persons exhibits a chronic lifestyle of unhappiness, resentment, and bitterness, without any serious acting out behavior. These individuals have conflicted marital situations and live their lives feeling hopeless and trapped. They resist psychotherapy, often aggravating therapists because of their tendency to undermine any suggestion with a defeated "I've tried it, and it doesn't work" attitude. Have them agree to do small, concrete homework assignments in the direction of change; then when they do not perform these assignments, talk about how they tend to not trust that any action on their part can lead to any real change. Help them see how they undermine themselves. Look for childhood experiences of being emotionally let down and abandoned, which has instilled in them a tendency to distrust not only relationships but also their own efficacy. Supportive, confrontive, and insight therapies all can be used to help them understand how they may have learned to "numb themselves" as a way of surviving a particularly difficult childhood and how they continue not to trust others and then act out impulsively when tension builds. Help them recognize when stress is accumulating so that they can find more adaptive ways to deal with it rather than to impulsively act out, leading to periodic depressed episodes as their acting-out behavior catches up with them.

This code pattern is most commonly associated with alcoholism, so individuals' chemical intake should be assessed even if the *MAC–R* scale is not elevated. Although these persons may express firm intentions to change their behaviors, the pattern is persistent and hard to change. Although they may show temporary improvement, many are unable to remain in treatment long enough to make more than superficial changes. They are likely to be superficially deferential when confronted or pressured in therapy, but these persons are likely to discontinue treatment or even leave town or change jobs to avoid coming to grips with their problems. In general, they run from others' expectations of them. Even so, a combination of warm support, firm limits, strategic therapy predictions, frequent contact, and environmental modifications may be significantly helpful.

243/423 Codes

The addition of Scale 3 adds hysterical defenses to the angry, self-defeating 24/42 code pattern. Consequently, these individuals will show some 23 code qualities, such as denial, "niceness," and self-sacrifice, yet simultaneously manifest the impulsiveness and anger associated with the Scale 4 elevation. Taken together, the profile suggests emotional overcontrol through repression and denial, especially concerning the expression of anger or rejection of others. Their anger will be expressed in roundabout ways through passive–aggressive behaviors and talking behind other people's backs. In some people, the anger will break through such that explosive, rageful episodes occur, the intensity of which is later denied. This is especially true if the *O-H* scale is elevated above a raw score of 17. With this code pattern, there is likely to be oral dependency, alcoholism, eating problems, and manipulativeness. Immaturity, egocentricity, and lack of insight into how others see them is common. These persons may establish relationships with marginally controlled, angry, acting-out individuals, thereby vicariously satisfying their own antisocial tendencies. It is as if these individuals are going through life manipulating others to get their emotional needs met, playing the right role, and fitting in to avoid rejection and conflict but distrusting others' responses to them, even if it is positive, projecting their own manipulativeness onto others.

Treatment. Look for childhood experiences of rejection or emotional abuse and, if Scales 4 and 3 are significantly elevated, physical abuse. These individuals have learned to role-play, thereby fitting into other people's expectations of them but not trusting others' responses to them if they are positive. Psychotherapy techniques can help them recognize when anger is building and to express it in adaptive, modulated, direct ways. Assertiveness training, catharsis, and ventilation would be important therapeutic modalities. Helping them recognize and express their rage toward an abusive caregiver could be useful in unblocking repressed feelings. Beware of medications that may be addictive, and carefully evaluate for chemical addition problems. These individuals lack insight and often express inconsistent verbalizations; therapies can be useful in helping them deal with "both sides" of their ambivalences. In some cases, this is primarily a depression profile, with the 43 elevations reflecting massive overcontrol, perhaps as a way of dealing with the depression. If depressive symptoms are evident, then an antidepressant medication could be indicated.

247/427/472/742 Codes (See Also 274/724 Codes)

This code pattern reflects an anxious, guilty, acting-out individual. Essentially, 27/72 persons are hyperresponsible "worriers," 24/42 individuals feel angry, defeated, and depressed; and 47/74 persons show compulsive, cyclical acting out followed by remorse and guilt. Taken together, these codes reflect a person who is hyperresponsible but self-defeating, anxious and guilty but acting out, clinging and dependent but emotionally distancing.

These individuals show an overreaction to any kind of security threats and respond with intense worry and anxious preoccupation. Obsessive–compulsive thoughts and behaviors are common with this code. Whenever something goes wrong in their life, they become extremely self-critical and catastrophize the situation, seeing themselves as failures and unworthy of being loved. Others tend to respond to them with reassurance and support, responding to their self-negation with reassurance. These individuals, however, have difficulty trusting the reassurance, and so it does little to calm them. The presence of 24 in the profile suggests self-defeating behaviors, which often occur as the anxiety and tension builds, making them unable to function effectively. They then act out in some way to relieve the tension and, as predicted by elevations on Scale 7, subsequently experience guilt, remorse, and self-dislike.

These individuals are extremely dependent but, perhaps because of fears of emotional closeness, tend to exhibit passive–dependent manipulativeness. Family or marital problems are likely, centered on angry feelings that this person has but is unable to express and feels guilty about. These individuals have substantial difficulty expressing anger because of guilt and fears of emotional abandonment. Consequently, their anger tends to be expressed passive–aggressively and in self-defeating acts, which often elicits protection, but also anger, from family members. These individuals tend to use guilt to manipulate others. They have a tendency to undermine other people's anger toward them by their own self-anger. This kind of behavior can often irritate their family members. Conceptually, one could think of a child, who feels hurt or abandoned by a caregiver, "breaking their own toys" as a way of punishing the caregiver. These individuals often feel that life is a strain and that they are getting a raw deal from life.

Depression, phobias, somatic complaints, anxiety, tension, worry, and feelings of social inadequacy usually are present. Frequently these individuals underachieve and are often extremely fearful to completely commit to anything because of fear of failure. Excessive alcohol use or episodic bouts of drinking or other substance abuse are quite likely (even when the *MAC–R* is not elevated) in attempts to alleviate their depression and their anxiety. This profile is highly associated with chemical addiction problems. Graham et al. (1999) reported suicidal ideation and discomfort with the opposite gender in association with this code pattern.

Men with this pattern are usually dependent and immature but verbally hostile. If married, the wife is strong, protective, and even dominating and/or minimally involved in a short-term marriage. These men often show a history of an extremely close relationship with their mother in which they were indulged but did not learn a sense of personal efficacy.

Women (particularly if Scale 5 is low) present themselves as weak, inferior, guilty, and submissive. Some get involved with older married men and end up marrying protective, older men, reflecting their needs for emotional security . Others virtually invite others to dominate them in a patronizing or deprecating way, almost as if they were atoning for guilt. Often their history shows a father who was hard-driving and successful.

When Scale 1 is coded fourth, they are likely to complain of numerous vague somatic symptoms. If Scale 3 is elevated, there is more overcontrol, hysterical role-playing, and denial.

Treatment. Often the precipitating event for this disturbance is a loss of a dependency support or a protective caretaker, and it may replicate childhood experiences of emotional abandonment. Additionally, these individuals typically overreact to minor problems and react to them as though they were emergencies. Even so, they are unlikely to be frank and open in discussing their problems, out of fear of trusting and then being abandoned, despite their clear discomfort. The profile has been described by Alex Caldwell as the "momma's boy" profile for men and as the "daddy's girl" profile for women. Typically, these individuals had caregivers who indulged them but also depended on them and were unreliable. Their parents typically were inconsistent, so these individuals never learned basic trust.

In psychotherapy, these individuals need much reassurance, but, as one would expect with Scale 4 coded third, they do not trust it. Although they seem to have a constant need for love and reassurance, they doubt that the love and reassurance can be trusted because they project their own manipulativeness onto others and therefore distrust the other's caring. Often this reflects childhood experiences of a caregiver who was highly involved with the client but who would unpredictably abandon the child because of narcissistic needs or psychiatric illness. The transference relationship and the tendency for these clients to put the therapist through trust tests will reflect their history of unpredictable emotional abandonments. Often these individuals initially seek psychotherapy to alleviate an immediate problem, such as getting the supportive person who has abandoned them back into their life. Cognitive restructuring, relaxation training, and insight therapy can be useful once these individuals begin to trust the therapist. Treatment prognosis may be poor because of reluctance to endure the anxiety involved in treatment. Firm, structured, goal-oriented therapy may be helpful in such situations.

248 Codes (Note: 284/824 and 482/842/824 Codes Have Different Interpretations)

It may be difficult to ascertain whether this profile reflects a stable 248 personality style or whether it reflects a 48/84 individual who recently is in trouble because of acting-out behavior, with resulting elevations on Scale 2. In either case, depression, sullen anger, and family and marital problems most likely will be present and such persons are less likely to engage in overt angry acting out than is likely with the pure 24/42 code patterns. Instead, they are more likely to withdraw into angry fantasy, feeling distrustful, alienated, and disaffiliated from others. Nevertheless, they fear loss of control over their impulses and may be quite concerned over their unusual and disturbing thoughts. Often they are seen by others as moody and unpredictable. Sexual difficulties of various sorts are quite likely. Suicidal ideation and multiple suicide attempts are frequently found.

Distrust is a central characteristic of the profile. It is manifested as a sense of alienation and disconnection from others as well as transitory episodes of diffuse paranoia. These individuals can experience periods of panic, which are manifested through irritable and hostile moods that are hard to predict by others. Although they verbalize a great deal of depression, it reflects more of a sense of emptiness and disconnection from others than the sense of real sadness and loss seen in other depression profiles. Further, the depression appears to be sensitive to situational changes rather than the enduring depression of, for example, a 278 profile. They verbalize feeling anxious, although the anxiety tends to be diffuse rather than focused and it may reflect their sense of inner emptiness and inner disorganization, as one would expect from the elevation on Scale 8. This code is a common one among mothers of child psychiatry clients, reflecting their difficulties with empathy and setting limits and boundaries.

Treatment. This pattern is found frequently in people who experience suicidal ideation and multiple suicide attempts; thus, suicide assessment should precede treatment. Suicide attempts generally occur during times of acute alienation, with a rageful sense that they have no one to turn to. These individuals tend to put the therapist through many trust tests, reflecting their fears of emotional abandonment and rejection. Look for childhood histories of rejection, abandonment, and cold cruelty. These individuals have experienced identity-damaging blows to their self-esteem and continue in the role of victim, often getting involved in relationships that are masochistic. Supportive, esteem-building psychotherapies, rather than insight-oriented therapies, are suggested. These individuals can become easily disorganized by demands of insight or analytical therapies, which require good ego functioning. Practical, goal-directive, supportive psychotherapies to help rebuild their self-esteem and develop coping skills that are not impulsively self-defeating are the most useful. Some individuals with this code pattern can show brief psychotic episodes.

The use of drugs and/or alcohol will increase their vulnerability to psychotic and impulsive-type behaviors. The code pattern tends to be associated with chemical addition proneness. Avoid group psychotherapy initially until trust develops. In the presence of severe depressive features, a sedating antidepressant could be useful in alleviating some symptoms.

25/52 Codes (See Also 275/725 Codes If Scale 7 Is Within 5 T-Score Points of Scale 5)

Men with this code are idealistic, inner-directed, unassertive, indecisive, and depressed. They are relatively noncompetitive, perhaps to the point of passivity. Acting out is not likely, and conflicts tend to be handled internally through intellectualization. Often they are anxious and withdrawn, show a history of somatic complaints, and may complain of being unable to think clearly. Typically, such persons are very self-aware to the point of being painfully self-conscious. They date infrequently and generally show relatively poor heterosexual adjustment. Most often this code is associated with Scale 7, 3, 4, or 0 as the third highest scale for men.

Women rarely obtain this code. They present as depressed, inwardly focused, prone to guilt, and duty-oriented and at the same time have identified with traditional male values and interests. An example might be a woman who enjoys outdoor activities, perhaps living and working on a farm, or a woman who is a research scientist who enjoys the company of men, who is practical and down to earth, but who is somewhat depressed, introspective, and withdrawn.

Male adolescents with this code usually are referred because of poor relations with their siblings or friends, shyness, extreme negativism, or hypersensitivity. Interpersonally shy, passive, and unassertive, these adolescents often show overintellectualization combined with perfectionism and meticulous concerns. Anxiety, guilt, hypersensitivity, self-condemnation, depression, and social awkwardness are usually present. Others often see them as not particularly masculine, and they frequently are teased by their peers.

Treatment. Treatment will be similar to that described for the Spike 2 code, and customary treatments for depression generally would be effective for this code pattern, although it may be necessary to also explore any gender-identity confusions. For men, assertiveness training and coaching in how to relate to women in close, intimate relations could be helpful. For women, exploring conflicts around their feminine identity could also be useful. Assertiveness training would also be important. Look for childhood experiences of an opposite gender parent identification and deficits of age-appropriate childhood carefreeness.

26/62 Codes

This is primarily a depression profile with underlying paranoid features in which the person feels their current predicament is due to the unfair and insensitive treatment by others. The elevation on Scale 6 predicts a touchiness, quickness to take offense, and tendency to feel victimized and therefore angry with others. These individuals have difficulty expressing resentments directly because they tend to store hurts. This leads to a self-fulfilling prophecy whereby their resentments lead to others' resenting them, confirming their view that others treat them unfairly.

Typical complaints are sad moods, crying spells, and other depression-related symptoms, such as worrying, somatic preoccupations, feelings of inferiority, sadness, and tiredness. These individuals appear critical and bitter, feeling trapped in their current situation, mistreated and victimized. They have poor coping skills and interpersonal difficulties typified by misinterpreting others' motives and tend to store rationalized resentments. Their interpersonal relations may also be hampered by their tendency to be rigid and critical, perhaps as a defense against being criticized or judged. Often they jump to conclusions, read malevolent meaning into neutral situations, and adopt a defensive "chip on the shoulder" attitude in an attempt to reject others before they are rejected. Unless Scale 6 is significantly elevated ($T > 65$), rarely is this a psychotic profile, although these individuals show underlying paranoid defenses, such as projection and reaction formation. If Scales 4 and 8 also are elevated above $T = 65$, the probability of psychosis is increased, however.

Treatment. Look for childhood experiences of feeling unfairly treated and/or prolonged periods of emotional deprivation. These individuals have learned a role of withdrawing into quiet, bitter silences to deal with their anger, perhaps because as children they saw the mistreating caregiver as impossible with which to deal. Conceptually, think of an individual who feels wounded and withdraws into a bitter, angry silence, for fear of exposing vulnerability. Consequently, psychotherapy should help them learn to express the underlying hurts by first rehearsing how to express anger directly without blame or judgment. These individuals tend to verbally attack and blame the person who is frustrating them, leading that person to become defensive, thus confirming their view that conflicts cannot be resolved. Help them learn how to ask for what they want before they are resentful, so that they can give up their martyr role. Help them see that confrontations can be productive and do not always need to be will breaking. Assertiveness and anger training, cognitive restructuring, and relaxation training could help them learn to express anger and their wants directly without judgment and blame. These clients feel vulnerable to the therapist and usually are on guard for being labeled by the therapist as somehow "mentally ill." They tend to be highly rational individuals who have difficulty letting go of emotional control, reflecting their fears of being criticized or judged. Consequently, techniques may be useful to help them let go of emotional control. These individuals are able to verbalize how disappointed they feel. Inherent in this reaction is a judgmentality and subtle blame, but they are unable to directly verbalize their anger.

27/72 Codes (See Also 273/723, 247/274, and 275/725 [for Men]; 27/72, Low 5 [for Women]; and 278/728 Codes)

This profile is typified by an anxious depression. A common code pattern, it reflects a hyperresponsible, prone-to-worry, constantly on edge, and apprehensive individual whose typical symptoms and complaints involve tension, depression, nervousness, anxiety, guilt, self-devaluation, and excessive painful introspection. Nonproductive ruminations are characteristic and usually accompanied by feelings of inadequacy, lack of self-confidence, reduced work efficiency, and insomnia. These persons focus on their personal deficiencies, even though their lives often show evidence of numerous personal achievements. They anticipate problems before they occur but tend to overreact to minor stresses with anxious preoccupations and somatic concerns, even without elevations on Scale 1. They tend to panic easily, catastrophizing minor setbacks as potentially leading to disaster and during such times can become clingingly overdependent. Perhaps as a defense against unpredictable loss, they develop rigid attitudes with strong concerns over issues of right and wrong, which are heightened if the L scale is also elevated. Sexual conflict and dysfunction are common with this code pattern. Often such individuals are overcontrolled and have difficulty expressing their feelings openly. The most common three-point codes are 270/720, 278/728, 273/723, and 271/721.

Typically, work interference and achievement motivation problems are noted; if a good achievement pattern is evident, it is usually accomplished in a compulsive way with a strict sense of responsibility. In interpersonal relations, they often show a pattern of dependency and lack of assertiveness. These individuals have a difficult time saying "no" to more responsibilities, but as responsibilities accumulate they feel overwhelmed and then are prone to becoming depressed and anxious. In some cases, they exhibit phobic symptoms and preoccupations. These individuals may also exhibit compulsive, meticulous, and perfectionistic trends. They tend to be self-blaming and self-punishing when things go wrong. Interestingly, the scholastic history of these clients is average or above. A high percentage of 27/72 code persons have a college education, and almost none act out in aggressive ways.

Suicidal ideation is common, and attempts are a real possibility with 27/72 code patterns, particularly if Scales 8 and 9 are elevated and Scale 1 or the *K* scale is low. In such cases, an evaluation of suicide potential is indicated.

Treatment. Prognostically, this is one of the most favorable code patterns, as one would expect with a compulsive, perfectionistic, serious, and responsible depressive individual. Moderate elevations on Scales 2 and 7 indicate motivation to change as well as a tendency toward introspection. Very high elevations (e.g., $T >$ 75), however, often mean that persons are so agitated and worried that they cannot focus sufficiently to profit from verbal psychotherapy, and other forms of intervention, such as psychotropic medications, may be necessary. Generally, 27/72 individuals are constrained about showing anger and are quick to feel guilt should they do so.

A suicide evaluation is necessary prior to treatment as this is a suicide-prone code pattern. Also, some clients can self-medicate with alcohol or chemical agents, even if the *MAC–R* scale is not elevated.

Look for a family history with early expectations of a high level of responsibility with a lack of age-appropriate carefreeness. It is the overcommitment to responsibilities that often can be the precipitating event for a 27/72 depressive episode, as can be a loss of dependency support or a perceived failure.

These individuals profit from many different treatment modalities, such as relaxation training, implosive therapy around their fears of failure, techniques to help them verbalize anger, psychotropic medication, and cognitive restructuring to help them switch off negative thoughts about the future. Help them deal with anger and sadness over the loss of childhood carefreeness, help them develop a sense of empathy for themselves as prematurely overburdened children, and encourage them to see how they continue to burden themselves with fear and responsibilities.

273/723 Codes

The addition of Scale 3 to the profile adds dependency to the anxious depression evidenced in the 27/72 code pattern. These persons often accumulate significant stress, usually by setting high standards for themselves, by their apparent strivings, and because they are easily led and highly dependent. When their stress accumulates, they readily seek help from others, and in their depression and worry, they become markedly and clingingly dependent. Their apparent helplessness, docility, and self-deprecating attitudes prompt others to want to save or protect them, and even experienced health care professionals must be careful not to get caught up in nonfunctional rescue behaviors. Sexual inhibition and guilt are also common, and marital problems are therefore likely. These individuals are naïve and immature and have difficulty with adult heterosexual relations. If Scale 1 is also elevated, the person is likely not only to have numerous anxiety-related somatic complaints but also to have substantial self-pity, self-blame, and social withdrawal, despite their desire to have others take care of them.

Treatment. History reporting is difficult because both Scales 3 and 7 predict extensive repression, denial, and lack of insight. Beware of "flights into health" as these individuals run away from treatment, returning when the anxiety and depressive symptoms recur. Assertiveness training to help them learn to recognize anger and express it directly, rather than internalizing it, would be a necessary focus of therapy. Look for childhood conditioning experiences of unpredictable, explosive caregivers or some kind of unpredictable emotional abandonments that instilled in them a tendency to repress and deny their feelings and never learn a sense of personal efficacy. Supportive therapies that can help them learn to self-soothe when flooded with anxiety could be useful. Also useful are reparenting-type therapies that offer encouragement, combined with setting practical, concrete goals to help them take emotional and personal risks so that they can learn self-confidence and the management of their tendency to panic. Training them to manage their anxiety and switch off negative thoughts could be useful adjuncts to therapy.

274/724 Codes (See Also 247/427/472/742 Codes If Scales 4 and 7 Are Within 5 T-Score Points of Each Other)

Conceptually, this code pattern reflects impulsive (high Scale 4) and self-defeating tension reduction that is associated with elevations on Scales 2 and 7. Consequently, these individuals will act out when they are anxious, often in self-defeating or self-destructive ways, wanting to be rescued. Anxiety, worry, and irritable depression are characteristic and are typically combined with feelings of inadequacy and low self-confidence. These individuals are quick to feel anxious and worried at any sign of failure. They show an exaggerated self-criticism whenever things go wrong, which tends to elicit reassurance and caretaking behaviors from others. The 24 combination predicts self-defeating impulsive behavior, whereas the 27 interaction predicts hyperresponsible strivings, ambition, and feelings of inadequacy. Taken together, this profile portrays individuals who undermine others' criticism by their own exaggerated self-criticisms.

Often such persons feel caught in situations over which they feel they have little control. These individuals have a very low threshold for threat, so minor irritants can become major issues for them, and they overreact to small stresses as if they were emergencies. They ruminate nervously over their life situation and may express resentment toward others in passive–aggressive ways.

Men with this profile often show histories of being emotionally rescued by their mothers and look to replicate this pattern later in their lives. Despite seeking such dependent relations, they nonetheless harbor resentment over the control that usually accompanies such relations. Women with this profile often have been particular objects of attention and pride by their fathers. Usually, they are self-effacing and try to look weak and submissive (particularly if Scale 5 is low). Their relations with others may show recurring difficulties, and they may have affairs with married men, perhaps searching for a replication of their dependent relations with their father figures.

This profile is associated with dependent behaviors and with substance abuse, even if the *MAC–R* scale is not elevated. The substance abuse may be an attempt to self-medicate the anxiety and depression.

Treatment. Usually, the precipitating event is the loss of some kind of parental figure and associated dependency support. These individuals demand much reassurance but, as expected with Scale 4 elevations, tend not to trust it, therefore, it has little long-term effect. Therapy should focus on helping them identify when stress accumulates and on helping them prepare alternative tension-reducing behaviors rather than impulsive self-defeating ones. Through taking a history, help them see how their past involves panicked, self-defeating ways of reducing tension and help them learn alternative coping strategies. Assertiveness training, skill building, and relaxation training, as well as thought stopping and cognitive restructuring, all could be useful in helping them lower their anxiety and learn more efficient coping skills.

Look for childhood experiences of emotional abandonment and the enduring of periods of high anxiety, as well as narcissistic and overinvolved caregivers. Look for conditioning experiences in their childhood of being overwhelmed by events with no one to turn to. It is particularly important to help them learn to self-soothe in the face of high anxiety.

275/725 (for Men) and 27, Low 5 (for Women) Codes

The addition of an elevated Scale 5 for men, or a low Scale 5 for women, increases difficulties with assertiveness and exaggerates the submissiveness already evidenced by the 27/72 code pattern. In addition, these individuals exhibit worried depression and excessive rumination. They have a chronic sense of failure and an enduring ambivalence about their self-worth. They present themselves as inadequate, weak, inferior, guilty, and passive, almost as though inviting others to be patronizingly superior. When Scale 4 is also low, unassertiveness, low sex drive, and an even greater adherence to rules and regulations than already evidenced in the 27/72 code pattern is likely. It is as if these persons are continually atoning in their depression by seeking relations in which others belittle them and are accustomed to such relations. Heterosexual difficulties are often present, as one would expect with someone who is so passive and worried and who anticipates failure and the loss of their loved one's respect.

Treatment. See treatment section under the 27/72 codes. The addition of Scale 5 for men suggests an even greater need for assertiveness training and self-esteem building. Therapy could also focus on their tendency to overanalyze their interpersonal relations to the point where they are immobilized by their own negative insights. Sex therapy and education can also be useful to help them be more assertive and involved in their sexual lives, if this is a problem area.

278/728 Codes (Note: 287/827 Codes Have Different Interpretations)

The addition of Scale 8 to the 27/72 code pattern reflects a damaged self-esteem and ruminations that are morbid and odd and indicate a damaged identity. These individuals are tense, anxious, depressed, extremely ruminative, and filled with self-doubt. Many report suicidal thoughts and attempts and have a history of previous psychiatric hospitalizations. Insomnia, obsessive thinking, somatic preoccupation, fears, and phobias are common, along with a focus on their failures. These individuals are psychological "scab pickers"; that is, they constantly analyze their weaknesses and vulnerabilities, anticipating failure and abandonment, perhaps in an effort to protect against them. Some of these people can be meticulous and perfectionistic, setting unreasonably high standards for themselves and others, and can feel intensely guilty when they fail to meet these standards. Others, however, can be disorganized and immobilized by their "internal noise," so that they are unable to function efficiently. Their excessive introspection and self-pressure often lead to difficulties in concentrating and reduced performance, which then lead to an increase in their depression and anxiety.

Clients with this profile typically show long histories of personal isolation or unusual relations. Particular difficulty exists in making emotional commitments, such as in establishing love relations with the opposite gender. Often these persons will focus on the minute details of such relations, analyzing what's "wrong" with their mate and oscillating between profound fear of rejection and concern that they are trapped with somebody whom they see as defective. This tends to be a projection of their own low self-esteem. Issues revolving around control, criticism, acceptance, and the expression of anger are common.

Suicide potential should be carefully evaluated with this code pattern, particularly when the K scale and Scale 1 are below $T = 50$ and/or when Scale 4 is also elevated. An elevation on Scale 9 would suggest an agitated aspect to the depression. If Scale 0 is elevated, the person's depression is more likely to be chronic and accompanied by shyness, introversion, and feelings of physical inferiority. When Scale 4 is low, passivity and submissiveness are also prominent, often accompanied by reduced sexual interests and sexual inadequacy. These individuals are passively dependent and insecure, often eliciting support through subtle manipulativeness. Women with 278/728 codes with low *T* scores on Scale 5 are particularly likely to feel a need to atone for themselves and may even provoke others to anger in this fashion. These women tend to berate themselves almost masochistically and to show various physical complaints involving headaches, backaches, and sexual difficulties.

Treatment. This code pattern predicts a pervasive unhappiness and anhedonia in which the sadness may not be immediately apparent to the therapist because these patients tend to present as more flat and disconnected. They are very ambivalent, often immobilized by even the smallest decisions. They show a blunting of expressions of affect, and they have difficulty dealing with feelings and being emotionally spontaneous. They are extremely introspective and sometimes appear to be excellent therapy candidates because of their insights and their tendency to analyze their own and others' feelings and behaviors in minute detail. However, there is a tendency for the observing ego to be in control, so that they exhibit little emotional spontaneity. Consequently, role-play therapies can be particularly useful because the role-plays provide an opportunity for the client to ventilate feelings. Their tendency to observe themselves—watching themselves as if in a movie—reflects their fear that spontaneity, allowing themselves to be "in the moment," will reveal their defectiveness and lead to abandonment.

These individuals have a very fixed, negative self-image, which makes therapy difficult. Although they may gravitate toward analytical-type therapies because of their tendency for introspection, these therapies may be contraindicated because of their tendency to endlessly intellectualize. They need to learn how to express anger, which tends to be overintellectualized, perhaps out of fear that expressing anger will lead to abandonment. Look for childhood experiences of humiliating putdowns, sexual abuse, and emotional abandonment in their primary relationships. Many described their caregivers' attitude toward them as rejecting, and many were only children. Forty-five percent of the Marks et al. (1974) sample reported that there were deaths in the immediate family, and many reported a notable physical illness in their parental home; 15% of fathers and 20% of mothers were sick, and 25% were ill during childhood. It is not surprising, then, that they are extremely apprehensive and constantly on edge, as if waiting "for the other shoe to drop."

Interestingly, 50% of the Marks, Seeman, and Haller (1974) sample reported extramarital relations. These individuals tend to be as critical of their spouses as they are of themselves, reflecting their low self-esteem. Assertiveness training, self-esteem building, and warm, supportive, motherly type reparenting therapies can be useful therapeutic modalities. Many individuals with this code pattern are diagnosed as borderline, especially when Scale 4 is elevated. Many of them develop peculiar and esoteric personal philosophies, perhaps as a way of finding meaning in their lives.

28/82 Codes (See Also 281/821, 284/824, and 287/827 Codes)

This code is associated with depression, social withdrawal, agitation, difficulty concentrating, and fear of losing control over one's impulses. In some cases, this profile reflects a psychotic depression. A common complaint among persons with 28/82 codes is forgetfulness and difficulties with concentration, with many feeling that they are "losing their mind," perhaps a reflection of their difficulties with thinking and processing information. If Scales 2 and 8 are both highly elevated, the likelihood of serious psychological problems is high and hallucinations or delusions may be present.

Others see these persons as tense, jumpy, keeping people at a distance, inefficient in making and carrying out plans, and somewhat peculiar in their thoughts and ideas, all correlates one would expect with an elevation on Scale 8. Suicidal thoughts are likely and should be evaluated as these individuals can often lose the will to live, exercise poor impulse control, and have specific suicidal plans.

These individuals show a profound fear of emotional involvement with others and have conflicts about emotional dependency and sexuality. Their histories typically show repeated hurts in childhood with emotional abandonment and neglect. There is less evidence of aggressive hostility directed toward them and more a sense of hostile neglect. Their self-esteem is low, and their identity is unstable. Heterosexual relations are usually minimal or involve problems or behaviors that are unusual.

Treatment. Establishing therapeutic relationships with such persons is difficult, and psychotherapy prognosis is typically poor. In fact, this is one of the more difficult of the code patterns in terms of actual therapeutic progress. Chemotherapy tends to be helpful and is recommended. Because these individuals often feel hopelessly defective, supportive, nurturing, reparenting types of therapies are most useful. They often have a history of many emotional hurts, and their fear of being hurt again prompts them to keep others—including therapists—at a distance. Assertiveness training, cognitive restructuring, relaxation training, and the slow development of a therapeutic relationship can be helpful. Too much uncovering therapy is contraindicated because of these individuals' fragile self-esteem and their tendency to interpret insights negatively. These individuals have great fears of emotional closeness, perhaps because of their repeated hurts and letdowns in childhood. Interpreting their fears of emotional abandonment by the therapist sometimes can be useful, although psychotherapy should be highly structured to help the client maintain a sense of control. These individuals tend to withdraw and isolate themselves from interpersonal relations and activities, which tends to exacerbate their symptoms. Gentle encouragement to form relationships and to reach out to others can also be useful in treatment. Help them to build a sense of empathy for themselves as emotionally wounded or hurt children so that they can develop a better self-image, rather than internalizing a negative self-image as a result of repeated letdowns. Individuals with 82/28 code patterns are more likely to evidence psychotic and even schizophrenic features in addition to the other behaviors described. Appropriate medications should be considered when there is evidence of psychosis as well as depression.

281/821 Codes

In addition to the general characteristics associated with the 28/82 code, these persons show numerous somatic complaints along with their tension. Usually, these are vague or medically atypical, as one would expect with elevations on Scale 8, and may involve tremors, thinking and concentration difficulties, or even somatic delusions. Sometimes the somatic delusions are part of a psychotic episode; in other cases, the psychosis does not fully develop. This code pattern may reflect a focus on somatic symptoms as an attempt to defend against a psychosis.

If Scale 3 is also elevated, then hysterical defenses are evident with attempts to reach out and evoke rescuing behavior from others, including the therapist. However, if the therapist responds, then the individual pushes the therapist away. This reflects the operation of distancing defenses, as one would expect with a 28/82 code pattern, and reaching out and clinging defenses, as one would expect with Scale 3 elevated.

Treatment. See 21/12 and 28/82 treatment sections. Although the addition of Scale 1 decreases the probability of actual suicide, nevertheless the suicide items on the MMPI–2 should be checked and suicidal ideation evaluated. Because of their control issues, beware of complaints of side effects of medications; medications should be given in small doses until the client is comfortable. Use therapies to have the individuals' physical symptoms "do the talking" as one way of helping them ventilate some of the anger around past hurts and emotional abandonments.

284/824 Codes

In addition to the 28/82 characteristics already noted, the simultaneous elevation of Scale 4 with the 28/82 code adds feelings of alienation and disaffiliation, distrust, other-directed anger and rebellion, and self-defeating behavior, as well as increasing the likelihood of suicidal, self-destructive behavior and substance abuse potential. Fears around loss of impulse control are strong, particularly if Scale 4 is above $T = 75$, and these individuals tend to be quite impulsive. Acting out can be self-destructive or directed outwardly toward others. This pattern frequently is found in people with suicidal ideation and multiple suicide attempts.

The elevation on Scale 2 acts as a suppressor of antisocial acting out in many cases. However, when acting out occurs, it is often sexual and/or bizarre. Many individuals with this profile have severe conflicts about sexuality, and some confuse sexuality and aggression. Severe social and marital maladjustment is likely. In some adults, this code is associated with schizoid or schizophrenic conditions, and in these cases the *F* scale is usually elevated. (If Scale 4 is within 5 *T*-score points of Scale 2 or 8, see the interpretation of the 482/842 codes).

In adolescents, this code may not represent the enduring pathology indicated for adults. Instead, this code more likely reflects the sullen rebelliousness and alienation from social groups that is found in many adolescents. Poor impulse control is present, as are unusual behaviors and mental inefficiency, but the underlying pathology is likely to be less severe. This code pattern predicts chemical abuse and addition, even if the *MAC–R* scale is not elevated.

Treatment. Some 248/482 individuals are really persons with 48/84 personality patterns who have recently gotten into some kind of trouble or difficulty, with their upset over being caught raising the elevation on Scale 2. In other cases, they are stable 248/482 personality patterns with chronic interpersonal difficulties, self-defeating and self-destructive behavior, and profound alienation and distrust. A history of rebellious acting-out behavior would suggest a 48/84 profile with a recently elevated Scale 2. Determining which of the two types of individuals are represented in this code pattern is important in planning a treatment strategy.

In either case, trust is a central issue. These individuals have experienced multiple blows to their self-esteem, leading to an angry, alienated individual who lacks empathy for others and sees the world from an extremely cynical perspective. Although these individuals reject emotional ties, at the same time they have an exaggerated need for affection. Some of these individuals tend to be diagnosed as psychotic with paranoid features, yet many do not evidence a gross or florid thought disorder. Rather, they experience a sense of paranoia that probably stems from their profound distrust.

Look for early childhood histories of caregiver rejection or domination. In the Marks et al. (1974) sample, none reported that their parents were affectionate. A larger proportion than average for other code patterns were illegitimate, and many were labeled behavior problems throughout their school career.

Conceptually, think of this code pattern as reflecting the "unwanted child," with resulting alienation and anger yet cravings for affection that cannot be trusted when received. Reparenting-type therapies that are long and require patience are probably the treatment of choice. Working on the transference would be an important component as these individuals feel that others "wear masks" and are untrustworthy, perhaps a projection of their own manipulativeness and role-playing. Help them see how they are impulsively self-defeating and self-destructive as a defense against emotional abandonment, and help them find more adaptive ways to cope with their sense of inner emptiness, rather than turning to chemical agents, sexually acting out, or other immediate tension reducers. These individuals tend to put the therapist through a number of trust tests, and if these tests are passed, then some progress can be made.

287/827 Codes

The interpretation is similar to the 278/728 code pattern, although there are some differences. The coding of Scale 8 first or second, rather than third, predicts more identity damage, alienation, and confusion and increases the likelihood of a psychotic or borderline diagnosis. Persons with this code show depression and anxiety and tangential thought processes, feel alienated from people, are unduly sensitive to criticism, and are distrustful of people in general. They almost always show significant mental difficulties, such as being unable to concentrate, episodes of dizziness, mental confusion, insomnia, and reduced ability to carry out duties and responsibilities. They may also show labile or inappropriate emotions, or even hallucinations or frank thought disorders. Characteristically, these individuals avoid close interpersonal relationships and are afraid of emotional involvement, generally because of fears of becoming dependent and then being abandoned. Conflicts over sexuality and self-assertion are often present.

Suicidal thoughts, preoccupations, and threats are likely and should be evaluated carefully, particularly if the *K* scale is below $T = 50$ and if Scales 9 and 4 are above $T = 65$. The likelihood of impulsiveness increases with these latter elevations. When suicides occur, they are often carried out in unusual or even bizarre ways.

Treatment. See treatment section under the 278/728 codes. Therapeutic modalities will be similar to the 278/728 code pattern. Because of their history of identity-damaging experiences and low self-esteem, therapy will be more difficult because of difficulties with trust and emotional closeness and a tendency to keep the therapist at a distance with odd, and even subtly hostile distancing, maneuvers. Look for childhood histories similar to the 278/728 individual with emotional withdrawal, humiliation, rejection, teasing, and putdowns. Some of these individuals have peculiarities or eccentricities, and some were slow to mature, resulting in vulnerability to being humiliated and put down by others. Many have internalized this negative self-image and continue to anticipate rejection and humiliation.

Chemotherapy is an important adjunct, medicating both their depression and any symptoms of a thought disorder. Although many of these individuals are not openly psychotic, they do evidence disruptive and tangential thought processes, inappropriate affect, and disorientation. Supportive psychotherapies are suggested, and once the patient has stabilized with the aid of chemotherapy, thought stopping, cognitive restructuring, assertiveness training, and relaxation training, as well as self-esteem building, can be effective.

29/92 Codes

These people can initially appear anxious or nervous and, without an MMPI–2, can be misdiagnosed as suffering from an anxiety disorder. Scale 2 cancels out the euphoria of Scale 9, and Scale 9 overrides the depression and sadness of Scale 2.

The result is an individual who is tense, moody, irritable, and ruminates excessively about their self-worth. During periods where Scale 9 appears to be dominating, they are excitable, positive, and even euphoric but can quickly become angry, upset, and despondent, triggered by small changes in their environment. One moment they can be joking and positive, although somewhat high-strung; then a small setback occurs, and they quickly get angry and catastrophize. Consequently, they show a constant moodiness and irritability that appears unstable and is frustrating for others around them with which to deal. Often these individuals evidence temper outbursts, and people often are surprised at the quickness with which they go from positive to negative. They can also present as inconsistent, "selling" an idea one minute and then denigrating it the next. It is almost as if one can track the operation of the manic and depressive defenses within the course of a few minutes. Most show histories of periods of serious depression.

Most often Scale 4 or 3 is the third highest elevation scale. Persons with 29/92 profile codes have a high energy level, but it is associated with depression or anxiety. Three types of persons generally obtain this code:

1. Persons with an agitated depression marked by overly expressive behaviors, such as weeping and wailing, depressive rumination, and a self-absorption that borders on pathological narcissism. As children, these persons may have had to be very emotional in order to get attention.
2. Persons who are trying to cope with underlying depression through using manic defenses. In some persons the grandiose thinking and denial may be sufficient to mask the depression. More commonly, however, these defenses are no longer effective. Often such persons turn to heavy drinking.
3. Persons with organic brain dysfunction who are somewhat aware of their reduced functioning and abilities and who are attempting to deny this to themselves and to hide this from others. Often these persons will show perplexity and agitation at their lack of abilities that previously were accomplished easily. They may attempt to regain control over their life environment through an excessive need for structure, perhaps even to the point of appearing ritualistic.

Treatment. Treatment initially should focus on stabilizing the individual through a mood-altering medication. If Scale 4 is elevated, this increases the likelihood of impulsiveness and self-defeating behavior, so that when the client is in a "down" mood, they can be quite self-defeating, "giving up" even if things are going well for them. When things start to go better, they can be foolhardy in an optimistic and positive way. If Scale 7 is elevated and coded third, then there is a great deal of fear of failure, and with it a resulting tendency to develop compulsive, repetitive types of behaviors. If Scale 8 is coded third, then there is more of an identity panic and fears of being disliked and found unworthy that can color the moodiness.

This generally is an addictive profile, particularly if the *MAC–R* scale is elevated. These individuals can experience blackouts and mood swings while under the influence of alcohol. The likelihood of aggressive behavior while drinking is high. Look for childhood experiences of being pressured constantly to achieve and succeed, with caregiver approval being dependent on high levels of success. Conceptually, think of the profile as representing an approach–avoidance conflict to caregiver success expectations. In some cases, there is a history of hyperactivity and aggression in childhood. Help the client deal with their fears of failure, set realistic goals, and learn through cognitive restructuring to not catastrophize over minor setbacks.

20/02 Codes

This code suggests a socially withdrawn and introverted person with a mild, but chronic and characterological depression. This depression is often related to poor interpersonal and social skills, combined with feelings of inferiority and shyness. Insomnia, guilt feelings, and worry are also often present. Both adults and adolescents with this profile type feel nervous and inhibited, particularly in social gatherings, and have few friends. Many also feel physically unattractive. Others likely see them as somewhat colorless and lacking in assertiveness, with a tendency to blend in with others and not draw attention to themselves. Passive and conventional, they are highly unlikely to be highly aggressive or delinquent. Conceptually, this profile can be characterized as the result of being parented by emotionally unresponsive parents. In other words, look for childhood histories in which primary caretakers were present but ignored the child unless there were direct requests for caretaking.

If Scales 4 and 8 are below $T = 65$, then the profile suggests a history of caregivers who provided adequate basic necessities but who were not solicitous and affectionate and touching in their caretaking behaviors. Consequently, these individuals may have learned to expect little or no emotional or physical contact from others and many have become used to their condition. In turn, they as caregivers will have difficulty providing tactile stimulation to their offspring.

With this code pattern, most often Scale 7 or 4 is the third highest scale. Common among mothers of children receiving psychological help, this code is often associated with only moderate improvement in treatment. Therapists see these mothers as in conflict about giving and are often fearful of emotional involvement with others. They tend to keep others at a distance, keeping a rigid check on their own emotions to avoid having demands placed on them or losing control of the situation (particularly if *K* is also elevated).

Treatment. The depression is clinically ingrained, and so these individuals have little motivation to change. They have adjusted to their depressive state, and engaging them in psychotherapy is difficult. Assertiveness training, role-playing, and social skill building could be beneficial in helping them with their social difficulties. If more long-term therapy is available, insight therapy can help them understand how growing up in an environment in which caregivers are caring but not emotionally expressive could have extinguished their desire for tactile contact.

Educating them on the need for physical stimulation toward their own offspring is often important. In some cases, it is possible to help them engage memories of feeling emotionally alone and help them mourn that they did not receive more active physical contact. If these individuals are willing to take antidepressant medications, they should be administered in small doses as these individuals have become used to their state and are disturbed by any changes in their equilibrium. Cognitive restructuring can also be helpful, so that they can learn to be more demanding and less withdrawing from conflict.

Scale 3 (*Hy*)

One way of defending against intolerably painful conditions is to deny that they exist. An even more effective way would be to switch the focus of attention away from pain onto something positive, even in the face of overwhelming pain. Scale 3 primarily measures the amount, type, and pervasiveness of such denial and/or positivization. For some individuals, this characteristic is a way of life and becomes part of their personality. In others, elevations reflect the individual's predominant way of coping with stress. Scale 3 primarily represents a neurotic or character style, and Scale 3 elevations generally predict against psychoticism, particularly when Scale 3 is one of the two most elevated scales in the profile.

High scores ($T \geq 65$) are obtained by persons who (a) are using repression and denial in many areas of their lives; (b) are quite conforming, naïve, and immaturely self-centered; and (c) have anxiety-related somatic concerns. Elevations on Scale 3 can reflect one or all of these characteristics. These individuals may be quite demanding of affection, approval, and support and have quite active social lives, although real intimacy is frightening to them. They tend not to be insightful into their own behaviors, as one would expect when denial, repression, and somatization are primary defense mechanisms.

Some of these persons may be exhibitionistic, reflecting their willingness to perform if it brings approval. Others may act out sexually and, depending on which other scales are elevated, even aggressively, as repressed sexual and aggressive feelings erupt in unpredictable ways. Aggressive acting out, however, is not likely if Scale 3 is the only scale elevated above $T = 65$.

Because of their strong need to be liked, high scorers on Scale 3 initially will respond quite enthusiastically to situations requiring commitment. Sooner or later, however, their difficulties dealing with conflict, in recognizing their own frustration, and in expressing it appropriately lead them to resent the demands placed on them. When angry, they tend to become passively resistant, even whining and complaining, and develop somatic problems that allow them to remove themselves from the situation or "have their symptoms do the ventilating."

Moderately high scores (T = 55–65) on Scale 3 are obtained by people who generally are optimistic and positive in their outlook on life. Often they are achievement oriented, socially involved, and outgoing. They tend to deny conflict, try hard to please others, and consequently are vulnerable to developing physical symptoms as accumulated stresses and resentments build. They can have areas in their lives where they deny or repress negative emotions, but others tend to see them positively because of their apparent "niceness" and agreeableness. Often they will develop transitory physical symptoms in response to stress.

Moderately low to very low scores ($T \leq 45$) generally reflect an individual who sees life "realistically" and may come across as somewhat caustic and blunt. Repression and denial are greatly reduced, perhaps used, and their interests tend to be overly narrowed. Some of these people are cynical and even misanthropic, seeing life as full of hardships. In a flat profile having an absence of any scale elevations above $T = 65$, low Scale 3 scores reflect individuals who see themselves as realistic and able to "call a spade a spade." They are not necessarily hostile, just blunt and lacking in typical courtesies or tact. They will not commit to something they do not want to do and will not give compliments unless they genuinely mean them, and even then they are expressed without embellishment or color. When other scales in the profile are significantly elevated, persons with low Scale 3 scores typically are painfully aware of their personal distress and have trouble excluding disturbing thoughts and impulses from their consciousness.

Spike 3

Spike 3 (i.e., no other clinical scale above $T = 65$) predicts overconventional individuals who have strong needs to be accepted and liked. They worry whether they will be unaccepted by their social group and become uncomfortable in confrontive situations that involve anger or self-assertiveness or when dealing with authority figures or situations (such as academic settings) in which they might be evaluated closely. In conversations, these people emphasize their optimism and good relations with others and gloss over or minimize any unusual or deviant behaviors in themselves. When anger is expressed, it may be expressed in inappropriate or impulsive ways because it is poorly integrated.

Their backgrounds often show an unhappy home and/or marital life, primarily with a father whom they saw as overly evaluative and rejecting. Women with Spike 3, particularly if Scale 5 is below $T = 40$, are particularly likely to be socialized into a traditional feminine role that is somewhat passive and which emphasizes socially acceptable facades. Often they are manipulative of men, perhaps being seductive without being conscious of it as a way of gaining approval and minimizing hostility. Because of their difficulties with intimacy, sexual problems are common, as is a lack of assertiveness accompanied by dependency and an inability to express anger openly. When Scale 0 is below $T = 45$, high Scale 3 individuals are even more extraverted and tend to be traditional—even superficial—in their orientations with many social skills.

Relations With Other Scales

Spike 3, High K Code

The addition of the *K* scale adds more overcontrol and a greater need to be emotionally controlled and to be seen as socially conforming. The need to be liked, accepted, and seen as conventional and the need to present oneself as having control of one's life are exaggerated substantially. Characteristically, these individuals show an almost rigid optimism, reflecting the need for emotional control, and resolutely maintain that things are fine even when surrounded by events that clearly are difficult. These people emphasize good relations and harmony with others and avoid (or become uncomfortable in) situations in which anger, disruptions, or hurt feelings are involved or in which they must exercise independent decision or power.

Treatment. The profile reflects a very well-defended individual. The stance in the world is one of denial and maintaining an even keel in the face of any emotional strife. Look for childhood conditioning experiences where they were scared by the intensity of their emotional response to some situation. Questions such as "Was there a time in your life when you felt surprised by the intensity of your emotional response to something?" may help explore previous frights by some event or series of events that led them to develop a determination not to allow emotions to knock them off balance. Many will show childhood histories of chaos and catastrophe within the family home, where the intense emotionality was frightening to them. Occasionally, however, an opposite history is seen where individuals grew up in homes where the expression of strong emotions was discouraged. In psychotherapy, use techniques to help them learn to become more comfortable with negative emotions, rehearsing situations in which they are able to express reasonable anger and frustration toward others. Help them deal with their fears of rejection and explore whether they experienced early rejections in their childhood that have conditioned them to go through life constantly wanting to please, avoid conflict, and minimize any intense negative emotionality.

31 Codes (See Also 13/31 Codes)

In contrast to the 13 code, people with a 31 pattern usually have symptoms that are relatively specific and even episodic in nature. Although they evidence insecurity and immaturity and develop physical symptoms as stress increases, they tend to use more denial than the 13 individual. The pessimistic, negative qualities evidenced in the 13 profile are reduced by the higher elevations on Scale 3, and these individuals even can be quite charming, manipulating people into taking care of them rather than coercing people like the 13 individuals tend to do.

Treatment. See treatment section under the 31/13 codes.

32 Codes (See Also 23 Codes If Scale 2 is Within 5 T-Score Points of Scale 3)

In contrast to 23 code patterns, these persons show less overt depression and more concern for their health, along with more repression, inhibition, and need for social approval. Fatigue, gastric complaints, headaches, and dizziness are common, although various other physical complaints may also be present. These symptoms are usually related to anxiety, depression, and attempts to overcontrol emotions. In some cases, the constant stress and tension on these individuals' physical systems leads to actual physical breakdowns.

Men with this profile pattern are usually in a clear state of anxiety (often mixed with depression) and may show an inability to concentrate in addition to physical symptoms. Typically, they are ambitious, conscientious, and serious about their responsibilities, and their concerns often center on business problems. They are concerned about appearing to be part of the mainstream and deny unacceptable impulses or interpersonal difficulties. They resist psychological interpretations of their physical problems and lack insight. Although reassurance about their physical condition can be helpful, it is difficult to engage these individuals in any kind of personality-changing psychotherapy. For men, Scale 1, 8, or 9 is most often the third highest scale.

Women with 32 codes most often have a history of marital difficulties (although divorces are rare), frequently lack desire for sexual relations with their husbands, and report lack of sexual enjoyment. Typically, they are depressed and complain about the infidelity or drinking of their husbands. Extremely sensitive to criticism or rebuff, many of these women will tolerate chronic unhappiness. Commonly, they feel inadequate and have significant self-doubt. Even so, they keep their feelings bottled up and under tight control. They may complain of fatigue and exhaustion (particularly if Scale 5 is also low) yet tend to be quite conscientious in their work. Physical symptoms of palpitation, sweating, insomnia, and vague complaints of pain are often reported. Sometimes this profile is associated with menopausal difficulties. For women, Scale 1, 4, or 8 is most likely to be the third highest scale.

Treatment. As caregivers, these individuals can be difficult because of their tendency to induce guilt and to demand caretaking behavior from their children. Consequently, their children can be angry and resentful, especially in adolescence. Assertiveness training, antidepressant medication, and relaxation training are useful, although antianxiety medications may be contraindicated as these individuals have a vulnerability to become dependency prone. If the *L* scale is elevated, then there is extreme denial, moral rigidity, and especially fear about being seen as psychologically "ill." Be aware of the client's difficulties in dealing with any negative transference; thus, subtle criticisms of other doctors could alert the therapist to some frustration with the client's current therapist. These individuals tend to focus on their physical complaints and resist psychological intervention. Treatments that focus on the individuals' symptoms, so that the symptoms can "do the ventilation," could help them learn to release emotionally. Look for childhood experiences of an early death of a caregiver and a resultant blocked mourning process. Have the client deal with the blocked anger and sadness around the loss. Walk through the client's fears that assertion or anger toward others will lead to their emotional abandonment. Help them develop a sense of empathy for themselves as children dealing with a painful loss by trying to be "brave" and positive in the face of great pain.

321 Codes

The addition of Scale 1 increases the hypochondriacal complaints and physical symptoms in response to stress. In addition to the characteristics of persons with 32 codes, these people show numerous hypochondriacal complaints, such as constipation, diarrhea, anorexia, insomnia, muscle tension, genital pain, palpitations, and exhaustion. Depression and worry are related to feelings of inferiority or even hopelessness. Disturbances in sleep and major changes in weight are quite common. These individuals deny socially unacceptable impulses, particularly of aggressiveness and the rejecting of others.

These people lack insight into themselves or others, and as a result they often find themselves in uncomfortable interpersonal situations. They tend to react to such frustrating situations by becoming intropunitively depressed, often in ways that hurt themselves further. For example, when stressed, they easily become depressed and hypochondriacal and take on the role of an invalid. This has the effect of making others around them feel guilty and therefore angry with them, aggravating their stress level. If Scale 8 is also elevated, there is greater difficulty with thinking, memory and concentrating, as well as difficulties with history reporting. If Scale 9 is low, clients will complain of loss of drive and energy.

The majority of clients who fit this profile tend to be female, and they frequently have recurring gynecological complaints and/or have had hysterectomies. It is interesting that one of the most frequent areas of manifestation of the disorder is sexual, with sexual difficulties reported as well as sexual acting out. In the original Marks and Seeman (1963) sample, 20% of the 321 women had abortions.

Men more often show gastric distress or ulcers. For both men and women, marital problems are likely, as are emotional conflicts about sex and sexual intimacy, with generally low sexual contact.

Treatment. These clients tend to come from families where the father was dominating and strict and where the mother, although affectionate, was also said to be strict. Interestingly, many of these clients have a history of taking care of an invalid caregiver, some who were physically ill and some who were mentally ill; consequently, some of these clients never marry as a result. Most often these patients were middle children, and school achievement generally was above average. They have internalized strict parental rules and inhibitions as well as their caregivers' moral rigidity. Close personal relations appear to present the biggest problem for these clients, who tend to keep others at an emotional distance. Treatment could help them deal with their approach–avoidance conflicts in relationships, perhaps dealing with their anger and sadness about early perceived rejection from overly punitive parental figures. In women, if Scale 5 is low, there is even greater passivity and fears of men's aggressive sexual impulses. If Scale 0 is elevated, there is an even greater tendency for the individual to want to "hide at home." Men are usually seen as extremely conscientious and tend to do well unless difficulties around assertiveness interfere with their career history.

34/43 Codes

Even though persons obtaining 34 codes often show clear differences from those obtaining 43 codes, the similarities warrant combined discussion. Both code patterns represent emotional instability in that the chronic, intense anger suggested by the elevation on Scale 4 is controlled, inhibited, and masked by needs for approval, closeness, and validation, prompting them to control and/or deny their angry impulses. The relative elevation of each scale will predict which defense is prominent; that is, whether the individual is more overcontrolled or whether the individual has a propensity toward impulsive acting-out behavior. The major characteristic of both code patterns is anger, with the 34 code persons showing sudden breakthroughs of strong feelings and persons with 43 codes tending to act out on a more continuous basis. The relative elevations of Scales 3 and 4 reflect the extent to which such persons will control and inhibit their anger and other impulses. If Scale 3 is higher, there is more inhibition; if Scale 4 is higher, there is more impulsive behavior.

Often these persons wish to be taken care of but also demand to be independent. That is, although they want to be dependent, they also find the expectancies and demands that accompany such a relationship to be irritating. Women with this code often place great emphasis on superficial aspects of their life and are impatient and demanding. They also often have mild episodic psychosomatic complaints, which are not incapacitating but rather a focus of discussion and complaint.

In 43 codes in which Scale 4 is distinctly higher than Scale 3, the anger is dominant, although typically bottled up for long periods and then expressed in rageful outbursts, particularly if alcohol is involved, sometimes even culminating in serious assault or murder, usually of family members. Many such persons appear to be quiet or even withdrawn for extended periods, and their impulsive, violent outbursts are a great surprise because the actual precipitating stress often is quite small. Their outbursts are typically not illogical or irrational (unless Scale 6 or 8 is also significantly elevated); rather, the anger has built internal pressure gradually over a long period of time. In some such persons, the violent outbursts occur in a cyclic pattern that alternates with long periods of socially appropriate behavior and is a pattern that is difficult to change.

Both code patterns suggest egocentricity and immaturity as well as anger. Both code patterns evidence marital disharmony and, in some cases, sexual acting-out behavior, as well as divorce, chemical addiction, and unstable relations with others. The central difficulties for both code patterns are in recognizing anger as it is developing and dealing with it in a modulated and timely fashion.

People with both profiles are role-players who want to fit in and be approved of and subtly manipulate others into getting that approval. Although conforming on the outside, they can show subtle impatience and criticalness of others, which is masked with a "nice" veneer. This can annoy and frustrate others, although the individual has little awareness of doing so.

Individuals with the 34/43 code pattern are sensitive to rejection and can respond angrily and impulsively when they feel rejected. Both code patterns project their own sensitivity to rejection onto others, so they have difficulty with the direct rejecting of others. Both code patterns tend to express anger and hostility in roundabout ways, such as talking behind people's backs, expressing anger in a sarcastic or joking way, or perhaps expressing anger in passive–aggressive ways. If Scale 3 is higher than Scale 4, there is more passive–aggressiveness, the subtle expression of anger through sarcasm and "joking humor," and with it, the denial of anger.

Persons with 34/43 codes tend to be very rule conscious and very sensitive to any kind of social disapproval. At the same time, Scale 4 attributes are manifested by the annoyance at being controlled or challenged in any way. Conceptually, think of an individual who follows the rules, is very sensitive to disapproval, wants to be seen as an upstanding, moral citizen, but then the Scale 4 impulses are acted out in roundabout, devious ways. If Scale 3 is higher than Scale 4, then the individual can actually dissociate from his or her acting-out behavior. If Scale 4 is greater than Scale 3, then there is more impulsive acting out with more conscious manipulativeness, which is then rationalized. If Scale 1 is also elevated, then the individual shows somatic symptoms, with a tendency to manipulate these symptoms for secondary gain. If Scale 2 is elevated, individuals may report depression, although they are more likely to evidence a sense of being trapped, bitter, and resentful. If Scale 9 is elevated, there are energized, approval-seeking behaviors, as well as the likelihood of more explosive behaviors and pressured activity with a tendency to overcommit.

Marital adjustment for 34/43 persons tends to be poor because of these individuals' tremendous sensitivity to rejection and their tendency to lack insight and to selectively report. Intimacy tends to be frightening for them, yet they need sexual approval, so sexual infidelity problems are common. The 34/43 codes are quite common among mothers and fathers of youngsters with behavior problems. Frequently, these caregivers subtly reinforce the acting-out behavior of their children as an indirect way of expressing anger at their spouse. For men, Scale 2, 5, or 6 is most often the third highest scale. For women, the third highest scale is most often Scale 2, 6, or 8.

Adolescents with 34/43 codes most often are seen professionally because of conflicts with caregivers and school authorities. Theft, drug use, school truancy, and running away from home are common, as are suicidal thoughts and sleep difficulties.

In 34 codes in which Scale 3 is distinctly higher, the person is likely to express angry feelings indirectly, or to vicariously express anger and rebellion through becoming involved with acting-out individuals. Generally, 34 individuals are more likely to be seen as conforming and socially poised. Women with this code often place great emphasis on superficial aspects of their life and are impatient and demanding. They are unlikely to seek treatment unless experiencing a recent rejection or some intense frustration, but they tend not to be self-referred for insight therapy. Because of their repression, denial, and overcontrol of anger, when outbursts occur, they are typically overaggressive but subsequently well rationalized.

Persons with 34 or 43 codes may have chronic problems with alcohol or substance abuse, even if the *MAC–R* scale is not elevated. Likewise, both 34 and 43 coded persons can evidence transitory paranoid episodes. This is not the fixed rational paranoia or the sense of emotional disintegration seen in individuals in which Scales 6 and 8 are elevated. Rather, it is a profound distrust that others are "telling them the truth." In many ways, this is a projection of their own tendency to role-play, to fit into others' expectations of them, and to selectively report.

Treatment. Look for childhood histories where they experienced rejection or were discounted by controlling and arbitrary caregivers. From an early age, these individuals learned to be survivors—that is, subtly manipulating others and telling white lies to get their needs met. In some cases, caregivers subtly encouraged their children to act out. In other cases, the profile reflects a shutting down of emotional spontaneity to fit in and avoid rejection from an explosive and arbitrary caregiver. Because these individuals are good role-players, often rehearsing their own role in new social situations, they tend to make good salespeople, particularly if they are from upper socioeconomic situations.

In treatment, these persons are very sensitive to disapproval or suggestions that they have a "mental disorder." If Scale 6 is also elevated, there is more tendency to deny anger and store resentments. Watch what the client denies, as it is often the source of his or her conflict. The 346/436 code pattern has been associated with individuals who become involved in long and angry divorce situations. Clients with this profile tend to be selective in reporting what is going on in their life, partly out of fear of disapproval from the therapist and partly because of their use of hysterical denial. These individuals are very sensitive to social disapproval; and although they may act out, they nevertheless want social approval. Help clients understand how painful it was to be discounted or rejected by their caregivers and help them ventilate rage toward the rejecting caregiver. Help them see how they protect others from the truth by selectively reporting and telling white lies and in the process seek to avoid rejection, which leads to more interpersonal difficulties. Help clients learn to express anger directly in a modulated fashion rather than passive–aggressively or explosively. Beware of their sensitivity to the therapist rejecting them.

345/435/534 Codes (See Also 34/43 Codes)

This is virtually always a male profile. The addition of Scale 5 predicts passivity and an increase in the sexual difficulties that persons with 34/43 codes already exhibit, as well as the other 34/43 characteristics. Men with this profile are immature in their relations with others and generally have fears around sexual intimacy. Often they feel a need for different kinds of sexual experiences and/or for more than usual sexual stimulation. Some have engaged in exhibitionism, voyeurism, or other kinds of sexual acting-out behavior. Others have homosexual fantasies (354 pattern), whereas others may act out homosexually (453 pattern). Some may express fears of being homosexual. When Scale 3 is higher than Scale 4, there is less likelihood that the feelings and desires have been acted on, particularly if the K scale is greater than $T = 50$. In these cases, there is more homosexual ideation rather than acting out.

Treatment. The essential difficulty for persons with 34/43 codes is the fear of emotional closeness because of fear of rejection. The addition of Scale 5 for men suggests even greater fears around sexual rejection from women. Treatment, therefore, should concentrate on helping these individuals deal with early caregiver rejection and/or discounting and their own fears of rejection. Because of the operation of hysterical defenses, these individuals may deny remembering painful rejections in their childhood and may also deny that they have any difficulty in asserting themselves. Assertiveness training and the building of self-esteem, as well as exploring their fears of intimacy in case they are rejected, would be appropriate foci of therapy. See also treatment section under the 34/43 codes.

346/436 Codes (See Also 36/63 Codes If Scale 6 is Within 5 T-Score Points of Scale 3 and 34/43 Codes)

The addition of Scale 6 to this code pattern increases the probability of clients building up rationalized resentments, denying anger, and externalizing their blame and anger. These individuals are extremely sensitive to rejection and to any loss of social approval. Outwardly, these individuals often are conforming, although some have histories of episodic extreme acting out followed by periods of overcontrolled behavior. Typically, such persons are hypersensitive to criticism and are tense and anxious as a result of their bottled up angry feelings, which are not well integrated. Usually, their anger is primarily at family members but is highly rationalized and justified in their own minds (e.g., self-righteous temper outbursts). Often they rigidly feel that they are "in the right" in any conflict and have little inclination to be forgiving (this is usually also reflected in *Pa3* being elevated).

These individuals show a rigid adherence to rules and "doing things the right way," with a tendency to be punitive if they feel that they have been wronged. At the same time, when their anger builds, they act it out through an explosive, highly rationalized outburst followed by overcontrol and denial. They tend to be very conscious of their appropriate social role and are often seen as sexually attractive by the opposite gender. They are also inhibited and lack psychological mindedness. In relationships, they tend to have difficulty articulating their wants and desires directly and tend to express their desires and resentments in a blaming and demanding way. Many establish long-standing, but often turbulent, relationships with acting-out individuals, thereby vicariously gratifying their own angry and rebellious impulses. Blame is a key part of their thinking style, perhaps reflecting their own fears of being blamed or judged. The 346/436 code pattern has been associated with unresolved divorce custody cases (see Caldwell, 1997).

Treatment. Look for childhood conditioning experiences, not only of rejection and being discounted by authoritarian caregivers but also of being judged, criticized, and in some cases, severely punished. Help them explore childhood memories of having been discounted or rejected and help them reengage the feelings of rejection and the accompanying blocked retaliatory rage.

Help them understand how they tend to repress and deny anger out of fear of rejecting others and, in turn, being rejected. Help them learn to ask for what they want before they are resentful, and help them see how they tend to use moral judgment as a way of manipulating others into giving them what they want. They tend to give others the subtle message of "You ought to do this; this is the morally right thing for you to do" and deny that they are making a request. By not making requests directly, they protect themselves from feeling controlled by any sense of obligation. This has the effect of angering others, which ends up being a self-fulfilling prophecy for 346/436 individuals. As they feel criticized or judged, they feel justified in protecting themselves by being hypervigilant.

35/53 Codes

This is generally a male profile about which there is limited empirical information. This pattern is obtained by educated histrionic men who are somewhat passive, fussy, and culturally, verbally, and aesthetically oriented. They tend to see themselves as well-adjusted, happy, calm, and self-confident, although others would see them as more clinging and demanding than they see themselves. They tend to develop physical problems in response to stress and are unlikely to act out in any aggressive way. Intellectually and artistically oriented, they present as somewhat inhibited and insecure with strong needs for attention and affection. Most show distinct moral and/or educational aspirations. If Scale 0 is also elevated, then they are likely to be shy, anxious, and socially uncomfortable. If the profile is within normal limits or just above the normal range, these men are likely to be seen as peaceable, nurturing, and gentle, although with a tendency toward self-absorption.

The 35/53 code is frequently seen in fathers of child psychiatry clients and is associated with the use of denial, repression, and passivity as a defense. Although appearing concerned with the family situation, these fathers tend to let the family concerns take second place to their own self-concerns and needs. In women, this two-point code is rare.

Scale 4 or 6 is usually the third highest scale. Interpretation is best accomplished by initially ignoring the elevated Scale 5, so as to treat the three-point code (e.g., 354 code) as though it were a two-point code (e.g., 34 code). Subsequently, the interpretations of the elevated Scale 5 can be added. If the third highest scale is highly elevated, it should be given particular consideration in interpreting the 35/53 profile.

Treatment. In men, look for a strong early son–mother identification and for childhood conditioning experiences of being subjected to periods of emotional pain, which were dealt with through the use of denial, repression, and positivization. These individuals often must learn to be more assertive and to recognize when anger is building, perhaps by paying attention to any increase in physical symptoms of stress. Recognizing and expressing anger appropriately tend to be major problems with this code pattern. These individuals are also unduly sensitive to criticism or rejection in their close relations and are somewhat self-absorbed about their needs for emotional gratification and approval. A common issue in therapy is learning to deal with the fears of rejection and disapproval.

36/63 Codes

Persons with 36/63 codes are extremely sensitive to anything that can be construed as a criticism and are extremely self-conscious about their social role. They want approval, and usually their polished and controlled demeanor and presentation reflects it. Underneath their veneer of almost exquisite correctness is an individual who is distrustful, tense, and even suspicious. Their feelings, however, tend to be ego-syntonic and denied. Underneath a surface of cooperation and conformity, these individuals harbor many long-standing feelings of anger and resentment toward their immediate family. Their anger tends to be rationalized and justified and is seen as self-protective.

In some cases, this profile is associated with brief psychotic episodes with paranoid jealousies, projections onto others, and self-righteous temper outbursts. Most of the time, however, this code is not associated with psychosis but rather a hysterical personality organization. The Scale 6 attributes manifest as an extreme sensitivity to criticism, an adherence to rigid values, and the tendency to use projection as a primary defense mechanism.

Frequently, these individuals also develop headaches or gastrointestinal complaints that reflect their overcontrol and tension. If the *L* or *K* scale is elevated, there is even more self-control, denial, rigidity, and inhibition. There is a tendency for any anxiety to be brief and situational and for the client then to project and blame others for his or her emotional upsets.

These individuals have very high expectations of themselves and for others around them. Some are religious in a rigid way, reflecting their overcontrol and their tendency to use moral judgments as a way of controlling others. If fact, many of these people are described as difficult to get along with because of their self-focus and their guarded posture.

Inhibitions and ambivalences around sexuality tend to be common for the 36/63 code pattern. Perhaps because of their need for approval, combined with their fear of criticism, these individuals often have a strong investment in being seen as attractive by members of the opposite gender. However, these individuals also have difficulties with emotional intimacy and intimate sexuality. Problems dealing with anger are central to the code pattern. As one would expect with an individual who basically craves approval and fears criticism, they go through life denying their anger so that it accumulates into rationalized resentments; then a small trigger can lead them to explode into a highly rationalized outburst.

Their lifestyle is characterized by self-control, the avoidance of criticism, and seeking of approval. As children, they tended to not act out, and many were seen as cooperative and conscientious. This two-point code is substantially more common among women than among men, and most often the third highest elevation is Scale 4 or 9. A high number of 36/63 women were cheerleaders and were well liked by their teachers.

When Scale 6 is higher than Scale 3 by 5 or more *T*-score points, then the person is likely to be more suspicious, more easily hurt, and more determined in striving for control, perhaps as a way of protecting him- or herself. Typically, such persons are quite rigid and defensive in their behaviors, and their control may take the form of egocentric striving for power and prestige, even including ruthless manipulations. When Scale 3 is higher than Scale 6, such persons are particularly unaware of their anger, even though this may be quite evident to others. Their self-focus and egocentricity are clearly present, usually along with hurt feelings. However, the pattern is more one of martyred acceptance and resignations rather than power struggles. If Scale 2 is coded third, then the individual manifests periods of angry self-pity and feelings of being unfairly treated and victimized.

Treatment. Look for childhood conditioning experiences of rigid, moralistic caregivers who shamed their children into conformity. In some cases, this may have been done through harsh and heavily justified punishments; in other cases, through strong criticisms and emotional rejection. These individuals appear to have identified strongly with their caregiver's values, and their retaliation response to any unjustifiable punishment has been blocked; instead, it is experienced through judging and shaming others whenever others behave in ways they feel are inappropriate.

These individuals tend to be quite defensive in the interview situation and often feel that history taking is a probe for what is "wrong with them." Consequently, they give histories that are socially correct and appropriate, which can be frustrating for the therapist. In fact, these individuals can aggravate others into expressing anger toward them because of their defensiveness in anticipation of criticism. It is as if they are constantly justifying themselves and blaming others, reflecting their fears of criticism and judgment. They tend to be highly rational individuals who want specific advice for specific problems. The central task in therapy is to help these clients come to terms with normal human emotions of anger, sexuality, jealousy, greed, and so on. It is as if early childhood experiences have taught them that these emotions are "wrong" and "bad" so that they do not have adequate avenues to engage or express them. Exploring early experiences of having been criticized or judged and then using techniques to help them express the anger at having been judged unfairly could begin the process of loosening up their emotional overcontrol.

37/73 Codes

Relatively uncommon, this code is associated with tension, anxiety, insomnia, chronic discomfort, and psychosomatic complaints, as well as with academic underachievement. Unresolved dependency yearnings, combined with feelings of inadequacy, often underlie these symptoms. However, these persons use repression that significantly hinders insight and will deny the existence of psychological problems. For both men and women, Scale 2, 4, or 1 is most often the third highest scale.

Conceptually, the profile reflects an individual who constantly is on edge, fearing abandonment, emotional letdown, or anger. The elevations of Scales 3 and

7 suggest major apprehension about dealing with conflict or confrontation, and thus they may be reluctant to assume responsibilities. Typically, these individuals have appropriate concerns that are excessive in intensity. Likable, these people go out of their way to please, often being ingratiatingly subservient in their attempts to elicit emotional support and minimize anger or conflict. Many report a free-floating anxiety and appear constantly on edge, jumpy, and immobilized by an anxiety without any specific attribution.

These individuals need constant reassurance and can be subtly manipulative to get their dependency needs met. Self-assertion is difficult, especially with family members. Somatic complaints are also common and tend to be reflected by at least some elevation on Scale 1. These individuals tend to be immobilized by guilt, especially if they are in any way impulsive or express sexual and/or aggressive feelings. It is as if they go through life constantly wanting approval and reassurance, fearful that if they express any anger or selfish desires they will be punished with emotional abandonment.

If Scale 2 is coded third, even more self-depreciation and derogation will be present. The subsequent anxiety likely will lead to insomnia, difficulties with concentration, and general inefficiency. If Scale 9 is elevated, anxiety tends to be focused on achievement failures and the loss of approval. If the *L* or *K* scale is elevated, there is even greater denial, lack of psychological mindedness, emotional constriction, and lack of insight.

Treatment. Look for childhood experiences of an explosive or even violent caregiver that terrified the individual as a child. As children, many were described as conforming, unobtrusive, and wanting to please adults. As adults, they tend to be highly conscientious, responsible, diligent, and anxious about any financial or security setbacks. Transitions tend to be particularly troubling for them, and they tend to do best in stable, structured, predictable environments. Relaxation training, implosion, and assertiveness training all can be useful for these individuals. They tend to be suggestible and make good hypnosis candidates. They are easily knocked off balance by strong emotions, so catharsis, although important, should be elicited slowly.

These clients also respond well to reassurance. Help them get a sense of empathy for themselves as children who were badly frightened, and help them develop a sense of control over their anxiety by rehearsing frightening situations in conjunction with relaxation therapy. Be aware that they tend to oscillate between acute anxiety states and hysterical denial in which there is a flight into health. Although they have a pleasant disposition with a strong need for the therapist's approval, they fear letting down their emotional guard; thus, therapy tends to proceed slowly. Gestalt therapy may be useful in helping the client get in touch with his or her denied and repressed feelings. If the therapist feels passive resistance from the client, usually it will be around the client's fears of being flooded by emotions engaged in the therapeutic process. Transference issues should be explored on a continuous basis.

38/83 Codes (See Also Scales 3 and 8)

This code is an uncommon one, particularly among men. The elevation on Scale 3 reflects hysterical defenses, hysterical personality organization, and a profile in the neurotic direction, whereas the elevation on Scale 8 reflects psychotic-like thought processes. The combination of these scales suggests an individual who may be defending against underlying psychotic thought processes with numerous hysterical defenses. Consequently, the symptoms, complaints, and personality traits of the 38/83 code reflect the interaction of these two processes.

As one would expect with elevations on Scale 8, these individuals are strange and peculiar, both in thought and action, and have difficulties in concentrating, thinking, and remembering clearly and in making minor decisions. Although they feel alienated, these people also have an exaggerated need for affection but are afraid of getting involved in dependent relationships. When they do attempt to achieve affectionate responses from others, they typically do so in immature ways that actually may serve to push others away.

Many complain of peculiar, if not bizarre, experiences. They tend to manifest loose thinking with intense and fluctuating moods that at times are inappropriate. When psychotic episodes are manifested, they generally come abruptly and are characterized by feelings of unreality, emotional inappropriateness, complaints of blurred vision, dizziness, numbness, and headaches. Some have brief, highly sexualized episodes, for which they have no memory later. Their psychotic episodes disappear fairly quickly once a sense of composure is regained. Conceptually, it is as if the hysterical defenses act as a "glue," with the thought disturbance erupting occasionally as the individual becomes threatened. In highly structured situations, these individuals function well and are unlikely to evidence autistic or psychotic-like thought processes. They do, however, present with dissociative symptoms, inappropriate affect, and bizarre preoccupations. Some of these individuals may report hallucinations that come and go, depending on their level of stress.

These individuals evidence substantial difficulty in the spontaneous flow of conversation and ideation. They seem easily blocked and distracted, so that the stream of conversation often is interrupted and the therapist may periodically wonder, "How did we get to talking about this?" This "blocking" may reflect the person's constant internal interruptions around emotionally charged material and associations. Often these persons have great difficulties with intimacy and have sexual preoccupations that are somewhat immature. Many become involved in bizarre religious and/or sexual preoccupations. Marked problems with the expression of anger are also common. Their emotional tone appears depressed, even if Scale 2 is not significantly elevated, although they appear more flat and disconnected than depressed. Their typical reaction to frustration is intropunitive, and they are also described as anxious, tense, and nervous, as well as ruminative and obsessional. Easily threatened, they are fearful individuals and many have phobias. When Scale 1 is elevated, there may be complaints of blurred vision, dizziness, numbness, and headaches (See 138/318 code). Scale 4, 1, 7, or 2 is most often the third highest scale in the profiles of persons with this code pattern.

Although these persons generally are not perceived by clinicians as somatizers, they nevertheless report a wide variety of physical complaints, often musculoskeletal difficulties and genitourinary problems. They seldom are the oldest children; most often they are the youngest. In the Marks and Seeman (1963) sample, childhood health was reported as good, as was academic achievement, with many of them doing above-average work in school and a large proportion educated beyond the high school level. For many, one or both caregivers were alcoholic; and some had a caregiver who was also mentally ill. Fathers tended to be affectionate yet dominating.

Treatment. Think of the profile as reflecting an approach–avoidance conflict in relationships to others. These persons have strong needs for affection yet harbor great fears of hostility and abandonment by others. It is important to proceed slowly with the therapy because insight therapy can have disorganizing effects on these individuals. Therapy works best initially with a supportive and practical here-and-now orientation. Highly structured situations with reparenting types of therapies are most effective with these individuals. These individuals need a great deal of structure in their relationship with the therapist. As one would expect with an elevation on Scale 3, watch for areas the client avoids in discussions because they may be a source of their conflicts. When they appear to become "loose" in their thinking or drift into religious or sexual preoccupations, explore whether they are feeling angry or upset with what is occurring in the therapy.

Once rapport has been established, look for childhood experiences where they were frightened and experienced blows to their self-esteem. Rageful alcoholic outbursts directed toward them or toward a loved one could have frightened them, leading to periods in which they escaped into fantasy and attempted to deal with the overwhelming event through positivization and repressive denial. Help them recognize when anger is building so that they find appropriate modulated ways to express it. Assertiveness training would be useful.

39/93 Codes

Usually these persons are energetic, gregarious, outgoing, apparently self-assured individuals, although they may be quite superficial (particularly if Scale 0 is below $T = 40$). They tend to be quite driven and ambitious, highly active, and talkative individuals. They often switch topics and consequently may be hard to interview, particularly when exploring an anxiety-loaded topic. Denial is associated with both Scale 3 and Scale 9. Scale 3 predicts overcontrolled "niceness" (oversocialized) and strong needs for approval. Scale 9 also predicts needs for approval. Taken together, the code pattern reflects an individual who feels such intense internal pressure for approval that anger tends to be overcontrolled. Sudden breakthroughs of strong feelings can occur that are infrequent in nature. Such explosive episodes are usually targeted at a specific person in their environment. These individuals are described as perfectionistic, demanding, and at times, explosive, even assaultive. Repression and denial are typical defenses.

In clinical situations, these persons show histories of episodic attacks of anxiety and acute distress, often accompanied by palpitations, tachycardia, or symptoms in the lower gastrointestinal tract. Often these symptoms are medically unusual or impossible. Typically, these somatic complaints respond well to symptomatic treatment combined with reassurance. These physical symptoms reflect not only massive overcontrol but also the shifting of attention away from anxiety-loaded topics onto somatic symptoms. If Scale 1 is elevated, there are numerous somatic complaints, which come and go according to the stress level.

Often the *MAC–R* scale is elevated, and these individuals have an addiction proneness. These individuals can be very "cause" oriented, taking leadership positions, which are an outlet for their energy and their needs for social approval. As caregivers, they tend to be controlling and have difficulty with anyone having different values.

Treatment. They show great conflict between needs for self-assertion and needs for approval. Look for childhood histories where caregivers dominated the individual, constantly pushing for performance and achievement. Help them develop goals for themselves, distinguishing between their internalized parental expectations and their own wants and desires. Help them understand how their needs to perform and achieve are understandable, given their caregivers demands for performance. It will be important to learn to express anger and frustration, recognizing when it is building, rather than denying it so that it leads to explosive episodes. They particularly must recognize unconscious resentment toward domineering caretakers.

These individuals tend to be anxious only episodically, so they often lack persistence in therapy. These individuals are so busy running away from their feelings that they do not give themselves a chance to engage negative emotionality, even though they need catharsis. The therapist must be aware of resisting the client's subtle demands for approval, which can be annoying. Often these individuals come across as boastful, eliciting flattery from others and sometimes flattering others in order to get approval back. Their behavior replicates their relationship with their caregivers. Rapport can develop if the therapist can find genuine ways to approve of the client's high energy, perseverance, and generally sunny and positive personality style. The client will need to develop an internalized reward system, rather than working so hard for others' approval.

30/03 Codes

This relatively unusual code may appear contradictory in that Scale 3 suggests needs for social connection and approval, whereas Scale 0 elevations suggest social withdrawal or avoidance. Taken together, the two scales suggest a passive, dependent, unassertive, and somewhat withdrawn individual who is unassumingly "nice" but quiet. Stress may lead these persons to develop episodic psychosomatic complaints, and this often is reflected in Scales 1 and 2, which frequently are the next most elevated scale. These individuals appear relatively comfortable with their level of adjustment. They generally avoid uncomfortable social situations, and their primary defenses appear to be repression and denial.

Treatment. Because these individuals tend not to experience much psychological or emotional distress, they probably do not seek treatment often; thus, there is little information on the 30/03 code pattern. Any anxiety they express, as hysterical defenses break down, tends to be transitory. Social skill building, anger recognition, and assertiveness training are suggested foci of therapy. Look for childhood experiences of hostility or other emotionally painful events that have led them to "shut down" emotions and be "brave" in the face of pain. In long-term therapy cases, help them re-experience any past frightening or painful events and learn to vent the appropriate anger around those events to unblock repressed anger and sadness.

Scale 4 (*Pd*)

Scale 4 is a heterogenous scale, and it is a mistake to assume that all persons with high Scale 4 scores are necessarily antisocial or even act out aggressively. In fact, Scale 4 elevations can also be obtained by individuals going through divorce or other situational stress, which has left them "numbing themselves" emotionally and/or experiencing anger and bitterness that is externalized. All individuals with Scale 4 elevations do have some commonalities, however. They are independent, dislike rules being imposed on them, are cautious about allowing others to get close to them emotionally, and experience problems with trust and the vulnerability that is necessary to experience true intimacy. All high Scale 4 persons can be manipulative, selectively report, and maintain an emotional distance to protect themselves from hurt and/or being let down.

Not all individuals elevated on Scale 4, however, are necessarily overtly fighting against authority, although many are. Some may be socially and emotionally alienated, perhaps going through a current stressful situation. An important variable is SES. Some educated and bright individuals who score high on Scale 4 act out in controlled, poised, and white-collar crime ways (e.g., a stock manipulator who pushes the limits of legality beyond "gray areas").

As with all MMPI–2 interpretation, a history is vital in order to put the current profile in context. A history of acting out, rebelliousness, anger, and emotional and social alienation would suggest that a current Scale 4 elevation is characterological. In the absence of such a history and in the presence of a current divorce or other alienating experience, a Scale 4 elevation would reflect a situational adjustment reaction of adult life. However, even an individual going through an adjustment reaction, with Scale 4 elevated, will still reveal alienation, anger that is externalized, and difficulties with emotional control and trust, even though these may not be enduring character traits.

High scores ($T \geq 65$) reflect anger, rebelliousness, and an irritation toward rules and regulations. Their anger may be against their family, authority and society in general, or both. This anger may be a situational response (e.g., divorce), or adolescent rebellion or may reflect the angry disaffiliation of being in a minority cultural group. When this is not the case, the pattern is likely to be long-standing and unlikely to change. However, the way in which individuals handle the resentment and asocial impulses may differ greatly, depending on elevations of other scales. The likelihood of the anger being acted out behaviorally is increased if Scale 9 is elevated, and the acting out is likely to be bizarre and senseless if Scales 8 and 9 are also elevated and the *K* scale is low. Generally, characterologically high Scale 4 persons show impulsiveness, poor interpersonal judgment, unpredictability, social alienation, and a reduced sense of responsibility and morals. They may evidence poor work and marital adjustment. They tend to sacrifice long-term goals for short-term desires and seem limited in their capacity to anticipate consequences. Social relations typically are shallow, and strong loyalties rarely are developed. Although these persons sometimes make good first impressions, their unreliability, self-orientation, manipulativeness, and resentment soon become apparent. Often these persons have come from homes where they felt uncared for and subsequently focus on their own immediate needs.

For individuals beyond age 40, an elevated Scale 4 most likely reflects longstanding interpersonal disaffiliation and antisocial behavior, whereas for individuals beyond age 60, such scores suggest alienation to the point of a sullen lack of involvement. When there is no clear life event that would prompt such anger, the Scale 4 characteristics are likely to be enduring and resistant to change.

Moderately high elevations ($T = 55–65$) are associated with adventurous- ness, risk taking, energy, sociability, independent thinking, and assertiveness. Generally, these traits are positive ones associated with being enterprising and showing initiative, drive, and independence. When these people are frustrated, however, these characteristics can turn into irritation, aggression, and socially maladaptive behavior. Even in these moderate ranges, individuals can show tendencies toward manipulation and selective reporting, which are more likely personality traits rather than clear psychopathology. For example, the telling of white lies to "protect people" from the truth and the ability to subtly manipulate others into doing "what's good for them anyway" would reflect the kinds of rationalizations in which a person with moderate Scale 4 scorers could engage.

Moderately low to very low scores ($T \leq 45$) are associated with conventionality, stability, passivity, and unassertiveness. These individuals are not adventurous and often are dependent and even rigid in their adherence to socially conforming traditions. Although they may be quite affectionate, frequently they are not assertive in seeking sexual interactions. In counseling, they are likely to seek reassurance concerning the attitudes that others have toward them.

Spike 4

Spike 4 occurs when Scale 4 is the only scale above $T = 65$ (or when Scale 4 is 10 or more *T*-score points above all the other scales in an elevated profile). These persons are impulsive, resentful, and rebellious and in general have difficulty accepting rules, regulations, and authority. The likelihood of legal difficulties is high. Although they may be quite gregarious (particularly if Scale 0 is low), their relations with others are shallow, superficial, and brief. Long-lasting, intimate relationships are unlikely because these persons have difficulties with empathy, as well as the responsibilities and demands that accompany enduring relationships. They are unable to maintain organized behaviors toward long-term goals and instead tend to focus on satisfying short-term desires. If Scale 0 is low, particularly as it approaches a *T* score of 30, these problems are likely to be more pervasive and severe, although there will be a social facade where the person gives an appearance of being suave and glib.

A low tolerance for frustration, an inability to delay gratification, and a generally hedonistic approach are often found, particularly if the *K* scale is low. Self-control of angry feelings may be poor, and conflicts with caregivers, family members, and authorities are common. If the *K* scale is above $T = 60$, and if the client is of above-average intelligence and education, these behaviors generally are likely to be well-controlled. Legal difficulties for these persons are more likely to be of the white-collar variety.

Sexuality, intimacy, and dealing with authorities are problem areas for these individuals. Extramarital relations and unusual or atypical sexual histories are common. Although they often verbalize guilt and even depression, this tends to be transitory and situational, rather than affecting their subsequent behavior. In cases in which there is a clear situational precipitant, the Spike 4 profile sometimes reflects an "emotional numbing" in response to a recent frustrating situation. Once the painful event has been explored in therapy, their profile changes and the underlying depression is manifested.

When there is a history of acting-out behavior, the profile is probably a characterological Spike 4 profile and therapy should concentrate on helping these individuals deal with their fundamental distrust of vulnerability. Look for childhood experiences of having been emotionally let down by caretakers who were arbitrary or controlling. From an early age, they learned to numb their feelings and to develop a "survivor" profile, in which manipulation and deviousness seemed necessary to get their basic emotional needs met.

These individuals usually distrust the therapist. Because they project their own manipulativeness onto the therapist, dealing with the transference on an ongoing basis is important. They tend to lose interest in psychotherapy once situational changes have occurred; long-term character change is possible only if they become engaged in the therapeutic process. These individuals most often have conflicted marriages, although surprisingly not often divorce. They tend to marry individuals who tolerate their acting-out behavior to some degree.

The profile is predictive of alcoholism, particularly if the *MAC–R* scale is elevated. Because they tend to be selective reporters, the extent of their alcohol or other substance abuse problems may not be ascertained easily. They tend to externalize their problems. An example would be individuals who are having a secret extramarital affair and, at the same time, are telling their spouse that their emotional distance is the spouse's fault. If long-term therapy is available, use techniques to unblock early childhood experiences of having felt emotionally let down and abandoned, and help the client develop a sense of empathy for themselves as a vulnerable child. Then help them see how they numb themselves emotionally in vulnerable situations, which prevents the development of intimacy. Teach them ways to control impulse pressures for the sake of long-term goals.

Relations With Other Scales

High 4, Low 5 Codes

In men, the low Scale 5 reflects a person's strong concerns about portraying himself as masculine, or even hypermasculine. Power, coarseness, and traditional masculine interests are emphasized. In working-class individuals without college education, this usually reflects a traditional masculine, macho orientation. In college-educated individuals, this pattern suggests a facade to cover up feelings of inadequacy, particularly toward women. In some cases, however, this pattern may simply reflect an educated male with nonaesthetic, traditional masculine values and interests. Regardless of educational levels, their relationship to women often is power-oriented, with attempts to control women, sometimes in a demeaning manner. The low Scale 5 increases the possibility of aggressive and impulsive acting-out behavior.

Women with a high 4, low 5 pattern are angry, often chronically so, but are unable to express these feelings directly. In women, the low Scale 5 tempers the overt acting out suggested by Scale 4 and their anger is more often indirect. Their anger is directed particularly at men, and heterosexual problems are to be expected. These women often are superficial in their relations and frequently have identified with cultural stereotypes of women who are demure, yielding, and alluring and play such roles to satisfy their need for affection and attention. Usually, they are demanding and dependent. Their anger toward men, however, prompts them to express their irritations in passive–aggressive fashion, frequently using sexual means to manipulate or control men. These women often provoke others to anger with such behaviors (particularly if Scale 6 is also elevated), but then pity themselves because they have been mistreated. When Scale 3 is also elevated, these women are particularly unaware of their impact on others and deny hostile feelings. Not surprisingly, marital and family problems are likely, as are sexual dysfunctions and lack of sexual enjoyment. Headaches and backaches are also frequent.

41/14 Codes (See 14/41 Codes)
42/24 Codes (See 24/42 Codes)
43/34 Codes (See 34/43 Codes)

45/54 Codes

Clients with this code pattern almost always are men because of the infrequency with which women elevate Scale 5 on the MMPI–2. This code pattern should be interpreted within the context of considering simultaneously the person's age, education, and gender.

For male adolescents, this code predicts temper tantrums or even violent outbursts. They dislike rules, regulations, and authority and often show histories of truancy, school suspension, and failing academic grades. This is particularly so when Scale 4 is higher than Scale 5. Male teenagers also tend to be passively unconventional, both in appearance and behavior. They clearly are rebelling against social conventions and show pleasure in defying and challenging rules and regulations. However, they are not likely to act out in obviously delinquent ways, although they do have low tolerance for frustration; even so, their impulsive behavior can get them into trouble, especially around chemical agents. The elevation on Scale 5 may act as a suppressor of the acting-out behavior that usually would be seen from the high Scale 4. However, some teenagers with this code pattern can act out overtly in antisocial ways, although they tend to be a minority. However, these teenagers are also gregarious, extraverted, and generally well-liked by their peers. Despite their problems, in therapy they show good rapport and ego strength and appear to have reasonably good prognoses.

Adults with this code, particularly those with fewer than 2 years of college, most often are narcissistic, self-directed persons who seem to delight in defying social conventions in appearance and in behaviors. The openness and even flagrant nature of their defiance will increase as Scale 4 goes higher, particularly if Scale 9 is also elevated. Their interests are often unusual and varied, and they seem to delight in their nonconformity. In some people, this code is associated with homosexuality. However, homosexuality cannot be predicted easily from this code pattern, and should individuals want to conceal their homosexuality, they could do so readily without flagging any of the validity scales.

Men with college education or above are less likely to be narcissistically nonconformist; instead, they are more likely to become involved in social protests, causes, or movements that have an antiestablishment focus. These men often are quite idealistic and self-aware and able to communicate their ideas clearly and effectively. Dominance and dependence are important issues for these persons. Although they engage in their nonconformist behaviors to reassure themselves of their independence and adequacy, they nonetheless want to belong and exhibit strong dependency needs. When Scale 3 is the next highest scale, the person is more overcontrolled and dependent or passive and less insightful (see 345/435/534 codes). When Scale 9 is the next highest scale, the person is more likely to be emphasizing actions, dominance, and control of situations and people.

Women with 45 and 54 codes most often have Scale 9 or 8 as the third highest scale. Typically, they have strongly rejected passivity as any part of their self-image. For some of these women, this constitutes an angry protest and/or the adoption of a masculine-like role in a lesbian relationship. In other women, particularly in rural areas, this profile indicates only a lifestyle that is not traditionally feminine, focusing instead on practical, mechanical, or other action-oriented work aspects of their subculture that requires active self- assertiveness.

Treatment. See also treatment section of the Scale 4 description. Typical presenting problems center on intimacy and anger problems, relationships, sexual problems, and acting out. In fact, some researchers associated this code pattern with male sex offenders (see Spike 4 treatment recommendations). The addition of Scale 5 for men suggests passivity and conflicts between their need for autonomy and their desires for closeness. Assertiveness training to help them express anger directly, rather than passive–aggressively, and impulse-control management to help them with their tendency for sexual acting out as a way of getting their emotional needs met would be appropriate foci in therapy. Look for a strong relationship with an opposite-gender parent figure in which the individual felt both controlled yet indulged. These individuals also need to learn how to be emotionally vulnerable in adult relations, so helping them deal with basic trust issues would be important.

46/64 Codes

This code is more common among women than among men. Most often Scale 2, 3, or 8 is the third highest scale in such profiles. Key features are anger, resentment, distrust, sullenness, irritability, hypersensitivity to criticism or to demands by others, and projection of blame onto others. These persons are quick to feel implied rejection or criticism, and they jump to conclusions on the basis of inadequate data and little forethought. Their thinking typically focuses on how they have been hurt or neglected, how others are "at fault," and how they can protect themselves or seek revenge. Their thinking is seldom oriented around their own role in creating difficult situations or problems. The histories of these people usually show social interaction problems, especially family conflicts with projection of blame onto family members, few close relations, divorce, and often drug use or alcoholism.

Older adolescents with this code virtually always have continuing and severe conflicts with their caregivers, as well as with authority figures in general, who see them as bitter, hostile, and deceitful. Self-indulgent undercontrol of impulses is characteristic, accompanied by acting without sufficient forethought or deliberation. Defiance, disobedience, negativism, and argumentativeness are common. Often they are frankly provocative of others but see no responsibility for their behaviors.

In men, the 46/64 code is often associated with psychotic or prepsychotic conditions (see 468/648 codes) or with borderline personalities (see 462/642 and 463/643 codes). Paranoid features of suspicion, distrust, and overgeneralization are common symptoms of the 46/64 code for both men and women. For men, when Scale 4 is higher than Scale 6, family and work difficulties are typical, along with anger being the predominant feature. When Scale 6 is higher than Scale 4, more blatantly paranoid features will predominate. Although these men generally control their anger and sullenly mull about it, they may show episodic vicious outbursts to the surprise of those around them. In women, the 46/64 code is sometimes associated with psychosis or prepsychosis (particularly if Scale 8 is high and *K* is low) but more often appears to be associated with passive–aggressive personality styles, primarily associated with anger at men (see high 4, low 5 codes). This is particularly so with 463/643 codes, in which lack of insight, indirect instigation of problems, and blame of others is highly likely to be present.

Treatment. These individuals tend to be difficult clients in therapy because they expect anger in others and with their defensive, challenging style, tend to provoke it, confirming their view that they need to be defensive! In the interview situation, they would view history taking as somehow looking for what is "wrong with them" and would tend to be defensive. They have difficulties empathizing with others, and their anger tends to come out as judgment and criticisms of the therapist, although usually evidenced in subtle, more passive–aggressive ways.

Despite being quite demanding, they resist openly asking for what they want; instead, they use "shoulds" and other guilt-inducing techniques to get their needs met. Look for childhood conditioning experiences of authoritarian and controlling caregivers who would use harsh punishments and judgment as a way of control. This tends to instill in them an extreme sensitivity to being controlled in any way, with resulting fears of closeness. They avoid making direct requests of others in case it leads to others having some kind of control over them. Conceptually, think of them as going through life constantly anticipating criticism, judgments, and being controlled and getting their needs met by being manipulative and judgmental. Not surprisingly, they usually go through life with a "chip on their shoulder" as if they have been let down and hurt, thus often provoking others into expressing the anger that these individuals expect from people. They come across as "itching for conflict" and are very defensive. Often they have conflicted relations with an opposite-gender caregiver.

If the therapist does not get "hooked" into arguing with these individuals, they can be good therapy candidates. Often they are very rational and analytical (perhaps reflecting their paranoid defensive structure), which can be an asset in psychotherapy. Explore with them childhood situations where they felt unfairly treated, humiliated, or emotionally let down in ways that were particularly unfair. Have them reexperience those events, helping them vent the rage toward the arbitrary caretaker. Supportive and directive therapies can be useful for these individuals. Help them learn how to express their wants directly, rather than manipulating others, and help them learn to express anger directly rather than passive–aggressively.

462/642 Codes

The addition of Scale 2 to the 46/64 code adds a sense of feeling trapped, defeated, angry, and bitter. The depression is manifested in negativism and in suicidal threats and attempts. Nevertheless, it is the characterological features of these individuals, rather than their depressive mood, which dominate the psychological picture and which present a striking contrast between this code pattern and other depressed clients. In other depressed profiles, there is more self-dislike and guilt, whereas in this code pattern there is anger directed outward with the sense that their current depression is due to other people and unreasonable situations. In addition to the anger and sensitivity associated with the 46/64 code, these persons are dramatically self-absorbed in agitated psychic distress and complain of nervousness, anxiety, and depression. Often this is a manipulative demand for attention, sympathy, and control. They tend to be demanding of others in subtle, guilt-inducing ways, which provokes anger in others. A diagnosis of borderline personality is frequent with this code.

These people are mistrustful, skeptical of others, and suspicious of their motivations. They are particularly resentful of, and have problems with, persons in authority and often project the blame for their problems onto these authority figures. They rationalize their difficulties as due to matters beyond their control or blame others. Sexual and marital maladjustment and conflict are likely.

Despite their discomfort with people in general, and their anger at authority, these people typically have an exaggerated need for affection and dependency (even more so if Scale 3 is also elevated). Much of their discomfort and anger apparently stems from fears of becoming vulnerable, overly dependent, and therefore controlled by others. Consequently, they often show a reduced sense of involvement with their families or coworkers. Interestingly, these clients are often the "baby" of the family. Typically, their school achievement is below average, although a large proportion of them eventually receive a college education.

Treatment. Look for childhood experiences of an alcoholic caregiver and for conditioning experiences of caregiver unfairness, control, and arbitrariness, usually with the opposite-gender caregiver. Because these individuals develop rationalized resentments and make subtle demands on others, help them learn to make direct requests and verbalize their anger before resentments build. They tend to become very "blame" involved so that marital arguments tend to center on "who said what to whom first" and "who is to blame." Help them learn to verbalize emotionally vulnerable hurts and angry feelings in a nonjudgmental way so that they can learn trust and vulnerability as well, learning that direct communication is more effective than passive–aggressive behavior.

463/643 Codes

The addition of Scale 3 to the 46/64 code pattern suggests more overcontrol, more neediness, and more superficial "niceness" and role-playing with the hostility and resentment showing up underneath. The elevation of each of these scales in relation to one another is important. If the code pattern is primarily a 46/64 code pattern with Scale 3 coded third and significantly lower than either Scale 4 or 6, then more of the classic 46/64 code attributes will be evident. If Scales 4, 6, and 3 are all elevated at about the same level, then the individual presents with a good social front, conforms to role expectations, and tends to present as socially correct, poised, and self-controlled. Their anger would more likely be expressed in circuitous ways, such as subtle judgments of others, paranoid sensitivities, and a quickness to feel hurt and rejected. They would tend to hold onto their resentments, pursuing retribution with controlled vigor for any slights or injustices that they feel have been perpetrated against them. Their anger is often particularly focused on family members but is highly rationalized and—in their eyes—well justified. This profile has been associated with individuals involved in long and bitter divorce custody battles (Caldwell, 1997).

Because of the repression and inhibition evidenced by the elevation on Scale 3, these people have marked difficulties with the expression of anger. They come across as judgmental, rationalizing their anger, and, especially if the *O-H* scale is elevated, can show brittle, angry eruptions that are justified as self-protective.

Extremely sensitive to anything that can be construed as a rejection, they have difficulties with the direct rejection of others and tend to feel justified in telling white lies to get their needs met. These individuals can also evidence a paranoid mistrust of others, reflecting their own tendency to role-play, which they expect from others. Their paranoia tends to be a rational, jealous, and possessive paranoia rather than a bizarre thought-disorder paranoia. Controlled and poised (especially if *L* and *K* are high) and sensitive to social etiquette, these individuals often subtly resist authority figures and resent being controlled or challenged in any way.

They demand affection and attention yet tend to distrust it, so that others feel that they are difficult to satisfy. Although very much wanting affection and approval, their behavior often is self-defeating in that their subtle demandingness and sensitivity to rejection tend to aggravate others into expressing the anger that these individuals' expect. This, then, aggravates others, which confirms these individuals view that emotional relationships are fraught with conflict and criticism.

Highly influenced by social reinforcement, they tend to be role-players, often seductive with the opposite gender. Marital maladjustment is likely. Women who also have Scale 5 scores below $T = 40$ often show much passivity, clinging dependence, and self-pity. Physical complaints such as menstrual irregularities, sexual dysfunction, headaches, and backaches are likely, perhaps reflecting the overcontrol.

Treatment. These individuals go through life craving attention and affection yet distrusting it when they get it, so that it is never satiating. Often they have had childhood conditioning experiences by a critical and/or rejecting caregiver who demanded strict conformity to appropriate social roles and values. Observe during psychotherapy how they will inhibit expressing unacceptable impulses, often denying feelings they appear to be expressing. Sometimes it is useful to educate them as to what are "normal" human emotions. Help them to express anger as it builds, rather than waiting until they feel "justified" in expressing it, by which time they are resentful and/or bitter. Help them ask for what they want without using moral judgments. For example, have them repeat "I would like you to give me ..." without having to justify it. Perhaps because their constant need to justify themselves reflects their childhood experiences of feeling criticized and blamed, they have learned that to make requests of others would lead to conflict. Ventilation, catharsis, and insight-oriented therapy all can be useful with these individuals, who tend to be quite rational and analytical.

468/648 Codes

This code suggests a severe, and probably chronic, emotional disorder, most likely paranoid schizophrenia if the person is a psychiatric inpatient. A *DSM-IV* Axis II diagnosis of antisocial personality disorder or antisocial features may be present with this code pattern. These individuals are suspicious, angry, hypersensitive, blameful, critical, argumentative, and evasive. They are easily hurt by criticism, tend to read malevolent meaning into situations, and can show psychotic distortion in their reality testing. They tend to ruminate angrily about real or imagined injustices done to them and may have delusions or ideas of reference. Their thinking often shows tangential or loose associations, along with elements of grandiosity, that reflect their paranoid sensitivity. These individuals are clearly seething with anger, which they rationalize as self-protective and justified. Primary defenses are acting out, projection, reaction formation, and rationalization. When they recognize their anger, it is well-rationalized and justified as self-protective.

Poor judgment, lack of insight, and impulsiveness typically accompany the anger. Assault, drug abuse/addiction, and suicide attempts are all moderately frequent, and any threats should be taken seriously. Problems in interpersonal, marital, and sexual adjustment are predicted. Reduced impulse control and increased overt problems are even more likely when the *K* scale is below $T = 50$, when Scale 8 is within 5 *T*-score points of Scales 4 and 6, and when Scale 9 is also above $T = 65$. However, with an elevated *K* scale and the *Es* scale also high, the paranoid anger can be more effectively organized and therefore potentially more dangerous because it may be less immediately obvious.

Treatment. This is a difficult code pattern to treat. These people are paranoid and often psychotically rageful. They distrust others, show defects of empathy, and feel emotionally isolated in a world they see as hostile and dangerous. Consequently, developing rapport is difficult. Initially, supportive empathizing psychotherapy could help them ventilate the injustices and hostilities that they feel have been directed against them. Because of their extreme distrust, the empathy must be real and not role-played by the therapist.

Look for childhood conditioning experiences of being treated with hostility, physical abuse, rejection, and cruelty, which has promoted their constant vigilance and self-protective cruelty toward others. Helping them ventilate some of their rage can be useful, although beware of it having a disorganizing effect on them. Reality testing and gentle, supportive therapy are recommended.

It is important not to be afraid of these individuals, even though they bristle with self-protective anger. If the therapist is unintimidated by the anger but is able to validate it for the client as understandable given the abuse of mistreatment he or she has felt, then rapport can develop. Medication can be useful, but it is important that individuals do not interpret it as criticism or judgment of them.

469 Codes (See 496/946 Codes)

47/74 Codes (See Also 247/427/274 and 478 Codes)

Profiles coded 47/74 usually have many other scales elevated close to both Scales 4 and 7, suggesting that this is not a homogenous group of individuals. Nevertheless, some specific attributes are associated with a 47/74 code pattern. Initially, the elevation on each of these scales seems paradoxical: Scale 4 predicts insensitivity, rebelliousness, acting out, and anger toward authority figures, whereas Scale 7 elevations suggest acquiescence, concern about others' responses, guilt, and anxiety. Typically, when these individuals seek treatment, Scale 7 attributes are being manifested so that the presenting complaint tends to be one of anxiety. When anxious, these individuals demand reassurance and are compliant, somewhat passive, and even ingratiating, although reassurance tends to have little long-term effect, as one would expect given the distrust indicated by the Scale 4 elevation.

The pattern predicts a cyclical acting-out pattern. First, tension and anxiety build; as stresses accumulate, the individual impulsively reduces tension in some manner that usually backfires; and then the individual become anxious, guilty, and self-recriminating, beginning the cycle of anxiety once again. Conceptually, the profile suggests a compulsive acting-out pattern in which tensions are reduced through impulsive ego-gratification followed by guilt and anxiety. Usually, the behaviors that reduce tension are self-indulgent, narcissistic ones yet are the ones that cause guilt and anxiety. The net effect is an approach–avoidance conflict toward their tension-reducing behaviors. Sexual acting out, gambling, or alcohol binging are examples of tension-reducing behaviors that often backfire and can produce guilt and remorse, leading to more tension, anxiety, and then, eventually, acting-out behavior.

Along with their cycles of guilt and acting out, these persons have substantial conflicts between dependence and independence. They are insecure and have strong needs for attention and reassurance, but because of their mistrust, reassurance tends not to work. The most common three-point codes are 274/472 and 478/748.

Treatment. Look for childhood histories of caregiver inconsistency with, at times, emotional abandonment and, at other times, emotional indulgence. These individuals have difficulty delaying immediate gratification because they distrust that pursuit of long-term goals will be effective. In some cases, the early childhood histories of unpredictable emotional letdowns and abandonments are such that individuals learn to "grab what they can" because they have learned to distrust caregiver consistency.

Helping clients set limits and predicting with them the kinds of situations that lead them to act out can be important in teaching them to anticipate stressful situations and learn alternative behaviors to their traditional acting-out ones. Help them to recognize when anxiety is building and what situations are particularly stressful. Rehearse with them alternative, non-acting-out, tension-reducing strategies.

Group therapy is effective for persons with this profile, where they can obtain support and specific strategies for dealing with acting-out impulses. Insight-oriented therapy could reawaken in them memories of specific moments in their childhood when they felt unpredictably abandoned. This will lead them to reexperience the anxiety and learn to self-soothe rather than act out.

478 Code (See Also 47/74 and 247/427/274 Codes)

This profile suggests impulsive and/or compulsive, alienated, acting-out behavior in order to immediately reduce tension. The elevation on Scale 4 suggests acting-out behavior, distrust, and alienation, whereas the elevation on Scale 7 suggests neurotic reassurance seeking, guilt, and anxiety. When both scales are elevated (see 47/74 codes), the profile predicts impulsive tension reduction, followed by guilt, anxiety, self-recrimination, and more acting-out behavior. When Scale 8 is also elevated, this adds low self-esteem and a history of self-esteem-damaging experiences. Consequently, this predicts more severe difficulties with closeness, intimacy, and trust.

Individuals with 478 elevations often experience sexual difficulties, such as sexuality and aggression confusion, and they tend to act out sexually. They experience approach–avoidance conflicts in their primary relationships. They seek closeness and reassurance, as predicted by the Scale 7 elevation, but at the same time distrust it and act out as a way of preserving emotional distance and control.

These individuals often exhibit addictive behaviors, as they find any experience that gives them relief from their anxiety and inner emptiness to be highly rewarding. In psychiatric settings, these individuals can exhibit delusions, hallucinations, loose associations, and disorientation. Some can be self-punishing and self-degrading. Therapists have also described some as complaining of depression and suicidal ideation.

Look for childhood experiences of ambivalent, angry caretakers, whose nurturing would tend to be unpredictable and self-serving rather than child-responsive.

Treatment. These individuals are anxious and seek reassurance but are highly distrustful, so therapists' reassurance has only limited success. These individuals tend to be manipulative and selectively report, even to the therapist, reflecting their deep underlying distrust. Consequently, trust building by the therapist is an important first step in therapy. This should be followed by teaching the patient how to recognize when anxiety is building and to find alternative self-soothing behaviors. Relaxation training, thought stopping, and cognitive restructuring, as well as implosion techniques, could be useful to help manage the anxiety. These individuals can profit from self-esteem building, which is often difficult to achieve, as they act out in ways that are self-esteem damaging. If more time is available, help them vent rage around unmet dependency needs due to unpredictable and at times hostile caretaking.

48/84 Codes (See Also 48/84 High F, Low 2; 482/842; 486/846; 487/847; and 489/849 Codes)

Adults with this code almost always show severe problems, usually as a major personality disorder or a psychotic process. Distrust is a central characteristic for this group and is characterized by a sense of profound alienation and disconnection from others. Persons with 48/84 code patterns have difficulties forming emotional attachments because of their profound mistrust and their difficulties with empathy. Often the *F* scale is elevated, reflecting their internal chaos. The *VRIN* scale may also be moderately elevated, but the elevation does not necessarily indicate that the profile is invalid. Not all persons with 48/84 patterns are psychotic, although some are. Some are frankly psychotic with hallucinations, delusional thinking, paranoid tendencies, and a significant likelihood of prior psychiatric hospitalization; others have borderline personality disorders. Others, although not clearly psychotic, will show episodic breakdowns in their reality testing with occasional ideas of reference and a diffuse paranoia.

Emotionally distant from others, these individuals are seen as peculiar in thought and action and show subtle communication problems. Unpredictable and moody, these individuals are difficult to relate to because their brooding and hostile mood changes do not appear to be always tied to specific external events. They show marked difficulties in their capacity for empathy. They evidence poor social judgment, nonconformity, and impulsiveness, and a high proportion of these individuals act out. Educational and occupational histories are marked by underachievement and marginal adjustments, with uneven performance and serious lapses in responsibility and concentration. These patients may report a history of sexual abuse.

Some of these individuals become social isolates or nomads, whereas others become involved in criminal activity. Men with this code are more likely to be involved in criminal behavior or sexual deviations. When crimes are committed by individuals with this code pattern, especially if Scale 6 and 9 are also elevated, they are often senselessly brutal, savage, and poorly planned and carried out and can involve sexual or homicidal attacks. Often the acting out is poorly thought through and impulsive, so that these individuals appear self-destructive in that they often are caught.

Women with this code pattern often have had unwed pregnancies (and are, themselves, the result of unwanted pregnancies) and have histories of establishing relationships with men who are "social losers" and who often are less competent than they are. They have low self-esteem and seem most comfortable with others who seem similarly less competent and are vulnerable to being abused. They appear to fear emotional closeness and may prefer to relate to others sexually, even though they do not find it particularly gratifying. There is a tendency to confuse sexuality and aggression.

In some elevated 48/84 codes, particularly outpatient educated samples, there is often no history of antisocial or even sexual acting-out behavior. Instead, the code pattern reflects more of a damaged self-esteem, profound distrust, difficulties with emotional closeness, and self-defeating behavior in relations with others. In these situations, the code also suggests periods of paranoid misinterpretation, moodiness, panic, and a tendency to keep others at an emotional distance. Bright, educated individuals may not necessarily have a marginal social adjustment but rather a chaotic emotional life. If the *K* scale is elevated and the *Es* scale is normal or above, then the "48-ness" generally is manifested in sexual difficulties, sexuality aggression confusion, and chaotic interpersonal relations, but less antisocial acting-out behavior.

For adults, this is a suicide-prone code pattern, reflecting the intensely damaged self-esteem, the anger, and the alienation of these individuals. Consequently, clinicians should note the client's responses to Items 150, 506, 520, and 524 on the MMPI–2. Chemical addiction is strongly associated with this code pattern.

In adolescents, this code is fairly common and reflects at least a moderate and perhaps quite severe, transient adjustment disorder. In other adolescents, however, it may reflect a prepsychotic process. These adolescents, like their adult counterparts, are angry, distrustful, and unhappy; show disturbances in thinking; have ongoing interpersonal difficulties; and are impulsive in nonconforming ways. They keep others at a distance, and some go out of their way to appear frightening or even disgusting to others. Typically, these adolescents are academic underachievers and can be delinquent, although some are just chemically addicted. Anorexia, hyperactivity, and histories of enuresis and encopresis are also often present.

Treatment. These individuals tend to come from disruptive, chaotic, abusive, and identity-damaging childhoods. Look for chronic family conflict, sexual abuse, alcoholism, and cruel neglect. Often they were "the bad apple" in the family, singled out for particularly abusive or harsh treatment, and the profile reflects this severely damaged sense of identity. Many of these persons learned quite early in life to view others as untrustworthy, rejecting, hostile, or dangerous and established an enduring attitude of distrust and protective withdrawal toward the world. Many also learned to protect themselves (and to alleviate their painful anticipation of rejection and hurt) by striking out first in anger and rebellion. Establishing a therapeutic alliance with such persons is difficult, and in treatment they often are evasive and may even deny that problems exist.

Treatment should proceed slowly as these individuals have great difficulty with trust. Many will put the therapist through trust tests, which often is self-defeating if the therapist is not aware of them. They tend to be manipulative, reflecting the central experience of their life, which is they cannot trust others for basic caring and respect.

Insight and dynamic therapies tend to be disorganizing to these individuals. A more effective form of psychotherapy might be reparenting, supportive therapies, which can also be empathic with respect to their early childhood experiences of neglect and cruelty. Self-esteem building is probably the most important foci of therapy. Helping them manage their life with practical advice and helping them develop coping strategies as stresses arise would be important focuses of therapy. Psychotropic medication also may be useful to "glue" them together should psychotic processes be evident. Be aware that many of these individuals use chemical agents as a way of self-medication.

48/84, High F, Low 2 Codes

In addition to the 48/84 characteristics, the low Scale 2 suggests persons who have become comfortable with their alienation from others. They tend to treat others as objects and often are aggressive, punishing, and controlling of others, often extremely so. If of above-average intelligence, they can be narcissistically manipulative of the guilt and anxiety in others. These individuals may complain of depression, but it is more a sense of emptiness and disconnection, which reflects their alienation and distrust, rather than depression. They have sexual difficulties, primarily with the confusion of aggression and sexuality. Some individuals with this pattern are clearly diagnosable as sociopaths. If Scale 7 is also low, then the lack of anxiety predicts a greater likelihood of sociopathic and unsocialized aggression.

Treatment. Although the client may report depression, the clinician will need to keep in mind that the client is primarily an alienated, angry, and emotionally disconnected individual. See treatment section under the 48/84 codes.

482/842/824 Codes

Distrust and alienation also characterize this code pattern, along with depression, anxiety, tension, irritability, and generalized mental distress. Similar to the 48/84 code pattern, these people show strong underlying distrust of people, a suspicious questioning of their motives, and a profound fear of emotional involvement. They are persistently perceived by clinicians as avoiding intimacy and maintaining a protective distance from others. At the same time, they show strong (even exaggerated) needs for affection. Their emotions are highly variable, and they are described as resentful, irritable, moody, depressed, and argumentative, as well as hostile.

Related to the 48/84 elevations, they are at times emotionally inappropriate and some will show ideas of reference. Their paranoia tends to be diffuse rather than fixed and rational. They tend to act out when stressed, and they are described as manipulative. They are extremely sensitive to any demands being placed on them and are often resentful and bitter.

Profound low self-esteem, anger, approach–avoidance conflicts in primary relationships, and a tendency to panic in emotional situations and to react with cruel, self-protective anger directed at others characterize these individuals' interpersonal relations. This profile is associated with severe marital discord and conflicts over emotional closeness and dependency. Inner conflicts about sexuality are also prominent. These individuals have difficulty expressing emotions in any modulated or adaptive way. It is not surprising, therefore, that suicide attempts are common and that many have severe suicidal ruminations.

Treatment. See also treatment section under the 48/84 codes. Similar to the 48/84 code pattern, these individuals often have disastrous early childhood histories. An overwhelming majority of these patients report histories of caregiver rejection and/or domination, and very few report that their caregivers were affectionate during their childhood. Look for illegitimate birth and/or a childhood in which they are labeled as behavior problems with school difficulties and uncompleted educations. This profile can be understood as the result of having been raised as an "unwanted child."

Supportive, rather than insight-oriented, therapy is suggested as the latter can be disorganizing to them. Reparenting kinds of therapies that help these clients understand that their response to closeness is understandable, given their early childhood experiences, could validate their inner reality. Help them learn to express anger in modulated and adaptive ways rather than in cruel and impulsive ways. Watch for the numerous ways that these individuals manipulate the therapist and put the therapist through trust tests, perhaps unconsciously seeking to replicate their rejection experiences with their caretakers. The prognosis in these cases is guarded. Psychotropic medications can be useful; however, beware of anti-anxiety medications that may be addictive as this is a highly addiction-prone code pattern.

486/846 Codes

In addition to the 48/84 characteristics, the descriptions listed under the 468/648 code pattern apply. However, when Scale 8 is higher than Scale 6, there is more likelihood of thinking difficulties, such as loose associations, fragmented thoughts, and poorer reality contact. Increased feelings of alienation and bizarre actions or fantasies are likely.

489/849 Codes

The addition of Scale 9 to a 84/48 code significantly changes the interpretation. Scale 9 adds an element of energy, which increases the likelihood of acting out in unsocialized, aggressive, and sometimes even bizarre ways. Behavioral agitation may be present, and assaultive, combative, or frankly violent behaviors are a distinct possibility, particularly if the *K* scale is low.

Superficially, these persons are often seen as exciting and adventurous with a wild, lawless side. The stereotype of a charismatic gang member fits the 489/849 code pattern description. Often these persons show a history of repeated aggressive behaviors where others have gotten hurt. Alcoholism and/or drug use is common with this code pattern and increases the possibility of unsocialized, poorly thought-out behavior. Although some of these individuals can appear superficially charming, friendly, and gregarious, the possibility for impulsive and bizarre explosive episodes is high. Especially if Scale 0 is low, these individuals can lead others—sometimes charismatically—into anti-social and anti-establishment acts; in some cases, these may even be bizarre and cruel.

These persons are sensitive to criticism or any blows to their self-esteem. In some cases, they are prone to unexpected violent outbursts and acts of cruel rage. In other cases, especially if the *K* scale is elevated, the violence can be cunningly organized and vindictive. Sexuality and aggression tend to be confused for these individuals, and they often have sadomasochistic and impersonal kinds of sexual relations. Sexually, these individuals are often promiscuous and some reveal sexual identity confusion.

Distrust is a primary feature of the profile. Although they may be charismatic, they have profound fears of emotional closeness. Projection, rationalization, externalization, and acting out are primary defenses. Some of these individuals develop a social veneer that is frightening to others and unusual or bizarre. Severe tattoos, body piercing, and flamboyantly bizarre clothing all would serve to draw attention to themselves as well as frightening people into keeping an emotional distance from them. They often are self-defeating in their acting out because their behaviors eventually cause them problems with authorities and a subsequent restriction of freedom. Even if bright, these individuals have poor and uneven achievement.

Treatment. Many have childhood histories where they were seen as the "bad apple" in the family and often experienced rejection and outright hostility toward them. They learned the role of a flamboyant rebel and pushed conflicts to an extreme, even if their behavior was self-defeating. Although many of these individuals can intimidate a therapist, it is important to develop a therapeutic alliance by not responding to their hostility and rejecting behavior. Help them understand their angry independence, given their childhood in which they felt they had to be survivors in dealing with rejecting and authoritarian caregivers. Help them find ways to deal with stress and tension rather than acting out as stresses accumulate. Often these individuals are particularly sensitive to anything that can be construed as authoritarian and/or rejecting, which makes setting limits difficult. Explore with them if these "hot buttons" come from childhood experiences with a rejecting authoritarian caregiver. Help them see how their behavior tends to be self-defeating and to learn more appropriate ways of dealing with stress. If catharsis is part of the treatment plan, be aware that they have difficulties controlling their emotions; first teach them how to "bring themselves down" once they become aggravated. Techniques to help them vent rage could be dangerous otherwise. Self-esteem building and reparenting kinds of therapies in which the therapist becomes the "good parent" while still setting limits could be useful.

49/94 Codes

This is a very heterogenous code pattern. Although many kinds of individuals can obtain elevations on Scales 4 and 9, all have difficulties with trust, emotional closeness, and long-term commitment to goals. They tend to be narcissistic, impulsive, manipulative, and power oriented and tend to see relationships in terms of power and control. Intelligent, educated 49/94 persons, however, are quite different from those who are less so. Many educated, successful people with elevations on Scales 4 and 9 are in positions of authority and tend not to act out antisocially; however, all 49/94 persons will tend to have difficulties with authority figures, long-term commitments, and long-term relations.

For adults and adolescents, this code is almost always associated with arousal seeking, self-indulgence, and a resentment of limits, rules, or regulations. Egocentric, narcissistic, and selfish, they typically are unwilling to accept responsibilities imposed on them, although they may expend significant energy to accomplish their own goals. Typically, they focus much activity on seeking pleasure, excitement, and short-term goals. Social standards and values can be easily flaunted, and they are likely to have markedly fluctuating values or to construct their own values to fit their needs. As stated earlier, however, some clever 49/94 persons bend and manipulate the rules without obviously breaking laws and regulations.

In brief interpersonal contacts and social situations, these persons often create favorable impressions because they seem full of energy and confidence and appear to have no insecurities or anxieties. Longer acquaintance, however, generally reveals them to be more shallow and superficial in their commitments to others and, in many cases, irresponsible and untrustworthy, thus alienating others. Poor marital adjustment is likely, and many engage in extramarital relations. The farther beyond age 20 the person is, the more enduring the pattern and the more maladjustment is indicated. In some cases, psychotic symptoms, such as paranoid ideation and hallucinations, or even paranoid psychotic episodes related to excessive drinking may be present.

Adolescents with this code predictably have a low tolerance for frustration, experience repeated conflicts with their caregivers, and are often truant from school. They generally show impulsive, reckless, and provocative behaviors, such as lying, cheating, or stealing. Drug and excessive alcohol use are common both for adolescents and adults and are reflected in the fact that their *MAC–R* scale is often elevated. Teenagers commonly get into trouble in legal or social ways that damage their family's reputation.

Both for adolescents and adults, manifestly delinquent, hostile, or antisocial behavior is less likely to occur if the *K* scale is above $T = 50$; if Scale 2, 7, or 0 is elevated; and if Scale 5 is elevated for men or low for women. A female 49/94 profile with a high Scale 5 would increase the likelihood of acting-out behavior. When Scale 0 is below $T = 50$, these clients are self-dramatizing, have a tendency for aggressive leadership and assertiveness, and gravitate toward leadership positions. Some socialized 49/94 persons become crusaders, often quite charismatically, although superficially so. In other cases, these individuals manipulate others into antisocial behaviors, rather than overtly acting out the behaviors themselves. For men, Scale 8, 5, or 3 is most often the third highest scale. For women, Scale 8, 3, or 6 is most often the third highest scale.

Treatment. These individuals are difficult to treat because they have an abnormally low capacity to experience anxiety, guilt, or stress. Consequently, they tend not to learn well from experience. Consistently, they are rated low on such adjectives as *tense*, *nervous*, *high-strung*, *anxious*, *shy*, and *inhibited*. They externalize blame and see their difficulties as due to other people and difficult situations. They have strong needs for immediate gratification and tend to present with a charismatic, colorful, adolescent-type of rebellious stance toward the world. In psychoanalytic terms, these people are governed by the pleasure principle, and they often are described as self-indulgent, egocentric, and narcissistic. Although some react with depression when confronted with the consequences of their behavior, this depression is of short duration and has little effect on their future behavior.

Although not all 49/94 persons are antisocial and not all show a lack of enduring adult pair bonding, some do appear incapable of establishing any kind of commitment to others. Even though many of these individuals achieve school success and are often brighter than average, they become underachievers; their self-defeating and acting-out behaviors undermine their success. The profile predicts marital conflict and sexual acting out. Look for childhood histories of dominating, narcissistic caregivers so that from an early age these individuals learn to be "survivors," numbing their vulnerable feelings and learning to manipulate others to get their needs met.

Working on the transference is an important part of the therapeutic process, as these individuals tend to project their own manipulativeness onto the therapist and assume that the therapist is somehow "playing a game or a role." Addressing the ongoing relationship with the therapist has the best chance of keeping them involved. For adolescents, settings with consistent, firm limits will be helpful. Psychotherapy also could help them learn to rehearse situations in which they are likely to act out and help them develop better tension-reduction mechanisms rather than impulsive acting-out ones. If they persevere in psychotherapy, then the therapist can perform a resocializing kind of reparenting therapy, becoming more limit setting as the transference takes hold.

493/943 Codes

In addition to the 49/94 features, Scale 3 predicts some temporary control of the acting out, along with at least a veneer of superficial niceness and social role-playing. Acting out, however, will still occur, although interspersed with periods of control and of socially appropriate behavior. These individuals have conflicts between their need for approval and their need for autonomy. With Scale 3 being coded third, their need for autonomy and immediate tension reduction tend to predominate over their need for approval. In a 493/934 code, acting out is likely to be less frequent and more often will be passive–aggressive and indirect in nature. However, if Scale 3 is within 5 *T*-score points of Scale 4, then many of the characteristics of the 34/43 code pattern may also be present. Some people with this code pattern may store up their anger, resulting in episodic explosive outbursts, usually directed at a family member. Usually the *O-H* scale is also elevated, reflecting the general overcontrol associated with this code pattern. If the *O-H* scale is not elevated, then there may be less explosive episodes and more irritability and anger as the 49/94 acting out predominates over the inhibition suggested by the elevation on Scale 3. In general, the 493/943 code pattern reflects individuals who are constantly searching for approval, success, and power. They are willing to play manipulative social roles and to justify bending the rules in order to get their needs met.

Treatment. Look for childhood experiences of caregivers who were constantly motivating the child to succeed and who tended not to give a great deal of approval when the child had setbacks or failures. Often the caregivers were self-centered and narcissistic themselves and saw the child's performance in life as a reflection of their own drives and aspirations.

These individuals need help recognizing when anger is building so they can express it directly rather than in a roundabout, passive–aggressive, or in some cases, explosive way. These individuals are usually quite unaware of their social role-playing and manipulations. Help them to distinguish between what their needs are versus their internalized caregiver expectations, and help them deal with their need for approval, which tends to be in conflict with their need for autonomy. It is important that the therapist give them much approval.

495/945 Codes (See Also 49/94 Codes)

The additional elevation of Scale 5 is sometimes associated with a person who is overtly and defiantly adopting an unusual sexual orientation (often homosexual). More often, however, Scale 5 is associated with a person who is well-educated and broadly experienced and whose impulsiveness and rebelliousness are tempered so that they are more socialized and better controlled than a pure 49/94 individual. They still will be nonconformist and will have difficulties in their close interpersonal relations, which are marred by distrust and acting out in the interpersonal and sexual arena. Sometimes these persons involve themselves in social causes that challenge traditions, particularly when Scales 4 and 9 are only moderately elevated. These persons dislike rules, regulations, or tight control by others and highly value their autonomy and self-interests.

Treatment. Men with 49/94 patterns in which Scale 5 is elevated tend to be more interested and responsive in psychotherapy than persons having only 49/94 codes. They tend to be better educated and more intellectually curious, verbal, and insightful. They are more amenable to being "coached," especially by a warm, approving psychotherapist who does not withdraw from the clients when they act out. Once the therapeutic relationship is established, helping them set limits so that they do not act out and helping them persevere toward long-term goals can be important therapeutic objectives. Look for childhood conditioning experiences similar to the 49/94 code pattern and treat accordingly. See also the treatment section under the 49/94 codes.

496/946 Codes

The addition of Scale 6 to the 49/94 code pattern changes it considerably because it predicts more paranoid sensitivity and vindictiveness and sometimes more organization. These individuals can be seriously assaultive, destructive, and even homicidal, especially if they feel they have been somehow wronged or treated with disrespect. They can pursue vengeance with a determination that might be lacking from a pure 49/94 individual. This code pattern also predicts difficulties dealing with anger, so that when anger occurs, it comes as a dangerous breakdown of brittle controls. If Scale 8 is also elevated, these individuals can pursue vengeance in bizarre, violent, and vindictive ways. Some may show brief psychotic episodes, and others can become more openly schizophrenic over time. Often childhood histories reveal controlling, arbitrary, and cruel caregivers who used strict punishment in attempts to "break the child's will." Consequently, these individuals show a strong response to any attempt to control or criticize them and go through life with a "chip on their shoulder," ready to argue and fight to protect their autonomy and sense of respect. Educated person with 496/946 patterns are argumentative, rationalizing, externalizing, and blaming. Less educated persons with 496/946 patterns still tend to be argumentative but more prone to act out violently and impulsively when threatened.

Treatment. Anger management strategies are most useful. Help them understand how their quickness to defend themselves and to "argue their position" perhaps comes from childhood experiences of having been controlled and constantly treated with disdain and disrespect from arbitrary caretakers. Help them recognize how authoritarian or strong-willed people can "push their buttons" into becoming argumentative and how their own tendency to be argumentative becomes self-defeating. Medication may be quite helpful, particularly if there are signs of psychosis.

498/948 Codes (See Also 489/849 Codes)

In addition to the 49/94 features, the likelihood of strange, unusual, bizarre, and/or violent behavior is quite high. In persons over the age of 20, this code usually represents major and enduring psychopathology. In adolescents, this code is more often associated with situational difficulties and an intense adolescent rebellion rather than the incipient or overt psychosis that is more often found in older persons with this code. Nevertheless, both adults and adolescents show intense feelings of alienation from others, family conflicts, high energy levels, difficulties with authority, and rebellious behaviors. They particularly fear feeling vulnerable, and in conversations they are likely to jump from topic to topic to avoid talking about emotional issues.

Treatment. See treatment section under the 489/849 codes.

40/04 Codes

This is a rare code pattern, as one would expect given that Scale 4 reflects acting out and a lack of conscience, whereas Scale 0 elevations are associated with individuals who rarely act out and who tend to be guilt-prone. Taken together, this code pattern predicts individuals who are both angry and interpersonally withdrawn. Typically, they do not express their anger openly, have difficulty in being appropriately assertive, and tend to sullenly hold onto grudges. Suspicious, resentful, and shy, they tend to be passively resistant.

These individuals tend to act out within the family rather than in antisocial ways. If they do act out in antisocial ways, they tend to be loners. However, this is generally not an acting-out profile but rather reflects an individual who has difficulties with emotional closeness and intimacy yet who does not experience psychological distress. Further interpretation depends on the three-point code or other configural analysis (e.g., high Scale 4, low Scale 5). Often it is helpful to omit Scale 0 in the three-point code and to then obtain interpretations based on the remaining two-point code, subsequently adding information from the elevated Scale 0.

Treatment. These individuals do not usually seek treatment. If they do, it likely would be around marital and relationship problems or the result of some self-defeating behavior. Relationship psychotherapy that would teach them how to relate intimately to others could be an effective therapeutic strategy if they are motivated to stay in therapy. As with all high Scale 4 codes, working on the transference should be done cautiously, although continuously, so that they remain involved and are able to discuss their trust issues openly.

Look for childhood histories of having caregivers who were emotionally distant and uninvolved, although not necessarily arbitrary or cruel. These individuals have learned the role of a loner, turning to their own resources in times of stress and not allowing themselves to engage and reveal normal vulnerable feelings.

Scale 5 (*Mf*)

Spike 5

High scores ($T \geq 65$) and Spike 5 codes in men suggest men who are introspective, inner-directed, and education-oriented and who have a wide range of interests, including aesthetic and contemplative preferences. Often these men are seen as idealistic and imaginative, quite socially perceptive, and interpersonally sensitive. In individuals with broad educational and cultural background, these characteristics are to be expected. In some men, however, this pattern may reflect a rejection of stereotypical masculine behaviors in favor of a relatively passive, noncompetitive style. Because Scale 5 in men is strongly correlated with education, intelligence, and cultural breadth, interpretations should take this into account. This scale tends to be at least moderately elevated for well-adjusted members of various occupational groups, such as social scientists, writers, artists, ministers, and teachers. High scorers, with no other scales elevated, tend to be relatively passive men (particularly if Scale 4 is low), and some are clearly effeminate in manner.

Elevation of Scale 5 is never in itself sufficient to suggest homosexuality, either overt or latent. Homosexuals who wish to conceal their orientation can do so with relative ease on this scale. Even so, when Scale 5 is above $T = 75$ and when education is fewer than 2 years of college or there is restricted cultural exposure, these men are likely to not have a traditional masculine lifestyle.

It is unusual for women to have high Scale 5 scores ($T \geq 65$) and Spike 5 codes because few women score above a *T* score of 60 on the MMPI–2. Nevertheless, women with an elevated Scale 5 tend to be assertive, competitive, tough-minded, and not particularly interested in appearing or behaving as other women do. Instead, they are more likely to be independent, self-confident, spontaneous, dominant, and even aggressive in thought and action. This may be expressed in pragmatic career and/or survival behaviors, in traditionally masculine sports or interest patterns, or in a dominant lesbian sexual orientation. Many of these women are quite uncomfortable when in situations where they are not in control.

If no other scales are elevated, then Scale 5 elevations in women can predict positive qualities associated with independence and assertiveness. Look also for elevations on the *GM* and *GF* scales. If the *GF* scale is also elevated, then the elevation on Scale 5 can suggest a healthy androgyny. The reverse is true for men, so that if Scale 5 is elevated and the *GM* scale is elevated, a healthy androgyny is suggested.

Moderately low scores (T = 35–45) are interpreted differently for men and women. Low Scale 5 men show a traditionally masculine pattern of interests and behaviors, and often their interests are narrowed almost exclusively to those areas. They are adventurous; prefer action to contemplation; prefer outdoor activities, sports, and competitive or mechanical activities; and often appear rugged and even coarse. Lower occupational achievement aspirations often accompany this pattern.

In women, moderately low scores (T = 35–45) suggest a woman who is sensitive and concerned about relationships, particularly with men. She likely tends to be nurturing and supportive, although this may also be accompanied by a submissiveness or even passivity. These women are typically concerned with presenting a neat, attractive, and feminine appearance in dress and demeanor, and often their interests are directed toward academic, home, or aesthetic areas. Most are attracted to sensitive men with whom they enjoy communicating. Professional and other college-educated women tend to obtain *T* scores in the 40 to 50 range on this scale.

When Scale 5 is very low ($T \leq 35$), men appear to virtually have a compulsion to appear masculine, perhaps to the point of being a caricature, and repeatedly manufacture exhibitions of strength and endurance in a narcissistic fashion. Such an overconcern for demonstrating one's masculinity is usually associated with underlying self-doubts. In male adolescents, low Scale 5 scores are associated with delinquency and school problems.

In women, very low scores ($T \leq 35$) usually reflect women who are emotionally constricted. They seem to need to reassure themselves of their self-worth through assuming numerous and frequent burdens, sometimes to an almost masochistic degree. If they are not sufficiently (in their own eyes) appreciated, they become filled with self-pity and often then inspire guilt in others in a guilt-finding fashion. Headaches, backaches, sexual dissatisfaction, and inability to enjoy sexual experiences are often found, and some of these women seem so caught up in a sense of duty that they are unable to allow themselves to enjoy pleasant experiences of any kind.

Relations With Other Scales

51/15 Codes (See 15/51 Codes)
52/25 Codes (See 25/52 Codes)
53/35 Codes (See 35/53 Codes)
54/45 Codes (See 45/54 Codes)

56/65 Codes

Little is known about persons with this code pattern, except that it is usually a male profile. In general, these men seem to be insecure and are afraid of emotional involvement with others. These men tend to be fussy, sensitive individuals who get their feelings hurt easily, take things personally, and have difficulties expressing anger directly. At times, their sensitivity could shade toward paranoia where they exhibit unreasonable jealousies and projections onto others. Somewhat passive, they would present as rational, intellectually oriented, somewhat aloof individuals who have difficulties with direct confrontations. When others place demands on them, they tend to become irritable. Many have high educational and career aspirations. Women, on the other hand, tend to be more abrasive, direct, judgmental and controlling.

Further information can be obtained if a third scale is elevated above $T = 65$ by temporarily disregarding Scale 5 and interpreting the other two scales as though they were a two-point code (e.g., a 564/654 code could be interpreted as a 46/64 code with an elevated Scale 5).

Treatment. Because they are sensitive to criticism or judgment, look for childhood histories of a caregiver who was quick to criticize or judge and/or quick to punish. These individuals appear to be going through life protecting themselves against criticism or judgment by becoming aloof and intellectually argumentative. Help them find ways to express anger more directly without the use of judgment. Help them ask for what they want directly, rather than waiting until they feel resentful or hurt before they express anger and before they make demands on others.

57/75 Code

Indecisive, *worrying*, *introspective*, *tense*, *unhappy*, and *needing reassurance* are terms that describe men with this code pattern. Men with less than a college education are particularly likely to experience anxious or depressive episodes characterized by obsessive rumination over self-inadequacies and shortcomings. Men with this code pattern are easily embarrassed and bashful, get their feelings hurt easily, and frequently feel inadequate in heterosexual relations. Women rarely obtain this code, but when they do, they are less aggressive and more self-analytical than would be expected just from a high Scale 5 elevation on its own. Even so, they are often intellectually competitive. For both men and women, the interpretations can be enhanced by considering also the two-point code that might result when Scale 5 is omitted.

Treatment. Because of their psychological mindedness (as predicted by the Scale 5 elevation) and their adherence to instructions (as predicted by the Scale 7 elevation), these individuals are good psychotherapy candidates. Insightful and introspective, they do well with insight therapy, as well as thought stopping, relaxation training, and ventilation and catharsis. Self-esteem building and assertion training are also useful.

58/85 Codes

Men with this code pattern are quite inner-directed and spend much time in thought, often engaging in philosophical musings or being concerned with abstract ideas about life's meaning. Most complain of feeling confused, unhappy, and alienated from others and of having home conflicts. This interpretation should be enhanced by considering the two-point code that may result when Scale 5 is omitted.

Greene (1991a) reported that men with this code pattern are likely to have family histories of alcohol abuse, mental illness, and physical abuse. Some of these men have psychiatric histories that began in childhood. Although many of them are not psychotic, they often report depression, paresthesia, and religious preoccupations. although some can be seen as creative, others are described as odd, eccentric individuals who have difficulties with emotional closeness. Sexual conflicts are common, as are family problems.

Women with this code display unusual thoughts and behaviors that often focus on issues of control of others in order to protect themselves. Typically, they feel alienated and are uncomfortable with others if they are not in control. Among female adolescents, this pattern would be associated with behavioral problems at home or school and/or legal difficulties.

Treatment. Self-esteem building, self-assertiveness training, and reparenting-type therapies are most effective. Avoid insight therapies, which tend to be disorganizing for these individuals or which can lead to seemingly endless intellectualizations.

59/95 Codes

For men, the presence of an elevated Scale 5 reduces the likelihood of overt acting out, perhaps because of the increased use of intellectualization, denial, and rationalization. Indeed, most men with this code do at least reasonably well academically. Emotional dependency and lack of self-assertiveness in intimate relations are the most likely problem areas. Men tend to be driven by needs for approval and require a great deal of reassurance in their intimate relations, particularly if Scale 3 is also elevated.

For women, an elevated Scale 5 increases the likelihood of overt aggressiveness. Whether this aggressiveness would be expressed verbally or behaviorally will depend on other factors. These women typically are energetic, competitive (particularly with men), confident, uninhibited, adventurous, and perhaps self-centered and irritable when their desires are thwarted or questioned.

For both men and women, these individuals tend to be quite comfortable with themselves and ordinarily do not report psychological problems or distress. Active, energetic, and easily bored, they describe themselves as self-confident and easygoing. Generally, Scale 0 is low, reflecting their social comfort and the fact that these individuals often make a good social impression. Even if the *MAC–R* scale is not elevated, these individuals can use chemical agents as a way of moderating their energy level. Further information can be derived by omitting Scale 5 and examining the resulting two-point code-pattern information.

Treatment. These individuals may need help in completing tasks and developing sustainable long-term goals. Men tend to be driven by needs for approval, often reflecting internalized caregiver expectations. For men, examining the mother–son relation can often help the client develop individual goals and complete the emancipation from their mother. Women are more likely to start projects but not necessarily finish them and may need to learn skills in managing or working with others harmoniously. Look for childhood histories of caregivers who were constantly motivating them to achieve and succeed. Persons with this code often internalize their caregiver expectations, and many have unconscious resentments of having been controlled and pushed.

50/05 Codes

Men with this code are introverted and generally retreat into personal or intellectual isolation, rather than reaching out to others. They are cautious, inhibited, withdrawn, and anxious in contacts with others and typically are overcontrolled and overideational. Socially, they are awkward and have difficulty in being assertive, and many have doubts about their own adequacy. They are embarrassed easily and rarely get into trouble because of acting-out behavior. Difficulties and discomfort in heterosexual relations are particularly common.

Women with this code are typically much less confident, spontaneous, vigorous, or assertive than ordinarily would be expected from an elevated Scale 5. Often these women have less education or are from a working-class or rural social background. For both men and women, further interpretation can be done by omitting Scale 5 and examining the resulting two-point code.

Treatment. Assertiveness training and enhancement of self-efficacy can be helpful. Many of these persons can profit from training and role-playing of specific social skills. Cognitive–behavioral approaches may help them examine their "self-talk," which is often overly self-critical and focuses on the likelihood of problems occurring.

Scale 6 (*Pa*)

Spike 6

High scores ($T \geq 65$) and Spike 6 codes reflect individuals who are suspicious, angry, and broodingly resentful and who overinterpret situations as "directed at them." Most often these behaviors are clearly paranoid, with ideas of reference, projection as a primary defense mechanism, poor reality testing, and delusions of persecution and/or grandeur. Some individuals, especially if they score high on the *K* and *Es* scales, can function well; however, they may show a paranoid sensitivity with unreasonable jealousies and occasional clear paranoid episodes, albeit without any enduring psychotic break.

Moderately high scores ($T = 55–65$) reflect individuals who are sensitive, whose feelings are easily hurt, and who have a tendency to misinterpret others' motives and to take things personally. Even in this moderate range, there is a clear use of paranoid defenses with projection, denial, reaction formation, and the development under stress of unreasonable jealousies. These people usually feel unfairly treated. In some cases, these paranoid traits can shade toward paranoid episodes, although without psychotic breaks. In unthreatening situations, these people can appear quite normal, but they will show difficulty in recognizing their anger and expressing it directly. They typically are subtly judgmental, easily hurt, and guarded and distrustful in their personal relations. They will tend to feel controlled by others' expectations of them and tend to develop rationalized resentments.

Very low scores ($T \leq 35$) are obtained by two widely divergent types of persons—those who lack personal sensitivity to others and those who are so suspicious and wary that they skillfully have avoided endorsing the items on Scale 6. The latter persons are essentially the same as those who score high on Scale 6, but they may be somewhat brighter and more cunning. Most persons with such low scores, however, are interpersonally insensitive, conventional, trusting, naïve, and gullible.

Scale 6 reflects three components of the dimension of paranoia. It reflects clear persecutory ideas as well as ideas of reference. Second, it reflects an exquisite sensitivity, with feelings of being treated unfairly. There is a strong tendency to take things personally and to misinterpret the motives of others as directed against the person. A third component is an element of self-righteousness in which the person feels indignant about the "bad" or "wrong" behavior evidenced by others and feels that behavior needs to be punished and exposed. These three components are well reflected in the Harris–Lingoes subscales.

Relations With Other Scales

61/16 Codes (See 16/61 Codes)
62/26 Codes (See 26/62 Codes)
63/36 Codes (See 36/62 Codes)
64/46 Codes (See 46/64, 462/642, 463/643, and 468/648 Codes)
65/56 Codes (See 56/65 Codes)

67/76 Codes

This rather infrequent code most often has Scale 2 or 8 as the third highest scale. Persons with this code are hypersensitive, tense, anxious, and often broodingly resentful. They are extremely concerned about criticism or disapproval and are especially preoccupied with failure. The code pattern reflects someone who is continually apprehensive about being judged, evaluated, and personally confronted. Consequently, they are constantly on edge, anticipating criticism. They typically have histories of strained or disrupted interpersonal relations in which they have felt wronged (usually because of misinterpretation on their part). Although they may feel quite inferior and/or guilty, they are also quick to judge others, perhaps as a defense against being judged and criticized. When both scales are above $T = 75$ and Scale 6 is higher than Scale 7, or even when the scores are similarly elevated, the possibility of decompensation from an obsessive–compulsive disorder into a psychotic episode is possible, although rare.

Treatment. Look for childhood experiences of being unpredictably shamed or judged, criticized, or even severely punished. Relaxation training, self-esteem building, and assertiveness training, as well as insight therapy, can be useful for these usually intelligent and rational individuals. In the presence of a history of extremely critical caregivers, help them realize how they understandably have become constantly on guard for criticism, sensitizing them to be somewhat quick to distort other people's motives and comments to them. Help them learn to express anger directly, as well as to express their vulnerable feelings. They tend to rationalize and project out of fear that being vulnerable will lead to judgment and criticism.

68/86 Codes (See Also 468/648, 486/846, and 489/849 Codes)

Most often Scale 7 or 4 will be the next highest scale. Both for adolescents and adults, the 68/86 code pattern suggests serious psychopathology and is usually accompanied by an elevation on the *F* scale and content scales. The *F* elevation usually reflects the large number of unusual experiences endorsed by the person. This is particularly so when a "paranoid valley" is present. The paranoid valley configuration occurs when Scales 6 and 8 are both above $T = 65$ and both are at least 10 *T*-score points above Scale 7. Even when several other scales are more elevated than Scales 6 and 8, the possibility of paranoid schizophrenia must be considered when a paranoid valley exists. Individuals with this pattern are more likely to have had prior psychiatric hospitalizations, reflecting recurrent episodes of illness.

The overall orientation of these clients toward others is one of suspicion and distrust; subsequently, they tend to have few or no friends. Others' motivations are regarded as highly suspect, and so these individuals have extremely difficult interpersonal relations with others; they tend to be most comfortable when alone. Not surprisingly, many of these persons are diagnosed as paranoid schizophrenics. They tend to be moody, hostile, unpredictable, negativistic, and at times emotionally inappropriate. They typically keep others at an emotional distance, often because of their irritability and anger, and tend to arouse in others dislike toward them. At the same time, they feel inferior and guilty. Many of these individuals are either an only child or the youngest in the family.

Difficulties in thought processes are marked by overgeneralizations, misinterpretations, and even frank delusions. Emotional inappropriateness, overideation, unrealistic ideas, suspicion, distrust, difficulties in concentrating, poor reality contact, confusion, and disturbed interpersonal relations are present, perhaps accompanied by depression or fears and phobias. The thought content of these persons is almost always unusual, if not bizarre, and they are often seen as odd or strange. Inner conflicts about sexuality are usually present, and feelings of sexual inadequacy are often a major problem area. Typically, they are socially withdrawn or isolated (most of these adults are single), and spend much time in self-absorbed fantasy. If married, their partner is likely to be emotionally deviant or alienated. Behaviorally, these people are unpredictable, particularly if Scale 4 (see 468/648 codes) or Scale 9 (see 689/986 codes) is also elevated.

Surprisingly, many adults with this profile show a history of being reasonably able to maintain employment, although episodes of fatigue, inefficiency, and difficulty concentrating may suddenly precede a psychotic episode that seems to occur without any clear precipitating event. Adolescents with this code often show violent tempers (particularly if K is below $T = 50$), have poor peer relations, spend much time in fantasy, do poorly academically, and show a family history of having received severe corporal punishment.

Look for caregivers who are rejecting or, at best, indifferent. School achievement will tend to be significantly below average. These individuals seem particularly sensitive to hostility and can respond with acute outbursts of rage if they perceive themselves as threatened. Some may collect weapons, reflecting their preoccupation with self-protection.

Treatment. Insight therapy tends to be contraindicated because these individuals can be easily disorganized. Supportive reparenting therapies are the most useful, as is teaching these individuals anger management. They can easily "go off on a tangent," ruminating about unfair aggression coming from others. Helping them regain composure and learning to deal with anger in appropriate ways are important goals. In the presence of a psychosis or psychotic-like symptoms, psychotropic medications would be important.

69/96 Codes (See Also See 698/968 Codes)

This is not a common profile pattern. However, when present, it indicates a paranoid grandiosity. The grandiosity is a reflection of inner insecurity and fears of inadequacy, whereas the paranoia reflects fears of being criticized and judged. For both men and women, Scale 4 or 8 is most often the third highest scale.

Persons with this code are tense and jumpy and overreact to minor situations as though they were emergencies or dangerous personal threats to them. These individuals have difficulties in the adequate expression of anger, which tends to be expressed in a brittle fashion. They often feel unfairly treated and persecuted. They are very sensitive to being controlled, and many have family conflicts and in-law problems. Because they are rigidly moralistic and judgmental, perhaps as a defense against being judged, they tend to be difficult individuals with which to get along. The

Caldwell Report has described this code pattern as the "left-out sibling," in which the individual has felt criticized and judged for not being "good enough" relative to the other siblings. They develop a lifestyle that reflects their inner conflict about needs for approval and acceptance and yet anger at being controlled and judged.

These clients tend to alternate between overcontrol of their feelings and being loud, excitable, irritable, and suspicious and seeming to have a need to continually explain (justify) why they are doing what they are doing. Family history may reveal an overly protective and affectionate mother who disciplined strictly, with a permissive but perhaps uninvolved father.

Both men and women have strong needs to be seen as attractive to the opposite gender. However, deeper intimacy is very frightening to them. These persons seem to fear emotional involvement and keep others at a distance. They are oversensitive to criticism, either open or implied, and have a chronic mistrust. Many also have an exaggerated need for affection.

Difficulties in thinking and concentrating are common, accompanied by perplexity and irritability. When their security is threatened, a grandiose, suspicious, manic-like panic may result, which can be accompanied by violence. This is even more likely if Scales 8 and 4 are also elevated.

Treatment. Argumentative, these clients have great difficulty exploring their intimate feelings with the therapist, perhaps out of fear of being judged. Many use chemical agents as a way of medicating their tension, even if the *MAC–R* scale is not elevated. They tend to be guarded and fear being judged by the therapist. They have strong needs to maintain control over their emotions.

Help them learn how to accept their own anger, which they tend to rationalize. Therapy techniques to help them verbalize anger can help them to become comfortable letting go emotionally in a safe environment. Explore their feelings of having been unfairly treated, and be aware that they may have difficulty expressing criticisms of their caregivers. Techniques to help them recognize situations in their lives where they felt unfairly treated and constantly defined as "not good enough" could help them vent some of their resentments and loosen up their general overcontrol.

These individuals, when slighted or when they feel wronged, can be dangerous in their quest for vengeance. Consequently, any threats should be taken seriously. A therapeutic alliance takes time to develop as these individuals are cautious about developing intimacy. It is important that the therapist not feel defensive when these individuals are critical of the therapist. If the client appears to feel hurt or angry, it is important for the therapist to gain a sense of empathy for how he or she has felt wronged or hurt rather than for the therapist to become defensive. These individuals can get involved in rational explanations of "who did what to whom first." Genuine concern for clients' hurt feelings, as well as helping them engage other situations in which they felt particularly wounded, could be productive in cases where transference issues appear to block therapeutic progress. Engaging these transference issues and having a sense of empathy for the client as a "disfavored" sibling with an understandable hypervigilance for unfairness could lead to rapid therapeutic progress.

698/968 Codes

In addition to the 69/96 characteristics, the addition of Scale 8 to this code pattern predicts confusion; mental perplexity; difficulties in thinking and concentrating; agitation; and possibly periods of intense, angry eruptions and psychotic breaks with reality. Tangential or loose associations are common, as are delusions, paranoid suspiciousness, and hallucinations. When Scale 8 is within 5 *T*-score points of Scale 6, see also 68/86 codes. Look also at the description of the 69/96 code patterns.

Treatment. See also the treatment sections of the 68/86 and 96/69 codes. These individuals may well need antipsychotic medication if there is evidence of florid psychotic thinking. Some may benefit from an anti-manic agent. Hostility will be a primary problem for these individuals, whose confusion, agitation, grandiosity, and paranoia can lead to serious interpersonal difficulties. It will be important for the therapist not to be frightened of the clients' anger, but to be soothing and the opposite of the kind of caregiver conditioning these individuals may have experienced. Look for early caregiver conditioning of being actively put down and disfavored relative to superior siblings, causing these individuals to feel damaged and disposed to "proving themselves."

60/06 Codes

This is a rare code pattern, and consequently little empirical information is available. Greene (1991a, 2000) reported that these individuals see themselves as calm, happy, well-adjusted, and in good physical health. They tend to see themselves as rational, clear thinkers with good judgment and memory. Others see them as honest, reliable, and loyal, although unassuming. They rarely complain of psychological or emotional distress.

As one would expect with a high Scale 0, they are extremely reserved, bashful, and easily embarrassed in social situations. With their elevation on Scale 6, they are extremely sensitive and easily hurt and tend to store rationalized resentments, having difficulties with assertiveness or the confronting of others. Women with this code pattern tend to experience feelings of inferiority about their physical attractiveness.

In elevated profiles, these individuals' sensitivities may shade toward paranoia, with the classic paranoid symptoms of unreasonable jealousy, ideas of reference, and the use of projection and reaction formation as primary defenses. Interestingly, when these individuals become paranoid, they tend not to show the fragmentation of thought processes typically seen with schizophrenia but rather a more fixed, rational paranoia.

Treatment. Look for childhood conditioning experiences of critical or even punitive caregivers who tended to use moral judgment and shaming as a way of controlling the child. These individuals need to be more assertive by articulating their wants and their frustrations, rather than allowing the buildup of rationalized resentments. Typically, they are quite unassertive and their feelings are easily hurt.

They tend to develop many resentments, which get acted out as hurts, silences, and sometimes a quiet, withholding cruelty (which reflects the depth of their hurt). Helping them to verbalize the anger could be an important therapeutic goal. Social skill building and assertiveness training could help in their reality testing. Educate them about how others tend to be insensitive and unaware of people's feelings more often than consciously intending to hurt them. Even though many of these individuals are not psychotic, their reality testing is distorted by their tendency to take things personally. Help them also to come to terms with their shyness, and if time is available, use techniques to help them ventilate anger about unreasonable criticisms they may have experienced in childhood.

Scale 7 (*Pt*)

Spike 7

High scores ($T \geq 65$) and Spike 7 codes are obtained by persons who are tense, anxious, and introspective and who evaluate themselves negatively to such a degree that it leaves them with feelings of insecurity, inadequacy, inferiority, and guilt. Typically, they lack self-confidence, are indecisive, and suffer from a constant sense of apprehensiveness. As Scale 7 is elevated, the person is increasingly likely to be rigid, self-critical, and perfectionistic and to show obsessive or compulsive patterns.

Moderately high scores (T = 55–65) scores in the absence of a significant *K* elevation would describe an individual who takes life seriously and who is prone to worry, with occasional anxious episodes, especially if stressors accumulate. Some people may exhibit obsessive–compulsive traits that are not debilitating or disorganizing. Others may exhibit specific fears and phobias. Moderately high scores in the presence of a significant *K* addition suggest an individual whose anxieties, fears, or phobias would be well contained and ego-syntonic.

Moderately low scores (T = 35–45) reflect an individual who is relaxed, comfortable, and without emotional distress. Most are self-confident and adaptable and are generally efficient and capable, although others may see them as unmotivated or undisciplined because of the lack of overt anxiety.

Treatment. Scale 7 is often the most frequent high point on profiles of individuals in college counseling centers. Typically, Scales 2 and 8 are also elevated (see 278/872 codes). It is important to examine the relative elevations of Scales 7 and 8. If Scale 7 is higher than Scale 8, especially if by 10 or more *T*-score points, the individual has a better prognosis than when Scale 8 is higher. If Scale 8 is significantly higher than Scale 7, the mental confusion and alienation evidenced by Scale 8 is more ego-syntonic. For example, in a videotape by the Caldwell Report, Alex Caldwell illustrated how Jeffrey Dahmer's MMPI was notable in that Scale 8 was significantly elevated but without any corresponding significant elevation on Scale 7. The psychotic-like thought processes suggested by the elevation on Scale 8 were apparently not leading to any great anxiety, a prognostically bad sign.

With Scale 7 elevations, look for childhood experiences in which the person experienced either a series of unpredictable negative events or a traumatic unpredictable event. In some cases, these individuals were sensitive and easily frightened children who were conscientious, responsible, and easily felt guilty.

Spike 7 codes are one of the easiest to deal with therapeutically because these individuals follow therapeutic advice and tend to be disciplined about the work of therapy. They tend to be honest and guilt prone. Relaxation training, self-esteem building, thought stopping, and catharsis all can be useful. Helping them deal with the guilt that is usually associated with the expression of anger would also be an important therapeutic strategy. Also help these individuals deal with their fears of failure and the resulting expectations of shame.

In unelevated profiles with Scale 7 significantly below $T = 50$, the task is essentially the reverse. Help these individuals develop a better sense of timeliness, and find ways to raise their level of anxiety so that they are more organized and efficient.

Relations With Other Scales

71/17 Codes (See 17/71 Codes)
72/27 Codes (See 27/72 Codes)
73/37 Codes (See 37/73 Codes)
74/47 Codes (See 47/74 Codes)
75/57 Codes (See 57/75 Codes)
76/67 Codes (See 67/76 Codes)

78/87 Codes

This code is frequent among individuals in acute psychological turmoil who are seeking psychological help, and Scale 2 or 4 is most often the next highest scale. (See 278/728 and 478/748 codes when Scale 2 or 4 is within 5 *T*-score points of Scale 8.) Persons with 78 and 87 codes are divided evenly between psychotic and neurotic diagnoses. In adults, when Scale 8 is higher than Scale 7, the likelihood of acute psychosis is greater.

Individuals with this code are filled with worry, anxiety, tension, and excessive rumination. Their excessive introspection and overideation may appear confused as well as highly emotional. They are unable to think or concentrate efficiently, and their distress is so great that insomnia and suicidal thoughts are highly likely. Suicidal potential should be evaluated. When Scale 8 is higher than Scale 7, suicide attempts are often bizarre and involve self-mutilation. Some individuals with this code show hallucinations or delusions, flat affect, and clear difficulties in maintaining reality contact. Some are preoccupied with health problems and report multiple somatic complaints. Others show notable impairment of functioning, but without psychotic behaviors.

Lacking in confidence, they are shy and feel inadequate and interpersonally sensitive, particularly where heterosexual relations are concerned. Poor sexual performance often occurs because of the excessive anxiety. Typically conscientious, their fears and excessive worry often lead them to have only mediocre or poor achievement. Many drink excessively in order to relax.

Although there are many similarities in the 78/87 code pattern, persons with 78 codes are less likely to show psychotic breaks, even though they are described as anxious, obsessive–compulsive, and schizoid. As expected from the Scale 7 elevation, they are extremely anxious and may show depersonalization and isolation from affect. They have a profoundly negative self-image. They are constantly "on edge," as if anticipating a disaster, and are extremely quick to feel criticized, judged, or somehow defective relative to others. Both 78 and 87 codes reflect a deep sense of being fundamentally damaged, and these persons appear to be constantly apprehensive that somehow they are going to be "discovered" and humiliated because of their perceived defects. Persons with 87 codes will show more psychotic-like symptoms and an even greater fixed belief that they are somehow damaged and defective. These individuals have such a strongly held belief that there is something "wrong with them" that a therapeutic relationship is difficult.

Treatment. Look for childhood histories of having been teased or put down, sexually abused, and having been somewhat immature and slow to develop. They may have been sickly or may have evidenced personal eccentricities, which left them vulnerable to being teased or put down by siblings or peers.

If Scale 4 is coded third, the sense of alienation is even greater, as is the possibility of impulsive acting out to reduce tension. If Scale 6 is coded third, these individuals are even more fearful of exposing their vulnerabilities in case they are somehow attacked and judged for being "defective." Young 78/87 adults often experience severe difficulties in college because of the problems they experience in emancipating from home. Their low self-esteem appears to give them little resilience in developing new supportive social relations outside their home environment.

Therapeutic strategies for this code pattern center on dealing with anger and self-esteem issues. Anger is often blocked because of the guilt and fear of rejection these people experience in expressing it. Assertiveness training, thought stopping, self-esteem building, and catharsis, especially around early childhood experiences of having been humiliated or put down, could all be a productive focus in therapy.

Psychotropic medication could be very helpful. It will be important to evaluate and monitor suicide risk in these codes.

79/97 Codes

This relatively uncommon code most often has Scale 8 or 4 as the next highest scale in the profile. These persons are anxious to the point of agitation. They are fearful, continually worried, overreact to events, and find it difficult to relax or to rid themselves of their almost constant rumination about their fears and inadequacies. Muscle spasms, backaches, and insomnia may also be present, reflecting their extreme tension. Some may complain of depression even if Scale 2 is not elevated, perhaps reflecting the emotional exhaustion that results from the constant anxiety and apprehensiveness.

Adolescents with this code appear to have strong needs for attention but fear losing control over themselves should they let go. Dependence–independence conflicts appear to be involved for these teenagers.

Treatment. The central issue for this code pattern is a profound fear of failure. Look for childhood conditioning experiences of disapproval and caregivers who demanded a great deal of achievement but were not rewarding enough. Conceptually, think of these individuals as having great needs to prove themselves and demanding perfection from themselves but at the same time constantly observing themselves to see how inadequate they are and how others could criticize them for their inadequacies. Consequently, they often approach life in an extremely defensive manner, extolling their virtues and preemptively protecting themselves against criticism. It is as if they oscillate between grandiosity and self-negation.

Self-esteem building, thought stopping, and relaxation training can be helpful. Implosion therapy also may be useful for these individuals to help them deal with their "worst fear" around failure and being publicly rejected "in shame" because of their failures. Usually, stories involved in the implosion therapy will center on fears of failure and resulting rejection.

70/07 Codes (See Also Scales 7 and 0)

This is an uncommon code, with Scale 2 or 8 as the third most often highest scale. Particularly when Scales 2 and 8 are within 5 *T*-score points of Scale 0 or 7, it is helpful to examine the two-point code that would result if Scale 0 were ignored temporarily.

Men with this code are shy, worried, and tense and feel inadequate regarding social skills and/or physical appearance. Many are introverted to the point of almost being nonverbal. Their lack of confidence and indecisiveness leaves them feeling confused, overcontrolled, and guilty. Their ruminations result in insomnia. Many had strong home conflicts centering on assertiveness or issues of dependence–independence, particularly with their mothers.

Women with this code show the same pattern as do men only if Scale 5 is below $T = 40$. Otherwise their problems are less severe but nonetheless center on issues of lack of confidence, self-consciousness, feelings of physical unattractiveness or inferiority, social insecurity, and difficulties in establishing comfortable relations with members of the opposite gender.

Treatment. Look for a childhood of having felt profoundly shy, with resulting fears of being teased or humiliated. Thought stopping, relaxation training, self-esteem building, social skill building, and even implosion therapy can help reduce their anxiety and self-doubts. Supportive, nonconfrontive therapy, as well as helping them learn to express anger without guilt, could be a useful therapeutic strategy.

Scale 8 (*Sc*)

Scale 8 elevations generally predict low self-esteem, difficulties with communication and the expression of anger, and difficulties with trust and intimacy.

Extremely high scores ($T \geq 85$) more often reflect acute situational stress or a severe identity crisis rather than the more chronic thought disturbances (such as in schizophrenia) indicated by scores in the $T = 70$–85 range. The indecision and mental confusion found in cases with such a markedly elevated Scale 8 is often dramatic and requires providing clear structure and support for the person to reduce the confusion being experienced.

Spike 8

Very high scores (T = 75–85) and Spike 8 codes reflect individuals who feel alienated and who are having difficulty in thinking clearly. They are unconventional in thought and action, perhaps even socially deviant, and are reluctant to become involved deeply in interpersonal relations. They have basic and disturbing concerns about who they are and where they fit in the world and basically feel that they do not belong. These individuals tend to feel somehow broken or damaged and therefore unlovable and lacking some essential ingredient of humanness that would allow them, like others, to become comfortable relating on an intimate level.

Difficulties in clearly communicating are likely and are due to their negatively self-absorbed preoccupation and intrusive or disorganized thoughts that interfere with clear and logical thinking. Although these people may give the appearance of being in reasonable reality contact, their conversations often have a quality of being just slightly off the mark. If the K scale is elevated so that much of the Scale 8 elevation is a result of K contribution, the person will have many areas of compensated and efficient functioning. Even so, the underlying negative self-image and difficulties with intimacy will still be a problem, and their problems will be manifested as subtle difficulties with closeness and communication.

High scores (T = 65–75) indicate persons who feel somewhat cutoff and distant from others and who feel uncomfortable with many interpersonal relations. Often their thinking is unconventional, focused on abstract or theoretical issues (such as the "meaning" of some aspect of life), and contains elements of dissatisfaction with themselves, others, and/or social values. If the Scale 8 element is largely due to the K addition, subtle signs of a negative self-image may be evidenced, but without any gross thought disturbance.

Low scores to very low scores ($T \leq 45$) are obtained by persons who generally are practical, conventional, and conservative in their behaviors and in their approach to life and who spend little effort in introspection or philosophical contemplation. Usually, these persons are conforming, responsible, dependable, and cautious but may also be unimaginative or even rigid.

Treatment. Conceptually, think of Scale 8 as reflecting the individual's poor sense of self-esteem and sense of feeling lovable by those for whom the individual cares. Consequently, elevations on Scale 8 suggest childhood conditioning experiences of being treated with hostility, perhaps even cruelty, and dislike. In behavioral terms, being treated with hostility by one's caretakers will lead not only to a tendency to treat others with hostility but also to other problems, such as sexuality and aggression confusion and a tendency to lash out when one feels vulnerable.

These individuals typically have many ways to keep others at a distance. In the normal to moderately elevated ranges, the therapist may notice individuals breaking the flow of conversation through a distancing remark, which usually occurs when they feel threatened or vulnerable or even when they are beginning to feel a sense of emotional connection. This self-protective distancing may reflect their fears that closeness can lead to rejection.

Scale 8 elevations suggest staying away from unstructured insight-oriented or psychodynamic kinds of therapies. These individuals need structure. They have difficulties "reading" others' emotions, which also suggests difficulties with empathy in their close relations. In the therapeutic relationship, they are prone to ruminate about the therapist's negative feelings toward them and can feel judged and painfully exposed if asked to explore painful childhood memories. Reparenting therapies from mothering-type therapists are most useful, providing they are done in a context of structure. Self-esteem building and cognitive restructuring are useful.

Relations With Other Scales

81/18 Codes (See 18/81 Codes)
82/28 Codes (See 28/82 Codes)
83/38 Codes (See 38/83 Codes)
84/48 Codes (See 48/84 Codes)
85/58 Codes (See 58/85 Codes)
86/68 Codes (See 68/86 Codes)
87/78 Codes (See 78/87 Codes)

89/98 Codes

Typically, the validity pattern with this code reveals low *L* and *K* scores with an elevated *F* scale, suggesting a candid, honest approach to the test questions against a backdrop of feelings of inferiority, inadequacy, low self-esteem, and a disorganized, manic thought process. Consequently, it is not surprising that this code primarily represents individuals with serious psychopathology, particularly with adults.

These persons are highly overideational and spend a great deal of time in fantasy, daydreams, and rumination. Tension, agitation, and insomnia may be present. Increased speech, behavioral restlessness, emotional lability, and flight of ideas are likely. In interpersonal situations, such as therapy sessions, they are highly distractible, jumping from topic to topic. Thus, therapeutic focusing is hindered because these persons seldom stay on a topic long enough to come to grips with it.

Discomfort in interpersonal relations is typical, most often involving those of the opposite gender. Poor heterosexual adjustment is likely. Most of these individuals are fearful of, and avoid, close interpersonal relations and distrust others' motives. Often they also have a history of high-achievement aspirations but show mediocre achievement. They are particularly likely to become disorganized under stress. As this code becomes more elevated, the likelihood increases that delusions and hallucinations (particularly of a religious nature) will occur and that a frankly psychotic picture will emerge. This code occurs more frequently in persons younger than age 27, and most often Scale 4, 7, or 6 is the next highest scale.

Clients with this profile experience episodes during which they are confused, hostile, demanding, manic, and panicky, as well as circumstantial. Talkative and high-strung, they are hard to follow and many can show paranoid ideation, which may be both persecutory and expansive with a religious content. Because they are extremely perfectionistic, any failures tend to be experienced as disastrous. Setbacks tend to be experienced by them as confirming their negative self-image.

They tend to be very self-critical and easily knocked off balance by rejection, especially from members of the opposite gender. The profile is often associated with an identity crisis, usually precipitated by a sexual rejection, with fears of being somehow damaged or fears that they are homosexual. Their heterosexual difficulties relate more to feelings of insecurity and inferiority rather than to difficulties with sexuality, per se.

Treatment. Individuals with this profile tend to be ambitious with high-achievement goals. They tend to be competitive with their siblings and easily feel inferior in comparing themselves with their siblings' successes. Look for childhood histories of feeling put down and disfavored relative to other siblings. Typically, these individuals are middle children. Precipitating circumstances are usually some kind of perceived failure or rejection, which throws them into a manic episode, perhaps with psychotic features, reflecting the person's deep underlying negative self-image. Medication is often necessary to deal with the agitation and mania and to help "glue" them back together. Look to see if they are using drugs and alcohol as a way of medicating themselves.

In therapy, these individuals develop a rapid transference, with strong demands on the therapist, perhaps recapitulating childhood yearnings to be favored and so undo their experience of feeling put down or disfavored. Self-esteem building in a structured environment would be an appropriate goal of therapy. These individuals have a very fixed negative self-image and strong desires to achieve and succeed but at the same time fear that they are unable to do so. Supportive, reparenting-type therapy, as well as reality-based therapies that could help them develop realistic goals for themselves, could also be useful.

80/08 Codes

Markedly aloof and socially withdrawn, these persons are very uncomfortable in interpersonal relations and avoid social interaction. They tend to spend a great deal of time in personal fantasy, and their social isolation tends to be so great that they often are alienated even from their own families. They tend to describe themselves as mildly depressed and anxious, and most report anhedonia. They describe their family life as conflicted and unsatisfying and report having trouble making decisions because they worry that others will be critical about the decisions they have made. They are easily frightened and many are phobic. Extremely uncomfortable in any type of social setting, they tend to give up easily when frustrated and avoid conflict whenever possible. Typically, they also feel worried, indecisive, anxious, and misunderstood by others. They often feel confused about what is bothering them or what they want (or expect) from others, and they lack assertiveness. In counseling sessions, they are likely to be largely nonverbal.

If a third scale is elevated within 5 *T*-score points of Scale 8 or 0, it is often helpful to ignore temporarily the elevation of Scale 0 and to interpret any two-point code that results. Scale 7 or 2 is most often the third highest scale elevation in this code pattern.

Treatment. Because they generally are nonverbal, psychotherapeutic relationships are initially difficult. The therapist must be patient and not push too hard, as they may interpret the pushing as hostile. Gentle, supportive esteem-building psychotherapy, along with assertiveness training and social skill training, could be useful once a therapeutic alliance is developed. These clients are sensitive to anything that could be construed as criticism or impatience. Establishing rapport could perhaps be done by asking them general questions about their ideas, what they enjoy, and their personal habits, being careful to not appear critical or "looking for what's wrong." These individuals tend to be so emotionally and socially isolated that they do not have the basic skills of relating; thus, even rudimentary rapport building could be therapeutic for them.

Scale 9 (*Ma*)

High scores ($T \geq 65$) are obtained by persons who are energetic, expansive, and emotionally excitable and who have high levels of both psychic energy and physical energy. Many of these people have an unusual capacity for sustained activity and effort, although as the scores surpass $T = 75$, the efforts more often become fragmented and scattered rather than organized. Along with their excess of energy, these people frequently take on more projects than they can complete. Generally they seem quite happy when they are so busy (sometimes euphoric) and may become depressed when their activities are constrained or if they feel in any way thwarted in their goal activity. In some persons, however, the energy is expressed more as tension, hyperactivity, self-centeredness, and irritability. In the extreme, these persons show clear verbosity, grandiosity, and difficulties in controlling or inhibiting their thoughts from becoming actions. This may represent efforts to ward off an impending depression.

Spike 9

Spike 9 clients are characterized as classic manic types. These individuals tend to be excitable, overproductive with pressured speech, superficially warm alongside a hostile joking humor, and quick-tempered. They can become overcommitted to many tasks and activities, many of which they are unable to complete. Reduced sleep, with reports of feeling "fine," would not be unusual. Typically, these individuals have drug and/or alcohol problems and this is often reflected by elevations on the *MAC–R* scale.

Moderately high scores ($T = 60–65$) suggest an energetic, outgoing, and active person who is likely seen by others as pleasant and efficient. Scores in this range are typical for college or postgraduate students because the energy level reflected in these scale scores is more commonly found among younger persons with high aspirations. Persons with scores in this range usually focus on their achievements to gain recognition and status and tend to be rather independent in thought and action.

Low scores to very low scores ($T \leq 45$) suggest a low energy level, lack of drive, listlessness, or even apathy. Although this may simply reflect temporary fatigue or illness, more often these low scores indicate a person who usually has low energy. Often these individuals are lacking in self-confidence and have reduced goals for themselves. Many find it difficult to expend extra effort on virtually any project. A very low score on Scale 9 ($T < 35$) suggests depression, even when Scale 2 is not markedly elevated. It should be noted, however, that Scale 9 scores decrease as persons get older, apparently reflecting normal aging processes. A low Scale 9 in a person younger than age 45 is unusual, and the causes should be explored further. In a normal-range profile, such a low Scale 9 score may reflect some medical problem and a physical exam is suggested.

As Scale 9 is elevated, individuals appear increasingly committed to their beliefs and tend to feel that they see more than others see. They have a sense of purpose and a grandiosity, which makes it hard to relate to them. Some control an underlying paranoia with feelings that others are trying to "hold them back" and that others are not "cooperating" in their many ideas. These individuals need a great deal of approval and tend to extol their own virtues. They are very self-focused and sensitive to being controlled, and resent any suggestion of control.

Treatment. Look for childhood histories of being dominated by caregivers who were either always motivating the child for greater successes and/or were attempting to control the child. Many of these individuals internalized their caregiver values and expectations and consequently have high needs for success. They are very ambitious and tend to become upset by any losses that limit their achievement potential. Medication often is needed in the presence of a clear manic episode.

Typically, the imminence of an achievement failure often is the precipitating event for the disturbance. They tend to be difficult to interview because of their lack of focus, denial, and evasiveness. They tend to see themselves as special or different from others, so it is hard to develop a therapeutic alliance. Give them a great deal of praise for their quick thinking, their abilities to see the connections between things, and their apparent intelligence. They tend to respond well to approval, and it is often of great importance to them to be seen as intelligent.

Once a therapeutic alliance has been established, help them develop more reasonable goals, and help them differentiate between their own wants and the internalized expectations of their caregivers and others. Also help them control their impulses and their tendency to switch careers and goals. The development of self-esteem and dealing with their fear of failure are primary goals of therapy.

Relations With Other Scales

High 9, High K Codes

When Scale 9 and the *K* scale are both above $T = 65$ (particularly if Scale 2 is below $T = 50$), these persons tend to be energetic, organized, managerial types, whose planning and organization prompt others to defer authority to them. These individuals often are excellent administrators, although some tend to be particularly autocratic or power oriented; ambiguity, indecision, or uncertainty are difficult for them to tolerate. They feel uncomfortable when they are not in control or in situations in which they feel uninformed or in which there is a lack of structure. Many of these individuals are highly competitive. As the *K* scale increases above *T* = 65, the likelihood increases that they feel driven to organize their lives and those around them and that to appear dependent, submissive, emotional, or out of control of situations would be extremely threatening and uncomfortable for them. Many reassure themselves by controlling and requiring others to be submissive and "in their place." Fundamentally, these individuals are basically insecure, clinging tenaciously to roles and appearances. In women, one may see additionally an almost exhibitionistic emphasis on physical attractiveness (particularly if Scale 5 is below *T* = 40) as an attempt at self-reassurance and control over others.

Treatment. The elevated *K* scale reflects overcontrol and difficulties with being emotionally expressive. Consequently, denial and evasiveness would be even greater in this profile than in a pure 9, low *K* individual. The therapist will have to multiply the intensity of what the individual is saying in order to get a sense of empathy for him or her. Help them see how their energy and organized efficiency are great assets, but also help them see that others do not have their level of energy and that their perfectionism and driven ambition may come across to others as demandingness and criticalness. By helping them accept that they are somehow "different" in terms of their energy level, they may be able to relax enough to develop some empathy for others. They are not aware of how their competitiveness and subtle bragging reflect intense needs for approval. Self-esteem building therapies, if the therapist approves of them so that clients can relax enough to be "in the moment," can be useful in helping them slow down.

91/19 Codes (See 19/91 Codes)
92/29 Codes (See 29/92 Codes)
93/39 Codes (See 39/93 Codes)
94/49 Codes (See 49/94 Codes)
95/59 Codes (See 59/95 Codes)
96/69 Codes (See 69/96 Codes)
97/79 Codes (See 79/97 Codes)
98/89 Codes (See 89/98 Codes)

90/09 Codes

This code is uncommon. Individuals with this code pattern describe themselves as being happy and well-adjusted, in good physical health, and experiencing few pains or physical discomforts. They tend not to be depressed and are often elated and excitable individuals. However, they also tend to be socially shy and withdrawn, even though they have adequate social skills. As one would expect with a Scale 9 elevation, they are described as egocentric and self-confident and can occasionally be grandiose. Sometimes these individuals are described as shy initially. However, once comfortable in a new social situation, the manic features may manifest themselves so that they then are described as energetic and dominant.

Often it is helpful with this code to ignore initially the elevated Scale 0 and then to interpret any two-point code that may result. Then use the elevated Scale 0 to modify the interpretation as necessary.

Treatment. See treatment section under the Spike 9 codes. Social skill building may also be useful.

Scale 0 (*Si*)

Spike 0

High scores ($T \geq 65$) and Spike 0 codes reflect a preference for being alone rather than with others, particularly if no other scale is elevated above $T = 65$. Elevations on Scale 0 above $T = 65$ suggest a person who is shy, interpersonally uncomfortable, insecure, introverted, and submissive. As the score approaches $T = 75$, this scale also suggests an absence of social supports, perhaps even an aloofness to a schizoid degree, and an enduring problem in establishing meaningful attachments with others. These characteristics are particularly striking with adolescents because they more often score low on Scale 0.

Moderately high scores ($T = 55$–65) may simply indicate a temperament style of being self-contained, autonomous, and quite adaptive in situations (e.g., college) requiring sustained periods of solitary activities.

Elevations of Scale 0 tend to reduce the likelihood of acting out indicated by other scale elevations (e.g., Scales 4 and 9) but may exacerbate the ruminations or self-absorption indicated by, for example, Scale 2, 7, or 8.

Moderately low to very low scores ($T \leq 45$) are obtained by persons who prefer generally to be with others and not by themselves. Most often they are outgoing, gregarious, friendly, and enthusiastic and have strong needs for affiliation, social recognition, and status. When scores are below $T = 35$, their social aggressiveness may prompt others to view them as opportunistic, manipulative, shallow, superficial, and even flighty. Impulse control problems may be present if Scales 4 and 9 are even mildly elevated, even though the low Scale 0 suggests a socialized veneer for their impulsive behaviors.

Usually, Spike 0 persons do not seek treatment for their shyness. Most often they have become accustomed to their level of shyness and are accepting of it. In situations in which shyness is a problem, social skill building, self-esteem building, and relaxation training therapies are most useful.

Relations With Other Scales

01/10 Codes (See 10/01 Codes)

02/20 Codes (See 20/02 Code)

03/30 Codes (See 30/03 Codes)
04/40 Codes (See 40/04 Codes)
05/50 Codes (See 50/05 Codes)
06/60 Codes (See 60/06 Codes)
07/70 Codes (See 70/07 Codes)
08/80 Codes (See 80/08 Codes)
09/90 Codes (See 90/09 Codes)

NORMAL CODE, HIGH *K* (*K*+)

The *K*+ profile for (Marks et al., 1974) is quite common in outpatient settings among people of upper SES and does not suggest the extent of psychopathology reflected by a similar profile in an inpatient setting. In an inpatient setting, this profile reflects a highly controlled, denying individual whose underlying psychological problems are suppressed.

On the basis of the new norms, the following adjustments to the Marks et al. (1974) rules are suggested. Research is needed to support these modifications. In inpatient settings the following criteria must be met: F must be below $T = 65$, L and K must be greater than F, six or more of the clinical scales must be below $T = 56$, and $K - F$ must be greater than 5 T-score points.

This profile often is produced by persons who are highly defensive about admitting psychological problems, which they view as personal weaknesses. Usually, they avoid situations in which their own performance might be compared unfavorably with others and are generally cautious, anxious, and inhibited. They are particularly influenced by others' evaluations of them and, as a result, are easily dominated, led, or controlled. Withdrawn from others, they often are seen as suspicious and fearful, with a strong schizoid component to their personality.

Whether as an inpatient or outpatient, these individuals need *K*-lowering therapies that help them become aware of their feelings. Once rapport has developed, help them ventilate and role-play, expressing anger, sadness, and even joy, so as to lower their overcontrol.

7

Interpreting the Content of the MMPI–2: Critical Items, Content Scales, and Subscales

CRITICAL ITEMS

The empirical keying or contrasted-groups methodology used by Hathaway in developing the eight basic clinical scales of the MMPI represented a significant innovation in personality inventory construction. Previous inventories relied on intuitive judgment to produce items related to a trait of interest and to combine them with other items thought to be related to the same trait to compose a scale. The items and scales thus composed tended to be highly face valid (i.e., the items tended to be obviously related to the trait to be measured). Unfortunately, they were often unsatisfactorily related to external criteria and were overly vulnerable to test-taking attitudes of the examinee that would bias responses and potentially distort the results of testing.

The new approach required only that items selected for inclusion differentiate between normal and abnormal criterion groups empirically. The authors of the MMPI gave little consideration to the content of individual items and were concerned only that the breadth of coverage for the original item pool was sufficient to sample a wide array of attitudes and behaviors. The justification for the new empirical strategy was provided in the classic manifesto of Meehl (1945a), "The Dynamics of 'Structured' Personality Tests."

In the decades following the release of the MMPI, clinical needs and advances in psychometric theory and methods have seen a return to attaching greater importance to test item content. The "dust-bowl empiricist" rationale for proscribing the examination of item content in the clinic was succinctly stated by Meehl (1945b): "The scoring does not assume a valid self-rating to have been given" (p. 147). But studies demonstrating comparable validities for personality assessment instruments developed under both rational and empirical strategies (Hase & Goldberg, 1967), and the appearance of sophisticated positions defending the importance of test item content (Goldberg & Slovic, 1967; Jackson, 1971), were instrumental in moderating Meehl's (1945) earlier position (Meehl, 1971, 1972). These developments were predated, however, by the needs of clinicians to explore the new inventory as part of and prelude to acquiring proficiency in its use and the pressing demands of clinical work to understand patients under investigation.

Caldwell (1991) has pointed out that the basic elements of the MMPI that are subject to interpretation may be located on a gradient of increasing obviousness or transparency, with the (a) the subtle components of the clinical scales and certain additional scales (e.g., *K* and, perhaps, *Mf*), (b) certain highly subtle empirically derived scales (e.g., *MAC/MAC–R* and *O-H*), and (c) the basic clinical scales having subtle components corresponding to three initial steps of this gradient. Intermediate steps would include empirically derived scales more generally, including the more obvious of the basic clinical scales. Still more obvious would be the obvious components of the basic clinical scales and scales whose developmental methodology emphasized internal consistency standards, such as the Wiggins' and MMPI–2 content scales. The top-most steps in this gradient would include scales composed of items with unusually low endorsement rates, such as *F* and *FB* scales, and the so-called critical items. It should not be surprising that the growth in the appreciation of test item content and its potential importance in the clinic should have originated with the distinction to which Wiener and Harmon (Wiener, 1948; Wiener & Harmon, 1946) called attention, between subtle and obvious content, and critical items.

Initially, clinicians sought access to the patient's responses to certain items thought to be clearly indicative of psychopathological disturbance. Grayson (1951) gathered a set of 38 items for use with a VA population. Endorsement of any of these items in the course of psychodiagnostic evaluation was considered sufficient to warrant more detailed clinical inquiry into the content area of the item, regardless of whether the MMPI profile appeared pathological. In some cases, these items were considered pathognomonic of a condition, such as delusions or suicidal ideation. In others, the item would serve as a red flag or a *stop sign*, forcing an interruption of the diagnostic process in order to explore the patient's grounds for its endorsement. These items thus came to be called *stop* or *critical items*. The history of critical items actually goes back to the Woodworth (1920) Personal Data Sheet, which included 10 "neurotic tendency items." These items were considered indicators of neurosis, regardless of the remainder of the individual's responses.

Although the Grayson items were widely adopted (Gravitz, 1968), particularly after being reprinted in *An MMPI Handbook* (Dahlstrom & Welsh, 1960), alert practitioners soon discovered that this group of items was overwhelmingly redundant with the *F* and *Sc* scales. Eighty-five percent (32/38) of these items were scored on one or both scales, 40% (16 items) on the *F* scale alone (Koss, 1979). Moreover, for 92% (35/38) of the items, the keyed response was "true." Thus, however salient the content of the individual items might be as a springboard for investigation within the interview, it became clear that the Grayson items placed undue stress on psychoticism, to the exclusion of other problem areas; that these items, like the *F* scale itself, were sensitive to gross deviancy and to a set on the patient's part to exaggerate or conceal psychological complaints; and that they were also vulnerable to an acquiescent response style, the inclination to mark items "true," regardless of their content.

Another set of critical items was selected by Caldwell (1969). Seeking a broader range of content, Caldwell chose 68 items, distributed among nine categories. As a set, the Caldwell critical items covered a wider range of problem areas than the Grayson items. Nevertheless, although not quite so dominated by psychoticism, with 56% (38/68) of the items overlapping the *F* and *Sc* scales (20 items, or 29%, on the *F* scale alone), these items remain relatively saturated with this source of variance (Friedman, Webb, & Lewak, 1989). These shortcomings were in addition to the greatest concern of all: that the Grayson and Caldwell critical items, with their origins in the rational–intuitive processes of their creators, had no demonstrated empirical relationships with the symptoms and complaints they enunciated. Critiques by Greene (1980) and R. G. Evans (1984) noted the occurrence of the Grayson and Caldwell critical items in normal groups, and other contradictory evidence for their validity.

Seeking to address the external validity of critical items, Lachar and Wrobel (1979) investigated the empirical correlates of a large number of items, including those appearing in the Grayson and Caldwell lists, nominated by clinicians as relevant to 14 common problem areas for psychiatric in- and outpatients. Lachar and Wrobel ultimately settled on 111 items, distributed into 11 content areas, of which 99 items achieved significant (.05) correlations with counterpart information on problems recorded in patient files; the remaining 12 items achieved acceptable correlations with closely related criteria.

An alternative approach was taken by Koss and Butcher (1973; Koss, Butcher, & Hoffmann, 1976) to ensure empirical correlates for critical items by identifying six crisis situations, each marked by a set of behaviors or complaints exhibited by patients at the time of their admission to the hospital. After defining the crisis group, Koss and Butcher asked clinicians to identify MMPI items that corresponded to the behaviors and complaints characteristic of each of the groups. Nominated items were then cross-validated on newly admitted patients, with noncrisis psychiatric patients serving as controls.

Despite the different methods used to develop the Lachar–Wrobel, Caldwell, and Koss–Butcher critical item sets, Table 7.1 suggests a high degree of similarity in the content of the items for each set, as well as roughly comparable areas of coverage. Each critical item list references distress and dysphoria, cognitive disruption, psychotic ideation, and substance abuse. (See Table A6 for the MMPI–2 items and scoring direction for the Koss–Butcher, Lachar–Wrobel, and Nichols critical item lists.)

A fourth list was developed by Nichols (1989) when he found many of the Lachar–Wrobel critical items categories insufficiently homogeneous and those of Caldwell and those of Koss and Butcher insufficiently numerous. For example, in his consultations for a neurologist, he wanted to be able to specify the kinds of somatic

TABLE 7.1

A Comparison of the Content Contained Within Three Sets of Critical Items

Lachar–Wrobel		*Caldwell*		*Koss–Butcher*	
Content Category	*No. Of Items (MMPI/ MMPI–2)*	*Content Category*	*No. Of Items (MMPI/ MMPI–2)*	*Content Category*	*No. Of Items (MMPI/ MMPI–2)*
Psychological discomfort					
Anxiety and tension	11/11			Acute anxiety	9/17
Depression and worry	16/16	Distress and depression	11/11	Depressed–suicidal Ideation	25/22
Sleep Disturbance	6/6	Suicidal thoughts	5/5		
Reality distortion					
Deviant beliefs	15/15	Ideas of reference, persecution, and delusions	10/1	Persecutory ideas	12/11
Deviant thinking and experience	11/10	Peculiar experience and hallucinations	9/9	Mental confusion	3/11
Characterological adjustment					
Substance abuse	4/3	Alcohol and drugs	4/3	Situational stress due to alcoholism	15/7
Antisocial attitude	9/9	Authority problems	5/5		
Family conflict	4/4	Family discord	7/7		
Problematic anger	4/4			Threatened assault	3/5
Sexual concern and deviation	8/6	Sexual difficulties	7/6		
Somatic symptoms	23/23	Somatic concerns	10/10		

complaints endorsed more precisely, both in terms of their specific content and in terms of the proportion of items endorsed within a specific content area, such as motor difficulties or genitourinary complaints. He was also discontented with the inclusion of items in categories implicating psychotic mentation that might reflect only "unusual" culturally based beliefs and experiences. For example, the item "Evil spirits possess me at times," although frequently scored on scales highly saturated with psychoticism (e.g., *F*, *Pa*, and *BIZ*) and potentially endorsed as an acknowledgment of the kind of hallucinatory or other anomalous experience common to psychotic states, may also be endorsed at relatively high frequency by members of certain religious sects or immigrants from countries wherein a belief in spirits, evil and otherwise, is more common than in the United States. Nichols therefore devised a new set of items based on both rational and statistical considerations. Categories were initially selected from large-scale item factor analyses on a very large Midwestern psychiatric sample. These categories were then refined by subdividing many of the somatic factors into more discrete classes of symptoms by eliminating categories that essentially duplicated the content of normed scales, such as fears and phobias, and by examining patterns of item overlap among content scales and the Caldwell, Koss–Butcher, and Lachar–Wrobel lists. Because of their established validity characteristics, virtually all of the items in the Koss–Butcher and Lachar–Wrobel sets were retained on the Nichols Critical Item List (NCIL). More than any of the alternative critical items lists, the NCIL permits a more specific assessment of both the range and the intensity of symptomatic expressions, particularly within the health/ somatic/neurological area. The NCIL for the MMPI–2 contains 217 items spread over four major classes and 23 specific item clusters.

Of the two chief controversies surrounding the use of critical items, one is conceptual, the other statistical. The conceptual issue is whether inventory items should be considered behavior samples or behavioral signs. According to Koss (1979), the earliest inventories viewed item responses as veridical self-reports or samples of behavior that could stand in lieu of actual interview or observational data, thereby providing a more efficient basis for clinical description. It was in part in reaction to this view, and the disappointing performance of previous inventories guided by it, that Hathaway chose to adopt an empirical approach to the composition on his scales. Abandoning the assignment of items to scales on the basis of judgments a priori, Hathaway left between-groups differences in endorsement frequency to identify each item as a sign of the criterion group, its significance to be determined by further investigation. Meehl's (1945b) enunciation of the empirical rationale emphasized the range of understandings various people might bring to test items and stressed the fact that a given statement was endorsed over the content of the statement itself. In his words, the empirical approach "consists simply in the explicit denial that we accept a self-rating as a feeble surrogate for a behavior sample, and substitutes the assertion that a 'self-rating' constitutes an intrinsically interesting and significant bit of verbal behavior, the nontest correlates of which must be discovered by empirical means" (Meehl, 1945, p. 297). According to Meehl (1945), the importance of a structured inventory response is not so much in its intrinsic semantic characteristics, its "face value," but the fact that certain kinds of people "tend to *say* certain things about themselves" (p. 298).

An unqualified allegiance to the sign approach would obviate the need for selection in gathering candidate items for the pool; any items would do. In their decision to formulate items out of their *clinical* experience, from psychiatric textbooks and interview forms and from previous personality and attitude scales, Hathaway and McKinley implicitly offered a bow to the traditional view. Their departure from it came only after the item pool was established, with the commencement of scale construction. As a result, most of the basic clinical scales of the MMPI are made up of a mix of items, some seeming to function more as samples, others apparently operating as signs. Dahlstrom (1969) called attention to this range in the way items may be understood, and his distinctions tend to parallel the distinction between obvious and subtle item content. That is, it is the obvious items that most readily conform to the behavior sample or self-report conception, whereas the subtle items, to the extent that they are valid, better fit into a conception of items as behavioral signs.

The statistical issue concerns the reliability of individual items and aggregates of items such as scales. If test-retest stability is the issue here, the MMPI–2 manual (Butcher et al., 1989, Appendexes D and I) makes it clear that over short time periods, at least, the temporal stability of the majority of individual items is at least as good as that of the most commonly used scales of the MMPI–2. Nevertheless, the endorsement of individual items may occur as a result of accident, confusion, misunderstanding, or similar inadvertence. The detailed probing of critical items, even when logistically feasible, does not always correct such mishaps or yield satisfactory information. Some respondents will deny valid endorsements by claiming disability or faux pas; many will feel excessively pressed and intruded on by close questioning of item responses. For these reasons, it is recommended that the psychologist begin any probing with the least threatening critical items and only then proceed to the most threatening content.

Proponents of the emphasis on item content (e.g., Butcher et al., 1990; Wiggins, 1966) have often focused on the internal consistency, typically measured by Cronbach's (1951) coefficient alpha, of item aggregates as an index of the adequacy of such aggregates for psychological measurement. Coefficient alpha operates as a measure of the homogeneity of item aggregates, or the degree to which the content of one item of an aggregate is similar in content to the other items included within it. Scales that have been developed using procedures designed to maximize internal consistency tend to bear a striking resemblance to aggregates derived from the factor analysis of test items (e.g., Johnson, Butcher, Null, & Johnson, 1984). In comparing scales, coefficient alpha will serve as an index of the degree of semantic spread that is observed as new items are added to a preexisting set. For example, starting with an item such as "My father is a good man," the addition of a second item, "I love my father," results in a very small enlargement of the semantic focus of the first item and a correspondingly slight decline in internal consistency. If to these two items one adds a third, "My mother is a good woman," the semantic focus is enlarged from positive sentiments about the father to similar sentiments toward parents. This will result in a further, and probably larger, increment of decline in internal consistency. The addition of a fourth item, "I enjoy children," broadens the focus yet again from parents to parents and children or perhaps to even "people in general" and may be associated with a still larger drop in internal consistency. A fifth addition, "I like mechanics magazines," would suggest a very sharp broadening of semantic focus to something like "liking things and people" and would be associated with a correspondingly sharp decline in coefficient alpha. Adding a sixth item, "I hate my whole family," might either augment both the focus of the aggregate and the value for internal consistency if it were scored "false" or essentially destroy its semantic coherence and internal consistency if scored "true." The main point is that internal consistency reflects the degree of semantic redundancy within a given set of items and, by implication, the personological redundancy (or strength, or robustness) of the attribute in the individual who achieves a high endorsement rate for the items in the set. However, coefficient alpha is always a declining function of the number of nonidentical items in a set. The point at which to close a given set to additional items is therefore at least somewhat arbitrary, and there is always at least some trade-off between internal consistency and test–retest stability because internal consistency favors short scales, whereas temporal stability favors long ones.

The internal consistency approach to scale development contrasts with the empirical or criterion keying approach, in which items are selected for inclusion on a given scale because they are associated with higher rates of endorsement by members of the criterion group than by groups such as normals. The values of coefficient alpha for empirically derived scales may vary considerably from one scale to the next but are generally modest in comparison with content-based scales. Each of the items included in an empirical scale is assumed to provide an increment of nonredundant criterion (e.g., diagnosis in the case of most of the basic MMPI scales) related variance that will make a unique contribution to the identification of cases similar to those composing the criterion group. Although it is true that such scales may possess considerable common variance and yield correspondingly high estimates of internal consistency (e.g., Scales 1, 7, and 8), such variance is not a goal of the method but an artifact of major sources of variation operating within the item pool at large. In some instances, large common variances may even attenuate the validity of empirically derived scales by reducing their specificity.

In this context, the NCIL might be seen as a compromise between the critical item approach and the content scale approach to the analysis of content. By forming critical items into relatively many but small sets, or "miniscales," the NCIL may be less vulnerable to interpretive hypotheses based on unintentional endorsements and yield a more pointed picture of a person's symptoms and complaints than is possible when pathological responses to a small cluster of items become obscured, given that such clusters become hidden in their parent scales.

Another set of small, highly homogeneous item clusters have been proposed as subscales for the MMPI–2 content scales (Ben-Porath & Sherwood, 1993; Sherwood & Ben-Porath, 1991), which we discuss later.

It is primarily in the context of other test data that sets of critical items, or any highly redundant cluster of items, have potential value to the clinician. Individual critical items and small sets thereof offer the clinician access to very highly focused components of the participant's self-report that may be obscured or lost in aggregates that approach the size of conventional scales, or even scales of high internal consistency, such as content scales. However, in the absence of supporting indicators in other features of the test, such as scale scores, profile codes, and the like, critical items are likely to overpredict the kinds of symptoms, problems, and concerns suggested by their content. It is significant that with the exception of the now rarely used Grayson items, all critical item lists subdivide their items into categories determined by content, thereby deemphasizing Grayson's initial conception of these items as stand-alone or stop items in favor of a conception that places critical items in a position intermediate between stop items and formally developed and normed scales.

Whatever their source, critical items afford the clinician a valuable if not always reliable channel of communication with the patient. Single and small sets of items are the means by which the patient can most directly address his or her concerns to the psychologist within the context of the MMPI–2. Although the various scales and indexes of the test serve to identify those problem areas that are of significance in the patient's current life and circumstances, it is only through single-item responses that the patient can call the clinician's attention to his or her specific problems. The clinician's access to some of these responses, in the form of critical items, can help to create a channel of communication that stands to facilitate empathy between therapist and patient and build a bridge between the phases of assessment and treatment.

CONTENT SCALES

As highly homogeneous collections of items with similar content, the content scales also provide a means by which the patient can communicate with the clinician. Because the most immediate access to the symptomatic behavior and concerns of the patient is through scales having a strong thematic character, content scales are designed in a way that allows them to respond directly to aspects of the examinee's self-presentation on the MMPI–2. As Wiggins, Goldberg, and Applebaum (1971) noted, the view that the MMPI constitutes "an opportunity for communication between S and the tester has much to commend it; not the least of which is the likelihood that this is the frame of reference adopted by the *S* [subject] himself" (p. 403).

In understanding the relationship between content scales and the clinical profile, it is helpful to recall the first two levels of Leary's (1956, 1957) multilevel interpersonal diagnostic scheme. He categorized as Level I data those which are concerned with how a person is described by others or the interpersonal pressure his symptoms, complaints, preoccupations, attitudes, and traits of character exert on them (i.e., his social "stimulus value"). Data at this level are objective and public and may or may not agree with the person's own view of him- or herself or situation. It is this level that is reflected in the MMPI/MMPI–2 clinical profile.

By contrast, Level II data are conscious descriptions of the person's phenomenological field, the report of his or her self-perceptions in terms of behavior, symptoms, traits, and relations with others. Content scales are especially sensitive to data at this level. Again, the person's self-report may well not coincide in its impact on or meaning to others with that anticipated by the person him- or herself.

These levels and their corresponding sets of scales reflect points of view and should not be considered mutually exclusive. Payne and Wiggins (1972) found generally excellent agreement between interpretations based on common clinical profile types and content-scale-derived personality descriptions. Butcher et al. (1990), Lachar and Alexander (1978), and Lachar, Dahlstrom, and Moreland (1986), among others, have also demonstrated meaningful and reliable Level I correlates of content scale scores.

Nevertheless, the redundancy of standard and content scales is far from perfect, and the ability to compare patterns of responses to the same item pool from both diagnostically and self-report-based perspectives adds a fruitful new dimension to MMPI/MMPI–2 interpretation. Each set of scales provides a useful context in which to consider the other. Comparisons between the two sets will often lead to the formulation of more detailed hypotheses regarding patterns of interpersonal functioning, psychodynamics, defensive operations and coping skills, adjustment and adaptation, and diagnosis than can be obtained from either set alone.

The original 13 content scales developed by Wiggins (1966) consisted of Poor Health (*HEA*), Depression (*DEP*), Organic Symptoms (*ORG*), Family Problems (*FAM*), Authority Conflict (*AUT*), Feminine Interests (*FEM*), Religious Fundamentalism (*REL*), Manifest Hostility (*HOS*), Poor Morale (*MOR*), Phobias (*PHO*), Psychoticism (*PSY*), Hypomania (*HYP*), and Social Maladjustment (*SOC*). Wiggins took as his starting point the 26 content categories identified by Hathaway and McKinley (1940), treating each as a prototype scale. Having as his goal scales that were internally consistent, moderately independent, and nonoverlapping, Wiggins then iteratively combined prototypes, reassigned items from one category to another, and created new categories before settling on the final 13 scales. The Wiggins content scales represented a culmination of combined rational and psychometric efforts. Final internal consistencies ranged from about .5 to .9, with a median midway between .7 and .8. Research throughout the 1970s and early 1980s uniformly supported the validity of the Wiggins content scales in many different populations. (For a description of the correlates for each of the 13 Wiggins content scales, see Wiggins, 1966, and Friedman, Webb, and Lewak, 1989.)

With the decision of the MMPI restandardization committee to replace 90 MMPI items with 107 new items came an opportunity to evaluate the content of the revised MMPI–2 item pool. Butcher et al. (1990) followed procedures similar to those of Wiggins in developing new content scales for the MMPI–2. Butcher identified 22 provisional categories of content from an examination of Hathaway and McKinley's original categories, the results of a large-scale replicated item factor analysis of the MMPI (Johnson et al., 1984), and a review of the newly written items for the MMPI–2. He then produced definitions for each category and, with Dahlstrom and Graham, assigned items to them. Provisional content scales were established from sets of items agreed to by at least two of these three authors. They then discussed the composition of each of the provisional scales, item by item, until consensus was reached. Twenty-one revised provisional scales remained after one was dropped for an insufficient number of items. These scales were then evaluated by means of deleted item–total correlations and deleted coefficients alpha to identify items that reduced the internal consistency of the revised provisional scales so that these items could be dropped. Four of the revised provisional scales were found to have unacceptably low internal consistencies and were dropped from further development. At this stage, however, a new provisional scale, Cynicism, was added and purified, as described, bringing the number of scales for continuing investigation to 18. Computation of the correlations between the purified scales and each of the remaining items in the MMPI–AX item pool was undertaken to add new items that strengthened these scales' internal consistencies but that had not heretofore been identified as belonging to the content domain of the scale. These purified and augmented scales were then subjected to a rational review to determine if the provisional scale name and definition needed adjustment and to identify and eliminate any items having an insufficient content affinity for their parent scales, even though their statistical association was strong. At this stage, two scales were combined and two others were dropped, leaving 15 scales. In the next step, a statistical and rational review enabled the identification of items more highly correlated with other scales and their elimination or reassignment. In this stage, overlapping items were permitted so long as the scales sharing items were conceptually related. In the final steps, uniform *T* scores were established and rational descriptions based on each scale's final item content were composed. Later, Ben-Porath and Sherwood (1993; Sherwood & Ben Porath, 1991) developed subscales for several of the content scales that they called *components*. The final MMPI–2 content scales are listed with their numbers of items and patterns of item overlap in Table 7.2. (See Table A.3 for a listing of the item composition and scoring directions for the MMPI–2 content and content component scales; see Appendix B for the uniform *T* score conversions from raw scores for these scales.)

Before describing the MMPI–2 content scales in detail, it may be helpful to compare the content domains of the MMPI and MMPI–2 with reference to the Wiggins and MMPI–2 content scale sets (see also Kohvtek, 1992a, 1992b). Table 7.3 presents the overlap between the MMPI–2 content scales and each of their components with the Wiggins content scales. Table 7.4 presents the correlations among groups of scales from the two sets having similar item content.

Despite the similarity of the two sets of scales, differences between them often appear on examination of those scales having similar names (see Table 7.5). For example, about half (16/33) of the MMPI–2 Depression scale (*DEP*) items are retained from the Wiggins *DEP* scale, but 6 (18%) of the original Wiggins *DEP* items now appear on the MMPI–2 Anxiety scale (*ANX*). Eight (24%) of the MMPI–2 *DEP* items are from the 107 newly written items for the MMPI–2, including three of four items bearing suicidal content. Of the 27 items on the Wiggins Manifest Hostility scale (*HOS*), 8 now appear on the MMPI–2 Anger scale (*ANG*) and 9 appear on the MMPI–2 Type A Behavior scale (*TPA*). Of the 36 items

TABLE 7.2

The MMPI–2 Content Scales With Numbers of Items and Patterns of Item Overlap

MMPI–2 Content Scale		*FRS*	*OBS*	*DEP*	*HEA*	*BIZ*	*ANG*	*CYN*	*ASP*	*TPA*	*LSE*	*SOD*	*FAM*	*WRK*	*TRT*
ANX	23		2											5	
FRS	23														
OBS	16													4	3
DEP	33							1			2			1	6
HEA	36														
BIZ	24												1		
ANG	16									3				1	
CYN	23								7	1				1	1
ASP	22									1					
TPA	19													2	
LSE	24													1	2
SOD	24														
FAM	25												1		
WRK	33														4
TRT	26														

TABLE 7.3

Item Overlap Between MMPI–2 Content and Component Scales and the Wiggins Content Scales

MMPI–2 Content and Component Scale	*HEA*	*DEP*	*ORG*	*FAM*	*AUT*	*FEM*	*REL*	*HOS*	*MOR*	*PHO*	*PSY*	*HYP*	*SOC*
HEA	13		20										
HEA1	4		1										
HEA2			10										
HEA3	3		1										
DEP		16							5				
DEP1		5							2				
DEP2		4											
DEP3		4							2				
DEP4		2											
FAM				10									
FAM1				5									
FAM2				2									
CYN					12			2	2		2		
CYN1					10								

continued on next page

MMPI–2 Content and Component Scale	HEA	DEP	ORG	FAM	AUT	FEM	REL	HOS	MOR	PHO	PSY	HYP	SOC
CYN2					2								
ASP				1	12			1					
ASP1					10								
ASP2					2								
ANG								8				1	
ANG1								3					
ANG2								4					
TPA								9				1	
TPA1								2					
TPA2								5					
LSE	1								6				
LSE1	1								5				
LSE2									1				
FRS										19			
FRS1										8			
FRS2										10			

TABLE 7.3 *(continued from previous page)*

MMPI-2 Content and Component Scale	*HEA*	*DEP*	*ORG*	*FAM*	*AUT*	*FEM*	*REL*	*HOS*	*MOR*	*PHO*	*PSY*	*HYP*	*SOC*
BIZ											19		
BIZ1											9		
BIZ2					2						8		
SOD										2	1		16
SOD1										1			3
SOD2										1			6
TRT		2							2				
TRT1		2							2		1		1
TRT2													
ANX	1	6	1						3	1		1	
OBS		1							1	1			
WRK		2	1						5			2	1

TABLE 7.4
Intercorrelations of Similar MMPI–2 and Wiggins Content Scales for Restandardization Men (and Women)

	MMPI–2 Somatic Content Scale		
	HEA	*ORG*	
HEA	79 (81)	82 (84)	
	MMPI–2 Distress Content Scale		
	PHO	*DEP*	*MOR*
FRS	91 (92)	38 (39)	39 (39)
DEP	39 (43)	89 (91)	79)80)
ANX	44 (47)	80 (83)	74 (77)
OBS	46 (49)	69 (75)	72 (79)
LSE	40 (41)	70 (73)	79 (83)
TRT	45 (48)	75 (76)	75 (76)
WRK	46 (46)	79 (82)	82 (85)
	MMPI–2 Cynicism and Psychotic Content Scale		
	AUT	*PSY*	
CYN	84 (86)	58 (64)	
BIZ	44 (46)	84 (82)	
	MMPI–2 Hostile Affect Scale		
	HOS		
ANG	79 (80)		
TPA	80 (78)		
	MMPI–2 Antisocial Content Scale		
	AUT		
ASP	88	(87)	
	MMPI–2 Interpersonal Content Scale		
	FAM	*SOC*	
FAM	82 (86)	23 (22)	
SOC	18 (19)	92 (92)	

TABLE 7.5
Similarities and Differences for the MMPI–2 and Wiggins Content Scales

MMPI–2		*Wiggins*	
Content Scale	*Abbreviation*	*Content Scale*	*Abbreviation*
Anxiety	ANX		
Fear	FRS	Phobias	PHO
Obsessiveness	OBS		
Depression	DEP	Depression	DEP
Health Concerns	HEA	Organic Symptoms	ORG
		Poor Health	HEA
Bizarre Mentation	BIZ	Psychoticism	PSY
Anger	ANG	Manifest Hostility	HOS
Cynicism	CYN	Authority Conflict	AUT
Antisocial Practices	ASP	(Authority Conflict)	(AUT)
Type A Behavior	TPA	(Hostility)	(HOS)
Low Self-Esteem	LSE	Poor Morale	MOR
Social Discomfort	SOD	Social Maladjustment	SOC
Family Problems	FAM	Family Problems	FAM
Work Interference	WRK		
Negative Treatment Indicators	TRT		
		Feminine Interests	FEM
		Religious Fundamentalism	REL
		Hypomania	HYP

on the MMPI–2 Health Concerns scale (*HEA*), 13 were formerly on the Wiggins Poor Health scale but 20, more than half of the items on the MMPI–2 *HEA* scale, were taken from the Wiggins Organic Symptoms scale (*ORG*). Nine items, including four with genitourinary content and three with bowel content, were among those dropped from the MMPI–2 item pool that were formerly on the Wiggins Poor Health scale.

These changes, although unsuspected from an examination of the names of the scales discussed, are apt to have significant consequences for the proper understanding of the MMPI–2 content scales, their interpretive implications, and their empirical correlates. In the case of the MMPI–2 *DEP* scale, the loss of its "anxiety" content and the addition of items denoting suicidal ideation can only strengthen its performance as a measure of depressive symptomatology. Although not necessarily a superior measure of somatic preoccupation or overconcern than its Wiggins predecessor, the MMPI–2 *HEA* scale, with its shift toward symptoms localized to the head and musculature and away from lower gastrointestinal and genitourinary content, must show a corresponding shift in its profile of empirical correlates. As a result of these and similar differences between the Wiggins and MMPI–2 content scales (described later), clinicians familiar with the Wiggins content scales cannot assume that their knowledge of the former set of scales can be reliably transferred to the content scales developed for the MMPI–2.

The reliability of the MMPI–2 content scales is uniformly high, with internal consistencies characteristically falling into the upper end of a range of .70 to .85 and 9-day test–retest stabilities falling in the center of the range of .80 to .90. We discuss the validity characteristics of the MMPI–2 content scales for each of the scales individually (Ben-Porath, McCully, & Almagor, 1993).

The MMPI–2 content scales are organized around four themes: internal symptoms; external or aggressive tendencies; a devalued view of the self; and general problem areas, including social style, family attachment, and attitudes toward work and psychotherapeutic treatment. The internal symptoms cluster—anxiety, fears, obsessiveness, depression, health concerns, and psychotic mentation—are oriented toward Axis I syndromes. The external or aggressive tendencies cluster is directed toward the evaluation of Axis II disorders. The devalued view of the self category contains only one scale: Low Self-Esteem (*LSE*). Although these themes may appear conceptually distinct, they are not independent in a statistical sense. Because the MMPI–2 is geared toward the detection and description of psychopathology, the item pool is highly biased in favor of items that report symptoms and problematic attitudes and behaviors. It should not, therefore, be surprising that face-valid scales drawn from this item pool show relatively high positive intercorrelations. The largest concentration of intercorrelations for the MMPI–2 content scales falls within a range of .40 to .49. The most highly intercorrelated scales include Anxiety (*ANX*), Obsessiveness (*OBS*), Depression (*DEP*), Low Self-Esteem (*LSE*), Work Interference (*WRK*), and Negative Treatment Indicators (*TRT*). The scales within the external–aggressive cluster are also highly intercorrelated.

Anxiety Scale (*ANX*)

The *ANX* scale contains 23 items, of which 18 are keyed "true." Among the MMPI–2 clinical scales, the *ANX* scale correlates most highly with Scale 7 (*Pt*) at .80 and with Welsh's *A* scale at .80. The primary theme in the scale is excessive worry against a background of nervous tension, disturbed sleep, and problems with attention and concentration. Subjective stress levels are already so high that decisions and disappointments are felt to carry the risk of total mental fragmentation and collapse; hence, the anxiety in question in the *ANX* scale is close to panic. High scorers feel "stressed out" and carry a strong sense of both dread and vulnerability. The anxiety in question in the *ANX* scale is also generalized; any and all events are seen as potentially disastrous and devastating, with tensing up and worrying providing the only insulation against the threat that a sudden unanticipated event will cause one to "go to pieces." The scale has a single item reporting somatic manifestations of anxiety: heart pounding and shortness of breath. Two of the items denote financial concerns.

Because the symptoms of anxiety as captured on the *ANX* scale tend to pervade conscious experience, they are associated with insight and a strong desire for relief. As a result, patients with high scores will generally have neither the means nor the inclination to conceal these symptoms (although they may feel reluctant to admit other symptoms, such as hallucinations).

Relations to Other Scales. Elevations on other scales in the presence of high *ANX* scores provide a basis for hypotheses about the object of anxiety and the circumstances most likely to provoke a sense of panic. For example, in the presence of an elevation on the Bizarre Mentation scale (*BIZ*), high *ANX* score may reflect particular concern about anomalous experience and psychotic disintegration. With a high *LSE* score, a high *ANX* score suggests particular apprehensions around self-devaluation, narcissistic injuries, the imminent withdrawal of dependency supports, and imperiled self-esteem. With a high *DEP* score, a high *ANX* score may suggest fears of a worsening of depressive experience, falling into despair, and a collapse into helplessness and hopelessness.

Fears Scale (*FRS*)

The *FRS* scale contains 23 items, of which 16 are keyed "true." It is one of the most independent of the content scales and achieves only modest correlations with a few of the standard MMPI–2 scales. In particular, the *FRS* and *ANX* scales correlate at only .35. The *FRS* scale has no counterpart among the standard clinical scales of the MMPI–2 and shares few items with them. As a result, the presence or absence of phobic symptoms cannot generally be inferred from the standard clinical profile.

Excessive fearfulness and more specific phobic concerns form the primary theme of this scale. The word *fear* and its cognates (*afraid*, *dread*, and *frightened*) appear in more than three fourths of the items. The several groups of items include (a) specific fears of classically phobic type (e.g., darkness, heights, and open and closed spaces); (b) animals (e.g., mice, snakes, and spiders); (c) natural phenomena (e.g., earthquakes, lightning, storms, fire, and water); (d) loss of physical integrity, especially through germs and tissue damage; and (e) admissions of general neurotic fearfulness and a low threshold for feeling fearful that is likely to be incapacitating. Ben-Porath and Sherwood (1993) found statistical justification for dividing the scale into two components: *FRS1*, Generalized Fearfulness, and *FRS2*, Multiple

Fears. In terms of the groups of *FRS* items described, *FRS1* encompasses most of the items in Groups a, d, and e, whereas most of the items contained in *FRS2* are from Groups b and c. The theme of *FRS1* is one of a broadly apprehensive tone in one's approach to daily life, one that places an emphasis on the dangers or potential harmfulness of objects and circumstances in the environment. Phobic anxiety appears to be the key empirical correlate of this component (Graham et al., 1999), as well as for *FRS* as a whole. *FRS2* contains no theme as such but is simply an enumeration of relatively common phobic objects and circumstances. Among the men of their outpatient sample, Graham et al. (1999) found indications of more serious psychopathology among high *FRS2* scorers, including hallucinations, diagnoses of schizophrenia, and treatment with antipsychotic medications. Low scores on the *FRS* scale connote fearlessness and the risk of reckless disregard for, or obliviousness to, danger, painful consequences or punishment such as may be found in manic-like pictures with euphoria, fearlessness, and poor judgment (high scores on Scale 9 and low scores on Scale 0 and *SOD*), or psychopathic recklessness (high scores on Scale 4, *FAM*, and *ASP* [*ASP* > *CYN*]). Low scores may also be associated with rigid attitudes regarding gender-role requirements in men, particularly macho masculinity (low scores on Scale 5 and high scores on *GM* [*GM* > *GF*]). Occasionally, low scores are seen in the context of "working" somatization pictures, with such physical complaints as abdominal pain, back pain, or visual problems.

The meaning of extreme scores on the *FRS* scale is highly dependent on other features of the content and clinical profiles. When elevated with Scale 7, especially the 273/723 profile, the *FRS* scale connotes phobic anxiety. In conjunction with profiles with peaks on the *HEA* scale (and perhaps Scale 3, *Hy4*, *Sc6*, and *HEA2*), elevations on the *FRS* scale connote a strong harm-avoidant orientation and strong fears of somatic injury, illness, or decay.

Relations to Other Scales. Both the *ANX* and *FRS* scales tap phenomena of apprehension. In the case of the *ANX* scale, the apprehension one feels is inchoate; one feels trepidation over the unpredictability of external and internal events that are feared to lead to disorganization and chaos. The defense against this feared breakdown in organization is active in the sense of involving preparation to contend with or absorb the threatened sudden event. With obsessive worry, one has a means of anticipating catastrophe in time to avert or avoid it. In the *FRS* scale, however, the apprehension is condensed onto a particular object or situation, or set thereof, the focus is on the avoidance of injury and harm, and the defense against these dangers is fundamentally passive: One seeks not to contend with the feared object or situation but to avoid it, and if unable to avoid, one might freeze or panic. The condensation of apprehension onto known objects and situations enables developmentally more advanced defense mechanisms to be brought to bear in the management of anxiety based on repression and displacement, measures which restore a sense of freedom from fear in those areas of life and functioning that do not risk exposure to phobic foci. This may explain, in part, why the correlation between the *FRS* and *ANX* scales is not greater. In some patients experiencing generalized and incapacitating fear or anxiety, an *FRS* score greater than $T = 70$ may be operating to mask more serious psychopathology. This is analogous to the familiar relationship between Scales 7 and 8 on the clinical profile in which the degree to which Scale 7 exceeds Scale 8, given the elevation of both scales, reflects the extent of struggle to contain psychotic expressions. In profiles with elevations on both the *ANX* and *FRS* scales, but in which the *FRS* score is higher, the effort to use more mature defensive measures against external and internal threats is suggested, whereas the reverse pattern would suggest a reliance on more primitive defenses. The *FRS* scale is more socially desirable and less negativistic than the *ANX* scale, another indication that it is associated with more mature modes of defensive functioning. Along with the Social Discomfort scale (*SOD*), the *FRS* scale is one of the least socially undesirable among the MMPI–2 content scales. In one type of defensive paranoid patients, the *FRS* scale may stand out as the only elevation of consequence among the content scales and be associated with an especially low Cynicism (*CYN*) score, suggesting a displacement of fears of others onto phobic objects. The patient strongly denies cynical and suspicious attitudes toward others but admits to a greater than average fearfulness of aspects of the nonhuman environment.

Obsessiveness Scale (*OBS*)

The *OBS* scale contains 16 items of which all are keyed "true." It is correlated with the *Pt* scale in the high .70s and with the *A* scale in the low .80s; it shares five items with each of these two scales. Although a few of the items do indeed seem classically obsessive in content, the modal item on this scale reflects indecision. The main theme, then, is one of overly busy but massively inefficient cognitive activity. Decision making becomes bogged down in detail, but this seems to occur against a background of timidity, if not dread, when faced with the necessity of taking practical action. Low scores on the *OBS* scale suggest an opposite trend, with decisions being made with self-confidence and dispatch. Very low scores may imply overconfidence and a hasty and incautious approach to decision making.

At this time, it is unclear what relation, if any, there is between the *OBS* scale and obsessive–compulsive disorder or, especially, obsessive–compulsive personality disorder. An appropriate scale for the identification of these disorders would need to include items having content related to such things as symmetry; checking; cleaning; ordering; perfectionism; concerns about contamination; overcontrol; restriction of affect; stinginess; overconscientiousness; preoccupation with details; and forbidden aggressive, sexual, or sacrilegious thoughts and actions, as well as with indecision. The content of the MMPI–2 does not include a sufficient number or variety of items in these areas, and not all of those that are included found their way onto the *OBS* scale (see, e.g., *FRS* Items 322 and 447). Hence, the *OBS* scale is a good example of a scale for which internal consistency strictures may have prevented the development of a scale having properties that would facilitate detection of obsessive syndromes. Notwithstanding these difficulties, Graham et al. (1999) did find that their high scoring outpatients did manifest "obsessive–compulsive tendencies," but did not report in what these tendencies consisted.

Relations to Other Scales. To maintain its relevance for the diagnosis of obsessional states and personality styles, it would seem important to require that the *OBS* scale exceed both the *ANX* and *FRS* scales by a margin of $T = 10$ to ensure that the *OBS* scale is not being pulled up by the variance it shares in common with the other two scales. (See also discussion of Harkness, McNulty, and Ben-Porath's, 1995, Aggressiveness [*AGG*] and Disconstraint [*DIS*] scales.) The negative implications of low *OBS* scores, such as impulsive decision making, are likely to be negligible, or at least not readily apparent, unless low *OBS* scores are accompanied by a low (preferably lower) *FRS* score. Correlations in the .50 to .65 range with measures of anger and hostility, such as Wiggins' Manifest Hostility scale (HOS), the MMPI–2 Anger scale (*ANG*), and the Type A Behavior scale (*TPA*), suggest that high *OBS* scores may indicate passive–aggressive motivation (i.e., using nonperformance through indecision, obsession, and preoccupation with detail as a means of coping with the demands and expectations of others and, in turn, engendering responses of impatience, frustration, and exasperation in them).

Depression Scale (*DEP*)

The *DEP* scale contains 33 items, of which 28 are keyed "true." Among the MMPI–2 clinical scales, the *DEP* scale correlates most highly with Scale 7 (*Pt*) at .81, and with Welsh's *A* scale at about .83. Sixteen of the items appeared on the Wiggins *DEP* scale. Six of the items scored on the Wiggins *DEP* scale now appear on the MMPI–2 *ANX* scale. Although the MMPI–2 and Wiggins *DEP* scales correlate at about .90, the improved separation between anxious and depressive content in the MMPI–2 content scales suggests that the current *DEP* scale is likely to have somewhat greater specificity and discriminant validity than its predecessor among the Wiggins scales, and evidence for the incremental validity of the *DEP* scale has been steadily accumulating (Barthlow, Graham, Ben-Porath, & McNulty, 1999; Ben-Porath, Butcher, & Graham, 1991; Wetzler, Khadivi, & Moser, 1998).

Ben-Porath and Sherwood (1993) subdivided the MMPI–2 *DEP* scale into four components: Lack of Drive (*DEP1*), Dysphoria (*DEP2*), Self-Depreciation (*DEP3*), and Suicidal Ideation (*DEP4*). The *DEP1* items report despair and a loss of pleasure, interest, and motivation in life. High scores reflect apathy, anhedonia, an inability to accomplish even the routine tasks of daily life, and a sense of having given up. By contrast, low scores suggest a zestful approach to daily life in which interests, aspirations, and plans for the future have a solid role. *DEP2* reflects dysphoric/depressed mood in the form of subjective unhappiness, especially a sense of brooding and feeling blue, and of being subject to moody spells. Four of the six items overlap the *D5* subscale (Brooding). The *DEP3* items reflect self-dissatisfaction, guilt and sense of moral failure, and a negative self-concept. High scorers admit to feelings of guilt, helplessness, hopelessness, regret/remorse, uselessness, and worthlessness. Low scorers deny such feelings. None of the DEP4 items appear on Scale 2. Although not all are explicitly suicidal in content, these items do carry the implication of a pessimism about the future that is so dire as to support a wish to die and thoughts of suicide. High scores raise the question of suicide potential, the need for its assessment, and the probable wisdom of initial precautions against suicidal acts or gestures. As Ben-Porath and Sherwood pointed out, *DEP1*, *DEP2*, and *DEP3* all lie close to aspects of diagnostic criteria for major depressive episode. The *DEP* scale is highly sensitive to the cognitive and attitudinal components of depressive syndromes. High scorers (following the component scales) report despair and a loss of interest and feelings of fatigue, apathy, and exhaustion (*DEP1*); they are unhappy, blue, and quick to cry (*DEP2*); they show a collapse in self-efficacy and self-regard to the point that they feel guilt-ridden, useless, unpardonably sinful, and condemned (*DEP3*); and they feel hopeless, wish for death, and contemplate suicide (*DEP4*). The empirical correlates of high *DEP* and component scores found by Graham et al. (1999) tend to confirm this description. Their outpatients tended to have histories of prior suicide attempts and psychiatric hospitalizations, and profuse depressive symptomatology, with hopelessness, suicidal ideation, and disturbed sleep. Although low scores on the *DEP* scale more clearly indicate the absence (or denial) of depressiveness than the presence of elated or expansive mood, some low scorers will be seen as defensive, euphoric, irritable, or overactive, especially in psychiatric settings.

Relations to Other Scales. The MMPI–2 *DEP* overlaps Scale 2 by only nine items, indicating that the two scales are likely to have significantly different patterns of empirical correlates. All of the overlapping items are found on the *D1* subscale (Subjective Depression), and eight of the nine appear on the *D5* subscale (Brooding), or 80% of that subscale. Convictions of worthlessness and futility, along with a view of the self as inadequate or inferior, are primary in the *DEP* scale but secondary in Scale 2. Conversely, the syndromal characteristics of depression, such as psychomotor retardation, the inhibition of aggression, and vegetative symptoms (e.g., sleep disturbance, anorexia, and weight loss making up an important part of Scale 2), are largely absent from the *DEP* scale. The relative elevations of the *DEP* scale and Scale 2, therefore, are helpful in determining both the type and severity of depressive phenomena. To the extent that the *DEP* scale exceeds Scale 2, a chronic condition with predominantly characterological features is suggested. To the extent that Scale 2 exceeds the *DEP* scale, vegetative symptoms and a less complicated symptom picture are characteristic. Streit, Greene, Cogan, and Davis (1993) found a markedly different pattern of correlates from the MMPI, Brief Psychiatric Rating Scale (BPRS), chemotherapy, and diagnoses at discharge for psychiatric patients, depending on whether Scale 2 was greater or less than Wiggins' *DEP* scale. Patients for which Scale 2 exceeded the *DEP* scale primarily had code patterns involving Scale 2; higher scores on the Wiggins Social Maladjustment scale; rated higher than the *DEP* > Scale 2 group on BPRS Somatic Concern, Emotional Withdrawal, Depressive Mood, and Blunted Affect; were treated with antidepressants and antipsychotics with equal frequency; and were generally given diagnoses of major depression, cyclothymia, adjustment disorder, histrionic personality disorder, and dependent personality disorder. By contrast, the group for which the *DEP* scale exceeded Scale 2 tended to produce code patterns in which Scale 8 was predominant and had higher scores on the Wiggins Family Problems, Authority Conflict, Manifest Hostility, Poor Morale, Psychoticism, and Hypomania scales. They also showed higher scores on the Welsh Anxiety, Navran Dependency, and MacAndrew Alcoholism (*MAC*) scales. On the BPRS, they had higher scores on Excitement. They were treated with antipsychotic medications almost three times as often as with antidepressants and were more often diagnosed with bipolar disorder, mania, alcohol abuse, antisocial personality disorder, and passive–aggressive personality disorder. The incidence of diagnoses of schizophrenia did not differ for the two groups. Although the Wiggins and MMPI–2 versions of the *DEP* scale share only about half of their items, their high intercorrelation and the very high internal consistencies (>.80 for both scales) would suggest a similar pattern of correlates. Hence, it is likely that the pattern of correlates reported by Streit et al. would not be markedly different had they used the MMPI–2 version of the *DEP* scale rather than the Wiggins version.

Health Concerns Scale (*HEA*)

The *HEA* scale contains 36 items, of which 14 are keyed "true." The amount of overlap between the *HEA* scale and Scale 1 (*Hs*) is very high at 21 items, more than two thirds of the *Hs* scale. The two scales correlate at .90. A majority of the items (20) appeared on the Wiggins Organic Symptoms scale (*ORG*); 13 appeared on the Wiggins Poor Health scale. The overlap with the *ORG* scale and the abandonment of most of the genitourinary and lower gastrointestinal items from the MMPI has made the *HEA* scale very different from its Wiggins predecessor. The continuity of content between the two scales is largely limited to items reflecting upper gastrointestinal symptoms and concerns over one's general health status (about five items each). Not surprisingly, in contrast to the Wiggins Poor Health scale, the *HEA* scale contains many items denoting complaints in and about the head, sensory and motor problems, and a few items reporting losses of consciousness. None of the items in these areas appeared on the Wiggins Poor Health scale. Complaints of pain and other somatic discomfort are more plentiful on the new *HEA* scale than on the Wiggins Poor Health scale. The greater variety of item content in the new *HEA* scale has been made explicit in the content component scales developed by Ben-Porath and Sherwood (1993). These are Gastrointestinal Symptoms (*HEA1*), a collection of mostly upper gastrointestinal items that report nausea, vomiting, stomach pain and discomfort (stomach-ache), and constipation; Neurological Symptoms (*HEA2*), items covering sensory and motor problems, losses of consciousness, and other head complaints; and General Health Concerns (*HEA3*), the items of which report poor health, and health worries and preoccupations.

Relations to Other Scales. The characterological features associated with Scale 1 are even more apparent in the *HEA* scale. This is because of the absence of any "dampening" effect of the *K* correction applied to Scale 1. That is, the addition of 0.5 *K* to the raw score for Scale 1 tends to attenuate its association with measures of dependency, hostility, and other traits. Implications for conflicts around dependency, demandingness and the management of the demands of others, the handling of anger and frustration, and related issues are highly similar for the *HEA* scale and the non-*K*-corrected version of Scale 1.

Bizarre Mentation Scale (*BIZ*)

The *BIZ* scale contains 24 items, of which all but 1 are keyed "true." Its pattern of overlap with the *F* scale (10 items), Scale 6 (8 items), and Scale 8 (8 items) would suggest that the *BIZ* scale is the content analogue of the 86/68 profile type. About one third of the items are paranoid in content. The *BIZ* scale is a measure of psychotic thought processes. Wetzler et al. (1998) found that the *BIZ* scale was highly specific in their sample but that it lacked sensitivity.

Ben-Porath and Sherwood (1993) divided the *BIZ* scale into two components: Psychotic Symptomatology (*BIZ1*), composed of items with frankly psychotic content reflecting positive or accessory symptoms characteristic of schizophrenia and other psychotic conditions (such as auditory, visual, or olfactory hallucinations; delusions of persecution and control; and other first-rank symptoms, like thought broadcasting and thought withdrawal). Nearly half of these items refer to paranoid symptomatology. The second component, Schizotypal Characteristics (*BIZ2*), contains items that are less obviously psychotic in content than *BIZ1* but are nevertheless unusual, odd, peculiar, and weird. These include ideas of reference, derealization, intrusive thoughts, and uncanny sensory experiences such as are sometimes seen in prodromal or residual phases of schizophrenia, dissociative conditions, and mood disorders with psychotic features.

The *BIZ* items are among the most obvious items on the MMPI–2, so respondents wishing to simulate (malinger) psychosis will be drawn to these items. Conversely, respondents seeking to avoid appearing psychotic on the *BIZ* scale (and on the MMPI–2 more generally) can do so easily, with one important exception. Because insight is often lacking in psychotic conditions, and in schizophrenia in particular, psychotic patients will commonly endorse at least a few of the *BIZ* items even when defensive motivation and guardedness are present. That is, for many patients, their lack of insight renders the psychopathological implications of certain items transparent to them, leading to the endorsement of items that guarded patients whose insight is better preserved would unhesitatingly avoid. For example, a paranoid schizophrenic patient who fears that hospital personnel have been co-opted by his primary persecutors to disable him with medications, and who therefore has every reason to attempt to convince his psychiatric captors that they have the wrong man, may see no reason not to endorse an item like "Someone has been trying to poison me." For this patient, the item may be said to be ego-syntonic, beyond the reach of his motivation to censor test expressions of psychopathology. Thus, high *BIZ* scores, especially when such scores are contributed to by the items of *BIZ1* (even scores above $T = 50$ on *BIZ1* should be considered high in defensive profiles), carry implications that are not limited to the content of those items endorsed. Among these are impaired insight, an inability to enter into collaborative relationships, and a grandiose sense of having been selected or appointed for a secret and lofty mission or endowed with special powers. Graham et al. (1999) found relatively frequent histories of physical (men) and sexual (women) abuse among their outpatients with high *BIZ* scores.

Relations to Other Scales. One of the more important uses of the *BIZ* scale is as an index to judge the degree to which psychotic content has contributed to elevations on the *F* scale, Scale 6, and Scale 8. It is not at all uncommon for Scale 8 to exceed the *BIZ* scale by a few standard deviations. Both Scales 6 and 8 have substantial depressive content and may easily elevate in depressive conditions as well as in the psychoses. Alienation and lowered self-esteem also may elevate Scale 8 in many different conditions. Reference to the *BIZ* scale in profiles showing elevations on the *F* scale, Scale 6, and Scale 8 can provide valuable guidance in interpretation by emphasizing the importance of psychotic thinking when such an emphasis can be supported by high *BIZ* (especially *BIZ1*) scores and by avoiding such emphasis when it cannot, thereby averting excessively pathological interpretations of Scale 8 elevations. The Low Self-Esteem scale (*LSE*) is very sensitive to the kinds of fixed, negative self-attitudes that often result in high Scale 8 scores. The relative elevations of the *BIZ* and *LSE* scales can thus provide a useful index of the relative contributions of psychotic experience and impaired self-esteem to high scores on Scale 8.

Anger Scale (*ANG*)

The *ANG* scales contains 16 items, of which all but 1 are keyed "true." Inexplicably, the *ANG* scale does *not* include Item 372, "I am not easily angered." It shares only two items with the standard validity and clinical scales of the MMPI–2, fewer than any other of the content scales. Eight of the items overlap the Wiggins Manifest Hostility scale. This scale is concerned with poorly controlled anger (Schill & Wang, 1990). High scorers are irritable and volatile people who underregulate crude affect, are intolerant of frustration, issue angry expressions at a high rate, and are prone to paroxysmal eruptions in the form of angry tirades and destructive outbursts. They have strong needs to discharge their ire, and if they feel constrained by external circumstances from discharging in expansive ways through temper tantrums, bouts of yelling and cursing, and the like, they will do so in more controlled ways through frequent bugging, nagging, picking, carping, quibbling, belittling, discrediting, deriding, needling, ridiculing, shaming, irritating, taunting, sadistic teasing, demanding, imposing, intruding, and being stubborn. As with the *ANX* scale, high *ANG* scores are associated with a high press for expression. Indeed, Graham et al. (1999) reported that their outpatients with high *ANG* scores were ill tempered and had histories of being physically abusive, especially the men. The patients also showed high rates of substance abuse and dependence. Ben-Porath and Sherwood (1993) divided the *ANG* scale into Explosive

Behavior (*ANG1*) and Irritability (*ANG2*). The *ANG1* items emphasize behavior over impulse; the opposite emphasis characterizes *ANG2*. This difference could also be conceived as a difference in the severity of anger arousal and dyscontrol between the two components. High *ANG1* scorers admit to explosive and violent episodes that have been directed to both persons and property and have likely resulted in injury and damage. The items are reminiscent of the criteria for intermittent explosive disorder. The high *ANG1* scoring outpatients studied by Graham et al. (1999) were seen as quite hostile, given to temper outbursts, with the men showing histories of convictions for domestic violence. Both the men and women had long histories of alcohol abuse, with the men showing long histories of marijuana abuse as well. Their histories were also positive for physical (men) and sexual (women) abuse. Low *ANG1* scores, then, emphasize the denial of undercontrolled violent expressions over the denial of anger per se. That is, the low *ANG1* scorer is more likely to be asserting better control than an absence of angry emotionality. High *ANG2* scorers admit to a great deal of anger and irritability, but they also experience a sense of distress and perplexity about their reactions that may in some degree support the inhibition of behavioral outbursts. The emotional tone of *ANG2* is more dysphoric than hostile. The combination of anger and inhibition themes in *ANG2* suggests that it may be responsive to partial or attenuated expressions of anger that are emitted within a context of self-justification, such as argumentativeness, disagreeableness, annoyance, frustration, stalling, pettiness, impatience, complaining, criticism, and passive–aggressive or passive–paranoid maneuvers. Graham et al. (1999) note that their high scoring *ANG2* outpatients were seen by their therapists as depressed and self-degrading.

Evidence for the construct validity of the *ANG* scale has been accumulating. For example, Clark (1994) found an association between *ANG* scores and an anger expression factor among male chronic pain patients. Kawachi, Sparrow, Spiro, Vokonas, and Weiss (1996) reported a significant relationship between *ANG* scores and risk for coronary heart disease (CHD) among older men in the VA Normative Aging Study.

Relations to Other Scales. The *ANG* items and its correlates seem to emphasize the press for discharge over hostile intent in the dynamics of anger, at least as anger is embodied in this scale. High scorers will not infrequently report a sense of being a helpless spectator to their major and minor discharges, viewing with a kind of horror their own destructiveness as they damage property or inflict physical or emotional pain and injury on others, and yet feeling unable to stop themselves. The gratification they report is in the release of anger, not in the damage occasioned by such release. For this reason, individuals scoring high on both the *DEP* and *ANG* scales may be at special risk for dramatic suicide, including provoked homicide and murder–suicide, when they are finally rejected by the partners that they "never meant to hurt." This pattern is especially associated with scores on *ANG2*, and the configurations *ANG2* greater than *ANG1*, and *TPA1* greater than *TPA2*. There are important implications of the relationship between the *ANG* scale and its sister scale, the *TPA* scale. The two scales are moderately highly correlated in the high .60s, but whereas the *ANG* theme is "hot," the *TPA* theme is "cool." The implications of this difference is taken up in the Type A Behavior scale description.

Cynicism Scale (*CYN*)

The *CYN* scale contains 23 items, all of which are keyed "true." Seventeen items overlap the Cook and Medley (1954) Hostility scale (*Ho*). As a dimension, cynicism covers a broad range of sentiments from naive altruism, an obtuse absence of skepticism regarding the motives of others, to normal prudent regard for one's vulnerability, to deceit, mendacity, and chicanery at the hands of others, to the unqualified misanthropic conviction that people are dishonorable, unprincipled, and corrupt, invariably acting out of motives that are selfish, perfidious, venal, or craven. The *CYN* scale models this dimension well, with high scorers asserting that others are to be distrusted because they act only from self-interest, resort to honesty only to avoid detection, and act friendly only because it makes others easier to exploit. They see life as a jungle in which one must be constantly on the look-out for any competitive advantage because they expect others will use any means at their disposal to claim such advantage for themselves, given the opportunity. They therefore have no qualms about resorting to deception, misinformation, hypocrisy, subterfuge, and manipulation to get away with whatever they can. They justify their expedient, if not exploitive, approach to others with the (projective) rationalization that others are equally selfish, dishonest, and amoral. Low scorers deny normal levels of skepticism regarding the good will of others by maintaining that they are completely trustworthy and driven solely by prosocial and altruistic motivations. At the same time, they portray themselves as bastions of benevolence, holders of an unshakable belief in the goodness of their fellow men and women. These sentiments are not infrequently expressed in the context of defensive response styles in which there is some focus on portraying oneself as enjoying consummately harmonious relationships, relationships in which conflict and ill will are unheard of. In some circumstances, such as when the *LSE* scale and other signs of dependency are high, low *CYN* scores can indicate an unusual aversion to giving others offense for fear that to do so might risk rejection or the loss of dependency supports. Low scores may also be achieved by paranoid defensiveness through the specific denial of paranoid attitudes (e,g., *Pa3* and *Pdf* [paranoid defensiveness] [Holroyd, 1964]). Such patients tend to produce highly defensive profiles, often with the *L* and *K* scales exceeding the *F* scale. The peak among the content scales in this configuration, as mentioned earlier, is often the *FRS* scale, possibly signifying the displacement of fears of others onto phobic objects.

Graham et al. (1999) described their high-scoring *CYN* outpatients as hostile and having paranoid ideation, but the men among them were also described as sad and depressed, and as having frequent nightmares and complaints of disturbed sleep. The women had histories of suicide attempts and made broadly negative impressions on their therapists, who described them as immature, antisocial, insightless, and unmotivated.

Ben-Porath and Sherwood (1993) divided the *CYN* scale into two components: Misanthropic Beliefs (*CYN1*) and Interpersonal Suspiciousness (*CYN2*). *CYN1* emphasizes a view of others as deceitful, selfish, untrustworthy, manipulative, unsympathetic, and disloyal. High scorers are likely to be "burned out" on relations with others and unwilling to exert significant efforts to improve them. *CYN2* emphasizes similar sentiments but includes a theme of feeling oneself to be a particular target of others cynical, hostile, manipulative, or exploitive actions, leading to suspicious and guarded reactions. It therefore has a more dysphoric tone than *CYN1*. The high *CYN2* scorer feels "under fire" and vulnerable to others, especially superiors, who are felt to be stingy with recognition and understanding and who are trying to disadvantage him or her.

Relations to Other Scales. Butcher et al. (1990) found rather different empirical correlates for men and women on the *CYN* scale. The restandardization men were rated as having temper tantrums, whining, demanding, nagging, and lying but also as lacking an interest in things. The women were rated as less hostile but more psychologically disturbed. They were described as suspicious, nervous and jittery, preoccupied with death/dying, apathetic, and showing poor judgement. The pattern suggests either that cynicism is more damaging to psychological functioning among women or that elevated *CYN* scores may be a consequence of more general or severe psychological disturbance among women. For men, in contrast, elevations on the *CYN* scale appear to reflect a more specific trait disturbance that is more localized to interpersonal relations. For either gender, the *CYN* scale is likely to interact with measures of dependency (e.g., *Si3* [Self–Other Alienation], *Do* [low], *GM* [low], *LSE*, and *LSE2*) and, where both are high, to signify higher levels of stress and discomfort in interpersonal functioning. Dependent high *CYN* scorers are in the position of being unable to trust those on whom they depend, and are therefore vulnerable to rapidly fluctuating levels of comfort as their psychological distance from significant others waxes and wanes. Too close and they feel the threat of engulfment and of losing autonomy; too distant and they feel vulnerable to abandonment, isolation, and loss.

Antisocial Practices Scale (*ASP*)

The *ASP* scale contains 22 items, all but 1 of which are keyed "true." It shares three items with *Pd2* (Authority Problems) and six with the *CYN* scale. The latter items assert that "most people" lie and cheat to get ahead in life, steal because others tempt them, and resort to honesty chiefly to avoid trouble. These and 10 additional items form Ben-Porath and Sherwood's (1993) first *ASP* component scale, Antisocial Attitudes (*ASP1*). The additional items endorse a code of silence with authorities, a disdain for the rule of law, a willingness to steal given the opportunity, sympathy for those who treat others rapaciously, and a kind of vengeful joy when others are "catching it." There is thus a strong implicit theme of defective empathy in this set of items and perhaps a tertiary theme of generalized rage at others. Although the data presented in Graham et al. (1999) do not implicate paranoid ideation among their high-scoring *ANT1* outpatients, the relatively high correlations between *ANG1* and *CYN2* (~.60) and *Pa1* (~.50) do suggest such trends. The five-item second component, Antisocial Practices (*ASP2*), consists of admissions of delinquencies in the past, including theft, truancy, school suspensions, and conflict with school and legal authorities. The imbalance in the length of the two *ASP* components is such that the full scale name is something of a misnomer because those items dealing with actual misbehavior (*ASP2*) come to only about one fourth of the full *ASP* scale. Moreover, *ASP2* is comparatively weakly associated with *ASP1* (about .30), a further indication that the relation of *ASP1*, and, to a lesser extent, *ASP* as a whole, to actual antisocial conduct is a tenuous one. Nevertheless, Graham et al. (1999) found that their high *ASP* outpatients frequently manifested antisocial features, including histories of arrest, hostility, antisocial behavior, acting out, low frustration tolerance, substance abuse, and physical abusiveness. In the case of high scores on *ASP2* these features were especially noteworthy, with multiple arrests, felony convictions, hostility, resentment, impulsiveness, poor frustration tolerance, temper outbursts, domestic violence, stormy and physically abusive interpersonal relationships, and diagnoses of antisocial personality disorder and substance abuse. These features were most commonly present in men but were also represented among their women outpatients, who also had histories of physical and sexual abuse, heroin abuse, family problems, and paranoid features.

Relations to Other Scales. The most important relative of the *ASP* scale is the *CYN* scale. Examination of the configuration of *CYN* versus *ASP*, *CYN1* versus *ASP1*, and *CYN2* versus *ASP2* permit fairly detailed inferences about individual sentiments and dynamics and may be especially useful in the interpretation of the 46/64 code patterns and its variants (462, 468, and 469). For all three comparisons, a positive slope (i.e., *CYN* < *ASP*, *CYN1* < *ASP1*, and *CYN2* < *ASP2*) favors a psychopathic over a paranoid bias, whereas a negative slope favors the opposite bias. The within-scale configurations (e.g., *CYN2* > *CYN1*) also may help to guide interpretive efforts when dealing with these issues.

Type A Behavior Scale (*TPA*)

The *TPA* scale contains 19 items, all of which are keyed "true." Three items overlap the *ANG* scale, one on *ANG1* and two on *ANG2*. Nine of the *TPA* items overlap the Wiggins HOS scale, and six items overlap the Cook and Medley (1954) *Ho* scale. The concept of the Type A or coronary-prone personality as operationalized in the Jenkins Activity Survey (JAS: Jenkins, Rosenman, & Friedman, 1967) included three components: Speed and Impatience, Job Involvement, and Hard Driving Competitiveness. The first focused on the time urgency aspect of the Type A syndrome; the second with the extent of occupational demands and the person's dedication or determination to meet or exceed them; and the third with a serious, competitive, and hard-driving self-concept. The items of the *TPA* scale fail to adequately cover this domain. First, the Job Involvement component is insufficiently represented with, at most, two items (Items 507 and 531). Second, the Hard Driving Competitiveness component is so heavily biased toward hostility that the themes of hostile competitiveness and self-imposed demands for performance tend to recede into the background. Indeed, the only correlate found among both the male and female outpatients studied by Graham et al. (1999) to be associated with high *TPA* scores was interpersonal hostility. In a report from the VA Normative Aging Study, Kawachi et al. (1998) found moderate to poor correlations between the *TPA* and JAS total (.36), Speed and Impatience (.46), Job Involvement (.12), and Hard Driving Competitiveness (.22) scores. However, they did find that *TPA* scores were associated with events related to CHD in a community-dwelling sample of older (mean age = 61 years) men. It should also be noted that the JAS was not related to the risk of CHD in a similar cohort (Kawachi et al., 1998).

Ben-Porath and Sherwood (1993) divided the *TPA* scale into Impatience (*TPA1*) and Competitiveness (*TPA2*) components. The *TPA1* items convey a sense of time urgency along with delay-stimulated irritability, such that having to wait in line, being interrupted, or having people on whom one depends fail do their work on time stirs one to annoyance, if not anger. The *TPA2* items convey less a spirit of competitiveness than of resentment, vengefulness, and sadism. High *TPA2* scorers admit to wanting to "win a point" against or pay back people who oppose them, opposing people for trivial reasons, relishing the misfortunes of people whom they dislike, feeling resentment when they feel taken in, and gloating over their competitive advantages. Two additional items appear thematically displaced from *TPA1* (Items 510 and 545), and a third refers to job overinvolvement (Item 531). Although both components carry themes of angry emotionality, the theme of *TPA1* is "hot" and closer to the irritable–angry emotionality of the *ANG* scale, whereas *TPA2* is "cool" and more calculating, controlled, hostile, vengeful, and sadistic than the *ANG* scale. Because TPA2 is the larger of the two components, containing half again as many items as *TPA1*, the quality of *TPA2* is imparted to the full *TPA* scale, making it "cooler" than the full *ANG* scale.

The question may be raised as to whether the *TPA* scale can be presumed to be a construct valid measure of the Type A syndrome. Although there can be little doubt that the scale has *some* construct valid variance if the JAS is held as the standard, it appears on the basis of the limitations of the *TPA* scale as a measure of Type A behavior described earlier, and from the lack of supportive construct-related evidence from empirical investigations that the *TPA* scale is unlikely to function as a sufficiently sensitive and specific measure to support construct-relevant predictions in the individual case. It may be possible, however, on rational grounds, to develop a configurally based indicator involving scores on the *TPA* scale, its components, and other scales in a way that would combine relevant sources of variance to maximize the success of predictions of Type A behavior. A group of hypotheses for this purpose follows.

Relations to Other Scales. Because of the overlap of three items between the *TPA* and *ANG* scales, as well as the similarity of the content between *ANG2* and *TPA1*, these two scales must be distinguished more extensively. As noted already, the *ANG* scale is the "hotter" of the two and the *TPA* scale the "cooler." That is, there is a more urgent press for the expression of affect involved in the *ANG* scale than in the *TPA* scale. The high *TPA* scorer is better controlled, more deliberate, more rigid, and less impulsive than the *ANG* scorer at comparable elevations. The high *TPA* scorer is also less dysphoric, less anhedonic, and less inclined to avoid or deny evidence of personal error or shortcomings than his or her high *ANG* counterpart. That is, the *TPA* scale is thematically more grandiose and narcissistic than the *ANG* scale. It is also more cynical, suspicious, self-justifying, disdainful, and control avoidant than the *ANG* scale. Although the high *ANG* scorer is more irritable, angry, and volatile than the high *TPA* scorer, his or her enmity toward others is less persistently sadistic and domineering; it involves a lesser determination to control and inflict emotional injury on others. The greater control inherent in the *TPA* scale is sufficient to create an impression of assertiveness at times when a comparable *ANG* score would create an impression of excessive anger.

As noted previously, one of the chief weaknesses of the *TPA* scale is the lack of item content related to job involvement. The Work Interference scale (*WRK*) does contain content that can be considered to be at least indirectly related to this aspect of the Type A construct. Of the 33 items on the *WRK* scale, 13 (39%) contain the word *work* or one of its cognates (e.g., *job*). The content of the *WRK* scale includes many items having clear relevance to job involvement and other components of the Type A construct, including eagerness or enthusiasm for work, concentration at work, self-confidence at work, perseverance, competitiveness, and coping with obstacles to work. Of these *WRK* items, about 8 are consistent with one or more of the JAS themes when endorsed in a manner consistent with the *WRK* key, and about 21 are consistent with the items on the JAS when scored in the direction opposite to those on the *WRK* scale. With this pattern in mind, it can be hypothesized that the sign value of high *TPA* scores for the Type A behavior pattern may be enhanced when *WRK* scores fall below $T = 60$. Given the extremity of the hostile implications of *TPA2*, it is likely that the Type A behavior pattern is more strongly suggested when scores on *TPA1* exceed those on *TPA2* than vice versa. Finally, given the high overlap between the *CYN* and *Ho* scales, which has been independently (of the JAS) shown to contain variance for coronary morbidity/mortality, *CYN* scores may support the inference of Type A dynamics when the *CYN* scale exceeds the *ASP* scale and when *CYN1* exceeds *CYN2*. *CYN* and *CYN1* scores that exceed *TPA2* scores might also have incremental value in identifying the Type A pattern.

Low Self-Esteem Scale (*LSE*)

The *LSE* scale contains 24 items, of which all but 3 are keyed "true." It is composed of items admitting personal and interpersonal shortcomings. The high scorer feels slower, less capable, less intelligent, less coordinated, less attractive, less likeable, less self-confident, less resolute, and in many more general ways less adequate than others. Indeed, the high *LSE* respondent feels so overwhelmingly flawed, incompetent, and inferior to others that the independent management of his or her life may seem out of the question, making him or her vulnerable to "charity case" dependent attachments onto others, in which dependency gratifications are paid for in the coin of self-abasement. It is the most sensitive of the content scales to ego-syntonic pathological dependency. The pattern of empirical correlates among the outpatients studied by Graham et al. (1999) appears to correspond closely to this description. However, they noted some relative differences in how their men and women were described. Both were described as depressed, but the men appeared more anxious and somatically focused with histories of physical abuse, whereas the women were seen as more sad, dependent, isolated from others, and with histories of suicide attempts.

Ben-Porath and Sherwood (1993) divided the *LSE* scale into Self-Doubt (*LSE1*) and Submissiveness (*LSE2*). The *LSE1* items are all negative self-attributions that are mostly phrased in such a way as to convey not self-doubt, but *conviction* that one is inferior and inadequate. That is, *LSE1* items assert negative self-attitudes that are relatively fixed and that sum to an overall negative or devalued identity. The *LSE2* items reflect passivity, a servile obedience to others, and by implication, an avoidance of responsibility. There is an interesting tension between the two components in that, when both are elevated, the high scorer seems to be saying, "I'll gladly do whatever you tell me to, but I'm so clumsy and incompetent that you can't expect me to do anything but bollix it up." This would, among other things, suggest an affinity between the *LSE* scale and interpersonal tactics, such as studied incompetence, that might be seen in some contexts as passive–aggressive and in others as self-defeating. However, the *LSE* scale carries a primary implication of a collapse in normal-range defensive operations in which the ordinary maneuvers to shore up self-esteem, to put the best face on one's actions and intentions, and to save face and seek acceptable excuses for one's shortcomings are abandoned. *LSE1* contributes most directly to this aspect of the *LSE* scale; *LSE2* extends the theme closer into the area of interpersonal interaction, where the renunciation of self-esteem culminates in an acceptance of the humiliation of servility.

Low scores on *LSE* suggest relative freedom from negative self-attitudes, especially in the context of interaction with others. Such scores affirm personal adequacy, self-confidence, competence, and independence. Within psychiatric populations, very low scores may reflect an inflated self-concept and possible grandiose ideation or delusions.

Relations to Other Scales. The *LSE* scale may be contrasted with the *DEP* scale in terms of the locus of control construct, with the *LSE* scale being more "external" than the *DEP* scale. Whereas the high *DEP* scorer feels worthless and is more active, demanding, and relatively extrapunitive, the high *LSE* scorer feels helpless and is more passive, dependent, and intropunitive. The *LSE* scale is highly intercorrelated with the *OBS*, *DEP*, *WRK*, and *TRT* scales. An underlying theme in each of these scales is an inability to perform. The *OBS* scale stresses the inability to make decisions and act on them, the *DEP* scale stresses the inability to mobilize sufficient personal resources to engage life, the *WRK* scale stresses the inability to produce output in the context of employment; and the *TRT* scale stresses the inability to rise above helplessness and despair in order to grapple with personal problems. Together, these scales form a quintet for which the theme of motivational disability may be almost as significant as their common core of negative emotionality. That is, the respondent showing peaks on these scales is reporting feeling like a "basket case": depleted, immobilized, blocked, helpless. As noted earlier, reference to the *LSE* and *BIZ* scales can be especially useful in the interpretation of high Scale 8 scores, with these two content scales reflecting the contributions of negative self-attitudes and psychotic thinking, respectively.

Social Discomfort Scale (*SOD*)

The *SOD* scale contains 24 items, of which 13 are keyed "true." Sixteen of the items overlap with the Wiggins Social Maladjustment scale (*SOC*). Eighteen (75%) of the *SOD* items overlap with Scale 0, and most of the nonoverlapping items express a preference for being alone; hence, the theme of interpersonal aversiveness is a good deal stronger in the *SOD* scale than in the *Si* scale. Like the *Si* scale, the *SOD* scale has a conspicuously bipolar character, with high scores connoting introversion and low scores connoting extraversion. Ben-Porath and Sherwood (1993) divided the *SOD* scale into two components: Introversion (*SOD1*) and Shyness (*SOD2*). *SOD1* emphasizes the avoidance of group and social situations, an aversion for interpersonal interaction, and a preference for being alone. Very low *SOD1* scores may reflect a drive to become "lost in the crowd" and an intolerance of being alone. Containing all of the items of the *Si2* subscale (Social Avoidance), *SOD1* is the more "behavioral" of the two components. *SOD2* is less than half the length of *SOD1* and emphasizes the more subjective and emotional features of the parent scale. It conveys a sense of discomfort, effort, difficulty, inhibition, and fear of embarrassment that pervades interactions with others, especially strangers, and in group situations. The high *SOD2* scorer is self-consciously lacking in social skill and, although not necessarily avoidant in the way characteristic of the high *SOD1* scorer, he or she is likely to be seen as reticent and standoffish. The low *SOD2* scorer, by contrast, manifests a uninhibited sociability, enjoys high social visibility, and impresses others as socially intrepid, forward, and mixing easily. All of the *SOD2* items are contained in the *Si1* subscale (Shyness/Self-Consciousness). The high *SOD* scorer, then, seeks to stay away from other people, whether individuals or groups, because he or she feels uneasy and awkward in such situations, and because being alone is said to feel happier. Thus, the high *SOD* scorer is not claiming loneliness, although this may represent a defensive denial of loneliness in some respondents. Low *SOD* scores, then, reflect a gregarious, outgoing style, the enjoyment of interaction, whether individually or in groups. Consistent with the opposite of social discomfort, the low *SOD* scorer evidences a high level of social comfort and confidence by being friendly, fun loving, talkative, participative, and flexible. Sizeable *SOD2–SOD1* differences tend to identify individuals who have difficulty feeling at ease either alone or in the company of others. Ben-Porath and Sherwood have suggested that a low *SOD1* scorer coupled with a high *SOD2* score may reflect an aspiration to be more socially involved and a desire for an increased sense of personal comfort and control in interaction. This pattern is somewhat akin to stage fright, in which others are not rigidly avoided but simply approached with a sense of anxious trepidation. Very low scores on both components suggest a glib but superficial interactional style and are consistent with those manic/hypomanic syndromes having high social hunger (and high social turnover) as a cardinal feature.

The Graham et al. (1999) outpatients with high *SOD* scores showed interpersonal sensitivity, shyness, and social awkwardness, but they were also often seen as depressed and having suicidal ideation. The men were described in terms suggesting more severe and pervasive (e.g., suspicious, resentful, self-degrading) problems than those used to describe the women.

Relations to Other Scales. In the context of high scores on Scale 2 and low scores on Scale 9, high *SOD* scores reflect the kinds of anergic withdrawal and social anhedonia seen in depressive syndromes. In profiles having primary elevations on the *F* scale and Scales 6 and 8, high *SOD* scores may indicate schizophrenia spectrum interpersonal aversiveness and social withdrawal, the avoidant wariness that is grounded in paranoid suspiciousness and concerns for one's personal safety, or both. *SOD* scores in a region of $T = 55–65$, when *SOD2* exceeds *SOD1*, are seen in borderline syndromes. Low *SOD* scores, especially when *SOD1* is low, can indicate warmth and a capacity for closeness with others when the *L* scale and Scales 2, 7, and 8 are relatively low; the *K* scale is in a $T =$ 55–65 range; and the raw *K* score exceeds the non-*K*-corrected raw score on the *Pt* scale. Low *SOD* scores in which *SOD1* exceeds *SOD2* are consistent with narcissistic (check scores on the *LSE* scale and Scale 9) and psychopathic (check scores on the *Pd2*, *ASP2* [*ASP* exceeds *CYN*], *Re*, and *GF* scales) features, as well as with manic/hypomanic states.

Family Problems Scale (*FAM*)

The *FAM* scale contains 25 items, of which 20 are keyed "true." The *FAM* scale contains 10 items that appeared on the Wiggins Family Problems scale and 6 that overlap the *Pd1* subscale (Familial Discord). *FAM* items are about evenly balanced between current family and family of origin. The relatively high correlations between the *FAM* scale and Scales 4 and 8 cannot be accounted for entirely by overlapping items, indicating that the *FAM* scale may have a wider array of personological correlates than might be expected on the basis of its item content alone. This impression is confirmed in the findings of Butcher et al. (1990) in their ratings data from the restandardization couples, and in the correlates Graham et al. (1999) found among their psychiatric outpatients. The restandardization spouses rated their high *FAM* partners in terms suggesting emotional instability and undercontrol; irritability, suspiciousness, hostility, and resentment; tension, worry, and fearfulness; dysphoric mood; dependency; and interpersonal ambivalence. The Graham et al. (1999) outpatients were seen as issuing from families in which emotional deprivation, discord, and abuse (men: physical; women: sexual) were common, but they were also described as depressed, hostile, resentful, and interpersonally sensitive.

The range and severity of these correlates is consistent with the view that positive emotional ties to family are essential to the kind of personal well-being that comes from feeling rooted in social life. A lack of sufficiently fostering primary relationships in childhood, and a stormy and contentious home atmosphere in particular, may bring about a level of personal deprivation and a pattern of negative social expectancies that leaves the individual ill-prepared for later developing the kinds of constructive relationships that lead to a sense of belongingness.

A substantially narrower set of correlates was found by Ben-Porath and Stafford (1993) in a forensic diagnostic sample of 113 men. Participants scoring high on the *FAM* scale tended to show a history of poor relationships with fathers, siblings, family, spouses, and friends; had more frequently lost physical and legal custody of their children; and had been arrested while previously on probation.

High *FAM* scorers not only feel deprived and mistreated by family but also appear to have acquired or augmented a set of dispositions that maintain both intrafamilial and more generalized enmity and insecurity into adulthood. They are apt to be seen by others as immature and overreactive people who harbor grave doubts and deeply negative attitudes toward themselves but who are equally mistrustful and disparaging of others. This pattern of correlates is reminiscent of the pattern of traits in BPD. It is also a pattern that is common to alcohol and other substance abuse.

Ben-Porath and Sherwood (1993) found two *FAM* components: Family Discord (*FAM1*) and Familial Alienation (*FAM2*). The content of *FAM1* stresses intrafamilial conflict and animosity, with members being seen as quarrelsome and disagreeable, oppressive and disapproving, annoying and ill-tempered. The theme is one of the family as an unpleasant, noxious environment from which one would like to escape. The male Graham et al. (1999) outpatients with high *FAM1* scores had histories of sexual abuse, and were described as hostile, depressed, intolerant of frustration, and getting on poorly with coworkers. The Graham et al. (1999) women had histories of suicide attempts and were described as "critical, argumentative, and grouchy" (p. 80).

Less than half the length of *FAM1*, *FAM2* stresses an emotional detachment from family. The items are phrased descriptively and have low emotional valences. They simply report factual states of affairs, which, in some respondents, would be associated with longing, loss, and anger, but in others with a sense of at least partial equanimity or indifference. In either case, high *FAM2* scores imply that respondents severed ties in order to cut their losses with their family because of its inability or disinclination to provide a center of belonging and emotional support. However, the empirical correlates that Graham et al. (1999) found among their outpatients suggest that for high *FAM2* scorers, the severing of emotional attachments to family is not followed by the formation of alternative attachments. Thus, these patients were described as lonely, having few or no friends, and self-destructive, either through suicide attempts (women) or through chronic alcohol and marijuana abuse (men). These investigators also found histories of physical (men) and sexual (women) abuse among high *FAM2* scorers.

Ben-Porath and Sherwood suggested that high scores on *FAM2* when *FAM1* is low indicate disengagement from family. This pattern would also seem to suggest a much greater sense of indifference, perhaps with some feeling of sorrow about the shortcomings of the family as a source of emotional provisions. The opposite pattern suggests the persistence of attachment in the midst of enmity and discord. When both components are elevated, a state of resentful alienation is suggested in which physical ties (i.e., association) have been severed but unresolved emotional attachments continue.

Relations to Other Scales. Despite the overlap between the *FAM* and *Pd1* scales, the two scales have somewhat different interpretive implications for the primary nature and locus of family conflict. As noted previously the *FAM* scale refers to current family and family of origin in about equal measure, whereas reference to the parental home more clearly dominates the content of the *Pd1* subscale, giving it a clear, albeit not strong, bias toward the family of origin. The *Pd1* subscale shows a relatively greater emphasis on the parents as restricting freedom, independence, and efforts toward emancipation. The *FAM* scale conveys a relatively greater sense of family turbulence, pathology, and estrangement. As a result, scores on the *FAM* scale exceeding those on the *Pd1* subscale may be a better reflection on current family relations, whereas the reverse pattern suggests that family strife may be largely confined to the parental home. The patient's age, family history, and current family circumstance, of course, may bear importantly on interpretations of ghe *Pd1* and *FAM* scales and the *FAM* component scales. Peak elevations on the *CYN* scale when the *FAM* scale is elevated imply distrust and dissatisfaction, if not enmity, with intimates that have apparently generalized to others. Distrust and dissatisfaction reach paranoid proportions when the *FAM* and *BIZ* scales are peaked. The pattern of high scores on the *FAM* and *ASP* scales when *ASP* exceeds *CYN* and *SOD* is low (and *SOD1* exceeds *SOD2*) appears to be the content scale equivalent of the psychopathic 49/94 profile type. Clinically, this pattern is associated with immaturity and substance abuse and with assaultiveness and destructiveness.

Work Interference Scale (*WRK*)

The *WRK* scale contains 33 items, of which 5 are keyed "false." As noted in the discussion of the *TPA* scale, almost 40% of the items contain the word *work* or one of its cognates. Of all the content scales, the *WRK* scale is the one most saturated with first-factor variance, achieving correlations with Welsh's *A* scale in the mid- to high .80s (eight items overlap with the *A* scale). It is, in effect, a general measure of distress and disability that has been trimmed to the context of work, emphasizing the kinds of problems that have adverse effects on productivity. As such, it reflects an admixture of content that includes defeatist and pessimistic attitudes; anergia and impersistence; indecision and distractibility; irritability and rebelliousness; bitterness and oppositionality; a lack of initiative and ambition; a lack of enthusiasm and competitiveness; a lack of self-confidence and self-esteem; and a proneness to tension, worry, and fearfulness. Thus, the interferences covered in the *WRK* scale include both interpersonal difficulties and the kinds of attitudes and symptoms that impair efficiency and impede output. Low scores, then, imply self-confidence, perseverance, an adequate fund of energy and the capacity to marshall one's abilities in the service of productivity on the job, a capacity for cooperative interactions with fellow employees (i.e., teamwork), and an ability to limit the influence of personal problems and symptoms on job performance. Graham et al. (1999) found that their high *WRK* scoring outpatients were described in terms indicative of depression, and as tending to lack ambition. The women presented as more passive and dependent; the men as more angry.

Relations to Other Scales. Because of its extensive shared variance with the first factor, the interpretive implications of the *WRK* scale are most likely to be realized when it exceeds the *A* scale in elevation. Although problems that may interfere with functioning in employment are suggested by elevations on the *WRK* scale alone, such elevations cannot be taken to indicate occupational malfunctioning *specifically*. The requirement that the *WRK* scale exceed the *A* scale strengthens the implication of specific work interferences to the extent of this difference. Recalling the high intercorrelations among the *OBS*, *DEP*, *LSE*, *WRK*, and *TRT* scales, scores on the *WRK* scale should always be compared with those on the other scales in this group as a means of gaining additional insight into the kinds of problems that may most threaten work performance.

Negative Treatment Indicators (*TRT*)

The *TRT* scale contains 26 items, of which 4 are keyed "false." It is highly correlated with the *DEP* scale (.77), with which it shares six items (23%), and the empirical correlates found by Graham et al. (1999) to describe high *TRT* scorers are highly similar (often identical) to those they found to describe high *DEP* scorers. As a whole, the *TRT* scale seems to reflect a depressive state in which apathy, despair, and helplessness reach such a level of severity as to result in immobilization. Ben-Porath and Sherwood (1993) divided the *TRT* into two components: Low Motivation (*TRT1*) and Inability to Disclose (*TRT2*). The *TRT1* items connote apathy, an external locus of control, and a tendency to quickly give up in the face of obstacles because of a depletion of personal resources. The high *TRT1* scorer feels helpless and motivationally destitute to the point that struggle against problems and adversity, or even the formulation of plans to do so, is felt to be futile and pointless, leaving no alternative but to give up. *TRT2* is less than half the length of *TRT1* and extends the theme of the futility of efforts at amelioration to the realm of discussion. All of the *TRT2* items reflect a disinclination to volunteer personal information and significant discomfort when one is asked to do so by others. The high *TRT2* scorer does not wish to reveal information about personal problems. Significantly, for women at least, the reasons for such disinclination and discomfort are suggested in the empirical correlates found by Graham et al. (1999) to characterize their high *TRT2* scoring female outpatients, including histories of both physical and sexual abuse, few or no friends, and prior suicide attempts and psychiatric hospitalization. Thus, for women, if not for men, high *TRT2* scorer may reason that confiding in others has not worked out well in the past and may only increase one's personal discomfort without offering any countervailing benefits.

Because both the item content and the empirical correlates of the *TRT* scale are so heavily biased toward depression (*all* of the empirical correlates from the restandardization couples' *TRT* ratings for women are contained within the *DEP* correlates for women; Butcher et al., 1990), it is most improbable that scores on the *TRT* scale or its components have much to contribute to estimates of prognosis for psychotherapeutic treatments. Indeed, it is doubtful that these scores can reliably contribute to questions of psychotherapeutic outcome even in depressive states. First, muteness can be a symptom of severe depression and, in this context, may be no more predictive of psychotherapeutic outcome than other vegetative symptoms of comparable severity. Second, the prognosis for psychotherapy in depression may be quite unstable, appearing guarded to poor in the depths of depressive episodes, only to improve markedly as symptoms such as insomnia, anorexia, and psychomotor retardation subside. Thus, *TRT* scores may better serve prediction and description in the area of depressive *severity* than as a specific and reliable indicator of negative prognostic factors for the psychotherapy of depression or any other conditions commonly treated psychotherapeutically. The interpretation of low scores on the *TRT* scale and its components is equally problematic. Because low *TRT* scorers are adequately motivated, self-confident, planful, and persistent, they are likely to be less distressed and therefore less motivated for psychotherapy. Others obtaining low scores may appear grandiose, inflated, overconfident, insouciant and unreflective in their approach to self-disclosure, and hence be potentially impervious to psychotherapeutic efforts even when tolerant of them. The mere capacity to disclose personal information affords no guarantee that the material revealed can be discussed productively, reflectively, or insightfully. Manic and psychopathic spectrum patients come easily to mind in this regard. Such patients, despite a tendency to obtain low and even very low *TRT* scores, may pose challenges to the psychotherapist that are every bit as forbidding as those posed by high *TRT* scorers. For these reasons, both the positive and the negative predictive power of the *TRT* scale is highly suspect. In a study of male inpatients undergoing treatment for chronic pain, for example, Clark (1996) found that although high *TRT* and *TRT1* scores predicted less improvement in physical capacities over the course of treatment, they predicted greater reductions in Beck Depression Inventory (BDI) scores, the latter effect being attributed to regression to the mean. *TRT* and *TRT1* scores also predicted higher levels of posttreatment dysfunction in these patients, indicating that high scorers were more impaired to begin with. *TRT2* was not significantly associated with changes related to treatment or with post-treatment functioning. Moreover, none of the *TRT* scales were related to premature termination of treatment. To be sure, the patients and treatment examined in this study are not typical of those psychotherapy and psychiatric settings in which the *TRT* scale may be routinely applied. However, until evidence of the validity of the *TRT* scale for its intended purpose is forthcoming from more traditional treatment venues, this scale should be interpreted conservatively and with due caution.

Relations to Other Scales. Recall that the *TRT* scale is one of a cluster of scales that also includes the *OBS*, *DEP*, *LSE*, and *WRK* scales. Of these, as noted earlier, the *TRT* scale is most closely associated with the *DEP* scale. Because the status of the *TRT* scale as a predictor of problems that favor a poorer prognosis for psychotherapeutic endeavors is unknown at this time, it is premature to speculate on patterns between the *TRT*, *DEP*, and other scales in this cluster.

GENERAL PRINCIPLES FOR THE INTERPRETATION OF CONTENT SCALES

Like the Wiggins content scales, scores on the MMPI–2 content scales are highly vulnerable to manipulation. The strong unithematic character of these scales, combined with the generally high obviousness or face validity of the items composing them, places them at the ready disposal of the respondent in accordance with his or her desires. This feature is both an asset and a liability for the assessment process. It is an asset in the sense that the homogeneity and obviousness of these scales make them suitable for a handshake across the item pool. Content scales are "user-friendly," facilitating communication between patient and clinician. Content scales, in effect, unburden the process of self-report and allow the patient greater freedom of movement within the item pool to reveal the kinds of symptoms, concerns, and attitudes considered most salient and problematic. These scales allow the patient to record the kinds of difficulties creating concern, to rank order their severity, and to contrast them with problem areas that have not given rise to concern, presumably those areas experienced by the patient to be conflict free and well within the patient's sphere of competencies to manage. In other words, the patient's control of all three features of a profile of scores—elevation, shape, and scatter—is far greater with the content scales than with other scale groupings, such as the standard clinical scales. MMPI/MMPI–2 data at the content level permit, if not encourage, a shared frame of reference between patient and clinician that, if seized by both, defines the assessment process as a collaborative enterprise; engages the trust of and promotes a sense of personal potency on the part of the patient; can be a stimulus to accurate empathy for the therapist; and can lead to a clear sense that the patient is speaking, the clinician is listening, and the two are in a state of communication. The obvious, homogeneous character of the content scales is a liability in the sense that the respondent who wishes to falsify, obscure, or otherwise present an inaccurate or deceptive account of his or her functioning and symptomatology will find few obstacles for doing so. This once again emphasizes the importance of properly preparing the patient for assessment by explaining the process and its purposes, seeking the patient's cooperation as a collaborator rather than as a subject by exploring ways that testing might help to answer questions of significance to the patient, and otherwise trying to advance the patient's individual purposes, as well as promising prompt and detailed test feedback. It is when the patient feels deprived of a stake in a collaborative relationship with the clinician and the outcome of the assessment that motivation to mislead the assessor and frustrate the goals of assessment is apt to be highest and the risk of a manipulative and deceptive response style are greatest. The patient wishing to present a distorted picture of adjustment may choose to exaggerate or minimize all manner of problems or may selectively emphasize some areas of difficulty and de-emphasize others. Some patients, typically among the most disturbed, will intentionally exaggerate or minimize some kinds of problems but inadvertently claim, or fail to claim, symptoms or complaints that disorder severity has placed outside the reach of conscious manipulation. Such cases can enormously confound and frustrate efforts at interpretation.

The extent of the patient's control of elevation in the content scales can create confusion and uncertainty to clinicians accustomed to following the distinction between elevations at or above $T = 65$ and those failing to reach this level. Among the standard clinical scales, the operation of the *K* scale, the internal corrections for some scales (e.g., Scale 2), and the inclusion of subtle item content for many scales tend to support a line of demarcation between the so-called normal and clinical ranges. The fact that the rate of endorsement for obvious items varies inversely with the endorsement rate for subtle items operates to push *T* scores up when an excess of subtle items are endorsed and to decelerate elevations when obvious items are overendorsed (Burkhart, Christian, & Gynther, 1978). For the content scales, however, these moderating factors are unavailable. As a consequence, content scale elevations are highly vulnerable to differences in response style, and both extremely high-ranging and extremely low-ranging content profiles are commonly seen. Reliance on a particular absolute elevation standard, such as $T = 65$, as an interpretive guideline is much more hazardous in the case of content scale elevations than it is for the standard clinical scales. Instead, the appropriate interpretation of content scales depends much more heavily on *relative* elevations, regardless of whether the average elevation of these scales is high or low.

Because of the extensive shared variation among the content scales, a substantial elevation on a given scale may be required before the variance that is shared with other, similar scales can be assumed to have been exhausted and that fraction of variance unique to the scale in question may be supposed to have "kicked in." The point at which this unique variance can be considered to be in play will vary with both its absolute level of elevation and with its elevation relative to other scales with which it shares variance. For example, consider a male patient obtaining scores of $T = 92$ on both the *ANX* and *DEP* scales. At this level, the items on the *ANX* scale have been exhausted, but five items on the *DEP* scale were marked in the nonscorable direction. It may, therefore, be tentatively assumed that this pattern of scores reflects the substantial contribution of the variance that the two scales share but a relatively larger fraction of variance that is unique to the *ANX* scale than that unique to the *DEP* scale. The clinician would, therefore, be justified in interpreting the *ANX* score more aggressively than the *DEP* score, even though the scales are equally elevated. Consider now a female patient with a score of $T = 69$ on the *ANX* scale and of $T = 83$ on the *DEP* scale. In this case, eight items from each scale were marked in the nonscorable direction, yet the difference in elevation suggests that these scores reflect the relatively greater contribution of unique variance in the *DEP* scale than that for the *ANX* scale. Thus, the clinician could, with some confidence, make the assumption that the *DEP* score reflects a true depressive phenomenon, whereas the *ANX* score may indicate no more that the kind of discomfort common to both anxiety and depression, even though the *ANX* scale is elevated into the "clinical range," and interpreted accordingly. Of course, it is unnecessary for any of the content scales to equal or exceed any particular level in order to be interpretable, provided that there are sufficient differences in elevation among these scales to suggest the operation of unique variances.

Similar considerations apply to very-low-ranging content scale scores. In the great majority of cases, such scores result from a defensive approach to the content of the MMPI/MMPI–2, in which an effort has been made to avoid all responses that might suggest maladjustment or psychopathology, and the clinician will have been alerted to this approach by the configuration of the *L*, *F*, and *K* scales. It is, nevertheless, important to consider how successful the respondent's efforts to avoid the revelation of psychopathology have been and, where a failure to do so is indicated, to attempt identification of possible causes for such failure. For example, consider a case in which all of the content scales except the *ANG* and *TPA* scales are below $T=40$. The *ANG* scale is at $T=43$, and the *TPA* scale is at $T=48$. Although such a profile suggests that the avoidance of pathological content has been largely realized, the avoidance of items reflecting angry or hostile content was relatively less successful. If expressions of anger and hostility are less well-contained on the MMPI/MMPI–2 than other problems, a question may be raised as to whether the control of such expressions in other areas of the respondent's life are also less than fully adequate. It may be that the respondent is comfortable endorsing a few of the *ANG* and *TPA* items out of a feeling that his or her ire, when present, is never less than fully justified. In this context, the respondent may feel that his failure to endorse these few items would amount to the admission of something having worse pathological implications: cowardice, tolerance for injustice, intolerable passivity, or a lack of principle. Consider another example, in which content scale scores range from a low of $T=30$ to a high of $T=47$, but with the *BIZ* scale having the highest score. Here, one may ask, given an obvious effort to avoid pathological content, why should failure occur on a scale having such egregious pathological implications. Because it is not unusual for psychotic ideation to underlie errors in judgment, including the kinds of social judgment that may be at play in completing the MMPI–2 (particularly in the context of ego-syntonic delusions), it is reasonable to consider the possibility of psychotic mentation in the search for an answer to this question. The reader may object, noting that a *T* score of 47 corresponds to a raw score of only a single item. But, however well-taken, this objection does not address the question of why one of this kind of item was endorsed and not an item with less severe implications. One might also object that a single-item endorsement could be the result of an accident in marking, a distraction, a lapse in attention, a manifestation of fatigue, a temporary misalignment of test booklet and answer sheet. Indeed, these possibilities should be admitted into consideration. But the endorsement of clearly pathological content in the context of a highly defensive test protocol is always worthy of further investigation.

The interpretation of content scale scores can often be enhanced in both clarity and precision by making reference to general moderators of test performance, such as factor scales *A* and *R*, and to other gross measures of deviance (e.g., *F* and *F* – *K*), defensiveness (e.g., *K*), and behavioral dyscontrol (e.g., *DIS* [Disconstraint]). For example, a person with a score of $T = 65$ on both the *DEP* and *K* scales may be much more disabled than a person with a score of $T = 65$ on the *DEP* scale and $T = 45$ on the *K* scale. In the first instance, the *K* scale may be suppressing the endorsement of items reflecting depression that might otherwise be made. In the same vein, the patient who scores $T = 70$ on the *BIZ* scale and $T = 75$ on the *F* scale may be more disabled by psychosis than one who obtains an identical *BIZ* score but a score of $T = 90$ on the *F* scale because the higher *F* score provides the *BIZ* scale greater "permission" to elevate. In other words, an individual elevating the *F* scale at $T = 90$ is likely endorsing a wide variety of unusual items but may not be responding preferentially to psychotic content. By contrast, in the context of a *BIZ* score at $T = 70$, a much lower *F* elevation would suggest a narrow focus on the psychotic content of the *F* scale, the content of which may be elaborated from the nonoverlapping items on the *BIZ* scale.

THE PERSONALITY PSYCHOPATHOLOGY FIVE (*PSY-5*)

The MMPI restandardization committee felt that the original MMPI item pool was inadequate to cover several assessment issues that the committee deemed important. These included suicidal ideation, substance abuse problems, accessibility to psychotherapeutic treatment, problems in the work setting, and others. The committee, therefore, generated many new items in order to expand the number of items with content related to these areas. The occasion of the restandardization afforded the committee members a rare and possibly unique opportunity to alter an item pool that had been fixed for nearly a half century. And given this opportunity, the members proceeded by a rational–deductive strategy, in which the formulation of new items was guided by the construct a desired future scale is intended to embody. But what of the assessor who is convinced of the merits of the rational strategy of scale construction but faced with an item pool that has been fixed, closed to new items and content? Harkness (1990) proposed that if new items could not be written in support of a construct that was not envisioned at the time the item pool became closed, the way was still open to rationally *select* items from the fixed pool to address new constructs. Specifically, Harkness proposed an approach he called *replicated rational selection*. Replicated rational selection remains a rational–deductive strategy in that the scale development process begins with the specification of the construct to be measured. It is at the next step that Harkness' strategy diverges from traditional methods. Instead of deducing new items to be written for the construct, items are selected from the established pool. The process remains deductive in that the selection of candidate items follows deductively from the construct to be measured. Whereas in the usual rational–

deductive sequence, items may be written by any number of contributors, from one to many, it is the essence of Harkness' procedure that many selectors, a couple of dozen or more, having been trained in the defining features of the construct, in both its convergent and discriminant aspects, nominate items to be scaled: hence his designation of the procedure as *replicated* rational selection. Candidate items are then evaluated for the degree to which each attained consensus within the group of selectors. Thus, items arrange themselves along a selection gradient that displays a range from items selected only sporadically among the cadre of selectors to those whose frequency of nomination approaches unanimity. Items for which adequate consensus is found are then subjected to expert and statistical scrutiny to ensure overall semantic consistency and adequate internal consistency reliability. No items can be added at this stage, but a few may be deleted because of ambiguous wording or keying, compound phrasing, items with a primary focus on others rather than the self, or the retention of some items leads to an unacceptable decrement in internal consistency. Following this stage, the scale is ready for empirical trials to assess its construct validity.

The PSY–5 (Harkness, McNulty, & Ben-Porath, 1995) is a set of five scales that are intended to model the domain of disordered personality. The scales are Negative Emotionality/Neuroticism (*NEN*), Psychoticism (*PSY*), Aggressiveness (*AGG*), Disconstraint (*DIS*), and Low Positive Emotionality/Extraversion (*LPE*). Table A.4 provides the scoring key for these scales, and Table B.12 presents the *T*-score conversions for the scales. Despite points of similarity with five-factor models of normal personality derived from the broader lexicon of trait descriptive terms (The Big Five), Harkness and McNulty (1994) argued that measures based on such models, like the Neuroticism, Extraversion, and Openness Personality Inventory (NEO–PI), are less than optimal as applied to the routine tasks of clinical assessment and description, particularly with personality disordered patients.

The correspondence between the normal-sample-based Five Factor Model (FFM), as represented by the scales of the NEO–PI–Revised (NEO–PI–R; Costa & McCrae, 1992a, 1992b, 1992c), and the PSY–5 is as follows, in descending order of their similarity:

FFM	PSY–5
Neuroticism	Negative Emotionality/Neuroticism
Extraversion	Low Positive Emotionality/Extraversion
Agreeableness	Aggressiveness (reversed)
Conscientiousness	Disconstraint (reversed)
Openness	—
—	Psychoticism

A recent investigation by Trull, Useda, Costa, and McCrae (1995) found substantial convergence between NEO–PI–R Neuroticism and Extraversion, including all six of the facets of each of these scales, and the *NEN* and *PEE* scales, respectively. But the extremity of the *AGG* scale rendered it a poor analogue for NEO–PI–R Agreeableness. Low *AGG* scores predicted only half of the Agreeableness facet scores and at only modest levels. The *AGG* scale was somewhat more strongly and consistently related to facets of NEO–PI–R Extraversion, especially Assertiveness and Activity. The *DIS* scale predicted (negatively) Agreeableness Straightforwardness and Compliance facet scores at modest levels, as well as the Deliberation and Dutifulness facets of NEO–PI–R Conscientiousness. Although none of the PSY–5 constructs correspond to *FFM* Openness, the *DIS* scale was correlated with NEO–PI–R Extraversion and Conscientiousness. Similarly, the *PSY* scale, which has no counterpart in the NEO–PI–R, was modestly related to most of the NEO–PI–R Neuroticism facets because of the negative emotionality shared by both scales (e.g., anxiety and anger).

Negative Emotionality/Neuroticism Scale (*NEN*)

The *NEN* scale contains 33 items, of which 6 are keyed "false." It is highly correlated with markers for the first factor, including the *A* scale (.87) and Scale 7 (.84), as well as with the *ANX*, *WRK*, *OBS*, and, importantly, *ANG* scales. Its overlap with the *A* scale, however, is confined to only six items. The largest subset of items reflect worry, nervousness, anxiety, tension, and stress. A second subset reflects anger and emotional undercontrol. Two smaller groups of items denote guilt and fears, respectively. The *NEN* scale reflects the sense of being so overwhelmed with the stress of worry, nervousness, fear, and guilt that one feels "at the end of one's rope" and "quick to fly off the handle." Two themes are implicit in the item content: (a) a pervasively unpleasant and aversive emotional life, one that feels both relentless and intrusive, leading to inner agitation, and (b) a feeling that one's controls have been taxed by this relentlessly aversive emotionality to the point of collapse. The high *NEN* scorer presents as helpless, dependent, needy, indecisive, and unstable. Relations with others are characterized by extreme passivity, fears of abandonment, and hypersensitivity to criticism. He or she may provoke exasperation in others as there may be repeated failures to take initiative to improve the situation and to act in his or her best interest. Borderline attachments to others, help-rejecting complainingness, and suicidal or self-mutilative behavior may be seen.

At the low end, the *NEN* scale reflects a relaxed and imperturbable emotionality that is so care- and worry-free as to suggest an impoverishment of internal experience and awareness, thus raising the question of repressiveness. In any case, at the extreme, low scores are likely to reflect an emotional life that is placid to the point of imperviousness.

Relations to Other Scales. As one more congener of the first factor, the *NEN* scale is related to distress across a wide range of manifestations.

Psychoticism Scale (*PSY*)

The *PSY* scale contains 25 items, of which 2 are keyed "false." The *PSY* scale is strongly correlated with measures of similar constructs, including the *BIZ* scale (.94), with which it shares 14 items, the *F* scale (.71), and Scales 8 (.69) and 6 (.65). Additional correlates include the *OBS* (.66) and *CYN* (.64) scales and the Morey, Waigh, and Blashfield (1985) Paranoid Personality Disorder scale (*PAR*; .64). The two largest groupings of items have active psychotic and active persecutory content, respectively. Additional subsets of items concern unusual experience/magical ideation, daydreaming, and suspiciousness. Harkness et al. (1995) describe the *PSY* scale as assessing "the gross verisimilitude of [one's] inner models of the outer social and object world" (p. 105). Thus, it is intended to reflect the extent to which the individual's ability to conform his or her thinking to consensual views of the external world and to the human action within it—and to correct elements of thinking and interpretation that render one's model of reality a poor fit to the actual external situation—is impaired. At moderate elevations (T = 55–65), the *PSY* scale may reflect little more than unusual beliefs or experiences, and perhaps a tendency to overindulge in daydreaming. Any elevation may be taken as a sign of reluctance to engage the world and other people in conventional terms. Even at mild and moderate elevations, the *PSY* scale reflects disharmony in one's relations with the physical and social worlds such that functioning is compromised and relationships are alienated. At these levels, the person may give the appearance of being "in the world but not of it." At higher elevations one encounters severe distortions in the way the individual interacts with his or her social and physical worlds, such that these interactions appear, respectively, hostile, provocative, offensive, inept or incompetent, irrelevant, bizarre, or self-defeating. At elevations greater than $T = 65$, however, true psychotic phenomena make an appearance, including Schneiderian symptoms, fixed persecutory if not frank delusional ideation, and suspiciousness. In general, the high *PSY* scorer presents as odd, peculiar, or weird in appearance, behavior, and belief. He or she appears to be preoccupied with fantasy and daydreaming and seems "out of touch with reality." Relations with others are apt to be minimal, distant, and covertly hostile, with a readiness to feel mistreated and resentful.

Low *PSY* scores are largely without symptomatic significance apart from the absence of those features associated with high scores. However, in terms of its guiding construct, one would expect low *PSY* scores to carry favorable implications regarding the individual's ability to detect and correct misimpressions in order to accommodate previous editions of his or her inner model of reality to newly apprehended features of the human and nonhuman environment.

Relations to Other Scales. Because the content of about 40% of the *PSY* items is persecutory or suspicious in character, reference can be made to the *Pa1* subscale (Ideas of External Influence) to estimate the contribution of paranoid ideation to *PSY* elevations.

Disconstraint Scale (*DIS*)

The *DIS* scale contains 28 items, of which the majority, 17, are keyed "true." It is moderately correlated with the *ASP* scale (.57), with which it shares eight items, and with the Morey et al. (1985) Antisocial Personality Disorder scale (.50). It overlaps negatively by nine items with the *GF* scale and seven items with the *Re* scale. The *DIS* scale is the only one of the PSY–5 scales for which age appears to be an important moderator, with scores tending to decrease with age (r = –.24; Harkness, Spiro, Butcher, & Ben-Porath, 1995). The largest subset of items reflects an expedient morality such that "anything goes." A somewhat smaller group of items admit delinquent conduct. Four additional groups of items concern sexual disinhibition, sensation seeking, activity, and fears (two items). The main theme is one of undermodulation of impulse, spontaneity, broad interests, cognitive and moral flexibility, insufficient delay of gratification, and an independence from familiar if not hackneyed rubrics. High scores, reflect an unconventional, disinhibited personality structure with insufficient delay and modulation of impulse, a nonconforming and rebellious attitude toward rules and regulations, sensation seeking, shallow and self-centered loyalties, a hedonistic moral compass, indifference to, if not disdain for, legal and ethical constraints, a fearless if not reckless disregard for potential physical hazards, and a tendency to sacrifice long-term goals for short-term satisfactions. The high *DIS* scorer may present initially as energetic and spontaneous, but on closer acquaintance comes to appear unreliable, reckless, and rebellious. Relations with parents and authority figures tend to be conflicted; relations with peers and others tend to be exploitive, promiscuous, and unstable. Impulsive and antisocial acting out, a lack of loyalty, repeated lying and neglect of obligations, and a lack of shame or remorse eventually may disrupt all but correctional relationships.

The low *DIS* scorer, by contrast, presents as conventional, conforming, and controlled. Relations with others may be quite smooth but distant, formalized, and routinized, with contacts limited to a small circle of like-minded friends. A high tolerance for boredom, sameness, and routine and a relatively rigid adherence to traditional moral standards, along with a willingness to judge others in terms of these standards, are characteristic. Very concerned with maintaining "proper" appearances, the low *DIS* scorer takes an overly deliberate if not perfectionistic, approach to problem solving.

Relations to Other Scales. The *DIS* scale appears to occupy the position formerly held by Block's (1965) Ego Control scale (*EC–5*; scoring reversed) in the MMPI environment. The restandardization entailed the loss of nearly a third of the *EC–5* items, with uncertain consequences for its adequacy as a marker for the second (or beta) factor of the MMPI/MMPI–2. With its emphasis on emotional inhibition, social withdrawal, and narrow interests, the *R* scale has been the traditional marker for this factor. An alternative marker for the same factor, the *EC–5* scale emphasized behavioral over emotional constraint, with particular reference to rule following and social conformity. The Harkness, McNulty, and Ben-Porath (1995) Disconstraint construct is very similar to *EC–5* (reversed) and shares a similar level of association with the *R* scale, about –.40. Because, like distress, emotional and behavioral controls are of pervasive significance in psychopathology, both the *R* and *DIS* scales may contribute to the interpretation of most other scales. Discussion of the *DIS* scale in relation to other scales is therefore highly selective.

In their discussion of the *DIS* scale, Harkness et al. (1995) called attention to the similarity between it and the personality disorder simplex found by Romney and Bynner (1992): Both had antisocial personality at one end and compulsive personality at the other. Although it is unknown whether and to what extent *DIS* scores (when low) are sensitive to obsessive–compulsive personality disorder, for reasons having to do with the pervasiveness of the constraint dimension across a variety of psychiatric conditions, scores on this scale may well contribute to the discrimination between obsessive–compulsive disorder and obsessive–compulsive personality disorder. Along with investigation of the correlates of both high and low *DIS* scores in relevant psychiatric samples, it may also be illuminating to examine configurational relationships of the *OBS* scale with the *DIS* scale. For example, are small (or negative) *OBS–DIS* differences associated with obsessive–compulsive personality disorder but not with obsessive–compulsive disorder, as might be expected, whereas larger differences in the context of high *OBS* scores (and, perhaps, a relatively large *FRS–DIS* difference) show the opposite pattern?

With high *DIS* scores and moderate to high *NEN* scores, one could anticipate contranormative approaches to coping with subjective discomfort, such as through alcoholism or other substance abuse. A recent study of the Boston VA normative aging sample by Harkness, Levenson, et al. (1995) found that the *DIS* (formerly *CON*) and *NEN* scales were the top-ranked variables contributing to the separation of problem and heavy drinkers from nonproblem drinkers. High *DIS* scores would synergize with low *LPE* scores to produce adventurousness, sensation seeking, and sometimes recklessness. In the context of low *NEN* scores and high *AGG* scores, this pattern would suggest the classic amoral/asocial psychopathic picture. Low *DIS* and high *NEN* scores would appear to coincide with immaturity and a lack of responsibility and to reflect those problems of impulse control in which impulsive action is reinforced by tension reduction. High *DIS* and high *PSY* scores may synergize to emphasize a readiness to indulge in fantasy (including bizarre fantasy) and daydreaming, especially when *LPE* scores are high.

Aggressiveness Scale (*AGG*)

The *AGG* scale contains 18 items, of which 3 are keyed "false." It is highly correlated with all of the scales within the aggressive tendencies cluster of the MMPI–2 content scales, ranging from a low of .45 for the *ANG* scale to a high of .55 for the *TPA* scale. Other correlates include the *R* scale (–.63); Scale 9 (.56); and the Narcissistic (*NAR*; .53), Histrionic (*HST*; .40), and Antisocial (*ANT*; .37) personality disorder scales of Morey et al. (1985). The *AGG* scale is unique among MMPI/MMPI–2 scales in tapping offensive or predatory aggression. For example, it is considerably less saturated with nonspecific variance, correlating with Welsh's *A* scale at –.01, than scales in the aggressive tendencies cluster whose correlations with the *A* scale are in the .45 to .60 range. In this respect, the *AGG* scale is much "cooler" than any of the other anger/hostility scales for the MMPI/MMPI–2, including the *ANG*, *TPA*, and Cook and Medley (1954) *HOS* scales. The content of the *AGG* scale emphasizes a theme of superiority and control avoidance, with additional subsets reflecting sadism and vindictiveness. *AGG* expressions of aggression, hostility, and control/domination are more apt to reflect cruelty than rage and are more apt to appear calculated, deliberate, methodical, and cold. By contrast, similar expressions from, for example, high scorers on the *ANG* and *TPA* scales are more likely to be seen as reactions to frustration or other provocation and as rash, unpremeditated, impulsive, and reckless or ill considered.

The *AGG* scale reflects the hostile urge to dominate, vanquish, and destroy others. Thus, it is predatory or sadistic aggression that is at stake in this scale rather the kind of (angry) aggression that is motivated by frustration in the *ANG* scale and in another of the PSY–5 scales, Negative Emotionality/Neuroticism (*NEN*). The self-concept is inflated, grandiose, and resentful, with a dread of being subject to the control of another and a willingness to act sadistically and vindictively in order to avoid such control. The *AGG* scale evokes several paranoid dynamisms, including the defense mechanism, identification with the aggressor, the tendency to see interactions as moves in a zero-sum game and, possibly, the authoritarian complex of submissiveness with superiors and tyrannical relations with subordinates. The high *AGG* scorer presents as controlling others through the threat of his or her temper. Relations with others are marked by aggressive efforts to control and dominate through fear and the threat of violence and by resentment, hostility, and sadism.

Low *AGG* scores will reflect less the absence of aggression, in the sense of approach, than of the hostile orientation toward power, domination, and sadism characteristic of high *AGG* scores. Thus, the low *AGG* scorer may manifest an aggressive, engaging style, but one that is less pressured and that accepts relations among others on horizontal, egalitarian terms, in which the mutual achievement of individual goals is not only conceivable but also expected. The low *AGG* scorer accepts both one-up and one-down positions in his or her relations with others, knowing that these are transitory and subject to a variety of constraints that limit arbitrary vertical action of superior on subordinate.

Relations to Other Scales. Assessment of the degree to which hostile expressions are likely to be calculated versus precipitate may be aided by reference to the relative elevations of the *AGG* and *ANG* scales. The *AGG* scale shares some common variance with three other PSY–5 scales, Disconstraint (*DIS*; .42) and Low Positive Emotionality/Extraversion (*LPE*; –.29), conceived as anergy, low activation, or low readiness to act, and Psychoticism (*PSY*; .33), reflecting an unrealistic view of self and others and one that overemphasizes issues of power and control. The shared variance between the *AGG* and *LPE* scales, along with the absence of variance in common with the *A* scale, suggests that the control, domination, and harm that issues from the high AGG scorer is associated with pleasure, enjoyment, and a sense of well-being. Selfish, self-centered, and yet envious of others, the high *AGG* scorer reflects a hostile narcissism that is heavily dependent on the attention and recognition of others. But the self-concept is so unrealistic, grandiose, and entitled that the desired reflections are forthcoming only under conditions of coercion. In this context, the combination of high *AGG* scores with high *DIS* scores or with high *PSY* scores would appear to be especially dangerous combinations. In the case of high *AGG* and high *DIS* scores, there is a synergy between sadistic motivation and deficits in behavioral control. Conjoint elevations on the *AGG* and *PSY* scales suggest a risk for hostile action in the context of disordered thinking, such as bizarre and violent fantasy, command hallucinations or ego-syntonic delusions, especially when *DIS* and *LPE* are high.

The *AGG* scales has an obvious bearing on the quality and dynamics of treatment relationships, especially when *DIS* scores are high and *NEN* scores are at least moderately high, with high scorers likely to violate treatment plans, fail to follow through on agreements, discontinue medication, and in other ways undermine therapeutic efforts.

In relation to low *AGG* scores, low *DIS* scores suggest underassertion, passivity, and a high threshold for resisting domination. In this context, elevations on the *NEN* scale (or similar distress scales, such as *A*, Scale 7, *ANX*, and *DEP*) may indicate patterns of behavior suggesting self-sabotage and self-defeat. Such a pattern would also be consistent with symptoms of obsessive–compulsive disorder. Low *AGG* scores with low *LPE* scores would seem to create a vulnerability to being played for a patsy by misplacing trust in others and approaching situations with a kind of credulous confidence that most others would avoid.

Low Positive Emotionality/Extraversion Scale (*LPE*)

The *LPE* scales contains 34 items, of which 5 are keyed "true." Correlates with other MMPI/MMPI–2 scales include Scales 2 (.79) and 0 (.76)—it shares 13 items with each—and with the *DEP* (.61) and *SOD* (.73) scales. Among the Morey et al. (1985) personality disorder scales, the *LPE* scale has positive correlations with the Avoidant (*AVD*; .68), Schizotypal (*STY*; .61) and Schizoid (*SZD*; .52) scales, and negative correlations with Narcissistic (*NAR*; –.71) and Histrionic (*HST*; –.64) scales. The largest subsets of items claim low energy and hedonic capacity, and social awkwardness/discomfort and withdrawal. Three smaller groups of items deny personal adequacy, persistence, and euphoria. The *LPE* scale reflects social disengagement and a lack of emotional buoyancy. High scorers suggest not so much the presence of unpleasant or aversive emotionality, as in the case of the *NEN* scale, as of a depleted, impoverished emotional life. Characteristic features include anhedonia, anergy, dissatisfaction, low self-esteem, and a tendency to give up quickly in the face of difficulty. Depending on the particular pattern of items endorsed, high *LPE* scores may reflect depressive withdrawal, schizoid underinvolvement, or both. The high *LPE* scorer is uncomfortable around other people and tends to avoid social situations. Relations with others are distant, although not hostile; rather, the high *LPE* scorer tends to react to others in an impassive way when interaction cannot be avoided. A defective pleasure parameter (Meehl's 1974, 1987, anhedonia) may be at the root of the high *LPE* scorer's impoverished emotional responsiveness.

The low *LPE* scorer presents as sociable, outgoing, visible, warm, and socially attractive if not charismatic. Relations with others are warm and easygoing, based on high self-esteem, freedom from debilitating stresses, distinct pleasure in interaction with others, and mutual respect for their rights and freedoms. The low *LPE* scorer describes high self-esteen, feeling liked and accepted by others, a quickness to feel pleasure and fulfillment, a deep reservoir of energy for the pursuit of goals, and a sense of happy connection with others that includes a desire for close and intimate relationships.

Relations to Other Scales. The *DIS* scale may be an important modifier of *LPE* scores, with low scores on both scales suggesting that the social buoyancy of the *LPE* scores is controlled and socially constructive. When *DIS* scores are high and *LPE* scores are low, the person's sociability is apt to be superficial and utilitarian. This combination suggests an especially high rate of social turnover, as the need for stimulation and novelty undermines loyalty and results in a lowered threshold for boredom in relationships. Conversely, low *DIS* scores in the context of high *LPE* scores reflects not only drastically curtailed social initiative, but also a high tolerance for predictability and sameness in relations with others. This is a formula for relationships that, however long-lived, remain shallow. With moderately high *AGG* scores, the low *LPE* scorer may be more dominant and controlling and have significant problems with joining others in compromise.

Effects of Response Styles on the *PSY–5* Scales

Given their method of construction, the *PSY–5* scales could not but have very high face validity. That is not to say, however, that their content will be obvious to the respondent. Whereas the items of the *NEN* and *PSY* scores obviously refer to psychopathological disturbance, a great many if not the majority of the items on the *DIS*, *AGG*, and *LPE* scores refer to normal-range individual differences and are therefore less socially undesirable, on the whole, than the *NEN* and *PSY* scales. To date, there have not been empirical investigations of the effects of response sets on the PSY–5 scales in order to gauge their susceptibility to manipulation, but on the basis of the correlates of these scales, some effects can be anticipated. Sets to exaggerate distress or psychopathology will tend to elevate the *NEN* scale, the *LPE* scale, and especially the *PSY* scale, whereas efforts to deny or conceal symptoms and maladjustment will tend to suppress the *NEN*, *PSY*, and *LPE* scales.

Like the MMPI–2 content scales, the great majority of the items on the *PSY–5* scales are keyed for the "true" response (the exception is the *LPE* scale for which about 85% of the items are keyed "false"). As a consequence, these scales are vulnerable to extremes in true–false responding. A high "true" percentage will sharply elevate the *AGG* scale, *NEN* scale, and especially the PSY scale, while keeping the *LPE* scale below $T = 50$. A high false percentage will sharply elevate the *LPE* scale, and confine scores on the other four scales to the average range or below.

8

Interpreting the Supplementary Scales

INTRODUCTION

Since the earliest days following the publication of the MMPI, investigators have selected the MMPI item pool as a source for the development of new scales for the measurement of a bewildering array of variables. Hathaway and McKinley's completion of the series of clinical scales based on pathological criterion groups produced no significant pause in scale development efforts. By the mid-1950s, these efforts had yielded a large number of scales, a plurality of which had been developed by graduates and doctoral advisees from the University of Minnesota or by their students in turn.

Following the example of the clinical scales, some of these efforts have been focused on psychopathological syndromes, or features of them, that were formerly unavailable in sufficient numbers to permit scale development. Examples of these include low-back pain, neurodermatitis, ulcer personality, alcoholism, and pedophilia. One series of scales was developed to discriminate several conditions—somatization reaction, depressive reaction, anxiety reaction, conversion reaction, and paranoid schizophrenia—not from a background sample of normals but from a reference group of general psychiatric patients (Rosen, 1962). Still other efforts sought scales to detect psychopathological syndromes but preferred a rational/statistical strategy over the empirical group contrast methodology that shaped the basic clinical scales of the MMPI. The DSM-III (American Psychiatric Association, 1980) personality disorder scales of Morey et al. (1985) are examples. However, the vast majority of new MMPI scales have been built to aid the measurement or prediction of an unusually broad range of abnormal and normal traits involving achievements, attitudes toward self and others, behavioral dispositions, styles of inventory response, and others. Dahlstrom et al. (1975) listed 455 scales. Their list was known to be incomplete at the time it was published and, among others, did not include any of the 89 basic clinical and validity scales and their derivatives that they listed in 1972. Thus, even in 1975, the total number of MMPI scales was almost certainly greater than the number of items on the test.

By far the greatest number of scales developed since the inception of the MMPI have not made their way to more than a handful of users. Many were probably never used by other than their authors. The reasons for the limited penetration of such scales are not hard to find, among them (a) scales developed for overly specific purposes; (b) the use of samples of inadequate size or representativeness; (c) inadequate or inappropriate contrast groups; (d) inadequate test–retest or internal consistency reliability; (e) inadequate concurrent or predictive validity; (f) failures on cross-validation or excessive cross-validation shrinkage; (g) excessive redundancy with preexisting and/or better validated scales; (h) excessive redundancy with the major sources of variation within the item pool (poor discriminant validity); (i) problems with construct definition or understanding; and (j) a host of other problems including awkward, obscure, or misleading scale names, uncertainties about the availability or appropriateness of norms, difficulties in retrieval (e.g., unpublished dissertations or reports in journals of limited circulation), and simple lack (or loss) of interest. Considering the time, personnel, and support required to mount and publish investigations justifying a scale's clinical or research application, it is not surprising that so few scales have been successful.

The formation of a standard "set" of supplementary scales occurred slowly. The initial stimulus was provided by the mention of some of the newer scales in the course of MMPI presentations at seminars, colloquia, and workshops by early publicists, especially Paul Meehl and Harrison Gough. A further important impetus was the inclusion of most of them in the Welsh and Dahlstrom (1956) compendium, *Basic Readings on the MMPI in Psychology and Medicine*, and the provision of norms for scoring them a year later (Hathaway and Briggs, 1957). To this point, users of the MMPI could select for scoring those scales that appeared to be applicable to their particular practices and populations, ignoring the rest. It was not until the 1960s and the advent of machine scoring that scores for these scales became routinely available as a set. The first automated MMPI scoring system was established at the Mayo Clinic, becoming operational in 1961, but The Psychological Corporation, the Consulting Psychologists Press, and many other commercial concerns made computer scoring services available shortly thereafter. These services ultimately formed what became known alternatively as the supplementary or research scales into a distinct set.

The first of the supplemental scales was actually Social Introversion (*Si*; Drake, 1946), which became formally incorporated as the last of the standard clinical scales only in 1951. The most frequently reported supplemental scales were 11 in number and usually presented in the following order: Welsh's (1956) factor scales *A* and *R*; Barron's (1953) Ego Strength scale (*Es*); Hanvik's (1949) Low Back Pain scale (*Lb*); H. L. Williams' (1952) Caudality scale (*Ca*); Navran's (1954) Dependency scale (*Dy*); Gough, McClosky, and Meehl's (1951) Social Dominance scale (*Do*); Gough, McClosky, and Meehl's (1952) Social Responsibility scale (*Re*); Gough's (1951) Prejudice scale (*Pr*); Gough's (1948a, 1948b) Social Status scale (*St*); and Cuadra's

(1956) Control scale (*Cn*). Although this series persisted for many years, scale development continued apace and many services expanded to accommodate and report scores on additional supplementary scales, notably, J. A. Taylor's (1953) Manifest Anxiety scale (*At* or *MAS*); Kleinmuntz' (1961a) College Maladjustment scale (*Mt*); MacAndrew's (1965) Alcoholism scale (*Alc* or *MAC*); and Megargee–Cook, and Mendelsohn's (1967) Overcontrolled–Hostility scale (*O–H*).

There is no doubt that this list scales, or any similar list of nonroutinely interpreted scales, are somewhat arbitrary. Few if any of them had proved themselves in routine clinical applications at the time they became aggregated into a semistandard panel of scores. Their attainment of this position of status rested on a combination of their reasonably scrupulous construction, and a degree of consensus among the MMPI opinion leaders at the time that these scales held promise for clinical decision making, application to research, or both.

The restandardization that led to the release of the MMPI–2 in 1989 created an opportunity to review an immense array of scales, those that had been available in 1975 (as compiled by Dahlstrom et al.) and those that had accumulated in the interim. Among the almost-limitless bases for the selection of a set of supplemental scales to succeed those that had become more or less standard for the MMPI environment was the effect of the 90 items that were not retained in the transition from the MMPI to the MMPI–2. The content of these discontinued items varied widely but disproportionately represented interests and hobbies (17 items); religion (16 items); interpersonal relationships (14 items); negative affects (12 items); and bodily functions, mostly urinary/excretory (9 items; Greene, 1991a). Thus, scales importantly or entirely (e.g., Wiggins, 1966, Religious Fundamentalism scale [*REL*]) consisting of such items would be ineligible for retention on the MMPI–2.

A potentially important factor guiding the selection of a new set of supplemental scales was the availability of research attesting to the validity of several scales that had accumulated during the preceding 40 years. Indeed, the majority of the scales chosen for the MMPI–2 supplemental scales (*A*, *R*, *Es*, *O-H*, *Do*, *Re*, *Mt*, and *MAC–R*) appear to have been selected on this basis. These scales and others are discussed in this chapter.

The sequence of supplemental scales for the MMPI–2 is as follows: *A*; *R*; *Es*; Back *F* or *F*-Back (*F*(*B*); Butcher et al., 1989); Tellegen's True Response Inconsistency (*TRIN*; Butcher et al., 1989); Tellegen's Variable Response Inconsistency (*VRIN*; Butcher et al., 1989); *O-H*; *Do*; *Re*; *Mt*; Peterson and Dahlstrom's (1992) Gender Role—Masculine (*GM*) and Gender Role—Feminine (*GF*); T. M. Keane, Malloy, and Fairbank's (1984) Post-Traumatic Stress Disorder (*PK*); Schlenger and Kulka's (1987) Post-Traumatic Stress Disorder (*PS*); and *MAC–R*.

Three of the supplemental scales were included to assess factors related to response style and cooperation in completing the MMPI–2: *VRIN*, *TRIN*, and *F*(B). These are discussed in chapter 2. The remaining scales—*GM*, *GF*, *PK*, and *PS*—were, like the supplementary scales for the MMPI, selected mostly because of their judged promise for augmenting the interpretive possibilities of the test and not on the basis of accumulated research supporting their validity.

These scales do not exhaust the MMPI–2 supplemental scales currently approved by the test's publisher. Several newer scales are already available, including Weed, Butcher, McKenna, and Ben-Porath's (1992) Addiction Potential (*APS*) and Addiction Acknowledgment (*AAS*) scales and Hjemboe, Almagor, and Butcher's (1992) Marital Distress scale (*MDS*). These are discussed later in this chapter. The item composition and scoring direction for the supplementary scales are reported in Table A.5; Tables B.13 and B.14 present the *T*-score conversions from the raw scores for these scales.

FACTOR SCALES *A* AND *R*

Welsh's purpose in developing the *A* and *R* scales was to provide a convenient means of locating respondents along the two primary dimensions that had been repeatedly identified in factor analyses of the basic clinical and validity scales of the MMPI. Although prior analyses had found varying numbers of factors, depending on the sample and the numbers of scales included in each, the primary dimension had consistently shown high positive loadings on Scales 7 and 8 and high negative loadings on the *K* scale. Thirty-nine items (38 keyed "true," 1 keyed "false") that achieved a 75% separation between the top and bottom 10% of the distribution of a preliminary scale (*G*) (Meehl & Hathaway, 1946) of both of two groups of male VA patients were chosen for the scale that Welsh called *A* for Anxiety. The *A* scale became, and remains, the most widely acknowledged marker for the first factor of the MMPI/MMPI–2.

The great response style debate that raged in the decade from 1955 to 1965 was largely concerned with whether the first factor of the MMPI should have a substantive (psychopathologic) or stylistic (test-taking attitude) interpretation. Although this controversy was never fully resolved, it cooled rapidly after Block (1965) demonstrated that even when the two main stylistic features of MMPI performance (social desirability and acquiescence) were controlled, the first and second factors of the MMPI continued to be associated with highly meaningful external correlates.

Among the clinical scales, the best marker for the first factor is Scale 7. It is therefore, instructive to compare the *A* scale with the *Pt* scale. The *Pt* scale is about 20% longer than the *A* scale; the two scales overlap by 13 items, or one third of the *A* scale. Of these, the content of five items is depressive, three items are anxious, two items are obsessive, two items suggest interpersonal aversion, and one item admits problems in concentration. Examining the scale as a whole, the *A* scale overlaps the *DEP* scale by nine items (four from *DEP2*), the *ANX* scale by seven items, and the *OBS* scale by five items. The *A* scale overlaps Scale 8 (*Sc*) by eight items, five of which are from the *Sc4* subscale (Lack of Ego Mastery, Conative). Thus, the content of the *A* scale emphasizes disturbed concentration and decision making, as well as dysphoria, anxiety, and worry. Other content emphasizes fatigue, discouragement, and lack of initiative; inadequacy, inferiority, and sensitivity; and a sense of deviance and isolation. All of the items are obvious and socially undesirable.

The empirical correlates for high scale *A* scorers among the Graham et al. (1999) outpatients tend to confirm the description given above, but suggested relatively severe symptomatology, with many of these patients having histories of previous psychiatric hospitalizations. They presented with multiple symptoms of depression and anxiety, and were seen as sad, depressed, insecure, hopeless, and self-degrading, with suicidal ideation.

Evaluation of the discriminative validity of scales developed for assessing distress syndromes must take the first factor into account, as this source of variance can readily create an appearance of validity in single-group comparisons. Provided that one group is more distressed than another, no matter what the exact phenomenological coloring of the distress in question (whether anxious, depressed, panicky, etc.), such scales will virtually always show evidence of convergent validity. That is, scales of this kind will evidence sensitivity to distress as such but will lack the specificity to discriminate one form of distress from another.

As the major marker for the first factor of the MMPI–2, the *A* scale plays an important dynamic role in determining the pattern of test findings. Among the basic clinical and validity scales, elevations on the *A* scale tend to suppress the *K* scale (and therefore the raw amounts of *K* added as corrections for five of the eight basic clinical scales), increase positive profile slope, and increase the probability that Scales 7 and especially 8 will figure in the code pattern. *A* elevations also exert widespread pressure on the content scales to enter the range above $T = 65$, with the heaviest influence on the *ANX*, *OBS*, *DEP*, *LSE*, *WRK*, and *TRT* scales. Among the supplementary scales, the *A* scale tends to exert positive pressure on the *Mt*, *PK*, and *PS* scales and negative pressure on the *GM* scale.

The major interpretive significance of high *A* scores is that the respondent readily admits distress and maladjustment. Duckworth and Anderson (1986) asserted that the *A* scale reflects short-term, situational (state) anxiety, in contrast to the *Pt* scale, which they believed represents long-term, characterological (trait) anxiety. Although their distinction is intriguing and worthy of investigation, the higher test–retest stabilities of *A* items, relative to those of the *Pt* scales, would argue against overconfident reliance on this hypothesis. On the other hand, as Duckworth and Anderson pointed out, the two scales show important differences in item content. The overlap between Scales 7 and 8 at 17 items is greater than that between Scale 7 and *A* and more than twice that between Scale 8 and *A*. This alone would suggest a tilt toward a trait interpretation of Scale 7 relative to *A*. The content of Scale 7 carries a greater emphasis on ingrained, global personal defects, such as feeling useless, lacking self-confidence, and being incapable. It also implicates more severe cognitive disruption, including problems with memory and comprehension, and fears of losing mental control, over and above the problems with concentration and indecision noted for the *A* scale. The content on Scale 7 reflecting acute emotional instability and irrational fearfulness is entirely absent from the *A* scale. Finally, the word *worry* (*-ied*, *-ing*) appears three times on the *A* scale but only once on Scale 7, whereas *anxiety* (*-ious*) appears twice on Scale 7 but only once on the *A* scale.

Regardless of the merits of assigning the *A* and *Pt* scales state and trait implications, respectively, Caldwell (1988) cautioned that differences in their elevations may be confounded by the *K* correction for the *Pt* scale. Thus, in comparing the scores on these two scales, it is recommended that the *A* scale be compared only with the non-*K*-corrected version of the *Pt* scale. However, because the *A* scale has fewer items and is less positively skewed than Scale 7, it tops out about 10 *T*-score points lower than the *Pt* scale. For example, the endorsement of two thirds of the items on both scales results in *T* scores of about 78 on Scale 7 but only about 70 on the *A* scale, with this difference increasing slightly as the proportion of the items endorsed on both scales moves higher. For this reason, especially when the *K* scale is not too far below the average range, the interpretation of the *A* scale may be undertaken confidently at somewhat lower levels of elevation than Scale 7 and protocols in which the *A* scale exceeds Scale 7 (usually in association with elevations on Scale 0) may have particular significance.

In general, high *A* scorers may be described as uncomfortable, unhappy, and apprehensive. The anxiety they experience appears to be directed more toward a sense of their own incompetence than toward a sense of external threat. Their worry over the adequacy of their performances renders them hesitant, distractible, and vacillating, and this in turn makes them subject to the influence and suggestion of others. Under stress, they tend to become confused, disorganized, and maladaptive. They cope with their feelings of inadequacy by being cautious, standing off, maintaining their distance, avoiding initiative and involvement, and inhibiting action. In interaction with others, they tend to be timid, awkward, passive, and easily rattled.

Provided that the pattern of validity indicators is not overly defensive, low *A* scorers may be described as showing confidence in their abilities, comfortable and friendly, expressive and assertive, taking initiative, active and readily involved, vigorous and forceful, versatile and achieving. In some cases, low *A* scorers are better described as egocentric, ostentatious, overconfident, outspoken, competitive, overbearing, manipulative, reckless, and impulsive.

The items for Welsh's *R* scale were selected by comparing the top and bottom 10% of the distribution of scores on Scale 2. Forty items that achieved separations of 60% or more in both VA patient groups compose the *R* scale (3 of these items were dropped in the transition to MMPI–2; the remaining 37 items are scored in the "false" direction). Despite marking the second major source of variation among the standard validity and clinical scales of the MMPI/MMPI–2, the *R* scale achieves no better than moderate correlations with any of these scales. Its highest correlations are with Scales 2 and 9, at .30 to .40 and at –.40 to –.45, respectively. Correlations in the range of .30 to .40 are also seen for *L*, *K*, and Scale 0. Notable item overlap occurs with Scales 2 (10 items [D-O, 6 items; D-S, 4 items]) and 0 (8 items).

The content of the *R* scale is fairly heterogeneous, including poor health and physical symptoms; inhibited if not blunted emotionality, particularly with respect to "negative" feelings and feelings of energy and excitement; a lack of enjoyment in and underesponsiveness to the potential stimulation of group membership and social interaction; the avoidance of conflict, competition, and social visibility; and a denial of activities and interest in pursuits that may occasion fatigue or stimulation. Taken as a whole, the content of the *R* scale suggests the suppression of emotionality and the avoidance of interactions with the human and nonhuman environment that may stimulate feeling, whether positive or negative, with the tendency to refer such feeling, when it occurs, to events in the somatic sphere.

Although *R* scores have been available for more than 40 years, surprisingly little is known of the interpretive significance of high and low scores. Interpretations tend to converge on some notion of *control*. In his choice of Repression as the designation for *R*, Welsh (1956) evidently favored a construct believed to operate in an unconscious fashion. Welsh (1956) based his choice on the kinds of mental disorders associated with high and low scores on the *R* scale: "The disorders exhibited by high R scorers are characterized by repression and denial; low R accompanies externalized and 'acting-out' behavior" (p. 280). More recent commentators have tended to reject the unconscious implications of Welsh's construct in favor of a kind of emotional control that is seen to operate within awareness. Thus, Duckworth and Anderson (1986) referred to the *R* scale as "a conscious repression scale (or suppression scale to be more accurate)" (p. 245) that reflects a coping style emphasizing limited insight, (conscious) denial and rationalization, and decisions to limit self-disclosure. Similarly, Caldwell (1988) favored an interpretation of the *R* scale as *constriction*, in which the person's "range of feelings is limited and whose emotional responsiveness is constricted across a wide spectrum" (p. 76).

As noted by Nichols and Greene (1995), a comparison of the pattern of MMPI/MMPI–2 scale correlates with *R* and *EC-5* (Ego Control), Block's (1965) second-factor scale (Ego Control), suggests an alternative but related interpretation of the *R* scale. Whereas the correlates of the *EC-5* scale suggest the modulation and containment of impulse and aggression, a narrowing of interests, and a deliberate, conforming, prosocial, and risk-averse approach to decision making and behavioral expression, the correlates of the *R* scale appear to reflect a more central locus of inhibition, one related to the strength of impulse and emotionality, and to openness to experience. Specifically, the high *R* scorer appears to be one who is uncomfortable with more than minimal levels of stimulation and emotionality and who therefore prefers to operate in circumstances that are conventional, predictable, familiar, and overlearned. Such preferences, in turn, suggest limitations in the individual's capacity to become aware of, identify, differentiate, and reflect on feelings and other emotional phenomena, and it is this that is the basis for the person's constricted expression of emotionality.

By contrast, low *R* scores suggest a ready access to feeling and impulse even if not impulsively expressed; an openness to experiencing them; a prodigal and unstable pattern of interests, a high tolerance for stimulation; a willingness to entertain unfamiliar or unconventional points of view; and an ability to endure ambiguity, uncertainty, and conflict. Extremely low scores may be associated with chaotic emotionality, in which the individual feels flooded with emotionality or even euphoria and is overinclusive and indiscriminate in his or her approach to expression.

Graham et al. (1999) reported only somatic symptoms and health preoccupation as broad empirical correlates of high *R* scores among their psychiatric outpatients.

EGO STRENGTH SCALE (*Es*)

Barron's (1953) Ego Strength scale was the product of an effort to predict the response of "psychoneurotic" outpatients to psychotherapy over a 6-month period. The 68 items that discriminated the 17 patients who improved ($M = 52.7$) from the 16 who did not ($M = 29.1$) became the *Es* scale and were subdivided by Barron into eight groups based on item content: physical functioning and physiological stability (11 items), psychasthenia and seclusiveness (10 items), attitudes toward religion (6 items), moral posture (11 items), sense of reality (8 items), personal adequacy/ability to cope (11 items), phobias/infantile anxieties (5 items), and miscellaneous (6 items). In the transition to the MMPI–2, the *Es* scale lost 16 items, distributed across the above groups, respectively, as follows: 1, 1, 5, 3, 1, 2, 0, and 3. Thirty-two of the 52 items are scored as "false"; 20 items are scored as "true."

Although neither the therapists nor the type of therapy received by the patients in Barron's (1953) sample was adequately described, others have characterized the treatment as psychoanalytically oriented (e.g., Dahlstrom et al., 1975; Graham, 1990). Because this form of therapy often places rather high intellectual demands on its patients, it is notable that Barron found moderate but consistent correlations between the *Es* scale and intelligence across a wide variety of measures. This confounding may, in part, help to account for the highly mixed character of the results of subsequent validity studies of the *Es* scale. As Greene (1991a) noted, "Various studies have reported positive, no, and inverse relationships between the Es scale and outcome in psychotherapy" (p. 187). It is also notable that moderate to high correlations between the *Es* scale and various measures of the first factor (e.g., *A* and *K*) have consistently been reported, raising the question of possible differences in initial severity of psychopathology between patients showing different therapeutic outcomes. In this context, Butcher et al. (1989) reported small but significant negative correlations between the *Es* scale and the total number of recent life changes and scores on the Social Readjustment Rating Scale (T. H. Holmes & Rahe, 1967). These data are consistent with the interpretation that patients with high *Es* scores show greater improvement in insight-oriented psychotherapy, in part because they are more intelligent and less disturbed than patients who score low.

An underappreciated part of the literature on the *Es* scale has examined physiological stability in response to stress (Alexander, Roessler, & Greenfield, 1963; Greenfield, Alexander, & Roessler, 1963; Greenfield, Roessler, & Crosley, 1959; Roessler, Alexander, & Greenfield, 1963; Roessler, Burch, & Childers, 1966; Roessler, Burch, & Mefford, 1967; Roessler & Collins, 1970; Roessler, Greenfield, & Alexander, 1964). Using dependent measures such as catecholamine excretion, finger blood volume, heart rate, muscle potential, and skin resistance, these investigators found that participants having high *Es* scores showed evidence of greater physiological organization in their responses to stressful events than did low *Es* scorers. In the physiological reactions of these participants, there was greater evidence of the preservation of hierarchical organization ("defense in depth"), with more peripheral reactions preceding in an orderly fashion those responses more appropriate for stresses of greater severity. They also showed greater speeds of recovery following the cessation of stress. The responses of low *Es* participants were more chaotic and extreme, with a loss of hierarchical patterning and delayed recoveries. These findings suggest that the more favorable psychotherapy outcomes seen in high *Es* patients may be rooted in the greater integrity of their physiological adaptation to life stresses such that they are better able to avoid overreaction and recover more readily from stresses and setbacks. By contrast, the coping styles of low *Es* scorers would appear to be encumbered by a lack of organization and a vulnerability to overreaction, leading to distracted attempts to assess the sources and meanings of stressors and rigid or poorly focused attempts at adaptation.

In summary, the *Es* scale appears to serve as a measure of both control and resiliency, factors that would seem to predict successful adaptation even in the midst of significant distress. In this sense, the *Es* scale may serve as an index of *stress tolerance*, and this may be, as Caldwell (1988) suggested, a more valuable focus for interpretive efforts than prognosis for psychotherapy. High *Es* scorers have been characteristically described as resourceful, independent, and self-reliant; as possessed of discipline and determination; as showing initiative, flexibility, and tolerance; and as creating an impression of competence and ability in others and being easily accepted by them. At times, they may be seen as aggressive, outspoken, and nonconforming if not rebellious toward authority. Thus, they would seem to be able to use psychotherapy to supplement their own problem-solving resources and to tolerate the self-scrutiny and confrontation that often occurs in this form of treatment without becoming upset. Low *Es* scorers are unstable, overreactive, and subject to confusion in the face of stresses; may be upset by seemingly minor matters; are less tolerant of other people, despite being suggestible and dependent; are inhibited, indecisive, and procrastinating; and are more rigid in their outlooks, in their choices of action, and in their approaches to problems. Graham et al. (1999) found that their low *Es* outpatients manifested an especially broad range of psychiatric symptoms, including depression, somatization, and psychoticism. They often had previous psychiatric hospitalizations, and were seen as insecure, hopeless, pessimistic, unambitious, and coping poorly with stress. The women often had histories of physical and sexual abuse, and of suicide attempts.

As noted earlier, the interpretation of the *Es* scale may be complicated by its covariation with the first factor, such that the *Es* scale and other scales having substantial first-factor variance may be mutually affected. For example, in psychiatric populations and among persons seeking mental health consultation, correlations between the *Es* and *K* scales are commonly in a range of .50 to .60. Thus, high (low) scores on one of these scales will tend to push scores on the other up (down). As a result, a relatively low *K* score when the *Es* score is substantially higher may lead to an underestimate of stress tolerance and adaptive functioning. Conversely, a relatively high *K* score when it substantially exceeds the *Es* score may reflect a desire to portray greater adequacy in coping with problems and stresses than is justified, depleted and precarious coping resources, or both. Caldwell (1988) suggested that differences between the *Es* and *K* scales of 10 or more *T*-score points may call for interpretive adjustments along the lines given here.

OVERCONTROLLED–HOSTILITY SCALE (*O–H*)

The stimulus for the development of the Overcontrolled–Hostility scale (Megargee et al., 1967) was the failure of 12 previously identified MMPI scales to achieve satisfactory identifications among a sample of male criminals who had been subdivided into extremely assaultive, moderately assaultive, and nonassaultive groups (Megargee and Mendelsohn, 1962). Moreover, there was a clear trend for the extremely assaultive criminals to score *lower* on these measures than the other two groups, suggesting that the controls (or levels of hostility) in the extremely assaultive group were, if anything, better than in the comparison groups. Megargee reasoned that the group of extremely assaultive criminals might contain a subgroup of individuals that, far from fitting the stereotype of the habitually aggressive and impulsive person who manifests a low threshold for responding with hostility to frustrating events and provocations, characteristically do *not* react to such instigations. He posited that extremely assaultive individuals could be divided into undercontrolled and overcontrolled types, with the overcontrolled group characterized by high levels of hostile impulse existing side by side with massive, rigid, and unconscious inhibitions against hostile expression. For these individuals, assaultiveness was an atypical response that would occur only rarely and unexpectedly, in circumstances of sufficient moment that the individual's normally hypertrophic defenses against the expression of hostility could be overcome. Whereas in the undercontrolled individual the hostile reaction was typically seen to be in some sense proportional to its instigation, the overcontrolled hostile reaction was often seen as poorly calibrated to instigating events, thereby increasing the importance of being able to identify the overcontrolled–hostile individual.

The *O-H* scale was derived to identify this overcontrolled hostile reaction type. Megargee et al. (1967) compared the responses of extremely assaultive ($n=14$), moderately assaultive ($n=25$), and nonassaultive ($n=25$) male prisoners and a group of noncriminal men ($n=46$). Item analysis yielded 55 items that separated the assaultive from the nonassaultive participants. These were then cross-validated on new samples of extremely assaultive, moderately assaultive, and nonassaultive prisoners. On the basis of the examination of prison records, Megargee et al. also compared the responses of prisoners who had histories of violence and were identified as conforming to the overcontrolled pattern with inmates with an undercontrolled pattern of violence. Thirty-one of the 55 items survived cross-validation to become the *O-H* scale. In the transition to the MMPI–2, the *O-H* scale lost three items. Of the remaining 28 items, 21 are scored as "false," 7 as "true."

Like most scales constructed using the method of contrasted groups, the item content of the *O-H* scale is quite heterogeneous, with few, if any, identifiable themes. An examination of the structure of the MMPI version of the *O-H* scale among 200 state penitentiary inmates found five factors (Walters & Greene, 1983), but subsequent analyses of other samples by R. L. Greene and D. S. Nichols (personal communication, March 1, 1999) cast doubt on the stability and coherence of the earlier solution. The *O-H* scale shares three items each with the *L*, *K*, and *Es* (scored in reverse) scales and four with the *S* and *Hy* scales. It also overlaps minimally with the MMPI–2 content scales; two items (scored in reverse) are shared with the *ANG* and *WRK* scales. Among psychiatric patients, the *O-H* scale is most highly correlated with scores on the *S*, *K*, *ANG* (negatively), and *TPA* (negatively) scales in a range of .50 to .60. As Greene (1991a) pointed out, it is unusual for a scale to share so few items with other scales, suggesting that the *O-H* scale may be tapping a unique source of variance. On the basis of an examination of item content, the high *O-H* scorer portrays him- or herself as (a) free of tension and internal conflict, although not of occasional worries and fears; (b) emotionally self-contained and impassive, if not underexpressive and imperturbable, and avoidant of stimulation and emotional or physical exertion (they deny impatience, irritability, and anger, portray themselves as relaxed, and are tolerant of boredom and frustrations); and (c) noncompetitive, as well as avoidant of willfulness and interpersonal conflict (but nonetheless socially interested and comfortable), and able to seek advice and assistance from others.

The research on this scale has generally been supportive of its construct validity among male prisoners when administered within the context of the full MMPI. Its validity among women and nonforensic psychiatric populations remains to be demonstrated. As expected, the research tends to support Megargee's distinction between persons prone to overcontrolled versus undercontrolled patterns of violence; it is much less clearly related to the propensity for violence as such, including murder. Group differences between violent and nonviolent groups have characteristically been small, compromising the predictive validity of the *O-H* scale as applied to the individual case when the purpose of the assessment bears on the issue of dangerousness. Quinsey, Maguire, and Varney (1983) found significant *O-H* differences in murderers classified as overcontrolled versus undercontrolled. In this context, again consistent with Megargee's view, mean differences between the two groups and effect sizes were substantial. These investigators also found that their overcontrolled murderers lacked assertiveness and suggested that assertiveness training might be indicated as a means of altering the overcontrolled–hostile pattern.

Given its origins, a major application of the *O-H* scale is in the classification of male prisoners convicted of violent offenses. That is, the value of the *O-H* scale primarily belongs in the postdictive context, providing a means for construing and classifying offenders following incidents of extreme assault. Because of the low base rates for violence in most other populations, it is unsuitable as a basis for predictions of assault, violence, or dangerousness. Data associating high *O-H* scores with violence in other than correctional populations are meager. Nevertheless, *O-H* scores may be suitable for inferring the presence or absence of a pattern of personality dynamics consisting of both hostile alienation and excessive inhibitions around the expression of aggressive or hostile impulses, both of which reside largely if not entirely outside of awareness. This pattern would appear to predict a vulnerability to accumulating resentments over time and to a potential for releasing them in an explosive manner when provocations are great or when controls are diminished (e.g., because of intoxication). Fixed cutting scores have not been developed for the *O-H* scale and Megargee et al. (1967) recommended that cutoffs be established setting by setting on the basis of local norms and the utilities attaching to false-positive versus false-negative decisions. For purposes of orientation, however, among White men, raw scores of 15 or greater should raise the question of overcontrolled personality dynamics, with scores of 18 clearly indicating such dynamics, particularly when test indicators of self-favorable responding and/or "false" percentage are no more than moderately elevated. Scores of 21 and above appear to be associated with strong external evidence of these dynamics, regardless of response style. There is some evidence that African Americans and women score somewhat higher on the *O-H* scale, suggesting the need to adjust these scores upward before inferring overcontrolled dynamics among members of these groups (Graham, 1977). Because the *O-H* scale reflects a syndrome (hostility/resentment + impulse overcontrol + lack of awareness of these), low scores are largely without interpretive significance. That is, a low score might signify the absence of any or all of these elements. Thus, person A might be inhibited and overcontrolled but neither hostile nor resentful, whereas person B might be hostile and resentful but neither inhibited nor overcontrolled.

DOMINANCE SCALE (*Do*)

The Dominance scale (Gough et al., 1951) grew out of a larger project investigating political participation. The 25 items of the *Do* scale for the MMPI–2 (28 for the MMPI) form a subset of the 60-item Dominance scale (*Do*) of the CPI. The developers gathered peer nominations from high school and college students, with each student nominating the five most and five least dominant of their peers. The item responses of high and low dominance nominees were compared. Care was taken to avoid confusing the construct of interest, dominance, with being domineering or autocratic and to ensure that peer ratings were based on nominees' actual behavior as opposed to how the peer thought the nominee might act, view him- or herself, and so on. Just how successful these efforts were in steering the nominations in the direction desired by the investigators is uncertain.

Although the CPI version of the *Do* scale is one of its better validated scales (Megargee, 1972), the MMPI/MMPI–2 version has stimulated surprisingly little research, although such research has been generally supportive. Correlations in a range of .55 to .60 with the *Es* scale suggest some overlap with this construct, and the pattern of overlap with other MMPI/MMPI–2 scales tends to reflect extraversion and the absence of anxiety.

The textual literature of the MMPI/MMPI–2 (e.g., Butcher & Williams, 1992; Friedman, Webb, & Lewak, 1989; Graham, 1990; Greene, 1991a) provides little insight into the core construct of the *Do* scale, but describes high scorers as showing comfort, poise, initiative, and influence in social relationships; being secure, self-confident, self-assured, efficient, resourceful, persevering, and able to concentrate;

and dutiful and having strong political opinions. Duckworth and Anderson (1986) described the high *Do* scorer as asserting that "he/she is able to take charge of his/her own life" (p. 273), an interpretation endorsed by Caldwell (1988) and Greene (1991a, 2000). Both the descriptions and the interpretation just given appear to converge on the *Do* scale, at least as measured in the MMPI/MMPI–2, as an indicator of *self-direction.* As a construct, self-direction would appear to encompass aspects of internal locus of control and independence of judgment, but without the implications of self-sufficiency or social distancing that these concepts sometimes carry. The high *Do* scorer tends to elicit the confidence and social approval of others that may move them in the direction of elevating the high scorer to positions of responsibility and leadership within the group. The outpatients with scores below $T = 40$ studied by Graham et al. (1999) often had histories of physical abuse (for women, also sexual abuse), and a broad range of symptoms, including depression, anxiety, somatization, and social awkwardness.

SOCIAL RESPONSIBILITY SCALE (*Re*)

Another product of their inquiry into political participation, Gough et. al. (1952) used methods similar to those used in the development of the *Do* scale for the construction of the *Re* scale. For samples of high school students and college members of fraternities and sororities, nominations by peers, teachers, or a high school principal identified individuals who rated as high in "a ready willingness to accept the consequences of [one's] own behavior, dependability, trustworthiness, and a sense of obligation to the group" (Gough et al., 1952, p. 74). Some effort was made to prevent the influence of extraneous characteristics, such as friendliness and popularity, on ratings of social responsibility, but it appears likely that the nominations were to at least some degree confounded with intelligence. The 30 items of the *Re* scale for the MMPI–2 (32 for the MMPI) form a subset of the 56-item Responsibility scale (*Re*) of the CPI.

The results of research with the CPI version of the *Re* scale are mixed, with studies based on ratings of responsibility faring less well than those comparing groups based on status or performance criteria (Megargee, 1972). Studies involving antisocial and delinquent groups have been more consistently supportive. The MMPI/MMPI–2 version of the *Re* scale has stimulated very little research, and none that has illuminated the construct measured by this version of the scale. More useful in this respect is the pattern of correlations with other MMPI scales, with moderate positive correlations being found with scales measuring academic achievement, intellectual efficiency, tolerance, and control and moderate negative correlations with scales measuring impulsivity, hostility, antisocial attitudes, and prejudice. The correlates relating to intelligence appear, at least in part, to be an artifact both of the samples and the peer nomination methodology of scale development. An unusual and interesting correlate of the *Re* scale is Brozek's (1955) Aging scale (*Ag*), consisting of items showing age differences in samples of high-ability college and middle-aged men. This correlate would tend to support the observations of Caldwell (1988) and Duckworth and Anderson (1986) that *Re* scores tend to increase with age.

The picture that emerges from an examination of the circumstances of its development, *Re* research to date, as well as the scale's internal MMPI/MMPI–2 correlates, suggests that the high *Re* scorer is a conventional and conforming but tolerant and even-tempered person who has benign expectations of others, exhibits self-control, is a "team player," and is able and willing to pledge allegiance to the collectives of which he or she chooses to be a part. The *Re* scale appears to measure a form of responsibility that is most likely to be manifested in institutional settings where creative demands are low. The institution may be as small as a family or club or as large as a multinational corporation. The high *Re* scorer appears to be one whose performance and achievement are best manifested in structured settings that place a premium on cooperation with others, persistence, and a "duty-bound" variety of conscientiousness. The core construct of the *Re* scale appears to be one of *dutifulness*. Thus, the responsible person is one on whom others can rely to observe and support the customs, norms, policies, and procedures and advance the goals of the institution with which the individual identifies. This would account for the wide use of the *Re* scale in employment screening (Butcher & Williams, 1992).

Duckworth and Anderson (1986) have put forward a conception of the *Re* scale (and one that has been cited with approval by Caldwell, 1988; Graham, 1990; and Greene, 1991a) that is similar to that offered here, but couched in terms of values. Duckworth and Anderson (1986) maintained that the *Re* scale "measures the acceptance (high score) or rejection (low score) of a previously held value system" (p. 279) and noted that the *Re* scale likely does not assist in identifying the nature of the particular value system that the person holds, is in transition from, or spurns. For persons under age 25, parental values are assumed to be those in question, whereas for persons over age 25, the person's current value system is not assumed to reflect parental values. According to this view, *Re* scores tend to decline during periods of transition, as previously held values become subject to increased reflection, examination, and questioning. Such periods may occur as a result of other life transitions, such as leaving home to attend college, the birth of a child, the recognition of a need to seek membership in a congregation for the benefit of a child's religious upbringing, a death in the family, shifts in occupation or employment (e.g., from sales to service), following natural disasters, and similar events. Such transitions often stimulate questions of value in their wake, just as they may lead to emotional upheaval, uncertainty, and weakened controls. Similarly, scores may fall as the person becomes disenchanted with the goals and practices of the organization to which he or she belongs.

Some of the research with delinquents reviewed by Megargee (1972) suggests that the lower ranges of the *Re* scale are more discriminating than the higher ranges. For example, in one study reviewed, a sample of delinquents with and without actual court contact showed mean *T* scores of 31 and 38, respectively. Duckworth and Anderson (1986) reported ranges consistent with this supposition. They stated that "persons with elevations [of $T = 50–65$] tend to accept their present value system and intend to continue using it. Persons with scores of 40 to 50 are questioning their present value system and those below 40 are rejecting their most recently held value system" (Duckworth & Anderson, 1986, p. 279). Guidelines for interpreting *Re* scores greater than $T = 50$ need further exploration and research. It appears likely, however, that as scores of about $T = 60$ are exceeded, the dispositions of high *Re* scorers may be less adaptive than scores of persons closer to the average range. Duckworth and Anderson speculated that higher ranging scores may be associated with a lack of imagination and an excessive, and perhaps excessively rigid, orientation to "oughts and shoulds," giving rise to attitudes that a high *Re* scorer's associates may find annoying. Similarly, scorers in this range may be overly quick to identify with authority, regardless of its moral/ethical standing, and to sacrifice the interests of others, both within and outside of the organization in the pursuit of narrow organizational goals. For example, one would expect the "company man" to have a considerably higher *Re* score than the "whistle blower," even though both might be seen as socially responsible.

Among the low *Re* scores studied by Graham et al. (1999), problems with substance abuse and dependence were especially prominent, and many of these outpatients had histories of one or more arrests. They were seen in largely antisocial terms, but also as resentful, suspicious, mistrustful, having family problems, and stormy relationships more generally.

COLLEGE MALADJUSTMENT SCALE (*Mt*); KEANE ET AL.'S POST-TRAUMATIC STRESS DISORDER SCALE (*PK*); AND SCHLENGER AND KULKA'S POST-TRAUMATIC STRESS DISORDER SCALE (*PS*)

These three scales are discussed together because of their extensive shared variance. All are saturated with the major source of variation within the MMPI–2 item pool, the first factor. They show considerable item overlap. In psychiatric samples, these scales are intercorrelated with each other and with the *A* and *Pt* scales (non-*K*-corrected raw scores) within a typical range of .85 to .95. As a result, all may be interpreted as global indexes of the individual's current level of distress, maladjustment, or psychopathology.

Kleinmuntz (1960, 1961a) developed the College Maladjustment scale (*Mt*) to identify college students with emotional problems of sufficient severity to impel them to seek treatment at a university mental health clinic. The item responses of students who sought counseling for emotional problems and remained for three or more sessions were compared with those of students referred to the same clinic for routine mental health screening for a teacher certification program and who reported no previous treatment for mental health problems. Forty-three items discriminated the maladjusted from the apparently adjusted students, of which 41 are retained in the MMPI–2; 28 items are scored as "true" and 13 as "false." In a follow-up study, Kleinmuntz (1961b) found that the *Mt* scale failed to adequately predict adjustment problems among entering college students during their 1st year and concluded that it is best suited to identifying current, as opposed to future, maladjustment.

On the basis of the *Mt* content, Kleinmuntz (1960) characterized the high scorer as an "ineffectual, pessimistic, procrastinating, anxious and worried person who tends to somatize and who finds that much of the time life is a strain" (p. 210). Low scorers, by contrast, would be considered effective, optimistic, conscientious, and free of emotional discomfort.

The similarity of the adjusted student group to groups that were provided an incentive to respond in a self-favorable manner to the items (e.g., Cofer et al., 1949) may tend to inflate scores on the *Mt* scale in persons inclined to modesty concerning their strengths, virtues, and other positive features of outlook, character, and demeanor. By contrast, scores may be suppressed by an inclination to claim such attributes. Thus, high *K* scores may suppress, and low *K* scores inflate, *Mt* scores.

Given the extensive shared variance between the *Mt* scale and better established markers for general maladjustment, such as the *A* and *Pt* (non-*K*-corrected) scales, and the lack of empirical data demonstrating any incremental advantages over the latter scales even in college or university settings, the continued use of the *Mt* scale has little or nothing to recommend it.

The two PTSD scales differ primarily in terms of the contrast groups used in their development. T. M. Keane et al. (1984) compared the items of 100 male VA Vietnam combat veterans for whom diagnoses of PTSD, often among other concurrent diagnoses, had been established on the basis of structured interviews and psychophysiological measurements with 100 veterans who carried diagnoses other than PTSD. The 49 items separating these groups, of which 46 remain in the MMPI–2, constitute the *PK* scale. Thirty-eight items are scored as "true," 8 as "false."

The empirical correlates found by Graham et al. (1999) to describe high *PK* scorers were, not surprisingly, identical to those found for high *A* scorers in most major respects.

Schlenger and associates (Schlenger & Kulka, 1987; Schlenger et al., 1989) compared the item endorsements of Vietnam veterans diagnosed with PTSD (without concurrent diagnoses) and nonpatient Vietnam veterans. They found 60 items that differentiated the two groups. These items constitute the *PS*, scale of which 47 are scored as "true" and 13 as "false."

Thus, whereas the development of the *PK* scale followed a method reminiscent of that used in the construction of the MacAndrew (1965) and Rosen (1962) scales, the *PS* scales issued from the more conventional criterion-normal control contrast method. Despite these differences in development, the two scales are correlated to the extent allowed by their reliabilities and share 26 items in common. One could fairly consider the latter set of items as a better validated measure of PTSD than either of its parent scales.

It remains uncertain how either of the PTSD scales may be used to contribute to the question of diagnosis. There are both empirical and conceptual reasons for doubts concerning the utility of these scales in the context of diagnosis. The chief empirical problem resides in the absence of research demonstrating incremental validity for the *PK* or *PS* scale over any of several other scales with which they share substantial variance. A study by Watson, Juba, Anderson, and Manifold (1990) found only a tenuous relationship between *PK* scores and a history of trauma in a sample of normal and patient Vietnam veterans. Thus, there is an urgent need for research comparing the diagnostic efficiency of the PTSD scales with older scales, such as Welsh's *A* scale. As one strategy for coping with the problem of the shared variance among the *A*, non-*K*-corrected *Pt*, *Mt*, *PK*, and *PS* scales, A. B. Caldwell (personal communication, June 29, 1999) has suggested scores on the PTSD scales be required to exceed scores on the *A* scale before diagnoses of PTSD are entertained. Although somewhat plausible, this suggestion also requires empirical investigation. Another empirical question that has received too little investigation concerns the specificity and positive predictive value of the *PK* and *PS* scales, especially when traumas other than those related to military combat are at stake. Finally, there is little evidence that either of the PTSD scales contributes to the discrimination of patients with anxiety disorders and patients with known traumatic histories, but the research that has become available to date is not encouraging (e.g., Miller, Goldberg, & Streiner, 1995).

What is possibly more troubling is that the status of the diagnosis of PTSD is itself controversial (Young, 1995). Apart from relatively minor terminological differences used to describe them, the symptoms of PTSD are typically indistinguishable from better established mood and anxiety disorders. This circumstance has necessitated that the differential diagnosis be reckoned on the basis of etiology (i.e., putative trauma) rather than presenting symptomatology. Yet the causal relationship between the "symptoms" of PTSD and reports of traumatic events is not established (e.g., Yehuda & McFarlane, 1995), and neither is the temporal stability for recall of traumatic events themselves, even when these are combat related (Southwick, Morgan, Nicolaou, & Charney, 1997). Moreover, Litz, Orsillo, Friedman, Ehlich, and Batres (1997) reported that in a sample of Somalia peacekeepers, noncombat factors, such as a lack of pride in military service and frustration with the mission, were as important in predicting symptoms of PTSD as combat experience. The presumption of a traumatic event as the etiological factor may not only shape the way familiar symptoms of depression, anxiety, panic, and so on are construed by both patients and clinicians so as to create confirmatory bias, it also tends to shift attention away from etiological factors, such as genetically influenced predispositions, that are better established as diatheses for such symptoms. Among veterans of military service, the population on which the vast majority of PTSD research has been conducted, the potential etiological influence of disability compensation has received inadequate research attention. Pending the clarification of these empirical and conceptual issues, the clinical utility of the *PK* and *PS* scales will remain uncertain.

GENDER ROLE—MASCULINE (*GM*) AND GENDER ROLE—FEMININE (*GF*) SCALES

In developing the gender-role scales, Peterson (1991; Peterson & Dahlstrom, 1992) sought to apply research and theory supporting a conception of masculinity and femininity as independent attributes of personality that could contribute to the understanding of both men and women. Her approach was intended as both a contrast and a supplement to the traditional bipolar measurement of masculinity–femininity embodied in the *Mf* scale of the MMPI/MMPI–2. The availability of scales for the independent measurement of masculinity and femininity would enable the identification of androgynous (high scores on both scales) and undifferentiated (low scores on both scales) gender-role styles. In addition, such scales would allow inferences regarding androgyny or a lack of gender-role differentiation, patterns that would otherwise be concealed by mid-range *Mf* scores. The ability to distinguish between androgynous and undifferentiated gender-role styles is, of course, of some significance clinically, as androgyny is typically aligned with favorable emotional adjustments, whereas a lack of gender-role differentiation is associated with more fragile and unstable adjustments.

Using the MMPI–2 restandardization sample, items were selected for each of the gender-role scales if endorsed by at least 70% of the members of one gender and by at least 10% fewer of the opposite gender. Items thus selected were then grouped into two scales. Those endorsed more commonly by men and less commonly by women compose the 47-item *GM* scale (19 items are scored as "true," 28 as "false"). Those with the opposite trend comprise the 46-item *GF* scale (15 items are scored as "true," 31 as "false"). Peterson's aspiration of independence for the *GM* and *GF* scales was substantially realized in that the scales were found to correlate at only –.10 in the restandardization sample (Peterson & Dahlstrom, 1992) and .05 in a large psychiatric sample (R. L. Greene, personal communication, March 6, 1998). Among members of the same psychiatric sample, correlations with the *Mf* and *GM* scales were –.39 and –.23, for men and women, respectively; correlations with the *Mf* and *GF* scales were .37 and .46, for men and women, respectively.

Although Peterson (1991) found some differences between men and women in the characteristics empirically associated with *GM* and *GF* scores, most are similar. High *GM* scores are associated with traditional attributes of masculine strength, such as self-confidence; forthrightness; goal persistence; and freedom from fears, worries, self-consciousness, and social inhibition. High *GF* scores are associated with traditional feminine attributes of social circumspection, agreeableness, trust, loyalty, and the avoidance of conflict and impropriety. The attributes associated with the *GM* scale appeared to fit both men and women more comfortably than those of the *GF* scales. Men with high *GF* scores appeared somewhat less comfortable than women with high *GM* scores, being often described as bossy, fault-finding, and given to outbursts of temper. But they were also more often described as religious and unlikely to engage in swearing. Somewhat surprisingly, both men and women with high *GF* scores were described as prone to misuse alcohol and nonprescription drugs. Peterson and Dahlstrom (1992) did not present empirical correlates for men or women scoring high or low on both the *GM* and *GF* scales.

The gender-role scales have not as yet stimulated much research, and the correlates reported by Peterson and Dahlstrom (1992) are in need of replication, especially those that are counterintuitive, like the abuse of alcohol and nonprescription drugs for the *GF* scale. Nevertheless, these scales would appear to serve a useful purpose, confirming the usual meanings that attach to very high or very low *Mf* scores and allowing tentative inferences concerning gender role when Mf scores fall into a middle range. Even in advance of further evidence bearing on the relations between the *GM* and *GF* scales and gender-role correlates, the moderate to high correlations between these scales and the *FRS*, *Es*, *LSE*, non-*K*-corrected *Pt*, *WRK*, *Si*, and *Do* scales and the *ASP*, *Re*, *MAC–R*, and *Pd2* scales, respectively, permit a glimpse of the general trend of correlates that are likely to be found for each, whether or not these may be seen to conform to gender-role expectations and stereotypes.

The alert reader will not have missed the apparent relationship between the *GM* and *GF* scales and the two major sources of variance in the MMPI–2 item pool. That is, the correlates of the *GM* scale appear substantially consistent with an absence of general maladjustment or subjective distress (first factor—low), whereas the correlates of the *GF* scale, at least for women, reflect emotional and behavioral control (second factor—high). From this perspective, one can better appreciate how high *GF* scores for men may more readily conflict with common masculine role expectations than high *GM* scores among women, whereas women may more readily achieve a comfortable balance between personal ambition and those traits such as loyalty and consideration that are necessary to maintain good relations with others. As in the case of other scales sharing considerable first-factor variance, the *GM* scale is relatively sensitive to distortion through response style, with a bias toward overreporting psychopathology tending to suppress scores and underreporting tending to elevate them.

Unfortunately, the utility of the gender-role scales does not extend to predictions regarding the respondent's pattern of leisure and occupational interests. Users of the MMPI long ago noted that *Mf* scores, even when relatively extreme, often afforded a misleading picture of interests. Because only about half of the *Mf* items carry interest-related content, men may achieve high *Mf* scores and still endorse many more traditional masculine interests than traditional feminine interests. Similarly, women may achieve high *Mf* scores and still endorse many more traditional feminine interests than traditional masculine interests. The *GM* and *GF* scales do little to clarify this matter. In the MMPI environment, the Serkownek (1975) subscales for the *Mf* scale provided scores for ascertaining the relative balance of masculine and feminine interests. However, these subscales were not retained in the MMPI–2. Martin and Finn (1992) have developed new *Mf* subscales, and it is hoped that these will eventually become available for routine use. These subscales are described in detail in chapter 3.

SUBSTANCE ABUSE MEASURES: THE MACANDREW ALCOHOLISM SCALE (*MAC/MAC–R*), THE ADDICTION POTENTIAL SCALE (*APS*), AND THE ADDICTION ACKNOWLEDGMENT SCALE (*AAS*)

Few scales in the history of the MMPI/MMPI–2 have been the subject of more research investigation than MacAndrew's (1965) Alcoholism scale (*MAC*). This research has been organized and summarized in several reviews (e.g., Apfeldorf, 1978; Friedman et al., 1989a; Gottesman & Prescott, 1989; Graham & Strenger, 1988; Greene & Garvin, 1988; MacAndrew, 1981; Megargee, 1985), to which the reader is referred for more detailed coverage of the *MAC* scale.

Several previous attempts to develop a scale for the prediction of alcoholism had been made in the 1950s (Hampton, 1951; W. O. Holmes, 1953; Hoyt & Sedlacek, 1958), but their development typically involved comparisons between alcoholic individuals and normals. Because discomfort and disturbance were more frequent in the alcoholic samples, the differentiating items tended to reflect general maladjustment rather than alcoholism as such. That is, previous alcohol scales tended to be saturated with nonspecific variance related to the first factor.

The method used by MacAndrew (1965) controlled this source of variation. He compared the item responses of 200 alcoholic outpatients with those of 200 psychiatric outpatients with problems other than alcoholism. Differentiating items were then cross-validated on another hundred members of each of these two groups. Fifty-one items survived cross-validation, of which 49 did not include content related to alcohol consumption. Although the two obvious items provided the best discrimination between his groups, MacAndrew decided not to include them on the final scale because they could be easily dissimulated. MacAndrew found that a cutting score of 24 correctly classified about 82% of both his initial and cross-validation samples. In the transition to the MMPI–2, four items (three with religious content) were dropped. Because of the tradition of interpreting the *MAC* scale on the basis of *raw* scores, these items were replaced with four new items that were found to discriminate alcoholic from nonalcoholic psychiatric patients (McKenna & Butcher, 1987); the revised scale was designated as the *MAC–R* scale. Thirty-eight of the items on the *MAC–R* scale are scored as "true," 11 as "false."

The use of raw cutting scores has been tellingly criticized by Gottesman and Prescott (1989). Because the base rate for alcoholism in MacAndrew's (1965) derivation research was 50%, his cutting score of 24 is likely to produce an excess of false positives in most clinical and nonclinical settings. For example, in their exhaustive review of studies on the *MAC* scale, Greene and Garvin (1988) reported weighted means for White alcoholic men and women of 28.41 (*SD* = 5.45) and 25.33 (*SD* = 4.28), respectively. The corresponding false negative rates were 20.4 and 46.5, respectively. They reported a weighted average for normal White men, the group from which White adult alcoholic men are most readily discriminated by the *MAC* scale, of 23.13 (*SD* = 4.31), with a false-positive rate of 26.5%. For White male psychiatric patients, the comparable figures are 23.30 (*SD* = 4.60), with a false-positive rate of 31.4%. For both of the latter groups, the weighted means are uncomfortably close to MacAndrew's recommended cutting score. Because the comparable scores for White normal and psychiatric women are about 2 raw score points below those of White men, their false-positive rate is correspondingly lower—about 20%. What little data are available for ethnic minorities suggests that ethnicity can exert a significant influence in the diagnostic efficiency of the *MAC* scale. Greene and Garvin found a weighted mean score of 26.32 (*SD* = 4.86) for the few available studies involving African American male psychiatric patients; for this group the rate of false positives reached 59.5%.

The foregoing values provide an inadequate picture of the ability of the *MAC* scale to identify alcoholic individuals, however. Studies of the *MAC* scale usually involve participant samples the composition of which is widely divergent from the typical base rates seen in both normal and psychiatric settings, when these can be determined at all. Gottesman and Prescott (1989) identified several groups for which classification on the basis of *MAC* scores is subject to large error rates. The first of these is members of the normal population, such as those that may be tested as a part of employment screening or in the course of child custody disputes. For such persons, the use of MacAndrew's (1965) recommended cutting score may result in as many as three to six times as many false positives as true positives. The situation for normal women is much worse. Because the base rate for alcoholism among women in the general population is only about half of that for men (roughly 4% vs. 8%), the likelihood that a positive (i.e., a score at or above even a cutting score favoring high specificity, such as 24) will be a true positive may drop to as low as 1 in 14. Gottesman and Prescott's discussion of the *MAC* scale in relation to adolescents and ethnic minorities is to similar cautionary effect. Moreover, the manipulation of cutting scores to reduce the proportion of false positives can only be achieved at the cost of increasing the number of alcoholic individuals who will go undetected. Even in settings with relatively high base rates for alcohol abuse, such as among psychiatric patients or correctional inmates, the development of local cutting scores is recommended to minimize misclassification.

To complicate matters further, Greene (1990a) reported that profile configuration also can significantly influence *MAC–R* scores. In his analysis, code patterns dominated by Scales 4, 6, and especially 9 tended to have substantially higher *MAC–R* scores than code patterns dominated by scales 1, 3, 7, and especially 2, for reasons that are elaborated later. As a result, for example, for any given cutting score, 49/94 code patterns will be associated with a relatively high false-positive rate and 27/72 code patterns will be associated with a relatively high false-negative rate. On the other hand, scores below such a cutting score in the first instance, or above it in the second, are significantly more likely to be true negatives and true positives, respectively.

Finally, there may be some false-negative cases that the *MAC/MAC–R* scale *should* miss. MacAndrew (1981) proposed a distinction between two kinds of alcoholism, reflecting "two fundamentally different character orientations" (p. 620). The first he designated as *primary alcoholics*, those true positives identified by the *MAC* scale. From these, he distinguished a much smaller group of *secondary or reactive alcoholics*, whom he described as "neurotics-who-also-happen-to-drink-too-much" (p. 620). In a study by Tarter, McBride, Buonpane, and Schneider (1978), the reactive alcoholic group not only scored significantly lower on the *MAC* scale ($M = 23.3$, $SD = 3.1$) than the primary alcoholic group ($M = 28.5$, $SD = 3.7$), they also reported less than half as many relatives with a history of heavy drinking and only one fourth as many symptoms of "minimal brain dysfunction" (accident proneness, lack of popularity with peers, unresponsiveness to discipline, vandalism, short attention span, fidgeting, inability to complete projects, inability to sit still, not working up to ability, ease of frustration, intolerance of delay, demanding of attention/affection, withdrawal, poor handwriting, overactivity, and impulsiveness). This finding raises the question of what it is that the *MAC/MAC–R* scale is measuring.

Although 30 years of research have amply attested to the validity of the *MAC* scale for identifying at least so-called primary alcoholics, there has been a steady accumulation of evidence (Allen, Faded, Rawlings, & Miller, 1991; Finney, Smith, Skeeters, & Auvenshine, 1971; Levinson et al., 1990; MacAndrew, 1981) that the *MAC* scale reflects a much broader and more fundamental bipolar personality dimension. Recall that because both the alcoholic and comparison groups used by MacAndrew (1965) to derive the *MAC* scale were psychiatric patients, his design may be presumed to have exerted significant control over the influence of first-factor variation. Under these circumstances, the next most pervasive source of variance in the MMPI item pool, the second factor, could have been influential in the separation of his groups. The finding of Schwartz and Graham (1979) that the *MAC* scale was significantly correlated with Wiggins' (1966) Authority Conflict (.61) and Hypomania (.55) content scales, with Welsh's *R* scale (–.62), and with Scale 9 (.55), all of which typically load on the second factor, confirms this expectation and is consistent with Greene's (1990b) finding, described earlier, that code pattern influences *MAC–R* scores. Hence, it should not be surprising that whatever variance possessed by the *MAC–R* scale that is specific to the abuse/nonabuse of alcohol is secondary to a personality/life style that constitutes a risk factor for such abuse. The consensus of the research to date suggests that the high *MAC–R* scorer is characterized as bold and energetic; self-confident and self-assertive; extraverted and sociable; uninhibited and impulsive; pleasure and sensation seeking; aggressive, rebellious, and resentful of authority; and having been arrested or in trouble with the law. Several studies (Fowler, 1975; Kranitz, 1972; Lachar, Berman, Grisell, & Schoof, 1976; Rhodes & Chang, 1978; Sutker, Archer, Brantley, & Kilpatrick, 1979) have reported that drug abusers of various kinds (mostly heroin addicts) typically produce scores on the *MAC* scale in the same range as alcoholics, and Graham (1978) found similar scores in a sample of pathological gamblers. The outpatients studied by Graham et al. (1999) tended to conform in most respects with previous expectations regarding the empirical correlates of high scorers. Their patients, 75% of whom were Caucasian, tended to have long histories of abusing alcohol, marijuana, and/or cocaine. Although both men and women were seen as antisocial, acting out, and having conflicts with authority, these characteristic appeared especially strong among their women patients, who often had histories of many arrests, misdemeanor and felony convictions, impulsiveness, and a low tolerance for frustration.

This cluster of traits is relatively stable over time. Hoffmann, Loper, and Kammeier (1974), for example, compared the MMPIs of 25 alcoholic men in treatment in a state hospital and the MMPIs these patients had completed as entering freshmen at the University of Minnesota. They found no differences in the *MAC* scores of these men, despite an average of 13 years between test administrations. A number of studies (Chang, Caldwell, & Moss, 1973; Gallucci, Kay, & Thornby, 1989; Huber & Danahy, 1975; Rohan, 1972; Rohan, Tatro, & Rotman, 1969) have reported that *MAC* scores show no change over the course of treatment or on follow-up. These findings, of course, provide yet another reason for caution in the interpretation of *MAC* scores. The risk of misidentification cannot, in general, be circumvented through the use of softened locutions such as "potential for alcoholism" or "addiction prone" as such attributions may be equally harmful in their consequences, particularly among normals such as job applicants.

Although there is little doubt of the validity of the *MAC/MAC–R* scale as a general measure of surgency, the bulk of research on its use for the detection of alcoholism or addiction proneness is equivocal, particularly for populations other than adult White men. Under these circumstances, the use of *MAC* scores for the prediction of substance abuse (or a liability thereto) in the individual case must be undertaken with caution. Friedman et al. (1989a) have suggested that the diagnostic efficiency of the scale may be enhanced by seeking support for the implications of *MAC* elevations among items with obvious content related to substance abuse, such as those found on the Addiction Acknowledgment scale (*AAS*). Although this suggestion is a plausible one, such a practice raises the question of the incremental validity of the *MAC* scale or any similar scale. What is the role of the *MAC* scale in the prediction of substance abuse if the examinee endorses test items that explicitly admit such abuse? This is a question for future research to address. It is possible, however, that if MacAndrew's (1981) distinction between primary and secondary alcoholism becomes substantially corroborated, the *MAC* scale may retain a useful role in the subclassification of alcoholic individuals who endorse item content admitting substance abuse.

MAC/MAC–R scores may also be used to modify the interpretation of scales such as *Pd* and *Ma*. Because both of the latter scales may be elevated into an interpretable range on the basis of their respective first-factor components, largely *Pd4* (Social Alienation), *Pd5* (Self-Alienation), and *Ma2* (Psychomotor Acceleration), the empirical correlates of the *Pd* and *Ma* scales may not apply, or may apply less strongly, when elevations on these scales are achieved on the basis of items distributed more widely across their subscales. In such cases, reference may be made to *MAC-R* scores, with high scores tending to support the application of the usual correlates associated with these scales and low scores emphasizing aspects of negative emotionality, such as dysphoria, guilt, agitation, and identity concerns. *MAC–R* scores may also moderate the interpretation of many other scales, such as *R*, *O–H*, and various of the content scales.

Weed et al. (1992) developed two new substance abuse measures, taking advantage of a wider range of item content related to substance use in the enhanced MMPI–2 item pool. The basic strategy for developing the Addiction Potential scale (*APS*) required that potential items discriminate a substance abuse sample from both the MMPI–2 restandardization sample and a mixed psychiatric sample. Participants from all the samples were subdivided on the basis of gender. Each item was subjected to four comparisons: male substance abusers versus male normals, male substance abusers versus male psychiatric patients, female substance abusers versus female normals, and female substance abusers versus female psychiatric patients. An initial item set was composed of 51 items that were found significantly discriminating in three of these four comparisons. Ten additional items were added on the grounds that they were strongly discriminating in two of the four comparisons and overlapped the *MAC* scale. Twenty-two items were then discarded because their endorsement frequencies were intermediate to those of normals and psychiatric patients, their content was obviously related to substance abuse, or they degraded the internal consistency of the remaining items. On cross-validation, the final 39-item *APS* scale achieved separations of about 1.5 *SD* units in the same four comparisons. In an independent replication, Greene, Weed, Butcher, Arredondo, and Davis (1992) found that the *APS* scale separated substance abusers from psychiatric patients at just under 1 *SD* unit, the shrinkage owing in part to an estimated 10% to 20% rate of substance abuse in the psychiatric sample. Twenty-three of the *APS* items are scored as "true," 16 as "false."

APS performed better than *MAC–R* in both the Weed et al. (1992) and Greene et al. (1992) studies, particularly among women, but it performed less well than *MAC–R* among the Graham et al. (1999) outpatients. It remains to be seen if any advantage favoring the *APS* scale over the *MAC–R* scale can be extended to the detection of substance abuse problems in patients with comorbid psychiatric disorders. Research is needed on both scales that incorporates the main features of MacAndrew's (1965) design, especially the comparison of alcoholic individuals having comorbid psychiatric disorders with nonalcoholic psychiatric patients.

Further research is also needed to evaluate the personality characteristics of high and low *APS* scorers and the patterns and implications of covariation between the *APS* score and other MMPI–2 scales and indexes. Such research would help to illuminate whether, like the *MAC–R* scale, the *APS* scale can be considered a general dimension of personality or is better treated as a measure the utility of which extends no farther than that anticipated at the time of its construction: a subtle measure of substance abuse.

The Addiction Acknowledgment scale (*AAS*) is a refinement of 14 initial items with content thought to be obviously related to substance abuse. Three of its items were deleted for degrading the internal consistency of the remaining items, and two items were added following a search of the total item pool for items with consistent content that achieved high point-biserial correlations with the 11-item core scale. Ten of the 13 items on this scale are scored as "true," 3 as "false." Weed et al. (1992) reported an internal consistency estimate (coefficient alpha) for the *AAS* scale of .74. Two recent reports (Rouse, Butcher, & Miller, 1999; Stein, Graham, Ben-Porath, & McNulty, 1999) provide evidence that the *AAS* scale is superior to the *MAC–R* and *APS* scales in the prediction of substance abuse among private and public mental health outpatients. For most comparisons across both studies, the *AAS* scale was associated with higher values for sensitivity, specificity, positive predictive power, negative predictive power, and correct classification rate than those for the *MAC–R* and *APS* scales for both women and men. Moreover, both studies found that the incremental variance that the *AAS* scale brought to predictions of substance abuse was substantial, whereas the incremental validity of the other two scales over the *AAS* scale was modest and, in the case of the *APS* scale, negligible. The correlates of high *AAS* scores among the Graham et al. (1999)

outpatients reflected diagnoses and histories of substance abuse for both men and women, but whereas the men were generally seen as depressed, insecure, and intropunitive, the women were described as antisocial, impulsive, argumentative, sarcastic, and cynical.

The *AAS* scale functions as a critical item list, but with the advantage of scaled scores, to detect substance abuse among persons who are able (insightful) and willing to admit such problems. The *APS* scale, on the other hand, functions much as other empirically derived scales, including the *MAC–R* scale. Like the *MAC–R* scale, its items are subtle in the sense of excluding items with content related to substance abuse, such as those on the *AAS* scale. Although intercorrelated at about .5, there is reason to think that conjoint use of the *AAS* and *MAC–R* scales (or *APS*) may be attended by an increase in diagnostic efficiency in the identification of substance abuse among nonpsychiatric patients and strong reason to anticipate differences in treatment readiness among substance abusers. When the *AAS* scale is high and the *MAC–R* scale (or *APS*) is unelevated, abuse may be largely situational and therefore carry a highly favorable prognosis. When the *AAS* and *MAC–R* scales (or *APS*) are both elevated, the presence of personality and lifestyle features disposing to substance abuse and the admission of such abuse combine to suggest a less favorable prognosis but a potential readiness to engage in treatment. When the *MAC–R* scale (or *APS*) is high but the *AAS* scale is unelevated, the prognosis for treatment is poor because of the person's reluctance to confide substance abuse.

MARITAL DISTRESS SCALE (*MDS*)

The availability of data gathered from couples in the course of the MMPI–2 restandardization project provided a suitable comparison group for a sample of 150 distressed couples involved in marital counseling. Test data for the distressed couples were gathered from 21 clinicians, most of whom practiced privately in the Minneapolis–St. Paul area. A few practiced in Scottsdale, Arizona.

An initial pool of potential items was selected on the basis of the strength of correlations between the 567 MMPI–2 items and scores on the 31-item Dyadic Adjustment Scale (DAS; Spanier, 1976) separately for the men and women in the marital counseling sample. The same correlations were then gathered from 392 of the couples from the restandardization sample. Significant (.001) correlations were found between the DAS scores and seventeen of the MMPI–2 items for the men and women of both the counselee and the restandardization normal couples. Of these 17 items, 2 were dropped for their failure to replicate in the 384 normal cross-validation couples and 1 was dropped for "extraneous content" (Hjemboe et al., 1992, p. 144), leaving a final scale of 14 items. Eight items are keyed in the "true" direction, 6 in the "false" direction.

Because the *MDS* scale overlaps substantially with Scale 4 (eight items), *Pd1* (Familial Discord; four items), and *FAM* (six items), Hjemboe et al. (1992) undertook multiple regression analyses to evaluate the relative value of the four scales in predicting DAS scores. The *MDS* scale emerged as the best predictor in both their clinical and nonclinical samples. Further analyses evaluated the performance of these four scales in contingency tables with respect to hit rate, positive predictive value, and sensitivity. The *MDS* scale was alone in exceeding the base rate in the overall accuracy of classification and in achieving a better than chance level of positive predictive value. However, none of these scales identified more than half of the participants scoring in the distressed range of the DAS. In attempting to account for this apparent lack of sensitivity, Hjemboe et al. compared the DAS scores of the true-positive and false-negative cases and found, as expected, that the DAS scores were significantly lower (poorer adjustment) for the former group than for the latter group. One hypothesis that is consistent with this finding is that *MDS* scores may be suppressed by an overall tendency to underreport psychopathology. That the social desirability ratings of the nine *MDS* items for which such ratings are available (Butcher et al., 1989) average only 2.53 (where neutral desirability is 5.00) would seem to lend plausibility to this hypothesis.

Although the *MDS* scale showed a higher than desirable false-negative rate and a lower than desirable true-positive rate at a T score of 60 on the basis of an estimated rate of marital maladjustment in the general population of 18%, the level of $T = 60$ did perform favorably in some of Hjemboe et al. (1992) other analyses. They suggested that an even lower score (e.g., $T = 58$) may improve predictive accuracy in outpatient and other settings having a higher base rate for problems in marital adjustment. On the other hand, in settings having a low base rate for persons of married (or the equivalent) status and/or a high base rate for general interpersonal conflict, the predictive accuracy of the *MDS* scale could fall off sharply. Perhaps in recognition of this problem, Butcher (1993) has suggested that the *MDS* scale be interpreted *only* when the examinee is a member of a couple.

Graham et al. (1999) found that their high *MDS*-scoring outpatients were depressed and interpersonally sensitive. They often had few or no friends, and tended to be described in terms suggesting anger and resentment as well as dysphoria.

For some purposes, however, the clinician may wish to disregard this limitation. One virtue of the *MDS* scale is its focus on discord within current, as opposed to past, family relationships. In this respect, it may provide a useful contrast with the *Pd1* subscale, which is biased toward discord within the family of origin. Thus, the two scales can be used along with *FAM*, configurally, to help refine hypotheses involving family conflict.

9

Interpretation and Report Writing

CLINICAL AND ACTUARIAL APPROACHES TO INTERPRETATION

Although specific detailed approaches to interpretation of MMPI–2 profiles are discussed in subsequent sections, it is first necessary to have a basic understanding of actuarial and clinical approaches to the interpretation of tests such as the MMPI–2. Misunderstanding the differences in these two approaches can lead a professional to make clinical errors.

Some mental health professionals rely solely on clinical approaches to test interpretation, even though the power of actuarial methods in psychological assessment has been demonstrated repeatedly and convincingly (e.g., Goldberg, 1965; Grove & Meehl, 1996; Marks & Seeman, 1963; Marks et al., 1974; Meehl, 1970; Quinsey, Harris, Rice, & Cormier, 1998; Sawyer, 1966). Clinical approaches to interpretations are those that come from a professional's personal and professional experience, and in this approach, clinicians base their conclusions on intuition, experience, and clinical judgement. For example, such a clinician may draw conclusions on the basis of a Draw a Person Test with little supporting empirical evidence. On the other hand, the clinician who uses actuarial data suspends making inferences from a test until the actuarial data are consulted, and interpretations are derived by following empirically validated rules, using clinical judgment to supplement these rules. In today's litigious society, psychology, like any other profession, must withstand the rigor of legal and public scrutiny. Clinicians who use tests to make important decisions that affect peoples' lives must be able to justify their decisions based on scientific data, relying solely on clinical judgement only when other methods are unavailable or impractical.

In the first half century of psychology, clinical judgement was considered to be the skill of central importance. Clinical judgement was based on professionally accrued experience with clinical information, such as presenting symptoms, personality attributes, and past history, and rested heavily on the internal norms about patients and people in general that the practitioner developed over time. Years and varieties of clinical experience were valued by clinicians because only then, it was believed, could one develop the depth of knowledge necessary to successfully consider the complex nuances that compose personality and psychopathology. Personality was felt to be too complex to be represented adequately and accurately by test scores. Results from psychological tests, although viewed as helpful adjuncts, were characteristically treated as secondary in importance as compared with an experienced clinician's judgments. In terms of persuasiveness, test data often yielded to clinical impressions.

In the face of such a long-standing tradition, the MMPI was developed in the 1940s largely as an empirical answer to the questions than began to be raised by the apparent unreliability of clinicians' judgments. The need for an objective and reliable measure of personality, independent of clinicians' personal impressions, became clear as empirical studies revealed the inadequacy of tests developed on the basis of clinicians' judgment alone. Although the MMPI was developed empirically, in the first several years of use, it often was interpreted without clear actuarial rules, and clinicians made many false assumptions when using it. For example, empirical conclusions were derived and validated for one population (e.g., psychiatric inpatients) but not validated for other populations (e.g., outpatients, adolescents, and marriage counselees). In these first few years of MMPI use, generalizations from one population to another were often made, even though empirical support for such generalization typically had not been demonstrated. Marks and his colleagues (e.g., Marks & Seeman, 1963) began the systematic empirical investigation of actuarial interpretation of the MMPI on which rests much of the literature on the MMPI, and now the MMPI–2.

Development of Actuarial Rules

In the 1950s, interpretations of the MMPI by practitioners emphasized the analysis of each scale in isolation and then attempted to combine each scale's interpretation clinically. Perhaps because the information from the covarying of so many scales was complex, clinical lore was generated at a quicker rate than research could verify. Although information from clinical interpretations added richness and breadth to the use of the MMPI, questions arose as to whether they added substantial error variance at the same time.

In 1954, Meehl recognized that skilled clinicians followed definable rules in their diagnosis decisions that could be articulated and taught. Furthermore, he discovered numerous studies showing that diagnostic judgments following objective, specifiable rules were superior in most instances to those of the clinicians. The result was his publication "Wanted—A Good Cookbook" (Meehl, 1956). In this article, Meehl (1956) proposed that an actuarial, rather than a clinical, approach should be used wherever possible. Subsequent research has supported this view repeatedly (e.g., Marks et al., 1974; Meehl, 1970). Although the term *actuary* is heard more in the context of the insurance business, it also is relevant to psychology, particularly to assessment. In the insurance industry, certain definable and measurable factors are statistically associated with risks. For example, age, blood pressure, lifestyle, longevity of parents, and occupation all are associated with risks of mortality, and that risk can be expressed in terms of a probability statement using mathematical relationships. Little judgment is involved. Insurance companies have found that when judgment is added (e.g., "But he seems to be particularly healthy"), the accuracy of predictions generally becomes worse.

The same findings have occurred in psychology (e.g., Goldberg, 1965; Meehl, 1954; Sawyer, 1966). Despite historical emphasis on clinical judgment, clinicians repeatedly have fared worse than the actuarial rules. In a meta-analysis of 20 studies of prediction using clinical and actuarial means, Meehl (1954) found that, "in about half of the studies, the two methods were equal; in the other half, the clinician is definitely inferior. No ... fully acceptable study puts him clearly ahead" (p. 119). Similarly, Sawyer analyzed 45 studies and substantiated Meehl's (1954) findings that the actuarial approaches showed clear and repeated superiority over clinical judgment in numerous situations with diverse types of data. Clearly the actuary is of greater assistance to the clinician than the clinician is to the actuary, at least in day-to-day clinical practice. Meehl (1970) stated that

> *it is difficult to come up with so much as one single research study in which the clinician's predictions are better than the statistical table or formula; in most studies the clinician is significantly worse* [italics added]. There are few domains of social science in which so sizeable a body of evidence is so consistently in the same direction. (p. 9)

Using the MMPI, actuarial approaches to personality description have shown a superiority over clinical judgments ranging from a 19% to 38% improvement in accuracy (Marks et al., 1974).

In their overview of clinical judgement difficulties, Quinsey et al. (1998) pointed out that people appear unable to adjust their predictions according to the interrelationships among predictive variables:

In practical terms, this means that people often think they have more information (or are using more information) than they actually have, they are therefore willing to make more extreme judgments than warranted, and they have more confidence than justified (Einhorn & Hogarth, 1978; Kahneman & Tversky, 1973; Wiggins, 1973). (p. 56)

Quinsey et al. (1998) further elaborated that

> when people are asked to make judgments on the basis of probabilistic data (as when a clinician tries to predict which persons will commit violence, or when a sports fan tries to predict which teams will have winning seasons), a variety of task features can lead them to make systematic and gross errors. Laboratory studies of probability learning and other tasks involving the combination of probabilistic data to arrive at a prediction have convincingly demonstrated that people make predictions on the basis of the frequencies of various individual events and not on their actual probabilities: Specifically, people do not take into account the opportunities an event has to occur, only how often it does occur (Estes, 1976). Thus, accuracy in judgment is possible

only when the alternative events have equal opportunities to occur. Needless to say, this rarely occurs under natural circumstances. In addition, accuracy in judgment is possible only when the various events are equally attended to and equally remembered. (pp. 55–56)

Actuarial Data and Base Rates

To understand actuarial approaches in prediction, personality description, psychological test interpretation, and diagnosis, one must first understand the differences and interrelations between cookbook and clinical and actuarial approaches to interpretation. Cookbook approaches describe any systematic approach, or recipe, for arriving at a diagnostic conclusion and/or personality formulation. Some cookbook approaches have been adapted to computers, such that the decision logic mimics an "automated clinician." Examples of this are the Minnesota report and the Caldwell report, both of which are based primarily, although not exclusively, on actuarial data. In other automated cookbooks systems, recipes for diagnosis and description are based primarily on clinical judgment or when actuarial and clinical approaches are mixed in unspecified ways.

The core concept of actuarial description is well described by Marks et al. (1974): "Actuarial descriptions consist of a set of descriptive attributes ... assigned to individuals on the basis of ... explicit ... rules derived from experimentally–statistically demonstrated associations between data (e.g. MMPI profiles) and the descriptive statements" (pp. 35–36). The demonstrated association between a set of data and certain personality descriptions implies some relation. That is, given scores are associated with certain personality traits or behaviors only if they exceed the ordinary base rate.

Base rates refer to the frequency with which a behavior or characteristic exists within a given population. Some behaviors have such a high base rate of occurrence that they cannot distinguish among people in meaningful ways, even though they may be true. These have sometimes been referred to as "Aunt Fanny" statements; that is, they are true about you, about me, and about my Aunt Fanny (Tallent, 1983). An example would be, "Sometimes I do not say all that is on my mind" or "My moods may change depending on what is happening in my life." Meehl (1973) also labeled this phenomenon the *Barnum effect* because many professionals apparently attempt to raise their appearance of credibility through frequent use of very high base-rate statements. For a good discussion about the Barnum effect and the validity of computer-based test interpretations, refer to Guastello and Rieke's 1990 article in *Psychological Assessment: A Journal of Consulting and Clinical Psychology*.

More meaningful are base rates that are less common, or even comparatively rare, and thus allow for distinguishing between individuals or groups of individuals. Sometimes the base rates are so low that one can "play the base rates" in arriving at a professional judgment or conclusion and have virtual certainty of being correct. For example, the incidence—or base rate—of suicide among 5-year-old girls attending kindergarten is virtually nil—certainly less than 1 in

100,000. Knowing nothing else about the person other than age, gender, and enrollment in public school, one could confidently predict an absence of suicidal risk with an accuracy rate of 99.999% or better—a rate that could hardly be improved on by the addition of any psychological test data. Consequently, development of a test to predict suicide in 5-year-old girls would be virtually impossible and would not usefully improve on a prediction made simply from the base-rate information alone. Psychological test data have the greatest potential for improving accuracy over the base-rate predictions (i.e., providing incremental validity) when the base rate is not extreme in either direction but is closer to 50-50.

Base rates change with different groupings and for different populations. For example, the base rate of suicide increases with age, reported depression, loss of social support or job, or history of recent suicide attempts. In another example, diagnosing brain disorder is extremely hazardous among executive candidates for senior job opportunities in business, simply because of the rarity. To do so in such a setting would require virtually overwhelmingly clear and convincing evidence of central nervous system dysfunction. The same diagnosis of brain disorder would be considered with far greater confidence when working with patients on a neurology inpatient ward simply because you are not "fighting the base rate" in your search for accuracy of diagnosis. In other words, the issue of base rates is primarily an issue of setting and recent history because scores often have different meaning depending on the setting. For this reason, MMPI–2 reports should not be written without knowing from which setting it came. An elevation on Scales 4 and 9, for example, would almost certainly predict antisocial behavior if obtained in a prison setting, but not necessarily if obtained from a college counselee.

The point, then, is that base rates for different disorders differ across groups, thereby directly affecting the description and prediction process. Thus, actuarial tables derived accurately for one group (e.g., medical patients) may be less accurate with other groups (e.g., psychiatric patients). For these reasons, careful thought must be given even when using actuarially based cookbook interpretations of the MMPI–2. Particular attention must be paid to recognizing when a given client differs from those on whom the actuarial interpretations were derived (Ehrenworth & Archer, 1985). Naïve applications of any system can result in situations such as a 24-year-old inpatient being diagnosed as suffering involutional depression simply because his MMPI–2 profile configuration suggested it.

Despite the power of the actuarial approach, it is still a "work in progress." The actuarial approach to MMPI–2 interpretation is indeed powerful, but only if the actuary has access to relevant data about the client. For these reasons, a cookbook or computerized interpretation system, although powerful and efficient, is not always sufficient. The MMPI–2 user should be particularly alert to the need to modify MMPI–2 clinical interpretations because of a person's age, intelligence, social or ethnic class, educational level, health status, medication influences, prior life traumas, and current situational difficulties. Such potent factors clearly must modify many interpretations made of MMPI–2 profile configurations because the existing knowledge does not yet allow these factors to be considered by the actuarial systems (Pancoast, Archer, & Gordon, 1988).

The Importance of Referrral Data

Because many MMPI–2 interpretive statements are empirically generated, individuals sharing the same code pattern will exhibit many of the same symptoms, complaints, behaviors, and personality traits. It is unlikely that individuals will obtain a valid elevated profile without exhibiting the primary typical characteristics associated with that profile. For example, persons with an elevated Scale 2 at a *T* score of 90 will be depressed, will exhibit varied symptoms of depression, and will be ruminative and guilt prone. However, the exact manifestations of these symptoms and complaints will vary across populations and will be modified by variables such as SES, intelligence, education, recent life events, and other personality traits. For example, most persons with 27/72 codes will be compulsive, depressed, perfectionistic, and worry prone. However, one individual with a 27/72 code may be more aware of anxiety and guilt and complain somewhat less of depression, whereas another may experience the depressive symptoms more intensely, with guilt and anxiety as secondary.

Elevations on the other clinical, supplementary, and content scales will aid in predicting these differences, but intelligence, education, and socioeconomic variables also will partly determine how individuals experience their symptoms and articulate their complaints. For example, an uneducated person with a 27/72 code likely would describe psychological problems in a different way than an educated individual of higher SES who had a similar 27/72 code. In another example, one individual, elevated on Scales 4 and 9, may be a successful businesswoman, charismatic, energetic, and enterprising, although impulse prone and with intimacy difficulties, whereas another woman with the same scores on Scales 4 and 9 may be a drug-addicted, marginally adjusted individual. They share many similarities: Both will find rules to be irritating; are likely to have difficulties with intimacy and long-term relationships, and will manifest impulse-control problems, difficulties with authority, and the postponement of gratification. These attributes will manifest themselves, however, quite differently. The successful businesswoman may have a higher intellectual and SES which will perhaps be reflected in her MMPI–2 by elevations on the *K* scale and on the *Es* scale, and perhaps on the *Ss* scale, all suggesting self-control, social poise, and sophistication. The educated, intelligent individual with a 49/94 code is more likely able to control her impulses well enough to effectively use her manipulative qualities, whereas the other individual with lower intelligence and lower ego strength is unable to use these qualities in socially adaptive ways.

Not factoring in the moderator variables, which often are reflected in elevations on some of the supplementary scales, can also lead to mistakes in MMPI–2 interpretation. For example, on seeing a 49/94 elevation at $T = 75$, the novice clinician may assume sociopathy and a life of crime, which is not necessarily true. In one case, an unskilled psychologist's report stated that there was evidence from the MMPI–2 results that the father, who was seeking visitation rights with his children subsequent to a divorce, exhibited antisocial criminal behaviors and personality traits. In fact, the father was a successful malpractice attorney, never in trouble with the law. A recovering alcoholic, he was prominent in the community as a leader of various causes. He had a tendency to externalize and had difficulties with impulse control. His children saw him as somewhat unreliable, although often warm and playful. He had managed, however, to create a successful business, channeling his aggressive, competitive impulses in mostly appropriate ways, except for difficulties in his marital life.

Not ascertaining the population from which the 49/94 code profile came led to a poorly worded report and an angry father who was able to cast doubt on the whole evaluation because a clearly refutable statement (about his "criminal tendencies") had been made by the psychologist in the report. Obtaining a referral question, a brief history and background information from the referral source would have helped to avoid such a mistake. The referring colleague might have requested an evaluation with a statement such as the following:

> Please evaluate this bright young attorney with a successful practice. He is recently divorced and in a custody dispute with his ex-wife. He is successful, but I'm wondering if there's any legitimacy to his wife's complaints that he's devious, manipulative, and controlling, even though others see him as successful, charming, and likeable. Can you evaluate him as part of the custody evaluation?

Thus, the report could have addressed the tendency for educated persons with 49/94 codes to come across as charming and poised, showing poor impulse control, but not necessarily as antisocial or manifesting criminal behavior. Therefore, MMPI–2 reports should never be written "blind," without any knowledge about an individual. At least a basic referral question is needed, as well as some population parameters. As described in chapter 10, psychologists are increasingly using computer-generated reports as an aid in their evaluations (Maruish, 1994), but most computer-generated reports incorporate extremely little background information, often only age, education, setting, and occasionally race. Currently, few computer-generated reports specifically address a particular referral question, although some computer reports vary their interpretations depending on whether the client is from a forensic setting, general medical setting, or an outpatient or inpatient mental health setting. Consequently, the psychologist must use clinical skills and information from other data to create a useful report and should not rely solely on a computer-generated report. It is the skill and judgment of the clinician that takes computer-generated statements and fits them for a particular individual, taking into consideration the referral question and the individual's history, achievements, and other intervening variables. Chapter 10 offers more detailed information about widely used computer-generated reports and presents several examples of these.

Another consideration is that patients sometimes obtain profiles that initially appear more pathological than is warranted once the referral question, current situation, and background information are obtained. For example, a client with an MMPI–2 profile peaking on Scale 4 with *T* scores about 70 may be going through a difficult divorce. Somewhat alienated and experiencing difficulties with trust, this individual may be responding understandably to his or her current difficulties. In another example, a client with a profile elevated on Scales 2 and 7 may show a chronic life history of compulsive, anxious, and depressive behaviors or the client may be responding to a recent catastrophic or unpredictable loss but have a history of fairly healthy adjustment.

A report using only an actuarial cookbook approach generally will describe the client accurately regarding current functioning, behaviors, and symptoms. The diagnosis, therapeutic suggestions, and the usefulness of the report may be compromised, however, unless the clinician simultaneously considers the referral question, current life situation, and background information. A key aspect of the background information is the client's demographic parameters because each demographic variable may influence, to some degree, how a particular set of scores is interpreted.

DEMOGRAPHIC VARIABLES

Age

As humans age, significant changes occur. People generally become less aggressive and less risk taking with age, as well as slightly more conservative. They also tend to worry more about health and illness and show some slight decrease in optimism. These changes are reflected in the empirical research on the effects of age on MMPI/MMPI–2 code patterns. Although age effects on the MMPI/MMPI–2 have been studied infrequently, the studies nevertheless confirm the general research on aging. One of the first large-scale studies (Aaronson, 1958), using 871 normals and the original MMPI, confirmed that with aging there is a tendency to become more preoccupied with health and illness, as well as somewhat more pessimistic. These issues were reflected in average increases in elevation of 5 or more *T*-score points on the *L* scale and Scales 1 and 2 for both men and women. Decreases in alienation and acting out and a slight decrease in energy were reflected in a similar drop in elevations on Scales 4 and 9 for both men and women.

Other findings using mostly the MMPI can be summarized as follows:

1. Psychopathology tends to diminish with age. Elevations across most scales drift down as a function of age by a significant, although small, number of *T* scores, except for the *L* scale and Scales 1 and 2, which tend to go up.
2. Scores on Scales 4 and 9 tend to decrease more than the other scales as a function of age, confirming the clinical observation that sociopaths "burn out" with age.
3. The *K* scale and Scale 0, scales which may have a genetic component (Caldwell, personal communication, June 1994), tend to stay stable across all groups over time.

More recently, Aaronson, Dent, Webb, and Kline (1996) demonstrated that endorsement of MMPI–2 critical items decreased with age, a finding which replicated the findings of Webb, Fowler, and Miller (1971) regarding critical items in the original MMPI. Both studies showed that as age increased, patients endorsed fewer items of overt pathology or distress and that this decrease was virtually linear from age 25 onward.

Two-point code-pattern frequencies likewise vary according to age. Webb's (1970a) analysis of over 12,000 patients showed that clients above age 27 obtained the following codes significantly more frequently than younger patients: 02/20, 12/21, 13/31, 23/32, 27/72, 34/43, and 36/63. Patients below age 27 obtained the following codes more frequently: 47/74, 48/84, 49/94, 68/86, 78/87, and 89/98. Although Webb's analysis has limited generalizability due to his use of a median split resulting in a cutoff at age 27, his point remains valid: Age is a moderator variable, with younger patients showing more acting out and psychotic code-patterns and older patients showing more anxious, depressed, and somatizing codes.

Gynther (1979) similarly observed that

> younger patients and normals obtain more peaks and higher scores on scales measuring nonconformity, rebelliousness, alienation, and energy level. Older patients and normals obtain more peaks and high scores on scales measuring concern with health, introversion, and to a lesser extent, scales involving depression and immaturity. (p. 64)

Age, then, can affect interpretation of profiles. For example, a profile with moderate elevations on the *D* or *Hs* scales from a person over age 70 might be interpreted less pathologically than the same profile from a young adult.

On the other hand, studies comparing the average *T* scores for various age categories in the MMPI–2 normative sample failed to show systematic scale variations by age (Dahlstrom & Tellegen, 1993; see also Fig. 1.1). Although there are definite aging effects on MMPI–2 scores, the effects vary, and by small amounts, so that age-corrected norms are difficult to generate and are probably not needed; an exception is for adolescents, which is accomplished by using the MMPI–A. The MMPI–2 is probably robust enough that the slight changes due to aging do not make a great deal of difference clinically except at the extremes.

Gender

Early in the development of the MMPI, different norms for men and women were developed because of the different patterns of endorsement of items for the two genders on some of the scales. In addition, Scales 3 (*Hy*) and 6 (*Pa*) were more often high point elevations for women, whereas Scales 1 (*Hs*) and 7 (*Pt*) were more often highest for men (Webb, 1971). Subsequently, it was also suggested that MMPI scale elevations had different correlates for the two genders (Dahlstrom et al., 1972). That is, elevations on Scale 6 did not necessarily mean the same for men as for women. However, little research has been published on whether gender differences occur in the empirical correlates of code patterns. Greene (1991a) stated that the dearth of research could reflect that gender differences are rarely found or that there has been an absence of research in this area.

The MMPI–2 also uses different *T* scores for men and women, although the gender differences appear to be less than with the original MMPI. What has not yet been adequately considered in interpreting MMPI–2 patterns are the gender-related specific situations that may need to be considered in understanding the clinical significance of an MMPI–2 profile. For example, spouse abuse is disproportionately an occurrence with wives, and the knowledge that a woman is being abused would make the anger reflected in an MMPI–2 pattern more understandable. Similarly, the frustrations of a competent, independent woman who is experiencing the glass ceiling in the business world could be reflected in portions of the MMPI–2 profile, reflecting the situation rather than enduring pathology. The clinician must be sensitive to such gender issues to effectively interpret MMPI–2 code patterns. Although the MMPI–2 is robust enough that it is not likely that these gender issues invalidate interpretation, more research is clearly needed.

Education

Beyond the matter of a basic comprehension of the MMPI–2 items, education also is associated with certain scale elevations. On the original MMPI, higher education levels were associated with decreases in elevation on the *F* and *Si* scales and increases on the *K* scale. Likewise, men with higher education showed fairly strong elevations on Scale 5 (*Mf*; Gulas, 1973), and women with similarly high education showed moderately low scores on Scale 5 (Dahlstrom et al., 1986; Graham & Tisdale, 1983). These patterns on Scale 5 are also associated with increased intelligence test scores, and generally these findings exist regardless of age or ethnic group membership (Dahlstrom et al., 1986). As Dahlstrom et al. (1986) noted,

> In general, then, all subjects who report some education beyond the level of high school graduation are more likely to answer the MMPI–2 in less deviant ways. Their scores are consistent with greater personal effectiveness, fewer interpersonal and emotional difficulties, and better morale. (p. 123)

This statement is consistent with the findings of Webb et al. (1971) that MMPI critical items were endorsed significantly less frequently as education increased, regardless of age.

The effects of education on scale elevations are quite different for the MMPI–2, as opposed to the MMPI, because the MMPI–2 normative group averaged almost 15 years of education, whereas the original normative sample had approximately 8 years of education. If the original "normals" deserved the sobriquet "Minnesota farmer," the new "normals" could be considered yuppies. Consequently, a typical individual taking the MMPI–2 will score lower on the *K* scale and Scale 5 and higher on the *L* scale than they would on the MMPI, as they are being compared with an educated normative group, whereas previously they were compared with a group of less educated individuals. In an attempt to counter the concern that the new "over"-educated normals would adversely affect code-pattern data, Butcher (1990a) grouped the MMPI–2 normative sample into five groups on the basis of education and examined mean *T* scores. His data suggested that education had no significant impact on *T*-score elevations because all five groups' mean profiles were around a *T* score of 50.

A. B. Caldwell (personal communication, May 6, 1990), however, has cautioned that the significant effects of education could alter codes to such a degree that it could compromise the validity of the MMPI–2 significantly. He has advised that MMPI–2 profiles be rescored onto an MMPI profile sheet to ensure scale pattern congruence. Clearly more research is needed with the MMPI–2 to determine if the effects of education, particularly on the *K* scale, lead to a resulting significant change in code patterns.

Race

Numerous studies reviewing the MMPI have shown significant differences between scores of African Americans and whites on the MMPI. Most often these differences have found the *F* scale and Scales 8 (*Sc*) and 9 (*Ma*) to be significantly higher in African Americans, with other studies also showing the *K* scale and Scale 5 (*Mf*) to be lower. Some evidence (Dahlstrom et al., 1986), however, strongly suggests that most of these apparent differences have resulted from influences of other variables, such as education, age, and rural/urban residence. At higher levels of SES, racial differences virtually disappeared. Within racial groups, scale score differences between higher and lower socioeconomic groups were much greater than any differences between racial groups. Clearly socioeconomic variables played a bigger role than the racial variable.

Even so, it is important to remember that African Americans, whether young or old, male or female, normal or institutionalized, generally obtain higher scores than whites on the *F* scale and Scales 8 (*Sc*), and 9 (*Ma*). Gynther (1979) suggested that these results appear to reflect differences in values and perceptions rather than differences in psychological adjustment. Many studies, according to Gynther, revealed that the principal factor distinguishing between African Americans and Whites was estrangement and mistrust of society, which was reflected on Scales 4 (*Pd*) and 8 (*Sc*). Indeed, Dahlstrom et al. (1986) noted that "by no means are all deviations (as reflected in elevated MMPI scores or in similar measures) evidence for disorder" (p. 202). Even so, these elevations and profile configurations are instructive. As Dahlstrom et al. (1986) concluded, "the MMPI may be useful in the task of characterizing the various coping and defense mechanisms to which minority individuals may resort in their efforts to deal with the special circumstances that they all too often encounter in America today" (p. 202).

Comparisons with Hispanics and other minority groups also suggest some differences in average MMPI scores. In reviewing these studies, Greene (1980) was not able, however, to discern any clear pattern of differences on the clinical scales, although some validity scale differences appeared on the *L* and *K* scales. His review suggested that the differences on the MMPI between Hispanic populations and Whites were less than the differences between African Americans and whites. Dahlstrom et al. (1986) made similar observations and additionally noted that acculturation generally reduced the differences between the MMPI scores of Hispanic and White populations.

Although caution should be used when interpreting MMPI–2 profiles from ethnic groups, Greene (1987), in a comprehensive review regarding ethnicity and the MMPI, suggested that too much has been made of average differences between ethnic groups' MMPI scores. His review suggested that there was a "failure to find a consistent pattern of scale differences between any two ethnic groups in any population" (Greene, 1987, p. 509). Instead, as he pointed out, "it appears that moderator variables such as socioeconomic status, education, and intelligence, as well as profile validity are more important determinants of MMPI performance than ethnic status" (Greene, 1987, p. 509). As Greene and Dahlstrom et al. both noted, researchers should focus on the empirical correlates associated with specific patterns and elevations on the MMPI–2 for various ethnic subpopulations, rather than reporting small mean differences between various poorly defined ethnic groups. Also, researchers need to establish whether a particular individual identifies with an ethnic group, rather than assuming that identification with the minority culture is defined by a person's race or surname, and assess the person's perception of estrangement from the majority culture at that time.

The MMPI–2 normative group consisted of a larger and somewhat more representative sample of ethnic minorities, so it is more appropriate for testing a broad range of ethnically diverse people than the MMPI. Shondrick, Ben-Porath, and Stafford (1992), for example, compared African American and White men who had been ordered by the court to take the MMPI–2 as part of their pretrial evaluation. The group mean profiles of both sets of defendants revealed few scale elevation differences between the groups. Scale 9 and the *CYN* and *ASP* scales were significantly more elevated for African Americans than for Whites, however. The differences were so slight that it is difficult to interpret, especially because the socioeconomic variables were not taken into account. The slight differences, however, are consistent with previous differences between African American and Whites found on the MMPI. More research is needed using the MMPI–2 and ethnic minorities, but the evidence suggests that the test is valid for use with ethnic minorities in the United States.

Socioeconomic Variables

The major dimensions that define SES in White participants can be matched only roughly to similar dimensions for participants who are African American or are from other ethnic groups. Thus, it is hazardous to make generalizations concerning MMPI–2 patterns that might be associated with socioeconomic variables (Dahlstrom et al., 1986). Even so, some patterns seem sufficiently consistent to warrant specific mention.

Normal participants from low socioeconomic groups, regardless of race or gender, tend to score higher on the *F* scale and on Scale 0 (*Si*) of the MMPI–2, whereas participants from higher socioeconomic backgrounds tend to score higher on the *K* scale (Dahlstrom et al., 1986; Duckworth & Anderson, 1986). For men, Scale 8 (*Sc*) decreases and Scale 5 (*Mf*) increases as SES increases, whereas for women, Scales 2 (*D*) and 5 (*Mf*) decrease as SES increases. SES is fundamentally composed of, and confounded with, such dimensions as education, age, gender, and ethnicity. Thus, it is no surprise that SES must provide a basic life pattern within which to interpret the MMPI–2. As noted earlier, although the MMPI–2 normative group had a mean level of education of 15 years, compared with 8 years for the MMPI normals, education as a variable does not significantly affect profile elevation. The exception to this was the *K* scale, for both men and women, and Scale 5, surprisingly only for men. Between socioeconomic groups generally, it is interesting that major differences emerged on the validity scales and Scale 5. The group with the lowest education (part high school) had higher *F* (about 8 *T*-score points) and *L* (about 5 *T*-score points) scores and lower *K* scores (about 9 *T*-score points) when compared with the group with the highest education level. How socioeconomic variables will affect interpretation will require further research.

INTERPRETIVE STEPS

Preparing a written report is an important part of many psychologists' work. Yet it is a procedure that has typically received insufficient emphasis in graduate schools, has been little researched, is often perceived as tedious to do, and consequently is often poorly done (Ownby, 1987). Writing a report involves two steps of which the first is the most important because, if it is done poorly, the second step becomes irrelevant. First, the psychologist needs to organize the raw data so that inferences can be developed from it, allowing for an accurate conceptualization of the testee. The second step involves crafting these inferences into a report that is empirically grounded and yet creates a picture of the testee that is accurate and useful to the reader.

Initially, most psychologists have difficulty in integrating the vast array of MMPI–2 data. At times, it can be daunting. Demographic and referral question variables are the backdrop against which 10 clinical and 9 (or more) validity scales covary across a wide possible range of *T* scores. When supplementary and content scales are added to the equation, sometimes yielding information that appears contradictory, it is little wonder that integrating the information in order to write an MMPI–2 report is seen as a complex and tedious task.

The following discussions include a step-by-step approach to interpreting an MMPI–2 profile as well as addressing actual report writing, outlining some common pitfalls, and suggested remedies so that MMPI–2 reports are empirically grounded yet capture the psychological richness of the individual described.

The interpretive steps outlined here assume that the interpretation is being made "blind," that is, without the benefit of other test data or clinical and historical data. Although this goes against usual and ethical clinical practice, MMPI–2 data is isolated from other data in this chapter in order to better explicate the interpretive process without the reader being burdened by the additional task of integrating other test data. Usually, however, MMPI–2 data is part of a complete battery of psychological tests and/or life history data, interview(s), and presenting complaints and referral questions.

The interpretation of the profile should be proceeded by the steps described in chapter 4. These steps include noting the test-taking time of the testee, as well as examining the answer sheet for erasures, omissions, and double-marked answers. Additionally, it is important to administer the appropriate version of the test (e.g., language and form) and to provide the testee with the appropriate instructions. Proper scoring techniques and conditions for testing are also described in chapter 4.

The actual interpretive task should begin with determining the setting in which the profile was administered. First, obtain basic demographic data, such as gender, age, ethnicity, and years of education, as well as referral question information. Is this a profile of a client from an inpatient setting or a prison setting? Is it a divorce/custody evaluation or a self-referred private practice individual? Is it a profile of an African American or someone from a different ethnic background? What is the client's age? Even when interpreting a profile "blindly," these demographic and referral information and moderator variables are necessary because they set the stage for the way a profile is interpreted. If the setting suggests that there is either no or great motivation toward positive or negative self-presentation, then the criteria for validity are affected. As described previously, there are no exact cutoff scores for determining validity. Rather, the clinician has to examine the entire profile, the setting, and any motivation to over- or understate problems in order to arrive at an interpretive understanding of the profile. For example, in a custody evaluation setting, an *L* score of $T = 65$, an *F* score of $T = 40$, and a *K* score of $T = 65$ would suggest a self-favorable presentation and a possibility that the test is invalid. In a private practice setting, however, a client with no motivation for a self-favorable presentation and who is presenting as out of touch with his or her feelings and having difficulty in relationships because of emotional overcontrol, the test may, in fact, be accurately reflecting a rigid and over-controlled, inhibited individual. Other validity indicators, such as the *Mp* and *Sd* scales, could help in determining the interpretation of such a profile.

The second step in profile interpretation is to verify that the client has answered the items in a consistent and accurate manner. If scores on the *VRIN* and *TRIN* scales, for example, are in the acceptable range, then the profile has been answered consistently. If they are not within the acceptable range, suggesting that they have been answered inconsistently, no other interpretable data are available.

If the profile is consistent and the elevations on the *F*, *F*B, *F*(P), *L*, *K*, *S*, and other supplementary validity scales are in the acceptable range, then the profile is valid. Sometimes profiles are not clearly invalid, although they suggest a positive or negative self-presentation. In these cases, the clinician has to determine whether the distorted self-presentation is intentional or unintentional. In either case, the clinician has to determine if the distortion in self-presentation is extreme enough to invalidate the test. For example, in some cases, individuals may present themselves in a somewhat favorable or unfavorable light, but the test can still be interpreted, with some caveats. An example would be a profile in which the *K* score of a custody evaluation client is at a *T* score of 63 and the *L* score is at a *T* score of 60. In examining the supplementary validity scales, the psychologist may determine that the individual "put his or her best foot forward" so that the test may underestimate any psychopathology. Nevertheless, the clinician may decide that the profile can be cautiously interpreted, especially because most child custody litigants show elevated *L* and *K* scores (Bathurst, Gottfried, & Gottfried, 1997). Recent research (see chap. 2) suggests that the *F(P)*, *F* – *K* Index, *Ds*, *Mp*, and *Sd* scales, among others, can be helpful in determining if the positive or negative self-presentation is conscious or unconscious.

Sometimes profiles are consistent, but clearly the individual is presenting with an overly unfavorable self-presentation. In settings in which there is little reason for the client to malinger, cautiously interpreting an exaggerated profile can be useful, even if only to obtain an understanding of how the client wanted to portray him- or herself to the clinician. Exaggerated profiles can serve as a road map for a dialogue with the client. For example, the clinician might state, "The way you answered the test suggests that you went out of your way to let me know how disturbed you feel, even to the point of overemphasizing some of your difficulties or fears. Did you do that intentionally or not? What difficulties or feelings did you want to make sure I knew about?" However, no profile should be interpreted if the *VRIN* and *TRIN* scales show clear-cut inconsistency and possible confusion.

The third step in interpreting a profile is to examine each of the clinical scale scores, noting each *T* score and determining if the profile is a recognizable code pattern. Chapter 4 describes in detail the method for coding a profile. Before mastery of the MMPI–2 has been achieved, it is difficult to recognize a code pattern and certainly difficult to know precisely what correlates go with a particular code pattern without looking it up. Once familiar with the MMPI–2, clinicians will find some codes easily recognizable. Usually two, three, or four of the clinical scales are clearly elevated above the rest and are at more or less the same level above a *T* score of 65. In this case, turn to chapter 6 and read the descriptors associated with a spike, two-, three-, or four-point code pattern.

The more distinctive and elevated the code pattern, the greater the confidence the clinician will have about the validity of the descriptive statements. For example, a profile in which Scales 2, 7, and 8 are all elevated at $T = 80$ and no other scales are elevated above 65 is a distinct and elevated code pattern. A profile in which Scales 2, 3, 4, 6, 8, 9, and 0 are all elevated between a *T* score of 64 and 66 is a moderately elevated and non-well-defined profile making it more difficult to interpret. The more distinct and elevated the code pattern, the more likely the code is the same as would be obtained had the original MMPI been administered (see chap. 4 for a discussion of code-pattern concordance issues). Moreover, the higher the elevation, the more confidence the clinician can have that the descriptive statements are both true and salient.

As recommended earlier, we suggest that all MMPI–2 profiles be translated back to an MMPI profile. Even although current research on the meaning of MMPI–2 code patterns is in progress, the vast majority of interpretive data is based on the original MMPI code patterns. In many cases, the MMPI and MMPI–2 code patterns will be the same. In cases in which they are different, the interpretive differences may not be that important (e.g., a 4896 code pattern on the MMPI–2, when replotted on to the MMPI, may be a 4986). Translating the

MMPI–2 back to an MMPI is a quick process (see chap. 4). If the MMPI–2 code pattern changes when plotted using MMPI norms, we recommend interpreting the MMPI code pattern. Although we recommend it, it is not standard practice at this time for most clinicians to do so. In most cases, if there is a lack of congruence between MMPI–2 and MMPI code patterns, the changes in interpretation are small and make little difference to the evaluation, recommendations, and treatment strategies. For example, if an individual obtains a 489 code on the MMPI–2 and a 4978 code on the MMPI, the interpretation will differ only slightly between the two profiles.

Once a code is identified, refer to the Code-Pattern Look-Up Table and write down the descriptions associated with the pattern. Beginning clinicians are often needlessly cautious about making strong inferences from the code-pattern data. This often reflects a distrust in the test and in the clinician's abilities. It is important to remember that it is very unlikely that an individual will obtain a valid elevated code pattern, particularly a well-defined one, and not exhibit the symptoms, complaints, and personality traits associated with that code. For example, an individual obtaining an MMPI–2 elevation on Scale 2 at a *T* score of 90 *will* be depressed and *will* exhibit the symptoms of depression, even if they are not (and this would be very rare) consciously aware and complaining of feeling depressed.

Psychologists are often apprehensive about copying from the textbook the descriptions associated with the code pattern. There is no danger of being accused of plagiarism, however, in copying the descriptions out of a cookbook, as these descriptions are empirically generated, and attempting to describe the individual in a different lexicon from that of the cookbooks might lead to interpretive errors. Some graduate students complain that writing reports this way leaves little room for clinical and interpretive skills. However, the skill of the clinician is needed in determining which descriptors fit for a particular individual and how to combine descriptors in complex profiles.

COMMON CODE PATTERNS

Over the past 5 decades of MMPI and MMPI–2 use, a number of commonly occurring scale configurations or code patterns have been described and have become part of the MMPI–2 lexicon. These commonly occurring *K*-corrected patterns (also described in chap. 6) are summarized here:

1. *Conversion V (see Fig. 9.1).* The Conversion V occurs when Scales 1 and 3 are greater than Scale 2 by 8 or more *T*-score points and when Scales 1 and 3 are at least a *T* score of 65. In the classic conversion V, other scales may be elevated, but not as high as Scales 1 and 3. The conversion V is a distinctive pattern with notable personality features (see 13/31 codes in chap. 6).
2. *Paranoid valley or psychotic V (see Fig. 9.2).* This profile occurs when Scales 6 and 8 are equal to or greater than Scale 7 by 8 or more *T*-score points and when Scales 6 and 8 are at or above a *T* score of 65.

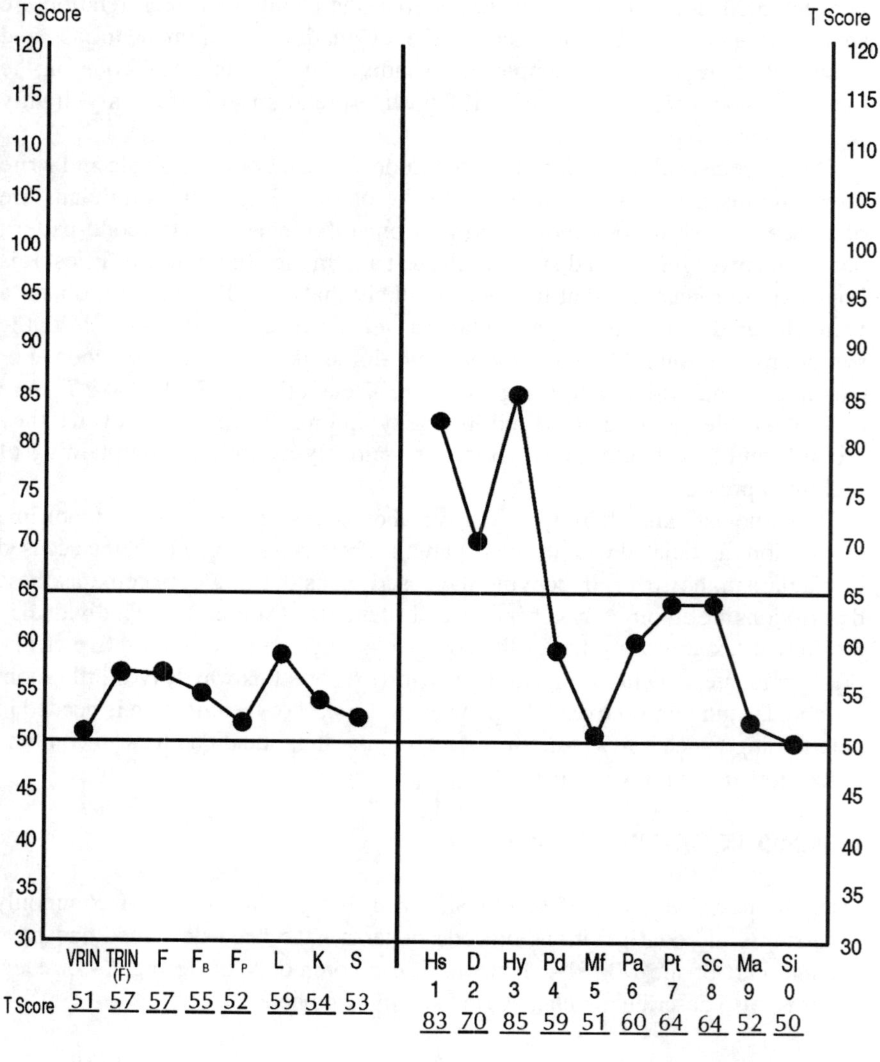

FIG. 9.1. Conversion V. Minnesota Multiphasic Personality Inventory–2, Basic Scales Profile Form. Copyright © by the Regents of the University of Minnesota 1942, 1943 (renewed 1970), 1989. Reproduced by permission of the publisher. All rights reserved "MMPI–2" and "Minnesota Multiphasic Personality Inventory–2" are trademarks owned by the University of Minnesota.

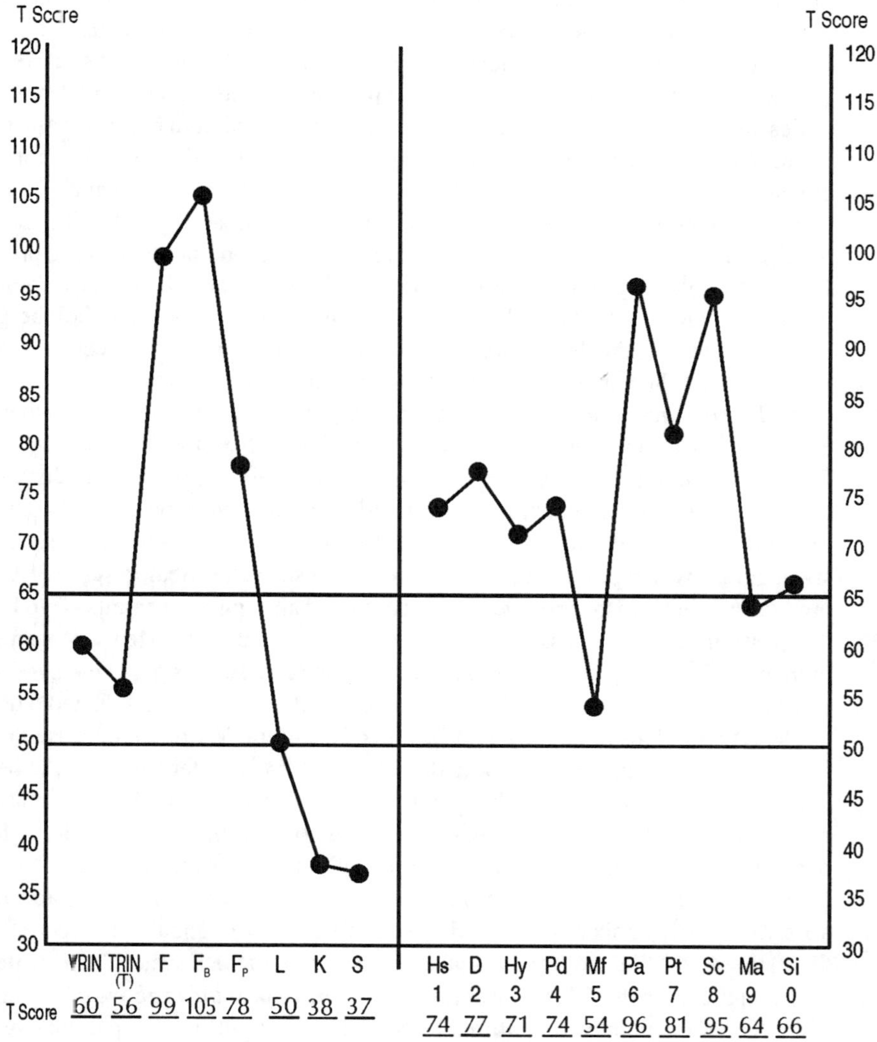

FIG. 9.2. Paranoid valley or psychotic V. Minnesota Multiphasic Personality Inventory–2, Basic Scales Profile Form. Copyright © by the Regents of the University of Minnesota 1942, 1943 (renewed 1970), 1989. Reproduced by permission of the publisher. All rights reserved "MMPI–2" and "Minnesota Multiphasic Personality Inventory–2" are trademarks owned by the University of Minnesota.

3. *Spike profiles (See Fig. 9.3).* A spike profile occurs when any scale is over 65, and higher than all other scales by at least 8 *T*-score points.

4. *Psychotic versus neurotic slope.* A vertical line through Scale 5 would divide the MMPI–2 profile roughly between the neurotic, left-hand, side of the profile and the psychotic, right-hand side of the profile. A positive slope occurs when the psychotic scales are elevated above 65 and the neurotic scales are below 65 (see Fig. 9.4). This predicts a psychotic adjustment. A negative slope occurs when the left, or neurotic, side of the profile is elevated and the psychotic scales are relatively low (see Fig. 9.5). This generally predicts a neurotic adjustment. No clinician, however, should assume that a profile indicates a psychotic or neurotic adjustment only by the slope of the profile. The neurotic-versus-psychotic-slope concept is useful only as a starting point in a diagnostic decision process that asks the question, "Am I looking at a neurotic or a psychotic profile?" Determining psychotic versus neurotic adjustment definitively is accomplished by referring to the scale elevations, scale configurations, the Goldberg index, and the *BIZ* scale, as well as the critical items, with all aspects being viewed within the context of the person's behavior and history.

5. *Passive–aggressive V in women (see Fig. 9.6).* This profile occurs when Scales 4 and 6 are elevated at or above $T = 65$ and Scale 5 is close to or below $T = 50$. The profile suggests a passive–aggressive personality disorder or trait disturbance. Because of its shape, it is often called the passive–aggressive V. The lower the Scale 5, the more passively self-defeating is the woman. The passive-aggressive V is associated with women because the low Scale 5 score often predicts passivity. In the presence of both paranoid and aggressive traits (46/64), this passivity becomes passive aggression and wounded pride. Men who score high on Scales 4 and 6, as well as Scale 5, are also often seen as passive–aggressive, angry, and hypersensitive; however, the elevations of Scales 4, 5, and 6 do not lend themselves to the characterization of the 46/64 V women because the Scale 5 is elevated in men. Men who do obtain a 46/64 V pattern are likely to be aggressive, paranoid, and possibly paranoid schizophrenic. Scale 5 in the "masculine" direction (low) would increase the likelihood of acting out, whereas high Scale 5 scores in men would have the effect of inhibiting overt acting out.

6. K+ *profile (See Fig. 9.7).* In this configuration, no clinical scales are above a *T* score of 65, and six or more clinical scales are below or equal to a *T* score of 56. In the *K*+ profile, the *L* and *K* scales are greater than the *F* scale. The *K* scale is also higher than the *F* scale by at least 5 *T- score points and is above a T* score of 60. The *K*+ profile was identified by Marks et al. (1974) in an inpatient psychotic population only. In other words, this profile occurred in patients whose test results were considered a false negative (test miss). The inpatient responder had gone through a minefield of test items and somehow managed to avoid raising a red flag on any of the clinical scales. In an inpatient setting, Marks et al. found that 48% of these responders were psychotic. Thus, if a *K*+ profile is obtained by a person in an inpatient setting, the clinician should describe the client's failure to report psychological pain and raise the likelihood of overcontrol, emotional shutdown, and conscious or unconscious denial of problems. This in-

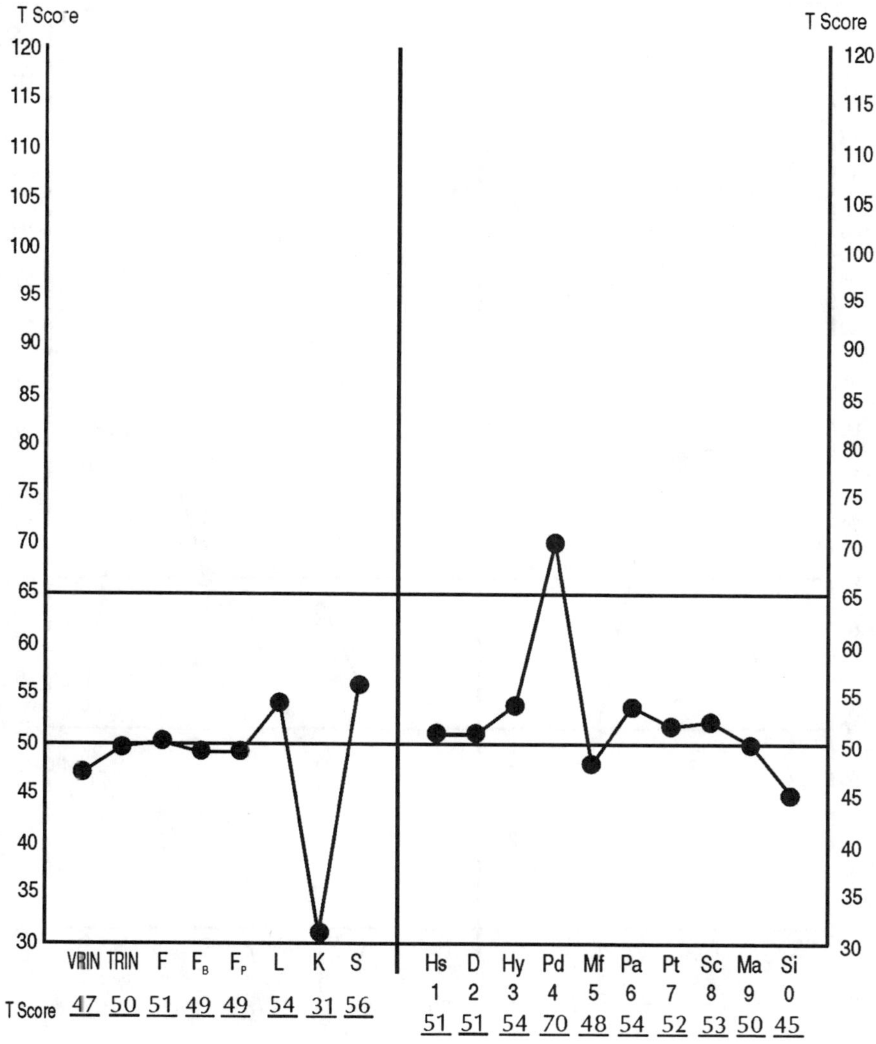

FIG. 9.3. Spike 4 profile. Minnesota Multiphasic Personality Inventory–2, Basic Scales Profile Form.

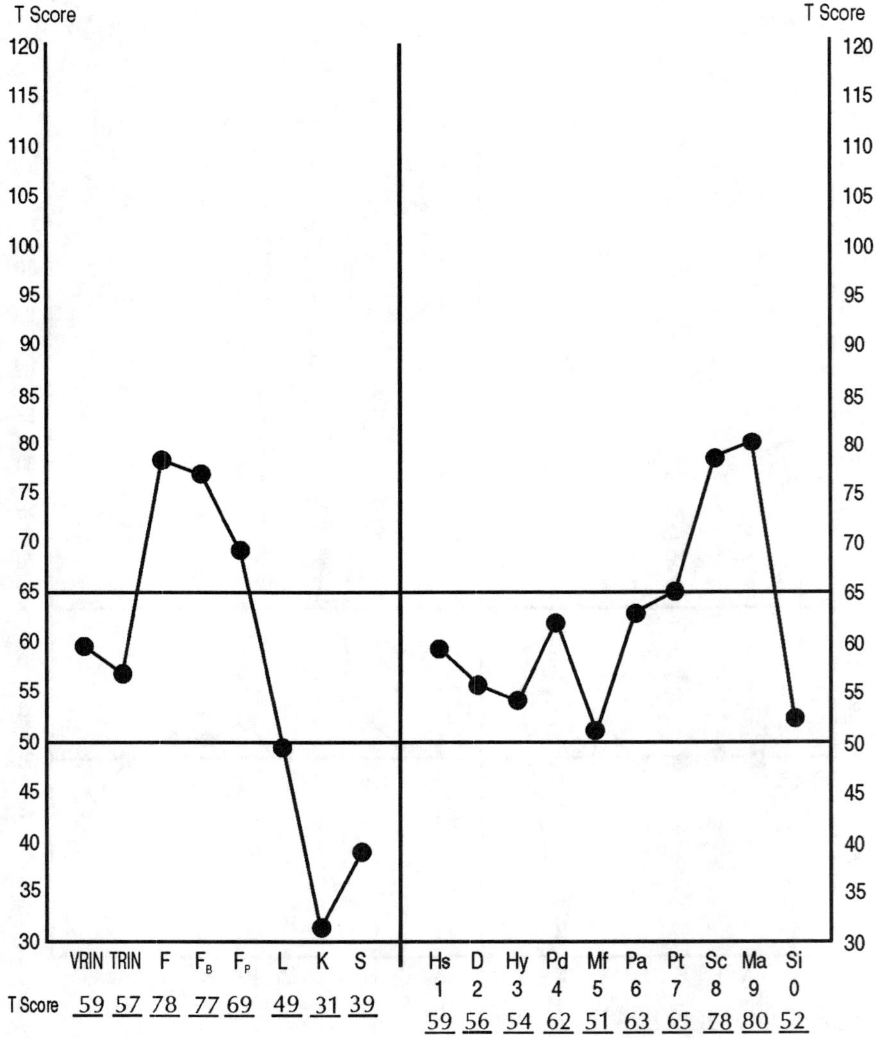

FIG. 9.4. Positive or psychotic slope. Minnesota Multiphasic Personality Inventory–2, Basic Scales Profile Form. Copyright © by the Regents of the University of Minnesota 1942, 1943 (renewed 1970), 1989. Reproduced by permission of the publisher. All rights reserved "MMPI–2" and "Minnesota Multiphasic Personality Inventory–2" are trademarks owned by the University of Minnesota.

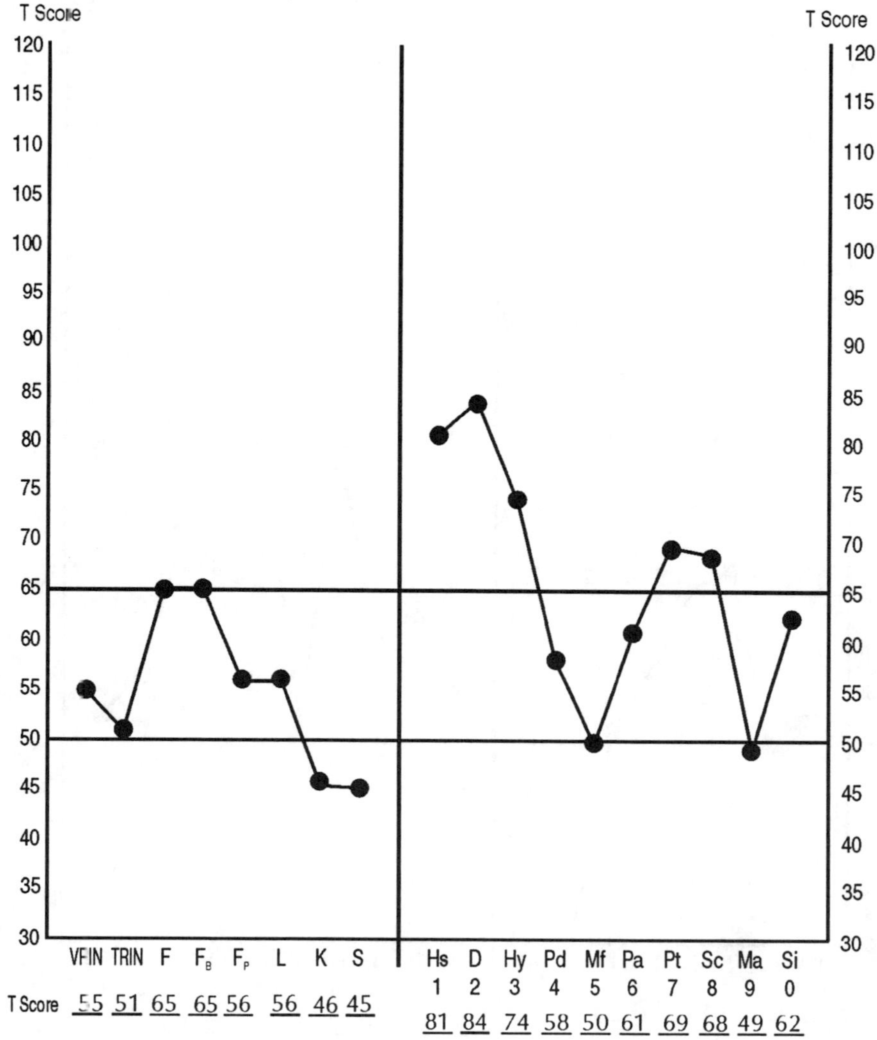

FIG. 9.5. Negative or neurotic slope. Minnesota Multiphasic Personality Inventory–2, Basic Scales Profile Form. Copyright © by the Regents of the University of Minnesota 1942, 1943 (renewed 1970), 1989. Reproduced by permission of the publisher. All rights reserved "MMPI–2" and "Minnesota Multiphasic Personality Inventory–2" are trademarks owned by the University of Minnesota.

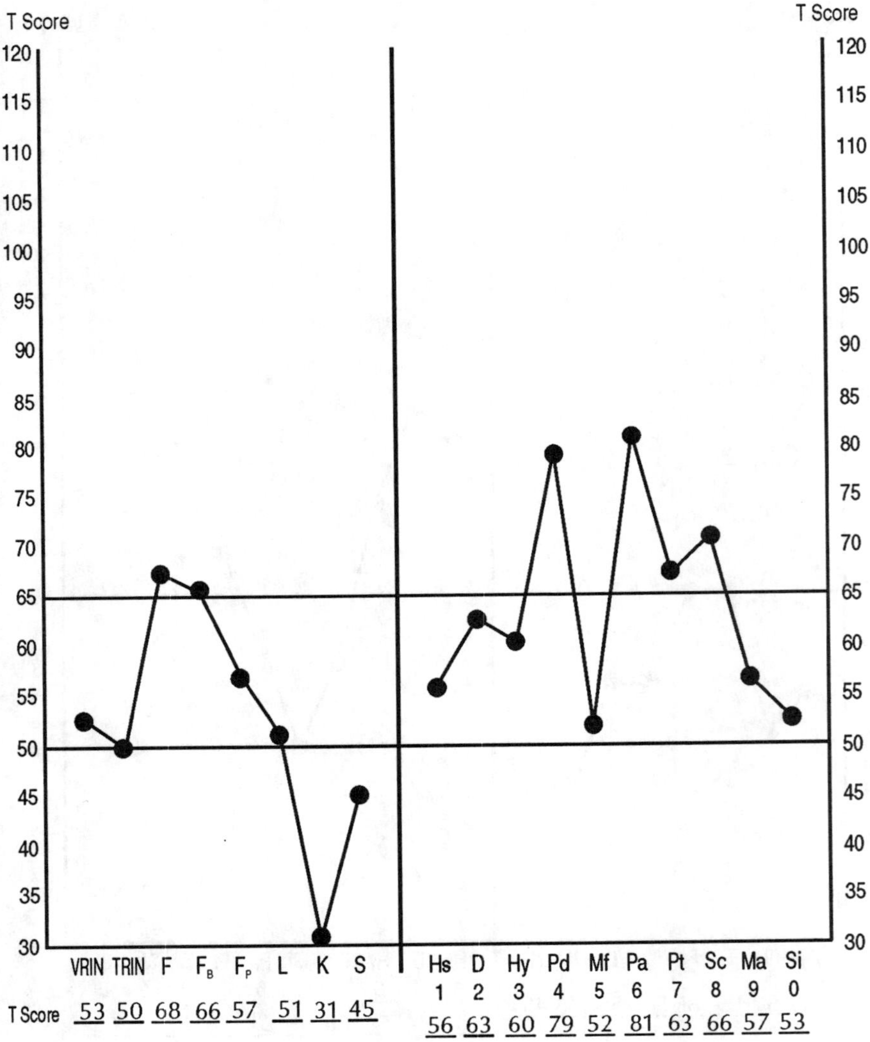

FIG. 9.6. Passive–aggresive V. Minnesota Multiphasic Personality Inventory–2, Basic Scales Profile Form. Copyright © by the Regents of the University of Minnesota 1942, 1943 (renewed 1970), 1989. Reproduced by permission of the publisher. All rights reserved "MMPI–2" and "Minnesota Multiphasic Personality Inventory–2" are trademarks owned by the University of Minnesota.

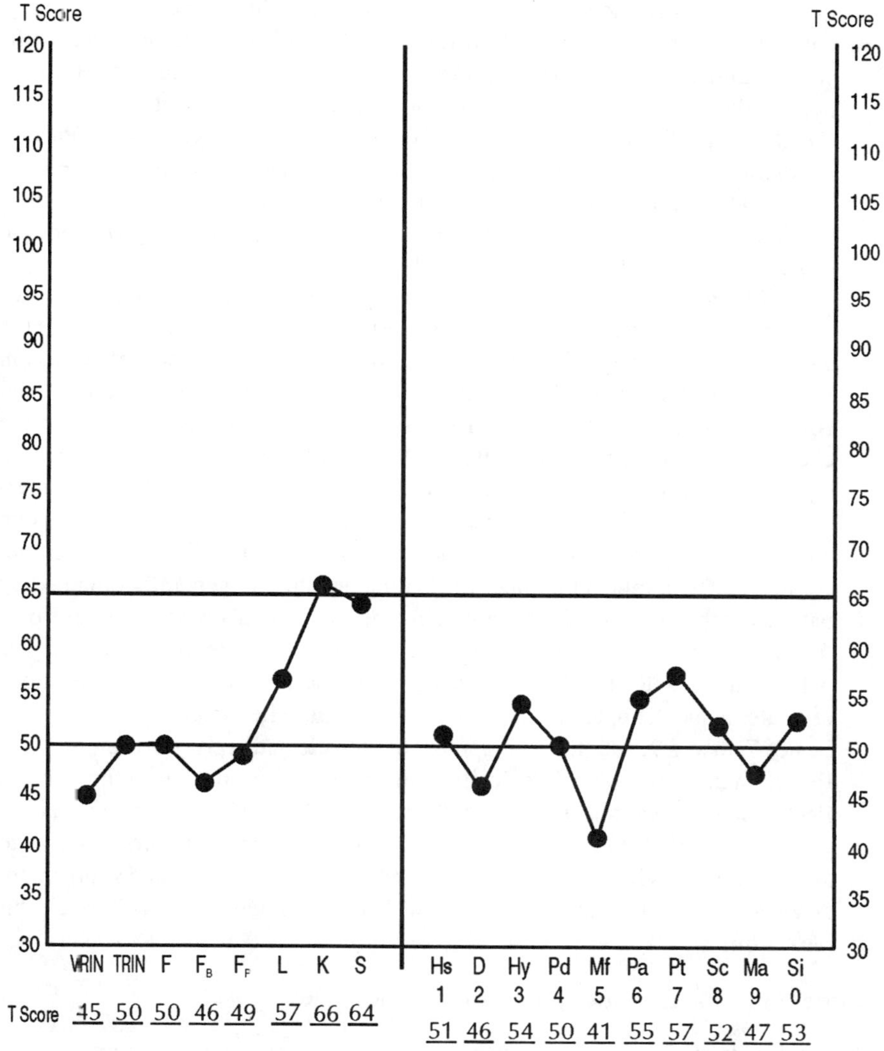

FIG. 9.7. *K* + profile. Minnesota Multiphasic Personality Inventory–2, Basic Scales Profile Form. Copyright © by the Regents of the University of Minnesota 1942, 1943 (renewed 1970), 1989. Reproduced by permission of the publisher. All rights reserved "MMPI–2" and "Minnesota Multiphasic Personality Inventory–2" are trademarks owned by the University of Minnesota.

formation should be integrated with what is known about the patient's history, behavioral observations, or other psychological test data. A possible way of dealing with the problem of a *K*+ profile is to ask clients to retake the test, answering the test from the perspective of how they feel at their worst. Psychologists are urged to remember that the *K*+ profile occurs in many different settings and in both men and women. However, the *K*+ correlates were derived specifically within a psychiatric inpatient setting; thus, caution should be used in applying these correlates to populations other than psychiatric inpatients (Duckworth & Barley, 1988). This kind of defensive profile without clinical elevations also often occurs in private practice settings and may suggest a well-adjusted, although somewhat overcontrolled individual. The supplemental validity scales such as *Mp*, *Sd*, and *SES* could help in determining whether the profile is intentionally or unintentionally self-favorable or due to SES.

7. *Floating profile (see Fig. 9.8).* In this profile, all or most scores on Scales 1–9 equal or exceed a *T* score of 65 and are usually accompanied by an extreme elevation on the *F* scale (Friedman, Webb, & Lewak, 1989; Newmark, Chassin, Evans, & Gentry, 1984). This profile is difficult to interpret, as no well-defined code pattern emerges for easy interpretation. Of all the code patterns, this is the code with the lowest congruence with MMPI profiles. The two highest scales are highly likely to be quite different when translated back to an MMPI. The interpretive process involves breaking down this complex profile into two-point code patterns, which lend themselves to being interpreted. It is likely, although not certain, that a significant number of floating profiles are generally obtained by patients with Borderline Personality Disorder. Individuals who obtain this profile experience a great deal of tension and turmoil, but no predominant defensive pattern emerges. Rather, they experience moodiness, reflected in the elevations of Scales 2 and 9; anxiety, tension, and self-doubt, reflected in the elevations of Scales 7, 8, and 9; and the development of somatic and repressive defenses, reflected in the elevations of Scales 1, 2, and 3, as well as episodic acting out, reflected in the elevations of Scales 4, 8, and 9. Slight changes in the code pattern from the MMPI–2 to the MMPI would make little significant difference as to how the profile is interpreted. The interpretation of the content and supplementary scales, as well as the critical items, will hone the interpretation of these complex profiles.

Code Patterns, Elevation, and Additional Scales

The code pattern (27, 49, etc.) defines a particular set of behaviors, symptoms, and experiential domains, irrespective of elevation. For example, people obtaining their highest scores on Scales 4 and 9 will generally be alienated from society, impulsive, and superficially charming but with a poor frustration tolerance. These characteristics will be fundamentally consistent across all 49 profile elevations, whether *T* scores are between 80 and 90 or between 65 and 80, and are even mildly applicable for *T*-score elevations between 59 and 65. In other words, the personality picture is basically similar for all 49s. However, the elevation of a profile predicts the intensity and severity of the symptoms. The higher the profile,

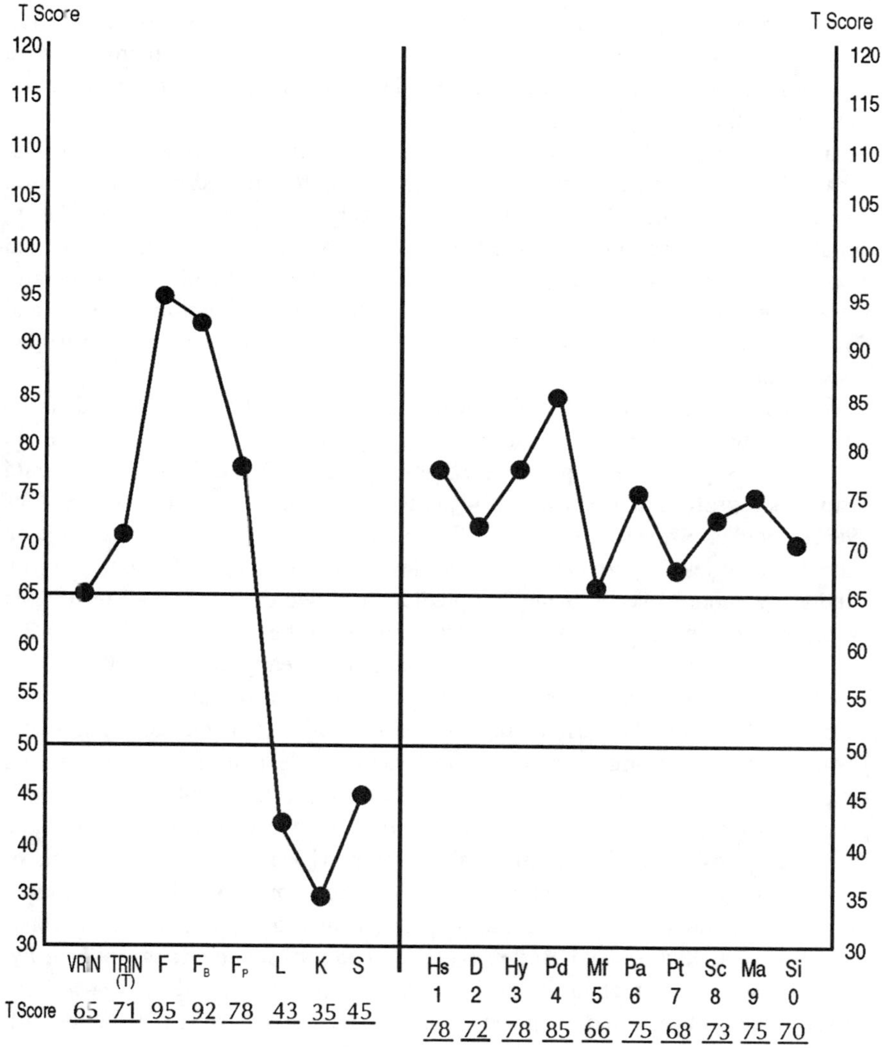

FIG. 9.8. Floating profile. Minnesota Multiphasic Personality Inventory–2, Basic Scales Profile Form.

the more severe the symptoms and the more a person's thoughts, feelings, and behaviors are likely to be dominated by the psychopathology predicted by the particular code pattern. For example, within the normal range, (e.g., Scales 4 and 9 at $T = 60$), the 49 code suggests some propensity for impulsivity and the probability of an energetic and potentially charming individual who exhibits some frustration intolerance and occasional difficulties with intimacy. However, many of these traits will be well within the normal range and will be exhibited more as personality traits rather than as psychopathology.

In another example, a 27 code above $T = 80$ is quite likely to reflect a person who is experiencing a severe, agitated depression that thoroughly permeates daily life. Another person with a 27 profile at $T = 65$ will likely show periods of despondency, agitation, and depression, followed by periods of feeling less depressed and anxious. Persons with a *T*-score elevation at 60 on Scales 2 and 7 will generally show good adjustment, with only occasional periods of agitation, anxiety, and down moods. Their personality style will likely be that of a prone-to-worry, responsible person.

In each case, the personality traits are the same, although the elevation predicts the intensity, duration, and pervasiveness of symptoms and pathological traits. In general, we suggest that a profile elevation between 60 and 64 predicts a mild disturbance, profiles between 65 and 74 predict a moderate disturbance, and profiles over 75 predict a severe disturbance. When a profile is severely elevated, a code pattern may be less important than just the elevation. For example, for someone who obtains a *T* score of 90 on Scale 2, a prediction of depression with all the classic symptoms of depression will fit, regardless of whether the code pattern is a 27, a 29, or a 28. However, elevations on the other scales help greatly in defining the kind of depression (anxious depression (27/72), psychotic depression (28/82), etc.).

Interpretations in the normal range of 50 to 59 rely less on the elevation of any particular scale and much more on the basis of code pattern and content and supplementary scales (see chaps. 7 and 8). For example, a 27 profile at $T = 60$ will predict a person who is prone to worry, experience anxiety over responsibility, be seen as responsible, and be cautious about taking risks; however, a diagnosis of depression is not certain, although possible. In other words, profiles in the normal range can be understood as identifying personality traits rather than psychopathology. Duckworth and Barley's (1988) caution, however, is noteworthy. Although within normal limits profiles may often correctly identify a healthy person, such profiles can often generate false negatives (i.e., overlook pathology), particularly within the following populations: (a) psychiatric inpatients whose *K* scores are greater than $T = 65$, (b) prisoners, and (c) participants with observed psychopathology but who lack insight or accurate self-appraisal. As a result, profiles of persons in psychiatric settings often need to be interpreted with caution if the validity scales suggest a self-favorable response set. In these situations, the interplay of defensiveness and psychopathology needs to be carefully teased out because the person's psychopathology may be aggravated by defensive overcontrol, denial, and a lack of appropriate emotional outlets, factors represented by the elevation on the validity scales. For example, a profile with both Scales 9 and

6 elevated at $T = 64$, with the L and K scales near $T = 60$, could reflect a controlled, rigid, tense, and brittle person who might become quite hostile, agitated, and even paranoid under stress. The moderate elevations on the validity scales add more overcontrol to an already overcontrolled and brittle 69 profile. Butcher (1990b) suggested that if all the clinical scales are between T scores of 60 and 64, content scales may be better sources of personality descriptions than are the clinical scales. Usually, however, information from all the scales is integrated in order to form a rich personality picture.

Usually, the content scale data confirm the code-pattern data and sharpen the interpretation. For example, a 278 profile might also exhibit elevations on the Anxiety (*ANX*) and Depression (*DEP*) content scales. Also, one would expect the Low Self-Esteem (*LSE*) and Work Interference (*WRK*) scales to be elevated, confirming the picture of a depressed, anxious, ruminative, procrastinating, low-self-esteem individual, a picture already painted by the 278 code. If in this hypothetical example, the *DEP* and *LSE* scales were not elevated, the description would change significantly. The 278 depression might be less characterological, more situational, less angry, and with a better prognosis. Although there is not much information available about the meaning of low clinical scale scores, or the lowest scale in a code pattern, these scores can also be a source of rich interpretive material (see chap. 3). For example, an individual scoring a spike 2 code (e.g., Scale 2 at $T = 85$) is likely experiencing a severe depression. If Scale 9 were also elevated at $T = 65$, the depression would exhibit different characteristics than if Scale 9 were elevated at $T = 40$. In the first example, the moderate elevation on Scale 9 would predict agitation, moodiness, and irritability, whereas in the second example, the elevation on Scale 9 at $T = 40$ would predict a more collapsed depression with low energy, low motivation, and less agitation. In another example, a 489 elevated code could be seen as more pathological if Scale 7 were below $T = 50$ than if Scale 7 were coded fourth, giving a 4897 profile. The low score on Scale 7 in such a code pattern would suggest that the callous, angry sociopathy of the 489 profile was unhindered by any anxiety, remorse, or guilt. Finally, the task is to look at critical items, which usually confirms the hypotheses already generated (see chap. 7). Critical items can also highlight aspects of statements already made about the individual. For example, an individual who is severely depressed and angry (24 code) might also be elevated on the *MAC–R* scale. The clinician may make a statement about the susceptibility of the individual to substance abuse and may then draw attention to this problem by quoting from the critical items: "The individual's response to Item 489, 'I have a drug or alcohol problem' (True) suggests a careful evaluation of his or her current alcohol use." This could also be done for suicide items or mental confusion items.

The next task is to organize the inferences into a written format that flows from paragraph to paragraph and captures the essential qualities of the testee. Graduate students and clinicians often have difficulty with report writing because they have difficulty conceptualizing the individual and organizing the inferences about him or her in a way that integrates contradictory descriptors to paint a realistic and accurate picture of the person. Once this is done well, writing the report is not difficult.

Organizing the Data

The next step in interpreting an MMPI–2 is to examine and organize the data gathered from the validity, clinical, content, and supplementary scales (and subscales), the code patterns, and the low-point elevations.

Most of the information collected will be consistent and fit together, but some of it will appear contradictory. For example, the clinician may have determined that a particular profile is valid, although slightly self-favorable; that the setting from which it came would predict some self-favorable responding (e.g., a custody setting); and that the individual has significant scale elevations (e.g., on Scales 4 and 9 at $T = 65$). Having identified in the Code-Pattern Look-Up Table some descriptors for a 49 profile, the clinician would likely draw inferences that the profile is that of someone who is generally energetic, positive, and superficially charming, although with some impulse problems and some difficulties with intimacy. If in this hypothetical case there was also an elevation on Scale 7 at $T=64$ and an elevation on Scale 2 at $T=60$, the information from the elevations on Scales 7 and 2 would appear contradictory to the earlier hypothesis generated for a 49 code. Integrating the contradictory data is difficult, and some clinicians are tempted to ignore it and write a report based only on the code-pattern data (in this case, the 49 data). A report written this way will be only partially accurate and be lacking in richness and complexity. The secondary elevations on Scales 7 and 2 would predict guilt, anxiety, and angry remorse over acting out behavior, and perhaps obsessive ruminations about how to avoid acting out, but little long-term behavioral change.

Some computer-generated reports use only code-pattern information, that is, information generated from the highest 1, 2, or 3 scales. Information from other scales that are elevated are then reported using single-scale descriptors, and often no attempt is made to integrate them into the body of the code-pattern description. For example, an individual with significant scale elevations on Scales 4 and 9 would be described using 49 descriptors. Statements associated with the mild elevations on Scales 2 and 7, suggesting that the individual had some proneness to worry, to be somewhat anxious and guilty, and for episodic "down" times, would be indicated later in the report but not integrated into the personality picture. The clinician reading the computer-generated report would be responsible for determining how these statements fit into the overall profile. Thus, it is the skill of the clinician to then integrate this contradictory data into a personality picture. (See chap. 10 for computer scoring and interpretive systems.)

After the clinician has determined profile validity and written down a series of descriptors generated from the code-pattern elevations and other elevated clinical scales and low-point scales, the next step is to examine the content and supplementary scales, as well as the Subtle–Obvious and Harris–Lingoes subscales. Usually the data from all the scales confirm the inferences generated from the code pattern. In some cases, however, the material is contradictory and these contradictions have to be understood and integrated into the assessment.

In selecting the appropriate descriptors for a particular code, there are several issues to consider. In many cases, the order of elevation of a two- or three-point code is not critical. For example, it is not critical whether the profile is a 13 or 31 code pattern. Although it is true, for example, that a 31 individual may exhibit more of the hysterical symptoms and less of the obviously negativistic and complaining attributes of the 13 individual, for most reports the order of the elevation is not critical. In other cases, however, the differences in elevations are very relevant, as in a 78 code versus an 87 code. A second issue in interpreting code patterns involves elevation. Most cookbooks provide interpretive data only for profiles above $T = 65$ but do not distinguish between various elevations above $T = 65$. It is up to the clinician to make appropriate adjustments in descriptors for the level of severity of disturbance. The more elevated the profile, usually the more severe, and sometimes acute, the disturbance.

Writing the Report

In beginning to use the MMPI–2, most clinicians have difficulty integrating the personality descriptors into a consistent report. A common error is to list in a report all the adjectives associated with elevations in the code pattern and single scales. Reports written in this manner present a string of disconnected adjectives, describing symptoms and behaviors that can confuse the reader. For example, a report based on the code pattern 278, all at $T = 80$ and with Scales 4 and 9 elevated at $T = 75$, might read as follows: "This individual is likely anxious, ruminative, depressed, and with low self-esteem (278 descriptor). He or she may also be hypomanic, acting out, and impulsive (94 descriptor)." Although these adjectives describe the individual, they are not integrated into a coherent picture and may be confusing. A more integrated description would describe an anxious, ruminative, depressed individual who also experiences mood swings and occasional acting out in self-defeating ways. The skill of the clinician is to understand, for example, how Scale 4 elevations in the context of 278 elevations predict self-defeating, negativistic behaviors and attitudes and how Scale 9 elevations predict moodiness and agitation, as well as increase the likelihood of impulsive, self-destructive behavior (as the depression and anger are energized by Scale 9).

When writing a report, begin by summarizing the *essence* of the profile. With what symptoms will the client present? Which symptoms or behaviors will be "glaring"? For example, a profile with the highest elevation on Scale 9 at $T = 90$ will predict hypomania. The symptoms will likely be obvious. Is this a profile that indicates primarily a depression? If so, what kind of depression? On the other hand, is it a profile of an acting-out, rebellious, angry person? If so, what kind of acting-out behaviors are suggested (sexual, passive–aggressive, self-defeating, etc.)? Is it a profile of a confused paranoid person? If so, is it a transitory psychotic disturbance or a longstanding one? How will the person's conflicts or personality characteristics likely manifest themselves in various situations, such as on the job or with family? What is it about the person's characteristics that prevents that person from achieving a resolution of the problems? The report should describe the code pattern before the remaining single-scale high-point and low-point information is discussed.

The following section is meant as a guide to beginning a report, often the most difficult part for psychologists. These statements are designed as *report openers*, which set the stage for the rest of the report. The first paragraph of the report should discuss the consistency and test-taking attitude and resulting validity of the profile. The second paragraph of the report should open with a statement describing the client's primary symptoms and complaints. The following descriptors/symptoms have been written as though the profile was at least moderately elevated ($T = 65$). Modifications in some of the language would be needed if the profiles were more or less elevated, even though the basic characteristics would remain the same.

Guidelines for Beginning a Report

Code pattern: Spike 1	*Descriptors/Symptoms*
Scale 1 elevated above $T = 65$ all other scales below *Hs2*.	1. Somatizing 2. Fearful 3. Immature 4. Passive 5. Psychologically unsophisticated

This is essentially a profile reflecting a [mild/moderate/severe] somatizing disorder in a dependent, fearful, immature, and passive individual with low psychological sophistication. Typically these individuals complain of [list symptoms]. Behaviors associated with this profile are [list behaviors]. Traits associated with this profile are [list traits].

Code pattern: 12	*Descriptors/Symptoms*
Scale 1 highest: Scale 2 added	1. Somatizing 2. Depressed 3. Despondent 4. Dependent 5. Passive 6. Moody

The profile suggests a [mild/moderate/severe] somatizing depression in a passive, dependent, and moody individual. Other symptoms associated with this profile are [list symptoms]. Behaviors associated with this profile are [list behaviors]. Traits associated with this profile are [list traits].

Code pattern: 13	*Descriptors/Symptoms*
Scale 1 highest Scale 3 added	1. Hysterical/somatizing 2. Overcontrolled 3. Psychologically naive 4. Dependent 5. "La belle indifference"

This profile, sometimes called *la belle indifference*, reflects a [mild/moderate/severe] somatizing disorder in an overcontrolled, psychologically naïve, and dependent personality. Other symptoms frequently associated with this profile are [list symptoms]. Behaviors associated with this profile are [list behaviors]. Traits associated with this profile are [list traits].

Code pattern: 14	*Descriptors/Symptoms*
Scale 1 highest Scale 4 added	1. Dependent 2. Manipulative 3. Immature 4. Passive–aggressive

The profile reflects a [mild/moderate/severe] disorder in a somatizing, dependent, manipulative, immature, passive–aggressive individual. Other symptoms often associated with the profile are [list symptoms]. Behaviors associated with this profile are [list behaviors]. Traits associated with this profile are [list traits].

Code pattern: 16	*Descriptors/Symptoms*
Scale 1 highest Scale 6 added	1. Somatizing 2. Paranoid 3. Suspicious 4. Angry 5. Blaming, externalizing

This is essentially a [mild/moderate/severe] somatizing disorder in a paranoid, suspicious, angry, and externalizing individual. Such persons typically show other symptoms such as [list symptoms]. Other symptoms often associated with the profile are [list symptoms]. Behaviors associated with this profile are [list behaviors]. Traits associated with this profile are [list traits].

Code pattern: 17	*Descriptors/Symptoms*
Scale 1 highest Scale 7 added	1. Somatizing 2. Anxious 3. Tense 4. Hyperresponsible 5. Preoccupied 6. Obsessive–compulsive traits and behaviors

The profile suggests a [mild/moderate/severe] somatizing disorder in an anxious, tense, preoccupied, and obsessive–compulsive individual. Other symptoms typically associated with such profiles are [list symptoms]. Behaviors associated with this profile are [list behaviors]. Traits associated with this profile are [list traits].

Code pattern: 18	*Descriptors/Symptoms*
Scale 1 highest Scale 8 added	1. Somatic 2. Confused 3. Schizoid 4. Immature 5. Possibly psychotic

The profile suggests a [mild/moderate/severe] somatizing disorder in a confused, immature, and schizoid individual. This person will likely show additional symptoms such as [list symptoms]. Behaviors associated with this profile are [list behaviors]. Traits associated with this profile are [list traits].

Code pattern: 19/91	*Descriptors/Symptoms*
Scale 1 highest Scale 9 added	1. Somatizing 2. Tense 3. Driven 4. Explosive

This profile suggests a [mild/moderate/severe] somatizing disorder in a tense, driven, hypomanic personality. Other symptoms often associated with such profiles are [list symptoms]. Behaviors associated with this profile are [list behaviors]. Traits associated with this profile are [list traits].

Code pattern: Spike 2	*Descriptors/Symptoms*
Scale 2 highest and above $T = 65$ All other scales below Scale 2	1. Vegetative symptoms [poor sleep, low sex drive, low energy] 2. Depression 3. Guilt 4. Anxiety 5. Low self-esteem

The profile suggests a [mild/moderate/severe] depression with vegetative symptoms of depression, disturbance in mood, feelings of guilt, anxiety, and low self-esteem. Other symptoms often associated with such profiles are [list symptoms]. Behaviors associated with this profile are [list behaviors]. Traits associated with this profile are [list traits].

Code pattern: 23	*Descriptors/Symptoms*
Scale 2 highest and above $T = 65$ Scale 3 above $T = 65$	1. Depression 2. Somatic symptoms 3. Low psychological mindedness 4. Immaturity 5. Secondary gain 6. Guilt inducing and self-sacrificing

The profile suggests a [mild/moderate/severe] depression in a dependent, somatizing, and immature individual. Other symptoms often associated with this profile are [list symptoms]. Behaviors associated with this profile are [list behaviors]. Traits associated with this profile are [list traits].

Code pattern: 24	*Descriptors/Symptoms*
Scale 2 highest and above $T = 65$ Scale 4 in second place and above $T = 65$	1. Angry 2. Self-defeating 3. Suicidal 4. Dependent 5. Manipulative

The profile suggests a [mild/moderate/severe] depression in an angry, self-defeating, dependent, and possibly suicidal individual. Other symptoms often associated with this profile are [list symptoms]. Behaviors associated with this profile are [list behaviors]. Traits associated with this profile are [list traits].

Code pattern: 25	*Descriptors/Symptoms*
Scale 2 highest and above $T = 65$ Scale 5 above $T = 65$ for men, below $T = 40$ for women]	1. Passive 2. Dependent 3. Hypersensitive 4. Indecisive

The profile suggests a [mild/moderate/severe] depression in a passive, dependent, and hypersensitive individual. Other symptoms also likely are [list symptoms]. Behaviors associated with this profile are [list behaviors]. Traits associated with this profile are [list traits].

Code pattern: 26	*Descriptors/Symptoms*
Scale 2 highest and above $T = 65$ Scale 6 in second place and	1. Depressed 2. Paranoid

above $T = 65$	3. Externalizing 4. Resentful 5. Bitter

The profile suggests a [mild/moderate/severe] depression in a hypersensitive, potentially paranoid, and externalizing individual. Other symptoms often associated with this profile are [list symptoms]. Behaviors associated with this profile are [list behaviors]. Traits associated with this profile are [list traits].

Code pattern: 27	***Descriptors/Symptoms***
Scale 2 highest and above $T = 65$ Scale 7 in second place and above $T = 65$	1. Anxiety 2. Depression 3. Guilt 4. Low self-esteem 5. Passiveness

This profile suggests a [mild/moderate/severe] anxious depression in a passive individual who is guilt-ridden and has low self-esteem. Other symptoms often associated with this profile are [list symptoms]. Behaviors associated with this profile are [list behaviors]. Traits associated with this profile are [list traits].

Code pattern: 28	***Descriptors/Symptoms***
Scale 2 highest and above $T = 65$ Scale 8 in second place and above $T = 65$	1. Depression 2. Anxiety 3. Agitation 4. Withdrawal 5. Inefficiency 6. Fears of emotional involvement 7. Possibly psychotic depression

This profile suggests a [mild/moderate/severe] depression in an anxious, withdrawn individual who is likely to complain of memory and concentration difficulties and have problems with general efficiency. Other symptoms often associated with this profile are [list symptoms]. Behaviors associated with this profile are [list behaviors]. Traits associated with this profile are [list traits].

Code pattern: 29	***Descriptors/Symptoms***
Scale 2 above $T = 65$ Scale 9 in second place and above $T = 65$	1. Labile 2. Explosive 3. Moody 4. Irritable 5. Mood disorder

This profile suggests a [mild/moderate/severe] affective disorder with irritability, lability, and possible explosiveness. Other symptoms often associated with this profile are [list symptoms]. Behaviors associated with this profile are [list behaviors]. Traits associated with this profile are [list traits].

Code pattern: Spike 3	***Descriptors/Symptoms***
Scale 3 above $T = 65$ All other scales below $T = 65$	1. Naive 2. Dependent 3. Somatizing 4. Immature 5. Self-centered 6. Lacking in insight

The profile suggests a [mild/moderate/severe] somatizing disorder in an immature, psychologically naive, dependent person. Other symptoms often associated with this pattern are [list symptoms]. Behaviors associated with this profile are [list behaviors]. Traits associated with this profile are [list traits].

Code pattern: 34	***Descriptors/Symptoms***
Scale 3 highest and above $T = 65$ Scale 4 in second place and above $T = 65$	1. Overcontrolled 2. Role Playing 3. Manipulative, impulsive 4. Explosive 5. Lacking in insight

The profile suggests a [mild/moderate/severe] overcontrolled personality disorder in a person who is likely to present as conforming and cooperative but will exhibit episodic, impulsive, and, at times, explosive episodes. Other symptoms often associated with this profile are [list symptoms]. Behaviors associated with this profile are [list behaviors]. Traits associated with this profile are [list traits].

Code pattern: 36	***Descriptors/Symptoms***
Scale 3 highest and above $T = 65$ Scale 6 in second place and above $T = 65$	1. Paranoid 2. Controlled 3. Conforming 4. Projecting 5. Denying

The profile suggests a [mild/moderate/severe] paranoid disorder in an individual who is typically overcontrolled, inhibited, and denying and who uses projection as a primary defense mechanism. Other symptoms often associated with this profile are [list symptoms]. Behaviors associated with this profile are [list behaviors]. Traits associated with this profile are [list traits].

Code pattern: 37	*Descriptors/Symptoms*
Scale 3 highest and above $T = 65$ Scale 7 in second place and above $T = 65$	1. Overcontrolled 2. Tense 3. Anxious 4. Passive 5. Ingratiating 6. Somatizing

The profile suggests a [mild/moderate/severe] anxiety disorder in a denying, psychologically naïve, anxious, and ingratiating individual who is likely to develop hysterical symptomatology in response to psychological stress. Other symptoms often associated with this profile are [list symptoms]. Behaviors associated with this profile are [list behaviors]. Traits associated with this profile are [list traits].

Code pattern: 38	*Descriptors/Symptoms*
Scale 3 highest and above $T = 65$ Scale 8 in second place and above $T = 65$	1. Confused 2. Sexually preoccupied 3. Possible hallucinations 4. Dissociative episodes

The profile suggests a [mild/moderate/severe] disturbance in an individual who will present as confused, sexually preoccupied, and dissociative and who may exhibit psychotic episodes. Other symptoms often associated with this profile are [list symptoms]. Behaviors associated with this profile are [list behaviors]. Traits associated with this profile are [list traits].

Code pattern: 39	*Descriptors/Symptoms*
Scale 3 highest and above $T = 65$ Scale 9 above $T = 65$	1. Hypomanic 2. Overcontrolled 3. Demanding 4. Attention seeking 5. Somatizing

The profile suggests a [mild/moderate/severe] hypomanic disturbance in an overcontrolled, demanding, approval-seeking, and somatizing individual. Such individuals are likely to exhibit explosive episodes whenever their goal-directed behavior is blocked. Other symptoms frequently associated with this profile are [list symptoms]. Behaviors associated with this profile are [list behaviors]. Traits associated with this profile are [list traits].

Code pattern: Spike 4	*Descriptors/Symptoms*
Scale 4 highest and above $T = 65$ No other scales elevated	1. Immature 2. Passively dependent 3. Manipulatively dependent 4. Angry 5. Can act out [depends on other scales]

The profile suggests a [mild/moderate/severe] personality disorder in an immature, passively dependent, manipulative, and angry individual.

Code pattern: 45 (men)	*Descriptors/Symptoms*
Scale 4 highest and above $T = 65$ Scale 5 in second place and above $T = 65$	1. Passive 2. Dependent 3. Manipulative 4. Potential sexual dysfunction 5. Passive–aggressive

The profile suggests a [mild/moderate/severe] disorder in an immature and dependent individual who is likely to have conflicts with unresolved dependency needs and will exhibit sexual and intimacy problems. The likelihood of a personality disorder should be considered. Other symptoms frequently associated with this profile are [list symptoms]. Behaviors associated with this profile are [list behaviors]. Traits associated with this profile are [list traits].

Code pattern: 45 (women)	*Descriptors/Symptoms*
Scale 4 highest and above $T = 65$ Scale 5 in second place and above $T = 65$	1. Aggressive 2. Acting out 3. Manipulative 4. Sexual acting-out problems

This is a rare profile in women. Women with this elevation are aggressive, act out, resist being controlled, and tend to have intimacy and sexual problems. Other symptoms frequently associated with this profile are [list symptoms]. Behaviors associated with this profile are [list behaviors]. Traits associated with this profile are [list traits].

Code pattern: 46	*Descriptors/Symptoms*
Scale 4 highest and above $T = 65$	1. Angry

Scale 6 in second place and above $T = 65$	2. Passive aggressive 3. Suspicious 4. "Victim" and "chip on the shoulder" attitude 5. Argumentative

The profile suggests a [mild/moderate/severe] disorder. Typically these individuals are angry, suspicious, and argumentative and maintain a "chip on the shoulder" attitude toward others. Typically, their lifestyle is that of a "victim," and they tend to be vigilant for any demands made on them. Other symptoms frequently associated with this profile are [list symptoms]. Behaviors associated with this profile are [list behaviors]. Traits associated with this profile are [list traits].

Code pattern: 47	***Descriptors/Symptoms***
Scale 4 highest and above $T = 65$ Scale 7 in second place and above $T = 65$	1. Low frustration tolerance 2. Impulsive tension reduction 3. Anxiety that leads to acting out 4. Immaturity 5. Dependent

The profile suggests a [mild/moderate/severe] personality disorder. Typical symptoms associated with this profile are a low frustration tolerance and a tendency to impulsively reduce anxiety and frustration through acting out behavior. Manipulatively dependent, they present with cyclical patterns of acting out. Other symptoms associated with this profile are [list symptoms]. Behaviors associated with this profile are [list behaviors]. Traits associated with this profile are [list traits].

Code pattern: 48	***Descriptors/Symptoms***
Scale 4 highest and above $T = 65$ Scale 8 in second place and above $T = 65$	1. Impulsive 2. Alienated 3. Distrustful 4. Lacking in empathy 5. Poor judgement and confusion 6. Drug and alcohol Problems 7. Sexual aggression

The profile suggests a [mild/moderate/severe] personality disorder in an alienated, acting-out, angry individual who exhibits empathy difficulties and sexuality and aggression confusion. Other symptoms often associated with this profile are [list symptoms]. Behaviors associated with this profile are [list behaviors]. Traits associated with this profile are [list traits].

Code pattern: 49	*Descriptors/Symptoms*
Scale 4 highest and above $T = 65$ Scale 9 in second place and above $T = 65$	1. Superficially charming 2. Impulsive 3. Acting out 4. Self-centered 5. Manipulative

The profile suggests a [mild/moderate/severe] personality disorder. Typically, these individuals are superficially charming, although often self-centered, impulsive, manipulative, and capable of acting out. Other symptoms often associated with this profile are [list symptoms]. Behaviors associated with this profile are [list behaviors]. Traits associated with this profile are [list traits].

Code pattern: Spike 6	*Descriptors/Symptoms*
Scale 6 highest and above $T = 65$ No other scales above $T = 65$	1. Suspicious 2. Overly sensitive 3. Self-righteous 4. Paranoid

The profile reflects a [mild/moderate/severe] elevation and suggests a paranoid individual who is likely to present as guarded, suspicious, and overly sensitive and may exhibit overt and subtle paranoid symptomatology. Other symptoms often associated with this profile are [list symptoms]. Behaviors associated with this profile are [list behaviors]. Traits associated with this profile are [list traits].

Code pattern: 67	*Descriptors/Symptoms*
Scale 6 highest and above $T = 65$ Scale 7 in second place and above $T = 65$	1. Tense 2. Overly sensitive 3. Fearful of criticism 4. Argumentative 5. Anger problems

This is a rare profile. The profile suggests a [mild/moderate/severe] disturbance with symptoms of tension, hypersensitivity, and fears of criticism and failure. Other symptoms often associated with this profile are [list symptoms]. Behaviors associated with this profile are [list behaviors]. Traits associated with this profile are [list traits].

Code pattern: 68D	*Descriptors/Symptoms*
Scale 6 highest and above $T = 65$ Scale 8 in second place and above $T = 65$	1. Marginal psychological adjustment 2. Intense feelings of inferiority and insecurity 3. Distrustful 4. Unstable 5. Possibly psychotic

This profile suggests a [mild/moderate/severe] disorder. Typically, these individuals exhibit marginal psychological adjustment, harbor intense feelings of inferiority and insecurity, and are suspicious and distrustful of others. They avoid deep emotional ties and are emotionally unstable. This is often a psychotic profile. Other symptoms often associated with this profile are [list symptoms]. Behaviors associated with this profile are [list behaviors]. Traits associated with this profile are [list traits].

Code pattern: 69	*Descriptors/Symptoms*
Scale 6 highest and above $T = 65$ Scale 9 in second place and above $T = 65$	1. Paranoid 2. Grandiose 3. High-strung 4. Explosive 5. Extremely sensitive to criticism

This profile suggests a [mild/moderate/severe] disturbance. Some individuals with this profile can exhibit paranoid traits. Often grandiose, they are high-strung and extremely sensitive to criticism. They tend to have difficulties with anger, are often explosive, and use projection as a defense mechanism. Other symptoms often associated with this profile are [list symptoms]. Behaviors associated with this profile are [list behaviors]. Traits associated with this profile are [list traits].

Code pattern: Spike 7	*Descriptors/Symptoms*
Scale 7 highest and above $T = 65$ No other scales above $T = 65$	1. Tense 2. Worried 3. Guilty 4. Poor self-image 5. Apprehensive 6. Compulsive 7. Possibly phobic

This profile suggests a [mild/moderate/severe] disorder in an anxious, tense, worried, guilty, and dependent individual. Many of these individuals exhibit obsessive–compulsive behaviors, and most have poor self-esteem. Other symptoms often associated with this profile are [list symptoms]. Behaviors associated with this profile are [list behaviors]. Traits associated with this profile are [list traits].

Code pattern: 78	*Descriptors/Symptoms*
Scale 7 highest and above $T = 65$ Scale 8 in second place and above $T = 65$	1. Worried 2. Low self-esteem 3. Tense 4. Withdrawn 5. Nervous 6. Insecure 7. Indecisive

This profile suggests a [mild/moderate/severe] disorder. Typically, these individuals exhibit extremely low self-esteem and are irritable, worried, insecure, and indecisive. Nervous and with strong feelings of inadequacy, many complain of depersonalization and many exhibit symptoms of withdrawal and apathy. Other symptoms often associated with this profile are [list symptoms]. Behaviors associated with this profile are [list behaviors]. Traits associated with this profile are [list traits].

Code pattern: Spike 9	*Descriptors/Symptoms*
Scale 9 highest and above $T = 65$ No other scale elevated above $T = 65$	1. Hypomanic 2. Emotionally labile 3. Flight of ideas 4. Good-humored euphoria 5. Irritable with outbursts of anger 6. Moodiness

This profile suggests a [mild/moderate/severe] disorder. Persons with this profile can exhibit good-natured euphoria, followed by mood lability, irritability, overcommitment to too many tasks and activities, and flight of ideas. Denial tends to be a major defense. Some are diagnosed as manic. Other symptoms often associated with this profile are [list symptoms]. Behaviors associated with this profile are [list behaviors]. Traits associated with this profile are [list traits].

Code pattern: 92	*Descriptors/Symptoms*
Scale 9 highest and above $T = 65$ Scale 2 in second place and above $T = 65$	1. Possible agitated depression 2. Insecure 3. Irritable and labile 4. Possibly alcoholic

This profile suggests a [mild/moderate/severe] disorder. It is difficult to determine whether this profile suggests a manic–depressive disorder or an agitated depression. Typically, these individuals are labile and irritable and may use chemical agents as a way of medicating their mood disorder. Other symptoms often associated with this profile are [list symptoms]. Behaviors associated with this profile are [list behaviors]. Traits associated with this profile are [list traits].

Code pattern: 98	***Descriptors/Symptoms***
Scale 9 highest and above $T = 65$ Scale 8 in second place and above $T = 65$	1. Confused, disoriented 2. Hyperactive 3. Emotionally labile 4. Poor sexual adjustment 5. Flight of ideas 6. Hostile

This profile suggests a [mild/moderate/severe] disturbance in a confused, disoriented, hyperactive, and emotionally labile individual. Typically, they have poor sexual adjustment and fears of intimacy. They often talk with a loud voice and can be hostile. Other symptoms often associated with this profile are [list symptoms]. Behaviors associated with this profile are [list behaviors]. Traits associated with this profile are [list traits].

Code pattern: 90	***Descriptors/Symptoms***
Scale 9 highest and above $T = 65$ Scale 0 in second place and above $T = 65$	1. Agitated 2. Introverted 3. Tense 4. Insecure

Not commonly seen, this profile suggests a [mild/moderate/severe] disturbance. Individuals with this profile tend to be tense, introverted, and withdrawn, although they are agitated and can exhibit hypomanic traits. Other symptoms often associated with this profile are [list symptoms]. Behaviors associated with this profile are [list behaviors]. Traits associated with this profile are [list traits].

You have now written an opening paragraph on the validity of the profile and the test-taking attitude of the respondent. You have begun the body of your report with an opening statement that summarizes the essence of the code pattern. Your next statements should go on to list other likely complaints, symptoms, conflicts, and so on for the code obtained from chapter 6. It is customary to report MMPI–2 data objectively, making statements such as "Typically, these individuals are depressed, ruminative, and anxious" (e.g., a 27 profile) or "Others are likely to describe these individuals as demanding, critical and unreasonable, although they are very sensitive to any demands placed on them" (e.g., a 46 profile). Reporting statistical data is also acceptable, although not mandatory in a report; for example, "A high percentage of these individuals tend to be unmarried and of those who are married, Marks and Seeman reported that 70% reported marital discord" (e.g., a 48 code). When writing an MMPI–2 report, it is not customary to integrate actuarial data obtained from the Code-Pattern Look-Up Table or a cookbook with data generated from the referral question, background and history, and current life situation of the individual being tested. This kind of integration is usually reserved for the discussion section of a test report. It is important that the reader of an MMPI–2 report understand that the report is being generated in a way that emphasizes empirical and actuarial data, even though it may include clinical or historical data.

Once you have described the symptoms, behaviors, defenses, and other correlates of the elevated code pattern, look up the correlates for the next highest scale in the configuration (see chap. 6). Repeat this for all the scales that are elevated above $T = 65$ in descending order of elevation. On completing of this task, look up the correlates for any scale below $T = 50$, if they are available (see chap. 3). For example, look at Fig. 9.9. The profile is that of a 26/62 code pattern. Look up the correlates for the 26/62 code above $T = 65$ in chapter 6. The next highest scale is Scale 7, which adds anxiety, self-doubt, guilt, and rumination to the symptom picture of a 26 trapped, depression. The next highest scale is Scale 0, which predicts introversion and social unease. There are no other scales above $T = 65$, but Scale 9 is below $T = 50$. This indicates low energy and intensifies the low-energy symptoms of depression but reduces the likelihood of acting out.

Organization of the Report

Reports should be organized into paragraphs that flow logically one from the other. The opening paragraph could have a separate heading, such as "Validity" or "Test-Taking Attitude." You may or may not, wish to formally label sections in your report. Different settings encourage or discourage such separate labels. After you have written a brief description of the validity and test-taking attitude, begin the interpretation section as a separate paragraph, which also may have a separate heading. You may label this second part of the report "Personality Profile" or "Symptoms, Behaviors, and Personality Traits." You may also have a third section labeled "Lifestyle and Family Background" (such as Caldwell does in the Caldwell Report) or a heading called "Background Experiences." Usually a fourth section is labeled "Diagnostic Impressions," in which the possible diagnoses associated with the profile are listed. A final section could be labeled "Treatment Recommendations." This section would contain treatment recommendations, warnings about possible suicidality, and suggestions for medication. Chapter 10 presents several computer reports with varied formats, any of which may appeal to the organizational inclinations of the reader.

It is not plagiarism to copy from any of the standard textbooks a list of symptoms, behaviors, and personality traits associated with a particular profile. These are generally empirically generated descriptors. The art of writing an MMPI–2 report comes in being able to integrate descriptors from all of the scales into a coherent report. It would be plagiarism, however, to copy verbatim a

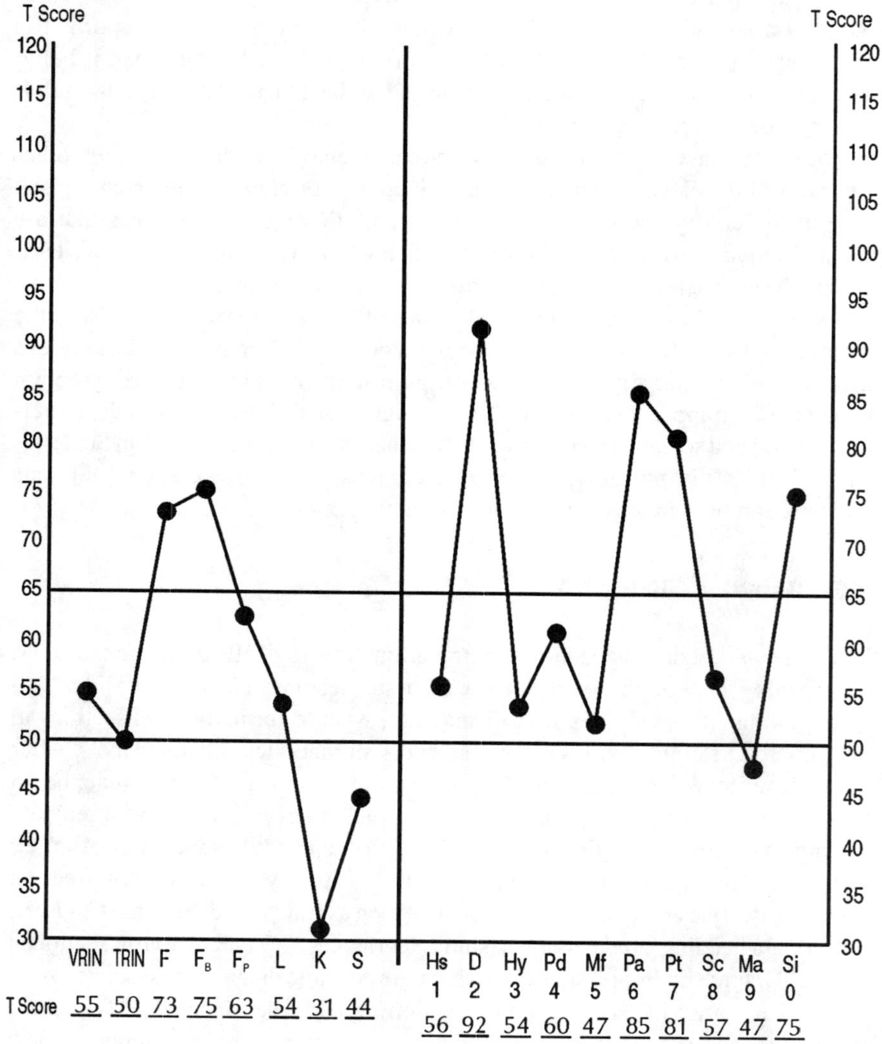

FIG. 9.9. 26 Code-Pattern. Minnesota Multiphasic Personality Inventory–2, Basic Scales Profile Form.

computer-generated report as if it were generated by the psychologist. However, quoting from a report is acceptable if appropriately acknowledged.

One way of organizing the data generated from an MMPI–2 is to break it down into a series of paragraphs, each dealing with a particular aspect of psychological functioning. The following list, adapted from Graham (1990), may serve as a guide in organizing a report:

1. Symptoms, complaints, and personality traits
2. Self-concept
3. Perception of the environment
4. Interpersonal relationships
5. Behaviors
6. Emotional control and response to stress
7. Psychological resources
8. Dynamics/etiology
9. Diagnostic impressions
10. Treatment implications

Symptoms, Complaints, and Personality Traits

After an opening statement that summarizes the essence of the profile, list all the symptoms and complaints associated with the code and then the symptoms and complaints associated with the other elevated clinical scales. Generate hypotheses from scales below $T = 50$ (e.g., Scale 4 at $T = 30$ suggests low aggressiveness and conformity). As part of the process of generating descriptors for this section, also look at the supplementary and content scales, as well as the various Harris–Lingoes and Subtle–Obvious Subscales. For example, if a profile is within the normal range and Scale 2 is at a *T* score of 60, the clinician may assume that a diagnosis of depression is not warranted. However, should the *DEP* scale be elevated above $T = 65$, then symptoms of depression and complaints of difficulties with concentration and memory would be warranted. Remember that symptoms are behavioral manifestations of the disorder that are noted by the clinician, whereas complaints emanate from the client. This paragraph should also describe personality traits associated with the profile. For example, 27s are hyper-responsible and prone to worry and respond to minor threats as if they are emergencies; high 4s are dependent and self-centered.

Self-Concept

Once you have described the symptoms, complaints, and personality traits, describe the way the person sees him or herself. In some cases, a sentence or two is all that is needed because the disturbance is mainly characterized by acting-out behavior or a projection of blame onto others with little self-awareness (e.g., a 49/94 profile), so the self-concept would tend to be egocentric and grandiose. In other cases, however, this will be a particularly important paragraph because the disturbance is primarily around self-image and self-dislike (e.g., 278/728, 86/68, and 89/98 profiles). This paragraph could start with a sentence such as, "Typically, these individuals see themselves as defective, damaged, and unlikable" (high scores on Scale 8). On the other hand, a statement about self-concept with an acting-out profile (49/94 or 46/64) might start off as follows: "The client is unlikely to see himself as responsible for his present difficulties. He is likely to see his difficulties as due to other people, difficult situations, or bad luck, and he will tend to project blame onto others."

Perception of the Environment

In this section, describe how the person sees the outside world. For example, 68/86 persons see it as hostile, dangerous, and confusing. High scorers on Scales 2 and 7 see the world as a frightening place, and they tend to overreact to situations as if they were emergencies. They see themselves as vulnerable to threat and loss of social approval. 48/84 persons see the world as hostile and uncaring, so they maintain a self-protective, angry, defensive style. They have difficulty empathizing with others and accurately interpreting other's responses to them. On the other hand, 46/64 individuals are vigilant for any demands being placed on them and they are likely to be guarded and protective of their autonomy, often feeling "cheated by life." As you read the descriptors in chapter 6, tease out the relevant sentences for each of your paragraphs.

It is not always necessary to organize your paragraphs according to this outline, but use the outline to make sure that you have covered as many facets of a personality description as possible.

Interpersonal Relationships

Given the previous perceptions of self and of others, describe how this affects the testee's interpersonal relationships. Descriptions of interpersonal relationships also will vary in length depending on the code pattern. For some profiles, a primary problem area will be interpersonal (e.g., in the 49/94 or 46/64 types), but for other profiles (e.g., 27/72) the problems are more of an intrapersonal nature. A possible opening statement for this paragraph could be, "The client's interpersonal relationships are apt to be characterized by painful misunderstandings (as in 78/87 elevations), exaggerated demands for affection (as in 46/64 elevations), or explosive irritability and narcissism (as in 49/94 elevations)."

Behaviors

People's behaviors result at least partly from their self-concept, perceptions of the environment, and interpersonal relationships. In a sense, interpersonal relationships are manifested in behaviors, so you may have already covered some of this in the preceding paragraph. A good opening sentence for this section might start as follows: "Typical behaviors associated with this profile are [list items]." For example, a person scoring high on Scale 2, with complaints of fatigue and with difficulties in concentration, guilt, anxiety, and sleeping will show behaviors such as apathy, a general loss in alertness and drive, and a slowed-down tempo. The behaviors you describe for a particular elevation ought to be linked in a meaningful way to the preceding symptoms, self-concept, and perception of the environment. Therefore, a person elevated on Scale 2 is likely to present with a slow interpersonal tempo, slow speech, and poor eye contact. Such a person would also likely withdraw from conflict and generally avoid assertive or purposeful behavior. Using a different example involving a Spike 4 elevation, you are unlikely to have a very long list of complaints because high scorers on Scale 4 often do not have complaints as such (although others may have many complaints about them). Often they are in therapy because of impulsive behavior that has led them into trouble or marital discord. In these cases, statements about their behaviors will predominate, so you might state

> They are likely to be in trouble because of sexual or other acting-out behavior problems. They are self-centered individuals who blame their problems on outside circumstances or difficult situations but rarely take responsibility for their behaviors. Typically, they are alienated people who exhibit an adolescent type of rebellion and nonconformity to accepted social norms and values. Rarely loyal, they see the world as a "dog-eat-dog" place where they have to have the "upper hand" in order to avoid being exploited. Typical behaviors are lying, impulsivity, poor frustration tolerance, and poor long-term planning. Marital difficulties are suggested, along with difficulties in accepting routine and conforming to structured work situations.

In sum, some code patterns generate a longer list of symptoms than complaints. Other codes generate longer lists of symptoms and complaints than descriptions of behaviors.

Emotional Control and Response to Stress

Whenever people experiences stress, typically they will show an increase in defensive behaviors, and therefore an increase in symptoms; as the stress increases, the maturity of their defensive behaviors decrease. The clinical and validity scales of the MMPI–2 are reflective of defensive behaviors. The clinical and validity scales of the MMPI–2 reflect not only the types of defenses that individuals are likely to use but also their level of coping skills and their levels of overall distress. Elevations on the *K* and *Es* scales suggest better coping ability than lower scores on these scales, especially if the clinical scales are elevated. High *F* and high *FB* scores, as well as elevations on Scales 6 and 8 and the *BIZ* scale, suggest distress and psychological disorganization. Low scores on Scale 0 generally indicate a broader array of social and interpersonal supports, as well as a history of comfortable socialization. Clinical scale configurations are often associated with varying amounts of emotional control or responses to stress. For some codes, increases in stress can lead to dangerous behaviors. For example, 68/86 types can become combative under stress, and 24/42 persons who have been threatening suicide can actually attempt it. High Scale 9 individuals can become increasingly manic or suddenly depressed under stress.

In this section, discuss what kind of stressors are most likely to lead to a breakdown of adaptive defenses. Table 9.1 offers some examples, drawn from our experiences, of stressors associated with particular code patterns.

Psychological Resources

Some of this section will overlap with the preceding section. Material for this section comes primarily from the code pattern and from scores on the validity scales, the *Es* scale, and the supplementary and content scales. High *Es* scores predict adequate psychological resources to deal with stress. For example, a person obtaining a 48/84 profile at an elevation of $T = 75$ with an *Es* *T* score of 65, a *K* *T* score of 65, and a *LSE* *T* score of 40, is probably coping with life better than a person with a 48/84 profile in which the *K* and *Es* scales are below $T = 50$ and the *LSE* scale is at $T = 75$. In the latter case, the sense of alienation and estrangement could result in impulsive and even bizarre acting out, whereas in the previous example, high *K* and *ES* scores would predict many areas of compensated functioning, with the alienation and estrangement being acted out in a more controlled way. However, it is nonetheless likely that in both cases the individual will be experiencing interpersonal conflicts, turmoil, and a lack of adequate emotional fulfillment in his or her interpersonal relationships. The individual with an elevated 48 code pattern, with high *K* and *Es* scores, is unlikely to present as psychotic or act out in impulsive ways because the *K* and *Es* scores predict control and the ability to handle stress. The more controlled 48 could be more potentially dangerous (e.g., Jeffrey Dahmer, who was able to lure his victims to their death with an apparent relaxed, easy charm). In another example, the higher the *F* score, in conjunction with lower *K* and *Es* scores, the less psychological resources a person has available to deal with the stress exhibited in the clinical profile elevation. Conversely, the higher the *K* and *Es* scores, the more coping resources that are available to the person.

The relationship between *K* elevations and psychological resources is curvilinear. The lower the *K* score, the less ego strength and the lower the self-concept. In the midranges, with the *K* scale at $T = 59–64$, a person has adequate psychological resources to deal with stress. At elevations over a *T* score of 65, a person is likely to be more rigid and out of touch with feelings, and therefore less flexible and less able to tolerate psychological self-exploration.

Dynamics/Etiology

Some report writers may divide their profile at this point with a heading such as "Dynamics/Etiology." In this section discuss any possible background and childhood experiences that may be associated with a particular code pattern. Marks et al. (1974) described typical background experiences associated with a particular code type. If these characteristics are available, then begin this section with a statement such as (in the case of a 48/84 code pattern), "Persons with this

TABLE 9.1
Code Patterns and Associated Stressors

Code Pattern	*Stressor*
27/72	Accumulation of responsibilities
28/82	Perceived withdrawal of emotional support from previously supportive person
43/34	Rejection or being discounted
46/64	Demands being placed on them
49/94	The imposition of controls on their behavior
93/39	Disapproval and/or being controlled

profile pattern often come from backgrounds in which there was deprivation, hostility, and sexual abuse." When there are empirical relevant background experiences, include them.

Diagnostic Impressions

This is probably the most difficult part of report writing because the MMPI–2 is neither diagnostically pure nor efficient. If one scale is particularly elevated over the others, then that scale usually determines or highly colors the diagnostic picture; even so, it is rare that one scale is uniquely more elevated than the others. Therefore, a definite diagnosis of depression, paranoia, personality disorder, and so on is not always possible using such an approach because several elevated scales will need to be considered. Therefore, the following guidelines to diagnosis are offered:

1. The highest scale predicts the type of diagnosis (Scale 2 = depression, Scale 7 = anxiety, Scale 9 = hypomania, etc.) when one scale is singularly elevated.
2. The slope of the profile suggests whether the diagnosis will fall in the neurotic or psychotic realm. Is it a neurotic slope (negative slope) or a psychotic slope (positive slope)?
3. Consider strongly those diagnoses actuarially associated most frequently with the two or three-point code or with the configuration (e.g., Conversion V). Where evidence exists, these have been listed under each code pattern in chapter 6.
4. Compute the Goldberg index. Is it in the psychotic or the neurotic direction? The Goldberg index is discussed in Table 9.2 and provides a description of how to properly use the Goldberg rules; the typical Goldberg index values associated with each code pattern are presented in Table 9.3.

TABLE 9.2

Notes for the Clinical Use of the Goldberg Rules

The Goldberg rules are a set of three linear indexes, each of which uses a combination of *K*-corrected MMPI–2 *T* scores in an equation for which a sign value (cutting score) has been established. The Goldberg rules were developed using *K*-corrected MMPI *T*-score values. Although there have been normative changes in the transition from the MMPI to the MMPI–2, the cutting scores for the Goldberg rules still appear to apply to the MMPI–2.

All of the Goldberg rules were developed using regression procedures on large data sets. Rules I and II were derived from 208 of the group profiles from Lanyon (1968), and Rule III (Index) emerged from the analysis of 861 individual male profiles collected from seven psychiatric centers (mostly Veterans Affairs [VA] and university hospital inpatients) previously used in Meehl and Dahlstrom's (1960) study of configural rules for discriminating psychotic from neurotic profiles. The methods and data on which these indexes are based have immediate implications for their use in clinical practice. The important point is that the Goldberg rules do not lend themselves to straightforward use in decisions involving the individual case. The differences in base rates between various kinds of settings (e.g., clinics, private practice, college counseling centers, VA hospitals, state mental hospitals, job screening, and prisons) will have large effects on the rate of correct decisions if the cutting scores for the three rules are held constant. Another thing to bear in mind is that the Goldberg rules show a different range of values for each of the common two- or three-point profile types (see Table 9.3, which shows index values for a sample of cases provided by Alex B. Caldwell and corresponding values for profiles in the Marks & Seeman, 1963 and Gilberstadt & Duker, 1965 code books). Take Goldberg Rule III, for example: Code patterns 138 and 86 are both associated with a high frequency of psychosis, yet the ranges of values for Rule III are almost completely nonoverlapping. The typical range of values for 138 profiles for Rule III is from 35 to 55, whereas that for 86 profiles is 65 to 90. Thus, decisions based solely on the Rule 111 cutting score of 45 will result in too many 86 profiles being called psychotic, whereas too few of the patients with 138 profiles will be called psychotic. As a result of these problems, the Goldberg rules are probably best thought of as a means of classifying large groups of patients or profile types rather than as a way of classifying individual profiles.

Let us now consider each rule separately:

Rule I: Normal Versus Deviant (*Hs* + 2*Pd* – *Ma*) Using *K*-Corrected *T* Scores

Scores above 123.5 are called deviant, whereas scores below 123.5 are considered normal. This rule probably performs best in populations or settings with a high base rate (say, at least 30%) for psychological normality, such as general medical patients, college counseling centers, police applicants, and Peace Corps volunteers. It should be applied with considerable caution to outpatients and should be avoided completely in inpatient psychiatric settings. Among the latter group, false negatives (patients erroneously classified as normal) occur at a particularly high rate among patients with code patterns in which Scale 9 is one of the two high points or as Scale 9 equals or exceeds $T = 65$. This rule appears to work better in outpatient settings when applied only to those profiles that do not fulfill the inclusion criteria for the normal *K*+ profile, that have no more than two scales greater than $T = 70$, and in which Scale 9 is no greater than third highest. In inpatient settings, Rule I may be thought of as a mania versus other indicator. Scores of 123 and below are obtained by patients with high activity levels who are less ambivalent, apathetic, and depressed than patients in general and who do not manifest a sense of inadequacy/inferiority (Lane & Lachar, 1979). Manic cases typically show Rule I below 123.5 and Rule III above 45.

Rule II: Psychiatric Versus Sociopathic Personality Disordered ($2Pd - Hy - Sc$) Using *K*-corrected *T* scores

Scores above 11 are considered sociopathic, whereas scores below 11 are called psychiatric. This rule corresponds roughly to the Diagnostic and Statistical Manual of Mental Disorders (4th ed.; American Psychiatric Association, 1994) distinction between Axis I (clinical syndromes) and Axis II (personality disorders). The assignment of separate axes to these two kinds of disorders by the American Psychiatric Association Task Force on Nomenclature and Statistics was decided on for the explicit purpose of encouraging, where appropriate, simultaneous classification. The implication for the practical utility of Rule II is that values exceeding the cutting score should serve to alert the clinician to the likely presence of a personality disorder rather than as a device to classify the individual patient. Rule II is relatively more sensitive in detecting those personality disorders lying at the more unstable end of the overcontrol–undercontrol continuum, such as antisocial and narcissistic personality disorder, while being correspondingly less sensitive to those at the more constricted end of this continuum, such as dependent or obsessive–compulsive personality disorders.

Classification accuracy is undoubtedly best for this rule in settings with high base rates for character pathology, such as prisons, and drug and alcohol treatment or rehabilitation programs. In clinic and psychiatric settings, this rule results in an intolerably high false-negative rate for neurotic and especially for psychotic conditions. The problem is that as Scale 4 reaches about $T = 80$, the profile tends to be classified as sociopathic, regardless of its total configuration. The 46/64 codetype is the outstanding miss for this rule but 48/84, 482/428, 274/742/472, 96/69, and 94 are also frequently misclassified as personality disordered.

Rule III: Neurotic Versus Psychotic ($L + Pa + Sc - Hy - Pt$) Using *K*-Corrected *T* Scores

Scores at 45 or above are considered psychotic, whereas scores below 45 are called neurotic. This rule is commonly referred to as the *Goldberg index*. Great caution should be exercised in applying this rule outside formal psychiatric settings. Because scores are obtained by subtracting the sum of two scales from the sum of three different scales, and because the average score for normals for each scale is near $T = 50$, the majority of individuals in unselected samples will obtain scores on the Goldberg index well within the psychotic range. It is, therefore, inappropriate to compute this index in presumptively normal samples, such as applicants for employment, general medical patients, and college counselees. Rule III is unique among the three Goldberg indexes in having some intelligible dynamic meaning in terms of the patient's psychological distance from others. High values are likely to reflect a marked distrust of others and strong needs for insulation, detachment and withdrawal in interpersonal relations. Low values suggest overattachment with dependency and clinging.

All of the profiles in the original data set were collected prior to 1960 and most prior to 1955, so it is very unlikely that affective disorders were fairly represented in the criterion diagnoses. Major depressions were almost certainly overrepresented in the neurotic group and underrepresented in the psychotic group at a period when schizophrenia was overdiagnosed in the United States. As a consequence, Rule III will almost certainly show greater sensitivity and specificity for schizophrenia than for affective disorders. Frequent misclassifications occur with the 278, 29/92, and 78/87 profile codes; 278s are misclassified as psychotic and as neurotic with about equal frequency, whereas 29/92s are called neurotic too often and 78/87s are called psychotic too often. Elevations on *L* and endorsements of most of the dozen or so somatic items on Scale 8 will result in some 13/31 profiles (especially those of female patients) being erroneously called psychotic . As suggested earlier, the 138 profile is the classic miss for Rule III, with the majority of patients with this code misclassified as neurotic.

Note. These notes on using the Goldberg rules were written by David S. Nichols and were reproduced with his permission.

5. When writing an MMPI–2 report, give a number of possible diagnoses associated with the code pattern. The MMPI–2 is usually administered as part of a test battery, so the clinician will have other test data, as well as extratest data, that will help him or her to make an accurate diagnosis. It is permissible when writing the MMPI–2 section of a test battery to state the typical diagnoses associated with the code pattern, although these diagnoses might not "survive" when the clinician is writing the actual diagnosis for an individual based on the complete test battery, history, and presenting problem. For example, a discussion section in a psychological evaluation may state, "Although the individual obtained an MMPI–2 profile that is typically associated with personality disorder diagnoses, the data from the other tests and the individual's history and clinical presentation do not suggest a personality disorder diagnosis." Usually, the code pattern is not diagnostically definitive and historical; behavioral and other test data can aid in making an accurate diagnosis. For example, an adolescent 89/98 profile might indicate a panic around a drug reaction or it might indicate a severe identity disturbance. Schizophrenia could be a possible diagnosis, but tell the reader what to look for in the client's history. Using the 89/98 adolescent as an example, the diagnosis section of an MMPI–2 report could contain a statement such as, "A history of schizophrenia in the family of origin would make the prognosis more guarded. If the history does not suggest a chemically induced disturbance or a recent blow to the individual's self-esteem, this profile could reflect a schizophrenic disorder." This kind of statement would be appropriate in the diagnostic section of the MMPI–2 part of a test battery but would probably be less appropriate in the final diagnostic section of a test battery, where a more definite diagnosis is usually required.

Treatment Implications

MMPI–2 users will have to use their clinical experience and the treatment literature (see treatment sections in chap. 6) to write this last section of the MMPI–2 report. The symptoms and complaints described will demand some kind of treatment modality. There are many empirically supported treatment approaches available for dealing with different kinds of psychopathology. For example, for depression, cognitive restructuring, self-esteem building, medication, and relaxation training have all proved effective (see also Lewak et al., 1990, for more treatment information).

The MMPI–2 can also provide some clues as to the client's treatability. Issues that are likely to arise in treatment, such as transference and defensive styles, and types of therapeutic intervention that are more or less likely to be effective should be included in this section if material is available. The *K* scale is generally a good indicator of therapy suitability. Extremely low *K* scores (below $T = 40$) suggest low self-esteem and low ego strength (and therefore psychological availability for treatment) but is often a poor prognosis because of a lack of psychological inner resources. *T* scores in the range of 50 to 65 typically predict a good therapeutic outcome, whereas *T* scores above 65 predict emotional rigidity and constriction. In

TABLE 9.3
Mean Goldberg (*N* – *P*) Index Values by Codetype

Codetype	*Caldwell Report Index Values a*	*Gilberstadt & Duker (1965)b*	*Marks & Seeman (1963)b*
123'a	34	18	
13' or 31'	32	24	40
231' or 213'	30	16b	30
26' or 62'	62		
27' or 72', basically 273' and not 274' or 278'	26	14	28
274', any order	36	26	36
278', any order	46	45	48
28' or 82'	58		58
29' or 92'	43		
321'	28		23
34' or 43'	40	33	
36' or 63'	53		
37', 73', or 137', any order	25	19[c]	
38', 83', or 138' any order	44	36	53
39' or 93'	37	34[d]	
4' and ('A – B)>10[e]	48	45	
46' or 64'	66		65[f]
48' or 84', not 489'[h]	58	56[g]	56
49' or 94', not 489'	49	45	53
489', any order	60		
68' or 86'	77	99[i]	92[i]
69' or 96'	70		78
78' or 87'	49	42	
89' or 98'	62	71	68
9', B < 70, 2 < 50[j]	54	55	

[a]Derived from a file sequential sampling of adult cases processed by the Caldwell Report. Cases included psychotherapy outpatients; psychiatric inpatients; workers' compensation and other forensic evaluations; parents in child custody cases; and a diversity of normals, including police and other job

applicants. For further information, write Alex B. Caldwell, Caldwell Report, 1545 Sawtelle Blvd., Los Angeles, CA 90025.

[b]Goldberg index values were derived from each corresponding adult psychiatric mean profile by codetype.

[c]Primed codes were used; the mean $N - P$ index values for unelevated profiles are usually quite similar, with no consistent pattern of differences.

[d]Codetype 1237'/2137'.

[e]Codetype 137' or 13'7.

[f]Codetype 139, 1 or 3 or $9 > T = 70$.

[g]$(A - B) > 10$ indicates scale 4 minus the next highest of the eight clinical scales is more than 10 points. Gilberstadt and Duker specified $4 > T = 70$ and no other scale $T = 70$.

[h]65 is the average of Codetype 46/64, mean $N - P$ index 78, plus Codetype 462/642, mean Index 52.

[i]Codetype 824(7).

[j]Codetype 482/842/824.

[k]High F scores were not excluded, nor was the $N - P$ index adjusted for excessive F elevations.

[l]$B < 70$ indicates the second highest of the eight clinical scales is below $T = 70$, and Scale 2 must be less than $T = 50$.

---

this case, a poor therapeutic outcome could be due to client difficulties in opening up. The *TRT* Content scale can also be useful in determining if the client is cynical about the effectiveness of "talk therapy" (see chap. 7).

Some code patterns reflect behaviors that are more amenable to treatment than other scales. For example, the 27/72 code predicts amenability to treatment because these individuals tend to be conscientious, reasonable, and follow treatment suggestions. On the other hand, elevations on Scale 4 predict a slow response to treatment, whether it is pharmacological or psychotherapeutic. Spike 4, 48/84, 46/64, 43/34, and 49/94 are all configurations that predict a relatively enduring personality picture that is difficult to change. The exception to this is when elevations on Scale 4 are the result of a recent letdown or psychological trauma, such as divorce or loss of job. In this case, a history of good adjustment prior to the precipitating circumstance would suggest a good response to treatment. A lifelong history of passive–aggressive or acting-out behavior in the presence of elevations on Scale 4, however, would suggest a slow treatment response. Beginning users of the MMPI–2 who have limited clinical experience should attempt to build a database of treatment suggestions by reading standard books on personality and psychopathology and associating them with basic configural code patterns (see also the Code-Pattern Look-Up Table for treatment suggestions).

Interpretation of "Complex Profiles"

Some profiles do not fit cleanly into a recognizable code pattern. In this case, you need to divide the profile into manageable, recognizable entities and then build a composite personality picture. The floating profile mentioned earlier (see Fig. 9.9), in which all the clinical scales are elevated at more or less the same *T*-score level, is an example of such a complex code configuration. It is used here as an example of how to break down a profile into entities. One strategy, adopted from Caldwell, is to divide the profile into highpoint pairs in order to generate a set of descriptors for each pair. First, write down, in order of elevations, all of the elevated scales. Using the example in Fig. 9.9, the following list is generated: 3162749580. Under each number, write the corresponding letter of the alphabet as far as the fourth highest elevation:

3 1 6 2 7 4 9 5 8 0

a b c d

Then divide the profile and interpret in high point pairs as follows: a-b, which is 3-1. Then interpret a-c, which is 3-6. Then interpret b-c, which is 1-6. After that, take the correlates for each of the scales in descending order. In this case, the anchor for the interpretation is the 3-1 (i.e., 13/31 two-point) code. Looking up the 13/31 code in chapter 6 reveals that these individuals tend to be somatizing, dependent, psychologically naive, and immature and as having difficulty facing anger directly. Descriptors for elevations on Scales 3 and 6 (see 36/63 code pattern in chap. 6) reveal persons who are hypersensitive to criticism, distrustful, and occasionally suspicious, with somatic symptoms. Looking up correlates for 1-6 reveals that these individuals tend to be rigid, grouchy, stubborn, hypersensitive to criticism, and quick to place blame on others.

The profile that emerges so far is that of a hypersensitive, somatizing, tense, possibly suspicious individual. Next, add the correlate for the single scales, starting with Scale 2. Elevations at this *T* score level suggest sadness, apathy, guilt, and depression. The anchor for the personality picture is the 13/31 profile, so the symptoms of depression will be manifested as somatic complaints, tension, and negativity, covered over with hysterical blandness. The correlates for Scale 7, the next highest scale, predict anxiety, tension, and guilt. Given the 13/31 backdrop, the person is unlikely to be aware of guilt and anxiety; rather he or she experiences it as tension and somatic complaints, especially when responsibilities accumulate. Correlates for the next highest scale, Scale 9, suggest agitation, lability, and impulsivity, but against the backdrop of the 3-1, 3-6, and 1-6 configuration, which suggests extreme inner tension and explosiveness. This is because the primary elevations form the basis of the personality picture, and the other scales modify that base. The 3-1 pattern contraindicates aggression. Consequently, the acting out associated with Scales 4 and 9 will be modified and expressed as passive resistance, self-defeating behavior, and manipulative dependency.

To begin the integration process, write down all of your descriptors. Attempt to group similar descriptors together. Any descriptors that are contradictory to the primary and secondary code configurations need to be integrated. In our experience, psychologists rarely go to this next step of attempting to understand how contradictory traits are integrated against the backdrop of a primary code pattern. This is where the skill of a psychologist is involved because most cookbooks do not give descriptors for 4-, 5-, or 6-point code patterns. A report that describes only the two- or three-point code is acceptable in most settings. However, learning to write reports that integrate contradictory data is the art of personality assessment. In complex profiles, the primary two or three scale elevations become the context within which the fourth, fifth, and all other individual clinical scales (including content and supplementary scales) are interpreted. Your purpose will be to make sense of the contradictions and to add those symptoms and descriptions that confirm each other so that you can use them in the report with a higher degree of certainty.

Scale 5

Elevations on Scale 5 (*Mf*) will modify the profile interpretation. For men, elevations on Scale 5 will mitigate against aggressive acting-out behaviors and will modify the scales that otherwise would predict such behaviors. Because elevated scores on this scale for men are associated with sensitivity, intellectual interests, and nonaggressiveness, it acts as a suppressor variable for acting-out behaviors. For example, a male profile elevated on Scales 4, 8, and 9, with Scale 5 elevated, would predict a charismatic, but self-centered, angry person whose acting-out is likely to be in indirect antisocial ways, such as through white-collar types of crime or unusual sexual behaviors. Scale 5 correlates with education and intelligence, so elevations on that scale will modify the profile in the same way that these demographic variables would.

Low Scale 5 scores in women (below a *T* score of 40) suggest a strong feminine identification and a rejection of competitive, aggressive values. This would increase the likelihood of passive–aggressiveness in profiles that would otherwise suggest direct anger. For example, in women, the addition of a low Scale 5 score to a 49/94 profile would suggest more sexual than antisocial acting-out behaviors in the same way that a high Scale 5 score would for a high 49 men.

Scale 0

Low scores on Scale 0 (*Si*) predict the need for and comfort with social interaction, and thus modify other aspects of profile interpretation. For example, for some codes (e.g., 278), interpersonal relationships and intimacy are a problem; when Scale 0 is additionally elevated, these interpersonal problems are even more striking. In another example, a 68/86 profile, Scale 0 is at or below $T = 50$ and would appear contradictory because the person apparently has a drive toward social interactions yet is hostile, guarded, and suspicious. Whether that suggests a better or worse prognosis is difficult to ascertain. Another example is that of 49/94 code pattern. When Scale 0 is elevated, the person is less likely to blatantly act out in aggressive fashion and is more likely to be sullenly asocial. If Scale 0 is low, the person would be more likely to act out but in socially skillful ways that may be effective in manipulating others.

Energizers and Suppressors

Some scales act as *energizer* variables, whereas other scales act as *suppressor* variables. An energizer variable is one that increases the likelihood that the attributes of a particular code pattern will be manifested behaviorally. For example, a 24/42 code, with Scale 9 coded third and above $T = 65$ would increase the likelihood of impulsive, self-destructive, or self-defeating behaviors. Similarly, elevations on Scales 4 and 8 would predict an angry, alienated, and confused individual. Adding Scale 9 coded third and above $T = 65$ would predict impulsive, antisocial, and bizarre acting-out behavior as the alienation and anger are energized by Scale 9. Scales 4, 8, and 9 can be considered energizers. Scale 4 predicts poor impulse control, and thus increases the likelihood that behaviors will get acted out impulsively. Elevations on Scale 8 also predict poor impulse control due to disordered thinking.

Suppressor variables are those that inhibit the likelihood of the attributes of a particular code being expressed in overt behaviors. Scales 2, 5, and 0 act as suppressor variables. For example, a 49/94 profile, with Scales 5 and 0 coded third and fourth, respectively, and above $T = 65$, would predict an angry person, but one who is not likely to act out. Rather, Scales 5 and 0 would suggest a sensitive individual who tends toward introversion and whose acting-out behavior would more likely manifest itself in some kind of intellectual rebelliousness, or perhaps in a controlled way, such as passive–aggressiveness or conflict within the family.

Strategies for Providing Feedback to the Client

Providing test feedback to clients can minimize apprehension around the issue of testing and, if done well, can enhance therapeutic effectiveness (see Finn & Tonsager, 1992; Lewak et al, 1990; and Pope, 1992). The language of psychopathology, which is the essence of the MMPI–2, is often judgmental and inappropriate for therapist–client sharing and for building a therapeutic alliance. This is because the MMPI–2 was conceived as a clinical instrument designed to identify problems. Most of the clinical scales were constructed with clinical groups to diagnose clinical problems characterized in clinical terms. The standard scales were developed originally not as measures of personality but as measures of clinical and nonclinical problems. Their mainstream use continues to be in evaluating abnormal, maladaptive, or undesirable aspects of personality and behavioral functioning rather than normal, adaptive, or desirable ones. Terms such as *hostile, dependent, secondary gain, demanding, manipulative,* and *acting out*, are commonly used in reports, although some clinicians have voiced concern that they are antithetical to building a therapeutic relationship (Erdberg, 1979; Finn & Tonsager, 1992). Some colleagues have characterized psychological testing reports as generally being written such that they are little more than character assassinations. Reports cannot readily be shown to clients because they are often judgmental in content in ways that conflict with the client's self-perception at that time and might even be harmful to the client's self-concept.

A therapeutic alliance is most likely to be forged if clients feel understood and their symptoms and fears are validated. In fact, Finn and Tonsager (1992) have shown that individuals provided with one feedback session from their MMPI–2 results can show improvement in symptomatology when compared with individuals who have had no feedback but have had a period of psychotherapy. Finn and Tonsager and Fisher (1994) have developed a concept of therapeutic assessment in which assessment is seen as a collaborative process, which, in itself, is therapeutic. Currently, there are few books available (e.g., Finn, 1996; Lewak et al., 1990) in which a feedback approach to MMPI–2 test data is outlined. It is remarkable that the most widely used and written-about personality test in the world has not been made more amenable for use as a feedback and treatment guide.

A phenomenological approach has been developed by Lewak et al. (1990) based on the unpublished formulations of Alex Caldwell. According to this approach, individuals are viewed as products of genetic and environmental factors. Maladaptive behavior is seen as a product of stress (fear) operating within an individual who has a diathesis (i.e., a predisposition or set of vulnerabilities) for the type of disorder that occurs. From their perspective, it is assumed that each person inherits a repertoire of available psychological defenses (antibodies) against stress. Under increased stress, those defenses that effectively reduce pressures become fixed and maintained in accordance with their reinforcing value. From this perspective, any particular defense could then be understood in the context of the stress that initially induced it.

Take, for example, Scale 1 (*Hs*). Persons with elevations on this scale are typically described as immature, dependent, psychologically naive, and preoccupied with somatic concerns. In the Lewak et al. (1990) approach, the judgmental terms *immature*, *psychologically naïve*, and so on make sense when seen from the perspective of a frustrated therapist whose task may be to rid the client of the habit of switching attention to physical health when other psychologically painful conflicts arise. Lewak et al. cautioned, however, that from the client's perspective, a concern about physical health may at one stage have been an adaptive response to a perceived overwhelming threat to his or her physical integrity. Staying in bed, worrying about deteriorating health, and being preoccupied with the availability of medical health care makes sense from the perspective of the client who is terrified of bodily damage or death. Lewak et al. have developed a way of giving feedback based on Caldwell's belief that eight clinical scales each reflect different basic patterns of fear-conditioned (defensive) avoidant behaviors. Scales 5 and 0 do not represent conditioned fear-avoidance responses but rather personality traits. The scales and their associated fears and defenses are summarized in Table 9.4. As shown in this table, for example, clients who score high on Scale 2 may have at some stage in life experienced inordinate pain over some significant and irretrievable loss. They may have responded by blocking further needs or wants in order to avoid further loss. Similarly, according to this view, clients with a Spike 9 profile fear failure. When stressed, such Spike 9 clients would respond by heightened activity in order to maintain their reward schedule and would constantly plan toward the future to avoid onset of loss (and depression).

According to this perspective, the more elevated a scale, and the more scales that are elevated in the profile, the more of the client's life will be devoted to self-protection by engaging in defensive behaviors. The scale will determine the class of stress to which a client is most susceptible, and the elevation predicts how much attention and energy is directed in a defensive posture. The client's history will usually reveal which early experiences have determined the situational events most likely to elicit the self-protective responses (defenses).

Which defenses are used should be understood in terms of the fears and anxieties motivating the client to engage in defensive behaviors. For example, high 7s fear unpredictable negative events. The defense of being obsessive compulsive, constantly attempting to anticipate the future (i.e., worrying), and feeling guilty when things go wrong make sense when understood as attempts to prevent future unpredictable negative events. The question then becomes, "What events could have conditioned such a fear?" Usually, taking a history will reveal that there are certain early traumatic experiences that may act like psychological "scar tissue" so that present situations that stimulate that "scar tissue" can lead to highly defensive behavior. For example, Marks et al. (1974) reported that 60% of the 31s in their sample experienced the death of a parent in childhood. Clearly, these individuals could be more vulnerable to an adult experience of loss than individuals who have not experienced the early loss of a parent.

In another example, 60% of the 28s in the same Marks et al. (1974) sample experienced a significant disruption in their family of origin (e.g., parental mental illness). Perhaps a significant disruption in the clients' adult life would make them more susceptible to feeling depressed and hopeless given their early experiences.

Most clients want feedback because feeling understood by a trained therapist can, in itself, be of substantial value (Erdberg, 1979; Finn & Tonsager, 1992). The general approach to giving feedback should be empathic in nature. The client's behavior should be understood in terms of the fears and anxieties motivating the client to engage in defensive behaviors. Using the fear paradigm previously described can be a good way of making client's present behaviors understandable to them.

Guidelines for Giving Feedback

The following general approach has been found useful in giving feedback to clients about their MMPI–2 profiles:

1. After the client is comfortably seated, the scored MMPI–2 profile is turned toward the client and he or she is told,

> You answered many questions, some of which may have seemed unusual or even peculiar to you. That is because the questions were designed for a broad variety of difficulties. All of the questions you answered were scored, and we divided your personality into 10 dimensions as follows ...

The client observes as the clinician counts from scale 1 to Scale 0. This allows the client to examine the shape of the graph.

2. Next, the client is told,

> Here, on the left side [the clinician points to the validity scales], are some scores that tell me the way in which you answered the test. For example, were you self-critical,

TABLE 9.4

MMPI–2 Scales and Associated Fear-Conditioned Defensive Responses

Scale	*Fear*	*Response*
1	Death, physical attack, illness, or pain	Maintaining physical integrity by overprotecting the body
2	Irretrievable and significant loss	Blocking wanting or needing in order to avoid further loss
3	Emotional pain	Positivizing unpleasant experiences by selectively blocking inputs (blindness, numbness)
4	Rejection, being unwanted, or abandoned	"Numbing out" emotional responding, not allowing oneself to get emotionally involved to avoid letdown
6	Humiliation, being criticized, evaluated	Maintaining constant vigilance against attack
7	Shock, unexpected events	Thinking ahead and worrying to anticipate onset of shock
8	Hostility, being disliked or despised by those on whom one depends	"Shutting down" cognitive processing to avoid unbearable reality
9	Deprivation or failure	Increasing activity level in an attempt to maintain reward schedule

Note. Based on Alex B. Caldwell's unpublished theory.

eager to tell me how you are feeling, or did you approach the test in a 'stiff upper lip' manner? Are you the kind of person that is open to sharing their feelings, or are you more private?

Be mindful not to share any information about how the validity scales operate so as to maintain the security of the test.

3. The client is then told that the lines at $T = 30$ and $T = 65$ represent statistical boundaries that define a range where most people score if they are not in any psychological pain or distress. Be careful to emphasize that an elevated profile indicates discomfort, pain, and distress, rather than deviance. Use discretion in sharing profile feedback; many people misinterpret their results when they see an elevated profile. If a profile is grossly elevated, the actual profile graph does not have to be shared with the client. Instead, the clinician can verbally outline the test results for the client.

4. Use everyday language to describe the profile. Remember that many clients are cautious and defensive, anticipating being judged. If they argue with you, then you have made them defensive, and you are defeating your purpose. If

at any stage the client disagrees with the feedback, see it as an opportunity to engage in a dialogue. For example, for clients with elevations on Scale 9, you might have told them that they have a great deal of energy, ambition, and drive, only to have them interrupt you to argue that those statements are not true. They may say they have no more energy than anybody else. Rather than becoming defensive, you should "go with the resistance" and give a response such as, "Tell me about your energy level" or "I would appreciate your helping me understand better about your ambitions." Once they have felt heard, proceed with the rest of the feedback. It is highly recommended that the feedback be woven into a dialogue, rather than having the client passively receive the information from the clinician. Some clients want to hear all of the feedback issues before responding, perhaps to see how accurate the test is, or perhaps to see what they "need to defend themselves against." Encourage a dialogue. Give the feedback as questions much more often than as statements of fact. Use the profile as a "road map" for asking the right questions (Lewak et al., 1990).

5. Continue with the rest of your feedback, interspersed with dialogue. Ask questions such as, "Perhaps you can give me an example of your energy level [or other characteristic]." Be empathic and understanding, and try to help clients see how any defensive, unhealthy behavior makes sense when understood in light of their history and their current difficulties. For example, a person scoring high on Scale 2 might be sad and despondent most of the time, and so it would be appropriate to inquire about any catastrophic losses that have left the client feeling hopeless and depressed. Watch for when clients shut off and stop listening because of anxiety or when they interrupt and divert their attention or the conversation to another topic. Allow them to take a "breather" because their interruptions or distractions are cues that they have assimilated as much information as they are ready to process, that the feedback is not accurate, or that it is being perceived as criticism. Try to organize your feedback by focusing periodically on a few anchor statements that you can explore as themes and that can lead to other statements if all progresses well. For example, persons scoring high on Scale 4 often respond to an initial feedback statement of "Your profile suggests that you are a survivor and that right now you are being cautious about letting yourself get emotionally involved in case you are let down and disappointed." The clinician could then say, "Are you being cautious? Why?" After the client has responded to this, other feedback can be explored, but the clinician can return to this basic theme later as it relates to other issues being discussed during the session. For example, in the case of high 4s, their difficulties in being intimate and trusting others could be discussed.

6. It is often useful at the end of the feedback session to ask the client to "summarize what you have heard from me today." This could be done in the last 10 min so that any misunderstandings can be clarified. Clinicians can modify their feedback, depending on the purpose of the MMPI–2 testing. In some cases, it may be used as part of the diagnostic and treatment planning process. In other cases, it may be used during the course of treatment. For example, a second MMPI–2 given some time into therapy may reveal that a client is feeling more

> despondent and self-disliking than had been indicated on the previous MMPI–2. This, shared with the client, could then open up questions such as, "Is the client responding to reawakened, old memories brought alive by the therapy?" or "Is therapy actually being counterproductive." On the basis of the feedback, the results could be used as a stimulus to refocus the therapy.

In brief treatment approaches, clients could be given feedback from the MMPI–2 so that specific behavioral corrective measures could be used to alleviate the present distress. For example, a client scoring high on Scales 2 and 7 could be given specific behavioral techniques for working on lowering anxiety without further psychological intervention if that is not desirable or possible.

Evaluating Feedback

The feedback process is most useful when envisioned as a joint exploration (clinician and client) of the client's current emotional and psychological status and a joint agreement about therapeutic strategies. It is important for the client to be given some way of evaluating feedback so that its accuracy can be validated. Remember that it is the explorative dialogue that forges a stronger therapeutic alliance (Finn & Tonsager, 1992). Joint treatment planning is more likely to enhance the treatment process than an arbitrary treatment approach. Do not get defensive if a client disagrees. Instead, you can explore the client's perspective because it is particularly valuable clinical data.

The approaches to sharing feedback with clients already described can be used whether the MMPI–2 has been administered and scored by you or whether a computer-generated MMPI–2 interpretive report (such as those presented in chap. 10) is used. The reader specifically interested in a computer-generated report designed for feedback to clients in referred to the Marks and Lewak Adult Feedback and Treatment Report presented in chap. 10.

10

Computerized Interpretation of the MMPI–2

COMPUTER-BASED TEST INTERPRETATION (CBTI)

Computer applications in psychology have grown remarkably during the last half of the 20th century. Initially used primarily for scoring test items on academic and psychological tests, computers increasingly have been used for more complex processes in ways that not only are more reliable than similar tasks done by humans but also more cost-effective.

At present, numerous procedures for CBTI are available, covering a number of psychological tests, including the MMPI–2, the Sixteen Personality Factor Questionnaire, the Rorschach Test, the Millon Clinical Multiaxial Inventory, the Personality Inventory for Children, and others (Fowler, 1985). Despite initial reluctance, the psychological and psychiatric community has shown an increasing acceptance of such computer uses. Indeed, by 1969 approximately one fourth of the eligible psychologists and psychiatrists in the United States used one such CBTI MMPI interpretation service (Fowler, 1969), and the proportion of such professionals using CBTI systems has continued to increase markedly (Spielberger & Piotrowski, 1990). Likewise computer-based interpretation and administration of psychological tests have gained increasing acceptance, as reflected by society at large (Carr & Ghosh, 1983; Greist, Klein, Erdman, & Jefferson, 1983; Spinhoven et al., 1993).

The extremely widespread use of CBTI systems has not been without controversy, however. The controversies have focused primarily on two areas: (a) whether CBTI systems have a demonstrated validity (Matarazzo, 1986; Moreland, 1985, 1990) and, relatedly, (b) whether psychological assessment is being supplanted inappropriately by formula-driven testing (Tallent, 1987).

The validity of CBTI systems would seem assured to the extent that such systems relied on actuarially derived data. Certainly, as discussed earlier in this book, the evidence overwhelmingly supports actuarially based clinical interpretation as compared with clinical interpretation. However, not all aspects of CBTI systems are actuarially based. Although most computer-generated MMPI–2 reports are somewhat actuarially based, they are only partially so, and the accuracy of their nonactuarial interpretations is only as good as the interpretive skills of the professional(s) who wrote the program.

Further, an actuarial system can consider only empirical data that have been incorporated into the system's algorithm, and the algorithms are limited by the population(s) on which the actuarial data have been derived. Because clinical situations frequently are far more complex, it is seldom the case that all relevant personal and contextual data will be considered by any CBTI system for interpreting the MMPI–2. Problems such as these prompted Rodgers (1972) to state, "I regard them [computerized interpretations] as basically dangerous except in the hands of a person who is sufficiently expert with the MMPI that he probably will not utilize the computer printout" (p. 245). Others, such as Eichman (1972) and Tallent (1987), have raised concerns that a computer report in the hands of a psychometrically unsophisticated professional might be substituted for clinical judgment, rather than supplementing it. In using CBTI reports, Fowler and Butcher's (1986) statement that "there must be a clinician between the computer and the client" (p. 95) seems clearly appropriate.

Despite these concerns, even early studies found that professional consumers rated CBTI MMPI reports as satisfactory in accuracy (Webb, 1970b; Webb, Miller, & Fowler, 1969; Webb et al., 1970). Subsequent studies (Moreland, 1985) likewise have supported the perceived validity of narrative reports generated by computers from the MMPI and the MMPI–2, even though the interrater reliability coefficients often have been so low as to limit estimates of validity. Other studies (Schuldberg, 1990; Watson et al., 1992) have examined whether scores obtained from persons who are administered the MMPI with a computer are comparable with their scores if they are administered the MMPI in booklet form. Overall, the scores were quite similar (Watson, Manifold, et al., 1990). The computer-based scores slightly underestimated their booklet counterparts on 8 of the basic 13 scales (Watson et al., 1992). This difference, although statistically significant in the large samples used, actually accounted for less than 1 *T*-score point of difference.

Despite these cautionary notes, it is clear that computer scoring and interpretation of the MMPI–2 is here to stay and, in fact, will likely increase in use. It has become evident that there are several distinct advantages of computer-generated psychological reports (Butcher, 1987a, 1994a; Spielberger & Piotrowski, 1990), including the following:

1. *Reliability.* The computer has far fewer bad days than humans, and the same input results in the same output.

2. *Memory.* The computer can store and more rapidly retrieve information with accuracy far more detailed than the human, at least if that human does not have ready access to a library.
3. *Objectivity.* Interpreter bias is minimized in computer-generated reports. Once the interpretation rules are programmed, they are applied automatically and regularly to specified cases, regardless of extraneous circumstances.
4. *Rapidity.* The speed of computer processing and printing is extremely great. It is simple for a computer to score, interpret, and print psychological reports from several thousand MMPI tests in 1 day, a feat far beyond human capability, or to interpret a single test within seconds of the test administration, saving valuable professional time.
5. *Cost-efficiency.* Because of these factors, the computer-generated reports are clearly cost- efficient and will undoubtedly become more so in the decades to come.

Of course, there are disadvantages as well (Butcher, 1987a, 1987b; Matarazzo, 1986; Spielberger & Piotrowski, 1990), including the following:

1. *Excessive generality.* Matarazzo (1986) pointed out that computer-generated reports rely on modal descriptions and do not do justice to the individual aspects of a person. However, as noted in chapter 9, the actuarial approach, based on just such descriptions, continues to regularly excel the skills of human clinicians. Even so, the relevant dimensions that modify interpretations of tests (e.g., SES, education, and recent job loss) are still not routinely included for consideration by most computerized interpretation programs.
2. *Algorithm limitations.* A related criticism, then, is that the objectivity and accuracy of the computer is only as good as the objectivity and accuracy of the person who developed and programmed the computer.
3. *Secrecy of the algorithms.* Because the CBTI system is proprietary, its algorithms generally are not shared with others. Some, perhaps most, systems employ a panel of expert consultants, who review the interpretive algorithms in private and then issue reassurances to the consumers that the interpretations appear valid.
4. *Potential for misuse.* Because of the ease of use, and the apparent reliability, there is an added possibility for overreliance on the reports, as well as the possibility of unqualified users having access to the data.
5. *Confusing abundance of packages.* Because of the large number of computer-assisted test-interpretation packages, the clinician often has difficulty in selecting among the offerings. This is made even more difficult because most of these packages were developed in a proprietary, businesslike fashion, and (unlike data in the public domain) the algorithms used by the computer in scoring and interpretations are private and not open to ordinary inspection or peer review.

Standards on the use of computers in psychological testing and assessment have been developed by the American Psychological Association (1986), and the reader is encouraged to become familiar with these. They are entitled *Guidelines for Users of Computer-Based Tests and Interpretations* and are available directly from the American Psychological Association (also printed as Appendix B in Butcher, 1987b). In these standards, the point is clearly made that the user of a computerized interpretation service remains just as professionally responsible as if that user had used that test without assistance from a computer.

COMPUTERIZED INTERPRETATION OF THE MMPI/MMPI–2

The MMPI was first computer-interpreted at the Mayo Clinic in Rochester, Minnesota (Rome et al., 1962), in what in retrospect was a fairly simple, scale-by-scale approach. At present, there are numerous sophisticated programs that interpret the MMPI–2 in a complex, configural fashion. Several examples of these are presented later. These presentations do not constitute an endorsement of these automated MMPI–2 interpretation services; they are presented simply as examples of the current state of the art to apprise the reader.

The following computer-generated reports are included to familiarize the reader with such reports. It must be remembered, however, that although these reports are reliable in that computers have better memories than people, they suffer from the disadvantages of not being capable of considering specific base-rate data about the clinician's unique practice or about various situational factors or other aspects of a referral question.

To partially solve the base-rate difficulties encountered within different populations, some CBTI programs for interpreting the MMPI–2 now generate different computer reports depending on the subpopulation to which a person is being compared. Thus, one may select a computer-generated MMPI–2 interpretation based on norms from a general mental health population, an alcohol and drug treatment population, a personnel system population, or a general medical population. Other population subsets undoubtedly will be developed as it becomes clear that base rates for that population differ in substantive ways from the basic norms for the MMPI–2.

To provide a comparison of the scoring and interpretation services, the same clinical case was sent to each of the four most widely used services for computerized interpretation of the MMPI–2. Along with the answer sheet, the following information was provided:

This MMPI–2 is from a 25-year-old Caucasian male with a high school education. He is single, never married, and was referred for a fitness evaluation regarding his working capacity. He was attacked by unknown muggers when he arrived at work and was also robbed. He had no psychiatric history prior to the incident, but was being treated for depression and posttraumatic stress disorder at the time of the present referral by his employer. He was taking an antidepressant at the time of the testing and wanted to return to work in his position as a building foreman.

CALDWELL REPORT
1545 SAWTELLE BOULEVARD
LOS ANGELES, CA 90025
(310) 478-3133
FAX (310) 479-5236

July 15, 1998

NAME: Mr. Jones

AGE: 25

SEX: Male

EDUCATION: 12 years

MARITAL STATUS: Single

REFERRED BY: Alan F. Friedman, Ph.D.

DATE TESTED: March 18, 1998

TEST ADMINISTERED: Minnesota Multiphasic Personality Inventory-2 (MMPI-2)

TEST TAKING ATTITUDE

Attention and Comprehension: His score on the Variable Response Inconsistency scale (VRIN) was quite unelevated; his item responses were highly self-consistent throughout the inventory. This suggests that he was clearly able to read and comprehend the test items, that he was attentive in considering his responses, and that he carefully matched the item numbers in the booklet to the corresponding numbers on the answer sheet. Therefore, his elevated score on scale F (rare answers) cannot be attributed to an inability to understand the content or to respond to the format of the inventory. This absence of substantial elevation on VRIN together with his only moderate elevation on the fake bad scale (Ds) suggest that his elevation on scale F was not due to a pervasive effort to "look sick" as well as not being due to a significant impairment of his ability to read and comprehend the items.

Attitude and Approach: Considering scales L, F, K, and Ds, his scores indicate that he made a great many atypical and rarely given responses to the inventory. His scores on the clinical scales may be overly elevated due to one or more of such factors as acute panic, severe psychopathology, deliberate exaggeration, or a plea for help (see other differentiating comments in this Test Taking Attitude section). The following report must be considered as highly tentative. It is intended for exploratory interview purposes to the extent that the general configuration of his profile and the following interpretations of it are accurate and appropriate.

A DIVISION OF CLINICAL PSYCHOLOGICAL SERVICES, INC.

He made a considerable number of atypical and rarely given responses to the items occurring in the last half of the inventory (scale F-back). These were consistent with his atypical responses to the earlier MMPI-2 items (scale F). His moderately elevated score on the F-back scale recommends some caution in the interpretation of deviant scores on the supplemental scales reported on the second page of extra scales (page 2, MMPI-2 subscales).

It should be noted that he obtained a high score on the Control scale (Cn). This anticipates considerable potential for disguising or concealing psychopathology in interviews. A presentation as "well put together" or as "having aggression under control" should not be taken at face value.

<u>Socio-cultural Influences vs. Conscious Distortion</u>: The supplemental validity scales suggest that the greater part of his elevation on the F scale is probably due to genuine emotional disturbance. Many confused and acutely disturbed patients, especially those in marginally and overtly psychotic states, do sincerely admit to large numbers of peculiar experiences and atypical complaints. A lesser part of his elevation on F may have been due to a too-ready willingness to report such a wide variety of symptoms and distresses; it would suggest a secondary contribution to his F score of a conscious overemphasis on his level of disturbance. Thus, although his item responses appear to have been distorted somewhat in the self-critical direction, his "fake sick" score (scale Ds) appears insufficient to reject his entire profile as malingered; the larger part of his elevation on F appears most likely due to a valid psychological disorder. In any case, the level of severity reflected in the following interpretation should be applied with care. This caution would be especially true if he were not of a relatively low level of currently attained, recently experienced, or self-perceived socioeconomic status that would correspond to his quite low status identification score (scale Ss)

SYMPTOMS AND PERSONALITY CHARACTERISTICS

The profile shows a moderate to severe depressive disorder. This may prove to be a psychotic depression or a schizo-affective schizophrenic decompensation. He tests as markedly fearful of emotional closeness with severe frustrations in his close relationships. He is apt to have many ways of keeping others at a distance. Pervasive insecurity, pessimism, and ambivalences are suggested along with complaints of confusion and loss of efficiency. Alcoholic remorse may be painfully distressing to him. Others would see him as disengaged and as very slow to involve himself in changing his current circumstances. Disturbances of sleep are very common with this pattern. Shy, introverted, and withdrawing, he would be quite insecure socially. His current functioning appears severely decompensated.

The profile has often been associated with physical symptoms that are secondary to the anxiety and expressive of the current conflicts. Conversion-like symbolizations of unreleased resentments, tensions, and aggressive impulses are particularly common. In similar cases such symptoms have also included dizziness, weakness, fainting, anorexia, atypical spells, and in rare cases paralyses. However, these atypical symptoms involved a displaced focus of anxiety rather than an effective solution or denial of it. In addition, the numerous physical preoccupations he expressed on the test suggest a wide variety of chronic somatic complaints lacking a sufficient organic basis. Gastrointestinal distress, headache, and fatigue would be typical, as would be excessive concern about his health and overreactions to minor physical dysfunctions. He is apt to get considerable "secondary gain" from his symptoms and to attribute many of his current difficulties to his health problems.

Repeatedly needing reassurances of being loved, he tests as immaturely emotional with many fears and inhibitions. His dependency needs would interfere with self-assertiveness and give him difficulties in handling acting out by family members.

He is likely to have been deeply hurt in past close relationships and to be distrustful and questioning of the motives of others. His underlying anger and resentment appear moderate to severe. The profile suggests that his lack of warmth and inappropriate actions would drive others away from him. Lacking in stable longterm goals, he is apt to tolerate frustrations poorly and to overreact to anything he interprets as a demand on him. Underneath his self-blame or when less depressed, he appears prone to rationalize resentments and to feel that his difficulties cannot really be relieved unless other people or circumstances change.

He obtained the so-called "burnt child" pattern type for which the phrase, "The burnt child fears the fire," has aptly characterized the chronic fears of emotional closeness and involvement. He is vulnerable to an impulsive marriage which could then reactivate his maternal dependency conflicts, increasingly as he would invite or provoke maternalistic behavior from his wife. Typical histories associated with this pattern have included uneven past achievements that were poor relative to the patient's intelligence and general potentials. His overall balance of masculine and feminine interests is within the normal range for his age and education.

DIAGNOSTIC IMPRESSION

The psychiatric diagnoses associated with this profile are mixed with diagnoses of depression being the most common. A secondary diagnosis reflecting chronic abuse of or dependence on alcohol may also be indicated. It should be re-emphasized that his profile is of very borderline validity and that such a diagnostic formulation is only tentative and speculative.

TREATMENT CONSIDERATIONS

The profile suggests a moderate suicide risk. Sedating phenothiazines and tricyclic anti-depressants have been used with most similar patients, often with best results from combinations of both. Any currently significant use of alcohol or drugs or past difficulties with them would predict a moderate to severe risk of increasing habituation and dependency on such chemical agents. His responses suggest a specific inquiry about alcoholic blackouts and episodes of heavy drinking. He tests as addiction prone, and the longterm risk of increasing dependence on alcohol and of related forms of chronic dependency on chemical agents tests as serious. The profile suggests that contact with relatives is apt to be of benefit in order to review the precipitating circumstances, adjustments to them that he may fail to mention, and ways of minimizing secondary gains. It should be noted that a minority of patients with this pattern have shown histories of cyclothymic fluctuation, and this possibility might need to be reviewed with family members or other informants. His responses suggest asking if he has been in trouble with the law. If currently involved, the stress of this could have precipitated or aggravated his symptoms or otherwise have led him to make professional contact. His responses suggest a careful review of his sexual history. If not already expressed in the interview, the therapist may wish to follow up the patient's "true" responses to the following items:

"I often hear voices without knowing where they come from."

"I hear strange things when I am alone."

Difficulties in trusting and in relating emotionally are likely to seriously handicap his response to treatment. Apathy and longterm schizoid trends would be prognostically negative signs. His shyness and persistent fears of losing emotional control would inhibit him from opening up in early interviews. He tests as prone to get others to tell him what to do, but ambivalent if not negativistic to decisions made for him by someone else. Although responsibility for decisions should be gently but firmly encouraged, he is apt to need extensive support in order to take initiative and to mobilize his energies. The shallowness of his longterm goals would also handicap his effort and persistence. He tests as prone to manipulate individual treatment passively if not overtly, and the character problems warn against involvement in his manipulations. He is particularly prone to provoke therapeutic rescue and then to back away abruptly from what he would fear as therapist demands on him and intolerable closeness in the treatment relationship. His ability to put up a facade and to hide his feelings from the therapist could also complicate treatment. If any administrative recommendations or decisions regarding his control of anger and aggression are required, a careful review of his history and records and, if appropriate, contact with others involved would be indicated. If he is currently going through an intense life crisis, then he may show fairly rapid and extensive emotional changes. Subsequent retesting is apt to be more than usually informative for reevaluating such shifts and for updating treatment directions and goals.

In many similar cases the precipitating circumstances involved personal "binds" that were partly due to the patients' ambivalences and to their avoidance of decisions and responsibility. Sexual fears and inhibitions may come up early in treatment, but the self-dislike that blocks self-assertiveness and risk-taking would be central to this. His awareness of the intensity of his hurt and angry feelings and of the indirectness of his ways of expressing them appears distorted. Discovery of his personal ways of keeping others at a distance---perhaps especially as he uses them on the therapist---is apt to be of direct benefit in treatment.

Thank you for this referral.

Alex B Caldwell

Alex B. Caldwell, Ph.D.
Diplomate in Clinical Psychology

ABC/ps

The preceding analysis is basically actuarial and probabilistic in nature in that the symptoms and personality characteristics presented in the report have been identified as disproportionately frequent among individuals obtaining similar scores and patterns of scores on the MMPI/MMPI-2 (tm). The diagnosis of any individual, however, needs to be based on the integration of information from personal contacts, the person's history, other test results, and whatever independent data are relevant and available.

This report has an overall focus on psychotherapy intake, differential diagnosis, treatment planning, and related personality-dependent determinations. It provides assistance in the diagnostic process by providing an extended set of clinical hypotheses, the largest part of the basis for which is data from traditional psychiatric settings. The application of these hypotheses to an individual requires independent confirmation of them by the clinician.

This report was prepared for our professional clientele. In most cases this is confidential information and legally privileged. The ongoing protection of this privilege becomes the responsibility of the professional person receiving the attached material from Caldwell Report.

CALDWELL REPORT
1545 SAWTELLE BOULEVARD
LOS ANGELES, CA 90025
(310) 478-3133
FAX (310) 479-5236

Name Mr. Jones

Date March 18, 1998

MMPI - 2 CRITICAL ITEMS

THE CIRCLED ITEMS WERE ANSWERED AS INDICATED IN THE PARENTHESES

Distress and Depression

5. I am easily awakened by noise. (True)
24. Evil spirits possess me at times. (True)
73. I am certainly lacking in self-confidence. (True)
130. I certainly feel useless at times. (True)
140. Most nights I go to sleep without thoughts or ideas bothering me. (False)
146. I cry easily. (True)
165. My memory seems to be all right. (False)
170. I am afraid of losing my mind. (True)
180. There is something wrong with my mind. (True)
233. I have difficulty in starting to do things. (True)
301. I feel anxiety about something or someone almost all the time. (True)

Suicidal Thoughts

75. I usually feel that life is worthwhile. (False)
150. Sometimes I feel as if I must injure either myself or someone else. (True)
234. I believe I am a condemned person. (True)
246. I believe my sins are unpardonable. (True)
303. Most of the time I wish I were dead. (True)]

Ideas of Reference, Persecution, and Delusions

42. If people had not had it in for me, I would have been much more successful. (True)
99. Someone has it in for me. (True)
138. I believe I am being plotted against. (True)
144. I believe I am being followed. (True)
162. Someone has been trying to poison me. (True)
228. There are persons who are trying to steal my thoughts and ideas. (True)
314. I have no enemies who really wish to harm me. (False)
333. People say insulting and vulgar things about me. (True)
336. Someone has control over my mind. (True)
361. Someone has been trying to influence my mind. (True)

Peculiar Experiences and Hallucinations

32. I have had very peculiar and strange experiences. (True)
60. When I am with people, I am bothered by hearing very strange things. (True)
96. I see things or animals or people around me that others do not see. (True)
198. I often hear voices without knowing where they come from. (True)
298. Peculiar odors come to me at times. (True)
311. I often feel as if things are not real. (True)
316. I have strange and peculiar thoughts. (True)
319. I hear strange things when I am alone. (True)
355. At one or more times in my life I felt that someone was making me do things by hypnotizing me. (True)

Sexual Difficulties

12. My sex life is satisfactory. (False)
34. I have never been in trouble because of my sex behavior. (False)
62. I have often wished I were a girl. (or if you are a girl) I have never been sorry that I am a girl. (Male:True; Female: False)
121. I have never indulged in any unusual sex practices. (False)
166. I am worried about sex. (True)
268. I wish I were not bothered by thoughts about sex. (True)

Authority Problems

35. Sometimes when I was young I stole things. (True)
50. I have often had to take orders from someone who did not know as much as I did. (True)
105. In school I was sometimes sent to the principal for bad behavior. (True)
240. At times it has been impossible for me to keep from stealing or shoplifting something. (True)
266. I have never been in trouble with the law. (False)

Alcohol and Drugs

168. I have had periods in which I carried on activities without knowing later what I had been doing. (True)
229. I have had blank spells in which my activities were interrupted and I did not know what was going on around me. (True)
264. I have used alcohol excessively. (True)

Family Discord

21. At times I have very much wanted to leave home. (True)
83. I have very few quarrels with members of my family. (False)
125. I believe my home life is as pleasant as that of most people I know. (False)
190. My people treat me more like a child than a grown-up. (True)
195. There is very little love and companionship in my family as compared to other homes. (True)
217. My relatives are nearly all in sympathy with me. (False)
288. My parents and family find more fault with me than they should. (True)

Somatic Concerns

2. I have a good appetite. (False)
10. I am about as able to work as I ever was. (False)
18. I am troubled by attacks of nausea and vomiting. (True)
47. I am almost never bothered by pains over my heart or in my chest. (False)
101. Often I feel as if there is a tight band around my head. (True)
111. I have a great deal of stomach trouble. (True)
141. During the past few years I have been well most of the time. (False)
164. I seldom or never have dizzy spells. (False)
175. I feel weak all over much of the time. (True)
224. I have few or no pains. (False)

A DIVISION OF CLINICAL PSYCHOLOGICAL SERVICES, INC.

MMPI™ & MMPI-2™

The Minnesota Multiphasic Personality Inventory™ The Minnesota Multiphasic Personality Inventory-2™

Starke R. Hathaway and J. Charnley McKinley

MMPI Code: 2 8 * 1 4 " 7 3 0 ' 6 - 5 9

MMPI-2 Code: 2 * 8 " 1 4 0 ' 3 7 6 - / 9 5

MMPI Basic Scale Profile

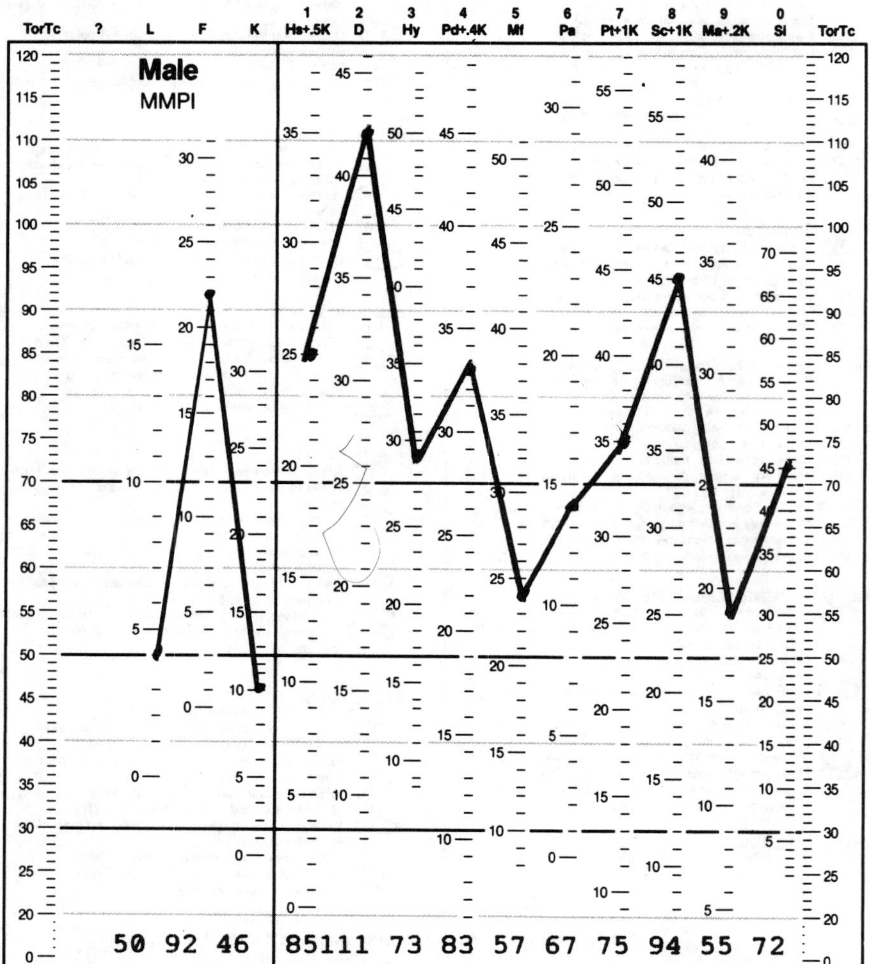

	?	L	F	K	1 Hs+.5K	2 D	3 Hy	4 Pd+.4K	5 Mf	6 Pa	7 Pt+1K	8 Sc+1K	9 Ma+.2K	0 Si
Raw Score	0	4	22	10	20	42	29	29	24	14	25	35	17	45
K to be added					5			4			10	10	2	
Raw Score with K					25			33			35	45	19	

Name Mr. Jones

Age 25 Marital Status Single

M Male

Education 12 years Date Tested 3/18/98

Referred by Alan F. Friedman, Ph.D.

Date Processed 07/15/98

MMPI-2 Basic Scale Profile

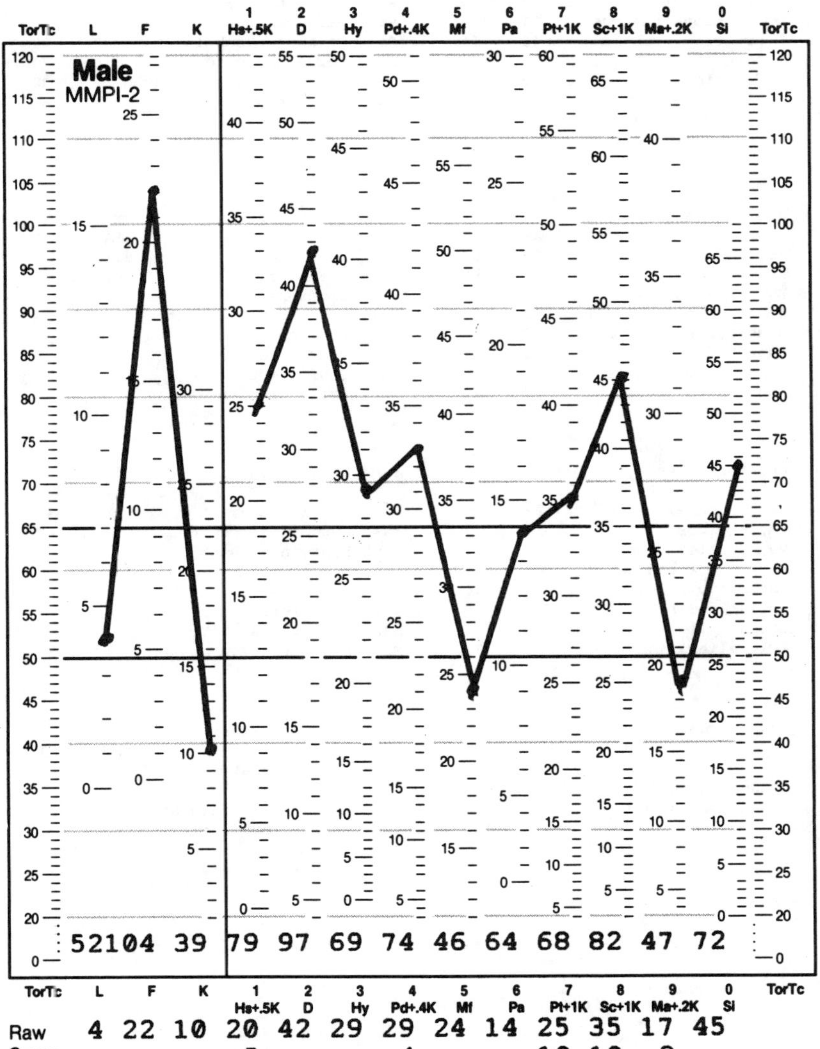

	L	F	K	1 Hs+.5K	2 D	3 Hy	4 Pd+.4K	5 Mf	6 Pa	7 Pt+1K	8 Sc+1K	9 Ma+.2K	0 Si
T or Tc	52	104	39	79	97	69	74	46	64	68	82	47	72
Raw Score	4	22	10	20	42	29	29	24	14	25	35	17	45
K to be added				5			4			10	10	2	
Raw Score with K				25			33			35	45	19	

Name: Mr. Jones
Referred by: Alan F. Friedman, Ph.D.
Date Tested: 3/18/98

Page 1 (MMPI-2)
Subscales

2-D and Subscales

		RAW	T
D	(full scale)	42	97
D-O	Depression, obvious	31	104
D-S	Depression, subtle	12	55
D1	Subjective depression	25	98
D2	Indecision-retardation	10	76
D3	Health pessimism	7	83
D4	Mental dullness	13	101
D5	Brooding, loss of hope	6	74

3-Hy and Subscales

		RAW	T
Hy	(full scale)	29	69
Hy-O	Hysteria, obvious	21	95
Hy-S	Hysteria, subtle	8	31
Hy1	Denies social anxiety	2	40
Hy2	Need for affection	2	32
Hy3	Lassitude - malaise	15	106
Hy4	Somatic complaints	8	77
Hy5	Inhibits aggression	0	25

4-Pd and Subscales

		RAW	T
Pd	(full scale)	29	74
Pd-O	Pd, obvious	17	79
Pd-S	Pd, subtle	12	56
Pd1	Family discord	7	84
Pd2	Authority problems	5	60
Pd3	Social disinhibition	2	39
Pd4	Social alienation	6	61
Pd5	Self-alienation	8	72

5-Mf and Subscales

		RAW	T
Mf	(full scale)	24	57
GM	Gender masculine	33	40
GF	Gender feminine	20	34

6-Pa and Subscales

		RAW	T
Pa	(full scale)	14	64
Pa-O	Paranoia, obvious	6	66
Pa-S	Paranoia, subtle	8	52
Pa1	Persecutory ideas	5	70
Pa2	Poignant sensitivity	4	62
Pa3	Moral righteousness	4	46

8-Sc and Subscales

		RAW	T
Sc	(full scale)	35	82
Sc1	Social alienation	10	80
Sc2	Emotional alienation	4	78
Sc3	Ego defect, cognitive	8	90
Sc4	Ego defect, conative	9	87
Sc5	Defective inhibition	2	54
Sc6	Sensorimotor dissociation	6	70

9-Ma and Subscales

		RAW	T
Ma	(full scale)	17	47
Ma-O	Hypomania, obvious	12	67
Ma-S	Hypomania, subtle	5	31
Ma1	Opportunism	2	50
Ma2	Psychomotor acceleration	7	58
Ma3	Imperturbability	2	41
Ma4	Ego inflation	3	50

0-Si and Subscales

		RAW	T
Si	(full scale)	45	72
Si1	Shyness and self-consciousness	11	68
Si2	Social avoidance	8	71
Si3	Alienation - self and others	6	53

Name: Mr. Jones
Referred by: Alan F. Friedman, Ph.D.
Date Tested: 3/18/98

Page 2 (MMPI-2)
Subscales

Major Clinical Variables

		RAW	T
ES	Ego strength MMPI estimated	29	25
ES	Ego strength MMPI-2 norms	22	30
MAC-R	Potential alcoholism	27	62
SAP	Teen drugs/alcohol	15	65
Mt	College maladjustment	32	82
N-P	Neurotic-psychotic profile balance		63

Validity & Stability

		RAW	T
VRIN	Response inconsistency	6	54
TRIN	T-F inconsistency	8	57F
F-back	Rare answers - back	8	75
F(p)	Psychiatric infrequency	5	77
Ds	Overemphasize-fake sick	24	76
Mp	Consciously fake good	8	45
Sd	Consciously fake good	6	32
Ss	SES identification	44	29
Ch	Correction for H	24	67
Rc	Retest-consistency	13	29
Ic	Retest-item change	32	64
Tc	Retest-score change	22	62

Interpersonal Style Variables

		RAW	T
ER-S	Ego resiliency	11	31
EC-5	Ego control	5	32
ORIG	Need novelty	51	84
INT	Abstract interests	43	39
Do	Need for autonomy	11	31
Dy	Need reassurances	22	60
Pr	Intolerance	21	77
Re	Value rigidity	9	21
Et	Ethnocentrism	12	52
St	Status mobility	12	32
R-S	Repression-sensitization	76	75
Lbp	Low back pain	9	51
O-H	Overcontrolled hostility	13	52
Ho	Cynical hostility	35	70
Ba	Good teamworker	37	29

Content Scales

		RAW	T
HEA	Health concerns	18	78
DEP	Depression	18	75
FAM	Family problems	13	71
ASP	Antisocial practices	13	62
ANG	Anger	13	74
CYN	Cynicism	16	62
ANX	Anxiety	19	82
OBS	Obsessiveness	5	50
FRS	Fears - phobias	3	48
BIZ	Bizarre mentation	5	60
LSE	Low self-esteem	6	55
TPA	Type A	10	53
SOD	Social discomfort	21	81
WRK	Work interference	20	74
TRT	Negative treatment indicators	16	70

Distress-Control

		RAW	T
A	Level of distress	21	65
R	Emotional constriction	20	61
Ca	Caudality-distress	20	76
Cn	Control-facade	29	72
So-r	Life as desirable	20	28
Th-r	Tired housewife	24	78
Wb-r	Worried breadwinner	18	70
PK	PTSD - patients	32	90
PS	PTSD - normals	44	92

Tryon, Stein & Chu Factor Scales

		RAW	T
TSC I	Introversion	16	63
TSC II	Body symptoms	18	84
TSC III	Suspicion	19	66
TSC IV	Depression	17	74
TSC V	Resentment	13	70
TSC VI	Autism	11	67
TSC VII	Tension	18	70

MMPI-2 ADULT INTERPRETIVE SYSTEM

developed by
Roger L. Greene, PhD
and PAR Staff

Client Information

Name :	Mr. Jones
Age :	25
Gender :	Male
Marital Status :	Never Married
Education :	12
Admin. Date :	03/18/1998

The interpretive information contained in this report should be viewed as only one source of hypotheses about the individual being evaluated. No decisions should be based solely on the information contained in this report. This material should be integrated with all other sources of information in reaching professional decisions about this individual. This report is confidential and intended for use by qualified professionals only. It should not be released to the individual being evaluated.

MMPI-2 Adult Interpretive System
Roger L. Greene
Mr. Jones

MMPI-2 PROFILE FOR VALIDITY AND CLINICAL SCALES

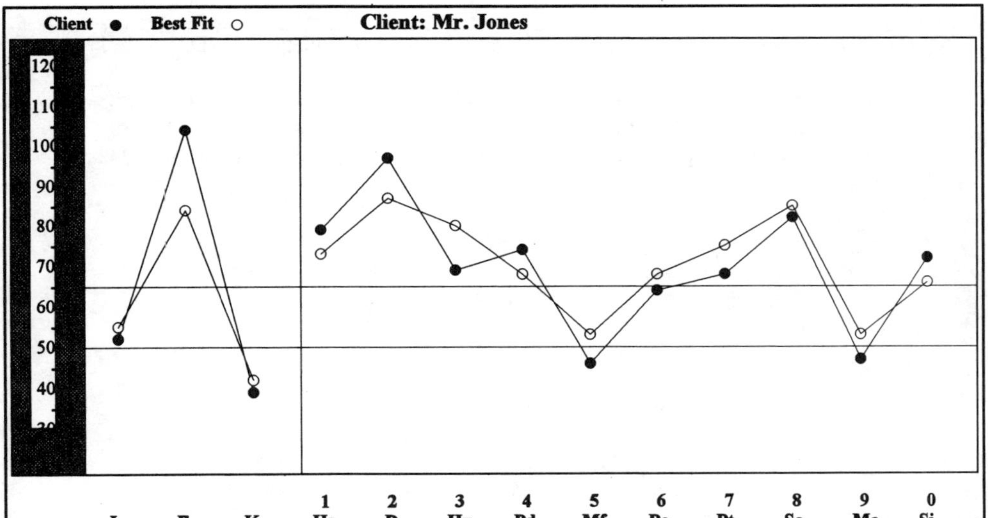

	L	F	K	1 Hs	2 D	3 Hy	4 Pd	5 Mf	6 Pa	7 Pt	8 Sc	9 Ma	0 Si
T Scores	52	104	39	79	97	69	74	46	64	68	82	47	72

MMPI-2 Adult Interpretive System
Roger L. Greene
Mr. Jones
Page:2

PROFILE MATCHES AND SCORES FOR STANDARD VALIDITY AND CLINICAL SCALES

Best Three Matches with Client's Profile:

Discriminant Function			Cohen's Index			Deviation Squared		
Codetype	Score	Prob	Codetype	rc	%ile	Codetype	D2	%ile
2-8/8-2	148.078	.911	Spike 8	0.792	90%	2-8/8-2-(3)	929	80%
1-2/2-1	145.217	.052	Spike 2-(3)	0.786	88%	2-8/8-2	932	80%
2-4/4-2	144.198	.019	1-2/2-1-(8)	0.920	86%	2-8/8-2-(1)	1032	74%

	Scale	Client's Profile	Best Fit Prototype Profile
Codetype:		2-8/8-2-(1)	2-8/8-2-(3)
rc:		0.961	0.952
D2:		1032	929
	L	52	55
	F	104++	84
	K	39	42
	1 Hs	79	73
	2 D	97+	87
	3 Hy	69-	80
	4 Pd	74	68
	5 Mf	46	53
	6 Pa	64	68
	7 Pt	68	75
	8 Sc	82	85
	9 Ma	47	53
	0 Si	72	66
Mean Clinical			
Elevation:		69	68
Scatter:		19	12
Client Age:		25	38
Men (Percent):		X	43%
Women (Percent):			57%

MMPI-2 Adult Interpretive System
Roger L. Greene
Mr. Jones

MMPI-2 PROFILE FOR CONTENT SCALES

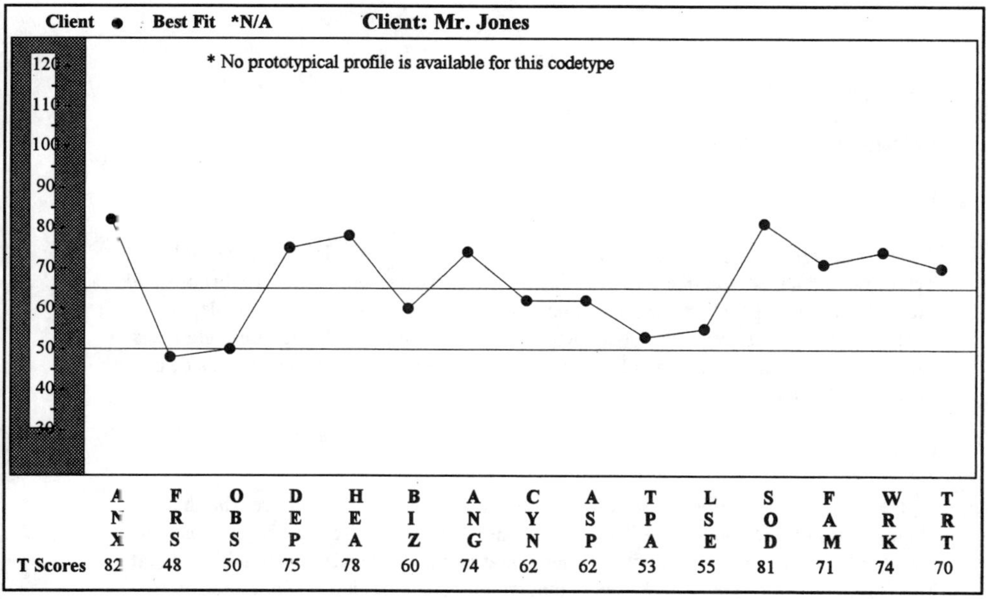

CONFIGURAL VALIDITY SCALES INTERPRETATION

He is admitting personal and emotional problems, requesting help with these problems, and is unsure of his own resources for dealing with them. As the elevation on the F scale increases, he is acknowledging that he is experiencing more problems and feeling worse or is overreporting his problems, perhaps to get help sooner.

CONFIGURAL CLINICAL SCALES INTERPRETATION

Codetype: 2-8/8-2-(3)

CLINICAL PRESENTATION:

Moods

He is experiencing moderate to severe emotional distress that is characterized by dysphoria and anhedonia. He is depressed, agitated, anxious, and guilty. He broods and ruminates over his problems and disappointments. He is also impatient, irritable, and angry. He does not seem to care what happens to him. He has difficulty initiating tasks or activities, and he has little hope of success if he does get started. He has lost his desire to work out his problems.

Cognitions

He has difficulty with concentration and memory problems. He believes that his judgment is not as good now as it was in the past. He lacks self-confidence. He is worried that there is something wrong with his mind, that he may be "losing his mind," and that he is about to "go to pieces." He thinks that strangers are looking at him critically. He generally feels worthless and inadequate. He avoids facing a crisis or difficulty and gives up quickly when things go wrong.

Interpersonal Relations

He is introverted and withdraws from and keeps others at a distance. He dislikes having people around him and spends most of his spare time by himself. He feels lonely even when he is with people. His withdrawal and isolation only serve to exacerbate his symptoms. He believes that no one seems to understand him. His family is critical of him, and he feels alienated from them.

Other Problem Areas

He reports a number of neurologic symptoms. His history and background should be reviewed carefully to determine a medical or neuropsychological evaluation is needed.
He is very likely to have suicidal ideation that should be evaluated carefully and monitored routinely. He may abuse substances. He has sleep difficulties.

TREATMENT:

His prognosis is generally poor. Psychopharmacologic interventions may be necessary to deal with his concerns that he may be "losing his mind," to help him sleep, and to elevate his mood. The probability of meaningful long-term change is low. Short-term, behavioral interventions that focus on his reasons for entering treatment will be most beneficial. Given the potential for abuse and suicide, use of psychotropics or sedatives should be carefully monitored.

POSSIBLE DIAGNOSES:

Axis I - R/O Mood Disorders
- 292.84 Substance-Induced Mood Disorder
- 296.xx Major Depressive Disorder
- 296.xx Bipolar I Disorder, Depressed
- 296.89 Bipolar II Disorder, Depressed

R/O Somatoform Disorders
- 300.81 Somatoform Disorder NOS

R/O Schizophrenia and Other Psychotic Disorders
- 295.40 Schizophreniform Disorder
- 295.70 Schizoaffective Disorder, Depressive Type

R/O Substance-Related Disorders
- 305.00 Alcohol Abuse
- 305.40 Sedative, Hypnotic, or Anxiolytic Abuse

R/O Other Cognitive Disorders
- 294.9 Cognitive Disorder NOS

Axis II - R/O Personality Disorders
- 301.22 Schizotypal Personality Disorder
- 301.82 Avoidant Personality Disorder
- 301.83 Borderline Personality Disorder

VALIDITY AND CLINICAL SCALES

VALIDITY SCALES

L T = 52

He responded frankly and openly to the items and is willing to admit to minor faults.

F T = 104

The profile should be interpreted with caution because the profile may be invalid. Scores elevated in this range suggest the following possibilities: 1) failure of the individual to understand the test items due to inadequate reading skills, visual problems, or poor contact with reality; 2) lack of cooperation resulting in a random or inconsistent pattern of responding to the test items; or 3) distortion due to confusion, delusional thinking, or other psychotic processes; 4) distortion or exaggeration of the severity of psychopathology in an attempt to derive secondary gain; or 5) a plea for help by an extremely anxious individual.

K T = 39

He has limited personal resources for coping with his problems and openly acknowledges significant psychological distress. He is likely to have a relatively poor self-concept, to be strongly dissatisfied with himself but lacking the skills necessary to change his situation, to be self-critical, and/ or to be extremely open and revealing. Scores in this range may also reflect low ego strength, a lack of insight into his motivation and behavior, and ineffectiveness in dealing with the problems of daily life. Prognosis for psychological intervention is usually guarded.

CLINICAL SCALES

1 Hs = 79

He is expressing excessive concern about the functioning of his body and is endorsing multiple vague somatic complaints. He is typically self-centered, dissatisfied, demanding of attention, complaining, and generally negative and pessimistic. He may use his somatic complaints to control and manipulate others. The prognosis for either psychological or medical intervention is guarded. Conservative medical treatment is usually recommended. He is highly skilled at frustrating and sabotaging the help of others and will often "shop" for physicians and/or therapists. Individuals with multiple bonafide physical disorders, particularly of an acute nature, will score in the lower end of this range (T scores = 65-75).

2 D = 97

He feels depressed, unhappy, sad, and pessimistic about the future. He often feels guilty and is self-critical. Suicidal ideation and potential should be evaluated carefully, as well as his responses to items 150, 303, 506, 520, and 524. He often feels inadequate, helpless, and lacking in self-confidence. Social withdrawal, poor concentration, appetite and sleep disturbances, and low frustration tolerance are possible. Increasingly higher scores are usually associated with an increase in the number and severity of depressive symptoms.

3 Hy = 69

He develops physical symptoms in response to stress and may use his complaints to avoid responsibility. He is often naive, immature, self-centered, and he denies any psychological problems. He lacks insight concerning the causes of his symptoms and his own motives and feelings.

He is frequently very demanding of affection and support, and may use indirect and manipulative means to get attention and affection. His social relationships are often superficial and immature. He is resistant to psychological interpretations and treatment, and any form of psychological intervention will be difficult. He often looks for simplistic, concrete solutions to his problems--solutions that do not require self-examination. He is unlikely to be psychotic.

4 Pd = 74

He is characterized as angry, belligerent, rebellious, resentful of rules and regulations, and hostile toward authority figures. He is likely to be impulsive, unreliable, egocentric, and irresponsible. He often has little regard for social standards. He often shows poor judgment and seems to have difficulty planning ahead and benefiting from his previous experiences. He makes a good first impression, but long-term relationships tend to be rather superficial and unsatisfying. Analysis of the Content Scales and/or the Harris-Lingoes Subscales may facilitate interpretation of scores within the lower end of this range (T scores 60-80).

5 Mf = 46

He has traditional masculine interests and activities.

6 Pa = 64

He tends to be sensitive to the opinions of others. He may be overly sensitive to criticism and overly responsive to the reactions of others toward him.

7 Pt = 68

He is worried, anxious, tense, and experiencing emotional discomfort. He may experience irrational fears and typically ruminates about his problems. Disabling guilt feelings may be present. Agitation may develop. He worries excessively and may have problems in concentration. Obsessions and compulsions may be present.

8 Sc = 82

He may be experiencing serious psychopathology that includes confused thinking, distorted perceptions, and other psychotic processes. Difficulties in logic and concentration, impaired judgment, and the presence of a thought disorder should be evaluated. The clinician should verify that measures of consistency and accuracy of item endorsement are within acceptable ranges.

9 Ma = 47

Scores in this range are considered to be within normal limits. Adolescents and college students tend to score in the upper end of this range (T scores of 54-57). Persons older than 55 years who score in the upper end of this range are likely to be overly energetic and active.

0 Si = 72

He is socially introverted, shy, reserved, insecure, and hard to get to know. He is often withdrawn and avoids interacting with other people. He often lacks self-confidence, has difficulty expressing his feelings openly, and shows frequent fluctuations in mood. He is sensitive to what others think.

ADDITIONAL SCALES

CONTENT SCALES

Since the content of the items on these scales is face-valid, it is important that scales or indices of overreporting and underreporting of psychopathology be evaluated carefully when interpreting these scales. Also, the deviant response for most of these items is true, so any patient who tends to respond "true" to items regardless of their content will elevate these scales. There are no data at this time for interpretation of low scores on these scales other than the absence of the qualities seen in high scores.

Anxiety (ANX) = 82

He is overtly anxious and reports the cognitive aspects of high levels of anxiety. He worries excessively and is very tense and nervous. These symptoms are readily apparent to him and others.

Fears (FRS) = 48

There is no interpretation of low scores on this scale.

Obsessiveness (OBS) = 50

There is no interpretation of low scores on this scale.

Depression (DEP) = 75

He is depressed and sees life as hopeless. He is likely to brood and cry easily. The possibility of suicide should be evaluated carefully, particularly if he has responded "true" to any of the items 150, 303, 506, 520, or 524.

Health Concerns (HEA) = 78

He reports a variety of specific and vague physical symptoms that are unlikely to be seen in actual physical illness. These physical symptoms involve a number of bodily systems and functions. He worries excessively about his health.

Bizarre Mentation (BIZ) = 60

There is no interpretation of low scores on this scale.

Anger (ANG) = 74

He may be reporting either that he is moody, irritable, and grouchy or that he actually physically expresses his anger. It is important to review the Component subscales and to check responses to items 540, 542, and 548 to distinguish how his anger is expressed.

Cynicism (CYN) = 62

There is no interpretation of low scores on this scale.

Antisocial Practices (ASP) = 62

There is no interpretation of low scores on this scale.

Type A (TPA) = 53

There is no interpretation of low scores on this scale.

Low Self-Esteem (LSE) = 55

There is no interpretation of low scores on this scale.

Social Discomfort (SOD) = 81

He chooses to isolate himself and to avoid interactions with others. He is extremely shy and uncomfortable in social situations. His social discomfort reflects more than simple introversion.

Family Problems (FAM) = 71

He sees his family as critical and unsupportive. His home life is not pleasant. Familial discord is a way of life for him.

Work Interference (WRK) = 74

He is reporting a number of behaviors that should have a negative impact on his ability to work. He is indecisive, moody, and grouchy. He has difficulty concentrating. Less than one-half of the items actually ask about behaviors seen in the work situation; instead, the behaviors displayed would be expected to have a detrimental effect on his ability to work.

Negative Treatment Indicators (TRT) = 70

He believes that treatment is unlikely to improve his condition, and he is not motivated to work to do so. He prefers to take medications rather than to talk about his problems with anyone. He tends to give up when facing a crisis or difficulty.

+++ END OF REPORT +++

MMPI-2*

The Minnesota Report:*

Adult Clinical System--Revised

Interpretive Report

James N. Butcher, PhD

ID Number 25

Male

Age 25

Never Married

12 Years of Education

Outpatient Mental Health Center

3/18/98

[5.5 / 1.0 / 1.0]

MMPI-2 VALIDITY PATTERN

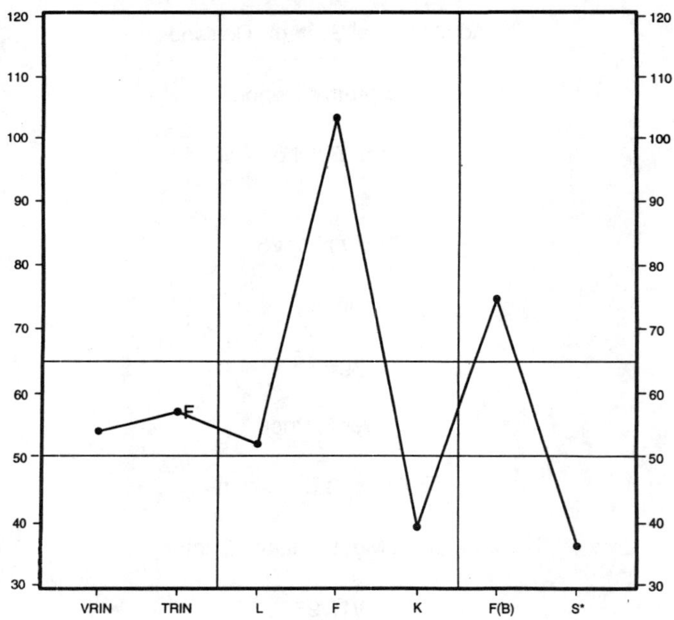

	VRIN	TRIN	L	F	K	F(B)	S*
Raw Score:	6	8	4	22	10	8	13
T Score:	54	57	52	104	39	75	36
Response %:	100	100	100	100	100	100	100

Cannot Say (Raw): 0
F-K (Raw): 12

Percent True: 42
Percent False: 58

*Experimental

PROFILE VALIDITY

His extremely elevated F score and low VRIN scale score suggest that his endorsement of extreme items is a result of careful item responding rather than an inconsistent response pattern. He apparently understood the item content and considers the symptoms descriptive of his current functioning.

His self-description as extremely disturbed requires further consideration because he has claimed many more psychological symptoms than most patients do. Two likely possibilities require further evaluation. It is possible that he is exaggerating his symptoms in order to gain attention or services. Sometimes an individual involved in litigation will produce this exaggerated clinical scale profile in order to win his case. If an exaggerated response set can be ruled out based on life circumstances, it may be that his extreme responding resulted from unusually severe psychological problems.

SYMPTOMATIC PATTERNS

This report was developed using the Hs, D, and Sc scales as the prototype. The client's MMPI-2 clinical profile suggests that he is presently experiencing many psychological problems. He is probably an extremely depressed and ineffective individual who is exhibiting personality deterioration at this time. He is likely to be quite confused and disoriented and to have inappropriate or blunted affect. He may appear tense, anxious, agitated, or hostile at times. Individuals with this profile are typically experiencing extreme physical symptoms, depressed mood, and cognitive disorganization. Symptoms of severe psychosis, such as delusions or hallucinations, are likely to be present.

He appears to feel very insecure. His life adjustment is chronically poor and he may drift from job to job or place to place. Social withdrawal is characteristic of his behavior. He has a great many vague physical concerns and may have somatic delusions.

In addition, the following description is suggested by the content of the client's item responses. He has endorsed a number of items suggesting that he is experiencing low morale and a depressed mood. He reports a preoccupation with feeling guilty and unworthy. He feels that he deserves to be punished for wrongs he has committed. He feels regretful and unhappy about life, and he seems plagued by anxiety and worry about the future. He feels hopeless at times and feels that he is a condemned person. He has difficulty managing routine affairs, and the items he endorsed suggest a poor memory, concentration problems, and an inability to make decisions. He appears to be immobilized and withdrawn and has no energy for life. He views his physical health as failing and reports numerous somatic concerns. He feels that life is no longer worthwhile and that he is losing control of his thought processes.

According to his response content, there is a strong possibility that he has seriously contemplated suicide. He has endorsed a number of items reflecting a high degree of anger. He appears to have a high potential for explosive behavior at times. He endorses statements that show some inability to control his anger. He may physically or verbally attack others when he is angry. His high endorsement of general anxiety content is likely to be important to understanding his clinical picture.

PROFILE FREQUENCY

Profile interpretation can be greatly facilitated by examining the relative frequency of clinical scale patterns in various settings. The client's high-point clinical scale score (D) occurs in 7.2% of the MMPI-2 normative sample of men. However, only 2.4% of the sample have D as the peak score at or above a T score of 65, and only 1.1% have well-defined D spikes. This elevated MMPI-2 profile pattern (2-8/8-2) is very rare in samples of normals, occurring in less than 1% of the MMPI-2 normative sample of men.

This high-point MMPI-2 score on the D scale is relatively frequent in various outpatient settings. In the NCS outpatient sample, the high-point clinical scale score on D occurs in 12.7% of the men. Moreover, 9% of the male outpatients have the D scale spike at or above a T score of 65, and 3.8% have well-defined D scale scores. This elevated MMPI-2 profile pattern (2-8/8-2) is found in 1.3% of the men in the NCS outpatient sample.

PROFILE STABILITY

The relative scale elevation of the highest scales in his clinical profile reflects high profile definition. If he is retested at a later date, the peak scores on this test are likely to retain their relative salience in his retest profile pattern. His high-point score on D is likely to remain stable over time. Short-term test-retest studies have shown a correlation of 0.75 for this high-point score. Spiro, Butcher, Levenson, Aldwin, and Bosse (1993) reported a 0.71 stability index for a large study of normals over a five-year test-retest period.

INTERPERSONAL RELATIONS

The client has not developed effective ways of dealing with others and feels very inadequate and socially alienated. Individuals with this profile type tend not to marry.

He is a very introverted person who has difficulty meeting and interacting with other people. He is shy and emotionally distant. He tends to be very uneasy, rigid, and overcontrolled in social situations. His shyness is probably symptomatic of a broader pattern of social withdrawal. Personality characteristics related to social introversion tend to be stable over time. His generally reclusive behavior, introverted lifestyle, and tendency toward interpersonal avoidance may be prominent in any future test results.

The content of this client's MMPI-2 responses suggests the following additional information concerning his interpersonal relations. He tends to approach social relationships with some caution and skepticism. He views his home situation as unpleasant and lacking in love and understanding. He feels like leaving home to escape a quarrelsome, critical situation and to be free of family domination. He feels intensely angry, hostile, and resentful of others, and he would like to get back at them. He is competitive and uncooperative, tending to be very critical of others. His social relationships are likely to be viewed by others as problematic. He may be visibly uneasy around others, sits alone in group situations, and dislikes engaging in group activities.

DIAGNOSTIC CONSIDERATIONS

The client can probably be diagnosed as having a Schizophrenic Disorder, possibly of a Disorganized or Undifferentiated type.

He appears to have a number of personality characteristics that have been associated with substance abuse or substance use problems. His scores on the addiction proneness indicators suggest that there is a possibility of his developing an addictive disorder. Further evaluation for the likelihood of a substance use or abuse disorder is indicated. In his responses to the MMPI-2, he has acknowledged some problems with excessive use or abuse of addictive substances.

TREATMENT CONSIDERATIONS

Individuals with this MMPI-2 clinical profile are experiencing significant adjustment problems for which they need treatment. This individual appears to have attitudes and beliefs centering on somatic symptoms that are chronic, intractable, and possibly delusional. His vague physical problems, social alienation, and general lack of trust in others make it difficult for him to view his problems objectively. Severe personality deterioration is apparent, and his treatment prognosis is likely to be poor.

Psychotherapy alone is not likely to be effective because he would probably have difficulty establishing a therapeutic relationship. His unusual thinking related to his bodily processes may also make him difficult to approach through psychological treatment methods. Psychotropic medications are usually considered the treatment of choice for individuals with this profile, but behavioral management or psychosocial therapy might also be attempted to decrease his somatic complaints and increase his interpersonal adjustment.

The client endorsed item content that seems to indicate low potential for change. He may feel that his problems are not addressable through therapy and that he is not likely to benefit much from psychological treatment at this time. His apparently negative treatment attitudes may need to be explored early in therapy if treatment is to be successful.

Examination of item content reveals a considerable number of problems with his home life. He feels extremely unhappy and alienated from his family. He reports that his home life is unpleasant and that he does not expect it to improve. Any psychological intervention will need to focus on his negative family feelings if progress is to be made.

In any intervention or psychological evaluation program involving occupational adjustment, his negative work attitudes could become an important problem to overcome. He has a number of attitudes and feelings that could interfere with work adjustment.

His acknowledged problems with alcohol or drug use should be addressed in therapy.

NOTE: This MMPI-2 interpretation can serve as a useful source of hypotheses about clients. This report is based on objectively derived scale indices and scale interpretations that have been developed in diverse groups of patients. The personality descriptions, inferences, and recommendations contained herein need to be verified by other sources of clinical information because individual clients may not fully match the prototype. The information in this report should most appropriately be used by a trained, qualified test interpreter. The information contained in this report should be considered confidential.

MMPI-2 BASIC AND SUPPLEMENTARY SCALES PROFILE

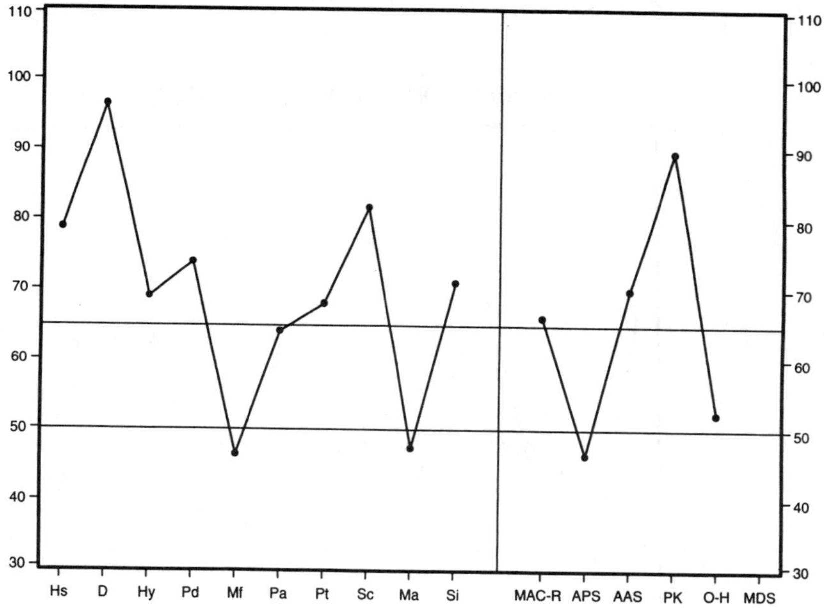

	Hs	D	Hy	Pd	Mf	Pa	Pt	Sc	Ma	Si	MAC-R	APS	AAS	PK	O-H	MDS
Raw Score:	20	42	29	29	24	14	25	35	17	43	28	22	7	32	13	*
K Correction:	5			4			10	10	2							
T Score:	79	97	69	74	46	64	68	82	47	71	66	46	70	90	52	*
Response %:	100	100	100	100	100	100	100	100	100	100	100	100	100	100	100	*

Welsh Code (new): 2*8"140'37+6-/95: F***"'+-L/:K#

Welsh Code (old): 2**8*14"730'6-59/ F*"'-L/K?:

Profile Elevation: 72.50

*MDS scores are reported only for clients who indicate that they are married or separated.

MMPI-2 CONTENT SCALES PROFILE

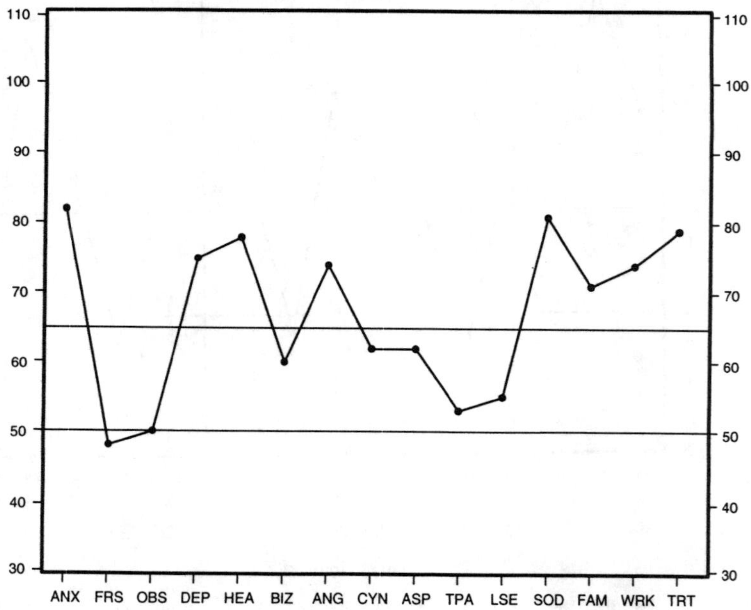

	ANX	FRS	OBS	DEP	HEA	BIZ	ANG	CYN	ASP	TPA	LSE	SOD	FAM	WRK	TRT
Raw Score:	19	3	5	18	18	5	13	16	13	10	6	21	13	20	16
T Score:	82	48	50	75	78	60	74	62	62	53	55	81	71	74	79
Response %:	100	100	100	100	100	100	100	100	100	100	100	100	100	100	100

SUPPLEMENTARY SCORE REPORT

	Raw Score	T Score	Resp %
Anxiety (A)	21	65	100
Repression (R)	20	61	100
Ego Strength (Es)	22	30	100
Dominance (Do)	11	31	100
Social Responsibility (Re)	9	30	100
Post-Traumatic Stress Disorder - Schlenger (PS)	44	92	100
Depression Subscales (Harris-Lingoes)			
Subjective Depression (D1)	25	98	100
Psychomotor Retardation (D2)	10	76	100
Physical Malfunctioning (D3)	7	83	100
Mental Dullness (D4)	13	101	100
Brooding (D5)	6	74	100
Hysteria Subscales (Harris-Lingoes)			
Denial of Social Anxiety (Hy1)	2	40	100
Need for Affection (Hy2)	2	32	100
Lassitude-Malaise (Hy3)	15	106	100
Somatic Complaints (Hy4)	8	77	100
Inhibition of Aggression (Hy5)	0	30	100
Psychopathic Deviate Subscales (Harris-Lingoes)			
Familial Discord (Pd1)	7	84	100
Authority Problems (Pd2)	5	60	100
Social Imperturbability (Pd3)	2	39	100
Social Alienation (Pd4)	6	61	100
Self-Alienation (Pd5)	8	72	100
Paranoia Subscales (Harris-Lingoes)			
Persecutory Ideas (Pa1)	5	70	100
Poignancy (Pa2)	4	62	100
Naivete (Pa3)	4	46	100
Schizophrenia Subscales (Harris-Lingoes)			
Social Alienation (Sc1)	10	80	100
Emotional Alienation (Sc2)	4	78	100
Lack of Ego Mastery, Cognitive (Sc3)	8	90	100
Lack of Ego Mastery, Conative (Sc4)	9	87	100
Lack of Ego Mastery, Defective Inhibition (Sc5)	2	54	100
Bizarre Sensory Experiences (Sc6)	6	70	100

Hypomania Subscales (Harris-Lingoes)			
Amorality (Ma1)	2	50	100
Psychomotor Acceleration (Ma2)	7	58	100
Imperturbability (Ma3)	2	41	100
Ego Inflation (Ma4)	3	50	100
Social Introversion Subscales (Ben-Porath, Hostetler, Butcher, & Graham)			
Shyness / Self-Consciousness (Si1)	11	68	100
Social Avoidance (Si2)	8	71	100
Alienation--Self and Others (Si3)	6	53	100

Uniform T scores are used for Hs, D, Hy, Pd, Pa, Pt, Sc, Ma, and the Content Scales; all other MMPI-2 scales use linear T scores.

EXPERIMENTAL CONTENT COMPONENT SCALES (Ben-Porath & Sherwood)

	Raw Score	T Score	Resp %
Fears Subscales			
Generalized Fearfulness (FRS1)	1	53	100
Multiple Fears (FRS2)	2	42	100
Depression Subscales			
Lack of Drive (DEP1)	9	89	100
Dysphoria (DEP2)	4	76	100
Self-Depreciation (DEP3)	2	55	100
Suicidal Ideation (DEP4)	1	62	100
Health Concerns Subscales			
Gastrointestinal Symptoms (HEA1)	2	70	100
Neurological Symptoms (HEA2)	1	47	100
General Health Concerns (HEA3)	6	89	100
Bizarre Mentation Subscales			
Psychotic Symptomatology (BIZ1)	1	55	100
Schizotypal Characteristics (BIZ2)	3	60	100
Anger Subscales			
Explosive Behavior (ANG1)	5	71	100
Irritability (ANG2)	7	72	100
Cynicism Subscales			
Misanthropic Beliefs (CYN1)	9	57	100
Interpersonal Suspiciousness (CYN2)	7	66	100
Antisocial Practices Subscales			
Antisocial Attitudes (ASP1)	9	57	100
Antisocial Behavior (ASP2)	4	67	100
Type A Subscales			
Impatience (TPA1)	4	57	100
Competitive Drive (TPA2)	5	56	100
Low Self-Esteem Subscales			
Self-Doubt (LSE1)	3	54	100
Submissiveness (LSE2)	0	41	100

Social Discomfort Subscales			
Introversion (SOD1)	14	76	100
Shyness (SOD2)	6	68	100
Family Problems Subscales			
Family Discord (FAM1)	5	60	100
Familial Alienation (FAM2)	5	84	100
Negative Treatment Indicators Subscales			
Low Motivation (TRT1)	6	77	100
Inability to Disclose (TRT2)	3	60	100

CRITICAL ITEMS

The following critical items have been found to have possible significance in analyzing a client's problem situation. Although these items may serve as a source of hypotheses for further investigation, caution should be used in interpreting individual items because they may have been checked inadvertently.

The percentages of endorsement for each critical item by various reference groups are presented in brackets following the listing of the item. The first endorsement percentage in the brackets "N" is the percentage of the MMPI-2 normative sample of 1,138 men who endorsed the item in the scored direction. Depending on the setting selected for the report, the endorsement percentage for the normative sample will be followed by the endorsement percentage of various clinical or research samples. The designation "Op" refers to a sample of 10,510 male outpatients (National Computer Systems, 1993).

Acute Anxiety State (Koss-Butcher Critical Items)

Of the 17 possible items in this section, 14 were endorsed in the scored direction:

2. I have a good appetite. (False)
   [N = 4.2; Op = 11.2]
3. I wake up fresh and rested most mornings. (False)
   [N = 31.5; Op = 48.4]
5. I am easily awakened by noise. (True)
   [N = 41.4; Op = 48.4]
10. I am about as able to work as I ever was. (False)
    [N = 15.3; Op = 31.4]
15. I work under a great deal of tension. (True)
    [N = 37.0; Op = 47.7]
28. I am bothered by an upset stomach several times a week. (True)
    [N = 8.1; Op = 19.2]
39. My sleep is fitful and disturbed. (True)
    [N = 11.4; Op = 29.1]
59. I am troubled by discomfort in the pit of my stomach every few days or oftener. (True)
    [N = 6.7; Op = 19.6]
140. Most nights I go to sleep without thoughts or ideas bothering me. (False)
     [N = 22.6; Op = 43.7]
208. I hardly ever notice my heart pounding and I am seldom short of breath. (False)
     [N = 30.0; Op = 32.1]
218. I have periods of such great restlessness that I cannot sit long in a chair. (True)
     [N = 30.1; Op = 39.2]
223. I believe I am no more nervous than most others. (False)
     [N = 15.6; Op = 31.0]
444. I am a high-strung person. (True)
     [N = 21.9; Op = 32.8]

469. I sometimes feel that I am about to go to pieces. (True)
[N = 14.8; Op = 37.0]

Depressed Suicidal Ideation (Koss-Butcher Critical Items)

Of the 22 possible items in this section, 14 were endorsed in the scored direction:

9. My daily life is full of things that keep me interested. (False)
[N = 14.4; Op = 34.1]
38. I have had periods of days, weeks, or months when I couldn't take care of things because I couldn't "get going." (True)
[N = 25.0; Op = 40.2]
65. Most of the time I feel blue. (True)
[N = 5.9; Op = 28.6]
71. These days I find it hard not to give up hope of amounting to something. (True)
[N = 30.7; Op = 42.0]
75. I usually feel that life is worthwhile. (False)
[N = 5.2; Op = 13.4]
92. I don't seem to care what happens to me. (True)
[N = 5.5; Op = 14.5]
95. I am happy most of the time. (False)
[N = 10.6; Op = 33.5]
215. I brood a great deal. (True)
[N = 14.6; Op = 25.8]
233. I have difficulty in starting to do things. (True)
[N = 35.2; Op = 39.3]
273. Life is a strain for me much of the time. (True)
[N = 16.0; Op = 35.5]
306. No one cares much what happens to you. (True)
[N = 13.0; Op = 14.9]
388. I very seldom have spells of the blues. (False)
[N = 25.0; Op = 46.6]
454. The future seems hopeless to me. (True)
[N = 4.8; Op = 15.8]
518. I have made lots of bad mistakes in my life. (True)
[N = 27.3; Op = 42.6]

Threatened Assault (Koss-Butcher Critical Items)

Of the 5 possible items in this section, 4 were endorsed in the scored direction:

37. At times I feel like smashing things. (True)
[N = 39.4; Op = 40.1]
85. At times I have a strong urge to do something harmful or shocking. (True)
[N = 18.5; Op = 22.6]

4. At times I feel like picking a fist fight with someone. (True)
[N = 16.0; Op = 20.2]
213. I get mad easily and then get over it soon. (True)
[N = 40.5; Op = 39.5]

Situational Stress Due to Alcoholism (Koss-Butcher Critical Items)

Of the 7 possible items in this section, 5 were endorsed in the scored direction:

125. I believe that my home life is as pleasant as that of most people I know. (False)
[N = 10.8; Op = 33.3]
264. I have used alcohol excessively. (True)
[N = 44.5; Op = 40.3]
502. I have some habits that are really harmful. (True)
[N = 27.8; Op = 29.8]
511. Once a week or more I get high or drunk. (True)
[N = 19.6; Op = 11.3]
518. I have made lots of bad mistakes in my life. (True)
[N = 27.3; Op = 42.6]

Mental Confusion (Koss-Butcher Critical Items)

Of the 11 possible items in this section, 6 were endorsed in the scored direction:

31. I find it hard to keep my mind on a task or job. (True)
[N = 13.3; Op = 33.6]
32. I have had very peculiar and strange experiences. (True)
[N = 23.8; Op = 30.7]
198. I often hear voices without knowing where they come from. (True)
[N = 1.7; Op = 4.1]
299. I cannot keep my mind on one thing. (True)
[N = 14.9; Op = 29.0]
316. I have strange and peculiar thoughts. (True)
[N = 14.9; Op = 22.8]
325. I have more trouble concentrating than others seem to have. (True)
[N = 18.9; Op = 34.1]

Persecutory Ideas (Koss-Butcher Critical Items)

Of the 15 possible items in this section, 6 were endorsed in the scored direction:

17. I am sure I get a raw deal from life. (True)
[N = 5.2; Op = 16.7]
124. I often wonder what hidden reason another person may have for doing something nice for me. (True)

[N = 29.2; Op = 33.5]
145. I feel that I have often been punished without cause. (True)
[N = 9.1; Op = 20.2]
216. Someone has been trying to rob me. (True)
[N = 2.6; Op = 2.7]
251. I have often felt that strangers were looking at me critically. (True)
[N = 23.8; Op = 28.8]
314. I have no enemies who really wish to harm me. (False)
[N = 11.6; Op = 21.7]

Antisocial Attitude (Lachar-Wrobel Critical Items)

Of the 9 possible items in this section, 7 were endorsed in the scored direction:

27. When people do me a wrong, I feel I should pay them back if I can, just for the principle of the thing. (True)
[N = 26.7; Op = 25.3]
84. I was suspended from school one or more times for bad behavior. (True)
[N = 17.3; Op = 25.2]
105. In school I was sometimes sent to the principal for bad behavior. (True)
[N = 30.9; Op = 40.1]
227. I don't blame people for trying to grab everything they can get in this world. (True)
[N = 39.9; Op = 50.9]
254. Most people make friends because friends are likely to be useful to them. (True)
[N = 23.8; Op = 26.5]
266. I have never been in trouble with the law. (False)
[N = 40.9; Op = 52.9]
324. I can easily make other people afraid of me, and sometimes do for the fun of it. (True)
[N = 7.7; Op = 8.3]

Family Conflict (Lachar-Wrobel Critical Items)

Of the 4 possible items in this section, 4 were endorsed in the scored direction:

21. At times I have very much wanted to leave home. (True)
[N = 31.9; Op = 41.0]
83. I have very few quarrels with members of my family. (False)
[N = 21.2; Op = 30.3]
125. I believe that my home life is as pleasant as that of most people I know. (False)
[N = 10.8; Op = 33.3]
288. My parents and family find more fault with me than they should. (True)
[N = 10.6; Op = 17.5]

Somatic Symptoms (Lachar-Wrobel Critical Items)

Of the 23 possible items in this section, 11 were endorsed in the scored direction:

18. I am troubled by attacks of nausea and vomiting. (True)
    [N = 1.1; Op = 5.9]
28. I am bothered by an upset stomach several times a week. (True)
    [N = 8.1; Op = 19.2]
33. I seldom worry about my health. (False)
    [N = 37.1; Op = 48.2]
40. Much of the time my head seems to hurt all over. (True)
    [N = 3.3; Op = 12.5]
57. I hardly ever feel pain in the back of my neck. (False)
    [N = 26.6; Op = 36.1]
59. I am troubled by discomfort in the pit of my stomach every few days or oftener. (True)
    [N = 6.7; Op = 19.6]
175. I feel weak all over much of the time. (True)
    [N = 4.2; Op = 17.2]
176. I have very few headaches. (False)
    [N = 14.6; Op = 26.9]
224. I have few or no pains. (False)
    [N = 18.2; Op = 32.9]
229. I have had blank spells in which my activities were interrupted and I did not know what was going on around me. (True)
    [N = 7.5; Op = 14.9]
464. I feel tired a good deal of the time. (True)
    [N = 24.5; Op = 39.1]

Sexual Concern and Deviation (Lachar-Wrobel Critical Items)

Of the 6 possible items in this section, 2 were endorsed in the scored direction:

12. My sex life is satisfactory. (False)
    [N = 26.7; Op = 42.0]
121. I have never indulged in any unusual sex practices. (False)
    [N = 36.9; Op 27.7=]

ITEM RESPONSES

1: 2   2: 2   3: 2   4: 2   5: 1   6: 2   7: 1   8: 2   9: 2   10: 2
11: 2   12: 2   13: 2   14: 1   15: 1   16: 1   17: 1   18: 1   19: 2   20: 1
21: 1   22: 1   23: 2   24: 2   25: 2   26: 2   27: 1   28: 1   29: 1   30: 1
31: 1   32: 1   33: 2   34: 1   35: 2   36: 1   37: 1   38: 1   39: 1   40: 1
41: 1   42: 2   43: 2   44: 2   45: 2   46: 1   47: 1   48: 2   49: 2   50: 1
51: 2   52: 1   53: 2   54: 2   55: 2   56: 2   57: 2   58: 1   59: 1   60: 2
61: 2   62: 2   63: 1   64: 2   65: 1   66: 1   67: 2   68: 2   69: 2   70: 2
71: 1   72: 2   73: 2   74: 2   75: 2   76: 1   77: 1   78: 1   79: 1   80: 2
81: 1   82: 2   83: 2   84: 1   85: 1   86: 2   87: 1   88: 1   89: 1   90: 1
91: 1   92: 1   93: 1   94: 2   95: 2   96: 2   97: 2   98: 1   99: 2   100: 2
101: 2   102: 1   103: 1   104: 2   105: 1   106: 2   107: 1   108: 2   109: 1   110: 1
111: 2   112: 2   113: 2   114: 2   115: 1   116: 1   117: 2   118: 2   119: 2   120: 1
121: 2   122: 1   123: 2   124: 1   125: 2   126: 1   127: 2   128: 2   129: 2   130: 2
131: 2   132: 2   133: 2   134: 1   135: 1   136: 2   137: 2   138: 2   139: 1   140: 2
141: 2   142: 1   143: 2   144: 2   145: 1   146: 2   147: 1   148: 2   149: 2   150: 2
151: 1   152: 2   153: 2   154: 2   155: 1   156: 1   157: 1   158: 1   159: 1   160: 2
161: 2   162: 2   163: 2   164: 1   165: 2   166: 2   167: 1   168: 2   169: 2   170: 1
171: 1   172: 2   173: 2   174: 2   175: 1   176: 2   177: 2   178: 2   179: 2   180: 2
181: 2   182: 2   183: 1   184: 1   185: 1   186: 1   187: 2   188: 2   189: 2   190: 2
191: 2   192: 1   193: 2   194: 2   195: 1   196: 1   197: 1   198: 1   199: 2   200: 2
201: 2   202: 1   203: 2   204: 2   205: 2   206: 2   207: 2   208: 2   209: 2   210: 1
211: 2   212: 2   213: 1   214: 1   215: 1   216: 1   217: 2   218: 1   219: 1   220: 2
221: 2   222: 1   223: 2   224: 2   225: 1   226: 2   227: 1   228: 2   229: 1   230: 2
231: 1   232: 1   233: 1   234: 2   235: 2   236: 2   237: 2   238: 2   239: 2   240: 2
241: 2   242: 2   243: 1   244: 2   245: 2   246: 2   247: 2   248: 2   249: 1   250: 1
251: 1   252: 2   253: 2   254: 1   255: 1   256: 2   257: 2   258: 2   259: 2   260: 1
261: 1   262: 2   263: 1   264: 1   265: 1   266: 2   267: 2   268: 2   269: 2   270: 2
271: 2   272: 1   273: 1   274: 2   275: 1   276: 1   277: 1   278: 1   279: 1   280: 2
281: 1   282: 2   283: 2   284: 2   285: 2   286: 1   287: 2   288: 1   289: 2   290: 1
291: 1   292: 2   293: 2   294: 2   295: 1   296: 2   297: 1   298: 2   299: 1   300: 1
301: 2   302: 1   303: 2   304: 2   305: 1   306: 1   307: 2   308: 1   309: 2   310: 2
311: 2   312: 1   313: 2   314: 2   315: 1   316: 1   317: 2   318: 1   319: 1   320: 2
321: 1   322: 2   323: 2   324: 1   325: 1   326: 2   327: 1   328: 2   329: 2   330: 2
331: 2   332: 2   333: 2   334: 2   335: 2   336: 2   337: 1   338: 1   339: 1   340: 2
341: 2   342: 2   343: 2   344: 1   345: 2   346: 1   347: 2   348: 2   349: 2   350: 1
351: 2   352: 1   353: 2   354: 2   355: 2   356: 2   357: 1   358: 2   359: 2   360: 2
361: 2   362: 1   363: 2   364: 2   365: 1   366: 2   367: 1   368: 2   369: 2   370: 2
371: 2   372: 2   373: 1   374: 1   375: 2   376: 2   377: 1   378: 1   379: 2   380: 1
381: 1   382: 1   383: 2   384: 2   385: 2   386: 1   387: 1   388: 2   389: 2   390: 1
391: 1   392: 2   393: 1   394: 2   395: 2   396: 2   397: 2   398: 2   399: 1   400: 1
401: 1   402: 2   403: 1   404: 1   405: 2   406: 1   407: 2   408: 2   409: 1   410: 2
411: 2   412: 1   413: 2   414: 1   415: 1   416: 2   417: 1   418: 1   419: 1   420: 2

421: 2	422: 1	423: 1	424: 2	425: 1	426: 2	427: 1	428: 1	429: 2	430: 1
431: 2	432: 2	433: 2	434: 1	435: 2	436: 1	437: 2	438: 2	439: 2	440: 1
441: 2	442: 2	443: 2	444: 1	445: 1	446: 2	447: 2	448: 2	449: 1	450: 2
451: 2	452: 1	453: 1	454: 1	455: 2	456: 1	457: 2	458: 2	459: 1	460: 1
461: 1	462: 1	463: 2	464: 1	465: 2	466: 2	467: 2	468: 2	469: 1	470: 2
471: 1	472: 2	473: 1	474: 2	475: 1	476: 2	477: 1	478: 2	479: 1	480: 1
481: 1	482: 2	483: 1	484: 2	485: 2	486: 1	487: 2	488: 1	489: 2	490: 2
491: 2	492: 2	493: 1	494: 2	495: 1	496: 2	497: 1	498: 2	499: 1	500: 1
501: 1	502: 1	503: 2	504: 1	505: 1	506: 2	507: 2	508: 2	509: 2	510: 2
511: 1	512: 2	513: 1	514: 2	515: 2	516: 2	517: 2	518: 1	519: 2	520: 2
521: 1	522: 2	523: 1	524: 2	525: 2	526: 2	527: 2	528: 1	529: 2	530: 2
531: 2	532: 2	533: 1	534: 2	535: 1	536: 1	537: 2	538: 2	539: 1	540: 2
541: 2	542: 1	543: 2	544: 2	545: 1	546: 2	547: 2	548: 1	549: 1	550: 1
551: 1	552: 2	553: 2	554: 2	555: 2	556: 1	557: 2	558: 2	559: 1	560: 2
561: 2	562: 1	563: 2	564: 2	565: 1	566: 2	567: 2			

End of Report

The Marks Adult Feedback and Treatment Report
for MMPI-2 and MMPI
by Philip A. Marks, Ph.D., and Richard W. Lewak, Ph.D.

A WPS TEST REPORT by Western Psychological Services
12031 Wilshire Boulevard
Los Angeles, California 90025-1251
Version: 2.010

NAME: MR. JONES
GENDER: MALE
AGE: 25
MMPI VERSION: MMPI-2

ID NUMBER: 1
EDUCATION(IN YEARS): 12
MMPI ADMIN DATE: 3/18/98
AF REPORT DATE: 8/15/98

THE FEEDBACK AND TREATMENT REPORT

This report is designed for professionals to provide clients with an understanding of their MMPI test results. It was developed from research and clinical experience with adults, ages 18 and older, earning at least low-middle level incomes who are seen in clinic or outpatient settings for a range of personal, marital, family and work-related reasons. It was developed to access results obtained from initial or pretreatment testing. The material may not be appropriate for other individuals or clients tested at different times or under other circumstances. It would not be appropriate for adolescents because it is based on K-corrected adult norms. Users of this report should be familiar with information contained in the "Therapist Guide to the MMPI and MMPI-2: Providing Feedback and Treatment" (WPS Product No. AE-4).

The report appears in three sections: Section 1 (NOTES TO PROVIDER), determines the validity of results, highlights salient characteristics of scores, and provides suggestions for treatment. This section is considered a professional-to-professional consultation and is for the provider's use only. Section 2 (ISSUES), describes the client's approach to the test and lists the client's uppermost thoughts, feelings, and concerns. This section is to be given directly to the client. The client is then asked to read and validate each statement as it applies to him or herself. Section 3 (SELF-HELP), offers suggestions for "homework" which, at the discretion of the provider, may be given to the client for practice at home.

> Users of the WPS TEST REPORT should be familiar with the interpretive guidelines, psychometric properties, and limitations of the MMPI and MMPI-2. Users should also be aware that empirical correlates available for the MMPI may not always apply to the MMPI-2.

MMPI-2 TEST REPORT ID NUMBER: 1 Page: 2
Code: 2*8"140'37+6-/95:# (F***"'+-L/:K#)

M M P I-2 P R O F I L E

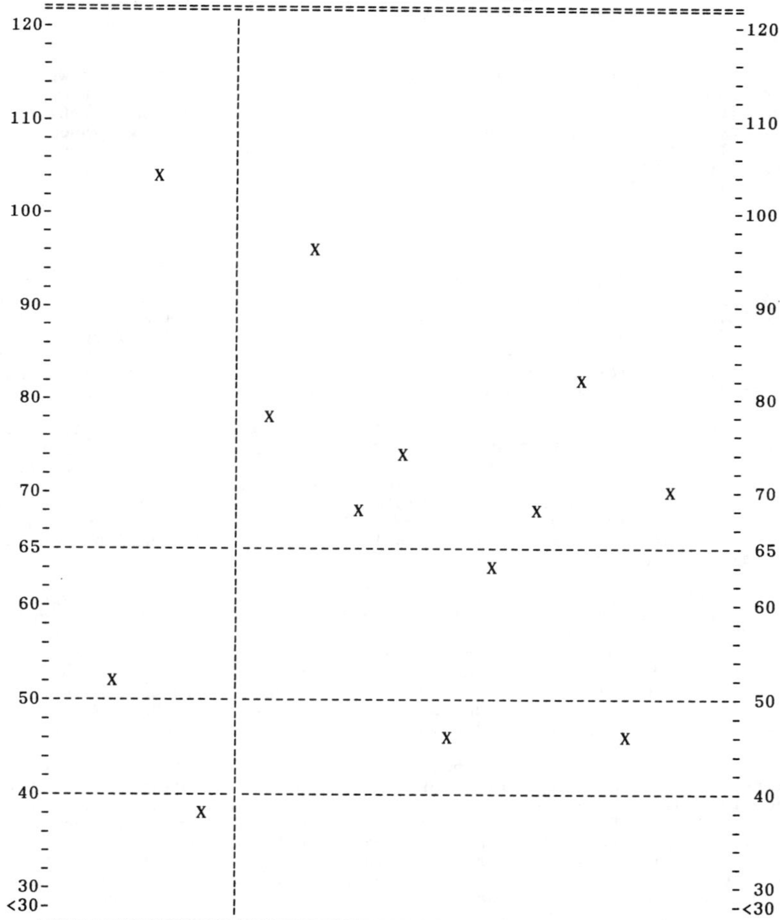

Scales	L	F	K	Hs [1]	D [2]	Hy [3]	Pd [4]	Mf [5]	Pa [6]	Pt [7]	Sc [8]	Ma [9]	Si [0]
T-Score	52	104	39	79	97	69	74	46	64	68	82	47	71

? Raw Score: 0

Scales	A	R	Es	OH	Do	Re	MAC-R	Fb	TRIN	VRIN
T-Score	65	61	30	52	31	21	66	75	57	54

ANX	OBS	DEP	FRS	HEA	BIZ	ANG	CYN	ASP	TPA	LSE	SOD	FAM	WRK	TRT
82	50	75	48	78	60	74	62	62	53	55	81	71	74	79

Code: 2*8"140'37+6-/95:# (F***"'+-L/:K#)

PROFILE VALIDITY

This is a markedly elevated profile of a client who has answered an improbable number of F scale questions, making the validity of the profile doubtful. This occurs because of scoring errors, or when the client has difficulty understanding the questions, or is answering them randomly, very deviantly, or obviously in a 'fake bad' direction. In any case, the test should probably be retaken. As presented, the report is tentative and should be verified using other sources.

NOTES TO PROVIDER

This patient's clinical scale scores correspond to the adult 2-8/8-2 codetype. Clients with this profile are depressed, typically feeling somehow broken, defective and unlovable. They complain of poor memory and of an inability to concentrate, make decisions and think clearly. They may also believe they are deteriorating or somehow falling apart. They may have been raised in families where they were treated with coldness and indifference, internalized as a negative self-image and proof of being defective.

The precipitating circumstance that often leads clients with this profile to seek treatment is that somebody who was previously supportive has withdrawn from the client and treated him in an uncaring or even hostile way. Such a client will probably not do well in explorative therapy, and may experience the uncovering of his intimate reactions as a confirmation of their negative self-image. He may do better with a nurturing and supportive approach that helps him feel acceptable and likable. Relaxation techniques are also useful.

Patients with this codetype are not homogeneous in their response to medication. Some respond well to a tricyclic anti-depressant or trazadone (Desyrel), which decreases their sense of defectiveness as the depression lifts. Other respond poorly to antidepressants, feeling an increase in agitation and confusion. Patients with this codetype and a history of parental neglect and hostility usually need a combination of antidepressan and phenothiazines in low dosages. For others, however, the use of antidepressants and anxiolytics in combination seems to be effective.

Studies of introversion have revealed that elevations of scale 0 are fairly stable over long periods of time. People who were shy and socially uncomfortable as children often remain so as adults. It is hypothesized that scores between 40T and 60T are determined genetically, but that scores elevated beyond 60T reflect a childhood characterized by an absence of outward human warmth and physical contact. Therapy for a client with an elevated score should concentrate on helping him find ways to accept and enjoy his shyness, rather than try to change or put himself down.

This client's responses to the MAC-R suggest the need to evaluate carefully the prospect of excessive drug or alcohol use.

The following pertain to elevations of supplementary and content scales. The provider should use personal judgment in integrating them with previous text, especially if they appear contradictory.

This A-anxiety score confirms that the client may be suffering from periods of anxiety and self-doubt, as well as difficulties concentrating and making decisions.

This client's R-repression score indicates difficulty recognizing and acknowledging psychological problems and conflicts. It suggests repression of feelings, which may be a result of unconscious drives, rather than a conscious attempt to distort feelings. Consequently, other scores may not be giving an accurate indication of the client's psychological status.

This ANG content score indicates problems with anger control. The client reports being irritable, grouchy, impatient, hot-headed, easily annoyed and stubborn. At times, he may feel like swearing and smashing things, and this may lead to episodic losses of self-control. The impulse to be physically abusive and act out when stressed is not uncommon.

This client's responses to the CYN content scale reveal that he has a cynical attitude towards others. He may see hidden negative motives behind the actions of others, and view the world as a "dog-eat-dog" place where people cannot be trusted. The client may have difficulties with emotional closeness and perceive being vulnerable as emotionally dangerous.

Individuals with similar ASP content scores report having poor judgment and engaging in impulsive antisocial behavior. They typically have had difficulties with authority figures and may have a recent past of breaking laws to achieve immediate gratification. If the client has not been in trouble with the law specifically, his distrust of authority may lead to "bending the rules" if not actually to breaking them.

SOD content scores in this range indicate feeling somewhat uneasy around others and preferring to be by oneself. In social situations, this client may feel awkward, and may look for places where he can hide and feel more comfortable. Shy and disliking of large groups of people he doesn't know, he probably feels at a loss for words when meeting someone new.

This FAM content score reveals a person reporting considerable family conflict and discord. The family is described as lacking in love, quarrelsome, and unpleasant. The person's childhood is seen as unhappy, lacking in affection and support, and perhaps as including periods of physical abuse.

This client's WRK responses reveal attitudes and behaviors that are likely to contribute to poor work performance. Clients with such scores may perform poorly at work because of difficulties in concentration, low self-confidence, and anxieties about making decisions. In some instances, these difficulties center around ambivalence regarding the choice of career, a lack of family support for the choice, and negative attitudes toward employer and co-workers.

This client's answers to the TRT suggest negative attitudes towards professionals offering help, which may interfere with the building of a therapeutic relationship. Frequently such clients feel that nobody can help or understand them, and thus they may not want to reveal their personal feelings and vulnerabilities. Often they throw in the towel rather than face up to a crisis or difficulty. The early building of rapport and the formation of an alliance is crucial, if somewhat difficult, in order for the client to

remain in treatment.

END OF NOTES TO PROVIDER

Dear MR. JONES,

The answers you gave to the statements on the MMPI-2 are recorded on scales that yield a personality profile. This profile is valuable because it provides one way of understanding your thoughts and your feelings. Appearing below are statements and information about you that are derived from your personality profile.

APPROACH TO THE INVENTORY

Your results indicate that you completed the test in the following manner:

The way you approached the test suggests that you try to avoid criticism for saying the wrong things.

You may be panicked about how much stress you are under right now. Your discomfort is probably so frightening that you are confused about what is happening, and you want guidance about what you can do.

You answered the questions in a very frank and open way, admitting how you feel and what troubles you without trying to put up a positive front.

ISSUES (Thoughts, Feelings, and Concerns)

Your profile suggests that the following issues are important to you. Please read each issue, then circle the number corresponding to how well it applies to you right now.

4	3	2	1	0
Very True	Mostly True	Partially True	Mostly False	False

1.	It is a very frightening time for you right now.......	4	3	2	1	0
2.	You may have dark moods that seem to come from nowhere when you feel sad, empty, and disconnected from others..	4	3	2	1	0
3.	You feel hopeless and dejected and blame yourself for feeling so bad................................	4	3	2	1	0
4.	You may also become tearful and despondent, feeling that life is not worth living........................	4	3	2	1	0
5.	You probably have headaches, stomach upsets, neckaches, or other symptoms, which cause you to worry that there is something wrong with you and that your body is letting you down...................................	4	3	2	1	0
6.	You may also have other concerns about your body, fearing that something is wrong with it, and that you are deteriorating physically and falling apart....	4	3	2	1	0
7.	At present you are having difficulties thinking, being unable to solve problems or make decisions effectively..	4	3	2	1	0

8.	It may be hard for you to keep your thoughts straight so that you know how you feel at any particular moment....................................	4	3	2	1	0
9.	You probably also have difficulty with your memory and attention..	4	3	2	1	0
10.	It is also hard for you to concentrate without other thoughts interrupting what you are trying to think about...	4	3	2	1	0
11.	You may be experiencing sleep problems, either having difficulty getting to sleep, or waking up early in the morning, long before you want to.........	4	3	2	1	0
12.	Upon waking in the morning you may feel unrested and exhausted, and find it hard to face another day...	4	3	2	1	0
13.	You spend a lot of energy trying to hold things together and fear that you feel too intensely, you might somehow fall apart........................	4	3	2	1	0
14.	It is hard for you to relate to others, and the way others react to you can be very confusing to you....................................	4	3	2	1	0
15.	It is difficult for you to get close to others because you feel unable to trust how you see people and how they might see you in return.................	4	3	2	1	0
16.	Generally, letting go of control and allowing people to know you can be very frightening.................	4	3	2	1	0
17.	You probably are frightened that if people get to know you, you will become vulnerable, and then they would humiliate or reject you.......................	4	3	2	1	0
18.	Because you are sensitive to anger or hostility from others, when you see that someone is angry with you, it is confusing, and you are not sure how to respond..	4	3	2	1	0
19.	Getting angry with people also is difficult for you..	4	3	2	1	0
20.	So if someone upsets you, you probably do not respond, even though you may feel angry and hurt......	4	3	2	1	0
21.	Right now your worries about your health take up most of your time and energy, and your body is a constant source of anxiety and fear..................	4	3	2	1	0
22.	These fears and worries may be taking their toll and leaving you feeling extremely defeated, pessimistic and bitter, and you may find yourself resigned to living the rest of your life in constant illness and pain..	4	3	2	1	0
23.	So much of your time is spent worrying about your physical well-being that it's hard for you to find other interests or things you can accomplish without incurring additional pain............................	4	3	2	1	0
24.	Symptoms such as headaches, stomachaches, weakness, fatigue, and shakiness are all very likely common right now..	4	3	2	1	0
25.	You are shy, sensitive, and extremely uncomfortable with strangers and with large groups of people you do not know......................................	4	3	2	1	0
26.	Right now it may be hard for you to know just whom you can trust and share your feelings with, because you are so easily hurt...............................	4	3	2	1	0
27.	Even with people you know and care about, you don't					

	feel the need to express your caring and love in a physical way....................................	4	3	2	1	0
28.	Very likely you also feel uncomfortable in confrontations with others and will go out of your way to avoid conflict...............................	4	3	2	1	0
29.	Men with your profile usually have a good balance between their "masculine" and "feminine" interests....	4	3	2	1	0
30.	You probably enjoy cultural, verbal, and aesthetic activities, but you also enjoy some traditionally masculine ones......................................	4	3	2	1	0
31.	You can be as comfortable in your relationships with men as in your relationships with women..............	4	3	2	1	0
32.	You probably don't need constant updates or feedback on the status of your relationships..................	4	3	2	1	0
33.	Some of your answers suggest that you may be using alcohol or drugs as a way of relaxing or enhancing your level of excitement............................	4	3	2	1	0
34.	In fact, people giving such answers are prone to becoming addicted to such agents, causing possible disruptions at home, at work, or with personal health.	4	3	2	1	0
35.	In some cases, they do not actually use such chemicals themselves, but have had close relatives who were at some time dependent on them..............	4	3	2	1	0
36.	You keep your emotional experiences private...........	4	3	2	1	0
37.	You are probably uncomfortable expressing emotions, and may find the exploration of your feelings somewhat intrusive..................................	4	3	2	1	0
38.	You have difficulty dealing with your anger..........	4	3	2	1	0
39.	When people bother you, there are times when it is almost impossible not to lash out at them............	4	3	2	1	0
40.	Perhaps you break things or strike others when you are angry...	4	3	2	1	0
41.	Often your impulsivity and hot-headedness get you into trouble..	4	3	2	1	0
42.	It is difficult for you to trust people..............	4	3	2	1	0
43.	It is hard for you to let down your emotional guard, and be vulnerable with others.........................	4	3	2	1	0
44.	You see the world as a place where people use each other and can rarely be trusted......................	4	3	2	1	0
45.	You believe that showing signs of weakness will only lead to being taken advantage of by others...........	4	3	2	1	0
46.	It is hard for you to ask for support because you fear it might be used against you.....................	4	3	2	1	0
47.	You may have had some difficulty with the law and with authority figures...............................	4	3	2	1	0
48.	You probably feel that many rules and laws are foolish, and should not apply to you.................	4	3	2	1	0
49.	You may also enjoy seeing others cleverly break the rules..	4	3	2	1	0
50.	You probably enjoy getting the better of people in authority..	4	3	2	1	0
51.	The world may seem like a "dog-eat-dog" place, where you have to have power over others so they can not get power over you...........................	4	3	2	1	0
52.	The family you grew up with very likely showed little love, warmth, or support for you..............	4	3	2	1	0
53.	You probably felt uncared for as a child.............	4	3	2	1	0

54.	You may have been physically abused by at least one member of your family............................	4 3 2 1 0
55.	In any event, you grew up feeling that in times of stress you had to rely on your own resources in order to pull through............................	4 3 2 1 0
56.	In your present family, you may feel quite alone, so it is hard to be vulnerable and turn to family members for support................................	4 3 2 1 0
57.	You may experience difficulties at work right now.....	4 3 2 1 0
58.	Such difficulties could arise from your fear that you are unable to make good decisions.................	4 3 2 1 0
59.	They could also be related to your tendency to examine the details and possible negative consequences of a decision, which can leave you feeling overwhelmed, tense, and ineffectual...........	4 3 2 1 0
60.	Your work difficulties may be related to concerns that you may not have made the right career choice....	4 3 2 1 0
61.	Concerns about your career may stem from feelings that your family and friends do not support and approve of your career decision....................	4 3 2 1 0
62.	Perhaps you also feel unhappy with you employer and your co-workers................................	4 3 2 1 0
63.	You may have doubts and concerns about receiving helpful care from doctors and mental health professionals......................................	4 3 2 1 0
64.	You may feel that treatment for your problems will not be beneficial, so you feel reluctant to open up and talk about them........................	4 3 2 1 0
65.	In fact, you may feel so pessimistic about treatment that you would rather live with things the way they are, even if they get worse, rather than deal with the frustration and possible pain of changing..	4 3 2 1 0

END OF ISSUES

SELF-HELP (Suggestions of Things You Can Do)

1. Whenever you feel as though a dark mood is coming over you, see if in fact you have not felt unfairly treated or treated in a mean or angry way. See if you can confront the person you feel has treated you so badly.

2. Often medication can be useful in reducing the sudden surges of these moods and the periods of confusion and anxiety. If you are receiving professional help, you should discuss this with your therapist.

3. Whenever you feel depressed and alone try not to push away the people you once felt close to. Perhaps you can tell them at these times that you are feeling bad and want to be alone and that it is not your intent to abandon or reject them.

4. Whenever someone is irritating you and you feel a fight is coming on, try to leave the situation for a few moments to cool off. You can always return after you have had some time to think it through.

5. Deal with anger as it builds, so you are not storing resentments towards others leading to angry outbursts that can backfire against you.

6. Learn also to recognize when tension is building, so that you can escape from a stressful situation before you blow up or become violent.

7. Find a way to blow off steam every day, so that you can approach the difficulties of life in an easier and more relaxed manner.

8. Get involved in some type of charitable organization where you can see the immediate effects of doing something helpful for others.

9. Be open with people you care for about how you feel, so you can see that not all emotional vulnerability leads to letdowns and hurt.

10. Notice when tension and frustration are building-up inside of you, and find ways to relieve these in ways that are not illegal and won't get you into trouble.

11. Make a list of the times in the past when you did something impulsive to feel better, but later it backfired and got you into trouble with others.

12. If you are using drugs, you may need to join a support group such as AA or CA to help you recognize and deal with your related difficulties.

13. If you are receiving professional help, you and your therapist should examine when you do use chemicals in order to find alternative ways of dealing with what stresses you.

14. Take an assertiveness class or work with your therapist to help you believe in yourself and your ability to make good decisions at work.

15. When making work decisions, try to stay focused on the problem you're working on, and don't get lost in all the details and worries about what could go wrong.

16. Examine your possibly negative attitude towards your co-workers. It may leave you vulnerable to their anger and contribute to their lack of support for you.

17. Take some time to evaluate whether you are really happy in your choice of career, and whether you feel supported in your career by your family and friends.

18. If you are receiving professional help, discuss with your therapist any letdowns or disappointments you have experienced with doctors or mental health professionals in the past.

19. Make a list of things that trouble you but you feel hopeless about changing. Take one at a time and see if you can change it for the better even if by a small amount.

END OF SELF-HELP

*** END OF REPORT ***

Appendix A: Scoring Keys and Norms for MMPI–2 Scales and Critical Items

The following tables are based on the materials made available by the publisher and include all of the changes to the existing MMPI–2 manual, which is currently being revised. Means and standard deviations presented for each scale are based on the contemporary normative sample of 1,138 men and 1,462 women.

TABLE A.1

Standard Validity Measures and Other Measures of Response Style

L—Lie (15 Items)

True

None

False

16 29 41 51 77 93 102 107 123 139 153 183 203 232 260

Men: $M = 3.53$, $SD = 2.28$ Women: $M = 3.57$, $SD = 2.08$

F—Infrequency (60 Items)

True

18 24 30 36 42 48 54 60 66 72 84 96 114 138

144 150 156 162 168 180 198 216 228 234 240 246 252 258

264 270 282 288 294 300 306 312 324 336 349 355 361

False

6 12 78 90 102 108 120 126 132 174 186 192 204 210

222 276 318 330 343

Men: $M = 4.53$, $SD = 3.24$ Women: $M = 3.66$, $SD = 2.91$

FB—Infrequency Back (40 Items)

True

281 291 303 311 317 319 322 323 329 332 333 334 387 395

407 431 450 454 463 468 476 478 484 489 506 516 517 520

524 525 526 528 530 539 540 544 555

False

383 404 501

Men: $M = 1.86$, $SD = 2.44$ Women: $M = 1.94$, $SD = 2.58$

K–Correction (30 Items)

True

83

False

29 37 58 76 110 116 122 127 130 136 148 157 158 167

171 196 213 243 267 284 290 330 338 339 341 346 348 356

365

Men: $M = 15.30$, $SD = 4.76$ Women: $M = 15.03$, $SD = 4.58$

VRIN—Variable Response Inconsistency (67 Item-Response Pairs)

For each of the following response pairs, add 1 point:

3T–39T	125T–195T	349T–515F
6T–90F	125F–195F	349F–515T
6F–90T	135F–482T	350F–521T
9F–56F	136T–507F	353T–370F
28T–59F	136F–507T	353F–370T
31T–299F	152F–464F	364F–554T
32F–316T	161T–185F	369F–421T
40T–176T	161F–185T	372T–405F
46T–265F	165F–565F	372F–405T
48T–184T	166T–268F	380T–562F
49T–280F	166F–268T	395T–435F
73T–377F	167T–243F	395F–435T
81T–284F	167F–243T	396T–403F
81F–284T	196F–415T	396F–403T
83T–288T	199T–467F	411T–485F
84T–105F	199F–467T	411F–485T
86T–359F	226T–267F	472T–533F
95F–388T	259F–333T	472F–533T
99F–138T	262F–275F	491T–509F
103T–344F	290T–556F	506T–520F
110T–374F	290F–556T	506F–520T
110F–374T	339F–394T	513T–542F
116T–430F		

Men: $M = 5.07$, $SD = 2.62$ Women: $M = 5.04$, $SD = 2.51$

Note: T = true; F = false

TRIN—True Response Inconsistency (23 Item-Response Pairs)

1) For each of the following response pairs, add 1 point:

3T–39T	65T–95T	209T–351T
12T–166T	73T–239T	359T–367T
40T–176T	83T–288T	377T–534T
48T–184T	99T–314T	556T–560T
63T–127T	125T–195T	

2) For each of the following response pairs, subtract 1 point:

9F–56F	140F–196F	262F–275F
65 F–95F	152F–464F	265F–360F
125F–195F	165F–565F	359F–367F

3) Then add 9 points to the total raw score:

Men: $M = 8.95$, $SD = 1.41$ Women: $M = 9.00$, $SD = 1.32$

Note. T = true, F = false.

Ds—Dissimulation (58 Items)

True

11	17	18	19	22	28	30	31	40	42	44
54	61	72	81	85	92	111	166	190	195	205
221	252	258	268	274	287	292	294	300	307	310
320	329	362	395	412	419	421	425	431	433	435
436	451	458	463							

False

57	75	83	108	125	188	278	318	404	429

Men: $M = 10.08$, $SD = 5.32$ Women: $M = 10.57$, $SD = 5.64$

F(p)—Infrequency–Psychopathology (27 Items)

True

66	114	162	193	216	228	252	270	282	291	294
322	323	336	371	387	478	555				

False

51	77	90	93	102	126	192	276	501

Men: $M = 1.16$, $SD = 1.38$ Women: $M = 1.03$, $SD = 1.26$

F(p1)—(14 Items)

True

66	114	162	193	216	228	252

False

51	77	90	93	102	126	192

Men: $M = 0.67$, $SD = 0.96$ Women: $M = 0.47$, $SD = 0.79$

F(p2)—(13 Items)

True

270 282 291 294 322 323 336 371 387 478 555

False

276 501

Men: $M = 0.49$, $SD = 0.80$ Women: $M = 0.56$, $SD = 0.84$

Mp—Positive Malingering (26 Items)

True

131 133 191 201 211 239 261 345 350 356 417

False

21 29 41 89 93 183 189 196 203 209 232 290 341 428 442

Men: $M = 9.70$, $SD = 3.52$ Women: $M = 8.35$, $SD = 3.26$

Sd—Social Desirability (33 items)

True

25 49 80 100 131 133 184 194 201 206 207

211 220 249 257 263 345 351 354 356 366 402

416 439

False

29 41 77 93 183 203 232 326 341

Men: $M = 12.92$, $SD = 3.74$ Women: $M = 12.11$, $SD = 3.32$

S—Superlative (50 Items)

True

121 148 184 194 534 560

False

15 50 58 76 81 87 89 104 110 120 123

154 196 205 213 225 264 279 284 290 302 337

341 346 352 373 374 403 420 423 428 430 433

442 445 449 461 486 487 523 538 542 545 547

Men: $M = 25.02$, $SD = 8.69$ Women: $M = 25.48$, $SD = 8.29$

S1—Belief in Human Goodness (15 Items)

True

None

False

50 58 76 81 104 110 120 225 284 346 352 374 403 445 538

Men: *M* = 7.30, *SD* = 3.83 Women: *M* = 7.90, *SD* = 3.75

S2—Serenity (13 Items)

True

148 194

False

87 89 154 196 279 337 341 433 442 545 547

Men: *M* = 6.08, *SD* = 2.73 Women: *M* = 5.49, *SD* = 2.62

S3—Contentment with Life (8 Items)

True

534 560

False

15 205 290 428 449 542

Men: *M* = 4.02, *SD* = 1.96 Women: *M* = 3.58, *SD* = 1.88

S4—Patience and Denial of Irritability or Anger (8 Items)

True

None

False

213 302 420 423 430 461 486 523

Men: *M* = 4.22, *SD* = 2.15 Women: *M* = 4.37, *SD* = 2.02

S5—Denial of Moral Flaws (5 Items)

True

121

False

123 264 373 487

Men: *M* = 2.91, *SD* = 1.38 Women: *M* = 3.61, *SD* = 1.28

Ss—Socioeconomic Status (73 Items)

True

2 41 139 151 160 203 217 224 232 362 385 427 456

False														
5	17	24	28	30	32	42	44	53	60	70	80	83		
101	109													
111	119	133	135	145	149	175	193	197	198	201	218	220	225	229
234	235	238	240	241	253	254	286	294	305	307	309	312	319	332
333	334	348	357	392	396	397	399	403	407	429	431	438	471	472

Men: $M = 57.27$, $SD = 6.37$ Women: $M = 56.81$, $SD = 6.50$

TABLE A.2

Standard Clinical Scales and Their Derivatives

Scale 1 (Hs)—Hypochondriasis (32 Items)

True

18	28	39	53	59	97	101	111	149	175	247			

False

2	3	8	10	20	45	47	57	91	117	141	143	152	164
173	176	179	208	224	249	255							

Raw scores without *K*:

Men: *M* = 4.92, *SD* = 3.87   Women: *M* = 5.93, *SD* = 4.51

Raw Score with K:

Men: *M* = 12.84, *SD* = 3.82   Women: *M* = 13.70, *SD* = 4.05

Scale 2 (D)—Depression (57 Items)

True

5	15	18	31	38	39	46	56	73	92	117	127	130	146
147	170	175	181	215	233								

False

2	9	10	20	29	33	37	43	45	49	55	68	75	76
95	109	118	134	140	141	142	143	148	165	178	188	189	212
221	223	226	238	245	248	260	267	330					

Men: *M* = 18.32, *SD* = 4.59   Women: *M* = 20.14, *SD* = 4.97

D-O—Depression–Obvious (39 Items)

True

15	18	31	38	39	46	56	73	92	127	130	146	147	170
175	215	233											

False

2	9	10	20	33	43	45	49	75	95	109	118	140	141
142	165	188	223	245	248	260	330						

Men: *M* = 7.72, *SD* = 4.29   Women: *M* = 8.75, *SD* = 4.88

D-S—Depression–Subtle (18 Items)

True

5	117	181

False

29 37 55 68 76 134 143 148 178 189 212 221 226 238 267

Men: $M = 10.60$, $SD = 2.61$ Women: $M = 11.39$, $SD = 2.44$

D1—Subjective Depression (32 Items)

True

31 38 39 46 56 73 92 127 130 146 147 170 175 215 233

False

2 9 43 49 75 95 109 118 140 148 178 188 189 223 260 267 330

Men: $M = 6.86$, $SD = 3.79$ Women: $M = 7.65$, $SD = 4.21$

D2—Psychomotor Retardation (14 Items)

True

38 46 170 233

False

9 29 37 49 55 76 134 188 189 212

Men: $M = 5.34$, $SD = 1.82$ Women: $M = 5.74$, $SD = 1.83$

D3—Physical Malfunctioning (11 Items)

True

18 117 175 181

False

2 20 45 141 142 143 148

Men: $M = 2.89$, $SD = 1.23$ Women: $M = 3.22$, $SD = 1.36$

D4—Mental Dullness (15 Items)

True

15 31 38 73 92 147 170 233

False

9 10 43 75 109 165 188

Men: $M = 2.42$, $SD = 2.09$ Women: $M = 2.55$, $SD = 2.21$

D5—Brooding (10 Items)

True

38 56 92 127 130 146 170 215

False

75 95

Men: *M* = 1.83, *SD* = 1.77 Women: *M* = 2.50, *SD* = 1.95

Scale 3 (Hy)—Conversion Hysteria (60 Items)

True

11 18 31 39 40 44 65 101 166 172 175 218 230

False

2 3 7 8 9 10 14 26 29 45 47 58 76 81
91 95 98 110 115 116 124 125 129 135 141 148 151 152
157 159 161 164 167 173 176 179 185 193 208 213 224 241
243 249 253 263 265

Men: *M* = 20.87, *SD* = 4.73 Women: *M* = 22.08, *SD* = 4.73

Hy-O—Hysteria–Obvious (32 Items)

True

11 18 31 39 40 44 65 101 166 172 175 218

False

2 3 8 9 10 45 47 91 95 115 125 141 152 159
164 173 179 208 224 249

Men: *M* = 4.78, *SD* = 3.61 Women: *M* = 5.67, *SD* = 4.21

Hy-S—Hysteria–Subtle (28 Items)

True

230

False

7 14 26 29 58 76 81 98 110 116 124 129 135 148
151 157 161 167 176 185 193 213 241 243 253 263 265

Men: *M* = 16.09, *SD* = 4.31 Women: *M* = 16.41, *SD* = 4.09

Hy1—Denial of Social Anxiety (6 Items)

True

None

False

129 161 167 185 243

Men: $M = 3.89$, $SD = 1.86$ Women: $M = 3.85$, $SD = 1.87$

Hy2—Need for Affection (12 Items)

True

230

False

26 58 76 81 98 110 124 151 213 241 263

Men: $M = 6.69$, $SD = 2.58$ Women: $M = 6.88$, $SD = 2.44$

Hy3—Lassitude–Malaise (15 Items)

True

31 39 65 175 218

False

2 3 9 10 45 95 125 141 148 152

Men: $M = 2.55$, $SD = 2.20$ Women: $M = 2.73$, $SD = 2.48$

Hy4—Somatic Complaints (17 Items)

True

11 18 40 44 101 172

False

8 47 91 159 164 173 176 179 208 224 249

Men: $M = 2.50$, $SD = 2.06$ Women: $M = 3.22$, $SD = 2.53$

Hy5—Inhibition of Aggression (7 Items)

True

None

False

7 14 29 115 116 135 157

Men: $M = 3.29$, $SD = 1.32$ Women: $M = 3.46$, $SD = 1.29$

Scale 4 (Pd)—Psychopathic Deviate (50 Items)													
True													
17	21	22	31	32	35	42	52	54	56	71	82	89	94
99	105	113	195	202	219	225	259	264	288				
False													
9	12	34	70	79	83	95	122	125	129	143	157	158	
160	167	171	185	209	214	217	226	243	261	263	266	267	

Raw scores without *K*:

Men: $M = 16.57$, $SD = 4.60$ Women: $M = 16.21$, $SD = 4.65$

Raw Score with K:

Men: $M = 22.69$, $SD = 4.63$ Women: $M = 22.22$, $SD = 4.52$

Pd-O—Psychopathic Deviate–Obvious (28 Items)													
True													
17	22	31	32	35	42	52	54	56	71	82	94	99	105
195	202	225	259	264	288								
False													
9	12	34	79	95	125	261	266						

Men: $M = 6.16$, $SD = 3.74$ Women: $M = 5.40$, $SD = 3.72$

Pd-S—Psychopathic Deviate–Subtle (22 Items)													
True													
21	89	113	219										
False													
70	83	122	129	143	157	158	160	167	171	185	209	214	217
226	243	263	267										

Men $M = 10.41$, $SD = 2.58$ Women: $M = 10.80$, $SD = 2.48$

Pd1—Familial Discord (9 Items)					
True					
	21	54	195	202	288
False					
	83	125	214	217	

Men $M = 1.78$, $SD = 1.52$ Women: $M = 2.05$, $SD = 1.65$

Pd2—Authority Problems (8 Items)

True					
35	105				
False					
34	70	129	160	263	266

Men: $M = 3.48$, $SD = 1.50$ Women: $M = 2.55$, $SD = 1.29$

Pd3—Social Imperturbability (6 Items)

True

None

False

70	129	158	167	185	243

Men: $M = 3.83$, $SD = 1.69$ Women: $M = 3.58$, $SD = 1.71$

Pd4—Social Alienation (13 Items)

True									
17	22	42	56	82	99	113	219	225	259
False									
12	129	157							

Men: $M = 3.93$, $SD = 1.90$ Women: $M = 4.18$, $SD = 1.89$

Pd5—Self-Alienation (12 Items)

True									
31	32	52	56	71	82	89	94	113	264
False									
9	95								

Men: $M = 3.39$, $SD = 2.08$ Women: $M = 3.35$, $SD = 2.07$

Scale 5 (Mf-m)—Masculinity–Femininity (Masculine; 56 Items)

True													
4	25	62	64	67	74	80	112	119	122	128	137	166	177
187	191	196	205	209	219	236	251	256	268	271			
False													
1	19	26	27	63	68	69	76	86	103	104	107	120	121
132	133	163	184	193	194	197	199	201	207	231	235	237	239
254	257	272											

Men: $M = 26.01$, $SD = 5.08$

Scale 5 (Mf-f)—Masculinity–Femininity (Feminine; 56 Items)													
True													
4	25	62	64	67	74	80	112	119	121	122	128	137	177
187	191	196	205	219	236	251	256	271					
False													
1	19	26	27	63	68	69	76	86	103	104	107	120	132
133	163	166	184	193	194	197	199	201	207	209	231	235	237
239	254	257	268	272									
Women: $M = 35.94$, $SD = 4.08$													

Martin–Finn Subscales for Scale 5 (Masculinity–Femininity)

Mf1—Denial of Stereotypic Masculine Interests (11 Items)										
True										
None										
False										
1	69	133	197	199	201	417	465	467	474	477
Men: $M = 4.98$, $SD = 2.29$					Women: $M = 8.20$, $SD = 1.96$					
Mf2—Hypersensitivity–Anxiety (13 Items)										
True										
166	196	205	219	251	256	268	271			
False										
63	184	194	237	239						
Men: $M = 5.04$, $SD = 2.66$					Women: $M = 6.12$, $SD = 2.65$					
Mf3—Stereotypical Feminine Interests (6 Items)										
True										
4	64	74	80	119	236					
False										
None										
Men: $M = 1.35$, $SD = 1.25$					Women: $M = 3.15$, $SD = 1.40$					
Mf4—Low Cynicism (6 Items)										
True										
None										
False										
26	27	76	104	193	254					
Men: $M = 4.13$, $SD = 1.44$					Women: $M = 4.44$, $SD = 1.35$					
Mf5—Aesthetic Interests (5 Items)										
True										
25	67	112	187	191						
False										
None										
Men: $M = 2.12$, $SD = 1.48$					Women: $M = 2.67$, $SD = 1.37$					
Mf6—Feminine Gender Identity (5 Items)										
True										

62 371[a] 384 426

False

272 371[b]

Men $M = 1.32$, $SD = 1.10$ Women: $M = 4.34$, $SD = 0.91$

[A]Men only. [B]Women only.

Mf7—Restraint (6 Items)

True

None

False

19 68 86 207 209 231

Men: $M = 3.68$, $SD = 1.48$ Women: $M = 4.26$, $SD = 1.35$

F – M —Composite Femininity–Masculinity (22 Items)

True

4 62 64 74 80 119 236 371a 384 426

False

1 69 133 197 199 201 272 371b 417 465 467 474 477

Men: $M = 7.66$, $SD = 2.79$ Women: $M = 15.69$, $SD = 2.63$

[A]Men only. [B]Women only.

Scale 6 (Pa)—Paranoia (40 Items)

True

16 17 22 23 24 42 99 113 138 144 145 146 162 234 259 271 277 285 305 307 333 334 336 355 361

False

81 95 98 100 104 110 244 255 266 283 284 286 297 314 315

Men: $M = 10.10$, $SD = 2.87$ Women: $M = 10.23$, $SD = 2.97$

Pa-O—Paranoia–Obvious (23 Items)

True

17 22 23 24 42 99 138 144 146 162 234 259 277 285 305 307 333 336 355 361

False

255 266 314

Men: $M = 2.55$, $SD = 2.19$ Women: $M = 2.76$, $SD = 2.33$

Pa-S—Paranoia–Subtle (17 Items)

True

16 113 145 271 334

False

81 95 98 100 104 110 244 283 284 286 297 315

Men: $M = 7.55$, $SD = 2.36$ Women: $M = 7.47$, $SD = 2.34$

Pa1—Ideas of External Influence (17 Items)

True

17 22 42 99 113 138 144 145 162 234 259 305 333 336

355 361

False

314

Men: $M = 1.74$, $SD = 1.66$ Women: $M = 1.79$, $SD = 1.67$

Pa2—Poignancy (9 Items)

True

22 146 271 277 285 307 334

False

100 244

Men: $M = 2.36$, $SD = 1.43$ Women: $M = 2.57$, $SD = 1.58$

Pa3—Moral Virtue (9 Items)

True

16

False

81 98 104 110 283 284 286 315

Men: $M = 4.84$, $SD = 2.09$ Women: $M = 4.95$, $SD = 2.09$

Scale 7 (Pt)—Psychasthenia (48 Items)

True

11 16 23 31 38 56 65 73 82 89 94 130 147 170

175 196 218 242 273 275 277 285 289 301 302 304 308 309

310 313 316 317 320 325 326 327 328 329 331

False

3 9 33 109 140 165 174 293 321

Raw scores without K:

Men: $M = 11.24$, $SD = 6.61$ Women: $M = 12.69$, $SD = 7.19$

Raw Score with K:

Men: $M = 26.54$, $SD = 4.82$ Women: $M = 27.72$, $SD = 5.07$

Scale 8 (Sc)—Schizophrenia (78 Items)

True

16 17 21 22 23 31 32 35 38 42 44 46 48 65
85 92 138 145 147 166 168 170 180 182 190 218 221 229
233 234 242 247 252 256 268 273 274 277 279 281 287 291
292 296 298 299 303 307 311 316 319 320 322 323 325 329
332 333 355

False

6 9 12 34 90 91 106 165 177 179 192 210 255 276
278 280 290 295 343

Raw scores without K:

Men: $M = 11.20$, $SD = 7.12$ Women: $M = 11.24$, $SD = 7.57$

Raw Score with K:

Men: $M = 26.50$, $SD = 5.73$ Women: $M = 26.27$, $SD = 5.93$

Sc1—Social Alienation (21 Items)

True

17 21 22 42 46 138 145 190 221 256 277 281 291 292
320 333

False

90 276 278 280 343

Men: $M = 2.72$, $SD = 2.42$ Women: $M = 3.11$, $SD = 2.59$

Sc2—Emotional Alienation (11 Items)

True

65 92 234 273 303 323 329 332

False

9 210 290

Men: $M = 1.05$, $SD = 1.04$ Women: $M = 1.12$, $SD = 1.09$

Sc3—Lack of Ego Mastery, Cognitive (10 Items)

True

31 32 147 170 180 299 311 316 325

False

165

Men: $M = 1.31$, $SD = 1.66$ Women: $M = 1.18$, $SD = 1.62$

Sc4—Lack of Ego Mastery, Conative (14 Items)

True

31 38 48 65 92 233 234 273 299 303 325

False

9 210 290

Men: $M = 2.13$, $SD = 1.85$ Women: $M = 2.17$, $SD = 1.95$

Sc5—Lack of Ego Mastery, Defective Inhibition (11 Items)

True

23 85 168 182 218 242 274 320 322 329 355

False

None

Men: $M = 1.42$, $SD = 1.43$ Women: $M = 1.57$, $SD = 1.57$

Sc6—Sensorimotor Dissociation (20 Items)

True

23 32 44 168 182 229 247 252 296 298 307 311 319 355

False

91 106 177 179 255 295

Men: $M = 1.90$, $SD = 2.04$ Women: $M = 2.07$, $SD = 2.20$

Scale 9 (Ma)—Hypomania (46 Items)

True

13 15 21 23 50 55 61 85 87 98 113 122 131 145
155 168 169 182 190 200 205 206 211 212 218 220 227 229
238 242 244 248 250 253 269

False

88 93 100 106 107 136 154 158 167 243 263

Raw scores without *K*:

Men: $M = 16.88$, $SD = 4.51$ Women: $M = 16.07$, $SD = 4.49$

Raw score with *K*:

Men: M = 19.95, SD = 4.28 Women: M = 19.09, SD = 4.26

Ma-O—Hypomania–Obvious (23 Items)

True

15 23 50 61 85 87 145 155 168 182 190 205 218 227

229 238 242 250 253 269

False

100 106 107

Men: M = 6.84, SD = 2.95 Women: M = 6.38, SD = 2.97

Ma-S—Hypomania–Subtle (23 Items)

True

13 21 55 98 113 122 131 169 200 206 211 212 220 244

248

False

88 93 136 154 158 167 243 263

Men: M = 10.04, SD = 2.68 Women: M = 9.69, SD = 2.60

Ma1—Amorality (6 Items)

True

131 227 248 250 269

False

263

Men: M = 1.97, SD = 1.29 Women: M = 1.56, SD = 1.20

Ma2—Psychomotor Acceleration (11 Items)

True

15 85 87 122 169 206 218 242 244

False

100 106

Men: M = 5.29, SD = 2.07 Women: M = 5.07, SD = 1.99

Ma3—Imperturbability (8 Items)

True

155 200 220

False

93 136 158 167 243

Men: M = 3.51, SD = 1.66 Women: M = 3.06, SD = 1.56

Ma4—Ego Inflation (9 Items)													
True													
13	50	55	61	98	145	190	211	212					
False													
None													
Men: $M = 3.04$, $SD = 1.53$						Women: $M = 3.09$, $SD = 1.64$							

Scale 0 (Si)—Social Introversion (69 Items)													
True													
31	56	70	100	104	110	127	135	158	161	167	185	215	243
251	265	275	284	289	296	302	308	326	328	337	338	347	348
351	352	357	358	364	367	368	369						
False													
25	32	49	79	86	106	112	131	181	189	207	209	231	237
255	262	267	280	321	335	340	342	344	345	350	353	354	359
360	362	363	366	370									
Men: $M = 24.74$, $SD = 8.84$						Women: $M = 26.90$, $SD = 9.46$							

Si1—Shyness/Self-Consciousness (14 Items)													
True													
158	161	167	185	243	265	275	289						
False													
49	262	280	321	342	360								
Men: $M = 4.80$, $SD = 3.44$						Women: $M = 5.31$, $SD = 3.69$							

Si2—Social Avoidance (8 Items)													
True													
337	367												
False													
86	340	353	359	363	370								
Men: $M = 3.12$, $SD = 2.33$						Women: $M = 2.75$, $SD = 2.19$							

Si3—Self–Other Alienation (17 Items)													
True													
31	56	104	110	135	284	302	308	326	328	338	347	348	358
364	368	369											

False

None

Men $M = 4.99$, $SD = 3.35$	Women: $M = 5.23$, $SD = 3.59$

TABLE A.3
MMPI–2 Content Scales and Content Component Subscales

ANX—Anxiety (23 Items)

True

15 30 31 39 170 196 273 290 299 301 305 339 408 415 463
469 509 556

False

140 208 223 405 496

Men: $M = 5.53$, $SD = 4.17$ Women: $M = 6.53$, $SD = 4.51$

FRS—Fears (23 Items)

True

154 317 322 329 334 392 395 397 435 438 441 447 458 468 471
555

False

115 163 186 385 401 453 462

Men: $M = 3.80$, $SD = 2.96$ Women: $M = 6.59$, $SD = 3.60$

FRS1—Generalized Fearfulness (12 Items)

True

317 322 329 334 395 435 441 447 468 471 555

False

186

Men: $M = .65$, $SD = 1.11$ Women: $M = 1.21$, $SD = 1.52$

FRS2—Multiple Fears (10 Items)

True

154 392 438 458

False

115 163 385 401 453 462

Men: $M = 3.59$, $SD = 2.04$ Women: $M = 5.54$, $SD = 2.27$

OBS—Obsessiveness (16 Items)

True

55 87 135 196 309 313 327 328 394 442 482 491 497 509 547
553

False

None

Men: M = 4.93, SD = 3.06 Women: M = 5.50, SD = 3.32

DEP—Depression (33 Items)

True

38 52 56 65 71 82 92 130 146 215 234 246 277 303 306
331 377 399 400 411 454 506 512 516 520 539 546 554

False

3 9 75 95 388

Men: M = 4.79, SD = 4.62 Women: M = 5.86, SD = 5.02

DEP1—Lack of Drive (12 Items)

True

38 71 92 399 400 512 516 539 554

False

3 9 75

Men: M = 1.72, SD = 1.82 Women: M = 1.98, SD = 1.99

DEP2—Dysphoria (6 Items)

True

56 65 146 215

False

95 388

Men: M = .87, SD = 1.17 Women: M = 1.07, SD = 1.33

DEP3—Self-Depreciation (7 Items)

True

52 82 130 234 246 377 411

False

None

Men: M = 1.21, SD = 1.41 Women: M = 1.30, SD = 1.43

DEP4—Suicidal Ideation (5 Items)

True

303 454 506 520 546

False

None

Men: M = .25, SD = .60 Women: M = .27, SD = .63

HEA—Health Concerns (36 Items)

True

11 18 28 36 40 44 53 59 97 101 111 149 175 247

False

20 33 45 47 57 91 117 118 141 142 159 164 176 179 181
194 204 224 249 255 295 404

Men: $M = 5.29$, $SD = 3.91$ Women: $M = 6.16$, $SD = 4.47$

HEA1—Gastrointestinal Symptoms (5 Items)

True

18 59 111

False

20 47

Men: M = .45, SD = .77 Women: M = .62, SD = .93

HEA2—Neurological Symptoms (12 Items)

True

44 53 101 149 247

False

91 142 159 164 179 255 295

Men: $M = 1.40$, $SD = 1.50$ Women: $M = 1.86$, $SD = 1.83$

HEA3—General Health Concerns (6 Items)

True

175

False

33 45 118 141 224

Men: $M = 1.15$, $SD = 1.24$ Women: $M = 1.18$, $SD = 1.29$

BIZ—Bizarre Mentation (23 Items)

True

24 32 60 96 138 162 198 228 259 298 311 316 319 333 336
355 361 466 490 508 543 551

False

427

Men: $M = 2.30$, $SD = 2.50$ Women: $M = 2.21$, $SD = 2.49$

BIZ1—Psychotic Symptomatology (11 Items)

True

24 60 96 138 162 228 336 355 361 508 551

False

None

Men: $M = .50$, $SD = .85$ Women: $M = .42$, $SD = .73$

BIZ2—Schizotypal Characteristics (9 Items)

True

32 259 298 311 316 319 333 466 543

False

None

Men: $M = 1.36$, $SD = 1.54$ Women: $M = 1.33$, $SD = 1.60$

ANG—Anger (16 Items)

True

29 37 116 134 302 389 410 414 430 461 486 513 540 542 548

False

564

Men: $M = 5.63$, $SD = 3.31$ Women: $M = 5.68$, $SD = 3.08$

ANG1—Explosive Behavior (7 Items)

True

37 134 389 414 540 548

False

564

Men: $M = 1.68$, $SD = 1.57$ Women: $M = 1.40$, $SD = 1.34$

ANG2—Irritability (7 Items)

True

116 302 430 461 486 513 542

False

None

Men $M = 2.71$, $SD = 1.91$ Women: $M = 3.09$, $SD = 1.92$

CYN–Cynicism (23 Items)

True

50 58 76 81 104 110 124 225 241 254 283 284 286 315 346

352 358 374 399 403 445 470 538

False

None

Men: $M = 9.50$, $SD = 5.35$ Women: $M = 8.73$, $SD = 5.16$

CYN1—Misanthropic Beliefs (15 Items)

True

58 76 81 104 110 241 254 283 284 286 352 374 399

470 538

False

None

Men: $M = 6.16$, $SD = 3.68$ Women: $M = 5.71$, $SD = 3.57$

CYN2—Interpersonal Suspiciousness (8 Items)

True

50 124 225 315 346 358 403 445

False

None

Men: $M = 3.34$, $SD = 2.17$ Women: $M = 3.02$, $SD = 2.10$

ASP—Antisocial Practices (22 Items)

True

26 35 66 81 84 104 105 110 123 227 240 248 250 254 269

283 284 374 412 418 419

False

266

Men: $M = 7.91$, $SD = 4.19$ Women: $M = 6.17$, $SD = 3.70$

ASP1—Antisocial Attitudes (16 Items)

True

26 66 81 104 110 123 227 248 250 254 269 248 283

284 374 418 419

False

None

Men: $M = 6.22$, $SD = 3.49$ Women: $M = 5.33$, $SD = 3.27$

ASF2—Antisocial Behavior (5 Items)

True

35 84 105 412

False

266

Men: $M = 1.63$, $SD = 1.39$ Women: $M = .80$, $SD = 1.03$

TPA—Type A (19 Items)

True

27 136 151 212 302 358 414 419 420 423 430 437 507 510 523
531 535 541 545

False

None

Men: $M = 8.08$, $SD = 3.68$ Women: $M = 7.41$, $SD = 3.34$

TPA1—Impatience (6 Items)

True

302 420 430 507 523 535

False

None

Men: $M = 2.74$, $SD = 1.73$ Women: $M = 2.62$, $SD = 1.64$

TPA2–Competitive Drive (9 Items)

True

27 151 212 358 419 423 510 531 545

False

None

Men: $M = 3.81$, $SD = 1.95$ Women: $M = 3.41$, $SD = 1.74$

LSE—Low Self-Esteem (24 Items)

True

70 73 130 235 326 369 376 380 411 421 450 457 475 476 483
485 503 504 519 526 562

False

61 78 109

Men: $M = 4.25$, $SD = 3.69$ Women: $M = 5.16$, $SD = 4.24$

LSE1—Self-Doubt (11 Items)

True

73 130 326 411 450 483 485 504

False

61 78 109

Men: $M = 2.06$, $SD = 1.97$ Women: $M = 2.33$, $SD = 2.19$

LSE2—Submissiveness (6 Items)

True

70 369 421 457 503 519

False

None

Men: $M = 1.25$, $SD = 1.41$ Women: $M = 1.78$, $SD = 1.68$

SOD—Social Discomfort (24 Items)

True

46 158 167 185 265 275 281 337 349 367 479 480 515

False

49 86 262 280 321 340 353 359 360 363 370

Men: $M = 7.65$, $SD = 4.77$ Women: $M = 7.53$, $SD = 4.80$

SOD1—Introversion (16 Items)

True

46 265 281 337 349 367 480 515

False

49 86 280 340 353 359 363 370

Men: $M = 4.7$, $SD = 3.46$ Women: $M = 4.23$, $SD = 3.27$

SOD2—Shyness (7 Items)

True

158 167 185 275

False

262 321 360

Men: $M = 2.51$, $SD = 1.84$ Women: $M = 2.93$, $SD = 2.04$

FAM–Family Problems (25 Items)

True

21 54 145 190 195 205 256 292 300 323 378 379 382 413 449
478 543 550 563 567

False

83 125 217 383 455

Men: $M = 5.32$, $SD = 3.52$ Women: $M = 6.14$, $SD = 3.77$

FAM1—Family Discord (12 Items)

True

21 54 190 205 256 323 378 382 449 478 563

False

83

Men: $M = 2.86$, $SD = 2.01$ Women: $M = 3.47$, $SD = 2.07$

FAM2—Familial Alienation (5 Items)

True

195 550

False

217 383 455

Men: $M = 1.06$, $SD = 1.13$ Women: $M = .97$, $SD = 1.10$

WRK—Work Interference (33 Items)

True

15 17 31 54 73 98 135 233 243 299 302 339 364 368 394
409 428 445 464 491 505 509 517 525 545 554 559 566

False

10 108 318 521 561

Men: $M = 7.30$, $SD = 4.98$ Women: $M = 8.51$, $SD = 5.45$

TRT—Negative Treatment Indicators (26 Items)

True

22 92 274 306 364 368 373 375 376 377 391 399 482 488 491
495 497 499 500 504 528 539 554

False

493 494 501

Men: $M = 4.70$, $SD = 3.71$ Women: $M = 5.02$, $SD = 3.98$

TRT1—Low Motivation (11 Items)

True

92 364 368 376 491 497 500 528 539 554

False	
494	
Men: *M* = 1.26, *SD* = 1.70	Women: *M* = 1.72, *SD* = 1.98

TRT2—Inability to Disclose (5 Items)	
True	
274 373 375 391 495	
False	
None	
Men: *M* = 1.62, *SD* = 1.31	Women: *M* = 1.52, *SD* = 1.35

Errata for Friedman et al., *Psychological Assessment of the MMPI-2*. Table A.4 should read as follows:

TABLE A.4

The Personality Psychopathology Five (PSY–5)

AGG—Aggressiveness (18 Items)

True

27 50 85 134 239 323 324 346 350 358 414 423

452 521 548

False

70 446 503

Men: *M* = 8.20, *SD* = 2.97 Women: *M* = 6.78, *SD* = 2.81

PSY—Psychoticism (25 Items)

True

24 42 48 72 96 99 138 144 198 241 259 315

319 336 355 361 374 448 466 490 508 549 551

False

184 427

Men: *M* = 3.59, *SD* = 2.77 Women: *M* = 3.41, *SD* = 2.76

Disconstraint (29 Items)

True

35 84 88 103 105 123 209 222 250

284 344 362 385 412 417 418 431 477

False

34 100 121 126 154 263 266 309 351

402 497

Men: *M* = 13.93, *SD* = 3.90 Women: *M* = 10.27, *SD* = 3.67

NEN—Negative Emotionality/Neuroticism (33 Items)

True

37 52 82 93 116 166 196 213 290 301 305 329 375 389 390

395 397

False

63 223 372 405 496 564

Men: *M* = 9.42, *SD* = 5.45 Women: *M* = 11.22, *SD* = 5.72

LPE—Low Positive Emotionality/Extraversion (34 Items)

TABLE A.4

The Personality Psychopathology Five (PSY–5)

AGG—Aggressiveness (18 Items)

True

27 50 85 134 239 323 324 346 350 358 414 423

452 521 548

False

70 446 503

Men: $M = 8.20$, $SD = 2.97$ Women: $M = 6.80$, $SD = 2.81$

PSY—Psychoticism (25 Items)

True

24 42 48 72 96 99 138 144 198 241 259 315

319 336 355 361 374 448 466 490 508 549 551

False

184 427

Men: $M = 3.58$, $SD = 2.74$ Women: $M = 3.42$, $SD = 2.76$

Disconstraint (29 Items)

True

35 84 88 103 105 123 209 222 250

284 344 362 385 412 417 418 431 477

False

34 100 121 126 154 263 266 309 351

402 497

Men: $M = 13.9$, $SD = 3.90$ Women: $M = 10.27$, $SD = 3.67$

NEN—Negative Emotionality/Neuroticism (33 Items)

True

37 52 82 93 116 166 196 213 290 301 305 329 375 389 390

395 397

False

63 223 372 405 496 564

Men: $M = 9.44$, $SD = 5.45$ Women: $M = 23.26$, $SD = 5.72$

LPE—Low Positive Emotionality/Extraversion (34 Items)

True

38	56	233	515	517						

False

9	49	61	75	78	86	95	109	131	174	188
189	207	226	231	244	267	318	330	340	342	343
353	356	359	370	460	531	534				

Men: *M* = 11.00, *SD* = 4.49 Women: *M* = *10.67, SD* = 4.18

True

38	56	233	515	517						

False

9	49	61	75	78	86	95	109	131	174	188
189	207	226	231	244	267	318	330	340	342	343
353	356	359	370	460	531	534				

Men: *M* = 11.00, *SD* = 4.49 Women: *M* = *10.67*, *SD* = 4.18

TABLE A.5
Supplementary Scales

A—Anxiety (39 Items)

True

31 38 56 65 82 127 135 215 233 243 251 273 277 289 301
309 310 311 325 328 338 339 341 347 390 391 394 400 408 411
415 421 428 442 448 451 464 469

False

388

Men: $M = 10.02$, $SD = 7.10$ Women: $M = 11.64$, $SD = 7.90$

R—Repression (37 Items)

True

None

False

1 7 10 14 37 45 69 112 118 120 128 134 142 168
178 189 197 199 248 255 256 297 330 346 350 353 354 359
363 365 422 423 430 432 449 456 465

Men: $M = 15.18$, $SD = 4.53$ Women: $M = 16.34$, $SD = 3.81$

Es—Ego Strength (52 items)

True

2 33 45 98 141 159 169 177 179 189 199 209 213 230
245 323 385 406 413 425

False

23 31 32 36 39 53 60 70 82 87 119 128 175 196
215 221 225 229 236 246 307 310 316 328 391 394 441 447
458 464 469 471

Men: $M = 37.34$, $SD = 4.46$ Women: $M = 34.37$, $SD = 4.90$

O-H—Overcontrolled–Hostility (28 Items)

True

67 79 207 286 305 398 471

False

1 15 29 69 77 89 98 116 117 129 153 169 171 293
390 400 420 433 440 460

Men: $M = 12.51$, $SD = 2.94$ Women: $M = 13.53$, $SD = 2.74$

Do—Dominance (25 Items)

True

55 207 232 245 386 416

False

31 52 70 73 82 172 201 202 220 227 243 244 275 309
399 412 470 473

Men: $M = 16.62$, $SD = 2.95$ Women: $M = 16.27$, $SD = 2.89$

Re—Social Responsibility (30 Items)

True

100 160 199 266 440 467

False

7 27 29 32 84 103 105 145 164 169 201 202 235 275
412 417 418 430 431 432 456 468 470

Men: $M = 20.09$, $SD = 3.89$ Women: $M = 21.02$, $SD = 3.36$

GM–Gender Role-Masculine (47 Items)

True

8 20 143 152 159 163 176 199 214 237 321 350 385 388 401
440 462 467 474

False

4 23 44 64 70 73 74 80 100 137 146 187 289 331 351
364 392 395 435 438 441 469 471 498 509 519 532 536

Men: $M = 37.87$, $SD = 4.87$ Women: $M = 28.83$, $SD = 6.51$

GF—Gender Role—Feminine (46 Items)

True

62 67 119 121 128 203 263 266 353 384 426 449 456 473 552

False

1 27 63 68 79 84 105 123 133 155 197 201 220 231 238
239 250 257 264 272 287 406 417 465 477 487 510 511 537 548
550

Men: $M = 27.93$, $SD = 4.72$ Women: $M = 37.68$, $SD = 3.88$

Mt—College Maladjustment (41 Items)

True

15 16 28 31 38 71 73 81 82 110 130 215 218 233 269

273 299 302 325 331 339 357 408 411 449 464 469 472

False

2 3 9 10 20 43 95 131 140 148 152 223 405

Men: $M = 11.30$, $SD = 6.44$ Women: $M = 12.31$, $SD = 6.99$

PK—Post-Traumatic Stress Disorder—Keane (46 Items)

True

16 17 22 23 30 31 32 37 39 48 52 56 59 65 82

85 92 94 101 135 150 168 170 196 221 274 277 302 303 305

316 319 327 328 339 347 349 367

False

2 3 9 49 75 95 125 140

Men: $M = 8.01$, $SD = 5.99$ Women: $M = 8.52$, $SD = 6.57$

PS–Post-Traumatic Stress Disorder–Schlenger (60 Items)

True

17 21 22 31 32 37 38 44 48 56 59 65 85 94 116

135 145 150 168 170 180 218 221 273 274 277 299 301 304 305

311 316 319 325 328 377 386 400 463 464 469 471 475 479 515

516 565

False

3 9 45 75 95 141 165 208 223 280 372 405 564

Men: $M = 10.49$, $SD = 7.98$ Women: $M = 11.82$, $SD = 8.96$

MAC-R—MacAndrew Alcoholism—Revised (49 Items)

True

7 24 36 49 52 69 72 82 84 103 105 113 115 128

168 172 202 214 224 229 238 257 280 342 344 387 407 412

414 422 434 439 445 456 473 502 506 549

False

73 107 117 137 160 166 251 266 287 299 325

Men: $M = 20.81$, $SD = 4.37$ Women: $M = 18.85$, $SD = 3.69$

APS—Addiction Potential (39 Items)

True

7 29 41 89 103 113 120 168 183 189 196 217 242 260 267

341 342 344 377 422 502 523 540

False

4 43 76 104 137 157 220 239 306 312 349 440 495 496 500

Men: $M = 23.37$, $SD = 3.69$ Women: $M = 23.13$, $SD = 3.71$

AAS—Addiction Admission (13 Items)

True

172 264 288 362 387 487 489 511 527 544

False

266 429 501

Men: $M = 2.86$, $SD = 2.05$ Women: $M = 1.98$, $SD = 1.76$

MDS—Marital Distress (14 Items)

True

21 22 135 195 219 382 484 563

False

12 83 95 125 493 494

Men: $M = 2.79$, $SD = 2.17$ Women: $M = 2.90$, $SD = 2.33$

TABLE A.6
Critical Item Sets

Koss–Butcher Critical Items Sets, Revised

Acute Anxiety State

2F	28T	208F	463T
3F	39T	218T	469T
5T	59T	223F	
10F	140F	301T	
15T	172T	444T	

Depressed Suicidal Ideation

9 F	92T	233T	411T	520T
38T	95F	273T	454T	524T
65T	130T	303T	485T	
71T	146T	306T	506T	
75F	215T	388F	518T	

Threatened Assault

37T
85T
134T
213T
389T

Situational Stress Due to Alcoholism

125F	511T
264T	518T
487T	
489T	
502T	

Mental Confusion

24T	180T	325T
31T	198T	
32T	299T	
72T	311T	
96T	316T	

Persecutory Ideas

17T	144T	241T	361T
42T	145T	251T	
99T	162T	259T	
124T	216T	314F	
138T	228T	333T	

Lachar–Wrobel Critical Item Sets

Anxiety and Tension

15T	261F	463T
17T	299T	
172T	301T	
218T	320T	
223F	405F	

Depression and Worry

2F	75F	273T	454T
3F	130T	303T	
10F	150T	339T	
65T	165F	411T	
73T	180T	415T	

Sleep Disturbance

5T	471T
30T	
39T	
140F	
328T	

Deviant Beliefs

42T	162T	333T
99T	216T	336T
106T	228T	355T
138T	259T	361T
144T	314F	466T

Deviant Thinking and Experience

32T	298T
60T	307T
96T	316T
122T	319T
198T	427F

Substance Abuse

168T
264T
429F

Antisocial Attitude

27T	240T
35T	254T
84T	266F
105T	324T
227T	

Family Conflict

21T
83F
125F
288T

Problematic Anger

85T
134T
213T
389T

Sexual Concern and Deviation

12F	268T
34F	
62T/F	
121F	
166T	

Somatic Symptoms

18T	47F	111T	176F	255F
28T	53T	142F	182T	295F
33F	57F	159F	224F	464T
40T	59T	164F	229T	
44T	101T	175T	247T	

Note. F = false; T = true.

Nichols Critical Item List

Health/Somatic/Neurological

Ill Health (5 Items)					
True					
None					
False					
	33	45	118	141	148
Weakness/Tiredness/Fatigue (Neurasthenia; 6 Items)					
True					
	175	464			
False					
	152	173	295	561	
Pain and Discomfort (8 Items)					
True					
	40	59	149		
False					
	47	57	176	224	459
Head Complaints (6 Items)					
True					
	40	97	101	149	536
False					
	176				
Cardiorespiratory (5 Items)					
True					
	36				
False					
	47	117	181	208	
Vascular (4 Items)					
True					
	44	294			
False					
	8	176			
Upper Gastrointestinal (8 Items)					

True								
	11		18		28		59	111
False								
	2		117		404			

Sweating (2 Items)								
True								
178	238							
False								
None								
Motor (9 Items)								
True								
23	172	182	476					
False								
91	106	177	179	295				
Sensory (7 Items)								
True								
53	252	247	298					
False								
204	249	255						
Memory and Concentration (11 Items)								
True								
31	147	299	308	325	472	475	533	565
False								
165	173							
Losses of Consciousness (7 Items)								
True								
23	168	182	229					
False								
142	159	164						

Anxiety and Depression

Acute Tension–Anxiety State (25 Items)

True

5 15 17 28 39 47 59 172 218 273 299 301 320

444 463 469

False

2 3 10 140 208 223 261 405 496

Phrenophobia (2 Items)

True

170 180

False

None

Depressed State (20 Items)

True

38 65 71 92 130 146 180 215 233 306 339 411 415 454

False

2 3 9 95 165 388

Sleep Disturbance (9 Items)

True

5 30 39 258 282 304 471

False

3 140

Suicidal Ideation (25 Items)

True

22 65 85 92 94 134 150 234 281 303 306 311 400 411 454

463 505 506 516 520 524 526 546 554

False

75

Thinking Disturbance

Unusual Experience (10 Items)

True

24 72 122 180 251 299 307 325

False

106 427

Active Psychotic Experience (10 Items)

True										
32	60	96	198	298	311	316	319	355	551	
False										
None										
Active Persecutory Experience (12 Items)										
True										
42	99	138	144	162	216	228	259	333	336	361
False										
314										
Miscellaneous										
Assaultive Impulse (12 Items)										
True										
37	85	134	150	213	324	389	513	540	542	548
False										
373										
Substance Abuse, Indirect (6 Items)										
True										
168	229	264	366							
False										
125	429									
Sexual Problems (8 Items)										
True										
74[a]	114	166	268	287						
False										
12	34	74[b]	121							

[A]For men only. [B]For women only.

Appendix B: MMPI–2 Uniform and Linear *T*-Score Conversions for Validity, Clinical, Supplementary, Content, Content Component, Subscales, and Special Scales

The following tables are based on the materials made available by the publisher and include all of the changes to the existing MMPI–2 manual, which is currently being revised. Linear *T* scores for Tables B.1, B.2, B.6, B.10, B.11, and B.12 have been computed directly from the means and standard deviations of the raw scores for each scale. They may vary by ± 1 *T*-score point from other sources.

MMPI–2 (Minnesota Multiphasic Personality Inventory–2): Manual for Administration, Scoring and Interpretation, revised. Minneapolis: University of Minnesota Press, in preparation. Reproduced by permission of the publisher.

TABLE B.1

Linear *T*-Score Conversions for Standard Validity Scales and Other Measures of Response Style for Men

Raw Score	L	F	FB	K	VRIN	TRIN	Ds	F(p)	$F(p_1)$	$F(p_2)$	Mp	Sd	S	S1	S2	S3	S4	S5	Ss	Raw Score
74																			76	74
73																			75	73
72																			73	72
71																			72	71
70																			70	70
69																			68	69
68																			67	68
67																			65	67
66																			64	66
65																			62	65
64																			61	64
63																			59	63
62																			57	62
61																			56	61
60																			54	60
59																			53	59

Raw Score	*L*	*F*	*F_B*	*K*	*VRIN*	*TRIN*	*Ds*	*F(p)*	$F(p_1)$	$F(p_2)$	*Mp*	*Sd*	*S*	*S1*	*S2*	*S3*	*S4*	*S5*	*Ss*	Raw Score
58																			51	58
57																			50	57
56																			48	56
55																			46	55
54																			45	54
53																			43	53
52																			42	52
51																			40	51
50													79						39	50
49													78						37	49
48							120						76						35	48
47							119						75						34	47
46							118						74						32	46
45							116						73						31	45
44							114						72							44
43							112						71							43
42							110						70							42
41							108						68							41

Raw Score	*L*	*F*	*FB*	*K*	*VRIN*	*TRIN*	*Ds*	*F(p)*	$F(p_1)$	$F(p_2)$	*Mp*	*Sd*	*S*	*S1*	*S2*	*S3*	*S4*	*S5*	*Ss*	Raw Score
40							106													40
39							104													39
38							102													38
37							101													37
36							99													36
35							97													35
34							95						60							34
33							93					105	59							33
32							91					102	58							32
31							89					100	57							31
30				81			87					97	56							30
29				79			86					94	55							29
28		122		77			84					92	53							28
27		119		75			82					89	52							27
26		116		72			80				96	86	51							26
25		113		70			78				93	83	50							25
24		110		68		101	76				91	81	49							24
23		107		66		98	74				88	78	48							23

Raw Score	L	F	FB	K	VRIN	TRIN	Ds	F(p)	$F(p_1)$	$F(p_2)$	Mp	Sd	S	S1	S2	S3	S4	S5	Ss	Raw Score
22		104		64	123	94	72				85	75	47							22
21		101		62	119	91	71				82	73	45							21
20		98		60	115	88	69				79	70	44							20
19		95	120	58	111	84	67				76	67	43							19
18		92	116	56	106	81	65				73	64	42							18
17		88	112	54	102	77	63				71	62	41							17
16		85	108	51	98	74	61				68	59	40							16
15	100	82	104	49	94	71	59				65	56	38	70						15
14	96	79	100	47	90	67	57				62	53	37	67						14
13	92	76	96	45	85	64	55				59	51	36	65	75					13
12	87	73	92	43	81	60	54				56	48	35	62	72					12
11	83	70	87	41	77	57	52	121			54	45	34	60	68					11
10	78	67	83	39	73	54	50	114			51	43	33	57	64					10
9	74	64	79	37	69	50	48	107			48	40	32	54	61					9
8	70	61	75	35	65	54	46	100			45	37	30	52	57		68			8
7	65	58	71	33	60	57	44	92	118		42	34		49	53	65	63			7
6	61	55	67	30	56	60	42	85	106	119	39	32		47	50	60	58			6
5	56	51	63		52	64	40	78	95	106	37	30		44	46	55	54	65		5

Raw Score	L	F	FB	K	VRIN	TRIN	Ds	F(p)	$F(p_1)$	$F(p_2)$	Mp	Sd	S	S1	S2	S3	S4	S5	Ss	Raw Score
4	52	48	59		48	67	39	71	85	94	34			41	42	50	49	58		4
3	48	45	55		44	71	37	63	74	81	31			39	39	45	44	51		3
2	43	42	51		39	74	35	56	64	69				36	35	40	40	43		2
1	39	39	46		35	77	33	49	53	56				34	31	35	35	36		1
0	35	36	42		31	81	31	42	43	44				31			30			0

TABLE B.2

Linear *T*-Score Conversions for Standard Validity Scales and Other Measures of Response Style for Women

Raw Score	*L*	*F*	*FB*	*K*	*VRIN*	*TRIN*	*Ds*	*F(p)*	$F(p_1)$	$F(p_2)$	*Mp*	*Sd*	*S*	*S1*	*S2*	*S3*	*S4*	*S5*	*Ss*	*Raw Score*
74																			76	74
73																			75	73
72																			73	72
71																			72	71
70																			70	70
69																			69	69
68																			67	68
67																			66	67
66																			64	66
65																			63	65
64																			61	64
63																			60	63
62																			58	62
61																			56	61
60																			55	60

Raw Score	L	F	FB	K	VRIN	TRIN	Ds	F(p)	$F(p_1)$	$F(p_2)$	Mp	Sd	S	S1	S2	S3	S4	S5	Ss	Raw Score
59																			53	59
58																			52	58
57																			50	57
56																			49	56
55																			47	55
54																			46	54
53																			44	53
52																			43	52
51																			41	51
50							120						80						40	50
49							118						78						38	49
48							116						77						36	48
47							115						76						35	47
46							113						75						33	46
45							111						74						32	45
44							109						72						30	44

Raw Score	L	F	FB	K	VRIN	TRIN	Ds	F(p)	$F(p_1)$	$F(p_2)$	Mp	Sd	S	S1	S2	S3	S4	S5	Ss	Raw Score
43							108						71							43
42							106						70							42
41							104						69							41
40							102						68							40
39							100						66							39
38							99						65							38
37							97						64							37
36							95						63							36
35							93						61							35
34							92						60							34
33							90					114	59							33
32							88					111	58							32
31							86					108	57							31
30				83			84					105	55							30
29				81			83					102	54							29
28				78			81					99	53							28
27				76			79					95	52							27
26				74			77				104	92	51							26

Raw Score	L	F	FB	K	VRIN	TRIN	Ds	F(p)	$F(p_1)$	$F(p_2)$	Mp	Sd	S	S1	S2	S3	S4	S5	Ss	Raw Score
25				72			76				101	89	49							25
24		120		70			74				98	86	48							24
23		116		67			72				95	83	47							23
22		113		65			70				92	80	46							22
21		110		63			68				89	77	45							21
20		106	120	61	118		67				86	74	43							20
19		103	116	59	114		65				83	71	42							19
18		99	112	56	109	118	63				80	68	41							18
17		96	108	54	105	111	61				77	65	40							17
16		92	104	52	101	103	60				73	62	39							16
15	105	89	101	50	96	95	58				70	59	37	69						15
14	100	86	97	48	92	88	56				67	56	36	66						14
13	95	82	93	46	87	80	54				64	53	35	64	79					13
12	91	79	89	43	83	73	53				61	50	34	61	75					12

Raw Score	L	F	F_B	K	VRIN	TRIN	Ds	F(p)	$F(p_1)$	$F(p_2)$	Mp	Sd	S	S1	S2	S3	S4	S5	Ss	Raw Score
11	86	75	85	41	79	65	51				58	47	33	58	71					11
10	81	72	81	39	74	58	49	120			55	43	31	56	67					10
9	76	68	77	37	70	50	47	113			52	40	30	53	63					9
8	71	65	73	35	65	58	45	105			49	37		50	60		68			8
7	67	61	70	32	61	65	44	97			46	34		48	56	68	63			7
6	62	58	66	30	57	73	42	89	120	115	43	31		45	52	63	58			6
5	57	55	62		52	80	40	81	107	103	40	30		42	48	58	53	61		5
4	52	51	58		48	88	38	73	95	91	37			40	44	52	48	53		4
3	47	48	54		44	95	37	65	82	79	34			37	41	47	43	45		3
2	43	44	50		39	103	35	57	69	67	31			34	37	42	38	37		2
1	38	41	46		35	111	33	49	57	55				32	33	36	33	30		1
0	33	37	42		30	118	31	41	44	43					29	31				0

TABLE B.3

Uniform and Linear *T*-Score Conversions for Standard Clinical Scales With *K* Corrections

	Men										Women										
Raw Score	Hs +0.5K	D	Hy	Pd +0.4K	Mf*[a]	Pa	Pt +1K	Sc +1K	Ma +0.2K	Si[a]	Hs +0.5K	D	Hy	Pd +0.5K	Mf[a]	Pa	Pt +1K	Sc +1K	Ma +0.2K	Si[a]	Raw Score
73																		120			73
72																		119			72
71																		118			71
70																		116			70
69										100								115		95	69
68										99								114		93	68
67								120		98								112		92	67
66								119		97							120	111		91	66
65								117		96							119	109		90	65
64								115		94							117	108		89	64
63								113		93							116	106		88	63
62								112		92							114	105		87	62
61								110		91							112	103		86	61
60								108		90							110	102		85	60
59							120	106		89							108	100		84	59
58							118	105		88							106	99		83	58

Uniform and Linear *T*-Score Conversions for Standard Clinical Scales With *K* Corrections

	Men										Women										
Raw Score	*Hs* +0.5*K*	*D*	*Hy*	*Pd* +0.4*K*	*Mf**[a]	*Pa*	*Pt* +1*K*	*Sc* +1*K*	*Ma* +0.2*K*	*Si*[a]	*Hs* +0.5*K*	*D*	*Hy*	*Pd* +0.5*K*	*Mf*[a]	*Pa*	*Pt* +1*K*	*Sc* +1*K*	*Ma* +0.2*K*	*Si*[a]	Raw Score
57							115	103		86							105	97		82	57
56					109		113	101		85							103	96		81	56
55		120			107		111	100		84							101	94		80	55
54		119			105		109	98		83							99	93		79	54
53		117			103		107	96		82		120					97	91		78	53
52		115			101		105	94		81		118	120				95	90		77	52
51		114		120	99		102	93		80		116	118				94	88		75	51
50		112	120	117	97		100	91		79		114	115	120			92	87		74	50
49		110	119	115	95		98	89		77		112	113	118			90	85		73	49
48		108	116	112	93		96	87		76		109	111	115			88	84		72	48
47		106	114	110	91		94	86		75		107	108	113			86	82		71	47
46		104	111	107	89		92	84		74	120	105	106	110			84	81		70	46
45		102	109	105	87		89	82		73	117	103	104	107			83	79		69	45
44	120	100	106	102	85		87	81		72	115	101	101	105	30		81	78	120	68	44
43	119	98	104	100	83		85	79	120	71	113	99	99	102	33		79	76	118	67	43
42	116	97	101	97	81		83	77	117	70	111	96	96	100	35		77	75	115	66	42
41	114	95	99	95	79		81	75	114	68	109	94	94	97	38		75	73	112	65	41
40	112	93	96	92	78		79	74	110	67	107	92	92	94	40		73	72	109	64	40
39	110	91	94	90	76		77	72	107	66	105	90	89	92	43		72	70	106	63	39

Uniform and Linear *T*-Score Conversions for Standard Clinical Scales With *K* Corrections

	Men										Women										
Raw Score	*Hs* +0.5*K*	*D*	*Hy*	*Pd* +0.4*K*	*Mf**[a]	*Pa*	*Pt* +1*K*	*Sc* +1*K*	*Ma* +0.2*K*	*Si*[a]	*Hs* +0.5*K*	*D*	*Hy*	*Pd* +0.5*K*	*Mf*[a]	*Pa*	*Pt* +1*K*	*Sc* +1*K*	*Ma* +0.2*K*	*Si*[a]	Raw Score
38	108	89	91	87	74		74	70	104	65	103	88	87	89	45		70	69	103	62	38
37	105	87	89	84	72		72	68	101	64	101	86	84	87	47		68	67	100	61	37
36	103	85	86	82	70		70	67	98	63	99	83	82	84	50		66	66	97	60	36
35	101	83	84	79	68		68	65	94	62	97	81	80	81	52		64	65	94	59	35
34	99	81	81	77	66		66	63	91	60	94	79	77	79	55		62	63	91	58	34
33	97	80	79	74	64		64	62	88	59	92	77	75	76	57		61	62	88	56	33
32	94	78	76	72	62		61	60	85	58	90	75	73	73	60		59	60	85	55	32
31	92	76	74	69	60		59	58	81	57	88	72	70	71	62		57	59	82	54	31
30	90	74	71	67	58	120	57	56	78	56	86	70	68	68	65	120	55	57	79	53	30
29	88	72	69	64	56	119	55	54	75	55	84	68	65	66	67	118	53	55	76	52	29
28	86	70	66	62	54	116	53	53	72	54	82	66	63	63	69	114	51	53	74	51	28
27	84	68	64	59	52	112	51	51	69	53	80	64	61	60	72	111	49	52	71	50	27
26	81	66	61	57	50	108	49	49	65	51	78	62	58	58	74	107	47	50	68	49	26
25	79	64	59	54	48	105	47	47	62	50	76	59	56	55	77	103	44	48	65	48	25
24	77	62	57	52	46	101	45	45	59	49	73	57	54	53	79	100	42	46	62	47	24
23	75	61	54	50	44	97	43	44	56	48	71	55	51	51	82	96	40	44	59	46	23
22	73	59	52	48	42	94	41	42	53	47	69	53	49	49	84	92	38	42	56	45	22
21	70	57	50	46	40	90	39	40	51	46	67	51	47	47	87	89	37	41	53	44	21

Uniform and Linear *T*-Score Conversions for Standard Clinical Scales With *K* Corrections

	Men										Women										
Raw Score	*Hs +0.5K*	*D*	*Hy*	*Pd +0.4K*	*Mf*[*a]	*Pa*	*Pt +1K*	*Sc +1K*	*Ma +0.2K*	*Si*[a]	*Hs +0.5K*	*D*	*Hy*	*Pd +0.5K*	*Mf*[a]	*Pa*	*Pt +1K*	*Sc +1K*	*Ma +0.2K*	*Si*[a]	*Raw Score*
20	68	54	47	44	38	86	37	39	49	45	65	49	45	45	89	85	35	39	51	43	20
19	66	52	45	42	36	83	35	37	47	44	63	47	43	43	92	81	33	37	49	42	19
18	64	50	43	40	34	79	33	36	45	42	61	46	41	41	94	78	32	36	47	41	18
17	62	47	42	38	32	75	32	34	43	41	59	44	39	39	96	74	31	34	45	40	17
16	59	45	40	37	30	72	30	33	41	40	56	42	38	37	99	70	30	33	43	38	16
15	57	42	38	35		68		32	39	39	54	40	36	36	101	67		32	41	37	15
14	54	40	37	34		64		31	38	38	51	38	35	34	104	63		31	39	36	14
13	51	38	35	32		61		30	36	37	49	36	34	32	106	59		30	37	35	13
12	48	36	34	31		57			35	36	46	34	32	30	109	56			35	34	12
11	45	34	33	30		53			33	34	43	32	32		111	52			33	33	11
10	42	32	32			49			31	33	40	30	31		114	49			31	32	10
9	39	30	31			46			30	32	38		30		116	45			30	31	9
8	37		30			42				31	35				118	42				30	8
7	34					39				30	33				120	39					7
6	33					37					30					37					6
5	31					34										34					5
4	30					32										32					4

Uniform and Linear *T*-Score Conversions for Standard Clinical Scales With *K* Corrections

	Men										Women										
Raw Score	*Hs +0.5K*	*D*	*Hy*	*Pd +0.4K*	*Mf*[a]	*Pa*	*Pt +1K*	*Sc +1K*	*Ma +0.2K*	*Si*[a]	*Hs +0.5K*	*D*	*Hy*	*Pd +0.5K*	*Mf*[a]	*Pa*	*Pt +1K*	*Sc +1K*	*Ma +0.2K*	*Si*[a]	*Raw Score*
3						31										31					3
2						30										30					2
1																					1
0																					0

[a]Linear *T* scores

TABLE B.4

Uniform and Linear *T*-Score Conversions for Standard Clinical Scales Without *K* Corrections

	Men										*Women*										
Raw Score	*Hs*	*D*	*Hy*	*Pd*	*Mf*[a]	*Pa*	*Pt*	*Sc*	*Ma*	*Si*[a]	*Hs*	*D*	*Hy*	*Pd*	*Mf*[a]	*Pa*	*Pt*	*Sc*	*M*[a]	*Si*[a]	*Raw Score*
72																		120			72
71																		118			71
70																		117			70
69										100								116		95	69
68								120		99								115		93	68
67								119		98								114		92	67
66								117		97								113		91	66
65								116		96								112		90	65
64								115		94								111		89	64
63								114		93								109		88	63
62								113		92								108		87	62
61								111		91								107		86	61
60								110		90								106		85	60
59								109		89								105		84	59
58								108		88								104		83	58
57								107		86								103		82	57
56					109			105		85								102		81	56

Uniform and Linear T-Score Conversions for Standard Clinical Scales Without K Corrections

	Men										Women										
Raw Score	*Hs*	*D*	*Hy*	*Pd*	*Mf*[a]	*Pa*	*Pt*	*Sc*	*Ma*	*Si*[a]	*Hs*	*D*	*Hy*	*Pd*	*Mf*[a]	*Pa*	*Pt*	*Sc*	*Ma*	*Si*[a]	*Raw Score*
55		120			107			104		84								100		80	55
54		119			105			103		83								99		79	54
53		117			103			102		82		120						98		78	53
52		115			101			100		81		118	120					97		77	52
51		114			99			99		80		116	118					96		75	51
50		112	120		97			98		79		114	115					95		74	50
49		110	119		95			97		77		112	113					94		73	49
48		108	116	120	93		104	96		76		109	111				98	93		72	48
47		106	114	117	91		103	94		75		107	108	120			97	92		71	47
46		104	111	115	89		101	93		74		105	106	118			95	90		70	46
45		102	109	113	87		100	92		73		103	104	116			94	89		69	45
44		100	106	111	85		98	91		72		101	101	113	30		93	88		68	44
43		98	104	109	83		97	90		71		99	99	111	33		91	87	120	67	43
42		97	101	106	81		95	88	120	70		96	96	109	35		90	86	119	66	42
41		95	99	104	79		94	87	118	68		94	94	106	38		89	85	116	65	41
40		93	96	102	78		92	86	115	67		92	92	104	40		87	84	114	64	40
39		91	94	100	76		91	85	112	66		90	89	102	43		86	83	111	63	39

Uniform and Linear T-Score Conversions for Standard Clinical Scales Without K Corrections

	Men										Women										
Raw Score	Hs	D	Hy	Pd	Mf[a]	Pa	Pt	Sc	Ma	Si[a]	Hs	D	Hy	Pd	Mf[a]	Pa	Pt	Sc	Ma	Si[a]	Raw Score
38		89	91	97	74		89	84	109	65		88	87	99	45		84	81	108	62	38
37		87	89	95	72		88	82	106	64		86	84	97	47		83	80	105	61	37
36		85	86	93	70		86	81	103	63		83	82	95	50		82	79	102	60	36
35		83	84	91	68		85	80	100	62		81	80	92	52		80	78	100	59	35
34		81	81	89	66		83	79	97	60		79	77	90	55		79	77	97	58	34
33		80	79	86	64		82	78	94	59		77	75	88	57		78	76	94	56	33
32	107	78	76	84	62		80	76	91	58	100	75	73	85	60		76	75	91	55	32
31	105	76	74	82	60		79	75	88	57	98	72	70	83	62		75	74	89	54	31
30	103	74	71	80	58	120	78	74	85	56	97	70	68	81	65	120	73	72	86	53	30
29	101	72	69	77	56	119	76	73	82	55	95	68	65	78	67	118	72	71	83	52	29
28	99	70	66	75	54	116	75	72	79	54	93	66	63	76	69	114	71	70	80	51	28
27	97	68	64	73	52	112	73	70	76	53	91	64	61	74	72	111	69	69	77	50	27
26	95	66	61	71	50	108	72	69	73	51	89	62	58	72	74	107	68	68	75	49	26
25	93	64	59	68	48	105	70	68	70	50	87	59	56	69	77	103	67	67	72	48	25
24	91	62	57	66	46	101	69	67	67	49	85	57	54	67	79	100	65	66	69	47	24
23	89	61	54	64	44	97	67	66	64	48	83	55	51	65	82	96	64	65	66	46	23
22	87	59	52	62	42	94	66	64	61	47	82	53	49	62	84	92	62	63	64	45	22

Uniform and Linear T-Score Conversions for Standard Clinical Scales Without K Corrections

	Men										Women										
Raw Score	Hs	D	Hy	Pd	Mf^a	Pa	Pt	Sc	Ma	Si^a	Hs	D	Hy	Pd	Mf^a	Pa	Pt	Sc	Ma	Si^a	Raw Score
21	85	57	50	60	40	90	64	63	58	46	80	51	47	60	87	89	61	62	61	44	21
20	83	54	47	57	38	86	63	62	56	45	78	49	45	58	89	85	60	61	58	43	20
19	81	52	45	55	36	83	61	61	53	44	76	47	43	55	92	81	58	60	55	42	19
18	79	50	43	53	34	79	60	60	51	42	74	46	41	53	94	78	57	59	53	41	18
17	77	47	42	51	32	75	58	58	49	41	72	44	39	51	96	74	56	58	51	40	17
16	75	45	40	49	30	72	57	57	47	40	70	42	38	49	99	70	55	57	49	38	16
15	73	42	38	46		68	56	56	45	39	69	40	36	47	101	67	53	56	47	37	15
14	71	40	37	44		64	54	55	43	38	67	38	35	45	104	63	52	55	45	36	14
13	69	38	35	42		61	53	54	42	37	65	36	34	43	106	59	51	53	43	35	13
12	67	36	34	40		57	52	52	40	36	63	34	32	41	109	56	50	52	41	34	12
11	65	34	33	38		53	50	51	38	34	61	32	32	39	111	52	48	51	40	33	11
10	63	32	32	36		49	49	49	37	33	59	30	31	37	114	49	47	50	38	32	10
9	61	30	31	34		46	47	48	35	32	57		30	35	116	45	46	48	36	31	9
8	59		30	33		42	46	46	33	31	56			33	118	42	44	47	34	30	8
7	57			31		39	44	45	31	30	54			31	120	39	43	45	32		7
6	54			30		37	42	43	30		52			30		37	41	43	30		6
5	52					34	41	41			49					34	39	42			5

Uniform and Linear T-Score Conversions for Standard Clinical Scales Without K Corrections

	Men										Women										
Raw Score	*Hs*	*D*	*Hy*	*Pd*	*Mf*[a]	*Pa*	*Pt*	*Sc*	*Ma*	*Si*[a]	*Hs*	*D*	*Hy*	*Pd*	*Mf*[a]	*Pa*	*Pt*	*Sc*	*Ma*	*Si*[a]	Raw Score
4	49					32	39	39			47					32	37	39			4
3	46					31	37	37			44					31	35	37			3
2	42					30	34	35			41					30	33	35			2
1	38						32	32			37						31	32			1
0	34						30	30			33						30	30			0

[a]Linear *T* scores

TABLE B.5

Linear *T*-Score Conversions for Harris—Lingoes Subscales for Men and Women

Men

Raw Score	D1	D2	D3	D4	D5	Hy1	Hy2	Hy3	Hy4	Hy5	Pd1	Pd2	Pd3	Pd4	Raw Score
32	116														32
31	114														31
30	111														30
29	108														29
28	106														28
27	103														27
26	100														26
25	98														25
24	95														24
23	93														23
22	90														22
21	87														21
20	85														20
19	82														19
18	79														18
17	77								120						17
16	74								116						16
15	71			110				106	111						15
14	69	98		105				102	106						14

TABLE B.5 (*Continued*)

Linear *T*-Score Conversions for Harris—Lingoes Subscales for Men and Women

								Men							
Raw Score	*Pd5*	*Pa1*	*Pa2*	*Pa3*	*Sc1*	*Sc2*	*Sc3*	*Sc4*	*Sc5*	*Sc6*	*Ma1*	*Ma2*	*Ma3*	*Ma4*	*Raw Score*
32															32
31															31
30															30
29															29
28															28
27															27
26															26
25															25
24															24
23															23
22															22
21															21
20					120										20
19					117										19
18					113										18
17					109					120					17
16					105					119					16
15					101					114					15
14		120			97			114		109					14

TABLE B.5 *(Continued)*

Linear *T*-Score Conversions for Harris–Lingoes Subscales for Men and Women

								Men							
Raw Score	*D1*	*D2*	*D3*	*D4*	*D5*	*Hy1*	*Hy2*	*Hy3*	*Hy4*	*Hy5*	*Pd1*	*Pd2*	*Pd3*	*Pd4*	*Raw Score*
13	66	92		101				97	101					98	13
12	64	87		96			71	93	96					92	12
11	61	81	116	91			67	88	91					87	11
10	58	76	108	86	96		63	84	86					82	10
9	56	70	100	82	91		59	79	82		98			77	9
8	53	65	91	77	85		55	75	77		91	80		71	8
7	50	59	83	72	79		51	70	72	78	84	73		66	7
6	48	54	75	67	74	61	47	66	67	71	78	67	63	61	6
5	45	48	67	62	68	56	43	61	62	63	71	60	57	56	5
4	42	43	59	58	62	51	40	57	57	55	65	53	51	50	4
3	40	37	51	53	57	45	36	52	52	48	58	47	45	45	3
2	37	32	43	48	51	40	32	48	48	40	51	40	39	40	2
1	35	30	35	43	45	34	30	43	43	33	45	33	33	35	1
0	32		30	38	40	30		38	38	30	38	30	30	30	0

TABLE B.5 (*Continued*)

Linear T-Score Conversions for Harris–Lingoes Subscales for Men and Women

								Men							
Raw Score	*Pd5*	*Pa1*	*Pa2*	*Pa3*	*Sc1*	*Sc2*	*Sc3*	*Sc4*	*Sc5*	*Sc6*	*Ma1*	*Ma2*	*Ma3*	*Ma4*	*Raw Score*
13		118			92			109		104					13
12	91	112			88			103		99					12
11	87	106			84			98	117	95		78			11
10	82	100			80		103	92	110	90		73			10
9	77	94	96	70	76	120	96	87	103	85		68		89	9
8	72	88	89	65	72	117	90	82	96	80		63	77	82	8
7	67	82	82	60	68	107	84	76	89	75		58	71	76	7
6	63	76	75	56	64	98	78	71	82	70	81	53	65	69	6
5	58	70	68	51	59	88	72	65	75	65	74	49	59	63	5
4	53	64	62	46	55	78	66	60	68	60	66	44	53	56	4
3	48	58	55	41	51	69	60	55	61	55	58	39	47	50	3
2	43	52	48	36	47	59	54	49	54	51	50	34	41	43	2
1	38	46	41	32	43	50	48	44	47	46	42	30	35	37	1
0	34	40	34	30	39	40	42	39	40	41	35		30	30	0

TABLE B5 (*Continued*)

Linear T-Score Conversions for Harris–Lingoes Subscales for Men and Women

								Women							
Raw Score	*D1*	*D2*	*D3*	*D4*	*D5*	*Hy1*	*Hy2*	*Hy3*	*Hy4*	*Hy5*	*Pd1*	*Pd2*	*Pd3*	*Pd4*	*Raw Score*
32	108														32
31	105														31
30	103														30
29	101														29
28	98														28
27	96														27
26	94														26
25	91														25
24	89														24
23	86														23
22	84														22
21	82														21
20	79														20
19	77														19
18	75														18
17	72								105						17
16	70								101						16
15	67			106				99	97						15
14	65	95		102				95	93						14

TABLE B.5 (*Continued*)

Linear *T*-Score Conversions for Harris–Lingoes Subscales for Men and Women

							Women								
Raw Score	*Pd5*	*Pa1*	*Pa2*	*Pa3*	*Sc1*	*Sc2*	*Sc3*	*Sc4*	*Sc5*	*Sc6*	*Ma1*	*Ma2*	*Ma3*	*Ma4*	*Raw Score*
32															32
31															31
30															30
29															29
28															28
27															27
26															26
25															25
24															24
23															23
22															22
21					119										21
20					115										20
19					111										19
18					108					120					18
17					104					118					17
16					100					113					16
15					96					109					15
14		120			92			111		104					14

TABLE B.5 (*Continued*)

Linear T-Score Conversions for Harris—Lingoes Subscales for Men and Women

								Women							
Raw Score	*D1*	*D2*	*D3*	*D4*	*D5*	*Hy1*	*Hy2*	*Hy3*	*Hy4*	*Hy5*	*Pd1*	*Pd2*	*Pd3*	*Pd4*	*Raw Score*
13	63	90		97				91	89					97	13
12	60	84		93			71	87	85					91	12
11	58	79	107	88			67	83	81					86	11
10	56	73	100	84	89		63	79	77					81	10
9	53	68	93	79	83		59	75	73		92			75	9
8	51	62	85	75	78		55	71	69		86	92		70	8
7	48	57	78	70	73		50	67	65	77	80	84		65	7
6	46	51	70	66	68	61	46	63	61	70	74	77	64	60	6
5	44	46	63	61	63	56	42	59	57	62	68	69	58	54	5
4	41	41	56	57	58	51	38	55	53	54	62	61	52	49	4
3	39	35	48	52	53	45	34	51	49	46	56	53	47	44	3
2	37	30	41	48	47	40	30	47	45	39	50	46	41	38	2
1	34		34	43	42	35		43	41	31	44	38	35	33	1
0	32		30	38	37	30		39	37	30	38	30	30	30	0

TABLE B.5 (*Continued*)

Linear T-Score Conversions for Harris—Lingoes Subscales for Men and Women

								Women							
Raw Score	*Pd5*	*Pa1*	*Pa2*	*Pa3*	*Sc1*	*Sc2*	*Sc3*	*Sc4*	*Sc5*	*Sc6*	*Ma1*	*Ma2*	*Ma3*	*Ma4*	*Raw Score*
13		117			88			106		100					13
12	92	111			84			100		95					12
11	87	105			81			95	110	91		80			11
10	82	99			77		104	90	104	86		75			10
9	77	93	91	69	73	120	98	85	97	81		70		86	9
8	72	87	84	65	69	113	92	80	91	77		65	82	80	8
7	68	81	78	60	65	104	86	75	85	72		60	75	74	7
6	63	75	72	55	61	95	80	70	78	68	87	55	69	68	6
5	58	69	65	50	57	86	74	65	72	63	79	50	62	62	5
4	53	63	59	45	53	76	67	59	65	59	70	45	56	56	4
3	48	57	53	41	50	67	61	54	59	54	62	40	50	49	3
2	43	51	46	36	46	58	55	49	53	50	54	35	43	43	2
1	39	45	40	31	42	49	49	44	46	45	45	30	37	37	1
0	34	39	34	30	38	40	43	39	40	41	37		30	31	0

TABLE B.6

Linear *T*-Score Conversions for Wiener–Harmon Subtle–Obvious Subscales for Men and Women

	Men										Women										
Raw Score	*D-O*	*D-S*	*Hy-O*	*Hy-S*	*Pd-O*	*Pd-S*	*Pa-O*	*Pa-S*	*Ma-O*	*Ma-S*	*D-O*	*D-S*	*Hy-O*	*Hy-S*	*Pd-O*	*Pd-S*	*Pa-O*	*Pa-S*	*Ma-O*	*Ma-S*	*Raw Score*
39											112										39
38	120										110										38
37	118										108										37
36	116										106										36
35	114										104										35
34	111										102										34
33	109										100										33
32	107										98		112								32
31	104										96		110								31
30	102		120								94		108								30
29	100		117								92		105								29
28	97		114	78	108						89		103	78	111						28
27	95		111	75	106						87		101	76	108						27
26	93		109	73	103						85		98	73	105						26
25	90		106	71	100						83		96	71	103						25
24	88		103	68	98						81		93	69	100						24

Linear *T*-Score Conversions for Wiener–Harmon Subtle–Obvious Subscales for Men and Women

	Men										Women										
Raw Score	*D-O*	*D-S*	*Hy-O*	*Hy-S*	*Pd-O*	*Pd-S*	*Pa-O*	*Pa-S*	*Ma-O*	*Ma-S*	*D-O*	*D-S*	*Hy-O*	*Hy-S*	*Pd-O*	*Pd-S*	*Pa-O*	*Pa-S*	*Ma-O*	*Ma-S*	*Raw Score*
23	86		100	66	95				105	98	79		91	66	97				106	101	23
22	83		98	64	92	95			101	95	77		89	64	95	95			103	97	22
21	81		95	61	90	91			98	91	75		86	61	92	91			99	93	21
20	79		92	59	87	87			95	87	73		84	59	89	87			96	90	20
19	76		89	57	84	83			91	83	71		82	56	87	83	120		92	86	19
18	74	78	87	54	82	79			88	80	69	77	79	54	84	79	115		89	82	18
17	72	75	84	52	79	76	116	90	84	76	67	73	77	51	81	75	111	91	86	78	17
16	69	71	81	50	76	72	112	86	81	72	65	69	75	49	79	71	107	87	82	74	16
15	67	67	78	47	74	68	107	82	78	69	63	65	72	47	76	67	103	82	79	70	15
14	65	63	76	45	71	64	102	77	74	65	61	61	70	44	73	63	98	78	76	67	14
13	62	59	73	43	68	60	98	73	71	61	59	57	67	42	70	59	94	74	72	63	13
12	60	55	70	41	66	56	93	69	67	57	57	53	65	39	68	55	90	69	69	59	12
11	58	52	67	38	63	52	89	65	64	54	55	48	63	37	65	51	85	65	66	55	11
10	55	48	64	36	60	48	84	60	61	50	53	44	60	34	62	47	81	61	62	51	10
9	53	44	62	34	58	45	80	56	57	46	51	40	58	32	60	43	77	57	59	47	9
8	51	40	59	31	55	41	75	52	54	42	48	36	56		57	39	72	52	55	44	8
7	48	36	56		52	37	70	48	51	39	46	32	53		54	35	68	48	52	40	7
6	46	32	53		50	33	66	43	47	35	44		51		52	31	64	44	49	36	6

Linear *T*-Score Conversions for Wiener–Harmon Subtle–Obvious Subscales for Men and Women

	Men										Women										
Raw Score	*D-O*	*D-S*	*Hy-O*	*Hy-S*	*Pd-O*	*Pd-S*	*Pa-O*	*Pa-S*	*Ma-O*	*Ma-S*	*D-O*	*D-S*	*Hy-O*	*Hy-S*	*Pd-O*	*Pd-S*	*Pa-O*	*Pa-S*	*Ma-O*	*Ma-S*	*Raw Score*
5	44		51		47		61	39	44	31	42		48		49		60	39	45	32	5
4	41		48		44		57	35	40		40		46		46		55	35	42		4
3	39		45		42		52	31	37		38		44		44		51	31	39		3
2	37		42		39		47		34		36		41		41		47		35		2
1	34		40		36		43		30		34		39		38		42		32		1
0	32		37		34		38				32		37		35		38				0

TABLE B.7

Linear T-Score Conversions for Finn–Martin Masculinity–Femininity Subscales

	Men								Women								
Raw Score	*Mf1*	*Mf2*	*Mf3*	*Mf4*	*Mf5*	*Mf6*	*Mf7*	*F-M*	*Mf1*	*Mf2*	*Mf3*	*Mf4*	*Mf5*	*Mf6*	*Mf7*	*F-M*	*Raw Score*
22								104								73	22
21								101								70	21
20								97								66	20
19								94								63	19
18								90								60	18
17								87								56	17
16								83								53	16
15								80								50	15
14								76								46	14
13		80						73		76						43	13
12		76						69		72						40	12
11	76	72						66	64	68						37	11
10	72	69						63	59	65						33	10
9	67	65						59	54	61						30	9
8	63	61						56	49	57						27	8
7	59	57						52	44	53						23	7

Linear *T*-Score Conversions for Finn–Martin Masculinity–Femininity Subscales

	Men								Women								
Raw Score	*Mf1*	*Mf2*	*Mf3*	*Mf4*	*Mf5*	*Mf6*	*Mf7*	*F-M*	*Mf1*	*Mf2*	*Mf3*	*Mf4*	*Mf5*	*Mf6*	*Mf7*	*F-M*	*Raw Score*
6	54	54	87	63			66	49	39	50	70	61			63	20	6
5	50	50	79	56	69	83	59	45	33	46	63	54	67	57	55	17	5
4	46	46	71	49	63	74	52	42	28	42	56	47	60	46	48	13	4
3	41	42	63	42	56	65	45	38	23	38	49	39	52	35	40	10	3
2	37	39	55	35	49	56	39	35	18	34	42	32	45	24	33	7	2
1	33	35	47	28	42	47	32	31	13	31	35	24	38	13	26	3	1
0	28	31	39	21	36	38	25	28	8	27	28	17	31	2	18	0	0

TABLE B.8

Linear T-Score Conversions for *Si* Subscales

	Men			Women		
Raw Score	Si_1	Si_2	Si_3	Si_1	Si_2	Si_3
17			86			83
16			83			80
15			80			77
14	77		77	74		74
13	74		74	71		72
12	71		71	68		69
11	68		68	65		66
10	65		65	63		63
9	62		62	60		61
8	59	71	59	57	74	58
7	56	67	56	55	69	55
6	54	62	53	52	65	52
5	51	58	50	49	60	49
4	48	54	47	46	56	47
3	45	49	44	44	51	44
2	42	45	41	41	47	41
1	39	41	38	38	42	38
0	36	37	35	36	37	35

TABLE B.9

Uniform *T*-Score Conversions for Content Scales

							Men								
Raw Score	*ANX*	*FRS*	*OBS*	*DEP*	*HEA*	*BIZ*	*ANG*	*CYN*	*ASP*	*TPA*	*LSE*	*SOD*	*FAM*	*WRK*	*TRT*
36					112										
35					110										
34					108										
33				100	106									98	
32				99	105									96	
31				97	103									94	
30				95	101									92	
29				94	99									90	
28				92	97									89	
27				90	95									87	
26				88	93									85	104
25				87	91								105	83	101
24				85	89						101	89	102	81	99
23	92	113		83	87	120		83			98	86	99	79	96
22	90	110		82	85	119		80	94		96	84	97	78	94
21	87	107		80	83	115		77	90		93	81	94	76	91
20	85	103		78	81	112		74	87		91	78	91	74	89
19	82	100		77	80	108		71	83	89	88	76	88	72	86
18	80	97		75	78	105		68	79	85	85	73	85	70	84
17	77	93		73	76	101		65	76	81	83	71	82	68	81

TABLE B.9 (*Continued*)

Uniform T-Score Conversions for Content Scales

	Men														
Raw Score	*ANX*	*FRS*	*OBS*	*DEP*	*HEA*	*BIZ*	*ANG*	*CYN*	*ASP*	*TPA*	*LSE*	*SOD*	*FAM*	*WRK*	*TRT*
16	75	90	87	71	74	98	86	62	72	77	80	68	80	67	79
15	72	87	84	70	72	94	82	59	69	72	77	65	77	65	76
14	70	84	80	68	70	91	78	56	65	68	75	63	74	63	74
13	67	80	77	66	68	88	74	54	62	64	72	60	71	61	71
12	65	77	73	65	66	84	70	52	58	60	70	58	68	59	69
11	62	74	70	63	64	81	67	51	55	56	67	55	66	57	66
10	60	70	66	61	62	77	63	49	53	53	64	54	63	56	64
9	57	67	63	59	60	74	59	48	51	50	62	52	60	54	61
8	55	64	59	58	58	70	56	47	49	48	59	50	57	52	59
7	53	60	56	56	56	67	53	46	47	46	57	49	55	50	56
6	52	57	53	55	53	63	50	44	46	44	55	47	52	48	54
5	50	54	50	53	51	60	48	43	44	43	53	45	50	46	52
4	47	51	47	51	48	57	46	41	42	41	51	43	47	44	49
3	45	48	44	48	44	54	43	40	40	38	48	41	44	41	47
2	42	45	41	45	41	51	40	38	37	36	45	39	41	39	43
1	39	41	37	41	37	46	36	35	34	32	41	35	37	36	39
0	35	35	33	36	33	39	32	32	30	30	35	32	33	33	35

TABLE B.9 (*Continued*)

Uniform *T*-Score Conversions for Content Scales

	Women															
Raw Score	*ANX*	*FRS*	*OBS*	*DEP*	*HEA*	*BIZ*	*ANG*	*CYN*	*ASP*	*TPA*	*LSE*	*SOD*	*FAM*	*WRK*	*TRT*	*Raw Score*
36					107											36
35					105											35
34					103											34
33				97	101									99		33
32				95	100									97		32
31				93	98									95		31
30				92	96									92		30
29				90	94									90		29
28				88	92									88		28
27				87	90									86		27
26				85	89									84	102	26
25				83	87								99	82	100	25
24				82	85						97	87	96	80	97	24
23	89	101		80	83	113		83			94	84	94	78	95	23
22	86	98		78	81	110		80	98		92	82	91	76	92	22

TABLE B.9 (*Continued*)

Uniform T-Score Conversions for Content Scales

								Women								
Raw Score	*ANX*	*FRS*	*OBS*	*DEP*	*HEA*	*BIZ*	*ANG*	*CYN*	*ASP*	*TPA*	*LSE*	*SOD*	*FAM*	*WRK*	*TRT*	*Raw Score*
21	84	94		77	79	108		77	94		89	80	89	73	89	21
20	81	91		75	77	105		75	91		86	77	86	71	87	20
19	79	88		73	76	102		72	88	94	84	75	83	69	84	19
18	76	85		72	74	99		69	85	90	81	72	81	67	82	18
17	74	81		70	72	96		67	82	86	78	70	78	65	79	17
16	71	78	87	68	70	93	88	64	79	81	76	68	75	63	77	16
15	69	75	83	67	68	90	84	61	75	77	73	65	73	61	74	15
14	66	72	79	65	66	87	80	58	72	73	70	63	70	59	72	14
13	64	68	75	63	64	84	76	56	69	69	68	60	68	57	69	13
12	61	65	71	62	63	81	72	54	66	64	65	58	65	55	67	12
11	59	62	67	60	61	79	68	53	63	60	62	56	62	54	64	11
10	56	59	63	58	59	76	64	51	59	56	60	54	60	52	61	10
9	55	56	59	57	57	73	60	50	56	53	57	52	57	51	59	9
8	53	53	56	55	55	70	56	48	54	50	55	51	55	50	57	8
7	51	51	53	54	53	67	53	47	52	48	54	49	52	48	55	7
6	49	48	50	52	51	64	50	46	49	45	52	48	50	46	53	6

TABLE B.9 (*Continued*)

Uniform *T*-Score Conversions for Content Scales

							Women									
Raw Score	*ANX*	*FRS*	*OBS*	*DEP*	*HEA*	*BIZ*	*ANG*	*CYN*	*ASP*	*TPA*	*LSE*	*SOD*	*FAM*	*WRK*	*TRT*	*Raw Score*
5	47	46	48	50	49	61	47	44	47	43	51	46	47	45	51	5
4	45	43	46	48	46	58	45	42	45	41	49	44	45	43	49	4
3	43	41	44	45	43	56	42	40	42	38	47	41	42	40	46	3
2	40	38	41	42	40	52	39	38	39	36	44	39	39	37	43	2
1	37	35	37	39	36	47	36	35	36	33	40	35	36	34	39	1
0	34	31	32	34	32	39	31	32	33	30	35	32	32	31	35	0

TABLE B.10

Uniform *T*-Score Conversions for the Content Component Scales for Men

Raw Score	FRS1	FRS2	DEP1	DEP2	DEP3	DEP4	HEA1	HEA2	HEA3	BIZ1	BIZ2	ANG1	ANG2	CYN1	Raw Score
16															16
15														74	15
14														71	14
13														68	13
12			106					120						65	12
11			100					114						63	11
10		81	95					107						60	10
9	120	76	89					100			99			57	9
8	116	71	84					94			93			55	8
7	107	66	79		91			87		120	86	83	72	52	7
6	98	61	73	93	83			80	89	114	80	77	67	49	6
5	89	56	68	85	76	120	109	74	81	102	73	71	61	46	5
4	80	52	62	76	69	112	96	67	72	91	67	64	56	44	4
3	71	47	57	68	62	95	83	60	64	79	60	58	51	41	3
2	62	42	51	59	55	79	70	54	56	67	54	52	46	38	2
1	53	37	46	51	48	62	57	47	48	55	47	45	41	35	1
0	44	32	40	42	41	45	44	40	40	44	41	39	35	33	0

TABLE B.10 (*Continued*)

Uniform *T*-Score Conversions for the Content Component Scales for Men

Raw Score	*CYN2*	*ASP1*	*ASP2*	*TPA1*	*TPA2*	*LSE1*	*LSE2*	*SOD1*	*SOD2*	*FAM1*	*FAM2*	*TRT1*	*TRT2*	*Raw Score*
16		78						82						16
15		75						79						15
14		72						76						14
13		69						73						13
12		66						71		95				12
11		63				95		68		90		107		11
10		60				90		65		85		101		10
9		57			76	85		62		80		95		9
8	71	55			71	80		59		75		89		8
7	66	52			66	75		56	74	70		83		7
6	62	49		68	61	70	83	53	68	65		77		6
5	57	46	74	63	56	64	76	50	63	60	84	71	75	5
4	53	43	67	57	50	59	69	47	58	55	76	66	68	4
3	48	40	59	51	45	54	62	45	52	50	67	60	60	3
2	43	37	52	45	40	49	55	42	47	45	58	54	52	2
1	39	35	45	39	35	44	48	39	41	40	49	48	45	1
0	34	32	38	34	30	39	41	36	36	35	40	42	37	0

TABLE B.11

Uniform T-Score Conversions for the Content Component Scales for Women

Raw Score	FRS1	FRS2	DEP1	DEP2	DEP3	DEP4	HEA1	HEA2	HEA3	BIZ1	BIZ2	ANG1	ANG2	CYN1	Raw Score
16															16
15														76	15
14														73	14
13														70	13
12	120		100					105						67	12
11	114		95					99						64	11
10	107	69	90					94						62	10
9	101	65	85					89			97			59	9
8	94	60	80					83			91			56	8
7	88	56	75		89			78			85	91	70	53	7
6	81	52	70	87	82			72	87	120	79	84	65	50	6
5	74	47	65	79	75	120	97	67	79	112	72	76	59	48	5
4	68	43	60	72	68	109	86	61	71	99	66	69	54	45	4
3	61	38	55	64	61	93	75	56	64	85	60	61	49	42	3
2	55	34	50	56	54	77	64	50	56	71	54	54	44	39	2
1	48	30	45	49	47	61	54	45	48	57	47	47	39	36	1
0	42		40	41	40	45	43	39	40	44	41	39	33	34	0

TABLE B.11 (*Continued*)

Uniform *T*-Score Conversions for the Content Component Scales for Women

Raw Score	*CYN2*	*ASP1*	*ASP2*	*TPA1*	*TPA2*	*LSE1*	*LSE2*	*SOD1*	*SOD2*	*FAM1*	*FAM2*	*TRT1*	*TRT2*	*Raw Score*
16		82						85						16
15		79						82						15
14		76						79						14
13		73						76						13
12		70						73	5	91				12
11		67				89		70		86		96		11
10		64				85		67		81		91		10
9		61			82	80		64		76		86		9
8	73	58			76	75		61		71		81		8
7	68	55			70	71		58	69	67		76		7
6	64	52		70	64	66	75	55	65	62		71		6
5	59	48	90	64	59	62	69	52	60	57	86	66	75	5
4	54	45	81	58	53	57	63	49	55	52	77	61	68	4
3	49	42	71	52	47	53	57	46	50	47	68	56	60	3
2	45	39	61	46	41	48	51	43	45	42	59	51	53	2
1	40	36	51	40	36	43	45	40	40	38	50	46	46	1
0	35	33	42	34	30	39	39	37	35	33	41	41	38	0

TABLE B.12

Linear *T*-Score Conversions for Personality Psychopathology Five (PSY–5) Scales for Men and Women

	Men					Women					
Raw Score	*AGG*	*PSY*	*DIS*	*NEN*	*LPE*	*AGG*	*PSY*	*DIS*	*NEN*	*LPE*	*Raw Score*
40											40
39											39
38											38
37											37
36											36
35											35
34					101					106	34
33				93	99				88	103	33
32				91	97				86	101	32
31				90	94				85	99	31
30				88	92				83	96	30
29			89	86	90			101	81	94	29
28			86	84	88			98	79	91	28
27			83	82	86			95	78	89	27
26			81	80	83			93	76	87	26
25			78	79	81			90	74	84	25
24			76	77	79			87	72	82	24
23		120	73	75	77		120	85	71	79	23
22		117	71	73	74		117	82	69	77	22
21		114	68	71	72		114	79	67	75	21
20		110	66	69	70		110	76	65	72	20
19		106	63	68	68		106	74	64	70	19
18	83	103	60	66	66	90	103	71	62	67	18
17	80	99	58	64	63	86	99	68	60	65	17
16	76	95	55	62	61	83	96	66	58	63	16
15	73	92	53	60	59	79	92	63	57	60	15
14	70	88	50	58	57	76	88	60	55	58	14
13	66	84	48	57	54	72	85	57	53	56	13
12	63	81	45	55	52	69	81	55	51	53	12
11	59	77	42	53	50	65	77	52	50	51	11
10	56	73	40	51	48	61	74	49	48	48	10

TABLE B.12 (*Continued*)

Linear *T*-Score Conversions for Personality Psychopathology Five (PSY–5) Scales for Men and Women

	Men					*Women*					
Raw Score	*AGG*	*PSY*	*DIS*	*NEN*	*LPE*	*AGG*	*PSY*	*DIS*	*NEN*	*LPE*	*Raw Score*
9	53	70	37	49	46	58	70	47	46	46	9
8	49	66	35	47	43	54	67	44	44	44	8
7	46	62	32	46	41	51	63	41	43	41	7
6	43	59	30	44	39	47	59	38	41	39	6
5	39	55	27	42	37	44	56	36	39	36	5
4	36	52	25	40	34	40	52	33	37	34	4
3	32	48	22	38	32	36	48	30	36	32	3
2	30	44	19	36	30	33	45	28	34	29	2
1		41	17	35	28	30	41	25	32	27	1
0		37	14	33	25		38	22	30	24	0

TABLE B.13

Linear *T*-Score Conversions for Supplementary Scales for Men

Raw Score	*A*	*R*	*Es*	*MAC–R*	*O-H*	*Do*	*Re*	*Mt*	*GM*	*GF*	*PK*	*PS*	*MDS*	*APS*	*AAS*	*Raw Score*
60												112				60
59												111				59
58												109				58
57												108				57
56												107				56
55												106				55
54												104				54
53												103				53
52			83									102				52
51			81									101				51
50			78									99				50
49			76	114								98				49
48			74	112								97				48
47			72	110					69			96				47
46			69	108					67	88	113	94				46
45			67	105					65	86	112	93				45
44			65	103					63	84	110	92				44

Table B.13 (*Continued*)

Linear *T*-Score Conversions for Supplementary Scales for Men

Raw Score	*A*	*R*	*Es*	*MAC–R*	*O-H*	*Do*	*Re*	*Mt*	*GM*	*GF*	*PK*	*PS*	*MDS*	*APS*	*AAS*	*Raw Score*
43			63	101					61	82	108	91				43
42			60	98					58	80	107	89				42
41			58	96				96	56	78	105	88				41
40			56	94				95	54	76	103	87				40
39	91		54	92				93	52	73	102	86		92		39
38	89		51	89				91	50	71	100	84		90		38
37	88	98	49	87				90	48	69	98	83		87		37
36	87	96	47	85				88	46	67	97	82		84		36
35	85	94	45	82				87	44	65	95	81		82		35
34	84	92	43	80				85	42	63	93	79		79		34
33	82	89	40	78				84	40	61	92	78		76		33
32	81	87	38	76				82	38	59	90	77		73		32
31	80	56	36	73				81	36	57	88	76		71		31
30	78	83	34	71			76	79	34	54	87	74		68		30
29	77	81	31	69			73	77	32	52	85	73		65		29
28	75	78	30	66	103		70	76	30	50	83	72		63		28

Table B.13 (*Continued*)

Linear *T*-Score Conversions for Supplementary Scales for Men

Raw Score	*A*	*R*	*Es*	*MAC–R*	*O-H*	*Do*	*Re*	*Mt*	*GM*	*GF*	*PK*	*PS*	*MDS*	*APS*	*AAS*	*Raw Score*
27	74	76		64	99		68	74		48	82	71		60		27
26	73	74		62	96		65	73		46	80	69		57		26
25	71	72		60	93	78	63	71		44	78	68		54		25
24	70	69		57	89	75	60	70		42	77	67		52		24
23	68	67		55	86	72	57	68		40	75	66		49		23
22	67	65		53	82	68	55	67		37	73	64		46		22
21	65	63		50	79	65	52	65		35	72	63		44		21
20	64	61		48	76	61	50	64		33	70	62		41		20
19	63	58		46	72	58	47	62		31	68	61		38		19
18	61	56		44	69	55	45	60		30	67	59		35		18
17	60	54		41	65	51	42	59			65	58		33		17
16	58	52		39	62	48	39	57			63	57		30		16
15	57	50		37	58	45	37	56			62	56				15
14	56	47		34	55	41	34	54			60	54	102			14
13	54	45		32	52	38	32	53			58	53	97		100	13
12	53	43		30	48	34	30	51			57	52	92		95	12

Table B.13 (*Continued*)

Linear *T*-Score Conversions for Supplementary Scales for Men

Raw Score	*A*	*R*	*Es*	*MAC–R*	*O-H*	*Do*	*Re*	*Mt*	*GM*	*GF*	*PK*	*PS*	*MDS*	*APS*	*AAS*	*Raw Score*
11	51	41			45	31		50			55	51	88		90	11
10	50	39			41	30		48			53	49	83		85	10
9	49	36			38			46			52	48	79		80	9
8	47	34			35			45			50	47	74		75	8
7	46	32			31			43			48	46	69		70	7
6	44	30			30			42			47	44	65		65	6
5	43							40			45	43	60		60	5
4	42							39			43	42	56		56	4
3	40							37			42	41	51		51	3
2	39							36			40	39	46		46	2
1	37							34			38	38	42		41	1
0	36							32			37	37	37		36	0

TABLE B.14

Linear *T*-Score Conversions for Supplementary Scales for Women

Raw Score	*A*	*R*	*Es*	*MAC-R*	*O-H*	*Do*	*Re*	*Mt*	*GM*	*GF*	*PK*	*PS*	*MDS*	*APS*	*AAS*	*Raw Score*
60												104				60
59												103				59
58												102				58
57												100				57
56												99				56
55												98				55
54												97				54
53												96				53
52			86									95				52
51			84									94				51
50			82									93				50
49			80									92				49
48			78									90				48
47			76						78			89				47
46			74						76	71	107	88				46
45			72	120					75	69	106	87				45

TABLE B.14 (*Continued*)

Linear *T*-Score Conversions for Supplementary Scales for Women

Raw Score	*A*	*R*	*Es*	*MAC-R*	*O-H*	*Do*	*Re*	*Mt*	*GM*	*GF*	*PK*	*PS*	*MDS*	*APS*	*AAS*	*Raw Score*
44			70	118					73	66	104	86				44
43			68	115					72	64	103	85				43
42			66	113					70	61	101	84				42
41			64	110				91	69	59	99	83				41
40			61	107				90	67	56	98	81				40
39	85		59	105				88	66	53	96	80		93		39
38	83		57	102				87	64	51	95	79		90		38
37	82	104	55	99				85	63	48	93	78		87		37
36	81	102	53	96				84	61	46	92	77		85		36
35	80	99	51	94				82	59	43	90	76		82		35
34	78	96	49	91				81	58	40	89	75		79		34
33	77	94	47	88				80	56	38	87	74		77		33
32	76	91	45	86				78	55	35	86	73		74		32
31	74	88	43	83				77	53	33	84	71		71		31
30	73	86	41	80			77	75	52	30	83	70		69		30
29	72	83	39	78			74	74	50		81	69		66		29

TABLE B.14 (*Continued*)

Linear *T*-Score Conversions for Supplementary Scales for Women

Raw Score	*A*	*R*	*Es*	*MAC-R*	*O-H*	*Do*	*Re*	*Mt*	*GM*	*GF*	*PK*	*PS*	*MDS*	*APS*	*AAS*	*Raw Score*
28	71	81	37	75	103		71	72	49		80	68		63		28
27	69	78	35	72	99		68	71	47		78	67		60		27
26	68	75	33	69	96		65	70	46		77	66		58		26
25	67	73	31	67	92	80	62	68	44		75	65		55		25
24	66	70	30	64	88	77	59	67	43		74	64		52		24
23	64	67		61	85	73	56	65	41		72	62		50		23
22	63	65		59	81	70	53	64	40		71	61		47		22
21	62	62		56	77	66	50	62	38		69	60		44		21
20	61	60		53	74	63	47	61	36		67	59		42		20
19	59	57		50	70	59	44	60	35		66	58		39		19
18	58	54		48	66	56	41	58	33		64	57		36		18
17	57	52		45	63	53	38	57	32		63	56		33		17
16	56	49		42	59	49	35	55	30		61	55		31		16
15	54	46		40	55	46	32	54			60	54		30		15
14	53	44		37	52	42	30	52			58	52	98			14
13	52	41		34	48	39		51			57	51	93		113	13
12	50	39		31	44	35		50			55	50	89		107	12

TABLE B.14 (*Continued*)

Linear *T*-Score Conversions for Supplementary Scales for Women

Raw Score	*A*	*R*	*Es*	*MAC-R*	*O-H*	*Do*	*Re*	*Mt*	*GM*	*GF*	*PK*	*PS*	*MDS*	*APS*	*AAS*	*Raw Score*
11	49	36		30	41	32		48			54	49	85		101	11
10	48	33			37	30		47			52	48	80		95	10
9	47	31			33			45			51	47	76		90	9
8	45	30			30			44			49	46	72		84	8
7	44							42			48	45	68		78	7
6	43							41			46	43	63		73	6
5	42							40			45	42	59		67	5
4	40							38			43	41	55		61	4
3	39							37			42	40	50		56	3
2	38							35			40	39	46		50	2
1	37							34			39	38	42		44	1
0	35							32			37	37	38		39	0

TABLE B.15

T Scores Below 30 for Six MMPI–2 Scales Based on MMPI–2 Normative Data

Men							Women							
Raw Score	*Es*	*Do*	*Re*	*GM*	*GF*	*Mf*	*Raw Score*	*Es*	*Do*	*Re*	*GM*	*GF*	*Raw Score*	*Mf*
30							30					30	56	1
29	31			32			29					28	55	3
28	29			30			28					25	54	6
27	27			28			27					22	53	8
26	25			26			26					20	52	11
25	22			24			25	31				17	51	13
24	20			22			24	29				15	50	16
23	18			19			23	27				12	49	18
22	16			17			22	25				10	48	20
21	13			15			21	23				7	47	23
20	11			13			20	21				4	46	25
19	9			11	31		19	19				2	45	28
18	7			9	29		18	17				–1	44	30
17	4			7	27		17	15				-3		

TABLE B.15 (*Continued*)

T Scores Below 30 for Six MMPI–2 Scales Based on MMPI–2 Normative Data

Men								*Women*						
Raw Score	*Es*	*Do*	*Re*	*GM*	*GF*	*Mf*	*Raw Score*	*Es*	*Do*	*Re*	*GM*	*GF*	*Raw Score*	*Mf*
16	2			5	25	30	16	13			30	-6		
15	0			3	23	28	15	10		32	29	-8		
14	–2			1	20	26	14	8		29	27	–11		
13	–5		32	–1	18	24	13	6		26	26	–14		
12	–7		29	–3	16	22	12	4		23	24	–16		
11	–9	31	27	–5	14	20	11	2	32	20	23	–19		
10	–11	28	24	–7	12	18	10	0	28	17	21	–21		
9	–14	24	21	–9	10	17	9	–2	25	14	20	–24		
8	–16	21	19	–11	8	15	8	–4	21	11	18	–26		
7	–18	17	16	–13	6	13	7	–6	18	8	16	–29		
6	–20	14	14	–15	4	11	6	–8	14	5	15	–32		
5		11	11	–17	1	9	5	–10	11	2	13	–34		
4		7	9	–20	–1	7	4	–12	8	–1	12	–37		
3		4	6		–3	5	3	–14	4	–4	10	–39		
2		0	3		–5	3	2	–16	1	–7	9	–42		
1		–3	1		–7	1	1	–18	–3	–10	7	–45		
0		–6	–2		–9	–1	0	–20	–6	–13	6	–47		

Note. Reproduced with the permission of L. Charles Ward, Veterans Affairs Medical Center, Tuscaloosa, Alabama.

Appendix C: Item Overlap and Intercorrelations Among the Standard MMPI–2 Validity and Clinical Scales in the Caldwell Clinical Data Set

MMPI–2 Scale	*L*	*F*	*K*	*1 (Hs)*	*2 (D)*	*3 (Hy)*	*4 (Pd)*	*5 (Mff)*	*5 (Mfm)*	*6 (Pa)*	*7 (Pt)*	*8 (Sc)*	*9 (Ma)*	*0 (Si)*
	S O	*S O*	*S O*	*S O*	*S O*	*S O*	*S O*	*S O*	*S O*	*S O*	*S O*	*S O*	*S O*	*S O*
L	–	1 0	1 0	0 0	2 0	0 0	0 0	1 0	1 0	0 0	0 0	0 0	2 0	0 0
F	–.154	–	1 0	1 0	2 0	1 0	4 0	2 0	2 0	9 0	1 0	15 0	1 0	0 0
K	.427	–.570	–	0 0	6 2	10 0	7 1	1 2	1 2	2 0	0 2	1 0	4 1	1 8
1 (Hs)	–.075	.624	–.508	–	9 1	20 0	1 0	0 0	0 0	1 0	2 0	4 0	0 0	1 0
2 (D)	–.045	.584	–.431	.818	–	13 0	7 0	2 0	2 0	2 0	13 0	9 1	1 4	7 1
3 (Hy)	.081	.363	–.702	.795	.724	–	10 0	4 0	3 1	4 0	7 0	8 0	4 2	1 7
4 (Pd)	–.307	.695	–.537	.538	.587	.387	–	2 1	1 2	8 0	6 0	10 0	6 1	5 6
5 (Mff)	–.079	–.042	–.022	.133	.217	.237	.067	–	52 4	2 0	1 0	1 3	3 0	6 3
5 (Mfm)	–.182	.086	–.159	.208	.272	.259	.196	.935	–	2 0	1 0	3 1	3 0	5 4
6 (Pa)	–.144	.714	–.426	.586	.594	.479	.663	.124	.221	–	4 0	13 0	4 2	1 4
7 (Pt)	–.313	.752	–.755	.770	.804	.499	.725	.146	.277	.696	–	17 0	3 0	8 1
8 (Sc)	–.270	.869	–.720	.767	.731	.481	.763	.049	.202	.748	.925	–	11 0	5 1
9 (Ma)	–.235	.488	–.522	.331	.125	.079	.469	–.121	.008	.386	.457	.557	–	1 5
0 (Si)	–.149	.638	–.641	.617	.731	.313	.539	.140	.207	.511	.798	.743	.141	–

Note. "S" indicates that the deviant response for the item is the same on both scales; "O" indicates that the deviant response is "true" on one scale and "false" on the other scale. *Mff* = Masculinity–Femininity (feminine); *Mfm* = Masculinity–Femininity (masculine). Reproduced with the permission of R. L. Greene.

Appendix D: *K*- and Non-*K*-Corrected *T*-Score Values for the MMPI–2 Basic Scales Based on the Original Minnesota Normative Group (*N* = 225 Men, 315 Women)

The following tables make it possible to score an MMPI–2 protocol using the original Hathaway–McKinley norms. This may be useful, for example, if one wants to compare an individual's MMPI–2 profile with that same individual's profile obtained earlier with the original MMPI. The *T*-score values are identical to the values originally published, except for those MMPI–2 basic scales (*F*, 1, 2, and 0) that are slightly shorter than the original scales; values for these scales were recomputed on the original normative samples. Scale 5 was also shortened, but because the original normative data are not available for this scale, the original values have been adjusted by a type of prorating.

TABLE D.1

K-Corrected *T*-Score Values for the MMPI–2 Basic Scales Based on the Original Minnesota Normative Group (*N* = 225 Men, 315 Women)

						Men							
Raw Score	*L*	*F*	*K*	*Hs+ 0.5K*	*D*	*Hy*	*Pd+ 0.4K*	*Mf*	*Pa*	*Pt +1K*	*Sc +1K*	*Ma +0.2K*	*Si*
72													
71													
70													
69													96
68													95
67													94
66													93
65													92
64													91
63													90
62													89
61													88
60													87
59											120		86
58											119		85
57										120	117		84
56										118	115		83
55						120				116	113		82
54						118		120		114	111		81
53						116		118		112	109		80
52						115		116		110	107		79
51						113		114		107	105		78
50						111		112		105	103		77
49						109	120	110		103	101		76
48						107	119	108		101	99		75
47						106	116	106		99	97		74
46						104	114	104		97	96		73
45						102	111	102		95	94	120	72
44					120	100	109	100		93	92	118	71
43					118	98	107	98		91	90	116	70
42					116	96	104	96		89	88	113	69
41					113	95	102	94		87	86	111	68
40					111	93	100	92		85	84	108	67
39				120	108	91	97	90		83	82	106	66
38				118	106	89	95	88		81	80	103	65
37				116	104	87	93	86		79	78	101	64
36				113	101	86	90	84		77	76	98	63

TABLE D.1 (*Continued*)

K-Corrected *T*-Score Values for the MMPI–2 Basic Scales Based on the Original Minnesota Normative Group (*N* = 225 Men, 315 Women)

						Men							
Raw Score	*L*	*F*	*K*	*Hs+ 0.5K*	*D*	*Hy*	*Pd+ 0.4K*	*Mf*	*Pa*	*Pt +1K*	*Sc +1K*	*Ma +0.2K*	*Si*
35		120		111	99	84	88	82		75	74	96	62
34		118		108	96	82	86	80		73	73	93	61
33		116		106	94	80	83	78		71	71	91	60
32		114		103	92	78	81	76	120	69	69	88	58
31		112		100	89	76	79	74	117	66	67	86	56
30		110	83	98	87	75	76	73	114	64	65	83	55
29		108	81	95	84	73	74	71	111	62	63	81	54
28		106	79	93	82	71	71	69	108	60	61	78	53
27		104	77	90	80	69	69	67	105	58	59	75	52
26		102	75	88	77	67	67	64	102	56	57	73	51
25		100	74	85	75	65	64	61	100	54	55	70	50
24		98	72	82	72	64	62	59	97	52	53	68	49
23		96	70	80	70	62	60	57	94	50	51	65	48
22		94	68	77	68	60	57	55	91	48	50	63	47
21		92	66	75	65	58	55	53	88	46	48	60	46
20		90	64	72	63	56	53	51	85	44	46	58	45
19		88	62	70	60	55	50	49	82	42	44	55	44
18		86	61	67	58	53	48	47	79	40	42	53	43
17		84	59	65	56	51	46	45	76	38	40	50	42
16		82	57	62	53	49	43	43	73	36	38	48	41
15	86	80	55	59	51	47	41	41	70	34	36	45	40
14	83	78	53	57	48	45	39	39	67	32	34	43	39
13	80	76	51	54	46	44	36	37	65	30	32	40	38
12	76	73	49	52	44	42	34	35	62		30	38	37
11	73	70	48	49	41	40	32	34	59			35	36
10	70	68	46	47	39	38	30	32	56			33	35
9	66	66	44	44	36	36		30	53			30	34
8	63	64	42	41	34	35			50				33
7	60	62	40	39	32	33			47				32
6	56	60	38	36	30	31			44				30
5	53	58	36	34		30			41				
4	50	55	35	31					38				
3	46	53	33	30					35				
2	44	50	31						33				
1	40	48	30						30				
0	36	46											

TABLE D.1 (*Continued*)

K-Corrected *T*-Score Values for the MMPI–2 Basic Scales Based on the Original Minnesota Normative Group (*N* = 225 Men, 315 Women)

Women													
L	*F*	*K*	*Hs* *+0.5K*	*D*	*Hy*	*Pd* *+0.4K*	*Mf*	*Pa*	*Pt* *+1K*	*Sc* *+1K*	*Ma* *+0.2K*	*Si*	*Raw Score*
													72
													71
													70
										120		96	69
									120	119		95	68
									118	118		94	67
									117	116		93	66
									115	115		92	65
									114	113		91	64
									112	112		90	63
									110	110		89	62
									109	109		88	61
									107	107		87	60
									106	106		86	59
					120				104	104		85	58
					118				102	103		84	57
					116				101	101		83	56
				120	114				99	100		82	55
				119	112				98	98		84	54
				117	110				96	97		80	53
				115	109				94	95		79	52
				113	107				93	94		78	51
				111	105				91	92		77	50
				109	103	120			89	91		76	49
				107	101	119			88	89		75	48
			119	105	100	116			86	87		74	47
			117	103	98	114			84	86		73	46
			115	102	96	111			83	84	120	72	45
			113	100	94	109			81	83	118	71	44
			111	98	93	107	30		79	81	116	70	43
			109	96	91	104	32		78	80	113	69	42
			107	94	89	102	34		76	78	111	68	41
			105	92	87	100	37		74	77	108	67	40
			103	90	86	97	39		73	75	106	66	39
			101	88	84	95	41		71	74	103	65	38
			99	86	82	93	43		69	72	101	64	37

TABLE D.1 (*Continued*)

K-Corrected *T*-Score Values for the MMPI–2 Basic Scales Based on the Original Minnesota Normative Group (*N* = 225 Men, 315 Women)

Women

L	*F*	*K*	*Hs* +0.5*K*	*D*	*Hy*	*Pd* +0.4*K*	*Mf*	*Pa*	*Pt* +1*K*	*Sc* +1*K*	*Ma* +0.2*K*	*Si*	*Raw Score*
			97	84	80	90	45		68	71	98	63	36
	120		95	82	79	88	48		66	69	96	62	35
	118		93	80	77	86	51		65	67	93	61	34
	116		91	78	75	83	53		63	66	91	60	33
	114		89	76	73	81	55	120	61	64	88	58	32
	112		87	75	72	79	57	117	60	63	86	56	31
	110	83	85	73	70	76	59	114	58	61	83	55	30
	108	81	82	71	68	74	61	111	56	60	81	54	29
	106	79	80	69	66	71	63	108	55	58	78	53	28
	104	77	78	67	64	69	66	105	53	57	75	52	27
	102	75	76	65	63	67	68	102	51	55	73	51	26
	100	74	74	63	61	64	70	100	50	54	70	50	25
	98	72	72	61	59	62	72	97	48	52	68	49	24
	96	70	70	59	57	60	74	94	46	51	65	48	23
	94	68	68	57	56	57	76	91	45	49	63	47	22
	92	66	66	55	54	55	78	88	43	47	60	46	21
	90	64	64	53	52	53	80	85	41	46	58	45	20
	88	62	62	51	50	50	82	82	40	44	55	44	19
	86	61	60	49	49	48	84	79	38	43	53	43	18
	84	59	58	47	47	46	86	76	36	41	50	42	17
	82	57	56	46	45	43	88	73	35	40	48	41	16
86	80	55	54	45	43	41	90	70	33	38	45	40	15
83	78	53	52	44	42	39	92	67	32	37	43	39	14
80	76	51	50	42	40	36	94	65	30	35	40	38	13
76	73	49	48	40	38	34	96	62		34	38	37	12
73	70	48	46	38	36	32	98	59		32	35	36	11
70	68	46	44	36	34	30	100	56		31	33	35	10
66	66	44	42	34	33		103	53		30	30	34	9
63	64	42	39	32	31		105	50				33	8
60	62	40	37	30	30		107	47				32	7
56	60	38	35				109	44				30	6
53	58	36	33				111	41					5
50	55	35	31				113	38					4
46	53	33	30				115	35					3
44	50	31					117	33					2
40	48	30					119	30					1
36	46						120						0

TABLE D.2

Non-*K*-Corrected *T*-Score Values for the MMPI–2 Basic Scales Based on the Original Minnesota Normative Group (N = 225 Men, 315 Women)

						Men							
Raw Score	*L*	*F*	*K*	*Hs*	*D*	*Hy*	*Pd*	*Mf*	*Pa*	*Pt*	*Sc*	*Ma*	*Si*
72													
71													
70													
69													96
68													95
67													94
66													93
65													92
64													91
63													90
62													89
61											120		88
60											118		87
59											117		86
58											115		85
57											114		84
56											113		83
55						120					111		82
54						118		120			110		81
53						116		118			109		80
52						115		116			107		79
51						113		114			106		78
50						111		112			105		77
49						109		110			103		76
48						107		108		103	102		75
47						106		106		102	101		74
46						104		104		100	99	120	73
45						102		102		99	98	119	72
44					120	100		100		98	97	117	71
43					118	98		98		96	95	115	70
42					116	96	120	96		95	94	112	69

TABLE D.2 (*Continued*)

Non-*K*-Corrected *T*-Score Values for the MMPI–2 Basic Scales Based on the Original Minnesota Normative Group (N = 225 Men, 315 Women)

						Men							
Raw Score	*L*	*F*	*K*	*Hs*	*D*	*Hy*	*Pd*	*Mf*	*Pa*	*Pt*	*Sc*	*Ma*	*Si*
41					113	95	119	94		93	92	110	68
40					111	93	116	92		92	91	108	67
39					108	91	114	90		91	90	106	66
38					106	89	111	88		89	88	104	65
37					104	87	108	86		88	87	101	64
36					101	86	106	84		86	86	99	63
35		120			99	84	103	82		85	84	97	62
34		118			96	82	101	80		84	83	95	61
33		116			94	80	98	78		82	82	93	60
32		114		113	92	78	96	76	120	81	80	90	58
31		112		110	89	76	93	74	117	79	79	88	56
30		110	83	108	87	75	91	73	114	78	78	86	55
29		108	81	106	84	73	88	71	111	77	76	84	54
28		106	79	104	82	71	86	69	108	75	75	81	53
27		104	77	101	80	69	83	67	105	74	74	79	52
26		102	75	99	77	67	81	64	102	73	72	77	51
25		100	74	97	75	65	78	61	100	71	71	75	50
24		98	72	94	72	64	75	59	97	70	70	72	49
23		96	70	92	70	62	73	57	94	68	68	70	48
22		94	68	90	68	60	70	55	91	67	67	68	47
21		92	66	88	65	58	68	53	88	66	65	66	46
20		90	64	85	63	56	65	51	85	64	64	63	45
19		88	62	83	60	55	63	49	82	63	63	61	44
18		86	61	81	58	53	60	47	79	61	61	59	43
17		84	59	78	56	51	58	45	76	60	60	57	42
16		82	57	76	53	49	55	43	73	59	59	54	41
15	86	80	55	74	51	47	53	41	70	57	57	52	40
14	83	78	53	72	48	45	50	39	67	56	56	50	39
13	80	76	51	69	46	44	47	37	65	54	55	48	38
12	76	73	49	67	44	42	45	35	62	53	53	45	37

TABLE D.2 (*Continued*)

Non-*K*-Corrected *T*-Score Values for the MMPI–2 Basic Scales Based on the Original Minnesota Normative Group (N = 225 Men, 315 Women)

						Men							
Raw Score	*L*	*F*	*K*	*Hs*	*D*	*Hy*	*Pd*	*Mf*	*Pa*	*Pt*	*Sc*	*Ma*	*Si*
11	73	70	48	65	41	40	42	34	59	52	52	43	36
10	70	68	46	62	39	38	40	32	56	50	51	41	35
9	66	66	44	60	36	36	37	30	53	49	49	39	34
8	63	64	42	58	34	35	35		50	48	48	37	33
7	60	62	40	56	32	33	32		47	46	47	34	32
6	56	60	38	53	30	31	30		44	45	45	32	30
5	53	58	36	51		30			41	43	44	30	
4	50	55	35	49					38	42	43		
3	46	53	33	47					35	41	41		
2	44	50	31	44					33	39	40		
1	40	48	30	42					30	38	38		
0	36	46		40						36	37		

TABLE D.2 (*Continued*)

Non-*K*-Corrected *T*-Score Values for the MMPI–2 Basic Scales Based on the Original Minnesota Normative Group (N = 225 Men, 315 Women)

							Women						
L	*F*	*K*	*Hs*	*D*	*Hy*	*Pd*	*Mf*	*Pa*	*Pt*	*Sc*	*Ma*	*Si*	*Raw Score*
													72
													71
													70
												96	69
												95	68
										120		94	67
										119		93	66
										118		92	65
										117		91	64
										116		90	63
										114		89	62
										113		88	61
										112		87	60
										111		86	59
					120					109		85	58
					118					108		84	57
					116					107		83	56
				120	114					106		82	55
				119	112					104		81	54
				117	110					103		80	53
				115	109					102		79	52
				113	107					101		78	51
				111	105					99		77	50
				109	103					98		76	49
				107	101				95	97		75	48
				105	100				94	96		74	47
				103	98				93	94	120	73	46
				102	96				91	93	119	72	45
				100	94				90	92	117	71	44
				98	93	120	30		89	91	115	70	43
				96	91	117	32		88	89	112	69	42
				94	89	115	34		86	88	110	68	41
				92	87	113	37		85	87	108	67	40
				90	86	110	39		84	86	106	66	39

TABLE D.2 (*Continued*)

Non-K-Corrected T-Score Values for the MMPI–2 Basic Scales Based on the Original Minnesota Normative Group (N = 225 Men, 315 Women)

Women													
L	*F*	*K*	*Hs*	*D*	*Hy*	*Pd*	*Mf*	*Pa*	*Pt*	*Sc*	*Ma*	*Si*	*Raw Score*
				88	84	108	41		82	84	104	65	38
				86	82	106	43		81	83	101	64	37
				84	80	103	45		80	82	99	63	36
	120			82	79	101	48		78	80	97	62	35
	118			80	77	99	51		77	79	95	61	34
	116			78	75	96	53		76	78	93	60	33
	114		97	76	73	94	55	120	75	77	90	58	32
	112		96	75	72	91	57	117	73	75	88	56	31
	110	83	94	73	70	89	59	114	72	74	86	55	30
	108	81	92	71	68	87	61	111	71	73	84	54	29
	106	79	90	69	66	84	63	108	69	72	81	53	28
	104	77	88	67	64	82	66	105	68	70	79	52	27
	102	75	86	65	63	80	68	102	67	69	77	51	26
	100	74	84	63	61	77	70	100	65	68	75	50	25
	98	72	82	61	59	75	72	97	64	67	72	49	24
	96	70	80	59	57	73	74	94	63	65	70	48	23
	94	68	79	57	56	70	76	91	62	64	68	47	22
	92	66	77	55	54	68	78	88	60	63	66	46	21
	90	64	75	53	52	65	80	85	59	62	63	45	20
	88	62	73	51	50	63	82	82	58	60	61	44	19
	86	61	71	49	49	61	84	79	56	59	59	43	18
	84	59	69	47	47	58	86	76	55	58	57	42	17
	82	57	67	46	45	56	88	73	54	57	54	41	16
86	80	55	65	45	43	53	90	70	52	55	52	40	15
83	78	53	63	44	42	51	92	67	51	54	50	39	14
80	76	51	62	42	40	49	94	65	50	53	48	38	13
76	73	49	60	40	38	47	96	62	49	52	45	37	12
73	70	48	58	38	36	44	98	59	47	50	43	36	11
70	68	46	56	36	34	42	100	56	46	49	41	35	10
66	66	44	54	34	33	40	103	53	45	48	39	34	9
63	64	42	52	32	31	37	105	50	43	47	37	33	8
60	62	40	50	30	30	35	107	47	42	45	34	32	7
56	60	38	48			32	109	44	41	44	32	30	6

TABLE D.2 (*Continued*)

Non-K-Corrected T-Score Values for the MMPI–2 Basic Scales Based on the Original Minnesota Normative Group (N = 225 Men, 315 Women)

Women													
L	*F*	*K*	*Hs*	*D*	*Hy*	*Pd*	*Mf*	*Pa*	*Pt*	*Sc*	*Ma*	*Si*	*Raw Score*
53	58	36	46			30	111	41	39	43	30		5
50	55	35	45				113	38	38	42			4
46	53	33	43				115	35	37	40			3
44	50	31	41				117	33	36	39			2
40	48	30	39				119	30	34	38			1
36	46		37				120		33	37			0

References

Aaronson, A. L. (1958). Age and sex influence on MMPI profile peak distributions in an abnormal population. *Journal of Consulting Psychology, 22*, 203–206.

Aaronson, A. L., Dent, O. B., Webb, J. T., & Kline, C. D. (1996). Graying of the critical items: Effects of aging on responding to MMPI–2 critical items. *Journal of Personality Assessment, 66*, 169–176.

Alexander, A. A., Roessler, R., & Greenfield, N. S. (1963). Ego strength and physiological responsivity: III. The relationship between the Barron Ego Strength scale to spontaneous periodical activity in skin resistance, finger blood volume, heart rate, and muscle potential. *Archives of General Psychiatry, 9*, 58–61.

Alker, H. A. (1978). Minnesota Multiphasic Personality Inventory. In O. K. Buros (Ed.), *Eighth mental measurements yearbook* (pp. 931–935). Highland Park, NJ: Gryphon Press.

Allen, J. P., Faded, V. B., Rawlings, R. R., & Miller, A. (1991). Personality differences associated with MacAndrew scores. *Psychological Reports, 66*, 691–698.

American Psychiatric Association. (1968). *Diagnostic and statistical manual of mental disorders* (2nd ed.). Washington, DC: Author.

American Psychiatric Association. (1980). *Diagnostic and statistical manual of mental disorders* (3rd ed.). Washington, DC: Author.

American Psychiatric Association. (1994). *Diagnostic and statistical manual of mental disorders* (4th ed.). Washington, DC: Author.

American Psychological Association. (1977). *Standards for providers of psychological services.* Washington, DC: Author

American Psychological Association. (1985). *Standards for educational and psychological testing.* Washington, DC: Author

American Psychological Association. (1986). *Guidelines for users of computer-based tests and interpretations.* Washington, DC: Author.

American Psychological Association. (1992). Ethical principles of psychologists and code of conduct. *American Psychologist, 47*, 1597–1611.

American Psychological Association. (1993). Guidelines for providers of psychological services to ethnic, linguistic, and culturally diverse populations. *American Psychologist, 48*, 45–48.

American Psychological Association. (1994). Guidelines for child custody evaluations in divorce proceedings. *American Psychologist, 49*, 677–680.

Anastasi, A. (1982). *Psychological testing* (5th ed.). New York: Macmillan.

Anderson, H. E., & Bashaw, W. L. (1966). Further comments on the internal structure of the MMPI. *Psychological Bulletin, 66*, 211–213.

Anderson, W. (1956). The MMPI: Low *Pa* scores. *Journal of Counseling Psychology, 3*, 226–228.

Anderson, W. P., & Kunce, J. T. (1984). Diagnostic implication of markedly elevated MMPI *Sc* scale scores for non-hospitalized clients. *Journal of Clinical Psychology, 40*, 925–930.

Anthony, N. (1971). Comparison of clients' standard, exaggerated and matching MMPI profiles. *Journal of Consulting and Clinical Psychology, 36*, 100–103.

Apfeldorf, M. (1978). Alcoholism scales of the MMPI: Contributions and future directions. *International Journal of the Addictions, 13*, 17–55.

Arbisi, P. A. & Ben-Porath, Y. S. (1995a, March) *Identifying changes in infrequent responding to the MMPI–2*. Paper presented at the 30th Annual Symposium on Recent Developments in the Use of the MMPI–2, St. Petersburg, FL.

Arbisi, P. A., & Ben-Porath, Y. S. (1995b). An MMPI–2 infrequent response scale for use with psychopathological populations. The Infrequency–Psychopathology scale, *F(p)*. *Psychological Assessment: A Journal of Consulting and Clinical Psychology, 7*, 424–431.

Arbisi, P. A., & Ben-Porath, Y. S. (1997). Characteristics of the MMPI–2 *F(p)* scale as a function of diagnosis in an inpatient sample of veterans. *Psychological Assessment: A Journal of Consulting and Clinical Psychology, 9*, 102–105.

Arbisi, P. A., McNulty, J. L., Ben-Porath, Y. S., & Boyd, J. (1999, April). *Detection of partial fake bad responding on the MMPI–2*. Paper presented at the 34th Annual Symposium on Recent Developments in the Use of the MMPI–2 and MMPI–A, Huntington Beach, CA.

Archer, R. P. (1984). Use of the MMPI with adolescents: A review of salient issues. *Clinical Psychology Review, 4*, 241–251.

Archer, R. P. (1987) *Using the MMPI with adolescents*. Hillsdale, NJ: Lawrence Erlbaum Associates.

Archer, R. P. (1988). Using the MMPI with adolescents. In C. D. Spielberger & J. N. Butcher (Eds.), *Advances in personality assessment* (Vol. 7, pp. 103–126). Hillsdale, NJ: Lawrence Erlbaum Associates.

Archer, R. P. (1992). *The MMPI–A: Assessing adolescent psychopathology*. Hillsdale, NJ: Lawrence Erlbaum Associates

Archer, R. P. (1997). *MMPI–A: Assessing adolescent psychopathology* (2nd ed.). Mahwah, NJ: Lawrence Erlbaum Associates.

Archer, R. P., Fontaine, J., & McCrae, R. R. (1998). Effects of two MMPI–2 validity scales on basic scale relations to external criteria. *Journal of Personality Assessment, 70*, 87–102.

Archer, R. P., & Gordon, R. A. (1991). [Correlational analysis of the MMPI–A normative data set]. Unpublished raw data.

Archer, R. P., Gordon, R. A., & Klinefelter, D. (1991). [Analyses of the frequency of MMPI and MMPI–A profile assignments for 1762 adolescent patients]. Unpublished raw data.

Archer, R. P., Griffin, R., & Aiduk, R. (1995). MMPI–2 clinical correlates for ten common codes. *Journal of Personality Assessment, 65*, 391–407.

Astin, A. W. (1959). A factor study of the MMPI Psychopathic Deviate scale. *Journal of Consulting Psychology, 23*, 550–554.

Astin, A. W. (1961). A note on the MMPI Psychopathic Deviate scale. *Educational and Psychological Measurement, 21*, 895–897.

Baer, R. A., Wetter, M. W., & Berry, D. T. R. (1992). Detection of underreporting of psychopathology on the MMPI: A meta-analysis. *Clinical Psychology Review, 12*, 509–525.

Baer, R. A., Wetter, M. W., & Berry, D. T. R. (1995). Effects of information about validity scales on underreporting of symptoms on the MMPI–2: An analogue investigation. *Assessment, 2*, 189–200.

Baer, R. A., Wetter, M. W., Nichols, D. S., Greene, R. L., & Berry, D. T. R. (1995). Sensitivity of MMPI–2 validity scales to underreporting of symptoms. *Psychological Assessment: A Journal of Consulting and Clinical Psychology, 7*, 419–423.

Bagby, R. M., Nicholson, R. A., Buis, T., Radovanovic, H., & Fidler, B. J. (1999). Defensive responding on the MMPI–2 in family custody and access evaluations. *Psychological Assessment: A Journal of Consulting and Clinical Psychology, 11*, 24–28.

Bagby, R. M., Rogers, R., & Buis, T. (1994). Detecting malingered and defensive responding on the MMPI–2 in a forensic inpatient sample. *Journal of Personality Assessment, 62*, 191–203.

Bagby, R. M., Rogers, R., Buis, T., & Kalemba, V. (1994). Malingered and defensive response styles on the MMPI–2: An examination of validity scales. *Assessment, 1*, 31–38

Bagby, R. M., Rogers, R., Buis, T., Nicholson, R. A., Cameron, S. L., Rector, N. A., Schuller, D. R., & Seeman, M. V. (1997). Detecting feigned depression and schizophrenia on the MMPI–2. *Journal of Personality Assessment, 68*, 650–664.

Bagby, R. M., Rogers, R., Nicholson, R. A., Buis, T., Seeman, M. V., & Rector, N. A. (1997). Effectiveness of the MMPI–2 validity indicators in the detection of defensive responding in clinical and nonclinical samples. *Psychological Assessment: A Journal of Consulting and Clinical Psychology, 9*, 406–413.

Ball, J. C., & Carroll, D. (1960). Analysis of MMPI Cannot Say score in an adolescent population. *Journal of Clinical Psychology, 16*, 30–31.

Barron, F. (1953). An ego-strength scale which predicts response to psychotherapy. *Journal of Consulting Psychology, 17*, 327–333.

Barthlow, D. L., Graham, J. R., Ben-Porath, Y. S., & McNulty, J. L. (1999). Incremental validity of the MMPI–2 content scales in an outpatient mental health setting. *Psychological Assessment: A Journal of Consulting and Clinical Psychology, 11*, 39–47.

Bathurst, K., Gottfried, A. W., & Gottfried, A. E. (1997). Normative data for the MMPI–2 in child custody litigation. *Psychological Assessment: A Journal of Consulting and Clinical Psychology, 9*, 205–211.

Bell, H. M. (1934). *Adjustment Inventory.* Stanford, CA: Stanford University Press.

Bem, S. L. (1974). The measurement of psychological androgyny. *Journal of Consulting and Clinical Psychology, 42*, 152–162.

Ben-Porath, Y. S. (1993, June). MMPI–2 items. *MMPI–2 and MMPI–A: News and Profiles, 4*, 7.

Ben-Porath, Y. S., & Butcher, J. N. (1989). Psychometric stability of rewritten MMPI items. *Journal of Personality Assessment, 53*, 645–653.

Ben-Porath, Y. S., Butcher, J. N., & Graham, J. R. (1991). Contribution of the MMPI–2 content scales to the differential diagnosis of schizophrenia and major depression. *Psychological Assessment: A Journal of Consulting and Clinical Psychology, 3*, 634–640.

Ben-Porath, Y. S., Hostetler, K., Butcher, J. N., & Graham, J. R. (1989). New subscales for the MMPI–2 Social Introversion scale. *Psychological Assessment: A Journal of Consulting and Clinical Psychology, 1*, 169–174.

Ben-Porath, Y. S., McCully, E., & Almagor, M. (1993). Incremental validity of the MMPI–2 content scales in the assessment of personality and psychopathology by self-report. *Journal of Personality Assessment, 61*, 557–575.

Ben-Porath, Y. S., & Sherwood, N. E. (1993). *The MMPI–2 content component scales: Development, psychometric characteristics and clinical application.* Minneapolis: University of Minnesota Press.

Ben-Porath, Y. S., Slutske, W. S., & Butcher, J. N. (1989). A real-data simulation of computerized adaptive administration of the MMPI. *Psychological Assessment: A Journal of Consulting and Clinical Psychology, 1*, 18–22.

Ben-Porath, Y. S., & Stafford, K. P. (1993, August). *Empirical correlates of MMPI–2 scales in a forensic diagnostic sample: An interim report.* Paper presented at the 101st Annual Convention of the American Psychological Association, Toronto, Ontario, Canada.

Bernreuter, R. G. (1933). The theory and construction of the Personality Inventory. *Journal of Social Psychology, 4*, 387–404.

Berry, D. T. R., Baer, R. A., & Harris, M. J. (1991). Detection of malingering on the MMPI: A meta-analysis. *Clinical Psychology Review, 11*, 585–598.

Berry, D. T. R., Wetter, M. W., Baer, R. A., Gass, C. S., Franzen, M. D., Youngjohn, J. R., Lomb, D. G., MacInnes, W. D., & Buchholz, D. (1995). Overreporting of closed-head injury symptoms on the MMPI–2. *Psychological Assessment: A Journal of Consulting and Clinical Psychology, 7*, 517–523.

Berry, D., Wetter, M., Baer, R., Larsen, L., Clark, C., & Monroe, K. (1992). MMPI–2 Random responding indices: Validation using a self-report methodology. *Psychological Assessment: A Journal of Consulting and Clinical Psychology, 4*, 340–345.

Berry, D. T. R., Wetter, M. W., Baer, R. A., Widiger, T. A., Sumpter, J. C., Reynolds, S. K., & Hallam, R. A. (1991). Detection of random responding on the MMPI–2: Utility of *F*, back *F*, and *VRIN* scales. *Psychological Assessment: A Journal of Consulting and Clinical Psychology, 3*, 418–423.

Bersoff, D. N., & Hofer, P. J. (1995). Legal issues in computerized psychological testing. In D. N. Bersoff (Ed.), *Ethical conflicts in psychology* (pp. 291–294). Washington, DC: American Psychological Association.

Blake, D. D., Penk, W. E., Mori, D. L., Kleespies, P. M., Walsh, S. S., & Keane, T. M. (1992). Validity and clinical scale comparison between the MMPI and MMPI–2 with psychiatric inpatients. *Psychological Reports, 70*, 323–332.

Blanchard, J. S. (1981). Readability of the MMPI. *Perceptual and Motor Skills, 52*, 985–986.

Bleuler, E. (1950). *Dementia praecox; or the group of schizophrenias.* New York: International Universities Press.

Block, J. (1965). *The challenge of response sets: Unconfounding meaning, acquiescence, and social desirability in the MMPI.* New York: Appleton-Century-Crofts.

Bond, J. A. (1986). Inconsistent responding to repeated MMPI items: Is its major cause really carelessness? *Journal of Personality Assessment, 50,* 50–64.

Bond, J. A. (1987). The process of responding to personality items: Inconsistent responses to repeated presentation of identical items. *Personality and Individual Differences, 8,* 409–417.

Box, G. E. P., & Cox, D. R. (1964). An analysis of transformations. *Journal of the Royal Statistical Society, 59,* 211–243.

Brauer, B. A. (1988). Substudies developed during the psychological instruments translation study. In R. C. Johnson, D. L. Smith, & S. Davies (Eds.), *A tradition of discovery.* Washington, DC: Gallaudet University, Gallaudet Research Institute.

Brauer, B. A. (1992). The signer effect on MMPI performance of deaf respondents. Journal of *Personality Assessment, 58,* 380–388.

Brozek, J. (1955). Personality changes with age: An item analysis of the MMPI. *Journal of Gerontology, 10,* 194–206.

Buechley, R., & Ball, H. (1952). A new test of "validity" for the group MMPI. *Journal of Consulting Psychology, 16,* 299–301.

Burkhart, B. R., Christian, W. L., & Gynther, M. D. (1978). Item subtlety and faking on the MMPI: A paradoxical relationship. *Journal of Personality Assessment, 42,* 76–80.

Buros, O. K. (Ed.). (1978). *The Eighth mental measurements yearbook.* Highland Park, NJ: Gryphon Press.

Butcher, J. N. (1979). Use of the MMPI in personnel selection. In J. N. Butcher (Ed.), *New developments in the use of the MMPI* (pp. 165–201). Minneapolis: University of Minnesota Press.

Butcher, J. N. (1987a). Computerized clinical and personality assessment using the MMPI. In J. N. Butcher (Ed.), *Computerized psychological assessment: A practitioner's guide* (pp. 161–197). New York: Basic Books.

Butcher, J. N. (Ed.). (1987b). *Computerized psychological assessment: A practitioner's guide.* New York: Basic Books.

Butcher, J. N. (1990a, August). Education level and MMPI–2 measured psychopathology: A case of negligible influence. *MMPI–2: News and Profiles, 1,* 2.

Butcher, J. N. (1990b). *Use of the MMPI–2 in treatment planning.* New York: Oxford University Press.

Butcher, J. N. (1992, October). International developments with the MMPI–2. *MMPI–2: News and Profiles, 3,* 4–5.

Butcher, J. N. (1993). *The Minnesota report: Adult clinical system—revised user's guide.* Minneapolis, MN: National Computer Systems.

Butcher, J. N. (1994a) Important considerations in the use of automated MMPI–2 reports. In J. N. Butcher & J. R. Graham (Eds.), *Topics in MMPI–2 and MMPI–A interpretation.* Minneapolis: University of Minnesota, Department of Psychology.

Butcher, J. N. (1994b). Psychological assessment of airline pilot applicants with the MMPI–2. *Journal of Personality Assessment, 62,* 31–44.

Butcher, J. N. (Ed.). (1996). *International adaptation of the MMPI–2.* Minneapolis: University of Minnesota Press.

Butcher, J. N., Dahlstrom, W. G., Graham, J. R., Tellegen, A., & Kaemmer, B. (1989). *Minnesota Multiphasic Personality Inventory–2 (MMPI–2): Manual for administration and scoring.* Minneapolis: University of Minnesota Press.

Butcher, J. N., & Graham, J. R. (1989). *Topics in MMPI–2 interpretation.* Minneapolis: University of Minnesota, Department of Psychology.

Butcher, J. N., Graham, J. R., Williams, C. L., & Ben-Porath, Y. S. (1990). *Development and use of the MMPI–2 content scales.* Minneapolis: University of Minnesota Press.

Butcher, J. N., & Han, K. (1995). Development of an MMPI–2 scale to assess the presentation of self in a superlative manner: The *S* scale. In J. N. Butcher & C. D. Spielberger (Eds.), *Advances in personality assessment* (pp. 25–50). Hillsdale, NJ: Lawrence Erlbaum Associates.

Butcher, J. N., & Hostetler, K (1990). Abbreviating MMPI item administration: What can be learned from the MMPI for the MMPI–2? *Psychological Assessment: A Journal of Consulting and Clinical Psychology, 2,* 12–21.

Butcher, J. N., Keller, L. S., & Bacon, S. F. (1985). Current developments and future directions in computerized personality assessment. *Journal of Consulting and Clinical Psychology, 53,* 803–815.

Butcher, J. N., Morfitt, R. C., Rouse, S. V., & Holden, R. R. (1997). Reducing MMPI–2 defensiveness: The effect of specialized instructions on retest validity on a job applicant sample. *Journal of Personality Assessment, 68*, 385–401.

Butcher, J. N., & Owen P. L. (1978). Objective personality inventories: Recent research and some contemporary issues. In B. Wolman (Ed.), *Clinical diagnosis of mental disorders* (pp. 475–546). New York: Plenum.

Butcher, J. N., & Pancheri, P. (1976). *A handbook of cross-national MMPI research.* Minneapolis: University of Minnesota Press.

Butcher, J. N., & Williams, C. L. (1992). *Essentials of MMPI–2 and MMPI–A interpretation.* Minneapolis: University of Minnesota Press.

Butcher, J. N., Williams, C. L., Graham, J. R., Archer, R. P., Tellegen, A., Ben-Porath, Y. S., & Kaemmer, B. (1992). *MMPI–A (Minnesota Multiphasic Personality Inventory—Adolescent) manual for administration, scoring, and interpretation.* Minneapolis: University of Minnesota Press.

Caldwell, A. B. (1969). *MMPI critical items.* Los Angeles: Author.

Caldwell, A. B. (1974, February). *Characteristics of MMPI pattern types.* Paper presented at the Ninth Annual Symposium on the MMPI, Los Angeles, CA.

Caldwell, A. B. (1977). *Questions people ask when taking the MMPI* (Special Bulletin No. 3). (Available from Caldwell Report, 1545 Sawtelle Boulevard, Suite 14, Los Angeles, CA 90025)

Caldwell, A. B. (1984, April). *Clinical decision making with the MMPI.* Workshop sponsored by the Advanced Psychological Studies Institute and Northwestern University, Chicago, IL.

Caldwell, A. (1988). *MMPI supplemental scale manual.* Los Angeles: Caldwell Report.

Caldwell, A. B. (1991). Commentary on the Minnesota Multiphasic Personality Inventory-2: A review. *Journal of Counseling and Development, 69*, 568–569.

Caldwell, A. B. (1997). *Forensic questions and answers on the MMPI/MMPI–2.* Los Angeles: Caldwell Report.

Calvin, J. (1975). *A replicated study of the concurrent validity of the Harris subscales for the MMPI.* Unpublished doctoral dissertation, Kent State University, Kent, OH.

Carkhuff, R. R., Barnett, L., & McCall, J. N. (1965). *The counselor's handbook: Scale and profile interpretations of the MMPI.* Urbana, IL: R. W. Parkinson.

Carr, A. C., & Ghosh, A. (1983). Response of phobic patients to direct computer assessment. *British Journal of Psychiatry, 142*, 60–65.

Carson, R. C. (1969). Interpretive manual to the MMPI. In J. N. Butcher (Ed.), *MMPI: Research developments and clinical applications* (pp. 279–296). New York: McGraw-Hill.

Chang, A. F., Caldwell, A. B., & Moss, T. (1973). Stability of personality traits in alcoholics during and after treatment as measured by the MMPI: A one-year follow-up study. *Proceedings of the American Psychological Association, 8*, 387–388.

Childs, R. A., Dahlstrom, W. G., Kemp, S. M., & Panter, A. T. (1992). *Item response theory in personality assessment: The MMPI–2 Depression scale* (Research Report No. 92-1). Chapel Hill: University of North Carolina, C. C. Thurstone Psychometric Laboratory.

Chojnacki, J. T., & Walsh, W. B. (1994). The consistency between scores of the Harris–Lingoes subscales of the MMPI and MMPI–2. *Journal of Personality Assessment, 62*, 157–165.

Christian, W. L., Burkhart, B. R., & Gynther, M. D. (1978). Subtle–obvious ratings of MMPI items: New interest in an old concept. *Journal of Consulting and Clinical Psychology, 46*, 1178–1186.

Clark, M. E. (1994). Interpretive limitations of the MMPI–2 Anger and Cynicism content scales. *Journal of Personality Assessment, 63*, 89–96.

Clark, M. E. (1996). MMPI–2 Negative Treatment Indicators, content and content component scales: Clinical correlates and outcome prediction for men with chronic pain. *Psychological Assessment: A Journal of Consulting and Clinical Psychology, 8*, 32–38.

Clavelle, P. R., & Butcher, J. N. (1977). An adaptive typological approach to psychiatric screening. *Journal of Consulting and Clinical Psychology, 45*, 851–859.

Clopton, J. R., & Neuringer, C. (1977). MMPI Cannot Say scores: Normative data and degree of profile distortion. *Journal of Personality Assessment, 41*, 511–513.

Cofer, C. N., Chance, J. E., & Judson, A. J. (1949). A study of malingering on the MMPI. *Journal of Psychology, 27*, 491–499.

Colby, F. (1989). Usefulness of the *K* correction in MMPI profiles of patients and non-patients. *Psychological Assessment: A Journal of Consulting and Clinical Psychology, 1*, 142–145.

Colligan, R. C., & Offord, K. P. (1987a). The MacAndrew Alcoholism scale applied to a contemporary normative sample. *Journal of Clinical Psychology, 43*, 291–293.

Colligan, R. C., & Offord, K. P. (1987b). Resiliency reconsidered: Contemporary MMPI normative data for Barron's Ego Strength scale. *Journal of Clinical Psychology, 43*, 467–472.
Colligan, R. C., & Offord, K. P. (1988). Contemporary norms for the Wiggins content scales: A 45-year update. *Journal of Clinical Psychology, 44*, 23–32.
Colligan, R. C., & Offord, K. P. (1991). Adolescents, the MMPI, and the issue of *K* correction: A contemporary normative study. *Journal of Clinical Psychology, 47*, 607–631.
Colligan, R. C., & Offord, K. P. (1992). Age, stage, and the MMPI: Changes in response patterns over an 85-year age span. *Journal of Clinical Psychology, 48*, 476–493.
Colligan, R. C., Osborne, D., & Offord, K. P. (1980). Linear transformation and the interpretation of MMPI *T* scores. *Journal of Clinical Psychology, 36*, 162–165.
Colligan, R. C., Osborne, D., Swenson, W. M., & Offord, K. P. (1983). *The MMPI: A contemporary normative sample.* New York: Praeger.
Colligan, R. C., Osborne, D., Swenson, W. M., & Offord, K. P. (1984). The MMPI: Development of contemporary norms. *Journal of Clinical Psychology, 40*, 100–107.
Colligan, R. C., Osborne, D., Swenson, W. M., & Offord, K. P. (1989). *The MMPI: A contemporary normative study of adults* (2nd ed.). Odessa, FL: Psychological Assessment Resources.
Comrey, A. L. (1958). A factor analysis of items on the MMPI Psychasthenia scale. *Educational and Psychological Measurement, 18*, 293–300.
Cook, W. W., & Medley, D. M. (1954). Proposed hostility and Pharisaic–Virtue scales for the MMPI. *Journal of Applied Psychology, 38*, 414–418.
Costa, P. T., Jr., & McCrae, R. R. (1992a). Normal personality assessment in clinical practice: The NEO Personality Inventory. *Psychological Assessment: A Journal of Consulting and Clinical Psychology, 4*, 5–13.
Costa, P. T., Jr., & McCrae, R. R. (1992b). Reply to Ben-Porath and Waller. *Psychological Assessment: A Journal of Consulting and Clinical Psychology, 4*, 20–22.
Costa, P. T., Jr., & McCrae, R. R. (1992c). *Revised NEO Personality Inventory (NEO–PI–R) and NEO Five-Factor Inventory (NEO–FFI): Professional manual.* Odessa, FL: Psychological Assessment Resources.
Coyle, F. A., Jr., & Heap, R. F. (1965). Interpreting the MMPI *L* scale. *Psychological Reports, 17*, 722.
Craig, R. J. (1984a). A comparison of MMPI profiles of heroin addicts based on multiple methods of classification. *Journal of Personality Assessment, 48*, 115–120.
Craig, R. J. (1984b). MMPI substance abuse scales on drug addicts with and without concurrent alcoholism. *Journal of Personality Assessment, 48*, 495–499.
Craig, R. J. (1984c). Personality dimensions related to premature termination from an inpatient drug abuse treatment program. *Journal of Clinical Psychology, 40*, 351–355.
Craig, R. J. (1988). Psychological functioning of cocaine free-basers derived from objective psychological tests. *Journal of Clinical Psychology, 44*, 599–606.
Cronbach, L. J. (1951). Coefficient alpha and the internal structure of tests. *Psychometrika, 16*, 297–334.
Cuadra, C. (1956). A scale for control in psychological adjustment (*Cn*). In G. S. Welsh & W. G. Dahlstrom (Eds.), *Basic readings on the MMPI in psychology and medicine* (pp. 235–254). Minneapolis: University of Minnesota Press.
Dahlstrom, W. G. (1969). Recurrent issues in the development of the MMPI. In J. N. Butcher (Ed.), *MMPI: Research developments and clinical applications* (pp. 1–40). New York: McGraw-Hill.
Dahlstrom, W. G. (1991). *Subtle–Obvious subscale correlates derived from partner ratings used in the MMPI–2 restandardization.* Unpublished manuscript, University of North Carolina, Chapel Hill, NC.
Dahlstrom, W. G. (1992a). Comparability of two-point high-point code patterns from original MMPI norms to MMPI–2 norms for the restandardization sample. *Journal of Personality Assessment, 59*, 153–164.
Dahlstrom, W. G. (1992b). The growth in acceptance of the MMPI. *Professional Psychology: Research and Practice, 23*, 1–4.
Dahlstrom, W. G. (1993). *Manual supplement: The items in the MMPI–2. Alterations in the wording, patterns of interrelationship and changes in endorsements.* Minneapolis: University of Minnesota Press.
Dahlstrom, W. G., & Archer, R. P. (in press). A shortened version of the MMPI–2. Assessment.

Dahlstrom, W. G., Archer, R. P., Hopkins, D. G., Jackson, E., & Dahlstrom, L. E. (1994). *Assessing the readability of the Minnesota Multiphasic Personality Inventory instruments—The MMPI, MMPI–2, MMPI–A* (MMPI–2/MMPI–A Test Report No. 2). Minneapolis: University of Minnesota Press.

Dahlstrom, W. G., & Dahlstrom, L. E. (Eds.). (1980). *Basic readings on the MMPI: A new selection on personality measurement.* Minneapolis: University Minnesota Press.

Dahlstrom, W. G., Lachar, D., & Dahlstrom, L. E. (1986). *MMPI patterns of American minorities.* Minneapolis: University of Minnesota Press.

Dahlstrom, W. G., & Moreland, K. L. (1983). Teaching the MMPI: APA-approved clinical internships. *Professional Psychology: Research and Practice, 14,* 563–569.

Dahlstrom, W. G., & Tellegen, A. (1993). *Manual supplement: Socioeconomic status and the MMPI–2. The relation of MMPI–2 patterns to levels of education and occupation.* Minneapolis: University of Minnesota Press.

Dahlstrom, W. G., & Welsh, G. S. (1960). *An MMPI handbook: A guide to use in clinical practice and research.* Minneapolis: University of Minnesota Press.

Dahlstrom, W. G., Welsh, G. S., & Dahlstrom, L. E. (1972). *An MMPI handbook: Vol. I. Clinical interpretation* (Rev. ed.). Minneapolis: University of Minnesota Press.

Dahlstrom, W. G., Welsh, G. S., & Dahlstrom, L. E. (1975). *An MMPI handbook: Vol. II. Research applications* (Rev. ed.). Minneapolis: University of Minnesota Press.

Damarin, F., & Messick, S. (1965). *Response styles as personality variables: A theoretical integration* (Technical Report No. ETS RB 65-10). Princeton, NJ: Educational Testing Service.

Dean, E. F. (1972). A lengthened Mini: The Midi-Mult. *Journal of Clinical Psychology, 28,* 68–71.

Drake, L. E. (1946). A social I.E. scale for the Minnesota Multiphasic Personality Inventory. *Journal of Applied Psychology, 30,* 51–54.

Drake, L. E., & Oetting, E. R. (1959). *An MMPI codebook for counselors.* Minneapolis: University of Minnesota Press.

Drake, L. E., & Thiede, W. B. (1948). Further validation of the Social I.E. scale for the Minnesota Multiphasic Personality Inventory. *Journal of Educational Research, 41,* 51–56.

Dubinsky, S., Gamble, D. J., & Rogers, M. L. (1985). A literature review of subtle–obvious items on the MMPI. *Journal of Personality Assessment, 49,* 62–68.

Duckworth, J. C. (1979). *MMPI interpretation manual for counselors and clinicians.* Muncie, IN: Accelerated Development.

Duckworth, J. C. (1991a). The Minnesota Multiphasic Personality Inventory–2: A review. *Journal of Counseling and Development, 69,* 564–567.

Duckworth, J. C. (1991b). Response to Caldwell and Graham. *Journal of Counseling and Development, 69,* 572–573.

Duckworth, J. C., & Anderson, W. (1986). *MMPI interpretation manual for counselors and clinicians* (3rd ed.). Muncie, IN: Accelerated Development.

Duckworth, J. C., & Anderson, W. (1995). *MMPI interpretation manual for counselors and clinicians* (4th ed.). Muncie, IN: Accelerated Development.

Duckworth, J. C., & Barley, W. D. (1988). Within-normal-limit profiles. In R. L. Greene (Ed.), *The MMPI: Use with specific populations* (pp. 278–315). Philadelphia: Grune & Stratten.

Edwards, A. L. (1957). *The social desirability variable in personality assessment and research.* New York: Dryden Press.

Edwards, A. L., Diers, C. J., & Walker, J. N. (1962). Response sets and factor loadings on sixty-one personality scales. *Journal of Applied Psychology, 46,* 220–225.

Edwards, D. W., Morrison, T. L., & Weissman, H. N. (1993). Uniform versus linear *T* scores on the MMPI–2/MMPI in an outpatient psychiatric sample: Differential contributions. *Psychological Assessment: A Journal of Consulting and Clinical Psychology, 5,* 499–500.

Edwards, D. W., Weissman, H. N., & Morrison, T. L. (1993). *Forensic case studies with additional data to resolve critical MMPI–2/MMPI differences.* Paper presented at the 101st Annual Convention of the American Psychological Association, Toronto, Ontario, Canada.

Edwards, E. L., Holmes, C. B., & Carvajal, H. H. (1998). Oral and booklet presentation of the MMPI–2. *Journal of Clinical Psychology, 54,* 593–596.

Ehrenworth, N. V., & Archer, R. P. (1985). A comparison of clinical accuracy ratings of interpretative approaches for adolescent MMPI responses. *Journal of Personality Assessment, 49,* 413–421.

Eichman, W. J. (1972). Minnesota Multiphasic Personality Inventory: Computerized scoring and interpreting services. In O. K. Buros (Ed.), *Seventh mental measurement yearbook* (pp. 253–255). Highland Park, NJ: Gryphon Press.

Einhorn, J. H., & Hogarth, R. M. (1978). Confidence in judgment: Persistence of the illusion of validity. *Psychological Review, 85*, 395–416.

Endicott, N. A., Jortner, S., & Abramoff, E. (1969). Objective measures of suspiciousness. *Journal of Abnormal Psychology, 74*, 26–32.

Erdberg, P. (1979) A systematic approach to providing feedback from the MMPI. In C. S. Newmark (Ed.), *MMPI clinical and research trends* (pp. 238–342). New York: Praeger.

Estes, W. K. (1976). The cognitive side of probability learning. *Psychological Review, 83*, 37–64.

Evans, C., & McConnell, T. R. (1941). A new measure of introversion–extroversion. *Journal of Psychology, 12*, 111–124.

Evans, R. G. (1984). Normative data for two MMPI critical item sets. *Journal of Clinical Psychology, 40*, 512–515.

Eysenck, H. J. (1967). *The biological basis of personality.* Springfield, IL: Thomas.

Eysenck, H. J., Wakefield, J. A., & Friedman, A. F. (1983): Diagnosis and clinical assessment: The *DSM–III*. *Annual Review of Psychology, 34*, 167–193.

Faschingbauer, T. R. (1974). A 166-item written short form of the group MMPI: The FAM. *Journal of Consulting and Clinical Psychology, 42*, 645–655.

Fine, H. K. (1973). Studying schizophrenia outside the psychiatric setting. *Journal of Youth and Adolescence, 2*, 291–301.

Finn, S. E. (1996). *Manual for using the MMPI–2 as a therapeutic intervention.* Minneapolis: University of Minnesota Press.

Finn, S. E., & Tonsager, M. E. (1992). Therapeutic effects of providing MMPI–2 test feedback to college students awaiting therapy. *Psychological Assessment: A Journal of Consulting and Clinical Psychology, 4*, 278–287.

Finney, J. C., Smith, D. F., Skeeters, D. E., & Auvenshine, C. D. (1971). MMPI alcoholism scales: Factor structure and content analysis. *Quarterly Journal of Studies on Alcohol, 32*, 1055–1060.

Fisher, C. T. (1994). *Individualizing psychological assessment.* Hillsdale, NJ: Lawrence Erlbaum Associates.

Fjordbak, T. (1985). Clinical correlates of high Lie scale elevations among forensic patients. *Journal of Personality Assessment, 49*, 252–255.

Foerstner, S. B. (1986). *The factor structure and stability of selected Minnesota Multiphasic Personality Inventory (MMPI) subscales: Harris and Lingoes subscales, Wiggins content scales, Wiener subscales, and Serkownek subscales.* Unpublished doctoral dissertation, University of Akron, Akron, OH.

Fowler, R. D. (1966). *The MMPI notebook: A guide to the clinical use of the automated MMPI.* Nutley, NJ: Roche Psychiatric Service Institute.

Fowler, R. D. (1969). Automated interpretation of personality test data. In J. N. Butcher (Ed.), *MMPI: Research developments and clinical applications* (pp. 105–126). New York: McGraw-Hill.

Fowler, R. D. (1975). *A method for the evaluation of the abuse prone patient.* Paper presented at the meeting of the American Academy of Family Physicians, Chicago, IL.

Fowler, R. D. (1985). Landmarks in computer-assisted psychological assessment. *Journal of Consulting and Clinical Psychology, 53*, 748–759.

Fowler, R. D., & Butcher, J. N. (1986). Critique of Matarazzo's views on computerized testing: All signs and no meaning. *American Psychologist, 41*, 94–96.

Friedman, A. F. (1982). Review of extraversion and introversion: An interactional perspective by Larry W. Morris. *Journal of Personality Assessment, 46*, 185–187.

Friedman, A. F. (1990, March). MMPI–2 concerns. *The APA Monitor*, p. 2.

Friedman, A. F., Gleser, G. C., Smeltzer, D. J., Wakefield, J. A., Jr., & Schwartz, M. S. (1983). MMPI overlap item scales for differentiating psychotics, neurotics, and nonpsychiatric groups. *Journal of Consulting and Clinical Psychology, 51*, 629–631.

Friedman, A. F., Webb, J. T., & Lewak, R. (1989a). *Psychological assessment with the MMPI.* Hillsdale, NJ: Lawrence Erlbaum Associates.

Friedman, A. F., Webb, J. T., Smeltzer, D. J., & Lewak, R. (1989b). *Workbook for Psychological Assessment With the MMPI.* Hillsdale, NJ.: Lawrence Erlbaum Associates.

Frueh, B. C., Gold, P. B., & de Arellano, M. A. (1997). Symptom overreporting in combat veterans evaluated for PTSD: Differentiation on the basis of compensation seeking status. *Journal of Personality Assessment, 68*, 369–384.

Fulkerson, S. C., & Willage, D. E. (1980). Decisional ambiguity as a source of "cannot say" responses on personality questionnaires. *Journal of Personality Assessment, 44*, 381–386.

Fuller, C. G., & Malony, H. N., Jr. (1984). A comparison of English and Spanish (Nuñez) translations of the MMPI. *Journal of Personality Assessment, 48*, 130–131.

Gallagher, B. J., & Jones, D. J. (1987). The attitudes of psychiatrists toward etiological theories of schizophrenia: 1975–1985. *Journal of Clinical Psychology, 43*, 438–443.

Gallucci, N. T. (1986). General and specific objections to the MMPI. *Educational and Psychological Measurement, 46*, 985–988.

Gallucci, N. T., Kay, D. C., & Thornby, J. I. (1989). The sensitivity of 11 substance abuse scales from the MMPI to change in clinical status. *Psychology of Addictive Behaviors, 3*, 29–33.

Gentry, T. A., Wakefield, J. A., Jr., & Friedman, A. F. (1985). MMPI scales for measuring Eysenck's personality factors. *Journal of Personality Assessment, 49*, 146–149.

Gilberstadt, H., & Duker, J. (1965). *A handbook for clinical and actuarial MMPI interpretation.* Philadelphia: Saunders.

Glaros, A. G., & Kline, R. B. (1988). Understanding the accuracy of tests with cutting scores: The sensitivity, specificity, and predictive value model. *Journal of Clinical Psychology, 44*, 1013–1023.

Goldberg, L. R. (1965). Diagnosticians vs. diagnostic signs: The diagnosis of psychosis vs. neurosis from the MMPI. *Psychological Monographs, 79*(9, Whole No. 602).

Goldberg, L. R., & Slovic, P. (1967). The importance of test item content: An analysis of a corollary of the deviation hypothesis. *Journal of Counseling Psychology, 14*, 462–472.

Gosling, F. G. (1987). *Before Freud: Neurasthenia and the American medical community, 1870–1910.* Urbana: University of Illinois Press.

Gottesman, I. I., & Prescott, C. A. (1989). Abuses of the MacAndrew MMPI Alcoholism scale: A critical review. *Clinical Psychology Review, 9*, 223–242.

Gough, H. G. (1947). Simulated patterns on the Minnesota Multiphasic Personality Inventory. *Journal of Abnormal and Social Psychology, 42*, 215–225.

Gough, H. G. (1948a). A new dimension of status: I. Development of a personality scale. *American Sociological Review, 13*, 401–409.

Gough, H. G. (1948b). A new dimension of status: II. Relationship of the *St* scale to other variables. *American Sociological Review, 13*, 534–537.

Gough, H. G. (1950). The *F* minus *K* Dissimulation index for the Minnesota Multiphasic Personality Inventory. *Journal of Consulting Psychology, 14*, 408–413.

Gough, H. G. (1951). Studies of social intolerance: III. Relationship of the *Pr* scale to other variables. *Journal of Social Psychology, 33*, 257–262.

Gough, H. G. (1954). Some common misconceptions about neuroticism. *Journal of Consulting Psychology, 18*, 287–292.

Gough, H. G. (1957). *Manual for the California Psychological Inventory.* Palo Alto, CA: Consulting Psychologists Press.

Gough, H. G. (1987a). *California Psychological Inventory: Administrator guide.* Palo Alto, CA: Consulting Psychologists Press.

Gough, H. G. (1987b). *Manual for the California Psychological Inventory* (Rev. ed.). Palo Alto, CA: Consulting Psychologists Press.

Gough, H. G., McClosky, H., & Meehl, P. E. (1951). A personality scale for dominance. *Journal of Abnormal and Social Psychology, 46*, 360–366.

Gough, H. G., McClosky, H., & Meehl, P. E. (1952). A personality scale for social responsibility. *Journal of Abnormal and Social Psychology, 47*, 73–80.

Gough, H. G., McKee, M. G., & Yandell, R. J. (1955). *Adjective check list analyses of a number of selected psychometric and assessment variables*, Officer Education Research Laboratory (Technical Memorandum No. OERL-TM-55-10).

Graham, J. R. (1977). Review of MMPI special scales. In P. McReynolds (Ed.), *Advances in psychological assessment* (Vol. IV, pp. 11–55). San Francisco: Jossey-Bass.

Graham, J. R. (1978, March). *MMPI characteristics of alcoholics, drug abusers, and pathological gamblers.* Paper presented at the 13th Annual Symposium on Recent Developments in the Use of the MMPI, Puebla, Mexico.

Graham, J. R. (1987). *The MMPI: A practical guide.* New York: Oxford University Press.

Graham, J. R. (1990). *MMPI–2: Assessing personality and psychopathology.* New York: Oxford University Press.

Graham, J. R. (1993). MMPI–2: *Assessing personality and psychopathology* (2nd ed.). New York: Oxford University Press.

Graham, J. R., Ben-Porath, Y. S., & McNulty, J. L (1999). *MMPI–2 correlates for outpatient community mental health settings.* Minneapolis: University of Minnesota Press.

Graham, J. R., Ben-Porath, Y. S., & McNulty, J. L. (1997). Empirical correlates of low scores on MMPI–2 scales in an outpatient mental health setting. *Psychological Assessment: A Journal of Consulting and Clinical Psychology, 9,* 386–391.

Graham, J. R., & Butcher, J. N. (1988, March). *Differentiating schizophrenic and major affective disorders with the revised form of the MMPI.* Paper presented at the 23rd Annual Symposium on Recent Developments in the Use of the MMPI, St. Petersburg, FL.

Graham, J. R., & McCord, G. (1985). Interpretation of moderately elevated MMPI scores for normal subjects. *Journal of Personality Assessment, 49,* 477–484.

Graham, J. R., Schroeder, H. E., & Lilly, R. S. (1971). Factor analysis of items on the Social Introversion and Masculinity–Femininity scales of the MMPI. *Journal of Clinical Psychology, 27,* 367–370.

Graham, J. R., & Strenger, V. E. (1988). MMPI characteristics of alcoholics: A review. *Journal of Consulting and Clinical Psychology, 56,* 197–205.

Graham, J. R., Timbrook, R. E., Ben-Porath, Y. S., & Butcher, J. N. (1991). Code-type congruence between MMPI and MMPI–2: Separating fact from artifact. *Journal of Personality Assessment, 57,* 205–215.

Graham, J. R., & Tisdale, M. J. (1983, April). *Interpretation of low 5 scores for women of high educational levels.* Paper presented at the 18th Annual Symposium on Recent Developments in the Use of the MMPI, Minneapolis, MN.

Graham, J. R., Watts, D., & Timbrook, R. E. (1991). Detecting fake-good and fake-bad MMPI–2 profiles. *Journal of Personality Assessment, 57,* 264–277.

Gravitz, M. A. (1968). Normative findings for the frequency of MMPI critical items. *Journal of Clinical Psychology, 24,* 220.

Grayson, H. M. (1951). *A psychological admissions testing program and manual.* Los Angeles: Veterans Administration Center, Neuropsychiatric Hospital.

Grayson, H. M., & Olinger, L. B. (1957). Simulation of "normalcy" by psychiatric patients on the MMPI. *Journal of Consulting Psychology, 21,* 73–77.

Greene, R. L. (1978). An empirically derived MMPI Carelessness scale. *Journal of Clinical Psychology, 34,* 407–410.

Greene, R. L. (1980). *The MMPI: An interpretive manual.* New York: Grune & Stratton.

Greene, R. L. (1982). Some reflections on "MMPI Short Forms: A Review." *Journal of Personality Assessment, 46,* 486–487.

Greene, R. L. (1985). New norms, old norms: What norms for the MMPI? [Review of the book *The MMPI: A Contemporary Normative Sample*]. *Journal of Personality Assessment. 49,* 108–110.

Greene, R. L. (1987). Ethnicity and MMPI performance: A review. *Journal of Consulting and Clinical Psychology, 55,* 497–512.

Greene R. L. (1988a). The relative efficacy of $F - K$ and the obvious and subtle scales to detect overreporting of psychopathology on the MMPI. *Journal of Clinical Psychology, 44,* 152–159.

Greene, R. L. (1988b). Summary. In R. L. Greene (Ed.), *The MMPI: Use with specific populations* (pp. 316–321). Philadelphia, PA: Grune & Stratton.

Greene, R. L. (1990a, March). *The effects of age, education, gender, and specific MMPI codetypes on the MacAndrew Alcoholism scale.* Paper presented at the annual meeting of the Society for Personality Assessment, San Diego, CA.

Greene, R. L. (1990b). Stability of MMPI scales scores across four codetypes over four decades, *Journal of Personality Assessment, 55,* 1–6.

Greene, R. L. (1991a). *The MMPI/MMPI–2: An interpretive manual.* Boston: Allyn & Bacon.

Greene, R. L. (1991b, July). *Some issues in assessing consistency of item endorsement on the MMPI–2.* Paper presented at the MMPI–2 Summer Institute, Colorado Springs, CO.

Greene, R. L. (2000). *The MMPI–2: An interpretive manual* (2nd ed.). Boston: Allyn & Bacon.

Greene, R. L., & Garvin, R. D. (1988). Substance abuse/dependence. In R. L. Greene (Ed.), *The MMPI: Use with specific populations* (pp. 159-197). San Antonio, TX: Grune & Stratton.

Greene R. L., Gwin, R., & Staal, M. (1997). Current status of MMPI–2 research: A methodologic overview. *Journal of Personality Assessment, 68*, 20–36.

Greene, R. L., Weed, N. C., Butcher, J. N., Arredondo, R., & Davis, H. G. (1992). A cross-validation of MMPI–2 substance abuse scales. *Journal of Personality Assessment, 58*, 405–410.

Greenfield, N. S., Alexander, A. A., & Roessler, R. (1963). Ego strength and physiological responsivity: II. The relationship between the Barron Ego Strength scale to the temporal and recovery characteristics of skin resistance, finger blood volume, heart rate, and muscle potential responses to sound. *Archives of General Psychiatry, 9*, 129–141.

Greenfield, N. S., Roessler, R., & Crosley, A. P. (1959). Ego strength and length of recovery from infectious mononucleosis. *The Journal of Nervous and Mental Disease, 128*, 125–128.

Greist, J. H., Klein, M. H., Erdman, H. P., & Jefferson, J. W. (1983). Computers and psychiatric diagnosis. *Psychiatric Annals, 13*, 785–792.

Grove, W. M., & Meehl, P. E. (1996). Comparative efficiency of informal (subjective, impressionistic) and formal (mechanical, algorithmic) prediction procedures: The clinical statistical controversy. *Psychology, Public Policy and Law, 2*, 293–323.

Guastello, S. J., & Rieke, M. L. (1990). The Barnum effect and validity of computer-based test interpretations: The human resource development report. *Psychological Assessment: A Journal of Consulting and Clinical Psychology, 2*, 186–190.

Gulas, I. (1973). MMPI–2 point codes for a "normal" college population: A replication study. *Journal of Psychology, 84*, 319–322.

Gynther, M. D. (1979). Aging and personality: An update. In J. N. Butcher (Ed.), *New developments in the use of the MMPI* (pp. 39–68). Minneapolis: University of Minnesota Press.

Hampton, P. J. (1951). A psychometric study of drinkers. *Journal of Psychology, 15*, 501–504

Hanvik, L. (1949). *Some psychological dimensions of low back pain.* Unpublished doctoral dissertation, University of Minnesota, Minneapolis.

Harkness, A. R. (1990). Phenotypic dimensions of the personality disorders (Doctoral dissertation, University of Minnesota, 1989). *Dissertation Abstracts International, 50*(12B), 5880B.

Harkness, A. R., Levenson, M. R., Butcher, J. N., Spiro, A., Ben-Porath, Y. S., & Crumpler, C. A. (1995, March). *Drinking and personality: MMPI–2 PSY–5 scales in the Boston VA's Normative Aging Study.* Paper presented at the 30th Annual MMPI–2 and MMPI–A Symposia, St. Petersburg, FL.

Harkness, A. R., & McNulty, J. L. (1994). The Personality Psychopathology Five (PSY–5): Issue from the pages of a diagnostic manual instead of a dictionary. In S. Strack & M. Lorr (Eds.), *Differentiating normal and abnormal personality* (pp. 291–315). New York: Springer.

Harkness, A. R., McNulty, J. L., & Ben-Porath, Y. S. (1995). The Personality Psychopathology Five (PSY–5): Constructs and MMPI–2 scales. *Psychological Assessment: A Journal of Consulting and Clinical Psychology, 7*, 104–114.

Harkness, A. R., Spiro, A., Butcher, J. N., & Ben-Porath, Y. S. (1995, August). *Personality Psychopathology Five (PSY–5) in the Boston VA Normative Aging Study.* Paper presented at the 103rd Annual Convention of the American Psychological Association, New York, NY.

Harrell, T. H., Honaker, L. M., & Parnell, T. (1992). Equivalence of the MMPI–2 with the MMPI in psychiatric patients. *Psychological Assessment: A Journal of Consulting and Clinical Psychology, 4*, 460–465.

Harris, R. E., & Lingoes, J. C. (1955, 1968). *Subscales for the MMPI: An aid to profile interpretation.* Mimeographed materials. Department of Psychiatry, University of California.

Hartshorne, H., & May, M. A. (1928). *Studies in deceit.* New York: Macmillan.

Hase, H. D., & Goldberg, L. R. (1967). Comparative validity of different strategies of constructing personality inventory scales. *Psychological Bulletin, 67*, 231–248.

Hathaway, S. R. (1939). The personality inventory as an aid in the diagnosis of psychopathic inferiors. *Journal of Consulting Psychology, 3*, 112–117.

Hathaway, S. R. (1947). A coding system for MMPI profiles. *Journal of Consulting Psychology, 11*, 334–337.

Hathaway, S. R. (1964). MMPI: Professional use by professional people. *American Psychologist, 19*, 204–210.

Hathaway, S. R. (1980). Scales 5 (Masculinity–Femininity), 6 (Paranoia), and 8 (Schizophrenia). In W. G. Dahlstrom & L. Dahlstrom (Eds.), (1980). *Basic readings on the MMPI: A new selection on personality measurement* (pp. 65–75). Minneapolis: University of Minnesota Press. (Original work published 1956)

Hathaway, S. R., & Briggs, P. F. (1957). Some normative data on new MMPI scales. *Journal of Clinical Psychology, 13*, 364–368.

Hathaway, S. R., & McKinley, J. C. (1940). A multiphasic personality schedule (Minnesota): I. Construction of the schedule. *Journal of Psychology, 10*, 249–254.

Hathaway, S. R., & McKinley, J. C. (1942). A multiphasic personality schedule (Minnesota): III. The measurement of symptomatic depression. *Journal of Psychology, 14*, 73–84.

Hathaway, S. R., & McKinley, J. C. (1943). *The Minnesota Multiphasic Personality Inventory manual.* Minneapolis: University of Minnesota Press.

Hathaway, S. R., & McKinley, J. C. (1983). *The Minnesota Multiphasic Personality Inventory manual* (Rev. ed.). New York: Psychological Corporation.

Hathaway, S. R., & Meehl, P. E. (1951). *An atlas for the clinical use of the MMPI.* Minneapolis: University of Minnesota Press.

Heaton, R., Grant, L., & Matthews, C. (1991). *Comprehensive norms for an expanded Halstead-Reitan Battery.* Odessa, FL: Psychological Assessment Resources.

Hedlund, J. L. (1977). MMPI clinical scale correlates. *Journal of Consulting and Clinical Psychology, 45*, 739–750.

Hedlund, J. L., & Won Cho, D. (1979). [MMPI data research tape for Missouri Department of Mental Health Patients.] Unpublished raw data.

Helmes, E., & Reddon, J. R. (1993). A perspective on developments in assessing psychopathology: A critical review of the MMPI and MMPI–2. *Psychological Bulletin, 113*, 453–471.

Hjemboe, S., Almagor, M., & Butcher, J. N. (1992). Empirical assessment of marital distress: The Marital Distress scale (*MDS*) for the MMPI–2. In C. D. Spielberger & J. N. Butcher (Eds.), *Advances in personality assessment* (Vol. 9, pp. 141–152). Hillsdale, NJ: Lawrence Erlbaum Associates.

Hoffmann, H., Loper, R. G., & Kammeier, M. L. (1974). Identifying future alcoholics with MMPI alcoholism scales. *Quarterly Journal of Studies on Alcohol, 35*, 490–498.

Hollrah, J. L., Schlottmann, R. S., Scott, A. B., & Brunetti, D. G. (1995). Validity of the MMPI subtle items. *Journal of Personality Assessment, 65*, 278–299.

Holmes, T. H., & Rahe, R. H. (1967). The Social Readjustment Rating Scale. *Journal of Psychosomatic Research, 11*, 213–218.

Holmes, W. O. (1953). *The development of an empirical MMPI scale for addiction.* Unpublished manuscript, San Jose State College, San Jose, CA.

Holroyd, R. G. (1964). Prediction of defensive paranoid schizophrenics using the MMPI (Doctoral dissertation, University of Minnesota, 1964). *Dissertation Abstracts, 25*, 2048.

Hovey, H. B., & Lewis, E. G. (1967). Semiautomatic interpretation of the MMPI. *Journal of Clinical Psychology, 23*, 123–134.

Hoyt, D. P., & Sedlacek, G. M. (1958). Differentiating alcoholics from normals and abnormals with the MMPI. *Journal of Clinical Psychology, 14*, 69–74.

Huber, N. A., & Danahy, S. (1975). Use of the MMPI in predicting completion and evaluating changes in a long-term alcoholism treatment program. *Journal of Studies on Alcohol, 36*, 1230–1237.

Hugo, J. (1971). Abbreviation of the Minnesota Multiphasic Personality Inventory through multiple regression (Doctoral dissertation, University of Alabama, 1991). *Dissertation Abstracts International, 32*, 123B.

Humm, D. G., & Wadsworth, G. W., Jr. (1935). The Humm–Wadsworth Temperament Survey. *American Journal of Psychiatry, 92*, 163–200.

Humphrey, D. H., & Dahlstrom, W. G. (1995). The impact of changing from the MMPI to the MMPI–2 of profile configurations. *Journal of Personality Assessment, 64*, 428–439.

Hunsley, J., Hanson, R. K., & Parker, C. H. K. (1988). A summary of the reliability and stability of MMPI scales. *Journal of Clinical Psychology, 44*, 44–46.

Hunt, H. (1948). The effect of deliberate deception on MMPI performance. *Journal of Consulting Psychology, 12*, 396–402.

Ihilevich, D., & Gleser, G. C. (1986). *Defenses mechanisms: Their classification, correlates, and measurement with the Defense Mechanism Inventory.* Owasso, MI: DMI.

Ihilevich, D., & Gleser, G. C. (1991). *Defenses in psychotherapy: The clinical application of the Defense Mechanism Inventory.* Owosso, MI: DMI.

Iverson, G. L., & Barton, E. (1999). Interscorer reliability of the MMPI–2: Should *TRIN* and *VRIN* be computer scored? *Journal of Clinical Psychology, 55*, 65–69.

Iverson, G., Franzen, M., & Hammond, J. (1993, August). *Examination of inmates' ability to malinger on the MMPI–2.* Poster session presented at the 101st Annual Convention of the American Psychological Association, Toronto, Ontario, Canada.

Jackson, D. N (1971). The dynamics of personality tests. *Psychological Review, 78*, 239–248.

Jaffe, A. M. (1992). Psychoanalytic approach to addictive disorders. In C. E. Stout, J. C. Levitt, & D. H. Ruben (Eds.), *Handbook for assessing and treating addictive disorders* (pp. 41–57). Westport, CT: Greenwood.

Jaffe, A. M., & Jaffe, K. L. (1992). Countertransference in the treatment of addictive disorders. In C. E. Stout, J. L. Levitt, & D. H. Ruben (Eds.), *Handbook for assessing and treating addictive disorders* (pp. 301–311). Westport, CT: Greenwood.

Jenkins, C. D., Rosenman, R. H., & Friedman, M. (1967). Development of an objective psychological test for the determination of the coronary-prone behavior pattern in employed men. *Journal of Chronic Disease, 20*, 371–379.

Jenkins, W. L. (1952). The MMPI applied to the problem of prognosis in schizophrenia (Doctoral dissertation, University of Minnesota, 1952). *Dissertation Abstracts, 12*, 381.

Johnson, J. H., Butcher, J. N., Null, C., & Johnson, K. N. (1984). Replicated item level factor analysis of the full MMPI. *Journal of Personality and Social Psychology, 47*, 105–114.

Kahneman, D., & Tversky, A. (1973). On the psychology of prediction. *Psychological Review, 80*, 237–251.

Katz, M. M. (1968). A phenomenological typology of schizophrenia. In M. M. Katz, J. O. Cole, & W. E. Barton (Eds.), *The role and methodology of classification in psychiatry and psychopathology* (PHS Publication No.1584, pp. 300–320). Washington, DC: U.S. Government Printing Office.

Kawachi, I., Sparrow, D., Kubzansky, L. D., Spiro, A., Vokonas, P. S., & Weiss, S. T. (1998). Prospective study of a self-report Type A scale and risk of coronary heart disease: Test of the MMPI–2 Type A scale. *Circulation, 98*, 405–412.

Kawachi, I., Sparrow, D., Spiro, A., Vokonas, P. S., & Weiss, S. T. (1996). A prospective study of anger and coronary heart disease: The Normative Aging Study. *Circulation, 94*, 2090–2095.

Keane, S. P., & Gibbs, M. (1980). Construct validation of the *Sc* scale of the MMPI. *Journal of Clinical Psychology, 36*, 152–158.

Keane, T. M., Malloy, P. F., & Fairbank, J. A. (1984). Empirical development of an MMPI subscale for the assessment of combat-related posttraumatic stress disorder. *Journal of Consulting and Clinical Psychology, 52*, 888–891.

Keiller, S. W., & Graham, J.R. (1993). The meaning of low scores on MMPI–2 clinical scales of normal subjects. *Journal of Personality Assessment, 61*, 211–223.

Kendrick, S., & Hatzenbuehler, L. (1982). The effect of oral administration by a live examiner on the MMPI: A split-half design. *Journal of Clinical Psychology, 38*, 788–792.

Kimlicka, T. M., Sheppard, P. L., Wakefield, J. A., & Cross, H. J. (1987). Relationship between psychological androgyny and self-actualization tendencies. *Psychological Reports, 61*, 443–446.

Kimlicka, T. M., Wakefield, J. A., & Friedman, A. F. (1980). Comparison of factors from the Bem Sex-Role Inventory for male and female college students. *Psychological Reports, 46*, 1011–1017.

Kimlicka, T. M., Wakefield, J. A., & Goad, N. A. (1982). Sex-roles of ideal opposite sexed persons for college males and females. *Journal of Personality Assessment, 46*, 519–521.

Kincannon, J. C. (1968). Prediction of the standard MMPI scale scores from 71 items: The Mini-Mult. *Journal of Consulting and Clinical Psychology, 32*, 319–325.

Kleinmuntz, B. (1960). Identification of maladjusted college students. *Journal of Counseling Psychology, 7*, 209–211.

Kleinmuntz, B. (1961a). The College Maladjustment scale (*Mt*): Norms and predictive validity. *Educational and Psychological Measurement, 21*, 1029–1033.

Kleinmuntz, B. (1961b). Screening: Identification or prediction? *Journal of Counseling Psychology, 8*, 279–280.

Kohutek, K. J. (1992a). The location of items of the Wiggins content scales on the MMPI–2. *Journal of Clinical Psychology, 48*, 617–620.

Kohutek, K. J. (1992b). Wiggins content scales and the MMPI–2. *Journal of Clinical Psychology, 48*, 215–218.

Koss, M. P. (1979). MMPI item content: Recurring issues. In J. N. Butcher (Ed.), *New development in the use of the MMPI* (pp. 3–38). Minneapolis: University of Minnesota Press.

Koss, M. P., & Butcher, J. N. (1973). A comparison of psychiatric patients' self-report with other sources of clinical information. *Journal of Research in Personality, 7*, 225–236.

Koss, M. P., Butcher, J. N., & Hoffmann, N. (1976). The MMPI critical items: How well do they work? *Journal of Consulting and Clinical Psychology, 44*, 921–928.

Kraepelin, E. (1893). *Psychiatrie* (4th ed.). Leipzig, Germany: Abel.

Kraepelin, E. (1919). *Dementia praecox and paraphrenia.* Edinburg, NY: Churchill Livingstone.

Kranitz, L. (1972). Alcoholics, heroin addicts and nonaddicts: Comparisons on the MacAndrew Alcoholism scale of the MMPI. *Quarterly Journal of Studies on Alcohol, 33*, 807–809.

Krishnamurthy, R., Archer R. P., & Huddleston, E. N. (1995). Clinical research note on psychometric limitations of two Harris–Lingoes subscales for the MMPI–2. *Assessment, 2*, 301–304.

Kunce, J., & Anderson, W. (1976). Normalizing the MMPI. *Journal of Clinical Psychology, 32*, 776–780.

Kunce, J., & Anderson, W. (1984). Perspectives on uses of the MMPI in nonpsychiatric settings. In P. McReynolds & G. J. Chelvne (Eds.), Advances in psychological assessment (Vol. 6, pp. 41–76). San Francisco: Josey-Bass.

Lachar, D. (1974). *The MMPI: Clinical assessment and automated interpretation.* Los Angeles: Western Psychological Services.

Lachar, D., & Alexander, R. S. (1978). Veridicality of self-report: Replicated correlates of the Wiggins MMPI content scales. *Journal of Consulting and Clinical Psychology, 46*, 1349–1356.

Lachar, D., Berman, W., Grisell, J. L., & Schoof, K. (1976). The MacAndrew Alcoholism scale as a general measure of substance abuse. *Journal of Studies on Alcohol, 37*, 1609–1615.

Lachar, D., Dahlstrom, W. G., & Moreland, K. L. (1986). Relationship of ethnic background and other demographic characteristics to MMPI patterns in psychiatric samples. In W. G. Dahlstrom, D. Lachar, & L. E. Dahlstrom (Eds.), *MMPI patterns of American minorities* (pp. 139–187). Minneapolis: University of Minnesota Press.

Lachar, D., & Wrobel, T. A. (1979). Validating clinicians' hunches: Construction of a new MMPI critical item set. *Journal of Consulting and Clinical Psychology, 47*, 1349–1356.

Ladd, J. S. (1998). The *F(p)* Infrequency–Psychopathology scale with chemically dependent inpatients. *Journal of Clinical Psychology, 54*, 665–671.

Lamb, D. G., Berry, D. T. R., Wetter, M. W., & Baer, R. A. (1994). Effects of two types of information on malingering of closed head injury on the MMPI–2: An analog investigation. *Psychological Assessment: A Journal of Consulting and Clinical Psychology, 6*, 8–13.

Landis, C., & Katz, S. E. (1934). The validity of certain questions which purport to measure neurotic tendencies. *Journal of Applied Psychology, 8*, 343–356.

Landis, C., Zubin, J., & Katz, S. E. (1935). Empirical evaluation of three personality adjustment inventories. *Journal of Educational Psychology, 26*, 321–330.

Lane, J. B., & Lachar, D. (1979). Correlates of broad MMPI categories. *Journal of Clinical Psychology, 35*, 560–566.

Lanyon, R. I. (1968). *A handbook of MMPI group profiles.* Minneapolis: University of Minnesota Press.

Lanyon, R. I., Dannebaum, S. E., Wolf, L. I., & Brown, A. (1989). Dimensions of deceptive responding in criminal offenders. *Psychological Assessment: A Journal of Consulting and Clinical Psychology, 1*, 300–304.

Lawton, M. P., & Kleban, M. H. (1965). Prisoners' faking on the MMPI. *Journal of Clinical Psychology, 21*, 269–271.

Leary, T. (1956). *Multilevel measurement of interpersonal behavior.* Berkeley, CA: Psychological Consultation Service.

Leary, T. (1957). *Interpersonal diagnosis of personality.* New York: Ronald Press.

Levinson, M. R., Aldwin, C. M., Butcher, J. N., de Labry, L., Workman-Daniels, K., & Bosse, R. (1990). The MAC scale in a normal population: The meaning of "false positives." *Journal of Studies on Alcohol, 51*, 457–462.

Levitt, E. E. (1989). *The clinical application of MMPI special scales.* Hillsdale, NJ: Lawrence Erlbaum Associates.

Levitt, E. E. (1990). A structural analysis of the impact of MMPI–2 on MMPI–1. *Journal of Personality Assessment, 55*, 562–577.

Lewak, R. (1993, March). *Low scores on Scale 6: A case history.* Paper presented at the annual convention of the Society of Personality Assessment, San Francisco, CA.

Lewak, R.W., Marks, P. A., & Nelson, G. E. (1990). *Therapist guide to the MMPI and MMPI–2: Providing feedback and treatment.* Muncie, IN: Accelerated Development.

Lilienfeld, S. O. (1999). The relation of the MMPI–2 *Pd* Harris–Lingoes subscales to psychopathy, psychopathy facets, and antisocial behavior: Implications for clinical practice. *Journal of Clinical Psychology, 55*, 241–255.

Little, J. W. (1949). *An analysis of the MMPI.* Unpublished master's thesis, University of North Carolina, Chapel Hill.

Little, K. B., & Fischer, J. (1958). Two new experimental scales of the MMPI. *Journal of Consulting Psychology, 22*, 305–306.

Litz, B. T., Orsillo, S. M., Friedman, M., Ehlich, P., & Batres, A. (1997). Posttraumatic stress disorder associated with peacekeeping duty in Somalia for U.S. military personnel. *American Journal of Psychiatry, 154*, 178–184.

Long, K. A., & Graham, J. R. (1991). The Masculinity–Femininity scale of MMPI–2: Is it useful with normal men? *Journal of Personality Assessment, 57*, 46–51.

Lubin, B., Larsen, R. M., & Matarazzo, J. (1984). Patterns of psychological test usage in the United States 1935–1982. *American Psychologist, 39*, 451–454.

Lubin, B., Larsen, R. M., Matarazzo, J. D., & Seever, M. F. (1985). Psychological test usage patterns in five professional settings. *American Psychologist, 40*, 857–861.

Lucio, E., & Reyes-Lagunes, I. (1994). MMPI–2 for Mexico: Translation and adaptation. *Journal of Personality Assessment, 63*, 105–116.

MacAndrew, C. (1965). The differentiation of male alcoholic outpatients from nonalcoholic psychiatric patients by means of the MMPI. *Quarterly Journal of Studies on Alcohol, 26*, 238–246.

MacAndrew, C. (1981). What the MAC scale tells us about men alcoholics: An interpretive review. *Journal of Studies on Alcohol, 42*, 604–625.

Marks, P. A., & Seeman, W. (1963). *The actuarial description of abnormal personality: An atlas for use with the MMPI.* Baltimore: Williams & Wilkins.

Marks, P. A., Seeman, W., & Haller, D. (1974). *The actuarial use of the MMPI with adolescents and adults.* Baltimore: Williams & Wilkins.

Martin, E. H. (1993). *Masculinity–femininity and the MMPI–2.* Unpublished doctoral dissertation, University of Texas, Austin.

Martin, E. H., & Finn, S. E. (1992). *Masculinity–femininity and the MMPI–2.* [Unpublished manuscript.]

Maruish, M. E. (1994). Introduction. In M. E. Maruish (Ed.), *The use of psychological testing for treatment planning and outcome assessment* (pp. 3–21). Hillsdale, NJ: Lawrence Erlbaum Associates.

Matarazzo, J. D. (1955). MMPI validity scores as a function of increasing levels of anxiety. *Journal of Consulting Psychology, 19*, 213–217.

Matarazzo, J. D. (1986). Computerized psychological test interpretations: Unvalidated plus all mean and no sigma. *American Psychologist, 41*, 14–24.

Matz, P. A., Altepeter, T. S., & Perlman, B. (1992). MMPI–2: Reliability with college students. *Journal of Clinical Psychology, 48*, 330–334.

McGrath, R. E., Powis, D., & Pogge, D. L. (1998). Code type–specific tables for interpretation of MMPI–2 Harris and Lingoes subscales: Consideration of gender and code type definition. *Journal of Clinical Psychology, 54*, 655–664.

McKenna, T., & Butcher, J. N. (1987, May). *Continuity of the MMPI with alcoholics.* Paper presented at the 22rd Annual Symposium on Recent Developments in the Use of the MMPI, Seattle, WA.

McKinley, J. C. (Ed.). (1944). *An outline of neuropsychiatry.* St. Louis, MO: John S. Swift.

McKinley, J. C., & Hathaway, S. R. (1940). A multiphasic personality schedule (Minnesota): II. A differential study of hypochondriasis. *Journal of Psychology, 10*, 255–268.

McKinley, J. C., & Hathaway, S. R. (1942). A multiphasic personality schedule (Minnesota): IV. Psychasthenia. *Journal of Applied Psychology, 26*, 614–624.

McKinley, J. C., & Hathaway, S. R. (1943). The identification and measurement of the psychoneuroses in medical practice. *Journal of the American Medical Association, 122*, 161–167.

McKinley, J. C., & Hathaway, S .R. (1944). The MMPI: V. Hysteria, hypomania, and psychopathic deviate. *Journal of Applied Psychology, 28*, 153–174.

McKinley, J. C., Hathaway, S. R., & Meehl, P. E. (1948). The MMPI: VI. The *K* scale. *Journal of Consulting Psychology, 12*, 20–31.

McLachlan, J. F. (1974). Test–retest stability of long and short MMPI scales over two years. *Journal of Clinical Psychology, 30*, 189–191.

McLaughlin, J. F., Helmes, E., & Howe, M. G. (1983). Note on the reliability of three MMPI short forms. *Journal of Personality Assessment, 47*, 357–358.

McNulty, J. L., Ben-Porath, Y. S., & Graham, J. R. (1998). An empirical examination of the correlates of well-defined and not defined MMPI–2 code types. *Journal of Personality Assessment, 71*, 393–410.

Meehl, P. E. (1945a). The dynamics of "structured" personality tests. *Journal of Clinical Psychology, 1*, 296–304.

Meehl, P.E. (1945b). An investigation of a general normality or control factor in personality testing. *Psychological Monographs, 59*(4, Whole No. 274).

Meehl, P. E. (1954). *Clinical versus statistical prediction: A theoretical analysis and a review of the evidence.* Minneapolis: University of Minnesota Press.

Meehl, P. E. (1956). Wanted—A good cookbook. *American Psychologist, 11*, 262–272.

Meehl, P. E. (1970). Psychology and criminal law. *University of Richmond Law Review, 5*, 1–30.

Meehl, P. E. (1971). Prefatory comment. In L. D. Goodstein, L. D. & R. I. Lanyon (Eds.), *Readings in personality assessment* (pp. 245–246). New York: Wiley.

Meehl, P. E. (1972). Reactions, reflections, projections. In J. N. Butcher (Ed.), *Objective personality assessment* (pp. 131–189). New York: Academic Press.

Meehl, P. E. (1973). *Psychodiagnosis: Selected papers.* Minneapolis: University of Minnesota Press.

Meehl, P. E. (1974). Hedonic capacity: Some conjectures. *Bulletin of the Menninger Clinic, 39*, 295–307.

Meehl, P. E. (1989). Paul E. Meehl. In G. Linzey (Ed.), *A history ofpsychology in autobiography* (Vol. 3, pp. 337–389). Stanford, CA: Stanford University Press.

Meehl, P. E., & Dahlstrom, W. G. (1960). Objective configural rules for discriminating psychotic from neurotic MMPI profiles. *Journal of Consulting Psychology, 24*, 375–387.

Meehl, P. E., & Hathaway, S. R. (1946). The *K* factor as a suppressor variable in the MMPI. *Journal of Applied Psychology, 30*, 525–564.

Megargee, E. I. (1972). *The California Psychological Inventory handbook.* San Francisco: Jossey-Bass.

Megargee, E. I. (1985). Assessing alcoholism and drug abuse with the MMPI: Implications for screening. In C. D. Spielberger & J. N. Butcher (Eds.), *Advances in personality assessment* (Vol. 5, pp. 1–39). Hillsdale, NJ: Lawrence Erlbaum Associates.

Megargee, E. I., Cook, P. E., & Mendelsohn, G. A. (1967). Development and validation of an MMPI scale of assaultiveness in overcontrolled individuals. *Journal of Abnormal Psychology, 72*, 519–528.

Megargee, E. I., & Mendelsohn, G. A. (1962). A cross-validation of twelve MMPI indices of hostility and control. *Journal of Abnormal and Social Psychology, 65*, 431–438.

Meloy, J. R., & Gacono, C. (1995). Assessing the psychopathic personality. In J. Butcher (Ed.), *Clinical personality assessment: Practical approaches* (pp. 410–422). New York: Oxford University Press.

Meyer, R. G. (1983). *The clinician's handbook: The psychopathology of adulthood and late adolescence.* Boston: Allyn & Bacon.

Miller, H. R., Goldberg, J. O., & Streiner, D. L. (1995). What's in a name? The MMPI–2 PTSD scales. *Journal of Clinical Psychology, 51*, 626–631.

Miller, H .R., & Streiner, D. L. (1985). The Harris–Lingoes subscales: Fact or fiction? *Journal of Clinical Psychology, 41*, 45–51.

Miller, H. R., & Streiner, D. L. (1986). Differences in MMPI profiles with the norms of Colligan et al. *Journal of Consulting and Clinical Psychology, 54*, 843–845.

Moreland, K. L. (1985). Validation of computer-based test interpretations: Problems and prospects. *Journal of Consulting and Clinical Psychology, 53*, 816–825.

Moreland, K. L. (1990). Some observations on computer-assisted psychological testing. *Journal of Personality Assessment, 55*, 820–823.

Moreland, K. L., & Dahlstrom, W. G. (1983). Professional training with and use of the MMPI. *Professional Psychology: Research and Practice, 14*, 218–223.

Morey, L. C., & Smith, M. R. (1988). Personality disorders. In R. L. Greene (Ed.), *The MMPI: Use with specific populations* (pp. 110–158). Philadelphia: Grune & Stratton.

Morey, L. C., Waugh, M. H., & Blashfield, R. K. (1985). MMPI scales for DSM–III personality disorders: Their derivation and correlates. *Journal of Personality Assessment, 49*, 245–251.

Navran, L. (1954). A rationally derived MMPI scale for dependence. *Journal of Consulting Psychology, 18*, 192.

Nelson, L. D. (1987). Measuring depression in a clinical population using the MMPI. *Journal of Consulting and Clinical Psychology, 55*, 788–790.

Nelson, L. D., & Cicchetti, D. (1991). Validity of the MMPI Depression scale for outpatients. *Psychological Assessment: A Journal of Consulting and Clinical Psychology, 3*, 55–59.

Nelson, S. E. (1952). The development of an indirect, objective measure of social status and its relationship to certain psychiatric syndromes (Doctoral dissertation, University of Minnesota, 1952). *Dissertation Abstracts, 12*, 782.

Newmark, C. S., Chassin, P., Evans, D., & Gentry, L. (1984). "Floating" MMPI profiles revisited. *Journal of Clinical Psychology, 40*, 199–201.

Nichols, D. S. (1988). Mood disorders. In R. L. Greene (Ed.), *The MMPI: Use with specific populations* (pp. 74–109). Philadelphia: Grune & Stratton.

Nichols, D. S. (1989). The Nichols critical item list. In A. F. Friedman, J. T. Webb, & R. W. Lewak, *Psychological assessment with the MMPI* (pp. 376–381). Hillsdale, NJ: Lawrence Erlbaum Associates.

Nichols, D. S. (1992a). Development and use of the MMPI–2: Content scales [Review of the book] *Journal of Personality Assessment, 58*, 434–437

Nichols, D. S. (1992b). Review of the Minnesota Multiphasic Personality Inventory–2. In J. J. Kramer & J. C. Conoley (Eds.), *The eleventh mental measurements yearbook* (pp. 562–565). Lincoln: University of Nebraska, Buros Institute of Mental Measurements.

Nichols, D. S. (1994). *A digest of the MMPI–2 PSY–5: Harkness, McNulty, and Ben-Porath's Personality Psychopathology Five (PSY–5).* Unpublished manuscript.

Nichols, D. S., & Greene, R. L. (1988, March). *Adaptive or defensive: An evaluation of Paulhus' two-factor model of social desirability responding in the MMPI with non-college samples.* Paper presented at the 23rd Annual Symposium on Recent Developments in the Use of the MMPI, St. Petersburg, FL.

Nichols, D. S., & Greene, R. L. (1991, March). *New measures for dissimulation on the MMPI/MMPI–2.* Paper presented at the 26th Annual Symposium on Recent Developments in the Use of the MMPI (MMPI–2/MMPI–A), St. Petersburg Beach, FL.

Nichols, D. S., & Greene, R. L. (1995). *MMPI–2 structural summary: Interpretive manual.* Odessa, FL: Psychological Assessment Resources.

Nichols, D. S., & Greene, R. L. (1997). Dimensions of deception in personality assessment: The example of the MMPI–2. *Journal of Personality Assessment, 68*, 251–266.

Nicholson, R. A., Mouton, G. J., Bagby, R. M., Buis, T., Peterson, S. A., & Buigas, R. A. (1997). Utility of MMPI–2 indicators of response distortion: Receiver operating characteristic analysis. *Psychological Assessment: A Journal of Consulting and Clinical Psychology, 9*, 471–479.

Nuñez, R. (1967). *Inventario multifasico de la personalidad.* MMPI-Espanol Mexico: El Manual Moderno, S.A.

Osborne, D. (1979). Use of the MMPI with medical patients. In J. N. Butcher (Ed.), *New developments in the use of MMPI* (pp. 141–163). Minneapolis: University of Minnesota Press.

Osborne, D., Colligan, R., & Offord, K. (1986). Normative tables for the *F* – *K* index of the MMPI based on a contemporary normal sample. *Journal of Clinical Psychology, 42*, 593–595.

Otto, R. K., Lang, A. R., Megargee, E. I., & Rosenblatt, A. I. (1988). Ability of alcoholics to escape detection by the MMPI. *Journal of Consulting and Clinical Psychology, 56*, 452–457.

Overall, J. E., & Gomez-Mont, F. (1974). The MMPI–168 for psychiatric screening. *Educational and Psychological Measurement, 34*, 315–319.

Ownby, R. L. (1987). *Psychological reports: A guide to report writing in professional psychology.* Brandon, VT: Clinical Psychology.

Page, J., Landis, C., & Katz, S. E. (1934). Schizophrenic traits in the functional psychoses and in normal individuals. *American Journal of Psychiatry, 13*, 1213–1225.

Pancoast, D. L., & Archer, R. P. (1988). MMPI adolescent norms: Patterns and trends across 4 decades. *Journal of Personality Assessment, 52*, 691–706.

Pancoast, D. L., & Archer, R. P. (1989). Original adult MMPI norms in normal samples: A review with implications for future developments. *Journal of Personality Assessment, 53*, 376–395.

Pancoast, D. L., Archer, R. P., & Gordon, R. A. (1988). The MMPI and clinical diagnosis: A comparison of classification system outcomes with discharge diagnoses. *Journal of Personality Assessment, 52*, 81–90.

Paolo, A. M., Ryan, J. J., & Smith, A. J. (1991). Reading difficulty of MMPI–2 subscales. *Journal of Clinical Psychology, 47*, 529–532.

Paulhus, D. L. (1984). Two-component models of socially desirable responding. *Journal of Personality and Social Psychology, 46*, 598–609.

Paulhus, D. L. (1986). Self-deception and impression management in test responses. In A. Angleitner & J. S. Wiggins (Eds.), *Personality assessment via questionnaires: Current issues in theory and measurement* (pp. 143–165). Berlin: Springer-Verlag.

Payne, F. D., & Wiggins, J. S. (1972). MMPI profile types and the self-report of psychiatric patients. *Journal of Abnormal Psychology, 79*, 1–8.

Peterson, C. D. (1991). *Masculinity and femininity as independent dimensions on the MMPI.* Unpublished doctoral dissertation, University of North Carolina, Chapel Hill.

Peterson, C. D., & Dahlstrom, W. G. (1992). The derivation of gender-role scales *GM* and *GF* for the MMPI–2 and their relationship to Scale 5 (*Mf*). *Journal of Personality Assessment, 59*, 486–499.

Pope, K. S. (1992). Responsibilities in providing psychological test feedback to clients. *Psychological Assessment: A Journal of Consulting and Clinical Psychology, 4*, 268–271.

Pope, K. S., Butcher, J. N., & Seelen, J. (1993). *The MMPI, MMPI–2, and MMPI–A in court: A practical guide for expert witnesses and attorneys*. Washington, DC: American Psychological Association.

Prokop, C. K. (1986). Hysteria scale elevations in low back pain patients: A risk factor for misdiagnosis? *Journal of Consulting and Clinical Psychology, 54*, 558–562.

Prokop, C. K. (1988). Chronic pain. In R. C. Greene (Ed.), *The MMPI: Use with specific populations* (pp. 22–49). Philadelphia: Grune & Stratton.

Putzke, J. D., Williams, M. A., Daniel, F. J., & Boll, T. J. (1999). The utility of *K*-correction to adjust for a defensive response set on the MMPI. *Psychological Assessment, 6*, 61–70.

Quinsey, V. L., Harris, G. T., Rice, M. E., & Cormier, C. A. (1998). Violent offenders: Appraising and managing risk. Washingotn, DC: American Psychological Association.

Quinsey, V. L., Maguire, A., & Varney, G. W. (1983). Assertion and overcontrolled hostility among mentally disordered offenders. *Journal of Consulting and Clinical Psychology, 51*, 550–556.

Rapport, L. J., Todd, R. M., Lumley, M. A., & Fisicaro, S. A. (1998). The diagnostic meaning of "nervous breakdown" among lay populations. *Journal of Personality Assessment, 71*, 242–252.

Raskin, R., & Novacek, J. (1989). An MMPI description of the narcissistic personality. *Journal of Personality Assessment, 53*, 66–80.

Rathvon, N., & Holmstrom, R. W. (1996). An MMPI–2 portrait of narcissism. *Journal of Personality Assessment, 66*, 1–19.

Reynolds, W. M., & Sundberg, N. D. (1976). Recent research trends in testing. *Journal of Personality Assessment, 40*, 228–333.

Rhodes, R. J., & Chang, A. F. (1978). A further look at the Institutionalized Chronic Alcoholic scale. *Journal of Clinical Psychology, 34*, 779–780.

Rodgers, D. A. (1972). Review of the MMPI. In O. K. Buros (Ed.), *Seventh mental Measurements yearbook* (pp. 243–250). Highland Park, NJ: Gryphon Press.

Roessler, R., Alexander, A. A., & Greenfield, N. S. (1963). Ego strength and physiological responsivity: I. The relationship of the Barron *Es* scale to skin resistance. *Archives of General Psychiatry, 8*, 142–154.

Roessler, R., Burch, N. R., & Childers, H. E. (1966). Personality and arousal correlates of specific galvanic skin responses. *Psychophysiology, 3*, 115–130.

Roessler, R., Burch, N. R., & Mefford, R. B. (1967). Personality correlates of catecholamine excretion under stress. *Journal of Psychosomatic Research, 11*, 181–185.

Roessler, R., & Collins, F. (1970). Personality correlates of physiological responses to motion pictures. *Psychophysiology, 6*, 732–739.

Roessler, R., Greenfield, N. S., & Alexander, A. A. (1964). Ego strength and response stereotypy. *Psychophysiology, 1*, 142–150.

Rogers, R., Bagby, R. M., & Chakraborty, D. (1993). Feigning schizophrenia disorders on the MMPI–2: Detection of coached simulators. *Journal of Personality Assessment, 60*, 215–226.

Rogers, R., Sewell, K. W., & Salekin, R. T. (1994). A meta-analysis of malingering on the MMPI–2. *Assessment, 1*, 227–237.

Rohan, W. P. (1972). MMPI changes in hospitalized alcoholics: A second study. Quarterly *Journal of Studies on Alcohol, 33*, 65–76.

Rohan, W. P., Tatro, R. L., & Rotman, S. R. (1969). MMPI changes in alcoholics during hospitalization. *Quarterly Journal of Studies on Alcohol, 30*, 389–400.

Rome, H. P., Swenson, W. M., Mataya, P., McCarthy, C. E., Pearson, J. S., Keating, F. R., & Hathaway, S. T. (1962). Symposium on automation procedures in personality assessment. *Proceedings of the Staff Meetings of the Mayo Clinic, 37*, 61–82.

Romney, D. M., & Bynner, J. M. (1992). A simplex model of five *DSM–III* personality disorders. *Journal of Personality Disorders, 6*, 34–39.

Roper, B. L., Ben-Porath, Y. S., & Butcher, J. N. (1991). Comparability of computerized adaptive and conventional testing with the MMPI–2. *Journal of Personality Assessment, 65*, 358–371.

Rosen, A. (1962). Development of MMPI scales based on a reference group of psychiatric patients. *Psychological Monographs, 76*(8, Whole No. 527).

Rothke, S. E., & Friedman, A. F. (1994). Response to Fox: Comment and clarification. *Assessment, 1*, 421–422.

Rothke, S. E., Friedman, A. F., Dahlstrom, W. G., Greene, R. L., Arrendondo, R., & Mann, A. W. (1994). MMPI–2 normative data for the $F - K$ index: Implications for clinical, neuropsychological, and forensic practice. *Assessment, 1*, 1–15.

Rothke S. E., Friedman, A. F., Jaffe, A. M., Greene, R. L., Wetter, M. W., Cole, P., & Baker, K. (In press). *Normative data for the F(p) scale of the MMPI–2: Implications for clinical and forensic assessment of malingering.* Psychological Assessment.

Rouse, S. L., Butcher, J. N., & Miller, K. B. (1999). Assessment of substance abuse in psychotherapy clients: The effectiveness of the MMPI–2 substance abuse scales. *Psychological Assessment: A Journal of Consulting and Clinical Psychology, 11*, 101–107.

Sawyer, J. (1966). Meaurement and prediction, clinical and statistical. *Psychological Bulletin, 66*, 178–200.

Schill, T., & Wang, S. (1990). Correlates of the MMPI–2 anger content. *Psychological Reports, 67*, 800–802.

Schinka, J. A., & Borum, R. (1993). Readability of adult psychopathology inventories. *Psychological Assessment: A Journal of Consulting and Clinical Psychology, 5*, 384–386.

Schinka, J. A., & LaLone, L. (1997). MMPI-2 norms: Comparisons with a census-matched subsample. *Psychology Assessment, 9*, 30715311.

Schlenger, W. E., & Kulka, R. A. (1987, August–September). *Performance of the Keane–Fairbank MMPI scale and other self-report measures in identifying post-traumatic stress disorder.* Paper presented at the 95th Annual Convention of the American Psychological Association, New York, NY.

Schlenger, W. E., Kulka, R. A., Fairbank, J. A., Hough, R. L., Jordan, B. K., Marmar, C. R., & Weiss, D. S. (1989). *The prevalence of post-traumatic stress disorder in the Vietnam generation: Findings from the National Vietnam Veterans Readjustment Study.* Research Triangle Park, NC: Research Triangle Institute.

Schuerger, J. M., Foerstner, S. B., Serkownek, K., & Ritz, G. (1987). History and validities of the Serkownek Subscales for MMPI Scales 5 and 0. *Psychological Reports, 61*, 227–235.

Schuldberg, D. (1990). Varieties of inconsistency across test occasions: Effects of computerized test administration and repeated testing. *Journal of Personality Assessment, 55*, 168–182.

Schwartz, M. F., & Graham, J. R. (1979). Construct validity of the MacAndrew Alcoholism scale. *Journal of Consulting and Clinical Psychology, 47*, 1090–1095.

Serkownek, K. (1975). *Subscales for Scales 5 and 0 of the MMPI.* Unpublished manuscript.

Sherwood, N. E., & Ben-Porath, Y. S. (1991). The MMPI–2 content component scales. *MMPI–2 News and Profiles, 2*, 9–11.

Shondrick, D. D., Ben-Porath, Y. S., & Stafford, K. P. (1992, May). *Forensic applications of the MMPI–2.* Paper presented at the 27th Annual Symposium on Recent Developments in the Use of the MMPI (MMPI–2 and MMPI–A), Minneapolis, MN.

Sieber, K. O., & Meyers, L. S. (1992). Validation of the MMPI–2 Social–Introversion subscales. *Psychological Assessment: A Journal of Consulting and Clinical Psychology, 4*, 185–189.

Sines, J. O. (1977). M-F: Bipolar and probably multidimensional. *Journal of Clinical Psychology, 33*, 1038–1041.

Sivec, H. J., Lynn, S. J., & Garske, J. P. (1994). The effect of somatoform disorder and paranoid psychotic role-related dissimulations as a response set on the MMPI–2. *Assessment, 1*, 69–81.

Southwick, S. M., Morgan, C. A., III, Nicolaou, A. C., & Charney, D. S. (1997). Consistency of memory for combat-related traumatic events in veterans of Operation Desert Storm. American *Journal of Psychiatry, 154*, 173–177.

Spanier, G. B. (1976). Measuring dyadic adjustment: New scales for assessing the quality of marriage and similar dyads. *Journal of Marriage and the Family, 38*, 15–28.

Spera, J., & Robertson, M. (1974, September). *104-item MMPI: The Maxi-Mult.* Paper presented at the 82nd Annual Convention of the American Psychological Association, New Orleans, LA.

Spielberger, C. D., & Piotrowski, C. (1990). Clinician's attitudes toward computer-based testing. *The Clinical Psychologist, 43*, 60–63.

Spinhoven, P., Labbe, M. R., & Rombouts, R. (1993). Feasibility of computerized psychological testing with psychiatric outpatients. *Journal of Clinical Psychology, 49*, 440–447.

Staal, M. A., & Greene, R. L. (1998). Classification accuracy in the measurement of MMPI/MMPI–2: Profile similarity. *Journal of Personality Assessment, 71*, 70–83.

Stein, K. B., (1968). The TSC scales: The outcome of a cluster analysis of the 550 MMPI items. In P. McReynolds (Ed.), *Advances in Psychological Assessment: A Journal of Consulting and Clinical Psychology* (Vol. 1, pp. 80–104). Palo Alto, CA: Science and Behavior Books.

Stein L. A. R., Graham, J. R., Ben-Porath, Y. S., & McNulty, J. L. (1999). Using the MMPI–2 to detect substance abuse in an outpatient mental health setting. *Psychological Assessment: A Journal of Consulting and Clinical Psychology, 11*, 94–100.

Strassberg, D. S. (1991). Interpretive dilemmas created by the Minnesota Multiphasic Personality Inventory–2 (MMPI–2). *Journal of Psychopathology and Behavioral Assessment, 13*, 53–59.

Streiner, D. L., & Miller, H. R. (1986). Can a short form of the MMPI ever be developed? *Journal of Clinical Psychology, 42*, 109–113.

Streit, K., Greene, R. L., Cogan, R., & Davis, H. G. (1993). Clinical correlates of MMPI depression scales. *Journal of Personality Assessment, 60*, 390–396.

Sutker, P. B., Archer, R. P., Brantley, P. J., & Kilpatrick, D. G. (1979). Alcoholics and opiate addicts: Comparison of personality characteristics. *Journal of Studies on Alcohol, 40*, 635–644.

Swenson, W. M., Pearson, J. S., & Osborne, D. (1973). *An MMPI source book: Basic item, scale and pattern data on 50,000 medical patients.* Minneapolis: University of Minnesota.

Tallent, N. (1983). *Psychological report writing* (2nd ed.). Englewood Cliffs, NJ: Prentice-Hall.

Tallent, N. (1987). Computer-generated psychological reports: A look at the modern psychometric machine. *Journal of Personality Assessment, 51*, 95–108.

Tanner, B. A. (1990). Composite descriptions associated with rare MMPI two-point codetypes: Codes that involve Scale 5. *Journal of Clinical Psychology, 46*, 425–431.

Tarter, R. E., McBride, H., Buonpane, N., & Schneider, D. U. (1978). Differentiation of alcoholics: Childhood history of minimal brain dysfunction, family history, and drinking pattern. *Archives of General Psychiatry, 34*, 761–768.

Tarter, R. E., & Perley R. N. (1975). Clinical and perceptual characteristics of paranoids and paranoid schizophrenics. *Journal of Clinical Psychology, 31*, 42–44.

Taylor, J. A. (1953). A personality scale of manifest anxiety. *Journal of Abnormal and Social Psychology, 48*, 285–290.

Taylor, S. E., & Brown, J. D. (1988). Illusion and well-being: A social psychological perspective on mental health. *Psychological Bulletin, 103*, 193–210.

Tellegen, A., & Ben-Porath, Y. S. (1992). The new uniform *T* scores for the MMPI–2: Rationale, derivation, and appraisal. *Psychological Assessment: A Journal of Consulting and Clinical Psychology, 4*, 145–155.

Tellegen, A., & Ben-Porath, Y. S. (1993). Code type comparability of the MMPI and MMPI–2: Analysis of recent findings and criticisms. *Journal of Personality Assessment, 61*, 489–500.

Tellegen, A., & Ben-Porath, Y. S. (1996). Evaluating the similarity of MMPI–2 and MMPI profiles: Reply to Dahlstrom and Humphrey. *Journal of Personality Assessment, 66*, 640–644.

Terman, L. M., & Miles, C. C. (1936). *Sex and personality: Studies in masculinity and femininity.* New York: McGraw-Hill.

Trull, T. J., Useda, J. D., Costa, P. T., & McCrae, R. R. (1995). Comparison of the MMPI–2 Personality Psychopathology Five (PSY–5), the NEO–PI, and the NEO–PI(R). *Psychological Assessment: A Journal of Consulting and Clinical Psychology, 7*, 508–516.

Van de Riet, V. W., & Wolking, W. D. (1969). *Interpretive hypotheses for the MMPI* [Mimeograph]. Gainesville: University of Florida.

Venn, J. (1988). Low scores on MMPI Scales 2 and 0 as indicators of character pathology in men. *Psychological Reports, 62*, 651–657.

Vestre, N. D., & Watson, C. G. (1972). Behavioral correlates of the MMPI Paranoia scale. *Psychological Reports, 31*, 851–854.

Wakefield, J. A., Jr., Bradley, P. E., Doughtie, E. B., & Kraft, I. A. (1975). Influence of overlapping and nonoverlapping items on the theoretical interrelationships of MMPI scales. *Journal of Consulting and Clinical Psychology, 43*, 851–856.

Wakefield, J. A., Sasek, J., Friedman, A. F., & Bowden, J. D. (1976). Androgyny and other measures of masculinity–femininity. *Journal of Consulting and Clinical Psychology, 44*, 766–770.

Wakefield, J. A., Wood, K. A., Wallace, R. F., & Friedman, A. F. (1978). A curvilinear relationship between extraversion and performance for adult retardates. *Psychological Reports, 43*, 387–392.

Wales, B., & Seeman, W. (1968). A new method for detecting the fake good response set on the MMPI. *Journal of Clinical Psychology, 24*, 211–216.

Walters, G. D. (1984). Identifying schizophrenia by means of Scale 8 (Sc) of the MMPI. *Journal of Personality Assessment, 48*, 390–391.

Walters, G. D. (1988). Schizophrenia. In R. L. Greene (Ed.), *The MMPI: Use in specific populations* (pp. 50–73). Philadelphia: Grune & Stratton.

Walters, G. D., & Greene, R. L. (1983). Factor structure of the Overcontrolled–Hostility scale of the MMPI. *Journal of Clinical Psychology,* 39, 560–562.

Walters, G. D., White, T. W., & Greene, R. L. (1988). Use of the MMPI to identify malingering and exaggeration of psychiatric symptomatology in male prison inmates. *Journal of Consulting and Clinical Psychology, 56*, 111–117.

Ward, L. C. (1991). A comparison of T scores from the MMPI and the MMPI–2. *Psychological Assessment: A Journal of Consulting and Clinical Psychology, 3*, 688–690.

Ward, L. C. (1994). MMPI–2 assessment of positive attributes: A methodological note. *Journal of Personality Assessment, 62*, 559–561.

Ward, L. C. & Dillon, E. A. (1990). Psychiatric symptoms of the Minnesota Multiphasic Personality Inventory (MMPI) Masculinity–Femininity scale. *Psychological Assessment: A Journal of Consulting and Clincal Psychology, 2*, 286–288.

Ward, L. C., Kersh, B. C., & Waxmonsky, J. A. (1998). Factor structure of the Paranoia scale of the MMPI–2 in relation to the Harris–Lingoes subscales and Comrey factor analysis. *Psychological Assessment: A Journal of Consulting and Clinical Psychology, 10*, 292–296.

Ward, L. C. & Perry, M. S. (1998). Measurement of social introversion by the MMPI–2. *Journal of Personality Assessment, 70*, 171–182.

Ward, L. C., & Ward, J. W. (1980). MMPI readability reconsidered. *Journal of Personality Assessment, 44*, 387–389.

Watkins, C. E., Jr. (1991). What have surveys taught us about the teaching and practice of psychological assessment? *Journal of Personality Assessment, 56*, 426–437.

Watson, C. G., Juba, M., Anderson, P. E. D., & Manifold, V. (1990). What does the Keane et al. PTSD scale for the MMPI measure? *Journal of Clinical Psychology, 46*, 600–606.

Watson, C. G., Manifold, V., Klett, W. G, Brown, J., Thomas, D. & Anderson, D. (1990). Comparability of computer- and booklet-administered Minnesota Multiphasic Personality Inventories among primarily chemically dependent patients. *Psychological Assessment: A Journal of Consulting and Clinical Psychology, 2*, 276–280.

Watson, C. G., Thomas, D., & Anderson, P. (1992). Do computer-administered Minnesota Multiphasic Personality Inventories underestimate booklet-based scores? *Journal of Clinical Psychology, 48*, 744–748.

Webb, J. T. (1970a, April). *The relation of MMPI two-point codes to age, sex and education in a representative nationwide sample of psychiatric outpatients.* Paper presented at the convention of the Southeastern Psychological Association, Louisville, KY.

Webb, J. T. (1970b). Validity and utility of computer-produced MMPI reports with Veterans Administration psychiatric populations. Proceedings of the 78th Annual Convention of the *American Psychological Association, 5*, 541–542.

Webb, J. T. (1971). Regional and sex differences in MMPI scale high-point frequencies of psychiatric patients. *Journal of Clinical Psychology, 27*, 483–486.

Webb, J. T., Fowler, R. D., & Miller, M. L. (1971, May). *Frequency of critical items by sex, age and education in psychiatric patients.* Paper presented at the meeting of the Midwestern Psychological Association, Detroit, MI.

Webb, J. T., Levitt, E. E., & Rojdev, R. S. (1993, March). *A comparison of the clinical use of MMPI–1 and MMPI–2.* Paper presented at the meeting for the Society of Personality Assessment, San Francisco, CA.

Webb, J. T., McNamara, K. M., & Rodgers, D. A. (1986). *Configural interpretations of the MMPI and CPI.* Columbus, OH: Ohio Psychology Publishing. (Original work published 1981)

Webb, J. T., Miller, M. L., & Fowler, R. D. (1969). Validation of a computerized MMPI interpretation system. *Preceedings of the 77th Annual Convention of the American Psychological Association, 4*, 523–524.

Webb, J. T., Miller, M. L., & Fowler, R. D. (1970). Extending professional time: A computerized MMPI interpretation service. *Journal of Clinical Psychology, 26*, 210–214.

Weed, N. C., Ben-Porath, Y. S., & Butcher, J. N. (1990). Failure of Weiner and Harmon Minnesota Multiphasic Personality Inventory (MMPI) Subtle scales as personality descriptors and as validity indicators. *Psychological Assessment: A Journal of Consulting and Clinical Psychology, 2*, 281–285.

Weed, N. C., Butcher, J. N., McKenna, T., & Ben-Porath, Y. S. (1992). New measures for assessing alcohol and drug abuse with the MMPI–2: The *APS* and *AAS*. *Journal of Personality Assessment, 58*, 389–404.

Welsh, G. S. (1948). An extension of Hathaway's MMPI profile coding system. *Journal of Consulting Psychology, 12*, 343–344.

Welsh, G. S. (1956). Factor Dimensions *A* and *R*. In G. S. Welsh & W. G. Dahlstrom (Eds.), *Basic readings on the MMPI in psychology and medicine* (pp. 264–281). Minneapolis: University of Minnesota Press.

Welsh, G. S., & Dahlstrom, W. G. (Eds.). (1956). *Basic readings on the MMPI in psychology and medicine.* Minneapolis: University of Minnesota Press.

Wetter, M. W., Baer, R. A., Berry, D. T. R., Robison, L. H., & Sumpter, J. (1993). MMPI–2 profiles of motivated fakers given specific symptom information: A comparison to matched patients. *Psychological Assessment: A Journal of Consulting and Clinical Psychology, 5*, 317–323.

Wetter, M. W., Baer, R. A., Berry, D., Smith, G. T., & Larsen, L. H. (1992). Sensitivity of MMPI–2 validity scales to random responding and malingering. *Psychological Assessment: A Journal of Consulting and Clinical Psychology, 4*, 369–374.

Wetzler, S., Khadivi, A., & Moser, R. K. (1998). The use of the MMPI–2 for the assessment of depressive and psychotic disorders. *Assessment, 5*, 249–261.

Wheeler, W. M., Little, K. B., and Lehner, G. F. J. (1951). The internal structure of the MMPI. *Journal of Consulting Psychology, 15*, 134–141.

Whitworth, R. H. (1988). Anglo- and Mexican-American performance on the MMPI administered in Spanish or English. *Journal of Clinical Psychology, 44*, 891–897.

Whitworth, R. H., & McBlaine, D. D. (1993). Comparison of the MMPI and MMPI–2 administered to Anglo- and Hispanic-American university students. *Journal of Personality Assessment, 61*, 19–27.

Wiederholt, J. L., & Bryant, B. R. (1986). *Gray Oral Reading Test* (Rev. ed.). Austin, TX: PRO-ED.

Wiederstein, M, (1986). *Construct validity for measuring Eysenck's dimensions of psychoticism and neuroticism with the MMPI.* Unpublished doctoral dissertation, California School of Professional Psychology, Fresno.

Wiener, D. N. (1948). Subtle and obvious keys for the MMPI. *Journal of Consulting Psychology, 12*, 164–170.

Wiener, D. N. (1956). Subtle and obvious keys for the MMPI. In G.S. Welsh & W.G. Dahlstrom (Eds.), *Basic readings on the MMPI in psychology and medicine* (pp. 195–204). Minneapolis: University of Minnesota Press.

Wiener, D. N., & Harmon, L. R. (1946). *Subtle and obvious keys for the MMPI: Their development* (VA Advisement Bulletin No. 16.). Minneapolis, MN: Regional Veterans Administration Office.

Wiggins, J. S. (1959). Interrelationships among MMPI measures of dissimulation under standard and social desirability instructions. *Journal of Consulting Psychology, 23*, 419–427.

Wiggins, J. S. (1964). Convergences among stylistic response measures from objective personality tests. *Educational and Psychological Measurement, 24*, 551–562.

Wiggins, J. S. (1966). *Substantive dimensions of self-report in the MMPI item pool. Psychological Monographs, 80*(22, Whole No. 630).

Wiggins, J. S. (1969). Content dimensions in the MMPI. In J.N. Butcher (Ed.), *MMPI: Research developments and clinical applications* (pp. 127–180). New York: McGraw-Hill.

Wiggins, J. S. (1973). *Personality and prediction: Principles of personality assessment.* Don Mills, Ontario, Canada: Addison-Wesley.

Wiggins, J. S, Goldberg, L. R., & Applebaum, M. (1971). MMPI content scales: Interpretive norms and correlations with other scales. *Journal of Consulting and Clinical Psychology, 37*, 403–410.

Willcockson, J. C., Bolton, B., & Dana, R. H. (1983). A comparison of six MMPI short forms: Code type correspondence and indices of psychopathology. *Journal of Clinical Psychology, 39*, 968–970.

Williams, C. L. (1983). Further investigation of the *Si* scale of the MMPI: Reliabilities, correlates, and subscale utility. *Journal of Clinical Psychology, 39*, 951–957.

Williams, H. L. (1952). The development of a caudality scale for the MMPI. *Journal of Clinical Psychology, 8*, 293–297.

Wong, M. R. (1984). MMPI Scale 5: Its meanings or lack thereof. *Journal of Personality Assessment, 48*, 279–284.

Woodworth, R. S. (1920). *Personal Data Sheet.* Chicago: Stoelting.

Wrobel, T. A. (1992). Validity of Harris and Lingoes MMPI subscale descriptions in an outpatient sample. *Journal of Personality Assessment, 59*, 14–21.

Wrobel, T. A., & Lachar, D. (1982). Validity of the Weiner subtle and obvious scales for the MMPI: Another example of the importance of inventory-item content. *Journal of Consulting and Clinical Psychology, 50*, 469–470.

Yehuda, R. & McFarlane, A. C. (1995). Conflict between current knowledge about posttraumatic stress disorder and its original conceptual basis. *American Journal of Psychiatry, 152*, 1705–1713.

Young, A. (1995). *The harmony of illusions: Inventing post-traumatic stress disorder.* Princeton, NJ: Princeton University Press.

Author Index

A

Aaronson, A. L., 421
Abramoff, E., 121
Aiduk, R., 181, 231
Aldwin, C. M., 409
Alexander, A. A., 395
Alexander, R. S., 346
Alker, H. A., 182n2
Allen, J. P., 409
Almagor, M., 354, 391, 412, 413
Altepeter, T. S., 49
Anastasi, A., 4
Anderson, D., 478
Anderson, H. E., 158n3
Anderson, P., 478
Anderson, P. E. D., 403
Anderson, W., 93, 105, 117, 119, 121, 128, 133, 142, 144, 155, 231, 392, 394, 400, 401, 425
Anderson, W. P., 132
Anthony, N., 43, 62
Apfeldorf, M., 406
Applebaum, M., 345
Arbisi, P. A., 37, 39, 40, 41, 42
Archer, R. P., 1, 6, 7, 8, 9, 22n5, 27, 51, 63, 74, 75, 105, 106, 157n2, 162, 168, 181, 231, 259, 409, 418
Arredondo, R., 2, 24n14, 35, 63, 411
Astin, A. W., 102
Auvenshine, C. D., 409

B

Bacon, S. F., 161
Baer, R. A., 30, 31, 35, 36, 37, 38, 44, 45, 46, 47, 49, 53, 54, 56, 60, 62, 63, 64
Bagby, R. M., 35, 40, 43, 44, 55, 61
Baker, K., 34, 40, 64, 65, 67
Ball H., 11, 68n4
Ball J. C., 26, 27
Barley, W. D., 438, 440
Barnett, L., 231
Barron, F., 7, 389, 395

*n denotes that name appears in Notes section of chapter.

Barthlow, D. L., 358
Barton, E., 29
Bashaw, W. L., 158n3
Bathurst, K., 428
Batres, A., 404
Bell, H. M., 4
Bem, S. L., 114
Ben-Porath, Y. S., 9, 10, 19, 20, 37, 39, 40, 41, 42, 54, 72, 78, 82, 86, 87, 88, 97, 98, 105, 106, 107, 108, 109, 110, 111, 123, 124, 136, 137, 138, 140, 146, 147, 148, 149, 150, 153, 161, 178, 179, 180, 181, 231, 232, 236, 263, 343, 344, 346, 347, 354, 355, 356, 357, 358, 359, 360, 362, 363, 364, 365, 366, 367, 369, 370, 371, 372, 374, 380, 382, 383, 384, 391, 392, 394, 396, 400, 402, 403, 410, 411, 425
Berman, W., 409
Bernreuter, R. G., 4
Berry, D. T. R., 30, 31, 35, 36, 37, 38, 44, 45, 46, 47, 49, 53, 56, 60, 62, 63
Bersoff, D. N., 167
Blake, D. D., 179
Blanchard, J. S., 168, 183n4
Blashfield, R. K., 382, 386, 388
Bleuler, E., 130
Block, J., 46, 383, 391, 394
Boll, T. J., 51
Bolton, B., 182n2
Bond, J. A., 31, 32
Borum, R., 169
Bosse, R., 409
Bowden, J. D., 114
Box, G. E. P., 19
Boyd, J., 42
Bradley, P. E., 152, 157n3
Brantley, P. J., 409
Brauer, B. A., 163
Briggs, P. F., 22n4, 63, 69n9
Brown, A., 26
Brown, J., 478
Brown, J. D., 25
Brozek, J., 400

Brown, J., 478
Brown, J. D., 25
Brozek, J., 400
Brunetti, D. G., 77, 78, 90, 125
Bryant, B. R., 169
Buchholz, D., 35, 45, 46
Buechley, R., 11, 68n4
Buigas, R. A., 40
Buis, T., 35, 40, 43, 44, 55, 61, 62
Buonpane, N., 408
Burch, N. R., 395
Burkhart, B. R., 76, 377
Buros, O. K., 182n2
Butcher, J. N., 1, 2, 9, 10, 11, 12, 14, 19, 20, 21, 22n7, 26, 27, 29, 30, 32, 35, 36, 37, 47, 48, 50, 52, 53, 54, 55, 63, 67n2, 70, 73, 74, 78, 82, 84, 85, 94, 103, 104, 105, 106, 111, 114, 115, 116, 117, 118, 121, 122, 126, 129, 130, 131, 135, 138, 143, 144, 145, 146, 147, 148, 150, 153, 155, 157n1, 161, 162, 163, 168, 169, 171, 174, 178, 180, 182n2, 187, 196, 203, 225, 231, 340, 343, 346, 358, 365, 371, 384, 390, 391, 395, 399, 401, 407, 409, 410, 411, 412, 413, 423, 478, 479, 480
Bynner, J. M., 383

C

Caldwell, A. B., 9, 14, 24n14, 43, 57, 59, 60, 74, 75, 86, 87, 88, 89, 90, 95, 96, 97, 98, 100, 106, 107, 108, 109, 110, 111, 112, 123, 124, 125, 126, 136, 137, 138, 139, 140, 143, 146, 147, 148, 150, 151, 164, 165, 179, 181, 204, 205, 231, 287, 303, 339, 340, 393, 394, 396, 400, 401, 404, 409, 424, 464
Calvin, J., 75
Cameron, S. L., 62
Carkhuff, R. R., 231
Carr, A. C., 477
Carroll, D., 26, 27
Carson, R. C., 231
Carvajal, H. H., 170
Chakraborty, D., 35
Chance, J. E., 47, 55, 204, 403
Chang, A. F., 409
Charney, D. S., 404
Chassin, P., 438
Childers, H. E., 395
Childs, R. A., 74
Chojnacki, J. T., 75, 106
Christian, W. L., 76, 377
Cicchetti, D., 78
Clark, C., 35, 36, 363
Clark, M. E., 375
Clavelle, P. R., 161
Clopton, J. R., 8, 26, 27, 67n1
Cofer, C. N., 47, 55, 204, 403
Cogan, R., 359
Colby, F., 51
Cole, P., 34, 40, 64, 65, 67
Colligan, R., 62, 63, 69n10, 91, 112, 113, 141
Colligan, R. C., 4, 6, 7, 18, 19, 22n6, 24n10, 51, 82, 105
Collins, F., 395
Comrey, A. L., 102, 129
Cook, P. E., 390, 397, 399
Cook, W. W., 366
Cormier, C. A., 414, 416
Costa, P. T., Jr., 380
Cox, D. R., 19
Coyle, F. A., Jr., 48
Craig, R. J., 105
Cronbach, L. J., 343
Crosley, A. P., 395
Cross, H. J., 114
Crumpler, C. A., 384
Cuadra, C., 389, 390

D

Dahlstrom, L. E., 1, 3, 4, 5, 6, 22n, 24n10, 26, 35, 47, 49, 50, 52, 53, 54, 61, 68n4, 80, 82, 83, 84, 85, 90, 91, 92, 93, 101, 102, 103, 104, 110, 111, 112, 113, 114, 118, 120, 121, 122, 126, 129, 130, 131, 134, 135, 141, 142, 144, 145, 152, 155, 156, 157, 168, 170, 173, 175, 231, 388, 390, 395, 422, 424, 425
Dahlstrom, W. G., 1, 3, 4, 5, 6, 7, 8, 9, 11, 12, 14, 15, 17, 19, 21, 22n, 22n7, 24n10, 24n11, 24n14, 26, 27, 29, 30, 32, 34, 35, 36, 37, 47, 48, 49, 50, 52, 53, 54, 61, 63, 64, 65, 67, 67n2, 68n4, 69n7, 70, 73, 74, 77, 80, 82, 83, 84, 85, 90, 91, 92, 93, 94, 100, 101, 102, 103, 104, 106, 110, 112, 113, 114, 115, 116, 117, 118, 120, 121, 122, 126, 129, 130, 131, 134, 135, 138, 141, 142, 143, 144, 145, 146, 147, 148, 150, 151, 152, 155, 156, 157, 157n1, 162, 163, 168, 169, 170, 171, 173, 174, 175, 176, 177, 178, 179, 180, 181, 184n7–8, 231, 339, 343, 346, 388, 389, 390, 395, 404, 405, 413, 422, 423, 424, 425
Damarin, F., 47
Dana, R. H., 182n2
Danahy, S., 409
Daniel, F. J., 51
Dannebaum, S. E., 26

Davis, H. G., 359, 411, 412
De Arellano, M. A., 40, 44
de Labry, L., 409
Dean, E. F., 182n2
Dent, O. B., 421
Diers, C. J., 47
Dillon, E. A., 118
Doughtie, E. B., 152, 157n3
Drake, L. E., 151, 152, 155, 159n5, 231
Dubinsky, S., 77
Duckworth, J. C., 9, 14, 24n14, 82, 93, 105, 117, 121, 128, 133, 142, 144, 155, 231, 392, 394, 400, 401, 425, 438, 440
Duker, J., 231, 464

E

Edwards, A. L., 21, 46, 47
Edwards, D. W., 180, 181
Edwards, E. L., 170
Ehrenworth, N. V., 418
Ehrlich, P., 404
Eichman, W. J., 478
Einhorn, J. H., 416
Endicott, N. A., 121
Erdberg, P., 471, 473
Erdman, H. P., 477
Estes, W. K., 416
Evans, C., 151
Evans, D., 438
Evans, R. G., 340
Eysenck, H. J., 130, 155

F

Faded, V. B., 409
Fairbank, J. A., 390, 403
Faschingbauer, T. R., 182n2
Fidler, B. J., 55
Fine, H. K., 132
Finn, S. E., 163, 406, 471, 472, 473
Finney, J. C., 409
Fischer, J., 92, 95, 97, 98, 100
Fisicaro, S. A., 43
Fjordbak, T., 48
Foerstner, S. B., 75, 115, 153
Fontaine, J., 51
Fowler, R. D., 231, 409, 421, 423, 477, 478
Franzen, M., 64
Franzen, M. D., 35, 45, 46
Friedman, A. F., 2, 11, 24n10, 24n14, 26, 34, 35, 40, 48, 49, 52, 60, 63, 64, 68n3, 68n4, 71, 79, 93, 114, 117, 121, 129, 130, 133, 143, 144, 152, 155, 157n3, 160, 173, 179, 231, 340, 346, 399, 406, 410, 438
Friedman, M., 366
Frueh, B. C., 40, 44
Fulkerson, S. C., 26, 31
Fuller, C. G., 162

G

Gacono, C., 107
Gallagher, B. J., 130
Galluci, N. T., 8, 409
Gamble, D. J., 77
Garske, J. P., 35
Garvin, R. D., 105, 406, 407
Gass, C. S., 35, 45, 46
Gentry, L., 438
Gentry, T. A., 79, 152, 157n3
Ghosh, A., 477
Gibbs, M., 132
Gilberstadt, H., 231, 464
Glaros, A. G., 67
Gleser, G. C., 79, 93, 120, 157n3
Goad, N. A., 114
Gold, P. B., 40, 44
Goldberg, J. O., 404
Goldberg, L. R., 339, 345, 414, 416
Gomez-Mont, F., 182n2
Gordon, R. A., 27, 105, 418
Gosling, F. G., 127
Gottesman, I. I., 406, 407, 408
Gottfried, A. E., 428
Gottfried, A. W., 428
Gough, H. G., 43, 44, 58, 60, 61, 62, 68n7, 69n7, 69n9, 69n10, 118, 134, 156, 389, 399, 400
Graham, J. R., 9, 11, 12, 14, 19, 22n7, 26, 27, 29, 30, 32, 35, 36, 37, 48, 52, 53, 54, 63, 65, 67n2, 70, 71, 72, 73, 74, 82, 84, 85, 86, 87, 88, 94, 97, 98, 103, 104, 105, 106, 107, 108, 109, 110, 114, 115, 116, 117, 118, 119, 122, 123, 124, 126, 129, 130, 134, 135, 136, 137, 138, 139, 140, 141, 143, 144, 145, 146, 147, 148, 149, 150, 153, 155, 157n1, 158n4, 163, 169, 171, 174, 178, 179, 181, 231, 232, 236, 263, 343, 346, 356, 357, 358, 359, 362, 363, 364, 365, 366, 369, 371, 372, 374, 390, 392, 394, 395, 396, 399, 400, 401, 402, 403, 406, 409, 411, 413, 423, 459
Grant, L., 65
Gravitz, M. A., 339
Grayson, H. M., 61, 339
Greene, R. L., 1, 2, 3, 7, 11, 22n5, 22n6, 24n14, 27, 28, 29, 30, 31, 34, 35, 36, 38, 39, 40, 44, 46, 50, 54, 55, 59, 60, 61, 62, 63, 64, 65, 67, 67n1, 67n3, 68n3, 68n5, 69n10, 71, 74, 75, 76, 77, 80, 81, 82, 83, 86, 87, 88, 89, 92, 93, 95, 96, 97, 98, 99, 100, 102, 103, 104,

105, 106, 107, 108, 109, 110, 113, 118, 120, 121, 123, 124, 125, 129, 133, 134, 136, 137, 138, 139, 140, 141, 142, 143, 144, 146, 147, 148, 149, 152, 153, 155, 158n4, 169, 172, 176, 177, 178, 182n2, 184n7, 187, 225, 319, 325, 340, 359, 390, 394, 395, 397, 398, 399, 400, 401, 405, 406, 407, 408, 409, 411, 422, 424, 425
Greenfield, N. S., 395
Greist, J. H., 477
Griffin, R., 181, 231
Grisell, J. L., 409
Grove, W. M., 414
Guastello, S. J., 417
Gulas, I., 423
Gwin, R., 176, 180
Gynther, M. D., 76, 144, 377, 422, 424

H

Hallam, R. A., 30, 31, 37
Haller, D., 33, 61, 83, 102, 105, 120, 127, 132, 133, 143, 164, 231, 272, 275, 337, 414, 415, 416, 417, 473
Hammond, J., 64
Hampton, 407
Han, K., 47, 53, 54, 55, 203
Hanson, R. K., 35, 49, 52, 83, 84, 94, 103, 117, 122, 130, 135, 145, 155
Hanvik, L., 389
Harkness, A. R., 358, 379, 380, 382, 383, 384
Harmon, L. R., 76, 81, 89, 99, 114, 115, 125, 126, 128, 149, 153, 339
Harrell, T. H., 179
Harris, G. T., 74, 414, 416
Harris, M. J., 35, 37, 44, 45, 46, 62, 63
Harris, R. E., 72, 75, 81, 85, 95, 103, 106, 114, 115, 122, 128, 153
Hartshorne, H., 47
Hase, H. D., 339
Hathaway, S. R., 3, 4, 5, 6, 7, 22n2–4, 24n9, 40, 47, 49, 50, 63, 69n9, 80, 83, 91, 92, 93, 101, 102, 103, 104, 110, 112, 113, 119, 120, 127, 128, 130, 131, 141, 144, 168, 173, 174, 343, 346, 391
Hathaway, S. T., 480
Hatzenbuehler, L., 170
Heap, R. F., 48
Heaton, R., 65
Hedlund, J. L., 62, 94, 133
Helmes, E., 7, 182n2
Hjemboe, S., 391, 412, 413
Hofer, P. J., 167
Hoffmann, H., 409
Hoffmann, N., 340
Hogarth, R. M., 416
Holden, R. R., 164
Hollrah, J. L., 77, 78, 90, 111, 112, 125, 150
Holmes, C. B., 170
Holmes, T. H., 395
Holmes, W. O., 407
Holmstrom, R. W., 104, 129
Holroyd, R. G., 364
Honaker, L. M., 176, 179
Hopkins, D. G., 168
Hostetler, K., 153, 162, 182n2
Hough, R. L., 403
Hovey, H. B., 231
Howe, M. G., 182n2
Hoyt, D. P., 407
Huber, N. A., 409
Huddleston, E. N., 74, 75, 157n2
Hugo, J., 182n2
Humm, D. G., 22n2
Humphrey, D. H., 178, 179, 181
Hunsley, J., 35, 49, 52, 83, 84, 94, 103, 117, 122, 130, 135, 145, 155
Hunt, H., 69n9

I

Ihilevich, D., 120
Iverson, G., 64
Iverson, G. L., 29

J

Jackson, D. N., 76, 339
Jackson, E., 168
Jaffe, A. M., 40, 64, 105
Jaffe, K. L., 105
Jefferson, J. W., 477
Jenkins, C. D., 366
Jenkins, W. L., 58
Johnson, J. H., 343, 346
Johnson, K. N., 343, 346
Jones, D. J., 130
Jordan, B. K., 403
Jortner, S., 121
Juba, M., 478
Judson, A. J., 47, 55, 204, 403

K

Kaemmer, B., 11, 12, 14, 19, 22n7, 26, 27, 29, 30, 32, 35, 36, 37, 48, 52, 63, 67n2, 70, 73, 74, 84, 85, 94, 103, 104, 106, 114, 115, 116, 117, 118, 122, 126, 130, 135, 138, 143, 144, 145, 146, 147, 148, 150, 155, 157n1, 163, 169, 171, 174, 178, 231, 343, 390, 395, 413
Kahneman, D., 416
Kalemba, V., 35, 40

Kammeier, M. L., 409
Katz, M. M., 77
Katz, S. E., 3
Kawachi, I., 363, 367
Kay, D. C., 409
Keane, S. P., 132,
Keane, T. M., 179, 390, 403
Keating, F. R., 480
Keiller, S. W., 71, 72, 85, 144
Keller, L. S., 161
Kemp, S. M., 74
Kendrick, S., 170
Kersh, B. C., 123, 124
Khadavi, A., 358, 361
Kilpatrick, D. G., 409
Kimlicka, T. M., 114
Kincannon, J. C., 182n2
Kleban, M. H., 61
Kleepsies, P. M., 179
Klein, M. H., 477
Kleinmuntz, B., 402
Klett, W. G., 478
Kline, C. D., 421
Kline, R. B., 67
Klinefelter, D., 105
Kohutek, K. J., 347
Koss, M. P., 339, 340, 342
Kraepelin, E., 130
Kraft, I. A., 152, 157n3
Kramitz, L., 409
Krishnamurthy, R., 74, 75, 157n2
Kubzansky, L. D., 367
Kulka, R. A., 390, 403
Kunce, J., 119, 128, 144
Kunce, J. T., 132

L

Labbe, M. R., 161, 477
Lachar, D., 24n10, 126, 143, 150, 231, 340, 346, 409, 423, 424, 425, 464
Ladd, J. S., 40
LaLone, 14, 15
Lamb, D. G., 35, 53
Landis, C., 3
Lane, J. B., 464
Lang, A. R., 56
Lanyon, R. I., 26, 464
Larsen, L., 31, 36
Larsen, L. H., 30, 37, 44, 53, 62
Larsen, R. M., 1
Lawton, M. P., 61
Leary, T., 345
Lehner, G. F. J., 80, 157n3
Levenson, M. R., 384
Levinson, M. R., 409
Levitt, E. E., 10, 74, 87, 95, 106, 107, 109, 124, 136, 137, 138, 146, 147, 148
Lewak, R., 2, 11, 24n10, 26, 34, 40, 48, 49, 52, 60, 68n3, 68n4, 71, 79, 94, 104, 105, 121, 129, 133, 134, 142, 143, 144, 155, 156, 160, 165, 173, 231, 232, 340, 346, 399, 406, 410, 438, 471, 472, 475
Lewis, E. G., 231
Lilienfeld, S. O., 106, 107, 109
Lilly, R. S., 114, 115, 153, 158n4
Lingoes, J. C., 72, 74, 75, 81, 85, 95, 103, 106, 114, 115, 122, 128, 153
Little, J. W., 122, 135, 145
Little, K. B., 80, 92, 95, 97, 98, 100, 157n3
Litz, B. T., 404
Lomb, D. G., 35, 45, 46
Long, K. A., 118, 119
Loper, R. G., 409
Lubin, B., 1
Lucio, E., 162
Lumley, M. A., 43
Lynn, S. J., 35

M

MacAndrew, C., 7, 390, 403, 406, 407, 408, 409, 410, 411
MacInnes, W. D., 35, 45, 46
Maguire, A., 398
Malloy, P. F., 390, 403
Malony, H. N., Jr., 162
Manifold, V., 403, 478
Mann, A. W., 2, 24n14, 35, 63
Marks, P. A., 33, 60, 61, 83, 93, 94, 102, 104, 105, 120, 121, 127, 129, 130, 132, 133, 134, 142, 143, 144, 155, 156, 164, 165, 231, 232, 236, 242, 272, 275, 283, 337, 414, 415, 416, 417, 464, 471, 472, 473, 475
Marmar, C. R., 403
Martin, E. H., 115, 116, 406
Maruish, M. E., 420
Matarazzo, J., 1
Matarazzo, J. D., 1, 197, 477, 479
Mataya, P., 480
Matthews, C., 65
Matz, P. A., 49
May, M. A., 47
McBlaine, D. D., 163
McBride, H., 408
McCall, J. N., 231
McCarthy, C. E., 480
McClosky, H., 389, 399, 400
McConnell, T. R., 151
McCord, G., 231
McCrae, R. R., 51, 380
McCully, E., 354
McFarlane, A. C., 404
McGrath, R. E., 74

McKee, M. G., 118, 134, 156
McKenna, T., 391, 407, 410, 411
McKinley, J. C., 3, 4, 5, 7, 22n3, 40, 49, 50, 80, 83, 90, 91, 92, 93, 101, 102, 103, 104, 110, 112, 113, 127, 128, 129, 141, 144, 168, 343, 346
McLachlan, J. F., 182n2
McLaughlin, J. F., 182n2
McNamara, K. M., 231
McNulty, J. L., 42, 72, 86, 87, 88, 97, 98, 106, 107, 108, 109, 110, 111, 123, 124, 136, 137, 138, 140, 146, 147, 148, 149, 180, 181, 231, 232, 236, 263, 356, 357, 358, 359, 362, 363, 364, 365, 366, 369, 371, 372, 374, 380, 382, 383, 392, 394, 396, 400, 402, 403, 411
Medley, D. M., 366
Meehl, P. E., 22n2, 47, 49, 50, 131, 144, 174, 338, 339, 342, 343, 389, 391, 399, 400, 414, 415, 416, 417
Mefford, R. B., 395
Megargee, E. I., 56, 390, 397, 399, 400, 401, 406
Meloy, J. R., 107
Mendelsohn, G. A., 390, 397, 399
Messick, S., 47
Meyer, R. G., 155
Meyers, L. S., 153, 154
Miles, C. C., 113
Miller, A., 409
Miller, H. R., 22n6, 75, 182n2, 404
Miller, K. B., 411
Miller, M. L., 421, 423, 478
Monroe, K., 36
Moreland, K. L., 1, 115, 153, 346, 477, 478
Morey, L. C., 104, 120, 382, 386, 388
Morfitt, R. C., 164
Morgan, C. A., III, 404
Mori, D. L., 179
Morrison, T. L., 21, 180, 181
Moser, R. K., 358, 361
Moss, T., 409
Mouton, G. J., 40

N

Navran, L., 389
Nelson, G. E., 60, 94, 104, 105, 121, 129, 134, 142, 144, 155, 156, 165, 231, 232, 471, 472, 475
Nelson, L. D., 78
Nelson, S. E., 47, 57, 58, 205
Neuringer, C., 8, 26, 27, 67n1
Newmark, C. S., 438
Nichols, D. S., 4, 6, 7, 8, 11, 22n2, 23n9, 30, 31, 36, 39, 44, 46, 54, 55, 59, 63, 86, 87, 88, 89, 95, 96, 97, 98, 99, 100, 102, 106, 107, 108, 109, 110, 118, 120, 121, 123, 124, 125, 129, 131, 133, 134, 136, 137, 138, 139, 140, 141, 142, 143, 146, 147, 148, 149, 152, 153, 340, 394, 398
Nicholson, R. A., 40, 43, 44, 55, 61, 62
Nicolaou, A. C., 404
Novacek, J., 144
Null, C., 343, 346
Nuñez, R., 162

O

Oetting, E. R., 231
Offord, K. P., 4, 6, 7, 18, 19, 22n6, 24n10, 51, 62, 63, 69n10, 82, 105, 112, 113, 141
Olinger, L. B., 61
Orsillo, S. M., 404
Osborne, D., 2, 4, 6, 7, 18, 19, 22n6, 24n10, 62, 63, 69n10, 82, 91, 105, 112, 113, 141, 231
Otto, R. K., 56
Overall, J. E., 182n2
Owen, P. L., 1
Ownby, R. L., 426

P

Page, J., 3
Pancheri, P., 163
Pancoast, D. L., 6, 7, 8, 22n5, 106, 418
Panter, A. T., 74
Paolo, A. M., 145, 169, 183n5
Parker, C. H. K., 35, 49, 52, 83, 84, 103, 117, 122, 130, 135, 145, 155
Parnell, T., 179
Paulhus, D. L., 25, 46, 47
Payne, F. D., 346
Pearson, J. S., 231, 480
Penk, W. E., 179
Perley, R. N., 120
Perlman, B., 49
Perry, M. S., 154
Peterson, C. D., 114, 390, 404, 405
Peterson, S. A., 40
Piotrowski, C., 161, 477, 478
Pogge, D. L., 74
Pope, K. S., 168, 187, 225, 471
Powis, D., 74
Prescott, C. A., 406, 407, 408
Prokop, C. K., 82, 97
Putzke, J. D., 51

Q

Quinsey, V. L., 398, 414, 416

R

Radovanovic, H., 55
Rahe, R. H., 395
Rapport, L. J., 43
Raskin, R., 144
Rathvon, N., 104, 129
Rawlings, R. R., 409
Rector, N. A., 43, 44, 55, 61, 62
Reddon, J. R., 7
Reyes-Lagunes, I., 162
Reynolds, S. K., 30, 31, 37
Reynolds, W. M., 1
Rhodes, R. J., 409
Rice, M. E., 414, 416
Rieke, M. L., 417
Ritz, G., 115
Robertson, M., 182n2
Robison, L. H., 35, 38, 64
Rodgers, D. A., 157n3, 231
Roessler, R., 395
Rogers, M. L., 77
Rogers, R., 35, 38, 40, 43, 44, 45, 55, 61, 62, 69n7
Rohan, W. P., 409
Rojdev, R. S., 10
Rombouts, R., 161, 477
Rome, H. P., 480
Romney, D. M., 383
Roper, B. L., 161
Rosen, A., 388, 403
Rosenblatt, A. I., 56
Rosenman, R. H., 366
Rothke, S. E., 2, 24n14, 34, 35, 40, 41, 42, 63, 64, 65, 67
Rotman, S. R., 409
Rouse, S. L., 411
Rouse, S. V., 164
Ryan, J. J., 145, 169, 183n5

S

Salekin, R. T., 35, 38, 43, 44, 45, 62, 69n7
Sasek, J., 114
Sawyer, J., 414, 416
Schill, T., 362
Schinka, J. A., 14, 15, 169
Schlenger, W. E., 390, 403
Schlottmann, R. S., 77, 78, 90, 111, 112, 125
Schneider, D. U., 408
Schoof, K., 409
Schroeder, H. E., 114, 115, 153, 158n4
Schuerger, J. M., 115
Schuldberg, D., 478
Schuller, D. R., 62
Schwartz, M. F., 409
Schwartz, M. S., 79, 157n3
Scott, A. B., 77, 78, 90, 111, 112, 125
Sedlacek, G. M., 407
Seelen, J., 168, 187, 225
Seeman, M. V., 43, 44, 55, 61, 62, 76
Seeman, W., 33, 83, 93, 102, 105, 120, 127, 130, 132, 133, 143, 164, 231, 236, 242, 272, 275, 283, 337, 414, 415, 416, 417, 464, 473
Seever, F., 1
Serkownek, K., 115, 153, 406
Sewell, K. W., 35, 38, 43, 44, 45, 62, 69n7
Sheppard, P. L., 114
Sherwood, N. E., 137, 140, 150, 344, 347, 355, 358, 359, 360, 362, 365, 367, 369, 370, 372
Shondrick, D. D., 425
Sieber, K. O., 153, 154
Sines, J. O., 114
Sivec, H. J., 35
Skeeters, D. E., 409
Slovic, P., 339
Slutske, W. S., 161
Smeltzer, D. J., 79, 93, 157n3, 231
Smith, A. J., 145, 169, 183n5
Smith, D. F., 409
Smith, G. T., 30, 31, 37, 44, 53, 62
Smith, M. R., 104, 120
Southwick, S. M., 404
Spanier, G. B., 412
Sparrow, D., 363, 367
Spera, J., 182n2
Spielberger, C. D., 161, 477, 478, 479
Spinhoven, P., 161, 477
Spiro, A., 363, 367, 382, 384
Staal, M., 176
Staal, M. A., 180
Stafford, K. P., 372, 425
Stein, K. B., 79
Stein, L. A. R., 411
Strassberg, D. S., 117
Streiner, D. L., 22n6, 75, 182n2, 404
Streit, K., 359
Strenger, V. E., 406
Sumpter, J., 31, 35, 38, 64
Sumpter, J. C., 30, 37
Sundberg, N. D., 1
Sutker, P. B., 409
Swenson, W. M., 4, 6, 7, 19, 24n10, 82, 91, 105, 112, 113, 141, 231, 480

T

Tallent, N., 417, 477, 478
Tanner, B. A., 118
Tarter, R. E., 120, 408
Tatro, R. L., 409
Taylor, J. A., 390
Taylor, S. E., 25

Tellegen, A., 7, 8, 9, 11, 12, 14, 17, 19, 20, 21, 22n7, 24n14, 26, 27, 29, 30, 32, 35, 36, 37, 48, 52, 63, 67n2, 70, 73, 74, 84, 85, 94, 103, 104, 106, 114, 115, 116, 117, 118, 122, 126, 130, 135, 138, 143, 144, 145, 146, 147, 148, 150, 155, 157n1, 163, 169, 171, 174, 178, 180, 231, 343, 390, 395, 413, 422
Terman, L. M., 113
Thiede, W. B., 152, 155, 159n5
Thomas, D., 161, 478
Thornby, J. I., 409
Timbrook, R. E., 53, 63, 65, 179
Tisdale, M. J., 423
Todd, R. M., 43
Tonsager, M. E., 471, 472, 473
Trull, T. J., 380
Tversky, A., 416

U

Useda, J. D., 380

V

Van de Riet, V. W., 231
Varney, G. W., 398
Venn, J., 85
Vestre, N. D., 121
Vokonas, P. S., 363, 367

W

Wadsworth, G. W., Jr., 22n2
Wakefield, J. A., Jr., 79, 93, 114, 130, 152, 155, 157n3
Wales, W. B., 76, 106
Walker, J. N., 47
Wallace, R. F., 155
Walsh, S. S., 179
Walsh, W. B., 75
Walters, G. D., 44, 131, 132, 133, 397
Wang, S., 362
Ward, L. C., 9, 72, 118, 123, 124, 154, 157n1, 168, 179
Watkins, C. E., Jr., 1
Watson, C. G., 121, 161, 403, 478
Watts, D., 53, 63, 65
Waugh, M. H., 382, 386, 388
Waxmonsky, J. A., 123, 124
Webb, J. T., 2, 10, 11, 24n10, 26, 34, 40, 48, 49, 52, 60, 68n3, 68n4, 71, 79, 121, 129, 133, 143, 144, 155, 160, 173, 231, 340, 346, 399, 406, 410, 421, 422, 423, 438, 478
Weed, N. C., 78, 391, 410, 411
Weiss, D. S., 367
Weiss, S. T., 363
Weissman, H. N., 21, 180, 181
Welsh, G. S., 1, 3, 4, 5, 6, 8, 22n, 26, 35, 49, 50, 52, 53, 54, 61, 68n4, 69n7, 80, 82, 83, 84, 85, 90, 91, 101, 104, 112, 113, 114, 118, 121, 122, 126, 129, 130, 131, 134, 135, 141, 144, 145, 155, 156, 157, 168, 170, 173, 174, 175, 231, 339, 388, 389, 390, 394, 395, 422, 423
Wetter, M. W., 30, 31, 34, 35, 36, 37, 38, 40, 44, 45, 46, 47, 49, 53, 54, 56, 60, 62, 63, 64, 65, 67
Wetzler, S., 358, 361
Wheeler, W. M., 80, 157n3
White, T. W., 44
Whitworth, R. H., 163
Widiger, T. A., 30, 31, 37
Wiederholt, J. L., 169
Wiederstein, M., 157n3
Wiener, D. N., 76, 81, 89, 99, 111, 114, 115, 125, 126, 128, 133, 149, 153, 339
Wiggins, J. S., 7, 46, 47, 56, 62, 82, 115, 147, 153, 204, 345, 346, 390, 409, 416
Willage, D. E., 26, 31
Willcockson, J. C., 182n2
Williams, C. L., 9, 20, 21, 54, 82, 105, 121, 129, 132, 144, 153, 231, 343, 346, 365, 371, 399, 401
Williams, H. L., 389
Williams, M. A., 51
Wolf, L. I., 26
Wolking, W. D., 231
Won Cho, D., 62, 133
Wong, M. R., 114, 153
Wood, K. A., 155
Woodworth, R. S., 4, 339
Workman-Daniels, K., 409
Wrobel, T. A., 75, 86, 87, 88, 96, 97, 99, 106, 107, 109, 110, 123, 126, 137, 138, 141, 147, 150, 340

Y

Yandell, R. J., 118, 134, 156
Yehuda, R., 404
Young, A., 404
Youngjohn, J. R., 35, 45, 46

Z

Zubin, J., 3

Subject Index

A

A scale, *see* Anxiety scale (*A*)
Abbreviated forms of MMPI-2, 161–162
Active persecutory experience, 576
Active psychotic experience critical items, 575–576
Actuarial and clinical approaches to interpretation, 414–415, *see also* Computer-based test interpretation
Actuarial data and base rates, 417–418
Actuarial rules, development of, 415–417
Acute anxiety state critical items, 341, 569
Acute tension-anxiety state critical items, 574–575
Ad (Admission) scale, 92
Addiction Acknowledgment/Addiction Admission scale (*AAS*), 410–412, 567–568
Addiction Potential scale (*APS*), 410–412, 567
Adolescents, 9–10, *see also* MMPI-A
Aesthetic Interest subscale, 116
Affection, need for, 96–97
Age, 105, 144, 196, 421–422
Aggression, 146, 341, 354, 569, 576, *see also* Anger; Hostility
  inhibition of, 98–99
Aggressiveness scale (*AGG*), 380–381, 384–387, 563
Agitated Hostility, 115
Alcoholism, 341, 404–411, 569, *see also* Drug abuse and addiction
Alienation, 109–111, 123, 136–137, 153, 154
familial, 106–107, 349
All-false response set, 51, 214–216
All-true response set, 209, 212–214
Alpha dimension, 46, 47, 57
American Sign Language (ASL) translation, 163
Amorality (*Ma1*), 146–147, 551, *see also* Psychopathy
ANG (Anger) scale, 139, 347, 358, 362–364, 367–368, 378, 384, 557
  ANG1 (Explosive Behavior), 350, 362–363, 557
  ANG2 (Irritability), 350, 363, 557
Anger, *see also* Aggression; Hostility
  critical items related to, 341, 571
  denial of, 53, 203–204
Antisocial attitude, *see also* *ASP*; *AUT*; Psychopathic Deviate scale (*Pd*)
  critical items related to, 341, 571
ANX (Anxiety) scale, 347, 348, 352–358, 377–378, 554
Anxiety and tension, 116, 127, 232, 341, 381, *see also* Fears; Psychasthenia scale (*Pt*)
  critical items related to, 341, 569, 570, 574–575
  denial of, 95–96, 108, 150
  lack of anticipatory, 102
  state *vs.* trait, 341, 392–393, 569, 574–575
Anxiety scale (*A*), 354, 391–394, 565
ASP (Antisocial Practices) scale, 107, 348–350, 352, 353, 365–366, 382, 558
  ASP1 (Antisocial Attitudes), 365, 366, 558
  ASP2 (Antisocial Behavior), 350, 366, 558–559
Assaultive impulse, 576
Audiotape version of MMPI-2, 160–161, 170, 171
Augmenting a profile, 184n7
AUT (Authority Conflict) scale, 346, 349
Authority problems, 341

Authority Problems (*Pd2*), 107–108, 365, 543–544
Avoidance, social, 153, 154

B

Base rates, 417–418
Behavioral signs/samples, items as, 342–343
Behaviors, *see also specific topics*
  anticipation of consequences of one's, 102
  paragraph in report on, 460–461
Belief in Human Goodness (*S1*), 53, 203, 537
Beliefs, *see also CYN* (Cynicism) scale, *CYN1* (Misanthropic Beliefs)
  deviant, 341, 570
BIZ (Bizarre Mentation) scale, 342, 348, 351–353, 355, 361–362, 370, 379, 381, 556
  BIZ1 (Psychotic Symptomatology), 351, 361–362, 557
  BIZ2 (Schizotypal Characteristics), 351, 361, 557
Blank items, *see* Cannot Say (*?*) score
"Blind" interpretation, 420, 426, 427
Borderline personality disorder (BPD), 140, 147, 438

C

Caldwell Critical Item Set, 340, 342
California Psychological Inventory (CPI), 68n7, 399
Cannot Say (*?*) score, 26–28, *see also* Omitted items
  interpretation, 26–28, 186–188
Cardiorespiratory complaints, critical items related to, 573
Carelessness scale, 28
CH (Correction for Hypochondriasis) scale, 81
Characterological adjustment, critical items related to, 341
Clinical scales, 3, *see also specific scales*
  development and use, 3, 70–73
Code pattern correspondence, MMPI/MMPI-2, 176–182
Code patterns/codetypes, 175–176
  common, 429–439
  defined, 176
  elevation, additional scales, and, 438, 440–441
  normal code, high K, 337, 432, 437, 438
  Spike 1 codes, 232–233
  high 1, low 4 codes (for men), 234
  high 1, low 5 codes (for women), 234
  12/21 codes, 234–235, 256, 444
  123/213/231/321 and 132/312/321 codes, 235–236, 243–244, 256–258, 283, 467
  1234/2134 codes, 237
  1237/2137 codes, 237–238
  128/218 codes, 238
  129/219 codes, 238–239
  120/210 codes, 239
  13/31 codes, 240–243, 281, 429, 444–445, 465, 467, 469
    conversion V code, 242, 429, 430
    with high K, 243
  134/316 codes, 244–245
  137 codes, 245–246, 467
  138/318 codes, 246–247, 465, 467
  139 codes, 247–248
  14/41 codes, 248–249, 445
  15/51 codes, 249–250
  16/61 codes, 250–251, 445
  17/71 codes, 251, 422, 445–446
  18/81 codes, 251–252, 446
  19/91 codes, 252–253, 446
  10/01 codes, 253
  Spike 2 codes, 254–255, 446
    with low 9, 255–256
  23/32 codes, 258–260, 281–282, 447
  24/42 codes, 260–262, 447, 461–462, 471
  243 codes, 262
  247/274/427/472/724/742 codes, 262–264, 269–270, 356, 467
  248 and 284/428/482/824/842 codes, 264–265, 274–275, 309–310, 465
  25/52 codes, 265–266, 447
  26/62 codes, 266–267, 447–448, 458, 467
  27/72 codes, 267–268, 408, 419, 421, 440, 459, 463, 467, 468
  273/723 codes, 269
  275/725 (for men) and 27, low 5 (for women) codes, 270–271
  278/728 and 287/827 codes, 271–273, 276, 441, 443, 465, 467
  28/82 codes, 273–274, 440, 463, 467
  281/821 codes, 274
  284/824 codes, 274–275
  29/92 codes, 276–278, 448–449, 455–456, 465, 467
  20/20 codes, 278–279
  Spike 3 codes, 280, 449
    with high K, 280–281
  34/43 codes, 284–286, 449, 463, 467, 468
  345/435/534 codes, 286–287
  346/436 and 463/643 codes, 287–288, 302–303
  35/53 codes, 288
  36/63 codes, 289–290, 422, 449–450, 467, 469
  37/73 codes, 290–291, 450, 467
  38/83 codes, 292–293, 450, 467

39/93 codes, 293–294, 450
30/03 codes, 294–295
Spike 4 codes, 297–298, 433, 451, 461, 467, 468
high 4, low 5 codes, 298
45/54 codes, 298–300, 451
46/64 codes, 300–301, 451–452, 460, 463, 465, 467, 468
462/642 codes, 301–302
468/648 codes, 304
47/74 codes, 305–306, 452
478 codes, 306
48/84 codes, 307–308, 452–453, 460, 462–463, 465, 467, 468
with high F and low 2, 309
486/846 codes, 310
489/849 and 498/948 codes, 310–311, 315, 441, 467
49/94 codes, 311–313, 373, 408, 419–421, 438, 440, 442, 453, 460, 463, 465, 467, 468, 470, 471
493/943 codes, 313–314
495/945 codes, 314
496/946 codes, 314–315
40/04 codes, 315–316
Spike 5 codes, 316
56/65 codes, 318
57/75 codes, 318–319
58/85 codes, 319
59/95 codes, 319–320
50/05 codes, 320
Spike 6 codes, 453
67/76 codes, 321–322, 453
68/86 codes, 322–323, 371, 454, 461, 467, 470
69/96 codes, 323–324, 454, 465, 467
698/968 codes, 325
60/06 codes, 325–326
Spike 7 codes, 326–327, 454–455
78/87 codes, 327–328, 453, 465, 467
79/97 codes, 328–329
70/07 codes, 329
Spike 8 codes, 330
89/98 codes, 465, 467
80/08 codes, 322–323
Spike 9 codes, 333, 455, 467, 472
high 9, high K codes, 334–335
93/39 codes, 463, 467
98 codes, 456
90/09 codes, 335–336, 456–457
Spike 0 codes, 336
Coding the profile, 173–176
"College educated" validity configuration, 226, 230
College Maladjustment scale (*Mt*), 402–404, 566
College students who seek psychotherapy, 402
Competitiveness, 366, 367
Competitiveness (*TPA2*), 350, 363, 368, 559
Complaints, paragraph in report on, 459
Computer-based administrations, 161
Computer-based test interpretation (CBTI), 477–480
Computer interpretation of MMPI/MMPI-2, 480–481
Computerized scoring, 172
Conation, defined, 138
Concentration, 574
Confusion, 341, 569
Consciousness, losses of, 574
Consistency of responding, 427, *see also TRIN*; *VRIN*
Constriction, *see* Repression scale (*R*)
Content scales, 345–354, *see also specific scales*
MMPI-2 and Wiggins, 346–348, 353–354
intercorrelations of similar, 347–352
item overlap, 347, 349–351
similarities and differences for, 347, 353
principles for interpretation of, 376–379
Control, 383, 394, 397–399, *see also* Impulse control; Repression scale (*R*)
emotional, 198, 202, 205, 226
paragraph in report on, 461–462
loss of, 139
Conversion symptoms, *see* Hysteria scale (*Hy*)
Conversion V code, 242, 429, 430
Coping ability, 198, 201–202, 226
Correction for Hypochondriasis scale (*CH*), 81
Correction scale, *see* *K* (Correction) scale
Criminals, 397–398, 440
Criterion keying method, 4–5
Critical items, 338–342
controversies surrounding the use of, 342–345
scoring keys and norms, 569–574
"Cry for help," 192, 225
CYN (Cynicism) scale, 203, 347–349, 352, 353, 357, 364–365, 557–558
CYN1 (Misanthropic Beliefs), 349, 365, 558
CYN2 (Interpersonal Suspiciousness), 350, 365, 558
Cynical Distress, 115
Cynical Distrust, 153
Cynicism, 101, 116, *see also* Superlative Self-Presentation scale (*S*), Butcher and Han subscales, *S1*
denial of, 120

D

Dahmer, Jeffrey, 326
Deception, *see* Other Deception Scale (*Od*)
Defensive responses, fear-conditioned, 472, 474
Defensiveness, 189, 202, *see also* "Most closed" validity configuration; Self-favorable scales; *specific defense mechanisms*

Demographic variables, 421–426, *see also* Socioeconomic variables
Denial, 93, 94, 217, 225
 of anxiety, 95–96, 108, 150
 of cynicism, 120
 of irritability and anger, 53, 203–204
 of physiologic symptoms, 92
 of resentment or suspicion, 96
Denial of Moral Flaws (*S5*), 53, 204, 537–538
Denial of Social Anxiety (*Hy1*), 95–96, 108, 541–542
Denial of Stereotypic Masculine Interests subscales, 115, 116
Denial scale (*Dn*), 92, 95
DEP (Depression) scale, MMPI-2, 347–349, 352–355, 358–360, 363, 369, 377–378, 441, 555
  DEP1 (Lack of Drive), 349, 358–359, 554
  DEP2 (Dyshporia), 349, 358–359, 555
  DEP3 (Self-Depreciation), 349, 358–359, 555
  DEP4 (Suicidal Ideation), 349, 358–359, 555
DEP (Depression) scale, Wiggins, 346, 348–353, 358–360
Dependency, pathological, 369
Depressed state critical items, 575
Depressed suicidal ideation critical items, 341, 569
Depression and worry, 102, 115, 153, 341, 375, *see also* Anxiety and tension
 critical items related to, 341, 570, 574–575
 differentiating various types of depression, 440, 441
 psychotherapy for, 375
Depression scale (*D*), 83–85, 359, 371, 539, *see also* Code patterns
 Harris-Lingoes subscales, 85–86
  D1 (Subjective Depression), 75, 86, 359, 540
  D2 (Psychomotor Retardation), 75, 86–87, 540
  D3 (Physical Malfunctioning), 75, 87, 540
  D4 (Mental Dullness), 75, 88, 137, 540
  D5 (Brooding), 75, 88–89, 358, 359, 541
 interpretation, 253–254, 359, 371
 Subtle—Obvious subscales (*D—S* and *D—O*), 89–90, 539–540
Deviant beliefs critical items, 341, 570
Deviant thinking and experience, critical items related to, 341, 571, 575
Diagnostic impressions, paragraph in report on, 463–467
Disabilities, participants with, 172
Disconstraint scale (*DIS*), 380, 382–387, 563
Dissimulation index, *see F—K*
Dissimulation scale (*Ds*, *Ds-r*, and *Ds-r2*), 43–46, 535
 interpretation, 195–196
Dissociation, sensorimotor, 140–141, 550
Distress, 191, 192, *see also* "Cry for help"; *specific topics*
 in a candid, self-critical person, 226, 228
 defending against, 142, *see also* Defensive responses
 subjective, 129
Distress scales, 89, 129, *see also specific scales*
Distrust, *see also* Paranoia; Trust
cynical, 153
Distrust (*Si5*), 153
Dominance scale (*Do*), 399–400, 565
Double-marked items, *see* Cannot Say (*?*) score
Drug abuse and addiction, 105, 108, 146, 406–412, *see also* Alcoholism
 critical items related to, 341, 571, 576
Dutifulness, 401
Dyadic Adjustment Scale (*DAS*), 412, 413
Dynamics/etiology section of report
 paragraph in report on, 462–463

E

Education, 196, 197, 202, 226, 230, 423–424, 426
Ego Control scale (EC-5), 383, 394
Ego strength, 462
 people experiencing problems but who have good, 222, 226
Ego Strength scale (*Es*), 226, 395–397, 461, 462
Emotional Alienation (*Sc2*), 136–137, 549
Emotional control, *see under* Control
Emotional deprivation, 102, 136
Emotionality, 380, 381, 384–388
Empirical approach to critical items, 342–343
Energizer variables, scales that act as, 470–471
Energy level, 138, *see also* Hypomania scale (*Ma*); Low Positive Emotionality/Extraversion scale (*LPE*)
Environment, perception of
 paragraph in report on, 460
Exaggeration, 43, 44, 195–196, 206, 428, *see also* Dissimulation scale; *F* (infrequency) scale; Malingering
Experimental booklet, 10–11
Explosive Behavior (*ANG1*), 350, 362–363, 557
Externalizing processes, 120, 123, 354
Extraversion, 108, 380–381, 384–388, *see also* Social Introversion scale (*Si*)

F

F—K (Dissimulation) index, 60–67
 interpretation, 66, 206–207

scores at lower and upper extremes of different diagnostic and participant groups, 65, 66
F-Back (*FB*) scale, 35–39, 226, 533
interpretation, 193–194
F-FB index, 59–60, 205
F (Infrequency) scale, 33–35, 342, 424, 425, 533
extreme elevation on, 192–193, 203, 438
interpretation, 35, 40, 191–193, 203, 371
relations with other scales, 40, 190, 192, 362, 371, 381
"Faking bad," 52, 53, 59, 61, 63, 77, *see also F* (Infrequency) scale; Malingering
"Faking good," 59, 61–63, *see also* Self-favorable scales; Underreporting
False response sets, 82
FAM (Family Problems) scale, MMPI-2, 348, 349, 352, 353, 560–561
FAM1 (Family Discord), 349, 372, 561
FAM2 (Familial Alienation), 349, 561
FAM (Family Problems) scale, Wiggins, 346, 350–353, 371
Familial Discord (*Pd1*), 106–107, 543
Family attachment, 354
Family conflict, 115
critical items related to, 341, 571
Family discord, 341
Fatigue, 138, 573
Fear-conditioned defensive responses, 472, 474
Fears, 127, 143, 232, *see also* Anxiety and tension; *FRS*; Phobic concerns; Psychasthenia scale (*Pt*)
Feedback (to client)
client's opportunity to evaluate, 476
guidelines for giving, 473–476
strategies for providing, 471–473
Feminine Gender Identity (*Mf6*), 116, 547
Feminine Interests scale (*FEM*), 346, 349
Femininity, 234, *see also* Gender differences; Masculinity—Femininity scale (*Mf*)
Five Factor Model (FFM), 380, 381
Floating profile, 438, 439
FM scale, *see* Gender Role—Feminine scale (*FM*)
Foreign translations of MMPI-2, 162–163
Form AX (experimental booklet), 10–11
F(p) (Infrequency-Psychopathology) scale, 39–42, 535
interpretation, 41–42, 194–195
subscales, 42, 535–536
Friedman Overlap scales (FOS), 158n3
FRS (Fears) scale, 348, 350, 352, 353, 355–357, 554
FRS1 (Generalized Fearfulness), 350, 355, 554
FRS2 (Multiple Fears), 350, 355–356, 554

G

Gamma dimension, 46–47, 57
Gastrointestinal concerns, upper, 573–574, *see also* Somatic symptoms and concerns
Gastrointestinal Symptoms (*HEA1*), 349, 360, 556
Gender differences, 422–423, *see also* Femininity; Masculinity—Femininity scale (*Mf*); *specific scales and specific topics*
Gender Role—Feminine scale (*FM*), 404–406, 566
Gender Role—Masculine scale (*GM*), 404–406, 566
Goldberg index, 463, 465, 467
Goldberg rules, clinical use of, 464–465
Grandiosity, 149–150
Group administration, 160–161
Guilt and remorse, 110, *see also* Amorality

H

Hallucinations and peculiar experience, 341, 342
Hard Driving Competitiveness, 366, 367
Harris-Lingoes subscales, 73–76, *see also specific subscales*
Hathaway system, 173–174
HEA (Health Concerns) scale, 98, 137, 140, 348, 349, 352–354, 360–361, 556
HEA1 (Gastrointestinal Symptoms), 349, 360, 556
HEA2 (Neurological Symptoms), 349, 360, 556
HEA3 (General Health Concerns), 349, 360, 556
HEA (Poor Health) scale, 98, 137, 140, 346, 349–353, 360–361
Head complaints, critical items related to, 573
Health Concerns, 115
Health problems, *see HEA*; Somatic symptoms and concerns
Homosexuality, 113–114, 299
HOS (Manifest Hostility) scale, 346, 347, 349, 352, 358, 362
Hostility, 115, 134, 139, 397–399, *see also* Anger; Psychopathic Deviate scale (*Pd*); *TPA*
Hostility scale (*Ho*), 364
Humms-Wadsworth Temperament Survey, 22n2
Hypersensitivity-Anxiety subscale, 116
Hypersensitivity/sensitivity, 102, 115, 120, 124
Hypersensitivity (*Si4*), 153
Hypochondriasis scale (*Hs*), 80–83, 360, 539, *see also* Code patterns

interpretation, 82, 232–233, 472
Hypomania scale (*HYP*), 146, 346, 349
Hypomania scale (*Ma*), 141–146, 371, 424, 471, 550–551, *see also* Code patterns
Harris-Lingoes subscales, 146
Ma1 (Amorality), 146–147, 551
Ma2 (Psychomotor Acceleration), 147, 551
Ma3 (Imperturbability), 148, 551
Ma4 (Ego Inflation), 149–150, 552
interpretation, 142–144, 333–334, 410, 440–441, 462, 471
Subtle—Obvious subscales (*Ma-S* and *Ma-O*), 149–151, 551
treatment implications, 334
Hysteria scale (*Hy*), 90–95, 541, *see also* Code patterns
Harris-Lingoes subscales, 95
Hy1 (Denial of Social Anxiety), 95–96, 108, 541–542
Hy2 (Need for Affection), 96–97, 542
Hy3 (Lassitude-Malaise), 97–98, 542
Hy4 (Somatic Complaints), 98, 542
Hy5 (Inhibition of Aggression), 98–99, 542
interpretation, 94, 279–280
Subtle—Obvious subscales (*Hy-S* and *Hy-O*), 95–96, 99–101, 108, 541

I

Ideas of External Influence (*Pa1*), 123, 382, 548
Ideas of reference, 115, 341
Ill health, *see also* Somatic symptoms and concerns
critical items related to, 573
Impatience, 53, 203–204, 366, 367, *see also* Patience and Denial of Irritability and Anger (*S4*)
Impatience (*TPA1*), 350, 363, 368, 559
Impulse control, poor, 102, *see also* Hypomania scale (*Ma*)
Inconsistent responding, *see TRIN*; *VRIN*
Infrequent item responses, *see F* (infrequency) scale; *F(p)* (Infrequency-Psychopathology) scale
Inner Directedness, 115
Insight, 197, 201, 217, *see also* Psychological mindedness; Psychotherapy, psychoanalytic/insight-oriented
Intelligence/IQ, and test administration, 171–172
Internal consistency, 343–344, *see also specific scales*
Interpersonal relationships, *see also FAM*; Social Maladjustment scale (*SOC*); *specific topics*
paragraph in report on, 460
Interpersonal Suspiciousness (*CYN2*), 350, 365, 558
Interpretation, *see also specific topics*
actuarial and clinical approaches to, 414–415
"blind," 420, 426, 427
Interpretative steps, 70–71, 426–429, *see also specific steps in interpretive process*
organizing the data, 442–443
Introspective-Critical (*Mf5*), 115, 158n4
Introversion, *see* Extraversion; Inner Directedness; Social Introversion
Invalid *F* scores, 191–193
Invalid profiles, 186–188, *see also* Validity, of profile
and report language, 209, 214
Irritability, 134
denial of, 53, 203–204
Irritability (*ANG2*), 350, 363, 557

J

Job applicants, 217, 225, 226, *see also* Work settings
Job Involvement, 366–367
Judgmental orientation, 124

K

K-correction procedures, 50–53, 120, 131, 173, 197, 360–361, 392, 393
K (Correction) scale, 49–53, 197, 425, 533–534, *see also* Code patterns; *F—K*
interpretation, 59, 197–198, 201–202, 225, 226, 396–397, 461, 462, 466
of very high scores, 52, 198, 202–203
low scores, 52–53, 198, 201, 204–205, 225, 462, 466
relations with other scales, 49–50, 52–54, 197, 198, 202–205, 217, 225, 226, 392, 396–397, 461, 462, *see also K*-correction procedures
treatment implications, 198, 200–202, 466, 468
K+ (normal code, high *K*) profile, 337, 432, 437, 438
Koss-Butcher Critical Item Set, 569–570

L

L (Lie) scale, 47–49, 56, 533
interpretation, 196–197, 199–200, 217, 225–226
relations with other scales, 56, 225–226
Lachar-Wrobel Critical Item Set, 570–572
Level I *vs.* Level II data, 345–346

Losses of consciousness, critical items related to, 574
Low Positive Emotionality/Extraversion scale (*LPE*), 380, 384–388, 563–564
Low scores on scales, 70–71, *see also specific scales*
LSE (Low Self-Esteem) scale, 348, 350–355, 362, 368–370, 441, 559
- *LSE1* (Self-Doubt), 350, 369, 559–560
- *LSE2* (Submissiveness), 350, 369, 560

Lying 46–47, *see also L* (Lie) scale

M

Ma scale, *see* Hypomania scale (*Ma*)
MacAndrew Alcoholism scale (*MAC/MAC-R*), 406–412, 567
Maladjustment, *see also specific topics*
general, 129
measuring, 34
Maladjustment Overlap scale (MOS), 158n3
Malingering, 34–35, 37–38, 41, 44–46, 62, 196, *see also* Dissimulation scale; *F* (infrequency) scale; "Faking bad"
Mania, *see* Hypomania scale
Manifest Hostility scale (*HOS*), 346, 347, 349, 352, 358, 362
Marital Distress scale (*MDS*), 412–413, 568
Masculine gender role, *see* Gender Role—Masculine scale (*GM*)
Masculinity—Femininity scale (*Mf*), 112–119, 425, 544–545, *see also* Code patterns
- interpretation, 118–119, 234, 316–317, 470
- Martin-Finn subscales, 115–116
  - *Mf1* Denial of Stereotypic Masculine Interests, 116, 546
  - *Mf2* Hypersensitivity-Anxiety, 116, 546
  - *Mf3* Stereotypical Feminine Interests, 116, 546
  - *Mf4* Low Cynicism, 116, 546
  - *Mf5* Aesthetic Interest, 116, 546
  - *Mf6* Feminine Gender Identity, 116, 546–547
  - *Mf7* Restraint, 547
  - *Mf10* Composite Masculinity—femininity, 547
- Serkownek subscales, 115, 158n4
  - *Mf1* (Narcissism-Hypersensitivity), 115
  - *Mf2* (Stereotypic Feminine Interests), 115, 158n4
  - *Mf3* (Denial of Stereotypic Masculine Interests), 115
  - *Mf4* (Heterosexual Discomfort-Passivity), 115, 158n4
  - *Mf5* (Introspective-Critical), 115, 158n4

Memory and concentration, critical items related to, 574
Mental confusion critical items, 341, 569
Minnesota T-S-E (Thinking-Social-Emotional) Inventory, 151–152
MMPI
- general description, 1–3
- historical development, 3–9
  - reasons for revision, 7–9, *see also* MMPI-2
- restandardization (MMPI-2), 9–10

MMPI/MMPI-2 code pattern correspondence, 176–182
MMPI-2
- forms of, 160–162, 182n2
- general description, 1–3
- item changes and deletions, 10–13
- reasons for developing, 7–9

MMPI-2 booklet, 10–12, 160
MMPI-2 restandardization project, 9–10
MMPI-A (Adolescent), 9–10, 27, 63, 65, 422
MOR scale, *see* Poor Morale scale (*MOR*)
Moral flaws, denial of, 53, 204
Moral virtue, 196, 204, *see also* Amorality
Moral Virtue (*Pa3*), 124–125, 548
"Most closed" validity configuration, 217–219, 225
"Most open" validity configuration, 209, 217, 218, 220, 225–230
Motivation, 193, 207, *see also* Test-taking attitude
Motor functioning, *see also* Psychomotor Acceleration (*Ma2*); Psychomotor Retardation (*D2*); Sensorimotor Dissociation (*Sc6*)
- critical items related to, 574

Mp scale, *see* Positive Malingering scale (*Mp*)
Mt scale, *see* College Maladjustment scale (*Mt*)

N

"Naive but non-defensive disturbed" configuration, 227
"Naive but open" validity configuration, 224, 226
Naïveté 196, 225, 472
Narcissism-Hypersensitivity (*Mf1*), 115
Narcissistic traits and narcissistic pathology, 104, 108, 144, 149
Negative Emotionality/Neuroticism scale (*NEN*), 380, 381, 384, 387, 563
Neurasthenia, 573, *see also* Fatigue
Neurological Symptoms (*HEA2*), 349, 360
Neurotic Overlap scale (NOS), 158n3
Neurotic triad, 70, 79
Neuroticism, 157n3, *see also* Negative Emotionality/Neuroticism scale (*NEN*)
Neuroticism, Extraversion, and Openness Personality Inventory—Revised (NEO-PI-R), 380–381

Neuroticism, Extraversion, and Openness Personality Inventory (NEO-PI), 380
Nichols Critical Item List (NCIL), 342, 344, 573–576
Nonoverlapping items, 79
Normalized *T*-scores, 18–19, *see also* *T*-scores
Normative sample, new MMPI-2, 12–16, *see also* MMPI, historical development

O

OBS (Obsessiveness) scale, 348, 351–354, 357–358, 369, 384, 554–555
Obsessive—compulsiveness, 127–129, 186, 384, *see also* Psychasthenia scale (*Pt*)
Omitted items, 8, *see also* Cannot Say (*?*) score
Openness, 380–381, *see also under* Validity scale configurations
Oral administration of MMPI, 170–171, *see also* Audiotape version of MMPI-2
ORG (Organic Symptoms) scale, 346, 349
Other Deception Scale (*Od*), 55
Overcontrolled-Hostility scale (*O-H*), 397–399, 565
Overlapping items, 79–80, 157n3, *see also specific scales*
Overreporting, 77, *see also* *F* (Infrequency) scale; "Faking bad"; Malingering

P

Pain and discomfort, *see also* Somatic symptoms and concerns
  critical items related to, 341, 573
Paranoia, 102, 109, 186, 341, 361, *see also* Code patterns; Psychoticism scale (*PSY*); Schizophrenia, paranoid; Trust, lack of
Paranoia scale (*Pa*), 119–122, 342, 362, 381, 422
  Harris-Lingoes subscales, 122–125
    Pa1 (Ideas of External Influence), 123, 382, 548
    Pa2 (Poignancy), 124, 548
    Pa3 (Moral Virtue), 124–125, 548
  interpretation of, 121, 320–321, 441
  Subtle—Obvious subscales (*Pa-S* and *Pa-O*), 125–126, 547–548
Paranoid personality, 120
Paranoid valley, 429, 431
Participants requirements, 168–172
Passive-aggressive V in women, 432, 436
Passivity, 115
Patience, 350, 363, 366–368, 559
Patience and Denial of Irritability and Anger (*S4*), 53, 203–204, 537
Persecutory ideas, *see also* Paranoia
  critical items related to, 341, 570, 576
Personality Psychopathology Five (*PSY-5*), 379–381, *see also specific scales*
  effects of response styles on, 387
Personality traits, paragraph in report on, 459
Phobias (*PHO*), 346, 349
Phobic concerns, 355, *see also* Psychasthenia scale (*Pt*)
Phrenophobia critical items, 575
Physical illness, 82, *see also* HEA; Hypochondriasis scale (*Hs*); *ORG*; Somatic symptoms and concerns
Physical Malfunctioning (*D3*), 75, 87, 540
Physical-Somatic Concerns (*Si6*), 153
Physiologic symptoms, admission *vs.* denial of, 92
Political participation, 399–400
Poor Morale scale (*MOR*), 346, 349
Positive Malingering scale (*Mp*), 55–57, 536
  interpretation, 204, 205
Post-Traumatic Stress Disorder scale—Keane (*PK*), 403–404, 566–567
Post-Traumatic Stress Disorder scale—Schlenger (*PS*), 403–404, 567
Posttraumatic stress disorder (PTSD), 38, 403–404
Problematic anger critical items, 341, 571
Profile plotting, 172–173
Profile(s)
  "complex," 468–470
  indeterminate, 188–189
Projection, 120, 123
Psychasthenia scale (*Pt*), 127–130, 354, 358, 391–393, 548–549, *see also* Code patterns
  interpretation, 128–129, 326, 392–393
  treatment implications, 326–327
Psychological discomfort, critical items related to, 341
Psychological mindedness, *see also* Insight
  lack of, 82, 217, 225
Psychological resources, paragraph in report on, 462
Psychomotor Acceleration (*Ma2*), 147, 551
Psychomotor Retardation (*D2*), 75, 86–87, 540
Psychopathic Deviate scale (*Pd*), 101–105, 471, 542–543, *see also* Code patterns
  Harris-Lingoes subscales, 106–111
    Pd1 (Familial Discord), 106–107, 543
    Pd2 (Authority Problems), 107–108, 365, 543–544
    Pd3 (Social Imperturbability), 95–96, 108–109, 544
    Pd4 (Social Alienation), 109–110, 123, 544
    Pd5 (Self-Alienation), 110–111, 544

interpretation, 103–105, 234, 295–296, 410, 459, 468, 471
relations with other scales, 103–105, 107–109, 234, 373, 410
Subtle—Obvious subscales (*Pd-S* and *Pd-O*), 111–112, 543
Psychopathy/psychopathic personality, 101, 102, 106, 107, 149, 150, 373, 465, *see also* Amorality; Disconstraint scale (*DIS*)
Psychosis, 192, 217, 342, 356, 361, 432, 575–576, *see also BIZ*; Schizophrenia
Psychotherapy, 198, 466, 468, *see also specific scales and codetypes*
attitudes toward, 354, 468
college students who seek, 402
for depression, 375
psychoanalytic/insight-oriented, 197, 200–202, 225, 226, 235, 395
Psychotic Overlap scale (POS), 158n3
Psychotic scales, 79, *see also specific scales*
Psychotic Symptomatology (*BIZ1*), 351, 361–362, 557
Psychotic tetrad, 53, 70, 79–80
Psychotic V, 429, 431
Psychotic *vs.* neurotic, 465
Psychotic *vs.* neurotic slope, 433–435
Psychoticism, 157n3, 342
Psychoticism scale (*PSY*), 346, 349, 380–382, 387, 563

Q

Questions during administration, answers to commonly asked, 164–168

R

R scale, *see* Repression scale (*R*)
Race, 424–425
Random response set, 31, 37–38, 209–211, *see also VRIN*
Re (Social Responsibility) scale, 400–402, 566
Reading ability and comprehension of items, 168–170
Reading items aloud, 170, *see also* Audiotape version of MMPI-2
Reality distortion, critical items related to, 341
Referral data, importance of, 419–421
Religious Fundamentalism scale (*REL*), 346, 349
Replicated rational selection, 379–380
Report openers, 443–444
Report writing, 443–444
Report(s)
guidelines for beginning, 444–458
organization of, 457, 459–468
Repression, 93, 94, 225
Repression scale (*R*), 383, 391–394, 565
Response style, measures of, 39, *see also specific scales*
Rigidity, 153

S

Scale 1, *see* Hypochondriasis scale (*Hs*)
Scale 2, *see* Depression scale (*D*)
Scale 3, *see* Hysteria scale (*Hy*)
Scale 4, *see* Psychopathic Deviate scale (*Pd*)
Scale 5, *see* Masculinity—Femininity scale (*Mf*)
Scale 6, *see* Paranoia scale (*Pa*)
Scale 7, *see* Psychasthenia scale (*Pt*)
Scale 8, *see* Schizophrenia scale (*Sc*)
Scale 9, *see* Hypomania scale (*Ma*)
Scale 0, *see* Social Introversion scale (*Si*)
Schizophrenia, paranoid, 38, 40–41, 361
Schizophrenia scale (*Sc*), 130–135, 362, 381, 392, 424, 471, 549, *see also* Code patterns
Harris-Lingoes subscales, 135–136
Sc1 (Social Alienation), 136, 549
Sc2 (Emotional Alienation), 136–137
Sc3 (Lack of Ego Mastery, Cognitive), 137–138, 549–550
Sc4 (Lack of Ego Mastery, Conative), 138–139, 550
Sc5 (Lack of Ego Mastery, Defective Inhibition), 139–140, 550
Sc6 (Sensorimotor Dissociation), 140–141, 550
interpretation, 131–133, 329–330, 471
treatment implications, 330–331
Schizotypal Characteristics (*BIZ2*), 351, 361, 557
Scoring, 172–173
Self-Alienation (*Pd5*), 110–111, 544
Self-concept, paragraph in report on, 459–460
Self-consciousness, 153, 154, 370
Self-critical person, distress in a candid, 226, 228
Self-criticism and self-devaluation, 97, 201, 235, 354, 369
Self-Depreciation (*DEP3*), 349, 358–359, 555
Self-direction, 400
Self-doubt, 127, 129, 235
Self-Doubt (*LSE1*), 350, 369, 559–560
Self-esteem
admitting serious problems while attempting to preserve, 221
low, 201, *see also* Depression scale (*D*), Harris-Lingoes subscales, *D5* (Brooding); *LSE*
Self-favorable scales and response sets, 46–47, 440, 442, *see also F—K*; *K*; *L*; Posi-

tive Malingering scale (*Mp*); Social Desirability scale (*Sd*); Superlative Self-Presentation scale (*S*)
Self—Other Alienation (*Si3*), 153, 154
Self-presentation, superlative, *see* Superlative Self-Presentation scale (*S*)
Sensitivity, *see* Hypersensitivity/sensitivity
Sensorimotor Dissociation (*Sc6*), 140–141, 550
Serenity (*S2*), 53, 203, 537
Sexual concern and deviation, 116
  critical items related to, 341, 571
Sexual problems, critical items related to, 576
Short forms of MMPI/MMPI-2, 162, 182n2
Shyness/Self-Consciousness (*Si1*), 153, 154, 370, 552, *see also* Social Introversion scale (*Si*)
Shyness (*SOD2*), 351, 370
Sign approach to critical items, 342–343
Situational stress due to alcoholism, critical items related to, 341, 569
Sleep disturbance critical items, 341, 570, 575
Social Alienation (*Pd4*), 109–110, 123, 544
Social Alienation (*Sc1*), 136, 549
Social anxiety, *see also SOD*
  denial of, 95–96, 108
Social Avoidance (*Si2*), 153, 154, 552
Social Desirability scale (*Sd*), 47, 56–57, 536
  interpretation, 204–205
Social I.E. scale, 152
Social Imperturbability (*Pd3*), 95–96, 108–109, 544
Social Introversion scale (*Si*), 116, 151–157, 425, 552, *see also* Code patterns
  Ben-Porath subscales, 153–154
    Si1 (Shyness/Self-Consciousness), 153, 154, 370, 552
    Si2 (Social Avoidance), 153, 154, 552
    Si3 (Self-Other Alienation), 153, 154, 552–553
  interpretation, 95–96, 108, 155–157, 336–337, 461, 470
  Serkownek subscales, 115, 153
    Si1 (Inferiority-Personal Discomfort), 153
    Si2 (Discomfort With Others), 153
    Si3 (Staid-Personal Rigidity), 153
    Si4 (Hypersensitivity), 153
    Si5 (Distrust), 153
    Si6 (Physical-Somatic Concerns), 153
Social maladjustment, 102
Social Maladjustment scale (*SOC*), 346, 349
Social Responsibility scale (*Re*), 400–402, 566
Socioeconomic Status scale (*Ss*), 57–59, 205, 538
Socioeconomic status (SES), 198, 202, 419, 425–426
Socioeconomic variables, 419, 425–426, *see also specific scales*
Sociopathy, *see* Psychopathy
SOD (Social Discomfort) scale, 95–96, 348, 351–353, 357, 370–371, 560
  SOD1 (Introversion), 351, 370, 371, 560
  SOD2 (Shyness), 351, 370, 560
Somatic Complaints (*Hy4*), 98, 542
Somatic symptoms and concerns, 93, 341, *see also HEA*; Hypochondriasis scale (*Hs*); Hysteria scale (*Hy*); *ORG*; Physical illness
  critical items related to, 341, 572–575
Speed and Impatience, 366, 367
Spike profiles, 432, *see also under* Code patterns
Stress, 341, 355, 569, *see also* Anxiety and tension
  response to, 472
    paragraph in report on, 461–462
Stress tolerance, 396, *see also* Ego Strength scale (*Es*)
Submissiveness (*LSE2*), 350, 369, 560
Subscales, *see also specific subscales*
  intercorrelations between, 74
Substance abuse, *see also* Drug abuse and addiction
  critical items related to, 341, 569, 571, 576
  indirect, 576
Subtle—Obvious subscales, 76–78, *see also specific subscales*
Suicidal ideation, feelings, and tendencies, 87, 97, 341, 364
  critical items related to, 341, 569, 575
Suicidal Ideation (*DEP4*), 349, 358–359, 555
Superlative Self-Presentation scale (*S*), 53–55, 203, 536
  Butcher and Han subscales
    S1 (Belief in Human Goodness), 53, 203, 537
    S2 (Serenity), 53, 203, 537
    S3 (Contentment With Life), 53, 203, 537
    S4 (Patience and Denial of Irritability and Anger), 53, 203–204, 537
    S5 (Denial of Moral Flaws), 53, 204, 537–538
  interpretation, 203–204
Supplemental scales, *see also specific scales*
  history and development, 388–391
Suppressor variables, scales that act as, 470–471
Suspicion, *see also* Interpersonal Suspiciousness (*CYN2*); Paranoia
  denial of, 96
Sweating, critical items related to, 574
Symptoms
  internal, 354
  paragraph in report on, 459

T

T-S-E (Thinking-Social-Emotional) Inventory, 151–152
T-score equivalents of percentages, 20, 21
T-scores, 71, 438
linear and uniform, 16–21, 23n9
normalized, 18–19
Test administration, psychiatric impairment and, 171
Test conditions, 167–168
Test hit/miss, 69n8
Test instructions, 163–167
Test setting/situation, 207–208, 427
Test-taking attitude, assessment of, 25–26, 193, *see also* Validity
Therapeutic alliance, 471, *see also* Psychotherapy
Thought disturbance, *see* Deviant thinking and experience; Psychosis; *specific topics*
Threatened assault critical items, 341, 569
Tiredness, *see also* Fatigue
critical items related to, 573
TPA (Type A Behavior) scale, 139, 347, 348, 350, 352, 353, 358, 364, 366–368, 378, 384
TPA1 (Impatience), 350, 363, 368, 559
TPA2 (Competitiveness), 350, 363, 368, 559
TR index, 28, 68n4
Traditional Feminine Interests, 115
Treatment implications, *see also* Psychotherapy; *TRT*; *specific scales and codetypes*
paragraph in report on, 466, 468
TRIN (True Response Inconsistency) scale, 30, 32–33, 48, 428, 534–535
interpretation, 33, 189–190
TRT (Negative Treatment Indicators), 348, 351–354, 369, 374–376, 561
TRT1 (Low Motivation), 351, 352, 561–562
TRT2 (Inability to Disclose), 351, 352, 562
Trust, 124
lack of, 96, 134, 153, *see also* Paranoia

U

Underreporting, 77, *see also* "Faking good"
Underreporting scales, 54–56, *see also* Self-favorable scales
Uniform *T* (UT) scores, *see* *T*-scores, linear and uniform
Unscorable items, *see* Cannot Say (*?*) score
Unusual experience critical items, 575
Upper gastrointestinal concerns, 573–574, *see also* Somatic symptoms and concerns

V

Validity
of profile, 169, 171, *see also* Invalid profiles; Validity scales
issues in determining, 67, 207–208, 427
psychiatric impairment and, 171
of scores, borderline, 191–192
Validity Pattern "A," 223, 226
Validity scale configurations, 209, 214, 217
most closed, 217–219, 225
most open, 209, 217, 218, 220, 225–230
naive but non-defensive disturbed, 227
naive but open, 224, 226
unusual or paradoxical, 226, 229
Validity scales, 3, 25–26, 59–67, *see also specific scales*
Vascular complaints, critical items related to, 573
Veterans, combat, 403–404
Violence, *see* Aggression
VRIN (Variable Response Inconsistency) scale, 28–32, 60, 428, 534
interpretation, 187–189

W

War veterans, 403–404
"Weakened will," 127
Weakness/tiredness/fatigue, *see also* Fatigue
critical items related to, 573
Welsh coding system, modified, 175
Wiggins content scales, *see* Content scales, MMPI-2 and Wiggins; *specific scales*
Work, *see also* Job applicants
attitudes toward, 354
Work settings, 208
Worry, *see* Anxiety and tension; Depression and worry
WRK (Work Interference) scale, 348, 351–354, 368, 369, 373–374, 561

Y

Yea/nay-saying, *see TRIN*

About the Authors

Alan F. Friedman, PhD, is a licensed clinical psychologist in full-time independent practice in Chicago and an Associate Clinical Professor in the Department of Psychiatry and Behavioral Sciences at Northwestern University Medical School where he has taught MMPI/MMPI-2 interpretation courses since 1983. Dr. Friedman specializes in psychological evaluations and consultations with mental health professionals, security specialists, human resource professionals, managers, executives, and attorneys interested in crisis prevention and management strategies for critical incidents. He regularly performs fitness for duty evaluations and threat assessments for small organizations and large multinational corporations and designs workplace violence prevention programs. Dr. Friedman is considered a leading expert in the threat assessment of potentially dangerous employees and routinely advises agencies and companies on risk management strategies. Recent clients of his include Commonwealth Edison, TDS Telecom, Honda of America Manufacturing, Inc., Wilson Sporting Goods, Northwestern University, FBI, Manufactured Home Communities, and the US Postal Service. He is a Fellow of the Society for Personality Assessment and a member of the American and Illinois Psychological Associations. He also serves as a consulting editor of the journal *Assessment* and acts as a litigation consultant and expert witness in cases of employment discrimination, criminal and disability matters, and child custody disputes. He is currently writing two books entitled *Evaluating Psychological Fitness for Duty* and *Managing the High Risk Employee*. Dr. Friedman can be contacted at 30 N. Michigan Avenue, Suite 1206, Chicago, IL 60602 (312) 368-4515, E-mail *dralanfriedman@cs.com*.

Richard Lewak, PhD, is a licensed clinical psychologist and Executive Director of the Del Mar Clinic in Del Mar, CA. Dr. Lewak specializes in marriage and family treatment and conducts forensic evaluations. He is the senior author of the book entitled *Therapist Guide to the MMPI & MMPI-2* and the co-author of the *Marks Adult Feedback and Treatment Report for the MMPI-2*. He regularly presents seminars on the clinical and forensic interpretation of the MMPI-2 as well as topics related to family and marital adjustment and well-being. As a member of the adjunct faculty, Dr. Lewak has taught MMPI-2 interpretation courses at the California School of Professional Psychology for the past 10 years. Dr. Lewak can be contacted at the Del Mar Clinic, 240 9th Street, Del Mar, CA 92014 (858) 755-8717.

James T. Webb, PhD, ABPP-CL, is President of Gifted Psychology Press, Inc., a company that publishes books dealing with social and emotional needs of gifted children and their families. Until 1995 he was Professor and Associate Dean at Wright State University's School of Professional Psychology, Dayton, Ohio. Previously, Dr. Webb directed the Department of Psychology at the Children's Medical Center in Dayton and was Associate Clinical Professor in the Departments of Pediatrics and Psychiatry at the Wright State University School of Medicine. Prior to that time, Dr. Webb was a member of the graduate faculty in psychology at Ohio University.

A Fellow of the American Psychological Association, he served for 3 years on the APA Council of Representatives. Dr. Webb is a Fellow of the Society of Pediatric Psychology and the Society for Personality Assessment. He has served on the Board of Directors for the National Association for Gifted Children and was President of the American Association for Gifted Children. Dr. Webb is a past-president of the Ohio Psychological Association, and was a member of its Board of Trustees for 7 years. Dr. Webb can be contacted at P.O. Box 5057, Scottsdale, AZ 85261 (602) 954-4200, E-mail *Giftedbook@aol.com*.

David S. Nichols, PhD, is recently retired from Oregon State Hospital-Portland (formerly Dammasch State Hospital), where he worked as a Clinical Psychologist for 27 years. He continues as Adjunct Professor at the School of Professional Psychology at Pacific University in Forest Grove, OR, where he has taught since 1979. He is a Diplomate of the American Board of Assessment Psychology and a Fellow of the Society for Personality Assessment. He serves as a consulting editor of *Assessment* and for the *Journal of Personality Assessment*. He is a self-described MMPI/MMPI-2 hobbyist and has done research and writing in this area for a quarter century. The author of some 30 reviews, articles, and monographs, he has offered numerous lectures and workshops on MMPI topics around the country and internationally. He is co-author, with Roger L. Greene, of the MMPI-2 Structural Summary, and is just completing *Essentials of MMPI-2 Interpretation*. He can be reached via E-mail: *Davemult@aol.com*.